MORE THAN MEETS THE EYE

THE LAST YEARS
OF
LEE HARVEY OSWALD

JOEL THOMAS GOLLAR

THIS WORK IS DEDICATED TO THOSE RESEARCHERS WHO HAVE DILIGENTLY TRIED TO PROVIDE A VALID PIECE OF THE PUZZLE IN REGARDS TO THE ASSASSINATION OF JOHN F. KENNEDY.

MORE THAN MEETS THE EYE
THE LAST YEARS OF LEE HARVEY OSWALD

CONTENTS

FOREWORD-----------PAGE 3
INTRODUCTION-----PAGE 6

NOTES----PAGE 9

CHAPTER 1---LEE AND HARVEY: PRE-MILITARY AND MILITARY CAREERS	16
CHAPTER 2---A BRIEF LIFE AS A CIVILIAN-	32
CHAPTER 3---THE "DEFECTION" AND COLD WAR CHESS GAMES	39
CHAPTER 4---THE "DEFECTOR" COMES IN FROM THE COLD	67
CHAPTER 5---THE MOVE TO DALLAS	81
CHAPTER 6---LEGITIMATE ASSOCIATES OR SET-UP CONSPIRATORS	100
CHAPTER 7---NEW ORLEANS: THE FINAL "ASSIGNMENT"	113
CHAPTER 8---THE MEXICO CITY CONNECTION	157
CHAPTER 9---THE RETURN TO DALLAS	165
CHAPTER 10--THE MOTORCADE AND THE SHOOTING	190
CHAPTER 11--THE TRAP IS SPRUNG	230
CHAPTER 12--DALLAS JAIL: FRIDAY	262
CHAPTER 13--DALLAS JAIL: SATURDAY	277
CHAPTER 14--THE SUNDAY SILENCING OF HARVEY	294
CHAPTER 15--BALLISTICS EVIDENCE IN THE TIPPIT SHOOTING	307
CHAPTER 16--THE PHOTOGRAPHIC SET-UP	309
CHAPTER 17--THE RIFLE SET-UP AND THE "HIDELL" CONNECTION	310
CHAPTER 18--FPFC: FBI FACT OR SET-UP FICTION	314
CHAPTER 19--NOTED HARVEY IMPOSTORS USED IN THE SET-UP	318
CHAPTER 20--WOUND EVIDENCE AND THE BIRTH OF THE MAGIC BULLET	321
CHAPTER 21--WITNESSES AND THEIR FATE	336

BIBLIOGRAPHY------- 340

BIOGRAPHY----------- 346

COPYRIGHT 2018 BY JOEL THOMAS GOLLAR
ALL RIGHTS RESERVED
ISBN: 069219035X
ISBN-13:978-0692190357

FAIR USE NOTICE: THIS WORK MAY CONTAIN EXCERPTS FROM MATERIAL WHICH HAS NOT BEEN AUTHORIZED BY THE COPYRIGHT OWNER. THIS WORK IS INTENDED TO SPUR FURTHER INVESTIGATION BY MORE EXPERIENCED RESEARCHERS AND CONSTITUTES A FAIR USE OF COPYRIGHTED MATERIAL AS PER 17 U.S.CODE 107.

FOREWORD

SHORTLY AFTER LUNCH ON FRIDAY, NOVEMBER 22ND, 1963, MY CLASSMATES AND I WERE INFORMED BY OUR TEACHER THAT SHOTS HAD BEEN FIRED AT THE PRESIDENTIAL MOTORCADE IN DALLAS. IN RETROSPECT SHE COULD NOT HAVE KNOWN AT THAT TIME THAT THE PRESIDENT HAD BEEN WOUNDED AND THAT THE WOUNDS WOULD PROVE TO BE FATAL. I WAS IN THE SIXTH GRADE. I WAS 12 YEARS OLD.

SCHOOL WAS DISMISSED ALMOST IMMEDIATELY. THE REMAINDER OF THAT FRIDAY AND SATURDAY WAS DEVOTED TO DIGESTING THE NEWS FROM DALLAS AND WASHINGTON. I RECALL THE NEAR-WEEPING WALTER CRONKITE AS HE ANNOUNCED THAT INDEED WHAT WAS FEARED WAS NOW APPARENTLY TRUE; THE PRESIDENT HAD DIED. I RECALL THE RESPONSES OF MY MOTHER AND OLDER SIBLINGS AS WELL.

ON SUNDAY MORNING, NOVEMBER 24TH, 1963, AMERICA WATCHED AS JACK RUBY FATALLY SHOT LEE HARVEY OSWALD. THE FOLLOWING DAY, STILL FASCINATED BY AN EVENT I HAD NOT YET FULLY GRASPED, I WATCHED THE FUNERAL PROCESSION SLOWLY MAKE ITS WAY TO THE CAPITAL ROTUNDA. TO THIS DAY I CAN STILL REMEMBER THE SOUND OF THE HOOVES OF THE RIDERLESS HORSE AS IT WAS RELUCTANTLY LEAD DOWN PENNSYLVANIA AVENUE.

LIFE SOON RETURNS TO NORMAL FOR A TWELVE YEAR OLD. IT WAS HOWEVER PALPABLY MORE DIFFICULT FOR OUR COUNTRY. AS THE MONTHS AND YEARS PASSED I COULD SENSE A CHANGE; A DISSATISFACTION WITH THE NEW PRESIDENT AND A GROWING SENSE OF CONCERN OVER THE ESCALATION OF OUR MILITARY PRESENCE IN VIETNAM.

IN MARCH 1967, NEW ORLEANS DISTRICT ATTORNEY JIM GARRISON REOPENED WHAT THE WARREN COMMISSION HAD HOPED CLOSED WHEN HE BROUGHT CLAY SHAW TO TRIAL. DUE I'M SURE TO MYYOUTH, I HARBOURED LITTLE INTEREST IN THAT PROCEEDING. IN THAT PRE-WATERGATE ERA OLDER CITIZENS AS WELL LIKELY SAW LITTLE REASON TO DOUBT THE COMMISSION'S FINDINGS.

THE NEW YEAR, 1968, ONLY ADDED TO THE GROWING SENSE THAT THE COUNTRY HAD SEEMINGLY ADOPTED VIOLENCE AS AN ALTERNATIVE TO THE BALLOT BOX AS A MECHANISM FOR CHANGE. THE ASSASSINATIONS OF ROBERT KENNEDY AND MARTIN LUTHER KING CEMENTED THE NOTION THAT IN A FIVE YEAR SPAN THE VERY SOUL AND DIRECTION OF THIS COUNTRY HAD CHANGED MARKEDLY.

I BELIEVE MARK LANE'S 1966 RELEASE OF RUSH TO JUDGEMENT WAS THE FIRST BOOK I PURCHASED ON THE ASSASSINATION. SINCE THAT TIME I HAVE READ AND COLLECTED OVER 180 ADDITIONAL BOOKS AND SEVERAL DVD'S AND VIDEOS REGARDING THE PRESIDENT'S DEATH.

THOSE WHO WERE AWARE OF MY INTEREST IN THE ASSASSINATION WOULD OFTEN ASK MY OPINION ON JUST WHAT HAD HAPPENED THAT WEEKEND AND OF OSWALD'S GUILT. BUT THE ISSUE WAS SO INCREDIBLY COMPLICATED AND THE EVENTS THAT OCCURRED SO SEEMINGLY UNBELIEVABLE THAT A VERBAL EXPLANATION WOULD HAVE LITERALLY TAKEN HOURS. IT WAS THEN THAT I DECIDED TO PUT THOUGHTS TO PAPER.

THE LITERATURE PUBLISHED OVER THE YEARS HAS RANGED FROM THE PROBABLE TO THE POSSIBLE TO THE UTTERLY RIDICULOUS IN REGARDS TO THE EVENTS THAT TOOK PLACE THAT WEEKEND IN DALLAS. ONE AUTHOR COULD NOT POSSIBLY RECONSTRUCT ALL THE EVENTS, NAME ALL THE NAMES, AND EXPLAIN JUST WHAT MECHANISMS HAD BEEN PUT INTO PLACE THAT WOULD CULMINATE IN THE

PRESIDENT'S DEATH AND THE ANNOINTING OF LEE HARVEY OSWALD AS THE LONE ASSASSIN.

I DECIDED THAT I WOULD NARROW MY FOCUS REGARDING THE ASSASSINATION. I INITIALLY ELECTED TO SIMPLY CONSTRUCT A DETAILED TIMELINE OF THE LIFE OF LEE HARVEY OSWALD STARTING WITH HIS PRE-MARINE CORP INVOLVEMENT WITH THE CIVIL AIR PATROL. I REVIEWED EVERY BOOK I HAD PREVIOUSLY READ, EVERY VIDEO/DVD, AND PERUSED DOCUMENTS AVAILABLE FROM THE CIA, FBI, THE DALLAS POLICE FORCE, THE WARREN COMMISSION, AND THE HSCA. WEB SITES SUCH AS MARY FERRELL'S, JFK LANCER, CLINT BRADFORD'S, THE EDUCATION FORUM, HISTORY-MATTERS, JOHN ARMSTRONG'S SITE, 22NOVEMBER1963.ORG.UK., AND THE NARA SITE PROVED INVALUABLE FOR MORE RECENTLY RELEASED DOCUMENTS. AS I PROGRESSED WITH MY INITIAL REVIEW OF THE MATERIAL AVAILABLE IN CONSTRUCTING THE TIMELINE OF OSWALD'S LATER YEARS I NOTICED THAT THERE WERE A VERY LIMITED NUMBER OF INDIVIDUALS WHO INTERACTED WITH OSWALD OUTSIDE THE CONFINES OF HIS NUMEROUS PLACES OF RESIDENCE. THESE INDIVIDUALS WERE HOWEVER VERY INFLUENTIAL, MANY WITH INTELLIGENCE TIES, AND SEEMINGLY ORCHESTRATED OSWALD'S EVERY MOVE AFTER HIS MARINE CORP ENLISTMENT AND HIS "DEFECTION." I DECIDED TO EXPAND SOMEWHAT ON MY TIMELINE AND TRY TO GATHER WHAT INFORMATION I COULD CONCERNING JACK RUBY, DAVID FERRIE, GEORGE DEMOHRENSCHILDT, GUY BANISTER, AND THEIR RELATIONSHIP WITH OSWALD. THIS OF COURSE NECESSITATED A <u>SECOND</u> REVIEW OF ALL THE BOOKS IN MY COLLECTION AND A <u>SECOND</u> PERUSAL OF THE DOCUMENTS AVAILABLE ON THE PREVIOUSLY MENTIONED WEBSITES.

AT THIS POINT I WAS SATISFIED THAT MY ORIGINAL ENDEAVOR, A DETAILED OSWALD TIMELINE, WAS COMPLETE AND INCLUSIVE OF THOSE INDIVIDUALS WHO WERE SEEMINGLY OSWALD'S ONLY ONGOING CONTACTS OUTSIDE HIS RELATIONSHIP WITH HIS WIFE AND RUTH PAINE. THERE WAS HOWEVER ONE NAGGING CONCERN. COULD THIS GROUP OF INDIVIDUALS HAVE PLANNED, COORDINATED, AND ENLISTED THE ASSISTANCE OF OTHERS IN WHAT PROVED TO BE A SUCCESSFUL ASSASSINATION OF THE PRESIDENT, THE ANNOINTING OF LEE HARVEY OSWALD AS THE ASSASSIN, AND THE SUBSEQUENT MANIPULATION OF THE INVESTIGATION THAT ENSUED? OR, WERE THESE INDIVIDUALS BEING GUIDED OR PERHAPS MANIPULATED BY OTHERS?

PONDERING THIS POSSIBILITY, OR MORE LIKELY PROBABILITY, I UNDERTOOK YET A <u>THIRD</u> REVIEW OF MY LIBRARY AND THE DOCUMENTS AVAILABLE ON THE VARIOUS WEBSITES. THIS TIME MY FOCUS OF ATTENTION INVOLVED THOSE WHO COULD INDEED HAVE ACCOMPLISHED WHAT THE OTHERS COULD NOT. DAVID ATLEE PHILLIPS, E. H. HUNT, CLAY SHAW, AND ROSCOE WHITE APPEARED TO BE THE NEXT HIERARCHIAL LEVEL CAPABLE OF MANIPULATING EVENTS LEADING UP TO THAT FATEFULL WEEKEND AND CAPABLE OF MANIPULATING OSWALD ON NOVEMBER 22ND. I AM NOT HOWEVER SUGGESTING THAT THEIR SCOPE OF INVOLVEMENT EXTENDED BEYOND THE SETUP OF OSWALD. IN FACT I BECAME MORE CONVINCED AFTER THE THIRD REVIEW THAT INDEED THEIR EFFORTS WERE LIMITED TO ESTABLISHING OSWALD AS THE ASSASSIN. AND, IN PHILLIPS' CASE, PARTICULAR EMPHASIS ON CONVINCING THE WARREN COMMISSION THAT OSWALD HAD INDEED VISITED MEXICO CITY IN THE FALL OF 1963.

AFTER THE THIRD REVIEW, I FELT FAIRLY COMFORTABLE IN MY THOROUGHNESS REGARDING OSWALD'S FINAL YEARS. ONE BOOK HOWEVER PROMPTED YET ANOTHER REWRITE. THIS WOULD BE MY 8TH REWRITE. THE BOOK WAS JOHN ARMSTRONG'S "HARVEY AND LEE." IN MANY WAYS HIS BOOK CORROBORATED MY THOUGHTS REGARDING OSWALD IN THAT IT WAS MY BELIEF THAT HE WAS INDEED A CIA OPERATIVE AND WAS INDEED SET-UP AS THE ASSASSIN OF THE PRESIDENT. OUR WORKS WERE ALSO SIMILAR IN THAT BOTH POINT TO HUNT AND PHILLIPS AS THOSE LIKELY TO HAVE ORCHESTRATED THE SET-UP OF OSWALD. SIMILARITIES HOWEVER DIVERGE REGARDING THE MANY INCIDENCES WHERE THERE WERE "OSWALDS" IN

TWO LOCALES AT THE SAME TIME. MY NOTION WAS THAT HUNT/PHILLIPS ARRANGED FOR INCRIMINATING IMPOSTORS TO POSE AS OSWALD.

ARMSTRONG TAKES THIS PREMISE TO AN ENTIRELY DIFFERENT LEVEL HE PROPOSES THAT THERE WERE INDEED TWO LEE HARVEY OSWALDS. ONE, WHO HE REFERS TO AS "**HARVEY**," A CIA FABRICATED IMPOSTOR THAT WOULD "DEFECT" TO RUSSIA, AND ANOTHER, WHO HE REFERS TO AS "**LEE**," WHO WAS BORN IN NEW ORLEANS, RAISED IN TEXAS, AND WAS LEGITIMATELY AND LEGALLY NAMED **LEE HARVEY OSWALD**. THEIR MILITARY ENLISTMENTS CLOSELY PARALLEL ONE ANOTHER AND THE EFFORTS BY THE CIA AND THE FBI TO MELD THE TWO DISTINCT PERSONAS INTO ONE LEE HARVEY OSWALD ENDURED THE TEST OF TIME AS IT WENT LARGELY UNCHALLENGED FOR ALMOST 50 YEARS. ARMSTRONG'S BOOK CHANGES EVERYTHING. HIS REMARKABLY DETAILED EFFORT LEFT ME NO CHOICE IN REGARDS TO WHETHER A 8TH VERSION OF MY WORK WAS NECESSARY.

I WILL TRY TO DISTINGUISH ARMSTRONG'S "**LEE**" FROM "**HARVEY**," THE OSWALD WHO WAS GUNNED DOWN BY RUBY ON NOVEMBER 24TH, 1963, AND FROM OTHER "OSWALDS" WHO MAY WELL HAVE BEEN UTILIZED BY THE SET-UP CONSPIRATORS TO FURTHER MUDDY THE WATERS IN THE WAKE OF THE ASSASSINATION.

THIS PAPER WILL NOT NAME ASSASSINS OR DOCUMENT THOSE RESPONSIBLE FOR THE PLANNING AND EXECUTION OF THE PRESIDENT'S DEATH. IT WILL HOWEVER CAST SERIOUS DOUBT AS TO THE LIKELIHOOD THAT THE MAN WE WOULD KNOW AS LEE **HARVEY** OSWALD WAS INDEED RESPONSIBLE FOR THAT EVENT.

NEW DOCUMENTS ARE BEING RELEASED EACH YEAR AND THE REMAINING DOCUMENTS ARE DUE TO BE RELEASED IN 2018. SOME WILL AFFECT THE PREMISES BROUGHT FORTH IN THIS WORK. BUT, I SUSPECT THEIR IMPACT WILL BE MINIMAL AS THE SCOPE OF THIS WORK IS NARROWLY FOCUSED AND IS NOT INTENDED TO BE A "FINAL WORD" ON THE PRESIDENT'S DEATH BUT A DETAILED EXAMINATION OF THE LAST YEARS OF LEE **HARVEY** OSWALD AND HIS RELATIONSHIP WITH **LEE** HARVEY OSWALD.

ALTHOUGH A BIBLIOGRAPHY IS INCLUDED IN THIS WORK, YOU WILL NOTE THE ABSENCE OF AN INDEX. IT WAS MY THINKING THAT A DETAILED TIMELINE WOULD SERVE AS AN "INDEX" OF SORTS IN THAT ONE COULD NOTE EXACTLY WHO, WHERE, AND PERHAPS MOST IMPORTANTLY, *WHEN* THE CAST OF CHARACTERS INVOLVED IN THIS SAGA INTERACTED WITH BOTH **LEE** AND **HARVEY**.

AT THOSE POINTS IN THE TIMELINE WHERE I NOTE EVENTS NOT OBTAINED FROM PUBLIC DOCUMENTS, I HAVE MADE EVERY ATTEMPT TO CREDIT AUTHORS (PARTICULARLY JOHN ARMSTRONG) WHOSE WORKS ARE PART OF THE BIBLIOGRAPHY. THERE ARE HOWEVER SOME EVENTS CITED WHERE NO CLEAR ORIGINAL SOURCE COULD BE DETERMINED. THESE EVENTS ARE CITED IN SO MANY PREVIOUS PUBLICATIONS THAT A "PAPER TRAIL" LEADING TO THE ORIGINATOR COULD NOT CLEARLY BE DETERMINED.

I CONSIDER THIS PAPER A WORK IN PROGRESS IN AN EFFORT TO PROVIDE A PIECE, ALBEIT VERY DETAILED PIECE, OF THE PUZZLE THAT SURROUNDS ANY RESEARCH OF THE PRESIDENT'S DEATH. MY HOPE IS THAT MY WORK WILL STIR THE INTEREST OF MORE EXPERIENCED RESEARCHERS.

INTRODUCTION

ON NOVEMBER 22ND, 1963, THE MILITARY AND EXECUTIVE LEADERSHIP OF OUR COUNTRY EFFECTIVELY BECAME EMPOWERED TO INITIATE A RAPID AND DRAMATIC CHANGE IN THE POLICIES EMBRACED BY THE KENNEDY ADMINISTRATION. THROUGH THEIR ACTIONS, THE YOUNG PRESIDENT AND HIS BROTHER HAD EMBITTERED MANY POWERFUL FACTIONS BOTH IN AND OUT OF THE NORMAL POLITICAL CIRCLES. SOME WOULD BENEFIT FROM THE POST-ASSASSINATION POLICY CHANGES WHILE OTHERS WOULD REAP BENEFITS OF A MORE PERSONAL NATURE.

BIG BUSINESS

THE OIL INDUSTRY'S GENEROUS OIL DEPLETION ALLOWANCE, 27.5%, HAD BEEN THREATENED BY THE PRESIDENT. IT WAS ESTIMATED THAT THE LOSS OF THIS ALLOWANCE WOULD COST TEXAS OILMEN $300 MILLION. THE SUCCESSION OF A VICE-PRESIDENT FROM AN OIL RICH STATE WOULD LIKELY PRESERVE THE A LLOWANCE. THE STEEL INDUSTRY HAD PREVIOUSLY SUCCUMBED TO THE PRESIDENT'S ORDER TO "ROLL BACK" THEIR $6 PER TON PRICE INCREASE. MORE POINTEDLY, TEXAS BUSINESS INTERESTS IN CUBA HAD BEEN CURTAILED OR NATIONILIZED BY CASTRO'S REGIME. POWERFUL ENTITIES SUCH AS LONE STAR CEMENT, TEXAS PETROLEUM COMPANY, KING RANCH, AND THE FREEPORT SULFUR COMPANY STOOD TO RECOVER THEIR LOST INTEREST IN CUBA IF CASTRO WERE REMOVED. LONE STAR CEMENT ALONE LOST 25 MILLION, TEXACO LOST 55 MILLION, EXXON LOST 71 MILLION AND SINCLAIR OIL LOST 13 MILLION. OTHER OIL COMPANIES ASSETS WERE FROZEN AS WELL. ESSO AND SHELL OIL WERE ALSO VICTIMS OF CASTRO'S APPROPRIATION OF U.S. ASSETS. IN ALL, OVER 1.9 BILLION DOLLARS WERE LOST BY U.S. COMPANIES AND INDIVIDUALS.

MILITARY / INDUSTRIAL ESTABLISHMENT

THIS ENTITY WOULD HAVE A CONSIDERABLY EASIER TASK IN REGARDS TO SELLING A WAR IN VIETNAM TO LBJ THAN TO THE RELUCTANT AND WARY JFK. THE DEFENSE INDUSTRY IN TEXAS WOULD BENEFIT GREATLY.

CIA PROPER

THE CIA WOULD BE IN A POSITION TO ESCALATE A COLD WAR THAT HAD BEEN THAWING THROUGH KENNEDY'S EFFORTS AT RAPROACHMENT WITH CUBA AND RUSSIA.

ORGANIZED CRIME

THE KENNEDY JUSTICE DEPARTMENT HAD MADE LIFE FOR MOB MEMBERS QUITE UNCOMFORTABLE WITH THEIR CONTINUED SUCCESS IN THE COURTROOM. A CHANGE IN POWER WOULD HOPEFULLY ALLOW AN ESCALATION IN EFFORTS TO RETURN CUBA TO ITS PRE-CASTRO STATUS AS A CASH-COW FOR THE MAFIA AND TO LESSEN THE EFFORTS OF THE JUSTICE DEPARTMENT TO WEAKEN THE ORGANIZED CRIME NETWORK.

ANTI-CASTRO CUBANS

THEY WOULD HOPE THAT A NEW ADMINISTRATION WOULD RESCIND THE "PLEDGE" JFK HAD MADE NOT TO INVADE CUBA AFTER THE 1962 CUBAN MISSLE CRISIS. THE PLEDGE HOWEVER WAS DEPENDANT UPON UNITED NATIONS INSPECTORS VERIFYING THE REMOVAL OF THE ICBM'S. SINCE CASTRO DENIED THE INSPECTORS ENTRY INTO CUBA, JFK'S "PLEDGE" WAS NON-BINDING.

RENEGADE BAY OF PIGS OPERATIVES

E. HOWARD HUNT, DAVID ATLEE PHILLIPS, DAVID FERRIE, GUY BANISTER, AND OTHERS WOULD HOPE THAT A NEW ADMINISTRATION WOULD TAKE A HARDER LINE AGAINST CUBA AND ALLOW THE CIA AN OPPORTUNITY TO RESTORE THE PRESTIGE THAT HAD BEEN LOST AT THE FAILED BAY OF PIGS LANDING. ALTHOUGH THE PRESIDENT TOOK FULL RESPONSIBILITY FOR THE FAILURE, HE PRIVATELY LAID THE BLAME ON THE CIA'S OVEREXUBERANT PROMISE OF SUCCESS.

THE ANTI-CASTRO CUBANS AND THE CIA OPERATIVES WHO ASSISTED THEM IN REGARDS TO THE FAILED BAY OF PIGS OPERATION BENEFITTED VERY LITTLE FROM THE EVENT AS VIETNAM QUICKLY BECAME THE FOCUS OF ATTENTION AND THE CUBA SITUATION DIMINISHED IN IMPORTANCE. ORGANIZED CRIME HOWEVER BENEFITED TO SOME DEGREE AS THE JUSTICE DEPARTMENT UNDER ATTORNEY GENERAL ROBERT KENNEDY PREDICTABLY LOST ITS PRE-ASSASSINATION FERVOR IN REGARDS TO ITS PURSUIT OF ORGANIZED CRIME KINGPINS.

J. EDGAR HOOVER

HOOVER COULD NOW AVOID BEING REPLACED AFTER THE 1964 ELECTION; AN ELECTION WHICH WOULD IN ALL LIKILIHOOD BE WON BY JFK.

LYNDON BAINES JOHNSON

LBJ COULD NOW AVOID BEING EMBARASSINGLY DROPPED FROM THE 1964 TICKET. AND, MUCH MORE IMPORTANTLY, AVOID A POSSIBLE PRISON SENTENCE FOR HIS RELATIONSHIPS WITH BOBBY BAKER AND BILLY SOL ESTES.

SEGREGATIONISTS

GROUPS THROUGHOUT THE SOUTH EQUATED THOSE FAVORING INTERGRATION WITH COMMUNISTS. THEIR EFFORTS TO USE THE "COMMUNIST THREAT" WAS LITTLE MORE THAN A THINLY-VEILED EXCUSE TO THWART THE EFFORTS OF CIVIL RIGHTS GROUPS FAVORING INTEGRATION. THEIR MINDSET WAS BEST DESCRIBED BY ROBERT DEPUGH, THE LEADER OF THE MINUTEMEN: "IF A COMMUNIST EVER COMES INTO OFFICE HE WILL BE REMOVED BY BALLOT OR BULLET."

NOT ONLY WERE THESE INDIVIDUALS AND GROUPS CHALLENGED BY THE PRESIDENT, BUT THEY COLLECTIVELY HAD THE POWER, THE MEANS, AND THE MOTIVES TO FACILITATE THE REMOVAL OF A PRESIDENT BY METHODS FAR REMOVED FROM THE MORE TRADITIONAL BALLOT BOX. THESE FACTIONS WOULD EXPECT THEIR INFLUENCE TO INCREASE, THEIR PROBLEMS TO LESSEN, AND THEIR POWER BASE TO EXPAND IN THE WAKE OF THE PRESIDENT'S SUDDEN AND DRAMATIC REMOVAL FROM OFFICE.

ONCE THE DECISION HAD BEEN MADE TO REMOVE THE PRESIDENT PRIOR TO THE 1964 ELECTION, THE PLANNING WOULD BEGIN. LEE **HARVEY** OSWALD WOULD BE CHOSEN BY RENEGADE CIA OPERATIVES FAMILIAR WITH HIS "DEFECTOR" BACKGROUND. ORGANIZED CRIME WOULD BE ENLISTED TO HIRE THE ACTUAL GUNMEN WITH THE ASSURANCE THAT **HARVEY** WOULD ULTIMATELY BE CAPTURED AS THE "LONE GUNMAN" PATSY. THE PLOT'S SUCCESS WOULD BE ENHANCED DRAMATICALLY BY THE LIKELIHOOD THAT THE CIA PROPER AND THE FBI WOULD VEHEMENTLY DENY ANY PAST INVOLVEMENT WITH **HARVEY**.

IT WAS TO BE THE PERFECT CRIME PERPETRATED NOT BY "A PATSY" BUT BY A <u>PERFECT</u> PATSY. THE SELECTION OF A PATSY WITH INTELLIGENCE TIES INSURED A LESS THAN COMPLETE INVESTIGATION. BUT, PERHAPS MORE IMPORTANTLY, THE SELECTION OF A PATSY WITH ALLEGED PRO-CASTRO, PRO-COMMUNIST TIES WOULD MOST CERTAINLY CEMENT A "NO-ACCOMPLICE" OUTCOME TO PREVENT AN OUTCRY FOR RETRIBUTION FROM THE AMERICAN PUBLIC THAT COULD HAVE LED TO A NUCLEAR SHOWDOWN WITH RUSSIA.

AND SO IT WAS. THE FBI AND THE CIA ALTERED, FABRICATED, AND SUPPRESSED EVIDENCE IN THEIR EFFORT TO ASSURE THE WARREN COMMISSION, AND THUS THE AMERICAN PUBLIC, THAT THERE HAD BEEN NO CONSPIRACY. LYNDON JOHNSON GRACIOUSLY EMBRACED THEIR CONCLUSIONS AND CAJOLED EARL WARREN INTO FORMALIZING THE COVER-UP WITH 26 VOLUMES OF WHAT YOU AND I WOULD BE EXPECTED TO ACCEPT AS THE TRUTH.

IN 1964, THE WARREN COMMISSION CONFIRMED THE FBI'S FINDINGS THAT LEE **HARVEY** OSWALD ALONE HAD KILLED THE PRESIDENT OF THE UNITED STATES. FOURTEEN YEARS LATER, THE HOUSE SELECT COMMITTEE ON ASSASSINATIONS DECIDED OTHERWISE. IN THEIR FINAL REPORT ON JULY 17TH, 1979, THE COMMITTEE ISSUED THIS STATEMENT:

"THE COMMITTEE BELIEVES, ON THE BASIS OF THE EVIDENCE AVAILABLE TO IT, THAT PRESIDENT JOHN F. KENNEDY WAS PROBABLY ASSASSINATED AS A RESULT OF A CONSPIRACY. THE COMMITTEE IS UNABLE TO IDENTIFY THE OTHER GUNMEN OR THE EXTENT OF THE CONSPIRACY."

THE SELECT COMMITTEE ALSO ALLOWED FOR 4 SHOTS HAVING BEEN FIRED; ONE FROM THE GRASSY KNOLL.

OVER 50 YEARS AFTER THE PRESIDENT'S MURDER, HISTORY IS FORCED TO EMBRACE TWO VERSIONS OF JUST WHO WAS RESPONSIBLE FOR FIRING THE FATAL SHOTS THAT WEEKEND IN DALLAS. HISTORY HOWEVER SHOULD REFLECT ONLY ONE VERSION; A VERSION AS CLOSELY TIED TO THE TRUTH AS IS POSSIBLE IN A CASE WITH SUCH ENORMOUS POLITICAL, SOCIAL AND EMOTIONAL RAMIFICATIONS.

IF THE HSCA BELIEVES THAT THERE WERE ADDITIONAL GUNMEN, SHOULD WE CONTINUE TO ACCEPT THE WARREN COMMISSION CONCLUSION THAT LEE **HARVEY** OSWALD WAS THE LONE GUNMAN? IN FACT, SHOULD WE EVEN ACCEPT THE HSCA ASSUMPTION THAT **HARVEY** WAS INDEED ONE OF THE GUNMEN BUT APPARENTLY HAD ACCOMPLICES?

SIR ARTHUR CONAN DOYLE SAID "IT IS A MISTAKE TO THEORIZE BEFORE ONE HAS DATA. INSENSIBLY, ONE BEGINS TO SUIT FACTS TO SUIT THEORIES INSTEAD OF THEORIES TO SUIT FACTS." IN THIS MANUSCRIPT I HAVE TRIED TO ADHERE TO THIS ADVICE BY RECONSTRUCTING AS ACCURATELY AS POSSIBLE A FACTUAL, MINUTE-BY-MINUTE ACCOUNT OF LEE **HARVEY** OSWALD'S LAST YEARS. ONLY THEN DID I TAKE THE LIBERTY TO SUPERIMPOSE PLAUSIBLE THEORIES OVER THE FACT-BASED TIMELINE.

WAS, AS THE WARREN COMMISSION INSISTS, LEE **HARVEY** OSWALD THE SOLE ASSASSIN? WAS, AS THE HSCA SUGGESTS, **HARVEY** ONLY ONE OF THE SHOOTERS? OR, AS ONE FOLLOWS THE TIMELINE, WAS **HARVEY** SIMPLY THE "PERFECT PATSY?" ONE ASSASSINATION RESEARCHER, NOTING THE COMPLEXITY OF THE EVENT, OFFERED THAT HE HOPED TO PROVIDE A "SMALL PIECE OF THE PUZZLE" FOR FUTURE RESEARCHERS. I HOPE TO DO THE SAME.

NOTES

LEE WILL BE USED TO IDENTIFY THE ACTIONS OR MOVEMENTS OF THE RELATIVELY TALLER AND STOCKIER (AS COMPARED TO **HARVEY**) **LEE** HARVEY OSWALD WHO WAS BORN IN NEW ORLEANS AND RAISED IN TEXAS. HE WAS LEGITIMATELY AND LEGALLY **LEE HARVEY OSWALD**. HIS MOTHER, MARGUERITE WAS TALL, THIN, DARK HAIRED, AND VERY ATTRACTIVE. SHE HAD LITTLE DIFFICULTY FINDING EMPLOYMENT. **LEE** WAS A GOOD STUDENT, SOMEWHAT BOISTEROUS, A FIGHTER, WAS KNOWN TO GET DRUNK ON OCCASSION, AND WAS LEFT HANDED. HE WAS NOT ONE TO DISCUSS POLITICS AND DID NOT SPEAK RUSSIAN. **LEE** WILL BE USED BY HUNT/PHILLIPS TO IMPLICATE **HARVEY** IN THE ASSASSINATION OF THE PRESIDENT.

HARVEY WILL BE USED TO IDENTIFY THE ACTIONS OR MOVEMENTS OF THE RELATIVELY SHORTER AND THINNER LEE **HARVEY** OSWALD WHO WAS OF EASTERN EUROPE HUNGARIAN DESCENT AND SPOKE FLUENT RUSSIAN. HIS FATHER AND AN UNCLE WERE FBI INFORMANTS IN NEW YORK CITY. **HARVEY** WAS A POOR STUDENT, QUIET, LISTENED TO CLASSICAL MUSIC, WAS AN AVID READER, NEVER FOUGHT, RARELY DRANK, AND WAS RIGHT HANDED. HE SPOKE QUITE OFTEN ABOUT COMMUNISM AND CRITICIZED THE UNITED STATES. HE WOULD, WITH CIA GUIDANCE, MELD HIS LIFE AND MILITARY CAREER WITH THAT OF THE REAL **LEE** HARVEY OSWALD FROM TEXAS. HE WOULD LATER "DEFECT" TO RUSSIA UNDER CIA/ONI GUIDANCE AND BE SHOT BY JACK RUBY ON NOVEMBER 24, 1963. **HARVEY** WAS, IN EFFECT, A CIA CREATED IMPOSTOR.

HARVEY'S IMPOSTOR "MOTHER" WILL OF COURSE ALSO BE NAMED MARGUERITE. TO AVOID CONFUSION, SHE HOWEVER WILL BE REFERRED TO AS "MARGUERITE." "MARGUERITE" HOWEVER IS SHORT, APPROXIMATELY 5 FEET TALL, OVERWEIGHT, GREY HAIRED, SOMEWHAT DOWDY IN APPEARANCE, AND FOUND IT DIFFICULT TO STAY EMPLOYED OFTEN WORKING IN BARS.

I WILL USE THE TERM "OSWALD" WHEN THERE IS SOME UNCERTAINTY AS TO WHETHER I AM DESCRIBING A SITUATION INVOLVING **LEE**, **HARVEY**, OR POSSIBLY SIMPLY A POORLY TIMED IMPOSTOR USED BY HUNT/PHILLIPS TO IMPLICATE **HARVEY**.

ARMSTRONG'S BOOK IS NOT A SIMPLE READ. ONE HAS TO BE WILLING TO LOOK THROUGH THE LOOKING GLASS. WHAT IS BLACK IS WHITE. WHAT IS WHITE IS BLACK. IN FACT, ALTHOUGH **HARVEY** IS ESSENTIALLY IMPERSONATING **LEE**, IT IS **LEE** WHO LATER IMPERSONATES **HARVEY** IN NUMEROUS ATTEMPTS TO IMPLICATE **HARVEY** IN THE SHOOTING OF THE PRESIDENT. THE "IMPERSONATED" **LEE** ESSENTIALLY "IMPERSONATES" THE VERY INDIVIDUAL WHO WAS CHOSEN TO IMPERSONATE HIM, **HARVEY**. IT IS WORTH REPEATING, ARMSTRONG'S BOOK IS NOT A SIMPLE READ.

AS MY BOOK PROGRESSED I FOUND MYSELF AT A LOSS TO EXPLAIN WHY ROBERT OSWALD WOULD OPENLY PORTRAY **HARVEY** AS HIS "BROTHER" WHEN INDEED IT WAS **LEE** WHO WAS HIS BROTHER. **LEE'S** HALF-BROTHER JOHN PIC WAS NOT COMPLETELY COERCED INTO ACCEPTING **HARVEY** AS HIS "BROTHER." HIS SUSPICION THAT **HARVEY** WAS NOT HIS REAL BROTHER WAS IN SHARP CONTRAST TO ROBERT'S ACCEPTANCE OF **HARVEY**. ONE IS ALSO SUSPICIOUS OF"MARGUERITE." IN ESSENCE, WE HAVE A "MARGUERITE" OSWALD WHO IS PRETENDING TO BE THE "MOTHER" OF A MAN, **HARVEY**, WHO IS HIMSELF MASQUERADING AS **LEE**. HOW WAS "MARGUERITE." COERCED INTO ACCEPTING **HARVEY** AS HER "SON?" IT IS EASY TO UNDERSTAND WHY **HARVEY** WAS WILLING TO ACCEPT ROBERT AS A "BROTHER," JOHN PIC AS A "HALF-BROTHER" AND "MARGUERITE" AS HIS "MOTHER." **HARVEY** WAS A CIA/ONI INTELLIGENCE OPERATIVE WHO WAS SIMPLY FOLLOWING HIS ASSIGNMENT BY CLOAKING HIMSELF WITH THE BACKGROUND OF **LEE** AND NOT ONLY "ADOPTING" **LEE'S** SIBLINGS BUT ADOPTING AN ENTIRELY DIFFERENT MOTHER, "MARGUERITE" TO COMPLETE HIS FABRICATED FAMILY.

ALTHOUGH **HARVEY'S** SELECTION BY THE INTELLIGENCE COMMUNITY TO IMPERSONATE **LEE** WAS LIKELY FOSTERED BY HIS FATHER AND UNCLE'S ROLE AS FBI INFORMANTS, IT WAS ALSO LIKELY SWAYED BY THE FACT THAT **HARVEY** COULD SPEAK RUSSIAN AND THAT THEY DID INDEED RESEMBLE ONE ANOTHER. WHAT I FIND AMAZING HOWEVER IS THEIR SELECTION OF "MARGUERITE" AS **HARVEY'S** "MOTHER." SHE COULD NOT BE MORE DISIMILAR IN APPEARANCE TO THE TALL, SLENDER, ATTRACTIVE MARGUERITE, **LEE'S** MOTHER. THERE IS HOWEVER ONE EXPLANATION FOR THEIR APPARENT OVERSIGHT IN THAT REGARD. THE CIA/ONI NEVER INITIALLY CONSIDERED THE POSSIBILITY THAT THEIR CREATION, "MARGUERITE" WOULD BE FORCED ON NOVEMBER 22ND, 1963 TO PLAY THE ROLE OF A LIFETIME: THE "MOTHER" OF A "SON" WHO HAD BEEN ACCUSED AS THE ALLEGED ASSASSIN OF THE PRESIDENT OF THE UNITED STATES.

WHEN ONE RUNS DOWN THE LIST OF CHARACTERS IN THIS COMPLEX EVENT, ONE HAS TO DECIDE WHICH PARTICIPANTS KNEW THAT **HARVEY** AND **LEE** WERE TWO DISTINCT INDIVIDUALS. ONE ALSO HAS TO DECIDE WHETHER THE PARTICIPANTS KNEW EITHER **LEE** OR **HARVEY** OR BOTH. IF THEY KNEW BOTH "OSWALDS" WERE THEY ACTIVE PARTICIPANTS AND OR ACCESSORIES IN THE SET-UP OF **HARVEY** BY VIRTUE OF THEIR SILENCE REGARDING **LEE**?

LET US LIST THE CAST OF CHARACTERS AND NOTE WHETHER THEY KNEW **LEE** OR **HARVEY** AND THE LIKELIHOOD OF THEIR BEING EITHER A WITTING OR AN UNWITTING ACCESSORY IN THE CIA/FBI EFFORTS TO BLEND THE TWO INDIVIDUALS.

JACK RUBY

HE KNEW **LEE** IN DALLAS, IN KEY WEST IN REGARDS TO GUN RUNNING TO CUBA, AND LIKELY IN NEW ORLEANS AS WELL. HE KNEW **HARVEY** IN NEW ORLEANS AND DALLAS. RUBY WAS A WITTING ACCESSORY AND QUITE POSSIBLY AN UNWITTING SET-UP CONSPIRATOR AS WELL SINCE HE MAY NOT HAVE BEEN COMPLETELY PRIVY TO WHAT WOULD APPEAR TO BE **HARVEY'S** INVOLVEMENT ON NOVEMBER 22ND, 1963.

DAVID FERRIE

HE CERTAINLY KNEW **HARVEY** IN NEW ORLEANS. HE ALSO KNEW **LEE** IN BOTH NEW ORLEANS AND DALLAS. FERRIE WAS A WITTING ACCESSORY. FERRIE, LIKE RUBY HOWEVER MAY NOT HAVE BEEN COMPLETELY PRIVY TO **HARVEY'S** ALLEGED INVOLVEMENT IN THE ASSASSINATION AND THUS AN UNWITTING SET-UP CONSPIRATOR.

JOHN PIC

HE WAS NOT TAKEN IN BY **HARVEY'S** AND "MARGUERITE'S" ATTEMPT TO MELD THEIR LIVES WITH HIS FAMILY. HE OBVIOUSLY KNEW BOTH MEN AND KNEW THAT "MARGUERITE" WAS NOT HIS MOTHER OR EVEN HIS STEP-MOTHER AND THAT **HARVEY** WAS NOT HIS STEP-BROTHER. PIC HOWEVER, DUE TO HIS STEP-BROTHER ROBERT'S INFLUENCE, RELUCTANTLY ACCEPTED HIS ROLE AND THUS BECAME A WITTING BUT LESS THAN ENTHUSIASTIC ACCESSORY.

DUTZ AND LILLIAN MURRETT

THEY WERE LIKELY WITTING ACCESSORIES AS THEY KNEW BOTH **HARVEY** AND **LEE** AND WERE AWARE THAT **HARVEY** WAS NOT THEIR NEPHEW AND "MARGUERITE" WAS NOT THE SISTER OF LILLIAN.

ROBERT OSWALD

MOST DEFINITELY A WITTING ACCESSORY AS HE NOT ONLY KNEW BOTH **LEE** AND **HARVEY** BUT WAS KEENLY AWARE THAT **HARVEY** WAS NOT HIS BROTHER AND THAT "MARGUERITE" WAS NOT HIS MOTHER.

MARILYN MURRETT

SHE ALSO WAS A WITTING ACCESSORY AS SHE KNEW BOTH **HARVEY** AND **LEE**. SHE ALSO KNEW THAT **HARVEY** WAS NOT HER COUSIN AND "MARGUERITE' NOT HER AUNT.

RUTH AND MICHAEL PAINE
THEY TOO WERE WITTING ACCESSORIES AS IT IS A CERTAINTY THAT THEY BOTH KNEW THE DISTINCTION BETWEEN **LEE** AND **HARVEY** AND WERE ACQUAINTED WITH BOTH MEN.

"MARGUERITE" OSWALD
MOST DEFINITELY A WITTING ACCESSORY AND AS AWARE THAT **LEE** WAS NOT HER SON AS SHE WAS AWARE THAT **HARVEY** WAS NOT HER SON. SHE WOULD ALSO BE AWARE THAT SHE WAS NOT THE MOTHER OF ROBERT, THE STEP-MOTHER OF JOHN PIC AND NOT THE SISTER OF LILLIAN MURRETT.

MARGUERITE OSWALD
SHE ALSO HAD TO HAVE BEEN AWARE THAT THERE WERE TWO LEE HARVEY OSWALDS AS SHE CERTAINLY WOULD NOTE ON NOVEMBER 22ND, 1963 THAT **HARVEY** WAS NOT HER SON AND THAT SHE BORE NO RESEMBLANCE TO "MARGUERITE." SHE WAS A WITTING ACCESSORY DUE TO HER SILENCE IN THE AFTERMATH OF THE ASSASSINATION.

CLAY SHAW
SHAW HAD CERTAINLY MET **HARVEY** IN NEW ORLEANS. BY VIRTUE OF HIS STATURE IN THE INTELLIGENCE COMMUNITY AND HIS FAMILIARITY WITH BANISTER AND FERRIE, IT IS QUITE LIKELY HE KNEW **LEE** AS WELL AND WAS A WITTING ACCESSORY.

GUY BANISTER
HE KNEW BOTH **HARVEY** AND **LEE** IN NEW ORLEANS. BANISTER WAS A WITTING ACCESSORY.

ROSCOE WHITE
KNEW BOTH **LEE** AND **HARVEY** AND WAS AN INVALUABLE WITTING ACCESSORY.

<u>LEE</u> HARVEY OSWALD
CERTAINLY KNEW OF **HARVEY** AND THAT **HARVEY** HAD BEEN TARGETED TO MELD HIS LIVE WITH HIS OWN. LIKE ROSCOE WHITE, HE WAS AN INVALUABLE AND WITTING ACCESSORY AND A SET-UP CONSPIRATOR.

LEE <u>HARVEY</u> OSWALD
CERTAINLY KNEW OF THE REAL **LEE** HARVEY OSWALD. HE MAY OR MAY NOT HAVE KNOWN THAT **LEE** WAS "HIDELL," BUT WAS UNFORTUNATELY A WITTING ACCESSORY TO HIS OWN DEMISE.

BEFORE WE PROCEED, IT IS IMPORTANT TO NOTE THAT ALTHOUGH INDIVIDUALS WERE WITTING ACCESSORIES TO THE **HARVEY**-TO-**LEE** TRANSFORMATION THIS DOES NOT IMPLY THAT THEY WERE PARTICIPATING IN THE SET-UP OF **HARVEY** AS THE ALLEGED PRESIDENTIAL ASSASSIN. THESE INDIVIDUALS WERE SIMPLY FULFILLING THEIR ROLES IN A CIA-SANCTIONED COLD WAR COUNTERINTELLIGENCE ACTIVITY TO SEND A "DEFECTOR" TO THE SOVIET UNION WHO COULD SPEAK RUSSIAN.

ARMSTRONG NOTES THE SUMMER OF 1947 AS PERHAPS THE FIRST TIME "MARGUERITE" AND **HARVEY** ARE KNOWN TO BE INHABITING THE SAME RESIDENCE. WAS THE INITIAL ARRANGEMENT BETWEEN "MARGUERITE" AND **HARVEY** DONE BY THE CIA OR DID THEIR INVOLVEMENT COME LATER? I WOULD HAVE TO THINK THAT IT ORIGINATED NO LATER THAN THAT YEAR BY VIRTUE OF THE FACT THAT THE NEW "OSWALD" FAMILY ("MARGUERITE" AND **HARVEY**) WAS CREATED BUT MORE IMPORTANTLY THAT THE MERGER OF **HARVEY**/"MARGUERITE" AND **LEE**/MARGUERITE STARTED AS WELL. MARGUERITE EKDAHL (OSWALD), **LEE'S** MOTHER, RENTED A HOME TO "MARGUERITE" AND HER "SON" **HARVEY** THAT SUMMER. THE SWITCH HAD BEGUN.

TO NOTE THIS LANDLORD/TENANT RELATIONSHIP AS A MERE COINCIDENCE WOULD BE RIDICULOUS. BUT, ONE MUST ALSO CONCEDE THAT THIS INITIAL BLENDING OF

ADDRESSES, SCHOOLS, NAMES, FAMILIES, WAS LIKELY DONE WITHOUT A DISTINCT PLAN FOR WHAT WOULD HAVE BEEN AN APPROXIMATELY 8 YEAR OLD YOUNG MAN NAMED **HARVEY**. HIS FATE AND WHAT WOULD BE EXPECTED FROM BOTH HE AND "MARGUERITE" WOULD COME LATER IN NEW YORK, NEW ORLEANS, TEXAS AND, IN **HARVEY'S** CASE, RUSSIA.

AS 1963 DRAWS NEAR HOWEVER THERE ARE NOW OTHER "PLANS" FOR THE RETURNED "DEFECTOR." THE SET-UP CONSPIRATORS HAVE ANNOINTED **HARVEY** AS THE APPARENT SOLE ASSASSIN IN THE PRESIDENT'S DEATH. "MARGUERITE" HAD MANAGED TO STAY AS CLOSE TO THE "SCRIPT" AS SHE WAS CAPABLE. HER INITIAL INVOLVEMENT WAS TO EXTEND ONLY TO THE POINT OF PORTRAYING HERSELF AS **HARVEY'S** MOTHER AND TO PROVIDE AN EXCUSE FOR HIS EARLY RELEASE FROM THE MARINE CORP PRIOR TO HIS "DEFECTION." WITH **HARVEY'S** SUCCESSFUL MISSION TO RUSSIA COMPLETE, THERE WOULD LIKELY BE LITTLE NEED TO PRESS "MARGUERITE" INTO THE SPOTLIGHT AGAIN: AT LEAST THAT WAS THE LIKELY NOTION AT THE CIA. BUT WITH **HARVEY'S** SET-UP AND DEATH AS THE ALLEGED ASSASSIN, SHE WOULD, MUCH TO THE ANXIOUS DISMAY OF THE CIA AND, TO A LESSER DEGREE THE FBI, HAVE TO BE TUTORED AND RE-REHEARSED REGARDING ALL ASPECTS OF HER LIFE AS WELL AS THE LIVES OF MARGUERITE, **LEE, HARVEY,** JOHN PIC, ROBERT OSWALD, AND THE MURRETS. WORK HISTORIES, SCHOOLS, MARRIAGES, HUSBANDS, DIVORCES, AND PLACES OF RESIDENCE WOULD HAVE TO BE BLENDED TO CONFORM TO THE COVER STORY OF A SINGLE LEE HARVEY OSWALD. IT WAS NOT A PROBLEM THE CIA/FBI FORESAW IN 1947, NOR WAS IT A TASK SUITED FOR THE WOMAN CHOSEN TO BE **HARVEY'S** MOTHER.

"MARGUERITE'S" TESTIMONY TO THE DPD, FBI, SECRET SERVICE, AND THE W.C. WOULD HAVE TO BE CAREFULLY "GUIDED" TO AID HER IN RECALLING ONLY THAT WHICH WOULD SUPPORT THE FBI/CIA/W.C. CONCLUSIONS AND PERHAPS JUST AS IMPORTANTLY NOT REVEAL WHAT WAS KNOWN AS THE "OSWALD PROJECT."

ONE HAS TO HAVE A CERTAIN AMOUNT OF SYMPATHY FOR "MARGUERITE." SHE LIED TO PROTECT A PROJECT SHE KNEW LITTLE IF ANYTHING ABOUT. SHE EMBRACED THE DESIRED NOTION THAT SHE WAS **HARVEY'S** MOTHER, THE MOTHER OF JOHN PIC (STEP-SON), AND ROBERT OSWALD, AND THE SISTER TO LILLIAN MURRET. SHE NEVER SWAYED FROM THE COVER STORY AFTER THE ASSASSINATION. COULD SHE HAVE BEEN, LIKE **HARVEY**, AN INTELLIGENCE OPERATIVE ALBEIT LOW-LEVEL? WE MAY NEVER KNOW.

MANY YEARS AGO WHEN I TITLED VERSION 1 OF MY WORK "MORE THAN MEETS THE EYE" I HAD LITTLE NOTION THAT NEARLY 30 YEARS LATER A WORK WOULD BE RELEASED THAT GENUINELY EMBRACED MY NOTION THAT **HARVEY** WAS A CIA CREATED ENIGMA. WHAT I WAS NOT PREPARED FOR HOWEVER WAS THAT THE MAN SILENCED BY JACK RUBY WAS AN IMPOSTOR. I WOULD TRULY LIKE TO SEE SOMEONE WITH THE RESEARCH SKILLS OF JOHN ARMSTRONG INVESTIGATE ROBERT OSWALD, DUTZ AND LILLIAN MURRETT, THEIR DAUGHTER MARILYN MURRETT, AND RUTH AND MICHAEL PAINE. THEY WERE ALL FULLY AWARE OF THE TWO **LEE HARVEY OSWALDS** AND REMAIN SILENT IN THAT REGARD TO THIS DAY. LOCATING AND INVESTIGATING **LEE** AND HIS MOTHER MARGUERITE WOULD BE INVALUABLE AS THEY VIRTUALLY DISAPPEARED AFTER THE ASSASSINATION.

THE TIMELINE NARRATIVE WILL BEGIN WITH **HARVEY** LEAVING NEW YORK IN THE SUMMER OF 1953 AND EVENTUALLY RETURNING TO NEW ORLEANS WITH HIS IMPOSTOR MOTHER "MARGUERITE." **LEE** AND HIS MOTHER MARGUERITE HOWEVER WILL REMAIN IN NEW YORK. I WILL HOWEVER ATTEMPT TO PREFACE THIS EVENT WITH A BRIEF SYNOPSIS OF WHAT ARMSTRONG OUTLINES AS HAVING TAKEN PLACE IN NEW YORK CITY PRIOR TO SEPTEMBER, 1953.

MAY 7TH, 1945
MARGUERITE OSWALD, **LEE'S** MOTHER, MARRIES EDWIN A. EKDAHL.

JANUARY 1947
MARGUERITE AND EDWIN EKDAHL ARE RESIDING AT HIS APARTMENT AT 1505 8TH AVENUE IN FORT WORTH, TEXAS.

JULY 7TH 1947
MARGUERITE EKDAHL (OSWALD) PURCHASES 101 SAN SABA IN BENBROOK, TEXAS. SHE IN TURNS RENTS THE HOME TO A "MARGUERITE" OSWALD AND HER SON **HARVEY**.

*DUE TO THEIR LANDLORD/TENANT RELATIONSHIP, IT IS ALMOST A CERTAINTY THAT MARGUERITE EKDAHL (OSWALD) MET "MARGUERITE" OSWALD THAT SUMMER. IT IS HOWEVER UNLIKELY THAT EITHER WERE AWARE OF THE FORCES AND EVENTS THAT WOULD SOON MELD THEIR LIVES AS WELL AS THE LIVES OF THE TWO YOUNG MEN KNOWN AS LEE HARVEY OSWALD. MARGUERITE LIKELY INTRODUCED HERSELF AS MARGUERITE EKDAHL. LITTLE WOULD BE MADE OF THEIR IDENTICAL GIVEN NAMES. ONE WOULD HAVE A SON NAMED **LEE OSWALD**, "MARGUERITE," A SON NAMED **HARVEY** OSWALD. EITHER THIS WAS A COINCIDENCE THE CIA WOULD EXPAND UPON AS THE YOUNG MEN GREW OLDER, OR A PLANNED FIRST STEP IN THE GRADUAL MELDING OF THE LIVES OF THE TWO YOUNG MEN AND THE TWO DISTINCTLY DIFFERENT FAMILIES.*

AUGUST 20TH, 1952
LEE AND MARGUERITE MOVE TO NEW YORK CITY FROM TEXAS WHERE THEY INITIALLY LIVE WITH JOHN PIC, **LEE'S** HALF-BROTHER AND HIS WIFE MARGARET AT 325 92ND ST. PIC, WHO WAS IN THE COAST GUARD, WAS STATIONED WITH THE PORT SECURITY UNIT AT ELLIS ISLAND, NEW YORK.

SEPTEMBER 1952
MARGUERITE AND **LEE** WOULD MOVE TO 1455 SHERIDAN, APT. F. MARGUERITE WOULD FIND EMPLOYMENT AT LERNER'S DRESS SHOP IN OCTOBER.

SEPTEMBER 30TH, 1952
HARVEY WOULD ENROLL IN P.S. #117. "MARGUERITE" HOWEVER WOULD LATER TELL THE W.C. THAT HER "SON" **HARVEY** HAD ENROLLED AT TRINITY EVANGELICAL LUTHERAN SCHOOL IN THE SEVENTH GRADE.

JANUARY 16TH 1953
HARVEY AND "MARGUERITE" WOULD MOVE TO 825 E. 179TH ST, APT. 3C. JANUARY 16TH WAS THE LAST DAY OF **HARVEY'S** ATTENDANCE AT P.S. #117.

FEBRUARY 7TH, 1953
MARGUERITE QUITS HER JOB AT LERNER'S DRESS SHOP.

FEBRUARY 17TH, 1953
MARGUERITE WOULD NOW FIND WORK AT MARTIN'S DEPARTMENT STORE.

FEBRUARY 1953
MARGUERITE AND **LEE** WERE VISITED BY JOHN PIC. THIS WOULD BE THE LAST TIME PIC WOULD SEE HIS HALF-BROTHER UNTIL THANKSGIVING 1962. HOWEVER THAT DAY HE WILL ACTUALLY BE GREETING **HARVEY** NOT **LEE**.

SPRING 1953
HARVEY IS PICKED UP BY AUTHORITIES FOR TRUANCY.

MARCH 23RD 1953
ACCORDING TO SCHOOL RECORDS, **LEE** IS ENROLLED IN P.S. #44 IN THE 7TH GRADE.

APRIL 15TH 1953

HARVEY IS SENT TO THE YOUTH HOUSE BECAUSE OF HIS TRUANCY. HE IS EVALUATED FOR 3 WEEKS. HE WILL NOW ATTEND P.S. # 611, A SMALL SCHOOL LOCATED AT THE YOUTH HOUSE.

APRIL 16TH 1953

ACCORDING TO ARMSTRONG, A "LEE OSWALD" IS SENT TO YOUTH HOUSE AFTER BEING PICKED UP BY AN OFFICER OF THE YOUTH DIVISION. THIS OBVIOUSLY COULD NOT BE **HARVEY** SINCE **HARVEY** HAD BEEN SENT TO THE YOUTH HOUSE THE PREVIOUS DAY. IF THIS "LEE OSWALD" IS **LEE** THEN, ACCORDING TO RECORDS, BOTH **LEE** AND **HARVEY** ARE IN YOUTH HOUSE. THE PHYSICAL DESCRIPTIONS HOWEVER OF "OSWALD" AS NOTED BY PSYCHIATRIST DR. MILTON KURIAN WHO INTERVIEWED "OSWALD" ON BEHALF OF A PROBATION OFFICER MOST CLOSELY DESCRIBE THE SHORT, 4'7", SLIGHTLY BUILT **HARVEY**.

MAY 1ST 1953

ACCORDING TO ARMSTRONG, YOUTH HOUSE PROGRESS REPORTS NOTE THAT THE "OSWALD" UNDER THEIR CARE IS "WELL DEVELOPED." ALSO, THIS SAME DATE, "OSWALD" IS EXAMINED BY YET ANOTHER YOUTH HOUSE PSYCHIATRIST WHO DESCRIBES "OSWALD" AS "WELL BUILT." THE WIDELY DIFFERENT PHYSICAL DESCRIPTIONS OF "OSWALD" IN YOUTH HOUSE LEND CREEDENCE TO THE NOTION THAT AT SOME TIME IN THE SPRING OF 1953 THAT BOTH **LEE** AND **HARVEY** WERE EITHER ADMITTED TO THE FACILITY OR EVALUATED AT THE FACILITY AS AN OUT-PATIENT.

MAY 7TH 1953

HARVEY IS RETURNED TO THE CUSTODY OF HIS "MOTHER"/CARETAKER "MARGUERITE."

*ACCORDING TO ARMSTRONG, "MARGUERITE" WAS INTERVIEWED BY JOHN CARRO, A PROBATION OFFICER AT THE YOUTH HOUSE. DURING THE INTERVIEW PRIOR TO **HARVEY'S** RELEASE, SHE MADE NUMEROUS ERRORS WHILE RECALLING HER FAMILY MEMBERS, HER MARRIAGE, HER EMPLOYMENT HISTORY, AND DETAILS OF HER "SON'S" PAST. "MARGUERITE'S" INABILITY TO ACCURATELY MELD HER AND **HARVEY'S** LIFE WITH MARGUERITE AND **LEE'S** LIFE HINTED THAT HER SELECTION AS **HARVEY'S** MOTHER MAY HAVE BEEN A POOR CHOICE. BUT, VERY LITTLE WAS AT STAKE NOW; ONLY THE RELEASE OF **HARVEY** FROM THE YOUTH HOUSE. IF SHE FALTERED NOW HOWEVER WOULD SHE PREDICTABLY ERR EVEN MORE SO WHEN THE STAKES WERE DRAMATICALLY HIGHER IN THE WAKE OF **HARVEY'S** SELECTION AS THE ACCUSED ASSASSIN OF THE PRESIDENT? IT WAS A DILLEMA THE CIA DID NOT ANTICIPATE AS THEIR USE OF **HARVEY** AND "MARGUERITE" WOULD LIKELY END AFTER **HARVEY** HAD RETURNED FROM RUSSIA.*

MAY 20TH, 1953

MARGUERITE LEAVES HER JOB AT MARTIN'S DEPARTMENT STORE.

A NEIGHBOR OF MARGUERITE'S NOTED THAT SHE WAS IRRITATED BY THE WAY THE NEW YORK CITY SCHOOL SYSTEM HAD BADGERED HER OVER THE TRUANCY OF HER SON **LEE**. LITTLE DID MARGUERITE KNOW THAT IT WAS THE TRUANCY OF **HARVEY** THAT HAD LIKELY TRIGGERED INQUIRIES REGARDING **LEE'S** ATTENDANCE.

AS PREVIOUSLY NOTED, WHILE **HARVEY** WAS ATTENDING P.S. #611 AT YOUTH HOUSE, DR. MILTON KURIAN INTERVIEWED **HARVEY** AND NOTES THAT HE IS 4'7" AND VERY THIN. BUT IN MAY 1953 P.S. #44 HEALTH RECORDS NOW SHOW **LEE** AS 5'4 1/2 INCHES AND 114 POUNDS. THE MELDING OF THE SCHOOL RECORDS OF **HARVEY** AND **LEE** HAS BEGUN. IT WAS QUITE LIKELY NOT DONE BY THOSE IN THE SCHOOL SYSTEM WITH A PARTICULAR AGENDA IN MIND. IT WOULD BE MADE TO APPEAR TO BE THE TYPE OF MISTAKE MADE WHEN TWO YOUNG MEN ATTEND THE SAME PUBLIC SCHOOL SYSTEM, HAVE MOTHERS WITH IDENTICAL NAMES, AND ARE BOTH KNOWN AS EITHER **LEE** OSWALD, **HARVEY** OSWALD, OR LEE HARVEY OSWALD. BUT THIS MELDING OF

RECORDS WAS INTENTIONAL. IT WAS THE DESIRE OF THE CIA/ONI TO GRADUALLY BLUR THE LINES BETWEEN **LEE** OSWALD AND THE RUSSIAN SPEAKING **HARVEY** OSWALD.

ON DECEMBER 2ND, 1963, THE ORIGINAL FAMILY COURT CASE FILE OF **HARVEY** OSWALD, #23979, WAS GIVEN TO THE SAIC OF THE FBI'S NEW YORK OFFICE, JOHN MALONE. IT WAS, AT JUDGE FLORENCE KELLEY'S INSISTANCE, TO BE TRANSFERRED TO THE W.C. THE CASE FILE INCLUDED BOTH SCHOOL RECORDS AND PSYCHIATRIC RECORDS. THE W.C. DID NOT RECEIVE THESE ORIGINAL RECORDS, THEY RECEIVED ONLY COPIES. THESE SAME RECORDS IN W.C. EXHIBIT FILES WERE ALSO COPIES. ONE WOULD HAVE TO QUESTION THE INTEGRITY OF THESE COPIES AND ALSO QUESTION WHY THE FBI, AS INSTRUCTED BY JUDGE KELLEY, DID NOT FORWARD THE _ORIGINAL_ CASE FILE TO THE W.C. IT IS ARMSTRONG'S OPINION THAT "COPIES" WERE GIVEN TO THE W.C. AFTER THE ORIGINALS HAD BEEN ALTERED TO MINIMIZE OR ELIMINATE THE DISCREPANCIES IN THE HEALTH RECORDS, THE PHYSICAL APPEARANCE, AND THE ATTENDANCE RECORDS OF BOTH **HARVEY** AND **LEE**. ONE COULD NOT BE 4'7 AND THIN WITH ABUNDANT DAYS OF ABSENCE AND AT THE SAME TIME BE 5'4 ½ INCHES TALL, WEIGH 117 POUNDS, AND APPARENTLY BE A STUDENT WHO ATTENDS CLASS REGULARLY.

IT IS WITH THIS UNCERTAINTY AND LATER ATTEMPT BY THE FBI – WITH A CERTAIN AMOUNT OF PRODING BY THE CIA OR ONI - TO "BLEND" **HARVEY** AND **LEE** THAT WE BEGIN OUR TIMELINE. WE WILL START WITH THE DEPARTURE OF **HARVEY** AND "MARGUERITE" FROM NEW YORK CITY. **LEE** AND HIS MOTHER WILL REMAIN IN NEW YORK CITY WHERE MARGUERITE WILL BE EMPLOYED BY LADY ORVA HOSIERY FROM MAY 1953 UNTIL DECEMBER 1953.

WITHOUT JOHN ARMSTRONG'S DILIGENT EFFORT WE WOULD KNOW LITTLE ABOUT THE CIA'S EFFORTS TO REPLACE **LEE** WITH **HARVEY** AND LITTLE ABOUT THE FBI'S EFFORTS TO TRY TO CONSOLIDATE THE LIVES OF THE TWO MEN IN THE DAYS AND WEEKS FOLLOWING THE ASSASSINATION.

CHAPTER 1: LEE AND HARVEY: PRE-MILITARY AND MILITARY CAREERS

JULY 1953
HARVEY AND "MARGUERITE" MOVE TO STANLEY, NORTH DAKOTA. **HARVEY** WOULD INTRODUCE HIMSELF TO LOCAL BOYS HIS AGE AS EITHER **"HARVEY"** OR **"HARV."**

SEPTEMBER 14TH 1953
MARGUERITE AND **LEE** REMAIN IN NEW YORK WHERE **LEE** ENTERS THE 8TH GRADE AT P.S. #44 MANHATTEN IN NEW YORK. HIS HEIGHT AND WEIGHT ARE NOTED TO BE 5'4 INCHES AND 115 POUNDS.

ARMSTRONG NOTES THAT THAT THERE WERE 5 P.S. #44 SCHOOLS IN NEW YORK.: ONE EACH IN MANHATTEN, THE BRONX, STATEN ISLAND, BROOKLYN, AND THE QUEENS. HE ALSO NOTES THAT THERE ARE SEVERAL JR. HIGH SCHOOLS AS WELL DISTRIBUTED BY THEIR BORROUGH LOCATIONS. NEW YORK WOULD PROVE TO BE AN IDEAL LOCATION TO MELD THE TWO OSWALDS.

FALL 1953
HARVEY AND "MARGUERITE" RETURN TO NEW ORLEANS. HE IS ENROLLED AS A PART-TIME STUDENT IN THE 8TH GRADE AT BEAUREGARD JR. HIGH SCHOOL. **HARVEY'S** RECORD ALSO SHOWS THAT HE HAD PREVIOUSLY ATTENDED P.S. #44, BYRON JUNIOR HIGH IN NEW YORK. P.S. #44 HOWEVER WAS KNOWN AS FARRAGUT JUNIOR HIGH. THEY MOVE INTO AN APARTMENT COMPLEX AT 126 EXCHANGE PLACE.

DECEMBER 25, 1953
MARGUERITE ENDS HER EMPLOYMENT AT LADY ORVA HOSIERY IN NEW YORK CITY.

EARLY JANUARY 1954
MARGUERITE AND **LEE** MOVE TO NEW ORLEANS. THEY MOVE IN WITH MARGUERITE'S SISTER LILLIAN MURRETT WHO RESIDES AT 757 FRENCH STREET.

JANUARY 13TH, 1954
HARVEY IS ENROLLED AS A FULL-TIME STUDENT AT BEAUREGARD JR. HIGH. HE IS ASSIGNED TO MYRA DAROUSE'S HOMEROOM. SHE WOULD RECALL **HARVEY** AS 4'6" TO 4'8" IN HEIGHT. SHE WAS 5'3 INCHES.

*EDWARD VOEBEL WAS **HARVEY'S** BEST FRIEND AT BEAUREGARD JR. HIGH. ONE DAY IN THE EARLY PART OF 1954, HE RAN TO FETCH MS. DAROUSE AS AN UPRIGHT PIANO HAD FALLEN AND TRAPPED **HARVEY** BENEATH IT. HE WOULD LATER RECALL NOT SEEING **HARVEY** AFTER JUNE OF 1954. **HARVEY** AND "MARGUERITE" WILL MOVE TO FT. WORTH THAT MONTH.*

JANUARY 1954
LEE IS ENROLLED AT BEAUREGARD JR. HIGH.

*BOTH **LEE** AND **HARVEY** ARE NOW IN NEW ORLEANS AND BOTH ARE ENROLLED IN THE SAME SCHOOL.*

FEBRUARY 1954
MARGUERITE AND **LEE** MOVE TO AN APARTMENT AT 1454 ST. MARYS.

FFEBRUARY 19TH, 1954
MARGUERITE STARTS EMPLOYMENT AT BURT'S SHOE STORE IN NEW ORLEANS. SHE WOULD LIST HER ADDRESS AS 1454 ST. MARYS. "MARGUERITE" HOWEVER IS APPARENTLY WORKING IN A BAR IN NEW ORLEANS.

JUNE 1954
HARVEY AND "MARGUERITE" MOVE TO A DUPLEX APARTMENT AT 2220 THOMAS PLACE IN FT. WORTH, TEXAS. "MARGUERITE" IS NOW EMPLOYED AS A PRACTICAL NURSE. BY NOVEMBER 22ND 1963, "MARGUERITE" HAD RETURNED TO THIS ADDRESS.

SEPTEMBER 7ᵀᴴ, 1954
LEE CONTINUES SCHOOL AT BEAUREGARD JR. HIGH IN NEW ORLEANS.

*ACCORDING TO ARMSTRONG, IN THE FALL OF 1954 **LEE** WAS INVOLVED IN A FIGHT WITH A ROBIN LEE RILEY IN WHICH HE <u>LOST A TOOTH</u>. THE FIGHT WAS WITNESSED BY EDWARD VOEBEL WHO HAD BEEN WITH **HARVEY** DURING THE PIANO EPISODE IN THE EARLY PART OF THE YEAR. **LEE'S** AUNT, LILLIAN MURRET REMEMBERED THE FIGHT AS WELL AS THE VISIT TO THE DENTIST. **LEE** HAD INDEED LOST A TOOTH. EDWARD VOEBEL KNEW BOTH **LEE** HARVEY OSWALD AND LEE **HARVEY** OSWALD. HE WOULD BE ONE OF THE VERY FEW PEOPLE OUTSIDE THE INTELLIGENCE COMMUNITY TO HAVE BEFRIENDED BOTH INDIVIDUALS. ACCORDING TO ARMSTRONG, VOEBEL HAD TAKEN ILL IN MAY OF 1971 AND TAKEN BY HIS FAMILY TO THE OCHSNER CLINIC. THE FAMILY WAS QUESTIONED AS TO WHETHER HE HAD BEEN EXPOSED TO ANY POISONS. THEY OF COURSE DENIED THAT HE HAD. HE PHONED HIS FAMILY THAT EVENING AND INFORMED THEM THAT WE WAS FEELING MUCH BETTER AND HOPED TO RETURN HOME THE NEXT DAY. HE DIED THE VERY NEXT DAY. HIS DEATH CERTIFICATE HOWEVER NOTES THAT HE DIED AT FOUNDATION HOSPITAL IN METAIRIE, LOUISIANA. VOEBEL'S FATHER FELT QUITE STRONGLY THAT HE DID NOT DIE BY NATURAL CAUSES. REMEMBER THE NAME OCHSNER CLINIC. WE WILL VISIT THIS ESTABLISHMENT LATER IN THE SUMMER OF 1963.*

*WHEN **HARVEY'S** BODY WAS EXHUMED IN 1981 NEITHER X-RAYS OR PHOTOS SHOWED A MISSING TOOTH, A CRACKED TOOTH, OR A CAPPED OR REPLACED TOOTH.*

FALL 1954
HARVEY ATTENDS THE 9ᵀᴴ GRADE AT STRIPLING JR. HIGH IN FT. WORTH BUT DOES NOT FINISH THAT FALL SEMESTER. ONCE AGAIN, **HARVEY** DOES NOT HAVE A TRANSCRIPT FROM HIS <u>PREVIOUS</u> SCHOOL, BEAUREGARD JR. HIGH IN NEW ORLEANS. THERE IS ALSO NO RECORD OF WHERE HIS STRIPLING JR. HIGH RECORD WAS <u>FORWARDED</u> TO.

*ARMSTRONG NOTES HE WAS TOLD BY FORMER STRIPLING JR. HIGH TEACHER FRANK KUDLARY THAT HE WAS VISITED BY 2 FBI AGENTS ONLY 20 HOURS AFTER THE ASSASSINATION. THEY CONFISCATED **HARVEY'S** STRIPLING SCHOOL RECORD. AS NOTED, **LEE** WAS ATTENDING BEAUREGARD JR. HIGH IN NEW ORLEANS IN THE FALL OF 1954. THE FBI COULD NOT ALLOW FOR RECORDS TO REMAIN IN CIRCULATION THAT WOULD CERTIFY THAT THE TWO YOUNG MEN WERE ATTENDING DIFFERENT SCHOOLS IN DIFFERENT CITIES.*

*THIS WOULD NOT BE THE ONLY EFFORT OF THE FBI TO MELD THE RECORDS OF **HARVEY** AND **LEE** BY ELIMINATING RECORDS THAT WOULD RAISE QUESTIONS IN REGARDS TO THEIR LOCALE. ANOTHER EFFORT WOULD BE ON DECEMBER 2ᴺᴰ, 1963 WHEN THE FBI FORWARDED TO THE W.C. ONLY DOCTORED <u>COPIES</u> OF **HARVEY'S** CASE FILE AND SCHOOL RECORDS WHEN THEY WERE SPECIFICALLY INSTRUCTED BY JUDGE FLORENCE KELLEY TO FORWARD THE ORIGINAL CASE FILE AND THE ORIGINAL SCHOOL RECORDS.*

*THE FBI, BY DEFAULT, WAS GIVEN THE UNENVIABLE TASK OF SUPRESSING THE DISCOVERY OF A **HARVEY** <u>AND</u> A **LEE** OSWALD. THIS DISCOVERY WOULD HAVE EXPOSED THE CIA'S PROJECT TO SUBSTITUTE **HARVEY** FOR **LEE** PRIOR TO **HARVEY'S** "DEFECTION" TO RUSSIA.*

*IT LIKELY IRKED HOOVER TO HAVE TO SUPRESS INFORMATION REGARDING A PROJECT SPONSORED BY THE CIA WHICH WOULD LATER APPEAR TO HAVE CULMINATED IN THE ASSASSINATION OF THE PRESIDENT. BUT, HOOVER WOULD HAVE LITTLE CHOICE AS HIS ORGANIZATION WOULD LATER UTILIZE **HARVEY** AS AN INFORMANT.*

OCTOBER 9ᵀᴴ, 1954
MARGUERITE LEAVES HER JOB AT BURT SHOES IN NEW ORLEANS.

NOVEMBER 1954
MARGUERITE AND **LEE** MOVE FROM 1454 ST. MARYS TO 1452 ST. MARYS IN NEW ORLEANS.
NOVEMBER 15TH, 1954
MARGUERITE STARTS WORK AT CHANDLER'S SHOE STORE IN NEW ORLEANS.
JANUARY 1955
LEE BEGINS THE SECOND HALF OF THE 9TH GRADE AT BEAUREGARD JR. HIGH IN NEW ORLEANS.
JANUARY 7TH, 1955
MARGUERITE LEAVES HER JOB AT CHANDLER'S SHOE STORE.
EARLY 1955
HARVEY AND "MARGUERITE" MOVE BACK TO NEW ORLEANS WHERE THEY RESIDE AT AN APARTMENT COMPLEX AT 126 EXCHANGE PLACE. BOTH APPLY FOR JOBS AT DOLLY SHOE COMPANY.

HARVEY WAS ISSUED A WORK PERMIT ON MARCH 10TH, 1955. NEITHER HIS WORK PERMIT NOR AN APPLICATION FOR DOLLY SHOE COMPANY WERE EVER LOCATED. IF THEY HAD BEEN FOUND, THEY WOULD HAVE SHOWN THAT LEE WAS ATTENDING BEAUREGARD JR. HIGH WHILE HARVEY WAS WORKING DURING THE DAY AT DOLLY SHOE. THIS OF COURSE COULD ONLY BE POSSIBLE IF THERE WERE TWO LEE HARVEY OSWALDS.

APRIL 12TH 1955
HARVEY IS FIRED BY DOLLY SHOE, AND "MARGUERITE" IS FIRED ON APRIL 14TH. SHE WILL RETURN TO WORKING AT BARS. THIS TIME SHE WILL WORK AT THE TRADE-WINDS BAR ON DECATUR ST.

ACCORDING TO ARMSTRONG, NONE OF "MARGUERITE'S" INCOME TAX RETURNS WERE EVER REVIEWED. HER JOBS AS A CARETAKER IN FAMILY HOMES AS WELL AS HER JOBS IN BARS WOULD HAVE RESULTED IN INCOME NOT LIKELY REPORTED TO THE GOVERNMENT. THE JOB AT DOLLY SHOE HOWEVER WOULD HAVE RESULTED IN REPORTED INCOME HAD SHE FILLED OUT THE BONDING FORMS REQUESTED BY DOLLY SHOE IN REGARDS TO HER JOB AS A CASHIER. REPORTED INCOME BY "MARGUERITE" WOULD NOT HAVE MATCHED REPORTED INCOME BY LEE'S MOTHER MARGUERITE WHO WAS NOW WORKING AT BURTS'S SHOE. EVEN THE ADDRESSES OF THE TWO WOMEN WERE DIFFERENT. MARGUERITE WAS RESIDING WITH LEE AT 1452 ST. MARYS, WHILE "MARGUERITE" AND HARVEY WERE RESIDING AT 126 EXCHANGE PLACE. IT IS AS CRITICAL FOR THE WORK RECORDS AND ADDRESSES OF THE REAL AND IMPOSTOR MOTHERS TO MESH AS IT IS FOR THE SCHOOL AND LATER MILITARY RECORDS OF LEE AND HARVEY TO MESH. THE FBI WAS ABLE, TO SOME DEGREE, INFLUENCE THIS BY STRICTLY CONTROLLING WHAT WAS GIVEN TO THE W.C. FOR REVIEW. THEY DID THIS BY SIMPLY NOT CONTACTING ANYONE WHO MIGHT SHED LIGHT ON THE POSSIBILITY OF TWO OSWALDS, DESTROYING ORIGINAL DOCUMENTS, AND/OR FORWARDING ALTERED "COPIES" OF THE ORIGINAL DOCUMENTS TO THE W.C. NO EMPLOYEES OF DOLLY SHOE WERE EVER INTERVIEWED BY THE W.C. IF THEY HAD, THEIR DESCRIPTION OF HARVEY (4'10", THIN, QUIET) WOULD HAVE BEEN MARKEDLY DIFFERENT FROM THE 5'4", HEAVIER, BOISTEROUS LEE. THEIR DESCRIPTION OF "MARGUERITE" WOULD ALSO HAVE BEEN MARKEDLY DIFFERENT FROM THAT OF MARGUERITE.

ARMSTRONG NOTES THAT IT WAS POSSIBLE, ACCORDING TO THE RECOLLECTION OF PFISTERER PRESIDENT LINDA FAIRCLOTH, THAT HARVEY WORKED AT PFISTERER BRIEFLY IN 1955. ARMSTRONG SURMISED THAT THIS WOULD HAVE BEEN EITHER BEFORE OR POSSIBLY AFTER HIS BRIEF EMPLOYMENT AT DOLLY SHOE.

APRIL 1955
"MARGUERITE" AND **HARVEY** MOVE OUT OF 126 EXCHANGE PLACE. ARMSTRONG NOTES THAT A "MARGUERITE OSWALD" WAS LISTED AS LIVING AT 120 NORTH TELEMACHUS IN A 1956 NEW ORLEANS PHONE DIRECTORY.

SPRING 1955
MARGUERITE AND **LEE** MOVE TO 126 EXCHANGE ALLEY IN NEW ORLEANS.

JUNE 1955
LEE GRADUATES FROM BEAUREGARD JR. HIGH.

JULY 1955
LEE MEETS DAVID FERRIE WHEN HE JOINS THE CIVIL AIR PATROL AT HIS HIGH SCHOOL. **LEE** LATER ATTENDED SOME MEETINGS AT LAKEFRONT BUT DID NOT JOIN THE CAP AT THAT TIME. LATER THAT SUMMER (JULY 27TH) HE JOINED THE CAP AT MOISANT AIRPORT. HE WAS ISSUED SERVICE NUMBER 48-4965. DAVID FERRIE INITIALLY SERVED AT THE LAKEFRONT CAP SQUADRON FROM SEPTEMBER, 1951 TO APRIL 1955. ALTHOUGH FERRIE WAS TERMINATED AS SQUADRON COMMANDER AT MOISANT ON DECEMBER 31ST,1954, HE APPARENTLY CONTINUED TO WORK WITH THE MOISANT SQUADRON DURING THE SUMMER AND FALL OF 1955. FERRIE INFLUENCED AND CLOSELY ASSOCIATED WITH CAP CADETS. HE BECAME A CONTROVERSIAL TOPIC WITH MANY OF THE PARENTS OF CAP CADETS. FERRIE'S HOMOSEXUAL INCIDENTS INVOLVING CADETS PROMPTED HIS EXPULSION FROM THE CAP IN LATE 1955. FERRIE ALSO URGED SEVERAL OF THE CADETS TO JOIN THE ARMED FORCES TO HELP FURTHER HIS CAUSE AGAINST COMMUNISM.

*IN A 1948 ARTICLE IN THE NEW YORK DAILY NEWS, THE CAP CONCEDED THAT A PLAN WAS BEING PROMOTED THAT WOULD INVOLVE ENROLLING CERTAIN PROMISING CAP RECRUITS IN THE ARMY'S COUNTER-INTELLIGENCE SCHOOL IN BALTIMORE, MARYLAND. MORE IMPORTANTLY IT NOTED THAT THESE SELECT RECRUITS "WOULD BE TAUGHT THE RUSSIAN LANGUAGE...MILITARY TACTICS....POLITICS...AND CHARACTERISTCS OF RUSSIAN PEOPLE." IN MY OPINION WHAT TOOK PLACE IN **LEE'S** SITUATION WAS SIMPLY TO REPLACE THE SOUTHERN-ACCENTED **LEE** WITH A CLOSELY RESEMBLING **HARVEY** WHO SPOKE RUSSIAN WITH LITTLE OR NO ACCENT. THIS "SWAP" IS INHERENTLY MORE LOGICAL THAN HAVING **LEE** LEARN A DIFFICULT LANGUAGE, RUSSIAN, IF IT IS THE INTENTION OF THE CIA/ONI TO SEND A LEE HARVEY OSWALD ON A BOGUS DEFECTION TO RUSSIA.*

EARLY SUMMER 1955
LEE STARTS WORK AT GERARD F. TUJAGUE, INC. HIS TASK WAS THAT OF A MESSENGER BOY FOR THE SHIPPING COMPANY. HE WOULD WORK THERE UNTIL JULY 1956. **LEE** AND MARGUERITE ARE VISITED BY HIS BROTHER, HER SON, ROBERT.

SEPTEMBER 8TH 1955
HARVEY IS ENROLLED AT WARREN EASTON HIGH SCHOOL AS A 10TH GRADER.

OCTOBER 10TH 1955
HARVEY QUITS SCHOOL AT WARREN EASTON HIGH SCHOOL.

EARLY 1956
HARVEY AND "MARGUERITE" MOVE TO SAN DIEGO, CALIFORNIA

MARCH 16TH 1956
MARGUERITE STARTS WORK AT GOLDRING'S DEPARTMENT STORE IN NEW ORLEANS.

JULY 1ST, 1956
HARVEY AND "MARGUERITE" RETURN TO TEXAS AND RESIDE AT 4936 COLLINGWOOD STREET, FT. WORTH, TEXAS.

JULY 1956
ROBERT OSWALD, **LEE'S** BROTHER, MOVES IN WITH HIS NEW "FAMILY." HE JOINS "MARGUERITE" AND **HARVEY** AT 4936 COLLINGWOOD STREET.

ROBERT WAS ENGAGED TO VADA MERCER. ACCORDING TO ARMSTRONG, HE NEVER INTRODUCED HER TO HIS "BROTHER" HARVEY OR HIS "MOTHER" THE SHORT, HEAVY "MARGUERITE." ACCORDING TO MRS. JAMES TAYLOR, THE MANAGER OF THE 4 PLEX APARTMENT, ROBERT LIVES AT THIS ADDRESS UNTIL HIS MARRIAGE TO VADA ON NOVEMBER 20TH, 1956. SHE WOULD ALSO CLAIM THAT "MARGUERITE" LIVED THERE UNTIL JULY 1ST, 1957.

JULY 31ST 1956
MARGUERITE QUITS HER JOB AT GOLDRING'S DEPARTMENT STORE.

JULY 1956
LEE LEAVES HIS JOB AT GERARD F. TUJAGUE, INC. AS BEST AS CAN BE DETERMINED, **LEE** JOINS THE MARINES THIS SAME MONTH.

SEPTEMBER 6TH 1956
HARVEY ENROLLS AT ARLINGTON HEIGHTS HIGH SCHOOL IN FORT WORTH. HIS ADDRESS IS NOTED AS 4936 COLLINWOOD STREET.

RICHARD GARRETT, A BOYHOOD FRIEND OF LEE, WOULD LATER TELL LIFE MAGAZINE THAT HE MET HARVEY AT ARLINGTON HEIGHTS. HE NOTED IN HIS INTERVIEW: "I REMEMBER I HAD TO LOOK DOWN TO TALK TO HIM (HARVEY) AND IT SEEMED STRANGE BECAUSE HE (LEE) HAD BEEN THE TALLEST, THE DOMINANT MEMBER OF OUR GROUP IN GRAMMAR SCHOOL……HE WAS VERY DIFFERENT FROM THE WAY I REMEMBERED HIM." GARRETT TOO HAD BEEN ABLE TO DISTINGUISH HARVEY FROM LEE.

SEPTEMBER 1956
MARGUERITE MOVES TO FT. WORTH, TEXAS. SHE WILL RESIDE AT 3830 W. 6TH, APT #3. ACCORDING TO LEE MCCRACKEN, WHO LIVED IN APT. #2, MARGUERITE LIVED AT THIS ADDRESS UNTIL JUNE 1957. MCCRACKEN, IN AN FBI INTERVIEW, NOTED THAT HE THOUGHT MARGUERITE WORKED AT CLYDE CAMPBELL'S MEN'S STORE IN FT. WORTH.

WE NOW HAVE MARGUERITE, HARVEY, AND "MARGUERITE" RESIDING IN FT. WORTH.

SEPTEMBER 28TH 1956
HARVEY QUITS THE 10TH GRADE AT ARLINGTON HEIGHTS HIGH SCHOOL.

OCTOBER 3RD 1956
ALLEGEDLY INSPIRED BY A PAMPHLET OF JULIUS AND ETHEL ROSENBERG AND THEIR CONSEQUENT EXECUTION IN 1953 FOR SPYING, **HARVEY** WROTE THE SOCIALIST PARTY OF AMERICA FOR INFORMATION ON THEIR YOUTH LEAGUE. HE DECLARED HE WAS A MARXIST.

OCTOBER 15TH 1956
HARVEY IS INTERVIEWED PRIOR TO HIS MARINE CORP ENLISTMENT. HIS HEIGHT AND WEIGHT ARE RECORDED AS 5'8" AND 135 POUNDS.

THESE MEASUREMENTS HOWEVER ARE MUCH MORE CONSISTENT WITH LEE'S PHYSIQUE.

OCTOBER 17TH 1956
WITH "MARGUERITE'S" CONSENT, **HARVEY** JOINS THE MARINES AT AGE 17.

OCTOBER 24TH, 1956
HARVEY SIGNS THE FORMS WHICH OFFICIALLY MAKE HIM A MARINE RECRUIT. ON A "REPORT OF MEDICAL HISTORY" FORM WAS WRITTEN "MASTOID OPERATION, 1945." IT HOWEVER LISTED NO SCARS FROM THIS SURGERY. **LEE** HAD A LONG SCAR ON HIS

NECK FROM HIS MASTOIDECTOMY IN 1946. **HARVEY** HAD NO SCAR SINCE HE HAD NOT HAD THIS SURGERY PERFORMED.

*JUST AS SCHOOL RECORDS WERE MANIPULATED, THE PHYSICAL DESCRIPTION OF **HARVEY** NOW CLOSELY PARALLELS THAT OF **LEE**. THE NOTED MASTOID OPERATION HOWEVER IS NOT CORROBORATED BY THE REQUISITE SCAR SINCE **HARVEY** DID NOT ACTUALLY HAVE MASTOID SURGERY.*

OCTOBER 26TH 1956

HARVEY ARRIVES IN SAN DIEGO, CALIFORNIA FOR COMMENCEMENT OF BASIC TRAINING. HE IS ASSIGNED TO 2ND RECRUIT TRAINING BATTALION. ONCE AGAIN, HIS HEIGHT AND WEIGHT ARE RECORDED AS 5'8 AND 135 POUNDS.

NOVEMBER 20TH, 1956

ROBERT OSWALD AND VADA ARE MARRIED.

JANUARY 18TH 1957

HARVEY COMPLETES BASIC TRAINING IN SAN DIEGO.

JANUARY 20TH 1957

HARVEY THEN GOES TO CAMP PENDLETON FOR COMBAT TRAINING AS PART OF "A" COMPANY, 1ST BATTALION, 2ND INFANTRY TRAINING REGIMENT.

*ALLEN R. FELDE, A FELLOW MARINE RECRUIT WHO SERVED WITH **HARVEY** IN BOTH BOOT CAMP AND COMBAT TRAINING, RECALLED THAT **HARVEY** WOULD LEAVE WITH OTHER RECRUITS WHEN GOING ON LIBERTY BUT WOULD THEN GO OFF ALONE ONCE THE DESTINATION WAS REACHED.*

FEBRUARY 18, 1957

ROSCOE WHITE JOINS THE MARINE CORP.

FEBRUARY 27TH 1957

HARVEY TAKES 18 DAYS LEAVE ALLEGEDLY TO VISIT "MARGUERITE" IN FT. WORTH. NEIGHBORS OF "MARGUERITE" HOWEVER DO NOT RECALL **HARVEY** VISITING HIS "MOTHER." **HARVEY** APPARENTLY WOULD RETURN TO CAMP PENDLETON WHERE HE WOULD REMAIN UNTIL MAY 13TH, 1957.

MARCH 1957

LEE ALSO TAKES LEAVE APPROXIMATELY THE SAME TIME AND VISITS MARGUERITE, ALSO IN FT. WORTH. SHE IS STILL RESIDING AT 3830 W. 6TH, AND STILL EMPLOYED BY CAMBELL'S MEN'S STORE. LEE MCCRACKEN, MARGUERITE'S NEIGHBOR NOTED THAT **LEE** HAD INDEED VISITED MARGUERITE DURING THIS TIME FRAME.

*ARMSTRONG'S BOOK NOTES THAT BY THIS TIME, **LEE** HAS APPARENTLY JOINED THE MARINES AS WELL. HE DOES HOWEVER NOT NOTE EXACTLY **WHEN** **LEE** JOINED. HE NOTES THAT **LEE** WAS APPARENTLY AT A MAC AIR FORCE FACILITY AT EL TORO CALIFORNIA FROM OCTOBER-DECEMBER 1956, AND AT CAMP PENDLETON IN JANUARY, 1957 ATTACHED TO THE 5TH MARINE DIVISION AS A RADIO COMMUNICATOR.*

*IF THIS IS TRUE THEN **LEE** WOULD HAVE HAD TO JOIN THE MARINES IN JULY OF 1956 AFTER HE QUIT HIS JOB AT GERARD F. TUJAGUE, INC. TO ALLOW FOR AN APPROXIMATELY 11 WEEK STINT IN BOOT CAMP.*

*THE PROBABILITY OF **LEE"S** MARINE ENLISTMENT IN JULY 1956 IS ALSO SUPPORTED BY FRANK DIBENEDETTO, A SUPERVISOR AT TUJAGUE. HE TOLD ARMSTRONG THAT HE BELIEVED IT WAS THE SUMMER OF 1956 AS "IT WAS HOT AND HE **(LEE)** SAID HE WAS QUITTING TO JOIN THE MARINES." GERALD TUJAGUE ALSO NOTED TO THE FBI THAT **LEE** HAD QUIT TO JOIN THE MARINES.*

*ROBERT OSWALD, IN AN FBI INTERVIEW, NOTED THAT HE HAD SEEN HIS BROTHER **LEE***

ONLY ONCE DURING **LEE'S** MARINE CORP ENLISTMENT.. HE NOTED THAT IS WAS ABOUT 4 MONTHS AFTER HIS (ROBERT'S) WEDDING TO VADA. **LEE** AND ROBERT HAD GONE HUNTING ON THIS VISIT AND ROBERT TOOK A PHOTO OF **LEE** HOLDING HIS HUNTING RIFLE. HE WAS HOLDING IT IN HIS <u>LEFT</u> HAND. **HARVEY** WAS <u>RIGHT</u> HANDED.

ARMSTRONG CONTENDS THAT WHEN **LEE** FINISHED THIS LEAVE PERIOD, HE NOW HAD IN HIS POSSESSION **HARVEY'S** MARINE CORP FILE. BUT, **HARVEY'S** ENLISTMENT PHOTOGRAPH HAD BEEN REPLACED BY A PHOTO OF **LEE** THAT HAD BEEN TAKEN ON DECEMBER 26TH, 1956 AT EL TORO. IT WOULD NOW BE **LEE** WHO REPORTS TO JACKSONVILLE, FLORIDA.

MARCH 18TH 1957
LEE REPORTS TO MARINE AVIATION DETACHMENT, NAVAL AIR TECHNICAL TRAINING CENTER IN JACKSONVILLE, FLORIDA FOR AVIATION FUNDAMENTAL SCHOOL CLASS P.

MAY 1ST 1957
LEE COMPLETES AVIATION FUNDAMENTAL SCHOOL. HE FINISHED 46 OUT OF 54 STUDENTS. HE IS PROMOTED TO PRIVATE 1ST CLASS.

LATE APRIL 1957
HARVEY COMPLETES COMBAT TRAINING AT CAMP PENDLETON HE DISPLAYED LEFT WING VIEWS AND CRITICIZED EISENHOWER'S HANDLING OF THE KOREAN SITUATION

MAY 6TH, 1957
LEE WAS THEN SENT TO KESSLER AIR FORCE BASE IN BILOXI, MISSISSIPPI WHERE HE ATTENDS RADAR SCHOOL. HE FINISHED 7TH IN HIS CLASS OF 30. HE SPENT HIS WEEKENDS IN NEW ORLEANS BUT ONLY VISITED HIS RELATIVES THERE ONE TIME. KEEP IN MIND HOWEVER THAT ALTHOUGH **LEE'S** MOTHER, MARGUERITE, WAS LIVING IN FT. WORTH. HIS AUNT, LILLIAN MURRETT WAS LIVING IN NEW ORLEANS.

MAY 13TH 1957
HARVEY (ACCORDING TO ARMSTRONG) ATTENDS AVIATION FUNDAMENTAL SCHOOL AT KEESLER AIR FORCE BASE IN BILOXI, MISSISSIPPI.

ACCORDING TO ARMSTRONG, **LEE** WAS ASSIGNED TO THE 3383RD STUDENT SQUADRON, GRADUATED FROM COURSE AB27073 IN CLASS 08057, AND WAS ASSIGNED MOS 6747.

HARVEY (ACCORDING TO THE W.C.) WAS ASSIGNED TO THE 3381 STUDENT SQUADRON, GRADUATED FROM COURSE AB27330 IN CLASS 24047 AND WAS ASSIGNED MOS 6741.

APRIL 23RD 1957
ROBERT AND VADA OSWALD MOVE TO 7313 DAVENPORT IN FT. WORTH.

JUNE 17TH 1957
LEE COMPLETED THE RADAR SCHOOL PROGRAM AT KEESLER AFB IN BILOXI.

JUNE 19TH – JULY 8TH 1957
LEE VISITS HIS MOTHER WHO IS STILL RESIDING AT 3830 W. 6TH, FT. WORTH TEXAS. MARGUERITE'S NEIGHBOR, LEE MCCRACKEN, RECALLED **LEE'S** VISIT TO HIS MOTHER.

JUNE 24TH 1957
HARVEY COMPLETES THE AVIATION FUNDAMENTAL SCHOOL PROGRAM AT KESSLER AFB IN BILOXI.

JUNE 25 – JULY 8TH
HARVEY TAKES 14 DAYS LEAVE. ONCE AGAIN HE VISITS HIS "BROTHER" ROBERT AND HIS "MOTHER", "MARGUERITE" IN FT. WORTH. "MARGUERITE" HAD MOVED FROM 4936 COLLINGWOOD TO 1031 W. 5TH IN FT. WORTH ON JULY 1ST.

JULY 9TH 1957
LEE IS TRANSFERRED TO THE MARINE AIR STATION AT EL TORO IN SANTA ANA, CALIFORNIA WHERE HE IS ASSIGNED TO THE 4TH REPLACEMENT BATTALION. ON MEDICAL/DENTAL PAPERWORK HE NOTED HIS MOTHER'S ADDRESS AS 3830 W. 6TH ST. FORT WORTH, TEXAS.

JULY 22ND, 1957
HARVEY REPORTS TO AVIATION ELECTRONICS SCHOOL IN MEMPHIS, TENNESSEE.

JULY 26TH, 1957
ROSCOE WHITE REPORTS FOR DUTY AT THE MARINE AIR STATION IN EL TORO.

*WE WILL INTRODUCE ROSCOE WHITE IN FURTHER DETAIL LATER IN THE TIMELINE. THIS IS THE FIRST OF MANY INSTANCES WHERE HE WILL BE IN CLOSE PROXIMITY TO EITHER **HARVEY** OR **LEE** OR BOTH MEN PRIOR TO NOVEMBER 22ND, 1963.*

AUGUST 1957
HARVEY COMPLETES THE AVIATION ELECTRONICS SCHOOL IN MEMPHIS.

*ARMSTRONG CONTENDS THAT IN SEPTEMBER, 1957, **HARVEY** WENT TO YELLOW SPRINGS, OHIO AND BRIEFLY ATTENDED ANTIOCH COLLEGE. RUTH PAINE, WHO WE WILL INTRODUCE LATER AS WE APPROACH NOVEMBER, 1963, GRADUATED FROM ANTIOCH COLLEGE IN 1955. SHE STUDIED RUSSIAN, AND WAS A MEMBER OF THE YOUNG FRIENDS MOVEMENT, AN ORGANIZATION THAT ENGAGED IN "PEN PAL" CORRESPONDENCE WITH RUSSIAN STUDENTS IN AN EFFORT TO INVITE THEM TO VISIT AND STUDY THE AMERICAN WAY OF LIFE. IT IS QUITE POSSIBLE, ACCORDING TO ARMSTRONG, THAT RUTHS PAINE'S FIRST MEETING OR CORRESPONDANCE WITH **HARVEY** OCCURRED IN 1957, NOT LATER IN 1963.*

AUGUST 22ND 1957
LEE DEPARTED SAN FRANCISCO ON THE USS BEXAR FOR ATSUGI, JAPAN, MARINE AIR CONTROL SQUADRON WHERE CIA SPONSORED U-2 FLIGHTS TOOK PLACE OVER RUSSIA AND CHINA. ROSCOE WHITE IS ABOARD THE BEXAR AS WELL.

SEPTEMBER 12TH 1957
LEE'S SHIP ARRIVES AT YOKOSUKA, JAPAN.

SEPTEMBER 13TH 1957
LEE ARRIVES IN ATSUGI, JAPAN WHERE HE IS ASSIGNED TO THE MACS1 SQUADRON MARINE AIR GROUP II, 1ST MARINE AIRCRAFT WING. ROSCOE WHITE IS SENT TO OKINAWA AND ASSIGNED TO OBSERVATION SQUADRON 2 OF MAG 16.

*ARMSTRONG'S BOOK DETAILS COMMENTS ABOUT **LEE** BY THOSE WHO SERVED WITH HIM AT ATSUGI. AS A RULE, THEY CONSISTENTLY DESCRIBED **LEE** AS AN AVID READER, ABOUT 35 POUNDS HEAVIER AND 3-4 INCHES TALLER THAN THE LATER ACCUSSED ASSASSIN **HARVEY**, AND THAT HE DID <u>NOT</u> DISCUSS POLITICS, STUDY RUSSIAN, OR READ COMMUNIST PERIODICALS. HE WAS KNOWN TO DRINK, SOMETIMES TO EXCESS. IT WAS HOWEVER NOTED THAT HE POINTEDLY DID NOT LIKE TO BE CALLED "**HARVEY**" OR "**HARV.**" HE WAS KNOWN TO FIGHT ANYONE WHO REFERRED TO HIM BY THAT NAME. **LEE** CLEARLY KNEW THAT IN ORDER FOR HIM TO BE RECALLED AS "**LEE**" AND **LEE** ONLY HE HAD TO DISTINGUISH HIMSELF FROM "**HARVEY.**" THOSE WHO KNEW **LEE** FOR AN EXTENDED PERIOD OF TIME WERE NOT INTERVIEWED BY THE W.C. THOSE WHO KNEW **LEE** ONLY FLEETINGLY HOWEVER WERE INTERVIEWED.*

SEPTEMBER 1957
"MARGUERITE" MOVES FROM 1031 W. 5TH, FT. WORTH, TEXAS TO THE HOTEL SENATOR AT 210 DAUPHINE STREET, NEW ORLEANS, LOUISIANA.

OCTOBER 1957

HARVEY ARRIVES IN NEW ORLEANS. HE TAKES A JOB AT PFISTERER DENTAL LAB LOCATED AT 227 DAUPHINE STREET. THE LAB IS ACROSS THE STREET FROM THE HOTEL SENATOR. **HARVEY** SOON BECOMES FAST FRIENDS WITH PALMER MCBRIDE, ONE OF THE DELIVERY BOYS. EMPLOYEES OF PFISTERER NOTED THAT **HARVEY** AND MCBRIDE OFTEN DISCUSSED AND ARGUED OVER WHICH WAS THE BETTER POLITICAL SYSTEM, CAPITALISM OR COMMUNISM. **HARVEY** ALSO MENTIONED THAT HE WOULD LIKE TO ASSASSINATE PRESIDENT EISENHOWER. THIS WAS A REMARK HE HAD MADE ONCE BEFORE DURING THE SUMMER OF 1953 WHEN HE WAS IN STANLEY, NORTH DAKOTA. ON A VISIT TO **HARVEY'S** APARTMENT, MCBRIDE WAS SHOWN **HARVEY'S** COLLECTION OF COMMUNIST BOOKS AND LITERATURE. MCBRIDE'S DESCRIPTION OF "MARGUERITE" WAS THAT OF A WOMAN WHO WAS HEAVY, SHORT, AND HAD GREY HAIR.

OCTOBER 1957

MARGUERITE LEAVES CAMPBELL'S MEN'S STORE IN FT. WORTH AND STARTS WORK FOR "WELCOME WAGON" FOR THE CITY OF FT. WORTH.

OCTOBER 27TH 1957

LEE ACCIDENTALLY WOUNDS HIMSELF IN THE LEFT HUMERUS JUST ABOVE THE ELBOW WITH AN ILLEGALLY POSSESSED 22 CALIBER DERRINGER. HE WAS TAKEN TO THE NAVAL HOSPITAL IN YOKOSUKU. THE WOUND WAS CLOSED, BUT THE SLUG WAS NOT REMOVED.

*FELLOW MARINES OWEN DEJANOVICH AND DANIEL P. POWERS BOTH NOTED IN WARREN COMMISSION TESTIMONY THAT THEY FELT THAT **LEE** HAD SHOT HIMSELF INTENTIONALLY.*

NOVEMBER 4TH 1957

LEE RETURNS TO THE HOSPITAL WHERE THE SLUG IS REMOVED AND THE WOUND STITCHED. **LEE** IS LEFT WITH TWO SCARS, ONE OF ENTRANCE AND ONE OF EXIT. AT **HARVEY'S** AUTOPSY ON NOVEMBER 24TH, 1963, THERE WAS NO NOTATION OF ANY SCARS ON HIS LEFT UPPER ARM. THERE WERE NO SCARS NOTICED BY MORTICIAN PAUL GROODY DURING THE PREPARATION OF **HARVEY'S** BODY FOR BURIAL.

NOVEMBER 20TH 1957 TO MARCH 6TH 1958

LEE AND HIS UNIT ARE IN THE SOUTH CHINA SEA AND THE PHILLIPINE ISLANDS ON BOARD THE USS TERRELL COUNTY. THEY ARE PARTICIPATING IN A MILITARY EXERCISE CODENAMED "PHIBLINK." IN JANUARY 1958, **LEE** IS ON BOARD THE LST CAYUGA COUNTY. IN FEBRUARY 1958, **LEE'S** UNIT WOULD BOARD THE USS WEXFORD COUNTY TO PARTICIPATE IN ANOTHER EXERCISE CODENAMED "OPERATION STRONGBACK."

DECEMBER 1957

BY THE CHRISTMAS SEASON OF 1957, MARGUERITE HAD LEFT "WELCOME WAGON" AND STARTED WORK AT PAUL'S SHOE STORE AT 606 HOUSTON IN FT. WORTH.

MARCH 7TH 1958

LEE'S UNIT SAILS BACK TO JAPAN ABOARD THE USS WEXFORD COUNTY.

MARCH 18TH 1958

LEE'S UNIT RETURNS TO YOKOSUKA, JAPAN AND THEN BUSSED TO ATSUGI, JAPAN.

MARCH 1958

DAVID FERRIE RETURNS TO THE CAP AT LAKEFRONT. THE NEW COMMANDER, ROBERT MORRELL, CONVINCES THE EXECUTIVE OFFICER OF LAKEFRONT TO OVERLOOK FERRIE'S PAST INDISCRETIONS.

SPRING 1958

HARVEY CONTINUES HIS EMPLOYMENT AT PFISTERER DENTAL LAB IN NEW ORLEANS. HE APPARENTLY CONTINUED TO VOICE HIS SUPPORT OF COMMUNISM. ACCOMPANIED BY PALMER MCBRIDE, THEY VISITED THE HOME OF WILLIAM WULF, A FRIEND OF

MCBRIDES. **HARVEY'S** LOUD AND VOCAL SUPPORT OF COMMUNISM PROMPTED WULF'S FATHER TO THROW HIM OUT.

EARLY 1958
MARGUERITE LEAVES PAUL'S SHOE STORE AND NOW WORKS FOR FAMILY PUBLICATIONS IN FT. WORTH.

APRIL 11TH 1958
LEE IS COURT-MARTIALED FOR HIS ILLEGAL POSSESSION OF A FIREARM WITH WHICH HE WOUNDED HIMSELF ON OCTOBER 27TH, 1957. HE IS FINED $50, BUSTED TO PRIVATE, AND ASSIGNED TO THE BRIG FOR 20 DAYS. THE BRIG SENTENCE HOWEVER IS SUSPENDED.

*PRIOR TO THE COURT-MARTIAL, **LEE** MET WITH CIVILIAN ATTORNEY FRANKLIN E. WARREN. **LEE** EXPLAINED TO WARREN WHAT HAD OCCURRED ON OCT 27TH WHEN HIS DERRINGER DISCHARGED WOUNDING HIM IN THE LEFT UPPER ARM JUST ABOVE THE ELBOW. **LEE** TOLD THE ATTORNEY THAT THE INCIDENT WAS NO ACCIDENT. WARREN TOLD **LEE** THAT HE DID NOT THINK THE CHARGES AGAINST HIM WARRANTED THE SERVICES OF AN ATTORNEY.*

*THE FINAL REPORT OF THE COURT-MARTIAL NOTED THAT THE WEAPON HAD ACCIDENTALLY DISCHARGED (THIS CONTRADICTS WHAT **LEE** HAD TOLD ATTORNEY WARREN), AND THAT THE INJURY "WAS SUSTAINED IN THE LINE OF DUTY." I FIND THIS PARTICULARLY INTERESTING SINCE THE REPORT ALSO STATED THAT HIS "POSSESSION OF THE WEAPON VIOLATED ARTICLE 92 OF THE UCMJ." HOW COULD POSSESSION OF A NON-GOVERNMENT ISSUED WEAPON RESULT IN AN INJURY THAT WAS "SUSTAINED IN THE LINE OF DUTY?"*

APRIL 14TH, 1958
LEE APPLIED FOR A 1 YEAR EXTENSION OF OVERSEAS DUTY THAT WOULD EXTEND HIS STAY UNTIL MAY, 1959.

MAY 1958
HARVEY AND "MARGUERITE" MOVE TO FT. WORTH, TEXAS. THEY WOULD LIVE AT 3006 BRISTOL ROAD. "MARGUERITE", ACCORDING TO ARMSTRONG, MAY HAVE WORKED FOR A SHORT PERIOD OF TIME AT WASHER BROTHERS DEPARTMENT STORE. **HARVEY** APPARENTLY WAS HIRED AT A SHOE STORE.

JUNE 20th 1958
LEE ALLEGEDLY POURS A DRINK OVER MARINE SERGEANT MIGUEL RODRIGUEZ AT A SQUADRON PARTY AT THE BLUEBIRD CAFÉ. IN WHAT WAS TO BE HIS 2ND COURT MARTIAL, **LEE** WOULD CLAIM THAT "MY DRINK FELL OUT OF MY HAND." THE COURT AGREED THAT THE DRINK INCIDENT WAS AN ACCIDENT.

JUNE 29TH 1958
AS A RESULT OF THE GUN INCIDENT AT ATSUGI AND THE RECENT INCIDENT AT THE BLUEBIRD CAFÉ, **LEE** WAS ALLEGEDLY PUT IN THE BRIG FOR A TOTAL OF 45 DAYS. HE WAS ALSO FINED $55. ONE INMATE SAW **LEE** ONLY ONCE IN THAT 45 DAY PERIOD AND HE NOTED THAT **LEE** WAS WEARING CIVILIAN CLOTHES AT THE TIME. NO OTHER INMATE COULD RECALL SEEING **LEE** EVEN ONCE.

SUMMER 1958
MARGUERITE IS NOW EMPLOYED AT COX'S DEPARTMENT STORE IN FT. WORTH.

JULY 12TH 1958
LEE IS TREATED FOR HEMORRHOIDS AT THE ATSUGI HOSPITAL.

JULY 18TH, 1958
LEE'S REQUEST FOR AN OVERSEAS EXTENSION IS REVOKED.

AUGUST 10TH 1958
LEE IS TREATED FOR AN APPARENT STD.

AUGUST 13TH 1958
LEE WAS APPARENTLY "RELEASED" FROM THE BRIG AND RETURNED TO ACTIVE DUTY.

AUGUST 28TH 1958
"MARGUERITE" BEGINS WORK AT A KING CANDY BOOTH AT THE FAIR RIDGLEA DEPARTMENT STORE IN FT WORTH.

ACCORDING TO ARMSTRONG, HARVEY HAS NOW ARRIVED AT ATSUGI.

*HARVEY'S ON-AGAIN-OFF-AGAIN MILITARY ENLISTMENT IS NOW IN "ON"MODE. HE COMPLETED AVIATION ELECTRONICS SCHOOL IN AUGUST 1957. BUT ACCORDING TO ARMSTRONG, HE DIDN'T RETURN TO DUTY UNTIL AUGUST 1958, AN ABSENCE OF 12 MONTHS. THIS SAME 12 MONTH PERIOD HOWEVER WAS A BUSY TIME FOR **LEE**. IN AUGUST 1957, HE LEAVES FOR ATSUGI, JAPAN. IN OCTOBER 1957 HE WOUNDS HIMSELF. IN APRIL 1958 HE IS COURT MARTIALED FOR THE SELF INFLICTED WOUND. IN JUNE 1958, HE HAS THE ALTERCATION WITH THE MARINE SERGEANT. AND, IN AUGUST 1958, HE RECEIVES HIS INITIAL TREATMENT FOR AN STD. THESE INCIDENTS OF COURSE WILL LATER BE ATTRIBUTED TO **HARVEY** WHO WAS STATESIDE VIRTUALLY THE ENTIRE TIME THAT **LEE** WAS IN ATSUGI.*

SEPTEMBER 1958
FIRST LT. WILLIAM TRAIL, WHO WAS ASSIGNED TO LEE'S MACS-1 UNIT NOTED THAT WHILE PREPARATIONS WERE BEING MADE TO DEPART FOR TAIWAN THAT LEE WAS STILL IN THE BRIG. LEE HOWEVER HAD BEEN "OFFICIALLY" RELEASED FROM THE BRIG ON AUGUST 13TH IF ONE ASSUMES THAT HE HAD ACTUALLY BEEN CONFINED. ARMSTRONG CONTENDS THAT LEE'S DETENTION WAS FOR THE SOLE PURPOSE OF DELAYING HIS DEPARTURE FROM ATSUGI SO THAT HE WOULD DEPART ATSUGI FOR TAIWAN WITH A DIFFERENT GROUP OF MARINES WHO DID NOT KNOW LEE.

SEPTEMBER 14TH 1958
HARVEY JOINS HIS UNIT ON BOARD THE USS SKAGIT, AN ATTACK CARGO SHIP. THEY ARE SET TO SAIL THIS DAY FROM YOKOSUKA, JAPAN TO THE SOUTH CHINA SEA.

SEPTEMBER 16TH 1958
LEE REPORTS TO THE INFIRMARY AT ATSUGI AND IS TREATED FOR A STD. HE WOULD RE-VISIT THE INFIRMARY ON THE 20TH, THE 22ND, THE 23RD, THE 24TH, AND THE 29TH OF SEPTEMBER.

*LEE REPORTEDLY HAD A "FLING" WITH A JAPANESE "HOSTESS AT THE QUEEN BEE NAMED MIDORII. ONE EVENING AT THE QUEEN BEE COST MORE THAN HIS ENTIRE MONTHLY SALARY. **LEE'S** ENCOUNTERS WITH THIS "HOSTESS" MAY HAVE RESULTED IN A MILD FORM OF GONORHHEA. HIS SERVICE RECORD ADDRESSED THIS MATTER BY NOTING "ORIGIN: IN LINE OF DUTY, NOT DUE TO OWN MISCONDUCT." THE HOSTESSES AT THE QUEEN BEE WERE KNOWN TO BE COLLECTING INFORMATION FOR THE JAPANAESE COMMUNIST ORGANIZATION IN JAPAN.*

*IT IS LIKELY THAT **LEE** WAS INTICING HOSTESSES WITH INFORMATION ON THE U-2 PROVIDED BY THE ONI, COURTESY OF THE CIA. ONE WOULD HAVE TO SURMISE THAT **LEE** WAS INDEED ON ASSIGNMENT THUS THE FINANCIAL ABILITY TO FREQUENT THE QUEEN BEE AND THE ABILITY OF HIS HANDLERS TO PROVIDE THE NOTATION REGARDING THE GONORHHEAL INFECTION IN HIS SERVICE RECORD THUS MINIMIZING THE EFFECTS OF WHAT WOULD NORMALLY BE A PUNISHABLE OFFENSE.*

*G. P. HEMMING, STATIONED WITH **LEE** IN JAPAN, WAS RECRUITED INTO THE ONI AND SUSPECTED **LEE** WAS AS WELL. IT WOULD NOT BE TOO FAR FETCHED TO INCLUDE*

*ROSCOE WHITE IN THIS RECRUITMENT EFFORT. WE WILL LEARN MORE ABOUT WHITE AND HIS IMPORTANCE IN THE FATE OF **HARVEY** IN LATER CHAPTERS.*

*IN SPITE OF THESE INCIDENTS, **LEE** WAS ABLE TO KEEP HIS SECURITY CLEARANCE. **LEE'S** MILITARY RECORDS REFLECT ONLY A CONFIDENTIAL CLEARANCE. HOWEVER MARINES WHO WORKED WITH **LEE** WOULD NOTE THAT THE <u>MINIMUM</u> CLEARANCE FOR HIS WORK WOULD BE A SECRET CLEARANCE.*

*LATER, FIRST LT. JOHN DONOVAN, WHO WORKED WITH **HARVEY** AT THE MARINE AIR FACILITY AT SANTA ANA, WOULD BE QUESTIONED BY THE WARREN COMMISSION. HE WAS AMAZED THAT HE WAS NOT ASKED SPECIFICALLY ABOUT THE U-2 OR **LEE'S** INVOLVEMENT WITH THAT OPERATION. **LEE** HAD INDEED WORKED WITH THE NEW MPS/6 HEIGHT-FINDING RADAR. DONOVAN EVEN WENT AS FAR AS TO ASK A COMMISSION LAWYER "DON'T YOU WANT TO KNOW ANYTHING ABOUT THE U-2?" HE WAS TOLD IN NO UNCERTAIN TERMS THAT HIS TESTIMONY WAS FINISHED.*

*BY ELIMINATING ANY DISCUSSION ABOUT **LEE** AND HIS **MARINE CORP** RELATIONSHIP WITH THE U-2, THE COMMISSION ESSENTIALLY ELIMINATED ANY FUTURE DISCUSSION OF **HARVEY'S** <u>CIVILIAN</u> RELATIONSHIP WITH THE U-2 AND ANY DISCUSSION OF **HARVEY'S** "DEFECTION" AND ITS POSSIBLE CONNECTION WITH GARY POWERS MAY 1960 U-2 FLIGHT.*

SEPTEMBER 19TH, 1958
HARVEY ARRIVES AT KAOHSIUNG, TAIWAN ABOARD THE USS SKAGIT.

SEPTEMBER 24TH, 1958
THE USS SKAGIT, WITH **HARVEY** ABOARD ARRIVES IN HONG KONG.

SEPTEMBER 25TH 1958
JOHN PIC, **LEE'S** HALF BROTHER, RE-ENLISTS IN THE AIR FORCE. HE LISTS HIS ADDRESS AS "C/O M. OSWALD, 3006 BRISTOL ROAD, FT. WORTH TEXAS."

*THIS HOWEVER IS THE ADDRESS OF THE IMPOSTOR "MARGUERITE." FOR PIC TO MAKE A MISTAKE OF THIS MAGNITUDE, ONE HAS TO SUSPECT THAT HE IS NOW ON BOARD WITH THE EFFORT TO MERGE **HARVEY** WITH **LEE**.*

SEPTEMBER 1958
ROSCOE WHITE IS GRANTED EMERGENCY LEAVE TO RETURN STATESIDE.

SEPTEMBER 30TH 1958
HARVEY'S UNIT, ON BOARD THE USS SKAGIT, ARRIVES IN PINGTUNG, NORTH TAIWAN.

OCTOBER 4TH 1958
HARVEY, WHILE ON GUARD DUTY IN TAIWAN, FIRED UPON MEN IN THE WOODS WHO WOULD NOT RESPOND TO HIS VERBAL "CHALLENGE" OF "WHO GOES THERE?" WHEN THE DUTY OFFICER. LT. CHARLES RHODES RACED TO THE SCENE HE FOUND **HARVEY** DISTRESSED AND VISIBLY SHAKEN.

OCTOBER 4TH 1958
LEE ONCE AGAIN VISITS THE INFIRMARY IN ATSUGI IN REGARD TO HIS STD.

OCTOBER 6TH 1958
HARVEY IS TRANSFERRED TO A REAR UNIT OF THE MACS-1 AT ATSUGI TO PREPARE FOR HIS RETURN STATESIDE.

*ARMSTRONG NOTES THAT **LEE'S** <u>MEDICAL</u> RECORDS CLEARLY SHOW THAT HE IS IN ATSUGI, WHILE **HARVEY'S** <u>MILITARY</u> RECORDS SHOW HIS SEPTEMBER 14TH THRU OCTOBER 5TH TRIP TO TAIWAN AND HONG KONG.*

*ARMSTRONG ALSO NOTES THAT THERE IS NO RECORD OF **HARVEY** BEING TRANSFERRED FROM TAIWAN BACK TO YOKOSUKA AND IN TURN ATSUGI. THE DISTANCE FROM PINGTUNG, NORTH TAIWAN TO YOKOSUKA IS APPROXIMATELY 1,000 MILES.*

IT IS IN TAIWAN THAT ARMSTRONG SUGGESTS THAT LEE <u>HARVEY</u> OSWALD ASSUMES THE IDENTITY OF <u>LEE</u> HARVEY OSWALD.

EARLY OCTOBER, 1958
JOHN PIC RECEIVED ORDERS TO JAPAN.

OCTOBER 1958
ACCORDING TO ARMSTRONG **HARVEY** WAS TRANSFERRED STATESIDE AND SENT TO THE MACS 9 FACILITY AT SANTA ANA, CALIFORNIA. IT IS NOT CERTAIN THE NUMBER OF THE QUANSET HUT HE WAS INITIALLY ASSIGNED TO.

*MACK OSBORNE, WHO WAS STATIONED WITH **HARVEY** AT SANTA ANA, NOTED THAT **HARVEY** TOLD HIM THAT WHILE IN JAPAN, HE HAD GOTTEN INTO A FIGHT AND STRUCK A MAN WITH A BOTTLE AND THAT HE HAD FOUGHT WITH A GUARD WHILE IN THE BRIG. **HARVEY**, WHO DID NOT FIGHT, HAD CLEARLY NOT PARTICIPATED IN EITHER OF THESE ACTS. IT WAS **LEE** WHO HAD INCIDENTS SUCH AS THESE. **HARVEY** WAS ATTEMPTING TO "BLUR THE LINES" BETWEEN HIS BEHAVIOUR AND **LEE'S**. HE ALSO TOLD OSBORNE THAT ONE DAY HE WOULD BE WELL KNOWN. ONE IS TEMPTED TO BELIEVE THAT THIS WAS IN REFERENCE TO HIS UPCOMING "DEFECTION."*

*SERGEANT ERWIN LEWIS WAS ALSO AT MACS 9 WITH **HARVEY**. HE NOTED THAT "IT WAS A MATTER OF COMMON KNOWLEDGE THAT LEE **HARVEY** OSWALD COULD READ, WRITE, AND SPEAK RUSSIAN."*

*SERGEANT DENNIS CALL, WHO SERVED WITH **HARVEY** AT SANTA ANA, NOTED THAT WHILE **HARVEY** WOULD NOT DISCUSS HIS LIFE PRIOR TO THE MARINE CORP, HE DID OFFEER THAT WHILE IN JAPAN HE HAD ACCIDENTLY SHOT HIMSELF IN THE FOOT. ONCE AGAIN, **HARVEY** WAS ATTEMPTING TO "MELD" THE TWO OSWALDS. BUT, HE MISTAKENLY "REMEMBERED" A <u>FOOT</u> WOUND ALTHOUGH **LEE** HAD ACCIDENTLY SHOT HIMSELF IN THE LEFT UPPER <u>ARM</u>.*

OCTOBER 6TH 1958
LEE MAKES A FOLLOW-UP VISIT TO THE INFIRMARY REGARDING HIS STD. HE IS PLACED ON GENERAL DUTY IN SUB-UNIT 1 OF MAG GROUP II, FLEET AIRCRAFT WING.

OCTOBER 7TH- 13TH 1958
LEE UNDERGOES A SIGMOIDOSCOPY ON OCTOBER 10TH. HE HAD BEEN DIAGNOSED WITH HEMORRHOIDS IN JULY. HIS HOSPITAL STAY WOULD LAST 1 WEEK. HE APPARENTLY ALSO RECEIVED ANOTHER FOLLOW-UP TREATMENT FOR HIS STD DURING THIS STAY.

OCTOBER 16TH 1958
LEE RECEIVES THE FIRST OF 2 FLU SHOTS PRIOR TO RETURNING TO THE U.S.

OCTOBER 24TH 1958
LEE HAS YET ANOTHER FOLLOW-UP VISIT FOR HIS STD.

OCTOBER 27TH 1958
LEE RECEIVES THE 2ND IN HIS SERIES OF FLU SHOTS.

OCTOBER 30TH 1958
JOHN PIC AND HIS WIFE ARRIVE IN FT. WORTH TEXAS TO VISIT HIS STEP-MOTHER, MARGUERITE. THE PICS ARE ENROUTE TO SAN FRANCISCO, CALIFORNIA WHERE HE IS TO CATCH A FLIGHT TO JAPAN. HE WOULD LATER TELL THE W.C. THAT HIS STEP-MOTHER WAS WORKING AT COX'S DEPARTMENT STORE IN FT. WORTH. HE WAS CORRECT IN THAT MARGUERITE WAS INDEED WORKING AT THAT DEPARTMENT

STORE. BUT, "MARGUERITE", WHOSE ADDRESS HE GAVE AS HIS OWN UPON RE-ENLISTMENT IN THE AIR FORCE ON SEPTEMBER 25TH, WAS WORKING AT THE KING CANDY COUNTER AT THE FAIR RIDGLEA DEPARTMENT STORE. ONCE AGAIN, AS ARMSTRONG POINTS OUT, PIC CONFUSED HIS REAL STEP-MOTHER MARGUERITE WITH HIS NOW TO BE ACCEPTED IMPOSTOR STEP-MOTHER "MARGUERITE."

*I THINK PIC EITHER UNDERESTIMATED THE IMPORTANCE OF AHDERING TO THE SCRIPT REGARDING MERGING **HARVEY** TO **LEE**, OR WAS SIMPLY HAVING THE SAME DIFFICULTY "MARGUERITE" HAD IN KEEPING THE EVER-CONFUSING STORYLINE STRAIGHT.*

OCTOBER 1958
ROSCOE WHITE REMAINS STATESIDE AND IS ASSIGNED TO THE 11TH MARINE REGIMENT AT CAMP PENDLETON, CALIFORNIA.

NOVEMBER 2ND, 1958
LEE LEAVES JAPAN TRAVELING ON THE USS BARRET FROM YOKOSUKO, JAPAN TO SAN FRANCISCO. THE VOYAGE WOULD TAKE 2 WEEKS.

NOVEMBER 10TH, 1958
JOHN PIC ARRIVES IN JAPAN

NOVEMBER 15TH, 1958
LEE'S SHIP ARRIVES IN SAN FRANCISCO FROM YOKOSUKO, JAPAN

. NOVEMBER 19TH, 1958
LEE BEGINS A LENGTHY LEAVE PERIOD. THIS LEAVE PERIOD WILL LAST 30 DAYS.

***LEE'S** WHERABOUTS DURING THIS ENTIRE LEAVE PERIOD ARE A BIT SKETCHY. ROBERT OSWALD TOLD THE FBI ON NOVEMBER 22ND, 1963 THAT HE AND **LEE** HAD HUNTED ON ROBERT'S IN-LAWS FARM IN FT. WORTH ON TWO OCCASSIONS. THE FIRST WAS MARCH 1957, THE SECOND WAS LIKELY DURING LATE NOVEMBER OR EARLY DECEMBER, 1958 WHEN **LEE** REVISITED FT. WORTH AFTER RETURNING FROM JAPAN.*

DECEMBER 5TH 1958
"MARGUERITE" SUSTAINED AN "INJURY" WHEN A BOX OF CANDY FELL OFF A SHELF AND HIT HER FACE AND NOSE. SHE WAS STILL WORKING FOR KING CANDY AT THE FAIR RIDGLEA DEPARTMENT STORE IN FT WORTH. SHE WAS EXAMINED ON DECEMBER 6TH AND AGAIN ON THE 8TH. THERE WERE NO FRACTURES OF HER NOSE NOR HER CERVICAL SPINE. BOTH AREAS WERE X-RAYED.

*ARMSTRONG POINTS OUT THAT NEITHER ROBERT NOR **LEE**, WHO WERE BOTH IN FT. WORTH AT THE TIME, ASSISTED "MARGUERITE" IN ANY WAY. IN FACT, THERE WAS NO INDICATION THAT SHE HAD BEEN VISITED AT <u>ANY</u> TIME BY HER "SONS" FROM OCTOBER 1956 THRU AUGUST 1959. THE EXPLANATION IS SIMPLE; THEY WERE NOT HER SONS. THEY WERE THE SONS OF THE TALL, DARK-HAIRED, THIN, MARGUERITE.*

DECEMBER 8TH 1958
LEE OPENS A SAVINGS ACCOUNT AT THE WEST SIDE STATE BANK IN FT. WORTH WITH A $200 DEPOSIT. HE WOULD LIST AS HIS ADDRESS THE MARINE CORP AIR STATION AT SANTA, ANA, CALIFORNIA WHERE HE WAS TO REPORT AT THE END OF HIS LEAVE PERIOD. HE DID <u>NOT</u> HOWEVER OFFER A LOCAL ADDRESS IN FT. WORTH.

*ONE COULD HARDLY EXPECT **LEE** TO LIST BOTH HIS MOTHER MARGUERITE'S ADDRESS AND "MARGUERITE'S" ADDRESS AS BOTH OF THEM WERE NOW LIVING IN FT. WORTH. ONE WOULD SUSPECT THAT **LEE** WAS AWARE OF THE IMPOSTOR "MARGUERITE" AND ALSO AWARE THAT IT WAS IMPERATIVE THAT HE BE ASSOCIATED ONLY WITH HIS REAL MOTHER MARGUERITE WHILE **HARVEY** WOULD BE ASSOCIATED WITH THE IMPOSTOR "MARGUERITE."*

DECEMBER 19TH 1958

LEE REPORTS TO MACS 3 IN EL TORO, CALIFORNIA.

ARMSTRONG'S BOOK, WITH BOTH **LEE** AND **HARVEY** AT NEARBY BASES IN CALIFORNIA, NOTES THE DISTINGUISABLE TRAITS AND CHARACTERISTICS THAT EACH OF OUR "OSWALDS" POSSESS.

LEE: IS NOW ABOUT 5'11 INCHES TALL AND WEIGHS ABOUT 150. HE IS KNOWN TO BE BOISTEROUS, AGGRESSIVE IN NATURE WITH A PENCHANT FOR FIGHTING AND DRINKING TO EXCESS ON OCCASION. HE IS AN AVID READER, DID NOT CARE TO DISCUSS POLITICS, NEVER DISCUSSED COMMUNISM, DID NOT POSSESS ANY COMMUNIST LITERATURE, AND DID NOT SPEAK, READ, OR WRITE RUSSIAN. HE APPARENTLY ENJOYED THE COMPANY OF WOMEN TO THE DEGREE THAT HE ACQUIRED AN STD WHILE OVERSEAS. HE WAS ALSO THE PROUD OWNER OF TWO DISTINCT SCARS IN HIS UPPER LEFT ARM AS THE RESULT OF THE ACCIDENTAL DISCHARGE OF AN UNAUTHORIZED WEAPON WHILE IN JAPAN AND HAS A BROKEN FRONT TOOTH. **LEE** WAS KNOWN TO BE A BETTER THAN AVERAGE SHOT WHEN USING A RIFLE. HIS SHOOTING SCORE WAS A 229, WHICH WOULD QUALIFY AS A HIGH SCORE IN THE "EXPERT" CATEGORY. **LEE'S** NICKNAME WAS "OZZIE."

HARVEY: IS ABOUT 5'8 INCHES TALL AND WEIGHS ABOUT 130 POUNDS. HE IS SCHOLARLY IN HIS DISCUSSIONS ABOUT COMMUNISM AND POLITICS, READS, SPEAKS, AND WRITES RUSSIAN, AND HAS IN HIS COLLECTION SEVERAL BOOKS ON COMMUNISM AND VARIOUS COMMUNIST PERIODICALS. HE IS QUIET, NOT KNOWN TO FIGHT, DOES NOT DRINK, AND APPARENTLY SPENT LITTLE TIME WITH WOMEN IN HIS OVERSEAS ASSIGNMENTS. HE LOVED CLASSICAL MUSIC, RUSSIAN RECORDS, AND AS A RESULT OF HIS LEFTIST LEANINGS OBTAINED THE NICKNAME "OSWALDOVICH." **HARVEY** WAS KNOWN TO BE A POOR SHOT. ON A QUALIFICATION SHOOTING WITH A RIFLE, **HARVEY** WOULD SCORE A 191, JUST 1 POINT ABOVE THE MINIMUM QUALIFYING SCORE FOR A MARKSMAN. MARKSMAN IS THE LOWEST CATEGORY OF QUALIFICATION WITH SHARPSHOOTER A GRADE HIGHER REQUIRING A SCORE OF 215, AND EXPERT THE HIGHEST CATEGORY REQUIRING A SCORE OF 225.

THE FBI WOULD CONSISTENTLY AVOID FORWARDING ANY DOCUMENTATION AND RECORDS OF FBI INTERVIEWS OF THOSE ACQUAINTED WITH MARGUERITE AND **LEE** TO THE W.C. THAT WOULD ENDANGER THEIR EFFORTS TO BLEND THE LIVES OF THE REAL **LEE** HARVEY OSWALD AND HIS MOTHER MARGUERITE WITH THE LIVES OF THE IMPOSTOR LEE **HARVEY** OSWALD AND HIS ALLEGED MOTHER, "MARGUERITE."

THE ABILITY OF THE W.C. TO REACH A CONCLUSION THAT WOULD STAND THE TEST OF TIME WAS DOOMED FROM THE START. ARMSTRONG IS CORRECT IN ASSUMING THAT <u>SOMEONE</u> KNEW THAT **LEE** AND **HARVEY** WERE TWO DISTINCT INDIVIDUALS AND CONVINCED THE FBI THAT IT WAS OF THE UTMOST IMPORTANCE THAT THEY "BLEND" THEIR LIVES AND MILITARY CAREERS IN A FASHION THAT SUITED A THIRD PARTY. THAT THIRD PARTY WAS THE CIA.

DECEMBER 20TH 1958

LEE, ACCORDING TO ARMSTRONG, WAS SENT TO A MARINE BASE AT LAKE MEAD, NEVADA. ALTHOUGH **LEE** HAD THE NAME "BENJAMIN" STENCILED ON HIS UNIFORM, HE APPARENTLY WENT BY THE NAME "HARVEY." HIS LAST NAME WAS KNOWN TO BE OSWALD, AND HE WAS KNOWN TO BE FROM TEXAS.

LEE HAD PREVIOUSLY SHOWN A STRONG DESIRE NOT TO BE REFERRED TO AS "HARVEY" OR EVEN' "HARV." HE WOULD THREATEN TO FIGHT ANYONE WHO HAD CALLED HIM BY EITHER OF THESE NAMES. AT LAKE MEAD HOWEVER HE SEEMED TO RELAX SOMEWHAT LIKELY BECAUSE HE KNEW THAT NO ONE HERE WOULD HAVE HAD ANY CONTACT WITH HARVEY AND THEREFORE WOULD NOT RECALL TWO "OSWALDS."

DECEMBER 22ND, 1958

LEE RETURNS TO EL TORO.

DECEMBER 22ND, 1958
HARVEY IS TRANSFERRED TO QUANSET HUT #34 AT THE MACS 9 FACILITY AT SANTA ANA, CALIFORNIA.

CHAPTER 2: A BRIEF LIFE AS A CIVILIAN

JANUARY 9TH, 1959
"MARGUERITE" VISITS A DR. MILTON GOLDBERG. SHE IS TRYING TO SEE IF SHE QUALIFIES FOR SOME SORT OF "COMPENSATION" FOR HER EARLIER INJURY.

JANUARY 19TH 1959
ACCORDING TO ARMSTRONG, **LEE** DEPARTS EL TORO ONCE AGAIN AND IS SENT TO VINCENT AIR FORCE BASE IN YUMA, ARIZONA.

JANUARY 23RD 1959
LEE RETURNS TO EL TORO.

JANUARY 30TH 1959
"MARGUERITE" RETURNS TO DR GOLDBERG'S OFFICE. THIS TIME SHE MENTIONS THAT "HER SON WANTED TO DEFECT TO RUSSIA."

*"MARGUERITE" MUST HAVE HAD SOME IDEA JUST WHAT WOULD TRANSPIRE REGARDING HER "SON" **HARVEY**. SHE MAY HOWEVER BEEN A BIT PREMATURE IN ANNOUNCING HIS DEPARTURE AS **HARVEY** WOULD NOT "DEFECT" UNTIL SEPTEMBER.*

1959
MARGUERITE RETURNS TO NEW ORLEANS. ACCORDING TO ARMSTRONG, SHE WOULD CONTINUE TO WORK IN VARIOUS CLOTHING STORES.

FEBRUARY 1959
"MARGUERITE" WOULD VISIT A SECOND DOCTOR. SHE WAS STILL SEEKING SOME SORT OF COMPENSATION FOR HER INJURY.

FEBRUARY 6TH, 1959
"MARGUERITE" FINALLY GETS WHAT SHE CONSIDERS HER JUST REWARD. SHE IS AWARDED $140 FOR 5 LOST WEEKS OF WORK. SHE WOULD ALSO CHANGE RESIDENCES MOVING TO 313 TEMPLETON DRIVE, FT. WORTH.

FEBRUARY 25TH 1959
HARVEY TOOK A RUSSIAN LANGUAGE APTITUDE TEST SHOWING LIMITED SKILLS IN THE LANGUAGE.

HIS LOW SCORE WAS LIKELY ORCHESTRATED BY HIM TO DISGUISE THE FACT THAT HIS RUSSIAN SPEAKING ABILITY WAS QUITE GOOD AS HE WAS FLUENT IN BOTH RUSSIAN AND HUNGARIAN.

*AFTER THE ASSASSINATION, LANGUAGE EXPERTS AT SOUTHERN METHODIST UNIVERSITY STUDIED TAPED RECORDINGS OF **HARVEY'S** VOICE. IT WAS THEIR OPINION THAT HIS NATIVE LANGUAGE WAS NOT ENGLISH.*

*WARREN COMMISSION COUNSEL J. LEE RANKIN WOULD LATER ATTEMPT TO "FIND OUT WHAT HE (OSWALD) STUDIED AT THE MONTEREY SCHOOL OF THE ARMY IN THE WAY OF LANGUAGES." APPARENTLY THERE WAS A STRONG SUSPICION BY COMMISSION MEMBERS THAT **HARVEY** HAD BEEN GIVEN <u>FORMAL</u> TRAINING IN RUSSIAN PRIOR TO HIS DISCHARGE.*

*FELLOW MARINE MACK OSBORNE, IN AN AFFADAVIT TO THE WARREN COMMISSION, STATED"I ONCE ASKED OSWALD (**HARVEY**) WHY HE DID NOT GO OUT LIKE THE OTHER MEN. HE REPLIED THAT HE WAS SAVING HIS MONEY...AND ONE DAY HE WOULD DO SOMETHING WHICH WOULD MAKE HIM FAMOUS. IT IS MY BELIEF THAT HE (**HARVEY**) HAD HIS TRIP TO RUSSIA IN MIND WHEN HE MADE THAT STATEMENT."*

HARVEY CONTINUED TO OPENLY READ EVERYTHING RUSSIAN, OPENLY LISTEN TO RUSSIAN RECORDS AND READ LEFT WING LITERATURE. WHEN HIS SUPERVISOR, CAPTAIN ROBERT BLOCK WAS INFORMED, HE DID NOTHING.

MARCH 1959
ACCORDING TO MARINE CORP RECORDS A "LEE HARVEY OSWALD" WAS DISCHARGED AT THE MARINE CORP STATION AT EL TORO. IF THIS IS TRUE, THEN THE OSWALD DISCHARGED WOULD HAVE HAD TO HAVE BEEN **LEE**.

MARCH 1ST 1959
HARVEY IS PROMOTED TO PRIVATE FIRST CLASS.

MARCH 11TH 1959
JACK RUBY IS INTERVIEWED BY THE FBI. HE AGREES TO THEIR REQUEST THAT HE BECOME AN INFORMANT FOR THE AGENCY. HIS CONTACT AGENT WAS CHARLES FLYNN.

MARCH 19TH 1959
HARVEY APPLIED TO ALBERT SCHWEITZER COLLEGE IN CHURWALDEN, SWITZERLAND. HE CLAIMED A PROFICIENCY IN RUSSIAN ON HIS APPLICATION

ARMSTRONG'S REMAKABLY DETAILED BOOK NOTES THAT THE COLLEGE'S SOLE SOURCE OF FUNDING WAS VIA THE "FRIENDS OF ALBERT SCHWEITZER COLLEGE" INCORPORATED IN NEW YORK STATE IN 1953. A PERCIVAL F. BRUNDAGE WAS PRESIDENT OF THE FRIENDS OF ASC FROM 1953 TO 1958. BRUNDAGE WAS A TOP NOTCH ACCOUNTANT. A NEW YORK TIMES ARTICLE IN 1973 NOTED THAT BRUNDAGE APPARENTLY ACTED ON BEHALF OF THE CIA IN ITS PURCHASE OF SOUTHERN AIR TRANSPORT IN MIAMI. SAT WAS A CIA FRONT AND WAS USED TO CARRY OUT VARIOUS CIA MISSIONS IN THE CONGO, CENTRAL AMERICA, AND THE CARIBBEAN. ARMSTRONG NOTES THAT THE COLLEGE, IN EXCHANGE FOR ITS COOPERATION WITH CERTAIN CIA ACTIVITIES, MAY WELL HAVE BEEN FUNDED IN PART BY THE CIA.

MARCH 23RD 1959
HARVEY TAKES THE TESTS REQUIRED TO OBTAIN A GED DIPLOMA.

SPRING 1959
HARVEY, WHO WAS STILL AT MACS 9 IN SANTA ANA, AND 3 OTHER MARINES VISITED TIJUANA, MEXICO. THEY VISITED THE FLAMINGO BAR AND ENDED THE EVENING IN A NEARBY HOTEL.

*ON THE WEEKEND OF THE ASSASSINATION, **HARVEY**, IN CUSTODY, FREELY ADMITTED TO HAVING BEEN IN TIJUANA. HE HOWEVER VEHEMENTLY DENIED EVER HAVING BEEN IN MEXICO CITY.*

APRIL 7TH 1959
THE RESULTS OF **HARVEY'S** GED TEST ARE RELEASED. HE HAD PASSED.

APRIL 28TH 1959
THE FBI VISITS RUBY IN REGARDS TO HIS CONFIDENTIAL INFORMANT STATUS.

MAY 9TH 1959
"MARGUERITE" CONTINUES TO VISIT PHYSICIANS REGARDING HER DECEMBER 1958 INJURY. THIS DAY SHE HAS X-RAYS PERFORMED AT THE FORT WORTH OSTEOPATHIC HOSPITAL.

MAY 27TH 1959
"MARGUERITE" WAS SENT BY THE INSURANCE COMPANY FOR A RE-EVALUATION AT THE GOLDBERG CLINIC. IN A LETTER TO THE INSURANCE COMPANY, DR. GOLDBERG NOTED "I COULD FIND NO ORGANIC CHANGES THAT COULD ACCOUNT FOR HER SYMPTOMS." NEEDLESSS TO SAY, LIBERTY INSURANCE SUSPENDED HER MONTHLY STIPEND FOR LOST WAGES.

*ARMSTRONG NOTES THAT "MARGUERITE'S" NUMEROUS ATTEMPTS TO HAVE HER MALADY DECLARED PERMANENT HAVE NOTHING TO DO WITH MONEY. HER PURPOSE IS TO GIVE THE MARINE CORP A REASON TO RELEASE HER "SON" **HARVEY** FROM ACTIVE DUTY PRIOR TO HIS UPCOMING "DEFECTION."*

MAY 1959

"MARGUERITE MOVES TO YET ANOTHER APARTMENT. THIS ONE IS LOCATED AT 3124 W. 5TH IN FT. WORTH.

JUNE 5TH 1959

THE FBI CONTACTS RUBY ONCE AGAIN.

JUNE 18TH 1959

THE FBI ONCE AGAIN CONTACTS RUBY.

JUNE 19TH 1959

HARVEY SENDS A $25.00 ENROLLMENT DEPOSIT TO ALBERT SCHWEITZER COLLEGE. IT WAS HIS LAST CONTACT WITH THE SCHOOL. HE WOULD START SCHOOL IN THE SPRING TRIMESTER COMMENCING APRIL 12TH, 1960 AND ENDING JUNE 27TH, 1960.

JUNE 28TH 1959

LEE IS NOTED TO HAVE CHECKED IN AT THE MCBEATH ROOMING HOUSE AT 2429 NAPOLEON AVENUE IN NEW ORLEANS. HE WAS TRYING TO JOIN ONE OF THE MANY CUBAN EXILE GROUPS IN NEW ORLEANS.

JULY 6TH 1959

HARVEY VISITS THE RED CROSS AT EL TORO AIR STATION. HE INFORMS THEM OF "MARGUERITE'S" INJURY AND IS TOLD TO FILL OUT AN APPLICATION FOR A "Q" ALLOTMENT. HE ALSO <u>INQUIRES</u> ABOUT OBTAINING A HARDSHIP DISCHARGE.

*AS ARMSTRONG POINTS OUT, **HARVEY**, IN ATTEMPTING TO "MELD" THE WORK HISTORIES OF THE REAL MARGUERITE AND HIS "MARGUERITE" MAKES 2 CRITICAL ERRORS. HE NOTES TO THE RED CROSS THAT "MARGUERITE" WAS INJURED AT COX'S DEPARTMENT STORE IN FT. WORTH AND THAT SHE HAD FILED SUIT AGAINST THE STORE. "MARGUERITE" HOWEVER WAS INJURED AT FAIR RIDGLEA DEPARTMENT STORE AND WAS WORKING FOR KING CANDY WHEN SHE WAS INJURED. SHE DID NOT FILE SUIT UNTIL AUGUST 11TH, NEARLY 5 WEEKS <u>AFTER</u> **HARVEY'S** VISIT TO THE RED CROSS.*

JULY 9TH 1959

"MARGUERITE" IS VISITED BY THE RED CROSS IN FT. WORTH. THEY WERE SENT ON BEHALF OF THE RED CROSS AT EL TORO AFTER **HARVEY** HAD VISITED THERE. SHE INFORMS THEM THAT SHE WISHES TO OBTAIN FOR HER "SON" **HARVEY** A HARDSHIP DISCHARGE DUE TO HER "INJURY."

JULY 10TH 1959

"MARGUERITE" IS ONCE AGAIN VISITED BY THE RED CROSS WHO OFFER THEIR ASSISTANCE IN REGARDS TO HER EFFORT TO OBTAIN A HARDSHIP DISCHARGE FOR HER "SON."

JULY 21ST 1959

FBI CONTACTS RUBY FOR THE FOURTH TIME SINCE HIS AGREEING TO BECOME A CONFIDENTIAL INFORMANT.

AUGUST 6TH 1959

RUBY IS CONTACTED BY THE FBI FOR THE 5TH TIME.

AUGUST 8TH 1959

RUBY ENTERS CUBA FLYING FROM NEW ORLEANS ACCORDING TO CUBAN TOURISM AUTHORITIES. HE WOULD VISIT SANTOS TRAFFICANTE WHO WAS INCARCERATED IN CUBA. RUBY WOULD VISIT TRAFFICANTE SEVERAL TIMES OVER THE NEXT 2 WEEKS. BUT THESE VISITS APPARENTLY TOOK PLACE AS A RESULT OF SEVERAL INDIVIDUAL TRIPS TO CUBA.

AUGUST 17TH 1959
HARVEY NOW FILES FOR A DEPENDANCY DISCHARGE ON THE GROUNDS THAT HIS "MOTHER" NEEDS HIS SUPPORT DUE TO AN INJURY SHE HAD SUSTAINED AT WORK ON DECEMBER 5TH, 1958.

AUGUST 18TH 1959
SANTOS TRAFFICANTE IS RELEASED FROM HIS QUARTERS AT TRESCARNIA, CUBA.

AUGUST 19TH 1959
THE REVIEWING OFFICER WHO ENDORSED **HARVEY'S** APPLICATION FOR DEPENDANCY DISCHARGE STATED: "A GENUINE HARDSHIP EXISTS IN THIS CASE. AND, IN MY OPINION, APPROVAL OF THE "Q" (QUARTERS ALLOTMENT) WILL NOT SUFFICIENTLY ALLEVIATE THIS SITUATION."

*IN ESSENCE, THE REVIEWING OFFICER WAS SUGGESTING THAT **HARVEY** BE GRANTED A DISCHARGE INSTEAD OF MERELY AWARDING FINANCIAL SUPPORT VIA THE "Q", QUARTERS ALLOTMENT. ONE WOULD SUSPECT THAT THE REWIEWING OFFICER'S OPINION WAS INFLUENCED BY THE ONI/CIA WHO HAD PLANS FOR THE SOON TO BE DISCHARGED **HARVEY**.*

*INTERESTINGLY AND NOT SURPRISINGLY, THE FORT WORTH RED CROSS DISAGREED WITH THIS ENDORSEMENT. THEY STATED A "Q"(QUARTERS) ALLOTMENT WAS ALL THAT WAS NECESSARY TO ASSIST MARGUERITE, NOT A HARDSHIP DISCHARGE FOR HER "SON" **HARVEY**.*

AUGUST 21ST 1959
RUBY, APPARENTLY HAVING RETURNED FROM CUBA, VISITS HIS DALLAS BANK AND ACCESSES HIS SAFETY DEPOSIT BOX.

AUGUST 27TH 1959
THE DEPENDANCY DISCHARGE BOARD RECOMMENDS THAT **HARVEY'S** REQUEST FOR HARDSHIP DISCHARGE BE APPROVED.

AUGUST 31ST 1959
FBI SA CHARLES W. FLYNN CONTACTS RUBY. THIS IS THE 6TH CONTACT BETWEEN THE FBI AND RUBY.

AUGUST 31ST 1959
LEE **HARVEY** OSWALD'S DEPENDANCY DISCHARGE IS APPROVED.

*IN 1978, THE HSCA INTERVIEWED LT. COLONEL BOLLISH KOZAK WHO HAD SERVED ON THE DEPENDANCY DISCHARGE BOARD THAT REVIEWED **HARVEY'S** REQUEST. HE NOTED THAT IT NORMALLY TOOK 3 TO 6 MONTHS FOR THIS PROCESS.*

*THE EFFORTS OF "MARGUERITE" AND **HARVEY** TO OBTAIN HIS DISCHARGE WERE ENHANCED BY THE EXTREMELY COOPERATIVE DISCHARGE BOARD. IT TOOK **HARVEY** ONLY 2 WEEKS TO RECEIVE APPROVAL FOR HIS DISCHARGE. UNDOUBTEDLY THE MARINE CORP WAS REQUESTED BY THE CIA TO EXPEDITE THE MATTER. THEY HAD PLANS FOR **HARVEY**.*

AUGUST 1959
LEE IS NOTED BY ARMSTRONG TO BE IN CORAL GABLES, FLORIDA. HE APPARENTLY IS WORKING WITH ANTI-CASTRO CUBAN FRANCISCO RODRIGUEZ TAMAYO WHO HEADED ONE OF THE CIA SPONSORED ANTI-CASTRO TRAINING CAMPS AT LAKE PONCHARTRAIN IN LOUISIANA.

SEPTEMBER 3RD 1959
HARVEY RECEIVES HIS DISCHARGE PHYSICAL. HE IS LISTED AS 5'11" AND 150 POUNDS. ALSO NOTED WAS A SCAR FROM A GUNSHOT WOUND TO THE LEFT ELBOW.

*THE SCAR NOTATION IS OF COURSE ONE THAT APPLIES TO **LEE**, NOT **HARVEY**. THE PHYSICAL HEIGHT AND WEIGHT ALSO MORE CLOSELY DESCRIBE **LEE**. THE MILITARY*

CONTINUES TO ASSIST IN REGARDS TO "MELDING" THE SERVICE RECORDS OF THE TWO "OSWALDS."

SEPTEMBER 4TH 1959

HARVEY IS INFORMED THAT HE WOULD BE RELEASED ON SEPTEMBER 11TH. HE ALSO APPLIES FOR A PASSPORT IN SANTA ANA AND RECEIVES PASSPORT #1733242 6 DAYS LATER ON SEPTEMBER 10TH. THE PASSPORT IS ISSUED BY THE LOS ANGELES PASSPORT OFFICE.

ONE HAS TO QUESTION WHY **HARVEY** WOULD EVEN NEED A PASSPORT IF HIS DEPENDANCY DISCHARGE WAS DESIGNED TO ALLOW HIM TO PERSONALLY ASSIST "MARGUERITE." IT IS QUITE OBVIOUS THAT NEITHER **HARVEY** NOR THE ONI/CIA HAD ANY INTENTION THAT **HARVEY** REMAIN IN FORT WORTH AFTER HIS DISCHARGE. IT IS ALSO OBVIOUS THAT BOTH "MARGUERITE" AND **HARVEY** WERE AWARE THAT HIS DISCHARGE WAS SOLELY FOR THE PURPOSE OF HIS UPCOMING "DEFECTION."

ARMSTRONG NOTES THAT THE PHOTO ATTACHED TO THE PASSPORT APPLICATION WAS NOT A PHOTO OF **HARVEY**, BUT A PHOTO OF **LEE**. **HARVEY** LISTED "MARGUERITE'S" DOB AS 3/7/1909. HE LISTED HIS "FATHER'S" DOB AS 8/12/1908. HIS MOTHER'S ("MARGUERITE'S") DOB WAS INCORRECT BY 2 YEARS; HIS "FATHER'S" DOB INCORRECT BY 12 YEARS. **LEE'S** FATHER'S ACTUAL DOB WAS 3/4/1896 AND **LEE'S** MOTHER'S DOB 7/19/1907. SINCE THE PHOTO ON THE APPLICATION WAS **LEE**, NOT **HARVEY**, IT WOULD SEEM THAT THOSE INVOLVED IN THE EVENTUAL "MORPHING" OF **HARVEY** TO **LEE** WOULD HAVE BEEN MORE PRECISE THAN ALLOWING **HARVEY** TO BE SO FAR OFF ON THE DATES OF BIRTH OF HIS "PARENTS." APPARENTLY JOHN PIC, "MARGUERITE" AND **HARVEY** ARE NOT THE ONLY ONES HAVING DIFFICULTY KEEPING THE STORY STRAIGHT. OH WHAT A TANGLED WEB WE WEAVE.

HARVEY DID NOT USE HIS BIRTH CERTIFICATE WHEN APPLYING FOR THE PASSPORT. HE USED A DOD1173 CARD. THIS CARD WAS A MARINE CORP RESERVE, I.E. "INACTIVE" ID CARD. BUT, HE SHOULD NOT HAVE RECEIVED THIS CARD UNTIL HIS DISCHARGE DATE OF SEPTEMBER 11TH, 10 DAYS _AFTER_ HE HAD APPLIED FOR THE PASSPORT. I STRONGLY SUSPECT THAT THIS CARD OR ANY IDENTICAL CARD MAY HAVE BEEN IN **LEE'S** POSSESSION AND A _COPY_ GIVEN TO **HARVEY** TO FURTHER HIS MORPHING INTO **LEE**. A "LEE HARVEY OSWALD" WAS DISCHARGED AT EL TORO IN MARCH 1959. THIS DOD CARD WAS FOUND AT THE SCENE OF THE TIPPIT SHOOTING IN ONE OF THE MANY WALLETS ATTRIBUTED TO **HARVEY** ON NOVEMBER 22ND, 1963. WE WILL ELABORATE ON THE WALLET(S) ISSUE LATER IN THE TIMELINE.

SEPTEMBER 5TH 1959

RUBY RETURNS TO HAVANA.

SEPTEMBER 11TH 1959

HARVEY IS DISCHARGED AT EL TORO IN SANTA ANA, CALIFORNIA WITH $219 SEVERENCE AND TRAVEL PAY. HE IS ALSO ISSUED A DOD ID CARD (DD1173) #N4271617. ACCORDING TO ARMSTRONG, THE PHOTO ON THE CARD IS A COMPOSITE. THE IMAGE IS COMPOSED OF THE LEFT HALF OF **LEE'S** FACE AND THE RIGHT HALF OF **HARVEY'S** FACE. THIS SAME PHOTO WILL RESURFACE ON AN ALTERED SELECTIVE SERVICE CARD ALLEGEDLY FOUND IN **HARVEY'S** WALLET ENROUTE TO THE DPD AFTER HIS ARREST. THE NAME ON THE CARD HOWEVER WOULD BE ALEK J. HIDELL. ANOTHER RARE BUT UNEXPECTED MISTAKE HAD BEEN MADE BY THE SET-UP CONSPIRATORS: SELECTIVE SERVICE CARDS DO NOT INCLUDE A PHOTO. **HARVEY** LISTS HIS DISCHARGE ADDRESS AS 3124 W. 5TH STREET, FT. WORTH, TEXAS. THIS IS THE ADDRESS OF "MARGUERITE."

ARMSTRONG NOTES THAT JUST PRIOR TO **HARVEY'S** EXPECTED ARRIVAL IN FT. WORTH THAT "MARGUERITE" HAD TOLD HER LANDLORD, GRACE CRANER, THAT HER "SON" WAS GOING TO BE IN TOWN FOR A FEW DAYS. ONCE AGAIN, "MARGUERITE" WAS FULLY AWARE THAT **HARVEY'S** DISCHARGE WAS EITHER FOR THE PURPOSE OF HIS "DEFECTION" OR HIS EARLY DEPARTURE FOR SCHOOL. IT HAD NO CONNECTION TO HER SUPPOSEDLY

DISABLING INJURY OR HE WOULD HAVE BEEN IN TOWN FOR MORE THAN "A FEW DAYS." THERE IS NO INDICATION THAT **HARVEY** VISITED "MARGUERITE" OR EVEN STOPPED IN FT. WORTH.

A MARINE NAMED BUCKNELL NOTED THAT THERE WERE SEVERAL OCCASSIONS WHERE HE AND **HARVEY** WERE INTERVIEWED FOR FUTURE COVERT OPERATIONS IN CUBA. KEEP IN MIND HOWEVER THAT AT THIS DATE, THE U.S. GOVERNMENT WAS HEDGING THEIR BETS ON THE OUTCOME OF CASTRO VS BATISTA IN CUBA. THE GOVERNMENT OFFERED SUPPORT TO <u>BOTH</u> OPPONENTS. **HARVEY** WAS CALLED BACK FOR FOLLOW-UP INTERVIEWS SEVERAL TIMES. BUCKNELL SAID **HARVEY** TOLD HIM HE KNEW THE MAN CONDUCTING HIS INTERVIEW. **HARVEY** ALSO TOLD BUCKNELL THAT HE WAS BEING DISCHARGED EARLY TO GO TO RUSSIA ON AN INTELLIGENCE OPERATION.

SEPTEMBER 11TH 1959
RUBY RETURNS FROM CUBA ACCORDING TO CUBAN AUTHORITIES.

SEPTEMBER 12TH 1959
LEE VISITS HIS BROTHER ROBERT IN FT. WORTH.

ROBERT TOLD THE W.C. THAT "LEE HARVEY OSWALD" VISITED HIM IN FT. WORTH BETWEEN THE TIME OF HIS DISCHARGE AND HIS TRIP TO NEW ORLEANS. **LEE** WAS DISCHARGED IN MARCH, 1959. **HARVEY** WAS DISCHARGED ON SEPTEMBER 11TH, 1959. ROBERT KNEW FULLY WELL THAT IT WAS **LEE**, NOT **HARVEY** WHO HAD VISITED HIM. HE WOULD HOWEVER LEAD THE W.C. TO THINK THAT IT WAS **HARVEY** WHO HAD BRIEFLY STOPPED IN FT. WORTH. **HARVEY** DID NOT VISIT EITHER HIS "BROTHER" ROBERT OR HIS "MOTHER" "MARGUERITE" ON HIS WAY TO NEW ORLEANS.

SEPTEMBER 12TH 1959
RUBY ONCE AGAIN TRAVELS TO CUBA FROM MIAMI ON PAN AM FLIGHT #415.

SEPTEMBER 13TH 1959
CUBAN TOURISM AUTHORITIES CLAIM THAT RUBY RETURNED FROM CUBA ON DELTA FLIGHT #750. HE CONTINUED ON TO NEW ORLEANS THE SAME DAY.

SEPTEMBER 14TH 1959
LEE CLOSES OUT HIS SAVINGS ACCOUNT AT THE WEST SIDE STATE BANK IN FT. WORTH. THE PROCEEDS FROM THE ACCOUNT TOTAL $203. HE WOULD ALSO REGISTER WITH THE LOCAL SELECTIVE SERVICE BOARD. HE IS ASSIGNED SELECTIVE SERVICE NUMBER 41-114-39-532 AND ISSUED A CARD.

SEPTEMBER 15TH1959
HARVEY, IF HE INDEED STOPPED, LEAVES FORT WORTH FOR NEW ORLEANS.

SEPTEMBER 16TH 1959
HARVEY BOOKS HIS TRIP TO FRANCE ON THE MARION LYKES. THE ONE-WAY FARE TO LE HARVE WAS $220.75.

HARVEY CONTACTED TRAVEL CONSULTANTS INC. IN NEW ORLEANS. ON HIS "PASSENGER IMMIGRATION QUESTIONNAIRE" HE NOTED THAT HE WOULD BE OVERSEAS FOR 2 MONTHS THE AGENCY WAS LOCATED IN THE SAME BUILDING AS THE OFFICES OF CLAY SHAW.

HARVEY, OR HIS ONI/CIA HANDLERS, WERE NOT WITHOUT A SENSE OF HUMOR. ON HIS QUESTIONNAIRE UNDER "OCCUPATION" **HARVEY** WROTE "SHIPPING EXPORT AGENT." **HARVEY** WOULD "EXPORT" HIMSELF ON A "SHIP" AS AN "AGENT" ONLY 16 DAYS LATER.

ARMSTRONG NOTES THAT IT MAY NOT HAVE BEEN **HARVEY** WHO FILLED OUT THE QUESTIONNAIRE. THE FORM ASKED FOR A RESIDENCE NEAR THE PORT OF EMBARKATION; IN THIS CASE NEW ORLEANS. **HARVEY**, OR WHOEVER FILLED OUT THE FORM, LISTED HIS

ADDRESS AS THE LIBERTY HOTEL IN NEW ORLEANS. **HARVEY** *HOWEVER DID NOT REGISTER AT THE HOTEL UNTIL SEPTEMBER 17TH. THE FORM REQUESTS THE NAME OF THE CITY WHERE THE PASSPORT WAS ISSUED. NEW ORLEANS WAS LISTED, BUT* **HARVEY'S** *PASSPORT HAD BEEN ISSUED IN LOS ANGELES.*

SEPTEMBER 17TH 1959
HARVEY REGISTERS AT THE LIBERTY HOTEL.

SEPTEMBER 19TH 1959
HARVEY BOARDS THE MARION LYKES.

CHAPTER 3: THE "DEFECTION" OF HARVEY AND COLD WAR CHESS GAMES

IT WAS WELL KNOWN IN INTELLIGENCE CIRCLES THAT THE U.S. WAS RUNNING A PROGRAM TO USE YOUNG MEN TO PENETRATE THE IRON CURTAIN. FROM 1958 THROUGH 1960, ELEVEN AMERICANS "DEFECTED" TO RUSSIA. THE CIA/ONI NORMALLY USED "COLLEGE TYPES" BUT THE RUSSIANS WERE SOON ABLE TO SPOT THESE TYPES OF RECRUITS. THE INTELLIGENCE COMMUNITY, CIA/ONI, THEN BEGAN USING YOUNG MEN WHO APPEARED TO BE "LONERS" AND "DISENCHANTED" WITH THE WESTERN WAY OF LIFE. IN THE EARLY 1960'S, THE STATE DEPARTMENT CONDUCTED A STUDY OF U.S. DEFECTORS. OTTO OTEPKA, IN CHARGE OF THE STUDY, WAS ATTEMPTING TO DETERMINE WHICH DEFECTORS WERE REAL AND WHICH WERE INTELLIGENCE PROJECTS. IN JUNE 1962, OTEPKA WAS FIRED FROM THE STATE DEPARTMENT. HE WAS REFUSED RE-ENTRY TO HIS OFFICE. WHEN ASKED IN 1971 JUST WHAT HIS STUDY DETERMINED REGARDING **HARVEY** HE REPLIED: "WE HAD NOT MADE UP OUR MINDS WHEN WE WERE THROWN OUT OF THE OFFICE." TWO EXAMPLES BELOW DETAIL TWO CASES INVOLVING THREE INDIVIDUALS WHO FIT THIS PROFILE. INTERESTINGLY ENOUGH, THEY ALSO HAVE CLOSE TIES TO **HARVEY'S** ARRANGED "DEFECTION" AND ITS CONSEQUENCES.

THE MITCHELL/MARTIN "DEFECTIONS" AND THE NSA-DANGLING, KGB-RECRUITMENT OF JACK EDWARD DUNLAP IN PARTICULAR DOVETAIL WITH **HARVEY'S** ASSIGNMENT. IT WOULD SEEM THAT THE CIA HAD A "PLAN B" HAD **HARVEY** ALONE NOT BEEN ABLE TO CONVINCE THE SOVIETS OF HIS LEGITIMACY. MITCHELL, MARTIN, AND DUNLAP WOULD HAVE, IN ALL LIKELIHOOD, STILL BEEN ABLE TO PROVIDE THE SOVIETS WITH THE NOTION THAT THEY HAD ENOUGH DATA TO "DOWN" A U-2.

A LOOK AT THE MITCHELL AND MARTIN "DEFECTIONS""

1951
BERNON MITCHELL AND WILLIAM H. MARTIN MET AS ENLISTED MEN IN KAMISEYA, JAPAN AT THE NAVY'S COMMUNICATION STATION.

1957
MITCHELL LEFT KAMISEYA AFTER HIS ENLISTMENT EXPIRED. MARTIN REMAINED IN JAPAN AFTER HIS ENLISTMENT EXPIRED AND WORKED IN A CIVILIAN JOB FOR THE ARMY.

1957
BOTH MITCHELL AND MARTIN WERE RECRUITED BY THE NSA AFTER THEIR NAVAL ENLISTMENTS EXPIRED.

1958
MARTIN AND MITCHELL BEGIN THEIR NSA EMPLOYMENT.

SEPTEMBER 1959
MARTIN EARNED AN "A" IN RUSSIAN AT THE UNIVERSITY OF ILLINOIS WHILE ON NSA ASSIGNMENT FOR A MASTERS DEGREE IN MATHEMATICS. IT WAS THERE THAT HE ASSOCIATED WITH COMMUNIST PARTY MEMBERS IN AN OBVIOUS EFFORT TO ENHANCE HIS COVER. MARTIN WOULD ATTEND GRADUATE SCHOOL AS WELL.

DECEMBER 1959
MARTIN AND MITCHELL VISIT CUBA.

MAY/JUNE 1960
MITCHELL SEES HIS PSYCHIATRIST AND TELLS HIM: "MAYBE I'LL SEE YOU AGAIN AND MAYBE I WON'T."

JUNE 25---JULY 11TH 1960
MITCHELL AND MARTIN FLY TO MEXICO CITY AND THEN TO HAVANA   THERE THEY BOARDED A SOVIET FREIGHTER TO RUSSIA.

JULY 26TH 1960
8 DAYS AFTER THEIR 1 WEEK LEAVE EXTENSION EXPIRED, THEIR NSA SUPERVISOR TRIED TO CONTACT THEM.

AUGUST 1ST 1960
THE PENTAGON ANNOUNCES THEIR DEFECTION.

AUGUST 30TH 1960
FRANCES E. WALTER, CHAIRMAIN OF THE HUAC LEARNS THAT ONE OF THEM (MITCHELL OR MARTIN) REQUESTED AND RECEIVED INFORMATION ABOUT POWERS U-2 FLIGHT BEFORE HE WAS DOWNED AND THAT BOTH MEN WORKED ON SOVIET COMMUNICATIONS ABOUT THE U-2 FLIGHTS.

SEPTEMBER 6TH 1960
AT THEIR PRESS CONFERENCE IN RUSSIA WHEN THEY WERE ASKED HOW THEY REACHED MOSCOW, MARTIN GRINNED AND DECLINED TO ANSWER STATING "OTHERS MAY WANT TO USE THE SAME ROUTE." AS WE WILL SEE, THIS SAME MEXICO, HAVANA, MOSCOW ROUTE WAS ONE **HARVEY** WOULD BE LED TO BELIEVE HE WOULD BE TAKING ON NOVEMBER 22, 1963 FOR ANOTHER ASSIGNMENT.THEY ALSO STATED THAT THEY WERE "DISENCHANTED" BY THE NSA ELECTRONIC INTELLIGENCE FLIGHTS THAT PENETRATED SOVIET BORDERS.

THE JACK EDWARD DUNLAP EPISODE

JACK DUNLAP WAS AN ARMY SERGEANT ASSIGNED TO NSA IN APRIL OF 1958 AS A CHAFFEUR. IN EARLY 1960, HE WAS PROMOTED TO CLERK/MESSENGER AT NSA. HIS JOB WAS TO COURIER HIGHLY CLASSIFIED DOCUMENTS BETWEEN VARIOUS DEPARTMENTS AT THE AGENCY.

IN JUNE 1960 WHILE STRUGGLING TO SUPPORT A FAMILY OF 7, HE BOUGHT A 30 FOOT CABIN CRUISER. OVER THE NEXT 3 YEARS, DUNLAP PURCHASED A HYDROPLANE, 2 CADILLACS, AND A JAGUAR. THE NSA APPARENTLY TOOK LITTLE NOTICE OF HIS NEW-FOUND WEALTH. AS A POINT, DUNLAP WAS INJURED DURING A YACHT CLUB REGATTA. THE NSA, PER PROTOCOL, SENT AN AMBULANCE TO TRANSPORT HIM TO FT. MEADE ARMY HOSPITAL FEARFULL OF WHAT HE MIGHT DISCLOSE UNDER ANESTHESIA. BUT THERE SEEMED TO BE LITTLE CONCERN AS TO HOW HE HAD THE NECESSARY FUNDS TO BE RACING YACHTS. WAS THE KGB USING DUNLAP? OR, WAS THE NSA/CIA USING DUNLAP AND THE KGB?

ON JULY 22ND 1963, DUNLAP COMMITTED SUICIDE. IT WAS HIS 3RD ATTEMPT SINCE JUNE 14TH OF THAT YEAR. AN FBI DOCUMENT DATED APRIL 21, 1966 STATED THAT DUNLAP HAD ACCESS TO FLIGHT SCHEDULES OF THE U-2 AND THAT IT WAS LIKELY THAT HE WAS INSTRUMENTAL IN THE SHOOT-DOWN OF POWERS' MAY 1960 FLIGHT.

ALTHOUGH MITCHELL AND MARTIN ARRIVED IN CUBA IN 1959, THEY DID NOT "DEFECT" TO RUSSIA UNTIL JULY 1960. THEIR CIA/NSA-SPONSORED "ASSISTANCE" TO THE SOVIETS WOULD APPEAR TO HAVE BEEN AFTER THE FAILED 1960 SUMMIT TALKS, AFTER THE POWERS' U-2 SHOOTDOWN, AND WOULD SEEMINGLY HAVE NO IMPACT ON THE SUCCESS OF OR THE ULTIMATE FAILURE OF THE TALKS. BUT, ONE MUST REALIZE THAT THEIR RECRUITMENT BY THE NSA OCCURRED IN 1957. THEIR RELATIONSHIP, AS WELL AS THAT OF JACK DUNLAP AND HIS EARLY 1960 NSA DANGLE WITH THE KGB, WOULD ALLOW THE THREE OF THEM TO JEOPARDIZE FUTURE U-2 FLIGHTS IF POWER'S FLIGHT WAS NOT SUCCESSFULLY SABOTAGED. IT WAS THE CIA'S DESIRE TO

CONTINUE TO ESCALATE THE COLD WAR REGARDLESS OF THE OUTCOME OF THE 1960 SUMMIT TALKS.

THE "DEFECTION" OF ROBERT WEBSTER

ANOTHER "DEFECTOR" PLAYED PROMINANTLY IN **HARVEY'S** "DEFECTION." AN ADDRESS IN MARINA OSWALD'S ADDRESS BOOK WAS RAN THRU CIA COMPUTERS AND THE ADDRESS WAS THAT OF ROBERT EDWARD WEBSTER'S LENINGRAD APARTMENT. HE WAS ANOTHER "DEFECTOR" WHO HAD TRAVELLED TO MOSCOW ON JULY 11, 1959 WHILE WORKING FOR THE RAND DEVELOPMENT CORPORATION. WEBSTER, LIKE **HARVEY**, ARRIVED AT THE U.S. EMBASSY AND NOTED HIS DESIRE TO DEFECT. IT WOULD BE RICHARD SNYDER, EMBASSY HEAD CONSUL, WHO WOULD MEET WITH WEBSTER.

THE STORYLINE ON WEBSTER WAS THAT HE WAS A "PLASTICS EXPERT." INTERESTINGLY THE TRADE SHOW WAS SPONSORED BY PERMINDEX, A CIA FRONT OPERATED BY CLAY SHAW'S INTERNATIONAL TRADE MART IN NEW ORLEANS. WEBSTER "DISAPPEARED" FOR 2 WEEKS IN OCTOBER DURING THE TRADE SHOW. HE RETURNED TO THE U.S. WITHIN WEEKS OF **HARVEY**. UNLIKE **HARVEY**, HE WAS DEBRIEFED/INTERROGATED FOR 2 WEEKS IN WASHINGTON UPON HIS RETURN. LIKE **HARVEY** HOWEVER, WEBSTER RETURNED WITH A RUSSIAN WIFE AND A BABY.

MARINA WAS ONE OF MANY RUSSIAN GIRLS "PAIRED" BY THE KGB WITH AMERICAN "DEFECTORS." WEBSTER HOWEVER WAS ALREADY MARRIED; **HARVEY** WAS NOT. MARINA, IN AN INTERVIEW YEARS AFTER THE ASSASSINATION, SAID SHE MET **HARVEY** WHILE HE WAS WITH AN AMERICAN EXHIBITION IN MOSCOW. **HARVEY** OF COURSE WAS <u>NOT</u> WITH AN AMERICAN EXHIBITION; IT WAS <u>WEBSTER</u> WHO "DEFECTED" WHILE VISITING RUSSIA WITH THE EXHIBITION. IT SEEMS MARINA CONFUSED THE MEETINGS OF HER KGB-INTENDED SUITORS.

WEBSTER WOULD LATER NOTE THAT IN HIS CONVERSATIONS WITH MARINA AT THE EXHIBITION THAT SHE SPOKE ENGLISH. IT IS WORTH NOTING THAT LATER, UPON HER ARRIVAL IN THE U.S., THAT MARINA WOULD PRIMARILY SPEAK ONLY RUSSIAN. ***HARVEY***, *WHILE IN RUSSIA, WOULD PRIMARILY SPEAK ONLY ENGLISH. HE WOULD HAVE LIKELY BLOWN HIS COVER HAD HE SPOKEN FLUENT RUSSIAN.*

INTERESTINGLY WEBSTER WOULD LATER TELL U.S. OFFICIALS THAT HE HAD NO CONTACT WITH ***HARVEY*** *WHILE IN RUSSIA. HOWEVER* ***HARVEY*** *MUST CERTAINLY HAVE BEEN AWARE OF WEBSTER'S VISIT TO RUSSIA SINCE IN 1961 HE INQUIRED ABOUT "THE FATE OF A YOUNG MAN NAMED WEBSTER." SINCE* ***HARVEY*** *HAD SERIOUS CONCERNS ABOUT WHAT LEGAL PROCEEDINGS HE WOULD BE SUBJECTED TO UPON HIS RETURN TO THE U.S., HE HOPED THAT INFORMATION ON WEBSTER'S STATUS WOULD SHED SOME LIGHT ON JUST WHAT HE COULD EXPECT AS A RETURNING "DEFECTOR."*

IT IS ALSO INTERESTING TO NOTE THT THE CIA WAS KEENLY AWARE OF SOVIET WOMEN'S INTEREST IN MARRYING U.S. CITIZENS. IN A MEMO ISSUED SHORTLY AFTER THE ASSASSINATION, THE CIA NOTED THAT "THE AGENCY WAS BECOMING INCREASINGLY INTERESTED IN WATCHING DEVELOP A PATTERN THAT WE HAD DISCOVERED IN THE COURSE OF OUR WORK; THE NUMBER OF SOVIET WOMEN MARRYING FOREIGNERS, BEING PERMITTED TO LEAVE THE USSR, THEN EVENTUALLY DIVORCING THEIR SPOUSES AND SETTLING DOWN ABROAD. WE VERIFIED AND NOTED SOMETHING LIKE ONE DOZEN SIMILAR CASES."

I SUSPECT, AS WE WILL SEE LATER, THAT RUTH PAINE'S BEFRIENDING OF MARINA UPON HER ARRIVAL IN THE U.S. WAS MORE OF AN ASSIGNMENT TO "MONITOR" MARINA SINCE THERE MAY HAVE BEEN SUSPICIONS THAT MARINA'S MARRIAGE TO ***HARVEY*** *AND HER DEPARTURE FROM RUSSIA WAS IN FACT A LOW-LEVEL INTELLIGENCE ASSIGNMENT GIVEN TO HER BY THE KGB.*

FINANCING OF TRIP TO MOSCOW

HARVEY'S SEVERANCE AND TRAVEL PAY FROM EL TORO TO FT. WORTH WAS $219. TO FINANCE A TRIP THAT WOULD TAKE HIM HALFWAY AROUND THE WORLD, THIS $219 SUM WOULD HAVE TO COVER:

THE TRIP FROM FORT WORTH TO NEW ORLEANS

A 2 NIGHT STAY AT THE LIBERTY HOTEL IN NEW ORLEANS

THE TRIP FROM NEW ORLEANS TO LE HAVRE, FRANCE

TRANSPORTATION FROM LE HAVRE TO SOUTHHAMPTON AND 1 NIGHTS STAY IN SOUTHHAMPTON

THE FLIGHT TO HELSINKI

5 DAYS STAY IN HELSINKI

TRAIN TRANSPORTATION FROM HELSINKI TO MOSCOW.

HARVEY TOLD CUSTOMS IN SOUTHHAMPTON THAT HE HAD $700 ON HIS PERSON. IF SO, HE WOULD HAVE HAD TO HAVE HAD A <u>MINIMUM</u> OF $1017 WHEN HE LEFT FORT WORTH. FOR ARGUMENTS SAKE, LET'S CONSERVATIVELY ESTIMATE HIS TRAVEL COST FROM EL TORO TO FT. WORTH AT $30 VIA A BUS. NOW WE HAVE A BALANCE OF $987. THE TRIP FROM FT. WORTH TO NEW ORLEANS ABOUT $25 VIA BUS. WE NOW HAVE A BALANCE OF $962. A 2 NIGHT STAY IN NEW ORLEANS, ABOUT $21, LEAVING A BALANCE OF $941 THE NEW ORLEANS LE HAVRE TRIP COST $221 LEAVING HIM A BALANCE OF $720. WE'LL ONCE AGAIN ESTIMATE THE FERRY FROM LE HAVRE TO SOUTHHAMPTON AT $20 FOR A BALANCE OF $700. UPON ARRIVAL IN SOUTHHAMPTON, **HARVEY** WOULD STILL HAVE TO FINANCE A 1 NIGHT STAY IN SOUTHHAMPTON, A FLIGHT TO HELSINKI AT A COST OF $112, A 5 NIGHT STAY IN 2 LUXURY HOTELS THERE, AND THE TRAIN TRIP TO MOSCOW COSTING $44. IF **HARVEY** WAS TRUTHFULL IN HAVING $700 UPON <u>ARRIVAL</u> IN SOUTHHAMPTON, HE COULD POSSIBLY HAVE COVERED THE TRAVEL EXPENSES INCURRED <u>AFTER</u> THAT POINT.

THE QUESTION OF COURSE IS WHERE DID HE GET THE ADDITIONAL $800 DOLLARS AS HIS PROJECTED BALANCE UPON <u>ARRIVAL</u> IN SOUTHHAMPTON WAS A <u>NEGATIVE</u> $100? HE COULD NOT HAVE LEFT THE MARINES WITH ONLY $219. HE WOULD HAVE HAD TO HAVE HAD AT LEAST $1017 AFTER LEAVING CALIFORNIA, $962 UPON LEAVING FT. WORTH, $720 UPON LEAVING NEW ORLEANS, AND THEN, AFTER PURCHASING THE CROSSING TICKET TO SOUTHHAMPTON, APPROXIMATELY THE $700 HE TOLD CUSTOMS HE HAD UPON ARRIVAL IN SOUTHHAMPTON.

THE W.C. NOTES THAT **HARVEY** <u>EARNED</u> $3452 DURING HIS 3 YEAR TERM IN THE MARINE CORP. THIS WOULD MAKE HIS ANNUAL SALARY $1150 PER YEAR. FEDERAL TAX RATES FOR 1959, **HARVEY'S** LAST YEAR IN THE CORP WOULD HAVE MEANT THAT HE PAID FEDERAL TAX OF $89 PER YEAR. THIS WOULD LEAVE A NET SALARY OF $3185 FOR THE 3 YEAR SPAN. HIS ROOM/BOARD WERE COVERED AS A MEMBER OF THE MARINE CORP. THE ONLY OTHER KNOWN INCOME IS THE MONEY ARMSTRONG CONTENDS HE EARNED AT PFISTERER DENTAL LABS IN NEW ORLEANS FROM OCTOBER 1957 TO MAY 1958. **HARVEY'S** MILITARY RECORD HOWEVER NOTES THAT HE IS IN JAPAN AT THIS TIME. NEEDLESS TO SAY, THERE IS NO RECORD OF HIS PAY AT PFISTERER. THE ONLY EXPENSE I COULD FIND WAS JUNE 1959 WHEN **HARVEY** SENT A $25 ENROLLMENT FEE TO ALBERT SCHWEITZER COLLEGE. IGNORING FOR THE MOMENT MONEY EARNED AS PFISTERER LABS – THE W.C. DID NOT INCLUDE THIS INCOME SINCE IT IS THEIR CONTENTION THAT **HARVEY** WAS IN JAPAN – AND SUBTRACTING THE $25 ENROLLMENT EXPENSE FROM HIS NET MARINE CORP PAY WE ARE LEFT WITH A BALANCE OF $3160. **HARVEY** SPENT NO MONEY ON VEHICLES, GAS, INSURANCE, AND MAINTENANCE ON ANY VEHICLES. THE $3160 NET, DIVIDED BY THE 3

YEAR SPAN, WOULD HAVE GIVEN **HARVEY** $1053 PER YEAR OR $20 PER WEEK FOR PERSONAL EXPENSES OVER A 3 YEAR SPAN. IF, AS EXPLAINED ABOVE THAT **HARVEY** WOULD HAVE TO HAVE HAD A MINIMUM OF $1017 UPON DEPARTING FT. WORTH TO HAVE TRUTHFULLY TOLD CUSTOMS THAT HE HAD $700 ON HIM UPON ARRIVAL IN ENGLAND. LET US RE-CALCULATE THE AMOUNT OF MONEY HE WOULD HAVE HAD FOR WEEKLY PERSONAL EXPENSES. IF WE SUBTRACT THE $1017 FROM $3160, WE ARE NOW LEFT WITH A NET BALANCE OF $2143 REMAINING FROM HIS MILITARY SERVICE. DIVIDING THIS AMOUNT BY THE 3 YEARS INVOLVED WE ARE LEFT WITH AN ANNUAL NET OF $714. THE $20 PER WEEK "SPENDING MONEY" IS NOW REDUCED TO $13.73. EVEN THE FRUGAL **HARVEY** WOULD HAVE HAD A DIFFICULT TIME ON THAT MEAGER ALLOWANCE.

WE WILL NOW RETURN TO THE TIMELINE

SEPTEMBER 20TH 1959
HARVEY LEAVES NEW ORLEANS AT 6:35 AM ON A FREIGHTER, THE SS MARION LYKES, FOR LE HAVRE, FRANCE. BILLY LORD AND **HARVEY** SHARED THE SAME CABIN FOR THE TRIP TO FRANCE. **HARVEY** TOLD LORD THAT HE HAD BEEN RECENTLY DISCHARGED FROM THE MARINES.

THE LYKES LINE WAS NOTED TO BE A PROPRIETARY INTEREST OF THE CIA.

SEPTEMBER 21ST 1959
ROBERT WEBSTER, WHO HAD "DISAPPEARED" FROM THE TRADE SHOW IN MOSCOW IN JULY 1959, SURFACES AND RENOUNCES HIS U.S. CITIZENSHIP. HE IS GRANTED SOVIET CITIZENSHIP.

OCTOBER 2ND 1959
RUBY IS CONTACTED ONCE AGAIN BY THE FBI. IT IS BELIEVED THAT HIS FBI INFORMANT STATUS ENDED THIS DATE.

ON FEBRUARY 27TH, 1964, HOOVER, IN A MEMO TO THE W.C., NOTED THAT INDEED RUBY HAD BEEN AN INFORMANT FOR THE FBI FROM MARCH 11TH TO OCTOBER 2ND, 1959. RUBY'S RELATIONSHIP WITH THE FBI WAS NOT REVEALED UNTIL 1971.

OCTOBER 1959
THE EVER MOBILE "MARGUERITE" MOVES ONCE AGAIN. SHE NOW RESIDES AT 1013 5TH AVENUE IN FT. WORTH.

OCTOBER 8TH 1959
THE SS MARION LYKES ARRIVES AT LE HAVRE, FRANCE AT 3:48 AM. IT IS UNCLEAR WHERE **HARVEY** SPENDS THE EVENING OF OCTOBER 8TH.

OCTOBER 9TH 1959
HARVEY CROSSES TO SOUTHHAMPTON, ENGLAND AND PRESUMABLY TAKES THE TRAIN TO LONDON. HE TELLS CUSTOMS OFFICIALS THAT HE WILL REMAIN IN ENGLAND ONLY 1 WEEK BEFORE GOING TO COLLEGE IN SWITZERLAND.

OCTOBER 10TH 1959
HARVEY SOMEHOW FLIES FROM LONDON TO HELSINKI. THERE IS ONLY 1 DIRECT FLIGHT, FINN AIR #852, <u>ARRIVING</u> AT 11:33 PM. THIS FLIGHT WOULD NOT HAVE ALLOWED TIME FOR CUSTOMS, IMMIGRATION, AND TRAVEL TO THE HOTEL TORNI WHERE HE CHECKED IN AT MIDNIGHT. **HARVEY** WILL STAY AT THE HOTEL TORNI ONLY 2 NIGHTS.

OCTOBER 12TH 1959
HARVEY REGISTERS AT THE KLAUS KURKI HOTEL IN HELSINKI. BOTH THE HOTEL TORNI AND THE KLAUS KURKI WERE HIGHLY RATED LUXURY HOTELS CONSIDERED TO BE HELSINKI'S FINEST.

OCTOBER 13TH 1959
HARVEY APPLIES TO THE SOVIET CONSULATE FOR A RUSSIAN VISA.

OCTOBER 14TH 1959
HARVEY IS AWARDED A 6 DAY VISA, VISA NUMBER 4173339.

FOR MOST AMERICANS, OBTAINING A VISA IN HELSINKI FOR TRAVEL TO RUSSIA WOULD NORMALLY TAKE 5-7 DAYS. BUT, THE SOVIET EMBASSY IN HELSINKI IS THE ONLY SOVIET EMBASSY IN EUROPE WHERE THE CONSUL IS EMPOWERED TO ISSUE A VISA ALMOST IMMEDIATELY. **HARVEY** *WAS LIKELY PRIVY TO THIS FACT VIA THE CIA WHO WAS LIKELY FOOTING THE BILL FOR THE EXPENSIVE HOTEL STAYS PRIOR TO* **HARVEY'S** *ENTRANCE TO RUSSIA WHERE HIS ACCOMODATIONS WOULD BE SPARTAN AT BEST.*

OCTOBER 15TH 1959
HARVEY LEAVES HELSINKI BY TRAIN FOR MOSCOW. HE CROSSES THE RUSSIAN BORDER AT VAINIKKALA, FINLAND.

OCTOBER 16TH 1959
HARVEY IS MET AT THE TRAIN STATION IN MOSCOW BY INTOURIST GUIDE RIMA SHIROKOVA. SHE ESCORTS HIM TO THE HOTEL BERLIN WHERE HE STAYS IN ROOM 320. HE TOLD HER HE DID NOT KNOW EVEN A SINGLE RUSSIAN WORD. THEY SPENT THE DAY TOURING MOSCOW.

OCTOBER 17TH 1959
HARVEY TELLS HIS INTOURIST GUIDE HE WANTS TO DEFECT. ONCE AGAIN THEY WOULD SPEND THE DAY SIGHTSEEING.

OCTOBER 18TH 1959
TODAY IS **LEE'S** ACTUAL BIRTHDAY. THE BIRTHDATE OF **HARVEY** IS NOT KNOWN. **HARVEY** AND RIMA WOULD CONTINUE THEIR SIGHTSEEING OF MOSCOW.

OCTOBER 19TH 1959
HARVEY IS INTERVIEWED BY RADIO MOSCOW. THIS INTERVIEW WAS RECORDED.

OCTOBER 21ST 1959
HARVEY WAS TOLD BY HIS INTOURIST GUIDE RIMA THAT HE WOULD NOT BE ALLOWED TO STAY IN RUSSIA. HIS REQUEST FOR CITIZENSHIP HAD BEEN DENIED AND HIS 6 DAY VISA HAD EXPIRED. IT WAS EXPECTED THAT HE WOULD BE ON A TRAIN DEPARTING FOR HELSINKI AT 8:00 THAT EVENING.

HARVEY'S *RESPONSE TO HIS EMINENT EXPULSION WAS QUICK AND DRAMATIC. HE ENGAGED IN A SUICIDE "ATTEMPT" THAT SAME AFTERNOON BY CUTTING HIS WRIST. THE CUT WOULD REQUIRE 4 STITCHES. HE IS ADMITTED TO BOTKIN HOSPITAL AT 4:00 PM. DURING HIS 7 DAY STAY, HE SPENT 3 DAYS IN THE PSYCHIATRIC WARD FOR EVALUATION.*

DURING HIS STAY, **HARVEY** *WAS INTERVIEWED BY RUSSIAN DOCTORS. ONE NOTED IN* **HARVEY'S** *CHART THAT THE PATIENT APPEARED TO UNDERSTAND RUSSIAN AND ANSWER QUESTIONS, BUT HE WOULD THEN QUICKLY COMMENT THAT HE DID NOT UNDERSTAND THE QUESTION ASKED.*

OCTOBER 25TH 1959
THE OCTOBER 19TH RECORDED INTERVIEW OF **HARVEY** IS BROADCAST ON RADIO MOSCOW.

OCTOBER 26TH 1959
A DISPATCH FROM THE U.S. EMBASSY TO STATE DEPARTMENT'S GENE BOSTER CITES ISSUES WITH ROBERT WEBSTER WHO HAD DEFECTED IN EARLY OCTOBER, <u>AND</u> **HARVEY**. **HARVEY** HOWEVER, ACCORDING TO THE W.C., WOULD NOT ATTEMPT TO "DEFECT" UNTIL OCTOBER 31ST.

OCTOBER 28TH 1959
HARVEY IS RELEASED FROM BOTKIN HOSPITAL.

OCTOBER 28TH 1959

HARVEY IS INTERVIEWED BY THE SOVIET PASSPORT OFFICE. HE IS TOLD THAT HIS REQUEST TO REMAIN IN RUSSIA WILL BE EVALUATED BY THE SUPREME SOVIET.

OCTOBER 31ST 1959

HARVEY CHECKS OUT OF THE HOTEL BERLIN AND INTO THE METROPOLE HOTEL, ROOM 214. HE WOULD LATER BE MOVED TO ROOM 233. ROOM 233 WAS, ACCORDING TO THE CIA, EQUIPPED WITH HIDDEN CAMERAS AND MICROPHONES.

THE OBSERVATIONS OF THE DOCTOR AT BOTKIN HOSPITAL MAY HAVE ALLERTED RUSSIAN AUTHORITIES ABOUT HARVEY'S ABILITY TO AT LEAST UNDERSTAND THE RUSSIAN LANGUAGE.

OCTOBER 31ST 1959

HARVEY, ACCORDING TO THE W.C. ARRIVED AT THE U.S. EMBASSY IN MOSCOW, THREW DOWN HIS PASSPORT, LOUDLY DENOUNCED THE U.S., AND INFORMED THE HEAD CONSUL, RICHARD E. SNYDER, THAT HE WAS RENOUNCING HIS CITIZENSHIP. BUT, AS PREVIOUSLY NOTED, THIS EVENT MAY HAVE TAKEN PLACE ON THE 26TH OF OCTOBER. HE ALSO STATED HE WOULD OFFER THE SOVIETS CLASSIFIED INFORMATION REGARDING HIS RADAR WORK INTHE MARINES, AND ALSO "SOMETHING OF SPECIAL INTEREST." THIS ITEM OF "SPECIAL INTEREST" IS NO DOUBT THE U-2. DURING THEIR ONGOING CONVERSATION REGARDING HARVEY'S ATTEMPT TO RENOUNCE HIS CITIZENSHIP, SNYDER RECALLED HIM STATING: "I WAS WARNED YOU WOULD TRY TO TALK ME OUT OF DEFECTING."

WHO WOULD HAVE WARNED HARVEY OF THIS PROBABILITY? IN ALL LIKELIHOOD HIS CIA SPONSORS. JEAN HALLETT WAS A RECEPTIONIST AT THE EMBASSY. SHE RECALLED HARVEY'S VISIT. SHE REMEMBERED THAT SNYDER AND THE EMBASSY SECURITY OFFICER ESCORTED HARVEY UPSTAIRS TO THE SECURE AREA. THIS IS WHERE THE OFFICES WERE LOCATED. HALLETT NOTED THAT SHE HERSELF HAD NEVER BEEN ALLOWED IN THE SECURE AREA. ONE WOULD HAVE TO WONDER WHY A "DEFECTOR" WOULD BE GIVEN ACCESS TO A SECURE AREA.

INTERESTINGLY SNYDER HAD PREVIOUSLY SENT A LETTER TO THE OFFICER IN CHARGE OF USSR AFFAIRS IN WASHINGTON ASKING ADVICE ON HOW TO DEAL WITH AN ATTEMPTED RENUNCIATION OF CITIZENSHIP. WAS HE ANTICIPATING HARVEY'S ARRIVAL? SNYDER IS BELIEVED TO HAVE BEEN A CIA AGENT WORKING UNDER DIPLOMATIC COVER DURING HIS POSTING TO THE U.S. EMBASSY IN MOSCOW.

JOHN MCVICAR, THE OTHER CONSUL AT THE EMBASSY, WOULD LATER NOTE IN A MEMO DATED 11/27/1963:"IT SEEMED TO ME THAT HE (HARVEY) HAD BEEN IN CONTACT WITH OTHERS BEFORE OR DURING HIS MARINE CORP TOUR WHO HAD GUIDED HIM AND ENCOURAGED HIM IN HIS ACTIONS."

MCVICAR ALSO NOTED THAT HE FELT THAT HARVEY, ON THAT DAY, APPEARED TO BE "FOLLOWING A PATTERN OF BEHAVIOR IN WHICH HE HAD BEEN TUTORED BY A PERSON OR PERSONS UNKNOWN. HE SEEMED TO BE USING WORDS HE HAD HEARD BUT DID NOT FULLY UNDERSTAND....". MCVICAR ALSO NOTED THAT HARVEY "SEEMED TO KNOW WHAT HIS MISSION WAS..."

THIS SAME SENSE THAT HARVEY HAD BEEN "COACHED" WOULD BE REPEATED IN DALLAS NEARLY 4 YEARS LATER BY CHIEF CURRY REGARDING HARVEY'S INTERROGATION SESSIONS FOLLOWING HIS ARREST. THE EMBASSY ALSO TELEGRAPHED THE STATE DEPARTMENT, THE CIA, THE FBI, AND THE OFFICE OF NAVAL INTELLIGENCE REGARDING HARVEY'S APPEARANCE AT THE EMBASSY. THE REPLY FROM ONI INSTRUCTED THE EMBASSY STAFF TO NEITHER PREVENT OR ENCOURAGE HARVEY'S ATTEMPT AT DEFECTION. IT DID HOWEVER ASK TO BE INFORMED OF "SIGNIFICANT DEVELOPMENTS IN VIEW OF CONTINUED INTEREST OF HQ, MARINE CORPS, AND U.S. INTELLIGENCE AGENCIES." THE CABLE WAS MARKED "INTELLIGENCE MATTER." THE ONI WAS

*NATURALLY INTERESTED IN **HARVEY'S** SUCCESS IN HIS NEW ROLE AS A CIA OPERATIVE. THE RUSSIANS FINALLY RELENTED AND ALLOWED **HARVEY** TO STAY.*

*THIS SAME EVENING **HARVEY** IS VISITED BY UPI BUREAU CHIEF ROBERT KORENGOLD. AFTER A BRIEF VISIT, KORENGOLD HAS UPI CORRESPONDENT ALINE MOSBY VISIT **HARVEY**. THE UPI DISPATCH WOULD BE THE INITIAL ANNOUNCEMENT OF **HARVEY'S** "DEFECTION." **HARVEY'S** "DEFECTION" DID NOT TRIGGER INVESTIGATIONS AT EITHER THE SANTA ANA MACS 9 OR AT MCAS WHERE **LEE** HAD BEEN STATIONED.*

OCTOBER 31ST 1959
A FT. WORTH REPORTER, JACK DOUGLAS, LOCATES ROBERT OSWALD. HE INFORMS HIM THAT HIS "BROTHER" **HARVEY** HAS "DEFECTED." ROBERT NOTES THAT HIS "BROTHER" HAD ATTENDED STRIPLING JUNIOR HIGH. HE IS CORRECT REGARDING HIS "BROTHER" **HARVEY**. BUT, HIS REAL BROTHER **LEE** HAD ATTENDED BEAUREGARD JR. HIGH IN NEW ORLEANS AT THE SAME TIME. LATER THAT DAY, ROBERT WAS INTEVIEWED BY OTHER REPORTERS. WHEN ASKED ABOUT THEIR "MOTHER", "MARGUERITE", ROBERT OFFERED A STERN "NO COMMENT."

LATE OCT 1959
THE NOMADIC "MARGUERITE" MOVES AGAIN. SHE NOW RESIDES AT 3616 HARLEY IN FT. WORTH.

NOVEMBER 1ST 1959
ROBERT OSWALD CABLES THE STATE DEPARTMENT REQUESTING THAT THEY HAVE HIS "BROTHER" **HARVEY** CONTACT HIM.

NOVEMBER 1ST 1959
AN ARTICLE ABOUT LEE **HARVEY** OSWALD'S "DEFECTION" WAS PRINTED IN THE FT. WORTH STAR-TELEGRAM. THE PICTURE OF COURSE IS OF **LEE** NOT **HARVEY**.

*ACCORDING TO ARMSTRONG, ARTICLES ABOUT **HARVEY'S** "DEFECTION" APPEARED IN MANY NEWSPAPERS THROUGHOUT THE COUNTRY. THERE WAS HOWEVER ONE EXCEPTION; NEW ORLEANS. THOSE IN NEW ORLEANS WHO KNEW BOTH A **HARVEY** AND A **LEE** COULD RAISE SERIOUS DOUBTS ABOUT THE SO-CALLED HISTORY OF **HARVEY**.*

NOVEMBER 2ND 1959
SECRETARY OF STATE CHRISTAN HERTER PERSONALLY CABLES THE U.S. EMBASSY IN MOSCOW ESSENTIALLY TELLING THE EMBASSY IT HAS NO RIGHT TO DENY **HARVEY** IF HE INDEED REQUESTS TO DENOUNCE HIS U.S. CITIZENSHIP.

*I SUSPECT THAT THE SECRETARY OF STATE IS ACTING PER REQUEST OF THE CIA TO **NOT** HAVE THE U.S. EMBASSY IN MOSCOW DISRUPT **HARVEY'S** "DEFECTION."*

NOVEMBER 3RD 1959
HARVEY WRITES A LETTER TO THE U.S. EMBASSY IN REGARDS TO HIS INITIAL VISIT TO THE EMBASSY ON OCTOBER 31ST.

NOVEMBER 8TH 1959
HARVEY WRITES HIS "BROTHER" ROBERT AS A RESULT OF THE NOVEMBER 1ST CABLE.

*INTERESTINGLY **HARVEY'S** LETTER OPENS WITH "WELL, WHAT SHOULD WE TALK ABOUT? THE WEATHER PERHAPS?" **HARVEY** WOULD INDEED HAVE LITTLE TO DISCUSS WITH ROBERT.*

NOVEMBER 9TH 1959
A TELEGRAM FROM **HARVEY'S** "HALF-BROTHER" JOHN PIC IS TAKEN TO **HARVEY'S** HOTEL BY THE U.S. EMBASSY. PIC HAD FINISHED HIS TOUR WITH THE COAST GUARD AND NOW WAS STATIONED IN JAPAN WITH THE AIR FORCE.

NOVEMBER 9TH 1959
THE FBI PLACES **HARVEY** ON THEIR "WATCH LIST." THE CIA PUT **HARVEY** ON THEIR "WATCH LIST" AS WELL. **HARVEY** WAS NOW ASSIGNED HT/LINGUAL MAIL INTERCEPT INDEX CARD #7-305. THIS OF COURSE WAS WINDOW DRESSING FOR THE CIA, BUT WOULD JUSTIFY THE CIA'S DESIRE TO READ ALL **HARVEY'S** MAIL. IT WOULD BE ONE METHOD OF MONITORING **HARVEY** AND HIS CORRESPONDANCE WITH HIS "BROTHER" ROBERT AND "MARGUERITE." THE FBI INDEED HAD SUSPICIONS **HARVEY** WAS USING A FALSE IDENTITY. IN THIS CASE, THE IDENTITY WOULD BE THAT OF **LEE**.

NOVEMBER 12TH 1959
THE U.S. EMBASSY IN MOSCOW REQUESTS THAT **HARVEY** COME TO THE EMBASSY IF HE WISHES TO REVOKE HIS CITIZENSHIP.

NOVEMBER 13TH 1959
HARVEY GRANTS AN INTERVIEW TO A UPI REPORTER, ALINE MOSBY.

*ARMSTRONG POINTS OUT THAT ONCE AGAIN **HARVEY** WOULD HAVE TO BE EXTREMELY CAREFULL IN HIS EFFORTS TO "BLEND" HIS LIFE TO THAT POINT WITH THAT OF **LEE**. HIS ANSWERS WERE ALWAYS GENERALIZED, AND HE WAS RELUCTANT TO ANSWER SPECIFIC QUESTIONS REGARDING HIS PAST. HE DID HOWEVER MAKE ONE GLARING MISTAKE. HE NOTED TO MOSBY THAT "WE MOVED TO NORTH DAKOTA." "WE" OF COURSE WOULD BE **HARVEY** AND "MARGUERITE." MOSBY RECORDED IN HER NOTES "N. DAKOTA" IN REGARDS TO **HARVEY'S** COMMENT. THIS APPARENTLY DISTURBED THE W.C. SINCE **LEE** HAD **NOT** BEEN TO NORTH DAKOTA. W.C. ATTORNEY LEE RANKIN REQUESTED FROM MOSBY HER <u>ORIGINAL</u> NOTES FROM THE INTERVIEW. HE WAS SENT A <u>TYPED TRANSCRIPT</u> OF HER NOTES. IN THE TYPED VERSION, "NORTH DAKOTA" HAD BEEN CHANGED TO "NEW ORLEANS." ONE WILL RECALL THAT THE <u>ORIGINAL</u> NEW YORK CITY FAMILY COURT CASE FILE OF **HARVEY** WAS TO BE GIVEN DIRECTLY TO THE W.C. THE FBI HOWEVER GAVE THE W.C. ALTERED <u>COPIES</u> OF THE CASE FILE. I SUSPECT THAT IT WAS THE FBI WHO ALTERED MOSBY'S HANDWRITTEN NOTES AND PREPARED THE TYPEWRITTEN COPIES FORWARDED TO THE W.C. IT APPEARS THAT THE INHERENT CONFUSION CREATED BY THE CIA IN CREATING **HARVEY** WOULD BE A MESS TO BE CLEANED UP BY THE FBI.*

***HARVEY** WAS VERY CAREFULL IN HIS RESPONSES TO HER QUESTIONS REGARDING HIS BACKGROUND. HE WOULD HAVE TO ANSWER ACCORDING TO THE "LEGEND" CREATED FOR HIM BY THE CIA. MILITARY ASSIGNMENTS, SCHOOL HISTORY, WORK HISTORY AND HIS RELATIONSHIP WITH HIS IMPOSTOR MOTHER "MARGUERITE" WOULD HAVE TO COINCIDE WITH THE CIA LEGEND.*

*MOSBY NOTED THAT **HARVEY** "SOUNDED TO ME AS IF HE HAD REHEARSED THESE SENTENCES" IN REGARDS TO HIS DEFECTION.*

NOVEMBER 14TH 1959
HARVEY IS INFORMED BY SOVIET OFFICIALS THAT HE MAY REMAIN IN RUSSIA AS A RESIDENT ALIEN BUT HE WILL NOT BE GRANTED CITIZENSHIP.

NOVEMBER 15TH 1959
"MARGUERITE" VISITS THE OFFICES OF THE FT. WORTH PRESS. A REPORTER, KENT BIGGLE, ARRANGES FOR HER TO CALL HER "SON" **HARVEY** AT HIS HOTEL IN MOSCOW. **HARVEY** IMMEDIATELY HUNG UP ON HER. HE WOULD HAVE LITTLE INCLINATION TO DEAL WITH "MARGUERITE" WHILE ON ASSIGNMENT IN RUSSIA.

*"MARGUERITE" AVOIDED HAVING HER PICTURE ASSOCIATED WITH ANY ARTICLES REGARDING THE "DEFECTION" OF **HARVEY**. THOSE WHO KNEW THE REAL MARGUERITE WOULD CERTAINLY BE ABLE TO DISTINGUISH THE SHORT, HEAVY, GREY-HAIRED "MARGUERITE" FROM **LEE'S** REAL MOTHER.*

NOVEMBER 16TH 1959
PRIOR TO HIS DEPARTURE FROM MOSCOW TO MINSK, **HARVEY** WAS INTERVIEWED BY PRISCILLA JOHNSON OF THE NORTH AMERICAN NEWS AGENCY. THE 4-5 HOUR INTERVIEW RESULTED IN A SOMEWHAT SYMPATHETIC ARTICLE IN WHICH SHE NEVER TOUCHED UPON **HARVEY'S** THREATS TO PASS ON RADAR SECRETS TO THE RUSSIANS. HOWEVER IN HER WARREN COMMISSION INTERVIEW SHE NOTED THAT "HE HOPED HIS EXPERIENCE AS A RADAR OPERATOR WOULD MAKE HIM MORE DESIRABLE TO THEM (THE SOVIETS)."

*THE OBVIOUS CHANGE OF HEART LIKELY STEMMED FROM THE FACT THAT JOHNSON HAD LINKS TO THE **CIA**. INDEED HER CIA FILE LISTS HER AS A "WITTING COLLABORATOR." SHE HAD PREVIOUSLY APPLIED TO THE CIA IN 1952 FOR EMPLOYMENT AS AN INTELLIGENCE ANALYST. SHE WAS LIKELY TOLD <u>NOT</u> TO INCLUDE HER LATER WARREN COMMISSION OBSERVATIONS IN HER INITIAL NOVEMBER 26TH, 1959 ARTICLE AS IT COULD COMPLICATE MATTERS FOR **HARVEY** WHEN HE EVENTUALLY RETURNED TO THE U.S AFTER COMPLETING HIS ASSIGNMENT AND POSSIBLY EXPOSE HIM TO CHARGES OF TREASON.*

*IT IS ALSO WORTH NOTING THAT IN HER 1959 ARTICLE SHE DESCRIBED **HARVEY** AS A "<u>NICE LOOKING SIX-FOOTER</u> WITH GREY EYES AND BROWN HAIR." ON NOVEMBER 24TH, 1963, THE ARTICLE WAS RE-RELELASED BUT NOW READ "**LEE**, A <u>YOUNG MAN</u> WITH GREY EYES AND BROWN HAIR." HAD JOHNSON IN HER ORIGINAL 1959 ARTICLE ERRED BY DESCRIBING **LEE** NOT **HARVEY**? IF SO, THE RE-RELEASED VERSION WOULD HAVE TO BE CHANGED SINCE IT WAS THE SHORTER, SOMEWHAT LESS ATTRACTIVE **HARVEY** WHO HAD BEEN ARRRESTED IN DALLAS AND THAT SHE HAD INTERVIEWED IN MOSCOW.*

NOVEMBER 17TH 1959
PRISCILLA JOHNSON SHARES HER INTERVIEW FINDINGS WITH J.V. MCVICKAR AT THE U.S. EMBASSY.

NOVEMBER 26TH 1959
HARVEY WRITES HIS "BROTHER" ROBERT ONCE AGAIN.

NOVEMBER 1959
HARVEY WAS PLACED ON A WATCH LIST OF PERSONS WHOSE MAIL GOING TO AND FROM THE U.S. WAS OPENED AND READ. HIS INCLUSION TO THE LIST WAS AT THE REQUEST OF JAMES ANGLETON, CIA CHIEF OF COUNTER-INTELLIGENCE. THE WATCH LIST WAS TITLED HT-LINGUAL. THE PROGRAM WAS ILLEGAL, BUT MORE IMPORTANT IS THE FACT THAT IT IS ONE YEAR <u>PRIOR</u> TO THE TIME THAT THE CIA NOTED TO THE WARREN COMMISSION THAT IT HAD OPENED A FILE ON **HARVEY**. THE CIA OPENED A 201 FILE ON A LEE HENRY OSWALD ON DECEMBER 9TH, 1960. IT WOULD BE ANGLETON WHO WOULD CONTROL THE FLOW OF INFORMATION FROM THE CIA TO THE W.C.

DECEMBER 1ST 1959
THE U.S. EMBASSY IN MOSCOW CABLES THE STATE DEPARTMENT NOTIFYING THEM THAT **HARVEY** HAS LEFT HIS HOTEL IN MOSCOW. **HARVEY** HOWEVER HAD NOT LEFT MOSCOW OR HOTEL METROPOLE. HIS INTOURIST GUIDE HAD GOTTEN HIM AN INEXPENSIVE ROOM IN THE TOP FLOOR OF THE HOTEL.

DECEMBER 17TH 1959
ROBERT OSWALD, **HARVEY'S** "BROTHER", RECEIVES A SHORT GOODBYE NOTE FROM **HARVEY** JUST PRIOR TO **HARVEY'S** DEPARTURE FOR MINSK.

DECEMBER 18TH 1959
"MARGUERITE" MAILS **HARVEY** A $20 CHECK TO HIS HOTEL IN MOSCOW.

DECEMBER 26TH 1959
HARVEY WRITES "MARGUERITE" FROM MOSCOW. HE APPARENTLY RETURNED THE CHECK AND NOW ASKS FOR CASH INSTEAD.

DECEMBER 29TH 1959
HARVEY SENDS IN A FORM TO THE MOSCOW CITY COUNCIL IN AN EFFORT TO OBTAIN AN IDENTITY CARD.

DECEMBER 1959
ROSCOE WHITE RE-ENLISTS IN THE MARINE CORP. HE WOULD LATER CLAIM THAT HE WAS RECRUITED BY THE CIA AT THIS TIME.

JANUARY 4TH 1960
HARVEY IS AWARDED RESIDENCY PERMIT #P.311479 ALLOWING HIM TO STAY IN RUSSIA FOR ONE YEAR. HE IS ALSO INFORMED THAT HE WILL BE RELOCATED TO MINSK..

JANUARY 5TH 1960
"MARGUERITE" SENDS HARVEY $20 IN CASH. HE HAD RETURNED THE PREVIOUSLY SENT CHECK AND REQUESTED CASH.

JANUARY 7TH 1960
HARVEY ARRIVES IN MINSK. HE IS TAKEN TO THE HOTEL MINSK. THERE HE IS MET BY ANOTHER INTOURIST GUIDE, ROZA KUZNETSOVA.

JANUARY 13TH 1960
HARVEY STARTS WORK AS A METAL WORKER AT THE BELORUSSIAN RADIO AND TELEVISION FACTORY.

JANUARY 14TH 1960
HARVEY IS ISSUED AN I.D. CARD FOR FOREIGNERS BY THE MOSCOW CITY GOVERNMENT.

JANUARY 22ND 1960
"MARGUERITE" SENDS HARVEY A $25 FOREIGN MONEY TRANSFER.

FEBRUARY 1960
"MARGUERITE" RECEIVES A CALL FROM AN FBI AGENT WHO IS ASSIGNED TO THE DALLAS FBI FIELD OFFICE. SHE WOULD RECALL HIS NAME AS "FANNAN." THE DALLAS OFFICE WOULD LATER STATE THAT THEIR INITIAL CONTACT WITH HER WAS NOT UNTIL APRIL 28, 1960 BY AGENT JOHN FAIN. HARVEY'S CORRESPONDANCE WITH "MARGUERITE" AND ROBERT WAS NOT ONLY BEING READ BY THE FBI'S MAIL INTERCEPT PROGRAM BUT ALSO BY THE CIA'S HT LINGUAL MAIL INTERCEPT PROGRAM.

FEBRUARY 25TH 1960
"MARGUERITE" RECEIVES THE LETTER SHE HAD PREVIOUSLY SENT TO HARVEY CONTAINING THE $20 IN CASH. IT WAS RETURNED UNOPENED.

MARCH 6TH 1960
"MARGUERITE" WRITES TEXAS CONGRESSMAN JIM WRIGHT REGARDING INFORMATION ON HER" SON" HARVEY.

MARCH 7TH 1960
"MARGUERITE", STILL CONCERNED OVER HER "SON'S" WHEREABOUTS, WRITES A LETTER TO THE SECRETARY OF STATE.

MARCH 16TH 1960
HARVEY IS MOVED TO AN APARTMENT BUILDING IN MINSK.

MARCH 17TH 1960
PRESIDENT EISENHOWER APPROVES THE CIA'S COVERT PLAN TO REMOVE CASTRO FROM POWER.

MARCH 21ST 1960
THE STATE DEPARTMENT SENDS COPIES OF "MARGUERITE'S" LETTER TO WRIGHT AND CONGRESSMAN WRIGHT'S LETTER TO HER TO THE AMERICAN EMBASSY IN MOSCOW.

50

APRIL 5ᵀᴴ 1960
A MEMO FFROM THE AMERICAN EMBASSY IN MOSCOW TO THE STATE DEPARTMENT STATED THAT "THE EMBASSY HAS HAD NO CONTACT WITH OSWALD (**HARVEY**) SINCE HIS DEPARTURE FROM THE METROPOLE HOTEL IN MOSCOW IN NOVEMBER 1959 AND HAS NO CLUE TO HIS PRESENT WHEREABOUTS."

APRIL 26ᵀᴴ 1960
A LETTER THIS DATE ARRIVES AT "MARGUERITE'S" RESIDENCE. IT IS TO INFORM **HARVEY** THAT HE IS BEING CONSIDERED FOR AN UNDESIRABLE DISCHARGE, PRESUMABLY AS A RESULT OF HIS "DEFECTION" AND REQUEST FOR SOVIET CITIZENSHIP.

APRIL 27ᵀᴴ 1960
FBI AGENT FAIN INTERVIEWS ROBERT OSWALD IN FORT WORTH, TEXAS. ROBERT INFORMS FAIN THAT "MARGUERITE" IS NOW LIVING IN WACO, TEXAS AT 1111 HERRING AVENUE. ROBERT APPARENTLY CONTACTS "MARGUERITE" WHO IN TURN CONTACTS FAIN AND AGREES TO AN INTERVIEW.

APRIL 28ᵀᴴ 1960
FBI AGENT FAIN INTERVIEWS "MARGUERITE" OSWALD IN FORT WORTH, TEXAS. "MARGUERITE" HOWEVER TELLS FAIN THAT HER "SON" **HARVEY** IS IN SWITZERLAND ATTENDING COLLEGE. IT IS WELL KNOWN BY THIS TIME THAT **HARVEY** IS IN RUSSIA.

COLD WAR CHESS GAMES

BEFORE **HARVEY"S** ARRIVAL IN RUSSIA, CIA CHIEF OF COUNTERINTELLIGENCE, JAMES JESUS ANGLETON, WAS CONCERNED ABOUT THE POSSIBLIITY OF A "MOLE" IN THE CIA HQ. THIS SUSPICION ROSE FROM THE FACT THAT A RELIABLE SOURCE IN RUSSIA HAD INFORMED HIS CIA CONTACT THAT U-2 SECRETS HAD BEEN COMPRIMISED. IT IS POSSIBLE THAT THE "MOLE" WAS ACTUALLY ONI/CIA OPERATIVES INVOLVED IN INTELLIGENCE GATHERING VIA THE U-2 PROGRAM BASED IN ATSUGI. THIS "COMPRIMISED" DATA WAS THEN FED TO **LEE** TO ESTABLISH HIS BONA FIDES TO THE JAPANESE HOSTESSESS WHO WERE KNOWN TO BE COLLECTING MILITARY INFORMATION FOR THE JAPANESE COMMUNIST ORGANIZATION; AN ORGANIZATION THE ONI WAS TRYING TO INFILTRATE. ONE HAS TO KEEP IN MIND THAT THE ONLY TRUE "SECRET" ABOUT THE U-2 WAS ITS **MAXIMUM OPERATING ALTITUDE CAPABILITY** (IN EXCESS OF 90,000 FEET, NOT THE 68,000 FEET PUBLISHED IN JANE'S BOOK OF AIRCRAFT), <u>AND</u> THE RECONNAISSANCE **FLIGHT PATHS** OVER MAINLAND RUSSIA.

IN THE EARLY 1950'S, B-36 BOMBERS WERE RETROFITTED FOR INTELLIGENCE FLIGHTS. THE BOMBERS WERE OFFICIALLY CREDITED WITH AN ALTITUDE CAPABILITY OF 40,000 FEET. THOSE CLOSELY FAMILIAR WITH THE PLANE NOTED THAT ITS TRUE ALTITUDE CEILING WAS ABOUT 60,000 FEET. THE B-36 WAS AN ENORMOUS PLANE OUTFITTED WITH 4 TURBOJETS. IF A PLANE OF THIS SIZE AND WEIGHT WITH A CREW OF 19 COULD REACH 60,000 FEET, ONE WOULD BE FOOLISH NOT TO THINK THAT A FEATHERWEIGHT GLIDER-LIKE U-2 WITH A CREW OF ONE COULD EASILY REACH ALTITUDES OF NEARLY 100,000 FEET; PARTICULARLY SINCE AT THE MIDWAY POINT OF A GIVEN OVERFLIGHT A U-2 WOULD BE MUCH LIGHTER DUE TO FUEL CONSUMPTION. IN SUPPORT OF THE LOFT CAPABILITIES OF THE U-2 IS A COMMENT MADE BY SAM BERRY WHO WORKED ALONGSIDE **LEE** IN THE RADAR HUT AT ATSUGI. BERRY NOTED "WE COULD TRACK THE U-2, SOMETIMES UP TO 100,000 FEET, AND THEN WE LOST THEM." OTHERS WOULD NOTE THAT U-2 PILOTS WOULD FREQUENTLY "REQUEST WINDS ALOFT AT 90,000 ANGELS." IN PILOT-SPEAK, 90,000 ANGELS IS 90,000 FEET.

IF THE U-2 WAS INDEED COMPRIMISED, ONE WOULD HAVE TO ASSUME THAT THE RUSSIANS HAD GAINED SOME KNOWLEDGE ABOUT EITHER THE <u>ACTUAL</u> OPERATING ALTITUDE THE U-2 USED IN ITS OVERFLIGHTS, OR HAD OBTAINED KNOWLEDGE ABOUT THE TYPICAL <u>FLIGHT PATHS</u> USED TO TARGET SENSITIVE RUSSIAN MILITARY

INSTALLATIONS. IRONICALLY, KNOWLEDGE OF THE ACTUAL OPERATING ALTITUDE OF THE U-2 WOULD HAVE BEEN OF LITTLE USE TO THE RUSSIANS. AT THAT TIME THEIR HEIGHT FINDING RADAR WAS INCAPABLE OF TRACKING U-2 FLIGHTS AT THEIR ROUTINE INTRUSION ALTITUDE OF ABOUT 75,000 FEET. THE RADAR WHICH THE SOVIETS USED AT THAT TIME WAS AMERICAN MADE AND SENT TO RUSSIA UNDER THE POST WORLD WAR II LEND-LEASE ACT. IT WAS UNABLE TO TRACK ANY PLANE IN EXCESS OF 40, 000 FEET.

EVEN IF THE SOVIETS HAD TRACKING CAPABILITY, THEIR MISSLE GUIDANCE SYSTEMS ON THEIR SAMS WAS INEFFECTIVE AT THOSE LOFTY ALTITUDES. ANOTHER FACTOR THE SOVIETS WOULD HAVE TO OVERCOME FOR A LEGITIMATE SHOOT-DOWN WOULD BE THE RADAR-JAMMING BEAM EMITTED BY THE U-2. IN THAT SAME REGARD, KNOWLEDGE OF SPECIFIC FLIGHT PATHS WOULD HAVE BEEN USELESS AS WELL WITHOUT THE ABILITY TO DOWN A PLANE. IT SEEMS THAT THE ONLY THING LIKELY COMPRIMISED ABOUT THE U-2 WAS THAT IT DID INDEED EXIST AND THAT IT WAS ROUTINELY USED FOR OVERFLIGHTS OF RUSSIAN TERRITORY. THIS WAS LIKELY ALL **LEE** WAS ALLOWED TO SHARE WITH THE JAPANESE COMMUNISTS. THE SOVIETS HOWEVER COULD NEVER PUBLICLY ACKNOWLEDGE THAT THE OVERFLIGHTS WERE TAKING PLACE SINCE THIS WOULD BE TANTAMOUNT TO ADMITTING THAT THEIR AIR SPACE COULD NOW BE ROUTINELY VIOLATED BY A PLANE THAT THEY WERE NOT ONLY UNABLE TO ACCURATELY TRACK, BUT ALSO SUCCESSFULLY SHOOT DOWN. THE FLIGHTS CONTINUED UP UNTIL THE SCHEDULED MAY 1960 TALKS AND NOW INCLUDED MILITARY AND CONSTRUCTION SITES AS WELL. THIS NECESSITATED A DIPLOMATIC APPROACH BY THE RUSSIANS IN REGARD TO ELIMINATING WHAT WAS A TREMENDOUS INTELLIGENCE GATHERING ADVANTAGE ENJOYED BY THE U.S.

BEFORE WE EXPLORE THE ESSENCE OF **HARVEY'S** "DEFECTION" TO RUSSIA, IT IS IMPORTANT TO SET THE STAGE FOR WHAT WAS HIS TRUE COLD WAR ASSIGNMENT. THERE ARE 3 DISTINCT ASPECTS TO DISCUSS:

(1) THE 1960 SUMMIT TALKS AND THE RUSSIAN OPEN SKY PROPOSAL
(2) **LEE'S** MILITARY BACKGROUND AND **HARVEY'S** "DEFECTION" TO RUSSIA
(3) THE DOWNING OF FRANCIS GARY POWERS U-2 PLANE

THE 1960 SUMMIT TALKS

AT THE JULY 1955 SUMMIT TALKS BETWEEN THE USSR AND THE U.S., EISENHOWER WANTED TO PROPOSE AN "OPEN SKIES" PROGRAM SINCE HE FELT THAT COVERT FLIGHTS OVER RUSSIA, IF DISCOVERED, COULD LEAD TO WAR. EISENHOWER STILL HARBORED CONCERNS THAT THE CIA WAS OVERESTIMATING, IN SPITE OF THEIR ASSURANCES, THE CAPABILITY OF THE U-2 TO FLY UNDETECTED. THE U-2 HAD TAKEN ITS FIRST TEST FLIGHT LESS THAN TWO WEEKS PRIOR TO THE JULY 1955 TALKS.

I FIND IT INTERESTING THAT JUST 5 YEARS LATER EISENHOWER'S SUCCESSOR, JFK, WOULD RECEIVE A SIMILAR ASSURANCE FROM THE CIA THAT THE BAY OF PIGS OPERATION WOULD BE AT WORST A LIMITED SUCCESS. ALTHOUGH BOTH PRESIDENTS WERE WARY OF THE BOLD ASSURANCES OFFERED BY THE AGENCY, BOTH MEN EVENTUALLY SUCCUMBED TO THE PROMISE OF COLD WAR VICTORIES OVER COMMUNISM.

THIS "OPEN SKIES" PROGRAM WOULD ALLOW U.S. AIRCRAFT TO "OVERFLY" RUSSIA. THESE OVERFLIGHTS WOULD UTILIZE RETROFITTED COMMERCIAL PLANES OR RECONNAISSANCE PLANES IN AN ATTEMPT TO LOCATE, MAP, AND QUANTIFY THEIR RELATIVE MILITARY STRENGTH AS WELL AS THE PROGRESS OF CONSTRUCTION AND AGRICULTURAL PROJECTS. THIS PROGRAM OF COURSE WOULD ALSO ALLOW THE SOVIETS TO OVERFLY AMERICAN SOIL AS WELL. WHY THE TRADE-OFF? ONE HAS TO BEAR IN MIND THAT SINCE THE IRON CURTAIN'S DRAMATIC DROP, OUR ACCESS TO INFORMATION ON NEARLY EVERY ASPECT OF SOVIET LIFE, BOTH CIVILIAN AND MILITARY, HAD SLOWED TO A TRICKLE. OUR DEMOCRATIC, OPEN STYLE OF

GOVERNMENT, THE FREEDOM THE PRESS AND THE MEDIA ENJOYED, AND OUR OPEN BORDERS WELCOMING IMMIGRANTS OF ALL COUNTRIES, CONTRASTED SHARPLY WITH THE SECRECY IN WHICH THE SOVIET UNION CONDUCTED ITS GOVERNMENTAL AFFAIRS. WITH THEIR STATE CONTROLLED COLD PRESS AND MEDIA AND TIGHTLY CONTROLLED BORDERS, CRUCIAL INFORMATION ON THEIR AGRICULTURAL, ECONOMIC, AND MILITARY STATUS WAS NOT EASILY OBTAINED. IN CONTRAST, MUCH OF THIS SAME INFORMATION REGARDING THE U.S WAS WIDELY PUBLISHED AND THEREFORE FREELY OBTAINED BY THE SOVIETS. THE INTELLIGENCE ADVANTAGE WAS CLEARLY THE SOVIETS'. AN "OPEN SKIES" PROGRAM WOULD LEVEL THE PLAYING FIELD FOR THE U.S. FULLY AWARE OF THIS STRATEGIC ADVANTAGE, THE SOVIETS WERE COOL TO THE U.S. PROPOSAL AT THE SUMMIT TALKS IN 1955.

THE RUSSIANS HAD YET ANOTHER REASON TO IGNORE EISENHOWER'S PROPOSAL EVEN IF THEY WERE ALLOWED RECIPROCAL PHOTOGRAPHIC OVERFLIGHTS OF THE U.S. THE SOVIETS LACKED PROVEN LONG RANGE BOMBERS AND LONG RANGE MISSLES. THE U.S HOWEVER WOULD NOT ONLY BE ABLE TO PHOTOGRAPHICALLY DOCUMENT TARGETS INSIDE THE SOVIET UNION, BUT WOULD LEGITIMATELY BE ABLE TO <u>REACH</u> THOSE TARGETS AS WELL.

EISENHOWER, EXPECTING THE REJECTION OF HIS PROPOSAL, HAD A TRUMP CARD; THE U-2. HE REPORTEDLY STATED DURING THE 1955 SUMMIT TALKS, "I'LL GIVE IT ONE SHOT, THEN IF THEY DON'T ACCEPT, WE'LL FLY THE U-2."

THE MAY 1960 SUMMIT TALKS WERE SCHEDULED IN PARIS BETWEEN THE U.S. AND THE SOVIETS. ON THE AGENDA ONCE AGAIN WAS A PROPOSAL FOR AN "OPEN SKIES" PROGRAM. AFTER THE U-2'S MAIDEN INCURSION INTO SOVIET AIR SPACE, COMPLETE WITH AN OVERFLIGHT OF THE SHIPYARDS OF LENINGRAD ON JULY 4TH, 1956, IT WAS FELT THAT IT WAS NO LONGER NECESSARY FOR THE U.S TO CONTINUE ITS PURSUIT OF SUCH A PROGRAM. THE INITIAL FLIGHT, LAUNCHED FROM WIESBADEN, WEST GERMANY, FLEW DIRECTLY OVER MOSCOW WITH NO SIGN THAT THE SOVIETS WERE EVEN AWARE OF THE DRAMATIC VIOLATION OF THEIR AIR SPACE.

AN "OPEN SKIES" PROGRAM NOW WOULD BE NOT ONLY BE TOTALLY UNNECESSARY AS FAR AS THE U.S. WAS CONCERNED, BUT WOULD DIMINISH WHAT WAS NOW A TREMENDOUS INTELLIGENCE GATHERING ADVANTAGE ENJOYED BY THE U.S. THE SOVIETS HOWEVER COULD NEVER PUBLICLY OR PRIVATELY ACKNOWLDEGE THAT THE OVERFLIGHTS WERE TAKING PLACE. THE RUSSIANS ONLY HOPE WAS THAT THE U.S WOULD ONCE AGAIN TENDER AN "OPEN SKIES" PROPOSAL SIMILAR TO THE ONE INTRODUCED BY THE U.S AT THE 1955 SUMMIT TALKS ***PRIOR*** TO THE SUCCESSFUL LAUNCH OF THE U-2 PROGRAM OR AT LEAST ENTERTAIN A SIMILAR PROPOSAL BY THE SOVIETS. THIS PRESENTED QUITE A DILEMMA FOR THE U.S. EISENHOWER COULD NOT SIMPLY GO TO THE SUMMIT TALKS AND REFUSE TO DISCUSS THIS SEEMINGLY INNOCUOUS PROPOSAL PARTICULARLY AS IT CLOSELY RESEMBLED THE VERY PROPOSAL <u>HE</u> PURSUED IN 1955. A REFUSAL TO EVEN *ADDRESS* THE PROPOSAL WOULD BE TANTAMOUNT TO ADMITTING THAT THE OVERFLIGHTS WERE INDEED TAKING PLACE. THE NEXT BEST SOLUTION WOULD BE TO SABOTAGE THE TALKS TO THE EXTENT THAT ANY MEANINGFUL DIALOGUE WOULD BE MOOT. WHAT WOULD TAKE PLACE ONLY 2 WEEKS PRIOR TO THE TALKS ACCOMPLISHED THIS OBJECTIVE PERFECTLY AND ALSO ALLOWED THE CIA TO TURN UP THE TEMPERATURE IN WHAT WAS BECOMING A SLOWLY "THAWING" COLD WAR.

DOWNING OF FRANCIS GARY POWERS U-2 PLANE

MAY 1ST 1960

POWERS U-2 FLIGHT IS SHOT DOWN 2 WEEKS BEFORE THE SCHEDULED SUMMIT TALKS IN PARIS. POWERS IS NOT ONLY CAPTURED ALIVE BUT A CONSIDERABLE AMOUNT OF THE U-2 WRECKAGE IS RECOVERED AS WELL.

IT IS INTERESTING TO NOTE THAT IN ALL THE PREVIOUS INCURSIONS BY THE U-2 INTO SOVIET AIRSPACE, THE PENETRATION WOULD ONLY BE A DISTANCE APPROXIMATELY HALFWAY INTO THE COUNTRY. THE PLANE WOULD THEN TURN AROUND AND RETURN TO ITS HOME BASE. POWERS' FATAL FLIGHT WOULD BE THE FIRST TO FLY COMPLETELY ACROSS THE COUNTRY. HIS FLIGHT WAS SCHEDULED TO DEPART FROM PERSHAWAR, PAKISTAN AND LAND IN BODO, NORWAY.

MAY 5TH 1960

WASHINGTON CONTINUES TO CALL POWER'S U-2 A NASA RESEARCH PLANE. KRUSCHEV HOWEVER ANNOUNCES THAT THE SOVIET UNION HAS SHOT DOWN A SPY PLANE.

MAY 7TH 1960

KRUSCHEV ANNOUNCES THAT THE PILOT IS "SAFE AND SOUND" AND THAT THE SOVIETS RECOVERED EQUIPMENT FROM THE WRECKED U-2. HE ALSO DISPLAYS PHHOTOGRAPHS TAKEN BY THE U-2 OF SOVIET FACTORIES, AIR FIELDS, AND OTHER STRATEGIC SITES.

AUGUST 17/18TH 1960

POWERS IS TRIED IN A SOVIET COURT. THERE IS EVIDENCE THAT **HARVEY** ATTENDED THE TRIAL AS WELL. IN PHOTOS AND FOOTAGE OF THE TRIAL THERE IS A YOUNG MAN SHOWN WEARING A SHIRT THAT LOOKS VERY SIMILAR TO THE ONE **HARVEY** WAS WEARING WHEN HE WAS PHOTOGRAPHED LATER IN MARCH OF 1961.

***HARVEY** HAD ALSO HIGHLIGHTED SEVERAL WORDS IN HIS ENGLISH-RUSSIAN DICTIONARY. THE WORDS "RADAR", "RANGE", AND EVEN MORE INTERESTING, THE WORD "EJECT" WERE UNDERLINED. THE IMPORTANCE OF THE WORD "EJECT" WILL BECOME CLEAR AS WE FURTHER EXPLORE THE FINAL MINUTES OF POWER'S FATEFUL U-2 FLIGHT.*

FEBRUARY 9TH 1962

POWERS IS EXCHANGED FOR RUSSIAN SPY RUDOLPH ABEL.

WHAT WE HAVE AT THIS POINT ARE THREE SEEMINGLY UNRELATED EVENTS; A LONG-PLANNED SUMMIT TALK BETWEEN THE U.S. AND RUSSIA, A "DEFECTION" BY AN EX-MARINE, AND THE DOWNING OF A U-2 RECONNAISSANCE PLANE.

SOLVING THE PUZZLE

ONE OF THE TWO KEYS TO LINKING THESE THREE EVENTS IS THE **AGENDA** AT THE 1960 SUMMIT TALKS; THE "OPEN SKIES" PROGRAM. FOR REASONS OUTLINED PREVIOUSLY, THIS PROPOSAL MUST BE AVOIDED AT ALL COSTS. THE SECOND KEY, SELF PRESERVATION BY A CIA THEN THREATENED BY BUDGETARY CUTS AND DOWNSIZING, ALSO PLAYS A DECISIVE ROLE IN THIS COLD WAR DRAMA. LET US MORE CLOSELY EXAMINE THE FLIGHT OF GARY POWERS THAT MAY IN 1960, **AND** INCLUDE **HARVEY** AS A PARTICIPANT.

OCTOBER 1959

HARVEY "DEFECTS" TO RUSSIA APPARRENTLY WITH SOME FINANCIAL AND LOGISTIC SUPPORT. HE STATES AT THE EMBASSY THAT HE HAD GIVEN THE SOVIETS INFORMATION ABOUT U-2 RADAR INSTALLATIONS. THIS COULD BE A REFERENCE TO THE ONI/CIA PROVIDED FALSE INFORMATION THAT **LEE** HAD PASSED TO THE SOVIETS VIA THE JAPANESE HOSTESSES WHILE STATIONED IN JAPAN, OR A REFERENCE TO NEW INFORMATION REGARDING THE U-2.

***HARVEY** WAS THE PERFECT "DANGLE." NEWTON S.MILAN, CHIEF OF OPERATIONS OF COUNTER-INTELLIGENCE NOTED THAT IN 1959, THE KGB WAS AT A CONSIDERABLE DISADVANTAGE IN REGARDS TO ITS ABILITY TO GATHER INFORMATION THAT WOULD NARROW THE TECHNOLOGY GAP THAT EXISTED BETWEEN THE U.S AND THE USSR. RADAR WAS A FOCUS OF THE KGB. **LEE'S** RADAR BACKGROUND WOULD MAKE **HARVEY** PARTICULARLY ATTRACTIVE TO THE SOVIETS.*

MAY 1960

POWERS LEAVES ON A U-2 MISSION FROM PESHWAR, PAKISTAN AT 6:26 AM. HE FEELS THAT THE FLIGHT IS ILL-TIMED DUE TO THE CLOSE PROXIMITY TO THE SUMMIT TALKS. IN FACT, THERE HAD BEEN ONLY **ONE** U-2 FLIGHT PENETRATING RUSSIAN AIR SPACE SINCE **HARVEY'S** ARRIVAL IN OCTOBER OF 1959. THAT FLIGHT WAS ON APRIL 9TH, 1960. POWERS WAS THE BACK-UP PILOT ON THAT FLIGHT.

POWERS' FLIGHT WAS DELAYED BY 26 MINUTES THAT SUNDAY MORNING WAITING FOR FINAL APPROVAL WHICH EISENHOWER INSISTED UPON FOR EACH FLIGHT. ENCRYPTED SIGNAL TRANSMISSION TO THE PESHAWAR FLIGHT STATION WAS GARBLED, SO THE OPERATOR AT ADANA DECIDED TO SEND THE "OK" PERMISSION NEEDED TO RELEASE POWER'S FLIGHT "IN THE CLEAR." IN ESSENCE, IT WAS NOT A CODED MESSAGE BUT SENT IN "PLAIN ENGLISH" MORSE CODE. NEEDLESS TO SAY, THE SOVIET COMMUNICATION INTERCEPT OPERATORS WOULD HAVE HAD NO DIFFICULTY IN INTERCEPTING THE MESSAGE AND TRANSLATING IT AS WELL

POWERS WAS FLYING U-2 PLANE # 360. THIS PARTICULAR U-2 HAD RUN OUT OF FUEL SHORT OF ITS LANDING SITE IN ATSUGI, JAPAN IN SEPTEMBER 1959. AS A RESULT, POWERS HAD LITTLE CONFIDENCE IN PLANE #360. OTHER PILOTS SHARED POWERS' CONCERNS. PLANE #360 WAS DUBBED A "HANGAR QUEEN" BY THOSE FAMILIAR WITH ITS FLIGHT CHARACTERISTICS. THE PLANE ORIGINALLY SCHEDULED TO BE THE ONE POWERS WOULD FLY WAS PULLED FROM SERVICE ON SATURDAY, 30 APRIL, JUST 1 DAY PRIOR TO POWERS DEPARTURE DATE.

POWERS NOTED THAT WHEN HE WAS INITIALLY ASSIGNED TO THE U-2 BASE AT ADANA, TURKEY THAT THE FLIGHTS SKIRTED THE SOVIET BORDER. HE NOTED THAT THE FLIGHTS WERE "NEVER PENETRATING, STAYING OFF THE COAST, OVER INTERNATIONAL WATERS." HE ALSO NOTED THAT THE MONITORING OF RUSSIAN MISSLE AND SPACE LAUNCHES WAS A TOP PRIORITY FOR U-2 SURVEILLANCE. THESE LAUNCHES HOWEVER NORMALLY TOOK PLACE AT NIGHT. POWERS LAST FLIGHT WAS UNIQUE IN TWO REGARDS: IT WAS A DAYLIGHT MISSION NOT CONNECTED WITH A NIGHTTIME SOVIET LAUNCH, AND IT WOULD NOT ONLY SIMPLY SKIRT THE SOVIET BORDER BUT WOULD FLY ACROSS THE COUNTRY.

AS IT STOOD, POWERS WAS ABOUT TO EMBARK ON THE FIRST SOUTH TO NORTH TRANS-RUSSIAN OVERFLIGHT ON BOARD THE LEAST RELIABLE PLANE IN THE U-2 PROGRAM AND THE RUSSIANS QUITE LIKELY KNEW HE WAS COMING

*POWERS, AT HIS CRUISING ALTITUDE FOR THIS FLIGHT, 70,500 FEET, IS STILL ABOVE THE RANGE OF SOVIET MISSLES. HOWEVER A NEAR-MISS BY A SURFACE-TO-AIR MISSILE, QUITE LIKELY LAUNCHED FROM THE TYURATAM MISSILE TEST RANGE, DAMAGES THE FRAGILE U-2'S TAIL SECTION. POWERS THEN FEELS A "DULL THUD" JUST BEHIND THE COCKPIT THAT PUSHES HIM FORWARD. POWERS' OUT OF CONTROL U-2 THEN LOSES **CONSIDERABLE** ALTITUDE. EAVESDROPPING BY THE NSA INDICATED THAT THE PLANE HAD TUMBLED TO 30,000 FEET. IT IS THEN, AND ONLY THEN, THAT HIS PLANE WAS EITHER HIT BY A RUSSIAN SA-2 MISSILE OR A SOVIET MIG 17 OR, SIMPLY CONTINUED TO LOSE ALTITUDE UNTIL HE CRASH LANDED WITHOUT THE SOVIETS MAKING A DIRECT HIT ON THE CRIPPLED U-2. AT HIS CRUISING ALTITUDE HE WAS SIMPLY TOO HIGH TO BE EITHER RELIABLY TRACKED OR SHOT DOWN.*

IT IS INTERESTING TO NOTE THAT POWERS NEVER SPECIFICALLY STATED THAT HIS PLANE HAD BEEN HIT BY A MISSLE FURTHER ADDING CREEDENCE TO THE NOTION THAT HE SIMPLY CRASH LANDED AFTER THE NEAR-MISS.

POWERS MANAGES TO ESCAPE HIS AIRCRAFT WITHOUT ACTIVATING THE EJECT MECHANISM. THE COCKPIT EJECT MECHANISM HAD A SLIGHT "DESIGN" FLAW. UPON EJECTION, IT WAS QUITE LIKELY THAT THE PILOT'S LEGS WOULD BE BADLY DAMAGED DUE TO THE SMALL OPENING ALLOWED FOR THE PILOT'S ESCAPE. A DELAYED SELF-DESTRUCT TIMER WAS ALSO ON BOARD THAT WOULD NORMALLY ALLOW THE PILOT TIME

TO EJECT SAFELY. LATER, ON SEVERAL U-2 FLIGHTS BY NATIONALIST CHINESE PILOTS FLYING OVERFLIGHTS FROM TAIWAN OVER MAINLAND CHINA, THE PILOTS, AFTER ACTIVATING THE SELF DESTRUCT DEVICE, WERE KILLED WITH LITTLE OR NO WRECKAGE RECOVERED. THE CIA MAINTAINED THAT THE SELF-DESTRUCT DEVICES WERE DESIGNED ONLY TO DESTROY THE CAMERA AND FILM, NOT THE ENTIRE PLANE. BUT, ALLEN DULLES HAD PREVIOUSLY GUARANTEED EISENHOWER THAT A U-2 PILOT WOULD NEVER SURVIVE A CRASH. ANDREW GOODPASTER, AN EISENHOWER AIDE, PUT IT MORE SUCCINCTLY: "WE HAD AN UNDERSTANDING THAT THE PLANE WOULD BE DESTROYED AND THAT IT WAS IMPOSSIBLE FOR THE PILOT TO SURVIVE."

EISENHOWER INITIALLY DENIES THAT THE FLIGHT TOOK PLACE. THEN, HE ADMITS THAT THE FLIGHT OCCURRED, BUT THAT IT WAS AN UNMANNED WEATHER PLANE UNDER THE CONTROL OF NASA. NASA THEN PROCLAIMED THAT INDEED ONE OF ITS PLANES HAD GONE DOWN NEAR TURKEY. THIS WAS INCREDIBLY INACCURATE SINCE THE PLANE WENT DOWN NEAR SMOLENSK, OVER 1000 MILES AWAY.

THE NEXT RELUCTANT ADMISSION WAS THAT THE U-2 WAS INDEED MANNED, BUT THAT THE PILOT HAD "OXYGEN DIFFICULTIES." THIS STORY WOULD HAVE HELD WATER HAD POWERS NOT SUCCESSFULLY FREED HIMSELF FROM THE PLUMETING U-2. TO EISENHOWER'S DISMAY, BOTH POWERS AND THE WRECKAGE ARE PARADED BEFORE THE CAMERAS BY A GLOWING KRUSCHEV.

EISENHOWER WAS AGITATED AND DISGUSTED TO THE POINT THAT HE REMARKED TO HIS SECRETARY, ANN WHITMAN, THAT HE CONSIDERED RESIGNING. ON MAY 20TH, A NATIONAL SECURITY COUNCIL MEETING TOOK PLACE. THE AGENDA WAS DOMINATED BY THE U-2/SUMMIT TALK FIASCO. CIA DIRECTOR DULLES STUNNED EISENHOWER BY COMMENTING THAT THE DECISION BY THE SOVIETS TO ABORT THE SUMMIT TALKS TOOK PLACE ONLY AFTER THE U.S. ADMITTED THAT PRESIDENTIAL APPROVAL WAS REQUIRED FOR ALL OVERFLIGHTS.

EISENHOWER'S FAITH IN REGARDS TO THE CIA'S ASSURANCE THAT NEITHER PLANE NOR PILOT WOULD BE RECOVERED IN A U-2 FLIGHT FAILURE WAS EERILY SIMILAR TO THE ASSURANCES THE CIA GAVE TO JFK THAT A GROUNDSWELL OF CIVILIAN SUPPORT WOULD ASSURE THE SUCCESS OF THE BAY OF PIGS INVASION.

IN BOTH INSTANCES, THE SEASONED EISENHOWER AND THE POLITICALLY NIEVE JFK WERE LEFT TO SHOULDER THE BLAME.

THE RUSSIANS QUESTION POWERS FOR THE REMAINDER OF THE MONTH OF MAY, 1960. **HARVEY** IS QUITE LIKELY PRESENT, WITNESSING THE INTERROGATING SESSIONS THROUGH A "PEEPHOLE" POWERS LATER DESCRIBES. AFTER HIS RELEASE, POWERS WOULD RELATE TO REPORTERS THAT OSWALD "HAD ACCESS TO OUR EQUIPMENT...KNEW THE ALTITUDES WE FLEW AT, HOW LONG WE STAYED OUT ON ANY MISSION, AND IN WHICH DIRECTION WE WENT." POWERS OF COURSE WOULD HAVE BEEN REFERRING TO **HARVEY**. IT WAS **LEE** HOWEVER WHO HAD THE U-2 BACKGROUND.

THE SOVIETS WOULD HAVE NEEDED **HARVEY'S** GUIDANCE TO ORCHESTRATE THE QUESTIONING AND TO DETERMINE POWERS' TRUTHFULLNESS UNDER QUESTIONING. POWERS WAS SHOWN A DETAILED MAP PLOTTING HIS **FLIGHT PATH** BUT WITH EMPTY BRACKETS (…………….) REGARDING HIS **ALTITUDE** AT VARIOUS POINTS ALONG THE PATH. WAS THE **ALTITUDE** THE INFORMATION **HARVEY** SUPPLIED THE RUSSIANS COURTESY OF THE CIA OR WERE THE RUSSIANS ATTEMPTING TO EXTRACT THIS FROM POWERS?

AN OFFICER WHO SERVED AT ATSUGI WITH **LEE** NOTED THAT **LEE** SHOWED AN "EXTRAORDINARY INTEREST" IN THE FLIGHT **PATHS** OF THE U-2 FLIGHTS IN FACT, THE APRIL 7TH 1960 FLIGHT THAT OCCURRED JUST PRIOR TO POWERS' FLIGHT WAS ABLE TO DOCUMENT THAT IT HAD BEEN PICKED UP VERY EARLY ON (ONLY 150 MILES INSIDE

RUSSIAN TERRITORY) IN ITS FLIGHT. THIS WOULD ONLY BE POSSIBLE IF THE RUSSIANS WERE AWARE OF THE FLIGHT **PATH** IN ADVANCE.

I WOULD OFFER ANOTHER EXPLANATION OF **HARVEY'S** ROLE IN THE INCIDENT. IF ONE INCLUDES THE 1957 NSA RECRUITMENT OF MITCHELL AND MARTIN AND THE 1958 NSA CAREER START FOR JACK EDWARD DUNLAP AND HIS SUBSEQUENT USE AS A DOUBLE-AGENT BY THE NSA, IT IS QUITE POSSIBLE THAT THE CIA, IN A COMPARTMENTALIZED "NEED TO KNOW" FASHION, ALLOWED **HARVEY** TO PROVIDE THE SOVIETS ONLY WITH THE SO CALLED "OFFICIAL" ALTITUDE OF THE U-2, 68,000 FEET. THE MAXIMUM <u>PUBLISHED</u> ALTITUDE OF THE U-2 WOULD LIKELY HAVE CHANGED LITTLE SINCE **HARVEY'S** DEPARTURE FROM THE MARINE CORP. IT IS QUITE LIKELY HOWEVER THAT THE FLIGHT **PATHS** WOULD HAVE CHANGED SINCE **LEE'S** DEPARTURE FROM JAPAN IN NOVEMBER 1958 DUE TO NEW RECONNAISSANCE TARGETS. **HARVEY'S** PROVIDING OF THE "OFFICIAL" **ALTITUDE** WOULD DOVETAIL WITH **LEE'S** EXPERIENCE AS A KNOWN U-2 RADAR OPERATOR. IT WOULD MORE LIKELY BE NSA EMPLOYEE JACK EDWARD DUNLAP WHO WOULD PROVIDE THE FLIGHT **PATH** AND **SCHEDULES**. MITCHELL AND MARTIN, WHO HAD REQUESTED INFORMATION ON POWERS' ILL-FATED FLIGHT **PRIOR** TO THE EVENT, WORKED FOR THE NSA AS SPECIALISTS IN SOVIET INTERCEPT COMMUNICATIONS ON THE U-2 FLIGHTS. THEY COULD HAVE PROVIDED COMMUNICATION FREQUENCIES UTILIZED BY THE U-2 FLIGHTS. EACH POINT ON THE INTELLIGENCE TRIANGLE, **HARVEY**, MITCHELL / MARTIN, AND DUNLAP COULD HAVE PROVIDED THE SOVIETS WITH INFORMATION THEY NEEDED; PATHS, FREQUENCIES, SCHEDULES AND ALTITUDE, TO "DOWN" A U-2

ALTHOUGH **HARVEY** COULD PROVIDE FALSE **ALTITUDE** CAPABILITIES, MITCHELL/MARTIN **COMMUNICATION FREQUENCIES**, AND DUNLAP **PATHS** AND **SCHEDULES**, IT WOULD STILL NOT BE POSSIBLE FOR THE SOVIETS TO SHOOT DOWN A U-2 AT ITS MAXIMUM ALTITUDE CAPABILITY OF APPROXIMATELY 100,000 FEET NOR AT THE 70,500 FEET ALTITUDE FOR THIS PARTICULAR FLIGHT. A <u>NEAR-MISS</u> HOWEVER BY A SOVIET SA-2 MISSLE ON POWERS' FLIGHT COULD DELIVER HIM TO A LOWER ALTITUDE MORE FAVORABLE FOR INTERCEPT BY SOVIET MISSILES OR MIG FIGHTER PLANES. KEEP IN MIND THAT THE ACTUAL <u>SCHEDULES</u> OF THE FLIGHTS WOULD BE THE LEAST OF THE SOVIET'S NECESSITIES. IF THEY WERE AWARE OF THE SUSPECTED FLIGHT <u>PATHS</u>, THEIR MISSILES AND HEIGHT FINDING RADAR WOULD BE ARMED AND ACTIVE ON A CONTINUOUS BASIS

BUT, THE RUSSIANS DESPARATELY WANTED TO KNOW POWERS **EXACT ALTITUDE** AT POINTS ALONG THE FLIGHT PATH TO DETERMINE THE ALTITUDE CAPABILITIES OF THEIR SAM MISSLES AND MIG 17'S.

WERE THEY SUCCESSFUL IN TRACKING AND SHOOTING POWERS DOWN DUE TO THEIR DEFENSE CAPABILITIES OR MERELY LUCKY? ACTUALLY THEY WERE A BIT OF BOTH. THE 70,500 FEET ALTITUDE CHOSEN FOR THIS PARTICULAR FLIGHT, NEARLY 1 MILE LESS THAN THE 75,000 FEET SAFE CEILING AND NEARLY 6 MILES LESS THAN THE U-2'S MAXIMUM ALTITUDE CAPABILITY OF 100,000 FEET, ALLOWED THE POSSIBILITY IF NOT THE PROBABILITY OF A NEAR-MISS BY A SOVIET SA-2. THE POSSIBILITY IS ENHANCED IF INDEED THE SOVIETS WERE AWARE OF THE **PATH** OF THIS PARTICULAR FLIGHT AND IF POWERS' PLANE SUFFERS A CONSIDERABLE ALTITUDE LOSS.

POWERS HOWEVER DID HOLD FIRM DURING HIS QUESTIONING IN THAT HE NEVER DEVIATED FROM THE PUBLISHED "MAXIMUM" ALTITUDE OF THE U-2; 68,000 FEET. CURIOUSLY, OR PERHAPS NOT, THE RUSSIAN INTERROGATION OF POWERS PERTAINED ONLY TO U-2 OPERATIONS OUT OF **ATSUGI**, JAPAN WHERE **LEE** HAD BEEN STATIONED. HE WAS <u>NOT</u> QUESTIONED IN REGARDS TO **PAKISTAN** WHERE HIS FLIGHT HAD ORIGINATED. FURTHER ADDING TO THE LIKELIHOOD OF **HARVEY'S** PRESENCE IN MOSCOW DURING THE POWERS' QUESTIONING IS THE FACT THAT **HARVEY'S** "DIARY" CONTAINED NO NOTATIONS FOR THE MONTH OF MAY, 1960. **HARVEY'S** STAY IN RUSSIA SPANNED 3 MAY DAYS: MAY 1ST 1960, 1961, AND 1962. OF THESE 3 MAY DAYS, THE ONLY ONE IN WHICH **HARVEY** IS UNACCOUNTED FOR IS MAY 1ST, 1960, THE <u>EXACT</u> DAY POWERS' U-2 IS DOWNED.

*IN A LETTER **HARVEY** HAD WRITTEN TO HIS "BROTHER" ROBERT JUST AFTER THE EXCHANGE OF POWERS FOR RUDOLPH ABEL IN FEBRUARY 1962, HE WROTE "HE (POWERS) SEEMED TO BE A NICE BRIGHT AMERICAN-TYPE FELLOW WHEN I SAW HIM IN MOSCOW." THIS WAS TO BE **HARVEY'S** ONLY REFERENCE TO THE U-2 INCIDENT.*

*HIS MISSION COMPLETED, **HARVEY** RETURNED HOME ON JUNE 13, 1962, 4 MONTHS AFTER POWERS' FEBRUARY 1962 SWAP FOR SOVIET SPY RUDOLPH ABEL.*

WHAT WAS THE OVERALL IMPACT OF THE U-2 INCIDENT? THE RUSSIANS, HARDLY SUSPECTING CIA SABOTAGE OF POWERS' SUMMIT-EVE FLIGHT, NOW CROWED THAT THEY WERE CAPABLE OF "DOWNING" A U-2. THE SOVIETS THOUGHT THAT THEY HAD ACHIEVED A COLD WAR PROPAGANDA COUP. LITTLE DID THEY SUSPECT THAT **HARVEY'S** CIA MISSION HAD BEEN TO REINFORCE THE ERRONEOUS NOTION THAT THE SOVIETS WERE FULLY CAPABLE OF DOWNING A U-2 AND THAT THEIR SUCCESS IN DOING SO HAD BEEN ASSISTED BY THE CHOICE OF A LESS THAN MAXIMUM ALTITUDE AND FLIGHT PATHS AND COMMUNICATION FREQUENCIES PROVIDED BY "DEFECTORS" MITCHELL, MARTIN, AND WEBSTER.

THE U-2 PROGRAM WOULD CONTINUE WITH FLIGHTS RESUMING ALMOST IMMEDIATELY. THESE FLIGHTS OF COURSE LIKELY TOOK PLACE AT THE U-2'S MAXIMUM OPERATIONAL ALTITUDE OF APPROXIMATELY 100,000 FEET; ONCE AGAIN WELL ABOVE SOVIET CAPABILITIES TO EITHER TRACK OR SHOOT DOWN THE CONTROVERSIAL SPY PLANE.

IT WAS IMPERATIVE THAT THE U-2 PROGRAM CONTINUE FOR THE IMMEDIATE FUTURE SINCE THE NEW <u>UNMANNED</u> CORONA SPY SATELLITES HAD YET TO BE PROVEN AS A RELIABLE REPLACEMENT FOR THE SUCCESSFUL BUT **MANNED** U-2 PROGRAM. A SINGLE PLANE WAS EXPENDABLE. A SINGLE PILOT WAS EXPENDABLE. THE U-2 PROGRAM IN ITS ENTIREITY WAS <u>NOT</u> EXPENDABLE; AT LEAST NOT YET.

THE 1960 SUMMIT TALKS PROVED TO BE ALL BUT MEANINGLESS DUE TO THE HEIGHTENED TENSION AFTER THE U-2 INCIDENT. THERE WAS NO DISCUSSION OF AN "OPEN SKIES" PROGRAM, NO GROUND WAS LAID FOR A NUCLEAR TEST BAN TREATY, AND CERTAINLY NO BREAK IN WHAT WAS NOW A RAPIDLY CHILLING COLD WAR CLIMATE.

KHRUSCHEV HIMSELF NOTED: "IT WAS AS THOUGH THE AMERICANS HAD DELIBERATELY TRIED TO PLACE A TIME BOMB UNDER THE MEETING, SET TO GO OFF JUST AS WE WERE ABOUT TO SIT DOWN WITH THEM AT THE NEGOTIATING TABLE." FOR THE CIA AND THE MILITARY/INDUSTRIAL ESTABLISHMENT, THE OVERALL OUTCOME GAVE BOTH THE CONGRESSIONAL CLOUT NECESSARY TO PUSH FOR INCREASED BUDGETING FOR SATELLITE RECONNAISSANCE, MISSILE CONSTRUCTION, AND AN OVERALL MILITARY BUILDUP.

INDEED, AFTER THE DOWNING OF POWERS' U-2, THE STOCKS OF COMPANIES MANUFACTURING MILITARY EQUIPMENT ROSE DRAMATICALLY IN RESPONSE TO AN EQUALLY DRAMATIC RISE IN MILITARY CONTRACTS AWARDED BY THE GOVERNMENT. THE COLD WAR WOULD OF COURSE CONTINUE TO ESCALATE CULMINATING IN THE OCTOBER, 1962 CUBAN MISSILE CRISIS.

EISENHOWER, IN HIS JANUARY 17, 1961 FINAL SPEECH BEFORE LEAVING OFFICE, OFFERED A WARNING TO BE WARY OF THE "MILITARY-INDUSTRIAL COMPLEX." I PONDER THAT WITH THIS COMMENT HE MAY HAVE REVEALED HIS SUSPICIONS THAT THE CIA DID INDEED SEND OUT THE ILL-TIMED U-2 FLIGHT AND QUITE LIKELY MADE ARRANGEMENTS THAT WOULD INSURE ITS DEMISE.

WITH THE NOTABLE EXCEPTION OF POWERS HAVING SURVIVED AND THE RECOVERY OF CONSIDERABLE WRECKAGE (MUCH TO WASHINGTON'S EMBARASSMENT AND THE CIA'S IRE) THE PLAN WORKED PERFECTLY. POWERS WAS EXPENDABLE, A SINGLE PLANE THAT HAD PREVIOUSLY CRASHED WAS EXPENDABLE, BUT, THE U-2 OPERATIONS WERE NOT SINCE IN THIS PRE- SATELLITE ERA, THE U-2'S PROVIDED 90% OF ALL HARD INFORMATION ON THE SOVIET'S MILITARY, AGRICULTURAL, AND INDUSTRIAL CAPABILITY.

IRONICALLY, **HARVEY'S** PRESENCE AT POWERS' INTERROGATION SESSIONS ALLOWED THE CIA TO DETERMINE IF POWERS HAD OFFERED MORE TO THE RUSSIANS THAN WAS COMMONLY KNOWN, OR MORE THAN HAD BEEN PROVIDED TO THEM BY **HARVEY**, BERNON MITCHELL, WILLIAM MARTIN, AND ROBERT WEBSTER.

POWERS' CAREER AS A CIA-OPERATIVE WAS AS DOOMED AS HIS FATAL FLIGHT HAD BEEN WHEN HE ELECTED NOT TO TAKE HIS OWN LIFE EITHER BY UTILIZING THE SUSPECT EJECTION DEVICE OR THE POISON ISSUED TO U-2 PILOTS. THE CIA'S CONCERNS HOWEVER WERE UNWARRANTED AS POWERS' NEVER STRAYED FROM THE PUBLICIZED "68,000 FEET" AS HIS MAXIMUM ALTITUDE

ALTHOUGH **HARVEY'S** RETURN TO THE U.S. WOULD BE WITHOUT FANFARE, IT WAS ALSO NOTABLY LACKING ANY FORM OF PROSECUTION IN SPITE OF HIS "DEFECTION" AND CONSEQUENT "REVELATION" OF RADAR AND U-2 INFORMATION TO THE SOVIETS. IT WAS OF COURSE WHAT ONE WOULD EXPECT FOR AN INTELLIGENCE OPERATIVE RETURNING FROM A SUCCESSFUL MISSION. **HARVEY'S** SUCCESSFUL "DEFECTION" AND POWERS' SUMMIT-CANCELLING SHOOT DOWN GAVE THE MANNED U-2 PROGRAM THE NEEDED ADDITIONAL TIME UNTIL THE UN-MANNED SATELLITE PROGRAM COULD BE RELIED UPON. IT ALSO GAVE THE CIA THE MUCH DESIRED ESCALATION OF THE COLD WAR AND SOME TEMPORARY RESPITE FROM BUDGET CUTTING AND DOWNSIZING.

POWERS HOWEVER WAS GIVEN QUITE A DIFFERENT RECEPTION. JOHN MCCONE, DIRECTOR CIA, CONVENED A THREE-MAN BOARD TO CONSIDER FORMAL CHARGES AGAINST POWERS FOR FAILING TO USE HIS PLANE'S DESTRUCT MECHANISM BEFORE BAILING OUT. THE NSA, BASED ON SOVIET COMMUNICATION INTERCEPTS, ARGUED THAT POWERS HAD AMPLE TIME TO DESTROY THE PLANE. MCCONE HOWEVER SENT KELLY JOHNSON OF LOCKHEED TO MOSCOW TO VIEW THE WRECKAGE OF THE U-2. JOHNSON DETERMINED THAT POWERS WOULD **NOT** HAVE HAD TIME TO DESTROY THE PLANE. THE THREE-MAN COMMITTEE, COMPOSED OF JUDGE E. BARRETT PRETTYMAN, AN ARMY GENERAL, AND CIA REPRESENTATIVE JOHN BROSS, EXONERATED POWERS OF ALL CHARGES. THE COMMITTEE WAS ESSENTIALLY WINDOW DRESSING.

THE CIA EITHER ELECTED TO DECIDE THAT THE EJECTION DEVICE SIMPLY FAILED IN DEFERENCE TO THE FACT THAT THEY FELT ASSURRED THAT POWERS HAD REVEALED NO ADDITIONAL U-2 SECRETS WITH **HARVEY** AS THEIR WITNESS THROUGHOUT THE POWERS' INTERROGATION SESSIONS **OR** THEY MAY HAVE THOUGHT IT BETTER NOT TO PRESS THE ISSUE FOR FEAR THAT POWERS WOULD PUBLICLY VOICE HIS CONCERNS THAT THE DEVICE WAS **NOT** DESIGNED TO ALLOW FOR A SAFE DESTRUCTION AND EJECTION SCENARIO BUT TO DESTROY EVIDENCE OF A <u>MANNED</u> RECONNAISSANCE FLIGHT BY KILLING THE PILOT.

THE **HARVEY** "DEFECTION", U-2 "DOWNING", AND CONSEQUENT MEANINGLESS 1960 SUMMIT TALKS IS IN ITSELF QUITE A POWERFUL ARGUMENT TO SUPPORT THE THEORY THAT **HARVEY** WAS A CIA OPERATIVE. INDEED, THERE WERE 30 SUCCESSFUL U-2 PENETRATIONS BETWEEN JUNE 1956 AND MAY 1ST, 1960. TWENTY-EIGHT OF THESE FLIGHTS TOOK PLACE <u>BEFORE</u> **HARVEY'S** OCTOBER 1959 DEFECTION TO RUSSIA. THE NEXT U-2 FLIGHT WOULD NOT BE UNTIL APRIL 9TH, 1960. IT WOULD ALSO BE SUCCESSFUL. THE NEXT FLIGHT, MAY 1ST, 1960 WAS SHOT DOWN. THIS WAS POWERS' FLIGHT.

ADDING FURTHER EVIDENCE THAT **HARVEY'S** RUSSIAN JOURNEY WAS SPONSORED BY AN INTELLIGENCE AGENCY WAS A DEPOSITION GIVEN TO THE HSCA IN 1978 BY JAMES B. WILCOTT. WILCOTT, A FORMER CIA FINANCE OFFICER, STATED THAT **HARVEY** HAD BEEN RECRUITED BY THE CIA FOR "THE EXPRESS PURPOSE OF A DOUBLE AGENT ASSIGNMENT IN THE USSR." WILCOTT HAD OVERSEEN THE FUNDING OF THIS PARTICULAR PROJECT IN WHICH **HARVEY** HAD BEEN A PARTICIPANT. THE PROJECT WAS KNOWN AS THE "OSWALD PROJECT." THE CODENAME FROR THE "OSWALD PROJECT" WAS RXZM.

WHEN ASKED WHAT HE MEANT BY THE TERM "AGENT", WILCOTT REPORTED THAT "HE (**HARVEY**) WAS A REGULAR EMPLOYEE RECEIVING A FULL-TIME SALARY FOR AGENT WORK FOR DOING CIA OPERATIONAL WORK." HE NOTED THAT THERE WERE AT LEAST 6 OR 7 OTHERS IN THE AGENCY WHO HE CONVERSED WITH THAT EITHER BELIEVED OR KNEW **HARVEY** TO BE A CIA AGENT. WILCOTT NOTED THAT JERRY FOX, CASE OFFICER FOR THE SOVIET RUSSIA BRANCH, WAS ONE OF THE CIA EMPLOYEES WHO KNEW **HARVEY** WAS INDEED A CIA AGENT. REID DENNIS, CHIEF OF SOVIET SATELLITE BRANCH AND CHINA BRANCH WAS ALSO NOTED AS ONE WHO RELATED TO WILCOTT THAT **HARVEY** WAS AN AGENT OF THE CIA. THERE WERE SEVERAL OTHERS NOTED BY WILCOTT: JOHN P. HOLTER, KAN TAKAI, CHESTER ITO, JIM DELANEY, BOB RENTNOR, LARRY WANTABI, AND TWO OTHERS WHOSE FULL NAMES WILCOTT COULD NOT RECALL. THIS WOULD TOTAL 10 MEN WHO WILCOTT FELT EXPRESSED A SENSE IF NOT A CERTAINTY THAT **HARVEY** WAS AN AGENT OF THE CIA. WILCOTT WOULD ALSO NOTE IN HIS HSCA INTERVIEW THAT 2-3 MONTHS AFTER THE ASSASSINATION THAT A CASE OFFICER APPEARED AT HIS WINDOW TO DRAW MONEY FOR A PROJECT. DURING THEIR CONVERSATION, WILCOTT NOTED THAT THE OFFICER SAID: "WELL JIM, THE MONEY THAT I DREW THE LAST COUPLE OF MONTHS OR SO WAS MONEY FOR THE OSWALD PROJECT OR FOR OSWALD." WHEN ASKED HOW MANY PEOPLE HE HAD SPOKEN TO AT THE CIA THAT "SPECULATED" THAT **HARVEY** WAS AN AGENT, WILCOTT REPLIED "DOZENS, LITERALLY DOZENS." THE HSCA INTERVIEW WAS CONDUCTED ON MARCH 22ND 1978. WILCOTT HOWEVER HAD DISCLOSED THE CIA/**HARVEY** CONNECTION IN 1968 AFTER HE HAD LEFT THE CIA THAT YEAR. WHEN ASKED WHY HE HAD WAITED 5 YEARS TO DO SO HE REPLIED: "I WAS AFRAID QUITE FRANKLY." WHEN ASKED IF HIS CO-WORKERS AT THE AGENCY DISCOVERED A POSSIBLE CIA ROLE IN THE ASSASSINATION WILCOTT REPLIED: "THEY SAID THINGS LIKE 'OSWALD (**HARVEY**) COULDN'T HAVE PULLED THE TRIGGER.....ONLY THE CIA COULD HAVE SET UP SUCH AN ELABORATE PROJECT'." FURTHER COMMENTING, WILCOTT ADDED THAT "THEY SAID THIS WAS THE WAY TO GET RID OF HIM…TO GET HIM INVOLVED IN THE ASSASSINATION THING AND PUT THE BLAME ON CUBA AS A PRETEXT FOR ANOTHER INVASION OR ANOTHER ATTACK AGAINST CUBA."

IT WAS ONLY A FEW MONTHS LATER, 18 AUGUST 1960, THAT A CORONA SATELLLITE WAS LAUNCHED AND WAS ABLE TO PHOTOGRAPH PARTS OF RUSSIA. THREE THOUSAND FEET OF FILM WAS TAKEN COVERING 1.6 MILLION SQUARE MILES OF THE SOVIET UNION. THIS ONE SATELLITE WAS ABLE TO PHOTOGRAPH MORE SURFACE AREA OF RUSSIA THAN ALL THE 23 OTHER U-2 FLIGHTS OVER RUSSIA COMBINED.

ONE WOULD THINK THAT POWERS' ILL-TIMED FLIGHT COULD HAVE WAITED 14 MORE WEEKS.

WHEN ONE FACTORS IN THE **KEY ELEMENTS**; THE "OPEN SKIES" PROGRAM TO BE TENDERED BY THE SOVIETS AT THE MAY 1960 SUMMIT TALKS, <u>AND</u> THE CIA'S DESIRE TO ESCALATE THE COLD WAR **PRIOR** TO THE LAUNCH OF THE LESS INTRUSIVE UNMANNED SATELLITES, **HARVEY'S** <u>**EXACT MISSION**</u> IN REGARDS TO HIS "DEFECTION" BECOMES EVEN MORE APPARENT. THE SCHEME IN ITS ENTIRETY COULD HARDLY HAVE OCCURRED BY MERE CHANCE.

IN FACT BY SENDING:

AN <u>UNRELIABLE PLANE</u> ON THE

<u>FIRST</u> OVERFLIGHT <u>COMPLETELY</u> ACROSS RUSSIA,

AUTHORIZED BY A RADIO MESSAGE SENT "<u>IN THE CLEAR</u>",

ON <u>MAY DAY</u> WHEN MILITARY AND COMMERCIAL TRAFFIC WOULD BE REDUCED ENABLING SOVIET RADAR OPERATORS TO CONCENTRATE THEIR EFFORTS TO TRACK THE U-2 AS SOON AS IT ENTERED SOVIET AIRSPACE,

ON THE <u>EVE</u> OF AN IMPORTANT SUMMIT TALK BETWEEN THE U.S. AND THE SOVIETS,

A MERE <u>14 WEEKS</u> BEFORE THE SWITCH TO SATELLITE RECONNAISANCE,

ONE WOULD HAVE TO CONCLUDE THAT THE FAILURE OF THIS FLIGHT AND THE 1960 SUMMIT TALKS WAS PLANNED. THE PRE-FLIGHT "CONTRIBUTIONS" OF **HARVEY**, WEBSTER, MARTIN AND MITCHELL ONLY INCREASE THE LIKELIHOOD THAT IT WAS THE DESIRE OF THE INTELLIGENCE COMMUNITY TO SCUTTLE THE SUMMIT TALKS AND HEIGHTEN COLD WAR TENSION.

THE JOURNAL *MILITARY AFFAIRS* NOTED: "THE ANOMALIES IN THE POWERS CASE SUGGEST THAT THE U-2 "INCIDENT" MAY HAVE BEEN STAGED. MOREOVER, THE MANAGEMENT OF THE CRISIS GIVES FURTHER WARRANT TO THE HYPOTHESIS THAT THE U-2 WAS A DEVICE DELIBERATELY CHOSEN TO DESTROY AN EMERGING DÉTENTE."

IRONICALLY, AFTER THE RUSE OF THE "WEATHER PLANE" HAD COLLAPSED, THE U.S. GOVERNMENT OFFERED AS AN EXCUSE FOR THE ILL-TIMED U-2 FLIGHT THAT <u>IT</u> BELIEVED IN THE PRINCIPLE OF "OPEN SKIES." WE SIMPLY DID NOT WANT THIS COURTESY TO BE EXTENDED TO THE RUSSIANS.

IT IS INTERESTING TO NOTE THAT **HARVEY** WAS TOLD BY ONI SPONSORS THAT HIS MISSION TO RUSSIA WAS "SPECIAL AND VITALLY IMPORTANT." HE WAS ALSO PROMISED A WELL PAYING OFFICIAL POSITION UPON HIS SUCCESSFUL RETURN TO THE U.S. HOWEVER THE BURDEN OF FULFILLING THIS PROMISE WOULD FALL UPON THE CIA NOT THE ONI AS THE CIA WOULD BE RUNNING **HARVEY** AT THAT TIME. HIS RETURN HOME OFFERED LITTLE HOPE THAT THIS PROMISE WOULD BECOME A REALITY. THE ONI NO LONGER NEEDED HIS SERVICES AS A CIVILIAN.

THE CIA HOWEVER, ALSO NO LONGER IN NEED OF HIS SERVICES, OFFERED HELP ONLY THROUGH GEORGE DEMOHRENSCHILDT'S PARENT-LIKE EFFORTS TO OBTAIN FOR **HARVEY** WHAT WERE ESSENTIALLY LOW PAYING JOBS. THE FBI WOULD LATER TAKE ON **HARVEY** AS A PAID INFORMANT. ALTHOUGH THIS DID INDEED HELP WITH EXPENSES, **HARVEY'S** ATTITUDE CONCERNING HIS FBI RELATIONSHIP WAS STRAINED.

ALTHOUGH THEY WERE USING HIM AS A PAID INFORMANT, THE FBI WOULD LATER HARASS HIM CONTINUOUSLY, ESPECIALLY AFTER THE "OSWALD" SIGHTINGS AROUSED THEIR SUSPICION THAT **HARVEY** MIGHT BE INVOLVED IN SOMETHING NOT OF THEIR MAKING. AS A RETURNING INTELLIGENCE OPERATIVE WHO HAD WORKED FOR BOTH THE ONI AND THE CIA IN MATTERS OF INTERNATIONAL CONSEQUENCE, THE DOMESTIC TASKS LATER TENDERED BY THE FBI MUST HAVE BEEN DISAPPOINTING FOR **HARVEY** IN THEIR SCOPE AS WELL AS THEIR LEVEL OF PRESTIGE. IN FACT, FBI DIRECTOR KELLY IN HIS 1987 AUTOBIOGRAPHY NOTED "DEALING WITH LEE **HARVEY** OSWALD WAS NO PICNIC FOR THE FBI."

LATER WE WILL SEE THAT **HARVEY** WAS INDEED A DISAPPOINTED AND FRUSTRATED INDIVIDUAL. HE HAD PERFORMED HIS ASSIGNMENTS WELL FOR THE ONI, THE CIA, AND THUS PRESUMABLY FOR HIS COUNTRY. FEELING SOMEWHAT ABANDONED – PARTICULARLY REGARDING FINANCIAL PROMISES THAT WERE NOT KEPT – INDIVIDUALS IN THE ONI/CIA PROPER SURELY HAD TO PAUSE MOMENTARILY AFTER THE ASSASSINATION WONDERING IF **HARVEY** COULD HAVE DONE IT OUT OF FRUSTRATION WITH HIS NOW STALLED INTELLIGENCE CAREER AND THE FINANCIAL BURDEN OF A RAPIDLY GROWING FAMILY. THE SET-UP CONSPIRATORS KNEW OTHERWISE. THEIR SUCCESSFUL SET-UP OF THE PERFECT PATSY WOULD BE FACILITATED BY A COMPLETE COVER-UP BY THE INTELLIGENCE COMMUNITIES OF THEIR RELATIONSHIPS WITH **HARVEY**. THOSE SAME INTELLIGENCE TIES WOULD INSURE THAT ANY INVESTIGATION INTO THE ASSASSINATION WOULD START AND END WITH A SOON TO BE ELIMINATED LEE **HARVEY** OSWALD.

OUR LAST ENTRY IN THE TIMELINE WAS APRIL 28TH, 1960.
WE WILL NOW RETURN TO THE TIMELINE
AS OF MAY 10, 1960.

MAY 10TH 1960
A MEMO FROM THE STATE DEPARTMENT TO THE MOSCOW EMBASSY NOTES THEIR INTENTION TO NOT ENCOURAGE "MARGUERITE" TO ATTEMPT TO CONTACT **HARVEY**. THIS WOULD EFFECTIVELY ISOLATE **HARVEY** FROM HIS" FAMILY."

JUNE 3RD 1960
AS A RESULT OF AGENT FAIN'S INTERVIEW WITH "MARGUERITE", HOOVER SENDS A MEMO TO THE STATE DEPARTMENT TITLED "LHO, INTERNAL SECURITY." THE MEMO STATED: "SINCE THERE IS A POSSIBILITY THAT AN IMPOSTER IS USING OSWALD'S BIRTH CERTIFICATE, ANY CURRENT INFO THE DEPARTMENT OF STATE MAY HAVE CONCERNING SUBJECT WILL BE APPRECIATED." HOOVER AT THIS POINT MAY HAVE SUSPECTED THAT **HARVEY** WAS AN IMPOSTOR AS A RESULT OF "MARGUERITE'S" LIE TO FAIN WHEN SHE TOLD HIM THAT SHE THOUGHT HER "SON" WAS IN SWITZERLAND WHEN SHE KNEW FULL WELL THAT **HARVEY** WAS IN RUSSIA. OR, DID HOOVER THINK THAT THE PERSON SUPPOSEDLY ATTENDING COLLEGE IN SWITZERLAND WAS AN IMPOSTOR SINCE **HARVEY** WAS KNOWN TO BE IN RUSSIA?

*ARMSTRONG NOTES THAT THERE WAS NEVER ANY EFFORT BY THE FBI TO LOCATE A SECOND "OSWALD." WITH THIS IN MIND, I AM INCLINED TO THINK THAT IT WAS HOOVER'S SUSPICION THAT THE OSWALD IN RUSSIA (**HARVEY**) WAS THE IMPOSTOR. HE HOWEVER WAS APPARENTLY NOT INCLINED TO PURSUE THE MATTER MOST LIKELY AT THE REQUEST OF THE CIA.*

JUNE 8TH 1960
"MARGUERITE" WRITES THE STATE DEPARTMENT ASKING FOR SOME PROOF AS TO WHETHER **HARVEY** HAD INDEED "SIGNED THE NECESSARY PAPERS RENOUNCING HIS CITIZENSHIP."

JUNE 10TH 1960
"MARGUERITE" WRITES THE MARINE CORP REQUESTING TO BE INFORMED OF THE CHARGES AGAINST **HARVEY** THAT IMPACT HIS DISCHARGE STATUS.

JUNE 17TH1960
THE MARINE CORPS REPLY TO "MARGUERITE" NOTED THAT **HARVEY'S** DISCHARGE STATUS HAD BEEN SUBJECT TO REVIEW DUE TO HIS "DESIRE FOR SOVIET CITIZENSHIP."

JUNE 18TH 1960
HARVEY OBTAINS A HUNTING LICENSE AND JOINS THE BELORUSSAN SOCIETY OF HUNTING. HE WOULD ALSO PURCHASE A 16 GAUGE SHOTGUN. HE WOULD FREELY ADMIT TO THIS PURHASE THE WEEKEND OF THE ASSASSINATION.

JULY 1ST 1960
"MARGUERITE" RETURNS TO FT. WORTH FROM WACO. SHE IS NOW RESIDING AT 1407 8TH AVENUE.

JULY 7TH 1960
JOHN T. WHITE OF THE STATE DEPARTMENT PASSPORT OFFICE WRITES TO " MARGUERITE" REGARDING HER CONCERNS ABOUT **HARVEY'S** CITIZENSHIP STATUS. THE LETTER ESSENTIALLY TELLS "MARGUERITE" THAT THE STATE DEPARTMENT HAS NOTHING CONCRETE FROM THE MOSCOW EMBASSY AS TO WHETHER **HARVEY** DID OR DID NOT OFFICIALLY DENOUNCE HIS CITIZENSHIP.

JULY 16TH 1960
"MARGUERITE" WRITES JOHN WHITE AGAIN INQUIRING AS TO WHEN AND WHERE **HARVEY** HAD APPLIED FOR HIS PASSPORT.

JULY 21ST 1960
JOHN WHITE REPLIES TO "MARGUERITE'S" QUERY NOTING THAT **HARVEY** HAD BEEN ISSUED HIS PASSPORT ON SEPT 10, 1959 AT THE LOS ANGELES, CALIFORNIA PASSPORT AGENCY.

AUGUST 1960
THE SOVIETS TRY DOWNED U-2 PILOT FRANCIS GARY POWERS FOR ESPIONAGE.

AUGUST 17TH 1960
THE MARINE CORP AMMENDS **HARVEY'S** DISCHARGE TO UNDESIRABLE.

SEPTEMBER 1ST 1960
"MARGUERITE" PREDICTABLY MOVES ONCE AGAIN. SHE NOW RESIDES IN BOYD, TEXAS.

*ARMSTRONG NOTES THAT AFTER 1960, ALL FBI EFFORTS TO TRACK A MARGUERITE OSWALD CONCENTRATED ON THE SHORT, HEAVY, GREY-HAIRED "MARGUERITE" NOT THE TALL, SLENDER MARGUERITE, THE REAL MOTHER OF **LEE** HARVEY OSWALD.*

SEPTEMBER 13TH 1960
THE MARINE CORP RESERVES ALSO RELEASES **HARVEY** WITH AN UNDESIRABLE DISCHARGE.

SEPTEMBER 1960
ROSCOE WHITE ATTENDS AT ARTILLERY SCHOOL AT FT. SILL, OKLAHOMA.

DECEMBER 9TH 1960
THE CIA OPENS FILE #289248, A 201 FILE ON A LEE **HENRY** OSWALD. THIS IS PRESUMABLY **HARVEY** WHO HAD "DEFECTED" ON OCTOBER 15TH, 1959, ALMOST 14 MONTHS EARLIER.

*THE 201 FILE WAS PROMPTED BY JAMES ANGLETON, CHIEF OF THE CIA'S CI/SIG (COUNTERINTELLIGENCE/SPECIAL INVESTIGATIONS GROUP.) BUT, THE FILE WAS MORE POINTEDLY OPENED BY ANN EGERTER WHO WORKED IN CI/SIG UNDER ANGLETON. THIS GROUP INVESTIGATED AGENCY PERSONNEL WHO WERE SUSPECTED OF HAVING BEEN "DOUBLED" BY THE SOVIETS. IN ESSENCE, A 201 FILE COULD BE OPENED ON ANYONE IN THE EMPLOY OF THE AGENCY AND/OR SUSPECTED AS BEING A COUNTER-INTELLIGENCE RISK. **HARVEY** WOULD SATISFY BOTH CRITERIA AS A CIA ASSET IN REGARDS TO HIS "DEFECTION", AND ALSO POTENTIALLY A SECURITY RISK IN REGARDS TO THE POSSIBILITY THAT HE WOULD BE SUBJECTED TO SOVIET EFFORTS TO "DOUBLE" HIM PRIOR TO HIS RETURN TO THE U.S.*

IN 1995, A CIA MEMO BY THE CIA'S C/I STAFF NOTED THAT THE 201 FILE ON LEE HENRY OSWALD WAS OPENED DUE NOT ONLY TO HIS "DEFECTION" ON OCTOBER 31ST, 1959, BUT ALSO DUE TO HIS APPARENT DESIRE TO RETURN TO THE U.S. INTERESTINGLY THE MEMO ALSO INCLUDES QUOTATION MARKS REGARDING THE "DEFECTION." THE QUOTATION

MARKS IMPLY THAT INDEED THE "DEFECTION" WAS NOT GENUINE. EQUALLY PROBABLEMATIC IS THE FACT THAT **HARVEY** WOULD NOT EXPRESS A DESIRE TO RETURN HOME UNTIL FEBRUARY 5TH, 1961, NEARLY 2 MONTHS LATER.

LATE 1960

LEE IS NOTED TO BE WORKING WITH CIA EXILE GROUPS IN AND AROUND MIAMI AND THE EVERGLADES. HE WAS WORKING IN THE TRAINING CAMPS PRIOR TO THE UPCOMING BAY OF PIGS INVASION OF CUBA.

JANUARY 4TH 1961

HARVEY REQUESTS THAT HIS SOVIET IDENTITY CARD BE EXTENDED. THE PASSPORT OFFICE HONORS HIS REQUEST AND EXTENDS HIS STAY UNTIL JANUARY 4TH,1962. HE DECLINED THEIR OFFER TO MAKE HIM A SOVIET CITIZEN.

JANUARY 20TH 1961

TWO MEN, 1 HISPANIC AND 1 CAUCASIAN, VISIT A FORD DEALERSHIP IN NEW ORLEANS. THEY TOLD THE SALESMAN OSCAR DESLATTE THAT THEY WANTED TO BUY 10 PICKUP TRUCKS. THEY NOTED THAT THEY WERE MEMBERS OF A PATRIOTIC CAUSE, THE FRIENDS OF DEMOCRATIC CUBA, AN <u>ANTI</u>-CASTRO GROUP, AND WISHED TO BUY THE TRUCKS AT "NO PROFIT" OR AT DEALER COST. THE LATIN GAVE THE NAME OF JOSEPH MOORE. THE CAUCASIAN IDENTIFIED HIMSELF AS "OSWALD." MOORE ASKED THAT THE NAME "OSWALD" GO ON THE PURCHASE DOCUMENTS. THE ALLEGED "<u>PRO</u>-CASTRO COMMUNIST" AND "DEFECTOR" **HARVEY** WAS STILL IN RUSSIA AT THE TIME AND WOULD NOT RETURN UNTIL JUNE 13, 1962. IT WAS LIKELY **LEE** PRESENT AT THE EVENT.

*THE FRIENDS OF DEMOCRATIC CUBA WAS FORMED ON JANUARY 6TH, 1961 ONLY 2 WEEKS PRIOR TO THE BOLTON FORD INCIDENT. THE <u>FOUNDER</u> OF THE FRIENDS OF DEMOCRATIC CUBA WAS GUY BANISTER. MORE INTERESTINGLY,THE VICE-PRESIDENT OF THE FDC WAS GERARD F. TUJAGUE. MR. TUJAGUE WAS THE OWNER OF GERARD F. TUJAGUE INC., FORWARDING COMPANY, A SHIPPING COMPANY IN NEW ORLEANS. **LEE** WAS EMPLOYED BY TUJAGUE'S COMPANY FROM NOVEMBER 10TH, 1955 TO JANUARY 14TH, 1956 AS A MESSENGER. RECALLING THAT DAVID FERRIE WAS ASSOCIATED WITH **LEE'S** CAP ACTIVITY IN THE SUMMER OF 1955, WE NOW HAVE 2 INDIVIDUALS WHO HAVE MET AND WERE FAMILIAR WITH **LEE**, FERRIE AND TUJAGUE, <u>PRIOR</u> TO THE JANUARY 1961 BOLTON FORD INCIDENT. BANISTER, AS ONE OF THE FOUNDING FATHERS OF THE FDC WILL LATER MEET, IF HE HAS NOT ALREADY DONE SO, **HARVEY** UPON HIS ARRIVAL IN NEW ORLEANS. DELPHINE ROBERTS, BANISTER'S NEW ORLEANS SECRETARY, WILL, IN A LATER INTERVIEW, NOTE THAT SHE FELT THAT **HARVEY** AND BANISTER ALREADY KNEW EACH OTHER WHEN **HARVEY** ARRIVED AT BANISTER'S OFFICE IN APRIL OF 1963. WITH BANISTER'S KNOWN ASSOCIATION WITH BOTH TUJAGUE AND FERRIE, IT IS QUITE LIKELY THAT HE HAD INDEED ALREADY MET **LEE** OR AT LEAST WAS MORE THAN PASSINGLY FAMILIAR WITH **LEE.** AND WITH HIS INTELLIGENCE TIES, BANISTER WAS LIKELY ONE OF THE FEW INDIVIDUALS WHO KNOW <u>BOTH</u> **LEE** AND **HARVEY**.*

BANISTER'S CLOSE ASSOCIATE IN NEW ORLEANS, DAVID FERRIE, HAD KNOWN **LEE** SINCE 1955 WHEN THEY WERE BOTH MEMBERS OF THE CAP. THIS PARTICULAR EVENT AT THE FORD DEALERSHIP IS INTERESTING SINCE **HARVEY** WAS, AT THE TIME, ON AN INTELLIGENCE MISSION FOR THE CIA IN RUSSIA, AND IT WAS IMPERATIVE THAT HIS "DEFECTOR / COMMUNIST" COVER NOT BE BLOWN. WHY WOULD THE FDC TRY TO ASSOCIATE **HARVEY** WITH A STAUNCHLY ORIENTED <u>ANTI</u>- CASTRO GROUP?

LATER, UPON HIS RETURN STATESIDE, **HARVEY** WILL BE "PAINTED" SEVERAL TIMES PRIOR TO HIS DEATH AS A <u>PRO</u>-CASTRO SYMPATHISER WITH A PREVIOUS "DEFECTION." THE OBVIOUS SET-UP AT THE FORD DEALERSHIP AT <u>THIS</u> PARTICULAR TIME SIMPLY DID NOT MAKE SENSE. THIS DID <u>NOT</u> APPEAR TO BE THE WORKINGS OF EITHER THE FBI, OR MORE POINTEDLY, THE CIA SINCE **HARVEY** WAS NOT IN THE COUNTRY AT THE TIME AND WAS IN ALL LIKELIHOOD PERFORMING A SERVICE FOR THE CIA IN THE SOVIET UNION. IN THAT

*SAME REGARD, I DO NOT DETECT ANY LOGICAL REASON FOR EITHER GUY BANISTER, DAVID FERRIE, OR GERARD TUJAGUE TO IMPLICATE **HARVEY** IN AN <u>ANTI</u>-CASTRO EFFORT AT THIS PARTICULAR TIME.*

*IF THIS ANTI-CASTRO IMPLICATION OF **HARVEY** REGARDING THE PURCHASE OF THE PICK-UP TRUCKS WAS NOT BEING RUN BY THE CIA PROPER OR THE FBI, WAS IT <u>SOLELY</u> THE IDEA OF BANISTER, FERRIE, OR TUJAGUE? THE ONLY OTHER GROUP LEFT TO CONSIDER IS THE GROUP I WILL LATER IDENTIFY AS THE SET-UP CONSPIRATORS. HOWEVER <u>THEIR</u> EFFORTS WOULD NOT BEGIN IN EARNEST UNTIL **HARVEY** HAD RETURNED STATESIDE IN JUNE OF 1962. AND, I DOUBT THAT THE ASSASSINATION PLANS WOULD HAVE PROGRESSED TO A POINT IN EARLY 1961 THAT IT WOULD BE A CERTAINTY THAT **HARVEY** WOULD BE THE PATSY.*

*AT THE TIME OF THIS WRITING, I CANNOT EXPLAIN DEFINITIVELY <u>WHY</u> SOMEONE WOULD IMPLICATE **HARVEY** AT <u>THIS</u> PARTICULAR TIME IN AN EVENT THAT WOULD AT FACE VALUE APPEAR TO BE ANTI- CASTRO IN NATURE. HOWEVER IT IS IMPORTANT TO KEEP IN MIND THAT <u>WHOEVER</u> ULTIMATELY ELECTED TO TIE **HARVEY'S** NAME TO THE ATTEMPTED PURCHASE OF THE TRUCKS WAS MAKING A <u>DELIBERATE</u> EFFORT TO TIE **HARVEY** TO AN <u>ANTI</u>-CASTRO CAUSE AT A TIME WHEN HE WAS IN FACT IN RUSSIA UNDER THE INTELLIGENCE GUISE OF A <u>PRO</u>-COMMUNIST "DEFECTOR." SOMEONE MAY HAVE BEEN VERY CARELESS ON JANUARY 20TH, 1961 AND IN ESSENCE JEOPARDIZED **HARVEY'S** COVER WHILE HE WAS IN RUSSIA ON ASSIGNMENT. OR, DID THEY KNOW THAT UPON **HARVEY'S** RETURN STATESIDE THAT HE WOULD BE USED AS AN INFILTRATOR/INFORMER BY THE INTELLIGENCE AGENCIES? LATER, THE ABILITY TO TRULY ESTABLISH WHETHER LEE **HARVEY** OSWALD WAS INDEED A PRO-COMMUNIST "DEFECTOR" WHO CHAMPIONED THE PRO-CASTRO FPFC OR WAS LEE **HARVEY** OSWALD SOMEONE TRYING TO ALIGN HIMSELF WITH THE ANTI-CASTRO MOVEMENT IN NEW ORLEANS AND DALLAS WOULD BE VIRTUALLY IMPOSSIBLE. PERHAPS THAT IN ITSELF WAS THE PURPOSE, ALBEIT PREMATURE, OF THE PICK-UP TRUCK PURCHASE INCIDENT.*

*IN LIGHT OF THIS CONFUSING AND PERHAPS PREMATURE EFFORT, MY SUSPICIONS CONTINUE TO LIE WITH THE TRIO OF BANISTER, FERRIE, AND TUJAGUE AS THE GROUP MOST LIKELY TO MAKE THIS TYPE OF INCRIMINATING EFFORT TO TIE **HARVEY** TO A PURCHASE OF TRUCKS THAT WOULD BE USED IN AN EFFORT TO OUST CASTRO. BUT, AT WHOSE BIDDING DID THEY DO THIS? WE WILL EXAMINE THIS LATER AS WE INTRODUCE THOSE MORE POINTEDLY RESPONSIBLE FOR THE SET-UP OF **HARVEY**.*

*IT IS INTERESTING TO NOTE THAT THIS IS ALMOST EXACTLY 2 YEARS <u>PRIOR</u> TO THE RIFLE/REVOLVER PURCHASE BY A "ALIK HIDELL" AND "A. HIDELL" RESPECTIVELY. THESE ALLEGED **HARVEY** ALIASES WOULD LATER BE USED BY THE SET-UP CONSPIRATORS TO TIE **HARVEY** TO THE PURCHASE OF WEAPONS ALLEGEDLY USED IN THE JFK/TIPPIT SHOOTINGS.*

JANUARY 26TH 1961

MARGUERITE" VISITS THE STATE DEPARTMENT IN WASHINGTON. SHE FREELY VOICES HER OPINION ON HER "SON'S" STATUS. HER COMMENTS TO A EUGENE BOSTER, A SPECIAL OFFICER IN CHARGE OF SOVIET AFFAIRS WERE PARTICULARLY POINTED: "I AM UNDER THE IMPRESSION THAT MY SON IS AN AGENT." DENMAN STANFIELD AND ED HICKEY ALSO ATTENDED THIS MEETING.

*WHEN TESTIFYING BEFORE THE WARREN COMMISSION IN 1964, SHE FURTHER ELABORATED ON HER VISIT TO WASHINGTON THAT JANUARY IN 1961: "HE HAS BEEN EXPLOITED ALL THROUGH THE PAPER AS A DEFECTOR……I KNOW A LITTLE ABOUT THE CIA AND SO ON, (POSSIBLY A MIS-SPOKEN REFERENCE TO **LEE'S** COUSIN MARILYN MURRETT) THE U-2, POWERS, AND THINGS THAT HAVE BEEN MADE PUBLIC. THEY (AGENTS) GO THROUGH ANY EXTREME FOR THEIR COUNTRY….FOR HIM TO MARRY A RUSSIAN GIRL AND BRING HER HERE,……I THINK THAT IS ALL PART OF AN AGENT'S DUTY."*

*THE MUCH MALIGNED "MARGUERITE'S" MUSINGS SHOWED SHE WAS MUCH MORE THAN JUST A CONCERNED "MOTHER." ONE HAS TO WONDER IF **HARVEY**, IN AN EFFORT TO LESSEN HER "WORRY"HAD GIVEN HER SOME MINIMAL INDICATION OF THE PURPOSE OF HIS TRAVELS. OR, DID SHE KNOW PRECISELY WHY HE HAD GONE TO RUSSIA?*

*"MARGUERITE" WAS, TO THE WARREN COMMISSION, A LOOSE CANNON. SHE WAS ALSO A LOOSE CANNON TO THE CIA. IN HER LATER VERBAL JOUSTING WITH COMMISSION ATTORNEY RANKIN SHE CONTINUED TO EMPHASIZE HER POINT THAT **HARVEY** WAS AN INTELLIGENCE AGENT. RANKIN TRIED GAMELY TO STEER HER TESTIMONY TOWARDS WHETHER **HARVEY** AND MARINA WERE IN LOVE. "MARGUERITE" CLOSED HER TESTIMONY WITH A VERY INSIGHTFULL COMMENT: "YES SIR, I THINK MY SON WAS AN AGENT. I CERTAINLY DO."*

*"MARGUERITE'S" INSISTANCE AS EARLY AS JANUARY 1961 THAT HER "SON" **HARVEY** WAS AN AGENT LEADS ME TO PERHAPS RECONSIDER JUST WHAT SHE KNEW REGARDING THE "OSWALD PROJECT." HER LATER TESTIMONY BEFORE THE W.C. RAISES THE SAME QUESTION. HER WILLINGNESS TO AT LEAST ATTEMPT TO ADHERE TO THE STORYLINE REGARDING THE **HARVEY**-TO-**LEE** TRANSFORMATION AND ACCEPTANCE OF ROBERT, JOHN PIC, AND THE MURRETTS AS RELATIVES TELLS ME THAT SHE WAS AT THE VERY LEAST BRIEFED IN REGARDS TO WHY SHE WAS ASKED TO BECOME "MARGUERITE." BUT, IF THAT WERE THE CASE, WHY WOULD SHE IN TURN JEOPARDIZE THE PROJECT BY PROCLAIMING THAT **HARVEY** WAS AN AGENT? ONCE AGAIN I MUST STATE THAT "MARGUERITE" MAY HAVE BEEN A SUITABLE CHOICE AS **HARVEY'S** CARETAKER, BUT LATER PROVE TO BE A POOR CHOICE WHEN HE WAS LATER ASKED TO "DEFECT" TO RUSSIA AND MOST CERTAINLY A POOR CHOICE WHEN PRESSED INTO SERVICE FOLLOWING THE ASSASSINATION TO OFFER A DETAILED FAMILY HISTORY THAT WAS IN ESSENCE A BLEND OF TWO DISTINCT FAMILIES BOTH WITH A VERY FRAGMENTED PAST.*

*IT IS IMPORTANT TO NOTE THAT THOSE CONSPIRATORS PLANNING THE ASSASSINATION AND THOSE SET-UP CONSPIRATORS RESPONSIBLE FOR PLACING THE BLAME ON **HARVEY** WERE NOT AT ALL CONCERNED ABOUT THE "CLEAN-UP" PROBLEM REGARDING **HARVEY** AND **LEE** AFTER THE DEATH OF THE PRESIDENT. THIS WOULD BE LEFT TO THE CIA AND TO A GREATER DEGREE TO THE FBI IF THOSE AGENCIES WERE TO SUCCESSFULLY DISTANCE THEMSELVES FROM **HARVEY**.*

JANUARY 26TH 1961

"MARGUERITE" PLACES A PHONE CALL TO THE WHITE HOUSE. THE CALL WAS NOTED IN EVELYN LINCOLN'S LOG OF OFFICIAL CALLS TO THE PRESIDENT.

JANUARY 30TH 1961

HARVEY ALSO WROTE A LETTER TO SECRETARY OF THE NAVY, JOHN CONNALLY, REGARDING HIS MARINE DISCHARGE. IT HAD BEEN CHANGED FROM "HONORABLE" TO "LESS THAN HONORABLE" DURING HIS STAY IN RUSSIA. HE ASKED TO HAVE THIS REVERSED SINCE HIS TRIP TO RUSSIA "ALWAYS HAD THE FULL SANCTION OF THE U.S. EMBASSY....AND HENCE THE U. S. GOVERNMENT." **HARVEY** NOTED THAT A "GROSS INJUSTICE" HAD BEEN DONE TO HIM BY VIRTUE OF THE "BELATED DISHONORABLE DISCHARGE" GIVEN TO HIM.

*IN THIS CORRESPONDANCE, **HARVEY** CAME PRECARIOUSLY CLOSE TO BLOWING HIS COVER AS IT IS DOUBTFUL THAT A TRUE "DEFECTION" WOULD HAVE THE BLESSING OF EITHER THE U.S. EMBASSY OR THE U.S. GOVERNMENT.*

FEBRUARY 1961

"MARGUERITE" RETURNS TO TEXAS WHERE SHE NOW RESIDES IN FT. WORTH AT 1612 HURLEY.

FEBRUARY 1ST 1961
THE STATE DEPARTMENT SENDS A CABLE TO THE U.S. EMBASSY IN MOSCOW REGARDING "MARGUERITE'S" VISIT AND REQUESTING INFORMATION ON THE "WELFARE WHEREABOUTS" OF HER "SON", **HARVEY.**

CHAPTER 4: THE "DEFECTOR" COMES IN FROM THE COLD

FEBRUARY 5TH 1961
HARVEY WRITES A LETTER TO THE U.S. EMBASSY STATING HIS DESIRE TO RETURN TO THE U.S. HE NOTES: "THAT IS, IF WE COULD COME TO SOME AGREEMENT CONCERNING THE DROPPING OF ANY LEGAL PROCEEDINGS AGAINST ME." HE ALSO REQUESTS THAT HIS PASSPORT BE RETURNED. THE LETTER ARRIVED AT THE EMBASSY ON FEB 13TH, 1961.

THIS WOULD OF COURSE BE A NATURAL CONCERN OF ANY "DEFECTOR"; PARTICULARLY ONE WHO HAD THREATENED TO TURN OVER RADAR SECRETS TO THE SOVIETS. ***HARVEY'S*** *WRITTEN CONCERNS WOULD SATISFY THE MAIL-READING RUSSIANS THAT HIS "DEFECTION" WAS REAL AND HIS VERBAL ASSURANCE FROM SNYDER, THE EMBASSY CONSUL, THAT THIS COULD BE ACCOMPLISHED – WITH APPROVAL OF THE STATE DEPARTMENT – WOULD BE WHAT **HARVEY** WOULD EXPECT TO HEAR AS A "DEFECTOR" RETURNING FROM AN INTELLIGENCE MISSION.*

HIS LETTER CLOSES WITH: "I HOPE THAT IN RECALLING THE RESPONSIBILITY I HAVE TO AMERICA THAT YOU WILL REMEMBER YOURS IN DOING EVERYTHING YOU CAN TO HELP ME SINCE I AM AN AMERICAN CITIZEN." I SUSPECT THAT HIS "RESPONSIBILITY TO AMERICA" WOULD INDEED BE A REFERENCE TO HIS INTELLIGENCE ASSIGNMENT IN THE SOVIET UNION.

FEBRUARY 23RD 1961
JOHN CONNALLY REPLIES TO **HARVEY'S** LETTER REGARDING HIS DISCHARGE. HE INFORMS HIM THAT HE IS NO LONGER SECRETARY OF THE NAVY.

FEBRUARY 28TH 1961
CONSUL SNYDER REPLIES TO **HARVEY'S** LETTER OF 2/5/61. HE REQUESTS THAT **HARVEY** COME TO MOSCOW FOR A PERSONAL INTERVIEW IN REGARDS TO HIS RETURNING TO THE U.S.

MARCH 1961
GEORGE DE MOHRENSCHILDT STARTS HIS WALKING TRIP THROUGH MEXICO AND CENTRAL AMERICA.

MARCH 4TH 1961
HARVEY AND MARINA MEET FOR THE FIRST TIME.

MARCH 5TH 1961
HARVEY WRITES THE EMBASSY ONCE AGAIN IN AN EFFORT TO EXPEDITE HIS RETURN TO THE U.S. IT SEEMS CONSUL SNYDER WISHES **HARVEY** TO RETURN TO MOSCOW FROM MINSK FOR AN INTERVIEW. BUT **HARVEY** REPLIES: "I SEE NO REASON FOR ANY PRELIMINARY INQUIRIES NOT TO BE PUT IN THE FORM OF A QUESTIONNAIRE AND SENT TO ME…….I HAVE NO INTENTION OF ABUSING MY POSITION HERE AND I AM SURE YOU WOULD NOT WANT ME TO."

IT'S APPARENT BY THE TONE OF ***HARVEY'S*** *LETTER TO CONSUL SNYDER THAT* ***HARVEY*** *FEELS THAT HE IS INDEED IN CONTROL OF THE HANDLING OF HIS RETURN TO THE U.S AND THAT HE ANSWERS TO A HIGHER POWER (NAVAL INTELLIGENCE AND THE CIA) THAN A MERE DIPLOMATIC CONSUL. ONE WOULD NOT EXPECT THIS TONE FROM A <u>TRUE</u> DEFECTOR NEEDING THE ASSISTANCE OF THE CONSUL TO RETURN HOME.*

MARCH 1961
"MARGUERITE" RECEIVES A LETTER FROM THE STATE DEPARTMENT INFORMING HER THAT **HARVEY** WISHES TO RETURN TO THE U.S.

MARCH 24TH 1961
SNYDER'S REPLY TO **HARVEY** WAS EQUALLY AS FIRM IN THAT HE STATES: "AS STATED IN OUR PREVIOUS LETTER, (2/28/61) A FINAL DETERMINATION OF YOUR

PRESENT AMERICAN CITIZENSHIP STATUS CAN ONLY BE MADE ON THE BASIS OF A PERSONAL INTERVIEW."

MARCH 24TH 1961

HARVEY MEETS WITH MARINA AT A TRADE UNION DANCE IN MINSK AT THE PALACE OF CULTURE

MARCH 30TH 1961

ACCORDING TO HOSPITAL RECORDS, **HARVEY** WAS ADMITTED TO THE 4TH CLINICAL HOSPITAL IN MINSK IN ITS EAR/NOSE/THROAT DIVISION.

APRIL 1ST 1961

HARVEY HAS ADENOID SURGERY.

APRIL 4TH 1961

CARLOS MARCELLO IS UNCEREMONIOUSLY DEPORTED FROM THE U.S. BY THE JUSTICE DEPARTMENT. HE IS SENT TO GUATAMALA AS THE ONLY PASSENGER ABOARD THE FLIGHT.

APRIL 10TH 1961

"MARGUERITE" IS INTERVIEWED BY THE FBI.

APRIL 11TH 1961

HARVEY IS RELEASED FROM THE HOSPITAL. HE AND MARINA FILE A NOTICE OF INTENTION TO MARRY WITH THE REGISTRAR'S OFFICE.

APRIL 13TH 1961

THE STATE DEPARTMENT CABLES THE EMBASSY IN MOSCOW REGARDING HOW TO HANDLE **HARVEY'S** REQUEST TO RETURN HOME. MORE POINTEDLY, THEY ADVISE THE EMBASSY TO PERSONALLY INTERVIEW **HARVEY**, MAKE NO PROMISES REGARDING HIS REQUEST THAT LEGAL PROCEEDINGS AGAINST HIM BE DROPPED, AND CONTINUE TO REPORT ANY NEW DEVELOPMENTS TO THE STATE DEPT.

APRIL 16-17TH 1961

THE DISASTROUS BAY OF PIGS INVASION TAKES PLACE.

GEORGE DEMOHRENSCHILDT FINDS HIMSELF IN GUATAMALA CITY DURING THE BAY OF PIGS INVASION. THE PRELIMINARY TRAINING AND THE INVASION ITSELF WAS LAUNCHED FROM GUATAMALA. HE WAS THERE FOR A 3 WEEK PERIOD.

APRIL 1961

ACCORDING TO ARMSTRONG, **LEE** WAS IN KEY WEST, FLORIDA. WILLIAM HUFFMAN, WORKING AT A MARINA ON STOCK ISLAND, FUELED A BOAT MANNED BY **LEE** AND SEVERAL CUBANS. HUFFMAN, A FBI INFORMANT, NOTIFIED THE MIAMI OFFICE OF THE FBI ABOUT THE VISIT ON NOVEMBER 25TH, 1963. NEEDLESS TO SAY, HIS REPORT WAS IGNORED BY THE FBI SINCE **HARVEY** WAS IN RUSSIA. AT THIS POINT, **LEE** WAS WORKING WITH JACK RUBY IN RUNNING STOLEN GUNS FROM FLORIDA TO CUBA.

APRIL 18TH 1961

MARINA IS AWARDED PERMISSION TO MARRY **HARVEY**.

APRIL 30TH 1961

HARVEY MARRIES MARINA ON THIS DATE AT 11:00 AM. IN MINSK AT THE CIVIL REGISTRAR'S OFFICE.

MAY 5TH 1961

HARVEY RE-INITIATES CONTACT WITH HIS "BROTHER" ROBERT VIA A LETTER AND INFORMS HIM OF HIS MARRIAGE TO MARINA.

EARLY MAY 1961

ACCORDING TO ARMSTRONG, DR. ENRIQUE LUACES, A PROFESSOR OF ENGINEERING AT THE UNIVERSITY OF SANTIAGO IN CUBA, IS INTRODUCED TO **LEE** AT SLOPPY JOE'S BAR IN HAVANA. **LEE** WAS INTRODUCED AS AN "ARMS EXPERT" AND SHOWED DR.

LUACES HIS PORTFOLIO OF RIFLES AND SMALL ARMS. ON NOVEMBER 23RD, 1963, LUACES WAS INTERVIEWED BY ARMY INTELLIGENCE IN PANAMA WHERE HE WAS RESIDING. DR. LUACES REMEMBERED THAT THE INDIVIDUAL INTRODUCED TO HIM IN MAY 1961 AS **LEE** HARVEY OSWALD. ONCE AGAIN, **HARVEY** IS IN RUSSIA. DR. LUACES WAS NOT QUESTIONED BY THE W.C.

MAY 25TH1961

A LETTER DATED ONLY "MAY 1961" BUT POSTMARKED MAY 16TH ARRIVES AT THE EMBASSY ON MAY 25TH IN REPLY TO SNYDER'S MARCH 24TH LETTER. IN THIS LETTER **HARVEY** IS STILL DEMANDING "GUARANTEES THAT I SHALL NOT BE PERSECUTED FOR ANY ACT PERTAINING TO THIS CASE." THE "ACT" OBVIOUSLY IS TREASON AS HIS "DEFECTION" INVOLVED GIVING UP RADAR SECRETS TO THE SOVIETS. **HARVEY** CONTINUES: "UNLESS YOU HONESTLY THINK THAT THIS CONDITION CAN BE MET, I SEE NO REASON FOR A CONTINUANCE OF OUR CORRESPONDANCE. INSTEAD I SHALL ENDEAVOR TO USE MY RELATIVES (MY UNDERLINE) IN THE U.S. TO SEE ABOUT GETTING SOMETHING DONE IN WASHINGTON."

*IN THIS LETTER, **HARVEY** INFORMS SNYDER THAT HE HAS MARRIED A RUSSIAN CITIZEN:"I WOULD NOT LEAVE HERE WITHOUT MY WIFE, SO ARRANGEMENTS WOULD HAVE TO BE MADE FOR HER TO LEAVE AT THE SAME TIME I DO."*

*ONCE AGAIN **HARVEY'S** REMARKS EMPHASIZE THE FACT THAT HE FEELS QUITE SECURE IN HIS STATUS AS A "DEFECTOR" WISHING TO RETURN HOME. NOW HE IS DEMANDING THAT HIS NEW WIFE BE INCLUDED IN THE TRAVEL PLANS AS WELL*

*THE "USE MY RELATIVES"COMMENT MAY HAVE BEEN A REFERENCE TO HIS "COUSIN" MARILYN MURRET. MORE ON HER INVOLVEMENT WHEN **HARVEY** RETURNS TO THE U.S. IT ALSO COULD HAVE BEEN A VEILED REFERENCE TO THE CIA. I AM INCLINED TO THINK IT WAS THE LATTER.*

MAY 26TH 1961

SNYDER CABLES THE STATE DEPARTMENT REQUESTING THEIR INPUT IN REGARDS TO **HARVEY'S** DEMANDS.

THE STATE DEPARTMENT, IN A CABLED REPLY TO THE U.S. EMBASSY IN MOSCOW, CLOSES WITH THE FOLLOWING NOTATION: "THE EMBASSY'S CAREFULL ATTENTION TO THE INVOLVED CASE OF MR. OSWALD IS APPRECIATED." THE CABLE WAS SIGNED BY SECRETARY OF STATE DEAN RUSK. THE WARREN COMMISSION CHOSE TO ELIMINATE THIS COMMENT BY THE SECRETARY OF STATE IN ITS FINAL REPORT.

*THE PASSPORT OFFICE IN WASHINGTON HOWEVER HAD PREVIOUSLY CABLED THE EMBASSY IN MOSCOW INFORMING THEM THAT **HARVEY'S** PASSPORT NOT BE RETURNED TO HIM UNTIL HIS TRAVEL PLANS TO THE U.S. WERE COMPLETE. APPARENTLY THE PASSPORT OFFICE DID NOT SHARE THE STATE DEPARTMENT'S DESIRE THAT **HARVEY** RETURN TO THE U.S AS QUICKLY AS POSSIBLE AND WITH AS LITTLE RED TAPE AS POSSIBLE.*

MAY 31ST 1961

HARVEY WRITES HIS "BROTHER", ROBERT. HE NOTES THAT HE NOW WISHES TO RETURN TO THE UNITED STATES.

JUNE 1ST 1961

HARVEY WRITES TO "MARGUERITE" AND TO ROBERT INFORMING THEM OF HIS MARRIAGE TO MARINA.

JUNE 5TH 1961

THE NOMADIC "MARGUERITE" MOVES ONCE AGAIN. SHE NOW RESIDES IN CROWLEY,TEXAS. SHE IS WORKING AT THE MCADAMS RANCH.

JUNE 1961
CARLOS MARCELLO SECRETELY AND ILLEGALLY RETURNS FROM GUATAMALA ON A PRIVATE PLANE PILOTED BY DAVID FERRIE.

JUNE 1961
OPERATION MONGOOSE IS LAUNCHED. MORE ON THIS IN CHAPTER 7.

JULY 5TH 1961
HARVEY LEAVES FOR MOSCOW AND ARRIVES ON JULY 8TH. HE VISITS THE U.S EMBASSY WITHOUT AN APPOINTMENT BUT FINDS THE EMBASSY CLOSED. HIS OLD PASSPORT IS DUE TO EXPIRE ON SEPTEMBER 10TH, 1961.

JULY 10TH 1961
MARINA FLYS TO MOSCOW TO JOIN **HARVEY**. **HARVEY** VISITS THE MOSCOW EMBASSY SO MARINA CAN INITIATE THE PROCESS FOR HER ENTRANCE VISA TO THE U.S. **HARVEY** RETURNS THE NEXT DAY AS WELL WITH MARINA. **HARVEY'S** SOON TO EXPIRE PASSPORT - SEPTEMBER 10TH- IS REVALIDATED AND RETURNED TO HIM.

JULY 14TH 1961
MARINA AND **HARVEY** RETURN TO MINSK

JULY 20TH 1961
HARVEY TURNS IN THE NECESSARY DOCUMENTS SO HE CAN OBTAIN AN EXIT VISA FROM RUSSIA.

JULY 24TH 1961
THE EMBASSY WRITES **HARVEY** REQUESTING COPIES OF HIS MARRIAGE CERTIFICATE AND MARINA'S BIRTH CERTIFICATE.

JULY 29TH 1961
MARINA WRITES TO **HARVEY'S** "BROTHER", ROBERT.

JULY 1961
ROSCOE WHITE IS ASSIGNED TO THE 1ST FIELD ARTILLERY GROUP LOCATED AT 29 PALMS, CALIFORNIA.

AUGUST 1ST 1961
"MARGUERITE" MOVES ONCE AGAIN. SHE IS NOW IN VERNON, TEXAS.

AUGUST 3RD 1961
HARVEY WRITES "MARGUERITE" TELLING HER THAT HE AND MARINA ARE IN THE PROCESS OF OBTAINING THEIR EXIT VISAS.

AUGUST 21ST 1961
MARINA PUTS IN A REQUEST FOR HER SOVIET EXIT VISA AND **HARVEY** SENDS THE PREVIOUSLY REQUESTED DOCUMENTS.

AUGUST 26TH 1961
DAVID FERRIE IS ARRESTED IN JEFFERSON PARISH, LOUISIANA. HE IS CHARGED WITH SEX CRIMES AGAINST 4 JUVENILE BOYS. ON AUGUST 29TH, FERRIE WILL BE CHARGED WITH INTIMIDATING A WITNESS IN REGARDS TO THESE CHARGES. FERRIE IS SUSPENDED BY EASTERN AIRLINES.

SEPTEMBER 18TH 1961
FBI AGENT FAIN TELEPHONES **HARVEY'S** "BROTHER", ROBERT IN AN EFFORT TO LOCATE THEIR "MOTHER", "MARGUERITE."

*ONE HAS TO QUESTION WHETHER BY THIS TIME THE FBI/FAIN HAS ANY CLUE THAT THE TWO PEOPLE THEY THINK ARE **HARVEY'S** "BROTHER" AND "MOTHER" ARE NOT AT ALL RELATED TO HIM. OR, ARE THEY AWARE OF THIS AND SIMPLY PURSUING THEM AS A*

ROUTINE MEASURE SINCE THEIR "SON" WAS A MARINE DEFECTOR? THEIR PURSUIT OF "MARGUERITE" VIA ROBERT MAY WELL BE SIMPLY WINDOWDRESSING.

SEPTEMBER 1961
ROSCOE WHITE IS ONCE AGAIN SENT OVERSEAS. HE IS STATIONED IN OKINAWA WITH THE 12TH ARTILLERY REGIMENT.

OCTOBER 4TH 1961
THE VISA PROCESS IS PREDICTABLY SLOW. **HARVEY**, IN A LETTER TO THE EMBASSY, TRIES TO ENLIST THEIR HELP BY NOTING IT WOULD BE "IN THE INTEREST OF THE U.S. GOVERNMENT AND THE AMERICAN EMBASSY, MOSCOW, TO LOOK INTO THIS CASE ON MY BEHALF."

*ONCE AGAIN, **HARVEY** SEEMS TO KNOW HE IS CAPABLE OF SOLICITING ASSISTANCE NOT NORMALLY AFFORDED A "DEFECTOR".*

OCTOBER 9TH 1961
MARINA FILES A PETITION TO THE U.S. IMMIGRATION AND NATURALIZATION SERVICE IN REGARDS TO HER TRAVEL TO THE U.S.

OCTOBER 1961
ACCORDING TO ARMSTRONG, **LEE** AND A MAN NAMED CELSO HERNANDEZ WERE QUESTIONED IN NEW ORLEANS BY LEVEE BOARD POLICER OFFICERS. **LEE** APPARENTLY BECAME ARGUMENTIVE WITH ONE OF THE OFFICERS AND CLAIMED TO BE WITH THE FAIR PLAY FOR CUBA COMMITTEE. THEY WERE TAKEN TO THE POLICE STATION AND QUESTIONED BY MARCEL CHAMPON, THE OFFICER IN CHARGE THAT EVENING. **LEE** WAS RELEASED. NO ONE FROM THE POLICE STATION WAS QUESTIONED BY THE W.C. **HARVEY** WAS STILL IN RUSSIA AND WILL OF COURSE LATER BE INVOLVED WITH THE FPFC COMMITTEE.

OCTOBER 22ND 1961
HARVEY WRITES TO BOTH "MARGUERITE" AND ROBERT.

NOVEMBER 1ST 1961
HARVEY WRITES THE U.S. EMBASSY IN MOSCOW.

NOVEMBER 8TH 1961
HARVEY WRITES "MARGUERITE" ASKING IF SHE HAS ANY OLD PICTURES OF THE TWO OF THEM. HE ALSO ASKS THE DATE OF BIRTH OF HIIS "BROTHER" ROBERT.

*APPARENTLY **HARVEY** NEEDED TO LEARN A BIT MORE ABOUT HIS "FAMILY" PRIOR TO HIS RETURN TO THE UNITED STATES.*

NOVEMBER 13TH 1961
THE U.S. EMBASSY IN MOSCOW, IN AN APPARENT ATTEMPT TO ANSWER **HARVEY'S** QUESTIONS AND CONCERNS IN HIS NOVEMBER 1ST INQUIRY, INFORM HIM THAT HIS RUSSIAN PASSPORT WILL NOT BE A PROBLEM IN REGARDS TO HIS RETURN TO THE U.S.

DECEMBER 1961
HARVEY'S CORRESPONDANCE WITH HIS "BROTHER" AND "MOTHER" CONTINUE. ON DECEMBER 10 AND DECEMBER 21 HE WRITES "MARGUERITE." ON DECEMBER 14 AND 20 HE WRITES ROBERT. BOTH ARE SENT CHRISTMAS CARDS AS WELL.

DECEMBER 25TH 1961
HARVEY AND MARINA ARE FINALLY GRANTED SOVIET EXIT VISAS.

LATE 1961
GEORGE DEMOHRENSCHILDT, A SOCIALITE IN THE DALLAS RUSSIAN SPEAKING COMMUNITY, HAS LUNCH WITH J. WALTON MOORE, DALLAS CIA DOMESTIC CONTACT

SERVICE. MOORE MENTIONED A FORMER MARINE, LEE **HARVEY** OSWALD, WAS WORKING IN MINSK WHERE DEMOHRENSCHILDT SPENT HIS CHILDHOOD. MOORE ASKED HIM TO LOOK INTO **HARVEY'S** STAY IN MINSK.

JANUARY 2ND, 1962

HARVEY WRITES "MARGUERITE" NOTING THAT HE AND HIS NEW WIFE HOPE TO RETURN TO THE U.S. IN MARCH. HE ALSO INFORMS HER THAT HE WILL NEED $800 FOR HIS AND MARINA'S RETURN TO THE U.S. HE REQUESTS THAT SHE CONTACT THE RED CROSS AND IN TURN HAVE THEM CONTACT THE INTERNATIONAL RESCUE COMMITTEE. "MARGUERITE" HOWEVER ONLY CONTACTS THE RED CROSS.

JANUARY 5TH 1962

THE U.S. EMBASSY IN MOSCOW WRITES **HARVEY** REQUESTING THAT HE RETURN TO THE U.S. WITHOUT HIS WIFE MARINA.

JANUARY 11TH 1962

MARINA IS ISSUED A RUSSIAN PASSPORT.

JANUARY 13TH 1962

HARVEY WRITES THE INTERNATIONAL RESCUE COMMITTEE REQUESTING $500 FOR HIS AND MARINA'S RETURN TO TEXAS.

*IN A LETTER TO THE WARREN COMMISSION, THE INTERNATIONAL RESCUE COMMITTEE NOTED THAT THEY HAD RECEIVED A LETTER FROM THE RED CROSS DATED 14 JANUARY 1962 TO WHICH WAS ATTACHED COPIES OF A LETTER FROM THE U.S. EMBASSY IN MOSCOW TO **HARVEY** (DATED DEC. 14TH, 1961) AND A LETTER ADDRESSED TO THE INTERNATIONAL RESCUE COMMITTEE (DATED JAN. 13, 1962) FROM **HARVEY**. THE LETTER FROM THE IRC TO THE WARREN COMMISSION WENT ON TO READ: "WHAT IS MOST PUZZLING... IS THAT THE LETTER FROM LEE HARVEY OSWALD DATED JAN 13, 1962 COULD HAVE REACHED THE U.S. BY JAN 14TH, 1962, AND THAT IT REACHED US VIA TEXAS...".*

*IT APPEARS THAT SOMEONE AT THE EMBASSY, FULLY AWARE OF THE RULE THAT REQUIRED A "TURN DOWN" FROM A CHARITABLE ORGANIZATION PRIOR TO A GOVERNMENT LOAN, WROTE TO THE IRC ON **HARVEY'S** BEHALF AND SENT IT – IN ALL LIKELIHOOD – VIA DIPLOMATIC POUCH. **HARVEY'S** LETTER TO THE IRC DIDN'T ARRIVE THERE UNTIL FEBRUARY, 1962.*

JANUARY 16TH 1962

HARVEY WRITES THE U.S. EMBASSY IN MOSCOW INFORMING THEM THAT HE WILL NOT RETURN TO THE U.S. WITHOUT MARINA.

JANUARY 26TH 1962

HARVEY ONCE AGAIN WRITES THE IRC. THIS TIME HIS REQUEST IS FOR $1,000.

FEBRUARY 6TH 1962

HARVEY RECEIVES HIS LOAN APPLICATION FORMS FROM THE U.S. EMBASSY IN MOSCOW.

*INTERESTINGLY, HAD THE EMBASSY SIMPLY WAITED FOR THE IRC TO REPLY TO **HARVEY'S** LETTER TO THAT ORGANIZATION, IT MAY WELL HAVE NOT BEEN NECESSARY FOR THE GOVERNMENT LOAN TO **HARVEY**. THE IRC WAS KNOWN TO BE A CONDUIT FOR DISPENSING CIA FUNDS. THE IRC MOST LIKELY WOULD HAVE BEEN MORE THAN HAPPY TO FUND THE DISGRUNTLED **HARVEY'S** RETURN.*

FEBRUARY 15th 1962

MARINA GIVES BIRTH TO JUNE, THEIR FIRST DAUGHTER. THIS PROMPTS ANOTHER LETTER TO THE EMBASSY IN MOSCOW. NOW THE TRAVEL ARRANGEMENTS WOULD NEED TO BE FOR THREE, NOT TWO.

FEBRUARY 17ᵀᴴ 1962
DAVID FERRIE IS CHARGED WITH EXTORTION IN THAT HE ATTEMPTED TO HAVE AN INDIVIDUAL INFLUENCE A WITNESS IN REGARDS TO THE MORALS CHARGE OF APRIL 26ᵀᴴ, 1961.

GEORGE LARDNER JR. NOTED THAT FERRIE HAD TOLD HIM THERE WAS NOTHING IMPROPER IN HIS RELATIONSHIP WITH YOUNG MEN. FERRIE NOTED THAT IT WAS HIS "HOBBY" TO GIVE "DESERVING YOUNGSTERS FROM BROKEN HOMES" A "BREAK IN LIFE."

AS THE INVESTIGATION INTO FERRIE'S ILLICIT ACTIVITIES GREW, THE NUMBER OF BOYS INVOLVED SWELLED TO 20. SEVERAL OF THE VICTIMS NOTED TO NEW ORLEANS POLICE THAT THEY HAD ACCOMPANIED FERRIE ON FLIGHTS HE PILOTED TO CUBA, HONDURAS, AND GUATEMALA.

FEBRUARY 1962
DAVID FERRIE JOINS GUY BANISTER'S INVESTIGATIVE STAFF IN NEW ORLEANS.

MARCH 7ᵀᴴ 1962
THE U.S. MARINE CORP RESERVES SENDS **HARVEY** HIS "LESS THAN DESIRABLE" DISCHARGE NOTICE.

MARCH 9ᵀᴴ 1962
JOSEPH NORBURY AT THE U.S. EMBASSY, MOSCOW INFORMS **HARVEY** THAT THEY ARE ONLY AUTHORIZED TO LOAN HIM $500 TO RETURN HOME.

*THIS WOULD BE THE THIRD EVENT THAT SHOULD HAVE PROMPTED A "LOOKOUT CARD" POSTING ON **HARVEY**. THE FIRST "TRIGGER" OF COURSE WOULD HAVE BEEN HIS "DEFECTION" ON OCTOBER 15ᵀᴴ, 1959. THE SECOND TRIGGER SHOULD HAVE BEEN THE APRIL 5ᵀᴴ, 1960 CABLE TO THE STATE DEPARTMENT FROM THE MOSCOW EMBASSY NOTING THAT THEY HAD NO IDEA OF **HARVEY'S** WHEREABOUTS AND HAD NOT KNOWN SINCE NOVEMBER 1959. EITHER THE STATE DEPARTMENT AND PASSPORT OFFICE WERE CONSISTANTLY INCOMPETENT REGARDING **HARVEY**, OR THEY WERE SIMPLY ACCOMODATING THE WISHES OF THE INTELIGENCE COMMUNITY WHOSE DESIRE WAS TO RETURN **HARVEY** TO THE U.S. WITH A MINIMUM OF FANFARE OR BUREAUCRATIC INTERFERRENCE.*

MARCH 16ᵀᴴ 1962
ENTRY VISA PROBLEMS ARISE FOR MARINA IN THE U.S. BUT, A LETTER FROM ROBERT OWEN OF THE STATE DEPARTMENT TO JOHN CRUMP IN THE STATE DEPARTMENT'S VISA OFFICE MAKES IT PERFECTLY CLEAR THE STATE DEPARTMENT'S STANCE ON **HARVEY'S** SITUATION. THE STATE DEPARTMENT'S LETTER TO THEIR VISA OFFICE SAID IT WAS "IN THE BEST INTEREST OF THE U.S. TO GET LEE H. OSWALD (**HARVEY**) AND FAMILY OUT OF THE SOVIET UNION AND INTO THE U.S. AS SOON AS POSSIBLE."

*DURING THE TIME FRAME IN WHICH **HARVEY** PURSUED HIS RETURN TO THE U.S., THE INS CONTACTED HIS "BROTHER" ROBERT ABOUT MARINA'S ENTRY AS WELL. ROBERT WOULD LATER TESTIFY BEFORE THE WARREN COMMISSION:"THE GENTLEMAN (INS) ADVISED ME HE ASSUMED LEE (**HARVEY**) WAS EMPLOYED <u>BY THE GOVERNMENT</u> IN SOME CAPACITY IN RUSSIA." A STATE DEPARTMENT DOCUMENT ALSO RAISED QUESTIONS AS TO WHETHER **HARVEY'S** "DEFECTION" WAS CIA SPONSORED. THE DOCUMENT COMMENTING ON THE HANDLING OF **HARVEY'S** RETURN NOTED: "THIS WAS IN LINE WITH THE PRACTICE CONTINUED THROUGHOUT THE OSWALD CASE, AS IN OTHER 'DEFECTOR' CASES." IF **HARVEY** WERE <u>TRULY</u> A DEFECTOR, THERE WOULD HAVE BEEN NO OBVIOUS NEED FOR THE 'DEFECTOR' QUOTATION MARKS.*

*I SUSPECT THAT **HARVEY'S** HANDLERS, (NAVAL INTELLIGENCE/CIA) WERE AWARE THAT THE TONE OF **HARVEY'S** LETTERS TO THE EMBASSY WERE PROOF THAT HE WAS BECOMING MORE IMPATIENT REGARDING HIS RETURN HOME. HIS MISSION HAD BEEN SUCCESSFULLY COMPLETED AND, IN HIS EYES, THERE WAS NO FURTHER REASON FOR HIS "DEFECTION" TO CONTINUE. COMMON SENSE WOULD TELL ONE THAT AN IRRITATED INTELLIGENCE AGENT IS A DANGEROUS INTELLIGENCE AGENT; ONE SUBJECT TO BLOWING*

*HIS COVER AND THE TRUE NATURE OF HIS ASSIGNMENT. INTERCESSION BY THE CIA, NAVAL INTELLIGENCE, AND THE STATE DEPARTMENT IN SPEEDING UP **HARVEY'S** RETURN WOULD SEEM LOGICAL.*

MARCH 22ND 1962

HARVEY WRITES THE DEPARTMENT OF THE NAVY PROTESTING HIS DISCHARGE STATUS. ARMSTRONG NOTES THAT **HARVEY** STATED "I HAVE NOT VIOLATED SECTION 1544, TITLE 18, U.S. CODE THEREFORE YOU HAVE NO LEGAL OR EVEN MORAL RIGHT TO REVERSE MY HONORABLE DISCHARGE FROM THE USMC."

*ARMSTRONG POINTS OUT THAT THE ABOVE CITED SECTION AND TITLE IS IN REGARDS TO PASSPORTS. IT HAS NOTHING TO DO WITH CHANGING MILITARY DISCHARGE STATUS. IT READS "WHOEVER WILLINGLY AND KNOWINGLY USES OR ATTEMPTS TO USE A PASSPORT DESIGNED FOR THE USE OF ANOTHER HAS VIOLATED THE LAWS OF THE UNITED STATES." WHY WOULD **HARVEY** CITE THIS UNLESS HE WAS AWARE THAT HE WAS INDEED IMPERSONATING THE REAL **LEE** HARVEY OSWALD AND THAT THEY HAD DIFFERENT BIRTH CERTIFICATES <u>AND</u> PASSPORTS.*

MARCH 1962

FERRIE, WITH MARCELLO'S ASSISTANCE, IS GIVEN A JOB TO ASSIST MARCELLO'S ATTORNEY, G. WRAY GILL.

APRIL 1962

LEE APPLIES FOR EMPLOYMENT AT THE TEXAS EMPLOYMENT COMMISSION IN FT. WORTH. HE IS SUBJECTED TO A BATTERY OF APTITUDE TESTS. **HARVEY** IS STILL IN RUSSIA.

APRIL 28TH 1962

HARVEY ONCE AGAIN WRITES THE NAVY TO DISPUTE HIS DISCHARGE STATUS.

MAY 10th 1962

A LETTER FROM JOSEPH NORBURY FINALLY YIELDS THE NEWS **HARVEY** HAS LONG AWAITED. NORBURY'S LETTER STATES "THE EMBASSY IS NOW IN A POSITION TO TAKE FINAL ACTION ON YOUR WIFE'S VISA APPLICATION."

MAY 13TH 1962

HARVEY APPLIES FOR A TRANSIT VISA AT THE DUTCH EMBASSY IN MOSCOW FOR HIS WIFE, MARINA. THE TRANSIT VISA IS ISSUED THE SAME DAY.

MAY 16TH 1962

THE STATE DEPARTMENT NOTIFIES THE FBI THAT **HARVEY** WILL SOON RETURN TO THE UNITED STATES.

MAY 1962

"MARGUERITE" MOVES FROM VERNON, TEXAS. SHE NOW RESIDED AT 316 EAST DONNELL IN CROWELL, TEXAS.

MAY 18TH 1962

FBI AGENT JOHN FAIN INTERVIEWS ROBERT OSWALD AND HIS WIFE, VADA.

MAY 22ND 1962

HARVEY AND FAMILY LEAVE MINSK FOR MOSCOW.

MAY 24TH1962

MARINA AND **HARVEY** VISIT THE U.S. EMBASSY WHERE THEY ARE INTERVIEWED AND COMPLETE THE LAST OF THE PAPERWORK PRIOR TO THEIR DEPARTURE.

MAY 30TH TO JUNE 3RD 1962

HARVEY AND FAMILY LEFT MOSCOW BY TRAIN AT 4:10 PM ON THE MOSCOW-BERLIN EXPRESS FOR ROTTERDAM. THE TRIP TO ROTTERDAM REQUIRED A BORDER CHECK AT HELMSTEDT ON THE EAST GERMAN BORDER. MARINA'S PASSPORT SHOWED THE REQUIRED STAMP. **HARVEY'S** PASSPORT SHOWED NO ENTRY STAMP THERE. HIS PASSPORT WAS STAMPED AT THE OLDENZAAL STATION IN HOLLAND ON JUNE 3RD. UPON ARRIVAL IN ROTTERDAM AT 11:22 AM ON JUNE 3RD, HE AND MARINA STAYED AT

A PRIVATE APARTMENT AT 250 MATHENESSERLAAN. THE APARTMENT WAS RECOMMENDED BY AN OFFICIAL OF THE U.S. EMBASSY IN MOSCOW. SINCE NEITHER MARINA NOR **HARVEY** KNEW ANYONE IN ROTTERDAM, IT IS LIKELY THAT THIS APARTMENT WAS A CIA SAFEHOUSE WHERE **HARVEY** WAS DEBRIEFED.

JUNE 4TH 1962

HARVEY AND FAMILY DEPARTED FROM THE PORT CITY OF ROTTERDAM ON THE SS MAASDAM ABOUT NOON.

JUNE 13TH 1962

HARVEY AND MARINA ARRIVED IN HOBOKEN, NEW JERSEY AT 1:00 P.M. **HARVEY'S** ONLY GREETER UPON ARRIVAL WAS SPAS T. RAIKEN OF THE TRAVELER'S AID SOCIETY OF NEW YORK. RAIKEN FOUND **HARVEY** UNCOOPERATIVE. RAIKEN ALSO NOTED THAT LOUIS JOHNSON, SENIOR INS OFFICER, NORMALLY WOULD HELP HIM IDENTIFY THOSE RETURNING TRAVELLERS THAT THE AID SOCIETY WOULD GREET. IN **HARVEY'S** CASE, RAIKEN SAID JOHNSON WAS SURLY AND QUITE RELUCTANT TO HELP. SEEMS THE INS NOT ONLY ALLOWED **HARVEY** AS A RETURNING "DEFECTOR / TRAITOR" TO ENTER THE U.S. WITHOUT INITIATING ANY LEGAL PROCEEDINGS, BUT THEY ALSO PREFERRED, OR WERE REQUESTED TO ALLOW **HARVEY** TO ARRIVE VIRTUALLY UNNOTICED.

*THE TRAVELLER'S AID SOCIETY ARRANGED TO PUT **HARVEY** AND FAMILY UP FOR 1 NIGHT IN THE TIMES SQUARE MOTOR HOTEL. **HARVEY** DID NOT HAVE ENOUGH MONEY TO RETURN TO HIS FAMILY IN TEXAS AND DEMANDED THAT MR.RAIKEN CONTACT THE STATE DEPARTMENT FOR THE NECESSARY FUNDS. MR. RAIKEN, QUITE UNDERSTANDABLY, IGNORED THIS UNUSUAL REQUEST AND INSTEAD CONTACTED **HARVEY"S** "BROTHER", ROBERT. **HARVEY**, ANNOYED BUT HAVING NO OTHER CHOICE, ACCEPTED THE $200 ROBERT WIRED HIM ON JUNE 14TH.*

*RAIKEN, WHILE WORKING WITH THE TRAVELER'S AID SOCIETY WAS ALSO THE SECRETARY-GENERAL OF THE AMERICAN FRIENDS OF THE ANTI-BOLSHEVIC NATIONS. THIS STAUNCHLY ANTI-SOVIET GROUP WAS CLOSELY TIED TO THE INTELLIGENCE COMMUNITY. IT WOULD SEEM THAT RAIKEN WOULD BE AN ODD CHOICE TO GREET **HARVEY** THE RETURNING "DEFECTOR" BUT A LOGICAL CHOICE TO WELCOME BACK A SUCCESSFUL INTELLIGENCE OPERATIVE. RAIKEN HAD BEEN A CIA CONTRACT EMPLOYEE SINCE 1957. HE APPLIED FOR FULL-TIME STATUS WITH THE CIA IN JANUARY 1967. RAIKEN WOULD LATER NOTE THAT **HARVEY** HAD TOLD HIM THAT HE WAS A MARINE GUARD AT THE EMBASSY IN MOSCOW. RAIKEN, SUBJECT TO HIS RECOLLECTION, NOTED THAT **HARVEY** HAD MENTIONED THAT HE DESERTED THE MARINE CORP WHILE IN RUSSIA OR HAD BEEN KIDNAPPED BY THE KGB. **HARVEY** OBVIOUSLY PREFERRED NOT TO DIVULGE THE DETAILS OF HIS "DEFECTION" TO RAIKEN.*

JUNE 1962

"MARGUERITE" RETURNS TO FT. WORTH AFTER SHE LEARNS HER "SON" **HARVEY** HAS RETURNED TO THE U.S. SHE MOVES INTO AN APARTMENT AT THE ROTARY APARTMENTS COMPLEX ON 1501 W. 7TH.

JUNE 1962

ACCORDING TO ARMSTRONG, **LEE** IS IN NEW ORLEANS WHERE HE LIVES IN A SMALL APARTMENT ABOVE THE COURT OF TWO SISTER'S RESTAURANT.

JUNE 14TH 1962

HARVEY AND FAMILY FLY TO FT. WORTH AT 4:15 PM ON DELTA FLIGHT 821. THEY WILL LIVE WITH HIS "BROTHER" ROBERT FOR ONE MONTH IN FORT WORTH AT 7313 DAVENPORT ST.

*ROBERT WOULD LATER NOTE UPON MEETING HIS "BROTHER" AT THE AIRPORT: "THAT HE (**HARVEY**) HAD BECOME RATHER BALD....SOMEWHAT THINNER....AND HAD PICKED UP 'SOMETHING OF AN ACCENT." ROBERT OF COURSE WAS DESCRIBING THE DISCREPANCIES BETWEEN HIS BROTHER **LEE** AND **HARVEY** WHO HAD NOW TAKEN OVER THE ROLE OF*

*LEE. **HARVEY**, OF HUNGARIAN DESCENT, HAD NOT "PICKED UP" AN ACCENT. ROBERT WAS ACUTELY AWARE THAT HIS RETURNING "BROTHER"WAS **HARVEY**, NOT **LEE**.*

JUNE 15TH 1962
HARVEY REPAYS ROBERT A PORTION OF THE $200 LOANED TO HIM FOR HIS RETURN TRIP TO THE U.S.

JUNE 18TH 1962
HARVEY REQUESTS PAULINE BATES, A STENOGRAPHER, TO TYPE THE 1962 "DIARY" THAT HE ALLEGEDLY WROTE WHILE IN RUSSIA. BATES WAS PAID $10.00.

HANDWRITING EXPERTS WOULD LATER NOTE THAT THE "DIARY" APPEARED TO HAVE BEEN WRITTEN IN ONLY ONE OR TWO SESSIONS AND NOT ON A DAILY BASIS OR EVEN A WEEKLY BASIS.

JUNE 1962
HARVEY IS INTERVIEWED BY ANNIE SMITH AT THE TEXAS EMPLOYMENT COMMISSION IN FORT WORTH.

*MS. SMITH WILL LATER RECALL HAVING INTERVIEWED A LEE HARVEY OSWALD ON 2 OCCASSIONS. IT IS MS. SMITH WHO WILL GIVE **HARVEY** THE NAME AND PHONE NUMBER OF DR. PAUL GREGORY. IT IS IMPORTANT TO NOTE HOWEVER THAT **HARVEY** WAS <u>NOT</u> GIVEN THE GATB TEST, A BATTERY OF APTITUDE TESTS NORMALLY REQUIRED OF APPLICANTS. THIS WAS MOST LIKELY DUE TO THE FACT THAT **LEE** HAD ALREADY TAKEN THE GATB TEST IN APRIL 1962 WHILE **HARVEY** WAS STILL IN RUSSIA. ANNIE SMITH WILL MEET AND INTERVIEW <u>BOTH</u> **HARVEY** AND **LEE**.*

JUNE 18TH 1962
HARVEY FILES A 5 PAGE PETITION WITH THE MARINE CORP DISCHARGE REVIEW BOARD REGARDING HIS "LESS THAN HONORABLE" DISCHARGE STATUS.

JUNE 20TH 1962
HARVEY MEETS DR. PAUL GREGORY. GREGORY, A PETROLEUM ENGINEER, TEACHES RUSSIAN AT THE LIBRARY IN FT. WORTH HE ALSO GIVES **HARVEY** A LETTER TESTIFYING TO **HARVEY'S** RUSSIAN LANGUAGE SKILLS.

*OVER LUNCH, GREGORY ASKS **HARVEY** WHAT HAD PROMPTED HIM TO GO TO RUSSIA. **HARVEY** REPLIED: "I WENT THERE ON MY OWN." GREGORY NOTED THAT **HARVEY** SEEMED SENSITIVE TO HIS QUESTION. GREGORY ALSO NOTED THAT IT WAS HIGHLY UNUSUAL THAT **HARVEY** WAS ABLE TO LEAVE RUSSIA WITH HIS WIFE, MARINA, IN TOW.*

*IN THE FALL OF 1954, PAUL GREGORY, THE SON OF DR. GREGORY, ATTENDED SCHOOL AT STRIPLING JR. HIGH IN FT. WORTH. HE AND **HARVEY** WERE IN THE 9TH GRADE.*

JUNE 20TH 1962
HARVEY RECEIVES A CALL FROM THE FBI. THEY WANT TO INTERVIEW HIM ON JUNE 26TH.

*THE HSCA DETERMINED THAT THE CIA'S DOMESTIC CONTACTS DIVISION DID NOT INTERVIEW **HARVEY** SINCE THEY CONSIDERED HIS DEFECTION OF "MARGINAL IMPORTANCE." IT IS MORE LIKELY THAT THEY DID INDEED INTERVIEW HIM <u>PRIOR</u> TO HIS RETURN TO THE U.S. AND THAT THIS TOOK PLACE IN ROTTERDAM PRIOR TO HIS RETURNING STATESIDE.*

JUNE 26TH 1962
AGENTS JOHN FAIN AND TOM CARTER INTERVIEW **HARVEY** AT THE FORT WORTH FBI OFFICE AT 1:00 PM. **HARVEY** REFUSES TO TAKE A POLYGRAPH TEST. **HARVEY** ALSO APPLIES AT COMMERCIAL EMPLOYMENT AGENCY FOR A JOB. HE STATES THAT HIS TRIP TO MOSCOW WAS DONE ON BEHALF OF THE STATE DEPARTMENT. THIS SAME DAY AGENT'S INVERVIEW VADA OSWALD, ROBERT'S WIFE.

*THIS IS AN UNCHARACTERISTIC MISTAKE BY **HARVEY**. THIS IS THE ONLY OCCASION I HAVE BEEN ABLE TO DOCUMENT IN WHICH **HARVEY** VERBALLY IMPLIES TO SOMEONE OTHER THAN EMBASSY OR STATE DEPARTMENT OFFICIALS THAT HIS "DEFECTION" WAS GOVERNMENT SPONSORED AND APPARENTLY MAKES NO EFFORT TO CORRECT THIS IMPLICATION. WE WILL HOWEVER SEE LATER, IN AUGUST OF 1963, THAT DURING A RADIO INTERVIEW/DEBATE, HE WILL VERBALLY ERR ONCE AGAIN IN REGARDS TO HIS "DEFECTION" BEING GOVERNMENT SPONSORED. THAT TIME HOWEVER HE QUICKLY CORRECTED HIMSELF FOR THE RECORD.*

JUNE 27TH 1962

HARVEY CONTACTS THE DALLAS INS OFFICE IN REGARDS TO OBTAINING CITIZENSHIP STATUS FOR HIS DAUGHTER JUNE.

JULY 6TH 1962

IN A REPORT MADE BY FBI AGENT JOHN FAIN OF DALLAS, TEXAS AFTER THE INITIAL JUNE 26TH INTERVIEW WITH **HARVEY**, FAIN NOTED THAT "OSWALD STATED THAT IN THE EVENT HE IS CONTACTED BY SOVIET INTELLIGENCE HE WILL PROMPTLY COMMUNICATE WITH THE FBI." HOWEVER **HARVEY** DECLINED TO ANSWER THE QUESTION (MY UNDERLINE) AS TO WHY HE MADE THE TRIP TO RUSSIA IN THE FIRST PLACE." **HARVEY** ALSO REPLIED TO FAIN THAT "HE DID NOT CARE TO RELIVE THE PAST." ALTHOUGH THE FBI IN WASHINGTON HAD A FILE ON **HARVEY**, FILE # 327-9250, WHICH CONTAINED INFORMATION SUPPLIED BY THE ONI, CIA AND THE STATE DEPARTMENT, IT IS APPARENT THAT THE FBI, AT LEAST AT THE LOCAL LEVEL, WAS UNAWARE THAT **HARVEY'S** "DEFECTION" WAS CIA/ONI SPONSORED.

***HARVEY'S** INVOLVEMENT IN THE INTELLIGENCE COMMUNITY WAS LIKELY KNOWN BY "MARGUERITE." **HARVEY** HOWEVER OFFERRED ONLY AN OCCASIONAL HINT. AFTER THE INTERVIEW BY THE FBI, **HARVEY** WAS QUESTIONED BY HIS "BROTHER" ROBERT AS TO WHAT THEY WANTED. **HARVEY** REPLIED: "THEY ASKED ME ....WAS I A SECRET AGENT." WHEN ROBERT ASKED **HARVEY** WHAT HE REPLIED, **HARVEY** REPLIED WITH A LAUGH: "WELL, DON'T YOU KNOW?" THE LOCAL FBI IN ALL LIKLIHOOD SUSPECTED THAT **HARVEY** WAS NOT A RETURNING "DEFECTOR" BUT INDEED HAD BEEN AN INTELLIGENCE OPERATIVE ON AN ASSIGNMENT WHEN HE VISITED RUSSIA. BUT, **HARVEY** WOULD NOT REVEAL THOSE INTELLIGENCE TIES TO AGENTS FAIN OR CARTER, NOR WOULD THE CIA SHARE THIS WITH THE FBI; PARTICULARLY IF SOMEONE IN THE CIA INTENDED TO USE **HARVEY** DOMESTICALLY WHICH WAS A VIOLATION OF THE CIA'S CHARTER..*

JULY 14TH 1962

HARVEY, MARINA, AND JUNE MOVE INTO "MARGUERITE'S" APARTMENT AT 1501 WEST 7TH STREET IN FORT WORTH.

JULY 17TH 1962

HARVEY STARTS HIS FIRST JOB AS A SHEET METAL WORKER AT LESLIE WELDING IN THEIR LOUV-R-PACK DIVISION.

JULY 17TH, 1962

JOHN PIC DEPARTS JAPAN AND IS ORDERED TO WILFRED HALL HOSPITAL AT LACKLAND AFB IN TEXAS.

JULY 1962

TENSION BETWEEN THE OSWALDS AND "MARGUERITE" PROMPT **HARVEY'S** AND MARINA'S MOVE TO AN APARTMENT AT 2703 MERCEDES STREET IN FORT WORTH

AUGUST 5TH 1962

HARVEY SUBSCRIBES TO THE WORKER.

AUGUST 7TH 1962

HARVEY STILL OWES THE STATE DEPARTMENT $435.71 FOR HIS FAMILY'S TRIP FROM MOSCOW TO NEW YORK. ON AUGUST 7TH, HE MAKES HIS FIRST PAYMENT OF $10. ON SEPTEMBER 1ST HE MAKES A $9.71 PAYMENT. ON OCTOBER 6TH, A $10 PAYMENT, AND ANOTHER $10 ON NOVEMBER 14TH. IN 13 WEEKS, HE REPAYS $39.71. HOWEVER ON DECEMBER 11TH, HE SENDS IN $190, AND ON JANUARY 9TH 1963 ANOTHER $100. HIS LAST

PAYMENT OF $106 IS MADE ON JANUARY 29TH, 1963. HIS INCOME FOR THAT PERIOD WAS $805 AND EXPENSES APPROX $527. THIS LEAVES $278, BUT ONE MUST ALSO ALLOW FOR THE $396 REPAID TO THE STATE DEPARTMENT. THIS LEAVES **HARVEY** $118 IN THE RED.

*THE WARREN COMMISSION ALLOWED FOR A SOMEWHAT MORE ROSY FINANCIAL PICTURE FOR **HARVEY**. THEY CONCLUDED THAT AT THE END OF JANUARY 1963, THAT **HARVEY** HAD LESS THAN $9.*

*I STRONGLY SUSPECT THAT **HARVEY'S** DEBT WAS BEING SERVICED BY THE CIA VIA GEORGE DE MOHRENSCHILDT. BOTH DE MOHRENSCHILDT'S WIFE JEANNE AND HIS SON-IN-LAW GARY TAYLOR BOTH NOTED, GARY TO THE FBI, THAT GEORGE HAD GIVEN **HARVEY** MONEY ON SEVERAL OCCASSIONS.*

*IN FACT, THE MONEY ORDERS OF JANUARY 29TH TOTALING $106 ARE SENT WITHOUT THE NAME OR ADDRESS OF THE PURCHASER. **HARVEY'S** ABILITY TO TRAVEL OUTSIDE THE U.S. HINGES ON HIS RETIREMENT OF THE STATE DEPARTMENT DEBT. IF HE WAS INDEED BEING PREPARED BY THE SET-UP CONSPIRATORS FOR ANOTHER "ASSIGNMENT" THAT COULD REQUIRE LEGITIMATE VISA-SANCTIONED TRAVEL OUTSIDE THE U.S., HE WOULD NEED TO PAY OFF THE STATE DEPARTMENT FIRST.*

*TO THIS DATE, THERE ARE STILL THOUSANDS OF PAGES OF DOCUMENTS YET TO BE RELEASED BY THE GOVERNMENT REGARDING **HARVEY**. INCLUDED ARE HIS ACTUAL TAX RETURNS FOR CALENDAR YEARS 1962 AND 1963. THE WARREN COMMISSION INSTEAD CHOSE TO SUPPLY A "RECORD OF ALL FUNDS THAT HE (**HARVEY**) AND HIS WIFE ARE REPORTED TO HAVE RECEIVED." THERE IS NO INDICATION AS TO THE SOURCE OF THE INCOME, ONLY A "NET SALARY" FIGURE LISTED. THE ONLY FATHOMABLE REASON TO WITHHOLD A DOCUMENT AS INNOCUOUS AS A TAX RETURN WOULD BE TO CONCEAL THE FACT THAT **HARVEY** DID INDEED RECEIVE A STIPEND AS A GOVERNMENT INFORMANT.*

AUGUST 1962

"MARGUERITE" MOVES YET AGAIN. THIS TIME SHE MOVES TO 808 SUMMIT IN FT. WORTH.

AUGUST 12TH 1962

HARVEY WRITES TO THE SOCIALIST WORKERS PARTY IN NEW YORK ABOUT MEMBERSHIP

*IT IS QUITE LIKELY THAT DURING HIS INITIAL INTERVIEW WITH AGENTS FAIN AND CARTER THAT **HARVEY** RELUCTANTLY AGREED TO BECOME AN <u>FBI</u> INFORMANT. THIS CONTACT WITH THE SOCIALIST WORKERS PARTY IS LIKELY IN CONJUNCTION WITH HIS FBI INFORMANT ROLE. IT IS HOWEVER POSSIBLE THAT IT WAS ORCHESTRATED BY HUNT/PHILLIPS IN REGARD TO THEIR SET-UP OF **HARVEY** AS A PRO-COMMUNIST.*

***HARVEY** HARBORED A CERTAIN DISTAIN FOR THE FBI. AFTER HIS WORK FOR THE CIA/ONI AS A "DEFECTOR", DOMESTIC TASKS ASSIGNED TO HIM BY THE FBI WOULD SEEM RELATIVELY PEDESTRIAN COMPARED TO HIS EARLIER WORK FOR THE OTHER INTELLIGENCE AGENCIES. THIS RESENTMENT FOR THE FBI WOULD NOT ONLY CONTINUE UNTIL NOVEMBER 24TH, 1963, BUT WOULD BE MARKEDLY EVIDENT DURING HIS INTERROGATION SESSIONS THAT WEEKEND.*

AUGUST 14TH 1962

FBI AGENT FAIN CONTACTS **HARVEY'S** "BROTHER" ROBERT IN AN EFFORT TO FIND OUT WHERE **HARVEY** IS LIVING. ROBERT INFORMS FAIN THAT **HARVEY** IS LIVING IN AN APARTMENT ON MERCEDES STREET. FAIN LATER THAT DAY WOULD HAVE A "CURBSIDE" INTERVIEW WITH **HARVEY** OUTSIDE HIS APARTMENT WHEN HE RETURNED FROM WORK.

AUGUST 16TH 1962

FBI AGENTS JOHN FAIN AND ARNOLD BROWN CONDUCT YET ANOTHER "CURBSIDE" INTERVIEW WITH **HARVEY**. HE STILL REFUSES TO ANSWER JUST WHY HE WENT TO RUSSIA.

*FAIN AND BROWN'S REPORT OF THE INTERVIEW NOTED THAT **HARVEY** STATED THAT HE WAS ASSURED HE WOULD <u>NOT</u> BE PROSECUTED UPON HIS RETURN FROM HIS "DEFECTION" TO RUSSIA; PRECISELY WHAT ONE WOULD EXPECT IF HE HAD BEEN SENT TO RUSSIA ON AN INTELLIGENCE ASSIGNMENT.*

MID AUGUST 1962
A LOCAL MEMBER OF THE DALLAS RUSSIAN SPEAKING COMMUNITY, GEORGE DE MOHRENSCHILDT, WAS ASKED BY DALLAS CIA BRANCH OFFICER J. WALTON MOORE TO "KEEP TABS ON **HARVEY**" FOR THEM. THEY HAD PREVIOUSLY DISCUSSED **HARVEY** IN LATE DECEMBER, 1961. MOORE NOTED THAT THE CIA HAD AN "INTEREST" IN **HARVEY** THAT HAD BEGUN <u>PRIOR</u> TO HIS ALLEGED DEFECTION. DEMOHRENSCHILDT HIMSELF HAD CIA CONNECTIONS DATING BACK TO HIS OSS DAYS AND WAS WELL KNOWN BY THE DALLAS CIA BRANCH OFFICER.

DEMOHRENSCHILDT WILL LATER SUGGEST TO **HARVEY** THAT SINCE MOST OF THEIR RUSSIAN SPEAKING FRIENDS LIVE IN OR NEAR DALLAS THAT HE CONSIDER MOVING THERE.

*THIS SUGGESTION MAY HAVE BEEN A MERE CONVENIENCE FOR DE MOHRENSCHILDT SINCE HE LIVED IN DALLAS. BUT I AM MUCH MORE INCLINED TO THINK THAT BOTH DEMOHRENSCHILDT AND MOORE WERE BEING USED IN THE SET-UP OF **HARVEY** AS WELL. E. HOWARD HUNT AND DAVID ATLEE PHILLIPS ARE THE "ARCHITECTS" IN THIS, THE INITIAL STAGE OF THE SET-UP OF **HARVEY**. IT WOULD HAVE BEEN A RELATIVELY SIMPLE PROCESS WHICH WOULD HAVE AROUSED LITTLE SUSPICION FROM EITHER MOORE OR DEMOHRENSCHILDT. MOORE WOULD HAVE HAD NO REASON NOT TO HONOR A REQUEST FROM PHILLIPS OR HUNT SINCE HE WOULD BE IN A POSITION TO KNOW THAT BOTH HUNT AND PHILLIPS WERE DEEPLY INVOLVED IN THE INFILTRATION OF PRO-CASTRO GROUPS AND PERHAPS WERE ENTERTAINING THE IDEA OF USING **HARVEY** IN AN "OFF THE RECORD" ROLE AS A DOMESTIC INFORMANT FOR THE AGENCY. DEMOHRENSCHILDT IN TURN WOULD HAVE NO REASON TO BE SUSPICIOUS OF THE REQUEST BY MOORE TO "KEEP TABS ON **HARVEY**." IT WOULD THEN BE THE UNSUSPECTING DEMOHRENSCHILDT WHO WOULD APPEAR TO BE THE GUIDING FORCE IN THE EARLY STAGES OF THE MANIPULATION OF **HARVEY**.*

*ON MARCH 29TH, 1977, IN AN INTERVIEW WITH EDWARD EPSTEIN, DEMOHRENSCHILDT NOTED THAT IT WAS THE CIA WHO REQUESTED AND SANCTIONED HIS CONTACT WITH **HARVEY**. LATER THAT DAY, DEMOHRENSCHILDT WAS FOUND SHOT TO DEATH. HE WAS TO MEET WITH GAETON FONZI AN INVESTIGATOR FOR THE HSCA THAT EVENING. THE "SUICIDE" WAS CARRIED OUT WITH A SHOTGUN. THE BARREL WAS APPARENTLY IN DEMOHRENSCHILDT'S MOUTH WHEN THE TRIGGER WAS PULLED.*

AUGUST 25TH 1962
HARVEY AND MARINA ATTEND A DINNER PARTY AT DR. PAUL GREGORY'S HOME. AT THE PARTY, DR. GREGORY INTRODUCES **HARVEY** TO HIS FRIENDS IN THE RUSSIAN COMMUNITY IN THE DALLAS/FORT WORTH AREA. **HARVEY** AND MARINA WERE INTRODUCED TO ANNA MELLER AND GEORGE BOUHE. MELLER AND BOUHE WOULD VISIT **HARVEY** AND MARINA QUITE OFTEN AFTER THIS INITIAL INTRODUCTION. THEY WOULD LATER INTRODUCE THE OSWALDS TO ELENE HALL, A DENTAL TECHNICIAN WHO WOULD HELP OBTAIN SOME MUCH NEEDED DENTAL WORK FOR MARINA.

AUGUST 28TH 1962
HARVEY PLACES AN ORDER FROM THE SOCIALIST WORKERS PARTY FOR PAMPHLETS TITLED "THE TEACHINGS OF LEON TROTSKY."

THIS AGAIN WOULD LIKELY BE A TASK ASSIGNED IN CONJUNCTON WITH HIS FBI INFORMANT ROLE.

LATE AUGUST 1962

"MARGUERITE" MOVES BACK TO THE ROTARY APARTMENTS IN FORT WORTH AND IS NOW RESIDING IN APARTMENT 301.

AUGUST 30TH 1962

HARVEY'S FBI CASE FILE WAS PLACED IN "INACTIVE STATUS."

*ALTHOUGH **HARVEY'S** CASE FILE WAS PLACED IN AN "INACTIVE" STATUS, IT IS QUITE LIKELY THAT ANOTHER FILE WOULD BE OPENED; A FILE THAT WOULD ACKNOWLEDGE THAT HE HAD NOW BECOME AN FBI INFORMANT.*

*IN A SPECIAL EMERGENCY MEETING OF THE WARREN COMMISSION HELD ON JANUARY 22ND, 1964, LEE RANKIN, GENERAL COUNSEL OF THE COMMISSION, WAS PROMPTED BY EARL WARREN TO REVEAL THE NECESSITY OF THE EMERGENCY SESSION. RANKIN RELATED TO THE STAFF THAT WAGGONER CARR, THE ATTORNEY GENERAL OF TEXAS, HAD CALLED HIM AT 11:10 THAT MORNING AND TOLD HIM THAT HE HAD LEARNED FROM HENRY WADE, DISTRICT ATTORNEY OF DALLAS COUNTY, THAT **HARVEY** WAS AN FBI INFORMANT. WADE HAD NOTED TO CARR THAT **HARVEY** HAD BEEN ON THE FBI PAYROLL FROM SEPTEMBER 1962 THRU NOVEMBER 1963 AT A MONTHLY RATE OF $200. WADE ALSO NOTED THAT THIS INFORMATION CAME FROM A FORMER FBI AGENT. THIS SEPTEMBER 1962 START DATE FOR **HARVEY** AS AN FBI INFORMANT DOVETAILS PERFECTLY WITH THE AUGUST 30TH 1962 DATE ON WHICH **HARVEY'S** <u>CASE FILE</u> WAS PLACED IN INACTIVE STATUS.*

*IN AN EFFORT TO FINALIZE SOME CONCLUSION REGARDING THE POSSIBILITY OF **HARVEY'S** FBI INFORMANT STATUS, ALAN BELMONT, ASSISTANT DIRECTOR TO THE FBI, APPEARED BEFORE THE COMMISSION ON MAY 6TH, 1964. HE OFFERED TO LEAVE **HARVEY'S** FILE WITH THE COMMISSION. RANKIN ADVISED THE COMMISSION TO <u>KEEP</u> THE FILE BUT <u>NOT</u> EXAMINE IT. RANKIN'S RATIONALE WAS TO ALLOW THE COMMISSION TO STATE IN ITS FINAL REPORT "WE HAVE SEEN EVERYTHING THAT THEY (THE FBI) HAVE." INCREDIBLY, EARL WARREN WOULD TAKE THIS "LOGIC" ONE STEP FURTHER BY STATING HIS DESIRE TO REFUSE TO EVEN <u>ACCEPT</u> THE FILE. WARREN'S RATIONALE IS EVEN MORE ALARMING THAN RANKIN'S AS HE STATES: "WELL, THE SAME PEOPLE WHO WOULD DEMAND THAT WE SEE EVERYTHING OF THIS KIND WOULD ALSO DEMAND THAT THEY BE ENTITLED TO SEE IT. AND, IF IT'S A SECURITY MATTER WE CAN'T LET THEM SEE IT." THE FILE WAS RETURNED TO THE FBI. THE COMMISSION WAS WILLING TO ACCEPT HOOVER AT HIS WORD THAT **HARVEY** WAS NOT AN INFORMANT.*

EARLY SEPTEMBER 1962

"MARGUERITE" MOVES TO A RESIDENCE AT 4800 HURLEY STREET IN FT.WORTH. .

SEPTEMBER 9TH 1962

THE OSWALDS VISIT ANNA MELLER AND HER HUSBAND TEOFIL AT THEIR HOME IN DALLAS. OVER LUNCH, **HARVEY** AND MARINA ALSO MEET DECLAN AND KATYA FORD. MR. FORD IS AN AMERICAN GEOLOGIST. HIS WIFE IS OF RUSSIAN DESCENT.

EARLY OCTOBER 1962

"MARGUERITE" MOVES YET AGAIN. SHE NOW RESIDES AT 1013 W. 5TH AVENUE IN APARTMENT 6 IN FT. WORTH.

CHAPTER 5: THE MOVE TO DALLAS

OCTOBER 7TH 1962
GEORGE DE MOHRENSCHILDT'S DAUGHTER, ALEX, AND HER HUSBAND, GARY TAYLOR, VISIT THE OSWALDS AND INVITE MARINA AND THEIR BABY TO MOVE TO DALLAS TO LIVE WITH THEM FOR A FEW DAYS. ALSO VISITING THE OSWALDS THIS DAY WERE FREQUENT WEEKEND VISITORS ANNA MELLER AND GEORGE BOUHE. THE OSWALDS WOULD ALSO MEET, FOR THE FIRST TIME, ELENE HALL AND HER EX-HUSBAND JOHN.

OCTOBER 8TH 1962
HARVEY LEAVES HIS JOB AT LESLIE WELDING AND MOVES TO DALLAS.

OCTOBER 9TH 1962
HARVEY VISITS THE DALLAS OFFICE OF THE TEXAS EMPLOYMENT COMMISSION WHERE HE IS INTERVIEWED BY DON BROOKS. BROOKS HAS THE FT. WORTH FILE ON "LEE HARVEY OSWALD" FORWARDED TO THE DALLAS OFFICE. IT IS HOWEVER **LEE'S** FILE THAT IS SENT TO HIM AS **HARVEY** WAS IN RUSSIA WHEN THE FT. WORTH FILE ON **LEE** WAS OPENED ON APRIL 12TH, 1962. **HARVEY** ALSO OPENS P.O. BOX 2915 UNDER THE NAME LEE H. OSWALD. LATER IT WILL BE ALLEGED THAT **HARVEY** LISTED AS "AUTHORIZED TO RECEIVE MAIL" AT THE P.O. BOX A "HIDELL" AND THE FPFC ORGANIZATION. **HARVEY** LISTS AS HIS ADDRESS ON THE P.O. BOX APPLICATION 3519 FAIRMONT STREET, THE ADDRESS OF ALEX TAYLOR, GEORGE DEMOHRENSCHILDT'S DAUGHTER.

*LATER, IN HIS LAST INTERROGATION SESSION ON SUNDAY NOVEMBER 24TH, **HARVEY** WILL ADMIT RENTING THIS PARTICULAR P.O. BOX UNDER HIS OWN NAME. BUT, HE WILL ALSO STATE THAT TO HIS KNOWLEDGE NO ONE OTHER THAN HIMSELF RECEIVED MAIL AT THIS BOX AND THAT HE DID NOT RECEIVE MAIL UNDER ANY OTHER NAME AT THIS BOX. HE WOULD GO ON TO STATE THAT NO ONE ELSE HAD ACCESS TO THE BOX OR THAT HE ALLOWED ANYONE ELSE TO USE THIS BOX. HE NOTED THAT HE ONLY BECAME INTERESTED IN THE FPFC AFTER HIS MOVE TO NEW ORLEANS.*

*THE LATER ADDITION OF "HIDELL" AND THE FPFC ORGANIZATION TO THE POSTAL BOX ARE LIKELY THE WORK OF SET-UP CONSPIRATORS HUNT/PHILLIPS. THE LATER FPFC ACTIVITY OF **HARVEY** IN NEW ORLEANS WHICH HE DID INDEED ADMIT TO WAS PROMPTED BY GUY BANISTER AND WILL PROVE TO BE NEITHER A LEGITIMATE CIA ASSIGNMENT NOR ONE THAT IS ASSOCIATED WITH HIS UNDERCOVER WORK AS AN INFORMANT FOR THE FBI. ALTHOUGH **HARVEY** MAY PERCEIVE HIS NEW ORLEANS FPFC ACTIVITIES AS PERTINANT TO A LEGITIMATE CIA ASSIGNMENT, IT WILL BE FOR THE SOLE PURPOSE OF INITIATING HIS SET-UP. **HARVEY** IS NOW IN THE INITIAL STAGE OF WHAT WILL PROVE TO BE A NEARLY 14 MONTH EFFORT BY THE SET-UP CONSPIRATORS TO PLACE HIM AT CENTER STAGE ON NOVEMBER 22ND, 1963.*

THE HIDELL AND FPFC ENTITIES WILL SERVE SEVERAL PURPOSES FOR THE SET-UP CONSPIRATORS:

- *TYING WEAPONS ALLEGEDLY USED ON NOVEMBER 22ND TO A "HIDELL"*
- *TYING "HIDELL" TO **HARVEY'S** MAILBOX, #2915*
- *TYING FPFC TO **HARVEY'S** MAILBOX, #2915*
- *TYING BOTH **HARVEY** AND "HIDELL" TO THE FPFC*
- *TYING **HARVEY** TO "HIDELL"*

OCTOBER 10TH 1962
HARVEY REVISITS THE EMPLOYMENT COMMISSION AND IS INTERVIEWED BY HELEN CUNNINGHAM. HE WAS TO LATER INTERVIEW AT HARRELL AND HAMILTON ARCHITECTS IN DALLAS FOR A JOB THAT PAID $1.50 PER HOUR.

OCTOBER 11TH 1962

HARVEY VISITS THE EMPLOYMENT OFFICE AGAIN. THIS TIME HE IS INTERVIEWED BY LOUISE LATHAM. SHE ARRANGES FOR AN INTERVIEW AT JAGGERS-CHILES-STOVALL IN DALLAS. ON THIS SAME DAY MARINA AND JUNE MOVE TO ELENE HALL'S HOME IN FORT WORTH.

OCTOBER 12TH 1962

HARVEY STARTS HIS FIRST DAY OF WORK AT JCS AS A PHOTO-PRINT TRAINEE. HIS PAY, $1.35 AN HOUR. THIS COMPANY PRINTED GOVERNMENT MAPS THAN INCLUDED FLIGHT DATA FROM THE U-2. IT WAS GEORGE DE MOHRENSCHILDT WHO ASSISTED **HARVEY** IN FINDING THIS JOB.

*THE GOVERNMENT, NEEDLESS TO SAY, REQUIRED STRICT SECURITY MEASURES AT JCS IN RETURN FOR THE MAP PRINTING CONTRACT. THIS HOWEVER APPARENTLY DID NOT PREVENT **HARVEY**, A KNOWN "DEFECTOR/TRAITOR" FROM OBTAINING EMPLOYMENT THERE. IN ALL LIKELIHOOD, AN "OK" FROM DE MOHRENSCHILDT WAS ALL THAT WAS REQUIRED IN REGARDS TO **HARVEY'S** ABILITY TO BE EMPLOYED AT THIS SENSITIVE SECURITY SITE. A FELLOW EMPLOYEE, DENNIS OFSTEIN, RECALLED THAT IT WAS **HARVEY** WHO EXPLAINED TO HIM WHAT A MICRODOT WAS. MICRODOTS WERE CONSIDERED AT THE TIME TO BE A RELATIVELY NEW INTELLIGENCE TECHNIQUE. THE WORDS "MICRO DOTS" WAS FOUND NEXT TO THE JCS ENTRY IN **HARVEY'S** ADDRESS BOOK. OFSTEIN ALSO NOTED THAT **HARVEY'S** RUSSIAN SPEAKING SKILLS WERE MUCH BETTER THAN HIS OWN. IN FACT, ROBERT OSWALD'S WIFE, VADA, NOTED THAT HE WAS HIRED BECAUSE HE COULD SPEAK RUSSIAN. OFSTEIN HAD STUDIED RUSSIAN FOR 1 YEAR AT THE DEFENSE LANGUAGE INSTITUTE AT MONTEREY, CALIFORNIA. HE SERVED IN THE ARMY IN THE ARMY SECURITY SERVICE AS A RUSSIAN LINGUIST.*

MY MILITARY CAREER WAS SIMILAR TO OFSTEIN'S. I SERVED AS A COMMUNICATION TECNICIAN IN THE NAVY. THE NAVY, LIKE THE ARMY HAD A INTELLIGENCE GATHERING APPARATUS, THE NAVAL SECURITY GROUP. THE AIR FORCE HAD A SIMILAR SECTION KNOWN AS AIR FORCE SECURITY SERVICE. ALL 3 BRANCHES OF THE SERVICE ANSWERED TO THE DEFENSE INTELLIGENCE AGENCY. THE DIA IN TURN SERVED THE INTELLIGENCE GATHERING NEEDS OF THE NSA. NAVY LINGUIST AT THE ROTA, SPAIN SITE WHERE I SERVED ALSO ATTENDED THE DEFENSE LANGUAGE INSTITUTE. I SUSPECT AIR FORCE LINGUIST USED THIS FACILITY AS WELL.

*INTERESTINGLY **HARVEY** AND THE U-2 ONCE AGAIN CROSS PATHS. THE ARMY MAP SERVICE WOULD SEND JCS LISTS OF NAMES TO BE TYPE-SET. THESE NAMES WOULD THEN BE ADDED TO MAPS AND INDEED TO PHOTOS TAKEN BY THE U-2. UP TO THIS POINT, THE NAMES WERE EITHER IN CHINESE OR RUSSIAN REFLECTING U-2 OVERFLIGHTS OF THOSE COUNTRIES. NOW THE NAMES WERE TO BE TYPE-SET IN SPANISH. THE NAMES IN SPANISH WERE TO BE ADDED TO U-2 PHOTOS OF CUBA. THE CUBAN MISSLE CRISIS WAS ABOUT TO SURFACE.*

*ROSCOE WHITE, WHO YOU REMEMBER HAD OVERSEAS MARINE CORP POSTINGS THAT PARALLED **HARVEY'S**, WAS NOW IN THE PROCESS OF FOLLOWING **HARVEY'S** STORYLINE ONCE AGAIN. WHITE WAS ABOUT TO BE AWARDED A HARDSHIP DISCHARGE FROM THE MARINES. UPON HIS RETURN STATESIDE, WHITE WOULD SETTLE IN DALLAS. HIS ARRIVAL IN DALLAS IS WITHIN 2 MONTHS OF **HARVEY'S**. ROSCOE WHITE WILL, IN THE MONTHS TO COME, BECOME THE DALLAS-BASED CONSPIRATOR TASKED WITH ASSISTING IN THE LOCAL SET-UP OF **HARVEY**.*

*IT IS MY OPINION THAT THE JOB AT HARRELL AND HAMILTON WAS PURPOSELY "SKIPPED" BY **HARVEY** AT THE REQUEST OF DE MOHRENSCHILDT. EVEN THOUGH THE JOB AT HARRELL AND HAMILTON PAID 15 CENTS MORE PER HOUR. IT WOULD HAVE BEEN A BIT TOO OBVIOUS IF **HARVEY'S** <u>FIRST</u> JOB IN DALLAS WERE AT THE SENSITIVE JCS FACILITY. THE CUBAN MISSLE CRISIS BEGAN ON THE 14TH, AND THE PRESIDENT'S PRIMETIME SPEECH TO THE NATION WAS ONLY 10 DAYS AFTER **HARVEY'S** EMPLOYMENT AT JCS.*

OCTOBER 14TH 1962
THE CUBAN MISSLE CRISIS BEGINS.

*ARMSTRONG ALSO NOTES THAT **HARVEY** STARTED WORK AT JCS JUST AS THE MISSLE CRISIS BEGAN. HIS ABILITY TO READ AND WRITE RUSSIAN WOULD LIKELY PROVE TO BE VALUABLE TO THE CIA IN REGARDS TO INTERPRETING ANY RUSSIAN MARKINGS ON EITHER THE MISSLES OR THE CRATES THAT THEY WERE SHIPPED IN.*

OCTOBER 15-19TH 1962
HARVEY RESIDES AT THE YMCA AT 605 NORTH ERVAY IN ROOM 415. HE CONSIDERED IT TOO EXPENSIVE AT $2.25 A NIGHT AND LEFT AFTER A 5 NIGHT STAY. HOWEVER IT IS NOT KNOWN WHERE HE RESIDED OCTOBER 9TH THRU OCTOBER 14TH.

OCTOBER 16TH 1962
MARINA AND JUNE TAKE PART IN A BAPTISMAL CEREMONY FOR BABY JUNE AT AN EASTERN ORTHODOX CHURCH IN DALLAS.

OCTOBER 29TH 1962
DALLAS FBI AGENT JOHN FAIN RETIRES AND **HARVEY'S** CASE FILE IS CLOSED. IT HAD BEEN PUT IN AN "INACTIVE STATUS" ON AUGUST 30TH. AGENT JAMES HOSTY, WHO REPLACES AGENT FAIN, OPENS A FILE ON MARINA OSWALD.

*IT IS IMPORTANT TO NOTE THAT IT IS THE "CASE" FILE THAT IS CLOSED. THE FILE DETAILING **HARVEY'S** WORK AS AN FBI INFORMANT WILL LIKELY REMAIN OPEN.*

OCTOBER 30TH 1962
HARVEY APPLIES FOR MEMBERSHIP IN THE SOCIALISTS WORKERS PARTY.

NOVEMBER 2ND 1962
ACCORDING TO THE W.C., **HARVEY** RENTS AN APARTMENT AT 604 ELSBETH STREET IN DALLAS. IT IS NOT CERTAIN HOWEVER WERE HE RESIDED FROM OCTOBER 20TH TO NOVEMBER 2ND AFTER LEAVING THE YMCA. GARY TAYLOR HOWEVER STATED TO THE W.C. THAT **HARVEY** STAYED AT THE COZ-I-EIGHT APARTMENTS ON NORTH BECKLEY.

*WE NOW HAVE TWO INSTANCES WHERE WE ARE NOT SURE OF THE WHEREABOUTS OF **HARVEY**; UPON ARRIVAL IN DALLAS ON THE 9TH THRU OCTOBER 14TH PRIOR TO BOARDING AT THE YMCA, AND ANOTHER GAP FROM OCTOBER 20TH TO NOVEMBER 2ND UNLESS GARY TAYLOR IS CORRECT REGARDING THE COZ-I-EIGHT APARTMENTS. THESE COMBINED PERIODS TOTAL 20 DAYS.*

NOVEMBER 3RD 1962
MARINA AND JUNE JOIN **HARVEY** IN THE APARTMENT AT 604 ELSBETH STREET. THE TAYLORS ASSIST IN THE MOVE.

NOVEMBER 8TH 1962
HARVEY RECEIVES NOTICE FROM THE SOCIALIST WORKERS PARTY NATIONAL SECRETARY FARRELL DOBBS THAT THEY ARE REJECTING HIS APPLICATION FOR MEMBERSHIP SINCE THERE IS NOT A CHAPTER IN DALLAS. THEY REQUIRED A MINIMUM OF 5 MEMBERS PRIOR TO STARTING A NEW CHAPTER.

NOVEMBER 8TH 1962
TENSION BETWEEN **HARVEY** AND MARINA ESCALATES. ONCE AGAIN GEORGE DE-MOHRENSCHILDT INTERVENES. AFTER TALKING WITH **HARVEY**, HE CONVINCES HIM TO ALLOW MARINA AND JUNE TO MOVE IN WITH TEOFIL AND ANNA MELLER. THE MELLERS HAD ALSO ASSISTED **HARVEY** IN OBTAINING HIS JOB AT JAGGERS-CHILES-STOVALL. MARINA AND JUNE WILL STAY WITH THE MELLERS UNTIL NOVEMBER 11TH.

*ANNA MELLER WOULD LATER NOTE THAT SHE HAD SEEN COMMUNIST LITERATURE IN **HARVEY'S** HOME. SHE STATED THAT SHE HAD RELATED THIS TO HER HUSBAND WHO IN TURN NOTIFIED THE FBI. THE FBI RESPONSE, ACCORDING TO TEOFIL MELLER, WAS: "OSWALD WAS ALL RIGHT."*

*ARMSTRONG NOTES THAT IN THE EARLY 1960'S, OVER 2 DOZEN RUSSIAN WOMEN MARRIED FOREIGNERS, WERE ALLOWED TO LEAVE THE COUNTRY, AND SOON AFTER DIVORCED THEIR HUSBANDS AND REMAINED IN PLACE. THE CIA WAS ABLE TO LINK SOME OF THESE WOMEN TO THE KGB. MARINA WAS CAPABLE OF SPEAKING EXCELLENT ENGLISH. WITH HER ABILITY TO MARRY **HARVEY** AND LEAVE RUSSIA IN WHAT WOULD HAVE TO BE CONSIDERED RECORD TIME, IT WAS LIKELY THAT THE CIA CONSIDERED MARINA TO BE A MEMBER OF THE KGB'S "HONEY TRAP" WHOSE TRAINING PREPARED HER TO MEET ENGLISH SPEAKING FOREIGNERS, MARRY THEM, RETURN TO THEIR NATIVE LAND AND FIND SOME RATIONALE FOR DIVORCE. MARINA'S "REASON" FOR DIVORCING **HARVEY** WOULD BE HER ALLEGATION THAT HE BEAT HER.*

NOVEMBER 11TH 1962

MARINA, AS SHE HAD APPARENTLY DONE IN HER STAY WITH THE TAYLORS, SOON BEGAN TRYING THE PATIENCE OF THE MELLERS AS WELL. SHE WAS ASKED TO MOVE OUT. MARINA AND JUNE THEN MOVED IN, PRESUMABLY WITH THE HELP OF THE DE MOHRENSCHILDTS ONCE AGAIN, WITH ANOTHER RUSSIAN REFUGE, KATIA FORD. AFTER THIS BRIEF STAY WITH MS. FORD, MARINA AND JUNE RETURNED TO THE ELSBETH ST. APARTMENT ON NOVEMBER 18TH TO RE-JOIN **HARVEY**.

NOVEMBER 21ST 1962

HARVEY AND MARINA SPEND A THANKSGIVING DAY HOLIDAY WITH **HARVEY'S** "BROTHER" ROBERT, AND JOHN PIC, HIS "HALF-BROTHER." THIS WILL BE THE LAST TIME ROBERT SEES **HARVEY** UNTIL NOVEMBER 22ND, 1963. IT IS HOWEVER THE FIRST TIME JOHN PIC HAS SEEN HIS "HALF-BROTHER" SINCE HIS "HALF-BROTHER" WAS 13 YEARS OLD. BEFORE THE W.C., PIC NOTED THAT "THE LEE HARVEY OSWALD I MET IN NOVEMBER OF 1962 WAS NOT THE LEE HARVEY OSWALD I HAD KNOWN 10 YEARS PREVIOUS." PIC IS ABLE TO DISTINGISH BETWEEN HIS HALF-BROTHER **LEE** AND THE YOUNG MAN HE MEETS THIS HOLIDAY HIS ALLEGED "HALF-BROTHER", **HARVEY**. IT APPEARS THAT ROBERT OSWALD AND "MARGUERITE" ARE WILLING TO ACCEPT **HARVEY** AS THEIR "BROTHER/SON." PIC APPARENTLY IS NOT.

*IT IS HOWEVER WORTH NOTING THAT "MARGUERITE" IS NOT PRESENT AT THIS "FAMILY" GET TOGETHER. SHE IS HOWEVER CURRENTLY RESIDING IN FT. WORTH AS WELL. IF JOHN PIC HAD SOME SUSPICION THAT **HARVEY** WAS NOT HIS HALF-BROTHER HE WOULD HAVE CERTAINLY REALIZED THAT THE SHORT, MATRONLY "MARGUERITE" DID NOT EVEN REMOTELY RESEMBLE HIS TALL, THIN, REAL MOTHER, MARGUERITE.*

HARVEY AND MARINA ARE DRIVEN FROM ROBERT'S HOME TO THE BUS STATION BY PAUL GREGORY. HE AND **HARVEY** HAD ATTENDED THE 9TH GRADE AT STRIPLING JR. HIGH IN THE FALL OF 1954. PAUL HAD STUDIED RUSSIAN AT THE UNIVERSITY OF OKLAHOMA. AFTER THE ASSASSINATION, IT IS NONE OTHER THAN PAUL GREGORY WHO OFFERS HIS SERVICE AS AN "INTERPRETER" FOR MARINA OSWALD. MARINA HOWEVER HAD LITTLE NEED FOR AN "INTERPRETER" AS SHE WAS CAPABLE OF SPEAKING FLUENT ENGLISH.

NOVEMBER 1962

ACCORDING TO ARMSTRONG, LYNN CURRY, A CAB DRIVER IN AUGUSTA, GEORGIA, PICKED UP A YOUNG MAN WHO INTRODUCED HIMSELF AS "**LEE** OSWALD." **LEE** WENT ON TO TELL CURRY THAT HE HAD BEEN IN THE MARINES, TRAVELED TO RUSSIA, HAD A RUSSIAN WIFE, SUPPORTED CASTRO, AND WAS ON HIS WAY TO NEW ORLEANS. **LEE** APPARENTLY INSISTED THAT CURRY WRITE DOWN HIS NAME AND TOLD CURRY HE WOULD BE HEARING MORE OF THAT NAME IN THE FUTURE. **HARVEY** IS HOWEVER IN DALLAS. **LEE** WOULD BECOME INSTRUMENTAL IN SETTING UP **HARVEY**.

DECEMBER 4th 1962
ROSCOE WHITE IS GRANTED A HUMANITARIAN DISCHARGE FROM THE MARINE CORP. WHITE HOWEVER NOTED IN HIS DIARY THAT HE LEFT THE MARINE CORP IN OCTOBER, 1962.

DECEMBER 6TH 1962
HARVEY SENDS A RESUME OF HIS PHOTOGRAPHY EFFORTS TO THE SOCIALIST WORKERS PARTY.

DECEMBER 15TH 1962
HARVEY SUBSCRIBES TO THE MILITANT AT A COST OF $1.

DECEMBER 19TH 1962
THE SOCIALIST WORKER PARTY DECLINES **HARVEY'S** OFFER OF HIS PHOTOGRAPHIC SKILLS. BUT, THEY PROMISE TO CONSIDER HIM FOR FUTURE PROJECTS.

DECEMBER 28TH 1962
HARVEY AND MARINA ATTEND A PARTY HOSTED BY DECLAN AND KATYA FORD TO CELEBRATE THE RUSSIAN NEW YEAR. THEY ARE TAKEN TO THE PARTY BY GEORGE AND JEANNE DEMOHRENSCHILDT. ACCORDING TO DEMOHRENSCHILDT, RUSSIAN JEWS IN ATTENDANCE AT THE PARTY WERE IMPRESSED BY **HARVEY'S** COMMAND OF THE RUSSIAN LANGUAGE. ONE ELDERLY GUEST WAS AMAZED BY HIS ABILITY TO SPEAK THE LANGUAGE NOT ONLY FLUENTLY BUT RAPIDLY.

LATE DEC 1962/EARLY JAN 1963
AT A HOUSE IN MONTERAY PARK IN LOS ANGELES, THERE WAS A FIGHT AMONG SOME CUBANS WITH SHOTS FIRED. AMONG THOSE LISTED IN THE ARREST RECORD WAS A "LEE HARVEY OSWALD."

*BORIS YARO, A PHOTOGRAPHER FOR THE L.A. TIMES WENT BACK TO THE MONTERAY PARK POLICE DEPARTMENT IN 1967 AND TRIED TO VIEW THE NEGATIVES OF THE POLICE PHOTOS TAKEN THAT DAY. THE NEGATIVES WOULD PRESUMABLY SHOW **HARVEY** IF HE WERE INDEED ARRESTED THAT DAY. THE NEGATIVES WERE GONE. THERE WAS NO SIGN-OUT FORM FOR THE NEGATIVES. IT IS QUITE LIKELY THAT THE "OSWALD" PHOTOGRAPHED WAS NOT **HARVEY** BUT AN IMPOSTER, POSSIBLY **LEE**, THUS THE NEED FOR THE DISAPPEARANCE OF THE NEGATIVES. THE REMAINDER OF THE ARREST RECORD, INCLUDING THE NAME "LEE HARVEY OSWALD" WAS INTACT. **HARVEY** WAS IN DALLAS WITH MARINA AND JUNE IN AN APARTMENT AT 604 ELSBETH STREET DURING THIS TIME FRAME. THIS EFFORT IS IN ALL LIKELIHOOD AN EFFORT – ALBEIT ILL-TIMED - OF THE SET-UP CONSPIRATORS.*

JANUARY 1ST 1963
HARVEY WRITES PIONEER PRESS SEEKING COPIES OF SPEECHES GIVEN BY CASTRO IN 1960 AND 1962.

JANUARY 1963
HARVEY SENDS $13.20 TO THE WASHINGTON BOOK STORE. HE REQUESTS SUBSCRIPTIONS TO 3 PERIODICALS; THE OGONEK, THE KROKODR, AND THE AGITATOR. INTERESTINGLY, HE ASKS THAT ALL 3 SUBSCRIPTIONS STOP IN DECEMBER 1963. THIS IS THE PLANNED DATE FOR THE C-DAY COUP IN CUBA.

JANUARY 14TH 1963
HARVEY SIGNS UP FOR A TYPING CLASS AT CROZIER TECHNICAL SCHOOL.

JANUARY 27TH 1963
AN ORDER FORM FOR A 38 CALIBER SMITH AND WESSON REVOLVER FROM SEAPORT TRADERS OF LOS ANGELES IS FILLED OUT BY A "A. J. HIDELL" WITH A $10 DOWN PAYMENT ON A $29.95 GUN PLUS $1.27 SHIPPING AND HANDLING. THE ADDRESS LISTED IS P.O. BOX 2915. THE ORDER/INVOICE HOWEVER IS NOT <u>FILLED</u> BY SEAPORT TRADERS UNTIL <u>MARCH 12, 1963</u> INDICATING THAT IT WAS LIKELY MUCH LATER WHEN THE ORDER FORM IS MAILED FROM DALLAS.

IT WILL BE NOTED LATER THAT THE ORDER FOR THE ALLEGED ASSASSINATION RIFLE IS ALSO <u>PLACED</u> ON MARCH 12TH,1963. IT WOULD APPEAR THAT THE DECISION TO MAIL-ORDER BOTH GUNS WAS MADE ON OR ABOUT THE SAME DAY. INDEED WE WILL ALSO SEE THAT <u>BOTH</u> WEAPONS <u>ARRIVE</u> IN DALLAS BETWEEN MARCH 20TH, 1963 AND MARCH 22ND, 1963.

ONE HAS TO KEEP IN MIND THAT ON JANUARY 29TH 1963, **HARVEY** MADE HIS LAST PAYMENT OF $106 TO THE STATE DEPARTMENT FOR HIS FAMILY'S TRIP FROM MOSCOW TO NEW YORK. WITH THAT DEBT RETIRED, WHY WOULD IT BE NECESSARY FOR **HARVEY** TO MAKE ONLY A $10 DOWNPAYMENT ON A $29.95 PISTOL UNLESS OF COURSE IT WAS NOT **HARVEY** WHO HAD INITIATED THE ORDER.

THE PURCHASE OF THE PISTOL (AND LATER THE RIFLE) COULD HAVE BEEN MADE BY <u>ANYONE</u> HAVING ACCESS TO **HARVEY'S** P.O. BOX, KNOWLEDGE OF **HARVEY'S** FINANCIAL SITUATION, AND KNOWLDEDGE OF THE FACT THAT THE NAME "HIDELL" HAD BEEN ADDED TO HIS P.O. BOX AS SOMEONE ALLOWED TO RECEIVE MAIL AT THAT PARTICULAR P.O. BOX. IN MY OPINION, IT IS HUNT, PHILLIPS, AND **LEE** WHO JOINTLY SHARED THIS KNOWLEDGE. THE HAND GUN COULD BE PICKED UP BY **LEE** WHO WOULD SIMPLY IDENTIFY HIMSELF AS "HIDELL."

THE PURCHASE AND LATER PICK-UP OF THE HANDGUN WAS LIKELY ORCHESTRATED BY DALLAS BASED SET-UP CONSPIRATOR ROSCOE WHITE. **HARVEY'S** MAIL-ORDERING OF GUNS TRACEABLE TO HIM, HAD HE BEEN THE REAL ASSASSIN IN BOTH THE JFK AND THE TIPPIT SHOOTINGS, WOULD HAVE BEEN FOOLISH AS HE COULD HAVE BOUGHT THEM AT <u>ANY</u> GUN/AMMO DEALER IN DALLAS WITHOUT AS MUCH AS A SIGNATURE AND NO PAPERTRAIL TO LATER INCRIMINATE HIM.

THE PURCHASE OF THE HANDGUN AND THE LATER PURCHASE OF THE RIFLE ARE THE FIRST INDICATIONS THAT THE END RESULT OF THE SET-UP OF HARVEY WOULD BE THE PERCEPTION THAT HE WAS THE SHOOTER IN BOTH THE JFK <u>AND</u> THE TIPPIT SHOOTINGS

JANUARY 1963

FRANK STURGIS, FUTURE WATERGATE BURGLER AND BAY OF PIGS VETERAN, FILES A REPORT TO THE FBI THAT HE HAD BEEN INVOLVED IN A FIGHT WITH LEE HARVEY OSWALD IN MIAMI. AT THE SAME TIME, ROBERT OSWALD, **LEE'S** BROTHER, RECEIVES A POST CARD FROM MIAMI POSTMARKED JAN 10TH, 1963. THE TYPED VERSION OF THE WRITING ON THE POST CARD IN THE W.C. READS AS FOLLOWS:

"DEAR ROBERT,

SORRY I TOOK SO LONG IN SAYING "THANK YOU" FOR THE NICE XMAS PRESENT YOU SENT JUNE. I WAS OUT OF TOWN FOR A FEW DAYS SO I DIDN'T KNOW ABOUT IT UNTIL AFTER XMAS.PLEASE SEND PIC MY REGARDS WHEN YOU WRITE HIM, I SEEM TO HAVE MISLAID HIS ADDRESS.

YOUR BROTHER, LEE
P.S. MARINA SAYS "HELLO"

PIC IS **LEE'S** HALF-BROTHER AND ALSO ROBERT'S HALF-BROTHER. STURGIS' FBI REPORT AND THE POST CARD LEND CREEDENCE TO THE NOTION THAT **LEE** WAS IN MIAMI IN MID JANUARY 1963 WHILE **HARVEY** REMAINED IN DALLAS.

FEBRUARY 1ST 1963

HARVEY WRITES THE STATE DEPARTMENT TO REQUEST A "PAID IN FULL" RECEIPT FOR HIS NOW RETIRED LOAN.

FEBRUARY 13TH 1963

HARVEY AND MARINA HAVE DINNER AT THE HOME OF GEORGE DEMOHRENSCHILDT AND HIS WIFE.

FEBRUARY 17TH 1963
MARINA, AT **HARVEY'S** INSISTANCE, WRITES THE SOVIET EMBASSY IN WASHINGTON. APPARENTLY WANTING TO RETURN HOME, SHE WRITES: "I BEG YOUR ASSISTANCE TO HELP ME RETURN TO HOMESTEAD THE USSR."

FEBRUARY 22ND 1963
MARINA AND **HARVEY** ARE INTRODUCED TO RUTH PAINE AT A PARTY HOSTED BY EVERETTE GLOVER A FRIEND OF GEORGE DE MOHRENSCHILDT.

*I SUSPECT THAT DE MOHRENSCHILDT WAS INTRODUCING MARINA, AND TO A LESSER DEGREE, **HARVEY** TO HER NEW CIA "SITTER." AS NOTED PREVIOUSLY, I SUSPECT THAT THE CIA/ONI HARBORED SOME NOTION THAT MARINA'S MARRIAGE TO **HARVEY** AND HER DEPARTURE FROM RUSSIA WAS INDEED A LOW-LEVEL INTELLIGENCE ASSIGNMENT IN RESPONSE TO THE ONI-SPONSORED RECRUITMENT OF "DEFECTORS" WHO WERE TRAINED AND THEN SENT TO RUSSIA AND EASTERN EUROPEAN NATIONS. THE DE MOHRENSCHILDTS' TRAVELLED FREQUENTLY AND WERE TO LEAVE FOR HAITI AT THE END OF APRIL WITH STOPS IN NEW YORK, PHILADELPHIA, AND WASHINGTON. THEY WOULD NOT RETURN UNTIL THE END OF MAY. RUTH PAINE WOULD SERVE AS AN UNOFFICIAL "PARENT" FOR **HARVEY** AND MARINA DURING DEMOHRENSCHILDT'S ABSENCE.*

*THE RELATIONSHIP BETWEEN THE DE MOHRENSCHILDTS AND THE PAINES MAY WELL HAVE EXTENDED BEYOND THE COMMON MONITORING TASK OF **HARVEY** AND MARINA. HOOVER WOULD LATER, ON OCTOBER 23, 1964, SEND A MEMO TO LEE RANKIN, COMMISSION COUNSEL. HOOVER REQUESTED THAT RANKIN NOT RELEASE FBI MEMOS ON THE TWO COUPLES. HOOVER NOTED THAT RELEASE OF THE FBI REPORTS "COULD CAUSE SERIOUS REPERCUSSIONS TO THE COMMISSION."*

MARCH 3RD 1963
ACCORDING TO THE W.C., **HARVEY** AND MARINA MOVE TO A NEW APARTMENT ON 214 WEST NEELY STREET. **HARVEY** HOWEVER WILL, IN CUSTODY, DENY HAVING LIVED AT 214 WEST NEELY STREET.

*A GREAT DEAL WILL HAPPEN BETWEEN MARCH 3RD (**HARVEY'S** ALLEGED MOVE TO 214 WEST NEELY) AND APRIL 24TH WHEN HE DEPARTS FOR NEW ORLEANS. ON MARCH 12TH THE ALLEGED ASSASSINATION RIFLE WILL BE ORDERED AS WELL AS AN ORDER FILLED FOR WHAT WAS LATER ALLEGED TO BE **HARVEY'S** PISTOL. BOTH ITEMS WILL ARRIVE IN DALLAS ON MARCH 25TH/26TH. THE BACKYARD PHOTO IS TAKEN ON MARCH 31ST AND ON APRIL 10TH A SHOT IS FIRED AT GENERAL WALKER'S RESIDENCE. THESE HIGHLY INCRIMINATING EVENTS ALL TAKE PLACE IN THE 52 DAY TIME FRAME IN WHICH **HARVEY** IS, ACCORDING TO THE W.C., RESIDING AT 214 WEST NEELY. THE INFAMOUS BACKYARD PHOTO, ALLEGEDLY OF **HARVEY** HOLDING A RIFLE AND PISTOL, WAS THOUGHT TO HAVE BEEN TAKEN AT 214 WEST NEELY. IN ESSENCE **HARVEY** WOULD DENY THE AUTHENTICITY OF THE PHOTO AND EVER HAVING LIVED ON WEST NEELY.*

MARCH 5TH 1963
HARVEY'S "BROTHER" ROBERT IS TRANSFERRED TO MALVERN, ARKANSAS.

MARCH 8TH 1963
THE SOVIET EMBASSY IN WASHINGTON, IN A REPLY TO MARINA, REQUESTS THAT SHE SUBMIT DETAILED PAPERWORK AND THAT THE PROCESSING TIME FOR HER REQUEST TO RETURN HOME COULD BE 5-6 MONTHS.

MARCH 11TH 1963
FBI AGENT HOSTY CALLS **HARVEY'S** PREVIOUS ADDRESS AT 604 ELSBETH IN AN ATTEMPT TO INTERVIEW MARINA. HE FINDS THE OSWALDS HAVE MOVED LEAVING NO FORWARDING ADDRESS.

ONE COULD LOGICALLY CONCLUDE THAT THIS PHONE CALL WAS PROMPTED BY MARINA'S EARLIER REQUEST TO RETURN HOME AS IT IS LIKELY IF NOT A CERTAINTY THAT HER CORRESPONDANCE WITH THE EMBASSY WAS READ BY THE FBI AND THE CIA.

MARCH 11TH 1963

HARVEY RECEIVES A "PAID IN FULL" NOTIFICATION FROM THE STATE DEPARTMENT REGARDING HIS EARLIER $435 LOAN.

SPRING 1963

ROSCOE WHITE MOVES TO THE OAK CLIFF SECTION OF DALLAS.

MARCH 12TH 1963

AN ORDER FOR A RIFLE FROM KLEIN'S SPORTING GOODS IN CHICAGO IS MADE BY A "A. HIDDELL". THE MAILING ADDRESS TO WHERE THE RIFLE IS TO BE SHIPPED IS P.O. BOX #2915, DALLAS, TEXAS. THE RIFLE COSTS $21.45 INCLUDING A 4X SCOPE, POSTAGE, AND HANDLING. A CLIP IS <u>NOT</u> INCLUDED IN THE ORDER.

THE RELEVANCE OF THE CLIP PROMPTS A PREMATURE LOOK AT THE NUMBER OF SHOTS FIRED AND THE TIME FRAME IN WHICH THEY WOULD HAVE TO HAVE BEEN FIRED.

IN HIS TESTIMONY BEFORE THE HSCA, A MR. WALDMAN FROM KLEIN'S SPORTING GOODS NOTED THAT THE SCOPE WOULD HAVE BEEN MOUNTED BY KLEIN'S IN-HOUSE GUNSMITH, WILLIAM SHARP. WHEN ASKED IF THE SCOPE WOULD BE CHECKED BY BORE SIGHTING OR ACTUAL FIRING OF THE RIFLE WITH THE MOUNTED SCOPE, HE REPLIED: "NO, IT IS UNLIKELY IN AN INEXPENSIVE RIFLE THAT HE (SHARP) WOULD DO ANYTHING OTHER THAN ROUGHLY ALIGN THE SCOPE WITH THE RIFLE."

THE SCOPE IS ALSO MOUNTED FOR A LEFT-HANDED SHOOTER. **HARVEY IS RIGHT-HANDED.** *THE ORDER FORM DOES NOT CONTAIN AN OPTION TO SELECT EITHER A LEFT-HANDED OR RIGHT-HANDED SCOPE MOUNTING. IF KLEIN'S WERE TO ERR ON THE SIDE OF PROBABILITY, THEY WOULD HAVE MOUNTED THE SCOPE FOR A RIGHT-HANDED SHOOTER SINCE APPROXIMATELY 84% OF PEOPLE ARE RIGHT-HANDED.*

NO CLIP WAS ORDERED FOR THE RIFLE. IT WOULD HAVE BEEN AN OPTIONAL PURCHASE FOR $7.50. IT HAS BEEN NOTED BY SEVERAL RESEARCHERS THAT ONE IS <u>UNABLE TO FIRE</u> THE RIFLE <u>WITHOUT A CLIP</u>. OTHERS HAVE NOTED THAT YOU <u>CAN</u>, BUT IT IS A <u>SLOW</u> AND <u>AWKWARD</u> PROCESS. BUT, FOR ARGUMENTS SAKE, LET'S ALLOW THE SHOOTER TO LOAD EACH ROUND <u>WITH</u> A CLIP AS THE W.C. CONVENIENTLY FAVORS THE NOTION THAT **HARVEY** *WAS INDEED IN POSSESSION OF A CLIP.*

THE IMPACT OF THE PRESENCE OR ABSENCE OF A CLIP CANNOT BE OVERSTATED. WITH THAT IN MIND, A PREMATURE LOOK AT THE FIRING SEQUENCE BOTH WITH AND WITHOUT A CLIP IS IN ORDER.

THE FIRST BULLET WOULD ALREADY BE IN THE CHAMBER. TWO MORE BULLETS, AFTER EJECTING THE SPENT CASINGS, WOULD BE LOADED VIA THE CLIP FOR EACH OF THE 2 ADDITIONAL SHOTS ALLOWED BY THE WARREN COMMISSION. THE FBI MARKSMEN EMPLOYED BY THE COMMISSION WOULD LATER DETERMINE THAT 2.4 SECONDS WAS A <u>MINIMUM</u> TIME <u>BETWEEN</u> SHOTS AND THEY WERE SHOOTING AT STILL TARGETS NOT A MOVING VEHICLE. KEEP IN MIND THAT THIS ALLOWED FOR <u>CLIP</u> <u>LOADING</u>. WITH CLIP LOADING YOU WOULD NOT HAVE TO PHYSICALLY PICK UP EACH BULLET AND MANUALLY LOAD EACH ONE FOR SHOTS 2 AND 3.
ELAPSED TIME IN SECONDS:

0.00----------------------SHOT 1
                            MANUALLY EJECT CASING /CLOSE THE BOLT / AUTO CLIP-LOAD

2.40----------------------SHOT 2
                            MANUALLY EJECT CASING / CLOSE THE BOLT / AUTO CLIP-LOAD

2.40----------------------SHOT 3

TOTAL TIME: 4.8 SECONDS

THIS IS A **BEST-CASE** SCENARIO FOR THE W.C. IN THAT IT ALLOWS FOR **ONLY 3 SHOTS**, ALLOWS FOR THE **MINIMUM** TIME FRAME POSSIBLE BETWEEN EACH OF THE SHOTS, AND ALLOWS FOR **CLIP-LOADING** VIA A CLIP THAT HAS NEVER BEEN PROVEN TO HAVE BEEN PURCHASED BY **HARVEY**. IT DOES **NOT** HOWEVER ALLOW FOR THE TIME TO RELOCATE THE TARGET WITH A SCOPE FOR SHOTS 2 AND 3.

LET US NOW REPEAT THE FIRING SEQUENCE BUT **NOT** ALLOW FOR CLIP LOADING. ASK YOURSELF HOW LONG WOULD IT TAKE TO LOWER THE RIFLE FROM THE FIRING POSITION, EJECT THE SPENT CASING, <u>PHYSICALLY PICK UP AND MANUALLY RE-LOAD ANOTHER BULLET</u>, CLOSE THE BOLT, AND RE-LOCATE THE MOVING TARGET? NOW DO THIS TWO TIMES; ONCE BETWEEN SHOTS 1 AND 2 AND AGAIN BETWEEN SHOTS 2 AND 3. WOULD THIS NOT ADD SECONDS TO THE 2.4 SECONDS THE FBI MARKSMEN NOTED AS THE <u>MINIMUM</u> TIME BETWEEN SHOTS IF ONE DID NOT USE A CLIP THEREFORE NECESSITATING, <u>MANUALLY</u> RELOADING THE RIFLE? KEEP IN MIND THAT THE ENTIRE FIRING SEQUENCE IS LIMITED TO **5.6** SECONDS ACCORDING TO THE COMMISSION. COULD ONE MANUALLY EJECT A SPENT SHELL, (SHOT 1), PHYSICALLY PICK UP A NEW BULLET, MANUALLY LOAD IT AND RE-LOCATE THE MOVING TARGET FOR SHOT 2, REPEAT THIS FOR SHOT 3 AND ADD ONLY .8 SECOND TO THE ENTIRE FIRING SEQUENCE? (4.8 SECONDS PLUS .8 SECONDS = 5.6 SECONDS)?

THE ACOUSTIC EVIDENCE IN THE HSCA INVESTIGATION NOTED THAT THERE WAS ONLY 1.6 SECONDS BETWEEN THE FIRST AND SECOND SHOTS. THIS OBVIOUSLY MAKES IT VIRTUALLY IMPOSSIBLE FOR **HARVEY** TO HAVE BEEN THE SOLE SHOOTER EVEN **WITH** THE BENEFIT OF A CLIP THAT WAS NEVER CONCLUSIVELY PROVEN TO HAVE BEEN ORDERED FOR THE RIFLE IN QUESTION.

IN FACT, IF ONE INCLUDES A **4TH** SHOT THAT MISSED THE LIMO ENTIRELY AND INFLICTED THE CONCRETE PROJECTILE WOUND ON JAMES TAGUE, THE FASTEST TIMING SEQUENCE EXTENDS TO **7.2** SECONDS (4.80 PLUS 2.40=7.2 SECONDS) EVEN IF ONE **ALLOWS** THE USE OF THE CLIP.

IF ONE INCLUDES THE 4TH SHOT FIRED, EXTENDING THE SHOOTING TIME FRAME TO A MIMIMUM OF 7.2 SECONDS, **HARVEY** COULD **NOT** HAVE BEEN THE SOLE SHOOTER.

IF ONE ALLOWS FOR THE 4TH SHOT AND **EXCLUDES** THE CLIP, IT WOULD HAVE BEEN AN IMPOSSIBILITY FOR **HARVEY** OR ANYONE ELSE TO HAVE BEEN THE SOLE SHOOTER THAT DAY IN DALLAS. ONCE AGAIN I WILL NOTE THAT FIREARMS EXPERTS HAVE STATED THAT MANUALLY LOADING THE MANNLICHER WITHOUT THE BENEFIT OF A CLIP TO BE A SLOW AND AWKWARD PROCESS.

IN ESSENCE, THE **ONLY** SCENARIO THAT EVEN REMOTELY WORKS FOR THE W.C. AND ALLOWS THAT **HARVEY** AND **HARVEY** ALONE FIRED ON THE MOTORCADE IN LESS THAN 5.6 SECONDS IS ONE THAT ALLOWS FOR **ONLY** 3 SHOTS **AND** THAT HE HAD THE **USE OF A CLIP.**

IRONICALLY, THE HSCA HAS **HARVEY** MISSING WITH THE FIRST SHOT, THE TAGUE SHOT, BY ABOUT 180 FEET. THIS WAS HIS **CLOSEST** SHOT IN TERMS OF DISTANCE FROM THE 6TH FLOOR TO THE PRESIDENTIAL LIMO. THEY WOULD HOWEVER INSIST THAT ON THE NEXT 2

SHOTS FROM *FURTHER* DISTANCES THAT *HARVETY* HAD APPARENTLY REGAINED A REMARKABLE DEGREE OF ACCURACY AND PROCEEDED TO INFLICT 8 WOUNDS ON 2 MEN WITH HIS LAST 2 SHOTS.

THERE WAS NO DOCUMENTATION THAT A CLIP WAS ORDERED OR USED BY EITHER *HARVEY*, AN "OSWALD" OR A "HIDDELL." AND, A DECEMBER 23RD, 1963 MEMO FROM CAPTAIN FRITZ TO CAPTAIN CURRY DOES NOT LIST A CLIP FOUND IN THE TSBD IN A LIST OF ALL EVIDENCE RELEASED BY THE DALLAS POLICE TO THE FBI. HOWEVER A <u>TYPED</u> FBI MEMO DATED 11-26-63 SHOWS A <u>HANDWRITTEN</u>, NOT TYPED NOTATION READING "RIFLE CLIP." BUT, THIS IS DATED, <u>ALSO</u> HANDWRITTEN, 8-13-65. THE CLIP HOWEVER IS INDEED MENTIONED IN THE WARREN COMMISSION PUBLISHED IN SEPTEMBER 1964. THE CLIP IS FOOTNOTED AND CITES TESTIMONY FROM LT. DAY AND CAPTAIN FRITZ. BUT, THE PAGES REFERENCED DO <u>NOT</u> MENTION THE CLIP. THERE IS NOTHING IN THE WARREN COMMISSION VOLUMES TO SUPPORT THE COMMISSION'S ALLEGATION THAT A CLIP WAS FOUND ON NOVEMBER 22ND, 1963 IN THE TSBD..

I THINK THE INCLUSION / EXCLUSION OF THE CLIP TROUBLED THE FBI AND THE COMMISSION. THE INCLUSION OF THE CLIP WOULD BE CRUCIAL IN AN EFFORT TO PROVE THAT THERE WAS AT LEAST A <u>POSSIBILITY</u> THAT *HARVEY* COULD HAVE FIRED THE 3 SHOTS IN THE 5.6 SECOND TIME FRAME ALLOWED. BUT, THERE IS NO RECORD OF *HARVEY* OR "HIDELL" ORDERING OR PURCHASING A CLIP. DID THE TIMING SEQUENCE OF THE SHOTS NECESSITATE AND OVERSHADOW THE INABILITY OF THE FBI AND THE COMMISSION TO NOTE WHEN AND WHERE THE CLIP WAS PURCHASED AND BY WHOM?

INTERESTINGLY, THE CLIP HELD 6 BULLETS. WITH AN ADDITIONAL BULLET ALREADY IN THE CHAMBER, THE RIFLE COULD IN EFFECT "HOLD" 7 BULLETS. I FIND IT DIFFICULT TO BELIEVE THAT AN ASSASSIN WOULD ONLY LOAD 4 BULLETS, 57% OF THE RIFLE'S CAPACITY, IN AN ATTEMPT ON THE PRESIDENT'S LIFE. THE COMMISSION SIMPLY DECIDED NOT TO ADDRESS THIS PROBLEM UNTIL <u>AFTER</u> THE REPORT HAD GONE TO PRESS.

THE CLIP IS DESIGNED TO FALL OUT THE BOTTOM OF THE RIFLE WHEN THE LAST BULLET IS CHAMBERED. AT 1:22, CAPTAIN WILL FRITZ WILL EJECT A LIVE ROUND FROM THE RIFLE FOUND ON THE 6TH FLOOR OF THE TSBD. IF ONLY 3 SHOTS WERE FIRED, RERESENTED BY THE 3 CASINGS FOUND ON THE 6TH FLOOR BENEATH THE ALLEGED SNIPER WINDOW, AND AN ADDITONAL UNFIRED ROUND WAS IN THE CHAMBER, THEN THE CLIP, IF INDEED USED, WOULD HAVE BEEN LOADED WITH 4 TOTAL ROUNDS. AFTER THE THIRD SHOT, THE CLIP SHOULD HAVE FALLEN OUT AFTER THE LAST, 4TH ROUND WAS CHAMBERED.

WHY WOULD *HARVEY* LEAVE BEHIND THE ALLEGED ASSASSINATION WEAPON, 3 EMPTY CASINGS, AND 1 LIVE ROUND IN THE RIFLE YET RETRIEVE THE NOW EMPTY CLIP AND TAKE IT WITH HIM? THE ONLY LOGICAL ANSWER IS THAT HE DIDN'T. THERE WAS NO CLIP.

MORE IMPORTANTLY, POSTAL RECORDS SHOW THAT THE MONEY ORDER USED TO ORDER THE RIFLE WAS PURCHASED EARLY THE MORNING OF MARCH 12TH. THE LETTER ITSELF WAS POSTMARKED AT 10:30 AM. BUT, *HARVEY'S* TIME SHEET SHOWED THAT HE HAD REPORTED FOR WORK AT JAGGERS-CHILES-STOVALL AT 8:00 AM THAT DAY. IF *HARVEY* WAS AT WORK, WHO BOUGHT THE MONEY ORDER PURCHASED BY A "A.HIDELL?" SINCE THE NAME "HIDELL" HAD BEEN ADDED AS "AUTHORIZED TO RECEIVE MAIL" AT *HARVEY'S* POST OFFICE BOX, THE INDIVIDUAL PURCHASING THE MONEY ORDER WOULD LIKELY USE THE NAME "HIDELL" THUS ALLOWING THEM TO PICK UP THE RIFLE UPON ITS ARRIVAL. I WOULD SUSPECT THAT THIS INDIVIDUAL WOULD BE THE LOCAL SET-UP CONSPIRATOR ROSCOE WHITE OR *LEE*. ARMSTRONG CONTENDS THAT "HIDELL" IS *LEE* AND PICKED UP BOTH THE HAND GUN AND THE RIFLE. I AM INCLINED TO AGREE.

AS POINTED OUT BY ARMSTRONG, FURTHER PROBLEMS CLOUD THE PURCHASE OF THE MONEY ORDER. THE MONEY ORDER, PURCHASED FROM THE POST OFFICE IN ZONE 1, WAS ENCLOSED IN AN ENVELOPE. THE ENVELOPE WAS POSTMARKED "MAR 12 10:30 AM DALLAS, TEX 12." IN ESSENCE THE MONEY ORDER WAS BOUGHT AFTER 8:00 AM IN ZONE 1 WHEN

THE POST OFFICE OPENED. THE LETTER HOWEVER WAS DROPPED INTO A MAILBOX IN POSTAL ZONE 12. THIS ZONE IS 3 ZONES WEST OF ZONE 1, DOWNTOWN DALLAS, WHICH WAS THE CLOSEST ZONE TO JCS WHERE **HARVEY** WORKED. A MAIL TRUCK THEN PICKED UP THE MAIL ORDER FROM THE ZONE 12 BOX AND TOOK IT TO THE INDUSTRIAL STATION OFFICE IN ZONE 12. THERE IT WAS POSTMARKED WITH THE ABOVE NOTED STAMP. WHY WOULD **HARVEY** PURCHASE A MONEY ORDER IN ZONE 1 THEN TRAVEL TO ZONE 12 TO MAIL IT? HIS WORK RECORD FOR THAT MORNING SHOWED THAT HE WAS AT JCS FROM 8:00 AM UNTIL 12:15. HE COULD NOT HAVE EITHER PURCHASED OR MAILED THE MONEY ORDER TO KLEIN'S. IF ARMSTRONG IS CORRECT, IT WOULD BE **LEE** WHO WOULD PERFORM THESE TASKS.

A NEW ORLEANS FBI INFORMANT, EUGENE DELAPPARRA, WOULD LATER REPORT HIS OBSERVATION OF 3 MEN IN A NEW ORLEANS RESTAURANT CONTROLLED BY CARLOS MARCELLO: "THE MEN......ONE A CERTAIN 'PROFESSOR' OF AN UNKNOWN NAME (DAVID FERRIE WAS KNOWN AS "THE PROFESSOR" IN NEW ORLEANS) WERE LOOKING AT AN AD FOR A FOREIGN-MADE RIFLE THAT SOLD FOR $12.98. MARCELLO'S <u>OTHER</u> FRIEND OBSERVED, "THIS WOULD BE A NICE RIFLE TO BUY TO GET THE PRESIDENT." APPARENTLY THE "OTHER FRIEND" WAS PRIVY TO THE UPCOMING EVENTS OF NOVEMBER 22ND AS WAS CARLOS MARCELLO.

THE RIFLE ORDERED FROM KLEIN'S SPORTING GOODS WAS AN m38 6.5 X 52MM MANNLICHER CARCANO MODEL #C20-T759. IT HAD A 17.5" BARRELL AND AN OVERALL LENGTH OF 36.INCHES. THE RIFLE THE WARREN COMMISSION LOGGED AS EXHIBIT 139 WAS NOTED TO BE SN C2766, HAS A 21.5" BARRELL, AND AN OVERALL LENGTH OF 40". THIS MODEL # WAS C20- 750. THESE DISCREPANCIES ALONE BREAK THE CHAIN OF POSSESSION TYING THE WARREN COMMISSION RIFLE TO THE ONE ALLEGEDLY ORDERED BY **HARVEY**.

BUT ANOTHER PROBLEM ARISES CONCERNING THE S/N ITSELF. MANNLICHER CARCANOS WERE MADE AT VARIOUS FACTORIES IN ITALY. EACH FACTORY WOULD UTILIZE ITS OWN NUMBERING SEQUENCE FOR THE RIFLES. IT IS THEREFORE QUITE POSSIBLE THAT THERE WERE SEVERAL CARCANOS WITH THE EXACT SAME SERIAL NUMBER. TRACING A PARTICULAR RIFLE WITH THE S/N 2766 EXCLUSIVELY TO **HARVEY** OR "HIDELL" WOULD BE NEXT TO IMPOSSIBLE WITH THE LIKLIHOOD OF OTHER RIFLES BEARING AN IDENTICAL SERIAL NUMBER.

MARCH 17TH 1963
MARINA SUBMITS AN APPLICATION TO THE SOVIET CONSULATE REQUESTING TO RETURN TO RUSSIA.

MARCH 20TH1963
THE PISTOL THAT WAS ALLEGEDLY USED TO KILL OFFICER TIPPIT, A .38 SPECIAL S&W VICTORY MODEL, SN V50210, IS SHIPPED TO "A.J. HIDELL", P.O. BOX 2915. THE RIFLE ALLEGEDLY USED IN THE PRESIDENTIAL ASSASSINATION IS SHIPPPED TO THIS SAME ADDRESS.

MARCH 24TH 1963
HARVEY WRITES THE SOCIALIST WORKERS PARTY ONCE AGAIN CONTINUING HIS PURSUIT OF MEMBERSHIP.

MARCH 25-26TH 1963
THE RIFLE ARRIVES AT THE POST OFFICE. THE PISTOL ARRIVES AT REA EXPRESS NEAR LOVE FIELD PRIOR TO ITS ARRIVAL AT THE POST OFFICE.

THE POST OFFICE WAS OF LITTLE HELP IN DETERMINING THOSE ACTUALLY INVOLVED IN THE PURCHASE AND, MORE IMPORTANTLY, THE <u>PICK-UP</u> OF THE RIFLE. THE PORTION OF THE P.O. BOX APPLICATION THAT LISTED AUTHORIZED PERSONS <u>OTHER</u> THAN THE APPLICANT TO RECEIVE MAIL WAS MISSING. DALLAS POSTAL INSPECTOR HARRY HOLMES TOLD THE WARREN COMMISSION THAT POSTAL REGULATIONS ALLOWED THE DISCARDING OF <u>THAT</u> PORTION OF THE APPLICATION WHEN THE BOX WAS <u>CLOSED</u>; IN THIS INSTANCE, MAY 14, 1963. THIS WOULD BE ONLY 55 DAYS AFTER THE RIFLE HAD ARRIVED AT THE POST OFFICE. BUT, THE POSTAL REGULATIONS ACTUALLY REQUIRED KEEPING THE <u>ENTIRE</u> APPLICATION FOR 2 YEARS <u>AFTER</u> THE BOX WAS CLOSED. BUT, MUCH MORE

IMPORTANTLY, A <u>SIGNED RECEIPT</u> FOR THE <u>PICKUP</u> OF THE RIFLE AT THE POST OFFICE OR THE PICKUP OF THE HANDGUN AT REA EXPRESS WAS NOT AVAILABLE EITHER. POSTAL REGULATIONS REQUIRED THE RETENTION OF RECORDS OF FIREARMS DELIVERY TO BE KEPT FOR <u>4 YEARS.</u> A RECEIPT <u>SIGNED BY **HARVEY**</u> WOULD HAVE PUT THE RIFLE IN HIS POSSESSION. HAD THE POST OFFICE BEEN ABLE TO PRODUCE THE ABOVE DOCUMENT, THE COMMISSION COULD HAVE <u>STRENGTHENED</u> THEIR CASE IN REGARDS TO PLACING THE RIFLE IN **HARVEY'S** POSSESSION. BUT, THESE TWO DOCUMENTS, THE RECEIPT AT THE POST OFFICE AND THE RECEIPT AT REA EXPRESS, <u>HAD</u> THEY BEEN PRODUCED, COULD ALSO HAVE RESULTED IN EXACTLY THE <u>OPPOSITE</u> EFFECT THE COMMISSION DESIRED IF <u>NEITHER</u> OF THE DOCUMENTS BORE THE SIGNATURE OF **HARVEY**. SO, BOTH DOCUMENTS WERE CONVENIENTLY DISCARDED PRIOR TO THE TIME OF THEIR SCHEDULED END DATE. WE WOULD BE LEFT WITH NO OTHER OPTION THAN TO TAKE THE FBI'S WORD THAT ALTHOUGH A "HIDELL" AND THE FPFC HAD BEEN AUTHORIZED TO RECEIVE MAIL AT **HARVEY'S** P.O. BOX THAT IT WAS **HARVEY** WHO PICKED UP BOTH WEAPONS;THE RIFLE AT THE POST OFFICE AND THE PISTOL AT REA EXPRESS..

IT IS INTERESTING THAT THE FBI, IN ITS INVESTIGATION OF THE WEAPONS USED ON NOVEMBER 22ND, COULD PRODUCE THE <u>ORDER FORMS</u> IN THEIR EFFORT TO TIE **HARVEY** TO THEIR <u>PURCHASE</u>. BUT THEY COULD <u>NOT</u> PRODUCE ANY DOCUMENTATION THAT WOULD SHOW THAT **HARVEY** WAS THE <u>ONLY</u> PERSON IN A POSITION TO <u>RECEIVE</u> THE WEAPONS.

WITH THE ADDITION, TEMPORARY AS IT WAS, OF A "HIDELL" AND THE FPFC AS AUTHORIZED TO RECEIVE MAIL AT THE P.O. BOX, A RIFLE COULD THEN HAVE BEEN ORDERED <u>WITHOUT</u> **HARVEY'S** KNOWLEDGE, DELIVERED TO THE P.O. BOX, THEN PICKED UP BY <u>ANYONE</u> WITH AN I.D. PORTRAYING THE RECIPIENT AS "HIDELL", <u>OR ANYONE</u> WITH FPFC CREDENTIALS. **LEE** MOST LIKELY HAD BOTH.

POSTAL INSPECTOR HARRY HOLMES' TESTIMONY WOULD FURTHER THE POSSIBILITY THAT SOMEONE OTHER THAN **HARVEY** COULD HAVE PICKED UP THE RIFLE ALLEGEDLY USED ON NOVEMBER 22ND. HOLMES NOTED THAT WHEN A PACKAGE ARRIVES ADDRESSED TO A PARTICULAR P.O. BOX THAT A NOTICE IS PLACED IN THE P.O. BOX <u>REGARDLESS</u> OF WHETHER THE <u>NAME</u> ON THE PACKAGE IS LISTED ON THE P.O. BOX APPLICATION. THE PERSON(S) WITH ACCESS TO THE BOX (AND PRESUMABLY ON THE APPLICATION) WOULD SIMPLY TAKE THE NOTICE TO THE PICK-UP WINDOW AND RECEIVE THE PACKAGE. EVEN MORE INCREDIBLE IS THE FACT THAT HOLMES ALSO OFFERED THAT THE PERSON WHO PRESENTS THE NOTICE IS <u>NOT</u> REQUIRED TO SHOW IDENTIFICATION. IT IS ASSUMED BY THE POST OFFICE, ACCORDING TO HOLMES, THAT WHOEVER HAS THE NOTICE IS ENTITLED TO THE PACKAGE. SIMPLY PUT, ALL ONE WOULD NEED TO DO IS OPEN THE BOX, TAKE THE NOTICE, GO TO THE WINDOW, AND PICK UP THE PACKAGE; NO IDENTIFICATION REQUIRED, ONLY ACCESS TO AND THE SIMPLE ABILITY TO OPEN THE BOX.

IN ALL LIKLIHOOD, THE PERSON PRESENTING HIMSELF AS "HIDELL" AND/OR PRODUCING FPFC CREDENTIALS, OR WITH NO IDENTIFICATION AT ALL, WAS AN OPERATIVE OF THE SET-UP CONSPIRATORS GROUP FURTHERING THEIR SET-UP OF **HARVEY** AS THE PRESIDENTIAL ASSASSIN AND THE ASSAILANT IN THE TIPPIT SHOOTING. THE PERSON MOST LIKELY TO PICK UP THE WEAPONS IN DALLAS WOULD BE EITHER ROSCOE WHITE OR MORE LIKELY **LEE**.

UNBEKNOWNST TO **HARVEY**, HE HAD BEEN LINKED TO BOTH "HIDELL" AND THE FPFC VIA THE PO. BOX. **LEE** HAD TIED HIM TO THE RIFLE AND THE HANDGUN PURCHASE, THE FPFC ORGANIZATION, AND A "HIDELL" IN A TIDY PORTRAIT SUITABLE FOR "FRAMING." THIS WOULD INDEED LATER PROVE TO BE A SUCCESSFUL STRATEGY FOR THE SET-UP CONSPIRATORS GROUP SINCE AN I.D. CARD ATTRIBUTED TO **HARVEY** THE DAY <u>AFTER</u> THE ASSASSINATION SHOWED **HARVEY** AS A MEMBER, AND "<u>HIDELL</u>" AS CHAPTER PRESIDENT OF THE NEW ORLEANS FPFC COMMITTEE. ALL SIDES OF THE "ACCESS TRIANGLE" TO THE P.O. BOX IN DALLAS HAD BEEN ESTABLISHED; **HARVEY**, "HIDELL", AND THE FPFC. ALL WOULD BE REPRESENTED ON THE SIMPLE I.D. CARD ALLEGEDLY IN

HARVEY'S POSSESSION ON NOVEMBER 23RD, THE DAY <u>AFTER</u> HIS ARREST. BUT, ANY SUPPORTING EVIDENCE OF THIS ACCESS TRIANGLE WOULD NOT BE AVAILABLE FOR SCRUTINY. IT HAD BEEN CONVENIENTLY LOST.

FOR THE SET-UP CONSPIRATORS, IT WAS SIMPLY A MATTER OF POINTING **HARVEY** IN THE RIGHT DIRECTION; A DIRECTION IN WHICH **HARVEY** HIMSELF HAD UNWITTINGLY WORSENED BY BEING UNABLE TO DISTINGUISH BETWEEN LEGITIMATE FBI INFORMANT SCENARIOS AND THE PROSPECT THAT HIS ROLE AS A LEGITIMATE CIA ASSET HAD BEEN NOTHING MORE THAN A RUSE BY THOSE (HUNT/PHILLIPS) MANIPULATING HIS ACTIONS AS PART OF THE SET-UP CONSPIRACY.

MARCH 26ST 1963
DALLAS FBI AGENT JAMES HOSTY REOPENS **HARVEY'S** FILE. HE HAD LEARNED, ON MARCH 14TH THAT AN FBI INFORMANT IDENTIFIED AS T-2 REPORTED THAT **HARVEY** HAD, <u>THE PREVIOUS AUGUST</u> SUBSCRIBED TO THE WORKER NEWSPAPER.

*I FIND THIS AN INTERESTING RESPONSE ON THE PART OF AGENT HOSTY. AS WAS NOTED PREVIOUSLY, AGENTS FAIN AND CARTER HAD THEIR INITIAL INTERVIEW WITH **HARVEY** ON JUNE 26TH, 1962 AT THE FBI OFFICE IN FORT WORTH. ON AUGUST 5TH, 1962, **HARVEY** SUBSCRIBES TO THE WORKER, AND ON AUGUST 12TH, **HARVEY**, WHO IS NOW LIKELY ON BOARD AS AN <u>FBI</u> INFORMANT, WRITES THE SOCIALIST WORKERS PARTY ABOUT MEMBERSHIP. **HARVEY** FOLLOWS THIS INQUIRY ON AUGUST 28TH 1962 BY WRITING TO THE SOCIALIST WORKERS PARTY FOR PAMPHLETS. FAIN, APPARENTLY NOT AT ALL CONCERNED ABOUT THIS, PLACES **HARVEY'S** FILE IN "INACTIVE" STATUS ON AUGUST 30TH 1962. ON OCTOBER 29TH OF 1962, FAIN CLOSES **HARVEY'S** CASE FILE WHEN HE RETIRES. IN DECEMBER OF 1962, **HARVEY** SUBSCRIBES TO THE MILITANT. NONE OF THESE OTHER THREE INCIDENTS SEEM TO WARRANT THE CONCERN OF AGENT FAIN. THIS WOULD MAKE SENSE IF **HARVEY** WERE INDEED ATTEMPTING TO INFILTRATE THESE ORGANIZATIONS AS PART OF HIS FBI INFORMANT/UNDERCOVER STATUS. NOW, ON MARCH 26TH, 1963, NEARLY 8 MONTHS AFTER **HARVEY'S** AUGUST 5TH LETTER TO THE SOCIALIST WORKERS PARTY IN REGARDS TO A SUBSCRIPTION, HOSTY DECIDES TO RE-OPEN **HARVEY'S** FILE AND USES THE BELATED INFORMATION PROVIDED BY INFORMANT T-2 OF **HARVEY'S** APPARENT SUBSCRIPTION TO THE WORKER NEWSPAPER AS THE REASON FOR DOING SO.*

*I AM MUCH MORE INCLINED TO THINK THAT HOSTY REOPENED HIS FILE FOR OTHER REASONS. **HARVEY** OPENED HIS FIRST DALLAS P.O. BOX ON OCTOBER 9TH, 1962. APPARENTLY SOMEONE OTHER THAN **HARVEY** LISTED AS "AUTHORIZED TO RECEIVE MAIL" A "HIDELL" AND THE FPFC COMMITTEE. THE FPFC COMMITTEE WAS <u>NOT</u> A PART OF THE FBI/**HARVEY** INFORMANT RELATIONSHIP. AS PREVIOUSLY NOTED IN LATE DECEMBER 1962 OR EARLY JANUARY 1963 THERE WAS A FIGHT AMONG SOME CUBANS INVOLVING GUNFIRE AT A HOUSE IN MONTERAY PARK IN LOS ANGELES. A "LEE HARVEY OSWALD" WAS AMONG THOSE LISTED ON THE ARREST RECORD. ON JANUARY 27TH, 1963, THE HANDGUN ALLEGEDLY USED TO SHOOT OFFICER TIPPIT WAS ORDERED BY A "A.J. HIDELL." ON MARCH 11TH 1963, HOSTY CALLS **HARVEY** ONLY TO FIND OUT THAT THE OSWALDS HAVE MOVED LEAVING NO FORWARDING ADDRESS. AND ON MARCH 12TH, 1963, THE RIFLE ALLEGEDLY USED TO SHOOT THE PRESIDENT WAS ORDERED BY A "A. HIDELL." BOTH THE HANDGUN AND THE RIFLE WERE DELIVERED TO P.O. BOX 2915, THE SAME P.O BOX OPENED BY **HARVEY** ON OCT 9TH, 1962. IT IS <u>THESE</u> EVENTS THAT ARE CONCERNING ENOUGH TO WARRANT AGENT HOSTY'S RE-OPENING OF **HARVEY'S** FILE PARTICULARLY SINCE HE HAS APPARENTLY LOST TRACK OF WHERE HE IS CURRENTLY RESIDING. THE EVENTS THAT PROMPT HOSTY TO REOPEN **HARVEY'S** FILE ARE THE WORK OF THE SET-UP CONSPIRATORS.*

*IT IS CRITICAL TO KEEP IN MIND THAT ALTHOUGH THEY MIGHT HAVE HAD <u>SUSPICIONS,</u> THE LOCAL DALLAS FBI WOULD NOT LIKELY HAVE HAD ANY DEFINITIVE <u>PROOF</u> THAT **HARVEY'S** "APPARENT" PRO-CASTRO FPFC CONNECTION (AS WITNESSED BY THE SET-UP CONSPIRATORS HAVING ADDED THE FPFC TO **HARVEY'S** P.O. BOX LISTING) WAS CIA-RELATED. AND, CERTAINLY NO IDEA THAT IT WAS SOLELY THE PRODUCT OF THE SET-UP*

CONSPIRATORS. IT IS HOWEVER INTERESTING TO NOTE THAT IN A 1996 INTERVIEW, HOSTY COMMENTED: *"I COULDN'T INTERVIEW OSWALD WITHOUT EXPLICIT PERMISSION FROM THE CIA. AND, THEY WEREN'T ABOUT TO GIVE IT AND I WASN'T ABOUT TO ASK FOR IT."* ALTHOUGH THE CIA "PROPER" HAD TASKED JAMES MCCORD TO START THE JOINT CIA/FBI COUNTER-INTELLIGENCE OPERATION AGAINST THE FPFC IN <u>NOVEMBER OF 1960</u>, THE <u>CIA</u> REPRESENTATIVE IN THIS JOINT INFILTRATION EFFORT WAS DAVID ATLEE PHILLIPS, AKA "MAURICE BISHOP." IT WAS IN ALL LIKELIHOOD PHILLIPS WHO HAD DECIDED THAT **HARVEY** WOULD BE LINKED TO BOTH "HIDELL" AND THE FPFC ON HIS INITIAL DALLAS P.O. BOX AS "AUTHORIZED TO RECEIVE MAIL." PHILLIPS, ALONG WITH HOWARD HUNT, WILL PROVE TO BE THE MOST INFLUENTIAL "GUIDING HANDS" IN REGARDS TO FACILITATING THE SET-UP OF **HARVEY**.

THE CIA HAD IN PLACE A MAIL INTERCEPT PROGRAM TITLED "HT-LINGUAL." ONE WOULD THINK THAT IF ITS PURPOSE WAS TO READ THE <u>MAIL</u> OF SUBVERSIVES THAT THIS SAME PROGRAM WOULD MONITOR <u>PACKAGES</u> AS WELL. IF **HARVEY** WAS A GENUINE RETURNED DEFECTOR WOULD NOT THE CIA HAVE INFORMED THE FBI OF THE PACKAGES CONTAINING THE ALLEGED ASSASSINATION WEAPON AND THE PISTOL ALLEGEDLY USED TO SHOOT TIPPIT?

MARCH 29TH 1963
ACCORDING TO ARMSTRONG, A YOUNG MAN WHO GAVE HIS NAME AS **LEE** HARVEY OSWALD, RECEIVED A HAIRCUT FROM BARBER JOHN ABBOTT IN SPARTA, WISCONSIN. **LEE** TOLD ABBOTT THAT HE HAD INTENDED TO GO TO WASSAU, BUT HAD GOTTEN OFF THE TRAIN PREMATURELY. THE PRESIDENT AND THE GOVENOR WERE TO DEDICATE A EITHER A LAKE OR A DAM AND **LEE** NOTED THAT HE HAD BEEN "FOLLOWING THEM AROUND" AND TAKING IN THEIR SPEECHES THROUGHOUT THE STATE. THIS WAS INDEED **LEE**, AS ABBOTT NOTED A SCAR BEHIND HIS LEFT EAR. **LEE** HAD UNDERGONE A MASTOIDECTOMY ON THE LEFT SIDE. **HARVEY** WAS AT WORK AT JCS IN DALLAS THIS DAY.

MARCH 30TH 1963
THE KENNEDY ADMINISTRATION LAUNCHES A CRACK-DOWN ON ANTI-CASTRO EXILE GROUP CAMPS AND ON THEIR RAIDS INTO CUBA. ALTHOUGH THE ANNOUNCEMENT IS MADE BY THE JUSTICE AND STATE DEPARTMENTS, THE FBI IS TASKED WITH ENFORCING THE STEPPED-UP MONITORING OF THESE GROUPS.

MARCH 31ST 1963
THE FAMOUS "BACKYARD" PHOTOS ALLEGED TO BE **HARVEY** ARE TAKEN. THEY ARE ALLEGEDLY TAKEN AT 214 WEST NEELY STREET, AN ADDRESS AT WHICH **HARVEY** DENIES EVER HAVING LIVED. THE CONTROVERSIAL PHOTOS ARE SUPPOSEDLY TAKEN BY MARINA AND SHOW **HARVEY** POSING WITH THE HANDGUN AND RIFLE ALLEGEDLY USED ON NOVEMBER 22ND AND COPIES OF THE WORKER AND THE MILITANT.

ROSCOE WHITE WAS ON THE DALLAS POLICE FORCE IN NOVEMBER 1963. HE WORKED IN THE PHOTOGRAPHY DEPARTMENT OF THE FORCE. HIS WIFE GENEVA NOTED THAT HE WAS CONSIDERED AN EXPERT IN "TRICK" PHOTOGRAPHY. THE SQUARE JAW NOTED ON THE BACK YARD PHOTOGRAPHS STRANGELY RESEMBLES THE CHIN OF ROSCOE WHITE. MANY RESEARCHERS ARE CONVINCED THAT THE BACKYARD PHOTOS ARE COMPOSITE PHOTOS AND THAT THEY WERE NOT ONLY CRAFTED BY ROSCOE WHITE, BUT THAT IT IS INDEED WHITE'S BODY, FROM THE CHIN DOWN, IN THE PHOTOS. LATER, MALCOLM THOMPSON, PREVIOUSLY PRESIDENT OF THE EVIDENCE PHOTOGRAPHER'S COUNCIL AND MAJOR JOHN PICKLAND OF THE CANADIAN DEPARTMENT OF DEFENSE WOULD BOTH OFFER THAT THE PHOTOGRAPHS WERE INDEED TAMPERED WITH AND LIKELY COMPOSITES. THE PHOTOS WERE OBVIOUSLY TAKEN ON A SUNNY DAY AS EVIDENCED BY THE SHADOWS. HOWEVER, ACCORDING TO THE WEATHER BUREAU, THE WEATHER IN DALLAS THAT DAY WAS RAINY WITH CONSIDERABLE CLOUDINESS.

MARCH 31ST 1963
HARVEY WRITES THE FPFC COMMITTEE TO REQUEST PAMPHLETS.

95

LATE MARCH 1963
ARMSTONG NOTES THAT **LEE** IS LIVING AT 1106 DICEMAN AVENUE IN DALLAS.

APRIL 2ND 1963
MICHAEL PAINE, RUTH PAINES ESTRANGED HUSBAND, DROVE TO DALLAS TO PICK UP THE OSWALDS. **HARVEY** AND MARINA WERE TO HAVE DINNER THAT EVENING AT RUTH PAINE'S HOME.

APRIL 6TH 1963
HARVEY WORKS HIS LAST DAY AT JAGGER-CHILES STOVALL.

APRIL 8TH 1963
HARVEY VISITS THE TEXAS EMPLOYMENT COMMISSION.

*A FLIGHT PLAN DATED THIS SAME DAY WAS FILED FOR A TRIP FROM NEW ORLEANS TO GARLAND, TEXAS. THE PILOT WAS DAVID FERRIE. THE 3 PASSENGERS WERE LISTED AS LAMBERT, DIAZ, AND A HIDELL. IF ARMSTRONG IS CORRECT IN HIS BELIEF THAT **LEE** IS HIDELL, THEN IT IS **LEE** WHO IS ABOARD THE FLIGHT. "LAMBERT" WAS AN ALIAS USED BY CLAW SHAW.*

APRIL 10TH 1963
A SHOT WAS FIRED AT GENERAL WALKER AT HIS HOUSE ON 4011 TURTLE CREEK BOULEVARD ABOUT 9:00 PM.

*THE <u>ONLY</u> WITNESS TO THE WALKER SHOOTING WAS A 14 YEAR OLD BOY NAMED WALTER COLEMAN. HE SAW 2 MEN SPEEDING DOWN THE ALLEY AT THE REAR OF WALKER'S HOUSE IN A LIGHT GREEN OR BLUE 1959 OR 1960 FORD. ANOTHER MAN GOT INTO A 1958 BLACK CHEVY AFTER PAUSING TO PUT SOMETHING ON THE BACKSEAT FLOORBOARD. COLEMAN WAS TOLD BY "AUTHORITIES" NOT TO DISCUSS WHAT HE HAD SEEN. COLEMAN LATER GAVE A STATEMENT TO THE FBI ESSENTIALLY REPEATING WHAT HE HAD TOLD THE LOCAL "AUTHORITIES." ALTHOUGH COLEMAN'S <u>INITIAL</u> STATEMENT CONTAINED NO REFERENCE TO **HARVEY**, **LEE**, OR EVEN A LEE HARVEY OSWALD, HIS LATER FBI REPORT IS TITLED <u>LEE HARVEY OSWALD.</u> COLEMAN TOLD THE FBI THAT NONE OF THE MEN RESEMBLED **HARVEY**. COLEMAN WAS NOT CALLED BY THE WARREN COMMISSION WHEN THEY ATTRIBUTED THE SHOOTING TO **HARVEY**. EVEN IF ONE WERE TO ASSUME THAT **HARVEY** WAS SOMEHOW INVOLVED IN THE SHOOTING, IT IS IMPORTANT TO NOTE THAT HE APPARENTLY HAD THE HELP OF AT LEAST 2 OTHER MEN. I FIND IT ODD THAT **HARVEY** WOULD ALLEGEDLY NEED **ASSISTANCE** IN TAKING **1 SHOT** ACROSS A BACK YARD AT A **STATIONARY** TARGET AT A DISTANCE LESS THAN 115 FEET AND **MISS**, AND YET ALLEGEDLY FIRE AT LEAST 3 SHOTS FROM A MINIMUM OF <u>177 FEET</u> AT A <u>MOVING</u> TARGET AND BE QUITE ACCURATE ON 2 OF THE THREE SHOTS. ONCE AGAIN, BALLISTICS COME INTO PLAY. AT THE TIME OF THE SHOOTING, THE MISSLE RECOVERED WAS A 30.06 CALIBER. PRESS REPORTS NOTED THAT THE DALLAS POLICE IDENTIFIED THE BULLET AS "STEEL JACKETED." THE AMMO ASSOCIATED WITH THE MANNLICHER ON NOVEMBER 22ND WAS <u>COPPER</u> JACKETED. THE MISSILE RECOVERED IN THE WALKER SHOOTING WAS LATER CHANGED TO A 6.5 CALIBER TO MATCH THE GUN ASSOCIATED WITH **HARVEY**. WALKER HIMSELF QUESTIONED THE DIFFERENCE IN THE BULLET CALIBER. THE WALKER BULLET DID <u>NOT</u> MATCH ANY OF THE MANNLICHER AMMO WHEN IT WAS LATER TESTED VIA NEUTRON ACTIVATION ANALYSIS. IN FACT, HOOVER HIMSELF IN A REPORT TO THE COMMISSION STATED: "THE BULLET RECOVERED IN THE ASSASSINATION ATTEMPT ON GENERAL WALKER DOES NOT MATCH EITHER CE399 (THE MAGIC BULLET) OR TWO FRAGMENTS RECOVERED FROM PRESIDENT KENNEDY'S LIMO. THE WARREN COMMISSION LINKING OF **HARVEY** TO THE GENERAL WALKER ASSASSINATION ATTEMPT IS SERIOUSLY WEAKENED."*

DPD LT. L.E. CUNINGHAM LEAD THE INVESTIGATION OF THE WALKER SHOOTING. HE VOICED HIS DOUBT REGARDING THE FAILED ATTEMPT: "THIS WAS A METHOD USED BY GENERAL WALKER TO GAIN ADDITIONAL PUBLICITY." IF AN ALLEGED COMMUNIST COULD BE TIED TO THE ATTEMPT TO SHOOT WALKER, IT WOULD SUPPORT LATER THE FAR RIGHT'S CONTENTIION THAT THE COMMUNIST PARTY WAS INSTRUMENTAL IN FURTHERING

THE CAUSE OF CIVIL RIGHTS, THE VERY RIGHTS THE SOUTHERN SEGREGATIONISTS OPPOSSED. TWO DAYS AFTER THE ASSASSINATION, WALKER STATED TO A GERMAN REPORTER THAT HE THOUGHT **HARVEY** HAD TAKEN THE SHOT ON APRIL 10TH. THE ONLY WAY HE COULD HAVE MADE A STATEMENT LIKE THIS ONLY 48 HOURS AFTER THE ASSASSINATION WAS IF HE HIMSELF HAD BEEN INVOLVED IN THE SO CALLED ATTEMPT ON HIS LIFE. WHEN ASKED BY THE W.C. IF HE HAD INDEED MADE THIS STATEMENT ONLY 2 DAYS AFTER THE PRESIDENT WAS SHOT HE DENIED IT.

THIS SHOOTING, **IF** IT COULD BE ATTRIBUTED TO **HARVEY**, WOULD HOWEVER AIDE THE SET-UP CONSPIRATORS IN THEIR EFFORT TO SHOW THAT HE HAD NOT ONLY A PROPENSITY FOR VIOLENCE, BUT WOUD RESORT TO VIOLENCE FOR POLITICAL REASONS **PRIOR** TO THE SHOOTING OF JFK AND OFFICER TIPPIT.

APRIL 10TH 1963

MARINA WOULD LATER CLAIM TO HAVE FOUND A LETTER, WRITTEN IN RUSSIAN, ON OR ABOUT THIS DATE.

*SS AGENT KUNKEL WOULD LATER NOTE THAT HE DID NOT RECEIVE THE LETTER FROM THE IRVING POLICE UNTIL DECEMBER 2ND, 1963. THE IRVING POLICE HAD SEARCHED THE PAINE RESIDENCE ON NOVEMBER 22ND. THE SS THEN CALLED THE PAINE RESIDENCE TO DISCUSS THE NOTE WITH MARINA. SHE DENIED ANY KNOWLEDGE OF THE INCRIMINATING NOTE. BUT, THE NEXT DAY, DECEMBER 3RD, SHE NOT ONLY RECALLED THE LETTER BUT CLAIMED IT WAS WRITTEN BY **HARVEY** PRIOR TO HIS ATTEMPT TO SHOOT GENERAL WALKER.*

THE LETTER READS AS FOLLOWS:

"THIS IS THE KEY TO THE MAILBOX WHICH IS LOCATED IN THE MAIN POST OFFICE IN THE CITY ON ERVAY STREET. THIS IS THE SAME STREET WHERE THE DRUGSTORE, IN WHICH YOU ALWAYS WAITED, IS LOCATED. YOU WILL FIND THE MAILBOX IN THE POST OFFICE WHICH IS LOCATED 4 BLOCKS FROM THE DRUGSTORE ON THAT STREET. I PAID FOR THE BOX LAST MONTH SO DON'T WORRY ABOUT IT.

SEND THE INFORMATION AS TO WHAT HAPPENED TO ME TO THE EMBASSY AND INCLUDE NEWSPAPER CLIPPINGS (SHOULD THERE BE ANYTHING ABOUT ME IN THE NEWSPAPERS.) I BELIEVE THE EMBASSY WILL COME QUICKLY TO YOUR ASSISTANCE ON LEARNING EVERYTHING.

I PAID THE HOUSE RENT ON THE 2ND SO DON'T WORRY ABOUT IT.
I RECENTLY ALSO PAID FOR WATER AND GAS.

THE MONEY FROM WORK WILL POSSIBLY BE COMING. THE MONEY WILL BE SENT TO OUR POST OFFICE BOX. GO TO THE BANK AND CASH THE CHECK.

YOU CAN EITHER THROW OUT OR GIVE MY CLOTHING, ETC., AWAY. DO NOT KEEP THESE. HOWEVER, I PREFER THAT YOU HOLD ON TO MY PERSONAL PAPERS (MILITARY, CIVIL, ETC.)

CERTAIN OF MY DOCUMENTS ARE IN THE SMALL BLUE VALISE.

THE ADDRESS BOOK CAN BE FOUND ON MY TABLE IN THE STUDY SHOULD YOU NEED SAME.

WE HAVE FRIENDS HERE. THE RED CROSS ALSO WILL HELP YOU.
I LEFT YOU AS MUCH MONEY AS I COULD, $60....YOU AND (JUNE) CAN LIVE FOR ANOTHER 2 MONTHS USING $10 PER WEEK.

IF I AM ALIVE AND TAKEN PRISONER, THE CITY JAIL IS LOCATED AT THE END OF THE BRIDGE THROUGH WHICH WE ALWAYS PASSED ON GOING TO THE CITY...."

*IF THIS LETTER IS INDEED **HARVEY'S** PREPARATION FOR HIS POSSIBLE CAPTURE AFTER THE WALKER SHOOTING, WHY WOULD HE NOT SIMPLY KEEP THE LETTER ON HIS PERSON AND GIVE IT TO MARINA AT THE JAIL? IF HE ISN'T CAPTURED, THERE IS NO REASON TO LEAVE FOR HER WHAT WOULD BE CONSIDERED A VERY INCRIMINATING LETTER. ONE CANNOT HELP BUT TO CONSIDER THE VERY REAL POSSIBILITY THAT THE LETTER WAS A PLANT. IF **HARVEY** COULDN'T BE TIED TO THE WALKER SHOOTING BALISTICALLY, HE COULD AT LEAST BE CIRCUMSTANTIALLY TIED TO THE SHOOTING BY THE LETTER AFTER HIS ARREST ON NOVEMBER 22ND.*

*INDEED THE WARREN COMMISSION CHOSE TO USE THE WALKER SHOOTING AS AN INDICATION THAT **HARVEY** HAD A PROPENSITY FOR VIOLENCE. IT IS INTERESTING TO NOTE THAT THE LETTER IS VERY GENERIC. IT WAS NEITHER DATED OR SIGNED. IT DOES NOT SAY WHAT CRIMES HE HAS COMITTED TO WARRANT HIS ARREST. I AM MUCH MORE INCLINED TO BELIEVE THAT THE LETTER WAS WRITTEN AND/OR DISCOVERED MUCH LATER THAN MARINA SUGGESTS.*

***HARVEY** APPARENTLY DID NOT INQUIRE ABOUT THE INCRIMINATING LETTER UPON HIS RETURN HOME THAT EVENING. MARINA CLAIMS TO HAVE HIDDEN THE NOTE IN A COOKBOOK. THE LETTER WAS LATER FOUND, ON DECEMBER 2ND, 1963 INSIDE OF ONE OF TWO RUSSIAN BOOKS GIVEN TO THE SECRET SERVICE BY IRVING POLICE. THEY HAD IN TURN GOTTEN THE BOOKS FROM RUTH PAINE.*

APRIL 10TH 1963

ACCORDING TO ARMSTRONG, JACK RUBY PLACES A CALL TO CLARENCE RECTOR, AN AUTOMOBILE TRANSPORTER IN SULPHUR SPRINGS, TEXAS. ON APRIL 17TH, THE DALLAS POLICE SOLD PATROL CAR #107 TO USED CAR DEALER ELVIS BLOUNT IN SULPHUR SPRINGS. RECTOR WOULD DELIVER THE CAR FROM DALLAS TO SULPHUR SPRINGS. LATER, EARLENE ROBERTS WILL IDENTIFY SQUAD CAR 107 AS THE CAR THAT BRIEFLY STOPPED AND SOUNDED THE HORN OUTSIDE HER ROOMING HOUSE AT APPROXIMATELY 1:00 PM ON NOVEMBER 22ND WHILE **HARVEY** CHANGED HIS CLOTHES.

APRIL 11TH 1963

ACCORDING TO ARMSTRONG, A ROBERT PRICE VISITS THE ESCAPADE LOUNGE IN HOUSTON. HIS WIFE DOLORES WORKED THERE AS A MANAGER. AFTER LUNCH JACK RUBY ARRIVES WITH THREE COMPANIONS. RUBY INTRODUCES ONE OF THE MEN TO PRICE AS **LEE** HARVEY OSWALD. RUBY AND HIS FRIENDS NOTED THAT THEY WERE "KILLING TIME" AS THEY AWAITED A PLANE TO TAKE THEM TO CUBA.

APRIL 11TH 1963

WHILE **LEE** IS IN HOUSTON WITH RUBY, **HARVEY** FILES FOR UNEMPLOYMENT PAY WITH THE TEXAS UNEMPLOYMENT COMMISSION IN DALLAS.

APRIL 13TH 1963

GEORGE DE MOHRENSCHILDT VISITS **HARVEY**. HE INQUIRES IF HE WAS INDEED INVOLVED IN THE ATTEMPT ON GENERAL WALKER. **HARVEY** DENIED HAVING BEEN THE SHOOTER.

APRIL 16TH 1963

HARVEY WRITES THE COMMUNIST, PRO-CASTRO FPFC COMMITTEE CLAIMING HE HAD BEEN SEEN HANDING OUT PAMPHLETS ON APRIL 5TH IN DALLAS WHILE WEARING A PLACARD AROUND HIS NECK READING "HANDS OFF CUBA –VIVA FIDEL." HE ALSO REQUESTS THAT HE BE SENT FPFC PAMPHLETS.

*THIS ACTIVITY, IF INDEED PROMPTED BY SET-UP CONSPIRATORS E.H. HUNT OR DAVID ATLEE PHILLIPS, WHO WE WILL SOON INTRODUCE IN DETAIL, WOULD LIKELY BE PERCEIVED BY **HARVEY** AS A LOGICAL EXTENSION OF HIS COMMUNIST "DEFECTOR" PERSONA THAT HAD BEEN EARLIER CREATED FOR HIM BY THE ONI/CIA IN ORDER TO SET THE STAGE FOR HIS PREVIOUS LEGITIMATE INTELLIGENCE MISSION TO RUSSIA.*

*ALTHOUGH THIS WOULD APPEAR TO BE HIS <u>FIRST</u> INVOLVEMENT WITH THE FPFC COMMITTEE, **HARVEY**, DURING HIS INTERROGATION SESSIONS ON THE WEEKEND OF 22 NOVEMBER, WOULD STATE THAT HE HAD NO INTEREST IN THE FPFC <u>UNTIL</u> HE REACHED NEW ORLEANS. INDEED HE WILL NOT BE ASKED BY GUY BANISTER TO FORM A NEW ORLEANS FPFC CHAPTER UNTIL MAY 26TH, 1963. HAD **HARVEY** SIMPLY FORGOTTEN ABOUT THIS CONTACT WITH THE FPFC <u>PRIOR</u> TO HIS DEPARTURE FOR NEW ORLEANS 8 DAYS LATER OR HAD THE SET-UP CONSPIRATORS WANTED TO ESTABLISH A LINK BETWEEN **HARVEY** AND THE FPFC IN <u>BOTH</u> DALLAS AND NEW ORLEANS? REGARDLESS, IN 8 DAYS **HARVEY** WOULD DEPART FOR NEW ORLEANS AND HIS RELATIONSHIP WITH THE FPFC WOULD BEGIN IN EARNEST.*

APRIL 16TH 1963
HARVEY'S UNEMPLOYMENT CLAIM IS REJECTED.

APRIL 19TH 1963
GEORGE DE MOHRENSCHILDT AND HIS WIFE JEANNE DRIVE TO NEW YORK, PHILADELPHIA, AND WASHINGTON, D.C.

APRIL 19TH 1963
THE N.Y. FPFC OFFICE MAILS THE REQUESTED PAMPHLETS, "THE CRIME AGAINST CUBA" BY CORLISS LAMONT TO **HARVEY**.

APRIL 20TH, 1963
JUDYTH VARY (NOT YET MARRIED TO ROBERT ALLISON BAKER III) ARRIVES IN NEW ORLEANS. SHE WILL STAY AT THE YWCA ON CLAIBORN AVENUE. VARY WAS A NATIONALLY PROCLAIMED HIGH SCHOOL SCIENCE STUDENT FROM BRADENTON, FLORIDA. HER ABILITIES ATTRACTED THE ATTENTION OF DR. ALTON OCHSNER WHO ARRANGED FOR HER TO DO A 1961 SUMMER INTERNSHIP AT THE ROSWELL PARK MEMORIAL INSTITUTE FOR CANCER RESEARCH IN BUFFALO, NEW YORK. AS A STUDENT AT ST. FRANCIS COLLEGE IN INDIANA, HER INTEREST REMAINED CANCER RESEARCH. SHE HAD ALREADY SUCCESSFULLY CONDUCTED EXPERIMENTS INDUCING CANCER BOTH IN FISH AND MICE AND NOW CONTINUED DEVELOPING MORE AGGRESSIVE HUMAN MELANOMAS, A TASK BEGUN DURING HER STINT AT THE ROSWELL INSTITUTE.

THIS PROJECT WOULD MARK A DRAMATIC DEPARTURE FROM HER EARLIER RESEARCH WITH FISH AND MICE. IN 1962, SHE ENROLLED AT THE UNIVERSITY OF FLORIDA. HER PARENTS HAD FORCIBLY REMOVED HER FROM ST. FRANCIS FEARING SHE WOULD FOLLOW THROUGH ON HER NOTION OF BECOMING A NUN. SHE WAS THEN INVITED TO NEW ORLEANS BY DR. OCHSNER. DR. OCHSNER HAD LURED HER TO NEW ORLEANS WITH THE PROMISE THAT AFTER WORKING AT HIS CLINIC HE COULD VIRTUALLY ASSURE HER ADMISSION TO MEDICAL SCHOOL AT TULANE. DR. OCHSNER, A KNOWN ANTI-COMMUNIST, WAS THE FOUNDER OF AND A KEY SUPPORTER OF THE INFORMATION COUNCIL OF THE AMERICAS WHICH HE FOUNDED IN 1961 AS A RESULT OF THE FAILED BAY OF PIGS OPERATION. HE SERVED AS BOTH THE CHAIRMAN AND THE PRESIDENT OF INCA.

THE EXTENT OF HIS ANTI-CASTRO SENTIMENTS ARE BLATANTLY DEMONSTRATED IN A FILM PROJECT UNDERTAKEN BY INCA TITLED "HITLER IN HAVANA." THE COUNCIL WAS AN ANTI-COMMUNIST PROPAGANDA ORGANIZATION. DR. OCHSNER SERVED ON MANY BOARDS OF DIRECTORS IN NEW ORLEANS WITH ANOTHER PROMINENT CIVIC LEADER CLAY SHAW. DR. OCHSNER WAS BOTH THE FOUNDER AND DIRECTOR OF THE OCHSNER CLINIC IN NEW ORLEANS.

*OCHSNER COUNTED AS HIS MORE FERVENT SUPPORTERS, WILLIAM B. REILY OF THE REILY COFFEE COMPANY AND BILL MONAGHAN, V.P. OF FINANCE AT STANDARD COFFEE. IT IS REILY COFFEE WHERE **HARVEY** WILL OBTAIN EMPLOYMENT IN NEW ORLEANS. OCHSNER ALSO OFFERED FINANCIAL SUPPORT TO ED BUTLER WHO WILL ENGAGE **HARVEY** IN A RADIO DEBATE WITH CARLOS BRINGUIER IN AUGUST 1963. THERE IS INDEED BOTH A*

*PHILOSOPHICAL AND FINANCIAL THREAD THAT CONNECTS THOSE WHO INTERACT EITHER DIRECTLY OR INDIRECTLY WITH **HARVEY** IN NEW ORLEANS. BANISTER, FERRIE, REILY, MONAGHAN, BUTLER, BRINGUIER, SHAW AND OCHSNER ARE ALL FERVENT ANTI-COMMUNIST. HOWEVER OCHSNER, REILY, MONAGHAN AND SHAW ARE LIKELY THE ONLY MEMBERS OF THE GROUP WHO COULD OFFER FINANCIAL ASSISTANCE TO AN ANTI-COMMUNIST CAUSE.*

APRIL 23RD 1963

LBJ ANNOUNCES JFK'S TRIP TO DALLAS. THE DALLAS TIMES HERALD NOTES LBJ'S ANNOUNCEMENT. **HARVEY** DEPARTS DALLAS FOR NEW ORLEANS. RUTH PAINE DRIVES HIM TO THE BUS STATION. MARINA AND JUNE WILL RETURN WITH MRS. PAINE TO THE PAINE'S RESIDENCE.

CHAPTER 6: LEGITIMATE ASSOCIATES OR SET-UP CONSPIRATORS?

BEFORE WE CONTINUE THE TIMELINE, LET US SET THE STAGE AND BOTH IDENTIFY AND FURTHER ELABORATE UPON THOSE WHO I FEEL WOULD PLAY MAJOR ROLES IN MANIPULATING **HARVEY** OVER THE NEXT 7 MONTHS. I HAVE CHOSEN THIS POINT IN THE TIMELINE TO DO SO SINCE THE MORE OVERT MANIPULATION OF **HARVEY** BEGINS WITH HIS ARRIVAL IN NEW ORLEANS. IN THE NEXT CHAPTER I WILL OUTLINE 2 SCENARIOS FOR **HARVEY**. IN SCENARIO I, THE SOON TO BE INTRODUCED PARTICIPANTS AND THEIR INVOLVEMENT WITH **HARVEY** IS, TO A DEGREE, LEGITIMATE AND IN LINE WITH THE ANTI-CASTRO EFFORTS OF THE TIME. IN SCENARIO II HOWEVER, SOME OF THE MAJOR PARTICIPANTS INVOLVED WITH **HARVEY** HAVE A MORE SINISTER MOTIVE. OTHERS UNWITTINGLY FALL PREY TO THE SAME MISCONCEPTIONS AS **HARVEY**. IS **HARVEY** BEING SET-UP FOR WHAT WILL TAKE PLACE ON NOVEMBER 22ND? IF SO, KEEP IN MIND THAT IN A CONSPIRACY OF THIS MAGNITUDE IT WOULD BE IMPERATIVE TO COMPARTMENTALIZE INDIVIDUAL ASPECTS OF THE OVERALL PLAN. WE WILL ONLY DEAL WITH THOSE ASPECTS AND THOSE INDIVIDUALS LIKELY RESPONSIBLE FOR KNOWINGLY GUIDING **HARVEY** TOWARD HIS ULTIMATE, UNFORTUNATE FATE, AND THOSE WHO WERE UNWITTINGLY USED IN THIS SAME EFFORT. THE "CHARACTERS" IN BOTH SCENARIOS REMAIN THE SAME. WHAT DIFFERS IS WHETHER THEIR INVOLVEMENT WITH **HARVEY** IS LEGITIMATE OR SOLELY FOR THE PURPOSE OF CREATING THE PERFECT PATSY FOR WHAT IS TO TAKE PLACE ON NOVEMBER 22ND. IN THE MURKY WORLD OF THE INTELLIGENCE COMMUNITY, THE LINES BLUR TO A DEGREE THAT THE PARTICIPANTS THESELVES MAY NOT HAVE KNOWN THEIR TRUE ROLE.

IT IS IMPORTANT HOWEVER TO MAKE A DISTINCTION BETWEEN THESE TWO GROUPS; THOSE WHO PARTICIPATED IN THE SET-UP OF **HARVEY** BUT DID NOT REALIZE THAT HE WOULD ULTIMATELY BE WRONGLY CHARGED WITH THE PRESIDENT'S DEATH, AND THOSE WHO PARTICIPATED IN THE SET-UP OF **HARVEY** KNOWING FULLY WELL THAT ON NOVEMBER 22ND **HARVEY** WOULD BE SUSPECT ONE.

LET US FIRST DISCUSS THOSE AWARE OF **HARVEY'S** PRESENCE IN NEW ORLEANS; CARLOS MARCELLO AND CLAY SHAW. WE WILL THEN INTRODUCE THOSE MORE PERSONALLY INVOLVED WITH **HARVEY** IN NEW ORLEANS; GUY BANISTER, AND DAVID FERRIE

NOTE: RATHER THAN INTRODUCE EACH PARTICIPANT IN SCENARIO I WHERE THEIR INVOLVEMENT WITH **HARVEY** IS THOUGHT TO BE LEGITIMATE AND THEN RE-INTRODUCE THEM IN SCENARIO II WHERE THEIR INVOLVEMENT WITH **HARVEY** IS SOLELY FOR THE PURPOSE OF ANNOINTING HIM AS THE PRESIDENTIAL ASSASSIN, I HAVE CHOSEN TO INTRODUCE THEM PRIOR TO **HARVEY'S** DEPARTURE FOR NEW ORLEANS. I WILL HOWEVER OUTLINE THEIR INVOLVEMENT IN RESPECT TO EACH SCENARIO AS WE DETAIL THEM INDIVIDUALLY IN FURTHER CHAPTERS.

CARLOS MARCELLO

IT IS HIGHLY LIKELY IF NOT A CERTAINTY THAT CARLOS MARCELLO WAS AWARE OF THE FACT THAT THERE WAS INDEED A MOVEMENT UNDERWAY TO ASSASSINATE JFK SOMEWHERE (CHICAGO, TAMPA, OR DALLAS) THAT FALL IN 1963. IN FACT MANY RESEARCHERS FIRMLY BELIEVE THAT THE ACTUAL SHOOTERS WERE CONTRACTED BY MARCELLO. ALSO, MARCELLO WOULD, VIA DAVID FERRIE BE AWARE OF **HARVEY** AND HIS SUMMER OF 1963 POSTURING IN NEW ORLEANS. THE SET-UP CONSPIRATORS WOULD WITHOUT DOUBT FIND SOMEONE TO TAKE THE FALL FOR THE PRESIDENT'S DEATH. MARCELLO, SANTOS TRAFFICANTE, AND JOHNNY ROSELLI NOT ONLY NEEDED A "PATSY", THEY NEEDED A *PERFECT* PATSY; ONE CAPABLE OF DRAWING ATTENTION TO GROUPS OTHER THAN ORGANIZED CRIME WHICH INDEED HAD AMPLE MOTIVE TO REMOVE THE PRESIDENT. THE CHOICE OF **HARVEY** AS THE INDIVIDUAL

WHO WOULD LATER BE PORTRAYED AS THE ASSASSIN WAS NOT HOWEVER LIKELY MADE BY THOSE PLANNING THE ACTUAL ASSASSINATION. THE CHOICE OF **HARVEY** WOULD HAVE BEEN MADE BY SOMEONE WITH AN INTELLIGENCE BACKGROUND WHO WOULD HAVE BEEN KNOWLEDGABLE OF **HARVEY'S** PAST CIA/ONI ASSOCIATION. CONSIDERING THE RELATIONSHIP THE CIA HAD ESTABLISHED WITH ORGANIZED CRIME IN REGARDS TO ASSISTANCE IN KILLING CASTRO, IT IS HIGHLY LIKELY THAT MARCELLO WOULD BE AWARE OF THE CARCINOGEN PROJECT DESIGNED TO ELIMINATE CASTRO. HIS "PIPELINE" REGARDING ONGOING EFFORTS BY THE CIA UP TO AND INCLUDING THE PLANNED DECEMBER 1963 C-DAY COUP WOULD HAVE BEEN HIS CLOSE FRIEND DAVID MORALES WHO RAN THE HUGE MIAMI CIA STATION.

CLAY SHAW

CLAY SHAW'S TIES TO THE INTELLIGENCE COMMUNITY DATE TO THE EARLY 1940'S. IN 1941 HE FOUND HIMSELF WITH THE U.S. ARMY WHERE HE WORKED FOR THE OSS AS A LIASON TO CHURCHILL. HE RETIRED FROM THE MILITARY IN 1946.

IN NEW ORLEANS SHAW JOINED A CIA PROPRIETARY COMPANY, THE MISSISSIPPI SHIPPING COMPANY. FROM MARCH 1946 TO SEPTEMBER 1965 HE WAS ASSOCIATED WITH THE INTERNATIONAL TRADE MART IN NEW ORLEANS WHERE HE EVENTUALLY WAS NAMED MANAGING DIRECTOR. THE TRADE MART WAS RUN BY A CIA OPERATIVE. FROM 1948 TO 1956, SHAW WAS A CIA CONTRACT AGENT IN THE DOMESTIC CONTACT SERVICE. HE FILED 30 REPORTS ON TRADE AND POLITICAL ACTIVITIES TO THE CIA. A REPORT WAS FILED BY SHAW REGARDING A 1949 MARCH THROUGH MAY TRIP THROUGH THE WEST INDIES, CENTRAL AMERICA, AND NORTHERN SOUTH AMERICA. HE ALSO REPORTED ON HIS JUNE 1957 TRIP TO SOUTH AND CENTRAL AMERICA AND THE CARIBBEAN.

IN 1952, SHAW AND THE CIA'S HOWARD HUNT WERE GIVEN CLEARANCE FOR A CIA PROJECT CODE-NAMED "QKEN CHANT." THIS PROJECT ALLOWED THE CIA TO RECRUIT CIVILIANS FOR FUTURE ACTIVITIES AND RELATIONSHIPS. WITHIN THIS PROGRAM SHAW RECRUITED GUY BANISTER IN AUGUST OF 1960.

IN 1959 SHAW WAS FLOWN BY DAVID FERRIE TO CUBA. SHAW WAS TO INVESTIGATE THE POSSIBILITY OF PROCESSING CUBAN NICKEL ORE AT FREEPORT SULPHUR, A CIA PROPRIETARY MINING OPERATION IN LOUISIANA. DAVID ATLEE PHILLIPS WAS ALSO INVOLVED IN THE FREEPORT SULPHUR PROJECT.

THE CENTRO MONDIALE COMMERCIALE, A CIA BACKED ORGANIZATION, WAS FORMED IN MONTREAL. IN 1961 IT MOVED ITS HEADQUARTERS TO ROME. SHAW WAS ON THE BOARD OF DIRECTORS. THE CMC HAS BEEN DESCRIBED AS A FRONT FOR RIGHT WING EXTREMISTS IN EUROPE.

AS LATE AS 1969, SHAW APPARENTLY REMAINED AN OPERATIVE IN THE CIA'S DOMESTIC OPERATIONS DIVISION. HIS SECURITY CLEARANCE WAS AT THE HIGHEST OF THE CIA'S 6 LEVELS. SHAW WAS A KNOWN ASSOCIATE OF DAVID ATLEE PHILLIPS, GUY BANISTER AND DAVID FERRIE. HE WAS ALSO FAMILIAR WITH **HARVEY** VIA BANISTER AND FERRIE.

SHAW, LIKE MARCELLO, WOULD ALSO LIKELY BE AWARE OF THE ASSASSINATION PLOT AGAINST JFK THAT PARTICULAR FALL. SHAW HOWEVER, UNLIKE CARLOS MARCELLO, MAY NOT BE AWARE OF THE SERIOUSNESS AND LIKLIHOOD OF THE EVENT ACTUALLY TAKING PLACE. SHAW WAS INDEED AWARE THAT **HARVEY** WAS BEING "MENTORED" IN NEW ORLEANS BY GUY BANISTER. BUTTHERE IS NO CERTAINTY THAT HE WAS PRIVY TO THE EVENTUAL OUTCOME OF THIS "MENTORING" BY BANISTER. SHAW WILL BE ARRESTED ON MARCH 1ST, 1967 BY JIM GARRISON EXACTLY 1 WEEK AFTER THE DEATH OF DAVID FERRIE. HE WILL BE CHARGED WITH CONSPIRACY TO COMMIT MURDER IN CONNECTION WITH THE ASSASSINATION OF THE PRESIDENT.

SHAW DIED ON AUGUST 15TH, 1974. HIS LAWYER, EDWARD WEGMAN, WAS TO BE CONTACTED IMMEDIATELY UPON SHAW'S DEATH. WEGMAN, RATHER THAN CALLING THE POLICE, CALLED A FUNERAL HOME. EMPLOYEES OF THE FUNERAL HOME ARRIVED PROMPTLY AND TOOK THE BODY OF SHAW TO THEIR FACILITY WHERE THEY PROCEEDED WITH THE EMBALMING PROCESS. THE EXACT CAUSE OF SHAW'S DEATH COULD NOT BE DETERMINED DUE TO THE EMBALMING.

GUY BANISTER

GUY BANISTER JOINED THE FBI IN 1934. IT HAS BEEN REPORTED THAT IN WORLD WAR II HE WAS A NAVAL INTELLIGENCE AGENT. IF SO, AFTER THE WAR HE EITHER RETURNED TO OR SIMPLY CONTINUED HIS FBI CAREER. OTHER RESEARCHERS HAVE NOTED THAT HE WAS EXEMPT FROM A MILITARY CALL-UP DURING THE WAR DUE TO HIS FBI STATUS. HE WAS CHIEF OF THE CHICAGO BRANCH OF THE FBI. HE RETIRED FROM THE FBI IN 1954. THAT SAME YEAR, HE BECAME INVOLVED IN THE CREATION OF THE ANTI-COMMUNIST LEAGUE OF THE CARIBBEAN. IT IS LIKELY THAT IT WAS HIS INVOLVEMENT WITH THIS ORGANIZATION THAT WOULD LEAD HIM TO HIS FIRST MEETINGS WITH FUTURE SET-UP CONSPIRATORS HUNT AND PHILLIPS. THE ACLC WAS INSTRUMENTAL IN ASSISTING HUNT AND PHILLIPS IN THEIR SUCCESSFUL 1954 OVERTHROW OF GUATAMALAN DICTATOR ARBENZ.

IN 1955 BANISTER BECAME SECOND IN COMMAND IN THE NEW ORLEANS POLICE DEPARTMENT. IN 1957 HE WAS RELEASED FROM THE NOPD DUE TO A DRUNKEN INCIDENT WITH A BARTENDER AT THE ABSINTHE HOUSE BAR. HE THEN STARTED A DETECTIVE AGENCY, "GUY BANISTER AND ASSOCIATES." HIS "DETECTIVE AGENCY" PROVIDED COVER FOR HIS CONTRACT WORK FOR THE FBI/CIA; MOST NOTABLY THE INFILTRATION OF PRO-CASTRO GROUPS AND THE SUPPORT OF ANTI-CASTRO GROUPS. BANISTER ALSO BELONGED TO THE JOHN BIRCH SOCIETY AND THE MINUTEMEN. HE ALSO PUBLISHED THE LOUISIANA INTELLIGENCE DIGEST, A RIGHT WING PERIODICAL. IN BANISTER'S MIND, AS WELL AS THOSE IN THE MINUTEMEN AND THE JOHN BIRCH SOCIETY, THERE WAS LITTLE OR NO DISTINCTION BETWEEN THOSE GROUPS SUPPORTING CIVIL RIGHTS AND INTEGRATION AND MEMBERS OF THE COMMUNIST PARTY. THIS WAS A PHILOSOPHY SHARED VEHEMENTLY BY BANISTER'S SECRETARY, DELPHINE ROBERTS.

ALTHOUGH BANISTER WAS DEEPLY INVOLVED WITH THE ANTI-CASTRO GROUPS IN NEW ORLEANS, HE WAS ALSO VERY MUCH INVOLVED IN THE PROCESS OF INFILTRATING LEFT-WING COLLEGE GROUPS. GEORGE HIGGENBOTHAM, BILL MITSCHE, AND SAMMY BAUMLER ALL CONFIRMED THE FACT THAT **HARVEY** WORKED FOR BANISTER. IN FACT, HIGGENBOTHAM WOULD LATER RELATE TO BANISTER HIS WITNESSING OF 3 MEN PASSING OUT PRO-CASTRO PAMPHLETS. BANISTER'S REPLY: "COOL IT. ONE OF THEM IS ONE OF MINE." ONE OF THE 3 MEN WAS **HARVEY**.

HARVEY HAD ALSO INFILTRATED THE NEW ORLEANS COMMITTEE FOR PEACEFUL ALTERNATIVES (NOCPA). THIS LEFT-WING GROUP WAS ESSENTIALLY A "BAN THE BOMB" ORGANIZATION. WITH BANISTER'S ASSISTANCE, **HARVEY** WOULD, IN HIS BRIEF NEW ORLEANS STAY, INFILTRATE/JOIN 4 ORGANIZATIONS SUPPORTING THE CIVIL RIGHTS/INTEGRATION MOVEMENT: THE FPFC, THE CONGRESS OF RACIAL EQUALITY, (CORE), THE NOCPA, AND THE ACLU. IT WAS BANISTERS INTENTION TO TAINT EACH OF THOSE GROUPS WITH AN "ALLEGED" COMMUNIST, **HARVEY**. IF SUCCESSFUL, HE COULD EFFECTIVELY UNDERMINE THE FUTURE SUCCESS AND CREDIBILITY OF THESE GROUPS BY ASSOCIATING THEM WITH COMMUNISM.

ALLEN AND DANIEL CAMPBELL WERE BROTHERS AND FORMER MARINES. THEY WERE RECRUITED BY BANISTER DURING THE SUMMER OF 1963 TO INFILTRATE PRO-CASTRO STUDENT GROUPS AT TULANE UNIVERSITY IN NEW ORLEANS. THEY ALSO PROVIDED TRAINING IN SMALL ARMS FOR CUBAN EXILES AT THE LOCAL EXILE TRAINING CAMPS.

THE CAMPBELLS' NOTED THAT WHEN BANISTER HEARD ABOUT **HARVEY'S** PRO-CASTRO POSTURING IN NEW ORLEANS HE JUST LAUGHED.

BANISTER'S NEW ORLEANS OFFICE WAS LOCATED AT 531 LAFAYETTE IN THE NEWMAN BUILDING. THE OTHER ENTRANCE TO THE BUILDING WAS AROUND THE CORNER AT 544 CAMP STREET. DELPHINE ROBERTS, BANISTER'S SECRETARY, NOTED THAT **HARVEY** SIMPLY WALKED IN ONE DAY IN MAY OF 1963 AND ASKED TO FILL OUT A FORM FOR ACCREDITATION AS ONE OF BANISTER'S AGENTS. NOTED OTHER AGENTS OR ASSOCIATES OF BANISTERS WERE DAVID FERRIE, CLAY SHAW, DAVID LEWIS, AND JACK MARTIN.

IN A LATER INTERVIEW ROBERTS NOTED:"I GAINED THE IMPRESSION THAT HE (**HARVEY**) AND GUY BANISTER ALREADY KNEW EACH OTHER. I PRESUMED THEN AND NOW AM CERTAIN THAT THE REASON FOR OSWALD (**HARVEY**) BEING THERE WAS THAT HE WAS REQUIRED TO ACT UNDER COVER." LATER, WHEN ROBERTS SPOTTED **HARVEY** PASSING OUT HIS FPFC LITERATURE SHE ASKED BANISTER ABOUT IT. HIS REPLY: "HE'S WITH US. HE'S ASSOCIATED WITH THE OFFICE."

ROBERT'S DAUGHTER USED A ROOM UPSTAIRS AT 544 CAMP ST. FOR PHOTOGRAPHIC WORK. SHE NOTED: "I GOT THE IMPRESSION OSWALD (**HARVEY**) WAS DOING SOMETHING TO MAKE PEOPLE BELIEVE HE WAS SOMETHING HE WASN'T....I AM SURE GUY BANISTER KNEW WHAT OSWALD (**HARVEY**) WAS DOING....".

JACK MARTIN HAD HIS OWN HISTORY OF INTELLIGENCE TIES. HIS BUSINESS CARD LISTED JOSEPH NEWBROUGH AND WILLIAM DALZELL AS PARTNERS. NEWBROUGH WAS A MEMBER OF THE CIA'S DOMESTIC CONTACT SERVICE. DALZELL HAD JOINED THE CIA IN THE EARLY 1950'S. MARTIN HIMSELF HAD JOINED THE CIA IN 1950 AND "RETIRED" IN 1958.

BANISTER LIKELY SUSPECTED THAT **HARVEY** MAY HAVE BEEN SERVING THE FBI AS AN INFORMANT DURING HIS STAY IN NEW ORLEANS. **HARVEY** COULD MONITOR BANISTER'S CIA-SANCTIONED GROUP AND REPORT ON HIS ANTI-CASTRO GUN DEALINGS TO THE LOCAL FBI AND CONSEQUENTLY THE FBI HQ IN WASHINGTON. THIS FBI SPONSORED MONITORING BY **HARVEY** WOULD MAKE ENLISTING BANISTER'S HELP IN THE SET-UP OF **HARVEY** A RELATIVELY EASY TASK FOR HUNT AND PHILLIPS AS IT WOULD BE THE FBI WHO WOULD TRY TO DISRUPT BANISTER'S CIA-SANCTIONED ANTI-CASTRO EFFORTS. BANISTER'S ROLE WOULD BE TWO-FOLD; TO STRENGTHEN AND PUBLICIZE **HARVEY'S** "PRO-CASTRO" POSTURING FOR HUNT/PHILLIPS, AND TO IMMERSE **HARVEY** IN THE INITIAL STAGES OF A BOGUS "ASSIGNMENT" THAT WILL BE USED TO MANIPULATE **HARVEY** ON NOVEMBER 22ND, 1963.

BANISTER HOWEVER WILL ALSO EMBARK ON A MANIPULATION OF **HARVEY** THAT PERHAPS SERVES EXCLUSIVELY THE PURPOSES OF THE JOHN BIRCH SOCIETY AND THE MINUTEMEN: TO TAINT THE LEFT-LEANING, PRO-INTEGRATION GROUPS FPFC, CORE, NOCPA, AND THE ACLU.

IN NEW ORLEANS, IT IS BANISTER WHO WILL ASSOCIATE **HARVEY** WITH BOTH THE "PRO-CASTRO" AND "ANTI-CASTRO" FACTIONS. BANISTER WAS INDEED AWARE THAT HE WAS INSTRUMENTAL IN "SHEEP-DIPPING" **HARVEY**, PARTICULARLY IN REGARD TO THE "CARCINOGENS" PROJECT. BANISTER'S PART IN THE SET-UP WOULD BE TO HELP CONVINCE **HARVEY** THAT THE "CARCINOGENS TO CUBA" EFFORT WAS A LEGITIMATE CIA PROJECT AND TO STRENGTHEN **HARVEY'S** "PRO-CASTRO" PROFILE IN NEW ORLEANS. I WOULD SUSPECT THAT BANISTER WAS AWARE OF THE PLANS TO ASSASSINATE JFK THAT FALL. I ALSO SUSPECT THAT HE UNDERSTOOD THAT **HARVEY** EITHER WOULD OR COULD BE ANNOINTED AS THE PRESIDENTIAL ASSASSIN IF THE HIT TOOK PLACE IN DALLAS. WE WILL REVISIT BANISTER'S UTILIZATION OF **HARVEY** IN TAINTING CIVIL RIGHTS GROUPS WHEN WE TAKE A CLOSER LOOK AT ONE OF THE

MOST MYSTERIOUS EPISODES IN **HARVEY'S** NEW ORLEANS STAY; THE INCIDENT IN CLINTON, LOUISIANA.

BANISTER DIED JUNE 6TH, 1964 OF "NATURAL CAUSES." ONE WEEK BEFORE HIS DEATH HE TOLD GUY JOHNSON, ONI CHIEF IN NEW ORLEANS: "IF I'M DEAD IN A WEEK, NO MATTER THE CIRCUMSTANCES, IT WON'T BE FROM NATURAL CAUSES."

JIM GARRISON, IN HIS 1967 INVESTIGATION, INTERVIEWED BANISTER'S WIDOW. SHE NOTED THAT WITHIN HOURS OF HIS DEATH THAT THERE WERE SEVERAL FILE CABINETS TAKEN FROM HIS OFFICE BY FEDERAL AGENTS. INDEX CARDS DESCRIBING THE FILING SYSTEM USED BY BANISTER SHED SOME LIGHT ON HIS INTERESTS. HIS CARDS REFERENCED FILES PERTAINING TO THE CIA, THE INTERNATIONAL TRADE MART, AND THE FPFC COMMITTEE. THE FPFC FILE CARD CONTAINED REFERENCES TO **HARVEY**. GARRISON WAS ABLE TO OBTAIN THE INDEX CARDS FROM THE LOUISIANA STATE POLICE. THERE IS NO REFERENCE TO OR MENTION OF BANISTER IN EITHER THE W.C. REPORT OR THE EVIDENTIARY 26 VOLUMES.

DAVID FERRIE

AFTER A NEARLY FOUR YEAR (1935-1938) ATTEMPT AT COLLEGE AT JOHN CARROLL UNIVERSITY, FERRIE ATTENDED ST. MARY'S SEMINARY IN CLEVELAND IN 1938. A NERVOUS BREAKDOWN HOWEVER TERMINATED HIS ATTEMPT AT THE PRIESTHOOD. HIS NEXT EFFORT WAS TO ATTEND BALDWIN-WALLACE, A TEACHER'S COLLEGE IN 1940. IN 1941, FERRIE, STILL APPARENTLY DETERMINED TO BECOME A PRIEST, ENTERED ST. CHARLES SEMINARY IN OHIO. HE ALSO JOINED THE OHIO CAP. HOWEVER IN 1944, HE WAS DISMISSED FROM ST. CHARLES. FERRIE ALSO TOOK FLYING LESSONS FROM 1942-1945 IN CLEVELAND AT SKY TECH AIRWAY SERVICE. IN 1947 HE JOINED THE CLEVELAND, OHIO SQUADRON OF THE CAP. IN 1949 FERRIE LEFT CLEVELAND AFTER HAVING TAKEN A GROUP OF CAP CADETS TO A HOUSE OF PROSTITUTION. HE WOULD RETURN TO CLEVELAND A FEW MONTHS LATER. IN APRIL 1950, FERRIE JOINED THE ARMY RESERVE. IN 1951, WITH HIS DISMISSAL FROM THE OHIO CAP ALMOST CERTAINLY AS A RESULT OF TRANSGRESSIONS WITH MINORS, FERRIE WAS ABLE TO OBTAIN A TRANSFER TO A LOUISIANA CAP UNIT IN SEPTEMBER OF 1951 WHERE HE MEETS **LEE**.

FERRIE WAS HIRED BY EASTERN AIRLINES IN 1951. HE WAS LATER FIRED IN SEPTEMBER 1961 AFTER BEING CHARGED WITH INDECENT BEHAVIOUR WITH 3 UNDERAGE MALES. EASTERN ALSO CHARGED FERRIE WITH MAKING VIOLENT REMARKS REGARDING PRESIDENT KENNEDY. GUY BANISTER APPEARED AT FERRIE'S HEARING IN MIAMI BEFORE THE AIRLINES REVIEW BOARD. G. WRAY GILL, CARLOS MARCELLO'S ATTORNEY, REPRESENTED FERRIE AT THE HEARING.

FERRIE'S STATUS NOT ONLY MERITED THE LEGAL EXPERTISE OF GILL, BUT ALSO THE INTEREST OF LOUSIANA CONGRESSMEN MORRISON AND LONG. BOTH MEN ATTEMPTED TO EXERT PRESSURE ON EASTERN'S LAWYERS TO FORGO THEIR DESIRE TO TERMINATE FERRIE.

FERRIE HAD TIES TO ORGANIZED CRIME, THE CIA, AND WAS A STRONG SUPPORTER OF ANTI-CASTRO GROUPS. AS A CRACK PILOT, HE HAD FLOWN MANY COVERT MISSIONS INTO CUBA AS A CONTRACT PILOT FOR THE CIA AND THE MANY ANTI-CASTRO GROUPS FOR WHICH THEY PROVIDED FINANCIAL AND LOGISTIC SUPPORT.

IN APRIL 1961, PRIOR TO HIS DISMISSAL BY THE AIRLINE, FERRIE TOOK A 3 WEEK "VACATION" FROM EASTERN AIRLINES. THIS "VACATION" COINCIDED WITH THE BAY OF PIGS INVASION.

ON APRIL 16TH 1961, FERRIE PILOTED A SMALL PLANE TO CUBA IN AN EFFORT TO SAMPLE SOME NEW RADIO SIGNALS EMINATING FROM THE MOUNTAINS IN CUBA. IT

WAS THOUGHT AT THE TIME THAT THE SOVIETS WERE CONSTRUCTING A MISSLE BASE IN CUBA IN RESPONSE TO OUR MISSLES IN TURKEY.

FERRIE'S FERVENT ANTI-COMMUNISM WAS COMBINED WITH AN OPENLY HOMO-SEXUAL LIFESTYLE. IT WAS THIS LIFESTYLE THAT COST HIM POSITIONS IN THE PRIESTHOOD, THE CIVIL AIR PATROL, AND EASTERN AIRLINES. FERRIE'S ANTI-COMMUNIST/ANTI-CASTRO LEANINGS AND OPEN HOMSEXUALITY WERE THE COMMON DENOMINATORS IN REGARDS TO HIS ASSOCIATION WITH CLAY SHAW.

FERRIE'S CIVIL AIR PATROL ACTIVITIES AND HIS RELATIONSHIP WITH **LEE** WAS NOTED BY CAP MEMBERS COLLIN HAMER, JOHN ORION, JOSEPH EHRLICHKER, JERRY PARADIS, GEORGE BOESCH, AND ANTHONY ATZENHOFFER. FERRIE MAINTAINED A DUAL ROLE WHILE IN NEW ORLEANS. HE WORKED UNDER GUY BANISTER STARTING IN FEBRUARY 1962, AND DID SOME PILOTING AND INVESTIGATIVE WORK FOR G.WRAY GILL, CARLOS MARCELLO'S ATTORNEY. INDEED FERRIE WAS IN THE COURT ROOM ON NOVEMBER 22ND 1963 WHILE THE COURTS WERE ATTEMPTING TO DECIDE WHETHER TO DEPORT MARCELLO. IT WOULD BE FERRIE WHO WOULD INTRODUCE **HARVEY** TO BANISTER UPON **HARVEY'S** ARRIVAL IN NEW ORLEANS.

FERRIE TOOK MOVIES OF THE ACTIVITIES AT THE LAKE PONCHARTRAIN CUBAN EXILE TRAINING SITE. ONE CLIP, LATER REVIEWED BY THE HSCA, WOULD SHOW FERRIE ALONG WITH **LEE**, DAVID ATLEE PHILLIPS, AND ANTONIA VECIANA.

LATER IN DALLAS, FERRIE'S FREQUENCY AT JACK RUBY'S CAROUSEL CLUB LED ONE WITNESS, BEVERLY OLIVER, TO WONDER IF HE WAS THE MANAGER.

THE AFTERNOON OF NOVEMBER 22ND, 1963, JACK MARTIN, AN ASSOCIATE OF GUY BANISTER, WOULD CALL THE NEW ORLEANS POLICE DEPARTMENT AND THE FBI AND STATE THAT FERRIE MIGHT BE INVOLVED TO SOME DEGREE IN THE ASSASSINATION. AS A RESULT, FERRIE WAS QUESTIONED BY THE NEW ORLEANS DISTRICT ATTORNEY ON NOVEMBER 25TH AND THE FBI AND THE SECRET SERVICE ON NOVEMBER 25TH AND 26TH. FERRIE DENIED KNOWING **HARVEY**. THE FBI HOWEVER FOUND EVIDENCE THAT FERRIE DID INDEED KNOW HIM BUT CLEARED HIM OF CONSPIRING WITH **HARVEY** IN REGARDS TO THE ASSASSINATION. THE **HARVEY**/FERRIE CONNECTION IS BOLSTERED BY FRED O'SULLIVAN OF THE NEW ORLEANS POLICE VICE SQUAD. HE STATED THAT FERRIE AND **HARVEY** WERE ACQUAINTANCES.

THE FBI APPARENTLY CONTINUED TO BE CONCERNED ABOUT FERRIE'S POSSIBLE INVOLVEMENT IN THE ASSASSINATION. HE WAS RE-INTERVIEWED ON DECEMBER 5TH. THEIR INVESTIGATION LASTED UNTIL DECEMBER 18TH, 9 DAYS AFTER THE FBI ISSUED ITS SUMMARY REPORT ON DECEMBER 9TH.

FERRIE, LIKE **HARVEY**, WAS ALSO LED TO BELIEVE THAT THE "CARCINOGENS TO CUBA" WAS INDEED A LEGITIMATE CIA EFFORT AND THAT THEY WERE A CRITICAL COMPONENT OF THE PROJECT. HE WOULD BE MORE DIRECTLY INVOLVED IN THE BOGUS "ASSIGNMENT" AS HE WOULD BE LED TO BELIEVE THAT HIS PICKUP OF **HARVEY** ON THE WEEKEND OF NOVEMBER 22ND WOULD BE SOLELY IN CONJUNCTION WITH HIS DELIVERY OF **HARVEY** AND THE CARCINOGENS TO CUBA VIA MEXICO. FERRIE'S ROLE, LIMITED TO BEING THE PILOT FOR **HARVEY**, WOULD BE SOMEWHAT BITTERSWEET FOR THE RABID ANTI-CASTRO FERRIE. FERRIE, WHO OFTEN BOASTED OF HIS OWN "CANCER RESEARCH", WOULD NOW HOWEVER THINK THAT HE WAS AT LEAST INVOLVED IN AN ASSIGNMENT THAT WOULD SEE HIS OWN FAILED EFFORTS REGARDING CANCER AND CARCINOGENS COME TO FRUITION.

FERRIE HOWEVER WOULD LATER PUT TOGETHER THE PIECES OF THE PUZZLE AND REALIZE THAT BOTH HE AND **HARVEY** HAD BEEN DECEIVED.

DAVID FERRIE DIED ON FEBRUARY 22ND, 1967, 5 DAYS AFTER THE ANNOUNCEMENT OF JIM GARRISON'S NEW ORLEANS BASED INVESTIGATION INTO THE ASSASSINATION AND THE DAY AFTER HE WAS RELEASED FROM PROTECTIVE CUSTODY. FERRIE PREDICTED HIS OWN FATE. THE FIRST DAY THE GARRISON INVESTIGATION WAS REPORTED IN THE NEWSPAPER, FERRIE CALLED LOU IVAN, AN ASSISTANT TO GARRISON, AND TOLD HIM: "YOU KNOW WHAT THIS DOES TO ME DON'T YOU…I'M A DEAD MAN."

ONE MAY QUESTION THE IMPORTANCE OF DAVID FERRIE IN THE EVENTS SURROUNDING THE ASSASSINATION: LBJ DID NOT. LBJ PHONED ACTING ATTORNEY GENERAL RAMSEY CLARK TO INFORM HIM OF FERRIE'S DEATH. A LATER FBI REPORT NOTED THAT LBJ WAS "VERY CONCERNED ABOUT THIS MATTER" AND WANTED A DETAILED REPORT OF THE CIRCUMSTANCES SURROUNDING FERRIE'S DEATH. ROBERTS WOULD LATER COMMENT ON FERRIE: "I BELIEVED HIS WORK WAS SOMEHOW CONNECTED WITH CIA RATHER THAN THE FBI." IT HAS ALSO BEEN REPORTED THAT ATTORNEY GENERAL ROBERT KENNEDY PHONED THE CORONER OF ORLEANS PARISH, DR. NICHOLAS CHETTA, CONCERNING FERRIE'S CAUSE OF DEATH.

THE SECRET SERVICE ALSO RECOGNIZED THE IMPORTANCE OF DAVID FERRIE AND HIS PROBABLE INVOLVEMENT WITH **HARVEY**. ON SUNDAY, NOVEMBER 24TH, 1963, MARINA WAS ASKED BY THE SECRET SERVICE IF SHE KNEW A "MR. FARRY." THIS IS THE DAY BEFORE GARRISON WOULD BRING IN FERRIE FOR QUESTIONING IN REGARDS TO THE ASSASSINATION.

*AT THIS POINT, I FIND IT OF THE UTMOST IMPORTANCE TO STRESS THAT I DO NOT CONSIDER DAVID FERRIE AS A WILLING AND INCLUSIVE MEMBER OF THE GROUP OF SET-UP CONSPIRATORS. HE WAS TOO LOW-LEVEL AN OPERATIVE, TOO EXCENTRIC, AND TOO PRONE TO BOASTING TO SAFELY AND KNOWINGLY BE INCLUDED IN A COVERT PLOT TO SET-UP **HARVEY**. HOWEVER AS WE WILL SEE, FERRIE DOES, ALBEIT UNKNOWINGLY, BECOME A MAJOR PARTICIPANT IN THE PROCESS OF SETTING UP **HARVEY**.*

*I DO HOWEVER FEEL THAT WITH HIS CLOSE ASSOCIATION TO BOTH BANISTER AND MARCELLO THAT HE MOST CERTAINLY WOULD HAVE BEEN AWARE OF THE ASSASSINATION PLANS THAT FALL. HE MAY NOT HOWEVER BEEN AWARE OF THE POSSIBILITY THAT THE EVENT WOULD TAKE PLACE IN DALLAS AND THAT **HARVEY** WOULD BE SUSPECT ONE.*

JACK RUBY

BORN IN CHICAGO, JACK RUBY WAS ONE OF MANY YOUTHS WHO RAN ERRANDS FOR AL CAPONE. DURING THE YEARS 1937-1940, HE BECAME INVOLVED IN THE LOCAL SCRAP IRON AND JUNK WORKER'S UNION. THE STATE OF ILLINOIS CONSIDERED THIS ORGANIZATION A FRONT FOR ORGANIZED CRIME. HE LEFT THE UNION IN 1940, AND WORKED VARIOUS JOBS UNTIL JOINING THE ARMY AIR CORP IN 1943.

RUBY SERVED IN THE MILITARY UNTIL FEBRUARY 1946. AFTER HIS DISCHARGE, HE REJOINED HIS PRE-MILITARY HOODLUMS IN CHICAGO AND WAS SENT TO DALLAS IN JUNE OF 1947 WITH A GROUP OF 25 ORGANIZED CRIME MEMBERS. THEIR MISSION WAS TO TAKE OVER THE GAMING AND JUKEBOX BUSINESS IN DALLAS. INITIALLY HE HELPED HIS SISTER, EVA GRANT, CO-MANAGE A CLUB CALLED THE SILVER SPUR.

IN 1947, RUBY WAS ALSO KNOWN TO BE AN INFORMANT FOR THE STAFF OF THEN CONGRESSMAN RICHARD NIXON. NIXON WAS A WELL KNOWN MEMBER OF HUAC, THE HOUSE UNAMERICAN ACTIVITIES COMMTTEE.

RUBY MANAGED SEVERAL CLUBS PRIOR TO THE CAROUSEL CLUB. IN THE EARLY 1950'S, HE MANAGED THE SINGAPORE CLUB. IN 1953, HE RAN A CLUB CALLED THE VEGAS CLUB. IN 1959 AND 1960 HE OPERATED THE SOVEREIGN CLUB WHICH CHANGED ITS NAME TO THE CAROUSEL CLUB IN 1960. HE WAS ALSO INVOLVED IN GAMBLING, DRUGS, AND PROSTITUTION. AS MANAGER OF THE CAROUSEL CLUB, HE CULTIVATED

FRIENDSHIPS WITH MANY DALLAS POLICEMEN AND WOULD ALWAYS ALLOW OFFICERS TO DRINK FREE AT HIS CLUB. IN TURN, RUBY ENCOUNTERED FEW PROBLEMS REGARDING HIS VIOLATIONS OF LIQUER AND DRINKING LAWS. HE ALSO MANAGED TO AVOID CHARGES INVOLVING INCIDENTS OF CARRYING CONCEALED WEAPONS AND ASSAULT. FROM 1949-1963, RUBY WAS ARRESTED 9 TIMES BUT NEVER CONVICTED.

IN 1957, RUBY SHIIPPED GUNS FROM KEMAH AND BAYTOWN, TEXAS TO HOLBOX ISLAND OFF THE NORTH COAST OF THE YUCATAN PENINSULA. FROM THERE THEY WERE SENT TO CUBA. RUBY'S APARTMENT WAS SEARCHED AFTER HIS ARREST FOR THE SHOOTING OF **HARVEY**. FOUND IN A SEPARATE STOREROOM WERE A BROWNING AUTOMATIC RIFLE, A CASE OF HAND GRENADES, A LARGE QUANTITY OF AMMO, AND A NUMBER OF M-16 RIFLES.

FROM MARCH 11TH TO OCTOBER 2ND 1959, RUBY SERVED AS A CONFIDENTIAL INFORMANT FOR FBI S.A. CHARLES FLYNN. RUBY MADE AT LEAST 2 TRIPS TO CUBA IN 1959 WHILE MONITORING GUN RUNNING ACTIVITIES TO CUBA FOR THE FBI. HE ENTERED CUBA ON AUGUST 8TH, DEPARTING ON SEPTEMBER 11TH. HE RE-ENTERED CUBA ON SEPTEMBER 12TH AND DEPARTED THE NEXT DAY, SEPTEMBER 13TH. HE CONTINUED TO NEW ORLEANS THAT SAME DAY. THE HSCA CONCLUDED THAT RUBY'S TRIPS TO CUBA WERE CONDUCTED AS A COURIER FOR ORGANIZED CRIME GAMBLING INTERESTS IN A LIKELY EFFORT TO OBTAIN THE RELEASE OF THE CUBAN-DETAINED SANTOS TRAFFICANTE.

RUBY, WHO WAS FAMILIAR WITH MARCELLO, BANISTER, FERRIE, **HARVEY**, AND **LEE** WOULD ALSO BE AN UNWITTING PARTICIPANT IN WHAT HE PERCEIVED AS A LEGITIMATE CIA EFFORT TO DELIVER CARCINOGENS TO CUBA VIA FERRIE AND **HARVEY**. RUBY'S ROLE WOULD BE TO PROVIDE **HARVEY'S** TRANSPORTATION FROM HIS BOARDING HOUSE TO REDBIRD AIRPORT FOR THE FIRST LEG OF HIS "ASSIGNMENT." RUBY'S EARLY MORNING NOVEMBER 22ND MEETING AT THE CABANA MOTEL (MORE ON THIS LATER), HIS ABOVE MENTIONED ASSOCIATIONS, AND THE DRAMATIC INCREASE IN HIS LONG DISTANCE CALLS PRIOR TO THE ASSASSINATION TEMPT ONE TO ASSUME THAT HE KNEW THAT THE PRESIDENT WOULD BE KILLED THAT DAY IN DALLAS. I AM NOT ABSOLUTELY CERTAIN THAT A RELATIVELY LOW-LEVEL ORGANIZED CRIME OPERATIVE WITH THE TEMPERMENT OF RUBY COULD BE TRUSTED WITH MAINTAING SECRECY PRIOR TO NOVEMBER 22ND. I AM HOWEVER OPEN TO THE POSSIBILITY THAT RUBY MAY HAVE BEEN UNDER THE IMPRESSION THAT AN ASSASSINATION "ATTEMPT" WOULD TAKE PLACE IN DALLAS, THUS THE "FIREWORKS" REMARK MADE BY HIM JUST PRIOR TO THE MOTORCADES ARRIVAL IN DEALEY PLAZA. WITH THAT IN MIND, I AM NOT CERTAIN THAT RUBY KNEW THAT AS NOVEMBER 22ND UNFOLDED THAT **HARVEY** WOULD BE ARRESTED BUT I AM CERTAIN THAT HE WAS NOT YET AWARE THAT HE WOULD LATER BE TASKED WITH SILENCING **HARVEY**.

ROSCOE WHITE

AT HIS HIGH SCHOOL GRADUATION SPEECH, WHITE SPOKE PASSIONATELY ABOUT THE "INTERNATIONAL COMMUNIST CONSPIRACY" AND WARNED THOSE ASSEMBLED ABOUT THE NEED FOR A STRONG U.S.DEFENSE POSTURE.

*THIS IS A PARTICULARLY WORLDLY VIEW FOR A FARMBOY FROM FOREMAN, ARKANSAS. HAD WHITE BEEN INDOCTRINATED IN THE SAME FASHION AS **LEE** HAD BEEN BY DAVID FERRIE DURING THEIR CIVIL AIR PATROL DAYS?*

WHITE JOINED THE MARINES ON FEBRUARY 19TH, 1957. ROSCOE WHITE AND **LEE** WERE BOTH MEMBERS OF MARINE WING 1 THAT EMBARKED FOR ATSUGI, JAPAN ON AUGUST 22ND, 1957 ABOARD THE USS BEXAR. ON SEPTEMBER 19TH, 1957, WHITE'S OUTFIT LEFT JAPAN FOR KAKDENA AIR BASE, OKINAWA. **LEE**, AFTER HIS SELF-INFLICTED GUNSHOT WOUND, WOULD REJOIN THE UNIT ON NOVEMBER 20TH.

IN NOVEMBER OF 1957, WHITE'S OUTFIT WAS STATIONED IN SUBIC BAY, PHILLIPINES. HIS UNIT WOULD RETURN TO OKINAWA IN MARCH 1958. WHITE WOULD RETURN STATESIDE IN OCTOBER 1958 AND BE STATIONED AT CAMP PENDLETON, CALIFORNIA. IN FEBRUARY OF 1960, WHITE WAS ASSIGNED TO FT. SILL, OKLAHOMA. IN MARCH 1961 WHITE RETURNED TO CAMP PENDLETON. IN SEPTEMBER 1961, WHITE WAS ONCE AGAIN SENT TO OKINAWA. IN OCTOBER 1962 WHITE RETURNED STATESIDE ONCE AGAIN. IN DECEMBER 1959, WHITE HAD RE-ENLISTED FOR 6 YEARS. BUT, ON DECEMBER 4TH, 1962, WHITE, LIKE **HARVEY**, WOULD OBTAIN A HARDSHIP DISCHARGE. HE WOULD MOVE TO DALLAS THE FOLLOWING WEEK. HIS HARDSHIP DISCHARGE WAS PRESUMABLY FOR THE SAKE OF HIS WIFE WHO HAD RECEIVED A HEAD INJURY AT WORK. HOWEVER THE HEAD INJURY, WHICH TOOK PLACE AT THE CATTLEMEN'S RESTAURANT, DID NOT OCCUR UNTIL AUGUST OF 1963, 8 MONTHS AFTER HIS HARDSHIP DISCHARGE. ON DECEMBER 12TH 1962, WHITE WOULD APPLY FOR A DALLAS POLICE DEPARTMENT POSITION.

IN THE SPRING OF 1963, WHITE WOULD MOVE TO THE OAK CLIFF SECTION OF DALLAS. HIS FIRST JOB WAS WITH AMERICAN NATIONAL INSURANCE COMPANY. ON OCTOBER 7TH OF 1963, WHITE WOULD JOIN THE DALLAS POLICE FORCE. FROM DECEMBER 4TH 1963 TILL FEBRUARY 25TH, 1964, WHITE WAS IN RECRUIT CLASS #79. HE BECAME A PATROLMAN (PROBATIONARY STATUS) ON OCTOBER 7TH, 1964 AND SHED HIS PROBATIONARY STATUS ON JANUARY 7TH, 1965. **HARVEY** RETURNED TO DALLAS FROM NEW ORLEANS ON OCTOBER 3RD, 1963, ONLY 4 DAYS PRIOR TO WHITE'S JOINING THE DALLAS POLICE FORCE.

WHITE'S DALLAS POLICE DEPARTMENT FILE CONTAINED ONLY INSURANCE PAPERS AND A BACKGROUND CHECK. THERE WAS NO INDICATION OF ANY ASSIGNMENTS WHILE ON THE FORCE. ON OCTOBER 17TH, 1965, WHITE LEFT THE DALLAS POLICE FORCE.

ROSCOE WHITE, THROUGH E. HOWARD HUNT OR DAVID ATLEE PHILLIPS, WOULD BE AWARE THAT A CARCINOGENS PROJECT WAS INDEED AN ONGOING AND LEGITIMATE CIA EFFORT. HOWEVER HE WOULD ALSO BE KNOWLEDGEABLE OF THE FACT THAT THE INVOLVEMENT OF FERRIE, RUBY AND **HARVEY** WAS, IN ITS ENTIRETY, A SET-UP THAT ONLY PARALLED A LEGITIMATE CIA OPERATION.

THE CARCINOGEN "ASSIGNMENT" WOULD APPEAR TO **HARVEY** AS A RETURN TO HIS FORMER LEVEL OF INTELLIGENCE WORK. THIS PROJECT WOULD BE OF THE SAME LEVEL OF IMPORTANCE AS WAS HIS "DEFECTION" TO RUSSIA. IT WOULD BE A VAST IMPROVEMENT OVER RECENT MUNDANE ASSIGNMENTS SUCH AS PASSING OUT PRO-CASTRO LEAFLETS AND SERVING AS AN INFORMANT FOR THE FBI. WHITE WAS QUITE LIKELY AWARE OF THE PLANS TO KILL JFK IN DALLAS. HE WOULD ALSO BE AWARE OF AND PARTICIPATE IN THE SET-UP OF **HARVEY**.

THE SELECTION OF **HARVEY** AS THE "ASSASSIN" AND THE CHOICE OF A PLAN THAT WOULD BE FATALLY INCRIMINATING TO HIM WAS LIKELY MADE BY SOMEONE DEEP IN THE INTELLIGENCE COMMUNITY, SOMEONE AWARE OF THE ONGOING CIA CARCINOGENS PROJECT, AND SOMEONE WHO KNEW THAT **HARVEY** WOULD ACT WITHOUT QUESTION REGARDING HIS NEW "ASSIGNMENT."

THIS BRINGS US TO MEXICO CITY-BASED E. HOWARD HUNT AND DAVID ATLEE PHILLIPS.

109

E. HOWARD HUNT

HUNT JOINED THE CIA ON NOVEMBER 23RD, 1949. IN DECEMBER OF 1950 HE ASSISTED IN ESTABLISHING THE CIA STATION IN MEXICO CITY. HE SERVED THERE UNTIL DECEMBER 1953. IN LATE 1953, HE WAS ASSIGNED TO THE BALKANS AT THE CIA'S SOUTHEAST EUROPE DIVISION. DURING 1953-54, HUNT WAS RECRUITED BY AND WORKED WITH DAVID ATLEE PHILLIPS IN AN EFFORT TO OVERTHROW PRESIDENT ARBENZ OF GUATAMALA IN WHAT WAS CALLED "OPERATION PB/ SUCCESS." THE OPERATION WAS RUN OUT OF A NAVY TRAINING CAMP AT OPA-LOCKA, FLORIDA. HUNT WAS INSTRUMENTAL IN INITIATING THE UPRISING IN SALAMA AGAINST ARBENZ. HE SERVED AS CHIEF OF POLITICAL ACTION IN THE OPERATION. BEFORE PB/SUCCESS WAS COMPLETED, HUNT WAS ASSIGNED TO TOKYO, JAPAN IN JUNE 1954 UNTIL EARLY JANUARY, 1957.

ON JANUARY 25TH, 1957, HUNT AND FAMILY MOVED TO MONTEVIDEO, URUGUAY WHERE HE SERVED AS CIA STATION CHIEF UNTIL APRIL 1960. HUNT WOULD HELP ORCHESTRATE A COUP ATTEMPT IN URUGUAY IN 1959. HUNT WAS CALLED TO WASHINGTON TO JOIN PHILLIPS IN A REUNION OF THE SUCCESSFUL GUATAMALAN PB/SUCCESS TEAM. THE NEW OPERATION INITIALLY SET UP SHOP IN MEXICO CITY IN JULY 1960. THIS TIME THE TARGET WOULD BE CASTRO. HUNT WOULD BE IN CHARGE OF POLITICAL ACTION AND PHILLIPS WOULD PROVIDE THE REQUISITE PROPAGANDA ARM OF THE OPERATION.

DURING LATE 1960 AND 1961, HUNT (UNDER ONE OF HIS ALIASES, EDUARDO) WAS ACTIVE IN THE CUBAN REVOLUTIONARY COUNCIL IN MIAMI AS PART OF THE PREPARATION FOR THE BAY OF PIGS INVASION. THE OPERATION HAD MOVED FROM MEXICO CITY TO THE MORE CONVENIENT MIAMI. HUNT ALSO HAD A CRC OFFICE IN NEW ORLEANS AT 544 CAMP STREET. ANOTHER ALIAS OF HUNT WAS INITIATED IN LATE SEPTEMBER OF 1960 WHEN HE WAS PROVIDED DOCUMENTATION IN THE NAME OF "EDWARD J. HAMILTON."

HUNT, ACCORDING TO RAFAEL TRUJILO'S SECURITY CHIEF, WAS IN THE DOMINICAN REPUBLIC JUST PRIOR TO THE MAY 1961 ASSASSINATION OF THE DOMINICAN DICTATOR.

DURING AUGUST-SEPTEMBER OF 1963, HUNT WAS TEMPORARY STATION CHIEF IN MEXICO CITY. LATER THAT SAME YEAR, HUNT SERVED DUTY IN WASHINGTON, D.C. IN CONNECTION WITH THE CIA'S DOMESTIC AFFAIRS DIVISION.

A 1966 MEMO TO COUNTER-INTELLIGENCE CHIEF JAMES ANGELTON FROM CIA DIRECTOR RICHARD HELMS READ IN EFFECT: "SOMEDAY WE WILL HAVE TO EXPLAIN WHAT HUNT WAS DOING IN DALLAS ON NOVEMBER 22ND, 1963." HUNT WAS KEENLY AWARE OF THE ASSASSINATION PLANS AND INSTRUMENTAL IN SETTING UP **HARVEY** AS THE ASSASSIN.

DAVID ATLEE PHILLIPS

PHILLIPS BEGAN WORKING FOR THE CIA IN 1950 IN SANTIAGO, CHILE AS A CONTRACT EMPLOYEE. HE WAS TASKED WITH POSING AS CIA CHIEF OF STATION. HE WAS A JOURNALIST AND BOUGHT A SMALL ENGLISH NEWSPAPER IN SANTIAGO, THE "SOUTH PACIFIC MAIL." IN 1954, HE WORKED WITH HOWARD HUNT ON THE GUATAMALAN ARBENZ COUP CODENAMED OPERATION PB/SUCCESS. PHILLIPS AND HUNT ORGANIZED THE PROPAGANDA CAMPAIGN USED IN THE COUP.

IN 1957, PHILLIPS WAS ASSIGNED TO BEIRUT, LEBANON. DURING 1958 AND 1959, HE WORKED UNDERCOVER IN HAVANA AS AN OWNER OF A PUBLIC RELATIONS AGENCY TITLED "DAVID PHILLIPS ASSOCIATES." HIS CASE OFFICER WAS DAVID MORALES. DURING HIS HAVANA STAY, PHILLIPS RECRUITED ANTONIO VECIANA AS AN INFORMANT. PHILLIPS WAS ALSO KNOWN TO USE THE NAME "JACK STEWART" DURING

HIS STAY IN HAVANA AND ALSO THE NAMES ANDREW F. MERTON AND LAWRENCE F. BARKER. OTHER NAMES ASSOCIATED WITH PHILLIPS ARE MICHAEL CHOADEN, BOB LEE, JOHN NADLEMAN, PAUL LANGEVIN, WALTER BRACTON, AND DAVID PADDACK.

IN MARCH OF 1960, PHILLIPS WAS ATTACHED TO THE CUBAN TASK FORCE IN WASHINGTON, D.C. IN REGARDS TO THE BAY OF PIGS PLANNING. HE WOULD BE TASKED WITH THE OPERATION OF RADIO SWAN, A HONDURAN OFF-SHORE RADIO STATION BROADCASTING PROPAGANDA TO CUBA. HE WOULD WORK WITH HUNT ON THIS PROJECT. PHILLIPS WOULD APPROACH VECIANA IN AN EFFORT TO ENLIST HIS HELP IN ANTI-CASTRO EFFORTS. IN NOVEMBER OF 1960, PHILLIPS WAS THE CIA'S HEAD MAN IN A COUNTER-INTELLIGENCE PROPAGANDA EFFORT AGAINST THE FPFC ORGANIZATION. THIS OPERATION ALSO INCLUDED JAMES MCCORD OF LATER WATERGATE FAME. THE FAILED BAY OF PIGS OPERATION IN APRIL 1961 AFFECTED PHILLIPS GREATLY. AS HE MONITORED THE FAILED EFFORTS OF THE INVADING FORCES, HE NOTED IN HIS BOOK THAT HE "FELT NAUSEOUS....THAT I BEGAN TO CRY...I CRIED FOR TWO HOURS."

IN AUGUST OF 1961, PHILLIPS WAS MOVED TO MEXICO CITY AS CHIEF OF COVERT ACTIONS AND LATER AS CHIEF OF CUBAN OPERATIONS. HIS MAIN FUNCTIONS WERE PROPAGANDA AND COUNTER-INTELLIGENCE. IN NOVEMBER OF 1961, PHILLIPS HAD VECIANA FORM AN ANTI-CASTRO GROUP WHICH WOULD LATER BECOME ALPHA 66. VECIANA WOULD BE ASSIGNED THE CIA CODENAME "AMSHALE-1".

ON SEPTEMBER 10TH, 1962 IN THE EARLY STAGES OF THE CUBAN MISSILE CRISIS, PHILLIPS HAD VECIANA'S ALPHA 66 GROUP ATTACK A BRITISH SHIP AND 2 CUBAN VESSELS OFF THE COAST OF CUBA. ON OCTOBER 5TH, PHILLIPS HAD VECIANA'S GROUP ATTACK A SOVIET SHIP IN HAVANA. IN LATE AUGUST/EARLY SEPTEMBER 1963, VECIANA WOULD TRAVEL TO DALLAS TO MEET WITH PHILLIPS. AS HE APPROACHED PHILLIPS (WHO HE KNEW BY PHILLIPS' ALIAS, MAURICE BISHOP), IN THE LOBBY OF THE SOUTHLAND BUILDING, HE WITNESSED PHILLIPS/BISHOP TALKING TO **HARVEY**. **HARVEY** WAS KNOWN TO REFER TO PHILLIPS AS "MR. B". VECIANA STATED THAT THEY DISCUSSED, WITH PARTICIPATION BY **HARVEY**, KILLING CASTRO. ARMSTRONG HOWEVER BELIEVES THAT VECIANA ACTUALLY WITNESSED **LEE** CONVERSING WITH PHILIPS, NOT **HARVEY**.

IN OCTOBER 1963, PHILLIPS BECAME CHIEF OF CUBAN OPERATIONS IN MEXICO CITY. HE ALSO WAS TASKED AS CHIEF OF PSYCHOLOGICAL OPERATIONS AT THE MIAMI CIA STATION. AS A RESULT, HE NOW PERSONALLY DIRECTED ALPHA 66. VECIANA HOWEVER REMAINED "OFFICIALLY" IN CHARGE OF THE GROUP. PHILLIPS TOLD VECIANA THAT HE WANTED TO "PUT KENNEDY'S BACK TO THE WALL" AND FORCE HIM TO TAKE ACTION ON CASTRO.

DAVID ATLEE PHILLIPS' EXPERIENCE AS A DISINFORMATION/PROPAGANDA SPECIALIST WOULD LIMIT HIS ROLE AND THAT OF HUNT IN THE ASSASSINATION PLOT TO THE SET-UP OF **HARVEY**.

WIN SCOTT, CIA'S MEXICO CITY CHIEF OF STATION, WOULD LATER NOTE: "IF THERE WERE A PRE-ASSASSINATION CIA OPERATION INVOLVING OSWALD AND CUBA, SUCH AN OPERATION, AT LEAST IN MEXICO CITY, WOULD ALMOST CERTAINLY HAVE BEEN DIRECTED BY DAVID PHILLIPS." ONE WOULD SUSPECT THAT THIS WOULD HOLD TRUE EVEN IF THE "OPERATION" WERE DESIGNED SOLELY TO SET-UP **HARVEY** AS THE FLEEING ASSASSIN ON NOVEMBER 22ND.

HUNT AND PHILLIPS ARE THE MASTERMINDS RESPONSIBLE FOR THE SET-UP OF **HARVEY**. BOTH PHILLIPS AND HUNT WOULD BE AWARE OF THE CARCINOGENS PROJECT AS A VIABLE CIA PROJECT. MORE IMPORTANTLY, THEY WOULD ALSO BE IN A POSITION TO REALIZE THAT **HARVEY'S** EARLIER LEGITIMATE ONI/CIA PROJECTS WITH THEIR "DEFECTOR" AND "PRO-CASTRO" POSTURING WOULD MAKE HIM AN IDEAL

CANDIDATE TO ENLIST FOR WHAT **HARVEY** WOULD PERCEIVE AS A LEGITIMATE OPERATION WHEN IN FACT, HIS "CARCINOGEN TO CUBA" ASSIGNMENT WOULD, ON THE AFTERNOON OF NOVEMBER 22ND, GIVE THE APPEARANCE OF AN "ASSASSIN" ON THE RUN TO CUBA.

AT THE TIME THAT **HARVEY** IS <u>ALLEGEDLY</u> IN MEXICO CITY TRYING TO ARRANGE <u>LEGITIMATE</u> TRAVEL VISAS THROUGH THE CUBAN AND MEXICAN EMBASSIES, HUNT AND PHILLIPS ARE RUNNING AN OSWALD IMPERSONATOR; **LEE**. WHAT IS LATER PERCEIVED BY THE WARREN COMMISSION AND OTHERS AS EVIDENCE OF **HARVEY'S** PHYSICAL PRESENCE IN MEXICO CITY IS NOTHING MORE THAN AN OPPORTUNITY FOR HUNT AND PHILLIPS TO RUN THE IMPOSTOR, **LEE**. IT IS THE IMPOSTOR WHO IS OVERLY RUDE AND IMPERTINANT AT THE EMBASSIES, NOT **HARVEY**. INDEED WE HAVE A **LEE** HARVEY OSWALD IMPERSONATING AN "IMPOSTOR" LEE **HARVEY** OSWALD. LATER YOU WILL SEE THAT THIS CONFRONTATIONAL ATTITUDE TOWARDS THE EMBASSY PERSONNEL BY **LEE** IS FOR NO OTHER PURPOSE THAN TO MAKE "OSWALD'S" VISITS TO THOSE EMBASSIES UNFORGETTABLE BY THE STAFF MEMBERS HE HAS CONTACT WITH.

IT IS IMPORTANT TO KEEP IN MIND THAT FROM SEPTEMBER 26TH TO OCTOBER 3RD, THERE IS NO HARD EVIDENCE REGARDING **HARVEY'S** WHEREABOUTS. IF THE MAN IN MEXICO CITY IS INDEED **LEE** AND NOT **HARVEY**, JUST WHERE IS **HARVEY**? I STRONGLY SUSPECT THAT BOTH HUNT AND PHILLIPS ARE NOT ONLY AWARE OF JUST WHERE HE IS, BUT MORE IMPORTANTLY WHERE HE IS NOT. **HARVEY'S** ABSENCE IS NOTED, BUT THERE IS NO CERTAINTY OF HIS LOCATION FOR THOSE 8 DAYS IN THE FALL OF 1963. THIS GIVES HUNT AND PHILLIPS THE PERFECT OPPORTUNITY TO RUN THE IMPOSTOR (**LEE**) AT THE EMBASSIES IN MEXICO CITY. WE WILL EXAMINE THIS TIME FRAME MORE CLOSELY IN A LATER CHAPTER.

BOTH PHILLIPS AND HUNT HAD THE CAPACITY, THE POSITION, AND THE MOTIVE TO GIVE BIRTH TO A SET-UP OF THIS COMPLEXITY <u>AND</u> TO SEE THAT THE DETAILS OF THE SET-UP WERE CARRIED OUT IN NEW ORLEANS, DALLAS, AND IN MEXICO CITY. INDEED **HARVEY**, ACCORDING TO THE SOON TO BE INTRODUCED JUDYTH BAKER, STATED THAT HIS CIA CONTACT WAS A "MR. B". PHILLIPS WAS KNOWN TO USE THE ALIAS, "MAURICE BISHOP." ROSS CROZIER, A CIA CASE OFFICER AT THE CIA'S MIAMI JMWAVE STATION WOULD LATER TELL THE HSCA THAT INDEED PHILLIPS USED THE NAME "MAURICE BISHOP."

HARVEY AND RUBY WOULD BE "BRIEFED" AS TO WHAT EVENTS WOULD TAKE PLACE ON NOVEMBER 22ND, THE DAY OF THE PRESIDENT'S VISIT, AND THE DAY THAT **HARVEY** WOULD DEPART ON HIS "ASSIGNMENT." THEY WERE LIKELY TOLD THAT THERE WOULD BE A **MOCK ATTEMPT** ON THE PRESIDENT'S LIFE, THAT THE SHOTS WOULD BE ATTRIBUTED TO A PRO-CASTRO ORGANIZATION, THAT FIREWORKS WOULD AIDE IN DISGUISING THE ORIGIN OF THE SHOTS, THAT THE FBI WOULD BE OCCUPIED WITH THEIR RESPONSE TO THE "ATTEMPT" ON THE PRESIDENT'S LIFE ALLOWING **HARVEY** MORE FREEDOM IN HIS DEPARTURE, AND THAT RUBY WOULD ASSIST BY PLANTING A BULLET TRACEABLE TO A RIFLE USED IN THE "ATEMPT." WHAT RUBY AND **HARVEY** WOULD **NOT** BE TOLD WAS THAT THE BULLET COURIERED BY RUBY WOULD BE TRACEABLE TO THE MANNLICHER, THAT THE MANNLICHER WOULD BE FOUND IN THE TSBD, THAT THE MANNLICHER WOULD BE TRACEABLE TO A "A. HIDDELL", AND THAT "HIDELL" WOULD BE TRACEABLE TO **HARVEY**.

TO REVIEW, IT IS PROBABLE IF NOT A CERTAINTY THAT MARCELLO AND PERHAPS EVEN SHAW ARE AWARE OF A LEGITIMATE CIA CARCINOGENS PROJECT. IT IS PROBABLE IF NOT A CERTAINTY THAT THEY ARE AWARE THAT THE "CARCINOGENS TO CUBA" ASSIGNMENT IN REGARDS TO **HARVEY** IS A PLOY. IT IS HOWEVER A NEAR <u>CERTAINTY</u> THAT NEITHER FERRIE, RUBY OR **HARVEY** ARE AWARE OF THE FACT THAT THE ENTIRE "ASSIGNMENT" IS A SET-UP.

PHILLIPS AND HUNT IN MEXICO CITY AND DALLAS, ROSCOE WHITE IN DALLAS AND NEW ORLEANS, **LEE** IN NEW ORLEANS, DALLAS, AND MEXICO CITY, AND GUY BANISTER IN NEW ORLEANS - AS IDENTIFIABLE MEMBERS OF THE SET-UP CONSPIRACY- ARE HOWEVER FULLY AWARE THAT THE ENTIRE CARCINOGENS PLOT IS INDEED A DECEPTION AND THAT NEITHER FERRIE, RUBY, OR **HARVEY** ARE COGNIZANT OF THIS FACT.

CHAPTER 7: NEW ORLEANS: THE FINAL "ASSIGNMENT"

THE SCENARIO WE ARE ABOUT TO DETAIL, **SCENARIO I**, INVOLVING A MRS. JUDYTH VARY BAKER WAS INCLUDED IN THE EXCELLENT "THE MEN WHO KILLED KENNEDY" SERIES AS SHOWN ON THE HISTORY CHANNEL.

BEFORE WE EXAMINE THIS SCENARIO AS PERCEIVED BY MS. BAKER INVOLVING **HARVEY** AND THE CIA AND MY MORE PLAUSIBLE VARIATION ON THIS SAME SCENARIO, SOME BACKGROUND IS IN ORDER REGARDING THE DEGREE TO WHICH THE CIA HELD IMPORTANT THE ELIMINATION OR REDUCTION IN EFFECTIVENESS OF FIDEL CASTRO.

AS EARLY AS SPRING 1959, PLANS WERE UNDERWAY TO ELIMINATE CASTRO. OPERATION ZAPATA, WITH VICE PRESIDENT NIXON AND THEN OILMAN GEORGE H.W. BUSH'S GUIDANCE, WAS TO USE BUSH'S ZAPATA OIL COMPANY AS A COVER FOR AN INVASION OF CUBA. EISENHOWER APPROVED A PLAN CODENAMED "PLUTO" TO UTILIZE A MULTI-PRONGED APPROACH TO FACILITATE CASTRO'S REMOVAL. THIS EFFORT FLOUNDERED AND BY NOVEMBER 1960 IT WAS DECIDED TO INVADE CUBA VIA WHAT WOULD LATER, IN APRIL OF 1961, BE KNOWN AS THE BAY OF PIGS INVASION. THIS ALSO FAILED, QUITE MISERABLY, FORCING THE CIA TO RESORT TO EVEN BOLDER EFFORTS, THE FIRST OF WHICH WAS OPERATION "MONGOOSE" ESTABLISHED IN NOVEMBER 1961. MONGOOSE WAS DESIGNED TO "HELP CUBA OVERTHROW THE COMMUNIST REGIME."

BY MARCH 1962, "OPERATION NORTH WOODS" WAS BEING CONSIDERED. THIS ANTI-CASTRO EFFORT WOULD INCLUDE HARRASSMENT, MOCK "ATTACKS" ON THE BASE AT GUANTANAMO, BOGUS ATTACKS ON U.S. PLANES, SHIPS, AND "TERRORIST" ATTACKS IN U.S. CITIES THAT COULD BE BLAMED ON THE CUBAN GOVERNMENT. THIS PROPOSAL WAS TENDERED BY GENERAL LYMAN LEMNITZER, JOINT CHIEFS OF STAFF. HE WOULD BE REPLACED BY THE PRESIDENT IN SEPTEMBER 1962. MORE ON THE GENERAL'S GRAND PLAN WILL FOLLOW.

THE OCTOBER 1962 CUBAN MISSILE CRISIS WOULD POTENTIALLY OFFER YET ANOTHER OPPORTUNITY TO OUST CASTRO. HOWEVER MUCH TO THE CIA'S AND THE JOINT CHIEFS' DISMAY, JFK CHOSE TO EMPLOY A NAVAL BLOCKADE RATHER THAN RISK AN INVASION THAT COULD HAVE EASILY ESCALATED TO A NUCLEAR WAR.

THERE WERE REPUTEDLY 18 VARIOUS PLANS UTILIZED TO ELIMINATE CASTRO UNDER WAY IN THE EARLY 1960'S. SOME OF THE MORE NOTABLE EFFORTS:

ZR RIFLE
(AKA EXECUTIVE ACTION) WITH OPERATIVES QJ/WIN (A LUXEMBOURG SMUGGLER) AND WI/ROGUE (A PARIS BANK ROBBER) AS THE ASSASSINS OR THE CONTRACTORS OF ASSASSINS

OPERATION MONGOOSE
A JOINT CIA, DEFENSE DEPARTMENT, AND STATE DEPARTMENT EFFORT TO OVERTHROW CASTRO.

OPERATION AMTRUNK
A SCENARIO WHICH HOPED FOR A MILITARY/POLITICAL OUSTER OF CASTRO BY RECRUITING AGENTS WITHIN THE CUBAN MILITARY

OPERATION AMLASH
RUN BY ROLANDO CUBELA, IT INCLUDED THE OPTION OF ASSASSINATION

OPERATION DUCK

ANOTHER SABOTAGE UNIT RUN BY THE CIA'S JMWAVE STATION.

OPERATION TRUEBLUE
THE BROADCASTING OF ANTI-CASTRO PROPAGANDA FROM FLORIDA.

OPERATION FREE RIDE
ONE-WAY AIRLINE TICKETS TO CARACAS OR MEXICO CITY WERE AIR-DROPPED OVER CUBA.

OPERATION GOOD TIMES
DISTRIBUTION OF A DOCTORED PHOTO OF AN OBESE CASTRO SHOWING HIM BETWEEN TWO VOLUMPTUOUS WOMEN.

OPERATION FULL-UP
SOVIET JET FUEL SUPPLIED TO CUBA WOULD BE CONTAMINATED WITH A BIOLOGICAL AGENT.

OPERATION BINGO
A FAKE ATTACK BY CUBA ON OUR GUANTANAMO BASE.

OPERATION ORTSAC
(CASTRO SPELLED BACKWARDS) IN OCTOBER 1962 THE GOVERNMENT LAUNCHED A FULL SCALE MOCK INVASION OF AN ISLAND IN THE CARIBBEAN INVOLVING 7,500 MARINES. THE INTENT OF THIS EXERCISE WAS TO SIMULATE THE TAKE OVER OF AN ISLAND COUNTRY AND THE RESULTANT OVERTHROW OF THAT GOVERMMENT. IN REALITY THIS "EXERCISE" WOULD BE ONE OF MANY OPTIONS IN RESPONSE TO THE CUBAN MISSLE CRISIS.

THE MOST IMPORTANT EFFORT OF ALL WOULD BE **OPERATION AMWORLD**, ALSO KNOWN AS THE **C-DAY COUP**. THE DEFINITIVE BOOK ON THIS COUP IS "ULTIMATE SACRIFICE" BY LAMAR WALDRON.

AMWORLD WAS A COUP PLANNED WITH THE ASSISTANCE OF JUAN ALMEIDA, THE COMMANDER OF CUBA'S ARMY. AMWORLD WAS SCHEDULED TO BE LAUNCHED ON DECEMBER 1ST, 1963. THE C-DAY COUP EVOLVED FROM WHAT WAS KNOWN AS THE CUBA CONTINGENCY PLANS GROUP. THIS GROUP WAS CREATED TO ADDRESS RESPONSES TO CASTRO'S POSSIBLE ATTEMPTS TO ATTACK U.S. FACILITIES AND OR U.S. POLITICAL FIGURES *IF* HE FOUND OUT ABOUT THE CIA/MAFIA ATTEMPTS TO REMOVE HIM. THE 10 DAY "COUNTDOWN" FOR THE C-DAY COUP WAS TO START ON NOVEMBER 22ND, 1963. THE CONTINGENCY PLANS GROUP WAS NOT MADE KNOWN TO THE WARREN COMMISSION SINCE QUESTIONS WOULD THEN ARISE AS TO THE *NEED* FOR A CONTINGENCY PLAN. IF IT COULD BE PROVEN THAT **HARVEY** HAD *LEGITIMATE* TIES TO CASTRO AND THAT HIS ALLEGED ASSASSINATION OF JFK WAS THE RESULT OF CASTRO'S KNOWLEDGE OF THE CIA/MAFIA PLOTS, IT WOULD HAVE NECESSITATED AN INVASION OF CUBA. WITH 13,000 RUSSIAN TROOPS ON THE GROUND IN CUBA, AN INVASION OF CUBA WOULD HAVE ESSENTIALLY BEEN AN INVASION OF RUSSIA.

IF THE PLOTTERS OF THE ASSASSINATION WANTED TO INSURE A GOVERNMENT COVER-UP AND THE ACCEPTANCE OF **HARVEY** AS THE LONE ASSASSIN VIA THE WARREN COMMISSION, THE ASSASSINATION WOULD HAVE TO TAKE PLACE PRIOR TO DECEMBER 1ST. JFK MAY HAVE BEEN OUR PRESIDENT, BUT THE NEW ADMINISTRATION AND ITS INTELLIGENCE AGENCIES WOULD NOT RISK WWIII IF IT WERE ALLEGED THAT **HARVEY** HAD TIES TO CASTRO. **HARVEY** WOULD HAVE TO BE TRANSFORMED INTO A DISGRUNTLED LONER WITHOUT ACCOMPLICES. THE TASK OF SELLING THIS "REALITY" TO A RELUCTANT WARREN COMMISSION FOR THE SAKE OF "NATIONAL SECURITY" WOULD FALL TO THE PERSUASIVE LBJ.

THE PRE-AMWORLD EFFORTS, FOR VARIOUS REASONS, FAILED TO PRODUCE THE DESIRED EFFECT; THE ELIMINATION OF THE CASTRO REGIME. AS A RESULT, THE CIA RESORTED TO "LESS CONVENTIONAL" MEANS.

THE SCOPE AND DIVERSITY OF THE CIA'S ATTEMPTS GREW IN INTENSITY IN THEIR EFFORT TO THWART THE PRESIDENT'S BACK-CHANNEL NEGOTIATIONS WITH CASTRO IN AN EFFORT TO ACHIEVE SOME DEGREE OF RAPPROACHMENT WITH THE CUBAN LEADER.

SOON AFTER THE PRESIDENT'S DEATH, THE EFFORT TO ACHIEVE MORE NORMAL RELATIONS WITH CUBA DIED A QUIET DEATH OF ITS OWN. THE CIA EFFORTS TO ELIMINATE CASTRO HOWEVER INCREASED IN INTENSITY.

AT THE TIME, THE CIA'S OPERATIONS DIVISION CONTAINED AN OFFICE OF MEDICAL SERVICES. THIS OFFICE, COMBINED WITH THE TECHNICAL SERVICE DIVISION OF THE CIA, TRIED NUMEROUS DEVICES AND CONCOCTIONS IN THEIR EFFORTS TO REDUCE THE INFLUENCE OF CASTRO IN CUBA. MANY OF THESE ATTEMPTS INCLUDED THE LIKELIHOOD OF CASTRO'S DEATH. SOME OF THE BETTER KNOWN AND WELL DOCUMENTED SCHEMES WERE:

1) SPRAYING CASTRO'S BROADCAST STUDIO WITH AN LSD-LIKE SUBSTANCE
2) IMPREGNATING A BOX OF CIGARS WITH A DRUG THAT WOULD CAUSE DISORIENTATION
3) DUSTING HIS SHOES WITH THALLIUM SALTS CAUSING HIS BEARD TO FALL OUT
4) CIGARS TREATED WITH LETHAL POISONS
5) AN EXPLODING CONCH SHELL AT HIS FAVORITE SNORKELING SPOT
6) A FUNGUS CONTAMINATED WET SUIT AND TUBERCULINE CONTAMINATED SNORKEL
7) A BALL POINT PEN WITH A HYPODERMIC NEEDLE CONTAINING BLACK LEAF 40.
8) A BACTERIAL PILL THAT WOULD MAKE HIM FATALLY ILL.
9) A MACHINE GUN HIDDEN IN A T.V. CAMERA

IN FACT, AS LATE AS NOVEMBER 22ND, 1963, DESMOND FITZAGERALD, CIA SPECIAL AFFAIRS, MET WITH ROLANDO CUBELA IN PARIS. CUBELA HAD, IN SEPTEMBER OF THAT YEAR, OFFERED HIMSELF AS A POTENTIAL CASTRO ASSASSIN FOR THE CIA. FITZGERALD GAVE CUBELA A FOUNTAIN PEN CONTAINING THE TOXIN BLACKEAF 40.

SINCE MOST IF NOT ALL OF THESE SCHEMES PROVED FRUITLESS, THE CIA'S TECHNICAL SERVICES DIVISION TURNED TO MORE DRASTIC MEASURES; THE DEVELOPMENT OF A CARCINOGEN THAT WOULD LEAD TO THE DEATH OF FIDEL CASTRO IN A FASHION UNTRACEABLE TO THE U.S INTELLIGENCE COMMUNITY. THE CIA HAD INDEED IN THE YEARS PRIOR TO CASTRO'S RISE TO POWER CONSIDERED DEVELOPING CARCINOGENS. A MEMO AS EARLY AS 1952 COMMENTED ON THE RADIAOACTIVE ELEMENT BERYLIUM: "THIS IS CERTAINLY THE MOST TOXIC INORGANIC, AND IT PRODUCES A PECULIAR FIBROTIC TUMOR AT THE SITE OF LOCAL APPLICATION."

THE OCHSNER CLINIC IN NEW ORLEANS EMPLOYED A DR. MARY SHERMAN. HER MENTOR AND FOUNDER OF THE CLINIC, DR. ALTON OCHSNER, WAS A KNOWN ANTI-COMMUNIST AND AN AVID SUPPORTER OF THE INFORMATION COUNCIL OF THE AMERICAS, AN ANTI-COMMUNIST PROPAGANDA ORGANIZATION. THE PHYSICIAN IN CHARGE OF THE PATIENT POPULATION AT THE MENTAL INSTITUTION IN JACKSON WAS ALSO A FERVENT ANTI-COMMUNIST.

THE RESEARCH INTO CARCINOGENS AT THE OCHSNER CLINIC WAS UNDER THE AUSPICES OF THE CIA'S TECHNICAL SERVICES DIVISION. THIS WAS THE SAME OFFICE RESPONSIBLE IN PART FOR SOME OF THE NOVEL APPROACHES PREVIOUSLY OUTLINED

IN AN EFFORT TO ELIMINATE CASTRO OR AT LEAST TO RENDER HIM INEFFECTIVE AS A LEADER IN CUBA.

THE PARTICULAR CARCINOGEN PURSUED BY THE OCHSNER CLINIC HAD, TO THIS POINT, ONLY BEEN TESTED ON MICE AND RATS. IT WOULD AT ONE POINT NEED TO BE TESTED ON HUMANS AS WELL PRIOR TO BEING CONSIDERED FOR USE AGAINST CASTRO.

IT IS INTERESTING TO NOTE THAT WHEN RUBY DIED OF CANCER ON JANUARY 3RD, 1967 THAT HE HAD PREVIOUSLY EXPRESSED HIS BELIEF THAT HE HIMSELF HAD BEEN INJECTED WITH CANCER CELLS. AL MADDOX, A DALLAS DEPUTY SHERIFF WAS ONE OF RUBY'S JAILERS. MADDOX RECALLED THAT A "DOCTOR." WOULD FREQUENTLY VISIT RUBY'S CELL. RUBY TOLD MADDOX: "WELL, THEY INJECTED ME FOR A CONDITION." HOWEVER RUBY WENT ON TO TELL MADDOX THAT THE INJECTIONS WERE CANCER CELLS. WHEN MADDOX ASKED RUBY IF HE TRULY BELIEVED THAT THE INJECTIONS WERE INDEED CANCER CELLS RUBY REPLIED: "I DAMN SURE DO."

LEST ONE PREMATURELY DISMISS THIS SCENARIO AS BEING TOO FAR FETCHED, REMEMBER THAT IN THIS COLD WAR ERA THE MILITARY, THE OSS, AND IN TURN THE CIA PURSUED MANY AVENUES OF BEHAVIOURAL MODIFICATION AND PSYCHOLOGICAL PROGRAMMING.

THE NAVY INITIATED "PROJECT CHATTER" IN 1947 IN WHICH THEY EXPERIMENTED WITH TRUTH SERUMS. "PROJECT BLUEBIRD", A MIND CONTROL EFFORT BASED ON HYPNOSIS STARTED IN 1949 AT THE EDGEWOOD ARSENAL IN MARYLAND. FORMER NORTH KOREAN POW'S WERE CHOSEN AS TEST SUBJECTS. "BLUEBIRD" ALSO EXPERIMENTED WITH OPIUM, HEROIN, AND MESCALINE. IN THE EARLY 1950'S, THE CIA ESSENTIALLY "INFILTRATED" PROGRAMS AT FT. DETRICK AND BEGAN RUNNING EXPERIMENTS OF THEIR OWN LIKING. "BLUEBIRD" EVOLVED INTO "OPERATION ARTICHOKE." IT WAS INITIATED IN LATE 1951 AND EARLY 1952 BY THE CIA'S TECHNICAL SERVICES SECTION, CHEMICAL DIVISION, AT FT. DETRICK, MARYLAND. ITS FOCUS NOW INCLUDED AMNESIA AND MARKED INTEREST IN UTILIZING LSD TO INDUCE AMNESIA. "ARTICHOKE" DELVED INTO DRUG ENHANCED INTERROGATION TECHNIQUES. "MK ULTRA" STARTED IN 1953 AS A COMPANION PROGRAM TO "MK DELTA" WHICH ALSO STARTED IN 1953. ALTHOUGH ELECTROSHOCK THERAPY AND SENSORY DEPRAVATION WERE ALSO EMPLOYED IN" MK ULTRA", LSD WAS THE DRUG OF CHOICE FOR MANY OF THE EXPERIMENTS. "MK ULTRA" WOULD PERFORM ITS EXPERIMENTS IN THE UNITED STATES AND CANADA WHILE "MK DELTA'S" CHARTER ALLOWED IT TO PURSUE EXPERIMENTS OVERSEAS. PROJECT "MK NAOMI", WHICH RAN CONCURRENTLY WITH "MK ULTRA" AND" MK DELTA", DEALT WITH THE DELIVERY OF MIND CONTROL DRUGS. IN 1955 SAN FRANCISCO WAS CHOSEN AS ANOTHER SITE WHERE "MK ULTRA" WAS RE-TITLED "MIDNIGHT CLIMAX" AND CONTINUED UNTIL 1963 AT WHICH TIME "MK ULTRA" WAS RETIRED BY A PROGRAM TITLED "MK SEARCH."

AT ITS PEAK, "ULTRA/MIDNIGHT CLIMAX" HAD 182 SUB-PROJECTS. IN SAN FRANCISCO, PROSTITUTES WERE PAID TO BRING BACK "CLIENTS" TO CIA SAFEHOUSES WHERE THE UNSUSPECTING MEN WERE GIVEN LSD. THEIR ACTIONS WERE THEN VIDEO TAPED. "MK ULTRA" WAS SUPERVISED BY GEORGE WHITE OF THE FEDERAL BUREAU OF NARCOTICS. "PROJECT PELICAN", AN OFFSHOOT OF "MK-ULTRA", WAS CONDUCTED AT THE NEW YORK STATE PSYCHIATRIC INSTITUTE AND USED CHILDREN AS YOUNG AS 6 YEARS OLD AS TEST SUBJECTS. OTHER LSD EXPERIMENTS WERE "PROJECT THIRD CHANCE" AND "PROJECT DERBY HAT." THE LSD EXPERIMENTS WERE CONDUCTED AT TWELVE U.S AND CANADIAN HOSPITALS, PRISONS, DUGWAY PROVING GROUND IN UTAH, AND AT FT. DETRICK. LSD EXPERIMENTS WERE ALSO CONDUCTED AT THE CENTER FOR ADDICTION RESEARCH IN LEXINGTON, KENTUCKY AND THE NEW YORK STATE PSYCHIATRIC INSTITUTE. THERE WERE 80 COLLEGES, PRIVATE INSTUTIONS, UNIVERSITIES, HOSPITALS/CLINICS, RESEARCH FACILITIES AND PRISONS USED AS FIELD EXPERIMENT SITES FOR MIND CONTROL DRUGS BY THE CIA, THE ARMY, AND

THE NAVY. THE MIND CONTROL EFFORTS OF THE CIA WOULD END IN JANUARY 1973 WHEN THEN CIA DIRECTOR HELMS DESTROYED ALL THE MK ULTRA FILES.

EXPERIMENTS INVOLVING CARCINOGENS, RADIATION, AND POTENTIAL BIOLOGIC WEAPONS WERE ALSO CONDUCTED DURING THIS PERIOD. IN 1952, AT THE OHIO STATE PENITENTIARY, NEARLY 400 INMATES WERE INJECTED WJITH HUMAN CANCER CELLS.. THIS PARTICULAR ENDEAVOR WAS PERFORMED BY THE NATIONAL INSTITUTE OF HEALTH.

"OPERATION WHITECOAT" WAS YET ANOTHER PROGRAM RAN FROM FT. DETRICK STARTING IN 1954. IT USED VOLUNTEERS FROM THE 7TH DAY ADVENTIST CHURCH. BIOLOGICAL TESTS WERE PERFORMED USING ANTHRAX AND OTHER VIRUSES SUCH AS QUEEN FEVER. THIS PROJECT INVOLVED OVER 2300 VOLUNTEERS. THE PUBLIC HEALTH SERVICE PERFORMED EXPERIMENTS ON BLACK MALES IN TUSKEEGEE ALABAMA AS THEY SIMPLY "MONITORED" THE MEN WITH KNOWN CASES OF SYPHILLIS OVER A 40 YEAR PERIOD.

THERE WERE ALSO RADIATION EXPERIMENTS DONE ON ORPHANS IN A CINCINNATI ORPHANAGE, AT BILLINGS HOSPITAL IN CHICAGO, AT VANDERBILT UNIVERSITY IN NASHVILLE, AT WRENTHAM STATE SCHOOL IN MASSACHUSSETTS, AT FERNALD SCHOOL, A BOY'S HOME IN MASSACHUSSETS, AT OAK RIDGE ARMY HOSPITAL, THE UNIVERSITY OF ROCHESTER, AND AT STATE PRISONS IN WASHINGTON AND OREGON. THESE EVENTS WERE LATER WELL DOCUMENTED AND THE DEPARTMENT OF DEFENSE, THE ATOMIC ENERGY COMMITTEE, AND THE CIA ADMITTED HAVING PERFORMED SUCH ACTS IN A MEASURE OF COLD WAR DESPERATION.

AN EXCELLENT BOOK ON THE VARIOUS PROGRAMS AND EXPERIMENTS RAN BY THE CIA IS.P. ALBARELLI, JR.'S BOOK "A TERRIBLE MISTAKE."

LEST ONE THINK THE CIA'S, THE DOD'S, AND THE AEC'S EFFORTS MINDBOGGLING, THE JOINT CHIEFS OF STAFF HAD EQUALLY DISTURBING NOTIONS OF HOW TO ELIMINATE CASTRO AND OR INVADE CUBA. ONE WAS A TOP SECRET PLAN CODENAMED "OPERATION NORTHWOODS." GENERAL LYMAN T. LEMNITZER, CHAIRMAN JCS, IN CONJUNCTION WITH THE JCS DECIDED THAT THE ONLY WAY TO INSURE THAT THE AMERICAN PUBLIC WOULD BACK A MILITARY INVASION OF CUBA WAS TO ARRANGE FOR AN "INCIDENT" THAT COULD BE FALSELY TIED TO THE CUBAN GOVERNMENT. ONE OF THE "INCIDENTS" PROPOSED WAS AN ATTACK ON GUANTANAMO, THE U.S. NAVAL BASE IN EASTERN CUBA, BY A GROUP OF CUBAN CIVILIANS DRESSED IN CUBAN ARMY UNIFORMS. ALSO CONSIDERED WAS AN EXPLOSION ON A U.S. NAVY SHIP ANCHORED AT GUANTANAMO WHICH WOULD ALSO BE BLAMED ON THE CUBAN GOVERNMENT. TERRORISTIC "INCIDENTS" WERE ALSO CONSIDERED: THE "HIJACKING" OF A CIVILIAN AIRLINER OR CRUISESHIP, AND EVEN A PLAN TO EXPLODE A DRONE CIVILIAN AIRLINER IN AN EFFORT TO CONVINCE THE WORLD THAT THE CUBAN GOVERNMENT HAD SHOT DOWN A CIVILIAN AIRCRAFT.

THE MOST DISTURBING OPTION PROPOSED BY THE JCS WAS DIRECTED AT NASA. THE PLAN CALLED FOR AN EXPLOSION ABOARD ASTRONAUT JOHN GLENN'S ROCKET ON HIS SCHEDULED FEBRUARY, 1962 ORBITAL MISSION. ONCE AGAIN, THE BLAME WOULD BE PLACED AT THE FEET OF THE CUBAN GOVERNMENT.

*IT IS CERTAINLY POSSIBLE THAT **HARVEY**, RUBY, AND FERRIE WERE LED TO BELIEVE THAT THE "FIREWORKS" RUBY WOULD LATER REFER TO ON NOVEMBER 22ND WERE INDEED AN "OPERATION NORTHWOODS" EVENT STAGED TO ARROUSE ANTI-CUBAN SENTIMENT JUST PRIOR TO THE EARLY DECEMBER AMWORLD INVASION OF CUBA. THE "FIREWORKS" COULD ALSO BE USED TO "MUDDY THE WATER" ACOUSTICALLY AND DISGUISE THE TRUE INTENTION OF THAT DAY: THE ASSASSINATION OF THE PRESIDENT. THE DETAILS REGARDING THE PLAUSABILITY OF THIS THEORY IF NOT THE PROBABILITY REGARDING A "OPERATION NORTHWOODS-TYPE" ATTEMPT WILL BE COVERED IN LATER CHAPTERS.*

ADMIRAL STANSFIELD TURNER WOULD LATER TESTIFY TO CONGRESS IN 1977 REGARDING THE CIA'S DOMESTIC ACTIVITIES. TURNER REVEALED THAT THE CIA FUNDED 159 SECRET RESEARCH FACILITIES ONE OF WHICH WAS THS OCHSNER CLINIC.

WITH THE MINDSET OF THE CIA, THE DOD, THE AEC, AND THE JCS FIRMLY ESTABLISHED, LET US EXAMINE THE **FIRST SCENARIO** THROUGH THE EYES OF JUDYTH VARY. WE WILL BEGIN THE STRANGE SUMMER OF 1963 WITH THE ARRIVAL OF JUDYTH VARY AND CONTINUE FROM HER PERSPECTIVE THROUGH THE FALL OF 1963 AND THE DEPARTURE OF BOTH HER AND **HARVEY** FROM NEW ORLEANS.

SCENARIO I

*A **LEGITIMATE** CIA PROJECT ENLISTS **HARVEY** TO DELIVER CARCINOGENS TO CIA OPERATIVES IN CUBA FOR THE PURPOSE OF ELIMINATING CASTRO. THIS IS LIKELY DONE IN CONJUNCTION WITH THE PLANNED "AMWORLD" COUP SCHEDULED FOR THE FIRST WEEK IN DECEMBER, 1963. ASSISTING **HARVEY** ARE GUY BANISTER, DAVID FERRIE, AND JUDYTH BAKER IN NEW ORLEANS, JACK RUBY IN DALLAS AND NEW ORLEANS, AND HOWARD HUNT AND DAVID ATLEE PHILLIPS IN MEXICO CITY AND DALLAS. MEDICAL GUIDANCE FOR THE PROJECT IS PROVIDED BY DR. ALTON OCHSNER AND HIS ASSOCIATE DR. MARY SHERMAN.*

WE WILL INTRODUCE AN ALTERNATE SCENARIO, **SCENARIO II,** LATER. I WILL NOTE THE SITUATIONS IN **SCENARIO II** THAT ARE LIKELY TO BE PERCEIVED DRAMATICALLY DIFFERENT THAN THEY WERE IN **SCENARIO I.**

*ALTHOUGH **SCENARIO I** IMPLIES THAT **HARVEY** IS INDEED INVOLVED IN A LEGITIMATE CIA ENDEAVOR TO INFUSE HIM INTO CUBA PRIOR TO THE C-DAY/AMWORLD COUP PLANNED FOR EARLY DECEMBER, 1963, I HAVE CHOSEN TO USE THIS MOMENT TO ALSO NOTE THE MORE LIKELY REASON FOR **HARVEY'S** TRANSFER TO NEW ORLEANS: THE SET-UP FOR THE EVENTS OF NOVEMBER 22ND. THAT CONCEPT WILL BE INTRODUCED IN MORE DETAIL IN **SCENARIO II** AFTER **HARVEY'S** DEPARTURE FROM NEW ORLEANS. IT IS, FROM A TIMEFRAME STANDPOINT, IMPORTANT TO INJECT AN ALTERNATE RATIONALE FOR **SCENARIO I** AT THIS POINT (**SCENARIO II**) RATHER THAN REPEAT THE ENTIRE NEW ORLEANS – MEXICO – DALLAS SEQUENCE FROM AN ENTIRELY DIFFERENT AND MORE PLAUSIBLE PERSPECTIVE, **SCENARIO II**. FROM THIS POINT FORWARD, THE EVENTS THAT TAKE PLACE IN BOTH SCENARIOS REMAIN THE SAME. IT IS THE PURPOSE OF THE EVENTS INVOLVING **HARVEY** AND OTHERS THAT VARIES DRAMATICALLY IN THE DISTINCTIVELY INDIVIDUAL SCENARIOS. IN ESSENCE, **SCENARIO I** IS **HARVEY'S** PERCEPTION. **SCENARIO II** IS **HARVEY'S** UNFORTUNATE REALITY.*

*IT IS POSSIBLE THAT **HARVEY'S** TRANSFER TO NEW ORLEANS WAS THE RESULT OF A LEGITIMATE CIA ASSIGNMENT TO WORK WITH AND QUITE LIKELY SIMULTANEOUSLY INFILTRATE THE ANTI-CASTRO SHAW, BANISTER, AND FERRIE GROUP IN NEW ORLEANS. THE CIA IN WASHINGTON WAS UNCERTAIN OF THE CAPABILITIES OR INTENTIONS OF THIS POWERFUL AND NOW RENEGADE GROUP OF OPERATIVES. **HARVEY'S** PRESENCE IN NEW ORLEANS WOULD BE PERCEIVED BY MOORE AND DEMOHRENSCHILDT AS A WAY TO ALLOW THE CIA PROPER TO MONITOR BANISTER'S GROUP. NEITHER MOORE OR DEMOHRENSCHILDT WOULD HAVE ANY SUSPICIONS OF THE REQUEST BY PHILLIPS OR HUNT NOR ANY INDICATION THAT THE MOVE WAS ALSO DESIGNED TO INITIATE THE SET-UP OF **HARVEY** (**SCENARIO II**) NOT THE FIRST STEP IN A LEGITIMATE EFFORT TO COURIER CARCINOGENS TO CUBA.*

*THIS MOVE, LIKE THE MOVE TO DALLAS, IS LIKELY PROMPTED BY THE MASTERMINDS RESPONSIBLE FOR THE SET-UP OF **HARVEY**; E. HOWARD HUNT AND DAVID ATLEE PHILLIPS. (**FURTHER EXPLAINED IN SCENARIO II**) THEY WOULD INITIATE THE PROCESS BY INFORMING DALLAS CIA BRANCH OFFICER J. WALTON MOORE. MOORE IN TURN WOULD RELAY THE REQUEST TO DEMOHRENSCHILDT WHO WOULD INFORM **HARVEY** OF THE NEW*

ORLEANS MOVE PRIOR TO HIS OWN APRIL 17TH DEPARTURE WITH HIS WIFE JEANNE FOR NEW YORK.

ALTHOUGH DE MOHRENSCHILDT WAS LIKELY BEING USED BY HUNT/PHILLIPS TO GUIDE **HARVEY** FIRST TO DALLAS AND THEN TO NEW ORLEANS, HE WAS ALSO INFLUENTIAL IN A POSITIVE WAY TOWARDS **HARVEY** AND HIS FAMILY. DEMOHRENSCHILDT'S INFLUENCE OVER **HARVEY** CANNOT BE OVERSTATED. HIS SON-IN-LAW, GARY TAYLOR, WOULD REMARK BEFORE THE WARREN COMMISSION THAT "WHATEVER HIS (DE MOHRENSCHILDT'S) SUGGESTIONS WERE, LEE (**HARVEY**) GRABBED THEM AND TOOK THEM WHETHER IT WAS WHAT TIME TO GO TO BED OR WHERE TO STAY." DE MOHRENSCHILDT HELPED **HARVEY** FIND JOBS AND ALSO FOUND A PLACE FOR MARINA AND JUNE IN HIS ABSENCE. NOW IT SEEMS THAT HUNT/PHILLIPS WANTED DEMOHRENSCHILDT FAR FROM DALLAS PRIOR TO NOVEMBER.22ND

DEMOHRENSCHILDT MAY HAVE BEEN THE ONLY PERSON WHO NOT ONLY <u>COULD HAVE</u>, BUT POSSIBLY <u>WOULD HAVE</u> SAVED **HARVEY** FROM WHAT WAS QUICKLY BECOMING A VERY TANGLED WEB OF DECEIT AND INCRIMINATING PRO-CASTRO POSTURING. DEMOHRENSCHILDT, HAD HE BEEN AWARE, WOULD HAVE QUESTIONED THE OBVIOUS DISCREPANCY BETWEEN **HARVEY'S** NEW ORLEANS "ASSIGNMENT" TO WORK WITH AND SIMULTANEOUSLY MONITOR BANISTER'S ANTI-CASTRO GROUP IN NEW ORLEANS FOR THE CIA (I.E. HUNT/PHILLIPS) WHILE AT THE SAME TIME BEING ENCOURAGED TO CONTINUE THE LEFTIST LEANINGS INITIATED WITH HIS CIA-SPONSORED RUSSIAN "DEFECTION" BY POSING AS A PRO-CASTRO FPFC ADVOCATE. DEMOHRENSCHILDT, IN HIS DEFENSE, HAD NO WAY OF KNOWING THAT THE TRUE PURPOSE OF **HARVEY'S** NEW ORLEANS "ASSIGNMENT" WAS THE FURTHERANCE OF HIS BEING SET-UP AS PRO-CASTRO PATRON. AND, MORE IMPORTANTLY, EXPOSING HIM TO THE INITIAL PHASE OF A BOGUS "CANCER PLOT" **(SCENARIO II)** THAT **HARVEY** WOULD MISTAKENLY BELIEVE TO BE HIS TRUE MISSION ON NOVEMBER 22ND.

LATER, A SECONDARY ROLE FOR **HARVEY** WILL EMERGE IN NEW ORLEANS AS WELL. HE WILL ALSO BE TASKED WITH THE ROLE AS AN INFORMANT FOR THE <u>FBI</u>. THEY WERE LEGITIMATELY INTERESTED IN MONITORING BANISTER'S GROUP IN NEW ORLEANS AS THE WHITE HOUSE HAD ORDERED A FBI CRACK-DOWN ON MILITANT ANTI-CASTRO GROUPS. MOST OF THESE GROUPS WERE FUNDED BY AND OFFERED LOGISTIC SUPPORT BY THE CIA. THE MONITORING OF BANISTER'S GROUP WOULD ALLOW THE FBI TO INFILTRATE THE GUN-RUNNING CONNECTION FROM DALLAS TO NEW ORLEANS TO MIAMI AND THEN TO CUBA. THIS HAD BEEN AGENT HOSTY'S PRIME FOCUS IN DALLAS. WITH **HARVEY** IN NEW ORLEANS, THE FBI COULD HOPEFULLY GATHER INFORMATION ON THE SECOND "LEG" OF THE GUN-RUNNING CORRIDOR TO CUBA

IN NEW ORLEANS, **HARVEY** WOULD BE HANDLED BY FBI AGENT WARREN DEBRUEYS WHO KEPT A C.I. (CONFIDENTIAL INFORMANT) FILE ON **HARVEY** DURING HIS STAY. HIS FILE WAS UNDER THE HEADING "ANTI-CASTRO ACTIVITIES." OREST PENA, OWNER OF THE HABANA BAR IN NEW ORLEANS AND ALSO AN FBI INFORMANT, WOULD LATER CLAIM THAT HE HAD SEEN **HARVEY** IN HIS BAR WITH CUBANS AND AGENT DEBREUYS. PENA WOULD ALSO NOTE THAT 10 DAYS <u>PRIOR</u> TO HIS TESTIMONY TO THE WARREN COMMISSION THAT DEBREUYS STATED TO HIM: "IF YOU EVER TALK ANYTHING ABOUT ME, I WILL GET RID....I'LL GET RID OF YOUR ASS." WILLIAM S. WALTER, A SECURITY CLERK AT THE FBI OFFICE IN NEW ORLEANS NOTED THAT **HARVEY** HAD BOTH A SECURITY <u>AND</u> AN INFORMANT FILE. DALLAS FBI AGENT WILL HAYDEN GRIFFIN STATED THAT **HARVEY** WAS DEFINITELY AN FBI INFORMANT.

HUNTER LEAKE, DEPUTY CHIEF OF THE NEW ORLEANS CIA OFFICE, NOTED THAT **HARVEY** HAD IN FACT PERFORMED TASKS FOR THE CIA AS WELL IN NEW ORLEANS IN THE SUMMER OF 1963. LEAKE OFFERED THAT HE HIMSELF PAID **HARVEY** FOR HIS EFFORTS THAT SUMMER ON BEHALF OF THE CIA.

TO SUMARIZE HARVEY'S TRANSFER TO NEW ORLEANS AND HIS STATUS:

HE WAS SENT TO NEW ORLEANS BY HUNT/PHILLIPS VIA J.WALTON MOORE AND GEORGE DE MOHRENSCHILDT. HE WOULD BE TOLD THAT HIS OFFICIAL ASSIGNMENT WAS TO WORK <u>WITH</u> GUY BANISTER REGARDING BOTH PRO AND ANTI-CASTRO GROUPS AND AT THE SAME TIME MONITOR BANISTER'S GROUP FOR THE CIA. MOORE, DEMOHRENSCHILDT, AND **HARVEY** WOULD <u>PERCEIVE</u> THIS AS A LEGITIMATE CIA ASSIGNMENT. HUNT AND PHILLIPS HOWEVER WOULD KNOW IT TO BE LITTLE MORE THAN AN EXCUSE TO GET **HARVEY** TO NEW ORLEANS WHERE THE INITIAL PHASE OF THE SET-UP WOULD BEGIN. **(SCENARIO II)**

BANISTER WILL ASSIST **HARVEY** IN ESTABLISHING HIS BONAFIDES BY ENCOURAGING HIM TO FORM A NEW ORLEANS CHAPTER OF THE FPFC AND ARRANGE BOTH STREET AND RADIO EVENTS TO PUBLICISE HIS LEFTIST LEANINGS. HE WOULD ALSO INTRODUCE **HARVEY** TO A CARCINOGENS PROJECT THAT WAS FRAUDULENT **(SCENARIO II)** AND <u>NOT</u> ASSOCIATED WITH A LEGITIMATE EFFORT ON THE PART OF THE CIA TO DEVELOP CARCINOGENS IN THEIR EFFORT TO ELIMINATE CASTRO.

HARVEY WOULD ALSO BE TASKED, <u>LEGITIMATELY</u> BY THE FBI TO MONITOR BANISTER'S GUN-RUNNING ACTIVITIES TO CUBA AND BANISTER'S EXTENSIVE INVOLVEMENT IN MONITORING AND INFILTRATING GROUPS FAVORABLE TO INTEGRATION.

BANISTER HOWEVER PROBABLY DID NOT REALIZE THAT HE WAS IN THE PECULIAR POSITION OF BEING "INFILTRATED" BY **HARVEY** AND THE FBI WHILE SIMUTANEOUSLY ASSISTING HUNT AND PHILLIPS IN THEIR SET-UP **(SCENARIO II)** OF **HARVEY**. IN THE POST-ASSASSINATION AFTERMATH HOWEVER BOTH AGENCIES AND BANISTER WOULD PREDICTABLY EXPEND A GREAT DEAL OF EFFORT IN DENYING ANY ASSOCIATION WITH **HARVEY**.

BANISTER WOULD ALSO UTILIZE **HARVEY** IN AN "OFF-THE-BOOKS" FASHION IN HIS EFFORTS TO INFILTRATE THE PREVIOUSLY MENTIONED GROUPS THAT FAVORED INTEGRATION AND THE FUTHERANCE OF CIVIL RIGHTS IN THE SOUTH. THE MINUTEMEN AND THE JOHN BIRCH SOCIETY WOULD USE THE THINLY-VEILED "COMMUNIST CONNECTION" IN THEIR ATTEMPT TO DISMANTLE ANY GROUP FURTHERING INTEGRATION.

NOTE

THIS IS AN APPROPRIATE TIME TO INTRODUCE A BOOK RECENTLY PUBLISHED IN 2015 BY JEFFREY H. CAUFIELD, M.D. HIS BOOK IS TITLED "GENERAL WALKER AND THE MURDER OF PRESIDENT KENNEDY." UNTIL THIS WORK WAS RELEASED, MY EXTENSIVE READING HAD TO A GREAT EXTENT EXPLAINED THE EXTENSIVE MANIPULATION OF **HARVEY** BY HUNT/PHILLIPS, GUY BANISTER, THE FBI, AND THE CIA. THE PRO-CASTRO POSTURING AND HIS FPFC ASSOCIATION ALSO MADE SENSE REGARDLESS OF WHETHER **HARVEY** WAS BEING GROOMED FOR A FUTURE LEGITIMATE ASSIGNMENT IN REGARDS TO THE DECEMBER 1963 C-DAY COUP OR WHETHER THIS CONTINUED "COMMUNIST-CONNECTION" WAS SIMPLY A WAY TO IMPLICATE CASTRO WHEN **HARVEY** WAS LATER ANNOINTED AS THE PRESIDENT'S ASSASSIN. WHAT WAS LESS CLEAR HOWEVER WAS **HARVEY'S** INFILTRATION OF CIVIL RIGHTS GROUPS; AN EFFORT ALMOST EXCLUSIVELY THE MAKING OF GUY BANISTER.

CAUFIELD'S WORK ADDS A NEW PERSPECTIVE TO THE CONFUSING "SHEEP-DIPPING" OF **HARVEY** IN NEW ORLEANS AND IMPLIES THAT A FACTION THAT HAD BEEN PREVIOUSLY OVERLOOKED, RADICAL RIGHT-WING SEGREGATIONISTS, MAY HAVE BEEN INSTRUMENTAL IN THE PRESIDENT'S DEATH. FEW BOOKS IN MY COLLECTION OF OVER 180 DISTINCT TITLES OPEN NEW DOORS TO SOLVING THE CRIME. CAUFIELD'S DILIGENT RESEARCH YIELDS WHAT IS IN MY OPINION ONE OF THE FEW GROUND-

BREAKING EFFORTS IN RECENT YEARS REGARDING THE ASSASSINATION. HIS THEORY WILL SHED NEW LIGHT ON WHAT TOOK PLACE, AND MORE IMPORTANTLY <u>WHY</u> IT TOOK PLACE WHEN WE DETAIL THE INCIDENT IN CLINTON, LOUISIANA IN A LATER CHAPTER.

OUR LAST ENTRY IN THE TIME LINE WAS APRIL 23RD, 1963. WE WILL NOW RETURN TO THE TIMELINE ON THE FOLLOWING DAY.

APRIL 24TH 1963
HARVEY ARRIVES IN NEW ORLEANS. IT IS NOT KNOWN WHERE HE STAYED FROM APRIL 24TH TO APRIL 28TH. IT IS POSSIBLE THAT HE STAYED AT THE YMCA. HOWEVER SINCE BANISTER IS HIS CONTACT PERSON I THINK THAT UPON ARRIVING IN NEW ORLEANS HE CONTACTED BANISTER WHO HAD HIM ROOM WITH DAVID FERRIE. I THINK IT IS LIKELY THAT HE STAYED AT DAVID FERRIE'S APARTMENT UNTIL APRIL 28TH. WITH **HARVEY'S** DEPARTURE, MARINA AND JUNE MOVE TO IRVING TO LIVE WITH RUTH PAINE AT 2515 FIFTH ST.

VARY/BAKER HOWEVER STATES THAT **HARVEY** *ARRIVED AFTER MIDNIGHT ON THE 25TH, THUS THE 26TH OF APRIL.*

APRIL 26TH 1963
THE CIA'S OFFICE OF SECURITY CONDUCTED AN EXPEDITE CHECK ON GEORGE DEMOHRENSCHILDT.

DEMOHRENSCHILDT'S RELATIONSHIP WITH THE CIA WOULD NOW BE ON TWO LEVELS. HE WOULD BE AIDED IN HIS PURSUIT OF OIL IN HAITI BY THE CIA PROPER IN WASHINGTON WHILE SIMULTANEOUSLY BEING USED TO "GUIDE" AND MONITOR **HARVEY'S** *ACTIVITIES FOR HUNT AND PHILLIPS. I SUSPECT THE EXPEDITE CHECK, ONLY <u>1 DAY</u> AFTER* **HARVEY** *LEFT FOR NEW ORLEANS, WAS ORDERED BY HUNT/PHILLIPS TO ESTABLISH DEMOHRENSCHILDT'S WHEREABOUTS.*

APRIL 26TH 1963
HARVEY VISITS THE LOUISIANA EMPLOYMENT SECURITY DIVISION IN HOPES OF OBTAINING EMPLOYMENT WHILE IN NEW ORLEANS. HE NOTED ON HIS PAPERWORK THAT HIS ADDRESS WAS 757 FRENCH ST. THIS HOWEVER IS THE ADDRESS OF **LEE'S** AUNT AND UNCLE, LILLIAN AND DUTZ MURRET. **HARVEY** HAD DROPPED LUGGAGE AT THEIR HOME THIS MORNING. HE IS INTERVIEWED BY JOHN RACHEL WHO REFERRED HIM TO THE GEORGE REPPEL STUDIO FOR A PHOTOGRAPHIC JOB. **HARVEY** DID NOT SHOW UP FOR HIS INTERVIEW AT THE STUDIO. HE WILL HAVE DINNER WITH DAVID FERRIE THIS EVENING.

THE MURRET'S DAUGHTER MARILYN, **LEE'S** *COUSIN, MAY HAVE BEEN INVOLVED IN* **HARVEY'S** *INITIAL RECRUITMENT INTO THE CIA. MARILYN WAS A LANGUAGE TEACHER AND TRAVELED EXTENSIVELY. INTERESTINGLY SHE MET* **LEE'S** *HALF-BROTHER, JOHN PIC, IN JAPAN IN SEPTEMBER 1959 WHERE SHE WAS TEACHING AND TOLD HIM THAT* **HARVEY** *WAS IN RUSSIA. HOW DID <u>SHE</u> KNOW? THE FIRST KNOWN PUBLIC ACKNOWLEDGEMENT OF* **HARVEY'S** *ARRIVAL IN RUSSIA WAS NOT UNTIL OCTOBER 31ST, 1959 WHEN A FT. WORTH REPORTER INFORMED ROBERT OSWALD OF* **HARVEY'S** *"DEFECTIION."* **HARVEY'S** *"FAMILY" WOULD HAVE HAD TO ASSUME AT <u>THAT</u> TIME THAT* **HARVEY** *WAS ENROLLED AT ALBERT SCHWEITZER COLLEGE IN SWITZERLAND. MARILYN QUITE LIKELY WAS A CIA CONTACT WHO WOULD REPORT ON HER VARIOUS TRAVELS UPON HER RETURN STATESIDE. THIS WAS QUITE A COMMON TECHNIQUE USED BY THE CIA WITH FRIENDLY BUSINESSMEN AND OTHERS WHOSE CAREERS FREQUENTLY LED TO TRAVEL IN PLACES DIFFICULT TO PLACE AGENTS. THE DOMESTIC CONTACTS DIVISION HANDLED THIS CHORE AFTER THE ASSASSINATION. THE FBI CONCLUDED THAT MURRET "WAS LINKED IN SOME MANNER WITH THE APPARATUS OF A PROFESSOR HAROLD ISAACS." ISAACS, A FORMER EDITOR AT NEWSWEEK, WAS ASSOCIATED WITH THE MIT'S CENTER FOR INTERNATIONAL STUDIES. THE CENTER WAS A CIA THINK TANK.*

APRIL 26TH, 1963
JUDYTH VARY MEETS **HARVEY** AT THE POST OFFICE IN NEW ORLEANS AT 10:00 AM.

THE MEETING WITH **HARVEY** AT THE POST OFFICE IS NOT AT ALL A CHANCE MEETING. **HARVEY** WAS LIKELY TOLD BY HUNT/PHILLIPS THAT SOMEONE IN NEW ORLEANS WITH LEGITIMATE RESEARCH EXPERIENCE WILL PROVIDE HIM WITH A CARCINOGEN THAT HE WILL LATER BE ASKED TO COURIER TO ANTI-CASTRO DISSIDENT DOCTORS IN CUBA. A PICTURE OF THE ATTRACTIVE VARY SUPPLIED BY HUNT/PHILLIP WOULD AID **HARVEY** IN IDENTIFYING VARY ON ONE OF HER FREQUENT TRIPS TO THE MAIN POST OFFICE.

ONE HAS TO ALSO CONSIDER THE POSSIBILITY THAT PERHAPS <u>VARY</u> WAS INSTRUCTED TO CONTACT **HARVEY**. HER RECOLLECTION OF THE ENCOUNTER HAS HER THANKING HIM FROM RETRIEVING HER DROPPED NEWSPAPER IN <u>RUSSIAN</u>. SHE WAS "STUNNED" WHEN HE REPLIED IN RUSSIAN. THE LIKELIHOOD OF VARY AND **HARVEY** ARRIVING IN NEW ORLEANS WITHIN 5 DAYS OF EACH OTHER, BOTH RESIDING AT YMCA/YWCA FACILITIES, AND SHARING THE SAME POST OFFICE FOR OUTSIDE COMMUNICATIONS IS SUSPICIOUSLY COINCIDENTAL. THEIR RUSSIAN INTRODUCTORY COMMENTS IS MORE IN LINE WITH A CLANDESTINE INTELLIGENCE FIRST ENCOUNTER THAN A RANDOM EVENT.

APRIL 27TH, 1963
VARY MOVES INTO A BOARDING HOUSE ON ST. CHARLES AVENUE. LATER THAT DAY, **HARVEY**, VARY AND FERRIE WOULD MEET FOR LUNCH. FERRIE COMMENTS TO VARY THAT HE IS FAMILIAR WITH DR. OCHSNER AND HIS CLINIC AND THAT DR MARY SHERMAN IS A "FRIEND." **HARVEY** INTRODUCED FERRIE TO VARY AS "DR. FERRIE."

APRIL 28TH 1963
HARVEY ESCORTS VARY TO A PARTY AT FERRIE'S APARTMENT. ALTHOUGH FERRIE ATTEMPTS TO INTRODUCE VARY TO DR. SHERMAN, OR "DR. MARY" AS FERRIE REFERS TO SHERMAN, VARY IS ABRUPTLY DISMISSED BY SHERMAN. THE SUSPICIOUS VARY ADMITTED TO HAVING SOME DOUBTS ABOUT THE CANCER PROJECT AND THE EFFORTS TO KILL CASTRO. FERRIE OFFERS TO HAVE SOMEONE VERIFY THAT THE PROJECT IS INDEED LEGITIMATE AND GOVERNMENT SANCTIONED. HE OFFERS TO INTRODUCE VARY TO GUY BANISTER.

VARY, TO HER CREDIT, SENSES THAT SOMETHING IS AMISS. SHE LIKELY IS UNCERTAIN THAT THE INVOLVEMENT OF A CAST OF CHARACTERS SUCH AS FERRIE AND **HARVEY** IN THIS TYPE OF HIGHLY CLASSIFIED RESEARCH EFFORT IS LEGITIMATE. HER DISMISSAL BY SHERMAN MAY HAVE REINFORCED THIS NOTION. IT IS ALSO POSSIBLE THAT DR. SHERMAN IS SOMEWHAT INSULTED AT HAVING TO TAKE UNDER HER WING THE MUCH YOUNGER VARY. VARY ALSO NOTED THAT **HARVEY** DID NOT DRINK AT THE PARTY. IT IS **LEE** WHO IS KNOWN TO DRINK.

APRIL 29TH 1963
DEMOHRENSCHILDT AND HIS WIFE RETURN TO DALLAS.

APRIL 29TH, 1963
HARVEY TAKES VARY TO BANISTER'S OFFICE ON CAMP STREET. BANISTER WOULD LESSEN VARY'S DOUBTS BY TELLING HER THAT BOTH **HARVEY** AND FERRIE WERE INDEED INVOLVED IN A SECRET GOVERNMENT PROJECT DESIGNED TO REMOVE CASTRO FROM POWER. **HARVEY** VISITS THE UNEMPLOYMENT OFFICE WHERE HE IS INTERVIEWED BY BOB HUNLEY.

APRIL 29TH 1963
HARVEY STAYS WITH HIS "AUNT AND UNCLE" LILLIAN AND DUTZ MURRET. THE MURRETS ARE THE AUNT AND UNCLE OF **LEE**. LILLIAN MURRET IS THE SISTER OF MARGUERITE, **LEE'S** MOTHER.

APRIL 30TH 1963
HARVEY AND VARY HAVE BREAKFAST AT THE ROYAL CASTLE RESTAURANT.

MAY 1ST, 1963
VARY'S FIANCE, ROBERT ALLISON BAKER III, ARRIVES IN NEW ORLEANS.

MAY 1ST 1963
THE EVER-MOBILE DE MOHRENSCHILDT AND HIS WIFE DEPART DALLAS AGAIN.

MAY 2ND 1963
VARY AND BAKER ARE MARRIED IN MOBILE, ALABAMA.

WE WILL, FROM THIS POINT FORWARD, REFER TO THE NEWLY MARRIED JUDYTH VARY AS VARY/BAKER TO LESSEN CONFUSION.

MAY 3RD 1963
VARY/BAKER'S NEW SPOUSE LEAVES NEW ORLEANS ABRUPTLY FOR HIS NEW JOB.

MAY 5TH, 1963
VARY/BAKER STATES THAT SHE MOVED INTO AN APARTMENT ON 1032 MARENGO STREET WITH SOME ASSISTANCE FROM **HARVEY**. APPARENTLY THE BOARDING HOUSE ON ST. CHARLES WAS ALSO A BROTHEL. IT WAS RAIDED AND VARY/BAKER WAS EVICTED.

MAY 5TH, 1963
HARVEY AND VARY/BAKER VISIT FERRIE'S APARTMENT AT 3330 LOUISIANA AVENUE PARKWAY. FERRIE FURTHER EXPOUNDS ON WHAT HE CALLS THE "PROJECT": THE DEVELOPMENT OF A CARCINOGEN TO BE USED TO KILL CASTRO. THE "PRODUCT" AS THE CARCINOGEN WAS DESCRIBED, WOULD BE DELIVERED TO DOCTORS IN CUBA WHO HAD ACCESS TO CASTRO BUT LITTLE REGARD FOR THE CASTRO REGIME.

*IT IS INTERESTING TO NOTE THAT THE ASTUTE VARY/BAKER OBSERVED THAT NOTHING ABOUT THE "PROJECT" WAS WRITTEN DOWN. THIS OF COURSE WOULD LATER ENHANCE THE WARREN COMMISSIONS ABILITY TO PAINT **HARVEY** AS A "LONER" WITH FEW INTERESTS OUTSIDE FURTHERING COMMUNISM IN CUBA. MORE IMPORTANTLY, IT WOULD ISOLATE THE BOGUS "ASSIGNMENT" **(SCENARIO II)** FROM THE CIA'S MORE LEGITIMATE EFFORTS. VARY/BAKER WOULD NOTE THAT FERRIE REFERRED TO HER AS THE "UNTRACEABLE" MEMBER OF THE PROJECT. SHE SUSPECTS THAT HE MEANS "UNTRACEABLE" TO THE CIA.*

MAY 6TH, 1963
VARY/BAKER IS INTRODUCED TO JACK RUBY AT FERRIE'S APARTMENT. FERRIE REFERS TO RUBY AS "SPARKY RUBENSTEIN." THIS SAME EVENING, ACCORDING TO VARY/BAKER, **HARVEY**, RUBY, AND FERRIE GO OUT FOR DINNER. SHE NOTES THAT RUBY, FERRIE, AND **HARVEY** SEEMED TO HAVE KNOWN EACH OTHER FOR SOME TIME.

MAY 6TH 1963
HARVEY ENLISTS THE HELP OF A-1 EMPLOYMENT SERVICES IN AN EFFORT TO FIND EMPLOYMENT.

MAY 7TH 1963
DE MOHRENSCHILDT AND HIS WIFE ARRIVE IN WASHINGTON, D.C. GEORGE MET WITH CIA STAFF OFFICER TONY CZAIKOWSKI AND A HAITIAN BANKER CLEMARD JOSEPH CHARLES. THEY WILL MAKE ONE BRIEF RETURN TO DALLAS ON MAY 25TH AND 26TH BEFORE DEPARTING FOR HAITI.

MAY 8TH, 1963
HARVEY, WITH VARY/BAKER IN TOW, MEETS WITH DR. OCHSNER AT CHARITY HOSPITAL. ACCORDING TO VARY/BAKER, **HARVEY** ENTERS FIRST. VARY/BAKER NOTED THAT DURING **HARVEY'S** VISIT WITH DR OCHSNER THAT OCHSNER EXPLAINED THE CARCINOGENS PROJECT AS AN EFFORT TO ELIMINATE CASTRO.

ON MONDAY, NOVEMBER 24TH, DAVID FERRIE WILL RETURN TO NEW ORLEANS AT 9:00 PM. HE WAS RETURNING FROM HIS FRIDAY, NOVEMBER 22ND DRIVE TO HOUSTON AND

GALVESTON. HE LEFT ONLY HOURS LATER AND DROVE TO HAMMOND, LOUSIANA WHERE HE STAYED AT HOLLOWAY SMITH HALL ON THE CAMPUS OF SOUTHEASTERN LOUSIANA COLLEGE. FERRIE STAYED WITH A FRIEND, THOMAS COMPTON. COMPTON, UNDER A DR. NICHOLS, PERFORMED FEDERALLY FUNDED RESEARCH IN NARCOTICS ADDICTION. THIS RELATIONSHIP BETWEEN COMPTON AND DR. NICHOLS IS STRIKINGLY SIMILAR TO VARY/BAKER'S RELATIONSHIP WITH DR. OCHSNER.

MAY 9TH1963

VARY/BAKER AND **HARVEY** GO TO A-1 EMPLOYMENT AGENCY TO LOOK FOR JOB OPENINGS.

MAY 10THTH 1963

HARVEY STARTED WORK FOR STANDARD COFFEE COMPANY, A SISTER COMPANY OF REILY COFFEE, AS A $1.50 AN HOUR MAINTENANCE MAN. HE WILL HOWEVER DO A ONE WEEK "INTERNSHIP" AT REILY COFFEE. HE LISTED HIS ADDRESS AT THE TIME OF HIS EMPLOYMENT AS 757 FRENCH STREET. THIS, ONCE AGAIN, IS THE ADDRESS OF HIS "AUNT", LILLIAN MURRET. AS REFERENCES ON HIS JOB APPLICATION, HE LISTED HIS "COUSIN" JOHN MURRETT, A SERGEANT ROBERT HIDELL, AND A LIEUTENANT J. EVANS. VARY/BAKER WILL START WORK AT STANDARD THIS VERY SAME DAY. SHE WILL WORK HOWEVER FOR WILLIAM MONAGHAN, REILY'S VICE-PRESIDENT, AS A PERSONAL SECRETARY. THEY ARE BOTH REFERRED TO STANDARD COFFEE BY THE SAME EMPLOYMENT SERVICE, A-1. BUT, THE POSITIONS AT STANDARD ARE ARRANGED BY DR. OCHSNER. **HARVEY** ALSO SENT FOR MARINA AND JUNE ON THIS DATE.

*THIS WAS LITTLE MORE THAN POSTURING FOR THOSE ASSISTING **HARVEY** AND VARY/BAKER IN THEIR "EMPLOYMENT" PURSUITS. **HARVEY** EXPLAINED TO VARY/BAKER THAT REILY WOULD REQUIRE A BACKGROUND CHECK ON ITS "NEW" EMPLOYEES. BUT, IF THE EMPLOYEE WAS A TRANSFER FROM STANDARD COFFEE, THEY WOULD NOT REQUIRE THAT EMPLOYEE TO UNDERGO AN ADDITIONAL CHECK. **HARVEY** KNEW THAT HE WOULD SOON BE TRANSFERRED TO REILY FROM STANDARD. HE ALSO KNEW THAT A LEGITIMATE BACKGROUND CHECK WOULD REVEAL HIS "DEFECTION", HIS DISHONORABLE DISCHARGE FROM THE MARINES, AND HIS RUSSIAN WIFE; HARDLY MARKS OF DISTINCTION THAT WOULD ENDEAR HIM TO WILLIAM B. REILY, A STAUNCH ANTI-COMMUNIST. **HARVEY'S** BACKGROUND CHECK WOULD HAVE TO BE FALSIFIED. STANDARD COFFEE'S V.P. OF FINANCE WAS BILL MONAGHAN. AS PREVIOUSLY MENTIONED, MONAGHAN, IN 1961, FORMED INCA WITH DR. OCHSNER AND ED BUTLER. HIS NEW SECRETARY, VARY/BAKER WAS INFORMED BY MONAGHAN THAT SHE WOULD PROVIDE **HARVEY** WITH A "CLEAN" BACKGROUND CHECK. HE WAS ABLE TO OBTAIN FOR HER COPIES OF THE FORMS THAT RETAIL CREDIT USED FOR THEIR BACKGROUND CHECKS. A-1 EMPLOYMENT SERVICE UTILIZED RETAIL CREDIT FOR THEIR BACKGROUND INQUIRIES. ONE HAS TO WONDER IF THIS WAS DONE TO PROVIDE WILLIAM B. REILY AT REILY COFFEE PLAUSIBLE DENIABILITY IN REGARDS TO **HARVEY'S** BACKGROUND, OR WAS REILY "OUT OF THE LOOP" AND NOT REGARDED BY OCHSNER AND MONAGHAN AS NEEDING-TO-KNOW THAT **HARVEY'S** EMPLOYMENT WAS SIMPLY A COVER TO PROVIDE HIM WITH MONEY AND ALSO ALLOW HIM FREE TIME TO ASSIST FERRIE, VARY/BAKER AND DR. SHERMAN ON THE "PROJECT."*

*WILLIAM B. REILY WAS COMMITTED TO CUBAN INTEREST, BUT NOT POLITICALLY INCLINED TO FAVOR CASTRO. HE SUPPORTED THE CUBAN REVOLUTIONARY COUNCIL AND THE CRUSADE TO FREE CUBA. REILY WAS ASSIGNED A CIA FILE AS AN ASSET AND HAD BEEN SINCE APRIL 1949. HIS BROTHER, EUSTOS REILY, WOULD DONATE HEAVILY TO INCA, AN ANTI-COMMUNIST ORGANIZATION FORMED BY DR. ALTON OCHSNER. WE WILL INTRODUCE DR. OCHSNER LATER AS THE SET-UP OF **HARVEY** UNFOLDS.*

MAY 10, 1963

HARVEY RENTS AN APARTMENT ON 4905 MAGAZINE STREET. THE APARTMENT IS 7 BLOCKS FROM VARY/BAKER'S MARENGO STREET APARTMENT. THE RENT IS $65 A MONTH, HIS LANDLORD A MRS. JESSE GARNER.

HARVEY WOULD LATER HOWEVER USE THE ADDRESS "4907 MAGAZINE STREET" AS HIS ADDRESS ON HIS FPFC FLYERS. HE WOULD ALSO RECEIVE MAIL AT THE 4907 ADDRESS. NINA GARNER, *HARVEY'S* LANDLADY, WOULD LATER NOTE THAT FBI AGENT MILTON KAACK VISITED HER REGARDING *HARVEY*. SHE WOULD ADD THAT THE FBI FREQUENTLY MONITORED THE HOUSE.

MAY 10TH 1963

RUTH PAINE DRIVES MARINA AND JUNE TO NEW ORLEANS TO JOIN **HARVEY**. MS. PAINE STAYS A FEW DAYS THEN RETURNS TO HER HOME IN IRVING ARRIVING ON MAY 14$^{TH.}$

MAY 11TH1963

VARY/BAKER MEETS WITH DR. SHERMAN AND DAVID FERRIE AT SHERMAN'S APARTMENT IN THE PATIO APARTMENT COMPLEX. ACCORDING TO VARY/BAKER, DR. SHERMAN DISCUSSED THE "PROJECT" AND FURTHER SOLICITED VARY/BAKER'S ASSISTANCE.

*THIS IS AN ABRUPT CHANGE IN REGARDS TO SHERMAN'S DEMEANOR TOWARDS VARY/BAKER AS SHE HAD "DISMISSED" VARY/BAKER AT THEIR INITIAL APRIL 28TH MEETING. SHERMAN WAS LIKELY TOLD BY DR. OCHSNER TO ACCEPT VARY/VAKER AS AN ASSISTANT. AS VARY/BAKER WAS SUSPICIOUS OF THE INCLUSION OF FERRIE/**HARVEY** IN WHAT WAS NOW TO HER INDEED A LEGITIMATE PROJECT, DR. SHERMAN SURELY FELT IMPOSED UPON BY DR. OCHSNER TO INCLUDE THE NOVICE RESEARCHER VARY/BAKER. ACCORDING TO VARY/BAKER, DR. SHERMAN EXPLAINS TO HER THAT THE PRESIDENT'S LIFE MAY HINGE ON THE SUCCESS OF THE "PROJECT." SHERMAN NOTES THAT THERE WERE INDEED PLANS TO KILL JFK AS A RESULT OF HIS PROMISE NOT TO INVADE CUBA. IF CASTRO IS NOT REMOVED WITHIN A CERTAIN TIME FRAME, IT IS JFK WHO WILL BE REMOVED ALLOWING FOR LBJ TO PURSUE THE REMOVAL OF CASTRO. THERE IS INDEED A CERTAIN AMOUND OF LOGIC IN SHERMAN'S STATEMENT. OPENING UP CUBA WOULD NO DOUBT PLEASE THE CIA/MAFIA, BUT IF IT WERE DONE WITH THE ASSISTANCE OF ORGANIZED CRIME, THE ADMINISTRATION MIGHT SOFTEN ITS WAR ON THE MAFIA.*

MAY 13TH 1963

HARVEY VISITS THE NEW ORLEANS POST OFFICE AND MAILS A NOTIFICATION CARD TO THE DALLAS POST OFFICE ASKING THEM TO CLOSE HIS OLD P.O. BOX, #2915. THE BOX IS CLOSED ON MAY 14TH.

MAY 17TH 1963

VARY/BAKER AND **HARVEY** ARE OFFICIALLY TRANSFERRED TO REILY COFFEE.

MAY 21ST 1963

HARVEY VISITS THE LOCAL BRANCH LIBRARY TO APPLY FOR A LIBRARY CARD.

MAY 22ND TO MAY 24TH, 1963

VARY /BAKER CONTINUES TO WORK ON THE "PROJECT" AT BOTH FERRIE'S AND DR SHERMAN'S RESIDENCES.

THE ROUTINE, ACCORDING TO VARY/BAKER, WAS HARVESTING THE MICE TUMORS ON WEDNESDAYS, PREPPING THE SPECIMENS ON THURSDAYS, THEN, ON FRIDAYS, THE SPECIMENS WERE EITHER TAKEN TO DR. SHERMAN'S APARTMENT OR A CLANDESTINE "DROP" IN A CAR PARKED NEAR THE ELI LILLY LAB. AFTER THE "DROP", A DRIVER WOULD ARRIVE AND TAKE THE CAR AND THE SPECIMENS TO BE IRRADIATED. THIS ROUTINE WOULD ASSIST IN ISOLATING FERRIE AND VARY/BAKER FROM THE MORE LEGITIMATE EFFORTS OF DRS. OCHSNER AND SHERMAN. THE WORK DONE AT FERRIE'S APARTMENT AND TAKEN TO DR. SHERMAN'S APARTMENT LIKELY NEVER SAW THE LIGHT OF DAY. THE SPECIMENS LEFT AT THE CAR "DROP" LIKELY NEVER PROGRESSED BEYOND THAT POINT AS WELL.

MAY 26TH 1963

HARVEY IS NOW INSTRUCTED BY SET-UP CONSPIRATOR GUY BANISTER TO ORGANIZE A NEW ORLEANS CHAPTER OF THE FPFC COMMITTEE.

VARY/BAKER NOTED THAT UNTIL THE SPRING SEMESTER ENDED AT TULANE UNIVERSITY, **HARVEY**, UNDER THE WATCHFUL EYE OF GUY BANISTER, WOULD PURSUE THE INFILTRATION OF LEFT WING PRO-CIVIL RIGHTS ACTIVISTS ON CAMPUS. SHE ALSO NOTED THAT <u>AFTER</u> THE SEMESTER ENDED, **HARVEY** INITIATED HIS PRO-CASTRO POSTURING. THIS IS INDEED SUPPORTED BY THE FACT THAT ON MAY 26TH, 1963, **HARVEY** WAS INSTRUCTED BY BANISTER TO START A NEW ORLEANS CHAPTER OF THE FPFC.

HARVEY WOULD VIEW THIS AS A LOGICAL EXTENSION OF WHAT HE HAD PERCEIVED AS A CIA- SPONSORED INFILTRATION OF THE FPFC THAT HAD INITIALLY STARTED IN DALLAS. KEEP IN MIND THAT THE DALLAS FPFC ACTIVITY WAS INITIATED BY HUNT/PHILLIPS. NEEDLESS TO SAY, THE NEW ORLEANS FPFC ACTIVITY WILL <u>NOT</u> BE A CONTINUANCE OF WHAT **HARVEY** SEES AS A "LEGITIMATE" ASSIGNMENT, BUT MERELY AN EXTENSION OF HUNT/PHILLIPS PLAN WHICH WE WILL VISIT IN **SCENARIO II.**

BANISTER, AT THIS POINT, IS KNOWINGLY MANIPULATING **HARVEY**. HE IS ATTEMPTING TO CONVINCE HIM THAT BY ENHANCING HIS BONAFIDES AS AN EX "DEFECTOR", DALLAS FPFC ACTIVITIST, AND NOW A NEW ORLEANS BASED FPFC ACTIVIST, THAT HE IS ACTUALLY HELPING HIM MAINTAIN HIS COVER; A COVER THAT HE WILL NEED TO MAINTAIN UNTIL THE AFTERNOON OF NOVEMBER 22ND.

BANISTER HAS DESIGNS FOR **HARVEY** THAT ARE OF HIS OWN MAKING. THESE PLANS INVOLVE BANISTER'S EFFORTS TO THWART THE EFFORTS OF CIVIL RIGHTS GROUPS IN LOUSISIANA. IT IS BANISTER'S DESIRE TO NOT ONLY FURTHER ADVERTISE **HARVEY** AS A "COMMUNIST" BUT MORE IMPORTANTLY TO BANISTER AND HIS SEGREGATIONIST GROUPS TO TIE **HARVEY** TO LEFT WING GROUPS THUS "TAINTING" LIBERAL GROUPS AS BEING INVOLVED WITH AND CONTROLLED BY COMMUNISTS.

ON MAY 26TH, **HARVEY** WROTE ONCE AGAIN TO THE FPFC HEADQUARTERS IN NEW YORK. THIS TIME HE ASKED FOR MORE LITERATURE AND INFORMED THEM HE WAS STARTING A NEW ORLEANS CHAPTER. HE WOULD "RECRUIT" ONLY 1 MEMBER TO HIS ORGANIZATION, AN "A. J. HIDELL," CHAPTER PRESIDENT.

THIS WOULD BE THE FIRST TIME **HARVEY** WOULD USE THE NAME "A.J.HIDELL." HOWEVER THE "HIDELL" SIGNATURE ON THE CARD IS <u>NOT</u> IN HIS HANDWRITTING ACCORDING TO THE FBI. **HARVEY** IS UNAWARE THAT THE NAME "HIDELL" WAS USED BY THE SET-UP CONSPIRATORS **(SCENARIO II)** TO ORDER THE INCRIMINATING HANDGUN AND RIFLE IN MARCH. HE DID <u>NOT</u> USE THE NAME AS AN ALIAS. ARMSTRONG IS CONVINCED THAT "HIDELL" IS ACTUALLY **LEE**. I SEE NO REASON TO REFUTE HIS CLAIM.

A REPLY FROM VINCENT LEE OF THE FPFC HEADQUARTERS ON MAY 29TH DISCOURAGED **HARVEY** FROM STARTING A NEW ORLEANS CHAPTER. MR. LEE NOTED THAT WITH "FEW MEMBERS AS SEEM TO EXIST IN THE NEW ORLEANS AREA" AND "OF THE RABID ANTI-CASTRO SENTIMENT IN NEW ORLEANS", HE WARNED **HARVEY** THAT NEW ORLEANS WAS NOT A LOCALE IN WHICH PROMOTING FPFC ACTIVITIES WOULD BE WELCOMED. HOWEVER IT IS IMPORTANT TO THE SET-UP CONSPIRATORS **(SCENARIO II)** THAT THE NEW ORLEANS CHAPTER BE PURSUED BY **HARVEY** AS THIS WOULD SET THE STAGE FOR HIS SOON TO COME ORCHESTRATED, AND MORE IMPORTANTLY, DOCUMENTED RUN-IN WITH THOSE LOCAL GROUPS WHO WERE VEHEMENTLY ANTI-CASTRO.

HARVEY'S "OFFICE" FROM WHICH HE RAN HIS 1 MAN FPFC CHAPTER WAS LOCATED AT 544 CAMP STREET. THIS WAS IN THE SAME BUILDING USED BY GUY BANISTER AS HIS OFFICE FOR A SMALL PRIVATE DETECTIVE AGENCY.

BANISTER LATER LEARNED THAT THE ADDRESS ON **HARVEY'S** FPFC LITERATURE WAS 544 CAMP ST. HE QUICKLY HAD HIM CHANGE IT TO 4907 MAGAZINE STREET WHERE **HARVEY** RECEIVED HIS MAIL. **HARVEY'S** ACTUAL RESIDENCE HOWEVER WAS 4905 MAGAZINE STREET. THIS WAS DONE TO MAINTAIN THE INTEGRITY OF BANISTER'S EFFORTS AND TO FURTHER CEMENT THE BONAFIDES OF **HARVEY** AS A PRO-CASTRO SUPPORTER. HAVING

THE PRO-CASTRO FPFC ADDRESS SHARE THE SAME BUILDING AS HIS LAFAYETTE STREET ANTI-CASTRO GROUP COULD WELL EXPOSE THE NEW ORLEANS FPFC PLOY FOR WHAT IT WAS; A THINLY-VEILED EFFORT TO COMBINE **HARVEY'S** PREVIOUS LEGITIMATE CIA "DEFECTOR" ASSIGNMENT IN RUSSIA, AND HIS HUNT/PHILLIPS INSPIRED BOGUS CIA INFORMANT ROLE AS A FPFC SUPPORTER, AND USE THESE TO MAINTAIN AND ENHANCE HIS COVER STORY FOR WHAT BOTH **HARVEY** AND DAVID FERRIE WERE LED TO PERCEIVE WOULD BE HIS NEXT LEGITIMATE ASSIGNMENT.

BANISTER WOULD OF COURSE BE CONCERNED THAT HIS MANIPULATION OF **HARVEY**, DRIVEN BY HIS DESIRE TO ASSOCIATE CIVIL RIGHTS GROUPS WITH KNOWN "COMMUNISTS" WOULD BE EXPOSED.

THE 544 CAMP ST. STAMP ON THE FPFC PAMPHLETS WAS PROBABLY AN INNOCENT EFFORT ON **HARVEY'S** PART TO LEGITIMIZE HIS FPFC CAUSE BY GIVING HIS FPFC "OFFICE" AN ADDRESS. IN FACT, IN HIS LETTER TO THE FPFC HQ, HE NOTED THAT HE HAD "BEEN THINKING ABOUT RENTING A SMALL OFFICE AT MY OWN EXPENSE." HE SIMPLY ASSUMED THAT SINCE BOTH HIS "CIA-SPONSORED" ASSIGNMENT TO WORK FOR AND SIMULTANEOUSLY INFILTRATE BANISTER'S RENEGADE ANTI-CASTRO GROUP IN NEW ORLEANS, AND HIS LEGITIMATE FBI-TASKED ASSIGNMENT TO MONITOR BANISTER'S GROUP WERE ESSENTIALLY BOTH GOVERNMENT (CIA AND FBI) SPONSORED, THAT THERE WAS LITTLE RISK IN USING THE 544 CAMP ST ADDRESS FOR HIS PRO-CASTRO FPFC LITERATURE. IT MIGHT ALSO EXPLAIN WHY HE CLAIMED HE DID NOT INCLUDE THE FPFC ON HIS NEW ORLEANS P.O. BOX AS "AUTHORIZED TO RECEIVE MAIL" IF HE WERE USING BANISTER'S OFFICE, MAIL FROM THE FPFC COULD BE SENT THERE.

THOSE MASTERMINDING THE SET-UP OF **HARVEY** (HUNT/PHILLIPS/ **SCENARIO II**) REALIZED THAT **HARVEY** COULD NOT ONLY BE THE "PATSY" FOR THE JFK ASSASSINATION BUT THAT HE WAS THE PERFECT PATSY WITH HIS PREVIOUS LEGITIMATE CIA ASSIGNMENT AND HIS FORMER "DEFECTOR" STATUS. **HARVEY** COULD NOT ONLY BE PORTRAYED AS THE SHOOTER IN THE ASSASSINATION, BUT ALSO INSURE A QUICK COVER-UP WITH FEW QUESTIONS ASKED BY THE UPPER ECHELONS AT THE CIA PROPER AND THE FBI. HIS ASSOCIATION WITH BOTH AGENCIES WOULD VIRTUALLY INSURE THAT THE BLAME FOR JFK'S ASSASSINATION WOULD START AND END WITH A LONE GUNMAN; LEE **HARVEY** OSWALD. BOTH AGENCIES WOULD QUICKLY AND PRUDENTLY DENY ANY INVOLVEMENT WITH **HARVEY**. IT WOULD INDEED BE THE PERFECT SETUP.

MAY 27TH 1963
HARVEY RECEIVES HIS LIBRARY CARD. HIS CARD IS # N8640.

MAY 29TH 1963
1000 FPFC LEAFLETS WERE ORDERED FROM JONES PRINTING CO. BY A "LEE OSBORNE" AT THE COST OF $9.89. ON MAY 31ST, "OSBORNE" WOULD RETURN AND MAKE A $4 DOWNPAYMENT ON THE ORDER.

THE PAMPHLETS WERE NOT PICKED BY **HARVEY** ACCORDING TO MYRA SILVER, A JONES PRINTING CO. EMPLOYEE. DOUGLAS JONES, THE OWNER OF THE COMPANY, DESCRIBED THE MAN WHO PICKED UP THE PAMPHLETS ON JUNE 4TH AS A "HUSKY- TYPE PERSON." ROSCOE WHITE HAD A HUSKY BUILD. ALTHOUGH THIS IN ITSELF CERTAINLY OFFERS NO CERTAINTY THAT THE MAN PICKING UP THE PAMPHLETS WAS INDEED ROSCOE WHITE, WE WILL SEE LATER THAT WHITE WILL, ALONG WITH **HARVEY**, RETURN TO DALLAS. WHITE WILL ARRIVE IN DALLAS ONLY 4 DAYS AFTER **HARVEY'S** RETURN FROM NEW ORLEANS. HE WILL ALSO JOIN THE DALLAS POLICE. WHITE'S ENLISTMENT ON THE DALLAS POLICE FORCE WILL LATER PROVE TO BE INVALUABLE TO THE SET-UP CONSPIRATORS (**SCENARIO II**) IN THEIR EFFORTS TO POSITION AND FURTHER INCRIMINATE **HARVEY** REGARDING THE EVENTS OF NOVEMBER 22ND.

A SECOND, PERHAPS MORE PLAUSIBLE IDENTIFICATION OF THE MAN WHO PICKED UP THE PAMPHLETS WAS OFFERED BY RESEARCHER HAROLD WEISBERG. HE TOOK PHOTOS TO

JONES PRINTING DEPICTING **HARVEY** AND FORMER FELLOW MARINE KERRY THORNLEY. EMPLOYEES IDENTIFIED THORNLEY AS THE PERSON WHO PICKED UP THE PAMPHLETS. THORNLEY WAS STRONGLY RIGHT WING AND ASSOCIATED WJITH BOTH BANISTER AND FERRIE.

MAY 31ST 1963

HARVEY AND VARY/BAKER MEET FERRIE AND DR. OCHSNER AT CHARITY HOSPITAL. ACCORDING TO VARY/BAKER, IT WAS PROPOSED THAT THEIR NEXT EFFORT WOULD BE TO TRANSFER CANCEROUS CELLS FROM MICE TO MONKEYS.

JUNE 2ND 1963

GEORGE DE MOHRENSCHILDT AND HIS WIFE ARRIVE IN HAITI.

JUNE 3RD 1963

HARVEY RENTS P.O BOX 30061 AT THE LAFAYETTE SQUARE STATION UNDER THE NAME L.H. OSWALD. THE PERSONS OTHER THAN **HARVEY** DESIGNATED TO RECEIVE MAIL AT THIS BOX WERE MARINA OSWALD AND ALLEGEDLY A "A.J. HIDELL."

IT IS IMPORTANT TO NOTE THAT HIS NEW ORLEANS P.O. BOX, BOX 30061 UNLIKE THE 1ST DALLAS P.O. BOX, DID NOT LIST THE FPFC AS A RECIPIENT OF MAIL. THE FPFC AND A P.O. BOX LINK HAD ALREADY BEEN ESTABLISHED IN DALLAS. IT WOULD BE UNNECESSARY FOR THE SET-UP CONSPIRATORS TO REPEAT THIS IN NEW ORLEANS. HOWEVER THE ALL IMPORTANT "HIDELL" LINK WOULD STILL BE MAINTAINED.

IN CUSTODY AFTER THE ASSASSINATION, **HARVEY** WOULD ADMIT TO HAVING LISTED ONLY HIMSELF AND MARINA ON THE P.O. BOX APPLICATION. HE DENIED LISTING AN "A.J. HIDELL", KNOWING A A.J. HIDELL, OR EVER USING THE NAME AS AN ALIAS. **HARVEY** HOWEVER MAY HAVE KNOWN OR KNOWN OF A **LEE** HARVEY OSWALD, BUT WAS LIKELY BEING TRUTHFULL WHEN HE NOTED THAT HE KNEW LITTLE ABOUT A "HIDELL."

ON JULY 23RD, 1963, FBI CONFIDENTIAL INFORMANT "NO T-1" INFORMED THE FBI THAT **HARVEY** HAD RENTED THE P.O. BOX. LATER, ON OCTOBER 23RD, 1963, THE SAME INFORMANT WILL INFORM THE FBI THAT **HARVEY** HAD REQUESTED THAT MAIL FROM THIS BOX BE FORWARDED TO 2515 W. 5TH, IRVING, TEXAS. THIS WAS TO START ON SEPTEMBER 26TH. IT IS ONLY AFTER THE W.C. PUBLISHES ITS WORK THAT WE FIND **HARVEY'S** APPLICATION FOR THE P.O. BOX. IT NOW LISTS BOTH MARINA AND AN "A.J. HIDELL" AS PERSONS ENTITLED TO RECEIVE MAIL AT THAT P.O. BOX. IT IS UNLIKELY THAT THE INFORMANT WOULD HAVE OMITTED THIS INFO IN HIS JULY 23RD AND OCTOBER 23RD REPORTS TO THE FBI. IT IS MUCH MORE LIKELY THAT THE RECIPIENTS WERE ADDED PRIOR TO PUBLICATION IN THE WARREN REPORT.

INTERESTINGLY, THE ADDRESS **HARVEY** FURNISHES THE POST OFFICE IS 757 FRENCH STREET. AT THE TIME, **HARVEY** WAS LIVING AT 4907 MAGAZINE STREET. THE FRENCH STREET ADDRESS IS THAT OF HIS "AUNT", LILLIAN MURRETT.

ON THIS DATE ALSO, 500 COPIES OF AN APPLICATION FORM, PRESUMABLY FOR FPFC APPLICANTS, IS PLACED. ONCE AGAIN, THE ORDER IS PLACED BY A "LEE OSBORNE." THIS TIME HOWEVER THE ORDER IS PLACED AT DIRECT MAIL ENTERPRISES. "OSBORNE" HOWEVER COMPLAINS THAT THE FORMS ARE TOO EXPENSIVE SO HE PLACES THE ORDER AT MAILER'S SERVICE ON 225 MAGAZINE. THE FPFC FORMS, AT A COST OF $9.34, ARE PICKED UP ON JUNE 5TH. **HARVEY'S** FPFC CARD AND HIS FPFC NEW ORLEANS CHAPTER CARD WERE BOTH IN HIS NAME, LEE **HARVEY** OSWALD. WHY WOULD BOTH THE LEAFLETS AND APPLICATIONS BE ORDERED UNDER AN ALIAS IF INDEED THEY WERE ORDERED BY **HARVEY**?

KEEP IN MIND THAT IN **HARVEY'S** PERCEPTION, HIS INITIAL AND ONLY CIA-SPONSORED "ASSIGNMENT" IN NEW ORLEANS WAS THE MONITORING /INFILTRATION OF BANISTER'S RENEGADE GROUP. HIS LEGITIMATE FBI ASSIGNMENT WAS TO GATHER INFORMATION ON

BANISTER'S CIA-SPONSORED ANTI-CASTRO GUN-RUNNING OPERATION ALONG THE CORRIDOR FROM DALLAS TO NEW ORLEANS TO MIAMI TO CUBA

*THE SET-UP CONSPIRATORS, HUNT/PHILLIPS, THROUGH BANISTER, WOULD BE RESPONSIBLE FOR PROMPTING **HARVEY'S** EFFORT TO ESTABLISH A NEW ORLEANS FPFC CHAPTER. AS A RESULT, THE SET-UP CONSPIRATORS WOULD ALSO BE RESPONSIBLE FOR THE ORDERING OF THE ADDITIONAL FPFC LITERATURE. JUST AS HIS FPFC ACTIVITY IN DALLAS FOR HUNT/PHILLIPS WAS WRONGLY PERCEIVED BY **HARVEY** AS LEGITIMATE, THE FPFC INCIDENTS IN NEW ORLEANS WOULD ALSO BE MANAGED BY AND FOR THE EVENTUAL PURPOSES OF THE SET-UP CONSPIRATORS. ALTHOUGH HE AND FERRIE WOULD PERCEIVE THE NEW ORLEANS FPFC ANTICS AS LEGITIMATE AND AS AN EFFORT TO STRENGTHEN HIS BONAFIDES FOR WHAT THEY THOUGHT WAS HIS NEXT CIA ASSIGNMENT, BANISTER, WHITE, HUNT, **LEE** AND PHILLIPS KNEW OTHERWISE MORE ON THIS IN **SCENARIO II.***

JUNE 4TH 1963

HARVEY MEETS WITH FERRIE AT GUY BANISTER'S OFFICE. ACCORDING TO VARY/BAKER, FERRIE GAVE **HARVEY** HIS (FERRIE'S) TULANE MEDICAL LIBRARY ACCESS CARD TO LOAN TO VARY/BAKER TO ALLOW HER ACCESS TO THE TULANE LIBRARY.

*THE LIBRARY CARD IS LIKELY THE SAME LIBRARY CARD THAT WILL CAUSE FERRIE TO PANIC THE WEEKEND OF NOVEMBER 22ND. FERRIE WILL BE TOLD BY HIS ROOMMATE LAYTON MARTENS THAT HIS (FERRIE'S) LIBRARY CARD HAD BEEN FOUND IN **HARVEY'S** POSSESSIONS UPON HIS ARREST.*

JUNE 5TH 1963

ACCORDING TO VARY/BAKER, RUBY RE-VISITS NEW ORLEANS. THE EVENING OF JUNE 8TH, VARY/BAKER, **HARVEY**, FERRIE, AND ANNA AND DAVID LEWIS ARE INVITED TO THE 500 CLUB COURTESY OF RUBY. VARY/BAKER WITNESSES **HARVEY** MEETING CARLOS MARCELLO WHO IS SEATED WITH HIS BROTHERS, SAMMY AND PETE. THERE IS HOWEVER NO ACCOUNTING FOR RUBY'S WHEREABOUTS FROM JUNE 5TH TO THE EVENING OF JUNE 8TH. RESEARCHERS SPECULATE THAT HE HAD ONCE AGIN BEEN FLOWN TO CUBA AS HE HAD DONE ON APRIL 11TH. IN BOTH INSTANCES, HE WAS UNABLE TO BE LOCATED, AT LEAST STATESIDE, FOR 72 HOURS.

JUNE 8TH 1963

MARINA VISITS NEW ORLEAN'S CHARITY HOSPITAL SEEKING TREATMENT. SHE IS 5 MONTHS PREGNANT WITH THEIR SECOND DAUGHTER, RACHEL.

JUNE 9TH 1963

RUBY RETURNS TO DALLAS.

JUNE 10TH 1963

HARVEY WRITES TO THE WORKER FOR PAMPHLETS. HE ALSO ENCLOSED A FPFC LEAFLET IN THE LETTER. **HARVEY** IS BEING MANIPULATED BY BANISTER TO ASSIST IN BANISTER'S EFFORT TO ASSOCIATE THE FPFC AND THE COMMUNIST PARTY.

JUNE 11TH 1963

THE PRESIDENT ANNOUNCED THAT HE WOULD PROPOSE A COMPREHENSIVE CIVIL RIGHTS BILL. THE 1954 SUPREME COURT RULING, BROWN V BOARD OF EDUCATION, WAS DESIGNED TO DESEGREGATE PUBLIC SCHOOLS. KENNEDY'S PROPOSAL WOULD BAN DISCRIMINATION REGARDING THE WORKPLACE AND IN ALL PUBLIC FACILITIES SUCH AS HOTELS, RESTAURANTS, THEATERS, ETC.

JUNE 16TH 1963

HARVEY DISTRIBUTES LEAFLETS BY THE DUMAINE ST. WHARF WHERE THE USS WASP IS DOCKED. ONE WAS A "HANDS OFF CUBA!" LEAFLET, THE OTHER A PAMPHLET TITLED "THE TRUTH ABOUT CUBA." OFFICER GIROD RAY OF THE HARBOUR POLICE INFORMED HIM THAT HE WOULD HAVE TO LEAVE THE WHARF AREA.

JUNE 17TH 1963
AGENT HOSTY IS INFORMED THAT **HARVEY** HAS CONTACTED THE WORKER. HOSTY REQUESTS THAT THE NEW ORLEANS FBI OFFICE VERIFY **HARVEY'S** PRESENCE IN NEW ORLEANS.

*KEEP IN MIND THAT HOSTY HAD REOPENED **HARVEY'S** FILE ON MARCH 26TH DUE IN PART TO THE FACT THAT ON MARCH 11TH, HE HAD CALLED HIS OLD ADDRESS ONLY TO FIND OUT THAT **HARVEY** HAD MOVED AND LEFT NO FORWARDING ADDRESS. UNTIL JUNE 17TH, HOSTY QUITE CANDIDLY DID NOT KNOW FOR CERTAIN WHERE **HARVEY** WAS OR WHAT HE WAS UP TO. IT IS POSSIBLE THAT THIS IS WHY THE SET-UP CONSPIRATORS USED THE ALIAS "LEE OSBORNE" WHEN ORDERING THE FPFC PAMPHLETS IN NEW ORLEANS. IF THEY HAD USED **HARVEY'S** REAL NAME, OR EVEN THE "HIDELL" ALIAS, IT WOULD HAVE TRIGGERED THE SAME FBI MONITORING PROCESS THAT INFORMED AGENT HOSTY THAT **HARVEY** HAD CONTACTED THE WORKER. IN SPITE OF THAT, HOSTY USED THIS WEAK ARGUMENT, **HARVEY'S** CONTACTING THE WORKER, AS HIS MAIN REASON FOR RE-OPENING HIS FILE.*

*THE USE OF **HARVEY'S** REAL NAME IN THE ORDERING OF THE FPFC PAMPHLETS WOULD MOST CERTAINLY HAVE TIPPED OFF THE FBI NOT ONLY TO HIS MOST RECENT WHEREABOUTS, BUT ALSO A REMINDER THAT HE WAS EMBARKING ON A PROJECT THAT HAD NOT BEEN LEGITIMATELY ASSIGNED TO HIM; AT LEAST BY THE FBI.*

*ALTHOUGH HUNT/PHILLIPS COULD NOT PREVENT THE EXPECTED RECRUITMENT BY AGENT FAIN OF **HARVEY** AS A DOMESTIC INFORMANT AFTER HE RETURNED TO DALLAS FROM RUSSIA, THEY WOULD HAVE <u>MUCH PREFERRED</u> THAT AGENT HOSTY REMAIN UNAWARE OF **HARVEY'S** WHEREABOUTS AS THEY PROCEEDED WITH THEIR SET-UP IN NEW ORLEANS.*

JUNE 22ND 1963
HARVEY VISITS THE LOUISIANA DIVISION OF EMPLOYMENT SECURITY TO LOOK FOR A JOB AND TO FILE AN INTERSTATE CLAIM FOR UNEMPLOYMENT FROM TEXAS.

JUNE 24TH 1963
HARVEY APPLIES FOR A NEW PASSPORT. HE LISTS CUBA AND THE SOVIET UNION AS TWO OF THE COUNTRIES HE INTENDS TO VISIT ALONG WITH POLAND. HE ALSO NOTED THAT HIS MEANS OF DEPARTING ON HIS JOURNEY WOULD BE THE LYKES SHIPPING LINE BASED IN NEW ORLEANS. HE HAD PREVIOUSLY UTILIZED THE LYKES LINE TO EMBARK ON HIS 1959 "DEFECTION" TO RUSSIA. HE TURNS IN THE STILL VALID 1959 PASSPORT FOR CANCELLATION. THE 1959 PASSPORT, ACCORDING TO ARMSTRONG, HAD A PHOTO OF **LEE**. THE 1963 PASSPORT WILL SHOW HOWEVER A PHOTO OF **HARVEY**.

INTERESTINGLY, HE LISTS HIS "AUNT", LILLIAN MURRET, AS THE PERSON TO BE NOTIFIED IN CASE OF HIS DEATH RATHER THAN HIS WIFE, MARINA. HE ALSO NOTES THAT HIS "DATE OF DEPARTURE" WOULD BE OCTOBER TO JANUARY FROM NEW ORLEANS.

JUNE 25TH 1963
HARVEY'S PASSPORT WAS ISSUED. THE PASSPORT INCLUDES A NOTATION THAT IT IS NOT VALID FOR TRAVEL TO CUBA.

*I FIND IT ONCE AGAIN REMARKABLE THAT A "DEFECTOR" WHO HAD OPENLY OFFERED TO GIVE UP RADAR SECRETS TO THE SOVIETS WOULD BE ABLE TO OBTAIN YET ANOTHER PASSPORT IN 24 HOURS. IT IS READILY APPARENT THAT NO "LOOK-0UT" CARD WAS ON FILE FOR **HARVEY** OR THE PASSPORT WOULD HAVE BEEN DELAYED FOR WEEKS IF GRANTED AT ALL*

***HARVEY'S** PASSPORT APPLICATION HAD GONE TO THE PASSPORT OFFICE OF THE STATE DEPARTMENT IN WASHINGTON. FRANCES KNIGHT WAS THE DIRECTOR OF THE OFFICE. KNIGHT WAS KNOWN FOR PLACING STRICT TRAVEL RESTRICTIONS ON LEFT-WING U.S. CITIZENS. APPARENTLY MS. KNIGHT WAS OVERRULED. ALSO, BY THIS TIME, THE FBI HAD*

*EXPANDED ITS SECURITY INDEX TO INCLUDE A "CUBAN SECTION." THIS SECTION INCLUDED THOSE CUBANS IN THE U.S. SUSPECTED OF BEING AGENTS AND ALSO THE NAMES OF THOSE WHO WERE MEMBERS OF ORGANIZATIONS THAT SUPORTED CASTRO. THERE WERE ALMOST 12,000 NAMES ON THE LIST, AND ANOTHER 20,000 NAMES ON TWO ADDITIONAL LISTS. BUT **HARVEY**, A FORMER "DEFECTOR" WHO HAD MADE WRITTEN CONTACTS WITH THE COMMUNIST PARTY USA, THE SOCIALIST WORKERS PARTY, THE FPFC, AND HAD PUBLICLY HANDED OUT FLYERS FOR THE FPFC AMAZINGLY DID NOT SHOW UP ON ANY OF THE 3 CUBAN SECTION LISTS. LOGIC WOULD DICTATE THAT THE FBI WOULD EITHER HAD TO HAVE BEEN REQUESTED BY ANOTHER INTELLIGENCE AGENCY (CIA) TO TURN A BLIND EYE TO **HARVEY'S** PRO-CASTRO ACTIVITIES, OR THAT THE FBI HAD PLANS TO UTILIZE HIS SERVICES AS WELL.*

JUNE 28TH 1963

A MR. PRECHTER FROM REILY COFFEE DISCUSSES WITH MR. WILL MONAGHAN **HARVEY'S** FREQUENT ABSENCES FROM HIS JOB. ACCORDING TO VARY/BAKER, PRECHTER TOLD MONAGHAN "I DON'T CARE WHAT HE'S DOING FOR GOD AND COUNTRY." PRECHTER HAD APPARENTLY GROWN TIRED OF MAKING EXCUSES FOR **HARVEY**.

*THIS IS INDEED REVEALING ON TWO LEVELS. ONE, PRECHTER'S DECISION TO APPROACH MONAGHAN RATHER THAN REILY REGARDING HIS PROBLEM WITH **HARVEY'S** ABSENCES MAY INDICATE THAT INDEED REILY WAS KEPT "OUT OF THE LOOP" IN REGARDS TO THE REASON FOR **HARVEY'S** PRESENCE IN NEW ORLEANS. TWO, THE "GOD AND COUNTRY" COMMENT MAY INDICATE THAT MONAGHAN MAY HAVE REVEALED, PROBABLY TO A MINIMAL DEGREE, THAT **HARVEY** WAS ON ASSIGNMENT AND INDEED WORKING FOR THE INTELLIGENCE COMMUNITY.*

JULY 6TH 1963

HARVEY IS INVITED BY HIS "COUSIN" EUGENE TO SPEAK TO THE STUDENTS AT THE JESUIT HOUSE OF STUDIES IN MOBILE, ALABAMA. EUGENE IS STUDYING TO BE A PRIEST.

JULY 10TH 1963

VARY-BAKER NOTES THAT SHE RECEIVED A CALL FROM A DR. BOWERS, AN ASSOCIATE OF DR. OCHSNER, ANNOUNCING A SUCCESSFULL INDUCTION OF CANCER IN THEIR MARMOSET MONKEYS. THE TRANSITION FROM MICE TO PRIMATES HAD APPARENTLY BEEN ACHIEVED.

JULY 16-17 1963

FERRIE ATTENDS HIS HEARING BEFORE EASTERN AIRLINES IN MIAMI.

JULY 19TH 1963

HARVEY HAS A CHECK CASHED AT MARTIN'S RESTAURANT. HE WOULD NORMALLY EAT HIS LUNCH AT MARTIN'S.

*ARMSTRONG NOTES THAT **LEE** WAS IN MEXICO CITY DURING JULY 1963 AND WAS NOTED TO BE AT A MEETING AT THE HOTEL LUMA. THE MEETING WAS ATTENDED BY RICHARD CASE NAGELL WHO WORKED FOR THE CIA AND WAS TASKED WITH INFILTRATING AND INVESTIGATING ANTI-CASTRO GROUPS SUCH AS BANISTER AND FERRIE'S GROUP IN NEW ORLEANS. NAGELL NOTED THAT THE DISCUSSION AT THE MEETING CONCERNED THE ASSASSINATION OF THE PRESIDENT.*

JULY 19TH, 1963

HARVEY IS FIRED FROM REILY COFFEE. HIS LAST DAY OF WORK WOULD BE MONDAY, JULY 20TH.

*ADRIAN ALDA, OWNER OF THE GARAGE ADJACENT TO REILY COFFEE, STOPPED BY TO WISH **HARVEY** WELL. **HARVEY'S** PARTING COMMENT TO ALBA MAY HAVE REVEALED HIS NOW MORE SECURE FINANCIAL SITUATION AS HE WAS IN ALL LIKELIHOOD A LEGITIMATE PAID INFORMANT FOR THE FBI AND LIKELY RECEIVING FINANCIAL ASSISTANCE FROM HUNT/PHILLIPS, VIA GEORGE DEMOHRENSCHILDT, ON BEHALF OF HIS "ASSIGNMENT" FOR THEM. **HARVEY'S** COMMENTED TO ALDA: "I HAVE FOUND MY POT OF GOLD AT THE END OF THE RAINBOW." HE ALSO RELATED TO ALDA THAT HE EXPECTED TO FIND*

EMPLOYMENT AT A NASA FACILITY NEAR NEW ORLEANS. INTERESTINGLY, 4 OTHER REILY COFFEE EMPLOYEES JOINED NASA SHORTLY AFTER **HARVEY** WAS FIRED. ALFRED CLAUDE, WHO HIRED **HARVEY** AT REILY'S, EMMETT BARBEE, HIS SUPERVISOR, JOHN D. BRANYON, AND DANTE MARCHINI ALL JOINED NASA WITHIN A FEW WEEKS OF **HARVEY'S** DEPARTURE. QUITE AN INTERESTING CAREER CHANGE FROM COFFEE TO AEROSPACE. **HARVEY** OBVIOUSLY THOUGHT HE WOULD BE JOINING THIS GROUP AS WELL. ADRIAN ALDA WAS ALSO A CIA CONTACT.

THE NASA CONNECTION EXTENDED TO DAVID FERRIE'S FRIENDS AS WELL. MELVIN COFFEY, WHO TRAVELLED WITH FERRIE TO HOUSTON/GALVESTON THE WEEKEND OF THE ASSASSINATION, LATER FOUND WORK AT THE CAPE CANAVERAL SPACE FACILITY. JAMES LEWALLEN, AN ASSOCIATE OF FERRIE, ALSO WENT TO WORK FOR NASA. I WOULD OFFER THAT THE TRANSITION FROM COFFEE TO AEROSPACE OR AN ASSOCIATION WITH DAVID FERRIE TO AEROSPACE WAS IN SOME WAY FACILITATED BY THE LIKELIHOOD THAT THE MEN INVOLVED EITHER HAD PREVIOUS OR CURRENT INTELLIGENCE TIES OR POSSESSED SECURITY CLEARANCES GRANTED WHILE IN THE MILITARY THEREBY "PRE-CLEARING" THEM FOR EMPLOYMENT AT NASA FACILITIES.

JULY 22ND 1963
HARVEY ONCE AGAIN FILES FOR UNEMPLOYMENT BENEFITS. HE ALSO APPLIES FOR A JOB AT MASON MARBLE AND GRANITE.

JULY 25TH 1963
HARVEY RECEIVES A NOTICE THAT HIS UNDESIRABLE DISCHARGE FROM THE MARINE CORPS HAD BEEN UPHELD AND WOULD NOT BE UGRADED TO HONORABLE

JULY 25TH 1963
VARY/BAKER MEETS WITH OCHSNER. HE INFORMS HER THAT THEY WILL NOW BE TESTING THE "PRODUCT" ON AFRICAN GREEN MONKEYS.

JULY 26TH 1963
A VISITOR TO THE ATOMIC ENERGY MUSEUM IN OAK RIDGE, TENNESSEE SIGNED IN AS "LEE H. OSWALD, USSR, DALLAS ROAD, DALLAS, TEXAS."

OBVIOUSLY WE HAVE A NUMBER OF PROBLEMS HERE. **HARVEY** IS LIVING IN NEW ORLEANS NOT DALLAS, THE HANDWRITING IS NOT **HARVEY'S**, AND THE "USSR" IS JUST TOO OBVIOUS. YET SOMEONE SEEMED TO KNOW THAT **HARVEY** HAD PREVIOUSLY LIVED IN DALLAS OR WOULD INDEED LATER RETURN TO DALLAS.

JULY 27TH 1963
THIS EVENING AT SPRING HILL COLLEGE IN MOBILE, ALABAMA, **HARVEY** SPEAKS TO HIS "COUSIN" EUGENE'S JESUIT STUDENTS ON CONTEMPORARY RUSSIA AND THE PRACTICE OF COMMUNISM.

JULY 29TH 1963
DALLAS FBI OFFICE AGENT HOSTY ONCE AGAIN REQUESTS THAT THE NEW ORLEANS OFFICE OFFER ASSISTANCE IN VERIFYING **HARVEY'S** PRESENCE IN NEW ORLEANS.

JULY 29TH 1963
VARY/BAKER MEETS **HARVEY** AT KATZENJAMMERS BAR NEAR REILY COFFEE. ACCORDING TO HER, HE STATED THAT WHILE IN NEW ORLEANS HE HAD COME INTO CONTACT WITH A CIRCLE OF POWERFUL ENTITIES THAT WERE CONTEMPLATING KILLING JFK. HE NOTED TO VARY/BAKER THAT THE GROUP CONSISTED OF POLITICIANS, BIG OIL INTERESTS, THE CIA, AND THE MILITARY.

JULY 31ST 1963
FBI AGENTS STAGE A RAID ON ANTI-CASTRO PARAMILITARY TRAINING CAMP NEAR LAKE PONCHARTRAIN IN LOUISIANA. THEY SEIZED DYNAMITE, MILITARY FIREARMS,

AND ORDINANCE AT A HOUSE OWNED BY WILLIAM MCLANEY. MCLANEY RAN A CASINO IN HAVANA BUT WAS DEPORTED BY CASTRO IN 1960. HE REPORTEDLY LOST OVER $7 MILLION DOLLARS WHEN HIS CASINO WAS TAKEN OVER BY THE CASTRO GOVERNMENT.

THE ACTUAL RAID WAS ON A HOUSE NEAR MANDEVILLE, LOUISIANA IN ST. TAMANY PARISH. THE FBI WOULD NOT REVEAL THE OWNER OF THE HOUSE. THE FBI REPORT WOULD HOWEVER NOTE THAT THE ARMAMENT SEIZED WERE "IN CONNECTION WITH AN INVESTIGATION OF AN EFFORT TO CARRY OUT A MILITARY OPERATION FROM THE U.S. AGAINST A COUNTRY WITH WHICH THE U.S. IS AT PEACE." THE OWNER OF THE HOUSE, AS LATER REPORTED BY COLUMNIST JACK ANDERSON, WAS WILLIAM MCLANEY. HE AND HIS BROTHER MIKE MCLANEY HAD OPERATED THE CASINO AT THE HOTEL NACIONAL IN HAVANA PRIOR TO CASTRO'S TAKEOVER IN 1959.

*THE FBI IN NEW ORLEANS MAY WELL HAVE BEEN TIPPED OFF BY **HARVEY** IN HIS LEGITIMATE FBI SPONSORED ROLE TO MONITOR THE CIA-BACKED SHAW/BANISTER/ FERRIE GROUP.*

JULY 31ST 1963
COMMUNIST PARTY USA FILLS **HARVEY'S** REQUEST FOR LITERATURE.

AUGUST 1ST 1963
HARVEY, IN A LETTER TO VINCENT LEE, NATIONAL DIRECTOR OF THE FPFC ORGANIZATION, COMMENTED THAT HIS LOCAL CHAPTER HAD BEEN "ATTACKED" BY "SOME CUBAN-EXILE 'GUSANOS' (WORMS)" WHILE HANDLING OUT FPFC LEAFLETS.

*THIS LETTER FURTHER CEMENTS THE NOTION THAT THE BRINGUIER INCIDENT WAS A SET-UP THAT **HARVEY** KNOWINGLY PARTICIPATED IN AS IT WOULD NOT OCCUR UNTIL 8 DAYS LATER ON AUGUST 9TH. IT IS INTERESTING TO NOTE HIS USE OF THE TERM "GUSANOS." IN 1962, THE CIA ADOPTED A CAMPAIGN TO CHANGE THE SYMBOL OF THE CUBAN RESISTANCE MOVEMENT FROM A FISH TO A WORM. THE SLOGAN WOULD ALSO BE CHANGED TO "GUSANO LIBRE", OR "FREE THE WORMS." **HARVEY** WAS LIKELY PRIVY TO THE EFFORT AND SAW FIT TO APPLY IT TO ANTI-CASTRO CUBANS OPERATING OUTSIDE CUBA.*

AUGUST 5TH 1963
HARVEY WAS INSTRUCTED BY BANISTER TO INITIATE A CONTACT WITH CARLOS BRINGUIER AN ANTI-CASTRO LEADER IN NEW ORLEANS. BRINGUIER BELONGED TO THE DRE. HE SERVED AS THEIR NEW ORLEANS DELEGATE. THE DRE WAS RUN BY THE CIA'S DAVID PHILLIPS. **HARVEY** VISITED BRINGUIER AT HIS CASA ROCA CLOTHING STORE AT 107 DECATUR.

AUGUST 5TH 1963
AN ARTICLE PUBLISHED IN A DALLAS PAPER OUTLINED HOW MILITARY INTELLIGENCE GROUPS, IN CONJUNCTION WITH THE FBI, PENETRATED GROUPS CONSIDERED SUBVERSIVE. THEY WOULD ENLIST YOUNG MEN TO JOIN THESE GROUPS AS INFORMANTS.

ON NOVEMBER 18TH, 1963, A YOUNG MAN NAMED JOHN GLENN TESTIFIED BEFORE BEFORE HUAC. GLENN HAD PREVIOUSLY BEEN A COLLEGE STUDENT WHEN HE DECIDED TO JOIN THE AIR FORCE. HIS LEFT WING POSTURING BEGAN UPON HIS DISCHARGE FROM THE AIR FORCE. GLENN REVEALED UNDER QUESTIONING THAT HE HAD JOINED THE FPFC IN THE FALL OF 1962. HE ALSO NOTED THAT HE TRIED TO TRAVEL TO CUBA VIA MEXICO. HE EVENTUALLY REACHED CUBA AND UPON THE EXPIRATION OF HIS VISA, VENTURED ON TO ALGERIA. HIS TESTIMONY BEFORE HUAC ESSENTIALLY PORTRAYED THE FPFC AS LITTLE MORE THAN A FRONT FOR COMMUNIST ACTIVITIES.

*THE PARALLELS BETWEEN GLENN AND **HARVEY** ARE NUMEROUS. BUT, THERE ARE ONLY THREE POSSIBILITIES REGARDING **HARVEY'S** INVOLVEMENT WITH THE FPFC IN NEW ORLEANS. WAS **HARVEY**, LIKE GLENN, A LEGITIMATE FBI INFORMANT INFILTRATING THE FPFC? OR, WAS HIS FPFC POSTURING SOLELY THE DESIGN OF HUNT/PHILLIPS? HAD*

*HUNT/PHILLIPS, AWARE OF THE FPFC PROGRAM, SIMPLY, THROUGH BANISTER, ENCOURAGED HIM TO FORM A RELATIONSHIP WITH AN ORGANIZATION WITH ALLEGED COMMUNIST TIES SOLELY FOR THE PURPOSE OF FURTHERING HIS LEGITIMACY IN REGARDS TO THE CUBA PROJECT? THE THIRD POSSIBILITY OF COURSE IS THAT HIS FPFC ACTIVITIES WERE LEGITIMATE IN REGARDS TO THE FBI AND HUNT/PHILIPS BUT FRAUDULENT IN REGARDS TO BANISTER'S ENCOURAGEMENT TO START A NEW ORLEANS BRANCH OF THE FPFC. I AM HOWEVER VERY MUCH INCLINED TO BELIEVE THAT THE NEW ORLEANS FPFC ACTIVITIES OF **HARVEY** WERE NOT ONLY THE WORK OF HUNT AND PHILLIPS BUT ALSO CONVENIENTLY ENHANCED BANISTER'S DESIRE TO ASSOCIATE AN ALLEGED COMMUNIST WITH CIVIL RIGHTS GROUPS. THE CONTINUED "SHEEP-DIPPING" OF **HARVEY** AS A "COMMUNIST" SERVED BOTH HUNT/PHILIPS AND BANISTER.*

AUGUST 6TH 1963

HARVEY RETURNED TO BRINGUIER'S STORE AND THEN OFFERED TO TRAIN BRINGUIER'S TROOPS. HE ALSO GAVE HIM A COPY OF HIS MARINE CORPS MANUAL.

*BRINGUIER WAS A HAVANA-SCHOOLED LAWYER, A MEMBER OF THE CUBAN BAR, AND A FORMER OFFICIAL IN THE CUBAN GOVERNMENT UNTIL HIS DEFECTION IN MAY OF 1960. HE LATER SUSPECTED THAT **HARVEY** WAS TRYING TO INFILTRATE HIS ANTI-CASTRO GROUP, THE DRE. IT IS IMPORTANT TO NOTE THAT THE DRE – CODE NAMED "AMSPELL"- WAS ALSO RUN BY THE CIA VIA DAVID ATLEE PHILLIPS.*

AUGUST 9TH 1963

BRINGUIER WAS INFORMED BY A CUBAN FRIEND, CELSO HERNANDEZ, THAT **HARVEY** WAS NOW HANDING OUT PRO-CASTRO FPFC LITERATURE IN THE 700 BLOCK OF CANAL STREET. BRUNGUIER, HERNANDEZ, AND ANOTHER CUBAN, MIGUEL CRUZ, CONFRONTED HIM AND SOON THE POLICE ARRIVED. BRUINGUIER AND **HARVEY** WERE ARRESTED FOR DISTURBING THE PEACE.

AUGUST 9TH 1963

VARY/BAKER IS FIRED FROM REILY COFFEE. ACCORDING TO WILLIAM MONAGHAN, HIS SECRETARY HAD SEEN VARY/BAKER TALKING TO **HARVEY** ON CANAL STREET WITH CARLOS BRINGUIER. IN ORDER TO ERASE ANY CONNECTION BETWEEN THE NOW APPARENTLY "PRO-CASTRO" **HARVEY**, VARY/BAKER, AND THE STAUNCHLY ANTI-CASTRO REILY COFFEE, VARY/BAKER WOULD HAVE TO BE DISMISSED.

AUGUST 10TH 1963

IN JAIL WHEN MOST WOULD CALL A LAWYER, **HARVEY** HAD LT. FRANCIS MARTELLO CALL THE FBI. **HARVEY** TOLD MARTELLO: "TELL THEM YOU HAVE LEE OSWALD IN CUSTODY." HE ALSO REQUESTED THAT LT. MARTELLO INFORM THE FBI THAT HE WOULD PREFER TO BE QUESTIONED BY AGENT WARREN DEBRUEY. AGENT DEBRUEY HOWEVER WAS NOT AVAILABLE. AGENT JOHN QUIGLEY WOULD BE TASKED WITH THE QUESTIONING OF **HARVEY**. ALBEIT A SATURDAY MORNING, QUIGLEY ARRIVED AND SPENT OVER 90 MINUTES WITH HIM. IN A NOTE HE PASSED TO MARTELLO WAS A NUMBER IDENTIFYING A MICHAEL JELISAVCIC. JELISAVCIC, EMPLOYED BY AMERICAN EXPRESS, WAS THE MANAGER OF THE AMERICAN EXPRESS OFFICE IN MOSCOW DURING **HARVEY'S** "DEFECTION" TO THE SOVIET UNIION.

LATER, NOT ONLY WAS THE TERM "AMEX" NOTED IN **HARVEY'S** ADDRESS BOOK SIX TIMES OR MORE, BUT JELISAVCIC'S NAME AND PHONE NUMBER APPEARED IN THE ADDRESS BOOK AS WELL. IN SEPTEMBER 1963, DEBRUEY WILL BE TRANSFERRED TO DALLAS. HE WILL LEAVE NEW ORLEANS ON SEPTEMBER 25TH, THE SAME DAY THAT **HARVEY** DEPARTS.

*LT. FRANCIS L. MARTELLO, WHO INITIALLY INTERVIEWED **HARVEY** WHILE HE WAS IN CUSTODY IN NEW ORLEANS, NOTED THAT **HARVEY** SHOWED HIM NUMEROUS FORMS OF IDENTIFICATION, BUT <u>ALL</u> IN THE NAME OSWALD, <u>NOT</u> HIDELL. I FEEL THAT THIS IS THE*

RESULT OF AN EFFORT BY HUNT/PHILLIIPS TO COMPARTMENTALIZE **HARVEY'S** BOGUS NEW ORLEANS FPFC ACTIVITY FROM HIS LEGITIMATE FBI ACTIVITY AS AN INFORMANT. BUT, MORE IMPORTANTLY, THE HIDELL FACTOR WAS A CARD BEST PLAYED BY HUNT/PHILLIPS <u>AFTER</u> THE ASSASSINATION WHEN IT WOULD BE USED TO TIE **HARVEY** TO THE PURCHASE OF THE HANDGUN AND THE RIFLE ALLEGEDLY USED THAT AFTERNOON.

QUIGLEY WAS FAMILIAR WITH **HARVEY'S** BACKGROUND. ON APRIL 18TH, 1961, THE FBI OFFICE IN DALLAS HAD REQUESTED THAT HE REVIEW **HARVEY'S** NAVY FILE AT THE NEARBY U.S. NAVAL AIR STATION IN ALGIERS, LOUISIANA. QUIGLEY NOTED THAT DURING HIS INTERVIEW WITH **HARVEY** THAT HE WAS RELUCTANT TO DISCUSS THE FPFC COMMITTEE: "WHEN I ASKED HIM SPECIFIC DETAILS WITH RESPECT TO HIS FPFC ACTIVITIES IN NEW ORLEANS AS TO WHERE MEETINGS WERE HELD, WHO WAS INVOLVED, WHAT OCCURRED, HE WAS RELUCTANT.....RETICENT...AND COMPLETELY EVASIVE." HE ALSO NOTED TO QUIGLEY THAT IT WAS "HIDELL" WHO HAD ASKED TO HIM TO PASS OUT THE FPFC PAMPHLETS AND THAT HE HAD <u>NOT MET</u> HIDELL, BUT HAD ONLY <u>SPOKEN</u> WITH HIM OVER THE PHONE AND A FEW BRIEF <u>MAIL</u> CORRESPONDANCES. ALTHOUGH HE TOLD THE FBI HE RECEIVED NO PAYMENT FOR HIS WORK DISTRIBUTING THE PAMPHLETS, HE WILL LATER TELL HIS LAWYER DEAN ANDREWS THAT HE RECEIVED $25 A DAY. **HARVEY'S** BEHAVIOR TOWARDS THE FBI IS EASILY EXPLAINED. AS HE SEES IT, THE FPFC ACTIVITY IN NEW ORLEANS, INCLUDING THE BRINGUIER INCIDENT, IS SOLELY FOR THE PURPOSE OF MAINTAINING HIS PRO-CASTRO COVER IN PREPARATION FOR WHAT HE AND FERRIE <u>PERCEIVE</u> AS HIS NEXT CIA INTELLIGENCE ASSIGNMENT. **HARVEY** HOWEVER DOES NOT REALIZE THAT BANISTER IS USING HIM TO "TAINT" THE LIBERAL FPFC BY VIRTUE OF HIS BEING A FORMER "COMMUNIST DEFECTOR."

HARVEY WOULD NOT DIVULGE WHAT <u>HE</u> PERCEIVED AS A LEGITIMATE CIA-SPONSORED PROJECT, ALBEIT A BOGUS ONE, **(SCENARIO II)** TO THE FBI.

INTERESTINGLY, QUIGLEY BURNED THE NOTES OF THE INTERVIEW. LATER, AFTER THE ASSASSINATION, THE FBI WOULD BURN YET ANOTHER REFERENCE TO **HARVEY**; THE LETTER HE DROPPED OFF AT THE DALLAS FBI OFFICE NOTING HIS AGITATION AT THE FBI FOR HARASSING HIS WIFE.

THIS INCIDENT AND CONSEQUENT ARREST WOULD ENABLE BOTH BANISTER AND **HARVEY** IN HIS ROLE AS A PRO-CASTRO SYMPATHISER, TO FURTHER DOCUMENT AS A MATTER OF PUBLIC RECORD **HARVEY'S** PRO-CASTRO TENDENCIES. ALBEIT FOR DIFFERENT REASONS, THIS WOULD BE USEFUL FOR BOTH PARTIES. **HARVEY'S** CALL TO THE FBI WOULD LIKELY BE TO EXPLAIN TO QUIGLEY THAT IT WAS <u>FORMER</u> FBI AGENT <u>BANISTER</u> WHO HAD INITIATED HIS CONTACT WITH BRINGUIER AND THAT THIS WAS NOT A DEVIATION FROM HIS FBI INFORMANT ROLE THAT HAD BEEN ESTABLISHED IN AUGUST 1962 IN DALLAS.

WITH HUNT/PHILLIPS AND BANISTER TRYING TO PUBLICLY DOCUMENT ON BOTH T.V. AND IN NEWSPRINT AN EVENT THAT WILL LATER IMPLICATE **HARVEY** AS A PRO-CASTRO PROPONENT, EVEN BAD PUBLICITY CAN HAVE ITS MERITS.

IT IS DOUBTFUL THAT THE NEW ORLEANS FBI OFFICE CONSIDERED THE FACT THAT THE NEW ORLEANS CHAPTER FPFC PLOY WAS USED SOLELY AS A MECHANISM BY WHICH BANISTER AND HUNT/PHILLIPS FURTHERED THE PORTRAYAL OF **HARVEY** AS A PRO-CASTRO SUPPORTER. **HARVEY'S** CONFRONTATION WITH BRINGUIER <u>AFTER</u> HIS ATTEMPT TO <u>JOIN</u> BRINGUIER'S GROUP WOULD RENDER HIM TOTALLY INEFFECTIVE IN ANY FURTHER ATTEMPTS TO MONITOR BRINGUIER'S ANTI-CASTRO ORGANIZATION.

WILLIAM GAUDET, THE EX-NEW ORLEANS CIA AGENT NOTED: "I DON'T THINK HE **(HARVEY)** KNEW EXACTLY WHAT HE WAS DISTRIBUTING...(WITH) THE FPFC DEAL WHICH WAS NOTHING BUT A FRONT AND WAS ONE OF THE DREAMS OF, I THINK, GUY BANISTER.." GAUDET WAS CORRECT.

GAUDET'S OBSERVATION WAS ECHOED BY OTHERS. UPON ARRIVAL AT THE JAIL, **HARVEY** IS INITIALLY INTERVIEWED BY SERGEANT HORACE AUSTIN. AUSTIN WOULD NOTE IN HIS REPORT "IT APPEARED AS THOUGH HE IS BEING USED BY THESE PEOPLE (CARLOS BRINGUIER) AND IS UNINFORMED AND KNOWS VERY LITTLE ABOUT THIS ORGANIZATION (FPFC) THAT HE BELONGS TO AND ITS ULTIMATE PURPOSE OR GOAL." ALSO PRESENT AT THE INTERVIEW WAS PATROLMAN WARREN ROBERTS, JR. IN HIS W.C. TESTIMONY ROBERTS STATED THAT "OSWALD ANWERED QUESTIONS IN A MECHANICAL MANNER…..HE WAS FREQUENTLY EVASIVE, AND WOULD NOT ANSWER QUESTIONS DIRECTLY."

HARVEY WAS NOW DEEPLY MIRED IN THE CONFLUENCE OF MULTIPLE GROUPS ORCHESTRATING HIS CONFLICTING MOVEMENTS; THE CIA, AS HE PERCEIVED IT THROUGH HUNT AND PHILLIPS, BANISTER, AND THE FBI. OF THESE 3 GROUPS, IT IS QUITE OBVIOUS THAT HUNT/PHILLIPS WILL PROVE TO BE THE MOST DANGEROUS TO **HARVEY** AS THEIR EFFORTS TO SET HIM UP **(SCENARIO II)** AND THE PLANS TO ASSASSINATE THE PRESIDENT GO FORWARD.

IT IS IMPORTANT TO NOTE THAT IT IS IN NEW ORLEANS WHERE MULTIFACETED ASPECTS OF THE ANTI-CASTRO MOVEMENT CONVERGE; A LARGE AND VOCAL CUBAN-LED ANTI-CASTRO MOVEMENT, ORGANIZED CRIME WITH THEIR CIA-BACKED EFFORTS TO ELIMINATE CASTRO, LOW-LEVEL DISGRUNTLED BAY OF PIGS OPERATIVES WHO HAD BEEN LED AND TRAINED BY THE CIA, AND STAUNCH ANTI-CASTRO PROPONENTS SUCH AS BANISTER AND HIS GROUP WHO CONTINUE TO MOUNT RAIDS INTO CUBA AGAINST CASTRO. THE PLOT TO ASSASSINATE JFK MAY OR MAY NOT HAVE BEEN NURTURED HERE, BUT THE CONSPIRACY TO SET-UP **HARVEY** AS THE PATSY MOST CERTAINLY INFLUENCED HIS BEHAVIOR WHILE IN NEW ORLEANS.

HARVEY WAS BAILED OUT BY A FRIEND OF THE MURRETS, A. MR. HECKMAN.

LT. MARTELLO WAS ASKED BY THE SECRET SERVICE FOR HIS ASSISTANCE IN IDENTIFYING RACISTS AND SEGREGATIONISTS IN NEW ORLEANS PRIOR TO THE PRESIDENT'S NEW ORLEANS VISIT ON MAY 4TH, 1962. MARTELLO SAW FIT TO MONITOR DELPHINE ROBERTS DURING THE PRESIDENT'S STAY. ROBERTS WOULD LATER BECOME BANISTER'S SECRETARY AT 544 CAMP ST. SHE AND BANISTER WERE BOTH RABID SEGREGATIONISTS.

JOHN PIC, **LEE'S** HALF-BROTHER, WAS LATER SHOWN PICTURES OF **HARVEY** PASSING OUT FPFC PAMPHLETS IN NEW ORLEANS BY W.C. ATTORNEY ALBERT JENNER. HE WAS UNABLE AND UNWILLING TO IDENTIFY **HARVEY** AS HIS BROTHER **LEE**. PIC WOULD CONTINUE TO BE THE ONLY MEMBER OF **HARVEY'S** "FAMILY" WHO WOULD REFUSE TO ACCEPT THE NOTION THAT **HARVEY** WAS INDEED HIS BROTHER **LEE**.

WHEN S.A. DEBRUEYS WAS LATER ASKED WHY **HARVEY** HAD ASKED TO BE INTERVIEWED BY HIM WHEN JAILED, HE REPLIED: "….HE MAY HAVE BEEN CONCERNED ABOUT BEING IN THE CUSTODY OF THE LOCAL POLICE AND PERHAPS THOUGHT IT WOULD BE SAFER IF THE 'FEDS' WERE AWARE OF HIS BEING INCARCERATED."

AUGUST 12TH 1963
BRINGUIER AND **HARVEY** APPEAR IN SECOND MUNICIPAL COURT IN NEW ORLEANS. BRINGUIER'S CHARGES ARE DISMISSED. **HARVEY** IS FINED $10.00. **HARVEY** SITS IN THE COURTROOM SECTION THAT IS RESERVED FOR BLACKS. THIS WAS LIKELY DONE AT THE REQUEST OF BANISTER AS IT CLEARLY ASSOCIATES A SO-CALLED COMMUNIST WITH A CIVIL RIGHTS CAUSE.

AUGUST 12TH 1963
VARY/BAKER VISITS DR. SHERMAN'S APARTMENT. ACCORDING TO VARY/BAKER, THE AFRICAN GREEN MONKEYS HAD SUCCESSFULLY BEEN INJECTED WITH THE CANCER CAUSING "PRODUCT." THE FOCUS WOULD NOW SWITCH TO THE INEVITABLE; THE EXPERIMENTS WOULD NOW BE CONDUCTED ON HUMANS.

AUGUST 13TH 1963

HARVEY VISITS THE UNEMPLOYMENT OFFICE IN NEW ORLEANS. HE HIRES 2 MEN TO ASSIST HIM IN PASSING OUT PAMPHLETS. HE ALSO WRITES THE AMERICAN COMMUNIST PARTY. HE ENCLOSED A CLIPPING OF HIS ENCOUNTER WITH CARLOS BRINGUIER ON AUGUST 9TH. HE ALSO REQUESTED ADDITIONAL PAMPHLETS.

AUGUST 16TH 1963

HARVEY IS ONCE AGAIN PASSING OUT LITERATURE WITH THE ASSISTANCE OF THE TWO MEN HIRED FROM THE TEMPORARY AGENCY. THIS TIME HE IS IN FRONT OF THE INTERNATIONAL TRADE MART. A FILM CREW FROM WDSU IN NEW ORLEANS FILMED THIS ACTIVITY AND IT WAS BROADCAST ON THE EVENING'S NEWSCAST.

*HARVEY'S PAMPHLET EFFORTS LASTED LESS THAN 20 MINUTES. IT WOULD NOT ONLY APPEAR TO BE UNWORTHY OF A FILM CREW BUT ALSO NOT WARRANT TIME ON THE EVENING NEWS. IT WOULD SEEM THAT THE FILM CREW WOULD HAVE HAD TO HAVE BEEN TIPPED OFF ABOUT THE EPISODE FOR IT TO HAVE BEEN ABLE TO CAPTURE THE BRIEF EVENT. INDEED IT MAY HAVE BEEN **HARVEY** WHO HAD INFORMED THE FILM CREW OF HIS THREE MAN DEMONSTRATION. HOWEVER IT IS JUST AS LIKELY IF NOT MORE LIKELY THAT THE TIP CAME FROM BANISTER.*

*THIS, ALONG WITH HIS ARREST ON AUGUST 9TH, WOULD FURTHER ESTABLISH HIM AS A PRO-CASTRO SUPPORTER. THIS PRO-CASTRO "POSTURING" BY **HARVEY** WOULD ADD CONSIDERABLE CREEDENCE TO THE NOTION THAT HIS POLITICAL LEANINGS WERE INDEED COMMUNISTIC AND HOPEFULLY EASE HIS PASSAGE INTO CUBA VIA MEXICO FOR WHAT HE PERCEIVED AS HIS NEXT CIA ASSIGNMENT.*

*ONE OF THE PAMPHLETS HE WAS PASSING OUT WAS TITLED "THE CRIME AGAINST CUBA." THIS FLYER WAS PUBLISHED IN NEW YORK AND DISTRIBUTED BY FASIC PAMPHLETS, A COMPANY ALSO BASED IN NEW YORK. ON THE 2ND PAGE UNDER THE 1961 COPYRIGHT THE PRINTING DATES WERE NOTED TO BE JUNE 1961 FOR THE FIRST PRINTING, AND DECEMBER 1961 FOR THE FOURTH PRINTING. HOWEVER, HIS PAMPHLETS SHOWED ONLY THE FIRST, JUNE 1961 PRINTING WHICH WOULD OBVIOUSLY HAVE BEEN SOLD OUT SINCE THE PAMPHLET WAS ALREADY IN ITS 4TH PRINTING BY DECEMBER 1961. BUT IN JUNE 1961, (FIRST PRINTING), **HARVEY** WAS STILL IN RUSSIA AND REMAINED THERE UNTIL AFTER THE DECEMBER 1961 FOURTH PRINTING. **HARVEY** COULD NOT HAVE ORDERED THE PAMPHLETS HE WAS DISTRIBUTING.*

*CORLISS LAMONT, THE WRITER OF THE PAMPHLET, RETAINED A XEROX COPY OF AN ORDER FOR THE FIRST PRINTING (THE PRINTING **HARVEY** WAS DISTRIBUTING). IT WAS NOT FROM **HARVEY** NOR WAS IT FROM CLAY SHAW, GUY BANISTER, OR EVEN DAVID FERRIE. IT WAS FROM THE CIA. THE ORDER FORM NOTES AS THE RECEIVING PERSONS ADDRESS:*

> *CENTRAL INTELLIGENCE AGENCY*
> *MAILROOM LIBRARY*
> *WASHINGTON 25, D.C.*

THE ORDER FORM ALSO LISTS ETHEL H. SMITH, CHIEF, ACQUISITIONS BRANCH, AS THE PERSON PLACING THE ORDER. THIS DOES INDEED SHOW AN INTEREST BY THE CIA IN LEFT-WING LITERATURE AS A PRELUDE TO INFILTRATION OF THOSE PARTICULAR GROUPS. AS IT WAS NOTED BEFORE, BOTH JAMES MCCORD AND DAVID ATLEE PHILLIPS HAD INITIATED INFILTRATION OF THE FPFC IN NOVEMBER OF 1960.

*HOWEVER ONE MUST STILL QUESTION HOW **HARVEY** ACQUIRED THESE PARTICULAR PAMPHLETS, THE JUNE 1961 PRINTING, IN AUGUST 1963. THE LOGICAL PIPELINE FROM THE CIA ORDER IN JUNE 1961 TO **HARVEY'S** DISTRIBUTION IN AUGUST 1963 WOULD BE VIA CIA AGENTS E. HOWARD HUNT AND DAVID ATLEE PHILLIPS TO GUY BANISTER, AND THEN TO **HARVEY**.*

AUGUST 17ST 1963

WILLIAM STUCKEY, A WEEKLY RADIO REPORTER ON STATION WDSU, VISITED **HARVEY** AT HIS RESIDENCE. HE HAD OBTAINED HIS NAME AND ADDRESS FROM CARLOS BRINGUIER. STUCKEY WANTED **HARVEY** TO VISIT THE STATION LATER THAT EVENING FOR AN INTERVIEW. HE ARRIVED AT 5:00 AS SCHEDULED. THE INTERVIEW LASTED 37 MINUTES, BUT WAS EDITED TO 4.5 MINUTES. IT AIRED ON STUCKEY'S SHOW THAT EVENING.

*STUCKEY WOULD LATER TESTIFY TO THE WARREN COMMISSION THAT THE DAY OF THE DEBATE HE HAD BEEN CONTACTED BY AN ANONYMOUS "NEWS SOURCE" WHO ENLIGHTENED HIM ABOUT **HARVEY'S** "DEFECTION" TO RUSSIA. THIS NEW INFORMATION WAS ALSO BROUGHT TO HIS ATTENTION BY ED BUTLER.*

AUGUST 19TH 1963

HARVEY CALLS STUCKEY AS REQUESTED AND AGREES TO A DEBATE WITH CARLOS BRINGUIER AND ED BUTLER, DIRECTOR OF THE INFORMATION COUNCIL OF THE AMERICAS.

*INDEED THE DEBATE COULD POSSIBLY ASSIST THE FBI IN GAUGING THE ATTITUDES OF ANTI-CASTRO GROUPS LIKE BRINGUIER'S. BY THE TIME OF THE DEBATE ON AUGUST 21ST, BRINGUIER WAS LIKELY AWARE OF AND WILLINGLY PARTICIPATING WITH BANISTER IN AN EFFORT TO DRAW ATTENTION TO AND PUBLICIZE **HARVEY'S** PRO-CASTRO SENTIMENTS. I WOULD SUBMIT THAT HE WAS KNOWINGLY ASSISTING BANISTER AND DAVID PHILLIPS IN THE EVENTUAL SET-UP OF **HARVEY**.*

***HARVEY'S** LEGITIMATE TIES TO THE INTELLIGENCE COMMUNITY, IN PARTICULAR THE CIA, WERE NEARLY UNINTENTIONALLY EXPOSED ON THIS OCCASION. DURING THE LIVE DEBATE, **HARVEY**, WHEN QUESTIONED AS TO HOW HE SUPPORTED HIMSELF IN RUSSIA, STAMMERED "WELL, I, UH, WELL, I WILL ANSWER THAT QUESTION DIRECTLY SINCE YOU WILL NOT REST UNTIL YOU GET AN ANSWER. I WORKED IN RUSSIA, **I WAS UNDER, UH, THE PROTECTION** OF THE, UH .... OF THE UH, **THAT IS TO SAY, I WAS NOT UNDER THE PROTECTION OF THE AMERICAN GOVERNMENT**, BUT THAT I WAS AT ALL TIMES AN **AMERICAN CITIZEN**." (BOLD ADDED) **HARVEY** HAD NEARLY EXPOSED HIS CIA INTELLIGENCE ROLE WHILE IN RUSSIA. A TRANSCRIPT OF THIS INTERVIEW RELEASED BY THE WARREN COMMISSON READS SOMEWHAT DIFFERENTLY. IT READS: "I WAS NOT UNDER, UH, THE PROTECTION OF THE, UH…OF THE UH, THAT IS TO SAY I WAS NOT UNDER THE PROTECTION OF THE AMERICAN GOVERNMENT." WHY WOULD **HARVEY**, IN THE COMMISSION TRANSCRIPT REPEAT THE "NOT" DISTINCTION? HE DIDN'T. HE CORRECTLY AND HONESTLY SAID INITIALLY "I WAS UNDER THE PROTECTION……". THE COMMISSION SIMPLY SAW FIT TO ELIMINATE HIS ERROR RATHER THAN REVEAL **HARVEY'S** SLIP OF THE TONGUE AND THE INTELLIGENCE TIE-IN (CIA/ONI) IT ALLUDED TO.*

*IT IS INTERESTING TO NOTE THAT BOTH OF **HARVEY'S** ADVERSARIES IN THE DEBATE, BRINGUIER AND BUTLER, WERE ASSOCIATED WITH GROUPS, THE DRE AND INCA RESPECTIVELY, THAT HAD TIES TO THE CIA.*

IN 1967, ON FEBRUARY 20TH, BRINGUIER WOULD MEET WITH J. EDGAR HOOVER. HE WOULD PROTEST TO HOOVER THAT NEW ORLEANS DISTRICT ATTORNEY JIM GARRISON IN HIS INVESTIGATION OF THE ASSASSINATION WAS ILLEGALLY HARASSING DAVID FERRIE. FERRIE WOULD DIE JUST 2 DAYS LATER.

***HARVEY'S** LEGITIMATE TIES TO THE FBI WERE ALSO NEARLY UNINTENTIONALLY EXPOSED ON ANOTHER OCCASSION. THE GARAGE NEXT TO REILY'S COFFEE PROVIDED TRANSPORTATION FOR THE FBI/CIA OFFICES IN THE VICINITY. ADRIAN ALBA, THE GARAGE MANAGER, SAW A WHITE ENVELOPE SLIPPED TO **HARVEY** BY AN FBI AGENT WHO WAS FAMILIAR TO ALBA. HE WITNESSED A SIMILAR EXCHANGE 2 DAYS LATER.*

*THE DEBATE WOULD BE THE 2ND TIME THAT STATION WDSU WOULD ACCOMMODATE **HARVEY** IN HIS ENDEAVOR TO EXPOUND UPON HIS APPARENT "PRO-CASTRO" LEANINGS. WDSU WAS OWNED BY EDGAR STEARNS, ANOTHER STAUNCH ANTI-COMMUNIST AND ALSO ONE OF THE FOUNDING MEMBERS OF INCA. DR. OCHSNER WAS PRESENT DURING THE DEBATE. IN FACT HIS VOICE COULD BE HEARD IN THE BACKGROUND ON A RECORDING MADE OF THE DEBATE. I WOULD SUBMIT THAT OCHSNER'S CONCERN WAS THAT **HARVEY** WOULD ACCIDENTLY MENTION, HOWEVER OBLIQUELY, THE "PROJECT."*

AUGUST 20TH 1963
HARVEY MAKES HIS USUAL VISIT TO THE NEW ORLEANS UNEMPLOYMENT OFFICE.

AUGUST 21ST 1963
THE FBI IN WASHNGTON CABLES OFFICES IN BOTH NEW ORLEANS AND DALLAS REQUESTING FURTHER INFORMATION ON **HARVEY**.

AUGUST 21ST 1963
HARVEY, BRINGUIER, AND BUTLER TAKE PART IN THE LIVE DEBATE MODERATED BY WILLIAM STUCKEY.

AUGUST 25TH 1963
AN ARTICLE IN THE NEW ORLEANS TIMES PICUYUNE NOTES THE ARRIVAL OF A LARGE SHIPMENT OF MONKEYS; 8,000 POUNDS OR APPROXIMATELY 100 EIGHTY POUND MONKEYS. THEY WERE TO BE SENT TO THE TULANE MEDICAL SCHOOL.

AUGUST 27TH 1963
HARVEY VISITS THE UNEMPLOYMENT OFFICE.

AUGUST 28TH 1963
HARVEY WRITES THE COMMUNIST PARTY USA ASKING ADVICE ON WHAT HIS APPROACH SHOULD BE IN HIS EFFORTS TO PROMOTE MARXISM.

THE EVENTS OF AUGUST 29TH AND 30TH ARE CONFUSING TO SAY THE LEAST. ONE VERSION IS OFFERED BY VARY/BAKER AND THE OTHER VERSION IS OFFERED BY ARMSTRONG. WE WILL ADDRESS VARY/BAKER'S VERSION FIRST.

AUGUST 29TH – AUGUST 30TH 1963
ACCORDING TO VARY/BAKER, WHO RELIED ON FERRIE FOR THIS VERSION OF THE DAYS EVENTS, **HARVEY**, FERRIE, AND CLAY SHAW, AS THE DRIVER OF HIS BLACK CADILLAC, TAKE THE "PRODUCT" TO THE STATE MENTAL INSTITUTION IN JACKSON. THE FIRST HUMAN EXPERIMENT WAS ABOUT TO TAKE PLACE. IF THE EXPERIMENTS WERE SUCCESSFUL, IT WOULD THEN BE **HARVEY** WHO WOULD BE TASKED TO TRANSPORT THE CARCINOGENS TO MEXICO CITY FOR THEIR DELIVERY TO CUBA WHERE THEY WOULD HOPEFULLY BE ADMINISTERED TO CASTRO BY A"TRUSTED" MEMBER OF HIS STAFF. THE GROUP ALLEGEDLY STOPPED IN CLINTON WHERE THEY PICKED UP AN ORDERLY WHO WORKED AT THE HOSPITAL IN JACKSON. THE TRIO PARKED IN FRONT OF THE COURT HOUSE FOR WORD THAT THE CONVOY WITH THE PRISONER(S) TO BE USED AS THE SUBJECTS HAD LEFT THE PRISON.

THE PHONE CALL FROM ANGOLA INFORMING SHAW THAT THE CARAVAN WITH THE PRISONER(S) WAS NOW ENROUTE TO THE HOSPITAL FINALLY CAME. THE CADILLAC AND THE CONVOY WOULD MEET JUST PRIOR TO ENTERING THE PRISON GATES AND WOULD ENTER AS A SINGLE ENTITY. **HARVEY** AND FERRIE THEN ALLEGEDLY TOOK THE "PRODUCT" TO THE CLINIC. THE "PRODUCT" HAD BEEN TRANSPORTED IN THERMOS BOTTLES. IT WOULD BE FERRIE WHO WOULD ADMINISTER THE CANCEROUS CELLS. AS HE PROCEEDED WITH THE INJECTIONS, **HARVEY** SUPPOSEDLY MADE HIS WAY TO THE PERSONNEL OFFICE WHERE HE FILLED OUT AN APPLICATON. A RESEARCH UNIT AT THE HOSPITAL WAS DIRECTED BY A DR. FRANK SILVA. DR.SILVA WAS CUBAN AND CAME TO THE U.S. IN 1955. DR. SILVA, UNDER THE AUSPICES AND

FINANCIAL SUPPORT OF THE CIA, HAD ALREADY PERFORMED STUDIES ON THE PRISON PATIENT POPULATION INVOLVING THE ADMINISTRATION OF LSD AND MESCALINE.

AS VARY/BAKER'S/FERRIE'S VERSION PLAYS OUT, IT IS **HARVEY** ALONG WITH SHAW AND FERRIE, WHO VISIT BOTH CLINTON AND JACKSON, LOUISIANA. **HARVEY'S** POTENTIAL EMPLOYMENT AT THE MENTAL INSTITUTION IN JACKSON WOULD BE IN LINE WITH HIS PERCEIVED ROLE AS THE CIA-SPONSORED COURIER OF THE CARCINOGENS FROM NEW ORLEANS TO THE MENTAL INSTITUTION IN JACKSON. **HARVEY** WOULD DELIVER THE CARCINOGENS TO THE PHYSICIAN IN CHARGE OF THE GENERAL PATIENT POPULATION, DR. FRANK SILVA. THE CARCINOGENS COULD THEN BE TESTED ON HUMANS AT THE INSTITUTION IN MUCH THE SAME WAY AS EXPERIMENTS HELD IN ALABAMA AND OHIO IN REGARDS TO STUDYING THE EFFECTS OF SYPHYLLIS AND RADIATION ON LIVE HUMAN SUBJECTS.

AFTER THE GROUP RETURNED TO NEW ORLEANS, VARY-BAKER NOTED THAT SHE HAD ASKED FERRIE JUST WHAT TYPE OF CANCER THE PRISONER HAD. IT SEEMS THAT SHE HAD PREVIOUSLY BEEN TOLD THAT THE SUBJECT WAS ALREADY TERMINALLY ILL. SHE WANTED TO BE ABLE TO DISTINGUISH THE "INDUCED" CANCER FROM THE PATIENT'S EXISTING CANCER. VARY-BAKER WAS SHOCKED WHEN FERRIE REPLIED THAT THE SUBJECT WAS NOT SUFFERING FROM CANCER. THE SUBJECT HAD BEEN CHOSEN BECAUSE HE WAS THE SAME AGE AND WEIGHT AS CASTRO. HE WAS ALSO CUBAN.

ARMSTRONG HOWEVER OFFERS AN ALTERNATIVE VERSION. IT IS BELIEVED BY ARMSTRONG THAT IT IS ACTUALLY **LEE** WHO MADE THE JACKSON/CLINTON TRIP. **LEE** HOWEVER DID NOT ENGAGE IN THE "CARCINOGENS TO CUBA" ANGLE TENDERED BY VARY/BAKER. THE FACT THAT VARY/BAKER HAD TO RELY ON FERRIE'S VERSION OF THE TRIP LENDS CREEDENCE TO ARMSTRONG'S NOTION THAT **HARVEY** DID NOT MAKE THIS TRIP. IT IS HOWEVER A NEAR CERTAINTY THAT SHAW AND FERRIE DID INDEED MAKE THE 2 DAY TRIP.

THE CLINTON TOWN MARSHALL, JOHN MANCHESTER, NOTED THAT THE DRIVER WAS CLAY SHAW. CORRIE COLLINS, A CASE WORKER AT THE RALLY ALSO IDENTIFIED THE DRIVER AS SHAW AND THAT HE WAS ACCOMPANIED BY DAVID FERRIE AND A "LEE HARVEY OSWALD."

IN 1978, THE HSCA INTERVIEWED JOHN MANCHESTER. MANCHESTER STATED THAT WHEN HE APPROACHED THE CADILLAC THAT DAY AND ASKED THE DRIVER TO IDENTIFY HIMSELF THAT THE DRIVER DID SO BY COMMENTING "CLAY SHAW FROM THE INTERNATIONAL TRADE MART."

CORE (CONGRESS FOR RACIAL EQUALITY) HAD CHOSEN AUGUST 30TH TO HOLD A VOTER REGISTRATION RALLY IN CLINTON. **LEE**, SEEKING SOME RELIEF FROM THE HOT VEHICLE, STOOD JUST OUTSIDE THE COURT HOUSE. A LONE BLACK WOMAN, APPARENTLY AGITATED, TOLD **LEE** THAT SHE WAS NOT ALLOWED TO REGISTER HAVING FAILED HER LITERACY TEST. **LEE** THEN WAGERED A BET THAT BECAUSE HE WAS WHITE THAT HE COULD REGISTER EVEN THOUGH HE WASN'T A RESIDENT OF THE PARISH. SO **LEE** GOT INTO LINE WITH THE ORDERLY FROM THE HOSPITAL.

DURING THE CONVERSATION THAT TOOK PLACE DURING THEIR 2 HOUR WAIT, **LEE** WAS TOLD THAT THERE WERE INDEED JOB OPENINGS AT THE MENTAL HOSPITAL. WHEN HE FINALLY REACHED THE REGISTRAR'S DESK, HE SHOWED AN ID AND WAS ALLOWED TO SIGN THE REGISTRAR'S LOG. **LEE**, APPARENTLY AMUSED THAT HE HAD WON HIS BET, DREW THE SUSPICION OF THE REGISTRAR, HENRY EARL PALMER, WHO NOW ASKED FOR A SECOND, CLOSER LOOK AT HIS ID. THE ID OF COURSE DID NOT SHOW **LEE** AS A CITIZEN OF EAST FELICIANA PARISH BUT OF ORLEANS PARISH. THE REGISTRAR WAS NOT AMUSED HOWEVER AND ERASED **LEE'S** SIGNATURE FROM THE LOG BOOK.

BOBBIE DEDON, THE RECEPTIONIST AT THE HOSPITAL NOTED THAT SHE TALKED TO **LEE** FOR 4 OR 5 MINUTES PRIOR TO SENDING HIM TO THE PERSONNEL OFFICE. A WOMAN EMPLOYED IN THE PERSONNEL DEPARTMENT OF THE HOSPITAL IN JACKSON LATER CLAIMED TO HAVE INDEED INTERVIEWED **LEE** AND TAKEN HIS APPLICATION. THIS APPLICATION WAS LATER NOTED AS MISSING BY EMPLOYEE MAXINE KEMP OF THE PERSONEL OFFICE AFTER THE GARRISON/SHAW TRIAL STARTED. BUT, SHE DID NOTE HOWEVER THAT THE APPLICATION WAS THERE AFTER THE ASSASSINATION. DEDON WAS INTERVIEWED BY THE HSCA IN 1978. SHE WAS SHOWN PHOTOS OF **HARVEY**. DEDON NOTED "THAT MAN REMINDS ME OF **LEE** HARVEY OSWALD...THEY FAVOR, AND THEN THEY DON'T FAVOR....THIS MAN HAS FULLER LIPS, AND THIS MAN HAS A WIRE MOUTH. HAIRCUTS ARE DIFFERENT. THEIR EARS ARE THE SAME." DEDON CLEARLY NOTED THE DIFFERENCES BETWEEN **LEE** WHO HAD VISITED HER, AND **HARVEY** WHO HAD NOT.

ARMSTRONG NOTES THAT IT IS **LEE** IN JACKSON AND CLINTON WHO IS IMPERSONATING **HARVEY**. BUT, ARMSTRONG ADMITS THAT HE DOES NOT UNDERSTAND THE ADVANTAGE OF OR THE REASON FOR THE SET-UP CONSPIRATORS CHOOSING TO LINK **HARVEY** TO CLINTON AND JACKSON

THE REMOVAL OF THE PERSONNEL INTERVIEW FILE FROM BOBBIE DEDON'S OFFICE BY EITHER THE SET-UP CONSPIRATORS, OR MORE LIKELY THE CIA PROPER, WOULD HOPEFULLY ELIMINATE ANY LATER POSSIBLE CONNECTION BETWEEN **LEE** AND **HARVEY** WHO WOULD LATER BE PERCEIVED AS THE PRESIDENT'S "ASSASSIN." HAD IT BEEN DESIRABLE TO CONNECT **HARVEY** TO THE MENTAL INSTITUTION IN JACKSON FOR LATER USE AS A POSSIBLE "CRAZED ASSASSIN" PLOY, IT WOULD HAVE BEEN NECESSARY TO LEAVE A "**HARVEY**" FILE IN PLACE. IT WOULD HAVE TAKEN LITTLE EFFORT FOR THE SET-UP CONSPIRATORS TO CONVERT THE JOB APPLICATION FILE TO A POTENTIAL "PATIENT" FILE. THE FACT THAT IT WAS LATER REMOVED INDICATES THAT IT WAS INDEED **LEE** IN CLINTON AND JACKSON AND NOT **HARVEY**. DISASSOCIATING BOTH **HARVEY** AND **LEE** FROM A LEGITIMATE CIA PROJECT TO CULTURE CARCINOGENS CARRIED A HIGHER PRIORITY THAN ANY BENEFIT THAT COULD BE GAINED FROM ASSOCIATING **HARVEY** WITH A MENTAL INSTITUTION.

I WOULD OFFER TWO OPINIONS. THE VISITS TO CLINTON AND JACKSON AS RELATED TO VARY/BAKER BY FERRIE WERE CRITICAL TO THE SET-UP CONSPIRATORS IN REGARDS TO CONVINCING THE NEW ORLEANS DUO OF VARY/BAKER AND **HARVEY** THAT THE "CARCINOGENS TO CUBA" PROJECT AND THEIR INVOLVEMENT WAS INDEED LEGITIMATE. A SECOND AND PERHAPS MORE IMPORTANT REASON FOR HAVING **LEE** VISIT CLINTON WAS THE CORE RALLY. THIS IS THE THEORY OF DR. JEFFREY CAUFIELD.

ASSOCIATING **HARVEY**, A FORMER RUSSIAN "DEFECTOR" AND AN ALLEGED PRO-CASTRO ADVOCATE TO A KNOWN LIBERAL CAUSE, CIVIL RIGHTS, WOULD REINFORCE THE WIDELY HELD NOTION IN THE SOUTH THAT CIVIL RIGHTS, INTEGRATION, AND VOTER REGISTRATION WERE INDEED COMMUNIST INSPIRED. THE PRESIDENT HAD PROPOSED THE CIVIL RIGHTS ACT IN JULY OF 1963. MORE IMPORTANTLY, IN LOUISIANA, THE SEGREGATIONIST-INSPIRED COMMUNIST CONTROL ACT WOULD HAVE SUBJECTED ANYONE ASSOCIATED WITH A KNOWN COMMUNIST, (i.e. **HARVEY**) TO POSSIBLE JAIL TERMS AND SUBSTANTIAL FINES. IF **HARVEY**, VIA **LEE'S** CLINTON EFFORTS, WERE LINKED TO CORE, THEIR CIVIL RIGHTS EFFORTS WOULD BE "TAINTED" BY AN ALLEGED COMMUNIST'S ASSOCIATION WITH THEIR CAUSE. EVEN IF BANISTER'S EFFORTS TO "SHEEP-DIP" **HARVEY** AS A PRO-CASTRO COMMUNIST WERE TOTALLY UNRELATED TO THE EVENTUAL SET-UP OF **HARVEY** AS THE PRESIDENTIAL ASSASSIN, BANISTER WOULD, AT A MINIMUM, HAVE USED **HARVEY** TO SUPPORT THE NOTION OF A COMMUNIST-LED CIVIL RIGHTS MOVEMENT. **LEE** WAS NOT IN JACKSON TO GET A JOB AT THE HOSPITAL. **LEE'S** SOLE PURPOSE WAS TO INFILTRATE CORE. AFTER THE ASSASSINATION, IT WOULD BE NECESSARY TO DIMINISH THE "CORE ANGLE" AND FURTHER THE "JOB PURSUIT" ANGLE.

AUGUST 30TH 1963

VARY/BAKER PUTS IN WRITING HER OBJECTIONS ABOUT USING SUBJECTS WHO ARE NOT ALREADY TERMINALLY ILL IN THE EXPERIMENTS. SHE THEN PERSONALLY DELIVERED THE NOTE TO DR. OCHSNER'S OFFICE. AFTER DEPARTING OCHSNER'S OFFICE, SHE THEN WENT TO DR. SHERMAN'S APARTMENT. THERE SHE RECEIVED A CALL FROM FERRIE WHO TOLD HER THAT OCHSNER WAS MARKEDLY IRRITATED AND WANTED TO SEE HER IMMEDIATELY. FERRIE ALSO TOLD VARY/BAKER THAT OCHSNER HAD NOTED TO HIM THAT BOTH SHE AND **HARVEY** "WERE EXPENDABLE." IMMEDIATELY AFTER HER CALL FROM FERRIE VARY/BAKER RECEIVES THE NOW DREADED CALL FROM OCHSNER. AFTER THREATENING HER OVER HER CARELESSNESS IN CREATING A PAPER TRAIL CONCERNING HER ISSUES WITH THE "PROJECT", HE THEN MORE CALMLY INFORMED HER THAT SHE WOULD HOWEVER NEED TO RETURN TO JACKSON THE FOLLOWING DAY TO CHECK ON THEIR "SUBJECT." VARY/BAKER WOULD LATER THAT EVENING BE TAKEN BY FERRIE TO OCHSNER'S OFFICE. THERE HE INFORMED HER THAT ONCE HER WORK AT JACKSON WAS DONE THAT SHE WOULD BE DISMISSED FROM THE "PROJECT."

AUGUST 31ST 1963

ACCORDING TO VARY/BAKER, SHE IS TAKEN BACK TO JACKSON BY **HARVEY**. AT THE HOSPITAL, VARY/BAKER EXAMINED BOTH SPECIMENS AND THE SUBJECT. SHE DETERMINED THAT THE "PRODUCT" HAD NOW PROVEN SUCCESSFUL ON HUMAN SUBJECTS.

*IT IS IMPORTANT TO NOTE THAT THIS IS NOT THE FIRST TIME THAT VARY/BAKER HAS REFERENCED **HARVEY'S** ABILITY AND WILLINGNESS TO DRIVE A MOTOR VEHICLE. THIS IS HOWEVER CONTRARY TO WHAT OTHERS HAVE NOTED, I.E. THAT **HARVEY** DID NOT DRIVE AND DID NOT POSSESS A VALID DRIVERS LICENSE. IS IT POSSIBLE THAT VARY/BAKER IN HER LATER RECOLLECTIONS CONFUSED **HARVEY** AND **LEE**? HAD SHE DURING HER STAY IN NEW ORLEANS BEEN EXPOSED TO BOTH **HARVEY** AND **LEE**? TO ME THIS IS THE ONLY LOGICAL EXPLANATION FOR HER "BLENDING" OF EVENTS MOST LIKELY PERFORMED BY BOTH **HARVEY** AND **LEE**.*

*FOR THE MOST PART I FIND VARY/BAKER'S RECOLLECTIONS PLAUSIBLE. BUT, IF ONE IS TO BELIEVE THAT SHE AND **HARVEY** HAD AN AFFAIR IN NEW ORLEANS I WOULD IN TURN FIND IT DIFFICULT TO BELIEVE THAT SHE WOULD CONFUSE **HARVEY** AND **LEE**. EITHER **HARVEY** COULD INDEED DRIVE, OR IT WAS **LEE** WHO TOOK VARY/BAKER TO JACKSON. TO THIS DAY, THE CLINTON/JACKSON EPISODE CONTINUES TO PUZZLE RESEARCHERS.*

DURING THE SUMMER OF 1963, **HARVEY** RESIDED IN NEW ORLEANS. **LEE** APPARENTLY SPENT TIME THERE AS WELL. ACCORDING TO ARMSTRONG, IN LATE SPRING, EDWARD GIRNIUS MET WITH CLAY SHAW IN REGARDS TO BROKERING WEAPONS. THE MEETING TOOK PLACE IN A DOWNTOWN OFFICE BUILDING NEAR SEARS & ROEBUCK. ONE OF THE MEN ACCOMPANYING SHAW WAS INTRODUCED TO GIRNIUS AS "**LEE**."

IN LATE JUNE OR EARLY JULY, ONCE AGAIN ACCORDING TO ARMSTRONG, VERNON W. BUNDY, WHO WORKED AT THE PONCHARTRAIN BEACH AUSEMENT PARK, WAS INTRODUCED BY A FRIEND TO BOTH DAVID FERRIE AND **LEE** OSWALD. IT WAS ALSO **LEE** WHO WAS PHOTOGRAPHED AND FILMED AT THE PONCHARTRAIN TRAINING CAMPS WHERE HE WORKED WITH DAVID FERRIE. IN EARLY AUGUST, IT IS **LEE** WHO IS NOTED BY ARMSTRONG TO HAVE VISITED THE HABANA BAR IN NEW ORLEANS. OREST PENA, THE BAR'S OWNER, NOTED THAT ON MANY OCCASSIONS BOTH FERRIE AND SHAW ALSO VISITED THE BAR.

LEE WAS ALSO KNOWN TO BE IN DALLAS THAT SUMMER WHILE **HARVEY** REMAINED IN NEW ORLEANS. DOROTHY MARCUM, WHO DATED RUBY THAT SUMMER OF 1963, NOTED THAT **LEE** WORKED FOR RUBY. WHEN **LEE** WOULD VISIT THE CAROUSEL CLUB, RUBY WOULD GREET HIM AS "OZZIE." THIS OF COURSE WAS THE NICKNAME GIVEN TO **LEE** IN JAPAN. ROBERT ROY, AN AUTO MECHANIC WHO SERVICED RUBY'S CAR, NOTED THAT HE HAD DRIVEN **LEE** TO THE CAROUSEL CLUB ON MORE THAN ONE

OCCASION THAT SUMMER. ACCORDING TO ARMSTRONG, WILLIAM CROWE, WALLY WESTON, DIXIE LYNN, AND KATHY KAY, ALL RUBY EMPLOYEES, NOTE **LEE'S** PRESENCE AT THE CLUB THAT SUMMER. CLIFF SHASTEEN, WHO OWNED A BARBERSHOP IN IRVING, TEXAS, HAD CUT **LEE'S** HAIR ON SEVERAL OCCASIONS. HE NOTED THAT **LEE** GOT A HAIRCUT ABOUT EVERY TWO WEEKS, AND, MORE IMPORTANTLY, HAD SHASTEEN CUT ONLY 1/16" OF HIS HAIR EACH TIME. I SUSPECT THAT THIS WAS DONE BY **LEE** IN AN ATTEMPT TO ALWAYS KEEP HIS HAIR APPROXIMATELY THE SAME LENGTH AS **HARVEY** WORE HIS.

SEPTEMBER 1ST 1963
HARVEY WRITES 2 MORE LETTERS; ONE TO COMMUNIST PARTY USA AND ONE TO THE SOCIALIST PARTY USA.

SEPTEMBER 2ND 1963
HARVEY AND MARINA VISIT HIS "UNCLE" CHARLES MURRET AND HIS WIFE LILLIAN..

SEPTEMBER 3RD 1963
VARY/BAKER, HER WORK ON THE "PROJECT" TERMINATED BY DR. OCHSNER, LEFT NEW ORLEANS WITH HER HUSBAND ROBERT. BOTH SHE AND ROBERT WOULD LATER START CLASSES AT THE UNIVERSITY OF FLORIDA IN GAINESVILLE. PRIOR TO HER DEPARTURE, SHE, **HARVEY**, AND FERRIE HAD WORKED OUT A "SYSTEM" BY WHICH THEY WOULD BE ABLE TO CALL EACH OTHER. **HARVEY'S** CODENAME WOULD BE "HECTOR."

SEPTEMBER 3RD 1963
HARVEY VISITS THE UNEMPLOYMENT OFFICE.

EARLY SEPTEMBER 1963
VARY/BAKER RECEIVES A PHONE CALL FROM FERRIE. **HARVEY**, ACCORDING TO FERRIE, HAD GONE BRIEFLY TO DALLAS TO CLARIFY ARRANGEMENTS FOR HIS TRIP TO MEXICO CITY. ACCORDING TO FERRIE, **HARVEY** NOTED THAT WHILE IN DALLAS HE MET WITH TWO MEN. ONE OF THE MEN WAS DESCRIBED BY **HARVEY** AS HIS "HANDLER", A "MR. B." MR. B. HAD, DURING THE CONVERSATION WITH **HARVEY**, SAID THAT HIS ACTUAL NAME WAS "BENTON." THE SECOND MAN WAS IDENTIFIED AS ANTONIO VECIANA, AN ANTI-CASTRO CUBAN THAT "MR.B." HAD RECRUITED AS AN INFORMANT IN 1959. VECIANA, ACCORDING TO **HARVEY** WHO HAD REPEATED THE STORY TO FERRIE AND IN TURN FERRIE REPEATED TO VARY/BAKER, HAD ADDRESSED "MR.B."AS "BISHOP." "BISHOP", OR "MAURICE BISHOP" WAS AN ALIAS USED BY DAVID ATLEE PHILLIPS.

*IT WAS NOT VECIANA'S FIRST VISIT TO DALLAS TO MEET WITH PHILLIPS. THIS VISIT HOWEVER WAS NOTABLY DIFFERENT. WHEN VECIANA APPROACHED PHILLIPS IN THE LOBBY OF THE SOUTHLAND BUILDING HE NOTED THAT PHILLIPS WAS CONVERSING WITH A YOUNG MAN. VECIANA WOULD, ON NOVEMBER 22ND, IDENTIFY **HARVEY** AS THE YOUNG MAN ENGAGED IN CONVERSATION WITH PHILLIPS. VECIANA WOULD LATER VERIFY THAT THIS MEETING TOOK PLACE AT THE SOUTHLAND BUILDING*

*IT IS WORTH NOTING THAT VARY/BAKER'S VERSION OF THE DALLAS VISIT AND HER VERSION OF **HARVEY'S** ALLEGED VISIT TO JACKSON AND CLINTON ARE VIA DAVID FERRIE. WAS FERRIE FABRICATNG STORIES FOR THE BENEFIT OF VARY/BAKER? WERE THE TWO EVENTS, JACKSON/CLINTON AND DALLAS NOTED TO VARY/BAKER BY FERRIE USING THE GENERIC "OSWALD" MONIKER ALLOWING VARY/BAKER TO ASSUME THAT IT WAS **HARVEY** AND TO DISGUISE THE FACT THAT **LEE** HARVEY OSWALD AND LEE **HARVEY** OSWALD WERE TWO DISTINCT INDIVIDUALS?*

*I AM MUCH MORE INCLINED, AS IS ARMSTRONG, TO BELIEVE THAT IT WAS ACTUALLY **LEE** WHO HAD MET WITH PHILLIPS AND **LEE** WHO HAD PASSED THIS INFORMATION ON TO FERRIE WHO IN TURN INFORMED VARY/BAKER OF THE DALLAS VISIT. IT IS ALMOST A CERTAINTY THAT FERRIE KNEW BOTH **LEE** AND **HARVEY**. OF COURSE IF FERRIE SIMPLY USED THE NAME "OSWALD" AND NOT MADE THE DISTINCTION BETWEEN **LEE** AND*

HARVEY *IN REGARDS TO JUST WHO HAD MADE THE DALLAS TRIP, THEN VARY/BAKER WOULD BE FREE TO DRAW HER OWN CONCLUSION THAT IT WAS **HARVEY** NOT **LEE**. IT IS IMPOSSIBLE TO BELIEVE THAT PHILLIPS WOULD HAVE MET WITH **HARVEY** IN PUBLIC, IN DALLAS, ONLY 3 MONTHS PRIOR TO AN ASSASINATION THAT WOULD BE BLAMED ON **HARVEY**. VECIANA WAS EITHER MISTAKEN ABOUT WHO ATTENDED THE MEETING IN DALLAS OR LYING. I AM HOWEVER QUICK TO NOTE THAT I AM INCLINED TO BELIEVE THAT HE WAS SIMPLY MISTAKEN. VECIANA WOULD BE ONE OF THE FEW PEOPLE WHO WOULD RISK LINKING PHILLIPS TO THE "BISHOP" ALIAS. HAVING TAKEN THAT CHANCE, HE WOULD LIKELY NOT BE RELUCTANT TO LINK **HARVEY** TO BISHOP/PHILLIPS EITHER PURPOSELY OR BY MISTAKE.*

*I AM INCLINED TO ACCEPT ARMSTRONG'S VERSION THAT IT WAS **LEE** WHO VISITED DALLAS AND MET WITH PHILLIPS AND VECIANA. IT IS INDEED **LEE** WHO IS IN NEED OF CLARIFICATION REGARDING HIS UPCOMING TRIP TO MEXICO CITY; A TRIP NO DOUBT PLANNED AND ARRANGED BY PHILLIPS AND HUNT.*

SEPTEMBER 1963
GENEVA WHITE, WIFE OF ROSCOE WHITE, IS EMPLOYED BY JACK RUBY AT THE CAROUSEL CLUB.

SEPTEMBER 9TH 1963
HARVEY RETURNED 3 LIBRARY BOOKS. THE BOOKS WERE OVERDUE. HE ALSO CASHED HIS UNEMPLOYMENT CHECK OF SEPTEMBER 3RD.

HARVEY *AT THIS TIME IS APPARENTLY STILL IN NEW ORLEANS WITH HIS PREGNANT WIFE AND BABY. THERE IS HOWEVER LITTLE DOCUMENTATION IN THE LITERATURE TO NOTE WITH ANY DEGREE OF CERTAINTY JUST WHAT **HARVEY** IS UP TO <u>AFTER</u> THE AIRING OF THE RADIO DEBATE WITH BRINGUIER ON AUGUST 21ST <u>UNTIL</u> SEPTEMBER 9TH WHEN HE RETURNS THE OVERDUE LIBRARY BOOKS. ALTHOUGH **HARVEY** OR AN "OSWALD" SHOWED UP AT THE UNEMPLOYMENT OFFICE ON AUGUST 27TH, THE FBI IS UNABLE TO VERIFY THE SIGNATURE AS **HARVEY'S**. THIS IS THE <u>FIRST</u> TIME THEY ARE UNABLE TO VERIFY HIS SIGNATURE ON CLAIM DOCUMENTS. THEY ARE ALSO UNABLE TO VERIFY HIS SIGNATURE ON HIS NEXT ALLEGED VISIT ON SEPTEMBER 3RD. ON SEPTEMBER 9TH HOWEVER, **HARVEY** CASHED HIS SEPTEMBER 3RD CHECK WHICH IS MAILED ON THE 6TH. THE FBI IS ABLE TO VERIFY THE SIGNATURE ON THIS CASHED CHECK AS **HARVEY'S**.*

SEPTEMBER 10TH 1963
HARVEY ONCE AGAIN VISITS THE UNEMPLOYMENT OFFFICE. THE FBI IS NOW ABLE TO VERIFY THE SIGNATURE ON THIS CLAIM AS **HARVEY'S**. ALSO ON THIS DATE, THE DALLAS FBI OFFICE OFFICIALLY TRANSFERS THE CASE FILE ON **HARVEY** TO NEW ORLEANS.

SEPTEMBER 13TH 1963
BUELL WESLEY FRAZIER STARTS WORK AT THE TSBD.

SEPTEMBER 13TH 1963
THE DALLAS MORNING NEWS ANNNOUNCES THE UPCOMING PRESIDENTIAL VISIT.

SEPTEMBER 16TH 1963
A SIGNATURE BY A "LEE OSWALD" WAS MADE IN A RESTAURANT LOG IN A HUBERTUS, WISCONSIN RESTAURANT. LATER THAT DAY A "LEE OSWALD, DALLAS" SIGNED A GUEST BOOK AT A NIGHTCLUB ABOUT 30 MILES FROM MILWAUKEE. JFK WAS TO VISIT WISCONSIN ONLY A FEW DAYS LATER.

*I TEND TO AGREE WITH ARMSTRONG THAT THESE TWO "SIGHTINGS" AND OTHERS THROUGHOUT THE COUNTRY OF A **LEE** OSWALD WHEN IT WAS CLEAR THAT **HARVEY** WAS IN NEW ORLEANS WITH HIS WIFE, WERE FOR THE SOLE PURPOSE OF SUGGESTING THAT IT WAS **HARVEY** WHO WAS STALKING THE PRESIDENT.*

SEPTEMBER 16TH 1963

IN A MEMO TO THE FBI, THE CIA NOTES THAT IT IS "GIVING SOME CONSIDERATION TO COUNTERING THE ACTIVITIES OF THE FPFC IN FOREIGN COUNTRIES…"

*IT IS READILY APPARENT THAT ONE OF THE COUNTRIES IN QUESTION IS MEXICO AND THAT THE CIA'S VEHICLE FOR THIS PARTICULAR EFFORT IS EITHER **HARVEY** OR MORE LIKELY **LEE** WHO WILL SOON ARRIVE IN MEXICO CITY. IT IS UNCLEAR AS TO WHETHER THE CIA SPECIFICALLY MENTIONS EITHER **HARVEY** OR **LEE** IN THIS MEMO. I WOULD OFFER HOWEVER THAT NEITHER **LEE** NOR **HARVEY** WERE SPECIFICALLY IMPLICATED, BUT THAT A "LEE HARVEY OSWALD" MAY HAVE BEEN. THIS WOULD ALLOW THE SET-UP CONSPIRATORS TO SEND **LEE** TO MEXICO CITY IN AN EFFORT TO FURTHER THE FRAMING OF **HARVEY** FOR THE PRESIDENT'S DEATH AND ALSO TO IMPLICATE CUBA AS WELL.*

SEPTEMBER 17TH 1963

HARVEY CHECKS WITH THE LOUSIANA DIVISION OF UNEMPLOYMENT SECURITY TO FOLLOW-UP ON HIS CLAIM FOR INTERSTATE UNEMPLOYMENT INSURANCE FROM TEXAS.

SEPTEMBER 17TH 1963

LEE OBTAINS MEXICAN TOURIST CARD FM- 8No.24085 IN NEW ORLEANS. THE CARD ISSUED IMMEDIATELY PRIOR TO HIS, CARD FM-8No.24084, IS ISSUED TO WILLIAM GAUDET, A CIA SOURCE OF INFORMATION VIA THE CIA'S DOMESTIC CONTACT DIVISION. GAUDET HAD BEEN EMPLOYED BY THE CIA IN THE 1940'S, 1950'S, AND CONTINUED HIS EMPLOYMENT INTO THE 1960'S.

*GAUDET MAY WELL HAVE BEEN A CIA "TAIL." GAUDET'S WORK AS AN INFORMER/OPERATIVE FOR THE CIA DATES BACK TO 1959 WHEN HE REPORTED ON JACK RUBY'S ACTIVITIES IN NEW ORLEANS. LATER HE WOULD REPORT TO THE CIA THE ACTIVITIES OF ANTI-CASTRO GROUPS IN NEW ORLEANS AS WELL AS THE ACTIVITIES OF GUY BANISTER, CLAY SHAW, DAVID FERRIE AND NOW **HARVEY**. GAUDET COULD VERIFY THAT **HARVEY** WAS IN CONTACT WITH THE FBI IN NEW ORLEANS AND THAT HE HAD SEEN HIM WITH BOTH GUY BANISTER AND DAVID FERRIE. THE CIA HIERARCHY IN WASHINGTON MUST HAVE QUESTIONED AND WONDERED WAS **HARVEY** THE SAME LEE **HARVEY** OSWALD THAT HAD SERVED THE CIA WITH HIS SUCCESSFUL SOVIET "DEFECTION" IN 1959? GAUDET ALSO EDITED A NEWSLETTER, THE LATIN AMERICAN TRAVELER. THIS WAS FINANCED BY INCA FOUNDER DR. ALTON OCHSNER. GAUDET WOULD LATER BE INTERVIEWED BY THE FBI ON NOVEMBER 27TH, 1963. HE WOULD DENY HAVING SEEN **HARVEY** IN NEW ORLEANS. BUT, HE WOULD TIE **HARVEY** TO DAVID FERRIE AND OFFER HIS OPINION THAT **HARVEY** WAS INDEED "A PATSY." THE WARREN COMMISSION LISTED ALL TRAVELERS WHO RECEIVED MEXICAN TOURIST CARDS THE SAME DAY AS **LEE**. THEY DID <u>NOT</u> HOWEVER LIST GAUDET. GAUDET WOULD LATER CLAIM THAT HE TRAVELLED TO MEXICO NOT BY BUS, BUT BY AIR.*

*THE W.C. INSISTS THAT IT IS **HARVEY** ENROUTE TO MEXICO CITY. ARMSTRONG HOWEVER CONTENDS THAT IT IS **LEE**. I TEND TO AGREE WITH THIS NOTION AND LATER EVENTS WILL SUPPORT THE PROBABILITY THAT IT WAS NOT **HARVEY** ABOUT TO EMBARK ON A JOURNEY TO MEXICO. BUT, DOES GAUDET REALIZE THAT HE IS TAILING **LEE** NOT **HARVEY**?*

SEPTEMBER 20TH 1963

RUTH PAINE ARRIVES IN NEW ORLEANS FOR WHAT SHE WOULD DESCRIBE AS A "VISIT." SHE OFFERS TO TAKE MARINA AND JUNE BACK TO TEXAS PRIOR TO THE ARRIVAL OF MARINA'S SECOND CHILD. **HARVEY** AGREES TO THIS PROPOSAL.

SEPTEMBER 23, 1963

MARINA, PREGNANT WITH AUDREY AND ACCOMPANIED BY JUNE, HER YOUNG DAUGHTER, DEPART NEW ORLEANS WITH RUTH PAINE TO RETURN TO DALLAS. MARINA AND HER DAUGHTER WILL RESIDE ONCE AGAIN WITH RUTH PAINE.

SEPTEMBER 23RD 1963

ACCORDING TO OLIN HAMILTON, A "**LEE** OSWALD" INTERVIEWED FOR A JOB AT A WAREHOUSE OF SEMTNER DRUG DEPOT. HAMILTON NOTED THAT "OSWALD" HAD BEEN SENT TO HIM BY THE TEXAS EMPLOYMENT COMMISSION. IT WOULD SEEM THAT THE SET-UP CONSPIRATORS WERE A BIT PREMATURE IN FINDING EMPLOYMENT FOR AN "OSWALD" IN DALLAS AS **HARVEY** WOULD NOT RETURN UNTIL OCTOBER 3RD. THIS "OSWALD" IS LIKELY **LEE** WHO WAS ALSO A BIT "PREMATURE" IN HIS INTERVIEW WITH HAMILTON. **LEE** NOTED THAT HE HAD A WIFE AND TWO CHILDREN TO SUPPORT. RACHEL OSWALD, **HARVEY'S** 2ND DAUGHTER WAS NOT BORN UNTIL OCTOBER 20TH, 1963.

SEPTEMBER 24TH 1963
RUTH PAINE, MARINA, AND HER DAUGHTER ARRIVE AT THE PAINE RESIDENCE IN DALLAS AT 1:30 PM.

SEPTEMBER 24TH 1963
HARVEY CLOSES OUT HIS NEW ORLEANS P.O. BOX 30061 AND LEAVES INSTRUCTIONS THAT HIS MAIL BE FORWARDED TO 2515 WEST 5TH STREET IN IRVING, TEXAS. THIS ADDRESS IS THAT OF RUTH PAINE. HE ALSO VISITS THE UNEMPLOYMENT OFFICE FOR THE LAST TIME. HE IS INTERVIEWED BY FREDERICK L. CHRISTEN. THE FBI IS ONCE AGAIN ABLE TO VERIFY THAT THE SIGNATURE ON THE CLAIM IS HIS.

SEPTEMBER 25TH 1963
HARVEY CASHES A $33 UNEMPLOYMENT CHECK AT A LOCAL WINN-DIXIE. THE CHECK HOWEVER IS NOT ENDORSED.

SEPTEMBER 25TH 1963
ACCORDING TO VARY/BAKER, AS RELATED TO HER BY **HARVEY**, HE AND A HISPANIC MAN ARE FLOWN BY PILOT HUGH WARD FROM NEW ORLEANS TO AUSTIN, TEXAS. HUGH WARD WAS AN ASSOCIATE OF GUY BANISTER IN NEW ORLEANS. HE WAS ACTIVE AS A PILOT OF GUNS AND AMMUNITION FROM NEW ORLEANS TO MIAMI AND THEN TO CUBA. AFTER A 2.5 HOUR FLIGHT, THE PLANE ARRIVES IN AUSTIN ABOUT NOON. **HARVEY** AND THE HISPANIC MAN THEN DRIVE TO THE TREK CAFE IN DOWNTOWN AUSTIN. AFTER **HARVEY** VISITS THE SELECTIVE SERVICE OFFICE, HE AND THE HISPANIC MAN RETURN TO THE AUSTIN AIRPORT WHERE HUGH WARD PROMPTLY FLEW THEM TO DALLAS. THEY ARRIVED IN DALLAS ABOUT 7:00 PM. IN DALLAS, **HARVEY** IS THEN PICKED UP BY TWO HISPANIC MEN AND IS THEN DRIVEN TO THE RESIDENCE OF SYLVIA ODIO. AFTER THE VISIT TO ODIO'S APARTMENT, THE LATINOS RETURNED **HARVEY** TO THE AIRPORT WHERE HUGH WARD PROMPTLY FLEW HIM TO HOUSTON. ARRIVING IN HOUSTON LATE THAT EVENING **HARVEY** WOULD THEN ALLEGEDLY PROCEED TO THE BUS STATION FOR THE RIDE FROM HOUSTON TO LAREDO, TEXAS DEPARTING AT 2:35 AM ON THE 26TH.

INDEED ON SEPTEMBER 25TH, A MAN IDENTIFYING HIMSELF AS "HARVEY OSWALD" APPEARED AT THE SELECTIVE SERVICE OFFICE IN AUSTIN, TEXAS. HE TALKED TO MRS. LEE DANNELLY, ASSISTANT CHIEF OF THE ADMINISTRATION DIVISION, FOR OVER 30 MINUTES CONCERNING UPGRADING HIS MARINE DISCHARGE FROM "OTHER THAN HONORABLE CONDITIONS" TO HONORABLE.

*ARMSTRONG CONTENDS HOWEVER THAT THE VISITOR TO AUSTIN IS **LEE** NOT **HARVEY**. ONCE AGAIN ONE HAS TO QUESTION THE VALIDITY OF VARY/BAKER'S INFORMATION. IS SHE GETTING A "COMPOSITE" STORY FROM **HARVEY** OR PERHAPS **LEE** VIA **HARVEY**? IF THE STORY ORIGINATED FROM **LEE**, IT WOULD EXPLAIN HOW <u>HE</u> GOT FROM DALLAS TO AUSTIN.*

*ARMSTRONG CONTENDS THAT **LEE** THEN FLEW FROM AUSTIN TO HOUSTON ON CONTINENTAL FLIGHT 214. THE FLIGHT LEFT AUSTIN AT 10:00 PM AND ARRIVED IN HOUSTON AT 10:42 PM. HE ALSO NOTES THAT IT WAS **LEE** WHO PURCHASED TICKET #112230 ON CONTINENTAL TRAILWAYS BUS #5133 FOR PASSAGE FROM HOUSTON TO LAREDO, TEXAS. THE DEPARTURE TIME FOR THE BUS WAS 2:35 AM ON THE 26TH.*

DE LESSEPS MORRISON WAS THE DEMOCRATIC MAYOR OF NEW ORLEANS FROM 1946 TO 1961. PRIOR TO DESEGREGATION, HE BUILT POOLS, PLAYGROUNDS AND RECREATION CENTERS FOR USE BY AFRICAN-AMERICANS IN SEGREGATED NEW ORLEANS. IN 1950 HE HIRED NEW ORLEANS FIRST BLACK POLICEMAN. IN SPITE OF THESE ACTS, HE WAS STILL CONSIDERED A SEGREGATIONIST. IN A RUN FOR GOVENOR IN 1959, HE CONTINUED TO SUPPORT SEGREGATION. IN 1960, 6 YEARS AFTER BROWN V BOARD OF EDUCATION, INTEGRATION FINALLY CAME TO THE NEW ORLEANS PUBLIC SCHOOL SYSTEM. MORRISON DID NOT OVERTLY STOP INTEGRATION OF THE SCHOOLS, BUT DID LITTLE TO PROTECT THE BLACK CITIZENS WHOSE CHILDREN WERE ENROLLING IN TWO OF THE CITIES ALL-WHITE SCHOOLS. MORRISON ENDEARED HIMSELF TO NEITHER SIDE REGARDING THE INTEGRATION OF THE NEW ORLEAN'S SCHOOLS. IN 1956 HE LOST THE GOVENOR'S RACE TO EARL LOVE. IN 1960 HE MADE ANOTHER RUN AT THE GOVERNORSHIP BUT LOST TO JIMMIE DAVIS. IN 1961 HE RESIGNED AS MAYOR AND WAS APPOINTED AMBASSADOR TO THE ORGANIZATION OF AMERICAN STATES BY PRESIDENT KENNEDY. HE MADE ONE FINAL RUN AT GOVENOR IN 1963 LOSING TO JOHN MCKEITNER. HE DIED IN A CHARTERED 2-ENGINE PLANE CRASH ON MAY 22, 1964 IN CIUDAD VICTORIA, MEXICO.

*THE PILOT OF DELESSEPS PLANE WAS HUGH WARD. NOT ONLY WAS WARD A PILOT, BUT HE WAS ALSO A PRIVATE INVESTIGATOR WITH BANISTER AND ASSOCIATES IN NEW ORLEANS. VARY/BAKER'S NOTING THAT WARD HAD PILOTED **HARVEY** FROM NEW ORLEANS TO TEXAS IS BUTTRESSED BY THE FACT THAT WARD DID INDEED WORK FOR AND WITH BANISTER. THE WRECKAGE FROM DELESSEP'S PLANE CRASH WAS NOT FOUND UNTIL THE FOLLOWING DAY. WHEN THE RESCUE TEAM ARRIVED, THEY WERE MET BY A NEWS TEAM FROM WDSU IN NEW ORLEANS WHO HAD CHARTERED A PLANE TO TRY TO "RE-TRACE" MORRISON'S FATEFULL FLIGHT. THE CAMERA CREW FILMED THE RECOVERY OF THE BODIES.*

RESEARCHERS HAVE QUESTIONED THE SIGNIFICANCE OF THE CRASH IN REGARDS TO WHETHER IT WAS SIMPLY AN UNFORTUNATE ACCIDENT OR YET ANOTHER SUSPICIOUS DEATH; ONE THAT TOOK PLACE DURING THE W.C. PROCEEDINGS.

SEPTEMBER 25TH 1963
ACCORDING TO THE WARREN COMMISSION **HARVEY** LIKELY LEFT NEW ORLEANS BY TRAILWAYS BUS #5121 AT 12:30 PM. HE WOULD ARRIVE IN HOUSTON AT 10:50 PM THAT SAME DAY.

*BUT, THERE ARE NO KNOWN WITNESSES TO IDENTIFY **HARVEY** ON THIS NEW ORLEANS TO HOUSTON PORTION OF HIS TRIP. EVEN THE WARREN COMMISSION NOTED THAT THERE WAS NO <u>FIRM</u> EVIDENCE OF THE MEANS BY WHICH **HARVEY** TRAVELED FROM NEW ORLEANS TO HOUSTON. INDEED IF ONE FOLLOWS ARMSTRONG'S THEORY, THERE IS NO FIRM EVIDENCE THAT **HARVEY** VISITED HOUSTON OR EVEN AUSTIN. I AM INCLINED TO ACCEPT ARMSTRONG'S NOTION THAT **HARVEY** LEFT NEW ORLEANS BY CAR AND WAS DRIVEN TO DALLAS. **LEE** HOWEVER WAS FLOWN FROM DALLAS TO AUSTIN, THEN FLEW COMMERCIALLY FROM AUSTIN TO HOUSTON FOR HIS BUS DEPARTURE FROM HOUSTON TO MEXICO CITY.*

SEPTEMBER 25TH OR 26TH 1963
ON THIS EVENING ABOUT 9:00 PM, THERE WERE 3 VISITORS TO SYLVIA ODIO'S APARTMENT AT THE MAGELLAN CIRCLE COMPLEX IN DALLAS; TWO HISPANICS AND ONE WHITE. THE HISPANICS IDENTIFIED THEMSELVES AS LEOPOLDO AND ANGELO. THE AMERICAN WAS INTRODUCED AS "LEON OSWALD."

THE VISITORS WERE TRYING TO RAISE FUNDS FOR JUNTA REVOLUCIONAMA, (JURE) AN ANTI-CASTRO UNIT. THE VISITORS ALSO NOTED THAT THEY HAD JUST ***<u>DRIVEN TO DALLAS FROM NEW ORLEANS</u>***. THE NEXT DAY MRS. ODIO GETS A PHONE CALL FROM LEOPOLDO ASKING HER THOUGHTS ON THE AMERICAN. LEOPOLDO COMMENTS: HE'S AN "EX-MARINE", "KIND OF NUTS", AND AN "EXPERT MARKSMAN" ....SAYS "WE SHOULD HAVE SHOT JFK AFTER THE BAY OF PIGS." AFTER THE ASSASSINATION, ODIO IDENTIFIED "LEON" AS **HARVEY**.

REGARDLESS OF WHOSE VERSION WE CHOOSE, VARY/BAKER'S VERSION OF **HARVEY** BEING **FLOWN** TO AUSTIN, DALLAS, THEN HOUSTON, THE COMMISSION'S VERSION THAT HE LIKELY LEFT NEW ORLEANS ON **BUS** #5121 ENROUTE TO HOUSTON TO CATCH THE BUS TO MEXICO CITY, OR THE VERSION TENDERED BY THE VISITORS TO SYLVIA ODIO'S APARTMENT THAT THEY HAD **DRIVEN** FROM NEW ORLEANS, ALL VERSIONS SEEM TO SUPPORT THE NOTION THAT **HARVEY** DID INDEED LEAVE NEW ORLEANS IN THE EARLY AFTERNOON OF SEPTEMBER 25TH.

HARVEY'S PRESENCE AT THE ODIO RESIDENCE IS POSSIBLE. IN FACT, THE HSCA ALLOWED THAT THE VISIT TO ODIO COULD HAVE BEEN ON THE 26TH, NOT THE 25TH. IF, ACCORDING TO THE W.C. **HARVEY'S** BUS ARRIVED IN HOUSTON AT 10:50 PM ON THE 25TH, IT IS UNLIKELY THAT **HARVEY** COULD HAVE LEFT NEW ORLEANS EITHER LATE MORNING OR EARLY AFTERNOON OF THE 25TH AND ARRIVED IN DALLAS BY 9:00 PM AS DALLAS IS ABOUT A 4 HOUR DRIVE FROM HOUSTON. BY ALL INDICATIONS, **HARVEY** LEFT NEW ORLEANS ON THE 25TH AND APPEARED AT THE ODIO'S THE EVENING OF THE 26TH.

IT IS IMPORTANT TO NOTE THAT IT IS THE **PHONE CALL** THE NEXT DAY BY LEOPOLDO THAT IS INCRIMINATING, **NOT** THE VISIT ITSELF. THE WHITE MALE (**HARVEY**) ACCOMPANYING LEOPOLDO AND ANGELO SAID VIRTUALLY NOTHING DURING THE ACTUAL MEETING AT THE ODIO'S APARTMENT THE PREVIOUS DAY.

HARVEY IS QUITE LIKELY UNDER THE IMPRESSION THAT HE IS CARRYING OUT HIS INFORMANT'S ROLE IN INFILTRATING YET ANOTHER ANTI-CASTRO GROUP. ALTHOUGH THIS "MEETING" IS QUITE SIMILAR TO THE ONE BANISTER HAD ARRANGED FOR **HARVEY** WITH CARLOS BRINGUIER'S DRE GROUP IN NEW ORLEANS, THE NEXT-DAY COMMENTS MADE BY LEOPOLDO; "EX-MARINE", "EXPERT MARKSMAN", AND OBVIOUSLY THE COMMENT ABOUT SHOOTING JFK, ARE SIMPLY TOO TRANSPARENT IN THEIR EFFORT TO MAKE **HARVEY'S** VISIT WITH SYLVIA ODIO ONE SHE WOULD VIVIDLY RECALL ON NOVEMBER 22ND.

MORE IMPORTANTLY, THESE COMMENTS ARE OF SUCH THAT THEY COULD BE USED LATER TO DIRECTLY IMPLICATE **HARVEY** IN THE JFK SHOOTING THUS THE COMMENTS WERE HELD UNTIL THE NEXT DAYS PHONE CALL AND NOT VOICED IN **HARVEY'S** PRESENCE.

IT IS ALSO IMPORTANT TO NOTE THAT ONE OF THE HISPANICS COMMENTED TO ODIO THAT THEY HAD DRIVEN TO DALLAS FROM NEW ORLEANS. THIS MAY WELL BE EXACTLY THE METHOD BY WHICH **HARVEY** ARRIVED IN DALLAS. IN SPITE OF VARY/BAKER'S CLAIM, HE MAY NOT HAVE VISITED AUSTIN OR PROCEEDED TO HOUSTON FOR THE BUS TRIP TO MEXICO CITY.

THE WARREN COMMISSION HOWEVER SIMPLY DECIDED THAT IT WAS NOT **HARVEY** AT THE ODIO APARTMENT BUT WILLIAM SEYMOUR. THIS IS A TACTIC THE COMMISSION ADOPTED THROUGHOUT THEIR HEARINGS. THEY REPEATEDLY CLAIMED THAT WITNESSES OF **HARVEY** "SIGHTINGS" WERE MISTAKEN.

BUT, IF THIS IS NOT **HARVEY** AT THE ODIO RESIDENCE, IT WOULD HAVE BEEN UNNECESSARY FOR LEOPOLDO TO HOLD HIS INCRIMINATING REMARKS UNTIL THE PHONE CALL THE FOLLOWING DAY. HE COULD HAVE SIMPLY MADE THE COMMENTS WITH WILLIAM SEYMOUR PRESENT. BUT ONCE AGAIN, THE COMMISSION CONTINUES TO IGNORE THE OBVIOUS; WHY IS SOMEONE BEING INTRODUCED AS "LEON OSWALD" AND VIRTUALLY PORTRAYED AS A POTENTIAL JFK ASSASSIN 2 MONTHS PRIOR TO DALLAS? IF IT IS NOT **HARVEY** AS THE COMMISSION CLAIMS, SHOULD THEY NOT AT LEAST RECOGNISE THE IMPLICATIONS OF SOMEONE TRYING TO IMPERSONATE AND POINTEDLY INCRIMINATE HIM IN THE JFK SHOOTING? EVEN MORE IMPORTANT IS THE NOTION OF TWO ANTI-CASTRO/ANTI-COMMUNIST ACTIVISTS SOLICITING FUNDS FOR THEIR EFFORTS WHILE BEING ACCOMPANIED BY AN ALLEGED PRO-CASTRO COMMUNIST.

*THE COMMISSION HAD TO MAKE A CHOICE; EITHER DISMISS SIGHTINGS OF **HARVEY** AT PLACES OTHER THAN THOSE ACCEPTED BY <u>THEIR</u> FINDINGS, OR ACKNOWLEDGE THE FACT THAT <u>SOMEONE</u> WAS MAKING A CONCERTED EFFORT TO IMPERSONATE HIM AND DIRECTLY IMPLICATE HIM IN THE SHOOTING OF THE PRESIDENT. IF SOMEONE IS INDEED MAKING AN ONGOING EFFORT TO INCRIMINATE **HARVEY** THROUGH THE USE OF IMPOSTORS, THEN YOU HAVE THE MAKINGS OF A CONSPIRATORIAL SET-UP.*

*HOOVER HIMSELF WAS CONCERNED REGARDING THE NON-HISPANIC VISITOR TO ODIO'S APARTMENT. HE PROMPTED THE FBI FIELD OFFICE IN DALLAS TO "DISAPPROVE HER ALLEGATION" BY VIRTUE OF "MENTAL ILLNESS." THE FBI ATTEMPTED TO SUPPORT THE COMMISSION CONCLUSION BY ISSUING A REPORT IDENTIFYING THE THREE VISITORS TO THE ODIO RESIDENCE. LATER HOWEVER, TWO OF THE MEN THE FBI CLAIMED TO BE ODIO'S VISITORS, WILLIAM SEYMOUR AND LAWRENCE HOWARD, WERE ABLE TO PROVE THAT THEY WERE <u>NOT</u> IN DALLAS AT THE TIME, AND THE THIRD MAN, LORAN HALL, STATED THAT HE HAD BEEN FORCED BY THE FBI TO GIVE A STATEMENT IN SUPPORT OF THEIR CONCLUSION. LATER, THE HSCA CONCLUDED THAT IT WAS INDEED **HARVEY** AT THE ODIO RESIDENCE.*

THE <u>NEXT-DAY</u> COMMENTS MADE BY LEOPOLDO ARE SO POINTEDLY DAMNING TO HARVEY IN REGARDS TO THE EVENTS OF NOVEMBER 22ND THAT I WILL AT THIS POINT CONCLUDE AND AGREE WITH THE HSCA THAT THE VISITOR TO SYLVIA ODIO'S RESIDENCE IS INDEED HARVEY. "LEOPOLDO" AND "ANGELO" WOULD HAVE TO BE CONSIDERED AS PERIPHERAL MEMBERS OF HUNT/PHILLIPS GROUP.

W.C. LAWYER WESLEY LIEBLER WOULD LATER NOTE: "THERE ARE PROBLEMS. ODIO MAY WELL BE RIGHT. THE COMMISSION WILL LOOK BAD IF IT TURNS OUT THAT SHE IS."

SOME RESEARCHERS BELIEVE THAT THE MAN IDENTIFYING HIMSELF AS "ANGELO" WAS ACTUALLY A FORMER MARINE NAMED EDWIN COLLINS. COLLINS HAS BEEN TIED TO BOTH THE KKK AND THE JOHN BIRCH SOCIETY IN THEIR EFFORTS TO THWART THE CIVIL RIGHTS EFFORTS IN THE SOUTH.

SEPTEMBER 26TH 1963
THE DALLAS MORNING NEWS ONCE AGAIN NOTES JFK'S NOVEMBER VISIT TO TEXAS.

SEPTEMBER 26TH 1963
LEE, ACCORDING TO ARMSTRONG, LEAVES HOUSTON ON TRAILWAYS BUS # 5133 ENROUTE TO MEXICO CITY AT 2:35 AM. HE CROSSES THE BORDER AT NUEVO LAREDO ON MEXICAN TOURIST CARD FM-8 NO.24085 AT ABOUT 1:45 PM. **LEE** WOULD NOW DEPART NUEVO LAREDO ON MEXICAN RED ARROW BUS # 516 ABOUT 2:15 PM. HEZIO MAYDON, THE BORDER INSPECTOR AT NUEVO LAREDO, DID NOT NOTE EITHER **LEE'S** TIME OF ENTRY INTO MEXICO **OR** HIS MODE OF TRANSPORTATION **INTO** MEXICO.

ON DECEMBER 2ND, 1963, THE MEXICAN CUSTOMS COMPILED A LIST OF ALL ENTRIES AND DEPARTURES ON OR ABOUT THE 26TH OF SEPTEMBER. LEE WAS NOT ON THE LIST. ON DECEMBER 5TH, HOOVER RECEIVES A REPORT FROM THE FBI'S SAN ANTONIO OFFICE STATING "INVESTIGATION TO DATE HAS FAILED TO ESTABLISH SUBJECT RETURNED TO U.S. ON OCTOBER 3RD LAST OR ENTERED MEXICO ON SEPTEMBER 26TH LAST."

ALBERT OSBORNE, AKA JOHN HOWARD BOWEN, AKA J. H. OWEN, IN HIS WARREN COMMISSION TESTIMONY WOULD DESCRIBE "OSWALD" AS "THIN AND BLONDE." OSBORNE TESTIFIED THAT HE SAT BESIDE "OSWALD" ON THE BUS TRIP TO MEXICO CITY. FELLOW PASSENGERS ON THE BUS NOTED THAT INDEED "OSWALD" SAT WITH A MAN WITH AN ENGLISH ACCENT. OSBORNE WAS BORN IN GRIMSEY, ENGLAND. ON THE BAGGAGE MAINIFEST, OSBORNE'S NAME WAS LISTED AS "JOHN BOWEN." THE FBI WOULD LATER INTERVIEW AN ALBERT OSBORNE WHO CLAIMED TO BE AN "ACQUAINTANCE" OF BOWEN. SEVERAL INTERVIEWS LATER, OSBORNE ADMITTED TO THE FBI THAT HE USED THE ALIAS "JOHN HOWARD BOWEN." OSBORNE STATED THAT HE WAS A "MISSIONARY." HE SEEMED TO TRAVEL AT WILL WITH NO APPARENT SOURCE OF INCOME TO FINANCE HIS

WANDERLUST. IT IS INTERESTING TO RECALL THAT THE NAME "OSBORNE" WAS USED IN REGARDS TO ORDERING FPFC LITERATURE IN NEW ORLEANS IN MAY AND JUNE OF 1963.

PASSENGERS ON THE BUS ALSO NOTED THAT "OSWALD" WAS QUITE SOCIAL ON THE TRIP. HE APPARENTLY INTRODUCED HIMSELF TO TWO AUSTRALIAN TOURISTS, PAMELA MUMFORD AND PATRICIA WINSTON, WHO BOARDED THE BUS ABOUT 7:30 PM IN MONTERREY, AND ENTERTAINED THEM WITH STORIES ABOUT RUSSIA AND THE MARINE CORP. A BRITISH COUPLE, DR. JOHN AND ANNA MCFARLAND, WOULD BE TOLD BY "OSWALD" THAT HE WAS THE SECRETARY OF THE FPFC IN NEW ORLEANS AND THAT HIS GOAL WAS TO TRAVEL TO HAVANA AND TO MEET CASTRO. THE SECRETIVE AND LESS THAN OUTGOING **HARVEY** WOULD HAVE BEEN UNLIKELY TO BEHAVE IN THIS MANNER. MUMFORD NOTED IN HER WARREN COMMISSION TESTIMONY THAT "OSWALD" NEVER MENTIONED HIS NAME ONCE."

INTERESTINGLY, THE HSCA QUOTES J. WESLEY LIEBLER, A WARREN COMMISSION ASSISTANT COUNSEL, AS NOTING: "THERE REALLY IS NO EVIDENCE THAT OSWALD (**HARVEY**) LEFT HOUSTON ON THAT BUS." LIEBLER IS CORRECT. IT WAS **LEE** WHO BOADED THE BUS IN HOUSTON AND PROCEED TO MEXICO CITY.

SCENARIO I IS BASED ON THE PREMISE THAT BOTH THE CARCINOGEN PROJECT AND THE ASSIGNMENT INVOLVING **HARVEY**, VARY/BAKER, BANISTER, FERRIE AND RUBY IS LEGITIMATE. HUNT AND PHILLIPS INVOLVEMENT IN THE PROJECT IS ALSO LEGITIMATE. MEDICAL RESEARCH AND GUIDANCE REGARDING THE CARCINOGENS IS PROVIDED BY DR. ALTON OCHSNER AND DR. MARY SHERMAN. **HARVEY'S** NOVEMBER 22ND DEPARTURE FOR CUBA VIA MEXICO IS IN CONJUNCTION WITH THE C-DAY COUP SCHEDULED FOR THE FIRST DAY OF DECEMBER, 1963.

WE WILL NOW EXAMINE WHAT I CONSIDER A SECOND, CONSIDERABLY MORE PLAUSIBLE SCENARIO INVOLVING BOTH **LEE** AND **HARVEY**, JUDYTH VARY/BAKER, DR. MARY SHERMAN, DR ALTON OCHSNER, GUY BANISTER, DAVID FERRIE, JACK RUBY, ROSCOE WHITE, DAVID ATLEE PHILLIPS, HOWARD HUNT, THE VISIT TO JACKSON, THE CIA AS **HARVEY** PERCEIVES IT, AND THE ATTEMPT TO USE CARCINOGENS TO ELIMINATE CASTRO.

SCENARIO II

IN THIS SCENARIO, THE PREVIOUSLY INTRODUCED CAST OF CHARACTERS REMAINS THE SAME. THEIR ROLES HOWEVER, IN SOME INSTANCES, CHANGE DRAMATICALLY. **HARVEY** WILL NO LONGER BE DEPARTING DALLAS ON NOVEMBER 22ND AS A PART OF THE AMWORLD/"C-DAY"COUP BUT WILL BE MANIPULATED IN SUCH A FASHION THAT HE NOW APPEARS TO BE THE FLEEING ASSASSIN RESPONSIBLE FOR THE DEATH OF THE PRESIDENT. THE SET-UP CONSPIRATORS GROUP, OF WHICH E. HOWARD HUNT AND DAVID ATLEE PHILLIPS ARE THE "PUPPETMASTERS", CHANCE COMPROMISING A LEGITIMATE CIA CARCINOGENS PROJECT IN ORDER TO SET-UP **HARVEY**. THE ALLEGED "ASSIGNMENT" INVOLVING **HARVEY** AS A COURIER FOR THE CARCINOGENS WITH ASSISTANCE FROM FERRIE AND RUBY TO DELIVER THOSE CARCINOGENS IS FRAUDULENT. HUNT AND PHILLIPS ENLIST THE HELP OF DR. ALTON OCHSNER WHO IN TURN INVOLVES THE UNWITTING DR. MARY SHERMAN AND JUDYTH VARY/BAKER IN ORDER TO ISOLATE THIS SET-UP "PROJECT" FROM THE LEGITIMATE EFFORTS AT THE CLINIC TO PRODUCE CARCINOGENS IN A COLD WAR EFFORT TO ELIMINATE CASTRO. ROSCOE WHITE AND **LEE** IN DALLAS/NEW ORLEANS ASSIST HUNT/PHILLIPS IN THE SET-UP EFFORTS. GUY BANISTER IN NEW ORLEANS ALSO ASSISTS IN THE SET-UP OF **HARVEY** ALTHOUGH I AM NOT CERTAIN THAT HE WAS PRIVY TO THE EVENTUAL OUTCOME OF HIS EFFORTS. RUBY AND FERRIE HOWEVER ARE NOT SET-UP CONSPIRATORS BUT ARE BEING USED TO FACILITATE THE SET-UP OF **HARVEY**. **HARVEY** IS CONVINCED THAT HIS DEPARTURE FROM DALLAS ON NOVEMBER 22ND IS IN CONJUNCTION WITH OPERATION AMWORLD, AKA THE C-DAY COUP. THE COUNTDOWN

FOR THE DECEMBER 1ST INVASION WAS TO START ON NOVEMBER 22ND. **HARVEY** WOULD HAVE LITTLE REASON TO QUESTION HIS DEPARTURE FROM DALLAS ENROUTE TO CUBA ON THE VERY DAY THE PRESIDENT VISITS DALLAS. I CONSIDER THIS SCENARIO CONSIDERABLY MORE PLAUSIBLE THAN **SCENARIO I**. IT IS BASED ON THREE HIGHLY LIKELY PREMISES:

THE PREMISE AND THE LIKELIHOOD THAT THE CIA'S MEDICAL SERVICES OFFICE, AN OFFSHOOT OF THE CIA'S OPERATIONS DIVISION, WAS INDEED RESEARCHING THE POSSIBILITY OF DEVELOPING A CARCINOGEN THAT COULD BE USED TO BRING AN UNTIMELY DEATH TO CASTRO IN SUCH A FASHION THAT IT WOULD BE UNTRACEABLE TO THE INTELLIGENCE COMMUNITY OF THE U.S.

THE PREMISE THAT THERE WAS INDEED A CONSPIRACY UNDERWAY TO ASSASSINATE PRESIDENT KENNEDY AND THAT THE AUTHORS OF THIS CONSPIRACY HAD NOT ONLY DESIGNED A PLAN THAT WOULD DRAW LITTLE ATTENTION TO THEMSELVES, BUT HAD NOW ALSO FOUND A "PERFECT PATSY" WHOSE "DEFECTOR", "PRO-CASTRO", AND "PRO-COMMUNISM" INTELLIGENCE FACADES WOULD GIVE AMPLE REASON FOR THE U.S. GOVERNMENT TO FINALLY EMBARK ON WHAT HAD BEEN DESIRED FOR SEVERAL YEARS; A SUCCESSFUL INVASION OF CUBA CULMINATING IN THE OVERTHROW OR DEATH OF CASTRO IF THE C-DAY COUP FAILED.

AND, THE **MOST CRITICAL PREMISE,** THAT ALTHOUGH THE CARCINOGEN PROJECT WAS A LEGITIMATE AND ONGOING CIA PROJECT, NEITHER DAVID FERRIE, JUDYTH VARY/BAKER, JACK RUBY OR **HARVEY** WERE INVOLVED. THEY WERE SIMPLY LED TO BELIEVE BY IDENTIFIABLE SET-UP CONSPIRATORS ROSCOE WHITE AND **LEE** IN DALLAS AND NEW ORLEANS, E.H. HUNT AND DAVID ATLEE PHILLIPS IN MEXICO CITY AND DALLAS, DR. ALTON OCHSNER IN NEW ORLEANS AND OTHER LESS INFORMED ASSISTANTS SUCH AS GUY BANISTER, THAT THEIR INVOLVEMENT WAS LEGITIMATE WHEN IN FACT THEIR INCLUSION WAS FOR THE SOLE PURPOSE OF GIVING THE IMPRESSION THAT ON THE AFTERNOON OF NOVEMBER 22ND, **HARVEY** WOULD APPEAR TO BE ATTEMPTING TO FLEE THE COUNTRY ENROUTE TO CUBA AS AN ALLEGED PRESIDENTIAL ASSASSIN NOT AS A COURIER ON WHAT **HARVEY** PERCEIVED AS A LEGITIMATE CIA ASSIGNMENT IN CONJUNCTION WITH THE DECEMBER C-DAY COUP.

IF WE RE-VISIT JUDYTH VARY/BAKER'S STORY IN **SCENARIO I** FOR A MOMENT WE WILL FIND NUMEROUS TIP-OFFS THAT INDICATE THAT WHAT SHE, FERRIE, RUBY AND **HARVEY** WERE INVOLVED IN COULD **NOT** HAVE BEEN PART OF A LEGITIMATE CIA RESEARCH PROJECT.

VARY/BAKER HERSELF NOTED THAT SHE WAS INITIALLY SKEPTICAL OF THE "PROJECT" AS EXPLAINED TO HER BY **HARVEY** AND FERRIE. HOWEVER IT IS GUY BANISTER WHO "CONFIRMS" FOR HER THAT THE "PROJECT" AND THEIR INVOLVEMENT IS INDEED "REAL."

IF WHAT VARY/BAKER, FERRIE, AND **HARVEY** WERE INVOLVED IN WERE INDEED PART OF A LEGITIMATE CASTRO ELIMINATION PROJECT, WOULD IT NOT HAVE BEEN CONDUCTED IN DR.OCHSNER'S OR EVEN DR.MARY SHERMAN'S LAB RATHER THAN IN FERRIE'S KITCHEN LAB?

IF THEIR INVOLVEMENT HAD BEEN LEGITIMATE, WOULD VARY/BAKER HAVE DELIVERED HER REPORTS AND HER TUMOR SAMPLES FROM THE MICE IN FERRIE'S LAB TO DR. SHERMAN'S APARTMENT OR THE "DROP" SPOT RATHER THAN TO THE OCHSNER CLINIC?

ONE WOULD HAVE TO CONCLUDE THAT DR. OCHSNER WAS AT LEAST OBLIQUELY INVOLVED IN THE SET-UP AS WELL AND INVOLVED THE UNWITTING DR. SHERMAN ONLY TO ISOLATE HIMSELF, THE CLINIC, AND LEGITIMATE CARCINOGEN RESEARCH FOR THE CIA FROM WHAT WAS OBVIOUSLY A FRAUDULANT EFFORT TO SET-UP

HARVEY. IT IS IMPERATIVE THAT VARY/BAKER, FERRIE, RUBY AND MOST IMPORTANTLY **HARVEY** CONSIDER THEIR TASK TO BE "LEGITIMATE." BUT, IT IS INFINITELY MORE IMPORTANT TO MAINTAIN THE INTEGRITY AND THE SECRECY SURROUNDING WHAT WAS LIKELY AN ACTUAL CIA-FUNDED PROJECT.

OCHSNER'S COMMENT TO VARY/BAKER AFTER SHE PUT IN WRITING HER CONCERNS ABOUT THE ETHICS OF TESTING THE CARCINOGENS ON PRISONERS IS REVEALING. ACCORDING TO VARY/BAKER, DR. OCHSNER NOTED TO FERRIE THAT BOTH SHE AND **HARVEY** WERE EXPENDABLE. I SUSPECT THAT THIS STEMMED FROM DR. OCHSNER'S DESIRE TO PROTECT THE SECRECY OF HIS LEGITIMATE CARCINOGEN PROJECT; A PROJECT THAT HE KNEW WOULD NEVER INVOLVE THE LIKES OF A CAST OF CHARACTERS COMPOSED OF **HARVEY**, JACK RUBY, AND THE UNFORGETABLE DAVID FERRIE.

DR. MARY SHERMAN MUST ALSO BE CONSIDERED. I FEEL FAIRLY CERTAIN SHE WAS USED BY DR. OCHSNER TO ISOLATE HIM FROM THE EVENTS TRANSPIRING IN DAVID FERRIE'S KITCHEN. SHE WOULD DIE IN A SUSPICIOUS FIRE IN JULY 1964.

VICTORIA HAWES RESIDED AT THE PATIOS APARTMENTS IN NEW ORLEANS. SHE NOTED THAT DR. SHERMAN WAS ALSO A RESIDENT. HAWES STATED THAT **HARVEY** WAS INDEED FRIENDLY TO AND ON SPEAKING TERMS WITH DR. SHERMAN. WHEN DR. SHERMAN'S BODY WAS DISCOVERED IN HER APARTMENT ON JULY 21ST, 1964, THE RIGHT SIDE OF HER BODY, HER RIGHT RIBS, AND RIGHT ARM HAD BEEN BURNED AWAY. IT IS QUITE LIKELY THAT INJURIES OF THIS NATURE WERE CAUSED BY SOMETHING MORE CATASTROPHIC THAN A MERE APARTMENT FIRE. RESEARCHERS HAVE SPECULATED THAT IN ALL LIKELIHOOD THERE HAD BEEN AN ACCIDENT INVOLVING THE LINEAR ACCELERATOR AT THE U.S. PUBLIC HEALTH SERVICE HOSPITAL WHERE SHE DID HER RESEARCH. HER RESEARCH OF COURSE WAS IN CONJUNCTION WITH DR. OSCHNER'S HIGHLY CLASSIFIED EFFORTS TO PRODUCE CARCINOGENS FOR THE CIA. TO MAINTAIN THE CLOAK OF SECRECY SURROUNDING "THE LAB", AS IT WAS KNOWN, HER BODY WAS MOVED TO HER APARTMENT WHERE SHE WAS LATER DISCOVERED AS A "VICTIM" OF AN APPARENT MURDER/ARSON FIRE.

THE POLICE REPORT OF HER DEATH CONTAINED NO MENTION OF THE CLINIC OR DR. OCHSNER. LIFE MAGAZINE DISCOVERED THAT DR. SHERMAN HAD DONATED MONEY TO DAVID FERRIE'S NEARBY ANTI-CASTRO TRAINING CAMP AND THAT SHE HAD ALSO TREATED SOME OF THOSE ATTENDING THE CAMP. JIM GARRISON, IN HIS INVESTIGATION, NOTED THAT DR. SHERMAN MAY HAVE BEEN ELIMINATED BECAUSE OF HER CONNECTION TO DAVID FERRIE. I AM MUCH MORE INCLINED TO BELIEVE THAT SHE WAS KILLED, IN WHAT WOULD APPEAR TO BE AN APARTMENT FIRE DUE TO HER FAMILIARITY WITH **HARVEY** AND HER MOST LIKELY FAMILIARITY WITH **LEE** IF SHE HAD INDEED TREATED TRAINEES AT FERRIE'S ANTI-CASTRO TRAINING FACILITY.

IT IS IMPORTANT TO COMMENT HERE THAT JUDYTH VARY/BAKER'S OBSERVATIONS WERE NOT INCORRECT. SHE WAS SIMPLY RELATING HER STORY UNDER THE SAME CLOUDED PERCEPTION THAT ENGULFED FERRIE, RUBY, AND MOST IMPORTANTLY, **HARVEY**. THEY ALL SHARED THE MISCONCEPTION DESIRED BY THE SET-UP CONSPIRATORS THAT THE CARCINOGENS PROJECT WAS NOT ONLY LEGITIMATE (WHICH IT LIKELY WAS), BUT MORE IMPORTANTLY THAT THEY WERE ALL ACTUALLY INVOLVED IN THE PROJECT AND THE DELIVERY OF CARCINOGENS TO CUBA WHEN THEY MOST CERTAINLY WERE NOT.

IN **SCENARIO II** HOWEVER, THE TRAVEL ARRANGEMENTS FOR **HARVEY'S** "ASSIGNMENT" WILL BE MODIFIED SOMEWHAT AFTER THE MEXICO CITY INCIDENT IN LATE SEPTEMBER.

HARVEY WOULD BE INFORMED, QUITE LIKELY BY HUNT OR PHILLIPS THAT HE WOULD BE MAKING HIS JOURNEY TO HAVANA WITH ASSISTANCE FROM CIA CONTRACT PILOT

AND ACQUAINTANCE DAVID FERRIE. **HARVEY** WOULD HAVE LITTLE REASON TO QUESTION THE CHOICE OF PILOT DAVID FERRIE AS HIS MEANS OF ARRIVING IN CUBA

SINCE **HARVEY** DIDN'T DRIVE, OR AT LEAST DID NOT POSSESS A VALID DRIVERS LICENSE NOR OWN A VEHICLE, THE FIRST LEG OF HIS UPCOMING JOURNEY TO HAVANA WOULD BE ARRANGED BY RUBY. ALTHOUGH THERE ARE SOME WHO WILL QUESTION WHETHER **HARVEY** HAD EVER <u>PHYSICALLY</u> MET JACK RUBY, HE WOULD CERTAINLY BE FAMILIAR WITH THE <u>NAME</u> RUBY AS IT WAS RUBY WHO ORCHESTRATED THE INITIAL LEG OF THE DALLAS TO NEW ORLEANS TO MIAMI TO CUBA GUN-RUNNING OPERATION IN SUPPORT OF ANTI-CASTRO REBELS STILL REMAINING IN CUBA. **HARVEY'S** TIME IN NEW ORLEANS INFILTRATING/WORKING WITH THE BANISTER GROUP FOR BOTH THE CIA AND THE FBI WOULD HAVE MADE IT VIRTUALLY IMPOSSIBLE FOR HIM NOT TO MAKE THE CONNECTION BETWEEN RUBY AND THE CACHES OF GUNS ARRIVING AT THE NEW ORLEANS CAMP STREET OFFICE OF GUY BANISTER. ONCE AGAIN, **HARVEY** WOULD HAVE LITTLE REASON TO QUESTION THE CHOICE OF RUBY AS THE PROVIDER OF TRANSPORTATION THAT WOULD EVENTUALLY TAKE HIM TO RED BIRD AIRPORT FOR WHAT HE PERCEIVED AS THE FIRST LEG OF HIS "ASSIGNMENT." FROM THERE A SMALL PLANE WOULD TAKE HIM TO HOUSTON OR PERHAPS GALVESTON THAT EVENING FOR HIS PICKUP BY DAVID FERRIE. THEY WOULD THEN DEPART FOR THE YUCATAN PENINSULA AND THEN ON TO CUBA TO DELIVER THE CARCINOGENS TO CIA OPERATIVES. THIS OF COURSE IS HOW THE "ASSIGNMENT" WAS PERCEIVED BY RUBY, FERRIE, AND **HARVEY**.

AS WE WILL SEE LATER IN MUCH MORE DETAIL ON THE AFTERNOON OF NOVEMBER 22ND, THIS SCENARIO WILL TAKE A DRAMATIC TURN FROM WHAT IS EXPECTED BY FERRIE, RUBY, AND **HARVEY**. THIS TURN WILL BE ORCHESTRATED BY SET-UP CONSPIRATORS ROSCOE WHITE AND **LEE**.

ROSCOE WHITE AND **LEE** WILL ARRANGE THE INTERCEPTION OF **HARVEY** IN DALLAS ON THE AFTERNOON OF THE ASSASSINATION. **HARVEY** WILL BE TAKEN TO THE TEXAS THEATER RATHER THAN DIRECTLY TO RED BIRD AIPROT. HE WILL BE DRIVEN NOT BY TIPPIT, BUT BY THE UNIDENTIFIED OFFICERS IN CAR #107. WHILE **HARVEY** PATIENTLY WAITS IN THE THEATER FOR HIS "CONTACT" WHO WILL PROVIDE THE RIDE TO REDBIRD AIRFIELD AND THE FLIGHT TO EITHER HOUSTON OR GALVESTON, THE SET-UP CONSPIRATORS MAKE THE FINAL PREPARATIONS THAT WILL SEAL THE UNSUSPECTING **HARVEY'S** FATE. THE ALLEGED ASSASSINATION RIFLE, "TRACEABLE" TO **HARVEY** IS FOUND IN THE BOOK DEPOSITORY, J.D. TIPPIT IS SLAIN RAISING THE SUSPICION THAT THE SHOOTER OF THE PRESIDENT WAS ALSO THE SHOOTER OF THE OFFICER, AND A BARRAGE OF DALLAS OFFICERS WILL CHASE A "DECOY" (**LEE**) INTO THE TEXAS THEATER WHERE **HARVEY** CALMLY WAITS, COMPLETELY UNAWARE THAT HE IS THE FOCUS OF ATTENTION FOR THE ENTIRE DALLAS POLICE AND SHERIFF'S OFFICE.

IF THE SET-UP CONSPIRATORS PLAN GOES AS EXPECTED, **HARVEY** WILL BE SILENCED IN THE TEXAS THEATER. AS WE WILL SEE IN LATER CHAPTERS, IF SOMETHING HAD GONE AWRY AND **HARVEY** HAD ACTUALLY MADE IT TO REDBIRD AIRFIELD FOR HIS LATER CONNECTION WITH DAVID FERRIE, NEITHER WOULD HAVE BEEN AWARE OF THE CIRCUMSTANTIAL EVIDENCE RAPIDLY ACCUMULATING THAT WOULD PAINT HIM AS THE PRESIDENTIAL ASSASSIN. THE UNWITTING DAVID FERRIE, THINKING HE WAS PICKING UP CIA OPERATIVE **HARVEY** FOR A LEGITIMATE CIA ASSIGNMENT, WOULD NOW BE PICKING UP **HARVEY** ALLEGED PRESIDENTIAL ASSASSIN. NEITHER FERRIE NOR **HARVEY** WOULD BE AWARE THAT THEY HAD BEEN DECEIVED. WE WILL GO INTO MUCH MORE DETAIL ON HOW **SCENARIO II** PLAYS OUT ON THE DAY OF THE ASSASSINATION AS THE TIMELINE UNFOLDS.

WITH A SET-UP OF THIS COMPLEXITY, IT WOULD BE A REASONABLE ASSUMPTION THAT OTHERS WERE INVOLVED. SOME WERE INVOLVED WITTINGLY, OTHERS UNWITTINGLY SUCH AS DR. MARY SHERMAN AND JUDYTH VARY/BAKER.

THERE WOULD BE "EXTRAS" WHO WOULD HAVE SMALLER, LESS CRITICAL ROLES IN THE SET-UP CONSPIRACY. THEIR INVOLVEMENT WOULD LIKELY BE SO SMALL AND SO SEEMINGLY INCONSEQUENTIAL THAT IT IS UNLIKELY THAT THEY WOULD BE ABLE TO DISTINGUISH WHETHER THEY WERE INVOLVED IN ASSISTING **HARVEY** ON WHAT HE PERCEIVED AS A LEGITIMATE CIA ASSIGNMENT, BEING USED TO FACILITATE THE SET-UP PLOT IN THE SAME MANNER AS FERRIE, RUBY, BANISTER, DR. SHERMAN, AND VARY/BAKER, OR SIMPLY GIVING A DOWN-ON-HIS-LUCK EX-MARINE A HELPING HAND.

ARMSTRONG'S BOOK WARRANTS A CLOSER LOOK AT SEVERAL OF THE PARTICIPANTS IN **BOTH** SCENARIOS. DAVID FERRIE MOST ASSUREDLY KNEW **LEE** FROM THE TRAINING CAMPS AND **HARVEY** FROM VISITS TO BANISTER'S OFFICE IN NEW ORLEANS. RUBY APPARENTLY KNEW **LEE** FROM BOTH DALLAS AND NEW ORLEANS, AND LIKELY KNEW **HARVEY** FROM NEW ORLEANS PRIOR TO THEIR FATAL MEETING ON NOVEMBER 22ND. GUY BANISTER KNEW BOTH **LEE** AND **HARVEY** IN NEW ORLEANS AS DID CLAY SHAW. I AM HOWEVER RELUCTANT TO STATE THAT THESE PARTICIPANTS IN WHAT WOULD BE THE EVENTUAL SET-UP OF **HARVEY** WERE AWARE THAT THE RESULT OF THEIR INVOLVEMENT WOULD BE THE ANNOINTING OF **HARVEY** AS THE PRESIDENTIAL ASSASSIN. BUT, THE POINT TO BE MADE IS THAT EACH OF THESE INDIVIDUALS KNEW THAT **HARVEY** AND **LEE** WERE TWO DISTINCT INDIVIDUALS.

WE SHOULD ALSO TAKE A MORE SKEPTICAL LOOK AT THE PAINE'S. IT IS A CERTAINTY THAT RUTH PAINE KNEW BOTH **LEE** AND **HARVEY**, AND ONE WOULD CONCLUDE THAT HER ESTRANGED HUSBAND MICHAEL KNEW BOTH MEN AS WELL.

THIS IS AN OPPORTUNE TIME TO EXAMINE HARVEY'S "FAMILY"AND THEIR INVOLVEMENT.

ROBERT OSWALD

ROBERT WAS **LEE'S** BROTHER. HE WAS NOT **HARVEY'S** BROTHER. HE OBVIOUSLY KNEW BOTH MEN AND APPARENTLY HAD AGREED TO PARTICIPATE WITH THE CIA IN THEIR EFFORT TO HAVE **HARVEY** "BECOME" **LEE** FOR A FUTURE INTELLIGENCE OPERATION, THE "DEFECTION" TO RUSSIA. IN THE AFTERMATH OF THE ASSASSINATION, HE REMAINED SILENT REGARDING HIS ASSISTANCE TO THE CIA IN THAT REGARD. HE WOULD LIKELY BE FORCED TO CONCLUDE THAT HIS INVOLVEMENT HAD LITTLE OR MORE LIKELY NOTHING TO DO WITH THE ASSASSINATION, BUT SIMPLY AN UNFORTUNATE COINCIDENCE AS A RESULT OF HIS EARLIER COOPERATION WITH THE CIA. HIS INVOLVEMENT MAY HAVE BEEN PERIPHERAL TO THE EVENTS OF NOVEMBER 22ND, BUT HIS RESULTANT SILENCE REGARDING HIS "RELATIONSHIP" TO **HARVEY** HELPED PROLONG THE CONFUSION REGARDING LEE **HARVEY** OSWALD.

JOHN PIC

JOHN WAS **LEE'S** HALF-BROTHER. HE WAS NOT **HARVEY'S** HALF-BROTHER. HE ALSO OBVIOUSLY KNEW BOTH MEN. BUT, UNLIKE HIS HALF-BROTHER ROBERT, HE WAS NOT WILLING TO BE TAKEN IN BY THE MELDING OF **HARVEY** INTO **LEE**. HE REMAINED SKEPTICAL IN HIS LATER INTRODUCTION TO **HARVEY** THAT THIS WAS INDEED HIS HALF-BROTHER, **LEE**. IT WOULD BE LEFT TO ROBERT TO CONVINCE JOHN THAT **HARVEY** WAS INDEED HIS HALF-BROTHER **LEE** OR CONVINCE HIM TO CONTINUE THE CHARADE DESPITE THE EVENTS OF NOVEMBER 22ND.

DUTZ AND LILLIAN MURRETT

THEY WERE THE UNCLE AND AUNT OF **LEE** NOT **HARVEY**. THEY APPARENTLY KNEW BOTH MEN AND HAD AGREED TO PARTICIPATE IN THE TRANSFORMATION OF **HARVEY** TO **LEE**. LIKE ROBERT, THEY MAINTAINED THE CLOAK OF SECRECY AFTER THE ASSASSINATION.

MARILYN MURRETT

MARILYN WAS THE COUSIN OF **LEE** NOT **HARVEY**. SHE WAS THE DAUGHTER OF DUTZ AND LILLIAN MURRETT. HER INTELLIGENCE TIES AND HER KNOWLEDGE THAT

HARVEY WAS SOON TO BECOME **LEE** LEADS ONE TO PONDER WHETHER SHE MAY HAVE BEEN THE ORIGINAL SOURCE FOR **HARVEY'S** NEW "FAMILY."

"MARGUERITE" OSWALD

IF THERE WERE A MYSTERY LADY IN THE ENTIRE EVENT IT WOULD BE "MARGUERITE." SHE WAS NOT ONLY **NOT** THE MOTHER OF **HARVEY**, BUT ALSO **NOT** THE MOTHER OF **LEE** EITHER. IN HER ROLE SHE WOULD UNDOUBTEDLY KNOW BOTH **HARVEY** AND **LEE**. BUT, LIKE HER "FAMILY" MEMBERS, "SON'S" ROBERT AND JOHN, SHE MAINTAINED HER SILENCE AFTER THE ASSASSINATION INSISTING THAT **HARVEY** WAS HER SON. CURIOUSLY THOUGH SHE ALSO PUBLICLY INSISTED THAT HER "SON" **HARVEY** WAS AN INTELLIGENCE AGENT. HER RECRUITMENT BY THE CIA IN THEIR EFFORT TO MERGE **HARVEY** INTO **LEE** BAFFLES ME AS SHE APPEARS TO BE A RISK IN REGARDS TO HER MENTAL STABILITY. OR PERHAPS THE POST ASSASSINATION "DAFFINESS" EXHIBITED BY "MARGUERITE" WAS JUST AN ACT. IT SO, IT WAS WELL PLAYED.

MARGUERITE OSWALD

BY VIRTUE OF HER DISAPPEARANCE IN THE AFTERMATH OF THE ASSASSINATION, ONE WOULD HAVE TO CONCLUDE THAT SHE WAS KEENLY AWARE THAT **HARVEY** WAS NOT HER SON AND THAT "MARGUERITE" WAS AN IMPOSTOR. HER WILLINGNESS TO REMAIN VIRTUALLY UNDISCOVERED AS THE REAL MARGUERITE OSWALD, MOTHER OF **LEE**, LENDS CREEDENCE TO THE NOTION THAT SHE WAS AWARE THAT BOTH SHE AND HER SON **LEE** WERE BEING IMPERSONATED AND THAT SHE TOO WAS PERIPHERALY INVOLVED IN AN INTELLIGENCE OPERATION THAT HAD GONE AWRY. I CANNOT RESIST THE IMPULSE TO IMPLY THAT MARGUERITE MAY HAVE BEEN OFFENDED BY THE CIA'S CHOICE OF "MARGUERITE" AS **HARVEY'S** "MOTHER." BY ALL INDICATIONS, MARGUERITE WAS MARKEDLY MORE ATTRACTIVE, TALLER, THINNER, AND MORE PERSONABLE THAN "MARGUERITE." **HARVEY** MAY HAVE RESEMBLED **LEE**, BUT "MARGUERITE" BORE NO RESEMBLENCE TO MARGUERITE. IN MY OPINION, THE INTELLIGENCE COMMUNITY TOOK A CONSIDERABLE RISK IN NOT CHOOSING A MORE PHYSICALLY COMPATIBLE "MARGUERITE."

*MARGUERITE VIRTUALLY DISAPPEARED AFTER **HARVEY'S** 1959 "DEFECTION." HER SISTER LILLIAN MURRET NOTED IN HER W.C. TESTIMONY THAT SHE HAD NOT SEEN HER SISTER SINCE SEPTEMBER 1959. MY LAST NOTATION OF MARGUERITE'S LOCATION PRIOR TO HER SEPTEMBER 1959 DEPARTURE FROM NEW ORLEANS IS HER ARRIVAL IN NEW ORLEANS FROM FT. WORTH EARLIER THAT CALENDAR YEAR. LILLIAN MURRET HOWEVER STUCK TO THE SCRIPT AS DID HER HUSBAND, HER DAUGHTER, MARILYN, ROBERY OSWALD, AND JOHN PIC. THEY SIMPLY IGNORED THE FACT THAT BY NOVEMBER 1963 THEIR SISTER/AUNT/MOTHER HAD BECOME 6 INCHES SHORTER AND GAINED A CONSIDERABLE AMOUNT OF WEIGHT.*

LEE HARVEY OSWALD

LEE, SON OF MARGUERITE, WAS INDEED RELATED TO BOTH ROBERT OSWALD AND JOHN PIC. HE WAS NOT ONLY COMPLETELY AWARE OF THE MELDING OF **HARVEY** INTO **LEE**, BUT INSTRUMENTAL IN IMPERSONATING **HARVEY** IN THE LATER STAGES OF THE SET-UP. I AM HOWEVER SOMEWHAT RELUCTANT TO IMPLY THAT HE KNEW PRECISELY HOW IT WOULD END FOR **HARVEY**, BUT I WOULD NOT RULEOUT THE POSSIBILITY THAT HE KNEW EXACTLY WHAT WOULD TAKE PLACE ON NOVEMBER 22ND. HE VIRTUALLY DISAPPEARED AFTER THE ASSASSINATION.

*IT IS MY PROFOUND WISH THAT SOMEONE WITH THE TENACITY OF ARMSTRONG FURTHER INVESTIGATE THE "FAMILY" OF **HARVEY**, THEIR RECRUITMENT BY THE INTELLIGENCE COMMUNITY, AND THE DEMISE OF **LEE** AND MARGUERITE AFTER THE ASSASSINATION. IT SEEMS THE MORE WE DISCOVER THE MORE WE REALIZE JUST HOW MUCH MORE THERE IS TO LEARN ABOUT THOSE WHO ASSISTED THE CIA IN THEIR EFFORT TO TRANSFORM **HARVEY** INTO **LEE**..*

IT IS IMPORTANT TO NOTE THAT EVEN THOUGH ROBERT OSWALD, JOHN PIC, THE MURRETTS, THE PAINES, AND BOTH MARGUERITE AND "MARGUERITE" MAINTAINED THEIR SILENCE IN REGARDS TO **HARVEY** AND **LEE**, IT DOES NOT IMPLICATE THEM IN THE SETUP OF **HARVEY** AS THE PRESIDENTIAL ASSASSIN. THEY SIMPLY PRESERVED THE INTEGRITY OF THE CIA INSPIRED **HARVEY-TO-LEE** TRANSFORMATION AS IT RELATED TO THE "DEFECTION" OF **HARVEY**. **LEE** AND ONLY **LEE** PARTICIPATED IN THE SET-UP OF **HARVEY** AS THE ASSASSIN.

IN THIS SCENARIO, **SCENARIO II,** THE SET-UP CONSPIRATORS USE **HARVEY'S** UNKNOWN WHEREABOUTS FROM APPROXIMATELY SEPTEMBER 26TH TO OCTOBER 3RD TO RUN AN IMPOSTOR IN MEXICO CITY. ACCORDING TO ARMSTRONG, THE IMPOSTOR IS **LEE**. THE PLANNED DEPARTURE OF **HARVEY** FOR CUBA WITH THE CARCINOGENS VIA DAVID FERRIE ARE ALL PART OF A SET-UP; A SET-UP QUITE LIKELY ORCHESTRATED BY E. HOWARD HUNT AND DAVID ATLEE PHILLIPS. THERE MAY HAVE BEEN A LEGITIMATE CARCINOGEN PROJECT ONGOING AT THE CIA, BUT FERRIE, RUBY, JUDYTH VARY/BAKER AND **HARVEY** ARE NOT INVOLVED. SUFFICE IT TO SAY THAT IN THIS SCENARIO, **SCENARIO II**, THE AFTERNOON OF NOVEMBER 22ND ENDS IN A DRAMATICALLY DIFFERENT FASHION FOR **HARVEY** AND THE UNSUSPECTING J.D. TIPPIT.

AT THIS POINT, WE WILL RETURN TO THE TIMELINE AS OF LATE SEPTEMBER, 1963 WITH LEE'S ARRIVAL IN MEXICO CITY.

WE WILL HOWEVER CONTINUE UNDER THE PREMISE OUTLINED IN **SCENARIO II**. TO SUMARIZE, I SUBMIT THAT THE CARCINOGEN PROJECT IS A LEGITIMATE CIA EFFORT. BUT, THE ATTEMPT TO CONVINCE **HARVEY** THAT HE HAS A ROLE IN THE PROJECT AND THE UPCOMING C-DAY COUP, AND THAT RUBY, FERRIE, BANISTER, VARY/BAKER, AND DR. SHERMAN ARE TO OFFER VARIOUS DEGREES OF ASSISTANCE IN COMPLETING THE PROJECT IS COMPLETELY FRAUDULENT. THE ENTIRE SCHEME IS DESIGNED TO ACCOMPLISH NOTHING MORE THAN TO GIVE THE APPEARANCE THAT THE ALLEGED PRESIDENTIAL ASSASSIN IS ABOUT TO FLEE THE COUNTRY ENROUTE TO CUBA ON THE DAY OF THE ASSASSINATION. THE SELECTION OF **HARVEY**, WITH TIES TO BOTH INTELLIGENCE AGENCIES, WAS DELIBERATE. HIS "PARTICIPATION" IN THE ASSASSINATION WOULD VIRTUALLY INSURE A COVER-UP BY BOTH THE CIA PROPER AND THE FBI AS THEY WOULD, IN THE AFTERMATH OF THE TRAGEDY THAT DAY, MAKE EVERY EFFORT TO DISAVOW ANY AND ALL CONNECTIONS TO THE ALLEGED PRESIDENTIAL ASSASSIN.

CHAPTER 8: THE MEXICO CITY CONNECTION

SEPTEMBER 27TH 1963
ACCORDING TO ARMSTRONG, **LEE** ARRIVES IN MEXICO CITY AT 10:00 AM AND CHECKS INTO ROOM 18 AT THE HOTEL DEL COMMERCIO AT 11:30 AM. HE REGISTERS AS "H.O. LEE." ACCORDING TO VARY/BAKER HOWEVER, IT IS **HARVEY** IN MEXICO CITY. **HARVEY**, BY VARY/BAKER'S ACCOUNTING, THEN WENT TO A "DROP POINT" WHERE HE WAS TO DELIVER THE "PRODUCT." THE TRANSFER HOWEVER DID NOT TAKE PLACE AS THE PICK-UP CONTACT NEVER ARRIVED AT THE SOUVENIR SHOP THAT HAD BEEN DESIGNATED AS THE DROP POINT. CONFUSED ABOUT WHAT PRECISELY TO DO NEXT SINCE HE WAS STILL IN POSSESSION OF THE "PRODUCT", **HARVEY** THEN CONSULTED HIS CONTACT. APPARENTLY HE HAD DECIDED THAT THE LOGICAL SOLUTION WAS TO GET TO CUBA IMMEDIATELY BEFORE THE "PRODUCT" EXPIRED.

*ONCE AGAIN, I FEEL THAT VARY/BAKER'S VERSION IS A COMPOSITE. IT IS EITHER FERRIE, **HARVEY**, OR **LEE** MELDING THE STORIES TOGETHER FOR HER CONSUMPTION. ALTHOUGH IT IS **LEE** WHO IS IN MEXICO CITY, IT APPARENTLY IS IMPORTANT THAT VARY/BAKER BELIEVE THAT IT IS **HARVEY**. THERE WILL BE LITTLE TIME FOR VARY/BAKER TO QUESTION **HARVEY** AFTER THE ASSASSINATION, AND THERE IS NO EVIDENCE THAT SHE ATTEMPTED TO CONTACT HIM WHILE IN CUSTODY IN DALLAS*

SEPTEMBER 27TH 1963
LEE ARRIVES AT THE CUBAN CONSULATE IN MEXICO CITY ABOUT 11:30 AM AND SHOWS CONSULATE ASSISTANT SILVIA DURAN A FILE WITH DOCUMENTS SHOWING THAT HE IS "LEE HARVEY OSWALD", THAT HE HAD BEEN TO RUSSIA, THE FPFC CARDS LISTING HIM AS A MEMBER OF THE NEW ORLEANS CHAPTER, HIS SOVIET LABOR CARD, HIS MARRIAGE CERTIFICATE, HIS PASSPORT, HIS COMMUNIST PARTY USA MEMBERSHIP CARD, AND THE NEWSPAPER PUBLICIZING HIS ARGUMENT WITH BRINGUIER AND THEIR SUBSEQUENT ARREST. **LEE** STATED THAT HE WANTED TO TRAVEL TO CUBA ON MONDAY, SEPTEMBER 30TH. DURAN TOLD **LEE** TO OBTAIN PHOTOS FOR HIS VISA APPLICATION, FILL OUT THE PROPER PAPERS, AND RETURN IN 1 WEEK. **LEE** WAS OUTRAGED. HE LEFT ONLY TO QUICKLY RETURN ABOUT 1:00 PM TELLING MS. DURAN THAT HE HAD BEEN TO THE SOVIET EMBASSY, SPOKEN TO VICE CONSUL OLEG NECHIPERENKO, AND THAT THEY APPROVED HIS REQUEST TO RETURN TO RUSSIA. HE WOULD NOW NEED ONLY A CUBAN VISA. DURAN CHECKED WITH THE SOVIET EMBASSY AND WAS TOLD WHAT SHE HAD EXPECTED; THAT **LEE'S** SOVIET VISA COULD TAKE MONTHS TO PROCESS. **LEE** ERUPTED ONCE AGAIN AND WAS THEN TOLD BY EUSEBIO AZCUE, THE CONSUL GENERAL TO LEAVE. **LEE** RETURNED ONE MORE TIME ABOUT 4:00 PM TO THE CUBAN EMBASSY AGAIN ARGUING WITH AZCUE. ABOUT 4:25 PM, AZCUE ONCE AGAIN CALLED THE SOVIET EMBASSY TO VERIFY **LEE'S** CONTENTION THAT A SOVIET VISA WAS IN THE MAKING. AT 4:45, THE SOVIET EMBASSY CALLED DURAN AND REPEATED WHAT THEY HAD PREVIOUSLY STATED; THAT IT WOULD TAKE MONTHS TO GET A SOVIET VISA. AFTER ENDURING **LEE'S"** ANTICS, ASCUE FINALLY HAD HIM THROWN OUT.

*IT IS INTERESTING TO NOTE THAT DURAN LATER POINTED OUT THAT SINCE THE MEXICAN GOVERNMENT WAS ANTI-COMMUNIST THAT AMERICANS WITH COMMUNIST SYMPATHIES WOULD TRY TO <u>HIDE</u> ANY INDICATION OF THEIR LEFTIST LEANINGS. SHE LATER NOTED: "IT WAS STRANGE. I MEAN CROSSING THE BORDER WITH ALL HIS PAPER...IT WAS NOT LOGICAL. I MEAN IF YOU'RE REALLY COMMUNIST YOU GO WITH JUST NOTHING, JUST YOUR PASSPORT, THAT'S ALL." **LEE** APPARENTLY DID JUST THE OPPOSITE. I AM INCLINED TO THINK THAT THIS IS JUST WHAT PHILLIPS' INTENDED; A VISIT BY **LEE** THAT WOULD INDEED ATTRACT ATTENTION THAT WOULD LATER BE ATTRBUTED TO A VISIT BY **HARVEY**. NO ONE WHO MET **LEE** AT THE CUBAN CONSULATE COULD LATER IDENTIFY HIM AS THE MAN ARRESTED IN DALLAS ON NOVEMBER 22ND.*

SEPTEMBER 28TH 1963
LEE ALLEGEDLY VISITED THE SOVIET EMBASSY THIS DAY AS WELL.

SEPTEMBER 28TH 1963
AN 11:51 AM PHONE CALL, ACCORDING TO CIA SURVEILLANCE, IS MADE TO THE SOVIET EMBASSY IN MEXICO CITY FROM THE CUBAN EMBASSY IN MEXICO CITY BY SYLVIA DURAN ON BEHALF OF A CALLER WHO HAD IDENTIFIED HIMSELF AS "LEE OSWALD."

*VICE CONSUL/KGB AGENT OLEG NECHIPORENKO HOWEVER INSISTS IN HIS BOOK THAT THE SOVIET EMBASSY WAS CLOSED THAT DAY, SATURDAY, SEPTEMBER 28TH. SYLVIA DURAN SUPPORTS THIS NOTION IN THAT SHE INSISTS THAT THE CUBAN EMBASSY WAS CLOSED THAT DAY AS WELL. EITHER THIS INTERCEPT REFLECTS A CALL MADE BY DURAN ON FRIDAY, 27 SEPTEMBER AT 4:25 PM NOT SATURDAY, 28 SEPTEMBER AT 11:51 AM AS THE CIA INTERCEPT CLAIMS, OR SOMEONE IS IMPERSONATING BOTH DURAN AND **HARVEY** THAT SATURDAY. THE LIKELY CANDIDATE FOR THIS CALL IS **LEE**.*

SEPTEMBER 29TH 1963
HARVEY, ONCE AGAIN ACCORDING TO VARY/BAKER, SAID HE TRIED TO CONTACT "MR.B." MR. "B" IS, AS NOTED PREVIOUSLY, MR. BISHOP, OR MAURICE BISHOP, AN ALIAS OF DAVID ATLEE PHILLIPS. **HARVEY** WAS TOLD HOWEVER THAT "BISHOP" HAD LEFT FOR WASHINGTON.

ACCORDING TO THE HSCA, PHILLIPS/"BISHOP" WAS INDEED IN WASHINGTON, D.C. FROM SEPTEMBER 30TH TO OCTOBER 7TH.

OCTOBER 1ST 1963
ACCORDING TO CIA SURVEILLANCE, TWO PHONE CALLS ARE MADE TO THE SOVIET EMBASSY IN MEXICO CITY; ONE AT 10:30 AM AND ANOTHER AT 10:45 AM. THE CALLER IDENTIFIES HIMSELF AS "LEE OSWALD." ACCORDING TO THE CIA, THIS "LEE OSWALD" SPOKE IN BROKEN RUSSIAN AND DISCUSSED HIS PREVIOUS VISIT TO THE EMBASSY ON SEPTEMBER 28TH AND HIS MEETING THAT DAY WITH A KGB AGENT VALERIY KOSTIKOV, AN AGENT WHO WAS A MEMBER OF THE KGB'S WAR PLANS AND ASSASSINATION SECTION KNOWN AS DEPARTMENT THIRTEEN.

ONCE AGAIN ONE HAS TO QUESTION THE VALIDITY OF THESE INTERCEPTS SINCE THEY REFER TO A SEPTEMBER 28TH MEETING WHEN IT IS WIDELY ACCEPTED THAT BOTH EMBASSIES WERE CLOSED THAT DAY TO THE PUBLIC.

*KOSTIKOV DESCRIBED **LEE** AS "25-27, BROWN HAIR, MEDIUM HEIGHT." AGENT NIKOLAI LEONOV ALSO NOTED RECEIVING A **LEE** OSWALD. LEONOV HOWEVER PLACES THE VISIT ON SUNDAY, SEPTEMBER 29TH, NOT SATURDAY, THE 28TH. BOTH MEN HOWEVER CLAIM THAT THEIR VISITOR CARRIED A SMALL HANDGUN.*

*WHEN CONSUL AZCUE WAS LATER SHOWN **HARVEY'S** PICTURE HE WAS CERTAIN THAT THE MAN IN THE PHOTO WAS **NOT** THE SAME MAN WHO HAD MADE SUCH A SPECTACLE AT THE EMBASSY. SILVIA DURAN HAD DESCRIBED THE MAN SHE HAD MET WITH AS ABOUT 5'6, BLONDE HAIR, BALDING, EARLY-MID THIRTIES. THIS MAN WAS CLEARLY NEITHER **HARVEY** NOR **LEE**. THE VISITOR TO THE SOVIET EMBASSY WAS NOT **HARVEY**. CONSUL AZCUE'S DESCRIPTION OF "OSWALD" CLOSELY PARALLELED. DURAN'S DESCRIPTION. BOTH WERE DEPOSED BY THE HSCA IN 1978. IN THE 1964 WARREN COMMISSION REPORT, DURANS' DESCRIPTION CONTAINED NO REFERENCE TO "OSWALD" AS BEING SHORT OR BLONDE. WHEN THE COMMISSION ASKED THE CIA FOR PHOTOS FROM THE SURVEILLANCE CAMERAS AT THE EMBASSY, THE PHOTO SENT WAS CLEARLY NEITHER **HARVEY** OR **LEE**. THE PHOTO THE COMMISSION WAS SHOWN WAS TAKEN ON WEDNESDAY OCTOBER 2ND AND WAS OF A HEAVYSET MALE ABOUT 35 YEARS OLD WITH LIGHT COLORED HAIR AND A RECEEDING HAIRLINE. **LEE** HOWEVER DEPARTED MEXICO CIY AT 8:30 AM THAT MORNING, TOO SOON TO HAVE BEEN PHOTOGRAPHED THAT DAY. THE COMMISSION ALSO ASKED*

FOR VOICE TAPES OF THE CIA-BUGGED SOVIET EMBASSY. THE VOICE ON THE TAPE WAS CLEARLY NOT **HARVEY**.

HOOVER WOULD LATER ADMIT TO LBJ THAT SOMETHING WAS AMISS. A PACKAGE WITH SURVEILLANCE PHOTOS AND TAPES WAS FLOWN TO WASHINGTON FROM MEXICO CITY ON NOVEMBER 23RD ARRIVING AT 4:00 AM. BY 10:00 AM, HOOVER WAS TELLING LBJ: "WE HAVE UP HERE THE TAPE AND THE PHOTO OF THE MAN WHO WAS AT THE SOVIET EMBASSY USING OSWALD'S NAME. THAT PICTURE AND THE TAPE DO NOT CORRESPOND TO THE MAN'S (**HARVEY'S**) VOICE, NEITHER TO HIS (**HARVEY'S**) APPEARANCE. IN OTHER WORDS, IT APPEARS THAT THERE IS A SECOND PERSON WHO WAS AT THE SOVIET EMBASSY DOWN THERE." AT THIS POINT HOOVER IS NOT ONLY OPEN TO THE POSSIBILITY OF A CONSPIRACY TO IMPLICATE **HARVEY** BUT ALSO A POTENTIAL CUBAN/RUSSIAN INVOLVEMENT IN THE PRESIDENTIAL ASSASSINATION.

THE DAY AFTER THE ASSASSINATION, THE CIA, DESIRING MS. DURAN ARRESTED, CABLED THE MEXICAN AUTHORITIES THIS MEMO:

> WITH FULL REGARD FOR MEXICAN INTERESTS, REQUEST YOU ENSURE
> HER ARREST IS KEPT ABSOLUTELY SECRET, THAT NO INFO FROM HER
> IS PUBLISHED OR LEAKED, THAT ALL SUCH INFO IS CABLED TO US, AND
> THE FACT OF HER ARREST AND HER STATEMENTS ARE NOT SPREAD TO LEFTIST
> OR DISLOYAL CIRCLES IN THE MEXICAN GOVERNMENT.

DURAN WAS KEPT IN CUSTODY FOR SEVERAL DAYS AND RELEASED ONLY <u>AFTER</u> SHE IDENTIFIED **HARVEY** AS THE MAN AT THE EMBASSY. AFTER SHE WAS RELEASED, SHE ONCE AGAIN SPOKE OF THE MAN AT THE EMBASSY <u>NOT</u> BEING **HARVEY**. THE CIA CABLED MEXICAN AUTHORITIES ONCE AGAIN REQUESTING HER ARREST ONLY 4 DAYS AFTER HER INITIAL RELEASE FROM CUSTODY. UPON HER 2ND RELEASE, A "WISER" SYLVIA DURAN HAD CHANGED HER STORY AND IDENTIFIED **HARVEY** AS THE MAN AT THE EMBASSY.

DURAN WOULD LATER NOTE THAT SHE WAS BEATEN DURING HER SECOND ARREST. THE BEATINGS WOULD FORCE DURAN TO NOT ONLY STATE THAT **HARVEY** HAD INDEED VISITED THE EMBASSY, BUT THAT SHE ALSO HAD HAD AN AFFAIR WITH HIM. SHE WOULD VEHEMENTLY DENY BOTH AFTER HER RELEASE.

DURAN WAS NEVER CONTACTED BY OR INTERVIEWED BY THE WARREN COMMISSION.

REGARDLESS OF THE FACT THAT THE "OSWALD" AT THE CUBAN CONSULATE WAS OBVIOUSLY AN IMPOSTER AND NOT **HARVEY**, THE CIA PROPER STILL FOUND IT NECESSARY TO LEAN ON SYLVIA DURAN TO CHANGE HER OPINION. THE CIA PROPER IN WASHINGTON, UNLIKE THE WARREN COMMISSION, AT LEAST REALIZED THAT AN IMPOSTOR IN MEXICO CITY WAS EVIDENCE OF SOME TYPE OF SET-UP ATTEMPT OF **HARVEY**. THE PROBLEM HOWEVER WAS THAT THEY DID NOT KNOW JUST <u>WHO</u> HAD ATTEMPTED TO SET HIM UP OR <u>WHY</u>. IT IS HIGHLY PROBABLE THAT HUNT AND PHILLIPS, THE SET-UP CONSPIRATORS BASED IN MEXICO CITY, TOOK ADVANTAGE OF THE FACT THAT FROM SEPTEMBER 26 TO OCTOBER 3RD 1963 THERE IS NO CONCRETE EVIDENCE OF THE WHEREABOUTS OF **HARVEY**. HUNT AND PHILLIPS COULD THEN USE THIS "GAP" IN **HARVEY'S** TIMELINE TO ARRANGE FOR AN "OSWALD", MOST LIKELY **LEE,** TO CONTACT BOTH THE CUBAN EMBASSY AND THE SOVIET EMBASSY AND TO LEAVE THOSE WHO CAME INTO CONTACT WITH "OSWALD" NO DOUBT THAT IT WAS **HARVEY** WHO WAS PURSUING TRAVEL TO RUSSIA VIA CUBA. THE TRAVEL PLANS TO MEXICO, CUBA, THEN ON TO RUSSIA THAT **HARVEY** WAS LED TO PERCEIVE AS INSTRUMENTAL IN HIS "ASSIGNMENT" ON NOVEMBER 22ND WOULD DOVETAIL PRECISELY WITH WHAT THE **HARVEY** IMPOSTOR HAD PURSUED DURING HIS CONTACTS WITH THE CUBAN AND RUSSIAN EMBASSIES. PHILLIPS, ACCORDING TO THE HSCA INVESTIGATION, WAS IN WASHINGTON FROM 30 SEPTEMBER TO OCTOBER 7TH, 1963. HIS ABSENCE FROM MEXICO CITY FOR 3 OF THE 6 DAYS THAT COVERED **HARVEY'S** ALLEGED VISIT TO MEXICO CITY WOULD NOT ONLY OFFER PHILLIPS A CERTAIN DEGREE OF DENIABILITY IN REGARDS TO THE UTILIZATION OF **LEE** TO IMPLICATE **HARVEY**, BUT HIS

ABSENCE WOULD DIMINISH THE ABILITY OF HIS STAFF – WITH THE EXCEPTION OF HUNT- TO DETERMINE THE TRUE IDENTITY OF THE VISITOR TO THE CUBAN AND SOVIET EMBASSIES.

THE "OSWALD IN MEXICO" SIGHTINGS CONTINUE.

CIA AGENT L. G. BARKER SENT A MESSAGE FROM MEXICO CITY TO WASHINGTON ON NOVEMBER 26TH, 1963. IT DESCRIBED A MEETING ON SEPTEMBER 18TH, 1963 BETWEEN AN "OSWALD" AND 2 MEN IN THE CUBAN CONSULATE OFFICE AS WITNESSED BY A GILBERT ALVARADO, A NICARAGUAN INTELLIGENCE INFORMANT.

THE TWO MEN WERE DESCRIBED AS A "TALL NEGRO WITH REDDISH HAIR" AND A "BLONDE-HAIRED HIPPIE." ACCORDING TO ALVARADO, $6,500 WAS REPORTEDLY GIVEN TO "OSWALD"BY THE NEGRO MAN APPARENTLY AS A PAYOFF FOR THE JFK ASSASSINATION. A COMMENT ATTRIBUTED TO THIS "OSWALD" BY ALVARADO: "YOU'RE NOT MAN ENOUGH....I CAN DO IT." WAS IN RESPONSE TO THE NEGRO'S INITIAL COMMENT "I WANT TO KILL THE MAN." BUT, A MESSAGE FROM DIRECTOR CIA TO WASHINGTON ON NOVEMBER 28TH REGARDING THIS INCIDENT NOTED THAT THE FBI HAD "RELIABLE INDICATIONS" THAT **HARVEY** WAS IN NEW ORLEANS AS LATE AS SEPTEMBER 19TH 1963, AND HAD APPLIED FOR UNEMPLOYMENT INSURANCE ON SEPTEMBER 17TH. A NOVEMBER 30TH, 1963 CIA CABLE TO WASHINGTON CLOSED THE DOOR ON WHAT WAS OBVIOUSLY ANOTHER SET-UP ATTEMPT BY THOSE WISHING TO FRAME **HARVEY**. IT NOTED THAT AFTER THE INTERROGATION OF ALVARADO BY MEXICAN AUTHORITIES THAT ALVARADO ADMITTED TO HAVING FABRICATED THE ENTIRE STORY.

THIS WAS THE SECOND TIME THAT THE CIA HAD ASKED MEXICAN AUTHORITIES TO INTERCEDE IN A SITUATION WHERE THERE WAS A **HARVEY** IMPOSTOR. THE OTHER INTERCESSION, ALSO IN MEXICO CITY, WAS THE SIGHTING OF AN "OSWALD" AT THE CUBAN EMBASSY BY SYLVIA DURAN. ONCE AGAIN WE HAVE TOO MANY "OSWALDS." THIS TIME HOWEVER THE CIA PROPER WOULD BE FORCED TO TAKE A DIFFERENT APPROACH. WITH THE FBI HAVING INTERJECTED THAT **HARVEY** WAS STILL IN NEW ORLEANS AT THE TIME OF THIS SIGHTING, THE CIA IN WASHINGTON HAD NO ALTERNATIVE BUT TO REFUTE ALVARADO'S CLAIM.

IT IS INTERESTING TO NOTE HOWEVER THAT ALVARDO'S STORY WAS NEVERTHELESS STRONGLY ENDORSED BY CIA OFFICIALS HOWARD HUNT AND DAVID ATLEE PHILLIPS. THIS WOULD NOT BE THE ONLY"MISTAKE" MADE BY THE TWO KEY SET-UP CONSPIRATORS DURING THE MONTHS PRIOR TO THE ASSASSINATION. THE MANY "TIMING" ERRORS MADE IN DALLAS REGARDING **HARVEY** AND IMPOSTORS WERE MADE BY EITHER ROSCOE WHITE OR **LEE** OR PERHAPS OTHER SET-UP CONSPIRATORS WITH A CONSIDERABLY LESSER DEGREE OF INVOLVEMENT AND EXPERIENCE. THE ENDORSEMENT OF THE SEPTEMBER 18TH "PREMATURE" SIGHTING OF "OSWALD" IN MEXICO CITY BY HUNT AND PHILLIPS HOWEVER WOULD BE AN OVERSIGHT NOT EXPECTED OF THESE EXPERIENCED COUNTER- INTELLIGENCE AGENTS.

THIS EPISODE ON SEPTEMBER 18TH COMBINED WITH THE EPISODE ON SEPTEMBER 26TH, ALSO IN MEXICO CITY, <u>AND</u> THE SYLVIA ODIO EPISODE SHOULD HAVE NOW ALERTED BOTH THE CIA PROPER AND THE FBI THAT EITHER **HARVEY** WAS ABOUT TO EMBARK ON A NON-SANCTIONED DEPARTURE FROM HIS PREVIOUSLY SANCTIONED INTELLIGENCE ROLES OR THAT HE WAS BLATANTLY BEING IMPERSONATED.

IT IS IMPORTANT TO NOTE THAT THIS "OSWALD" <u>FAILED</u> IN HIS EFFORTS TO OBTAIN <u>LEGITIMATE</u> VISAS AT THE EMBASSIES IN MEXICO CITY AND IN TURN <u>LEGAL</u> PASSAGE TO RUSSIA VIA CUBA. THIS "FAILURE" WAS NOT ONLY DELIBERATE, BUT WAS INDEED THE VERY REASON THAT THE SET-UP CONSPIRATORS PROMPTED **LEE** TO BEHAVE IN SUCH A FASHION THAT WOULD VIRTUALLY INSURE THAT THE NECESSARY VISAS FOR PASSAGE TO CUBA AND RUSSIA WOULD NOT BE APPROVED.

NOW THAT A **LEE** HARVEY OSWALD HAD BEEN REBUKED BY THE EMBASSIES, LEE **HARVEY OSWALD** WOULD NOW HAVE TO FIND <u>ANOTHER</u> METHOD IN WHICH TO TRAVEL TO RUSSIA VIA CUBA. THE DALLAS TO HOUSTON TO GALVESTON TO YUCATAN, MEXICO TO CUBA ITENERARY ARRANGED BY THE SET-UP CONSPIRATORS FOR THE NOVEMBER 22ND "ASSIGNMENT" FOR THE UNSUSPECTING **HARVEY** AND HIS PILOT DAVID FERRIE WOULD, IF THE HOPED FOR SHOOTOUT IN THE TEXAS THEATER FAILED TO OCCUR, BE PERCEIVED BY THOSE INVESTIGATING THE ASSASSINATION AS AN <u>ALTERNATIVE</u> METHOD OF TRAVEL FOR **HARVEY** IN LIGHT OF THE PREVIOUSLY PURPOSELY FAILED EFFORTS TO OBTAIN PASSAGE INTO CUBA BY **LEE** IN MEXICO CITY. WHAT **HARVEY** AND FERRIE WOULD ACCEPT AS LEGITIMATE TRAVEL PLANS THAT NOVEMBER AFTERNOON FOR THEIR ALLEGED "CARCINOGENS TO CUBA"MISSION WOULD NOW BE VIEWED BY LOCAL DALLAS AUTHORITIES AS THE EFFORT OF AN ALLEGED PRESIDENTIAL ASSASSIN TO FLEE THE COUNTRY.

INDEED, U.S. NEWS AND WORLD REPORT WOULD TAKE THE BAIT. IN THEIR DECEMBER 9TH, 1963 ISSUE, THEY NOTED: "...WHAT WAS THE REASON FOR OSWALD'S VISIT TO MEXICO...WAS OSWALD PLANNING THE ASSASSINATION THEN AND PREPARING HIS ESCAPE ROUTE?"

THE CHOICE OF NOVEMBER 22ND AS THE DEPARTURE DATE FOR **HARVEY'S** BOGUS "ASSIGNMENT" WILL BE AN EASY SELL BY THE SET-UP CONSPIRATORS TO **HARVEY**. HIS INTELLIGENCE ALLEGIANCE IS TO THE CIA, OR AT LEAST TO THE CIA AS HE KNOWS IT, (HUNT/PHILLIPS), IN REGARD TO HIS "ASSIGNMENT." **HARVEY** HAD SHOWN, AND WILL CONTINUE TO EXHIBIT HOSTILITY AND RESENTMENT TOWARDS THE FBI REGARDING THEIR RELATIVELY MENIAL INFORMANT ASSIGNMENTS AND THEIR CONSTANT HARASSMENT OF HIS WIFE. **HARVEY** IS LIKELY TOLD BY THE SET-UP CONSPIRATORS THAT NOVEMBER 22ND PRESENTS AN <u>IDEAL</u> OPPORTUNITY FOR HIM TO LEAVE THE COUNTRY ON "ASSIGNMENT" AS THE FBI WILL BE OCCUPIED WITH SECURITY SURROUNDING THE PRESIDENTIAL VISIT.

INTERESTINGLY, MARINA CLAIMED THAT SHE HAD ASKED **HARVEY** TO BUY HER A BRACELET IN MEXICO CITY. THE BRACELET HE LATER GAVE HER WAS "MADE IN JAPAN" AND PURCHASED IN DALLAS AT THE N.L. GREEN STORE ON OCTOBER 3RD. **HARVEY** GAVE HER POST CARDS ON HIS <u>RETURN</u> TO DALLAS RATHER THAN MAIL THEM FROM MEXICO CITY. HE DID NOT RETURN WITH ANY OF THE "MEXICAN RECORDS" MARINA HAD ASKED FOR. HAD **HARVEY** SHARED WITH MARINA THE <u>POSSIBILITY</u> OF A TRIP TO MEXICO BUT PURCHASED THE GIFTS IN DALLAS AS A RESULT OF <u>NOT</u> HAVING MADE THE TRIP? THESE SMALL BUT MEANINGFUL OVERSIGHTS BY **HARVEY** ADD CREEDENCE TO THE NOTION THAT ALTHOUGH IT IS <u>POSSIBLE</u> THAT SET-UP CONSPIRATORS HUNT AND PHILLIPS HAD LURED **HARVEY** TO MEXICO CITY FOR THE PURPOSE OF ARRANGING THE INCRIMINATING "OSWALD" ANTICS AT THE EMBASSIES, THAT IT IS NEITHER A CERTAINTY NOR A <u>NECESSITY</u> FOR **HARVEY** TO HAVE VISITED MEXICO CITY THAT FALL. HUNT/PHILLIPS COULD HAVE PROCEEDED WITH THE "OSWALD" IMPERSONATORS OR WITH **LEE** <u>WITHOUT</u> **HARVEY'S** ACTUAL PRESENCE IN MEXICO. IN FACT, WITH NO HARD EVIDENCE OF **HARVEY'S** WHEREABOUTS FROM SEPTEMBER 26TH TO OCTOBER 3RD, IT WOULD HAVE MADE HUNT AND PHILLIP'S TASK THAT MUCH EASIER.

ACCORDING TO VARY/BAKER HOWEVER **HARVEY**, UNABLE TO SUCCESSFULLY DELIVER THE "PRODUCT" TO HIS CONTACT AND UNABLE TO MANIPULATE AN URGENT TRIP TO CUBA WITH THE DECAYING "PRODUCT" IS TOLD BY THE MEXICO CITY CIA STATION TO RETURN TO DALLAS. HE WOULD HAVE BEEN TOLD TO DO SO BY E. HOWARD HUNT AS PHILLIPS, "MR.B", IS IN WASHINGTON. **HARVEY** HAD APPARENTLY BEEN TOLD THAT DUE TO A HURRICANE APPROACHING CUBA THAT HE WOULD HAVE BEEN LESS LIKELY TO MEET WITH HIS CONTACTS ONCE HE ARRIVED IN CUBA. VARY/BAKER WOULD WISELY NOTE THAT WITH **HARVEY'S** RETURN TO DALLAS THAT BOTH SHE AND **HARVEY** WERE NOW NO LONGER A PART OF ANY "CARCINOGENS TO CUBA" PLAN. SHE WOULD HOWEVER BE ONLY <u>PARTIALLY</u> CORRECT AS **HARVEY** WAS TOLD THAT HE COULD BE CALLED UPON TO GO TO MEXICO AT ANY TIME. HIS VISIT HOWEVER WILL HAVE, AS VARY/BAKER PREDICTED, NO CONNECTION TO THE CARCINOGEN PLOT. IT WILL I SUSPECT BE ON NOVEMBER 22ND 1963.

*ONCE AGAIN, VARY/BAKER'S VERSION APPEARS TO BE A COMPOSITE OF **LEE'S** VISIT TO MEXICO CITY TO INCRIMINATE **HARVEY**, AND WHAT SHE IS TOLD BY EITHER FERRIE, **HARVEY**, OR **LEE** REGARDING **HARVEY'S** FICTITIONAL VISIT.*

OCTOBER 2ND 1963

ACCORDING TO THE W.C. **HARVEY** DEPARTS MEXICO CITY BY BUS AT 8:30 AM. ON TRANSPORTES DEL NORTE BUS # 332. HIS FARE IS $20.30. THE BUS WOULD ARRIVE IN MONTEREY ABOUT 9:15 PM. PASSENGERS THEN BOARDED BUS #373 WHICH DEPARTED AT 9:50 PM.

*WHAT **HARVEY**, **LEE** OR EVEN "OSWALD"(S) WERE UP TO IN SEPTEMBER 1963 IS CONFUSING TO SAY THE LEAST:.*

AS EARLY AS SEPTEMBER 18TH, AN "OSWALD" IS REPORTEDLY IN MEXICO CITY.

*BUT THE FBI FEELS THAT **HARVEY** IS STILL IN NEW ORLEANS AS LATE AS SEPTEMBER 19TH.*

***HARVEY** ALLEGEDLY LEFT NEW ORLEANS BY BUS ON SEPTEMBER 24TH FOR HOUSTON.*

*THEN **HARVEY** IS ALLEGEDLY SEEN IN AUSTIN, TEXAS ON SEPTEMBER 25TH.*

*ON SEPTEMBER 25TH, **HARVEY** APPEARS AT SYLVIA ODIO'S APARTMENT IN DALLAS.*

***HARVEY** OR "OSWALD" THEN ALLEGEDLY LEAVES HOUSTON FOR MEXICO CITY ON SEPTEMBER 26TH.*

*AND, **HARVEY, LEE,** OR AN "OSWALD" ALLEGEDLY CHECKS INTO A HOTEL IN MEXICO CITY ON SEPTEMBER 27TH.*

***HARVEY'S** WHEREABOUTS BETWEEN SEPTEMBER 26TH AND OCTOBER 3RD 1963 IS A MYSTERY. EITHER HE WAS IN <u>ALL</u> THE LOCALES ATTRIBUTED TO HIM, <u>NONE</u> OF THE LOCALES, OR, MORE LIKELY PHYSICALLY PRESENT AT ONLY A <u>PORTION</u> OF THE SIGHTINGS. I FEEL THAT THE MEXICO CITY VISITS TO THE EMBASSIES WERE EITHER PERFORMED BY IMPOSTERS ON BEHALF OF THE SET-UP CONSPIRATORS HUNT AND PHILLIPS OR THE VISITOR WAS, AS ARMSTRONG NOTES, **LEE**. I FEEL THAT IT IS MORE LIKELY THAT THE AUSTIN, TEXAS VISIT WAS BY **LEE** AND THE SYLVIA ODIO VISIT WAS ACTUALLY MADE BY **HARVEY** PRIOR TO RENTING THE ROOM AT THE YMCA IN DALLAS ON OCTOBER 3RD, 1963. IT IS <u>POSSIBLE</u> THAT **HARVEY** WAS INDEED IN MEXICO CITY DURING THIS TIMEFRAME, BUT DID <u>NOT</u> VISIT THE EMBASSIES. THE SET-UP CONSPIRATORS, IN THIS PARTICULAR INSTANCE, HUNT AND PHILLIPS COULD HAVE LURED **HARVEY** TO MEXICO CITY FOR WHAT HE WOULD PERCEIVE AS A LEGITIMATE CIA-SPONSORED MEETING IN REGARD TO HIS LATER DELIVERY OF CARCINOGENS TO CUBA. HUNT/PHILLIPS COULD THEN USE **HARVEY'S** PHYSICAL PRESENCE IN MEXICO CITY AS AN OPPORTUNITY TO RUN THE IMPOSTOR/ OR **LEE** AT THE EMBASSIES. BUT, I DO NOT BELIEVE THIS IS THE CASE.*

*IN SEPTEMBER, 1964, JUST <u>DAYS</u> BEFORE THE WARREN COMMISSION REPORT WAS TO GO TO PRESS, MARINA FOUND A MEXICAN BUS TICKET STUB IN A SPANISH-LANGUAGE MAGAZINE. HOWEVER ONE MUST CONSIDER THE BACKGROUND OF THE JOURNALIST WHO JUST "HAPPENED" TO BE WITH MARINA WHEN SHE "FOUND" THE TICKET STUB. THE JOURNALIST WAS PRISCILLA JOHNSON. THIS WAS THE SAME PRISCILLA JOHNSON WHO INTERVIEWED **HARVEY** SHORTLY AFTER HIS ARRIVAL IN RUSSIA. EVEN THE FBI HAD SUSPICIONS OF JOHNSON WHEN THEY DISCOVERED HER TIES TO THE CIA, THE STATE DEPARTMENT, AND HER RELATIONSHIP WITH THE U.S. EMBASSY IN MOSCOW. THE ROOM IN WHICH THE TICKET STUB WAS FOUND WAS SEARCHED <u>PRIOR</u> TO JOHNSON'S ARRIVAL. NO STUB WAS FOUND. THE STUB HOWEVER <u>WAS</u> FOUND ALMOST IMMEDIATELY <u>AFTER</u> HER ARRIVAL.*

*DURING THE MONTHS AFTER THE ASSASSINATION WHEN MARINA WAS KEPT IN CUSTODY, NUMEROUS REQUESTS FOR INTERVIEWS WERE DENIED. "MARGUERITE" WAS NOT ALLOWED TO SEE HER. A LAWYER REPRESENTING **HARVEY** WAS NOT ALLOWED TO SEE HER. THE CIA HOWEVER MADE AN EXCEPTION FOR PRISCILLA JOHNSON EVEN THOUGH THE FBI QUESTIONED WHETHER SHE WAS INDEED A <u>SUSPECT</u> IN THE ASSASSINATION. THE PRIVELIGED MS. JOHNSON WOULD SURFACE ONCE AGAIN IN LATER YEARS WHEN SHE WOULD AUTHOR A BOOK TITLED "MARINA AND LEE".*

*NEARLY 10 MONTHS AFTER **HARVEY'S** DEATH, THE TICKET STUB WOULD BE YET ANOTHER ATTEMPT BY THE CIA TO PROVE THAT IT WAS INDEED **HARVEY** PURSUING TRAVEL TO RUSSIA VIA CUBA. APPARENTLY IT WAS STILL CRITICAL FOR THE CIA TO ATTEMPT TO PROVE THAT IT WAS INDEED **HARVEY** IN MEXICO CITY IN SPITE OF THE TESTIMONY OF THE EMBASSY EMPLOYEES AND THE CIA'S OWN PHOTO AND VOICE INTELLIGENCE GATHERING THAT VIRTUALLY CERTIFIED THAT IT WAS <u>NOT</u> **HARVEY**. FOR THE CIA IT WAS A POST-ASSASSINATION DILLEMA; EITHER <u>EXPLAIN</u> WHY THERE IS LITTLE CREDIBLE EVIDENCE TO PROVE THAT THE VISITOR TO THE EMBASSIES, THE PERSON PHOTOGRAPHED OUTSIDE THE SOVIET EMBASSY, AND THE PERSON WHOSE VOICE IS RECORDED BY THEIR OWN EAVESDROPPING METHODS IS **HARVEY**, OR <u>ADMIT</u> THAT **HARVEY** WAS <u>NOT</u> IN MEXICO CITY AND THAT THERE WAS A CONCERTED EFFORT BY <u>SOMEONE</u> TO IMPERSONATE HIM IN MEXICO CITY THAT FALL. AN IMPOSTOR IN MEXICO CITY INHERENTLY CARRIES WITH IT THE MAKINGS OF A SET-UP. EVIDENCE OF A SET-UP IMPLIES A CONSPIRACY.*

*SO, HOW DO WE SUMARIZE THE EVENTS IN MEXICO CITY? WAS **HARVEY** INDEED IN MEXICO CITY THAT FALL OR WAS IT MERELY THE IMPOSTOR/**LEE** BEING RUN BY SET-UP CONSPIRATORS HUNT AND PHILLIPS? I AM INCLINED TO DOUBT THAT **HARVEY** WAS IN MEXICO CITY THAT LATE SEPTEMBER / EARLY OCTOBER OF 1963. **HARVEY** HIMSELF DENIED EVER HAVING BEEN IN MEXICO CITY AT HIS 1ST INTERROGATION SESSION ON NOVEMBER 22ND. THE LIMITED AMOUNT OF INFORMATION RETAINED FROM THESE INTERROGATION SESSIONS SHOW THAT **HARVEY**, WHEN QUESTIONED, WAS CONSISTENTLY QUITE CANDID IN HIS WHEREABOUTS AT ANY GIVEN TIME. IT WOULD BE INTERESTING TO FIND OUT IF HE WAS ASKED HIS WHEREABOUTS DURING THE TIME HE WAS ALLEGEDLY IN MEXICO CITY SINCE HE DENIED EVER HAVING BEEN THERE. I AM HOWEVER INCLINED TO AGREE WITH ARMSTRONG THAT IT WAS **LEE** WHO HAD TAKEN THE TRIP TO MEXICO CITY.*

*THE CIA SURVEILLANCE, BOTH PHOTOGRAPHIC AND AUDIO, IN MEXICO CITY REVEALED NO ONE WHO EITHER REMOTELY LOOKED LIKE **HARVEY** OR SOUNDED LIKE HIM. IN FACT, THE DESCRIPTIONS DO NOT FAVOR **LEE** EITHER. HOOVER BELIEVED, AND IN TURN PHONED LBJ TO INFORM HIM, THAT BOTH THE TAPES AND THE PHOTOS TAKEN IN MEXICO CITY "DO NOT CORRESPOND TO THE MAN'S (**HARVEY'S**) VOICE, NEITHER TO HIS APPEARANCE." EMBASSY STAFF AT THE CUBAN EMBASSY WERE ALSO CERTAIN THAT THE "OSWALD" THEY ENCOUNTERED WAS NOT **HARVEY**.*

*ALTHOUGH **HARVEY** APPARENTLY LEFT NEW ORLEANS ON SEPTEMBER 25TH, IT WAS **LEE** AT THE SELECTIVE SERVICE OFFICE IN AUSTIN, TEXAS ON THE 25TH. IT WAS HOWEVER **HARVEY** AT SYLVIA ODIO'S RESIDENCE ON SEPTEMBER 26TH. THERE IS LITTLE INFORMATION ON **HARVEY'S** WHERABOUTS FROM SEPT 26TH UNTIL OCT 3RD WHEN HE CHECKS INTO A DALLAS YMCA UNLESS ONE IS ABSOLUTELY CERTAIN THAT HE IS INDEED IN MEXICO CITY. THIS 8 DAY GAP REMAINS A MYSTERY. BUT, **HARVEY'S** ABSENCE CONVENIENTLY GIVES THE SET-UP CONSPIRATORS HUNT AND PHILLIPS A UNIQUE OPPORTUNITY TO RUN THE "OSWALD" IMPOSTOR IN MEXICO CITY. KEEP IN MIND THAT AT THIS POINT, **LEE** IS A **HARVEY** "IMPOSTOR." WITH **HARVEY'S** WHEREABOUTS UNCERTAIN, THE MEXICO CITY SEGMENT WITH AN IMPOSTER GETS A MUCH NEEDED CREDIBILITY BOOST. I WOULD BE REMISS IF I DID NOT TENDER THE NOTION THAT HUNT, PHILLIPS, AND FELLOW SET-UP CONSPIRATORS ROSCOE WHITE AND **LEE** KNEW <u>EXACTLY</u> WHERE **HARVEY** WAS THOSE 8 DAYS. WITH HUNT AND PHILLIPS KNOWLEDGE THAT **HARVEY** WAS INDEED INCOMMUNICADO, IT WOULD NOT ONLY BE A SIMPLER TASK TO RUN THE "OSWALD" IMPOSTER (**LEE**) IN MEXICO CITY, BUT AT LEAST PLAUSIBLE TO THOSE WHO WOULD LATER*

*INVESTIGATE EVENTS SURROUNDING THE ASSASSINATION THAT IT <u>COULD</u> HAVE BEEN **HARVEY** IN MEXICO CITY, <u>NOT</u> AN IMPOSTOR..*

*IT IS IMPERATIVE TO KEEP IN MIND THAT WITH PHILLIPS AS CHIEF OF COVERT ACTIONS AND CHIEF OF CUBAN OPERTIONS, THAT HE WAS IN A UNIQUE POSITION TO CONTROL BOTH PHOTOS AND VOICE TAPES OF THE PERSON PRESENTING HIMSELF AS "OSWALD" IN MEXICO CITY. PHOTOGRAPHS AND AUDIO SURVEILLANCE LATER PROVED THAT THE PERSON IN QUESTION WAS **NOT** LEE **HARVEY** OSWALD. PHILLIPS KNEW THIS AND AS A RESULT HAD TO RELY SOLELY ON "VISUAL" CONTACTS WITH AN "OSWALD" IN AN ATTEMPT TO PLACE **HARVEY** IN MEXICO CITY AS PART OF THE SET-UP.*

*PHILLIPS ATTEMPTED TO COERCE WITNESSES TO SUPPORT "VISUALLY" WHAT HE WOULD NOT, AND PERHAPS MORE IMPORTANTLY, <u>COULD</u> NOT VALIDATE WITH VIDEO SURVEILLANCE, PHOTOGRAPHS, OR AUDIO TAPES. PHILLIPS' EFFORTS DID NOT STOP WITH EMBASSY PERSONNEL. ON NOVEMBER 23RD,1963, PHILLIPS HAD A LUNCHEON ENGAGEMENT WITH CARL MIGDALE. MIGDALE WAS CHIEF OF U.S. NEWS AND WORLD REPORT'S MEXICO CITY BUREAU. PHILLIPS CONTINUED THE **HARVEY**-IN-MEXICO-CITY PUSH BY NOTING TO MIGDALE: "THANK GOD THAT WE REPORTED ON OSWALD BEING HERE IN SEPTEMBER OTHERWISE MY ORGANIZATION MIGHT BE IN DANGER OF BEING ELIMINATED."*

SENATOR RICHARD SCHWEIKER, A MEMBER OF THE SENATE INTELLIGENCE COMMITTEE'S EXAMINATION OF CIA ACTIVITY IN REGARD TO THE ASSASSINATION WAS NOTHING LESS THAN PRECISE WITH HIS APPRAISAL OF THE MEXICO CITY AFFAIR. HE EXPRESSED HIS OPINION THAT IF THE "OSWALD" VISITS TO MEXICO CITY DID INVOLVE A RENEGADE ELEMENT OF THE CIA THAT IT WOULD NOT BE HARD TO SEE WHY BOTH THE SURVEILLANCE PICTURES AND TAPES WOULD DISAPPEAR SHORTLY AFTER THE ASSASSINATION.

*HUNT AND PHILLIPS WOULD MAKE EVERY EFFORT TO <u>INSINUATE</u> THAT **HARVEY** WAS PRESENT IN MEXICO CITY THE FALL OF 1963. THEY WOULD HOWEVER MANIPULATE, ERASE OR FALSIFY THE VERY MECHANISMS (PHOTOGRAPHIC, CABLE, AND TELEPHONE INTERCEPTS) BY WHICH THEY COULD HAVE OFFERED <u>PROOF</u> OF **HARVEY'S** ACTUAL PRESENCE AT THE CUBAN AND SOVIET EMBASSIES. THE SET-UP OF **HARVEY** WAS PREDICATED ON THE HOPE THAT INVESTIGATORS WOULD BE WILLING TO ACCEPT THE MERE <u>POSSIBILITY</u> OF **HARVEY'S** PRESENCE IN MEXICO CITY AND ITS IMPLICATIONS WHEN BOTH HUNT AND PHILLIPS KNEW THAT THIS WAS NOT THE CASE.*

*LBJ WAS LEFT TO DRAW HIS OWN CONCLUSIONS ABOUT MEXICO CITY. THE CIA WOULD CONTEND, WITHOUT VERIFIABLE, UNBIASED, PROOF THAT **HARVEY** HAD INDEED VISITED THE EMBASSIES AND ENGAGED BOTH THE SOVIETS AND CUBANS IN WHAT COULD BE PERCIEVED AS AN ASSASSINATION PLOT AGAINST THE PRESIDENT. HOOVER HOWEVER WOULD CONTEND THAT THE VISITOR TO BOTH EMBASSIES WAS AN IMPOSTOR DESIGNED TO IMPLICATE **HARVEY**, THE CUBAN AND THE SOVIET GOVERNMENTS, AND THAT THE LIKELY PERPETRATORS OF THIS HOAX WAS THE CIA. THIS MAY HAVE BEEN SELF SERVING ON HOOVER'S PART, BUT IT MAY ALSO HAVE BEEN ONE OF THE FEW TRUTHS SPOKEN BY HOOVER REGARDING THE ASSASSINATION.*

CHAPTER 9: THE RETURN TO DALLAS

OCTOBER 3ᴿᴰ 1963

ACCORDING TO THE WARREN COMMISSION, **HARVEY**, ON TRANSPORTES DEL NORTE BUS #373, CROSSES INTO LAREDO, TEXAS FROM NUEVO LAREDO, MEXICO ABOUT 2:00 AM. HE LEAVES LAREDO ABOUT 3:00 AM AND CONTINUES TO SAN ANTONIO ARRIVING THERE AT 6:20 AM ON GREYHOUND BUS #1265. HE LEAVES SAN ANTONIO AT 7:10 AM ON BUS 1265. HOWEVER MEXICAN IMMIGRATION RECORDS STATE THAT "OSWALD" LEFT MEXICO BY AUTO. THIS WAS LIKELY **LEE'S** METHOD OF DEPARTING MEXICO AS IT WAS APPARENTLY HIS METHOD OF ENTERING MEXICO. **LEE** ALSO NOTED, UPON LEAVING MEXICO, THAT HIS DESTINATION WAS NEW ORLEANS, NOT DALLAS.

*ROGELIO GUEVAS AND RAMON GONZALES, THE DRIVERS OF THE BUS ON THE MEXICO CITY TO MONTERREY TRIP WERE NOT ABLE TO IDENTIFY **HARVEY** AS A PASSENGER ON THEIR BUS. RAUL TIJERNA, WHO SOLD "OSWALD" A TICKET IN LAREDO, DID NOT IDENTIFY **HARVEY** FROM PHOTOGRAPHS. THE BUS DRIVER FROM LAREDO TO SAN ANTONIO, J.C. ROBINSON, COULD NOT IDENTIFY THE PASSENGER AS **HARVEY**. BEN JULIAN, THE DRIVER OF THE SAN ANTONIO TO DALLAS LEG COULD NOT IDENTIFY **HARVEY** AS A PASSENGER EITHER.*

OCTOBER 3ᴿᴰ 1963

HARVEY ARRIVED IN DALLAS FROM HIS ALLEGED TRIP TO MEXICO AT 2:20 PM. AFTER CALLING THE PAINE RESIDENCE AND NOTIFYING MARINA AND RUTH PAINE OF HIS RETURN TO DALLAS, HE FILED A CHANGE OF ADDRESS WITH CLAIMS CLERK HENRY MCCLUSKEY AND ALSO REGISTERED FOR UNEMPLOYMENT WITH HARRY SANDERSON. DON BROOKS, A PLACEMENT INTERVIEWER WITH THE TEXAS EMPLOYMENT COMMISSION ARRANGES TWO JOB INTERVIEWS FOR **HARVEY**. HE IS INFORMED BY THE NEW ORLEANS OFFICE THAT **HARVEY** HAS LEFT NEW ORLEANS. **HARVEY** WOULD APPARENTLY SPEND THIS EVENING AT THE YMCA.

A PHONE CALL IS PLACED TO THE SOVIET EMBASSY IN BROKEN ENGLISH/SPANISH. THE CALLER CLAIMS TO BE "LEE HARVEY OSWALD." THE CALL IS PLACED AT 3:39 PM. **HARVEY** *IS IN DALLAS AT THE EMPLOYMENT COMMISSION OFFICE. IT IS UNLIKELY HOWEVER THAT THIS IMPOSTOR IS **LEE** AS **LEE** HAS APPARENTLY ALREADY RETURNED TO TEXAS.*

OCTOBER 3ᴿᴰ 1963

AN "OSWALD" WAS NOTED TO HAVE APPLIED FOR A JOB AT STATION KPOY IN ALICE SPRINGS, TEXAS ABOUT 6:00 PM. HE WAS TOLD TO RETURN THE NEXT DAY TO SPEAK WITH THE MANAGER. ALICE IS 400 MILES SOUTH OF DALLAS. **HARVEY** IS IN DALLAS. ALICE HOWEVER IS ONLY 90 MILES NORTH OF LAREDO. THIS IS LIKELY **LEE**.

A WAITRESS AT THE B.F. CAFÉ IN FREER, TEXAS, NOTED THAT AT ABOUT 7:00 PM, A MAN RESEMBLING **HARVEY**, A WOMAN IN HER EARLY 20'S, AND A CHILD ABOUT 2 YEARS OF AGE, VISITED HER CAFÉ. THE MAN RESEMBLING **HARVEY** ASKED ABOUT WORK IN THE FREER AREA. HE WAS REPORTEDLY DRIVING A GREY PLYMOUTH OR DODGE, EITHER A 1952 OR 1953 MODEL. THE WOMAN, ACCORDING TO THE WAITRESS, HAD SHOULDER LENGTH BLONDE HAIR AND WEIGHED ABOUT 110 POUNDS. THE MAN MAY HAVE RESEMBLED **HARVEY**, BUT THE WOMAN BORE LITTLE RESEMBLENCE TO MARINA WHO WAS 8 ½ MONTHS PREGNANT. ONCE AGAIN **HARVEY** IS IN DALLAS; **LEE** HOWEVER WOULD SPEND THE NIGHT IN ALICE AND IS LIKELY THE VISITOR TO THE CAFÉ.

OCTOBER 4ᵀᴴ 1963

ANOTHER "OSWALD" SIGHTING WAS NOTED IN ALICE. TWO MECHANICS AT HILL MACHINERY COMPANY NOTED A MAN WHO USED NAME "OSWALD" ON A JOB APPLICATION. THE "OSWALD" ALSO REFERENCED HIS MARINE CORP DUTY ON THE APPLICATION. LEO SEPULVEDA AND M.B. POPE DESCRIBED THE MAN AS BEING ABOUT 5'8" AND 150 POUNDS. THEY NOTED THAT HE DROVE AN OLD PLYMOUTH OR CHEVY

SEDAN. **HARVEY** WAS IN DALLAS AT THE TIME. ONCE AGAIN, THE "OSWALD" WAS LIKELY **LEE**.

OCTOBER 4TH 1963

HARVEY APPLIES FOR A JOB AT PADGETT PRINTING COMPANY, SEVERAL BLOCKS FROM THE PARADE ROUTE. HE DID NOT GET THE JOB. HE ALSO APPLIES FOR A JOB AS A PHOTOGRAPHER, FILING AN APPLICATION WITH THE JOBCO EMPLOYMENT AGENCY LOCATED IN THE ADOLPHUS HOTEL. AT THE END OF THE DAY, **HARVEY** HITCHHIKES TO RUTH PAINE'S HOME IN IRVING. HE WOULD STAY WITH THE PAINE'S THROUGH THE EVENING OF THE 6TH OF OCTOBER.

*PADGETT'S PLANT SUPERINTENDENT, THEODORE GANGEL, NOTED ON THE BACK OF **HARVEY'S** JOB APPLICATION: "BOB STOVALL DOES NOT RECOMMEND THIS MAN. HE WAS RELEASED BECAUSE OF HIS RECORD AS A TROUBLEMAKER, HAS COMMUNISTIC TENDENCIES." BOB STOVALL WAS ONE OF THE FOUNDERS OF JAGGERS-CHILES-STOVALL WHERE **HARVEY** WORKED FROM OCTOBER 1962 TO APRIL 1963. QUITE AN ODD COMMENT FROM A FIRM THAT DID CLASSIFIED MAP WORK FOR THE GOVERNMENT AND YET SAW FIT TO <u>HIRE</u> **HARVEY** DESPITE HIS "DEFECTOR" STATUS. STOVALL'S COMMENTS, REGARDLESS OF HIS INTENTIONS, WOULD REINFORCE THE PERSONA THE SET-UP CONSPIRATORS DESIRED FOR **HARVEY**.*

OCTOBER 4TH 1963

SONNY STEWART, THE MANAGER OF STATION KPOY IN ALICE SPRINGS, TEXAS WAS VISITED BY A "LEE OSWALD", HIS "WIFE" AND A BABY "JUNE" ABOUT 1:30 PM. THEY ARRIVED IN A 1953 MODEL CAR. ALICE SPRINGS IS 400 MILES FROM DALLAS. THIS "OSWALD" SAID HE HAD JUST COME FROM MEXICO AND WAS LOOKING FOR EMPLOYMENT. MR. STEWART SUGGESTED TO "OSWALD" THAT HE TRY STATION KBOP IN PLEASANTON, TEXAS. "OSWALD" APPARENTLY MADE THE TRIP AS HE VISITED THE STATION AND SPOKE WITH DR. BEN PARKER. WHEN TOLD THERE WERE NO OPENINGS FOR A RADIO ANNOUNCER, "OSWALD" THEN DROVE NORTHWARD TO DALLAS.

*THE WARREN COMMISSION MAINTAINS THAT **HARVEY** DID INDEED RETURN TO DALLAS ON THURSDAY AFTERNOON, OCTOBER 3RD. IF THIS IS INDEED THE CASE, THEN SOMEONE IS IMPERSONATING BOTH **HARVEY** <u>AND</u> MARINA IN AND AROUND ALICE, TEXAS ON OCTOBER 3RD AND 4TH.*

OCTOBER 4TH 1963

ABOUT 10:00 PM, ATTORNEY CARROLL JARNIGAN VISITED THE CAROUSEL CLUB. JARNIGAN LATER STATED TO THE DALLAS PD THAT RUBY AND "OSWALD" WERE CONVERSING IN AN ADJACENT BOOTH ON THAT DAY. ON DECEMBER 5TH, HE FOLLOWED UP HIS PREVIOUS STATEMENT VIA AN EIGHT PAGE SUMMARY OF HIS OBSERVATION OF "OSWALD" AND RUBY AT THE CLUB. THIS STATEMENT WAS FOR THE BENEFIT OF THE FBI. JARNIGAN WAS NOT CALLED BEFORE THE WARREN COMMISSION. **HARVEY** WAS AT THE PAINE'S RESIDENCE THAT EVENING. JARNIGAN LIKELY SAW **LEE** WHO HAD JUST RETURNED TO DALLAS. JARNIGAN NOTED THAT "OSWALD" STATED TO RUBY THAT HE HAD "JUST GOT IN FROM NEW ORLEANS." THIS WOULD MESH WITH THE NEW ORLEANS DESTINATION HE HAD NOTED ON HIS IMMIGRATION PAPERWORK UPON RETURNING FROM MEXICO.

*IT IS THIS SAME DATE THAT THE SHORT HAIRED, STOCKY "OSWALD" IS PHOTOGRAPED OUTSIDE THE SOVIET EMBASSY IN MEXICO CITY. IT WOULD BE THE 2ND TIME THAT HE IS PHOTOGRAPHED. WITH **LEE** HAVING RETURNED FROM MEXICO CITY AND NOW IN DALLAS AND **HARVEY** IN IRVING, ONE IS LEFT TO PONDER THE IDENTITY OF <u>THIS</u> "OSWALD."*

OCTOBER 5TH 1963

AN ARTICLE IN THE DALLAS MORNING NEWS AGAIN NOTES THE PRESIDENTIAL VISIT SCHEDULED FOR NOVEMBER.

OCTOBER 6TH 1963

MRS. LOWELL PENN OWNED LAND ON THE OUTSKIRTS OF DALLAS. SHE SAW "OSWALD" THAT DAY WITH 2 MEN, "ONE LATIN OR CUBAN" FIRING A RIFLE ON HER

PROPERTY. LATER, A CARTRIDGE FROM A 6.5 MANNLICHER WAS FOUND BUT THE FBI DETERMINED IT HAD <u>NOT</u> BEEN FIRED FROM THE GUN THAT **HARVEY** HAD ALLEGEDLY USED TO ASSASSINATE THE PRESIDENT. **HARVEY** SPENT THIS DAY AT THE PAINE RESIDENCE. THIS WAS LIKELY **LEE** AT THE PENN PROPERTY.

OCTOBER 7TH 1963

HARVEY RENTS A ROOM FROM MARY BLEDSOE AT 621 MARSALIS STREET UNDER HIS OWN NAME, L. H. OSWALD. THE RENT WAS $7 A WEEK. HE WOULD RETURN TO THE YMCA TO GATHER HIS OTHER BAG. LATER THAT AFTERNOON HE PHONES MARINA TELLING HER OF HIS NEWLY RENTED ROOM.

OCTOBER 7TH 1963

HARVEY'S "SHADOW", IDENTIFIED SET-UP CONSPIRATOR ROSCOE WHITE, JOINS THE DALLAS POLICE DEPARTMENT. THIS TAKES PLACE ONLY 4 DAYS AFTER **HARVEY** RETURNS TO DALLAS FROM NEW ORLEANS AFTER ALLEGEDLY TAKING A TRIP TO MEXICO CITY. WHITE, WHO JOURNEYED TO JAPAN ON THE USS BEXAR WITH **LEE**, ALSO RETURNED TO THE STATES THE SAME MONTH AS **LEE.**

ROSCOE WHITE'S POLICE PERSONNEL FILE CONTAINED VERY FEW CLUES AS TO EXACTLY WHAT HIS ASSIGNMENTS WERE OR TO WHAT DIVISION HE WAS ASSIGNED. HIS WIFE GENEVA WAS NOT AWARE OF HIS POLICE DEPARTMENT POSITION EITHER. WHITE WOULD NOT ATTEND THE POLICE ACADEMY UNTIL JANUARY 1964, OVER 3 MONTHS <u>AFTER</u> HE OFFICIALLY JOINS THE FORCE.

*WHITE WOULD STAY WITH THE DPD UNTIL OCTOBER 18TH, 1965. HIS FILE CARD IN THE PERSONNEL DEPARTMENT OF THE DPD LISTED <u>ONLY</u> HIS HIRE DATE AND THE DATE HE RESIGNED. THERE IS NO NOTATION OF <u>WHERE</u> HE WORKED OR <u>WHAT DIVISION</u> HE WAS ASSIGNED TO. HE DIED IN 1971 AT THE AGE OF 36 OF BURNS FROM AN EXPLOSION. HIS WIDOW, GENEVA, HAD BEEN A DANCER AT JACK RUBY'S CAROUSEL CLUB. IN 1975, GENEVA WHITE PRODUCED YET A 3RD PHOTO OF "OSWALD" IN THE NOW- FAMOUS BACKYARD POSE WITH THE RIFLE AND SIDEARM. THE DPD HAD CLAIMED IN NOVEMBER 1963 THAT ONLY <u>TWO</u> PHOTOS HAD BEEN FOUND. GENEVA WOULD ALSO PRODUCE AS PART OF HER LATE HUSBAND'S POSSESSIONS, A PICTURE OF **HARVEY'S** DEPARTMENT OF DEFENSE ID CARD. LATER, AFTER **HARVEY'S** ARREST IN DALLAS, WE WILL SEE THAT **HARVEY'S** POSSESSION OF THIS PARTICULAR TYPE OF DEPARTMENT OF DEFENSE I.D. CARD MAY HAVE BEEN AN INDICATOR THAT HE WAS INDEED A CIVILIAN ON ASSIGNMENT DURING HIS RUSSIAN "DEFECTION."*

OCTOBER 8TH 1963

HARVEY INTERVIEWS FOR A JOB WITH JAMES HUNTER AT SOLID STATE ELECTRONICS COMPANY. HE WAS INFORMED OF THE OPENING BY MR. R.L. ADAMS OF THE TEXAS EMPLOYMENT COMMISSION.

OCTOBER 8TH 1963

CIA MEXICO CITY STATION CHIEF WIN SCOTT SENDS A CABLE TO CIA LANGLEY SUMMARIZING A VISIT BY AN "OSWALD" TO MEXICO CITY. SCOTT REQUESTS A NAME TRACE. INCLUDED IN THE CABLE WAS A TELEPHONE TRANSCRIPT OF "OSWALD'S" CONVERSATIONS WITH THE SOVIET EMBASSY AND THE PHOTOGRAPH OF THE 35 YEAR OLD, BALDING, HEAVYSET, AMERICAN MALE WHO OBVIOUSLY WAS NOT **HARVEY** OR **LEE**.

*SCOTT DOES NOT HOWEVER CLAIM THAT THE MAN IN THE PHOTO IS **HARVEY**. MORE IMPORTANTLY, HE DOES NOT MENTION VISITS TO THE CUBAN EMBASSY BY THIS "OSWALD." EITHER THIS WAS AN INCREDIBLE OVERSIGHT BY A NORMALLY METICULOUS SCOTT, OR WAS HE NOT INFORMED OF THE CUBAN ASPECTS OF "OSWALDS" VISIT TO MEXICO CITY AS OF THIS DATE. I AM VERY MUCH INCLINED TO BELIEVE THAT SCOTT'S EXCLUSION OF "OSWALD'S" CUBAN ACTIVITIES WAS EITHER THE RESULT OF DAVID PHILLIPS' EXCLUSION OF THIS INFORMATION TO SCOTT, OR PHILLIPS' REQUEST THAT SCOTT NOT DOCUMENT THE CUBAN ASPECT IN THE CABLE TO CIA HEADQUARTERS.*

OCTOBER 9TH 1963
HARVEY APPLIES FOR A JOB AT BURTON-DIXIE VIA HIS REFERRAL BY R.L. ADAMS OF THE TEXAS EMPLOYMENT COMMISSION.

*PRIOR TO THIS DATE BUT AFTER **HARVEY'S** OCTOBER 31, 1959 EPISODE AT THE U.S. EMBASSY IN MOSCOW, A "FLASH" HAD BEEN ISSUED BY THE FBI REGARDING **HARVEY**. IN ESSENCE **HARVEY** WAS NOW ON THE FBI'S SECURITY WATCH LIST.*

*THE FBI'S SECURITY WATCH ON **HARVEY** WAS LIFTED ON OCTOBER 9TH, 1963. THIS IS ONLY 13 DAYS AFTER THE DALLAS MORNING NEWS ANNOUNCED THE PRESIDENT'S NOVEMBER VISIT AND ONLY 6 DAYS AFTER "OSWALD" RETURNED FROM MEXICO CITY. MORE IMPORTANTLY, THE LIFTED SECURITY WATCH IS 1 DAY PRIOR TO THE CIA'S NOTIFYING THE FBI THAT "OSWALD" HAD BEEN IN MEXICO CITY AND THAT HE HAD CONTACTED THE SOVIET AND CUBAN EMBASSIES.*

*IT IS APPARENT THAT SOMEONE IS NOT ONLY INTERESTED IN KEEPING WIN SCOTT OUT OF THE "OSWALD"/MEXICO CITY LOOP, BUT PERHAPS MORE INTERESTED IN MINIMIZING OR ELIMINATING THE POSSIBILITY OF FBI INTRUSION ON WHAT WOULD TAKE PLACE ON NOVEMBER 22ND. IN ESSENCE, IT APPEARS THAT THE CIA (OR AT A MINIMUM HUNT AND PHILLIPS) WAS HOPEFULL THAT THE FBI WOULD CEASE IT'S MONITORING OF **HARVEY** BY VIRTUE OF THE IMPLICATION THAT **HARVEY** WAS WORKING UNDERCOVER FOR THE AGENCY IN MEXICO CITY. THE LIKELY PERPETRATOR OF THE MANIPULATION WOULD BE DAVID ATLEE PHILLIPS.*

OCTOBER 10TH 1963
HARVEY VISITS THE JOBCO EMPLOYMENT AGENCY IN DALLAS. HE LISTS GEORGE DE MOHRENSCHILDT AS "CLOSEST FRIEND" ON THE AGENCY FORMS. HE WAS LATER TO APPLY FOR A JOB AT DeVILBISS COMPANY.

OCTOBER 10TH 1963
A REPLY TO WIN SCOTT'S NAME TRACE REQUEST ON A LEE OSWALD IS RECEIVED FROM CIA HEADQUARTERS IN LANGLEY. THE REPLY WAS FROM SAM KARAMESSINES, AN ASSISTANT TO CIA DIRECTOR RICHARD HELMS. KARAMMESSINES CLAIMS THAT THE LATEST INFORMATION CIA HEADQUARTERS HAD WAS INFORMATION IT HAD RECEIVED FROM THE STATE DEPARTMENT IN MAY 1962 WHEN **HARVEY** WAS STILL IN RUSSIA. THIS WAS SIMPLY NOT TRUE. CIA HEADQUARTERS HAD 2 REPORTS FROM THE FBI; ONE NOTING **HARVEY'S** LEFTIST ACTIVTIES IN DALLAS DATED 24 SEPTEMBER 1963, AND ANOTHER ON HIS FPFC ACTIVITIES AND HIS RUN IN WITH THE DRE/CARLOS BRINGUIER IN NEW ORLEANS DATED OCTOBER 4TH, 1963. THE "LATEST" INFORMATION CIA HEADQUARTERS HAD ON **HARVEY** WAS NOT 16 MONTHS OLD AS IT STATED TO SCOTT, BUT ONLY A WEEK OLD. SCOTT WAS DECEIVED. THIS CABLE FROM HEADQUARTERS TENDS TO SUPPORT THE NOTION THAT SCOTT WAS DENIED INFORMATION ON **HARVEY** BY BOTH PHILLIPS IN MEXICO CITY AND CIA HEADQUARTERS IN LANGLEY.

OCTOBER 10TH 1963
WILLIAM SOMERSETT, A MIAMI POLICE/FBI INFORMANT WAS VISITED BY JOSEPH MILTEER IN MIAMI. A RIGHT-WING EXTREMIST FROM QUITMAN, GEORGIA, MILTEER WAS A MEMBER OF THE NATIONAL STATES RIGHT PARTY, THE CONGRESS OF FREEDOM, THE WHITE CITIZENS COUNCIL, AND THE CONSTITUTION PARTY.

OCTOBER 11TH 1963
A CHANGE OF ADDRESS CARD WAS SENT TO THE NEW ORLEANS POST OFFICE. IT WAS POSTMARKED IN NEW ORLEANS ON OCTOBER 11TH, 1963.

*KEEP IN MIND THAT **HARVEY** HAD ALREADY FILLED OUT A CHANGE OF ADDRESS CARD IN NEW ORLEANS IN LATE SEPTEMBER PRIOR TO HIS DEPARTURE FOR HIS ALLEGED MEXICO CITY TRIP. NOT ONLY WOULD HE NOT NEED TO FILLOUT A 2ND CARD, BUT BY OCTOBER 11TH, THE POSTMARK DATE, **HARVEY** HAD ALREADY RETURNED TO DALLAS HAVING ARRIVED ON OCTOBER 3RD. SOMEONE ELSE MUST HAVE SIGNED AND MAILED THE 2ND*

CARD. IN HIS WARREN COMMISSION TESTIMONY, POSTAL INSPECTOR HARRY HOLMES NOTED THAT THIS PARTICULAR CARD WAS NOT SIGNED BY **HARVEY**. COMMISSION LAWYER WESLEY LEIBLER NOTICED THIS DISCREPANCY AS WELL. HE NOTED "MY PROBLEM IS THAT OSWALD **(HARVEY)** WAS NOT IN NEW ORLEANS ON OCTOBER 11TH, HE WAS IN DALLAS." ONCE AGAIN, EVIDENCE OF TWO "OSWALDS." JIM GARRISON'S COMMENT ON THIS MATTER SUMS UP THE OBVIOUS: "WHO SAYS THAT LONE ASSASSINS HAVE NO FRIENDS?"

OCTOBER 11TH TO OCTOBER 18TH 1963

DAVID FERRIE VISITS GUATAMALA ON BEHALF OF CARLOS MARCELLO IN REGARDS TO MARCELLO'S FRAUDULENT GUATAMALAN BIRTH CERTIFICATE AND PASSPORT. MARCELLO'S DEPORTATION TRIAL IS SCHEDULED FOR NOVEMBER 1ST.

OCTOBER 12TH 1963

AFTER ONLY 6 DAYS, **HARVEY** IS EVICTED FROM HIS ROOMING HOUSE ON MARSALIS STREET BY HIS LANDLADY MARY BLEDSOE.

*A POLICE REPORT DATED 10/11/63 AT 11:30 PM LISTED AS THE "COMPLAINANT" A MARY BLEDSOE, 621 NORTH MARSALIS STREET. THE OFFENSE WAS "DISTURBING THE PEACE." THE OFFICERS WRITING THE REPORT WERE J.C.WHITE AND B. W. HARGIS. THE NAMES ON THE REPORT WERE J. R. RUBENSTEIN OF 1303 ½ COMMERCE AND ALEK HIDELL OF 621 NORTH MARSALIS. IF THIS WERE INDEED JACK RUBY, WHY WOULD HE HAVE SHOWN AN I.D. OR PERHAPS TOLD THE OFFICERS HE WAS J.R. RUBENSTEIN? WOULD NOT ONE OF THE OFFICERS HAVE RECOGNIZED RUBY? IF THIS WERE INDEED **HARVEY**, WHY GIVE THE NAME ALEK HIDELL OR SHOW AN I.D. WITH THIS NAME WHEN HE HAD INDEED RENTED THE ROOM UNDER THE NAME L. H. OSWALD? **HARVEY** NEVER USED THE NAME "HIDELL" AS AN ALIAS. BUT, WE HAVE ONLY TWO CHOICES: EITHER THE TWO MEN WERE INDEED **HARVEY** AND JACK RUBY AND GAVE THE OFFICERS FALSE NAMES IN DEFERENCE TO THE UPCOMING "ASSIGNMENT" FOR **HARVEY**, OR BOTH MEN WERE IMPOSTERS AND USED "RUBENSTEIN", RUBY'S REAL NAME, AND "HIDELL" IN AN EFFORT TO SHOW THAT RUBY AND **HARVEY**, VIA THE "HIDELL" MONIKER WERE ACQUAINTED. NORMALLY I COULD ATTACH SOME SIGNIFICANCE TO AN EPISODE OF THIS NATURE THAT WOULD INDEED BENEFIT THE SET-UP CONSPIRATORS. IN THIS INSTANCE I CANNOT. I DO HOWEVER FEEL THAT THE TWO MEN INVOLVED WERE JACK RUBY AND **LEE**. IT WAS **LEE** WHO WAS INDEED ALEK HIDELL.*

OCTOBER 14TH 1963

AN **"OSWALD"** APPLIES FOR A JOB AT WERNER LUMBER COMPANY ON INWOOD ROAD. HE TOLD THE PERSONNEL MANAGER THAT HE HAD SERVED 2 TERMS IN THE MARINES WITH HIS LAST TERM ENDING SEPTEMBER 1963. HE ALSO STATED THAT HE HAD A CAR.

HARVEY WAS DISCHARGED FROM THE MARINES ON SEPTEMBER 11TH, 1959. HE WAS NOT KNOWN TO DRIVE, AND HE DID NOT OWN A CAR OR POSSESS A DRIVERS LICENSE. IT IS INTERESTING TO NOTE THAT INWOOD ROAD IS THE DIRECT ROUTE FROM THE TRADEMART TO THE AIRPORT. WAS THIS WAS TO BE AN ALTERNATIVE SITE FOR THE ASSASSINATION IF BY CHANCE HARVEY DID NOT FIND EMPLOYMENT AT THE TSBD? OR, WAS IT SIMPLY TO PORTRAY HARVEY AS SEEKING TO FIND EMPLOYMENT AT SITES ALONG THE ROUTE THE PRESIDENT WOULD TRAVEL THAT DAY? I AM VERY MUCH INCLINED TO BELIEVE THAT THIS VISIT WAS NOT BY HARVEY, BUT BY LEE.

*EARLENE ROBERTS WAS THE HOUSEKKEEPER FOR GLADYS JOHNSON AT 1026 NORTH BECKLEY. ROBERTS' SISTER, BERTHA CHEEK WAS A REAL ESTATE AGENT. CHEEK WAS A FRIEND OF JACK RUBY WHO HAD AT ONE POINT OFFERED HER AN OPPORTUNITY TO BECOME A CO-OWNER OF THE CAROUSEL CLUB. ONE HAS TO CONSIDER THE POSSIBILITY THAT IT WAS RUBY, THROUGH REAL ESTATE AGENT CHEEKS, WHO HELPED **HARVEY** FIND A NEW RESIDENCE AFTER HE WAS EVICTED FROM HIS MARSALIS STREET RESIDENCE FOLLOWING AN INCIDENT POSSIBLY INCITED BY RUBY AND **LEE**/ALEK HIDELL.*

OCTOBER 14TH 1963

RUTH PAINE LEARNS OF POSSIBLE WORK AT THE TSBD FROM A NEIGHBOR, LINNIE MAE RANDLE, WHOSE BROTHER, BUELL WESLEY FRAZIER, IS EMPLOYED THERE. FRAZIER HAD BEEN HIRED ON SEPTEMBER 13TH. MRS. PAINE CALLS ROY TRULY AT THE TSBD TO ARRANGE FOR AN INTERVIEW FOR **HARVEY**. **HARVEY** MOVES YET AGAIN ON THIS DATE. HE NOW RENTS A ROOM FROM GLADYS JOHNSON AT 1026 NORTH BECKLEY UNDER THE NAME "O.H. LEE." HIS RENT IS $5 A WEEK.

AMONG ITEMS RECOVERED FROM **HARVEY'S** ROOM ON NOVEMBER 22ND WAS A RUSSIAN MADE SHORTWAVE RADIO. HE APPARENTLY LISTENED EACH EVENING ACCORDING TO GLADYS JOHNSON'S HUSBAND. THE RADIO HOWEVER WAS NOT ASSIGNED AN EXHBIT NUMBER BY THE WARREN COMMISSION. THIS AMAZING "OVERSIGHT" IS STRIKINGLY SIMILAR TO THE FBI'S LATER EFFORTS TO CHANGE **HARVEY'S** MINOX CAMERA TO A LIGHT METER.

KEEP IN MIND THAT THE SUCCESS OF THE SET-UP OF **HARVEY** AS THE ASSASSIN WAS NOT CONTINGENT ON HIS BEING EMPLOYED AT THE TSBD. AN "ASSASSIN" WHO SIMPLY HAD ACCESS TO AND FAMILIARITY WITH A MOSTLY EMPTY BUILDING ON THE PARADE ROUTE THAT HE COULD HAVE "SCOUTED" WHILE BEING SHOWN AROUND DURING AN INTERVIEW, COMBINED WITH A RIFLE FOUND THERE THAT COULD BE TRACED VIA THE "HIDELL" MONIKER TO **HARVEY'S** P.O. BOX MAY HAVE BEEN ENOUGH TO INCRIMINATE **HARVEY**. HIS WORKING THERE MAY HAVE SIMPLY BEEN A STROKE OF GOOD FORTUNE FOR THOSE PLOTTING HIS SET-UP. IN FACT, ON THE AFTERNOON OF THE ASSASSINATION, RUTH PAINE COMMENTED THAT SHE DIDN'T KNOW THE TSBD OCCUPIED A BUILDING ON ELM STREET. SHE THOUGHT **HARVEY** WORKED IN THE WAREHOUSE, LOCATED AT ANOTHER SITE ON MCKINNEY AVENUE 2-3 BLOCKS BEYOND THE RAILROAD YARDS.

OCTOBER 15TH 1963

HARVEY FILLS OUT AN APPLICATION AND IS INTERVIEWED FOR A TEMPORARY JOB AT THE TSBD BY ROY TRULY.

THIS VERY SAME DAY, R. L. ADAMS OF THE TEXAS EMPLOYMENT COMMISSION CALLED THE PAINE RESIDENCE REGARDING THE POSSIBILITY OF **HARVEY** OBTAINING A PERMANENT JOB AT TRANS TEXAS AIRWAYS. THE JOB WOULD PAY $310 PER MONTH, $100 MORE THAN THE TEMPORARY TSBD JOB. ADAMS NOT ONLY REQUESTED THAT **HARVEY** CONTACT HIM, BUT ALSO CALLED AGAIN THE NEXT MORNING AND WAS TOLD THAT **HARVEY** HAD ACCEPTED A JOB AT THE TSBD. ALTHOUGH ADAMS DID NOT STATE WHO SPECIFICALLY HE TALKED TO AT THE TIME OF HIS TWO CALLS, ONE WOULD HAVE TO SUSPECT THAT IT WAS RUTH PAINE. SHE WAS SEPARATED FROM HER HUSBAND AT THE TIME, AND IT IS UNLIKELY THAT MARINA WOULD ANSWER THE PHONE IF RUTH PAINE WERE PRESENT. IF MARINA DID INDEED TAKE THE CALLS, IT IS LIKELY THAT ADAMS WOULD HAVE RECALLED HER ACCENT.

WHEN RUTH PAINE TESTIFIED TO THE W.C. SHE WAS QUESTIONED 4 DISTINCT TIMES REGARDING THE 2 PHONE CALLS TO HER RESIDENCE ABOUT THE TRANS TEXAS AIRWAYS JOB. SHE DENIED ANY KNOWLEDGE OF THE CALLS INITIALLY. BY THE 4TH QUERY, SHE FINALLY CLAIMED SHE DID "RECALL SOME REFERENCE OF THAT SORT."

OCTOBER 16TH 1963

HARVEY STARTS WORK AT THE TSBD. HIS HOURS WOULD BE 8:00 AM TO 4:45 PM AT A SALARY OF $1.25 AN HOUR. HIS LUNCH BREAK IS FROM 12:00 NOON TO 12:45 PM.

MANY BELIEVE THAT RUTH AND MICHAEL PAINE WERE INVOLVED IN THE SET-UP OF **HARVEY** BY VIRTUE OF RUTH'S ASSISTANCE IN OBTAINING EMPLOYMENT FOR HIM AT THE TSBD. IT IS INDEED DIFFICULT TO REFUTE MICHAEL PAINE'S TIES TO THE INTELLIGENCE COMMUNITY. AS AN ENGINEER HE DID HIGHLY CLASSIFIED WORK FOR BELL HELICOPTER. RUTH'S FATHER AND BROTHER-IN-LAW BOTH WORKED FOR THE AGENCY FOR INTERNATIONAL DEVELOPMENT; BASICALLY A CIA COVER ORGANIZATION. RUTH'S SISTER SYLVIA HOKE WAS A STAFF PSYCHOLOGIST FOR THE CIA. SYLVIA'S HUSBAND, JOHN HOKE

*BECAME A CIA CONTACT EMPLOYEE IN AUGUST OF 1963. BUT, I AM MUCH MORE INCLINED TO BELIEVE THAT RUTH AT LEAST WAS GENUINELY INTERESTED IN **HARVEY'S** WELFARE AS WELL AS THE WELFARE OF HIS GROWING FAMILY. SHE, ALONG WITH GEORGE DEMOHRENSCHILDT, WERE WHAT ONE MIGHT CONSIDER THE CIA'S "SUPPORT GROUP" IN THEIR EFFORTS TO HELP **HARVEY** ACCLIMATE HIMSELF TO "CIVILIAN" LIFE AFTER HIS ASSIGNMENT IN RUSSIA. IT IS QUITE LIKELY THAT DEMOHRENSCHILDT AND PERHAPS RUTH PAINE WERE BEING USED TO FACILITATE THE SET-UP OF **HARVEY**. I AM HOWEVER SOMEWHAT MORE SUSPICIOUS OF MICHAEL PAINE'S INVOLVEMENT WITH **HARVEY**.*

OCTOBER 16th 1963

MEXICO CITY STATION CHIEF WIN SCOTT TRIES YET AGAIN TO GATHER MORE INFORMATION ON **HARVEY** FROM CIA HEADQUARTERS IN LANGLEY. HE REQUESTS A PHOTO OF **HARVEY**. BY THIS TIME, SCOTT HAD LEARNED OF THE CUBAN EMBASSY VISIT BY AN "OSWALD." HE DID NOT HOWEVER LEARN THIS FROM PHILLIPS BUT FROM HIS PERSONAL TRANSLATOR. HE NEVER RECEIVED THE REQUESTED PHOTO OF **HARVEY**.

*IT SEEMS THAT EVERY EFFORT WAS BEING MADE BY PHILLIPS IN MEXICO CITY AND COUNTERINTELLIGENCE COHORTS AT LANGLEY TO KEEP WIN SCOTT COMPLETELY IN THE DARK NOT ONLY ABOUT **HARVEY**, WHO HAD <u>NOT</u> VISITED MEXICO CITY, BUT ALSO ABOUT **LEE** WHO HAD.*

OCTOBER 18TH 1963

HARVEY VISITS MARINA COURTESY OF A RIDE FROM BUELL FRAZIER. AWAITING **HARVEY** IS A SURPRISE BIRTHDAY PARTY. HE WOULD BE 24 YEARS OLD.

OCTOBER 18TH-20TH 1963

JOSEPH MILTEER, ALONG WITH A LEE MCCLOUD AND EARL LINDER, MET FBI INFORMANT SOMERSETT AT THE MAROTT HOTEL IN INDIANAPOLIS, INDIANA. THE MEN WERE ATTENDING A NATIONAL CONVENTION OF THE CONSTITUTION PARTY. SOMERSETT NOTED THAT THERE WAS A DISCUSSION OF AN UPCOMING PLAN TO KILL THE PRESIDENT. PLAN "A" WAS TO INCLUDE AN ATTEMPT IN PALM BEACH. PLAN "B" WAS TO INCLUDE AN ATTEMPT IN WASHINGTON, D.C.

OCTOBER 20TH 1963

MARINA GIVES BIRTH TO HER SECOND DAUGHTER, AUDREY MARINA RACHEL OSWALD, AT PARKLAND HOSPITAL.

OCTOBER 21ST 1963

HARVEY VISITS MARINA, JUNE, AND HIS NEW DAUGHTER, RACHEL.

OCTOBER 22ND 1963

MARINA IS RELEASED FROM THE HOSPTAL AND RETURNS TO THE PAINE'S RESIDENCE.

OCTOBER 23RD 1963

HARVEY ATTENDS A "U.S. DAY" RALLY AT THE DALLAS MEMORIAL AUDITORIUM WHERE THE GUEST SPEAKER IS GENERAL EDWIN WALKER.

*ONCE AGAIN **HARVEY** EXHIBITS THE SAME POLITICAL EXTREMISM THAT HE DISPLAYED WITH HIS PRO AND ANTI-CASTRO POSTURING IN NEW ORLEANS.*

OCTOBER 25TH 1963

HARVEY, AT THE INVITATION OF MICHAEL PAINE, ATTENDS A LOCAL MEETING OF THE ACLU AT SOUTHERN METHODIST UNIVERSITY.

***HARVEY** GAVE A SHORT SPEECH AT THE MEETING. ON THE RIDE HOME WITH PAINE, HE NOTED THAT HE WOULD NOT JOIN THE ACLU.*

OCTOBER 25TH 1963

WHILE **HARVEY** IS IN DALLAS, **LEE** IS INQUIRING ABOUT AN APARTMENT IN BATON ROUGE. MRS. ALDEANE MAGEE, WHO HAD A GARAGE APARTMENT FOR RENT, MET WITH A MAN WHO INTRODUCED HIMSELF AS HARVEY **LEE** OSWALD. **LEE** WAS ACCOMPANIED BY A WOMAN WHO WAS PREGNANT. BUT MARINA OSWALD, **HARVEY'S** WIFE, HAD GIVEN BIRTH TO HER 2ND DAUGHTER 5 DAYS EARLIER.

OCTOBER 26TH 1963

LEE VISITS THE SPORTS DROME RIFLE RANGE IN DALLAS. MALCOM PRICE, WHO WORKED AT THE RANGE, WAS ASKED BY **LEE** TO RANGE SIGHT A RIFLE. PRICE FIRED THE RIFLE PRIOR TO TURNING THE RIFLE OVER TO **LEE** WHO THEN TOOK 3 SHOTS. **LEE** THEN PICKED UP THE 3 EMPTY SHELL CASINGS AND DEPARTED WITH THE RIFLE. ONE HAS TO WONDER IF THESE WERE THE SHELL CASINGS LATER FOUND IN THE TSBD.

OCTOBER 29TH 1963

JERRY BRUNO, JFK'S PERSONAL ADVANCEMAN, FLEW TO DALLAS TO MEET WITH GOVENOR CONNALLY TO DISCUSS DETAILS OF THE UPCOMING PRESIDENTIAL TRIP. THEY ARGUED STRONGLY ABOUT THE PARADE ROUTE AND THE LUNCHEON SITE. BRUNO FELT THAT THE ROUTE, UNLIKE THE <u>TRADITIONAL</u> PARADE ROUTE WHICH HAD BEEN USED <u>SINCE 1936</u>, WOULD SLOW THE MOTORCADE TO SUCH SPEEDS THAT IT COULD ENDANGER THE SAFETY OF THE PRESIDENT. AS THE ARGUMENT CONCLUDED, BRUNO STATED THAT CONNALLY GOT ON THE PHONE APPARENTLY IN DISCUSSION WITH THE WHITE HOUSE. BRUNO NOTED THAT CONNALLY STATED TO HIM THAT THE WHITE HOUSE AGREED WITH <u>HIS</u> MOTORCADE ROUTE AND THE LUNCHEON SITE. BRUNO WOULD NOTE <u>AFTER</u> THE ASSASSINATION THAT CONNALLY HAD DECEIVED HIM; THE WHITE HOUSE HAD <u>NOT</u> AGREED TO CONNALLY'S PLAN AT ALL. BRUNO WOULD ALSO NOTE THAT IN HIS 3 YEARS AS ADVANCE MAN THAT THERE HAD <u>NEVER</u> BEEN ANOTHER OCCASION WHERE THE LOCAL PLANNING PARTY DID NOT ACCEPT HIS CONCERNS FOR THE PRESIDENT'S SAFETY.

ONE MAY BE WILLING TO ACCEPT THE GOVENOR'S CONCERNS OVER <u>WHERE</u> THE LUNCHEON WAS HELD, BUT I FIND IT EXTREMELY UNUSUAL AND DISCONCERTING THAT THE GOVENOR WOULD NOT ONLY ARGUE AGAINST A PARADE ROUTE THAT HAD TRADITIONALLY BEEN USED IN DALLAS FOR <u>27 YEARS</u> , BUT ALSO MAKE WHAT WAS APPARENTLY A FRAUDULENT PHONE CALL TO THE WHITE HOUSE.

*CONNALLY'S NICKNAME WAS "LBJ." IT DID HOWEVER STAND FOR "LYNDON'S BOY JOHN." CONNALLY'S INSISTANCE ON THE TRADEMART CEMENTED THE ROUTE OF THE MOTORCADE. THE ROUTE OF THE MOTORCADE CEMENTED THE FACT THAT THE PRESIDENT WOULD PASS DIRECTLY IN FRONT OT THE TSBD. BUT I FEEL THAT THERE IS ALSO AN ADDED SIGNIFICANCE TO HAVING THE LUNCHEON AT THE TRADE- MART. THERE WERE TWO SECURITY ISSUES REGARDING THE TRADEMART. ONE WAS THE NUMEROUS ENTRANCES/EXITS AND THE SECOND WAS THE EXTENSIVE "CAT WALK" ABOVE THE TRADEMART FLOOR. SINCE EARLIER ATTEMPTS TO MURDER THE PRESIDENT WERE THWARTED IN CHICAGO AND TAMPA, DALLAS WOULD HAVE TO BE A SUCCESS. IF THE ASSASSINATION IN DEALEY PLAZA HAD TO BE ABORTED, THE TRADEMART COULD AND WOULD BE PLAN B. IT WOULD HAVE HOWEVER NECESSITATED ANOTHER "PATSY"OR POSSIBLY FINDING EMPLOYMENT FOR **HARVEY** AT THE TRADEMART.*

OCTOBER 29TH 1963

AGENT HOSTY INTERVIEWS A NEIGHBOR OF THE PAINES, DOROTHY ROBERTS.

OCTOBER 30TH to NOVEMBER 1st 1963

DAVID FERRIE ONCE AGAIN VISITS GUATAMALA ON BEHALF OF CARLOS MARCELLO.

OCTOBER 31ST1963

AN "OSWALD" APPLIES FOR A JOB AT THE STATLER HILTON IN DOWNTOWN DALLAS.

173

THE APPLICATION NOTED THAT APPLICANT, "OSWALD" WAS MARRIED, HAD 2 CHILDREN, AND SPOKE RUSSIAN. ONCE AGAIN, IT IS LIKELY **LEE** AT THE HILTON AS **HARVEY** HAD BEEN HIRED BY THE TSBD ON OCTOBER 16TH AND WAS AT WORK THAT DAY: YET ANOTHER "TIMING" ERROR BY LOCAL SET-UP CONSPIRATORS.

NOVEMBER 1ST 1963
AN FBI REPORT STATES THAT **HARVEY** CASHED A CHECK FOR $33 AT AN A&P GROCERY STORE IN IRVING THE EVENING OF OCTOBER 31ST.

NOVEMBER 1ST 1963
HARVEY RENTS P.O. BOX 6225 IN DALLAS ON THIS DATE UNDER HIS NAME. HE RENTED THE BOX FOR 2 MONTHS AT $1.50 A MONTH. IT WAS ALLEGED THAT LISTED UNDER "NAME OF FIRM OR CORPORATION" TO BE USING THE BOX WERE THE FPFC AND THE ACLU. **HARVEY**, IN SPITE OF WHAT HE HAD TOLD MICHAEL PAINE ON OCTOBER 25TH, SENDS IN HIS APPLICATION FOR MEMBERSHIP TO THE ACLU. RUTH PAINE IS VISITED BY FBI AGENT JAMES HOSTY. DURING THE VISIT, MARINA, WHO IS STAYING WITH PAINE, ASKS HOSTY NOT TO BOTHER **HARVEY** AT WORK SINCE HE HAD TROUBLE KEEPING JOBS AND THOUGHT HE LOST THEM "BECAUSE THE FBI IS INTERESTED IN HIM."

MICHAEL PAINE WOULD LATER NOTE THAT HE THOUGHT **HARVEY** JOINED THE ACLU BECAUSE HE THOUGHT IT WOULD PROVIDE FREE LEGAL REPRESENTATION. **HARVEY** MAY HAVE CONSIDERED THAT HIS UPCOMING "ASSIGNMENT", IF NOT SUCCESSFUL, WOULD INDEED REQUIRE LEGAL COUNSEL PARTICULARLY IF HE WERE CAPTURED.

ANOTHER POSSIBILITY, PERHAPS EVEN MORE PLAUSIBLE, IS THAT THE ACLU WAS ENCOURAGED BY BANISTER IN HIS CONTINUED EFFORT TO USE **HARVEY'S** "COMMUNIST" PERSONA TO PAINT THE ACLU AS NOT JUST A PRO-INTEGRATION ORGANIZATION BUT ONE THAT ALSO OPENLY ENTERTAINED "COMMUNIST" MEMBERS.

IT IS INTERESTING TO COMPARE JUST WHO **HARVEY** ALLEGEDLY LISTED AS "AUTHORIZED TO RECEIVE MAIL" ON HIS <u>FIRST</u> DALLAS POST OFFICE BOX OPENED ON OCTOBER 9TH 1962, COMPARED TO HIS <u>LAST</u> DALLAS POST OFFICE BOX ON NOVEMBER 1ST, 1963. THE <u>FIRST</u> BOX ALLEGEDLY LISTED THE FPFC ORGANIZATION <u>AND</u> A "HIDELL." KEEP IN MIND THAT BOTH THE HANDGUN IN **HARVEY'S** POSSESSION UPON HIS ARREST AND THE ALLEGED RIFLE USED IN THE ASSASSINATION WERE ORDERED BY A "HIDELL." WHEN **HARVEY** RETURNS TO DALLAS ON OCTOBER 3RD, 1963, HE LATER, ON NOVEMBER 1ST OPENS HIS <u>SECOND</u> DALLAS POST OFFICE BOX. HOWEVER LISTED ON <u>THIS</u> BOX AS "NAME OF FIRM OR CORPORATION" TO BE USING THE BOX HE ALLEGEDLY LISTS THE FPFC ORGANIZATION AND THE ACLU. THERE IS NO INCLUSION OF "HIDELL." WITH THE INCRIMINATING FIREARMS ALREADY ORDERED BY THE SET-UP CONSPIRATORS, MOST LIKELY **LEE**, UNDER THE GUISE OF A "HIDELL" IN JANUARY AND MARCH 1963, THE SET-UP CONSPIRATORS APPARENTLY SAW NO NEED TO LIST "HIDELL" AS A RECIPIENT OF MAIL ON <u>THIS</u> BOX. BUT, PERHAPS EVEN MORE INTERESTING IS THE <u>NEW</u> INCLUSION OF THE ACLU. IT IS INTERESTING TO NOTE THAT IT WAS RUTH PAINE'S ESTRANGED HUSBAND MICHAEL WHO, ON OCTOBER 25TH, INVITED **HARVEY** TO AN ACLU MEETING. WE WILL SEE LATER THAT IT IS INDEED THE ACLU WHO **HARVEY** WILL SEEK FOR LEGAL COUNSEL ON NOVEMBER 22ND AFTER HE IS UNABLE TO CONTACT A JOHN ABT.

THE INCLUSION OF THE ACLU AS A RECIPIENT OF MAIL AT THIS NEW DALLAS POST OFFICE BOX MAY HOWEVER HAVE BEEN SOLELY FOR THE PURPOSE OF FRAUDENTLY IMPRESSING UPON **HARVEY** THAT WITH THE "CARCINOGENS TO CUBA PROJECT" THERE WOULD CERTAINLY BE SOME RISK IN HIM BEING DETAINED BY AUTHORITIES ENROUTE TO CUBA. IF SO, HE WOULD INDEED NEED LEGAL COUNSEL FROM THE ACLU AS THE INTELLIGENCE COMMUNITY WOULD NOT BE ABLE TO RENDER ASSISTANCE. ONE DOES INDEED HAVE TO CONSIDER WHETHER HUNT AND/OR PHILLIPS <u>DIRECTLY</u> IMPRESSED UPON **HARVEY** THE NEED FOR THE ACLU ATTACHMENT TO HIS NEW P.O. BOX OR UTILIZED THE SERVICES OF MICHAEL PAINE. THIS BEING SAID, ONE HAS TO DECIDE WHETHER MICHAEL PAINE WAS A

WILLING, LOW-LEVEL PARTICIPANT IN THE SET-UP OF **HARVEY**, OR MERELY A CONDUIT FOR THE EFFORTS OF HUNT/PHILLIPS. THE RESEARCH COMMUNITY IS SOMEWHAT DIVIDED ON THIS POINT.

THE POST OFFICE HOWEVER ONCE AGAIN PREVENTS US FROM DETERMINING IF THERE WERE INDEED OTHERS WITH ACCESS TO THIS, **HARVEY'S** LAST P. O. BOX. AS WAS THE CASE IN HIS FIRST DALLAS P.O. BOX, THE ONE TO WHICH THE RIFLE WAS DELIVERED, THE POST OFFICE HAD AGAIN "LOST" THE PORTION OF THE APPLICATION AUTHORIZING "OTHER" PERSONS TO RECEIVE MAIL AT THAT PARTICULAR BOX. IF, IN BOTH INSTANCES, CIA/FBI CONTACTS HAD BEEN LISTED UNDER THE "OTHERS" PORTION OF THE APPLICATION, IT WOULD HAVE INDEED BEEN "PRUDENT" FOR THE POST OFFICE TO "LOSE" THOSE PORTIONS AT THE REQUEST OF THOSE AGENCIES TO AVOID ACKNOWLEDGEMENT OF THE FACT THAT **HARVEY** HAD INDEED BEEN AN INTELLIGENCE INFORMANT. PERHAPS EVEN MORE IMPORTANTLY, HAD ROSCOE WHITE'S NAME BEEN LISTED OR EVEN AN ALIAS USED BY SET-UP CONSPIRATOR WHITE ON THE FIRST POST OFFICE BOX AS "OTHER" IN REGARDS TO RECEIVING MAIL, IT WOULD HAVE BEEN A SIMPLE TASK FOR WHITE TO ORDER THE WEAPONS AND RETRIEVE THEM FROM THE POST OFFICE WITHOUT THE KNOWLEDGE OF **HARVEY**. **LEE** HOWEVER ALSO HAD ANOTHER OPTION. HE COULD HAVE SIMPLY ORDERED THE WEAPONS AS "HIDELL" AND RETRIEVED THEM BY SHOWING AN I.D. IDENTIFYING HIMSELF AS "HIDELL." I AM INCLINED TO BELIEVE THIS WAS THE METHOD CHOSEN BY **LEE** IN REGARDS TO THE RIFLE/HANDGUN AT THE FIRST DALLAS P.O. BOX, THUS NEGATING THE NECESSITY TO INCLUDE "HIDELL" ON THE SECOND DALLAS P.O. BOX. ONCE AGAIN, ARMSTRONG CONTENDS THAT IT IS **LEE** WHO IS "HIDELL." I AM INCLINED TO AGREE.

THE RECORD KEEPERS AT KLEIN'S SPORTING GOODS IN CHICAGO WOULD FARE FAR BETTER THAN THE POSTAL SERVICE IN THEIR ABILITY TO RETAIN DOCUMENTS PERTINENT TO "HIDELL" AND THE RIFLE PURCHASE. THE MONEY ORDER FROM "HIDELL" WAS DEPOSITED ON MARCH 13TH, 1963 AS PART OF A BANK DEPOSIT OF $13,827.98 BY KLEIN'S. THIS WOULD REPRESENT PROCEEDS FROM HUNDREDS OF MAIL-ORDER SALES. HOWEVER, UNLIKE THE POST OFFICE, KLEIN'S MANAGED NOT ONLY TO SAVE THE "HIDELL" COUPON ORDERING THE MANNLICHER, BUT ALSO THE ENVELOPE IN WHICH IT WAS MAILED. THEIR "ZEALOUSNESS" WOULD PROVE TO BE QUITE CONVENIENT FOR THE SET-UP CONSPIRATORS.

IT IS FAIRLY OBVIOUS BY NOW THAT PAPERWORK TRAILS THAT INCRIMINATE **HARVEY** ARE PRESERVED. THOSE TRAILS THAT MAY INCRIMINATE THE FBI, THE CIA, OR THAT REVEAL THE INTENTIONS OR IDENTITIES OF THE SET-UP CONSPIRATORS ARE LOST.

HARVEY HAD, IN HIS NOTEBOOK, THE FOLLOWING NOTATION:

> NOV.1, 1963
> FBI AGENT (RI-11211)
> JAMES P. HOSTY
> MU 8605
> 1114 COMMERCE ST.
> DALLAS

SINCE HOSTY DID INDEED VISIT THE PAINE'S RESIDENCE THAT DAY, FRIDAY, NOVEMBER 1$^{ST.}$ (KEEP IN MIND THAT **HARVEY** OFTEN VISITED THE PAINE'S ON FRIDAYS AFTER WORK) **HARVEY** APPARENTLY HAD AN APPOINTMENT TO MEET WITH HOSTY THAT SAME DAY. IN ALL LIKELIHOOD, IT WAS IN AN EFFORT BY HOSTY TO RE-ESTABLISH A WORKING RELATIONSHIP WITH **HARVEY** WHO HAD RETURNED FROM NEW ORLEANS ON OCT 3RD. **HARVEY** WOULD NOW BE PASSED FROM NEW ORLEANS AGENT DEBREUYS TO DALLAS-BASED JAMES HOSTY AS HIS FBI CONTACT. THIS TIME **HARVEY** WOULD BE TASKED WITH FOCUSING HIS UNDERCOVER INTELLIGENCE EFFORTS ON THE DALLAS BRANCH OF THE ANTI-CASTRO GROUP THE DRE.

NOVEMBER 2ND 1963
DEWEY BRADFORD TOLD THE FBI HE SAW "OSWALD" AT MORGAN'S GUNSHOP IN FORTH WORTH ATTEMPTING TO BUY AMMO. THIS "OSWALD" SAID HE HAD BEEN IN THE MARINES AND WAS NOTED TO BE "RUDE AND IMPERTINENT."

*THERE IS NO RECORD OF ANY AMMO EVER BEING PURCHASED AND NONE FOUND IN **HARVEY'S** POSSESSION AFTER THE ASSASSINATION. SINCE **HARVEY** WAS AT THE PAINE'S FOR THE WEEKEND, THIS "OSWALD" WAS LIKELY **LEE**.*

NOVEMBER 2ND 1963
HARVEY SENDS OUT 3 CHANGE OF ADDRESS CARDS. ONE WAS SENT TO THE FPFC, ONE TO THE MILITANT, AND ONE TO THE WORKER.

NOVEMBER 2ND, 1963
THE PRESIDENT WAS SCHEDULED TO VISIT CHICAGO WHERE HE WOULD TAKE PART IN A MOTORCADE. THREE DAYS PRIOR TO THE VISIT, AN FBI INFORMANT CALLED THE CHICAGO FIELD OFFICE REVEALING THAT THERE WAS AN ASSASSINATION PLAN IN THE WORKS. TWO OF THE CONSPIRATORS WERE ARRESTED. TWO ACCOMPLICES HOWEVER REMAINED AT LARGE. THE PRESIDENT'S VISIT WAS CANCELLED. BOTH THE SS AND THE FBI BURIED ANY FORMAL DOCUMENTATION OF THE ATTEMPT. ANOTHER INDIVIDUAL HOWEVER WAS NOT SO FORTUNATE. THOMAS ARTHUR VALLEE WAS ARRESTED ON NOVEMBER 2ND. THE DAY PRIOR, HIS APARTMENT WAS SEARCHED AND SS AGENTS FOUND 2 RIFLES AND AMMO. VALLEE SHARED CONSIDERABLE SIMILARITIES WITH **HARVEY**. HE WAS A FORMER MARINE PREVIOUSLY STATIONED IN JAPAN AND CONSIDERED A "LONER." HE WAS EMPLOYED AT IPP LITHO-PLATE. THE LOCATION OF THE BUSINESS ON WEST JACKSON BOULEVARD WAS, LIKE THE TSBD IN DALLAS, ON THE ROUTE OF THE PRESIDENT'S PLANNED MOTORCADE IN CHICAGO. HAD THE PLOT IN CHICAGO NOT BEEN DISCOVERED BY THE FBI INFORMANTS IT IS LIKELY THAT VALLEE WOULD HAVE SUFFERED THE SAME FATE AS **HARVEY**. HE WOULD NOT HAVE LIVED BEYOND THAT WEEKEND, AND HIS NAME WOULD BE INDELIBLY WRITTEN IN THE HISTORY BOOKS.

NOVEMBER 2ND 1963
AT A LINCOLN-MERCURY DEALERSHIP IN DALLAS, SALESMAN ALBERT BOGARD WROTE THE NAME "LEE OSWALD" ON A BUSINESS CARD. ON A TEST DRIVE WITH BOGARD, "OSWALD" DROVE AT SPEEDS UP TO 70 MPH. ANOTHER SALESMAN, ORAN BROWN, ALSO WROTE DOWN THE NAME "OSWALD" AS A POTENTIAL CUSTOMER.

IF BOGARD WOULD NOT LATER RECALL THE DRIVER'S NAME, HE WOULD CERTAINLY REMEMBER THE TEST DRIVE. "OSWALD" WAS HEARD TO HAVE MUTTERED "MAYBE I'M GOING TO HAVE TO GO BACK TO RUSSIA TO BUY A CAR." "OSWALD" ALSO COMMENTED THAT HE WOULD "BE COMING INTO A LOT OF MONEY SOON" AND THAT "WORKERS IN RUSSIA RECEIVED BETTER TREATMENT."

*THE WARREN COMMISSION HOWEVER QUOTES BOTH RUTH PAINE AND MARINA TO PROVE THAT **HARVEY** COULD NOT HAVE BEEN AT THE DEALERSHIP THAT AFTERNOON. BUT, ONCE AGAIN, THE COMMISSION IGNORES THE SIGNIFICANCE OF THE FACT THAT THIS IS YET ANOTHER INCIDENCE OF SOMEONE POSING AS **HARVEY** AND PARTAKING NOT ONLY IN A MEMORABLE TEST DRIVE BUT MAKING INCRIMINATING COMMENTS AS WELL.*

BOGARD WAS FOUND DEAD IN HIS CAR AT A DRAG STRIP IN HALLSVILLE, TEXAS ON FEBRUARY 14TH, 1966. THE DEATH WAS NOTED TO BE A SUICIDE BY CARBON MONOXIDE POISONING.

NOVEMBER 4TH 1963
AGENT HOSTY CALLS THE TSBD TO VERIFY **HARVEY'S** EMPLOYMENT THERE.

NOVEMBER 5TH 1963

HOSTY RETURNS TO RUTH PAINE'S HOUSE IN AN ATTEMPT TO FIND OUT THE ADDRESS OF **HARVEY'S** RESIDENCE. HE IS ACCOMPANIED BY AGENT GARY S. WILSON.

NOVEMBER 5TH 1963
ACCORDING TO ARMSTRONG, MARVIN N. LLOYD STOPPED BY THE CAROUSEL CLUB AND OVERHEARD A CONVERSATION BETWEEN JACK RUBY AND **LEE.** DURING THE CONVERSATION, RUBY SAID TO **LEE** "YOU'VE JUST SIMPLY GOT TO HAVE THE BALLS TO DO IT; IT SIMPLY TAKES BALLS." **LEE'S** PRESENCE WAS ALSO NOTED BY WILBRYN LICTCHFIELD WHO WANTED TO TALK TO RUBY ABOUT BUYING ONE OF HIS CLUBS. **HARVEY** IS AT WORK AT THE TSBD.

*ONE COULD SPECULATE THAT RUBY WAS REFERRING TO THE ASSASSINATION OR EVEN TO THE LATER SHOOTING OF EITHER J.D. TIPPIT OR **HARVEY** AFTER THE ASSASSINATION. BUT, I AM NOT CONVINCED THAT RUBY IS AWARE OF WHAT WILL ULTIMATELY TAKE PLACE ON NOVEMBER 22ND REGARDING THE PRESIDENT. WITH THAT IN MIND, I DON'T THINK THE COMMENT WAS IN REFERENCE TO **LEE'S** SHOOTING OF TIPPIT AND I AM NOT CONVINCED THAT AT THIS POINT THAT RUBY IS AWARE OF THE UPCOMING EFFORT TO CONVINCE HIM TO SHOOT **HARVEY**.*

NOVEMBER 6TH 1963
AN "OSWALD" VISITED A GUNSHOP IN IRVING TEXAS ABOUT 3:00 PM ONLY TO FIND OUT IT WAS NOW A FURNITURE SHOP. "OSWALD" BROUGHT HIS "WIFE" IN AND TWO GIRLS APPROXIMATELY THE AGES OF JUNE AND RACHEL. THEY CONVERSED IN A "FOREIGN LANGUAGE." MARINA WOULD LATER STATE THAT SHE HAD NOT BEEN THERE. A MRS. WHITWORTH, WHO WITNESSED THE VISIT, TOLD "OSWALD" OF THE LOCATION OF THE IRVING SPORTS SHOP. THIS VISIT WAS ALSO WITNESSED BY A FRIEND OF MRS. WHITWORTH, A GERTRUDE HUNTER. BOTH WOMEN RECALLED THEIR VISITOR DEPARTING IN A 1957 OR 1958 FORD OR PLYMOUTH.

NOVEMBER 6TH 1963
AN "OSWALD" ALLEGEDLY BRINGS A RIFLE TO DIAL RYDER'S IRVING SPORTS SHOP TO THAVE 3 HOLES DRILLED FOR A SCOPE. THE WORK TICKET WAS ASSIGNED TO AN "OSWALD." THE CHARGE WAS $1.50 PER HOLE AND $1.50 FOR A BORE SIGHTING FOR A TOTAL OF $4.50.

*THE RIFLE ALLEGEDLY USED BY **HARVEY** ONLY NEEDED 2 HOLES TO MOUNT A SCOPE. IN FACT, AS WE HAVE POINTED OUT PREVIOUSLY, THE GUN **HARVEY** ALLEGEDLY ORDERED WAS SHIPPED WITH THE SCOPE ALREADY MOUNTED.*

ON NOVEMBER 24TH, 1963, WAFF-TV IN DALLAS WOULD RECEIVE AN ANONYMOUS PHONE CALL SAYING AN "OSWALD" HAD A GUN SIGHTED. THE FBI RECEIVED A PHONE CALL CITING THE SAME.

NOVEMBER 6TH 1963
HARVEY VISITS THE DALLAS PUBLIC LIBRARY, OAK CLIFF BRANCH. HE CHECKS OUT "THE SHARK AND THE SARDINES", A BOOK WRITTEN BY JUAN ARAWELO, THE FORMER PRESIDENT OF GUATAMALA.

ON / ABOUT NOVEMBER 7TH 1963
AN "OSWALD" APPLIES FOR A JOB AT THE ALLRIGHT PARKING GARAGE.

*ONCE AGAIN, **HARVEY** HAD ALREADY BEEN HIRED BY THE TSBD ON OCTOBER 16TH.*

NOVEMBER 8TH 1963
A BARBER IN IRVING OWNED BY CLIFF SHASTEEN IS VISITED BY AN "OSWALD" ACCOMPANIED BY A 14 YEAR OLD BOY. THEY BOTH MADE "LEFTIST REMARKS." "OSWALD" THEN VISITED HUTCH'S SUPER MARKET, A NEARBY GROCERY, AND ASKED THE MANAGER LEONARD HUTCHINSON TO CASH A CHECK FOR $189 MADE OUT TO "HARVEY OSWALD." MARINA WOULD LATER QUESTION WHERE **HARVEY** WOULD GET A CHECK FOR THAT AMOUNT OF MONEY. TSBD EMPLOYEES WERE PAID IN CASH.

*LEE VISITED SHASTEEN'S BARBERSHOP EVERY OTHER WEEK. **HARVEY** WAS KNOWN BY FELLOW EMPLOYEES TO GET HAIRCUTS VERY INFREQUENTLY. IT WAS LIKELY **LEE** WHO HAD ATTEMPTED TO CASH THE CHECK AT HUTCH'S MARKET.*

A LETTER DATED NOVEMBER 8TH, 1963 READ AS FOLLOWS:

DEAR MR. HUNT,

I WOULD LIKE INFORMATION CONCERNING MY POSITION. I AM ASKING ONLY FOR INFORMATION. I AM SUGGESTING THAT WE DISCUSS THE MATTER FULLY BEFORE ANY STEPS ARE TAKEN BY ME OR ANYONE ELSE.

THANK YOU, LEE HARVEY OSWALD

*THERE IS MUCH SPECULATION ABOUT THIS LETTER. SOME RESEARCHERS BELIEVE THAT IT WAS INTENDED FOR OIL BARON H.L. HUNT. HUNT'S SPECIAL ASSISTANT JOHN CURINGTON CLAIMS HE FOUND THE LETTER IN HUNT'S INCOMING MAIL BOX. I AM HOWEVER MORE INCLINED TO BELIEVE THAT IT IS TO E. HOWARD HUNT AND IS REGARDING WHAT **HARVEY** PERCEIVES AS HIS UPCOMING NOVEMBER 22ND DEPARTURE FOR CUBA WITH THE ASSISTANCE OF PILOT DAVID FERRIE. APPARENTLY **HARVEY** NEEDS FURTHER CLARIFICATION ON <u>EXACTLY</u> WHAT IS TO TAKE PLACE REGARDING WHAT HE PERCEIVES AS HIS LEGITIMATE CIA ASSIGNMENT TO DELIVER CARCINOGENS TO CUBA AND HIS POSSIBLE FURTHER TRAVEL TO RUSSIA. AN "ASSIGNMENT" OF THIS NATURE AND COMPLEXITY WOULD PROMPT THE EVER-CAUTIOUS **HARVEY** TO SEEK CLARIFICATION ON ANY AND ALL DETAILS. IN THIS CASE, THE TRAVEL ARRANGEMENTS WOULD BE OF PARTICULAR CONCERN SINCE HE HAD NOT YET OBTAINED A DRIVER'S LICENSE MUCH LESS HAVE THE ABILITY TO PILOT THE SMALL PLANES THAT WOULD BE USED FOR HIS ENTRY INTO CUBA VIA MEXICO. ONE MUST ALSO CONSIDER THE POSSIBILITY THAT THE BRIEF NOTE WAS FROM **LEE** TO E. HOWARD HUNT. **LEE** TOO WOULD LIKELY HAVE CONCERNS REGARDING HIS CONTINUING ROLE IN THE SET-UP OF **HARVEY**.*

NOVEMBER 9TH 1963

WILLIAM SOMERSETT, A MIAMI POLICE AND FBI INFORMANT, MET WITH JOSEPH A. MILTEER, THE RIGHT WING EXTREMIST FROM QUITMAN, GEORGIA. MILTEER WAS PRESIDENT OF THE GEORGIA KKK. SOMERSETT, HAVING INFILTRATED THE STATES RIGHTS PARTY AND THE CONSTITUTION PARTY, SECRETLY RECORDED A CONVERSATION WITH MILTEER IN HIS, SOMERSETT'S, APARTMENT IN MIAMI. ON THE TAPE, MILTEER TALKED FREELY ABOUT THE IMPENDING PRESIDENTIAL ASSASSINATION.

MILTEER:
"THE MORE BODYGUARDS HE HAS, THE EASIER IT IS TO GET HIM."

SOMERSETT:
"WELL HOW THE HELL DO YOU FIGURE WOULD BE THE BEST WAY TO GET HIM?"

MILTEER:
"FROM AN OFFICE BUILDING WITH A HIGH-POWERED RIFLE."

SOMMERSETT:
"DO YOU THINK HE KNOWS HE'S A MARKED MAN?"

MILTEER:
"I'M SURE HE DOES…..YES."

SOMERSETT:
ARE THEY REALLY GOING TO TRY AND KILL HIM?"

MILTEER:
"OH YEAH, IT'S IN THE WORKS."

SOMERSETT:
"HITTING THIS KENNEDY....I'LL TELL YOU IS GOING TO BE A HARD PROPOSITION...
BELIEVE YOU MAY HAVE FIGURED IT OUT HOW TO GET HIM FROM AN OFFICE
BUILDING AND ALL THAT, BUT I DON'T KNOW HOW THEM SECRET SERVICE...
THEY'D NEVER COVER ALL THEM OFFICE BUILDINGS AND ANYWHERE HE'S GOING.
DO YOU KNOW WHETHER THEY'D DO THAT OR NOT?"

MILTEER:
"IF THEY HAVE ANY SUSPICIONS THEY WILL OF COURSE, BUT WITHOUT SUSPICION,
THE CHANCES ARE THEY WOULDN'T. YOU WOULDN'T HAVE TO TAKE A GUN UP
THERE....TAKE IT UP IN PIECES....ALL THOSE GUNS COME KNOCKED DOWN AND
YOU CAN TAKE THEM APART."

SOMERSETT:
"BOY, IF THAT KENNEDY GETS SHOT WE GOT TO KNOW WHERE WE'RE AT."

MILTEER:
"YES, IT'S COMING."

SOMERSETT:
"BECAUSE YOU KNOW, BOY THAT'S GONNA BE, YOU KNOW THAT WOULD BE A
REAL SHAKE IFTHEY DO THAT."

MILTEER:
"THEY WOULDN'T LEAVE ANY STONE UNTURNED THERE....NO WAY."

SOMERSETT:
"OH, HELL NO."

MILTEER:
"HELL, THEY WILL PICK UP SOMEBODY WITHIN HOURS AFTER IF ANYTHING
LIKE THAT WOULD HAPPEN JUST TO THROW THE PUBLIC OFF."

SOMERSETT:
"YEAH THAT'S RIGHT. WELL SOMEBODY IS GOING TO HAVE TO GO TO JAIL IF HE
GETS KILLED."

NOVEMBER 9TH 1963
ACCORDING TO RUTH PAINE, SHE HAD TAKEN **HARVEY** AND MARINA TO THE TEXAS
DRIVER'S BUREAU SO THAT **HARVEY** COULD APPLY FOR A LEARNER'S PERMIT. THE
OFFICE HOWEVER WAS CLOSED. THE REMAINDER OF THE DAY WAS SPENT AT THE
PAINE RESIDENCE.

NOVEMBER 9TH/ 10TH 1963
FERRIE AND MARCELLO SPEND THE WEEKEND AT MARCELLO'S CHURCHILL FARM.
MARCELLO'S DEPORTATION CASE IS BEING TRIED IN FEDERAL COURT IN NEW
ORLEANS.

NOVEMBER 9TH—NOVEMBER 17TH 1963
DURING THIS TIME FRAME "OSWALD" WAS SEEN ALMOST EVERY DAY AT EITHER THE
SPORTSDROME RIFLE RANGE IN DALLAS OR AT A RANGE IN IRVING. THIS PARTICULAR
"OSWALD" FIRED AT OTHER PEOPLES TARGETS, BEHAVED OBNOXIOUSLY, AND FIRED
A 6.5 ITALIAN CARBINE THAT EMITTED A "BALL OF FIRE" WHEN FIRED. EXPERIENCED
RIFLEMEN AT THE RANGES NOTED THAT THE GUN WAS <u>NOT</u> A MANNLICHER <u>AND</u>
THAT THIS "OSWALD" PICKED UP <u>EVERY</u> SPENT SHELL.

*IF THIS WERE INDEED **HARVEY**, WHY WOULD HE BOTHER TO PICK UP THE SPENT SHELLS WHILE <u>PRACTICING</u>, BUT <u>NOT</u> AT THE TSBD AFTER HE ALLEGEDLY SHOT THE PRESDENT <u>OR</u> AT THE SCENE OF THE TIPPIT SHOOTING WHERE THE SPENT SHELLS WOULD HAVE HAD TO BEEN MANUALLY REMOVED FROM HIS PISTOL AND INTENTIONALLY STREWN ABOUT THE CRIME SCENE SINCE THE HANDGUN **HARVEY** HAD IN HIS POSSESSION AT THE TIME OF HIS ARREST WAS A REVOLVER, NOT AN AUTOMATIC?*

*INTERESTINGLY, THE FBI REPORT ON THE SHELLS PICKED UP IN THE TSBD NOTED THAT THE SHELLS HAD DOUBLE MARKINGS AS THOUGH THEY HAD BEEN LOADED <u>TWICE</u>. THIS COULD EXPLAIN THE RETRIEVING OF THE SPENT SHELLS BY AN "OSWALD" AT THE SHOOTING RANGE IN AN EFFORT TO FACILITATE THE SET-UP OF **HARVEY** AS THE TSBD SHOOTER. ARMSTRONG CONTENDS THAT THE VISITOR TO THE SPORTSDROME IS **LEE**.*

NOVEMBER 11TH 1963
ACCORDING TO ARMSTRONG, HARVEY WADE, A BUILDING INSPECTOR FROM EAST RIDGE, TENNESSEE, NOTED **LEE** AT THE CAROUSEL CLUB. BILL DEMARR ALSO NOTED **LEE** IN THE AUDIENCE AND HAD ASKED HIM TO ASSIST HIM IN HIS ACT WHICH INVOLVED MEMORY RECALL ON THE PART OF DEMARR.

NOVEMBER 12TH 1963
ACCORDING TO ARMSTRONG, **LEE** AND JACK RUBY VISITED CONTRACT ELECTRONICS WHERE THEY CONVERSED WITH DONALD STUART AND CHARLES ARNDT REGARDING ELECTRONIC EQUIPMENT. **LEE** WAS NOTED TO HAVE A TATTOO ON HIS LEFT FOREARM. **HARVEY** DID NOT HAVE ANY TATTOOS. HE WAS ALSO AT THE TSBD AT THE TIME OF THE VISIT TO THE ELECTRONICS STORE.

NOVEMBER 13TH 1963
HARVEY VISITS THE DALLAS FBI OFFICE ABOUT NOON ON OR ABOUT THIS DATE WITH A NOTE FOR AGENT HOSTY SUGGESTING THAT IF HOSTY DIDN'T STOP BOTHERING HIS WIFE HE WOULD "TAKE APPROPRIATE ACTION AND REPORT THIS TO THE PROPER AUTHORITIES." NANNY LEE FENNER, THE RECEPTIONIST, NOTED HOWEVER THAT SHE RECALLED THAT THE MESSAGE READ IN PART "I WILL EITHER BLOW UP THE DALLAS POLICE DEPARTMENT OR THE FBI OFFICE IF YOU DON'T STOP BOTHERING MY WIFE."

*I SUSPECT THAT TO **HARVEY** THE "PROPER AUTHORITIES" WOULD BE THE CIA. HIS DECLINING TOLERANCE LEVEL FOR WHAT HE DEEMED AS HARASSMENT BY THE FBI WOULD NEARLY PUSH HIM TO JEOPARDIZE WHAT HE CONSIDERED HIS CIA COVER. THE LETTER WAS NOTED BY THOSE WHO READ IT TO HAVE A "THREATENING" TONE.*

*HOSTY HOWEVER LATER INSISTED THAT IF THE NOTE HAD CONTAINED A DIRECT THREAT THAT HE WOULD HAVE ACTED ON IT IMMEDIATELY. HE ALSO INSISTED THAT THE NOTE WAS FOLDED AND THEREFORE IMPOSSIBLE FOR FENNER TO HAVE READ IT. I SUSPECT HOSTY'S DESIRE TO DOWNPLAY THE CONTENTS OF THE NOTE AS AN EFFORT TO DIMINISH CRITICISM OF HIS NOT HAVING BROUGHT **HARVEY** IN FOR QUESTIONING IF INDEED THE NOTE WAS AS THREATENING AS CLAIMED.*

*THE WARREN COMMISSION WAS NEVER INFORMED OF THE NOTE OR ITS LATER DISPOSAL. HOSTY WAS CHASTISED AFTER THE ASSASSINATION FOR NOT BEING MORE CONCERNED REGARDING THE ACTIVITIES OF **HARVEY**. INTERESTINGLY WHEN HOSTY TESTIFIED BEFORE THE COMMISSION HE NOTED THAT HE DID NOT MAKE **HARVEY** A PRIORITY CASE BECAUSE **HARVEY** WAS "NOT EMPLOYED IN A SENSITIVE INDUSTRY." APPARENTLY **HARVEY'S** WORK AT JAGGERS-CHILES-STOVALL IN DALLAS FROM OCTOBER 12TH, 1962 TO APRIL 6TH, 1963 WAS FORGOTTEN BY HOSTY.*

*AT APPROXIMATELY 6:00 PM ON SUNDAY, NOVEMBER 24TH, 1963, AGENT HOSTY WILL BE CALLED TO THE OFFICE OF DALLAS FBI CHIEF GORDON SHANKLIN. HOSTY IS GIVEN THE ORIGINAL NOTE FROM **HARVEY** AND THE MEMO HE HAD WRITTEN IN REGARDS TO THE THREATENING NOTE. HOSTY WAS TOLD IN NO UNCERTAIN TERMS TO "GET RID OF IT."*

HOSTY THEN TORE UP THE NOTE AND FLUSHED IT DOWN A TOILET IN A NEARBY MEN'S ROOM. THE ORDER TO DESTROY THE NOTE HAD COME FROM HOOVER.

THE NOTE IS PROBLEMATIC FOR THE FBI. ALTHOUGH IT <u>COULD</u> HAVE BEEN USED TO SHOW THAT **HARVEY** HAD A PROPENSITY FOR VIOLENCE, IT WAS LIKELY MORE IMPORTANT FOR THE FBI TO ELIMINATE IT DUE TO THE FACT THAT HE WAS NOT ARRESTED AFTER THE THREAT OR EVEN QUESTIONED. DAVID ATLEE PHILLIPS WOULD LATER CLAIM THAT THE NOTE HAD INCLUDED A NOTATION REGARDING THE DPD OR THE FBI. IN 1977, PHILLIPS IN TESTIMONY BEFORE THE HSCA ADMITTED THAT HE HAD FABRICATED THE PORTION OF THE NOTE REGARDING THE FBI AND THE DPD. APPARENTLY THE FBI RECEPTIONIST NANNY GENNER HAD LIED AS WELL.

NOVEMBER 13TH 1963
FBI AGENT DON ADAMS, BASED IN THOMASVILLE, GEORGIA, IS TASKED WITH PERFORMING A BACKGROUND INVESTIGATION ON JOSEPH MILTEER WHO RESIDES IN QUITMAN, GEORGIA.

NOVEMBER 14TH 1963
THE WHITE HOUSE GAVE ITS APPROVAL FOR THE TRADE MART AS THE SIGHT FOR THE LUNCHEON. SECRET SERVICE AGENTS FORREST SORRELS AND WINSTON LAWSON DRIVE OVER A POSSIBLE ROUTE FROM LOVE FIELD TO THE TRADEMART.

NOVEMBER 15TH 1963
THE DALLAS TIMES HERALD ANNOUNCES THE TRADE MART AS THE SITE OF THE LUNCHEON.

NOVEMBER 15TH 1963
A MAN ASKS HUBERT MORROW ABOUT A JOB AS A PARKING ATTENDANT AT THE SOUTHLAND HOTEL PARKING GARAGE AT 1208 COMMERCE STREET IN CENTRAL DALLAS. MORROW WRITES DOWN HIS NAME AS "OSBORNE" BUT WAS CORRECTED BY THE MAN TO WRITE "OSWALD." "OSWALD" ALSO ASKED HOW TALL THE HOTEL WAS AND WHAT KIND OF VIEW IT HAD OF DALLAS. **HARVEY** WAS AT WORK AT THE TSBD. THIS WAS MOST LIKELY **LEE**.

THIS WILL BE THE THIRD TIME AN "OSWALD" HAS APPLIED FOR A JOB SINCE **HARVEY'S** 0CTOBER 16TH HIRE BY THE TSBD. HOWEVER THE NEAR MISTAKE OF MORROW RECORDING THE NAME AS "OSBORNE" BEFORE BEING CORRECTED TO CHANGE IT TO "OSWALD" MAY BE MORE REVEALING THAN IT APPEARS. DURING **HARVEY'S** STAY IN NEW ORLEANS, THERE WERE 2 OCCASSIONS, MAY 29TH AND JUNE 3RD, WHERE ORDERS WERE PLACED FOR FPFC PRINTINGS AT JONES PRINTING COMPANY. BOTH THESE ORDERS WERE PLACED BY A "LEE OSBORNE." IT IS QUITE POSSIBLE THAT THIS PARTICULAR "OSWALD" INTIALLY SAID TO MORROW THAT HIS NAME WAS "OSBORNE" AND THEN QUICKLY HAD TO CORRECT IT TO "OSWALD."

IN THE DAYS IMMEDIATELY PRIOR TO THE ASSASSINATION, THE LOCAL SET-UP CONSPIRATORS HAD APPARENTLY GOTTEN QUITE CARELESS IN THEIR EFFORTS TO FURTHER THE SET-UP OF **HARVEY**. THIS MAY HAVE BEEN YET ANOTHER EXAMPLE OF A LAPSE IN THE EXPERTISE AND ATTENTION TO DETAIL REQUIRED OF SUCH AN ELABORATE SCHEME. ONCE AGAIN, THE LIKELY CANDIDATE FOR THIS ENDEAVOR WOULD BE **LEE**.

IN INSTANCES WHERE "OSWALD" APPEARED TO BE TWO PLACES AT ONCE, THE WARREN COMMISSION SIMPLY STATED THAT IT WAS <u>NOT</u> **HARVEY**. THEY NEVER PURSUED JUST <u>WHO</u> HAD IMPERSONATED HIM OR <u>WHY</u>. THE "IMPOSTERS", AND OR **LEE** BEING ORCHESTRATED BY HUNT/PHILLIPS MADE MANY MISTAKES:

1. **HARVEY** DID NOT OWN A CAR NOR DID HE POSSESS A VALID DRIVERS LICENSE
2. THE ALLEGED ASSASSINATION RIFLE DIDN'T NEED A FIRING PIN.
3. THE ALLEGED ASSASSINATION RIFLE NEEDED ONLY 2 HOLES FOR THE SCOPE NOT 3.

4. THE ALLEGED ASSASSINATION RIFLE WAS ORDERED <u>WITH</u> A SCOPE.
5. BYSTANDERS NOTED THAT THE GUN USED AT THE RIFLE RANGES WAS <u>NOT</u> A MANNLICHER-CARCANO
6. "OSWALD" APPLIED FOR 3 JOBS AFTER **HARVEY** HAD BEEN HIRED BY THE TSBD.

IT IS INTERESTING TO NOTE THAT VIRTUALLY ALL THSE SIGHTINGS TAKE PLACE <u>AFTER</u> THE ANNOUNCEMENT (SEPTEMBER 26TH) OF JFK'S TRIP TO DALLAS <u>AND</u> **HARVEY'S** DEPARTURE FROM NEW ORLEANS ON SEPT 25TH, 1963. THE SET-UP PLOT WAS IN ITS FINAL STAGE. EITHER THE SET-UP CONSPIRATORS WERE EXTREMELY CARELESS IN ALLOWING "OSWALD" TO BE IN DIFFERENT LOCATIONS AT THE SAME TIME, OR THEY WERE NOT AT ALL CONCERNED ABOUT THE POSSIBILITY OF **HARVEY** BEING PERCEIVED AS PART OF A LARGER CONSPIRACY WITH NUMEROUS ACCOMPLICES. ALTHOUGH THE SET-UP CONSPIRATORS COULD EXPECT THE WARREN COMMISSION, THE CIA, AND THE FBI TO ADOPT A "LONE-GUNMAN" THEORY AND SUPPRESS ANY EVIDENCE OF A LARGER CONSPIRACY, ALL THREE PARTIES WOULD BE LEFT WITH THE NAGGING REALIZATION THAT BOTH THE CUBANS AND THE RUSSIANS <u>MAY</u> HAVE BEEN INVOLVED. IT WOULD BE THIS LINGERING SUSPICION BY THE INTELLIGENCE COMMUNITY AND THE WHITE HOUSE THAT WOULD HOPEFULLY, FOR THE SET-UP CONSPIRATORS, PROMPT AN INVASION OF CUBA AND THE OVERTHROW OF CASTRO.

NOVEMBER 16TH 1963
THE DALLAS TIMES HERALD LISTS MAIN ST. AS THE PARADES PRIMARY ROUTE BUT DOES <u>NOT</u> SHOW THE SHARP MAIN TO HOUSTON TO ELM TURNS.

NOVEMBER 16TH 1963
ACCORDING TO RUTH PAINE, **HARVEY** ONCE AGAIN RETURNS TO THE DRIVERS LICENSE BRANCH TO OBTAIN A LEARNER'S PERMIT. BUT, THE LONG LINE OF APPLICANTS BEFORE HIM DISCOURAGED HIM FROM STAYING.

NOVEMBER 16TH 1963
DR. HOMER WOOD AND HIS SON STERLING WERE TARGET SHOOTING AT THE SPORTS-DROME RIFLE RANGE. BOTH WITNESSED A MAN WHO RESEMBLED **HARVEY**. LATER, WHEN SHOWN A PHOTO OF THE RIFLE THAT **HARVEY** ALLEGEDLY USED TO SHOOT THE PRESIDENT, DR. WOOD'S SON NOTED THAT BOTH THE SLING AND THE SCOPE AS DIFFERENT FROM WHAT HE HAD SEEN AT THE RIFLE RANGE.

NOVEMBER 16TH, 1963
AGENT ADAMS ENCOUNTERS MILTEER ENGAGING IN WHAT WAS APPARENTLY MILTEER'S SATURDAY AFTERNOON HABIT; HANDING OUT EXTREMIST PAMPHLETS IN HIS HOMETOWN OF QUITMAN, GEORGIA. ADAMS COLLECTS COPIES OF THE PAMPHLETS IN CONJUNCTION WITH HIS BACKGROUND INVESTIGATION OF MILTEER.

NOVEMBER 16TH-17TH 1963
FERRIE AND MARCELLO ONCE AGAIN SPEND THE WEEKEND AT MARCELLO'S FARM. MARCELLO'S TRIAL IS NEAR ITS CONCLUSION.

NOVEMBER 17TH 1963
MARINA ASKS RUTH PAINE TO CALL **HARVEY** AT HIS NORTH BECKLEY ROOMING HOUSE. SHE WAS TOLD THAT THERE WAS NO "LEE OSWALD" LIVING THERE. **HARVEY** HAD LISTED HIS NAME AS "O.H. LEE" AT THE ROOMING HOUSE.

NOVEMBER 17TH 1963
LEE ONCE AGAIN VISITS THE SPORTS DROME RIFLE RANGE.

NOVEMBER 18th 1963
THE MOTORCADE ROUTE IS APPROVED BY THE LOCAL DALLAS HOST COMMITTEE AND WHITE HOUSE REPRESENTATIVES. FORREST SORRELS, CHIEF OF THE DALLAS SECRET SERVICE UNIT, MODIFIES THE PARADE ROUTE. HE ADDS THE MAIN-TO-HOUSTON

RIGHT HAND TURN AND THE SECURITY-BREACHING 120 DEGREE TURN FROM HOUSTON TO ELM.

NOVEMBER 18ᵀᴴ 1963

THE RUSSIAN EMBASSY IN WASHINGTON RECEIVED A LETTER FROM A "LEE H. OSWALD" OF DALLAS. IN THE LETTER, "OSWALD" NOTES HIS MEETING IN MEXICO CITY WITH VALERY KOSTIKOV AS EARLIER OUTLINED IN THE OCTOBER 1ˢᵀ, 1963 ENTRY IN THE TIMELINE. THE LETTER CONTINUES WITH A REFERENCE TO "OSWALD'S" FAILED EFFORTS TO REACH CUBA.

*IF NOT WRITTEN BY **HARVEY**, WHICH IS LIKELY, THE LETTER CERTAINLY ACHIEVES ITS PROBABLE INTENTION: A FURTHER EFFORT TO LINK HIM TO THE SOVIETS AS WELL AS THE CUBANS. THIS LETTER WAS TYPEWRITTEN. EARLIER CORRESPONDANCES FROM "OSWALD" TO THE EMBASSY WERE HANDWRITTEN. IF ONE ACCEPTS THE LIKELY PROBABILITY THAT THE ENTIRE MEXICO CITY EPISODE WAS THE DESIGN OF SET-UP CONSPIRATORS PHILLILPS AND HUNT, THIS PARTICULAR CORRESPONDANCE WOULD THEN BE A MERE CONTINUANCE OF THAT PREVIOUS EFFORT.*

*THE SOVIETS HOWEVER WOULD NOT ALLOW THE "SET-UP" TO STAND. THE LETTER OF NOVEMBER 18ᵀᴴ (ACTUALLY DATED NOVEMBER 19ᵀᴴ) WAS NOT ONLY NOT DIGNIFIED WITH A REPLY, BUT WAS LATER RETURNED TO THE U.S. STATE DEPARTMENT ALONG WITH OTHER CORRESPONDANCE FROM EITHER **HARVEY** AND/OR "OSWALD." THE SOVIETS WOULD NOT IDLY STAND BY AND BE PAINTED AS ACCESSORIES TO THE PRESIDENT'S DEATH.*

NOVEMBER 18ᵀᴴ, 1963

THE PRESIDENT WAS SCHEDULED TO APPEAR IN TAMPA, FLORIDA THIS DAY. A SS MEMO DATED NOVEMBER 8ᵀᴴ DESCRIBED A WHITE MALE, 20 YEARS OF AGE, AND A SLENDER BUILD WHO HAD, IN OCTOBER, 1963, STATED THAT IT WAS HIS INTENTION TO ASSASSINATE THE PRESIDENT. IT WAS NOTED IN THE TAMPA TRIBUNE THAT THE SUSPECT UNDER SUSPICION IN TAMPA WAS GILBERTO LOPEZ, A CUBAN-AMERICAN. LOPEZ WAS 23 YEARS OLD AND HAD PREVIOUSLY DEFECTED TO CUBA ONLY TO RETURN. LOPEZ SHARED OTHER SIMILARITIES WITH **HARVEY**. HE TOO WAS INVOLVED WITH THE FPFC AND HAD ALSO HAD AN ALTERCATION WHILE PASSING OUT FPFC LITERATURE. THIS WAS SUBSEQUENTLY REPORTED IN THE NEWSPAPER. LOPEZ HAD ALSO APPARENTLY ATTEMPTED TO ENTER CUBA VIA MEXICO CITY. LOPEZ WAS ALSO EMPLOYED IN TAMPA IN A BUILDING THAT OVERLOOKED THE PLANNED PRESIDENTIAL MOTORCADE ROUTE. HE WAS HOWEVER DETAINED IN TAMPA DURING THE PRESIDENT'S VISIT. WITH ATTEMPTS FOILED IN BOTH CHICAGO AND NOW TAMPA, THE STAGE WAS SET FOR DALLAS. ONE WOULD EXPECT SECURITY IN DALLAS TO BE DRAMATICALLY INCREASED. IT WAS HOWEVER NOT THE CASE. THE DPD WAS NOT INFORMED OF THE PLANNED ATTEMPTS IN EITHER CHICAGO OR TAMPA.

HISTORY IS NOW DESTINED TO BE WRITTEN NOT WITH THE NAME THOMAS ARTHUR VALLEE OR GILBERTO LOPEZ, BUT WITH THE NAME LEE **HARVEY** OSWALD. THE SIMILARITIES SHARED BY THE 3 SITES AND THE MARKED SIMILARITIES BETWEEN LOPEZ AND **HARVEY** ARE TOO IMPROBABLE TO BE ATTRIBUTED TO MERE CHANCE. THE PRESIDENT WAS DESTINED TO BE ELIMINATED IN THE FALL OF 1963 AND ONE OF THE 3 MEN AND ONE THESE 3 CITIES WOULD FOREVER BEAR THE UNDESERVED GUILT.

NOVEMBER 19ᵗʰ 1963

THE PARADE ROUTE IS DESCRIBED IN THE DALLAS TIMES-HERALD AND THE DALLAS MORNING NEWS. THE MAIN-TO-HOUSTON-ELM TURN IS MENTIONED ONLY IN THE TIMES-HERALD.

THE 120 DEGREE MAIN-HOUSTON-ELM TURN WAS NECESSARY FOR A NUMBER OF REASONS:

1) TO DRAMATICALLY SLOW THE MOTORCADE

2) TO BRING IT CLOSER TO THE TSBD
3) TO BRING IT CLOSER TO THE SHOOTERS ON THE GRASSY KNOLL LAND THE OVERPASS

CHIEF CURRY, FORREST SORRELS, CHIEF OF THE DALLAS S.S. UNIT, AND WIN LAWSON, S.S. ADVANCE MAN, MADE A "DRY RUN" OVER THE PARADE ROUTE. WHEN THE CAR REACHED THE MAIN AND HOUSTON INTERSECTION, CURRY POINTED FURTHER DOWN MAIN STREET AND COMMENTED "AND AFTERWARDS THERE'S ONLY THE FREEWAY." CURRY THEN PROCEEDED TO TURN <u>LEFT</u> NOT <u>RIGHT</u> ONTO HOUSTON. HAD HE TURNED <u>RIGHT</u> AND FOLLOWED THE ROUTE ACTUALLY USED ON NOVEMBER 22ND, IT WOULD HAVE PAINFULLY OBVIOUS TO SORRELS AND LAWSON THAT A <u>RIGHT</u> TURN FROM MAIN TO HOUSTON WOULD HAVE NECESSITATED AN EVEN MORE DANGEROUS 120 DEGREE LEFT TURN ONTO ELM IN ORDER TO REACH THE FREEWAY ENROUTE TO THE TRADE MART. CURRY DELIBERATELY MISLEAD THE SECRET SERVICE REGARDING THE ROUTE THAT WOULD BE TAKEN ON NOVEMBER 22ND; A ROUTE THAT WOULD TAKE THE PRESIDENTIAL LIMO DIRECTLY IN FRONT OF THE TSBD. ACCORDING TO JERRY BRUNO, JFK'S ADVANCE MAN, IT WAS GOVENOR CONNALLY WHO WAS VEHEMENT ABOUT THE LUNCHEON BEING AT THE TRADE MART. BOTH THE S.S AND THE WHITE HOUSE HAD PREVIOUSLY PREFERRED THE WOMEN'S BUILDING. THE ROUTE TO THE WOMEN'S BUILDING WOULD HAVE HAD THE MOTORCADE CONTINUE ON MAIN STREET AT A FREEWAY-LIKE SPEED WITHOUT THE SECURITY COMPRIMISING TURNS ONTO HOUSTON AND ELM. BOTH KENNY O'DONNELL AND BILL MOYERS TOLD BRUNO THAT CONNALLY WOULD CANCEL THE TRIP IF THE LUNCHEON WAS NOT AT THE TRADE MART. CONNALLY EMPHASIZED HIS ADAMANT NON-NEGOTIABLE CHOICE TO BRUNO BY STATING "EITHER WE SELECT THE STOPS AND RUN THE TRIP OR THE PRESIDENT CAN STAY HOME."

NOVEMBER 20TH 1963

TSBD SUPERINDENDANT ROY TRULY AND HIS FOREMAN BILL SHELLEY ARE SHOWN A MAUSER AND A 22 CALIBER RIFLE BY WARREN CASTER AT THE TSBD.

NOVEMBER 20TH 1963

BONNIE RAY WILLIAMS, A TSBD LABORER, WOULD LATER NOTE THAT THE WORKERS HAD STARTED ON THIS DATE TO RE-SURFACE THE FLOOR ON THE 6TH FLOOR OF THE TSBD. THEY HAD RECENTLY DONE THIS SAME TYPE OF REPAIR ON THE 5TH FLOOR. THE 6TH FLOOR REPAIR STARTED ON THE WEST END OF THE BUILDING, SO THE BOXES OF BOOKS HAD TO BE MOVED TO THE EAST SIDE OF THE BUILDING.

WITH WORKERS INVOLVED IN THE RESURFACING OF THE <u>6TH</u> FLOOR, WHY WOULD THE ALLEGED ASSASSIN CHOOSE THIS FLOOR INSTEAD OF THE LESS TRAFFICKED, COMPLETED <u>5TH</u> FLOOR OR A LOWER FLOOR?

NOVEMBER 20TH 1963

RALPH YATES, A SERVICEMAN FOR THE TEXAS BUTCHER SUPPLY COMPANY, WOULD, ON NOVEMBER 26TH, RELATE TO THE FBI THAT HE PICKED UP A HITCHHIKER ON WEDNESDAY, NOVEMBER 20TH AT ABOUT 10:30 A.M NEAR THE BECKLEY ST. ENTRANCE TO THE THORNTON FREEWAY. YATES STATED IN HIS REPORT THAT THE MAN WAS "CARRYING A PACKAGE WRAPPED IN BROWN WRAPPING PAPER ABOUT 4-4 ½ FEET LONG…..THE MAN SAID THE PACKAGE CONTAINED CURTAIN RODS." THE REPORT WENT ON TO SAY THAT "THE MAN ASKED YATES IF HE THOUGHT A MAN COULD ASSASSINATE THE PRESIDENT, ASKED IF IT COULD BE DONE FROM THE TOP OF A BUILDING OR HIGH UP…THE MAN THEN PULLED OUT A PHOTO WHICH SHOWED A MAN WITH A RIFLE….THE MAN THEN ASKED IF HE THOUGHT THE PRESIDENT WOULD CHANGE HIS ROUTE." THE REMAINING PORTION OF THE REPORT CONTINUES WITH "YATES LET THE MAN OFF AT THE CORNER OF ELM AND HOUSTON ……YATES STATED THAT THE MAN WAS IDENTICAL TO LHO."

THE PICTURE SHOWN TO YATES, THE COMMENT REGARDING ASSASSINATING THE PRESIDENT, THE COMMENT REGARDING THE ROUTE CHANGE AND THE PICKUP POINT ON BECKLEY AND THE DEPARTURE POINT FOR HIS PASSENGER AT HOUSTON AND ELM ARE

SIMPLY TOO PATENTLY INCRIMINATING TO SERVE ANY OTHER PURPOSE THAN TO
CONNECT **HARVEY** TO THE EVENTS OF NOVEMBER 22ND. WITH THIS IN MIND, I WOULD
CONCLUDE THAT THE MAN YATES PICKED UP, IF INDEED HE HAD PICKED HIM UP ON THE
20TH, WAS AN IMPOSTOR; INDEED A VERY WELL INFORMED IMPOSTER IN REGARDS TO
WHAT WOULD TAKE PLACE ON FRIDAY. THE IMPOSTOR WAS LIKELY **LEE**. **HARVEY** WAS AT
WORK AT THE TSBD THAT DAY.

IT INTERESTING TO NOTE THAT THE "CURTAIN ROD" STORY OFFERED BY YATES,
COMBINED WITH THE "CURTAIN ROD" THAT BUELL FRAZIER WILL CLAIM **HARVEY**
CARRIED TO WORK ON NOVEMBER 22ND WILL BE THE 2ND TIME IN A 3 DAY PERIOD THAT
HARVEY HAD ALLEGEDLY TAKEN CURTAIN RODS TO WORK.

THE YATES REPORT IS IMPORTANT BECAUSE OF THE DESCRIPTION OF THE PACKAGE
LENGTH. THE "4-4 ½ FEET LONG" DESCRIPTION WOULD CERTAINLY ALLOW THE
POSSIBILITY THAT THE RIDER WAS <u>NOT</u> CARRYING CURTAIN RODS BUT A RIFLE. HOWEVER,
A CLOSER LOOK AT BUELL FRAZIER'S QUESTIONING REGARDING HIS NOVEMBER 22ND
RIDE WITH **HARVEY** MAKES ONE WONDER IF PERHAPS FRAZIER'S TESTIMONY WASN'T
ALTERED SINCE THE FBI HAD NOT YET BEEN APPROACHED BY YATES. YATES WILL NOT BE
INTERVIEWED UNTIL NOVEMBER 26TH. HAD YATES BEEN INTERVIEWED <u>FIRST</u>, **HIS**
DESCRIPTION OF THE LENGTH OF THE PACKAGE ON NOVEMBER 20TH WOULD HAVE
TRUMPED FRAZIER'S DESCRIPTION OF A PACKAGE ON NOVEMBER 22ND; A DESCRIPTION
WHICH MADE IT VIRTUALLY IMPOSSIBLE FOR THE PACKAGE THAT DAY TO HAVE
CONTAINED THE ALLEGED ASSASSINATION RIFLE.

FRAZIER WAS QUESTIONED LATE FRIDAY AFTERNOON, NOVEMBER 22ND AND THEN
RETURNED TO HIS HOME IN IRVING. LATER THAT EVENING FRAZIER WAS ARRESTED. THE
DALLAS POLICE SEARCHED HIS HOME AND TOOK AS SUSPECTED EVIDENCE A RIFLE, SOME
AMMO, AND A CLIP. BOTH FRAZIER AND HIS SISTER WERE TAKEN DOWNTOWN AND
QUESTIONED AGAIN. ABOUT 9:00 P.M. THAT EVENING, FRAZIER WAS RELEASED FOR THE
2ND TIME. HE WAS NEARLY HALF-WAY HOME WHEN THE SQUAD CAR DRIVING HIM WAS
INSTRUCTED TO BRING HIM BACK FOR YET A 3RD VISIT TO THE POLICE STATION. FRAZIER
WAS RELEASED ABOUT 12:10 A.M. SATURDAY MORNING. SINCE YATES REPORT HAD NOT
YET BEEN TAKEN, THE LOCAL AUTHORITIES NEEDED <u>SOMEONE</u> TO CERTIFY THAT **HARVEY**
HAD INDEED TAKEN THE ALLEGED ASSASSINATION WEAPON TO WORK AT SOME POINT IN
TIME. I STRONGLY SUSPECT THAT IT WAS "SUGGESTED" TO FRAZIER THAT THE PACKAGE
HARVEY CARRIED TO WORK THE MORNING OF NOVEMBER 22ND WAS AT LEAST OF THE
<u>SHAPE</u> IF NOT THE <u>SIZE</u> OF A RIFLE.

IN 2013, ONE OF THE MANY ASSASSINATION SPECIALS AIRED SHOWED AN INTERVIEW WITH
FRAZIER. THIS PARTICULAR SEGMENT WAS SHOWN ON "THE DAY KENNEDY DIED" ON THE
SMITHSONIAN CHANNEL. FRAZIER NOTED THAT DURING ONE SESSION WITH CAPTAIN
FRITZ THAT FRITZ PULLED HIS ARM BACK AS IF HE WERE GOING TO STRIKE HIM SINCE HE
WOULD NOT SIGN PAPERS STATING THAT **HARVEY** HAD INDEED CARRIED A RIFLE TO
WORK THAT DAY. ACCORDING TO FRAZIER, FRITZ HAD THREATENED TO ARREST HIM AS A
CONSPIRATOR IN THE DEATH OF THE PRESIDENT. THAT FRIDAY MAY HAVE GONE MUCH
BETTER FOR FRAZIER HAD ONLY YATES COME FORWARD THAT DAY RATHER THAN
NOVEMBER 26TH.

FRAZIER ALSO WENT ON TO NOTE IN THE SMITHSONIAN SEGMENT: "SO THEY DID A ROLE
CALL AND THE ONLY BODY THAT WASN'T THERE WAS LEE OSWALD. AND I DIDN'T KNOW
WHAT TO THINK BECAUSE SOMETIMES......EH....I REMEMBER THAT MORNING HE DID NOT
TAKE HIS LUNCH."WHY THE SEEMINGLY AWKWARD TRANSACTION FRONM DISCUSSING
"ROLL CALL" TO **HARVEY'S** LUNCH? FRAZIER WAS, NEARLY 50 YEARS LATER, SEEMINGLY
STILL OBLIGATED TO GIVE THE W.CD. WHAT THEY DESPERATELY NEEDED: A METHOD BY
WHICH **HARVEY** INTRODUCED THE SO-CALLED ASSASSINATION RIFLE INTO THE TSBD. IT
WAS STILL IMPERAATIVE TO THE W.C. THAT **HARVEY** TOOK A RIFLE TO WORK THAT DAY
AND NOT HIS LUNCH. FRAZIER RELUCTANTLY RECOGNIZED THIS POINT AND AWKWARDLY
PROMOTED IT.

*IF THE PRESSURE PUT ON FRAZIER DIDN'T ACHIEVE THE DESIRED EFFECT – **HARVEY'S** METHOD OF INTRODUCING RIFLE TO THE TSBD – THE SET-UP CONSPIRATORS WOULD HOPE THAT YATES BAITING BY THE HITCHHIKER WOULD ENTICE HIM TO COME FORWARD WTH A STORY THAT COULD CONCEIVABLY BE MORE PLAUSIBLE IN REGARDS TO ASSOCIATING **HARVEY**, THE RIFLE, AND THE TSBD.*

*BUT, AS WE HAVE HAD NUMEROUS "OSWALD" SIGHTINGS WHEN **HARVEY** WAS KNOWN TO BE ELSEWHERE, WE NOW HAVE **HARVEY** AND/OR AN IMPOSTOR TAKING THE RIFLE/CURTAIN RODS TO HOUSTON AND ELM ON TWO DIFFERENT DAYS. THE ONLY THING CONSISTANT IN THOSE TWO EFFORTS WAS THE USE OF THE CURTAIN ROD ALIBI.*

*HAD THE FBI BEEN AWARE OF YATES STORY ON NOVEMBER 22ND, IT LIKELY WOULD NOT HAVE PRESSED FRAZIER 3 TIMES ON THAT FRIDAY IN AN EFFORT TO PUT THE ALLEGED ASSASSINATION WEAPON IN THE TSBD VIA **HARVEY** ON HIS RIDE TO WORK WITH FRAZIER THAT MORNING.*

*THIS IS YET ANOTHER INSTANCE IN WHICH THE SET-UP CONSPIRATORS OVERZEALOUS EFFORTS TO FRAME **HARVEY** PROVED TO BE MORE PROBLEMATIC FOR THE COMMISSION THAN INCRIMINATING TO **HARVEY**. YATES WOULD RETURN TO THE DALLAS FBI OFFICE ON DECEMBER 10TH TO REPEAT HIS STORY AND SIGN AN AFFADAVIT REGARDING HIS STATEMENT. THE FBI WOULD EXPEND A GREAT DEAL OF EFFORT TO DISCREDIT YATES WHOSE STORY NOW CONFLICTED WITH THE STORY SOLICITED FROM THE RELUCTANT FRAZIER. THERE WAS NO NEED FOR **HARVEY** TO ALLEGEDLY BRING THE RIFLE TO THE TSBD ON BOTH WEDNESDAY AND FRIDAY.*

AFTER A JANUARY 4TH, 1964 VISIT TO THE FBI OFFICE, YATES WAS SENT TO WOODLAWN, A PSYCHIATRIC FACILITY. ACCORDING TO HIS WIFE, THIS WAS FOLLOWED BY A STAY AT ANOTHER STATE HOSPITAL, A V.A. HOSPITAL, AND FINALLY AT YET ANOTHER STATE HOSPITAL. HE WAS SUBJECTED TO SHOCK TREATMENTS AND A VARIETY OF MOOD ALTERING DRUGS. YATES DIED ON SEPTEMBER 3RD 1975 AT THE AGE OF 39.

NOVEMBER 20TH 1963

LEE WAS DRIVEN TO RED BIRD FIELD IN DALLAS BY A MALE AND A FEMALE. THE UNIDENTIFIED MALE AND FEMALE TRIED TO RENT A CESSNA 310 FROM WAYNE JANUARY, A PARTNER IN AMERICAN AVIATION COMPANY, TO FLY TO THE YUCATAN ON FRIDAY, NOVEMBER 22ND. THEY ALSO NOTED THAT THEY WANTED TO RETURN TO RED BIRD ON SUNDAY, NOVEMBER 24TH. THE COUPLE ASKED ABOUT FUEL CONSUMPTION AND THE POSSIBILITY OF FLYING TO A FURTHER LOCATION. (CUBA?)

LEE WAITED IN THE CAR WHILE THEY TALKED TO JANUARY. JANUARY TURNED DOWN THE CHARTER BECAUSE THEY DIDN'T SEEM DRESSED IN A FASHION THAT INDICATED TO HIM THAT THEY HAD THE MONEY FOR THE CHARTER. THE COUPLE DROVE A 1947 MODEL BLACK CAR. THEY BECAME AGITATED WHEN HE TURNED THEM DOWN. HOWEVER SOMEONE ELSE AT RED BIRD APPARENTLY TOOK THEIR UNUSUAL CHARTER. ON FRIDAY AFTERNOON, NOVEMBER 22ND, A SMALL AIRCRAFT WAS STANDING BY THE PERIMETER FENCE AT RED BIRD. IT WAS FUELED-UP WITH ENGINES REVING. NEIGHBORS CALLED THE POLICE DUE TO THE NOISE.

HARVEY NORMALLY ATE BREAKFAST AT THE DOBBS RESTAURANT ON NORTH BECKLEY BETWEEN 7 AND 7:30 AM. THE MORNING OF THE RED BIRD INCIDENT HOWEVER, **LEE** ARRIVED AT 10 AM ACCORDING TO WAITRESS MARY DOWLING. **LEE** COMPLAINED ABOUT HIS ORDER AND CREATED A FUSS NOTICED BY AN OFFICER. THE OFFICER WAS J. D. TIPPIT. THIS INTERESTING SCENARIO WAS ALSO LIKELY ARRANGED BY ROSCOE WHITE, THE DALLAS-BASED SET-UP CONSPIRATOR. WITH TIPPIT'S PENCHANT FOR NOT LOOKING AT PEOPLE TO WHOM HE WAS SPEAKING, **LEE'S** OUTBURST WOULD LIKELY SOLICIT AT LEAST MORE THAN A GLIMPSE IN THE DIRECTION OF THE IMPOSTER FROM TIPPITT. THE FBI REPORT OF THE RED BIRD AIRPORT INCIDENT SAID IT TOOK PLACE IN LATE JULY 1963. WAYNE JANUARY VEHEMENTLY DENIED THIS.

IT WOULD BE IMPERATIVE THAT TIPPIT ASSOCIATE A FACE (ALBEIT THE FACE OF LOOKALIKE **LEE**) WITH THE NAME "OSWALD" IT IF WERE DECIDED THAT TIPPIT WOULD BE INSTRUMENTAL IN LEADING THE CONTINUED POLICE SEARCH FOR **HARVEY** BY VIRTUE OF HIS FATAL ENCOUNTER WITH **LEE** ON NOVEMBER 22ND. CONVERSELY, IT WOULD ALSO BE IMPORTANT FOR **LEE** TO RECOGNIZE TIPPIT IF THEIR ENCOUNTER RESULTED IN THE NEED TO ELIMINATE TIPPIT IF **HARVEY** WERE NOT ALREADY APPREHENDED OR SHOT. AS YOU WILL SEE, TIPPIT'S DEATH IS NECESSITATED BY THE FACT THAT **HARVEY** WAS STILL ALIVE. IT WAS, IN MY OPINION, THE SET-UP CONSPIRATORS DESIRE THAT **HARVEY** WOULD BE SHOT IN THE TSBD. IF NOT THERE ON THE BUS RIDE TO HIS ROOMING HOUSE. THEIR FIRST TWO OPTIONS HAD FAILED. IN ORDER TO ENHANCE THE POSSIBILITY THAT **HARVEY** WOULD BE SHOT IN THE TEXAS THEATER, IT WOULD REQUIRE AN EVENT THAT WOULD PUT THE DPD ON HAIR-TRIGGER ALERT; THE DEATH OF A FELLOW OFFICER.

HARVEY NORMALLY RODE TO WORK WITH BUELL FRAZIER. HE WOULD WALK TO FRAZIER'S SISTER'S HOUSE WHERE FRAZIER LIVED <u>AFTER</u> HAVING BREAKFAST AT THE DOBBS RESTAURANT. THEY WOULD ARRIVE AT THE TSBD TO COMMENCE WORK AT THEIR NORMAL TIME OF 8:00. I HAVE NOT IN MY EXTENSIVE READING FOUND ANY INDICATION THAT **HARVEY** WAS OFF WORK EITHER WEDNESDAY MORNING, NOVEMBER 20TH OR THURSDAY, NOVEMBER 21ST. ONCE AGAIN, **HARVEY** APPEARS TO BE IN TWO PLACES AT ONCE. IF **HARVEY** IS AT WORK AT THE TSBD, THE PERSON SITTING IN THE CAR AT REDBIRD AIRFIELD ON THE 20TH IS AN IMPOSTOR, MOST LIKELY **LEE**. CONSEQUENTLY, THE MAN AGITATED BY HIS BREAKFAST ORDER AT THE DOBBS RESTAURANT THAT SAME MORNING IS ALSO AN IMPOSTER, MOST LIKELY **LEE**.

THE ATTEMPTED CHARTER FROM WAYNE JANUARY AND THE SUBSEQUENT SUCCESSFUL CHARTER FROM AN UNKNOWN PROVIDER WAS SIMPLY TO PROVIDE WHAT WOULD <u>APPEAR</u> TO BE A MEANS OF ESCAPE FOR THE MAN WHO WOULD SOON BE CONSIDERED THE ALLEGED PRESIDENTIAL ASSASSIN. THIS METHOD OF TRAVEL WOULD COMPLEMENT THE FACT THAT **LEE**, IN HIS INCRIMINATING VISIT TO MEXICO CITY, WAS UNABLE TO OBTAIN LEGITIMATE TRAVEL VISAS AT THE CUBAN AND SOVIET EMBASSIES. I WOULD STRONGLY CONSIDER THE POSSIBILITY THAT THE MAN WHO ENTERED THE HANGAR AND TALKED TO JANUARY WAS SET-UP CONSPIRATOR ROSCOE WHITE. THE WOMAN REMAINS UNIDENTIFIED. ONCE AGAIN, **HARVEY** WAS AT WORK AT THE TSBD THAT DAY. THE BOOKKEEPER AT THE TSBD, A.S. AIKEN, LATER PROVIDED PAYROLL RECORDS SHOWING THAT HE WORKED HIS NORMAL 8 TILL 4:45 SHIFT THAT DAY

IF THE PERSON IN THE CAR AT RED BIRD AIRFIELD IS <u>NOT</u> **HARVEY**, THEN THE SET-UP CONSPIRATORS' INTENTION IS TO HAVE INVESTIGATORS <u>PERCEIVE</u> THAT HE HAD ATTEMPTED TO MAKE ARRANGEMENTS TO FLEE THE COUNTRY AND MAKE HIS WAY TO MEXICO THEN ON TO CUBA AND PERHAPS RUSSIA AS WELL.

THE SET-UP CONSPIRATORS WERE APPARENTLY NOT ONLY QUITE COMFORTABLE IN THE USE OF **HARVEY** IMPOSTORS- PARTICULARLY **LEE**- BUT ALSO SEEM TO HAVE LITTLE CONCERN THAT THEIR "OSWALD" WOULD OVERPLAY THE ROLE. MORE AMAZING THOUGH IS THAT THEY SEEMINGLY HAVE LITTLE CONCERN THAT THEIR "OSWALD" IS OFTENTIMES SIGHTED AT PLACES AND AT TIMES THAT WOULD BE DIFFICULT CONSIDERING **HARVEY'S** WORK SCHEDULE. **HARVEY** DID NOT MISS ONE DAY OF WORK DURING HIS EMPLOYMENT AT THE TSBD. BUT, PERHAPS IT IS LESS A MATTER OF LACK OF CONCERN BUT MORE A MATTER OF COMPETENCY BY THOSE WHO LIKELY BORE THE RESPONSIBILITY FOR THE RUNNING OF THE DALLAS IMPOSTORS. MISTAKES OF THIS MAGNITUDE WOULD NOT LIKELY BE MADE BY EITHER HUNT OR PHILLIPS. IT IS HOWEVER POSSIBLE THAT ROSCOE WHITE AND **LEE'S** EFFORTS LACKED THE ATTENTION TO DETAIL THAT BOTH HUNT AND PHILLIPS WOULD HAVE OFFERED.

ANOTHER AIRCRAFT INCIDENT TOOK PLACE THAT SAME WEEK IN NOVEMBER. HANK GORDON, ACTUALLY AN ALIAS AS HE FEARED FOR HIS LIFE, WAS A MECHANIC WHO FORMERLY WORKED AT RED BIRD FOR WOBURN INCORPORATED. HE WAS ASKED TO

RETURN TO DALLAS TO SERVICE A DOUGLAS DC-3 THAT WAS TO BE SOLD. GORDON MET THE BUYER, NOTING THAT THE BUYER WAS WELL DRESSED WITH A MILITARY APPEARANCE. THE BUYER'S PILOT WAS IN HIS LATE 30'S, AND ALSO REFLECTED A MILITARY APEARANCE. THE BUYER'S PILOT TOLD GORDON THAT HE WAS BORN IN CUBA AND THAT THE BUYER WAS AN AIR FORCE COLONEL. THE BUYER'S PILOT ALSO REVEALED THAT HIS EXPERIENCE WITH THE DC-3 WAS OBTAINED AS A PILOT IN CASTRO'S AIR FORCE.

ON THURSDAY, NOVEMBER 21ST, 1963 OVER LUNCH, THE PILOT REMARKED: "HANK, THEY ARE GOING TO KILL YOUR PRESIDENT." GORDON, NOT QUITE KNOWING WHAT TO SAY, ASKED: "YOU MEAN PRESIDENT KENNEDY?" THE PILOT NODDED HIS HEAD. HE WENT ON TO TELL GORDON THAT HE WAS A MERCENARY PILOT HIRED BY THE CIA FOR THE BAY OF PIGS INVASION. HE DETAILED THE LEVEL OF HURT, ANGER, AND EMBARASSMENT SHARED BY THOSE WHO HAD PLANNED THE OPERATION WHICH HAD FAILED MISERABLY. GORDON ASKED HIM: "IS THAT WHY YOU THINK THEY'LL KILL THE PRESIDENT?" THE PILOT ANSWERED: "THEY ARE GOING TO KILL ROBERT KENNEDY AND ANY OTHER KENNEDY WHO GETS INTO THAT POSITION……YOU WILL SEE."

BY LUNCH TIME ON FRIDAY NOVEMBER 22ND, ALL THAT WAS LEFT WAS FUELING THE PLANE. GORDON, NOTING A COMMOTION AT THE TERMINAL BUILDING, HEADED IN THAT DIRECTION. A FRIEND, NOTICING GORDON, PULLED UP TO HIM AND ASKED HIM: "HAVE YOU HEARD……THE PRESIDENT HAS BEEN SHOT." GORDON WENT BACK TO THE PLANE WHERE THE PILOT WAS LOADING BAGGAGE. THE PILOT TOLD HIM HE HAD BEEN TOLD BY THE FUEL TRUCK DRIVER ABOUT THE SHOOTING. THE PILOT SOMBERLY LOOKED AT GORDON AND COMMENTED: " IT'S ALL GOING TO HAPPEN JUST LIKE I TOLD YOU." THE "BUYER" OF THE DC-3 WAS PURCHASING THE PLANE FOR HOUSTON AIR CHARTER, A FRONT FOR THE CIA LOCATED ON AIRPORT BOULEVARD IN HOUSTON. ONE HAS TO WONDER IF THIS PLANE WAS USED TO EXTRACT THE ACTUAL SHOOTERS FROM DALLAS THAT DAY.

REDBIRD AIRPORT, SOUTH OF DALLAS, WAS OWNED BY SOUTHWEST AIRCRAFT CORPORATION. SOUTHWEST AIRCRAFT WAS CONSIDERED TO BE A CIA PROPRIETARY COMPANY.

SYLVIA JANUARY, WAYNE JANUARY'S WIDOW, WOULD LATER ADMIT THAT IT WAS INDEED HER HUSBAND WHO HAD TAKEN PART IN THE DC-3 INCIDENT. HE HAD HOWEVER THOUGHT IT WISE TO USE THE ALIAS HANK GORDON IN LIGHT OF THE SERIOUSNESS OF THE INCIDENT.

NOVEMBER 20TH 1963
THE DALLAS MORNING NEWS ONCE AGAIN DESCRIBES THE PARADE ROUTE. NO REFERENCE IS MADE TO A HOUSTON-ELM ROUTE.

NOVEMBER 20TH 1063
ROSE CHERAMIE, AKA MELBA YOUNGBLOOD, WAS A FORMER STRIPPER AND DRUG COURIER AT THE PINK SLIPPER CLUB IN DALLAS. RUBY WAS PART OWNER OF THE CLUB. SHE HAD BEEN STRUCK BY A CAR WHILE HITCHHIKING ON HIGHWAY 190 JUST OUTSIDE EUNICE, LOUISIANA. THE DRIVER OF THE VEHICLE THAT HAD STRUCK HER, FRANK ODUM, DROVE HER TO MOOSA MEMORIAL HOSPITAL. THE STAFF AT THE HOSPITAL SUSPECTED DRUG ABUSE AND CALLED THE LOUISIANA STATE POLICE.

ON NOVEMBER 20TH 1963, SHE WAS PICKED UP BY LT. FRANCIS FRUGE OF THE LOUISIANA STATE POLICE AT MOOSA HOSPITAL. FRUGE THEN TOOK HER TO THE JAIL IN EUNICE. THAT EVENING, HER WITHDRAWAL FROM HEROIN PROMPTED FRUGE TO HAVE HER SEEN BY A LOCAL PHYSICIAN, DR. DEROUIN. SHE WAS THEN TAKEN TO THE EAST LOUISIANA STATE HOSPITAL IN JACKSON ON NOVEMBER 21ST AND ADMITTED ABOUT 6:30 AM. ON THE DRIVE TO THE HOSPITAL, SHE TOLD LT. FRUGE THAT SHE HAD BEEN TRAVELLING FROM FLORIDA TO LOUISIANA WITH TWO HISPANIC MEN WHO HAD BEEN DISCUSSING A PLOT TO ASSASSINATE JFK. SHE WAS QUESTIONED AGAIN BY LT. FRUGE. SHE TOLD FRUGE THAT THE MEN SHE HAD BEEN TRAVELLING WITH HAD

GOTTEN INTO AN ARGUMENT AT A BAR, THE SILVER SLIPPER. SHE CLAIMED SHE LEFT THE BAR ALONE AND WAS HITCHING WHEN SHE WAS STRUCK BY THE CAR. THE BAR MANAGER, MAC MANUAL, SAID HE HAD THROWN HER OUT OF THE BAR. CHERAMIE WENT ON TO DETAIL THAT SHE WAS TO TRAVEL TO HOUSTON WITH THE MEN AND COMPLETE A DRUG DEAL. SHE ALSO NOTED THAT A JACK RUBENSTEIN WAS INVOLVED IN THE DRUG DEAL. SHE GAVE FRUGE THE NAME OF A SEAMAN AND A SHIP IN HOUSTON. LT. FRUGE VERIFIED THE INFORMATION THRU U.S.CUSTOMS. SHE ALSO STATED THAT RUBY (RUBENSTEIN) AND **LEE** HAD KNOWN EACH OTHER. IN SEPTEMBER 1965, SHE WAS ONCE AGAIN FOUND ON THE SIDE OF A ROAD NEAR BIG SANDY, TEXAS. THIS TIME SHE WAS DEAD. AN AUTOPSY DETERMINED THAT SHE HAD BEEN SHOT IN THE HEAD AND THAT A VEHICLE HAD RUN OVER HER HEAD AS WELL.

EARLY AM NOVEMBER 21ST 1963

MARITA LORENZ, A CIA CONTACT, NOTED THAT SHE HAD SEEN RUBY, FRANK STURGIS, **LEE** AND HOWARD HUNT IN EITHER JIM BRADEN OR MORGAN BROWN'S HOTEL ROOM AT THE CABANA HOTEL SHORTLY AFTER 2:00 AM. BRADEN HAD LEGALLY CHANGED HIS NAME TO JIM BRADEN AND A CALIFORNIA DRIVERS LICENSE OBTAINED SEPTEMBER 10TH, 1963 REFLECTED THIS NEW MONIKER. HE WAS FORMERLY KNOWN AS EUGENE HALE BRADING OR JAMES BRADEN. BRADEN WAS ARRESTED IN THE DAL-TEX BUILDING SHORTLY AFTER THE ASSASSINATION. MORGAN BROWN, BRADEN'S COMPANION, WILL CHECK OUT OF THE HOTEL AT 2:00 PM, 90 MINUTES AFTER THE ASSASSINATION ON THE 22ND. RUBY CALLED LARRY CRAFARD AT THE VEGAS CLUB FROM THE HOTEL AT 2:00 AM.

NOVEMBER 21ST 1963

HARVEY ASKS FOR A RIDE FROM BUELL WESLEY FRAZIER TO IRVING TO VISIT MARINA AFTER WORK. HE NOTED TO FRAZIER, AT LEAST ACCORDING TO FRAZIER, THAT HE NEEDED TO GET SOME CURTAIN RODS. MARINA WOULD NOTE LATER THAT IT WAS THE FIRST TIME HE HAD BROKEN HIS ROUTINE AND CAME ON THURSDAY RATHER THAN THE CUSTOMARY FRIDAY. SHE WENT ON TO SAY THAT HE TOLD HER: "HE WANTED TO MAKE HIS PEACE WITH HER." MARINA HOWEVER NEGLECTED TO MENTION THAT **HARVEY** DID NOT VISIT THE PREVIOUS WEEKEND.

*THIS PARTICULAR DEPARTURE FROM HIS NORMAL ROUTINE WAS IN DEFFERENCE TO THE FACT THAT **HARVEY** BELIEVED HE WOULD BE DEPARTING THE COUNTRY THE NEXT DAY ENROUTE TO CUBA AND PERHAPS RUSSIA ON WHAT HE BELIEVED WAS A LEGITIMATE CIA ASSIGNMENT. THIS WOULD BE HIS FIRST POST "DEFECTION" ASSIGNMENT THAT WOULD INVOLVE TRAVEL OUTSIDE THE U.S. IF ONE DISCOUNTS THE LIKLIHOOD THAT IT WAS **HARVEY** IN MEXICO CITY. SINCE THIS "ASSIGNMENT" INVOLVED THE VERY REAL POSSIBILITY OF CAPTURE, **HARVEY** NOT ONLY MADE THIS UNUSUAL THURSDAY NIGHT VISIT, BUT, AS YOU WILL SEE, ON FRIDAY MORNING, HE WILL ALSO LEAVE $170, HIS WALLET, AND HIS WEDDING RING ON MARINA'S DRESSER.*

NOVEMBER 21ST 1963

THE PRESIDENTIAL ENTOURAGE ARRIVES AT THE HOTEL TEXAS IN FT. WORTH. THE PRESIDENT AND HIS WIFE ARE ASSIGNED SUITE 850.

EARLY AM, NOVEMBER 21ST 1963

RUBY WAS NOTED TO BE ON THE 6TH FLOOR OF THE RECORDS BUILDING. THIS BUILDING IS ACROSS FROM THE TSBD AT THE CORNER OF HOUSTON AND ELM. RUBY, IN HIS USUAL FASHION, WAS HANDING OUT CARDS FOR HIS CAROUSEL CLUB TOUTING HIS HEADLINE STRIPPER, JADA. AS HE WAS LEAVING, RUBY INTRODUCED HIMSELF TO ASSISTANT DISTRICT ATTORNEY BEN ELLIS. ELLIS NOTED LATER THAT RUBY HAD SAID TO HIM "YOU PROBABLY DON'T KNOW ME NOW, BUT YOU WILL."

DID RUBY KNOW MORE THAN I ANTICIPATED? OR, WAS HE SIMPLY AWARE THAT HE MAY BE CALLED UPON BY ORGANIZED CRIME TO PERFORM A "TASK" THAT WEEKEND?

NOVEMBER 21ST 1963
HARVEY COMPLETES HIS USUAL DAILY WORK AT THE TSBD AND RIDES TO THE PAINE RESIDENCE WITH BUELL FRAZIER. ACCORDING TO MARINA, **HARVEY** RETIRED FOR THE EVENING AT ABOUT 9:00 PM.

NOVEMBER 21ST 1963
A MUCH DISPUTED MEETING WAS ALLEGEDLY HELD THIS EVENING AS CLINT MURCHISON HOSTED A GATHERING AT HIS HOME IN DALLAS. IT WAS NOTED TO BE HELD IN HONOR OF J. EDGAR HOOVER. OVER THE COURSE OF THE EVENING, THE EVENT WAS ATTENDED BY FORMER PRESIDENT RICHARD NIXON, HOOVER OF COURSE, AND MURCHISON'S OIL ASSOCIATES H. L. HUNT. ALSO ATTENDING WAS GEORGE BROWN AND EMORY ROBERTS, SAIC OF THE PRESIDENT'S VISIT TO TEXAS. MADELEINE BROWN, LBJ'S MISTRESS, ALSO ATTENDED THE PARTY. SHE WOULD LATER NOTE THAT AS THE GATHERING WAS ABOUT TO DISPERSE, LBJ ARRIVED. HE ARRIVED AT APPROXIMATELY 1:00 AM, NOVEMBER 22ND. HIS PRESENCE DRAMATICALLY CHANGED WHAT HAD BEEN A JOVIAL ATMOSPHERE. BROWN NOTED THAT AS LBJ EXITED A HASTILY ARRANGED MEETING BEHIND CLOSED DOORS THAT HE WAS LIVID. SHE ALSO NOTED THAT WHEN HE APPROACHED HER HE LEANED IN AND SAID "AFTER TOMORROW, THOSE GODDAMN KENNEDYS WILL NEVER EMBARRASS ME AGAIN.....THAT'S NO THREAT....THAT'S A PROMISE."

NOVEMBER 21ST 1963
JACK RUBY HAD A LATE DINNER AT THE EGYPTIAN RESTAURANT AND LOUNGE WITH THE OWNER JOSEPH CAMPISI. CAMPISI WAS CONSIDERED TO BE THE CANDIDATE LIKELY TO SUCCEED JOE CIVELO AS CARLOS MARCELLO'S CHIEF OPERATIVE IN DALLAS. RUBY'S ROOMMATE, GEORGE SENATOR, WOULD OFFER LATER THAT CAMPISI WAS ONE OF RUBY'S "THREE CLOSEST FRIENDS." CAMPISI WAS THE FIRST TO VISIT RUBY IN JAIL AFTER RUBY HAD KILLED **HARVEY**. CLOSE TO MIDNIGHT, RUBY MET LAWRENCE V. MEYERS AND JEAN AESE (AKA JEAN WEST) IN THE BON VIVANT ROOM AT THE CABANA MOTEL. RUBY'S MEETING WITH MEYERS AND JEAN AESE ENDED ABOUT MIDNIGHT. RUBY HOWEVER TOLD AN EMPLOYEE OF HIS THAT HE STAYED AT THE HOTEL UNTIL ABOUT 2:00 AM.

EARLY AM NOVEMBER 22ND 1963
THE CELLAR COFFEE HOUSE WAS ONLY A FEW BLOCKS FROM THE RICE HOTEL IN HOUSTON. ALTHOUGH THEY DID NOT HAVE A LIQUOR LICENSE, THEY WERE KNOWN TO SERVE ALCOHOL TO REGULAR PATRONS. THEY ALSO OFFERED A LATE NIGHT BUFFET. IT HAD BEEN HOURS SINCE MOST OF THE SS AGENTS HAD EATEN, SO EIGHT AGENTS WENT TO THE CLUB ACCORDING TO THE W.C. AGENT CLINT HILL STAYED UNTIL AT LEAST 2 AM, 6 OTHER AGENTS STAYED UNTIL 3 AM, AND AGENT PAUL LANDIS STAYED UNTIL 5 AM. ALTHOUGH THE NOTION THAT THE AGENTS HAD BEEN DRINKING HEAVILY IS WIDELY DISPUTED, THEY NEVERTHELESS HAD TO REPORT TO DUTY AT 8 AM.

NOVEMBER 22ND 1963
AT 2:15 AM, **LEE** ARRIVES AT THE LUCAS B&B RESTAURANT. THE RESTAURANT IS ONLY TWO DOORS FROM THE VEGAS CLUB. AT 2:30 AM, RUBY AND A WOMAN NAMED "GLORIA" MET LARRY CRAFARD AT THE VEGAS CLUB. RUBY THEN WALKED TO THE LUCAS B&B RESTAURANT WHERE HE MET WITH **LEE**. WAITRESS MARY LAWRENCE WAS LATER INTERVIEWED BY DALLAS DETECTIVE P.M. DAVIS AND R.W. WESTPHAL. SHE NOTED THAT SHE WAS CERTAIN THAT THE MAN WHO ENTERED THE RESTAURANT WAS "OSWALD" (**LEE**) AND THAT HE HAD REMARKED TO HER THAT HE WAS WAITING FOR JACK RUBY. LAWRENCE HAD KNOWN RUBY FOR 8 YEARS. LAWRENCE WAS NOT INTERVIEWED BY THE W.C.

CHAPTER 10: THE MOTORCADE AND THE SHOOTING

EARLY AM FRIDAY, NOVEMBER 22ND 1963

THE DALLAS MORNING NEWS SHOWS A <u>MAP</u> OF THE PARADE ROUTE. IT DOES <u>NOT</u> INCLUDE THE MAIN-HOUSTON-ELM STREET TURN

ON NOVEMBER 16TH, THE DALLAS TIMES HERALD <u>NOTED</u> A MAIN STREET ONLY ROUTE BUT DID <u>NOT</u> SHOW A <u>MAP</u> OF THE ROUTE.

ON NOVEMBER 19TH, BOTH THE HERALD AND MORNING NEWS DID <u>DESCRIBE</u> THE MAIN-HOUSTON-ELM STREET TURNS. <u>NEITHER</u> PAPER HOWEVER SHOWED A <u>MAP</u> OF THE ROUTE.

ON NOVEMBER 20TH, <u>NEITHER</u> PAPER INCLUDED THE MAIN-HOUSTON-ELM TURN <u>NOR</u> DID THEY SHOW A PARADE ROUTE <u>MAP</u>.

ON NOVEMBER 21ST, THE HERALD DID SHOW A <u>MAP</u> WHICH INDEED INCLUDED THE MAIN-HOUSTON-ELM TURN.

ON NOVEMBER 22ND, THE MORNING NEWS <u>DID</u> SHOW A <u>MAP</u> BUT IT DID <u>NOT</u> INCLUDE THE MAIN-HOUSTON-ELM TURN.

THE DALLAS MORNING NEWS FRONT PAGE WAS USED AS AN EXHIBIT BY THE WARREN COMMISSION. THE AREA OF THE FRONT PAGE WHERE THE <u>MAP</u> HAD BEEN LOCATED WAS REPLACED BY A LARGE SOLID GREY SQUARE. THE COMMISSION APPARENTLY DID NOT WANT TO CALL ATTENTION TO THE FACT THAT AS OF FRIDAY MORNING, THE OFFICIAL PARADE ROUTE DID <u>NOT</u> INCLUDE THE SECURITY-BREACHING 120 DEGREE TURN IN FRONT OF THE TSBD; AT LEAST IN THE DALLAS MORNING NEWS.

*THE IMPORTANCE OF THIS OMISSION CANNOT BE OVERSTATED. THE W.C. CONTENDS THAT **HARVEY'S** ALLEGED ASSASSINATION ATTEMPT WAS SPAWNED IN PART BY THE REALIZATION THAT THE MOTORCADE WOULD PASS DIRECTLY BELOW HIS PLACE OF EMPLOYMENT, THE TSBD. BUT THE NEWSPAPERS HOWEVER ARE VERY INCONSISTANT IN NOTING THE FATAL TURN AS DEMONSTRATED ABOVE.*

EARLY AM, NOVEMBER 22ND 1963

VICE-PRESIDENT JOHNSON AND JFK ARGUED LOUDLY IN THE PRESIDENTIAL SUITE AT THE TEXAS HOTEL IN FT. WORTH. THE ARGUMENT REVOLVED AROUND LBJ'S INSISTANCE THAT HIS POLITICAL ENEMY, SENATOR RALPH YARBOROUGH, RIDE WITH JFK IN THE MOTORCADE. THIS WOULD ALLOW GOVENOR CONNALLY AND LBJ TO RIDE IN THE FOLLOW-UP CAR. JFK REFUSED TO HONOR LBJ'S REQUEST AND INSISTED THAT CONNALLY RIDE WITH HIM.

IT IS INTERESTING TO NOTE THAT CONNALLY, UPON BEING SHOT, CRIED OUT "OH, NO, OH MY GOD, THEY ARE GOING TO KILL US ALL!" THE USE OF THE WORD "THEY" WOULD IMPLY THAT CONNALLY'S IMMEDIATE AND OBVIOUSLY UNREHEARSED UTTERANCE REVEALED A CLUE THAT HE MAY HAVE BEEN AWARE THAT THIS WAS NOT THE WORK OF A "LONE GUNMAN." IN HIS TESTIMONY BEFORE THE WARREN COMMISSION, CONNALLY WOULD NOTE IN REGARDS TO THE TIMING OF THE SHOTS: "THE THOUGHT IMMEDIATELY PASSED THROUGH MY MIND THAT THERE WERE EITHER 2 OR 3 PEOPLE INVOLVED IN THIS OR SOMEONE WAS SHOOTING WITH AN AUTOMATIC RIFLE."

HIS CHOICE OF THE WORDS "KILL US ALL" WOULD ALSO LEAD ONE TO THINK THAT HE MAY HAVE FEARED THAT THE ACCURACY OR THE INTENTIONS OF THE SHOOTERS HAD SOMEHOW BEEN CHANGED. KEEP IN MIND THAT CONNALLY HAD DISTANCED HIMSELF POLITICALLY FROM BOTH THE LIBERAL DEMOCRATIC PRESIDENT AND SENATOR

YARBROUGH. WAS CONNALLY'S "KILL US ALL" COMMENT AN AKNOWLEDGEMENT OF THE SHARPLY DIVIDED TEXAS DEMOCRATIC PARTY? WHEN ONE COMBINES THE SEATING ARRANGEMENT ARGUMENT BETWEEN LBJ AND JFK WITH THE PECULIAR OUTCRY OF CONNALLY, IT IS NOT DIFFICULT TO IMAGINE THE POSSIBILITY IF NOT THE PROBABILITY THAT BOTH LBJ AND CONNALLY WERE AWARE THAT THE MOTORCADE WOULD ALTER THEIR POLITICAL FUTURES DRAMATICALLY AND BRING ONE MAN'S PRESIDENCY TO A VIOLENT END.

7:00 AM FRIDAY
PATROLMAN J.D. TIPPIT REPORTS TO THE OAK CLIFF SUBSTATION.

EARLIER THAT MORNING, TIPPIT HAD TOLD HIS 14 YEAR OLD SON "NO MATTER WHAT HAPPENS TODAY, I WANT YOU TO KNOW THAT I LOVE YOU." HIS SON, ALLEN, NOTED THAT THIS WAS VERY UNCHARACTERISTIC OF HIS FATHER.

APPROXIMATELY 7:18 AM FRIDAY
HARVEY OVERSLEEPS AND APPARENTLY SKIPS HIS USUAL BREAKFAST AT THE DOBBS RESTAURANT. HE THEN LEAVES THE PAINE HOUSE WHERE MARINA IS STAYING. HE LEAVES $170 AND, ACCORDING TO THE WARREN COMMISSION, HIS WALLET IN A DRESSER DRAWER AND HIS WEDDING RING IN A CUP ON MARINA'S DRESSER. HE WALKS THE 100 YARDS OR SO TO LINNIE MAE RANDLES'S HOME WHERE HER BROTHER BUELL FRAZIER RESIDES.

7:22 AM FRIDAY
HARVEY ARRIVES AT THE RANDLE'S HOME. PRIOR TO APPROACHING THE KITCHEN WINDOW HE, ACCORDING TO LINNIE MAE RANDLE, PLACED A PACKAGE ON THE REAR SEAT OF BUELL FRAZIER'S CAR. RANDLE'S MOTHER, ELSIE WILLIAMS, NOTED HOWEVER THAT **HARVEY** WAS NOT CARRYING A PACKAGE AS HE APPROACHED THE CAR.

7:25 AM FRIDAY
FRAZIER AND **HARVEY** LEAVE RANDLE'S HOUSE FOR WORK. WHEN HE AND FRAZIER ENTERED THE CAR, FRAZIER ASKED HIM WHAT WAS IN THE PACKAGE. **HARVEY**, ACCORDING TO FRAZIER, REPLIED "THOSE ARE THE CURTAIN RODS."

*ONCE IN CUSTODY IT IS DIFFICULT TO VERIFY **HARVEY'S** COMMENTS REGARDING THE "PACKAGE" HE ALLEGEDLY PLACED ON THE BACK SEAT OF FRAZIER'S CAR THAT MORNING SINCE THERE WAS NO OFFICIAL RECORD KEPT OF HIS INTERROGATION. BUT, IT WAS NOTED BY THOSE ATTENDING THE INTERROGATION SESSIONS THAT HE DENIED CARRYING ANYTHING OTHER THAN HIS LUNCH TO WORK THAT DAY. INTERESTINGLY, THERE WERE 9 PHOTOS TAKEN THE MORNING OF NOVEMBER 23RD AT **HARVEY'S** ROOMING HOUSE BY BLACK STAR PHOTOGRAPHER GENE DANIELS. THE PHOTOS SHOW A CO-OWNER OF THE HOME, MRS ARTHUR JOHNSON, SUPERVISING HER HUSBAND HANGING CURTAIN RODS IN **HARVEY'S** ROOM. MRS. JOHNSON INSISTS THAT THE ROOM DID INDEED HAVE CURTAINS AND THE OBVIOUSLY NECESSARY CURTAIN RODS. BUT, THE PREVIOUS EVENING, FRIDAY NOVEMBER 22ND, THEY HAD BEEN TAKEN DOWN WHEN THE VISITING NEWSMEN DESCENDED UPON THE PROPERTY. ONE HAS TO WONDER IF THE CURTAINS, INNOCENTLY REMOVED BY THE UNWITTING MRS. JOHNSON PRIOR TO THE NEWSMENS ARRIVAL FURTHERED THE NOTION THAT THE ROOM WAS INDEED IN NEED OF CURTAINS AND THEREFORE CURTAIN RODS. A "CURTAIN-LESS" ROOM WOULD HAVE SUPPORTED BUELL FRAZIER'S CONTENTION THAT **HARVEY** MAY HAVE HIS SMUGGLED THE ALLEGED ASSASSINATION RIFLE INTO THE TSBD UNDER THE GUISE OF CURTAIN RODS THAT FRIDAY.*

*I HAVE NOT READ ANYWHERE OF ANY WITNESSES REPORTING **HARVEY** CARRYING A PACKAGE FROM THE TSBD TO HIS ROOMING HOUSE ON FRIDAY, NOVEMBER 22ND AFTER THE MID-DAY SHOOTING. AND, NO CURTAIN RODS WERE FOUND AT THE TSBD. ONE WOULD HAVE TO ASSUME THAT THE CURTAIN RODS WERE EITHER TAKEN BY **HARVEY** TO THE ROOMING HOUSE BEFORE NOVEMBER 22ND (IF INDEED HE PROVIDED THEM AT ALL) OR THAT THE CURTAIN ROD STORY WAS SIMPLY REPEATED BY **HARVEY** THAT MORNING IN SUPPORT OF WHAT HE HAD TOLD FRAZIER THE PREVIOUS DAY AS TO HIS EXCUSE FOR HIS GOING TO MARINA'S ON THURSDAY RATHER THAN FRIDAY.*

HARVEY, BY ALL INDICATIONS, WAS NOT ONE TO ALLOW ANYONE TO BECOME TOO FAMILIAR WITH HIS PERSONAL LIFE. HE HAD ARGUED WITH MARINA OVER WHAT SHE THOUGHT WAS HIS USE OF AN ALIAS WHEN HE RENTED HIS ROOM AT THE ROOMING HOUSE AND HIS NOT HAVING VISITED THE WEEKEND BEFORE. WITH HIS PERCEIVED "DEPARTURE" FOR HIS ASSIGNMENT SCHEDULED FOR FRIDAY, **HARVEY** LIKELY USED THE CURTAIN ROD STORY AS AN EXCUSE IN HIS RELUCTANCE TO SHARE WITH BUELL FRAZIER THE PROBLEMS BETWEEN HE AND MARINA AND TO DISGUISE THE FACT THAT HE WOULD NOT BE GOING TO THE PAINE'S RESIDENCE ON FRIDAY, NOVEMBER 22ND. THE PACKAGE **HARVEY** CARRIED TO WORK THAT FRIDAY, IF IT WERE ANYTHING OTHER THAN HIS LUNCH, WAS ONLY TO SUPPORT THE EXCUSE HE HAD GIVEN TO FRAZIER FOR HIS THURSDAY RATHER THAN FRIDAY VISIT TO MARINA.

ALTHOUGH WE MAY NEVER KNOW WHAT WAS IN THE PACKAGE **HARVEY** CARRIED TO WORK THAT DAY, IT IS A VIRTUAL CERTAINTY THAT HE WAS NOT CARRYING THE ALLEGED ASSASSINATION RIFLE THAT FRIDAY MORNING AS THE WARREN COMMISSION CLAIMS. BOTH FRAZIER AND RANDLE TESTIFIED THAT THE LONGEST THE PACKAGE COULD HAVE BEEN WAS 27-28 INCHES LONG. THE MANNER IN WHICH HE CARRIED THE PACKAGE, AS DESCRIBED BY FRAZIER, WOULD HAVE MADE IT IMPOSSIBLE FOR THE PACKAGE TO HAVE BEEN THE MANNLICHER. THE CARBINE, IN ITS SHORTEST POSSIBLE LENGTH, WAS ALMOST 35 INCHES LONG. FRAZIER, BEFORE THE COMMISSION, DEMONSTRATED HOW **HARVEY** CARRIED THE PACKAGE: ONE END CUPPED IN HIS HAND, THE OTHER END IN THE PIT OF HIS ARM.

IN HIS DEMONSTRATION, IN WHICH HE USED THE ALLEGED ASSASSINATION WEAPON IN ITS SHORTEST LENGTH, 35 INCHES, THE TOP END OF THE PACKAGE PROTRUDED ABOVE HIS SHOULDER NEARLY TO HIS EAR. FRAZIER WAS NEARLY 6'1. **HARVEY** WAS SEVERAL INCHES SHORTER. ONE WOULD HAVE TO ASSUME THAT THE SAME PACKAGE CARRIED BY THE SHORTER **HARVEY** WOULD HAVE REACHED WELL ABOVE HIS EAR IF CARRIED IN THE FASHION DESCRIBED BY FRAZIER.

IT IS HOWEVER RANDLE'S DESCRIPTION THAT I FIND MORE REVEALING. IN HER TESTIMONY BEFORE THE WARREN COMMISSION SHE NOTED THAT **HARVEY** GRIPPED THE PACKAGE AT THE TOP WITH HIS RIGHT HAND AND THAT THE BOTTOM OF THE PACKAGE ALMOST TOUCHED THE GROUND. REVISITING FRAZIER'S OBSERVANCE OF **HARVEY** CARRYING THE SAME PACKAGE INTO THE TSBD, FRAZIER NOTED THAT **HARVEY** HAD THE TOP OF THE PACKAGE CUPPED IN HIS ARM PIT AND THE BOTTOM CUPPED IN HIS HAND. WITH THE TOP OF THE PACKAGE FIRMLY HELD IN PLACE BY HIS UPPER ARM AGAINST HIS SIDE, THE PACKAGE WOULD APPEAR TO FRAZIER AS BEING RIGID. IT WOULD OF COURSE ALSO HAVE APPEARED TO BE RIGID TO RANDLE AS THE PACKAGE WOULD HAVE HUNG BY **HARVEY'S** SIDE. I STRONGLY SUSPECT THAT **HARVEY** DID INDEED HAVE HIS LUNCH IN THE BOTTOM OF THIS ODD SHAPED PACKAGE. HE SIMPLY USED A BAG LONG ENOUGH THAT IT GAVE THE APPEARANCE OF BEING SOMEWHAT RIGID WHEN HELD IN THE TWO MANNERS DESCRIBED BY FRAZIER AND RANDLE.

HARVEY SIMPLY NEED A PACKAGE OF THE DIMENSIONS THAT COULD POSSIBLY HAVE HELD CURTAIN RODS AS TO AVOID ANY FURTHER QUESTIONING BY FRAZIER AS TO THE TRUE REASON FOR HIS THURSDAY VISIT TO MARINA. THE BOTTOM DIAMETER OF THE BAG, AS DESCRIBED BY FRAZIER AND RANDLE, WAS ABOUT 6-8 INCHES ACROSS; THE DIAMETER ONE WOULD EXPECT TO ACCOMMODATE THE SANDWICHES **HARVEY** BROUGHT TO WORK THAT DAY.

ALTHOUGH THE PHYSICAL DESCRIPTION OF THE PACKAGE BY FRAZIER AND RANDLE IS A BIT ODD FOR A LUNCH SACK, IT WOULD HAVE BEEN AN IMPOSSIBILITY FOR THE PACKAGE TO HAVE CONTAINED THE ALLEGED ASSASSINATION RIFLE.

IT IS INTERESTING TO NOTE THAT THE BAG ALLEGEDLY USED TO CARRY THE RIFLE ALLEGEDLY USED TO SHOOT THE PRESIDENT WAS NOT PHOTOGRAPHED AT THE LOCATION WHERE IT WAS SUPPOSEDLY FOUND; NEAR THE 6TH FLOOR WINDOW. THE

MANNLICHER AND THE SHELL CASINGS WERE INDEED PHOTOGRAPHED WHERE THEY WERE FOUND. THE BAG HOWEVER WAS ONLY SHOWN AS AN "OUTLINE" SUPERIMPOSED OVER A PHOTOGRAPH TAKEN NEAR THE 6TH FLOOR WINDOW ADJACENT TO THE ALLEGED "SNIPER'S NEST."

WARREN COMMISSION TESTIMONY SHEDS LITTLE LIGHT ON ORIGIN OR ACTUAL INITIAL LOCATION OF THIS BAG:

ROGER CRAIG, DEPUTY
WHEN ASKED IF THERE WAS A LARGE SACK LYING ON THE FLOOR REPLIED: "NO, I DON'T REMEMBER SEEING ANY."

ROBERT LEE STUDEBAKER, DPD PHOTOGRAPHER
WHEN ASKED IF THE SACK WAS IN ANY OF THE EVIDENCE PICTURES HE TOOK THAT DAY REPLIED "NO, IT DOESN'T SHOW IN ANY OF THE PICTURES."

JOHN HICKS, DPD DETECTIVE
WHEN ASKED IF HE SAW A SACK IN ITEMS REMOVED FROM THE TSBD REPLIED "NO SIR, I DID NOT."

GERALD HILL, DPD SERGEANT
NOTED THAT THE ONLY SACK HE SAW WAS "A SMALL SACK THAT APPEARED TO BE A LUNCH SACK."

DESPITE THE DISCREPANCIES BETWEEN THE SACK AND THE MANNLICHER AND THE DISCREPANCIES NOTED IN THE LENGTH OF THE SACK ITSELF:

1) LACK OF OIL ON THE SACK VERSUS THE "WELL OILED" MANNLICHER
2) THE LENGTH NOTED BY FRAZIER, RANDLE (ABOUT 2 FEET) AND STUDEBAKER, (3.5-4 FEET)

THE WARREN COMMISSION NEVERTHELESS FOUND IT IMPERATIVE TO UTILIZE THE CURTAIN ROD STORY TO SHOW HOW **HARVEY** COULD HAVE BROUGHT THE ALLEGED ASSASSINATION WEAPON INTO THE TSBD.

7:30 AM FRIDAY
W. STARK IS THE OWNER OF THE TOP TEN RECORD STORE AT 338 W. JEFFERSON. WHEN HE ARRIVED AT THE STORE, **LEE** WAS WAITING OUTSIDE. **LEE** BOUGHT A TICKET TO A "DICK CLARK CARAVAN OF STARS" ROCK AND ROLL SHOW THAT WAS TO BE HELD THAT EVENING IN DALLAS. **LEE** THEN LEFT THE STORE AND CAUGHT A BUS. A SHORT TIME LATER, **LEE** RETURNED TO THE STORE AND BOUGHT A 2ND TICKET. ON HIS 2ND VISIT, J.D. TIPPIT WAS ALSO IN THE STORE.

*WAS **LEE'S** SECOND TICKET PURCHASE NECESSAARY IN ORDER TO ALLOW TIPPIT TO ONCE AGAIN LAY EYES ON THE MAN WHO WOULD ENCOUNTER HIM AT 10TH AND PATTON LESS THAN 6 HOURS LATER? LEE HAD ALREADY DONE THIS ON WEDNESDAY AT THE DOBB'S RESTAURANT. BUT, KEEP IN MIND THAT IT WAS A HABIT OF TIPPITS TO NOT DIRECTLY LOOK PEOPLE IN THE EYE WHEN CONFRONTING THEM. THIS HABIT ALONE LIKELY PROMPTED THE NECESSITY OF <u>TWO</u> ENCOUNTERS BETWEEN TIPPIT AND LEE IN LESS THAN 48 HOURS.*

7:30 AM FRIDAY
TIPPIT LEAVES THE OAK CLIFF STATION AND IS ENROUTE TO HIS NORMAL PATROL AREA, DISTRICT 78.

7:55 AM FRIDAY
FRAZIER AND **HARVEY** ARRIVE AT TSBD.

*JACK DOUGHERTY SAW **HARVEY** ENTER THE TSBD THROUGH A BACK DOOR. DOUGHERTY NOTED THAT **HARVEY** WAS NOT CARRYING A PACKAGE OF <u>ANY</u> TYPE. IF **HARVEY** WAS*

INDEED CARRYING ONLY HIS LUNCH AS HE CLAIMED, HE COULD HAVE PUT IT IN THE POCKET OF THE JACKET HE WAS WEARING.

*FRAZIER NOTED THAT **HARVEY** WALKED QUICKLY TO THE TSBD. HE ALSO NOTED THAT HE DID NOT ACTUALLY SEE HIM ENTER THE BUILDING SINCE HE REMAINED IN THE CAR FOR A FEW MINUTES TO "GUN" THE MOTOR AND CHARGE HIS BATTERY. THE LOT WHERE FRAZIER PARKED IS 3 BLOCKS NORTH OF THE TSBD ON NORTH RECORD AT MCKINNEY AVENUE. NO ONE INSIDE THE BUILDING RECALLED SEEING **HARVEY** ENTER WITH ANY TYPE OF PACKAGE. DID **HARVEY** HIDE A PACKAGE OUTSIDE THE BUILDING OR GIVE IT TO SOMEONE PRIOR TO ENTERING? THE CONTENTS OF AND THE SIGNIFICANCE OF WHO EVENTUALLY RECEIVED A PACKAGE – IF INDEED THERE WAS ONE - CANNOT BE UNDERESTIMATED UNLESS OF COURSE THE PACKAGE WAS WHAT **HARVEY** CLAIMED: HIS LUNCH.*

8:00 AM FRIDAY
ROY TRULY, TSBD SUPERINTENDANT, NOTICES **HARVEY** IN THE BUILDING.

8:15 AM FRIDAY
JUNIOR JARMAN, WHOSE WORK IS PRIMARILY ON THE FIRST FLOOR, SEES **HARVEY**.

9:30 AM FRIDAY
LEE ENTERS A JIFFY STORE LOCATED AT 310 SOUTH INDUSTRIAL BOULEVARD. FRED MOORE, THE STORE CLERK, ASKS FOR AN I.D AS **LEE** IS ABOUT TO BUY 2 BOTTLES OF BEER. MR. MOORE IS PRESENTED WITH A TEXAS DRIVERS LICENSE *TAKEN FROM A BILLFOLD* WITH THE NAME "LEE OSWALD" OR POSSIBLY "H. LEE OSWALD."

*KEEP IN MIND THAT ACCORDING TO THE WARREN COMMISSION **HARVEY** LEFT HIS WALLET ON MARINA'S DRESSER EARLIER THAT MORNING PRIOR TO LEAVING FOR WORK AND THAT HE DID NOT HAVE A DRIVERS LICENSE NOR WAS HE KNOWN TO DRINK.*

9:56 AM FRIDAY
DISPATCH SENDS TIPPPIT TO THE ALUMINUM MANUFACTURING COMPANY AT 2800 EAST ILLINOIS AVENUE TO INVESTIGATE A SITUATION.

10:00 AM FRIDAY
LEE RETURNS TO THE SAME JIFFY STORE TO BUY TWO PIECES OF PECO BRITTLE AND ANOTHER BEER AS MOORE RECALLS.

*__HARVEY'S__ WORKDAY STARTED AT 8:00 AM THAT MORNING. EITHER HIS EMPLOYER, THE TSBD, HAS A LIBERAL BREAK POLICY WHICH INCLUDES THE CONSUMPTION OF ALCOHOL, OR **HARVEY** COULD NOT HAVE POSSIBLY MADE TWO VISITS TO THE JIFFY STORE IN HIS FIRST TWO HOURS ON THE CLOCK. BESIDES, THE JIFFY STORE IS OVER 1 MILE FROM THE TSBD. **HARVEY** WOULD HAVE HAD TO EITHER TAKE A BUS THAT WAS SCHEDULED PERFECTLY TO ALLOW FOR THESE VISITS, OR WOULD HAVE HAD TO TAKE AN EXPENSIVE, RELATIVE TO HIS PURCHASES, CAB RIDE FOR EACH VISIT. THE FIRST VISIT OBVIOUSLY IS THE MORE TROUBLING SINCE **LEE** DISPLAYED A WALLET WHILE THE WARREN COMMISSION CLAIMS **HARVEY** LEFT HIS WALLET ON MARINA'S DRESSER LESS THAN TWO HOURS BEFORE.*

*THE SET-UP CONSPIRATORS WERE NOT ONLY ONCE AGAIN CARELESS, BUT APPARENTLY ALLOWED FOR A SIGHTING OF A LEE HARVEY OSWALD AT A TIME WHEN **HARVEY** COULD NOT HAVE POSSIBLY BEEN ANYWHERE BUT AT THE TSBD.*

10:00 AM FRIDAY
TSBD EMPLOYEE EDDIE PIPER ARRIVES AT WORK. HE NOTICES **HARVEY** ON THE FIRST FLOOR.

10:15 AM FRIDAY
HANK NORMAN, A TSBD EMPLOYEE, NOTES THAT **HARVEY** IS ON THE 1ST FLOOR.

10:17 AM FRIDAY
TIPPIT CLEARED HIMSELF TO DISPATCH FROM THE 9:56 CALL AT 2800 EAST ILLINOIS AVENUE.

10:30 AM FRIDAY
MIAMI POLICE/FBI INFORMANT WILLIAM SOMERSETT RECEIVED A PHONE CALL FROM JOSEPH MILTEER WHO, ACCORDING TO THE FBI IN WASHINGTON, WAS IN DALLAS. THE ATLANTA FIELD OFFICE HOWEVER WOULD CONTEND THAT MILTEER WAS AT HOME IN QUITMAN, GEORGIA. MILTEER COMMENTED: "WELL I'M DOWN HERE IN JACK RABBIT COUNTRY....I DON'T THINK YOU WILL EVER SEE YOUR BOY AGAIN IN MIAMI." MILTEER HIMSELF ADMITTED TO SOMERSETT THAT HE WAS INDEED IN DALLAS.

MILTEER WAS PHOTOGRAPHED IN THE CROWD AT HOUSTON AND ELM JUST MOMENTS PRIOR TO THE SHOOTING. THIS WOULD INDEED SUPPORT THE FBI IN WASHINGTON'S NOTION THAT HE WAS IN DALLAS.

CAPTAIN CHARLES SAPP OF THE MIAMI POLICE INTELLIGENCE BUREAU ALERTED BOTH THE FBI AND THE SECRET SERVICE ABOUT MILTEER'S COMMENTS OF 18-20 OCTOBER IN INDIANAPOLIS, AND THE TAPED CONVERSATION MILTEER HAD WITH WILLIAM SOMERSETT ON NOVEMBER 9TH IN MIAMI. THE SECRET SERVICE DETAIL ASSIGNED TO JFK'S DALLAS TRIP WAS APARENTLY NOT INFORMED. MILTEER IS NOT MENTIONED IN THE COMMISSION'S 26 VOLUMES

10:30 AM FRIDAY
OFFICER TIPPIT STOPS FOR A BRIEF COFFEE BREAK WITH OFFICER WILLIAM ANGLIN AT THE REBEL DRIVE-IN.

10:30 AM FRIDAY
RUBY ARRIVES AT THE DALLAS MORNING NEWS AND TALKS TO 2 GIRLS IN THE RECEPTION AREA.

10:40 AM FRIDAY
A GREEN AND WHITE FORD PICKUP TRUCK STALLS ON ELM STREET NEAR THE RAILROAD OVERPASS. OFFICERS WHOSE PRIMARY FUNCTION WAS TO PROVIDE SECURITY FOR THE MOTORCADE ARE DISTRACTED BY THE TRUCK'S PRESENCE AND EFFORTS TO HAVE IT MOVED. THE TRUCK HAD, ON THE DOORS, "AIR CONDITIONING" STENCILED IN BLOCK LETTERS WITHIN AN OVAL BACKGROUND IN A "HALF-MOON" DESIGN.

10:40 AM FRIDAY
TIPPIT IS DISPATCHED TO EAST ANN ARBOR AND CORRIGAN.

10:45 AM FRIDAY
TIPPIT IS CLEARED FROM THE 10:40 DISPATCH.

10:50 AM FRIDAY
THE STALLED PICKUP TRUCK WAS WITNESSED BY JULIA ANN MERCER. LATER THAT DAY SHE GAVE A SWORN DEPOSITION TO DALLAS COUNTY SHERIFFS. MERCER'S DEPOSITION NOTES THAT SHE WITNESSED A MAN, LATE 20'S, WHITE MALE, EXIT THE PASSENGER SIDE OF THE TRUCK AND REMOVE WHAT APPEARED TO BE A GUN CASE FROM THE BED OF THE TRUCK. SHE ALSO NOTED THE MAN WAS WEARING A GREY JACKET, BROWN SLACKS, AND A PLAID SHIRT. HE ALSO WORE A WOOL STOCKING CAP WITH A TASSEL ON TOP. THE MAN THEN WALKED UP THE HILL TOWARDS THE OVERPASS AT THE TOP OF THE HILL SOON TO BE KNOWN AS THE GRASSY KNOLL. THE DRIVER OF THE TRUCK REMAINED BEHIND THE WHEEL. THIS MAN WORE A GREEN JACKET, WAS HEAVY SET, AND APPEARED TO BE IN HIS MID 40'S. MERCER WAS INTERVIEWED BY THE FBI ON NOVEMBER 25TH AND AGAIN ON NOVEMBER 27TH. IN BOTH REPORTS HOWEVER SHE WAS UNABLE TO IDENTIFY RUBY AS THE DRIVER OF THE TRUCK OR **HARVEY** AS THE MAN WHO REMOVED THE GUN CASE. SHE WOULD LATER IN JANUARY 1968, CLAIM TO JIM GARRISON THAT HER 3 STATEMENTS TO AUTHORITIES WERE ALTERED AND THAT SHE HAD IDENTIFIED THE DRIVER AS JACK RUBY. BUT, RUBY CLAIMS TO HAVE BEEN AT THE DALLAS MORNING NEWS AT

VIRTUALLY (10:30-11:00AM) THE SAME TIME. EITHER RUBY CONVENIENTLY CHOSE 10:30 AS HIS ARRIVAL TIME AT THE PAPER TO DISPUTE HIS BEING BEHIND THE WHEEL OF A STALLED TRUCK IN DEALY PLAZA OR MERCER IS MISTAKEN.

11:00 AM FRIDAY
BUELL WESLEY FRAZIER NOTES **HARVEY'S** PRESENCE ON THE 1ST FLOOR.

11:30 AM FRIDAY
OFFICER TIPPIT TAKES AN ABREVIATED LUNCH BREAK AT HIS HOME WITH HIS WIFE AND SON.

11:30 AM FRIDAY
AFTER HAVING BREAKFAST, RUBY PLACES HIS REGULAR AD FOR THE CAROUSEL CLUB WITH DON CAMPBELL OF THE DALLAS MORNING NEWS. RUBY CLAIMS HE WAS STILL THERE WHEN THE NEWS BROKE OF THE SHOOTING AND THEN FOR SOME TIME AFTERWARDS.

THERE IS STRONG EVIDENCE HOWEVER THAT RUBY LEFT THAT BUILDING BRIEFLY <u>PRIOR</u> TO THE ARRIVAL OF THE MOTORCADE.. THE DALLAS NEWS BUILDING IS LOCATED AT THE CORNER OF HOUSTON AND YOUNG STREETS, ONLY 4 BLOCKS FROM DEALEY PLAZA, APPROXIMATELY A 4 MINUTE WALK. HUGH AYNSWORTH, A REPORTER FOR THE PAPER, AND SEVERAL OTHER EMPLOYEES INCLUDING DON CAMPBELL, NOTED THAT RUBY HAD NOT BEEN SEEN FROM ABOUT 12:20 UNTIL ABOUT 12:45. IN FACT, TV REPORTER WES WISE NOTED THAT HE HAD SEEN RUBY NEAR THE TSBD ONLY MINUTES AFTER THE 12:30 SHOOTING. WISE WOULD LATER BECOME MAYOR OF DALLAS, THE WARREN COMMISSION ELECTED NOT TO CALL WISE TO TESTIFY.

11:40 AM FRIDAY
AIR FORCE ONE ARRIVES AT LOVE FIELD.

ACCORDING TO LIVE T.V. REPORTS, THERE ARE "LITERALLY HUNDREDS OF POLICE PATROLLING AT LOVE FIELD AND POLICE ON THE ROOFS OF EVERY BUILDING." ONE WOULD QUESTION WHY THIS SAME LEVEL OF ROOFTOP PROTECTION WAS NOT UTILIZED ALONG THE PARADE ROUTE.

11:42 AM FRIDAY
HARVEY NOTICES THE CROWD GATHERING ON THE STREET AND ASKS A FELLOW WORKER ON THE 6TH FLOOR WHAT THE COMMOTION WAS ABOUT. THE WORKER TOLD HIM THAT THE PRESIDENT WOULD SOON BE PASSING BY.

HARVEY WAS CERTAINLY AWARE OF THE PRESIDENT'S VISIT TO DALLAS. BUT, HE MAY NOT HAVE BEEN AWARE THAT WITH THE MAIN-HOUSTON-ELM TURN THAT THE MOTORCADE WOULD PASS DIRECTLY IN FRONT OF THE TSBD.

11:50 AM FRIDAY
JFK, THE FIRST LADY, AND JOHN AND NELLIE CONNALLY ENTER THE PRESIDENTIAL LIMO.

11:51 AM FRIDAY
OFFICER TIPPIT LEAVES HIS RESIDENCE TO RETURN TO HIS PATROL CAR. HE REPORTS TO DISPATCH "78 CLEAR."

11:55 AM FRIDAY
THE MOTORCADE LEAVES THE AIRPORT.

11:55 AM FRIDAY
BONNIE RAY WILLIAMS, HAROLD NORMAN, AND DANNY ARCE, WHO HAD BEEN WORKING THAT MORNING ON THE 6TH FLOOR, TOOK THE ELEVATOR DOWN TO RETRIEVE THEIR LUNCHES.. WILLIAMS SAID **HARVEY** CALLED TO HIM TO SEND THE ELEVATOR BACK UP. EDDIE PIPER TOLD THE WARREN COMMISSION THAT HE SPOKE TO **HARVEY** ON THE <u>1ST</u> <u>FLOOR</u> SHORTLY AFTER 12:00. **HARVEY** HAD TOLD HIM " I'M

GOING UP TO EAT." THE LUNCH ROOM, WITH BOOTHS AND A COKE MACHINE, WAS ON THE 2ND FLOOR.

12:05 PM FRIDAY
BONNIE RAY WILLIAMS GOES BACK UP TO THE 6TH FLOOR TO WATCH THE MOTORCADE AND EAT HIS LUNCH.

12:13 PM FRIDAY
CAROLYN ARNOLD TOLD THE FBI THAT SHE HAD SIGHTED **HARVEY** IN THE HALLWAY ON THE 2ND FLOOR AT THIS TIME.

12:15 PM FRIDAY
THE STALLED PICKUP TRUCK IS PUSHED AWAY BY ANOTHER TRUCK AS AN AMBULANCE IS EN ROUTE TO HOUSTON AND ELM TO TRANSPORT THE VICTIM OF A "SEIZURE" TO PARKLAND HOSPITAL.

THERE HAD BEEN AN EARLIER ASSASSINATION ATTEMPT ON CASTRO IN CHILE. THE ATTEMPT INVOLVED NUMEROUS SHOOTERS AND A STALLED VEHICLE IN AN EFFORT TO SLOW CASTRO'S VEHICLE. A "PATSY", WHO WAS SUPPOSED TO BE KILLED AFTER THE UNSUCCESSFUL ATTEMPT, WAS TO BE IMPLICATED BY FAKED PHOTOS AND DOCUMENTS. IN DALLAS, THE STALLED PICK-UP TRUCK AND THE AMBULANCE RUN WERE APPARENTLY DESIGNED TO NOT ONLY DISTRACT THE OFFICERS ON SITE, BUT ALSO TO ASSIST IN SLOWING THE MOTORCADE AS IT PASSED THRU THE KILL ZONE; THE STRETCH OF ELM STREET LOCATED PRECISELY BETWEEN THE AMBULANCE AT HOUSTON AND ELM, AND THE STALLED TRUCK ON ELM NEAR THE RAILROAD OVERPASS. BOTH VEHICLES WOULD VACATE THE AREA ONLY A FEW MINUTES PRIOR TO THE ARRIVAL OF THE MOTORCADE. BUT, IT IS IMPORTANT TO NOTE THAT AT 12:30 PM WHEN THE PRESIDENTIAL LIMO REACHED ELM AND HOUSTON THAT IT WAS OVER 5 MINUTES BEHIND SCHEDULE. THE MOTORCADE WAS SCHEDULED TO ARRIVE AT THE TRADE CENTER FOR THE LUNCHEON AT 12:30. HAD THE MOTORCADE BEEN ON SCHEDULE, IT WOULD HAVE BEEN A NEAR CERTAINTY THAT IT WOULD HAVE BEEN SLOWED IF NOT COMPLETELY STOPPED EITHER BY THE STALLED TRUCK OR BY THE AMBULANCE WHICH DID NOT DEPART THE SCENE UNTIL 12:24.

IN ADDITION TO THE DISTRACTIONS OFFERED BY THE AMBULANCE AND THE TRUCK, A TRAIN PASSED OVER ELM ST. ON THE RAILROAD OVERPASS ONLY 3 MINUTES AFTER THE MOTORCADE HAD PASSED. THE TRAIN WOULD HAVE CONTRIBUTED CONSIDERABLY TO THE NOISE AND COULD HAVE MADE AURALLY LOCATING THE SOURCE OF THE SHOTS VIRTUALLY IMPOSSIBLE. THE TRAIN COULD ALSO HAVE BEEN A METHOD BY WHICH SHOOTERS COULD HAVE BEEN EXTRACTED FROM THE SITE. THEIR PARTICIPATION AND ESCAPE WOULD HAVE LIKELY BEEN VIRTUALLY UNNOTICED.

SECRET SERVICE PLANNING FOR THE MOTORCADE INCLUDED ORDERS THAT SHOULD HAVE PREVENTED ANY TRAINS FROM USING THE ELM ST. OVERPASS FOR A CONSIDERABLE TIME FRAME BOTH BEFORE AND AFTER THE TIME THAT THE MOTORCADE WOULD HAVE PASSED.

12:15 –12:18PM FRIDAY
CAROLYN ARNOLD, THE TSBD VICE PRESIDENT'S SECRETARY, LATER TOLD "CONSPIRACY" AUTHOR ANTHONY SUMMERS: "ABOUT A QUARTER OF AN HOUR BEFORE THE ASSASSINATION….ABOUT 12:15, *IT MAY HAVE BEEN LATER*….I WENT TO THE LUNCHROOM ON THE 2ND FLOOR….**HARVEY** WAS SITTING IN ONE OF THE BOOTHS….HE WAS ALONE…AND HAVING LUNCH."

THE MOTORCADE WAS TO PASS HOUSTON AND ELM ABOUT 12:25 AND THEN PROCEED TO THE TRADE MART WHERE IT'S SCHEDULED ARRIVAL TIME WAS 12:30.

12:17 PM FRIDAY
OFFICER TIPPIT NOTIFIES DISPATCH THAT HE WOULD "BE OUT OF THE CAR A MINUTE CORNER BONNIEVIEW AND KIEST."

12:20 PM FRIDAY
BONNIE RAY WILLIAMS WENT DOWNSTAIRS FROM THE 6TH FLOOR WHERE HE IS JOINED BY HAROLD NORMAN AND JAMES JARMAN TO WATCH THE MOTORCADE FROM THE 5TH FLOOR. BOTH NORMAN AND JARMAN HAD BOTH EATEN THEIR LUNCHES IN THE SECOND FLOOR "DOMINO" ROOM AS DID **HARVEY**.

12:21 PM FRIDAY
OFFICER TIPPIT "CLEARED" HIMSELF BACK INTO SERVICE WITH DISPATCH.

12:22 PM FRIDAY
THE AMBULANCE ARRIVES AT THE CORNER OF HOUSTON AND ELM TO PICK UP THE VICTIM OF AN APPARENT SEIZURE.

12:24 PM FRIDAY
THE AMBULANCE CONTACTS DISPATCH TO INFORM THEM THAT THEY ARE ENROUTE TO PARKLAND.

ENROUTE THE AMBULANCE CREW DETERMINED THAT THE MAN WAS NOT SUFFERING A SEIZURE. WHEN THEY ARRIVED AT PARKLAND, THE VICTIM, IN THE CHAOS FOLLOWING THE ARRIVAL OF THE PRESIDENTIAL LIMO SIMPLY WALKED OUT OF THE EMERGENCY ROOM AT PARKLAND WITHOUT RECEIVING ANY TREATMENT. HE WAS LATER IDENTIFIED AS JERRY BOYD BELKNAP, AN EMPLOYEE OF THE DALLAS MORNING NEWS..

IN THE WEEKS PRIOR TO THE ASSASSINATION, THE AMBULANCE COMPANY ASSIGNED TO THE MOTORCADE MADE OVER 10 "FALSE-ALARM" RUNS TO THE CORNER OF HOUSTON AND ELM. IN EACH INSTANCE THERE WAS NO VICTIM UPON THEIR ARRIVAL. ONE WOULD HAVE TO SUSPECT THAT THE CONSPIRATORS WERE TRYING TO GAUGE JUST HOW LONG IT WOULD TAKE AN AMBULANCE TO ARRIVE THAT MORNING IF IT WERE TO SERVE, AS DID THE BROKEN DOWN PICKUP, AS A DISTRACTION TO LOCAL LAW ENFORCEMENT OFFICERS AND, MORE IMPORTANTLY, AS VEHICLES THAT WOULD, HAD THE MOTORCADE BEEN ON TIME, DRAMATICALLY SLOWED THE MOTORCADE IF NOT COMPLETELY STOPPED IT ON ELM STREET.

AMBULANCE DRIVER AUBREY RIKE NOTED THAT THE CALLS WERE ALL MID-DAY AND THE CALLERS REQUESTED THAT THE AMBULANCE RESPOND TO DEALEY PLAZA "IN FRONT OF THE FOUNTAIN." THIS IS WHERE THE "SEIZURE" VICTIM WAS FOUND ON THE MORNING OF THE 22ND. RIKE LATER NOTED THAT HE WONDERED IF SOMEONE WAS TIMING THE AMBULANCES' NUMEROUS TRIPS TO DEALEY PLAZA.

12:25 PM FRIDAY
CAROLYN ARNOLD SEES **HARVEY** ON THE 1ST FLOOR NEAR THE FRONT DOOR OF THE TSBD. HE HAD JUST FINISHED HIS LUNCH ON THE 2ND FLOOR.

KEEP IN MIND THAT THE MOTORCADE WAS APPROXIMATELY 5 MINUTES LATE. IT WAS TO HAVE BEEN AT THE TRADE MART AT 12:30. IT WAS TO HAVE PASSED THE TSBD AT 12:25. MRS. ARNOLD WAS NOT CALLED TO GIVE TESTIMONY TO THE W.C.

12:25 PM FRIDAY
RUBY HAD INVITED AN IRS INFORMANT TO **"WATCH THE FIREWORKS."** THEY WATCHED THE MOTORCADE PASS THE CORNER OF MAIN AND HOUSTON.

*AS NOTED EARLIER, BOTH RUBY AND **HARVEY** MAY WELL HAVE BEEN LED TO BELIEVE THAT THERE WOULD BE AN ASSASSINATION "ATTEMPT" THAT DAY. THIS ATTEMPT WOULD BE CONSIDERED A "DIVERSIONARY TACTIC" AND SERVE TWO PURPOSES: TO FURTHER OCCUPY THE FBI ALLOWING **HARVEY** AMPLE COVER TO INITIATE HIS FIRST LEG OF TRAVEL IN REGARDS TO HIS BOGUS "CUBAN ASSIGNMENT" AND AS AN OPPORTUNITY TO TIE AN <u>ATTEMPT</u> ON THE PRESIDENT'S LIFE TO PRO-CASTRO SUPPORTERS THUS OFFERING A RATIONAL FOR THE PLANNED DECEMBER 1ST INVASION OF CUBA. THIS TACTIC WOULD INCLUDE THE FIRING OF SHOTS IN THE <u>DIRECTION</u> OF THE MOTORCADE. THE SHOTS, AS*

RUBY AND **HARVEY** WOULD UNDERSTAND, WOULD BE TRACED TO A PRO-CASTRO SYMPATHIZER. THIS PROCESS DOVETAILS PERFECTLY WITH THE TYPES OF "FALSE FLAG" INCIDENTS DISCUSSED AS PART OF OPERATION NORTHWOODS. IT WOULD BE **HARVEY** AND RUBY'S UNDERSTANDING HOWEVER THAT NO ONE IN THE MOTORCADE WOULD BE INJURED. RUBY WILL LATER FACILITATE THE IMPLICATION OF THE PRO-CASTRO "ASSASSIN" BY PLANTING A BULLET AT PARKLAND. RUBY MAY NOT REALIZE THAT THE PRO-CASTRO SYMPATHIZER THAT HE IS IMPLICATING IN THE "ATTACK" ON THE MOTORCADE IS **HARVEY** NOR IS IT A CERTAINTY HE WOULD BE PRIVY TO THE FACT THAT THE BULLET PLANTED AT PARKLAND WOULD BE TIED TO A RIFLE TRACED TO **HARVEY** AND THAT THE RIFLE WOULD BE FOUND IN THE TSBD.

RUBY'S USE OF THE TERM "FIREWORKS" MAY WELL HAVE BEEN LITERAL SINCE MANY IN DEALY PLAZA LATER DESCRIBED THE ACTUAL GUNFIRE AS SOUNDING LIKE FIREWORKS. THE USE OF FIREWORKS WOULD MAKE IT MORE DIFFICULT TO LOCATE THE ORIGIN OF SHOTS BOTH FROM THE TSBD AND, MORE IMPORTANTLY, FROM SITES IN FRONT OF THE PRESIDENTIAL LIMO. IT IS ALSO POSSIBLE THAT RUBY SIMPLY USED THE TERM "FIREWORKS" IN REFERENCE TO WHAT HE BELIEVED WOULD BE VICTIM-LESS SHOTS THAT WOULD BE FIRED IN THE DIRECTION OF THE MOTORCADE AS IT PASSED THROUGH DEALY PLAZA.

THERE WERE 45 "EARWITNESSES" WHO WERE LATER INTERVIEWED BY THE FBI OR THE WARREN COMMISSION. THEIR IMPRESSIONS ARE AS FOLLOWS:

WITNESSES IN THE MOTORCADE

SS AGENT WIN LAWSON-------IN LEAD CAR---------------"SOUNDED LIKE A FIRECRACKER"

SS AGENT SAM KINNEY---------DRIVING PRESIDENTIAL FOLLOW-UP CAR "FIRECRACKER-LIKE SOUND"

SS AGENT ROY KELLERMAN--FRONT SEAT PRESIDENTIAL LIMO----------"A REPORT LIKE A FIRECRACKER"

SS AGENT CLINT HILL----------- PRESIDENTIAL FOLLOW-UP CAR------"A NOISE SOUNDED LIKE A FIRECRACKER"

K. T. O'DONNELL-----PRESIDENTIAL FOLLOW-UP CAR-----"A FIRECRACKER-LIKE NOISE"

SS AGENT JOHN READY-----------PRESIDENTIAL FOLLOW-UP CAR--------"SOUNDED LIKE FIRECRACKERS"

SA WARREN TAYLOR---------PRESIDENTIAL FOLLOW-UP CAR-----------------A BANG WHICH SOUNDED LIKE A FIRECRACKER"

SS AGENT ROBERT GREER-----RESIDENTIAL LIMO DRIVER---------------------"FIRST SHOT A FIRECRACKER"

MAYOR EARLE CABELL----IN THE DIGNITARY CAR------------"FIRECRACKER-LIKE NOISES"

CLIFF CARTER-----IN VICE-PRESIDENT FOLLOW-UP CAR--"A FIRECRACKER-LIKE NOISE"

SS AGENT GLEN BENNETT-----—IN PRESIDENTIAL FOLLOW-UP CAR----"SOUNDED LIKE A FIRECRACKER"

JAMES DARNELL-------IN CAMERA CAR #1---"2ND SHOT SOUNDED LIKE A FIRECRACKER"

SS AGENT GEORGE HICKEY-—-IN PRESIDENTIAL FOLLOW-UP CAR "A FIRECRACKER-LIKE NOISE"

THOMAS DILLARD--------IN CAMERA CAR 1--------------"SOUNDED LIKE A 'FIRECRACKER'

SS AGENT EMORY ROBERTS----PRESIDENT'S FOLLOW-UP CAR-----"REMINDED ME OF A FIRECRACKER"

ON RAILROAD OVERPASS

GEORGE DAVIS--"FIRECRACKERS"
ROYCE SKELTON---------------------------------------"NOISE I THOUGHT WAS FIRECRACKERS"

NEAR OVERPASS

S.M. HOLLAND--"SOUNDED LIKE FIRECRACKERS"
DPD OFFICER JAMES FOSTER-----------------"THOUGHT FIRST SHOT WAS FIRECRACKER"

ON ELM OR HOUSTON, OR AT ELM AND HOUSTON

JUDY JOHNSON--"SOUNDED LIKE FIRECRACKERS"
MARY ANN MITCHELL--------------------------------------"FIRST SHOT LIKE A FIRECRACKER"
GAYLE NEWMAN--"SHOT SOUNDED LIKE A FIRECRACKER"
MAURICE ORR--"I THOUGHT OF FIREWORKS"
AUBREY SUGGS---"SOUNDED LIKE FIRECRACKERS"
PEARL SPRINGER---"FIRECRACKERS"
DPD E. L. SMITH--"THOUGHT OF FIRECRACKERS"
JEAN NEWMAN----------------------------""I HEARD WHAT I THOUGHT WAS A FIRECRACKER"
BILL NEWMAN---"IT SOUNDED LIKE A FIRECRACKER"
J. W. ALTGENS---"FIRECRACKER-LIKE NOISE"
HOWARD BRENNAN-----------------------------"AS IF SOMEONE IS SHOOTING FIRECRACKERS"
HUGH BETZNER--"SOUNDED LIKE FIRECRACKERS"
DPD EUGENE BARNETT---------------------------------------"SOUNDED LIKE FIRECRACKERS"
BILLIE CLAY------------------------"THOUGHT THE SHOTS WERE FIRECRACKERS OR BACKFIRE"
RUBY HENDERSON---"SOUND SIMILAR TO FIRECRACKERS"

IN FRONT OF TSBD

BILL SHELLEY--"NOT REAL LOUD, LIKE FIRECRACKERS"
BETTY THORNTON---"I THOUGHT OF FIREWORKS"
VIRGIE RACKLEY---""I THOUGHT OF FIRECRACKERS"
BILL LOVELADY---"LIKE FIRECRACKERS"

IN TSBD

BONNIE RAY WILLIAMS--------------------------------"THOUGHT THEY WERE FIRECRACKERS"
SANDRA STYLES--"HEARD FIREWORKS"
VICTORIA ADAMS--"SOUNDED LIKE FIRECRACKERS"
YOLA D. HOPSON--"THOUGHT THEY WERE FIRECRACKERS"
BETTY FOSTER--"HEARD SOMETHING LIKE FIREWORKS"

OTHER BUILDINGS

LILLIAN MOONEYHAM (2ND FLOOR CRIMINAL COURTS BUILDING)"I THOUGHT A FIRECRACKER HAD GONE OFF"

ON MAIN STREET

JAMES TAGUE--"SOUNDED LIKE A FIRECRACKER"

*IN THE CONFUSION IMMEDIATELY FOLLOWING THE PASSING OF THE MOTORCADE, **HARVEY** WOULD DEPART THE SCENE WITH THE MISCONCEPTION THAT THE REPORTS HEARD IN DEALY PLAZA WERE THE DIVERSIONARY "FIREWORKS." BOTH HE AND RUBY WOULD VERY SOON FIND OUT OTHERWISE.*

THERE ARE SEVERAL WITNESSES WHO PLACE INDIVIDUALS ON THE 6TH FLOOR OF THE TSBD JUST PRIOR TO THE SHOOTING.

CHARLES BRONSON
SHOOTING HOME MOVIES, HE NOTES TWO MEN IN THE SOUTHEASTERN CORNER OF THE 6TH FLOOR.

CAROLYN WALTHER
SHE NOTED 2 MEN IN AN UPPER FLOOR WINDOW. ONE, HOLDING A RIFLE, WAS EITHER LIGHT-HAIRED OR BLOND. THE OTHER MAN WAS WEARING A BROWN SUIT COAT.

ARNOLD ROWLAND
HE ALSO SAW 2 MEN ON THE 6TH FLOOR OF THE TSBD. ONE HE NOTED WAS WEARING A WHITE OR LIGHT COLORED SHIRT WITH DARK HAIR. THIS SAME MAN WAS ALSO HOLDING A RIFLE WITH A SCOPE.

RUBY HENDERSON
SHE ALSO SAW 2 MEN IN AN UPPER FLOOR WINDOW. ONE WAS WEARING A DARK SHIRT, THE OTHER A WHITE SHIRT.

RICHARD CARR
NOTED A MAN WEARING A BROWN COAT, GLASSES, AND A HAT LOOKING OUT THE TOP FLOOR OF THE BUILDING.

COUNTY JAIL INMATES
SEVERAL INMATES NOTED TWO MEN ON THE 6TH FLOOR JUST PRIOR TO THE SHOOTING.

THIS PARTICULAR MORNING, **HARVEY** IS WEARING A LONG SLEEVE REDDISH-BROWN PLAID SHIRT. **LEE** IS WEARING A WHITE T-SHIRT. IT IS ARMSTRONG'S BELIEF THAT IT IS INDEED **LEE** IN THE TSBD AND HE IS ACCOMPANIED BY A MAN IN A BROWN SUIT.

12:30 PM FRIDAY
SHOTS ARE FIRED IN DEALEY PLAZA.

BEFORE WE PROCEED WITH THE EVENTS THAT TOOK PLACE DURING THE SHOOTING, LET US TAKE A CLOSER LOOK AT THE MAKE-UP OF THE MOTORCADE ITSELF.

ADVANCE CAR
1/2 MILE IN FRONT OF MOTORCADE AND DRIVEN BY DALLAS POLICE CAPTAIN P. LAWRENCE.

PILOT CAR
DPD CAR---1/4 MILE IN FRONT OF THE MOTORCADE AND DRIVEN BY DEPUTY CHIEF LUMPKIN. ALSO IN THE CAR DETECTIVES F.M.TURNER, B.L. SENKEL, LT. COLONEL GEORGE WHITMEYER, COMMMANDER OF AN ARMY INTELLIGENCE UNIT AT THE DALLAS DISTRICT U.S. ARMY COMMAND, AND JACOB PUTERBACH FROM THE WHITE HOUSE.

LEAD CAR
DPD CAR--NORMALLY A CONVERTIBLE TO GIVE THE OCCUPANTS A

WIDER VIEW. THE LEAD CAR ON NOVEMBER 22ND WAS A <u>CLOSED SEDAN</u>. THE LEAD CAR WAS DRIVEN BY POLICE CHIEF CURRY. ALSO IN THE CAR, SHERIFF BILL DECKER AND SS AGENTS SORRELS AND LAWSON. THE CAR WAS 400 YARDS AHEAD OF THE PRESIDENTIAL LIMO.

PRESIDENTIAL LINCOLN
DRIVEN BY SS AGENT WILLIAM GREER. ALSO IN THE CAR AGENT ROY KELLERMAN, THE PRESIDENT AND HIS WIFE AND GOVENOR CONNALLY AND HIS WIFE.

GREER WAS A REPLACEMENT DRIVER FOR SA TOM SHIPMAN WHO HAD DIED OF AN APPARENT HEART ATTACK AT CAMP DAVID ON OCTOBER 14TH, 1963. HE WAS ALONE AT THE TIME. SA SHIPMAN WAS 51 YEARS OLD AT THE TIME OF HIS DEATH.

S.S. FOLLOW-UP CAR
THE DRIVER AGENT IS SAM KINNEY. ALSO IN/ON THE CAR ARE AGENTS EMORY ROBERTS, CLINT HILL, WILLIAM MCINTYRE, JOHN READY, PAUL LANDIS, GEORGE HICKEY AND GLEN BENNETT. ALSO ON BOARD ARE PRESIDENTIAL AIDES DAVE POWERS AND KENNY O'DONNELL.

VICE-PRESIDENT'S CAR
VP JOHNSON AND HIS WIFE, SENATOR RALPH YARBROUGH, AGENT RUFUS YOUNGBLOOD, AND DRIVER TEXAS HIGHWAY PATROL OFFICER HURCHEL JACKS.

VICE-PRESIDENT SS FOLLOW-UP CAR
DRIVEN BY TEXAS STATE POLICE OFFICER J.H. RICH. ALSO IN THE CAR, V.P. AIDE CLIFF CARTER AND 3 SECRET SERVICE AGENTS, JERRY KIVETT, WOODY TAYLOR, AND LEM JOHNS.

8) DIGNITARY CAR #1
9) NATIONAL PRESS POOL CAR
10) CAMERA CAR #1 (MOVIE CAR)
11) CAMERA CAR #2 (STILL PHOTOGRAPHERS)
12) CAMERA CAR #3 (STILL PHOTOGRAPHERS)
13) DIGNITARY CAR #2
14) DIGNITARY CAR #3
15) DIGNITARY CAR #4
16) STAFF CAR
17) BUS #1
18) LOCAL PRESS CAR
19) BUS #2
20) EXTRA CAR #1
21) WESTERN UNION CAR
22) WHITE HOUSE SIGNAL CORPS CAR
23) EXTRA CAR #2
24) BUS #3
25) POLICE CAR

*THE CARS IN THE MOTORCADE ARE, AS ONE WOULD EXPECT, DARK IN COLOR. THE VICE-PRESIDENT'S CAR HOWEVER WAS **LIGHT BLUE** AND JOHNSON'S SS FOLLOW-UP CAR IS **WHITE**. ONE CAN'T HELP BUT TO CONSIDER THAT THIS STARK DIFFERENCE IN COLOR AS COMPARED TO THE PRESIDENTIAL LIMO AND THE PRESIDENTIAL SS FOLLOW-UP CAR WOULD SERVE SHOOTERS IN DISTINGUISHING THE "TARGET" CAR FROM ONE CONTAINING THE VICE-PRESIDENT OR HIS SS DETAIL.*

SHERIFF BILL DECKER GAVE OUT SOME DISTURBING INSTRUCTIONS TO HIS OFFICERS THAT DAY:

HE INSTRUCTS PLAINCLOTHES OFFICERS, DETECTIVES, AND WARRANT MEN TO TAKE NO PART IN THE SECURITY OF THE MOTORCADE.

HE INSTRUCTS UNIFORMED OFFICERS THAT THEY ARE TO STAND WITH THEIR <u>BACKS TO THE CROWD AND TO FACE THE MOTORCADE.</u>

HE DECIDED THAT THE DALLAS POLICE WOULD END THEIR SECURITY SUPERVISION FOR THE MOTORCADE AT MAIN AND HOUSTON, AND <u>NOT</u> INCLUDE THE HOUSTON TO ELM TO DEALY PLAZA PORTION.

SECRET SERVICE AGENTS WERE TOLD BY THE ASSISTANT SPECIAL AGENT IN CHARGE OF THE WHITE HOUSE DETAIL (WHO WAS IN CHARGE OF THE PLANNING OF THE DALLAS TRIP) <u>NOT</u> TO RIDE ON OR NEAR THE REAR OF THE PRESIDENTIAL LIMO. THIS WORD WAS RELAYED TO SHIFT LEADER EMORY ROBERTS WHO WAS IN CHARGE OF THE SECRET SERVICE FOLLOW-UP CAR. VIDEO SHOT AT LOVE FIELD BY STATION WFAA PRIOR TO THE START OF THE MOTORCADE DOES INDEED SHOW ROBERTS MOTIONING TO TWO AGENTS, DON LAWTON AND HENRY RYBKA. THESE ORDERS WERE GIVEN BY SS AGENT WINSTON G. LAWSON. THE AGENTS JOGGING ON EACH SIDE OF THE LIMO ARE INSTRUCTED <u>NOT</u> TO RIDE ON THE BACK OF THE PRESIDENTIAL LIMO BUT TO RIDE IN THE ALREADY FULL FOLLOW-UP CAR. ONE OF THE AGENTS, SA HENRY RYBKA CLEARLY SHOWS HIS FRUSTRATION AS HE REPEATEDLY RAISES AND LOWERS HIS ARMS IN DISBELIEF.

THERE WERE SEVERAL EXTREMELY UNUSUAL MOTORCADE CHANGES INVOKED BY THE SECRET SERVICE THAT DAY. THE MOTORCYCLE ESCORT WAS TOLD TO STAY <u>BEHIND</u> THE PRESIDENTIAL LIMO, NOT TO FLANK IT AS WAS CUSTOMARY. ONE OF THE TWO PRESIDENTIAL AIDES, EITHER TED CLIFTON OR GODFREY MCHUGH, WOULD NORMALLY RIDE BETWEEN THE AGENTS IN THE FRONT SEAT OF THE PRESIDENTIAL LIMO. MCHUGH WAS RELEGATED TO DIGNITARY CAR #3. THIS PUT HIM **10 CARS** FURTHER BACK IN THE MOTORCADE THAN NORMAL. REAR ADMIRAL GEORGE BURKLEY, THE **PRESIDENT'S PHYSICIAN** WAS IN BUS #3. THIS WOULD PUT HIM **20 VEHICLES BEHIND THE PRESIDENT**. CECIL STOUGHTON, A WHITE HOUSE PHOTOGRAPHER, NORMALLY RODE IN THE SS FOLLOW-UP CAR. HE ROUTINELY TOOK BOTH STILL PHOTOS AND MOVIE FILMS FROM THIS LOCATION WHILE IN A MOTORCADE. THIS DAY HOWEVER HE WAS ASSIGNED TO CAMERA CAR #2, 6 CARS BEHIND HIS USUAL MOTORCADE LOCATION AND 1 CAR BEHIND PHOTOGRAPHER ROBERT JACKSON.

IN HOUSTON THE DAY PRIOR, THERE WERE <u>12</u> MOTORCYCLES IN THE POLICE ESCORT. SIX RIDERS WERE ON EACH SIDE OF THE PRESIDENTIAL LIMO. ON NOVEMBER 22ND IN DALLAS, THE MOTORCYCLE OFFICERS WERE CUT TO <u>FOUR</u>, TWO ON EACH SIDE OF THE LIMO. MORE IMPORTANTLY, RATHER THAN CYCLISTS AT EACH OF THE FOUR CORNERS OF THE LIMO, THEY WERE INSTRUCTED TO POSITION THEMSELVES NO FURTHER FORWARD THAN THE REAR OF THE LIMO. AT THE TIME OF THE 12:30 SHOOTING, THE LEADING CYCLISTS WERE ACTUALLY FLANKING THE FOLLOW-UP CAR. THESE ORDERS WERE GIVEN BY SS AGENT WINSTON G. LAWSON.

WHEN REQUESTED BY THE ASSASSINATIONS RECORD REVIEW BOARD, THE SECRET SERVICE REVEALED THAT THEY HAD DESTROYED RECORDS OF THE MOTORCADE OF NOVEMBER 22ND, 1963. THEY HAD VIOLATED AT LEAST 15 SS POLICIES REGARDING PRESIDENTIAL PROTECTION IN THE MOTORCADE THAT DAY IN DALLAS.

THE <u>SEQUENCE</u> OF THE VEHICLES IN THE MOTORCADE WAS ALSO DRAMATICALLY DIFFERENT FROM WHAT WAS NORMALLY USED. INSTEAD OF THE PRESS CAMERA CARS OR TRUCKS BEING <u>IN FRONT</u> OF THE PRESIDENTIAL LIMO THEY WERE PLACED <u>FAR BACK</u> IN THE MOTORCADE. PHOTOGRAPHER TOM DILLARD RAN THE PHOTO DEPARTMENT AT THE DALLAS MORNING NEWS. HE NOTED THAT THE PRESS PHOTOGRAPHERS NORMALLY RODE IN A FLATBED TRUCK OR OPEN CAR DIRECTLY <u>IN FRONT</u> OF THE LIMO TO CAPTURE PRESIDENTIAL REACTIONS TO THE CROWD. THE PRIVILEGE OF RIDING IN THE CAR OR

TRUCK WAS ROTATED. FOR ONE LEG OF A MOTORCADE TRIP THE STILL PHOTOGRAPHERS WOULD GET THE CHOICE LOCATION DIRECTLY IN <u>FRONT</u> OF THE PRESIDENT'S LIMO. ON THE NEXT LEG, THE MOVIE PHOTOGRAPHERS WOULD THEN TAKE THEIR TURN. ON NOVEMBER 22ND 1963, THESE TYPICAL ARRANGEMENTS WOULD BE CHANGED DRAMATICALLY

DILLARD STATED LATER: "THE SAD THING NEWS-WISE WAS THAT THE CUSTOM ALWAYS WAS THAT A SELECTED GROUP OF PRESS PEOPLE – PHOTOGRAPHERS – WERE TO RIDE IN A FLAT BED TRUCK IN FRONT OF THE PRESIDENT. THAT WAS STANDARD PROCEDURE IN ALL PRESIDENTIAL PARADES....IT WAS UNDERSTOOD THAT THE FLATBED WAS GOING TO BE THERE, BUT AT THE LAST MOMENT IT WAS CANCELLED." ALL PREVIOUS TRIPS, INCLUDING FLORIDA HAD PRESS PHOTOGRAPHERS VERY CLOSE IN FRONT AND BEHIND JFK'S LIMO.

ROBERT JACKSON, A DALLAS TIMES HERALD PHOTOGRAPHER, WAS IN THE MOTORCADE IN THE FIRST OF THE 3 CAMERA CARS. THESE CARS WOULD BE NUMBERS 9, 10, AND 11 IN THE MOTORCADE. THE PRESIDENTIAL LIMO WAS CAR #3 IF ONE INCLUDES THE PILOT CAR AS #1 AND THE LEAD CAR AS #2. THE <u>CLOSEST</u> CAMERA CAR TO THE PRESIDENTIAL LIMO WAS 6 CARS <u>BEHIND</u> THE PRESIDENT.

JACKSON'S CAR HAD JUST MADE THE TURN ONTO HOUSTON FROM MAIN WHEN THE <u>1ST SHOT</u> WAS FIRED. AT THE <u>COMPLETION</u> OF THE SHOOTING, JACKSON'S CAR WAS STILL ON HOUSTON, FACING THE FRONT OF THE TSBD WHICH WAS ABOUT 25 FEET IN FRONT OF HIM. HE STATED: "I SAW THE RIFLE……APPROXIMATELY HALF OF THE WEAPON…AND JUST AS I LOOKED AT IT, IT WAS DRAWN **<u>FAIRLY SLOWLY</u>** (MY EMPHASIS) BACK INTO THE BUILDING." MALCOLM COUCH, A CAMERAMAN IN THE SAME CAR WITH JACKSON, RECALLED YELLING: "LOOK UP IN THE WINDOW! THERE'S THE RIFLE!" HE WENT ON TO NOTE THAT HE SAW ABOUT A FOOT OF A RIFLE, THE BARREL, EXTENDING FROM THE WINDOW THEN SLOWLY BROUGHT BACK INTO THE WINDOW.

MUCH ATTENTION HAS BEEN PAID TO THE 120 DEGREE HOUSTON TO ELM <u>TURN</u> AS BEING A MAJOR INDICATOR THAT THE ASSASSINATION WAS ASSISTED BY GOVERNMENT OFFICIALS EITHER LOCAL OR FEDERAL. IT WAS A SECRET SERVICE POLICY THAT <u>NO</u> TURNS WOULD BE GREATER THAN <u>90 DEGREES</u> SINCE THIS WOULD NECESSITATE SLOWING AN OPEN MOTORCADE TO DANGEROUSLY SLOW SPEEDS. ALTHOUGH THE TURN DID INDEED HAVE THE EFFECT OF DRAMATICALLY SLOWING THE MOTORCADE AND BRINGING IT CLOSER TO THE TSBD, I THINK IT WAS THE <u>SEQUENCE</u> OF THE VEHICLES IN THE MOTORCADE THAT CONTRIBUTED MOST TO THE SUCCESS OF THOSE WISHING TO HAVE THE REAL SHOOTERS REMAIN UNDOCUMENTED ON FILM AND YET HAVE THE ALLEGED SHOOTER HOPEFULLY CAPTURED ON FILM OR AT LEAST THE RIFLE BARREL CAPTURED ON FILM.

ASK YOURSELF THESE TWO QUESTIONS: AT THE TIME OF THE <u>SHOOTING</u>, WHERE WERE THE <u>PROFESSIONAL</u> STILL PHOTOGRAPHERS AND MOVIE CAMERA MEN **AND** WHERE WERE THE <u>AMATEUR</u> PHOTOGRAPHERS AND MOVIE TAKERS?

THE <u>AMATEURS</u> WERE ON ELM STREET IN THE KILL ZONE FLANKING THE PRESIDENTIAL LIMO. THE <u>PROFESSIONAL</u> PHOTOGRAPHERS/CAMERA MEN WERE STILL ON HOUSTON, CONVENIENTLY FACING THE TSBD WHERE THEY WOULD HOPEFULLY NOTICE AND FILM OR PHOTOGRAPH A RIFLE "DRAWN FAIRLY SLOWLY" BACK INTO AN UPPER WINDOW.

IT IS QUITE EVIDENT THAT THE INTENTION OF THOSE RESPONSIBLE FOR THE ACTUAL SHOOTING, WITH ASSISTANCE FROM THOSE DECIDING THE SEQUENCE OF THE CARS IN THE MOTORCADE, WAS THAT FEW IF ANY <u>AMATEUR</u> PHOTOGRAPHS OR FILMS WOULD YIELD EVIDENCE OF SHOTS FROM IN <u>FRONT</u> OF THE LIMO. BUT, THEY SINCERELY HOPED THAT THE <u>PROFESSIONAL</u> PHOTOGRAPHERS WOULD CAPTURE A RIFLE "DRAWN FAIRLY SLOWLY" (OBVIOUSLY IN AN EFFORT TO ALLOW THE PHOTOGRAPHERS MORE TIME TO CAPTURE A PICTURE) BACK INTO AN UPPER WINDOW WHERE THEY WOULD LATER PLACE **HARVEY**.

ALTHOUGH THE EASIER AND CLOSER SHOT FOR AN ASSASSIN WOULD HAVE BEEN FROM A WINDOW ON THE LEFT (WEST) SIDE OF THE TSBD, THE CHOICE OF A WINDOW ON THE RIGHT (EAST) SIDE OF THE BUILDING FOR THE PROTRUDING RIFLE WOULD PUT THE INCRIMINATING "DRAWN FAIRLY SLOWLY" RIFLE _DIRECTLY_ IN FRONT OF THE PROFESSIONAL PHOTOGRAPHERS FOR HOPEFULL CAPTURE ON FILM. THE SET-UP CONSPIRATORS EFFORT TO DRAW ATTENTION TO A EAST SIDE SIXTH FLOOR WINDOW MAY HAVE BEEN SOMEWHAT OVERDONE. AMOS LEE EUINS TOLD OFFICER D.V. HARKNESS THAT JUST _PRIOR_ TO THE SHOOTING HE SAW "THIS PIPE THING STICKING OUT THE WINDOW." HE WENT ON TO NOTE THAT _AFTER_ THE 1ST SHOT, HE LOOKED UP AT THE WINDOW AND SAW A RIFLE WITH ONE HAND ON THE BARREL AND THE OTHER ON THE _TRIGGER_ STICKING _OUT_ THE WINDOW. EITHER YOU HAVE A VERY BOLD AND FOOLISH ASSASSIN OR A PAINFULLY OBVIOUS ATTEMPT TO DRAW ATTENTION TO THE SIXTH FLOOR OF THE TSBD.

BOBBY JOE DALE, A MOTORCYCLE OFFICER IN THE MOTORCADE MADE AN INTERESTING OBSERVATION. HE NOTED THAT THERE SEEMED TO BE MORE CONCERN ABOUT THE _TIMING_ ELEMENT IN THIS MOTORCADE THAN IN OTHERS HE HAD BEEN IN. HE WENT ON TO ADD THAT TIME WAS GIVEN _CONTINUOUSLY_ OVER THE RADIO TO CHECK THE PROGRESS OF THE MOTORCADE, BUT THAT THERE WAS NO REASON GIVEN FOR THE HEIGHTENED CONCERN ABOUT TIME. IF THE TEAMS OF SHOOTERS WERE MONITORING THE PROGRESS OF THE MOTORCADE VIA POLICE RADIOS, THE _EXACT_ LOCATION OF THE MOTORCADE AS OPPOSSED TO ITS _SCHEDULED_ PROGRESS WOULD HAVE BEEN INVALUABLE.

IT IS IMPERATIVE TO KEEP IN MIND THAT THE MOTORCADE WAS RUNNING LATE; ABOUT 5-7 MINUTES LATE. THE MOTORCADE WAS SCHEDULED TO ARRIVE AT THE TRADE MART AT 12:30. ACCORDING TO THE WARREN COMMISSION, A SS AGENT IN THE MOTORCADE RADIO'D THE TRADE MART AT APPROXIMATELY 12:25 STATING THAT THEY SHOULD ARRIVE IN ABOUT 5 MINUTES

WITH THE MOTORCADE DUE TO BE AT THE _TRADE MART_ AT 12:30, IT SHOULD HAVE PASSED THE TSBD ABOUT 12:25. HAD **HARVEY** BEEN THE SHOOTER, HE WOULD LIKELY HAVE BEEN AT HIS SNIPER'S PERCH NO LATER THAN 12:20, _NOT_ IN THE BREAK ROOM EATING LUNCH.

THE BEST CASE SCENARIO FOR THE SET-UP CONSPIRATORS WOULD BE TO HAVE **HARVEY** _ENROUTE_ FROM THE UPPER LEVEL FLOORS OF THE BUILDING AND THE LUNCH ROOM IMMEDIATELY AFTER THE SHOTS WERE FIRED. IT COULD THEN BE NOTED THAT HE WAS FLEEING THE "ASSASSIN'S PERCH."

SINCE THE _EXACT_ LOCATION OF **HARVEY** AT THE TIME OF THE SHOOTING IS CRUCIAL TO HIS SET-UP, I SUSPECT THAT HIS "HANDLERS", i.e. THE SET-UP CONSPIRATORS, PROMPTED HIM TO BE NEAR THE PAY PHONE IN THE LUNCHROOM FOR INSTRUCTIONS REGARDING HIS UPCOMING TRANSPORTATION TO REDBIRD AIR FIELD. OR, IF THE SET-UP CONSPIRATORS AND THE SHOOTING TEAMS WERE MONITORING THE PROGRESS OF THE MOTORCADE, **HARVEY** COULD BE INSTRUCTED BY PHONE TO PROCEED TO THE 6TH FLOOR JUST _PRIOR_ TO THE ARRIVAL OF THE PRESIDENTIAL LIMO ON ELM STREET AND THEN QUICKLY RETURN TO THE LOWER LEVEL AFTER THE PRESIDENT'S LIMO HAD PASSED. WERE THE SET-UP CONSPIRATORS CONFIDENT THAT BY MERELY KEEPING **HARVEY** _INSIDE_ THE TSBD THAT THIS WOULD BE ADEQUATE IN ASSURING HIS ALLEGED COMPLICITY IN THE SHOOTING? IF ONE ADDS IN THEIR EARLIER EFFORTS TO TIE HIM TO THE PRO-CASTRO FACTIONS AND THEIR EFFORTS TO TIE HIM TO THE GUNS VIA "HIDELL", IT IS QUITE POSSIBLE THAT THE SET-UP CONSPIRATORS WERE INDEED OF A MIND SET THAT THE SET-UP IN ITS _ENTIRETY_ WOULD BE OF A MAGNITUDE TO FRAME **HARVEY** EVEN WITH THE LATE ARRIVAL OF THE PRESIDENTIAL LIMO; PARTICULARLY IF THEY COULD MANIPULATE HIS LOCATION ONLY MOMENTS BEFORE THE ACTUAL SHOOTING. IN MY OPINION THEY EITHER TOOK A CONSIDERABLE RISK IN CHANCING THAT **HARVEY** WOULD BE PHOTOGRAPHED GAWKING OUT OF AN UPPER FLOOR WINDOW _NOT_ ON THE 6TH FLOOR OR STANDING IN _FRONT_ OF THE TSBD, OR THEY WERE CONFIDENT THAT THE TESTIMONY OF

*ANY WITNESSES WHO PLACED **HARVEY** IN A POSITION THAT POSITIVELY <u>EXCLUDED</u> HIM FROM BEING THE SHOOTER WOULD BE ALTERED.*

*MORE ON A PHOTOGRAPH DEPICTING **HARVEY** IN FRONT OF THE TSBD AT THE TIME OF THE SHOOTING AS WE PROCEED WITH THE TIMELINE.*

*IT WAS SIMPLY A MATTER OF CONNECTING THE DOTS…….RIFLE IN AN UPPER WINDOW OF THE TSBD……**HARVEY** EMPLOYED AT THE TSBD……RIFLE ALLEGEDLY TRACEABLE TO A"HIDELL"… "HIDELL" ALLEGEDLY SHARING THE SAME MAILBOX AS **HARVEY**……*

*ALTHOUGH THE PROFESSIONAL PHOTOGRAPHERS DID NOT CAPTURE THE ALLEGED ASSASSIN ON FILM, THEIR COMMENTS ALONE ASSISTED THE SET-UP CONSPIRATORS IN THEIR EFFORTS TO PORTRAY **HARVEY** AS THE TSBD SHOOTER. ON THE OTHER HAND, THE AMATEURS WOULD CAPTURE STILLS AND MOVIES THAT WOULD INDICATE PRECISELY WHAT THE CONSPIRATORS HOPED TO AVOID; SHOTS FROM THE FRONT OF THE LIMO. AS THE PRESIDENTIAL LIMO SPED TOWARD PARKLAND, POLICE CHIEF CURRY ORDERED: "GET SOMEONE UP IN THE RAILROAD YARD AND CHECK THOSE PEOPLE." CURRY ALSO ORDERED: "GET MEN ON TOP OF THE UNDERPASS." SHERIFF DECKER THEN ISSUED A SIMILAR COMMAND: "STAND BY MEN! ALL UNITS AND OFFICERS VICINITY OF STATION REPORT TO THE RAILROAD TRACK AREA JUST NORTH OF ELM." BOTH MEN WERE IN THE CAR IMMEDIATELY IN <u>FRONT</u> OF THE PRESIDENTIAL LIMO. THEIR INITIAL COMMENTS FOLLOWING THE SHOOTING OFFERED FIRM OPINIONS AS TO WHERE THE TWO TOP LAW ENFORCEMENT OFFICERS IN DALLAS THOUGHT THE SHOOTER (S) WERE LOCATED.*

ADDING CREEDENCE TO THE NOTION THAT SOME OF THE SHOTS ORIGINATED FROM GROUND LEVEL IN THE PLAZA WERE THE COMMENTS MADE BY SENATOR RALPH YARBOROUGH. IN A LATER INTERVIEW HE NOTED THAT AS THE MOTORCADE CONTINUED THROUGH THE PLAZA: "I SMELLED GUNPOWDER. I ALWAYS THOUGHT THAT WAS STRANGE BECAUSE, BEING FAMILIAR WITH FIREARMS, I NEVER COULD SEE HOW I COULD SMELL THE POWDER FROM A RIFLE HIGH IN THAT BUILDING."

ANOTHER PROMINENT WITNESS WHO QUESTIONED THE ORIGIN OF THE SHOTS WAS NAVY COMMANDER THOMAS ATKINS. ATKINS WAS AN OFFICIAL PHOTOGRAPHER FOR THE WHITE HOUSE. HE WAS 6 CARS BEHIND JFK'S LINCOLN. HIS VEHICLE HAD JUST MADE THE MAIN-TO-HOUSTON TURN WHILE THE PRESIDENTIAL LIMO HAD ALREADY MADE THE HOUSTON-TO-ELM TURN AND WAS APROACHING THE OVERPASS. HE COMMENTED THAT: "THE SHOTS CAME FROM BELOW AND OFF TO THE RIGHT SIDE FROM WHERE I WAS. I NEVER THOUGHT THE SHOTS CAME FROM ABOVE. THEY DID NOT SOUND LIKE SHOTS COMING FROM ANYTHING HIGHER THAN STREET LEVEL." ATKINS LATER MADE A FILM ENTITLED "THE LAST TWO DAYS." HE WAS NOT QUESTIONED BY THE WARREN COMMISSION NOR WAS HIS FILM VIEWED BY THE COMMISSION.

SEYMOUR WEITZMAN WAS THE FIRST OFFICER TO ENTER THE RAILROAD YARD BEHIND THE FENCE ON THE GRASSY KNOLL. WHEN QUESTIONED BY THE WARREN COMMISSION ABOUT OTHERS BEHIND THE FENCE HE REPLIED: "YES SIR, THERE WERE OTHER OFFICERS, SECRET SERVICE AS WELL." THERE WERE <u>NO</u> SECRET SERVICE AGENTS ASSIGNED TO DEALEY PLAZA THAT DAY. LATER, WEITZMAN DESCRIBED ONE MAN AS BEING OF MEDIUM HEIGHT AND DARK HAIR. WHEN SHOWN PICTURES OF FRANK STURGIS AND BERNARD BARKER, LATER OF WATERGATE FAME, WEITZMAN NOTED: "YES, THAT'S HIM….YES, THAT'S THE SAME MAN." HE HAD IDENTIFIED BERNARD BARKER. WEITZMAN WAS NOT THE ONLY OFFICER TO ENCOUNTER "SECRET SERVICE" AGENTS THAT AFTERNOON. SERGEANT D.V. HARKNESS WENT TO THE REAR ENTRANCE OF THE TSBD AND FOUND SOME "SECRET SERVICE" AGENTS THERE. HE WENT ON TO COMMENT: "I DIDN'T GET THEM IDENTIFIED. THEY TOLD ME THAT THEY WERE SECRET SERVICE."

THE "AGENT" WEITZMAN ENCOUNTERED SHOWED HIM WHAT IS KNOWN AS A "COMMISSION BOOK" IDENTIFYING HIM AS AN AGENT OF THE SECRET SERVICE. ABRAHAM BOLDEN, A MEMBER OF THE WHITE HOUSE SS DETAIL NOTED THAT AT THAT TIME IT WAS

FELT THAT ONE OF THE AGENTS WHO ACCOMPANIED THE PRESIDENT TO DALLAS HAD EITHER <u>LOST</u> HIS COMMISSION BOOK OR HAD IT <u>STOLEN</u> FROM HIM IN THE EARLY MORNING HOURS PRIOR TO THE ASSASSINATION AT THE FT. WORTH PRESS CLUB WHERE SEVERAL AGENTS HAD GONE FOR DRINKS. THE AGENTS RERPORTEDLY HAD BEEN DRINKING AND REMAINED AT THE PRESS CLUB UNTIL NEARLY 3:00 AM. TWO AGENTS REPORTEDLY CONTINUED THEIR REVELRY BY VISITING THE CELLAR, AN ALL NIGHT CLUB. IN JANUARY 1964, THE SS ANNOUNCED THAT IT WAS "UPDATING" THE COMMISSION BOOKS. ACCORDING TO AGENT BOLDEN, THE BOOKS WERE "UPDATED" TO DISGUISE THE LIKELIHOOD THAT THE SS IDENTIFICATION SHOWN TO SHERIFF WEITZMAN IMMEDIATELY FOLLOWING THE SHOOTING WAS ONE EITHER LOST OR STOLEN THE NIGHT BEFORE OR THE EARLY MORNING OF THE ASSASSINATIION FROM AN AGENT. IT IS HOWEVER INTERESTING TO NOTE THAT <u>PRIOR</u> TO THE ASSASSINATION IT WAS THE CIA'S TECHNICAL SERVICES DIVISION WHO PROVIDED THE WHITE HOUSE WITH ALL FORMS OF IDENTIFICATION. IT WOULD NOT HAVE BEEN NECESSARY FOR SS AGENT(S) TO BE RELIEVED OF THEIR ID'S PRIOR TO THE MOTORCADE TO PROVIDE THOSE PRESENTING THEMSELVES AS SS AGENTS ON THE KNOLL WITH FALSE SS ID'S. THE SET-UP CONSPIRATORS, HUNT/PHILLIPS COULD HAVE SIMPLY PROVIDED THOSE IMPOSTORS ON THE KNOLL WITH AUTHENTIC SS DOCUMENTS COURTESY OF THE CIA'S TECHNICAL SERVICES DIVISION.

THERE WERE 3 "TRAMPS"ROUSTED FROM A RAILROAD CAR IN THE EARLY AFTERNOON SHORTLY AFTER THE ASSASSINATION. MANY RESEARCHERS CONTEND THAT TWO OF THE "TRAMPS" WERE E. HOWARD HUNT AND FRANK STURGIS. THE 3RD MAN WAS THOUGHT TO BE CHARLES HARRELSON, A CONTRACT KILLER. OTHER RESEARCHERS HAVE NOTED THAT THE TRAMP RESEMBLING HUNT IS ACTUALLY CHAUNCEY HOLT. IF IT IS INDEED HOLT, IT DOES LITTLE TO LESSEN THE SUSPICION THAT THE "TRAMPS" WERE NOT TRULY "TRAMPS." HOLT HAD CONNECTIONS TO ORGANIZED CRIME AND WAS A CIA ASSET WHO WORKED ON THE OPERATION MONGOOSE PROJECT. HOLT WAS ALSO AN ACCOUNTANT FOR MEYER LANSKY. HOLT WAS CONSIDERED AN ACCOMPLISHED FORGER OF DOCUMENTS. IF THE SS COMMISSION BOOKS DISPLAYED IN DEALY PLAZA WEREN'T STOLEN GENUINE DOCUMENTS, IT IS POSSIBLE THAT THEY WERE THE WORK OF HOLT IF NOT THE CIA'S TECHNICAL SERVICES DIVISION. HOLT CONTENDS HOWEVER THAT THE TRAMP FELT TO BE FRANK STURGIS IS ACTUALLY CHARLES ROGERS, AN ASSOCIATE OF CARLOS MARCELLO. ROGERS, DURING WWII, WAS LINKED TO THE ONI, AND LATER AFTER THE WAR, JOINED THE CIA. IF E. HOWARD HUNT AND FRANK STURGIS WERE INDEED TWO OF THE THREE "TRAMPS" ARRESTED IN DALLAS THAT AFTERNOON, HUNT, ALONG WITH STURGIS, WOULD COMPRISE 2 OF THE 4 WATERGATE CO-CONSPIRATORS IN DALLAS ON THE DAY OF THE ASSASSINATION. IF ONE INCLUDES BERNARD BARKER AS ONE OF THE "SECRET SERVICE" ENCOUNTERED ON THE GRASSY KNOLL, THEN YOU HAVE 3 WATERGATE CO-CONSPIRATORS IN DALLAS THAT DAY. THE 4TH CO-CONSPIRATOR, ALBEIT UNINDICTED, WAS OF COURSE RICHARD NIXON. NIXON WAS IN DALLAS UNTIL 11:00 AM THAT FRIDAY IN NOVEMBER. HE DEPARTED ON AMERICAN AIRLINES FLIGHT #82. THE PRESIDENT WOULD BE SHOT 90 MINUTES LATER. NIXON HAD ARRIVED IN DALLAS ON WEDNESDAY NOVEMBER 20TH. HE WAS INTERVIEWED BY A REPORTER FROM THE DALLAS TIMES HERALD WHO WROTE: "THE FORMER V.P ARRIVED IN DALLAS WEDNESDAY NIGHT TO ATTEND A BOARD MEETING OF PEPSI-COLA COMPANY WHICH IS REPRESENTED BY HIS N.Y. LAW PARTNERSHIP." IN COMMISSION EXHIBIT #1973 TAKEN ON FEBRUARY 28TH, 1964, NIXON TOLD THE FBI: "THE ONLY TIME I WAS IN DALLAS, TEXAS DURING 1963 WAS TWO DAYS <u>PRIOR</u> TO THE ASSASSINATION OF JFK." NIXON NOTED THAT HE LEFT DALLAS ON WEDNESDAY NOVEMBER 20TH. LATER, IN AN EARLY 1967 INTERVIEW, NIXON TOLD JULES WITCOMER THAT HE ARRIVED IN DALLAS ON THURSDAY THE 21ST AND LEFT ON THE 22ND.

LATER, RICHARD SPRAGUE, A WARREN COMMISSION COUNSEL, EXAMINED THE CORPORATE RECORDS OF PEPSI-COLA. HE FOUND THERE WAS <u>NO</u> BOARD MEETING IN DALLAS IN 1963. THOSE OF US OF AGE REMEMBER <u>EXACTLY</u> WHERE WE WERE THAT FATEFULL DAY. NIXON APPARENTLY COULD NOT.

IN FEBRUARY 1968, NIXON AND HIS CLOSEST ADVISORS WATCHED ROBERT KENNEDY ANNOUNCE HIS CANDIDACY FOR THE PRESIDENCY. NIXON WAS NOTED TO HAVE REMARKED RATHER SOMBERLY "WE'VE JUST SEEN SOME TERRIBLE FORCES UNLEASHED." COULD NIXON HAVE BEEN REFERRING TO HIS LIKELY SUSPICION THAT WHAT TOOK PLACE IN DALLAS IN 1963 WAS NOT THE MAKING OF A LONE ASSASSIN? INDEED IF THE "LONE ASSASSIN" WAS DECEASED, JUST WHO WERE THE STILL EXISTANT "TERRIBLE FORCES" NIXON WAS REFERRING TO? I WOULD OFFER THAT NIXON WAS LIKELY REFERRING TO MILITARY AND INDUSTRIAL INTERESTS AND THE CIA WHO, IN 1968, WERE CLEARLY ORCHESTRATING THE VIETNAM WAR. ROBERT KENNEDY, IF ELECTED, WOULD HAVE PUT AN END TO U.S. INVOLVEMENT IN VIETNAM. I SUSPECT THAT NIXON KNEW THAT THE "TERRIBLE FORCES" HE HAD REFERRED TO WOULD ACT WITHOUT HESITANCY TO ASSURE THAT THEIR POLICIES WOULD NOT BE CHANGED IN REGARDS TO VIETNAM.

THERE WERE NUMEROUS WITNESSES TO THE EVENTS IN DEALEY PLAZA

VICTORIA ADAMS
WAS ON THE 4TH FLOOR OF THE TSBD: "IT SEEMED AS IF IT CAME FROM THE RIGHT (WEST) BELOW RATHER THAN THE LEFT (EAST) ABOVE."

EMMETT J. HUDSON
WAS SITTING ON THE STAIRS LEADING UP THE KNOLL: "YOU COULD TELL THE SHOTS WERE COMING FROM ABOVE AND KIND OF BEHIND."

SAM HOLLAND
A RAILROAD WORKER ON THE OVERPASS. HE SAW A PUFF OF SMOKE ABOVE THE PICKET FENCE. HIS TESTIMONY WAS IGNORED BY THE COMMISSION. HE ALSO HEARD 4 SHOTS. THE COMMISSION RECORDED THAT HE HAD HEARD BUT 3 SHOTS.

CAROLYN WALTHER
SHE STOOD ON HOUSTON STREET. SHE SAW 2 MEN ON THE 4THOR 5TH FLOOR OF THE TSBD. ONE WORE A WHITE SHIRT, HAD LIGHT HAIR, AND A RIFLE. THE OTHER WAS WEARING A BROWN SUIT. THE COMMISSION IGNORED HER TESTIMONY.

ARNOLD ROWLAND
HE SAW 2 MEN; 1 WITH A LIGHT SHIRT AND RIFLE ON THE 6TH FLOOR.

RONALD FISHER
WAS ON THE CORNER OF HOUSTON AND ELM. IN HIS COMMISSION TESTIMONY HE NOTED: "THEY (THE SHOTS) APPEARED TO COME FROM JUST WEST OF THE SCHOOL BOOK DEPOSITORY BUILDING."

JEAN HILL
HE WAS ON ELM STREET FACING THE GRASSY KNOLL. SHE SAW SMOKE RISING FROM BEHIND THE FENCE. THECOMMISSION IGNORED HER TESTIMONY.

MARY MOORMAN
SHE STOOD BESIDE JEAN HILL AND TOOK A PICTURE SHOWING WHAT MANY BELIEVE TO BE A SNIPER IN A POLICE UNIFORM. HER PICTURE WAS NEVER VIEWED BY THE COMMISSION.

BILL AND GAYLE NEWMAN
WERE ON THE SIDEWALK IN FRONT OF THE KNOLL. BILL NEWMAN WOULD NOTE IN A T.V. INTERVIEW: "ITHOUGHT THE SHOTS WERE COMING FROM DIRECTLY BEHIND US." NEITHER WERE INTERVIEWED BY THE COMMISSION. IN THE INTERVIEW, WHICH TOOK PLACE SHORTLY AFTER THE SHOOTING, MR. NEWMAN ALSO STATED THAT THE HEAD SHOT HIT THE PRESIDENT IN THE RIGHT TEMPLE. THE NEWMANS WERE ON THE CURB AND THE CLOSEST TO THE LIMO AT THE MOMENT OF THE FATAL HEAD SHOT.

LEE BOWERS JR.
WAS IN THE RAILROAD TOWER. HE SAW BEHIND THE FENCE: "A FLASH OF LIGHT OR SMOKE OR SOMETHING WHICH CAUSED ME TO FEEL THAT SOMETHING OUT OF THE ORDINARY HAD OCCURRED THERE."

OCHUS CAMPBELL
HE RELATED TO THE FBI: "I HEARD SHOTS BEING FIRED FROM A POINT WHICH I THOUGHT WAS NEAR THE RAILROAD TRACKS LOCATED OVER THE VIADUCT ON ELM ST."

ED HOFFMAN
HE WAS ON THE OVERPASS. HE SAW A STOCKY MAN IN A DARK SUIT WEARING A HAT, TIE, AND OVERCOAT FIRE A SHOT TOWARDS ELM ST.THEN RUN BEHIND THE FENCE AWAY FROM THE TSBD CARRYING A RIFLE. THE MAN THEN THREW THE RIFLE TO ANOTHER MAN NEAR THE TRACKS.THE 2ND MAN, IN LIGHT OVERALLS AND A RAIL WORKERS CAP, CAUGHT THE GUN, DISMANTLED IT, AND PUT IT IN A RAIL-WORKERS TOOLBAG. HE THEN WALKED TOWARD THE RAIL TOWER AND EXITED THE NORTH END OF THE PARKING LOT. THE MAN IN THE SUIT THEN WALKED EAST IN THE PARKING LOT WHERE – WHEN CONFRONTED BY OFFICER JOE MARSHALL SMITH – HE SHOWED SECRET SERVICE CREDENTIALS. SMITH DID NOT DETAIN THE MAN AND THE MAN THEN PROCEEDED TOWARDS A LIGHT GREEN 1962 RAMBLER STATION WAGON. THE VEHICLE EXITED THE NORTH END OF THE PARKING LOT BY THE RAILROAD TOWER .ED HOFFMAN WAS NOT INTERVIEWED BY THE WARREN COMMISSION.

GORDON ARNOLD
HE HAD PARKED NEAR THE RAIL TOWER THEN WALKED BEHIND THE PICKET FENCE. HE WAS TOLD TO LEAVE BY A MAN WITH A BADGE WHO SAID HE WAS A SECRET SERVICE AGENT. THERE WERE NO SECRET SERVICE ON THE KNOLL THAT DAY. ARNOLD SAID HE "FELT" A BULLET FLY BY HIM; "IT WENT RIGHT PAST MY LEFT EAR." ARNOLD WENT ON TO SAY HE HAD HIT THE GROUND WHEN 2 POLICEMEN APPROACHED HIM..ONE KICKED HIM AND TOLD HIM TO GET UP. HIS CAMERA WAS THEN OPENED AND THE FILM REMOVED.

JEAN NEWMAN
SHE TOLD THE FBI THAT WHEN SHE REALIZED THE REPORTS SHE HEARD WERE SHOTS, SHE IMMEDIATELY TURNED AND LOOKED UP THE HILL TO THE NORTH TOWARD THE PARKING LOT.

HARRY WEATHERFORD
A DALLAS DEPUTY SHERRIFF, WROTE IN HIS REPORT ON NOVEMBER 23RD:
"I WAS RUNNING TOWARDS THE RAILROAD YARDS WHERE THE SOUND SEEMED TO COME FROM."

PAUL LANIS JR.
THE SECRET SERVICE AGENT ON THE RIGHT RUNNING BOARD OF THE CAR IMMEDIATELY <u>BEHIND</u> THE PRESIDENTIAL LIMO STATED: "MY REACTION AT THE TIME WAS THAT THE SHOTS CAME FROM SOMEWHERE TOWARDS THE FRONT, RIGHT-HANDED SIDE OF THE ROAD…"

FORREST SORRELS
SECRET SERVICE AGENT IN CHARGE OF THE DALLAS OFFICE WAS IN THE LEAD CAR. HE STATED: "THE NOISE FROM THE SHOTS SEEMED LIKE THEY MAY HAVE COME FROM BACK UP ON THE TERRACE THERE."

CLYDE HAYGOOD
DALLAS POLICE OFFICER TOLD THE COMMISSION THAT WHEN THE SHOTS WERE FIRED HE RAN TO THE RAILROAD YARD BEHIND THE KNOLL.

SEYMOUR WEITZMAN
A DALLAS SHERIFF'S DEPUTY REPORTED: "I RAN IN A NORTHWEST DIRECTION AND SCALED A FENCE TOWARD WHERE WE THOUGHT THE SHOTS CAME FROM." HE ALSO TOLD THE COMMISSION THAT HE ENCOUNTERED A MAN WHO CLAIMED HE WAS SECRET SERVICE. THE MAN SHOWED WEITZMAN AN I.D. AND STATED: "HE HAD EVERYTHING UNDER CONTROL."

AURELIO ALONZO AND ANNE DONALDSON
REPORTERS FOR THE DALLAS MORNING NEWS. THEY WOULD LATER WRITE: "SUDDENLY THERE WAS A HORRIBLE, EAR-SHATTERING NOISE COMING FROM BEHIND US AND A LITTLE TO THE RIGHT." ALONZO TOLD A TEXAS OBSERVER REPORTER: "THE SOUND SEEMED TO BE COMING FROM ABOVE OUR HEADS. WE LOOKED UP AND BEHIND US. THERE ARE SOME TREES THERE AND SOME CEMENT STRUCTURES."

ED JOHNSON
A REPORTER FOR THE FORT WORTH STAR-TELEGRAM WROTE ON 11/23: "SOME OF US SAW LITTLE PUFFS OF WHITE SMOKE THAT SEEMED TO HIT THE GRASSY AREA IN THE ESPLANADE THAT DIVIDES DALLAS MAIN DOWNTOWN STREETS."

HAROLD ELKINS
DALLAS DEPUTY SHERIFF STATED: "I IMMEDIATELY RAN TO THE AREA FROM WHICH IT SEEMED LIKE THE SHOTS HAD BEEN FIRED. THIS IS AN AREA BETWEEN THE RAILROAD AND THE TSBD."

JOE MARSHALL SMITH
SMITH WAS A DALLAS POLICE OFFICER. HE RAN, ACCOMPANIED BY DEPUTY SHERIFF SEYMOUR WEITZMAN, TO THE GRASSY KNOLL AFTER THE SHOOTING. THERE HE ENCOUNTERED A MAN BEHIND THE FENCE. SMITH DREW HIS PISTOL. THE MAN STATED TO SMITH THAT HE WAS "SECRET SERVICE" AS HE REMOVED HIS CREDENTIALS FROM HIS HIP POCKET.

AS NOTED EARLIER, THERE WERE NO SECRET SERVICE AGENTS STATIONED ON THE KNOLL THAT DAY. ALL THE SECRET SERVICE AGENTS WERE ON BOARD VEHICLES IN THE MOTORCADE. THE COMMISSION DID NOT ACKNOWLEDGE THIS ENCOUNTER WHEN THEY QUESTIONED OFFICER SMITH. LATER HOWEVER SMITH WOULD NOTE: "HE LOOKED LIKE AN AUTO MECHANIC. HE HAD ON A SPORT SHIRT AND SPORTS PANTS. BUT, HE HAD DIRTY FINGERNAILS, AND HANDS THAT LOOKED LIKE AN AUTO MECHANIC'S HANDS. AFTERWARDS IT DIDN'T RING TRUE FOR SECRET SERVICE. HE HAD PRODUCED CORRECT IDENTIFICATION...I SHOULD HAVE CHECKED THE MAN CLOSER."

ED HOFFMAN MAINTAINS THAT THE SHOOTER WORE A HAT, TIE AND SUIT AND THAT HE ALSO WITNESSED OFFICER SMITH'S – WITH PISTOL DRAWN – ENCOUNTER WITH THIS MAN. BUT SMITH WOULD NOTE THAT THE MAN HE ENCOUNTERED WORE A SPORT SHIRT AND SLACKS. EITHER HOFFMAN IS MISTAKEN IN HIS OBSERVATION FROM 230 YARDS AWAY OR HE WRONGLY IDENTIFIED SMITH AS THE OFFICER WHO ENCOUNTERED THE MAN IN THE HAT, TIE, AND SUIT. NONETHELESS THERE ARE 4 KNOWN WITNESSES, SEYMOUR WEITZMAN, OFFICER SMITH, SERGEANT D.V. HARKNESS, AND GORDON ARNOLD WHO ENCOUNTERED MEN WHO EITHER PRODUCED SECRET SERVICE CREDENTIALS OR VERBALLY CLAIMED TO BE SECRET SERVICE AGENTS.

W.W. MABRA / ORVILLE SMITH
THESE DALLAS OFFICERS WERE ATTEMPTING TO SEARCH THE AREA OF THE PARKING LOT BEHIND THE GRASSY KNOLL. A MAN IN A DALLAS P.D. UNIFORM APPROACHED THEM AND TOLD THEM THAT HE HAD BEEN ASSIGNED TO PATROL THE RAILROAD YARD. HE STATED TO MABRA AND SMITH: "I WAS STATIONED IN THE RAILYARD AND HAD THIS ENTIRE AREA IN VIEW. NOBODY CAME THIS WAY." BOTH MABRA AND SMITH

DISCONTINUED THEIR SEARCH OF THE AREA. POLICE RECORDS LATER SHOWED THAT THERE HAD <u>NOT</u> BEEN AN OFFICER ASSIGNED TO THAT AREA.

BEVERLY OLIVER, WHO WAS STANDING ON THE SOUTH SIDE OF ELM ACROSS FROM THE KNOLL, WALKED ACROSS ELM AS SOON AS THE MOTORCADE HAD PASSED. SHE HAD FILMED PORTIONS OF THE MOTORCADE. ON THE KNOLL WERE DALLAS OFFICERS P.T. DEAN AND "GENEVA'S HUSBAND", ROSCOE WHITE. OLIVER WHO WORKED AS A "SINGER" AT THE COLONY CLUB ADJACENT TO RUBY'S CAROUSEL CLUB, RECOGNIZED ROSCOE WHITE WHO OFTEN FREQUENTED CLUBS LIKE THE COLONY AND THE CAROUSEL WHERE HIS WIFE GENEVA WORKED. ON MONDAY, NOVEMBER 25TH UPON ARRIVAL AT THE COLONY CLUB, OLIVER WAS CONFRONTED BY FBI AGENTS WHO DEMANDED HER FOOTAGE OF THE MOTORCADE. SHE WONDERED HOW <u>THEY</u> KNEW SHE HAD SHOT MOVIE FILM ON THE 22ND OF THE MOTORCADE. SHE WAS CONVINCED THAT THE FBI WAS TIPPED-OFF BY ROSCOE WHITE, OUR DALLAS-BASED SET-UP CONSPIRATOR, OR POSSIBLY OFFICER P.T. DEAN

JAMES TAGUE
WOUNDED BY A FRAGMENT FROM A PIECE OF CURBING CAUSED BY A MISSED SHOT. HE NOTED THAT "SHOTS CAME FROM THE BUSHES."

DANNY ARCE
TSBD EMPLOYEE STATED THAT THE "SHOTS CAME FROM THE RAILROAD TRACK YARDS."

MARION BAKER
DPD OFFICER WHO WILL SOON CONFRONT **HARVEY** IN THE TSBD, NOTED THIS ABOUT THE SHOTS: "WELL, TO ME, IT SOUNDED HIGH AND I IMMEDIATELY KIND OF LOOKED UP AND I HAD A FEELING THAT IT CAME FROM THE BUILDING EITHER RIGHT IN FRONT OF ME (TSBD) OR FROM THE ONE ACROSS TO THE RIGHT OF IT."

THE BUILDING "JUST TO THE RIGHT OF IT (TSBD)" IS THE DAL-TEX BUILDING.

MARY WOODWARD
A STAFF WRITER FOR DALLAS MORNING NEWS WAS STANDING ON THE KNOLL SHE NOTED IN HER NEWSPAPER ARTICLE THAT WEEKEND: "SUDDENLY THERE WAS A HORRIBLE EAR-SHATTERING NOISE COMING FROM BEHIND US AND A LITTLE TO THE RIGHT."

ROGER CRAIG
A DALLAS COUNTY DEPUTY SHERIFF TOLD THE COMMISSION HE RAN "ACROSS HOUSTON STREET, ACROSS THE PARKWAY, ACROSS ELM STREET, AND RAN UP TO THE RAILROAD YARD."

JOE MOLINA
TSBD EMPLOYEE WHO WAS STANDING ON THE STEPS OF THE TSBD NOTED THAT HE THOUGHT THE SHOTS "CAME FROM THE WEST SIDE."

LUKE MOONEY
A DALLAS COUNTY DEPUTY SHERIFF, INCLUDED IN HIS WRITTEN REPORT THAT HE "STARTED RUNNING ACROSS HOUSTON STREET, DOWN ACROSS THE LAWN TO THE TRIPLE UNDERPASS AND UP THE TERRACE TO THE RAILROAD YARDS. WE THOUGHT THEY (THE SHOTS) CAME FROM THAT DIRECTION."

EDGAR SMITH
A DPD OFFICER TOLD THE WARREN COMMISSION THAT HE "RAN DOWN HOUSTON AND THEN RAN DOWN ELM AND WENT TO A PARKING AREA BEHIND THE CONCRETE STRUCTURE."

DOLORES KOUNAS

IN HER FBI STATEMENT SHE NOTED: "IT SOUNDED AS THOUGH THE SHOTS WERE COMING FROM THE VICINITY OF THE VIADUCT."

BILL SHELLEY
SHELLEY, A TSBD SUPERINTENDANT, WAS STANDING ON THE TSBD STEPS. HE NOTED THAT THE SHOTS "CAME FROM THE WEST."

*IT IS INTERESTING THAT IN CAPTAIN FRITZ'S ROUGH NOTES TAKEN DURING THE INTERROGATION SESSIONS THAT HE WRITES "OUT WITH SHELLEY" AS **HARVEY'S** RESPONSE WHEN ASKED WHERE HE WAS STANDING WHEN THE SHOTS WERE FIRED.*

BUELL WESLEY FRAZIER
ALSO A TSBD EMPLOYEE, NOTED THAT HE THOUGHT THE SHOTS "CAME FROM THE RAILROAD OVERPASS."

CHERYL MCKINNEN
WAS STANDING BESIDE BILL NEWMAN: "TURNED IN HORROR TOWARD THE BACK OF THE GRASSY KNOLL WHERE IT SEEMED THE SHOTS ORIGINATED."

SS AGENT LEM JOHNS
"THE FIRST TWO (SHOTS) SOUNDED LIKE THEY WERE ON THAT SIDE OF ME TOWARDS THE GRASSY KNOLL."

OTIS N. WILLIAMS
"I THOUGHT THESE BLASTS OR SHOTS CAME FROM THE DIRECTION OF THE VIADUCT."

DOROTHY GARNER
ON THE 4TH FLOOR OF THE TSBD: "THE SHOTS OR REPORTS CAME FROM A POINT TO THE WEST OF THE BUILDING."

BILL LOVELADY
LOVELADY WORKED AT THE TSBD. HE WAS STANDING ON THE FRONT STEPS AT THE TIME OF THE SHOOTING. WHEN ASKED BY THE WARREN COMMISSION WHERE HE THOUGHT THE SHOTS CAME FROM HE REPLIED: "TO MY RIGHT, BETWEEN THE UNDERPASS AND THAT BUILDING RIGHT ON THE KNOLL."

*JAMES ALTGENS, AN AP PHOTOGRAPHER, TOOK 3 PHOTOS OF THE MOTORCADE. HIS SECOND PHOTO, WHICH HAS BEEN REPRODUCED IN A NUMBER OF BOOKS ON THE ASSASSINATION, SHOWS THE PRESIDENTIAL LIMO AND IN THE BACKGROUND, THE ENTRANCE TO THE TSBD. ON THE TOP STEP OF THE DEPOSITORY IS A MAN WEARING A DARK PLAD SHIRT WITH THE TOP 2 BUTTONS UNDONE OR MISSING AND A T-SHIRT UNDERNEATH. THE MAN LOOKS A GREAT DEAL LIKE **HARVEY**. HE ALSO LOOKS A GREAT DEAL LIKE BILLY LOVELADY, ALSO A TSBD EMPLOYEE. IF THIS IS INDEED **HARVEY**, IT PRESENTS QUITE A DILEMMA FOR THE W.C. SINCE THE PHOTO WAS TAKEN ONLY SECONDS BEFORE THE FATAL HEAD SHOT. THE PHOTO WAS PUBLISHED ON NOVEMBER 22ND NATIONALLY INCLUDING THE WASHINGTON POST.*

ON NOVEMBER 23RD, LOVELADY WAS VISITED BY THE FBI WITH A COPY OF THE ALTGEN'S PHOTO. THE FBI REPORTED THAT LOVELADY "IMMEDIATELY IDENTIFIED HIMSELF IN THE ABOVE-MENTIONED PHOTOGRAPH."

ON FEBRUARY 29TH, 1964 HOWEVER LOVELADY NOTED TO THE FBI THAT ON THE DAY OF THE ASSASSINATION THAT HE WAS "WEARING A RED AND WHITE VERTICAL STRIPED SHIRT." THE SHIRT HE DESCRIBED WAS ALSO SHORT-SLEEVED. THIS CLEARLY IS <u>NOT</u> THE SHIRT THAT IS BEING WORN BY THE YOUNG MAN IN QUESTION IN THE ALTGEN'S PHOTO. THE FBI ALSO PHOTOGRAPHED LOVELADY IN THE VERTICAL STRIPED SHIRT HE CLAIMED HE WORE TO WORK ON NOVEMBER 22ND.

*THE SHIRT IN THE ALTGEN'S PHOTO LOOKS NEARLY IDENTICAL TO THE SHIRT **HARVEY** WAS WEARING WHEN ARRESTED RATHER THAN THE "RED AND WHITE VERTICAL STRIPED SHIRT" LOVELADY NOTED. .*

*THE FACIAL FEATURES SEEM TO SUPPORT THE NOTIION THAT IT IS INDEED LOVELADY IN THE PHOTO. I AM HOWEVER TROUBLED BY THE FEBRUARY 29TH FBI INTERVIEW IN WHICH LOVELADY CLAIMS TO HAVE WORN A VERTICAL STRIPED SHIRT TO WORK ON NOVEMBER 22ND. SHORTLY AFTERWARD HE CHANGED THIS TO A LARGE RED/GREY PLAID SHIRT. WHY THE INITIAL DECEPTION? WAS LOVELADY BEING TRUTHFULL INITIALLY AND LATER COERCED INTO DESCRIBING A SHIRT CLOSER IN APPEARANCE TO THE ONE IN THE ALTGEN'S PHOTO? ADMITTEDLY THE LATER SHIRT IS CLOSER IN APPEARANCE TO THE SHIRT IN THE PHOTO, BUT THE SHIRT IN THE PHOTO DOES NOT SHOW THE DISTINCTIVE LARGE 2-3 INCH BLOCKS THAT THE LOVELADY PLAID SHIRT DISPLAYS. I AM NOT INCLINED TO LABEL THE MAN IN THE ALTGEN'S PHOTO AS LOVELADY. NEITHER OF THE TWO MARKEDLY DIFFERENT SHIRTS HE CLAIMED TO WEAR TO WORK THAT DAY RESEMBLE THE SHIRT IN AN ENLARGED VERSION OF THE PHOTO. I AM HOWEVER LESS RELUCTANT TO CLAIM THAT THE MAN IN THE PHOTO IS **HARVEY**. I AM INCLINED TO AGREE WITH SOME RESEARCHERS THAT THE MAN IN THE PHOTO IS A COMPOSITE: **HARVEY'S** FACIAL FEATURES BUT WITH THE HAIRLINE ALTERED TO MORE CLOSELY RESEMBLE LOVELADY'S HAIRLINE.*

*I WOULD STRONGLY URGE YOU TO VISIT A FASCINATING WEBSITE, WWW.OSWALD-INNOCENT.COM FOR FURTHER DETAILS REGARDING THE ALTGEN'S PHOTO. I AM CERTAIN THAT YOU WILL COME TO THE SAME CONCLUSION. THE REMOVAL OF THE POSSIBILITY OF **HARVEY'S** PRESENCE ON THE TSBD STEPS WAS NOT LIMITED TO THE ALTGEN'S PHOTO. FURTHER FILMS AND STILLS TAKEN AT THE DPD ATTEMPT TO INCLUDE LOVELADY'S PRESENCE WEARING THE RED/GREY PLAID SHIRT. THE RESULTS ARE NOT ONLY FUTILE SINCE THAT SHIRT BEARS LITTLE RESEMBLENCE TO THE ONE WORN IN THE ALTGEN PHOTO, BUT BY TODAY'S STANDARDS, THE MANIPULATION OF THE FOOTAGE IS AMATEURISH AT BEST. IF NOTHING ELSE, IT SHOWS THE LEVEL OF DESPERATION REGARDING THE NEED TO HAVE THE MAN ON THE STEPS IDENTIFIED AS LOVELADY <u>NOT</u> **HARVEY**.*

GEORGE HICKEY
A SS AGENT IN THE PRESIDENTIAL FOLLOW-UP CAR. HE NOTED THAT THE FIRST SHOT "SEEMED TO BE AT GROUND LEVEL." HE ALSO STATED THAT THE NEXT 2 SHOTS "APPEARED TO ME COMPLETELY DIFFERENT IN SOUND THAN THE FIRST REPORT." MORE IMPORTANTLY HE NOTED THAT THE 2ND AND 3RD REPORTS/SHOTS "WERE IN SUCH RAPID SUCESSION THAT THERE SEEMED TO BE PRACTICALLY NO TIME ELEMENT BETWEEN THEM."

IF HARVEY IS IN THE TSBD, WHY A FRONTAL HEAD SHOT?

*THROUGH THE COURSE OF READING OVER 180 BOOKS REGARDING THE PRESIDENTIAL ASSASSINATION IT HAS BEEN MY CONTENTION THAT **HARVEY** WAS INDEED WHAT HE CLAIMED, A PATSY. I HAVE READ LITTLE TO DETER MY THINKING THAT HE WAS SET-UP AS THE LONE ASSASSIN. IN SPITE OF THAT, I HAVE, AS HAVE MANY OTHER RESEARCHERS, LABORED OVER THE PROBLEM INHERENT IN PLACING **HARVEY** AS THE ALLEGED ASSASSIN ON THE 6TH FLOOR OF THE TSBD YET HAVING A SHOOTER TAKE THE FATAL HEAD SHOT FROM THE <u>FRONT</u> OF THE VEHICLE. IF INDEED **HARVEY** WAS THE VICTIM OF A SET-UP THAT WOULD LEAVE HIM AS THE SOLE SHOOTER THAT DAY, WOULD THAT NOT BE JEOPARDIZED BY HAVING THE LAST, FATAL SHOT FIRED FROM THE <u>FRONT</u>? THE FRONTAL NECK WOUND ASIDE, WHY WOULD THE CONSPIRATORS RESPONSIBLE FOR THE PLACEMENT OF THE SHOOTERS UTILIZE A SCHEME THAT WOULD BE AT SUCH ODDS WITH THOSE RESPONSIBLE FOR THE SET-UP OF **HARVEY** ON THE 6TH FLOOR OF THE TSBD?*

I HAVE GIVEN A GREAT DEAL OF THOUGHT TO THIS SEEMINGLY INCONGRUENT AND OFTEN QUESTIONED DILEMMA AND WILL OFFER MY OPINION AS TO WHY THOSE

CONSPIRATORS RESPONSIBLE FOR THE SHOOTING SEQUENCE TOOK FRONTAL SHOTS THAT WOULD SERIOUSLY DAMAGE THE CREDIBILITY OF THE SET-UP CONSPIRATORS IN THEIR EFFORTS TO ISOLATE **HARVEY** ON THE 6TH FLOOR **BEHIND** THE PRESIDENTIAL LIMO.

SERIOUS RESEARCHERS HAVE NO DOUBT REPEATEDLY VIEWED THE ZAPRUDER FILM. INDEED, THEY HAVE LIKELY WATCHED IT FORWARD, BACKWARD, IN SLOW MOTION, FRAME-BY-FRAME, AND WITH AND WITHOUT DIGITAL ENHANCEMENT. MANY WILL POINT OUT THAT _PRIOR_ TO THE FATAL AND DRAMATIC HEAD SHOT THAT THE PRESIDENT MOVES SLIGHTLY _FORWARD_ AND SLIGHTLY TO HIS _LEFT_. THIS MOVEMENT IS ATTRIBUTED TO EITHER THE BACK SHOT OR MORE LIKELY TO A HEAD SHOT FROM THE REAR THAT TOOK PLACE VIRTUALLY AT THE SAME TIME AS THE MORE NOTICEABLE FRONTAL HEAD SHOT THAT FORCED THE PRESIDENT BACKWARDS AND TO HIS LEFT.

WHAT I FIND CRITICAL HOWEVER IS NOT THE PRECISE LOCATION OF THE PRESIDENT IN THE LIMO JUST PRIOR TO THE FATAL HEAD SHOT, BUT THE LOCATION OF _MRS. KENNEDY_ AND HER SPATIAL RELATIONSHIP TO THE PRESIDENT JUST PRIOR TO THE FRONTAL HEAD SHOT. MRS. KENNEDY IS TURNED TO HER RIGHT AND BENT FORWARD TOWARD HER SLUMPING HUSBAND. HER HEAD NEARLY TOUCHES THAT OF THE PRESIDENT. IT IS CRITICAL TO KEEP IN MIND THAT JUST PRIOR TO THE DRAMATIC FRONTAL HEAD SHOT THERE IS NO VISIBLE INDICATION THAT THE PRESIDENT HAS SUFFERED ANY WOUND THAT WAS NOT SURVIVABLE. TO INSURE WHAT THE CONSPIRATORS WOULD CONSIDER A "SUCCESSFUL" ASSASSINATION PLOT, THERE WOULD HAVE TO BE A SHOT INFLICTED UPON THE PRESIDENT THAT WOULD LEAVE LITTLE DOUBT AS TO HIS INABILITY TO SURVIVE AND THIS SHOT WOULD HAVE TO BE EASILY DISCERNABLE TO _ALL_ THE SHOOTERS.

AS THE SHOOTING SEQUENCE UNFOLDED, THE SHOOTER(S) LOCATED TO THE _REAR_ OF THE PRESIDENTIAL LIMO WERE LIKELY AWARE THAT ANOTHER SHOT WOULD BE REQUIRED TO ENSURE A SUCCESSFUL ATTEMPT ON THE PRESIDENT'S LIFE. THEY WERE ALSO ACUTELY AWARE THAT THE SHOT MUST COME FROM THE REAR OF THE LIMO IF INDEED **HARVEY** WERE TO BE ANNOINTED AS THE SOLE ASSASSIN. THE PROBLEM THE SHOOTERS _BEHIND_ THE LIMO FACED HOWEVER WAS THE POSITION OF _MRS. KENNEDY_ IN RELATION TO HER HUSBAND JUST PRIOR TO THE LAST AND FATAL HEAD SHOT. A FATAL HEAD SHOT FROM THE _REAR_ OF THE LIMO WOULD NOW PLACE THE FIRST LADY IN JEOPARDY DUE TO HER ALIGNMENT WITH THE PRESIDENT. TIME WAS RUNNING OUT FOR THE SHOOTERS BOTH TO THE REAR AND THE FRONT OF THE LIMO. THE MOTORCADE, NOW AWARE THAT SOMETHING HAD GONE DRAMATICALLY WRONG, WOULD SURELY ACCELERATE AND RAPIDLY APPROACH THE OVERPASS. THE WINDOW OF OPPORTUNITY TO DELIVER A FATAL SHOT WAS QUICKLY CLOSING FOR THE SHOOTER(S) _BEHIND_ THE PRESIDENTIAL LIMO. IT WAS, DUE TO THE POSSIBILITY OF WOUNDING THE FIRST LADY, TOO LATE TO DELIVER A FATAL HEAD WOUND FROM THE REAR.

IT IS INTERESTING TO NOTE THAT LBJ HAD LOBBIED THE PRESIDENT TO HAVE THE FIRST LADY RIDE WITH HIM AND LADY BIRD. ONE WEEK BEFORE THE DALLAS TRIP, JFK HAD TOLD SENATOR GEORGE SMATHERS OF FLORIDA: "WELL, YOU KNOW HOW LYNDON IS……JOHNSON WANTS JACKIE TO RIDE WITH HIM….." HAD LBJ'S WISHES BEEN GRANTED, THE SHOOTING SEQUENCE WOULD _NOT_ HAVE REQUIRED SHOOTERS IN FRONT OF THE LIMO TO TAKE THE FATAL HEAD SHOT THUS STRENGTHENING THE CASE FOR A TSBD/**HARVEY** SOLE ASSASSIN SCENARIO.

THOSE RESPONSIBLE FOR THE SHOOTING SEQUENCE WERE LEFT WITH LITTLE CHOICE; THE LAST SHOT AVAILABLE THAT WOULD INSURE A FATAL OUTCOME FOR THE PRESIDENT TO THE EXCLUSION OF ALL OTHERS IN THE LIMO, PARTICULARLY HIS WIFE, WOULD HAVE TO BE TAKEN FROM THE FRONT. IT WAS NOT LIKELY THE FIRST CHOICE OF THE CONSPIRATORS, BUT THEY CERTAINLY REALIZED THAT THERE WAS AT LEAST THE _POSSIBILITY_ THAT A FATAL FRONTAL SHOT WOULD BE REQUIRED OR THERE WOULD NOT

HAVE BEEN A TEAM OR TEAMS LOCATED TO THE FRONT OF THE PRESIDENTIAL LIMO AS IT NEARED THE OVERPASS.

*I TRULY FEEL THAT THOSE RESPONSIBLE FOR THE SHOOTING SEQUENCE WOULD PERCEIVE A FATAL FRONTAL SHOT AS A CALCULATED RISK. I QUALIFY THE RISK AS "CALCULATED" SINCE I BELIEVE THAT THEY KNEW THAT THE PREPONDERANCE OF "EVIDENCE" WOULD <u>STILL</u> POINT TO THE TSBD, THE 6TH FLOOR, **HARVEY**, AND THE MAIL-ORDERED RIFLE. IT WAS THE SHOOTERS' RESPONSIBILITY TO ENSURE, FOR THE LACK OF A BETTER TERM, A "KILL." IT WOULD BE THE RESPONSIBILITY OF THE SET-UP CONSPIRATORS TO "ERASE" ANY EVIDENCE OF FRONTAL SHOOTERS BY MANIPULATING THE AUTOPSY, THE PHOTOS, THE X-RAYS, AND THE FINDINGS OF THE WARREN COMMISSION.*

CHIEF JESSE CURRY HOWEVER WOULD LEAVE LITTLE DOUBT AS TO WHERE HE THOUGHT THE FATAL HEAD SHOT HAD BEEN FIRED FROM. IN HIS WARREN COMMISSON TESTIMONY, CURRY WOULD NOTE "BY THE DIRECTION OF THE BLOOD AND BRAINS FROM THE PRESIDENT FROM ONE OF THE SHOTS, IT WOULD SEEM THAT IT WOULD HAVE HAD TO BE FIRED FROM THE FRONT RATHER THAN BEHIND."

CLINT HILL, THE SS AGENT WHO CLIMBED ONTO THE BACK OF THE PRESIDENTIAL LIMO NOTED "BLOOD, BRAIN MATER AND BONE FRAGMENTS EXPLODED FROM THE BACK OF THE PRESIDENT'S HEAD AND SPLATTERED ALL OVER ME....ON MY FACE, MY CLOTHES, IN MY HAIR." THIS IS IN STARK CONTRADICTION TO THE ZAPRUDER FILM WHICH SHOWS THE "PINK ORB" OF BLOOD AND BRAIN MATTER FROM THE FATAL WOUND TO THE <u>FRONT</u> OF THE PRESIDENT'S SKULL NOT TO THE <u>REAR</u>. IF THE FATAL HEAD SHOT HAD BEEN FROM THE REAR, AT A <u>MINIMUM</u>, THE FIRST LADY WOULD HAVE HAD BLOOD AND BRAIN MATTER COVERING HER UPPER TORSO. HOWEVER IF ONE VIEWS THE STILL PHOTO OF HER AND RFK EXITING AIR FORCE ONE IN WASHINGTON, YOU WILL NOTE THAT VIRTUALLY ALL THE BLOOD/BRAIN STAINS ARE LOCATED ON THE <u>LOWER</u> HALF OF HER SKIRT AND ON HER GLOVES. THE PICTURE OF HER WITH LBJ AS HE IS SWORN INTO OFFICE SHOWS THIS AS WELL.

THERE ARE SEVERAL BOOKS AND WEBSITES THAT CONTEND THAT THE ZAPRUDER FILM HAS BEEN ALTERED; FRAMES DROPPED, FRAMES REVERSED, BACKGROUND DISCREPANCIES, MOVEMENTS OF BYSTANDERS THAT DEFY PHYSICS, AND TIMING DISCREPANCIES THAT WHEN COMBINED MAKE THE FORENSIC VALUE OF THE FILM ESSENTIALLY ZERO. THIS IS BEYOND THE SCOPE OF THIS WORK, BUT I STRONGLY ENCOURAGE ONE TO SIMPLY DO A WEB SEARCH AND DECIDE IF THIS SOURCE OF EVIDENCE HAS ALSO BEEN ALTERED TO FIT THE CONCLUSIONS OF THE W.C.

BOTH MALCOLM KILDUFF, WHITE HOUSE PRESS OFFICIAL, AND TOM ROBINSON, A BETHESDA MORTICIAN, DESCRIBED THE ENTRY POINT OF THE FATAL HEAD SHOT AS THE RIGHT FRONT TEMPLE.

IT IS FELT THAT THE FIRST SHOT, OR AT LEAST THE FIRST SHOT THAT HIT THE PRESIDENT, WAS FIRED FROM THE FRONT; EITHER FROM THE OVERPASS OR THE KNOLL. THIS IS, I THINK, SUPPORTED BY THE NOTION THAT MANY WITNESSES NOTED THAT THE PRESIDENTIAL LIMO BRAKED TO A STOP OR NEAR STOP AT THE <u>COMMENCEMENT</u> OF THE SHOOTING SEQUENCE. IF ONE WERE BEING FIRED UPON FROM THE <u>REAR</u>, YOU WOULD INSTICTIVELY <u>ACCELERATE</u>. HOWEVER IF YOU SENSED THAT YOU WERE BEING FIRED UPON FROM THE <u>FRONT</u>, WOULD YOU NOT INSTINCTIVELY <u>BRAKE</u> TO AVOID CLOSING THE DISTANCE BETWEEN YOUR VEHICLE AND THE SHOOTER?

WE WILL NOW RETURN TO THE TIMELINE AS OF
12:31 PM, 1 MINUTE AFTER THE SHOOTING

12:31 PM FRIDAY

LEE AND THE MAN IN THE BROWN SUIT LEAVE TH 6TH FLOOR OF THE TSBD VIA THE REAR STAIRS. **LEE,** ACCORDING TO ARMSTRONG, STOPS AT THE SECOND FLOOR AND ENTERS THE OFFICE OF THE TSBD. THE MAN IN THE BROWN SUIT CONTINUES TO THE 1ST FLOOR AND EXITS THE BUILDING VIA ONE OF THE REAR DOORS.

12:32 PM FRIDAY

POLICE CHIEF CURRY AND SHERIFF DECKER WERE BOTH IN THE LEAD CAR IMMEDIATELY IN FRONT OF THE PRESIDENTIAL LIMO. THEIR TRANSMISSIONS TO DISPATCH REVEAL THEIR SUSPICIONS AS TO THE LOCATION OF SHOOTERS:

CHIEF CURRY: "…GET MEN UP ON THAT OVERPASS. SEE WHAT HAPPENED UP THERE. MAKE ALL MEN AVAILABLE TO THE RAILROAD YARD AND DETERMINE WHAT HAPPENED….."

SHERIFF DECKER: "MOVE ALL AVAILABLE MEN OUT OF MY OFFICE INTO THE RAILYARD TO TRY TO DETERMINE WHAT HAPPENED IN THERE."

12:32 PM FRIDAY

POLICEMAN MARION BAKER, WITH GUN DRAWN, AND ROY S. TRULY, SUPERINTENDANT AT THE TSBD, ENTER THE TSBD. THEY HAD INITIALLY TRIED TO CALL FOR THE ELEVATORS BUT THEY WERE STUCK ON THE 5TH FLOOR. THEY THEN RAN UP TO THE SECOND FLOOR. BAKER ENCOUNTERS **HARVEY** IN THE SECOND FLOOR LUNCH ROOM. HE CALLS HIM OUT AND **HARVEY** EXITS THE LUNCH ROOM WHERE HE IS THEN FACE TO FACE WITH BAKER. TRULY IDENTIFIES **HARVEY** AS AN EMPLOYEE OF THE TSBD.

*TRULY'S COMMISSION TESTIMONY ABOUT HIS CONFRONTATION WITH **HARVEY** HARDLY DESCRIBED THE DEMEANOR OF A MAN WHO HAD JUST ALLEGEDLY SHOT A PRESIDENT. TRULY NOTED: "HE DIDN'T SEEM TO BE EXCITED OR OVERLY AFRAID OR ANYTHING. HE MIGHT HAVE BEEN A LITTLE BIT STARTLED LIKE I MIGHT HAVE BEEN IF SOMEONE CONFRONTED ME, BUT I CANNOT RECALL ANY CHANGE IN EXPRESSION OF ANY KIND ON HIS FACE." WHEN QUESTIONED BEFORE THE W.C., TRULY WAS ASKED IF **HARVEY** HAD ANYTHING IN EITHER HAND. HE REPLIED "NO." ALLEN DULLES THEN ASKED TRULY "DID HE HAVE A COKE?" TRULY REPLIED "NO SIR, NO DRINK AT ALL." DULLES LIKELY QUESTIONED TRULY CONCERNING THE COKE AS A RESULT OF MRS. REID'S TESTIMONY THAT **LEE** WAS IN POSSESSION OF A COKE WHEN SHE ENCOUNTERED HIM IN THE TSBD OFFICE. **HARVEY** HAD ALREADY EATEN HIS LUNCH AND DRANK THE COKE THAT HE HAD PURCHASED SHORTLY AFTER 12:00. THE W.C. VERSION OF **HARVEY'S** ACTIVITY IMMEDIATELY AFTER THE SHOOTING AND PRIOR TO HIS DEPARTURE FROM THE TSBD HAD HIM DRINKING A COKE. MRS. REID HOWEVER HAD WITNESSED **LEE** DRINKING THE COKE.*

12:33 PM FRIDAY

LEE, UPON ENTERING THE REAR DOOR OF THE TSBD OFFICE, ENCOUNTERS MRS. ROBERT REID SUPERVISOR OF THE CLERICAL STAFF OF THE TSBD. SHE HAD JUST ENTERED THE OFFICE VIA THE FRONT DOOR. SHE NOTED THAT HE HAD ON A WHITE SHIRT, NO JACKET, AND HELD A BOTTLE OF COKE IN HIS RIGHT HAND. **LEE** WALKED PAST MRS. REID AND EXITED THE TSBD OFFICE VIA THE FRONT DOOR.

12:33 PM FRIDAY

HARVEY PICKS UP HIS GREY JACKET AND LEAVES THE TSBD VIA THE FRONT STAIRS. LINNIE MAE RANDLE HAD ALSO NOTED THAT **HARVEY** HAD BEEN WEARING A GREY JACKET WHEN HE MET WITH BUELL FRAZIER FOR HIS RIDE TO WORK THAT MORNING. **HARVEY** IS CONFRONTED BY SOMEONE LOOKING FOR THE NEAREST PAY PHONE. HE WOULD LATER DESCRIBE THE MAN AS A "CREW CUT SS AGENT." THE MAN WAS LATER IDENTIFIED AS WFAA-TV NEWSMAN PIERCE ALLMAN.

*SOME RESEARCHERS HAVE NOTED THAT AS **HARVEY** EXITED THE TSBD THAT RUBY HANDED HIM A PISTOL. THIS WAS WITNESSED BY 3 WOMEN WHO WORKED IN A SEWING*

ROOM AT MCKELL'S SPORTSWEAR IN THE DAL-TEX BUILDING. ONE WOMAN, MRS. LOUIS VELEZ, STATED THAT SHE TOLD HER MOTHER, MRS. EVELYN HARRIS ABOUT THE INCIDENT. MRS. HARRIS WAS INTERVIEWED BY THE FBI ON NOVEMBER 30TH, 1963. THE 3 WOMEN WHO WITNESSED THE TRANSACTION WITH THE PISTOL WERE FAMILIAR WITH JACK RUBY. THEY HOWEVER WERE <u>NOT</u> INTERVIEWED BY THE FBI OR THE DPD. IF THIS EVENT HAD INDEED TAKEN PLACE, IT WOULD HAVE ARMED **HARVEY** <u>PRIOR</u> TO BOARDING THE BUS AT 12:39 AND EXPLAINED WHY 2 OFFICERS BOARDED THAT PARTICULAR BUS AND ASKED IF ANYONE WAS CARRYING A WEAPON. IT WOULD ALSO HINT THAT PERHAPS RUBY HAD BEEN ENLISTED NOT TO <u>ASSIST</u> **HARVEY** THAT WEEKEND IN HIS EFFORT TO GO TO CUBA, BUT TO EXPEDITE THE <u>SILENCING</u> OF **HARVEY** <u>PRIOR</u> TO HIS EVENTUAL ARREST IN THE TEXAS THEATER.

CONFLICTING DEPARTURES BY **HARVEY** FROM THE TSBD ARISE AT THIS POINT. OFFICER ROGER CRAIG WOULD LATER, ABOUT 5:00 PM FRIDAY, TELL CAPTAIN FRITZ THAT HE SAW "OSWALD" EXIT THE BACK OF THE TSBD, RUN DOWN THE GRASSY KNOLL AND INTO A LIGHT GREEN RAMBLER STATION WAGON AT APPROXIMATELY 12:40. HE DESCRIBED "OSWALD" AS 5'9, 145 POUNDS, BROWN HAIR, AND WEARING A WHITE SHIRT. **HARVEY** OF COURSE WAS WEARING A REDDISH-BROWN SHIRT. CRAIG WOULD LATER DESCRIBE TO THE W.C. THE MAN'S CLOTHING AS A LIGHT TAN SHIRT AND MEDIUM BLUE TROUSERS. **HARVEY** WAS WEARING GREY SLACKS AND THE PREVIOUSLY MENTIONED DARK REDDISH-BROWN SHIRT. WHEN **HARVEY** IS LATER INFORMED OF CRAIG'S SIGHTING BY CAPTAIN FRITZ HE REPLIES: "THE STATION WAGON BELONGS TO MRS. PAINE...DON'T TRY TO DRAG HER INTO THIS...SHE HAD NOTHING TO DO WITH IT." ONE HAS TO WONDER JUST WHAT **HARVEY** WAS REFERRING TO WITH HIS "IT" COMMENT. ONE ALSO HAS TO WONDER IF **HARVEY** WAS AWARE OF THE FACT THAT **LEE** WOULD BE EXTRACTED FROM THE SCENE AND THAT IT WOULD BE VIA A VEHICLE BELONGING TO RUTH PAINE.

WE NOW HAVE 3 LIGHT COLORED 1961/1962 RAMBLER STATION WAGONS:

ED HOFFMAN
LIGHT GREEN 1962 BEHIND THE STOCKADE FENCE IN THE RAILWAY PARKING LOT

RICHARD CARR
LIGHT COLORED 1961/1962 ON RECORD STREET (1 BLOCK EAST OF HOUSTON)

DEP. SHERIFF ROGER CRAIG
LIGHT GREEN OR NEAR WHITE

ALTHOUGH THERE SEEMS TO BE SOME CONSISTANCY IN THE <u>DESCRIPTION</u> OF THE RAMBLER, THE <u>OCCUPANTS</u> OF THE CAR VARY IF ONE SEQUENCES THE OBSERVANCE OF THE CAR:

ED HOFFMAN
APPROXIMATELY 12:31, THE GRASSY KNOLL SHOOTER AND A DRIVER

RICHARD CARR
APPROXIMATELY 12:36, THREE OCCUPANTS, MOST LIKELY THE GRASSY KNOLL SHOOTER, THE DRIVER, AND A THIRD MAN CARR DESCRIBES AS THE 6TH FLOOR TSBD SHOOTER

DEP. SHERIFF CRAIG
APPROXIMATELY 12:40, A DRIVER AND **LEE** WHO ENTERS THE VEHICLE FROM THE GRASSY KNOLL

IT IS QUITE POSSIBLE THAT IT IS THE SAME RAMBLER IN ALL 3 INSTANCES. HOFFMAN NOTES THAT THE RAMBLER WAGON BEHIND THE STOCKADE FENCE LEFT THE NORTH END OF THE RAIL YARD, WENT BEHIND/NORTH OF THE TSBD AND TURNED RIGHT/SOUTH ON

HOUSTON. CARR NOTES THAT A RAMBLER WAGON WAS SITTING FACING NORTH ON RECORD STREET. HOFFMAN'S WAGON, WHICH WAS PROCEEDING SOUTH ON HOUSTON, COULD HAVE TURNED LEFT ON COMMERCE AND NORTH ON RECORD WHERE CARR WITNESSED THE MAN HE DESCRIBED AS THE 6TH FLOOR SHOOTER ENTER THE WAGON. THE WAGON WOULD HAVE THEN PROCEEDED NORTH ON RECORD, LEFT ON ELM, AND PICKED UP **LEE** AT THE FOOT OF THE GRASSY KNOLL. AN EXCELLENT BOOK ON THIS TOPIC IS CASEY QUINLAN AND BRIAN EDWARD'S BOOK "BEYOND THE FENCE LINE." THEY OFFER COMPELLING EVIDENCE THAT INDEED THE SAME RAMBLER WAGON PROVIDED AN "EXTRACTION" OF THE GRASSY KNOLL SHOOTER, THE 6TH FLOOR TSBD SHOOTER, AND A FINAL STOP ON ELM STREET TO PICK UP **LEE**.

HARVEY RESIDED AT 4905 MAGAZINE STREET IN NEW ORLEANS FROM MAY 10TH TO SEPTEMBER 25TH, 1963. NEIGHBORS NOTED THAT THAT A WOMAN IN A TWO-TONE BLUE STATION WAGON HAD VISITED THE OSWALDS ON TWO DIFFERENT OCCASSIONS SEVERAL MONTHS APART. THE NEIGHBORS STATED THAT THE WOMAN HAD BROUGHT MRS. OSWALD AND HER SMALL DAUGHTER TO THE APARTMENT AND THAT SEVERAL MONTHS LATER SHE RETURNED AND PICKED UP MRS. OSWALD AND THE CHILD.

RUTH PAINE DID INDEED BRING MARINA AND JUNE TO NEW ORLEANS ON MAY 10TH. SHE ALSO RETURNED ON SEPTEMBER 23RD TO TAKE THEM BACK TO DALLAS. THIS WOULD THEN TIE RUTH PAINE TO A TWO-TONE <u>BLUE</u> STATION WAGON AS LATE AS SEPTEMBER 1963. RUTH PAINE WAS ALSO LINKED TO A TWO-TONE LIGHT GREEN RAMBLER WAGON BUT THERE IS SOME UNCERTAINTY AS TO WHETHER SHE WAS IN POSSESSION OF THIS PARTICULAR WAGON IN NOVEMBER OF 1963.

IT IS QUITE OBVIOUS THAT THE PERSON OBSERVED BY OFFICER CRAIG WAS NOT **HARVEY** AS **HARVEY** WAS 7 BLOCKS TO THE EAST AT THIS POINT. CRAIG HAD OBSERVED **LEE'S** ESCAPE. BUT IF **LEE** LEFT VIA THE FRONT ENTRANCE AS ARMSTRONG NOTES, JUST WHO WAS THIS "OSWALD?" OFFICER CRAIG WAS NOT MISTAKEN IN REGARDS TO HIS NOTION THAT **LEE** <u>APPEARED</u> TO HAVE EXITED THE REAR OF THE TSBD. KEEP IN MIND THAT **LEE** HAD LEFT THE TSBD AT 12:34. HE WAS NOT PICKED UP UNTIL ABOUT 12:40. CRAIG HAD NOTED **LEE** RUNNING FROM THE WEST SIDE OF THE TSBD, DOWN THE GRASSY KNOLL AND <u>ASSUMED</u> THAT HE HAD EXITED FROM THE REAR OF THE BUILDING. **LEE** MAY WELL HAVE BEEN WAITING TOWARDS THE BACK/WEST SIDE OF THE TSBD <u>UNTIL</u> THE RAMBLER WAGON CAME INTO VIEW. THE HURRIED FASHION IN WHICH "OSWALD" WOULD BE SEEN LEAVING THE SCENE OF THE ASSASSINATION BY OFFICER CRAIG WOULD ADD CREEDENCE TO THE NOTION THAT **HARVEY** WAS INDEED THE PRESIDENT'S ASSAILANT. **HARVEY** HOWEVER WOULD PROCEED BY HIS USUAL MODE OF TRANSIT, PUBLIC TRANSPORTATION, TO HIS BOARDING HOUSE WHERE HE WOULD DEPART AWAITING HIS ANTICIPATED RIDE TO REDBIRD AIR FIELD. AS HAS BEEN DOCUMENTED, THERE WERE NUMEROUS SIGHTINGS OF AN "OSWALD" <u>PRIOR</u> TO THE ASSASSINATION. THE SIGHTINGS THAT DID <u>NOT</u> ADHERE TO WHAT THE COMMISSION FOUND WERE SIMPLY DISMISSED. HOWEVER THIS SIGHTING WAS IMMEDIATELY <u>AFTER</u> THE SHOOTING AND BY A WITNESS WHO WOULD NORMALLY BE CONSIDERED QUITE RELIABLE. **LEE'S** DEPARTURE FROM THE TSBD, IF OBSERVED BY WITNESSES, WOULD GIVE **HARVEY** TIME TO TRAVEL VIA HIS <u>NORMAL</u> MODES OF TRANSPORTATION; BUS, TAXI, AND A RIDE FROM A CAR NUMBERED 107. ACCORDING TO THE SET-UP CONSPIRATORS PLAN, **HARVEY** WAS NOT TO HAVE HIS <u>FIRST</u> ENCOUNTER AS A SUSPECT (ALLOWING FOR THE INITIAL 12:32 MEETING WITH OFFICER BAKER AND TSBD SUPERINDENDANT ROY TRULY) WITH LAW ENFORCEMENT UNTIL <u>AFTER</u> HE HAD APPARENTLY SLAIN OFFICER TIPPIT AND <u>AFTER</u> HE WAS MORE POINTEDLY ANNOINTED AS THE PRESIDENTIAL ASSASSIN. WITH THAT IN MIND, ONE HAS TO CONSIDER THE UPCOMING ENCOUNTER ON THE MARSALIS STREET BUS AS YET ANOTHER "TIMING" MISTAKE. BUT, THE SOONER **HARVEY** COULD BE DISPOSED OF THE BETTER.

OFFICER CRAIG'S POLICE CAREER AND PERSONNAL LIFE TOOK A SERIES OF TURNS FOR THE WORSE AFTER THE ASSASSINATION. HE STEADFASTLY REFUSED TO CHANGE HIS OPINION OF WHAT HE PERCEIVED AS **HARVEY** FLEEING THE TSBD. IN 1967 HE WAS FIRED FROM THE POLICE FORCE FOR TALKING TO REPORTERS. A FEW YEARS LATER, HE WAS

FIRED AT, THE BULLET GRAZING HIS HEAD. IN 1973 HE WAS RUN OFF THE ROAD. IN 1974 HIS CAR WAS BOMBED. IN 1975 HE WAS SHOT IN THE SHOULDER. THAT SAME YEAR IT WOULD ALL COME TO AN END FOR OFFICER CRAIG. HE ALLEGEDLY COMMITTED SUICIDE AT THE AGE OF 39. ON MAY 15TH, HE LEFT A SUICIDE NOTE TO HIS FATHER WHICH READ "I AM TIRED OF THE PAIN."

12:33 PM FRIDAY

HARVEY, HAVING EXITED THE FRONT ENTRANCE OF THE TSBD, THEN WALKS 4 BLOCKS TO THE EAST UP ELM STREET WHERE HE WILL SOON CATCH AN ONCOMING MARSALIS STREET BUS.

12:34 PM FRIDAY

LEE EXITS THE TSBD BUILDING VIA THE FRONT DOOR. **LEE** WOULD THEN WALK WEST ON ELM AND LINGER AT THE WEST/REAR SIDE OF THE TSBD. ACCORDING TO ARMSTRONG, HE WAS WAITING FOR THE MAN IN THE BROWN SUIT TO RETURN WITH A CAR AND PICK HIM UP. THE MAN IN THE BROWN SUIT, ACCORDING TO RICHARD CARR, WAS WALKING SOUTH ON HOUSTON. WHEN HE ARRIVED AT COMMERCE STREET, HE TURNED EAST AND WALKED AN ADDITIONAL BLOCK TO RECORD STREET WHERE HE ENTERED A 1961 OR 1962 NASH RAMBLER STATION WAGON. THE DRIVER OF THE CAR, ACCCORDING TO RICHARD CARR, WAS A "YOUNG NEGRO MAN." AS **LEE** LEFT THE TSBD, HE ENCOUNTERED NBC CORRESPONDANT ROBERT MACNEIL WHO WAS LOOKING FOR A PHONE. **LEE** POINTED TO PIERCE ALLMAN WHO IN TURN POINTED TO A DESK PHONE IN AN ADJACENT OFFICE.

*IF THIS TIMELINE IS CORRECT, THEN BOTH **HARVEY** AND **LEE** EXIT THE TSBD WITHIN APPROXIMATELY 2 MINUTES OF EACH OTHER. THERE ARE HOWEVER CONSIDERABLE DIFFERENCES IN THEIR DIRECTION AND THEIR ATTIRE:*

***LEE** IS WEARING A LIGHT SHIRT OR T-SHIRT, WEARING NO JACKET, AND HEADED WEST ON ELM STREET.*

***HARVEY** IS WEARING A WHITE T-SHIRT, A REDDISH-BROWN LONGSLEEVE SHIRT, CARRYING HIS GREY JACKET, AND HEADED EAST ON ELM STREET.*

12:36 PM FRIDAY

THE PRESIDENTIAL LIMO ARRIVES AT PARKLAND HOSPITAL.

12:40 PM FRIDAY

HARVEY BOARDS A BUS, MARSALIS #1213 AT ELM AND FIELD STREETS. THE BUS HOWEVER IS SLOWED IN TRAFFIC. THE BUS NORMALLY WOULD TRAVEL WEST TOWARDS THE TSBD , LEFT ON HOUSTON FROM ELM, THEN TOWARDS HIS ROOMING HOUSE.

*IF **HARVEY** HAD INDEED SHOT THE PRESIDENT IT IS DOUBTFULL THAT HE WOULD BOARD A BUS THAT WOULD RETURN HIM TO THE SCENE OF THE CRIME.*

CECIL MCWATTERS, DRIVER OF MARSALIS BUS #1213 IN HIS SWORN AFFADAVIT ON NOVEMBER 22ND STATED "I PICKED UP A MAN ON THE LOWER END OF TOWN ON ELM AROUND HOUSTON." HE NOTED THE PICK-UP TIME AT ABOUT 12:40 PM. MCWATTERS ASKED A WOMAN PASSENGER "IF SHE KNEW THE PRESIDENT HAD BEEN SHOT?' HE THEN STATED "SHE THOUGHT I WAS KIDDING. I TOLD HER IF SHE DID NOT BELIEVE ME TO ASK THE MAN BEHIND HER THAT HE HAD TOLD ME THE PRESIDENT WAS SHOT IN HIS TEMPLE. THE MAN WAS GRINNING AND NEVER DID SAY ANYTHING." MCWATTERS WENT ON TO STATE "I DON'T KNOW WHERE I LET THE MAN OFF. THIS MAN LOOKS LIKE THE #2 MAN I SAW IN THE LINE-UP TONIGHT. THE TRANSFER #004459 IS A TRANSFER FROM MY BUS WITH MY PUNCH MARK."

*MCWATTERS IS CORRECT IN NOTING THAT THE MAN WHO RESEMBLED **HARVEY** BOARDED HIS BUS AT ABOUT 12:40. HE IS HOWEVER APPARENTLY DESCRIBING SOMEONE WHO ONLY RESEMBLED **HARVEY** AND WHO QUITE POINTEDLY INCRIMINATED **HARVEY** WITH HIS*

"GRINNING"REGARDING THE SHOOTING OF THE PRESIDENT. THE MAN'S NOTING THAT THE PRESIDENT HAD BEEN "SHOT IN THE TEMPLE" CURIOUSLY SUPPORTS A SHOT FROM THE FRONT AND IS SUPPORTED BY MALCOLM KILDUFF, THE WHITE HOUSE PRESS SPOKESMAN WHO CLEARLY POINTS TO HIS RIGHT TEMPLE WHEN HE ANNOUNCES THE PRESIDENT'S DEATH AT 1:32.

HARVEY *HOWEVER <u>BOARDED</u> THE BUS AT 12:39 **NOT** AT "ELM AROUND HOUSTON" AS MCWATTERS STATED BUT 4 BLOCKS <u>EAST</u> OF ELM AND HOUSTON AT THE INTERSECTION OF ELM AND GRIFFIN. HE THEN <u>DEPARTED</u> THE BUS 2 BLOCKS WEST OF THIS POINT ON ELM BETWEEN NORTH AUSTIN ST. AND LAMAR AT 12:43. THE **HARVEY** LOOK-ALIKE THAT MCWATTERS PICKED UP WAS NOT ONLY IN THE IMMEDIATE VICINITY OF THE TSBD BUT ALSO CURIOUSLY WELL INFORMED ABOUT THE LOCATION OF THE HEAD WOUND OF THE PRESIDENT.*

*THE BUS TRANSFER **HARVEY** RECEIVED FROM MCWATTERS WAS FOUND IN HIS SHIRT POCKET WHEN HE WAS ARRESTED. THIS IS FURTHER PROOF THAT HE DID <u>NOT</u> CHANGE SHIRTS UPON ARRIVAL AT HIS ROOMING HOUSE. HE ONLY CHANGED HIS SLACKS. THE SHIRT HE WORE TO WORK THAT FATEFULL MORNING WAS THE SAME ONE HE WAS ARRESTED IN.*

12:40 PM FRIDAY

OFFICER TIPPIT ARRIVES AT GLOCO SERVICE STATION AT 1502 NORTH ZANGS BOULEVARD.

THIS TIME IS AN APPROXIMATION. SEVERAL WITNESSES NOTED THAT TIPPIT <u>LEFT</u> THE SERVICE STATION AFTER HAVING BEEN THERE ABOUT 10-12 MINUTES OR SO. HIS APPROXIMATE TIME OF DEPARTURE WAS NOTED TO BE ABOUT 12:51 PM. WHEN ONE SUBTRACTS THE NOTED TIME ON THE SCENE AT THE SERVICE STATION, THE APPROXIMATE TIME OF ARRIVAL WOULD HAVE BEEN ABOUT 12:40 PM.

12:40 PM FRIDAY

LEE RUNS FROM THE WEST/REAR SIDE OF THE TSBD TOWARDS ELM AND WHISTLES LOUDLY. THE RAMBLER STATION WAGON DRIVEN BY THE DARK SKINNED MAN AND HIS PASSENGERS, THE GRASSY KNOLL SHOOTER AND THE 6TH FLOOR SHOOTER, STOPS. **LEE** RUNS DOWN THE SLOPE OF THE KNOLL AND HURRIEDLY ENTERS THE VEHICLE. THE CAR PROCEEDS WEST ON ELM.

FREELANCE PHOTOGRAPHER JIM MURRAY TOOK A PHOTOGRAPH SHOWING A NASH RAMBLER STATION WAGON PASSING IN FRONT OF THE TSBD. THE HERTZ SIGN ON THE ROOF OF THE TSBD WAS ALSO CAPTURED IN THE PHOTO. THE CLOCK INCORPORATED IN THE SIGN SHOWS A TIME OF 12:40.

THERE ARE NUMEROUS RESEARCHERS WHO BELIEVE THAT THE MAN IN THE BROWN COAT (THE 6TH FLOOR SHOOTER) WEARING HORN-RIMMED GLASSES WAS THE LONGTIME ASSOCIATE OF LBJ, MAC WALLACE. MADELEINE BROWN, WHO HAD A LONG RUNNING AFFAIR WITH LBJ FELT THAT WALLACE WAS INDEED ONE OF THE SHOOTERS. BILLY SOL ESTES, ACCORDING TO BROWN, WAS ALSO CONVINCED THAT WALLACE WAS ONE OF THE SHOOTERS THAT DAY IN DALLAS. WALLACE HAD A REPUTATION AS A "HIT MAN" AND INDEED WAS FOUND GUILTY OF MURDERING A GOLF PRO IN AUSTIN, JOHN KINSER, WHO WAS INVOLVED WITH LBJ'S SISTER, JOSEFA. WALLACE WAS, AT THE SAME TIME, ALSO INVOLVED WITH LBJ'S SISTER. LBJ WAS QUICK TO BAIL WALLACE OUT. HE HAD HIS ATTORNEY SUBMIT A BRIEF CONSISTING OF ONLY ONE PAGE. THE JUDGE AWARDED WALLACE A 5 YEAR SUSPENDED SENTENCE. HE DID NOT SPEND ONE DAY IN JAIL.

JOHNSON INSIDERS ALSO BELIEVE THAT WALLACE MURDERED HENRY MARSHALL WHO WORKED FOR THE U.S.D.A. MARSHALL WAS INVESTIGATING BILLY SOL ESTES REGARDING LAND DEALS IN TEXAS THAT WERE CONSIDERED "SKETCHY" AT BEST. A CONVICTION OF ESTES WOULD HAVE MOST CERTAINLY IMPLICATED LBJ AND FURTHER DIMINISHED HIS CHANCES TO REMAIN ON THE 1964 PRESIDENTIAL TICKET. ESTES, IN 1984 BEFORE A GRAND

JURY, STATED THAT LBJ HAD INDEED ARRANGED FOR THE MURDER OF MARSHALL. SOME SPECULATE THAT IT WAS NOT OUT OF THE REALM OF POSSIBILITIES THAT LBJ COULD HAVE SERVED TIME IN PRISON FOR HIS MERE INVOLVEMENT WITH ESTES EVEN IF HIS CONTRACTING OF WALLACE HAD NOT COME TO THE SURFACE.

THE DPD DUSTED THE 6TH FLOOR OF THE TSBD FOR PRINTS. IN EACH CASE WHERE PRINTS WERE FOUND THERE WERE ABLE TO ASSOCIATE THE PRINTS WITH TSBD EMPLOYEES OR OTHERS KNOWN TO HAVE HANDLED BOXES ON THE 6TH FLOOR. THERE WAS HOWEVER ONE PRINT THAT COULD <u>NOT</u> BE LINKED TO KNOWN VISITORS OR WORKERS ON THE 6TH FLOOR. IN 1998 THIS 1963 PRINT WAS COMPARED TO A 1951 PRINT FROM AN ARREST RECORD. THE COMPARISON WAS PERFORMED BY NATHAN DANBY, A CERTIFIED LATENT FINGERPRINT EXAMINER. MR. DANBY WAS ABLE TO FIND 14 IDENTICAL ELEMENTS BETWEEN THE PRINT FOUND ON THE 6TH FLOOR OF THE TSBD ON NOVEMBER 22ND, 1963 AND THE 1951 ARREST PRINT CARD. ONLY 12 IDENTICAL ELEMENTS ARE REQUIRED FOR A "MATCH." THE FINGERPRINT CARD FROM THE 1951 ARREST WAS THAT OF MAC WALLACE.

12:41 PM FRIDAY
RUBY RETURNS TO THE DALLAS MORNING NEWS. HE WOULD LATER CLAIM HOWEVER THAT HE HAD GONE IMMEDIATELY TO HIS APARTMENT AFTER THE SHOOTING. HE WAS NOTED BY THOSE WHO SAW HIM TO BE VERY QUIET AND DOLE.

12:43 PM FRIDAY
RUBY LEAVES THE DALLAS MORNING NEWS.

*RUBY IS NOW LIKELY AWARE THAT THE DIVERSIONARY "FIREWORKS" WERE ACTUAL GUNSHOTS. I DO NOT FEEL HOWEVER THAT HE HAS ANY REASON TO SUSPECT **HARVEY** AS A SHOOTER.*

12:43 PM FRIDAY
HARVEY, AFTER TRAVELLING 2 BLOCKS IN THE SLOWED TRAFFIC, EXITS THE BUS WITH A TRANSFER AT ELM BETWEEN NORTH AUSTIN STREET AND LAMAR STREET.

*THE BUS DRIVER, CECIL MCWATTERS NOTED THAT **HARVEY** WAS CARRYING A JACKET. ROY MILTON JONES, A PASSENGER, ALSO NOTED THAT **HARVEY** WAS CARRYING A JACKET. MARY BLEDSOE, **HARVEY'S** FORMER LANDLADY NOTED THAT HE WAS WEARING A LONG-SLEEVED BROWNISH SHIRT. ALTHOUGH THE COMMISSION INSISTS THAT THE MAN IN QUESTION IS **HARVEY**, THEY ALSO INSIST THAT **HARVEY** <u>WAS NOT</u> WEARING <u>OR</u> CARRYING A JACKET WHEN HE LEFT THE TSBD BUT WEARING A WHITE T-SHIRT AS DESCRIBED BY MRS. REID WHO HAD ENCOUNTERED HIM IN THE TSBD OFFICE. MRS. REID HOWEVER HAD ENCOUNTERED **LEE,** NOT **HARVEY**.*

*MARY BLEDSOE LATER DESCRIBED THE SHIRT AS HAVING A HOLE IN THE RIGHT ELBOW AND MISSING MOST OF THE BUTTONS. WHEN SHOWN THE SHIRT THAT **HARVEY** WAS WEARING WHEN ARRESTED SHE SAID IT WAS THE SAME SHIRT HE WAS WEARING ON THE BUS. THIS CASTS SERIOUS DOUBT AS TO WHETHER **HARVEY** HAD CHANGED HIS SHIRT WHEN HE STOPPED AT HIS ROOMING HOUSE AT 1:00 PM. BLEDSOE ALSO DESCRIBED THE PANTS HE WAS WEARING ON THE BUS AS GREY.*

*SHORTLY AFTER **HARVEY** LEFT THE BUS TWO POLICE OFFICERS BOARDED AND ASKED EACH PASSENGER IF THEY WERE CARRYING A WEAPON. ACCORDING TO ARMSTRONG, THESE MEN HAVE NEVER BEEN IDENTIFIED AND THERE ARE NO DALLAS POLICE OR FBI REPORTS THAT INDICATE THAT ANY OTHER BUS OTHER THAN THE BUS BOARDED BY **HARVEY** WERE EVER SEARCHED IN THIS FASHION. ALTHOUGH THIS IS THE SECOND TIME IN THE LAST 12 MINUTES THAT **HARVEY** HAD BEEN CONFRONTED OR PURSUED BY A POLICE OFFICER, IT MAY HAVE BEEN THE FIRST "OPPORTUNITY" FOR THE SET-UP CONSPIRATORS TO ELIMINATE **HARVEY**.*

*I FIND IT INTERESTING THAT THEY QUESTIONED PASSENGERS AS TO WHETHER THEY WERE CARRYING A WEAPON. WAS **HARVEY** TOLD TO BRING HIS PISTOL TO WORK THAT DAY? IF HE HAD DONE SO, IT MAY HAVE COST HIM HIS LIFE HAD HE STILL BEEN ON THE BUS. WE ARE ONLY TWO MINUTES OR LESS AWAY FROM THE 12:45 APB THAT CLOSELY DESCRIBES HIM. DID HE SIMPLY FORGET THE PISTOL NECESSITATING A TRIP TO HIS ROOMING HOUSE OR WAS HE RELUCTANT AND CAUTIOUS IN NOT BRINGING THE PISTOL TO WORK THAT PARTICULAR DAY AND INTENDED TO RETRIVE IT PRIOR TO HIS ANTICIPATED RIDE TO RED BIRD AIRFIELD? YET, AS PREVIOUSLY NOTED, ANOTHER POSSIBILITY IS THAT HE WAS INDEED GIVEN A PISTOL BY RUBY AS HE EXITED THE TSBD, AND THE OFFICERS WERE AWARE OF THAT HAVING TAKEN PLACE. THE PISTOL, WHICH LATER WOULD BE NOTED TO HAVE A BENT FIRING PIN, WOULD HAVE RENDERED **HARVEY** DEFENSELESS HAD HE BEEN CONFRONTED ON THE BUS OR LATER IN THE TEXAS THEATER. **HARVEY'S POSSESSION OF A NON-FUNCTIONING PISTOL IMMEDIATELY AFTER THE PRESIDENTIAL SHOOTING IS OF PARAMOUNT IMPORTANCE**. THE MURDER OF OFFICER TIPPIT WAS DESIGNED TO INCITE THE DPD. THERE WOULD BE NO FURTHER NEED TO SACRIFICE A SECOND INNOCENT OFFICER IN A SHOOTOUT WITH **HARVEY**. **HARVEY'S** POSSESSION OF A MALFUNCTIONING PISTOL WAS DESIGNED TO INSURE HIS SILENCING AT THE EARLIEST POSSIBLE ENCOUNTER WITH ANY TYPE OF LAW ENFORCEMENT <u>AFTER</u> HE HAD TAKEN POSSESSION OF THE WEAPON.*

12:45 PM FRIDAY

AN APB IS BROADCAST BY DISPATCHER GERALD HENSLEE WITH A PHYSICAL DESCRIPTION MARGINALLY FITTING **HARVEY**: "UNKNOWN WHITE MALE, APPROXIMATELY 30, SLENDER BUILD, HEIGHT 5'10, WEIGHT 165 REPORTED TO BE ARMED WITH WHAT IS BELIEVED TO BE A 30 CALIBER RIFLE." THE APB IS ISSUED BY POLICE INSPECTOR HERBERT SAWYER.

*IT IS THOUGHT THAT THE APB WAS BASED ON A DESCRIPTION PROVIDED BY HOWARD BRENNAN. A ROLL CALL OF TSBD EMPLOYEES WAS TAKEN BETWEEN 12:35 AND 12:45 AND IT WAS REPORTED THAT **HARVEY** WAS THE <u>ONLY</u> ONE OF 73 TSBD EMPLOYEES MISSING. ACTUALLY 4 OTHER EMPLOYEES DID NOT RETURN UNTIL 3 PM OR LATER THAT DAY. JACK REVILL, HEAD OF DPD CRIMINAL INTELIGENCE DIVISION, SUBMITTED A LIST OF EMPLOYEES OF THE TSBD THAT AFTERNOON. THE FIRST EMPLOYEE ON THE LIST WAS "LEE HARVEY OSWALD." **HARVEY'S** ADDRESS WAS LISTED AS 605 ELSBETH.*

***HARVEY** HAD HOWEVER MOVED FROM THAT ADDRRESS ON APRIL 24TH, 1963 WHEN HE DEPARTED FOR NEW ORLEANS. IN FACT, UPON HIS RETURN TO DALLAS, HE HAD <u>TWO</u> MORE <u>CURRENT</u> ADDRESSES THAN THE OLD PRE-NEW ORLEANS ELSBETH STREET ADDRESS. THE ELSBETH ST. ADDRESS WAS <u>NOT</u> GIVEN TO HIS EMPLOYERS AT THE TSBD. SO, HOW DID REVILL COME TO ASSOCIATE THE ELSBETH ST. ADDRESS WITH **HARVEY** ON THE LIST OF TSBD EMPLOYEES? REVILL STATED TO THE COMMISSION THAT ON NOVEMBER 22ND, A MEMBER OF THE ARMY 112 MILITARY INTELLIGENCE GROUP RODE WITH HIM FROM DEALEY PLAZA TO THE POLICE STATION. LATER IT WOULD BE NOTED THAT THE 112 MILITARY INTELLIGENCE GROUP HAD AN OPEN FILE ON A "HARVEY OSWALD." THE ADDRESS IN THE ARMY FILE WAS 605 ELSBETH ST. ONE WOULD HAVE TO SURMISE THAT REVILL OBTAINED THE ERRONEOUS ADDRESS FROM ARMY INTELLIGENCE. LT. COLONEL ROBERT E. JONES, 112 MILITARY INTELLIGENCE GROUP, LATER TESTIFIED TO THE HSCA THAT ON NOVEMBER 22ND HE RECEIVED A CALL FROM THE DALLAS MILITARY INTELLIGENCE OFFICE STATING THAT A "A.J. HIDELL" HAD BEEN ARRESTED. JONES THEN WAS ABLE TO LOCATE A FILE ON A "A.J. HIDELL" WHICH CROSS-REFERENCED A FILE FOR "HARVEY OSWALD." IT SEEMS ARMY INTELLIGENCE WAS INDEED AWARE THAT A "HARVEY OSWALD" HAD BEEN TIED TO THE NAME "HIDELL." THE WARREN COMMISSION HAD ASKED FOR <u>ALL</u> MILITARY FILES ON **HARVEY**. BUT, THEY WERE NOT SHOWN THE HIDELL OR THE "HARVEY OSWALD" FILES KEPT BY ARMY INTELLIGENCE.*

DID THE ROLE CALL PROMPT THE APB? NOT LIKELY SINCE THE INCLUSION OF THE RIFLE IN THE APB WOULD NOT BE A DIRECT RESULT OF A MERE ROLE CALL OF ABSENT EMPLOYEES. SO, ONE WOULD HAVE TO CONCLUDE THE APB STEMMED FROM HOWARD BRENNAN'S DESCRIPTION.

HOOVER HOWEVER, IN A JANUARY 14TH, 1964 LETTER TO THE COMMISSION, ADMITTED THAT THE INITIAL DESCRIPTION ISSUED IN THE APB WAS "INITIATED ON THE BASIS OF A DESCRIPTION FURNISHED BY AN UNIDENTIFIED CITIZEN WHO HAD OBSERVED AN INDIVIDUAL APPROXIMATING OSWALD'S DESCRIPTION RUNNING FROM THE TSBD AFTER THE ASSASSINATION." I QUESTION THE PROBABILITY OF AN APB BEING SENT OUT FOR A PERSON WANTED IN CONNECTION WITH THE SHOOTING OF THE PRESIDENT OF THE UNITED STATES WITHOUT SOMEONE OBTAINING THE NAME OF THE CITIZEN PROVIDING THE DESCRIPTION. THE APB DESCRIBING **HARVEY** WAS CONVENIENTLY ISSUED "ANNONYMOUSLY" FOR THE SOLE PURPOSE OF "JUMPSTARTING" THE SEARCH FOR **HARVEY**. IT IS INTERESTING TO NOTE THAT THE DESCRIPTION ALSO INCLUDED THE REMARK "RUNNING FROM THE TSBD AFTER THE ASSASSINATION." **HARVEY** WAS NEVER NOTED TO HAVE BEEN RUNNING AFTER THE SHOOTING. BUT, **LEE** WAS NOTED TO HAVE BUN DOWN THE HILL FROM THE LEFT/WEST SIDE OF THE TSBD FOR HIS PICKUP BY THE RAMBLER STATION WAGON. THE PHYSICAL DESCRIPTIION IN THE APB ALSO IS A MUCH CLOSER FIT TO **LEE** THAN **HARVEY**. WAS THE APB BASED ON THE SIGHTING OF **LEE** AND HIS DEPARTURE RATHER THAN **HARVEY**?

WHAT IS TRULY PROBLEMATIC WITH THE 12:45 APB IS THAT IT NOTES THE SUSPECT IS REPORTED TO BE ARMED WITH A "30 CALIBER RIFLE." NEITHER **LEE** NOR **HARVEY** LEFT THE BUILDING WITH A RIFLE.

IN FACT, INSPECTOR SAWYER'S TESTIMONY BEFORE THE COMMISSION LEAVES EVEN MORE DOUBT AS TO WHO HAD PROVIDED THE DESCRIPTION THAT LED TO THE 12:45 APB BROADCAST. WHEN ASKED BY COMMISSION COUNSEL DAVID BELIN: "DO YOU KNOW ANYTHING ABOUT HIM (THE WITNESS), WHAT WAS HE WEARING?" SAWYER REPLIED: "I DON'T KNOW WHAT HE WAS WEARING." SAWYER'S COMMENTS BECOME EVEN MORE INCREDULOUS AS HE CONTINUES: "I REMEMBER THAT HE WAS A WHITE MAN AND THAT HE WASN'T YOUNG AND HE WASN'T OLD....HE WAS THERE...THAT IS THE ONLY THING I CAN REMEMBER ABOUT HIM." WHEN ASKED IF HE (THE WITNESS) WAS TALL OR SHORT, SAWYER REPLIES: "I CAN'T REMEMBER THAT MUCH ABOUT HIM. I WAS REAL HAZY ABOUT THAT." SOMEHOW I FIND THIS SUSPICIOUSLY LACKING FOR A S0-CALLED "INSPECTOR."

IT IS INTERESTING TO NOTE THAT REGARDLESS OF THE SOURCE OF THE DESCRIPTION IN THE APB THAT THE APB INCLUDES NO MENTION OF EITHER HAIR COLOR, AND PERHAPS MORE IMPORTANTLY, NO MENTION OF CLOTHING WORN. COULD THE "ANONYMOUS" SOURCE HAVE BEEN PRIVY TO THE NOTION THAT **HARVEY** WOULD, AFTER ALLEGEDLY SHOOTING THE PRESIDENT, STOP BY HIS APARTMENT AND CHANGE HIS CLOTHING? COULD THE "ANONYMOUS" SOURCE HAVE BEEN IN A POSITION TO SUPPLY THE DESRIPTION THAT WOULD INITIATE THE SEARCH? I WOULD HAVE TO OFFER THAT THIS APB, WITHOUT THE NORMAL CLOTHING OR HAIR DESCRIPTION, WAS INDEED RELAYED TO INSPECTOR SAWYER BY AN UNKNOWN MALE. THE "UNKNOWN MALE" HOWEVER WOULD INDEED BE KNOWN TO OUR DALLAS-BASED SET-UP CONSPIRATOR, ROSCOE WHITE, IF IT WERE NOT INDEED WHITE HIMSELF WHO PROVIDED THE DESCRIPTION TO INSPECTOR SAWYER.

WHITE WOULD RECOGNIZE THE IMPORTANCE OF NOT SUPPLYING A CLOTHING DESCRIPTION TO SAWYER EITHER PERSONALLY OR VIA HIS "WITNESS" SINCE HE MAY NOT HAVE BEEN CERTAIN AS TO JUST WHAT CLOTHES **HARVEY** WOULD WEAR TO WORK THAT DAY, OR, MORE IMPORTANTLY, WHAT CLOTHING CHANGE **HARVEY** MIGHT MAKE PRIOR TO DEPARTING FOR THE FIRST LEG OF HIS PERCEIVED "ASSIGNMENT." WHITE COULD ALSO HAVE BEEN ACUTELY AWARE THAT **LEE** WOULD LIKELY BE WEARING CLOTHING DISSIMILAR TO **HARVEY'S** THUS THE AVOIDANCE OF A CLOTHING DESCRIPTION TO SAWYER.

INSPECTOR SAWYER'S INCREDIBLE INABILITY TO REMEMBER ANYTHING OF NOTE ABOUT THE WITNESS SUPPLYING HIM WITH A DESCRIPTION ON WHICH HE BASES HIS APB IS EXTREMELY BOTHERSOME. I WOULD NOT HESITATE TO SUGGEST THAT SAWYER'S

*INABILITY TO OFFER ANYTHING MORE THAN HIS RECOLLECTION OF THE WITNESS BEING A "WHITE MAN" WHO "WAS THERE" AS NOTHING MORE THAN A THINLY VEILED EXCUSE TO AVOID DISCLOSING THAT IT WAS ROSCOE WHITE OR SOMEONE HANDPICKED BY WHITE WHO HAD PROVIDED HIM WITH THE DESCRIPTION THAT WOULD PROMPT THE FIRST APB FOR **HARVEY**.*

ON JANUARY 9TH, 1964, SAWYER WOULD PROVIDE THE FBI WITH THE NAME OF THE SOURCE WHO HAD PROVIDED HIM WITH THE DESCRIPTION. THE NAME HOWEVER WAS NEVER MADE PUBLIC.

*A CIA CABLE OF EARLY OCTOBER 1963, ONE WEEK PRIOR TO **HARVEY'S** OCTOBER 16TH EMPLOYMENT AT THE TSBD NOTED **HARVEY'S** HEIGHT AND WEIGHT AS 5'10" AND 165 LBS. ON HIS JOB APPLICATION ON OCTOBER 15TH HOWEVER, **HARVEY** LISTED HIS HEIGHT AND WEIGHT AS 5'9" AND 150 LBS. ROY TRULY, THE TSBD SUPERINTENDANT USED **HARVEY'S** JOB APPLICATION AS THE BASIS FOR HIS LATER DESCRIPTION TO CAPTAIN WILL FRITZ. THE PATHOLOGISTS WHO CONDUCTED **HARVEY'S** AUTOPSY NOTED THAT HE WAS 5'9, 150 LBS; EXACTLY WHAT **HARVEY** HAD HIMSELF OFFERED ON HIS TSBD JOB APPLICATION. BUT THE HEIGHT/WEIGHT DESCRIPTION PROVIDED TO INSPECTOR SAWYER BY THE "UNKNOWN" WITNESS HOWEVER MATCHES EXACTLY WHAT WAS ON THE CIA CABLE IN EARLY OCTOBER. ONCE AGAIN, I SUBMIT THAT THE "WITNESS" WHO GAVE INSPECTOR SAWYER THE DESCRIPTION PROMPTING THE 12:45 APB WAS ROSCOE WHITE OR SOMEONE ASSISTING WHITE. WHITE, VIA HUNT AND PHILLIPS, WOULD HAVE BEEN PRIVY TO THE HEIGHT AND WEIGHT DESCRIPTION GIVEN IN THE EARLY OCTOBER CIA CABLE.*

*I FIND IT INTERESTING THAT THE "5'10" AND 165 POUND" DESCRIPTION IN THAT APB MORE CLOSELY DESCRIBES **LEE** RATHER THAN **HARVEY**. THE INCLUSION OF THE "30 CALIBER RIFLE" AS BEING THE WEAPON WITH WHICH THE SUSPECT HAD APPARENTLY ARMED HIMSELF WITH IS ALSO INTERESTING IF NOT EXTREMELY PREMATURE SINCE NO WEAPONS HAD BEEN FOUND BY 12:45. SINCE **HARVEY** WOULD BE ASSIGNED THE MANNLICHER AS HIS APPARENT "WEAPON OF CHOICE", I WOULD NOT DISMISS THE POSSIBILITY THAT PERHAPS TO THE SET-UP CONSPIRATORS THIS WAS AN OPPORTUNITY TO PERHAPS ELIMINATE **LEE** AS WELL VIA THE APB.*

SANDY SPEAKER, HOWARD BRENNAN'S FOREMAN, LATER NOTED AN ABRUBT CHANGE IN BRENNAN IN THE WEEKS FOLLOWING THE ASSASSINATION. SHE NOTED: "THEY TOOK HIM OFF FOR ABOUT 3 WEEKS. I DON'T KNOW IF THEY WERE SECRET SERVICE OR FBI BUT THEY WERE FEDERAL PEOPLE. HE CAME BACK A NERVOUS WRECK AND WITHIN A YEAR HIS HAIR HAD TURNED SNOW WHITE. HE WOULDN'T TALK ABOUT THE ASSASSINATION AFTER THAT. HE WAS SCARED TO DEATH. THEY MADE HIM SAY WHAT THEY WANTED HIM TO SAY." SUFFICE IT TO SAY, BRENNAN'S INITIAL DESCRIPTION APPARENTLY DIFFERED FROM WHAT THE MYSTERIOUS 12:45 APB NOTED AND WHAT THE FBI HAD DESIRED.

*THE WARREN COMMISSION WOULD STATE THAT BRENNAN "IDENTIFIED OSWALD (**HARVEY**) AS THE PERSON IN THE LINE-UP WHO BORE THE CLOSEST RESEMBLANCE TO THE MAN IN THE WINDOW...." BRENNAN WAS NEARLY 90 YARDS FROM THE TSBD AT THE TIME THE SHOTS WERE FIRED. BRENNAN ATTENDED THE 3RD LINEUP HELD AT 6:20 PM ON FRIDAY, THE 22ND.*

12:46 PM FRIDAY
THE JUDGE PRESIDING OVER CARLOS MARCELLO'S DEPORTATION TRIAL ANNOUNCES THE PRESIDENTIAL SHOOTING TO THOSE IN ATTENDANCE. HE RECESSES THE COURT FOR 1 HOUR.

12:46 PM FRIDAY
TIPPIT IS STILL AT THE GLOCO SERVICE CENTER AT 1502 NORTH ZANGS BLVD. BUT, HE REPORTS TO DISPATCH THAT: "I'M ABOUT KIEST AND BONNIEVIEW." HE AND OFFICER 87, RONALD NELSON, ARE INSTRUCTED TO "MOVE INTO CENTRAL OAK CLIFF" BY DISPATCHER MURRAY JACKSON.

KEEP IN MIND THAT TIPPIT HAD REPORTED TO DISPATCH AT 12:17 THAT HE WAS "OUT OF THE CAR A MINUTE, 4100 BLOCK CORNER KIEST AND BONNIEVIEW." HE HAD ALSO "CLEARED" BACK INTO SERVICE AT 12:21 PM, PRESUMABLY STILL AT KIEST AND BONNIEVIEW. AT 12:46 PM HE STILL CLAIMS TO DISPATCH THAT HE IS AT KIEST AND BONNIEVIEW. BUT, WITNESSES NOTE THAT HE ARRIVED AT THE GLOCO SERVICE STATION AT 1502 NORTH ZANG AT APPROXIMATELY 12:40 PM. THE DISTANCE FROM KIEST AND BONNIEVIEW TO THE GLOCO SERVICE STATION IS ABOUT 9 MILES OR ABOUT A 15 MINUTE DRIVE. IF TIPPIT "CLEARED" BACK INTO SERVICE AT 12:21 PM, HE WOULD HAVE LITTLE DIFFICULTY ARRIVING AT THE SERVICE STATION AT APPROXIMATELY 12:40, OR 19 MINUTES LATER AS NOTED BY WITNESSES.

AL AND LOU VOLKLAND, WHO WERE FAMILIAR WITH TIPPIT, NOTED THAT THEY DROVE BY THE SERVICE STATION AND WAVED AT TIPPIT. THEY ALSO NOTED THAT HE SEEMED TO BE WATCHING TRAFFIC CROSSING THE RIVER FROM DOWNTOWN OVER THE VIADUCT.

IN MY OPINION, TIPPIT NEEDED SOME TIME TO DO HIS ORIGINAL "ERRAND" FOR JACK RUBY; I.E. TAKE **HARVEY** TO RED BIRD AIRFIELD. BY TELLING DISPATCH THAT HE IS MILES (9 MILES /15 MINUTES) SOUTHEAST OF HIS ACTUAL LOCATION, HE WILL HAVE TIME TO COMPLETE HIS ERRAND AND FULLFILL THE WISHES OF DISPATCH THAT HE MOVE INTO CENTRAL OAK CLIFF. TIPPIT'S PRESENCE AT THE GLOCO SERVICE CENTER PLACES HIM IN AN IDEAL LOCATION TO OBSERVE THE ARRIVAL OF **HARVEY** ON THE MARSALIS STREET BUS AS IT CROSSES THE TRINITY RIVER ENROUTE TO HIS BOARDING HOUSE. THERE ARE HOWEVER TWO PROBLEMS; **HARVEY IS NOT ON THE MARSALIS STREET BUS** AND **THE BUS IS TIED UP** IN THE POST-ASSASSINATION TRAFFIC ON ELM STREET BETWEEN POYDRAST AND LAMAR STREETS. GLOCO EMPLOYEES EMMETT HOLLINGSHEAD AND J.B. LEWIS WITNESS TIPPIT'S PRESENCE AT THE STATION. THEY NOTED THAT HE STAYED ABOUT 10-12 MINUTES.

12:47 PM FRIDAY
HARVEY WALKS 3 BLOCKS SOUTH ON LAMAR AND HAILS WILLIAM WHALEY'S TAXI AT THE GREYHOUND BUS STATION AT COMMERCE AND LAMAR. ACCORDING TO THE WARREN COMMISSION HOWEVER WHALEY'S LOG BOOK SHOWS THE TRIP LOGGED IN THE 12:30 TO 12:45.TIME SLOT.

WHALEY, IN TESTIMONY TO THE COMMISSION, NOTED THAT **HARVEY** DIDN'T APPEAR NERVOUS OR IN A HURRY. IN FACT HE HAD EVEN OFFERED TO GIVE UP THE CAB TO AN ELDERLY WOMAN. THE FRUGAL **HARVEY** WOULD LATER ADMIT THAT IT WAS THE FIRST TIME HE HAD EVER HIRED A TAXI. WHALEY WOULD ALSO NOTE THAT **HARVEY** WAS WEARING A REDDISH-BROWN SHIRT AND HAD A BLUISH-GREY JACKET THAT NEARLY MATCHED HIS PANTS.

APPROXIMATELY 12:47 PM FRIDAY
THE FUTILE LIFESAVING EFFORTS OF THE PARKLAND PHYSICIANS CEASED. PRESIDENT JOHN FITZGERALD KENNEDY SUCCUMBED TO THE FATAL HEADWOUND. THE OFFICIAL TIME OF DEATH HOWEVER WILL BE FIXED AT 1:00 PM BY DR. MALCOLM PERRY.

APPROXIMATELY 12:47 PM FRIDAY
A LIVE T.V. REPORT FROM THE TRADEMART LUNCHEON SITE STATED "THE ATTEMPTED ASSASSINS, WE NOW HEAR IT WAS A MAN AND A WOMAN WHO FIRED THE SHOTS, WERE ON THE LEDGE OF A BUILDING NEAR THE HOUSTON STREET UNDERPASS."

12:47 PM FRIDAY
OFFICER NELSON, IN SPITE OF DISPATCH'S REQUEST, DOES NOT GO TO CENTRAL OAK CLIFF BUT INSTEAD DRIVES DIRECTLY TO THE TSBD. THIS WOULD LEAVE ONLY TIPPIT IN CENTRAL OAK CLIFF.

12:48 PM FRIDAY
ACCORDING TO ARMSTRONG, THE NASH RAMBLER STATION WAGON WITH **LEE** ON BOARD ARRIVES AT THE TIDY LADY LAUNDRY AT THE CORNER OF DAVIS AND NORTH CLINTON. AFTER MAKING A PHONE CALL IN WHICH HE, ACCORDING TO JOHN AND ODA

PENNINGTON, SPOKE IN SPANISH, **LEE** THEN LEFT ON FOOT AND PROCEEDED SOUTH ON CLINTON TOWARDS JEFFERSON BOULEVARD.

12:49 PM FRIDAY
A PATROL CAR CALLS DISPATCH INQUIRING IF THERE WAS A CLOTHING DESCRIPTION IN THE 12:45 APB. DISPATCH REPLIES THAT THERE WAS NOT, AND REPEATS THE PREVIOUS 12:45 APB.

12:50 PM FRIDAY
THE MARSALIS ST. BUS CROSSES THE HOUSTON STREET VIADUCT AND PASSES THE GLOCO SERVICE STATION WHERE TIPPIT EXPECTS IT TO STOP. HE IS EXPECTING **HARVEY** TO EXIT THE BUS. THE BUS HOWEVER DOES NOT STOP. TIPPIT NOW HAS TO WONDER WHETHER **HARVEY** IS ON THE BUS AND DID NOT EXIT, OR IS HE SIMPLY NOT ON BOARD THE BUS.

12:50 PM FRIDAY
TIPPIT LEAVES THE GLOCO SERVICE CENTER RATHER HURRIEDLY AS WITNESSES NOTED. HE WOULD DRIVE ONE BLOCK EAST THEN TURN SOUTH ON LANCASTER.

12:54 PM FRIDAY
DISPATCH CALLS TIPPIT: "YOU ARE IN THE OAK CLIFF AREA ARE YOU NOT?" TIPPIT ANSWERS DISPATCH SAYING HE IS AT "LANCASTER AND 8TH". HE IS TOLD BY THE DISPATCHER: "YOU WILL BE AT LARGE FOR ANY EMERGENCY THAT COMES IN." HE THEN PROCEEDS SOUTH ON LANCASTER AND RIGHT ON EAST JEFFERSON.

12:54 PM FRIDAY
HARVEY LEAVES WHALEY'S TAXI IN THE 700 BLOCK OF N. BECKLEY AT NEELY STREET AFTER HAVING WHALEY DRIVE <u>PAST</u> HIS ROOMING HOUSE AT 1026 N. BECKLEY, 3 BLOCKS NORTH OF HIS EXIT POINT FROM THE CAB.

LATER IN CUSTODY, **HARVEY** *WOULD CONFIRM THAT HE HAD INDEED TAKEN BOTH THE BUS RIDE AND WHALEY'S TAXI RIDE ENROUTE FROM THE TSBD TO HIS ROOMING HOUSE.*

12:55 PM FRIDAY
A SECOND PATROL CAR, 349 MANNED BY PATROLMAN C.R. GALBREITH, CALLS DISPATCH INQUIRING ABOUT A CLOTHING DESCRIPTION. DISPATCH ONCE AGAIN GIVES A NEGATIVE REPLY AND REPEATS THE 12:45 APB.

IT IS READILY APPARENT BY NOW THAT AT LEAST 2 PATROLMEN ARE QUESTIONING THE LACK OF A CLOTHING DESCRIPTION IN THE SUSPICIOUS 12:45 APB.

12:55 PM FRIDAY
DISPATCH CALLS TIPPIT REQUESTING HIS LOCATION. TIPPIT DOES NOT RESPOND.

12:56 PM FRIDAY
TIPPIT PAUSES AT JEFFERSON AND MARSALIS AWATING THE SOUTH BOUND MARSALIS ST. BUS. HE IS GIVING **HARVEY** ONE LAST CHANCE TO EXIT THE BUS IF INDEED **HARVEY** IS ON THE BUS. THE BUS HOWEVER DOES NOT STOP AT MARSALIS AND JEFFERSON.

12:58 PM FRIDAY
CAPTAIN WILL FRITZ AND SHERIFF BILL DECKER ARRIVE AT THE TSBD AND ORDER THE BUILDING SEALED. THEY ARE ACCOMPANIED BY DETECTIVES SIMS AND BOYD.

1:00 PM FRIDAY
HARVEY REACHES HIS ROOMING HOUSE AND CHANGES HIS SLACKS AND POSSIBLY HIS SHIRT. HE WILL DEPART WEARING A DARK REDDISH-BROWN SHIRT AND GREY SLACKS.

IN CAPTAIN FRITZ'S SKETCHY NOTES TAKEN DURING ONE OF **HARVEY'S** *INTERROGATION SESSIONS, HE NOTED THAT WHEN* **HARVEY** *WAS ASKED WHAT HE DID AT HIS ROOMING HOUSE, HE REPLIED: "CHANGED HIS TROUSERS AND HIS SHIRT THEN WENT TO THE*

PICTURE SHOW." IT IS IMPORTANT TO NOTE THAT **HARVEY** DOES <u>NOT</u> MENTION DONNING A JACKET AS WELL. IT IS ALSO IMPORTANT TO NOTE THAT THE COMMENT REGARDING THE SHIRT IS WHAT FRITZ <u>SAID</u> THAT **HARVEY** REPLIED TO HIS QUESTION OF WHAT HE DID AT HIS ROOMING HOUSE. I AM NOT CONVINCED THAT **HARVEY** CHANGED HIS SHIRT. THE FINDING OF CECIL MCWATTERS' BUS TRANSFER IN THE POCKET OF THIS PARTICULAR SHIRT WHEN **HARVEY** WAS ARRESTED ATTEST TO THE NOTION THAT **HARVEY** WORE THE SAME SHIRT FROM HIS DEPARTURE FROM THE PAINES' RESIDENCE EARLY THAT AM UNTIL HIS AFTERNOON ARREST IN THE TEXAS THEATER. WEATHER IN DALLAS HAD CLEARED. WITH BOTH A T-SHIRT <u>AND</u> A LONG SLEEVE SHIRT, **HARVEY** APPARENTLY FEELS THERE IS NO NEED FOR A JACKET. HE DOES APPARENTLY EITHER NEWLY ARM HIMSELF WITH A REVOLVER OR CONTINUES TO CARRY THE REVOLVER THAT WAS REPORTEDLY HANDED TO HIM BY RUBY AS HE EXITED THE TSBD.

ALTHOUGH THERE ARE MANY QUESTIONS CONCERNING **HARVEY** AND HIS TIES TO THE MANNLICHER-CARCANO, THERE IS LITTLE DOUBT THAT WHEN ARRESTED HE WAS INDEED IN POSSESSION OF A REVOLVER. TWO ITEMS THAT AN "ASSASSIN" WOULD NEED TO EXPEDITE A SUCCESSFUL ESCAPE FROM A CRIME SCENE WOULD BE MONEY AND A FIREARM. KEEP IN MIND HOWEVER THAT **HARVEY** HAD LEFT $170 ON MARINA'S DRESSER THAT MORNING. HAD **HARVEY** FELT THE NEED TO "ESCAPE" AFTER THE ASSASSINATION, HE WOULD <u>NOT</u> HAVE LEFT THAT MUCH MONEY WITH MARINA (LEAVING HIM WITH LESS THAN $15 DOLLARS) AND WOULD HAVE TAKEN THE REVOLVER TO WORK EARLIER THAT DAY.

ALTHOUGH IT WOULD NOT BE CRITICAL FOR THE SET-UP CONSPIRATORS THAT **HARVEY** BE ARMED WITH A HANDGUN <u>PRIOR</u> TO THE MOTORCADE SHOOTING, IT WOULD BE <u>CRUCIAL</u> THAT HE BE ARMED <u>AFTER</u> THE SHOOTING IF HE WERE TO BE IMPLICATED IN OFFICER TIPPIT'S DEATH. ODDLY ENOUGH, IT WOULD LIKELY BE RUBY WHO WOULD ASSIST THE SET-UP CONSPIRATORS BY SUGGESTING TO **HARVEY** THAT HE CARRY SOME SORT OF PROTECTION FOR HIS RISKY "ASSIGNMENT" TO TRANSFER THE CARCINOGENS TO CUBA. RUBY, WHO ROUTINELY CARRIED A SIDEARM, WOULD INSIST THAT EITHER **HARVEY** HIMSELF BE ARMED, OR AT LEAST TAKE THE PISTOL TO REDBIRD WHERE HE COULD, IF HE WISHED, LATER TRANSFER POSSESSION OF THE PISTOL TO DAVID FERRIE IF HE HIMSELF FELT UNCOMFORTABLE CARRYING AND POSSIBLY USING THE FIREARM ENROUTE TO CUBA.

RUBY'S REQUEST THAT **HARVEY** CARRY SOME SORT OF PROTECTION DURING HIS JOURNEY TO CUBA WOULD IN ESSENCE "ARM" THE MAN WHO WOULD SOON BE CONSIDERED THE ALLLEGED PRESIDENTIAL ASSASSIN. IT WILL ALSO ALLOW THE SET-UP CONSPIRATORS TO IMPLICATE HIM AS THE SHOOTER OF OFFICER TIPPIT AS WELL. MORE IMPORTANTLY, THE MERE <u>POSSESSION</u> OF THE HANDGUN AFTER THE PRESIDENTIAL SHOOTING WOULD INCREASE GREATLY THE LIKLIHOOD THAT **HARVEY** WOULD EITHER BE KILLED BY THE UNIDENTIFIED POLICE ON THE BUS, OR LATER IN THE TEXAS THEATER.

AT THE TEXAS THEATER, DALLAS POLICE WOULD HAVE, AS FAR AS THEY KNEW, ALREADY LOST ONE OFFICER TO THE SUSPECT IN THE THEATER. THEY WOULD NOT HESITATE WITH EVEN THE SLIGHTEST PROVOCATION TO SHOOT FIRST AND PREVENT THE POSSIBLE SHOOTING OF YET ANOTHER OFFICER. IT WAS EXACTLY WHAT ROSCOE WHITE, **LEE**, AND THE SET-UP CONSPIRATORS HAD PLANNED FOR IF HE WERE ABLE TO ESCAPE THE TSBD AND NOT BE SLAIN ON THE BUS RIDE TO HIS ROOMING HOUSE BY THE TWO UNIDENTIFIED POLICE OFFICERS.

IN CUSTODY, **HARVEY** WOULD ADMIT TO HAVING PURCHASED A PISTOL IN FORT WORTH "SEVERAL MONTHS AGO." HE WAS HOWEVER ADAMANT ABOUT <u>NOT</u> REVEALING JUST <u>WHERE</u> THE GUN WAS PURCHASED. EITHER RUBY'S ARMING OF **HARVEY** WAS DONE IN AN EFFORT TO ASSIST IN THE <u>CAPTURE</u>, PREFERABLY FATALLY, OF **HARVEY** AS AN ALLEGED PRESIDENTIAL ASSASSIN OR RUBY PERCEIVED IT AS PROVIDING SOME SEMBLANCE OF PROTECTION FOR **HARVEY** ON HIS "ASSIGNMENT."

SINCE IT WAS CRUCIAL TO THE OVERALL PLANS OF THE SET-UP CONSPIRATOR THAT **HARVEY** WOULD INDEED BE ARMED AT THE EARLIEST POSSIBLE MOMENT AFTER THE ASSASSINATION, I BELIEVE THAT **HARVEY** DID NOT "PURCHASE" THE GUN AS HE CLAIMED, BUT THAT IT WAS PROVIDED TO HIM AT SOME POINT BY RUBY PROMPTING **HARVEY'S** REFUSAL TO REVEAL JUST WHERE HE HAD OBTAINED THE FIREARM..
IT IS ALSO WORTH NOTING THAT IF **HARVEY** HAD PURHASED THE PISTOL IN FT. WORTH, THERE WOULD BE LITTLE NEED FOR HIM TO MAIL ORDER A 2ND PISTOL ON MARCH 12TH, 1963

AS WE WILL SEE LATER, IT IS THE <u>TYPE</u> OF PISTOL TAKEN FROM **HARVEY** IN THE TEXAS THEATER THAT WILL CAUSE PROBLEMS FOR THE SET-UP CONSPIRATORS, NOT WHO HAD SOLD OR GIVEN HIM THE HANDGUN ALLEGEDLY USED TO MURDER TIPPIT.

THE WARREN COMMISSION CONTAINS PHOTOS OF THE PISTOL THAT SHOW A BADLY WORN, BENT FIRING PIN ON THE HANDGUN **HARVEY** HAD IN HIS POSSESSION WHEN CAPTURED IN THE THEATER. AN FBI REPORT NOTED THAT THE FIRING PIN HAD BEEN "ALTERED." IF THIS WERE INDEED THE CASE, **HARVEY** WOULD HAVE HAD DIFFICULTY IN SHOOTING OFFICER TIPPIT HAD HE BEEN THE ACTUAL SHOOTER IN THAT FATAL INCIDENT. MORE POINTEDLY, IT WOULD HAVE PREVENTED **HARVEY** FROM DEFENDING HIMSELF ON THE BUS OR IN A POSSIBLE THEATER SHOOTOUT WITH THE ARRESTING OFFICERS. THIS IS PRECISELY WHAT THE SET-UP CONSPIRATORS HAD IN MIND; IT WAS NOT INTENDED THAT **HARVEY** BE CAPTURED ALIVE. IT WOULD BE THEIR LAST CHANCE TO SILENCE HIM PRIOR TO BEING TAKEN INTO CUSTODY.

IT IS INTERESTING TO NOTE THAT RAYMOND KRYSTINIK, A RESEARCH ENGINEER AT BELL HELICOPTER AND A CO-WORKER OF MICHAEL PAINE, RUTH PAINE'S ESTRANGED HUSBAND, NOTED BEFORE THE WARREN COMMISSION THAT WHEN IT WAS BROADCAST THAT **HARVEY** HAD BEEN ARRESTED WITH A GUN THAT MICHAEL PAINE SAID: "HE IS NOT EVEN SUPPOSED TO HAVE A GUN." IT IS POSSIBLE THAT **HARVEY** MAY HAVE CONFIDED IN PAINE REGARDING HIS CIA "ASSIGNMENT." THIS WOULD NOT ONLY EXPLAIN WHY IT WAS PAINE WHO HAD INVITED **HARVEY** TO AN ACLU MEETING ON OCTOBER 25TH, BUT ALSO ADD CREEDENCE TO THE POSSIBILITY THAT MICHAEL PAINE HAD INTELLIGENCE TIES AS WELL. BOTH PAINE AND **HARVEY** WOULD UNDERSTAND THAT IF ANYTHING WERE TO GO WRONG ON **HARVEY'S** "ASSIGNMENT" THE AGENCY WOULD DISAVOW ANY RELATIONSHIP BETWEEN THE INTELLIGENCE COMMUNITY AND **HARVEY**. HE WOULD HAVE TO OBTAIN HIS OWN COUNSEL THUS THE VISIT TO THE ACLU. BUT, PAINE WAS LIKELY UNAWARE OF THE SET-UP OF **HARVEY** THUS QUESTIONING WHY HE WAS ARMED THAT DAY.

ROSCOE WHITE AND **LEE** PLAY KEY ROLES IN THE SET-UP CONSPIRATORS DIVERSION OF **HARVEY** FROM WHAT **HARVEY** PERCEIVED AS HIS NEXT LEGITIMATE ASSIGNMENT FOR THE CIA. THEIR SUBSTITUTION OF CAR #107 FOR TIPPIT AND THEIR DELIVERY OF **HARVEY** TO THE THEATER <u>NOT</u> THE AIRPORT WOULD SEAL **HARVEY'S** FATE.

THERE IS LITTLE DOUBT AMONG RESEARCHERS THAT RUBY STALKED **HARVEY** AFTER HIS ARREST. NOW ONE NEEDS TO DECIDE WHETHER RUBY'S PROVIDING **HARVEY** WITH A DAMAGED HANDGUN EITHER UPON HIS DEPARTURE FROM THE TSBD OR AT AN EARLIER DATE WAS THE EFFORT OF ONE ASSISTING **HARVEY** ON HIS "ASSIGNMENT" OR WAS RUBY INDEED PART OF THE SET-UP CONSPIRATORS PLAN TO SILENCE **HARVEY** AS SOON AS POSSIBLE. ONE HAS TO CONSIDER THE POSSIBILITY THAT HAD **HARVEY** BEEN SHOT ON THE BUS, THAT IT THEN WOULD NOT HAVE BEEN NECESSARY TO SHOOT OFFICER TIPPIT IN AN EFFORT TO INCITE THE DPD AND PUT THEM IN A CLASSIC "SHOOT FIRST AND ASK QUESTIONS LATER" SCENARIO.

I AM INCLINED AT THIS POINT TO RECONSIDER RUBY'S ROLE. IT OF COURSE WOULD BE DIFFICULT TO PROVE, BUT I DO INDEED THINK THAT HE IS NOT ASSISTING **HARVEY**, BUT ASSISTING THE SET-UP CONSPIRATORS. BUT, IS HE AWARE OF THIS? IF HE IS NOT AWARE THAT HIS "ARMING" OF **HARVEY** IS DESIGNED TO SILENCE **HARVEY**, HE WILL SURELY REALIZE IT AFTER **HARVEY** IS IN CUSTODY WHEN HE IS THEN TASKED WITH HIS OWN

"ASSIGNMENT" TO ELIMINATE **HARVEY**. RUBY'S MANIPULATION BY OTHERS IS SECONDARY ONLY TO **HARVEY'S** MANIPULATION.

1:00 PM FRIDAY
SECRET SERVICE AGENT SORRELLS RETURNS FROM PARKLAND AND GETS A DESCRIPTION OF THE "SHOOTER" FROM HOWARD BRENNAN WHO WAS SITTING ON A WALL OPPOSITE THE TSBD ON ELM STREET WHEN THE SHOTS WERE FIRED. THE APB HOWEVER HAD ALREADY GONE OUT AT 12:45.

1:00 PM FRIDAY
SS AGENT ROY KELLERMAN IS INFORMED BY DR. BURKLEY OF THE PRESIDENT'S DEATH. THE PRESIDENT'S DEATH IS CONFIRMED BY THE PRIEST WHO ADMINISTERED THE LAST RITES AND ANOTHER PRIEST WHO HAD BEEN CALLED TO PARKLAND.

*THE NEAR HOUR FROM APPROXIMATELY 1:00 PM WHEN **HARVEY** ARRIVES AT HIS ROOMING HOUSE, TO APPROXIMATELY 1:52 PM WHEN HE IS ARRESTED IN THE TEXAS THEATER IS THE LAST HOUR HE WILL SPEND AS A FREE MAN. THIS DAY WILL END DRAMATICALLY DIFFERENT FROM WHAT HE HAD BEEN LED TO EXPECT.*

1:02 PM FRIDAY
ACCORDING TO EARLENE ROBERTS, **HARVEY'S** LANDLADY, A BLACK CAR WITH 2 OFFICERS STOPPED IN FRONT OF HER ROOMING HOUSE AND TOOTED THE HORN TWO TIMES. SHE NOTED THE NUMBER OF THE CAR TO BE EITHER 106, 107, OR 207 SHE WAS CONSISTANT IN THAT IT WAS A 3 DIGIT NUMBER NOT TWO DIGITS AS WAS TIPPIT'S SQUAD CAR # 10. THE CAR THEN EASED AWAY FROM THE CURB AND TURNED LEFT ONTO ZANG BOULEVARD.

ACCORDING TO ARMSTRONG, THE FBI ATTEMPTED TO LOCATE ALL DPD CARS AND THEIR LOCATIONS AT 1:00 PM ON THAT DAY. CAR NUMBER 107 WAS NOT LISTED IN THE REPORT. AS NOTED EARLIER, JACK RUBY HAD PLACED A CALL TO CLARENCE RECTOR, AN AUTOMOBILE TRANSPORTER IN SULPHUR SPRINGS, TEXAS ON APRIL 10TH. ON APRIL 17TH, THE DALLAS POLICE SOLD PATROL CAR #107 TO USED CAR DEALER ELVIS BLOUNT IN SULPHUR SPRINGS. RECTOR DELIVERED THE CAR FROM DALLAS TO SULPHUR SPRNGS.

*ARMSTRONG BELIEVES, AND I CONCUR, THAT THESE TWO UNIDENTIFIED MEN IN CAR #107 ARE THE SAME TWO UNIDENTIFIED POLICEMEN WHO BOARDED THE MARSALIS ST. BUS SHORTLY AFTER **HARVEY** EXITED AT 12:43 PM. THEY ARE MONITORING **HARVEY'S** MOVEMENTS. IT IS APPARENT BY NOW THAT TIPPIT HAS NOT LOCATED **HARVEY**. IF HE HAD, **HARVEY** WOULD LIKELY BE ON HIS WAY TO THE AIRFIELD. IT WILL BE UP TO THE UNIDENTIFIED OFFICERS IN CAR 107 TO PROVIDE **HARVEY** WITH HIS RIDE TO THE THEATER RATHER THAN RED BIRD AIRFIELD.*

1:03 PM FRIDAY
TIPPIT THEN DRIVES 9 BLOCKS WEST ON JEFFERSON AND STOPS AT THE TOP TEN RECORD STORE ON 338 WEST JEFFERSON BOULEVARD TO USE THE TELEPHONE. HE HAS NOT LOCATED **HARVEY** AND HE NEEDS SOME GUIDANCE AS TO WHAT TO DO NEXT.

1:03 PM FRIDAY
HARVEY DEPARTS HIS ROOMING HOUSE.

CHAPTER 11: THE TRAP IS SPRUNG

HARVEY'S FINAL JOURNEY STARTS AT APPROXIMATELY 1:03 PM WITH HIS DEPARTURE FROM HIS ROOMING HOUSE ENROUTE TO THE TEXAS THEATER WHERE HE IS CAPTURED AT APPROXIMTELY 1:52 PM THIS TRIP IS FRAUGHT WITH CONTRADICTIONS. COULD HE HAVE WALKED FROM HIS ROOMING HOUSE TO THE 10TH AND PATTON SITE OF TIPPIT'S SHOOTING IN TIME TO SHOOT TIPPIT? DID HE ACTUALLY SHOOT TIPPIT? HOW DID **HARVEY** GET TO THE TEXAS THEATER WHERE, ACCORDING TO BUTCH BURROUGHS, HE ENTERED "SHORTLY AFTER 1:00" OR APPROX IMATELY 1:08. THE THEATER IS ABOUT 13 BLOCKS FROM HIS ROOMING HOUSE. COULD HE HAVE WALKED THIS DISTANCE IN 5 MINUTES? WOULD THE DISTANCE NOT HAVE NECESSITATED RUNNING WHICH WOULD INDEED HAVE ATTRACTED THE ATTENTION OF OTHERS? WAS **HARVEY** INDEED CAPABLE OF RUNNING 13 CITY BLOCKS IN 5 MINUTES?

LET US CONTINUE THE TIMELINE WITH **HARVEY** LEAVING HIS ROOMING HOUSE AND WITH OFFICER TIPPIT MAKING A PHONE CALL FROM THE TOP TEN RECORD STORE. BOTH TIMES ARE NEARLY IDENTICAL AT APPROXIMATELY **1:03 PM**

1:03 PM FRIDAY

LEWIS CORTINAS, A STORE EMPLOYEE, AND THE TOP TEN RECORD STORE OWNER, J.W. STARK STATED THAT THE PHONE CALL TIPPIT MADE WAS BRIEF AND THAT TIPPIT SAID NOTHING WHILE ON THE PHONE. STARK CONTINUED NOTING THAT TIPPIT "WALKED OFF FAST, HE WAS UPSET OR WORRIED ABOUT SOMETHING."

*IN MY OPINION THE PHONE CALL IS TO JACK RUBY'S RESIDENCE AT 223 SOUTH EWING. IT IS ONLY 6 SHORT BLOCKS FROM RUBY'S APARTMENT TO 10TH AND PATTON WHERE TIPPIT WILL VERY SOON MEET HIS FATE. IT IS TIPPIT'S DESIRE TO INFORM RUBY THAT HE DID NOT WITNESS **HARVEY** EXITING THE MARSALIS STREET BUS FROM HIS VANTAGE POINT AT THE GLOCO SERVICE STATION. IT WOULD ALSO BE TIPPIT'S DESIRE TO INFORM RUBY THAT WITH THE FRENZY SURROUNDING THE SHOOTING IN DEALEY PLAZA THAT HE WOULD NOT HAVE TIME TO FIND **HARVEY** AND DRIVE HIM TO REDBIRD AIRFIELD. BOTH CORTINAS AND STONE NOTED THAT TIPPIT HOWEVER SAID NOTHING DURING THE PHONE CALL. THERE ARE THREE POSSIBILITIES THAT COME INTO PLAY THAT WOULD EXPLAIN WHY TIPPIT SAID NOTHING WHILE ON THE PHONE: EITHER THE CALL WENT UNANSWERED, THE LINE WAS BUSY, OR THE CALL WAS INDEED PICKED UP AND THE RECIPIENT OF TIPPIT'S CALL TOLD TIPPIT TO SAY NOTHING AND FOLLOW THE NEW INSTRUCTIONS ABOUT TO BE GIVEN TO HIM THEN HUNG UP.*

*I FEEL THAT THE PERSON ANSWERING THE CALL FROM TIPPIT HOWEVER WAS NOT RUBY. I WOULD OFFER THAT THE PERSON GIVING TIPPIT HIS LATEST INSTRUCTIONS WAS EITHER ROSCOE WHITE OR POSSIBLY **LEE**.*

*WHITE OR **LEE** WOULD NOW PROCEED TO TELL TIPPIT IN NO UNCERTAIN TERMS TO DRIVE TO 10TH AND PATTON WHERE HE WOULD PICK UP HIS PASSENGER, **HARVEY**. TIPPIT WOULD CORRECTLY ASSUME THAT IF **HARVEY** HAD NOT OBTAINED A BUS RIDE TO HIS RESIDENCE FROM THE TSBD THAT HE LIKELY CROSSED THE RIVER IN A TAXI INSTEAD. WHITE OR **LEE** WOULD CLOSE THE VERY BRIEF ONE-WAY CONVERSATION BY POINTEDLY INSTRUCTING TIPPIT TO MEET **HARVEY** ON 10TH NEAR PATTON.*

ASIDE FROM THE FACT THAT RUBY KNEW A GREAT NUMBER OF DALLAS POLICE OFFICERS, THERE IS MORE POINTED PROOF THAT RUBY KNEW J.D. TIPPIT. HAROLD R. WILLIAMS WAS ARRESTED IN DALLAS IN NOVEMBER 1963 IN AN EARLY MORNING RAID ON THE MIKADO CLUB IN DALLAS. WILLIAMS, WORKING AS A CHEF, WAS ARRESTED AND PLACED IN THE BACK SEAT OF AN UNMARKED CAR. THE DRIVER OF THE CAR WAS J.D. TIPPIT. SITTING IN THE FRONT SEAT WITH TIPPIT WAS RUBY. WILLIAMS WAS FAMILIAR WITH RUBY SINCE

RUBY SUPPLIED THE MIKADO CLUB WITH DANCERS. WILLIAMS STATED THAT TIPPIT CALLED HIS FRONT SEAT PASSENGER "RUBE."

AFTER THE ASSASSINATION WHEN PICTURES OF TIPPIT WERE PUBLISHED, WILLIAMS STARTED TALKING ABOUT WHAT HE HAD SEEN THE NIGHT OF HIS ARREST. HE WAS RE-ARRESTED BY THE DALLAS POLICE AND TOLD NOT MENTION THAT EVENING AGAIN.

1:04 PM FRIDAY
LEE IS WALKING <u>WEST</u> ON EAST 10TH STREET. HE IS TWO BLOCKS NORTH OF RUBY'S APARTMENT AND 4 BLOCKS EAST OF 10TH AND PATTON. HE IS WEARING A WHITE T-SHIRT AND A LIGHT COLORED SHORT JACKET. HE WOULD CONTINUE TO WALK <u>WEST</u> AND CROSS SOUTH MARSALIS STREET.

1:04 PM FRIDAY
HARVEY IS STANDING AT THE BUS STOP AT THE CORNER OF ZANG AND NORTH BECKLEY.

*ACCORDING TO THE WARREN COMMISSION, IT TOOK **HARVEY** NEARLY SIX MINUTES TO COVER THE MERE 4/10'THS OF A MILE (3.5 BLOCKS) FROM HIS 12:54 EXIT OF WHALEY'S CAB TO HIS 1:00 ARRIVAL AT HIS ROOMING HOUSE. THE COMMISSION STATED THAT IT WAS .85 MILES (10 BLOCKS) FROM HIS ROOMING HOUSE TO THE SITE OF THE TIPPIT SHOOTING. WITH HIS DEPARTURE FROM THE BUS STOP ESTIMATED TO BE AT 1:04, **HARVEY** WOULD HAVE ARRIVED AT THE SITE OF THE TIPPIT SHOOTING AT APPROXIMATELY 1:21 IF HE WALKED AT THE SAME PACE AS HE DID FROM WHALEY'S CAB <u>TO</u> HIS ROOMING HOUSE. THIS IS AS MUCH AS 6 MINUTES <u>AFTER</u> TIPPIT WAS SHOT AND ABOUT 4 MINUTES AFTER THE CALL WAS PLACED TO DISPATCH BY T.G. BOWLEY INFORMING THEM THAT AN OFFICER HAD BEEN SHOT.*

*D.A. BILL ALEXANDER HAD DOUBTS AS TO WHETHER **HARVEY** COULD HAVE ARRIVED AT THE TIPPIT SHOOTING IN THE TIME FRAME ALLOWED: "HE (**HARVEY**) WOULD HAVE TO HAVE DOUBLE-TIMED A BIG PART OF THE WAY THUS DRAWING ATTENTION TO HIMSELF. SOMEBODY WOULD HAVE SEEN HIM. **I DON'T KNOW HOW HE GOT THERE AND NOBODY ELSE DOES EITHER."***

*USING THE SAME 3.5 BLOCKS/6 MINUTES RATIO, IT WOULD HAVE TAKEN **HARVEY** 12 MINUTES TO WALK THE 7 BLOCKS FROM 10TH AND PATTON TO THE TEXAS THEATER HAD HE SHOT TIPPIT. THIS WOULD PLACE HIM AT THE THEATER AT 1:27. BUT, AS WE WILL SEE, **HARVEY** ARRIVED AT THE THEATER AT APPROXIMATELY 1:08 PM ACCORDING TO BUTCH BURROUGHS. THE SECRET SERVICE DETERMINED THAT IT WOULD HAVE TAKEN A SOMEWHAT SHORTER 10 MINUTES TO WALK FROM 10TH AND PATTON TO THE THEATER THUS PUTTING **HARVEY** AT THE THEATER AT 1:25.*

*IF **HARVEY** HAD WALKED 14 BLOCKS FROM THE CORNER OF ZANG AND NORTH BECKLEY <u>DIRECTLY</u> TO THE THEATER WITHOUT SHOOTING TIPPIT AND WE USE THE SAME 3.5 BLOCKS/6 MINUTE RATIO AS THE W.C. OFFERED ABOVE, THE WALK WOULD HAVE TAKEN 24 MINUTES TO COVER THE 14 BLOCK DISTANCE. HE WOULD HAVE THEN ARRIVED AT THE THEATER AT 1:28, 20 MINUTES LATER THAN HIS ACTUAL ARRIVAL TIME OF APPROXIMATELY 1:08 ACCORDING TO BUTCH BURROUGHS.*

*HARVEY COULD NOT HAVE <u>WALKED</u> FROM ZANG AND BECKLEY TO 10TH AND PATTON IN TIME TO HAVE BEEN TIPPIT'S SHOOTER AT APPROXIMATELY 1:15. AND, QUITE OBVIOUSLY, HAD THE TIPPIT SHOOTING TAKEN PLACE PRIOR TO 1:15, AS NOTED BY WITNESSES WE WILL MEET SHORTLY, **HARVEY'S** PRESENCE AT THE SCENE WOULD REMAIN AN IMPOSSIBILITY.*

HARVEY COULD NOT HAVE ARRIVED AT THE TEXAS THEATER AT 1:08 IF HE HAD INDEED BEEN TIPPIT'S ASSAILANT AT 1:15.

THIS BEING SAID, **HARVEY** *ALSO COULD NOT HAVE <u>WALKED</u> FROM ZANG AND NORTH BECKLEY <u>DIRECTLY</u> TO THE THEATER AND ARRIVE AT THE TIME HE WAS NOTED TO HAVE ARRIVED WHICH WAS APPROXIMATELY 1:08.*

IN MY OPINION, **HARVEY** *IS PICKED UP BY THE UNIDENTIFIED BLACK #107 SQUAD CAR THAT HAD SOUNDED THE HORN IN FRONT OF HIS ROOMING HOUSE AND THEN DRIVEN <u>DIRECTLY</u> TO THE TEXAS THEATER FROM THE CORNER OF ZANG AND NORTH BECKLEY. HE IS TOLD BY THE OCCUPANTS OF THE CAR THAT HE WILL MEET HIS CONTACT FOR HIS RIDE TO THE AIRPORT AT THE THEATER.* **HARVEY** *DOES NOT QUESTION THE FACT THAT HIS DRIVER IS NOT TIPPIT. HE DOES NOT QUESTION THE FACT THAT HE IS NOT BEING TAKEN DIRECTLY TO RED BIRD AIRFIELD. HE WAS SIMPLY WAITING FOR WHAT HE THOUGHT WAS A DPD SQUAD CAR (PRESUMABLY DRIVEN BY TIPPIT) TO PROVIDE HIM WITH A RIDE TO HIS NEXT STOP. THE NEXT STOP HOWEVER HAS BEEN CHANGED FROM RED BIRD AIRFIELD TO THE TEXAS THEATER.*

1:05 PM FRIDAY
JAMES ANDREWS, AN INSURANCE SALESMAN, IS DRIVING WEST ON 10TH STREET 2 BLOCKS WEST OF ZANG BOULEVARD. HE IS SUDDENLY FORCED TO THE SIDE OF THE STREET BY TIPPIT'S PATROL CAR. TIPPIT THEN RAN BACK TO ANDREW'S CAR, LOOKED INSIDE AT THE AREA BETWEEN THE FRONT AND BACK SEATS, THEN HURRIEDLY RETURNED TO HIS CAR, TURNED AROUND, AND DROVE EAST ON 10TH ST.

TIPPIT COULD HAVE BEEN LOOKING FOR **HARVEY.** *BUT IN MY OPINION HE HAD ALREADY BEEN TOLD TO PICK UP* **HARVEY** *AT 10TH AND PATTON. ANDREWS WAS DRIVING WEST ON 10TH AND WAS WEST OF ZANG. PATTON WOULD BE EAST ON 10TH AND ALSO EAST OF ZANG. IT IS ALSO POSSIBLE THAT TIPPIT IS LOOKING FOR THE RIFLE THAT WAS MENTIONED IN THE INITIAL 12:45 APB AS HE LOOKED AT THE BACKSEAT AND REAR FLOOR AREA.*

APPROXIMATELY 1:05 PM FRIDAY
DEPUTY SHERIFF LUKE MOONEY DISCOVERS THE SO CALLED "SNIPER'S NEST." THERE WERE 3 SHELL CASINGS ON THE FLOOR ALONG THE WALL BELOW THE WINDOW.

DEPUTY SHERIFF ROGER CRAIG WOULD LATER NOTE THAT THE 3 CASINGS WERE SIDE-BY-SIDE AND ALL FACING THE SAME DIRECTION; AN UNLIKELY SCENARIO IF THEY HAD BEEN RANDOMLY STREWN ABOUT AFTER BEING EJECTED FROM THE ALLEGED ASSASSINATION RIFLE.

1:08 PM FRIDAY
HARVEY *ENTERS THE TEXAS THEATER.*

LITTLE DOES **HARVEY** *SUSPECT THAT THIS IS THE SET-UP CONSPIRATORS LIKELY TERMINATION POINT FOR BOTH HE AND HIS ALLEGED "CARCINOGENS TO CUBA" ASSIGNMENT. THERE IS NO ONE IN THE THEATER TO MEET HIM. HE IS NOT ONLY RUNNING SOLO, BUT, UNBEKNOWNEST TO BOTH HIM <u>AND</u> JACK RUBY, HE IS BEING PURSUED NOT ONLY AS THE KILLER OF A POLICE OFFICER, BUT WANTED FOR QUESTIONING IN THE SLAYING OF THE PRESIDENT*

AT THE TIME **HARVEY** *ENTERED THE THEATER, THE TICKET SELLER, JULIA POSTAL, WAS NOT IN THE TICKET BOOTH. THIS 1:08 ARRIVAL TIME WOULD CORRELATE WITH THE* **"SHORTLY AFTER 1:00"** *TIME THAT BUTCH BURROUGHS SUSPECTS AS THE TIME THAT* **HARVEY** *ENTERED THE THEATER AND WENT UP TO THE BALCONY. LATER IN CUSTODY,* **HARVEY** *WOULD OFFER THAT HE WENT STRAIGHT FROM HIS ROOMING HOUSE TO THE THEATER. HE DID NOT HOWEVER REVEAL <u>HOW</u> HE HAD ARRIVED THERE. I ONCE AGAIN SUGGEST THAT HE WAS DRIVEN THERE BY THE TWO UNIDENTIFIED MEN IN THE BLACK SQUAD CAR MARKED 107.*

1:08 PM FRIDAY

PATROLMAN C.M. BARNHART, #261, CONTACTS DISPATCH. HE IS THE 3RD PATROLMAN TO INQUIRE ABOUT A CLOTHING DESCRIPTION. ONCE AGAIN DISPATCH REPLIES NEGATIVELY ON A CLOTHING DESCRIPTION AND REPEATS THE 12:45 APB DESCRIPTION.

1:08 PM FRIDAY
TIPPIT CALLS DISPATCH BUT DISPATCH DOES NOT RESPOND. A FEW SECONDS LATER TIPPIT TRIES ONCE AGAIN TO CONTACT DISPATCH. DISPATCH ONCE AGAIN DOES NOT RESPOND.

1:10 PM FRIDAY
WILLIAM SCOGGINS IS SITTING IN HIS CAB NEAR THE CORNER OF 10TH AND PATTON EATING HIS LUNCH. TIPPIT SLOWLY CROSSES THE INTERSECTION HEADING EAST ON 10TH ST. SCOGGINS NOTICES A MAN WALKING WEST ON 10TH TOWARDS THE POLICE CAR. THE MAN IS WEARING A LIGHT COLORED SHORT JACKET, DARK PANTS, AND A LIGHT COLORED SHIRT. THE MAN OBSERVED BY SCOGGINS IS **LEE**. **HARVEY** IS AT THE TEXAS THEATER. HE IS WEARING GREY PANTS, AND A REDDISH-BROWN SHIRT

1:10 PM FRIDAY
HARVEY LEAVES THE BALCONY AND ENTERS THE NEARLY EMPTY LOWER LEVEL OF THE THEATER. HE SITS NEXT TO 18 YEAR OLD JACK DAVIS.

1:11 PM FRIDAY
TIPPIT CROSSES 10TH STREET AT PATTON.

1:12 PM FRIDAY
TIPPIT SLOWLY DRIVES EAST ON 10TH. **LEE** NOTICES TIPPIT'S CAR SLOWLY APPROACHING HIM FROM THE WEST AND ABRUPTLY TURNS AROUND AND STARTS WALKING EAST ON 10TH. THIS MOVE ALONE ENHANCES THE PROBABILITY THAT TIPPIT SUSPECTS HE HAS FOUND **HARVEY**.

1:12 PM FRIDAY
DAVIS NOTES THAT **HARVEY** MOVES FROM HIS SEAT IN THE THEATER ONLY TO SIT NEXT TO ANOTHER MAN.

1:13 PM FRIDAY
TIPPIT NOTICES THE SUDDEN REVERSAL OF **LEE'S** DIRECTION AND SLOWLY EASES HIS CAR TO THE CURB. TIPPIT MOTIONS FOR OR CALLS OUT FOR **LEE** TO COME OVER TO THE CAR. **LEE** LEANS FORWARD, PLACING HIS HANDS ON THE PASSENGER WINDOW SILL AND CONVERSES WITH TIPPIT. AGENT ROBERT BARRETT WOULD LATER NOTE THAT SOMEONE TOLD HIM THAT **LEE** HANDED SOMETHING TO TIPPIT. IT WILL HOWEVER NOT BE **LEE'S** WALLET. IT WILL BE ONE CONTAINING IDENTIFICATION PERTAINING TO **HARVEY** AND HIDELL.

*THE PASSENGER WINDOW AS SHOWN IN PHOTOS OF DPD DUSTING THE CAR FOR PRINTS SHOWS THAT THE WINDOW WAS ONLY DOWN ABOUT 2-3 INCHES. **LEE** LIKELY GAVE THE WALLET TO TIPPIT THROUGH THE OPEN WING VENT WINDOW.*

1:14 PM FRIDAY
TIPPIT EXITS THE SQUAD CAR AND WALKS TOWARDS THE FRONT OF THE VEHICLE. HE MAY BE QUESTIONING THE CONTENTS OF THE WALLET HANDED TO HIM BY **LEE**. THE WALLET WILL LATER SHOW IDENTIFICATION FOR BOTH A "LEE HARVEY OSWALD" AND AN "A.J. HIDELL." TIPPIT IS LIKELY WONDERING WHETHER HE HAS FINALLY LOCATED **HARVEY** OR HE HAS SOME CONCERN REGARDING THE HIDELL IDENTIFICATION.

1:15 PM FRIDAY
TIPPIT IS FATALLY SHOT BY **LEE**.

*ONCE AGAIN, THE W.C. STATES THAT **HARVEY** WALKED FROM ZANG AND NORTH BECKLEY TO 10TH AND PATTON. IT WOULD HAVE TAKEN HIM 17 MINUTES TO WALK THE 10 BLOCKS. IF **HARVEY** WAS STANDING AT THE BUS STOP AT ZANG AND NORTH BECKLEY AT 1:04 JUST*

PRIOR TO BEING PICKED UP BY THE BLACK CAR #107 AND DECIDED TO <u>WALK</u> TO 10TH AND PATTON, HE WOULD NOT HAVE ARRIVED UNTIL 1:21 PM; TOO LATE TO HAVE SHOT TIPPIT.

THIS FATAL RENDEZVOUZ POINT WOULD BE FAR ENOUGH AWAY FROM THE NUMEROUS SQUAD CARS THAT WOULD SOON BE ON THEIR WAY TO THE TEXAS THEATER NOW THAT **HARVEY** HAD BEEN DRIVEN THERE BY THE MYSTERIOUS CAR #107.

JACK RUBY'S APARTMENT AT 323 S. EWING IS 2 BLOCKS SOUTH AND ALSO 4 BLOCKS <u>EAST</u> OF THE SITE OF THE TIPPIT SHOOTING. AS MENTIONED PREVIOUSLY, I FEEL STRONGLY THAT TIPPIT CONNECTED WITH ROSCOE WHITE OR POSSIBLY **LEE** WHEN HE PLACED THE 1:03 PHONE CALL TO RUBY'S APARTMENT FROM THE RECORD STORE. **LEE** WOULD EASILY HAVE HAD TIME TO MAKE THE 6 BLOCK WALK (ABOUT 1/2 MILE) FROM RUBY'S APARTMENT TO 10TH AND PATTON <u>AFTER</u> THE 1:03 PHONE CALL FROM TIPPIT. HE WOULD HAVE HAD APPROXIMATELY 13 MINUTES TO WALK 6 BLOCKS, A COMFORTABLE BLOCK EVERY 2.2 MINUTES PACE.

TIPPIT'S EXPECTATION THAT HE WOULD ENCOUNTER **HARVEY** WOULD ALLOW FOR THE CASUAL MANNER IN WHICH HE ALLOWED **LEE** TO LEAN ON THE PASSENGER WINDOW SILL TO TALK JUST PRIOR TO HIS (TIPPIT'S) EXITING OF THE SQUAD CAR. IN ALL LIKLIHOOD, THE DISCUSSION CONCERNED WHETHER TIPPIT – THINKING HE IS CONVERSING WITH **HARVEY** - STILL HAD TO DELIVER **HARVEY** TO RED BIRD AIRPORT. IT WAS NOW TIME FOR THE SET-UP OF **HARVEY** AS TIPPIT'S ASSAILANT. TIPPIT HAD SOME FAMILIARITY WITH **LEE** AS A RESULT OF THE ENCOUNTER AT THE DOBBS RESTAURANT. PERHAPS THIS IS WHY HE HAD AT THE TIME OF THE SHOOTING, <u>NOT</u> DRAWN HIS SIDEARM. UNFORTUNATELY FOR TIPPIT, HE THOUGHT HE HAD NO REASON TO BE WARY OF **HARVEY**. HE DID HOWEVER NEED TO BE WARY OF **LEE**. TIPPIT MAY HAVE FUMED OVER WHITE'S/**LEE'S** INSISTANCE THAT HE, IN SPITE OF ORDERS FROM DISPATCH AND THE FRENZY SURROUNDING THE ASSASSINATION, NEVERTHELESS DRIVE **HARVEY** TO REDBIRD AIRFIELD. BUT, TIPPIT WOULD CERTAINLY NOT BE EXPECTING THE EVENTUAL OUTCOME OF THIS CONVERSATION. NOR WOULD HE BE EXPECTING THAT HIS CONVERSATION WAS WITH **LEE**, NOT **HARVEY**.

ON SEPTEMBER 2ND, 1956, TIPPIT AND FELLOW OFFICER DALE HANKINS CONFRONTED A LEONARD GARLAND IN A NIGHTCLUB IN WEST DALLAS. TIPPIT HAD ASKED GARLAND TO ACCOMPANY HIM OUTSIDE THE CLUB. GARLAND STOOD, POINTED HIS PISTOL AT TIPPIT, AND PULLED THE TRIGGER. FORTUNATELY FOR TIPPIT, GARLAND NEGLECTED TO RELEASE THE SAFETY. BOTH OFFICERS FIRED A TOTAL OF 7 SHOTS RESULTING IN GARLAND'S DEATH. THIS MORE RAPID AND EFFECTIVE RESPONSE BY TIPPIT MAY WELL HAVE BEEN PROMPTED BY AN EVENT EARLIER THAT SAME YEAR. ON APRIL 28TH, TIPPIT WAS STABBED TWICE WHILE ATTEMPTING TO SUBDUE AN ICE PICK WIELDING HUSBAND WHO HAD APPARENTLY THREATENED TO KILL HIS WIFE. IRONICALLY, TIPPIT WAS AWARDED A CERTIFICATE OF MERIT FOR "OUTSTANDING JUDGEMENT AND QUICK THINKING DURING 1956." IN MY OPINION HIS "QUICK THINKING" NEARLY COST HIM HIS LIFE TWICE IN A 4 MONTH SPAN.

FELLOW OFFICERS NOTED THAT THE LATER INCIDENT PROMPTED TIPPIT TO BE VERY CAUTIOUS WHEN APPROACHING POTENTIAL SUSPECTS. ON NOVEMBER 22ND, 1963, LESS THAN 45 MINUTES AFTER THE ASSASSINATION OF THE PRESIDENT, WITH THE ENTIRE DALLAS POLICE FORCE ON HIGH ALERT, WOULD TIPPIT HAVE APPROACHED AN UNFAMILIAR ARMED "SUSPECT" BASED ON A BROADCAST AT 12:45 AND REPEATED AT 12:49 AND 1:08 AS CASUALLY AS HE APPARENTLY DID? EITHER THE CAUTIOUS TIPPIT HAD CHOSEN A MOST UNOPPORTUNE AND UNEXPECTED TIME TO THROW CAUTION TO THE WIND, OR HE WAS FAMILIAR WITH THE MAN WHO WAS ABOUT TAKE HIS LIFE. IT IS A CERTAINTY THAT TIPPIT KNEW ROSCOE WHITE. TIPPIT'S WIFE WAS A BRIDESMAID IN ROSCOE AND GENEVA WHITE'S WEDDING. IT HAS NEVER BEEN <u>CONCLUSIVELY</u> ESTABLISHED THAT TIPPIT ACTUALLY KNEW **HARVEY** OR EVEN **LEE** OTHER THAN THE INCIDENT WITH **LEE** AT THE DOBB'S RESTAURANT ON NOVEMBER 20TH.

SINCE 1959, TIPPIT HAD BEEN VERBALLY REPRIMANDED ON 4 OCCASSIONS FOR LEAVING HIS PATROL CAR WITHOUT INFORMING DISPATCH. TODAY'S VIOLATION WOULD BE HIS LAST.

TIPPIT'S CAPTAIN, CAPTAIN SOLOMEN, NOTED THAT HE THOUGHT THE REASON TIPPIT WAS KILLED WAS BECAUSE WHEN TIPPIT TALKED TO OR INTERROGATED SOMEONE HE WOULD NEVER LOOK DIRECTLY AT THEM. HE WOULD LOOK AWAY OR LOOK OFF SOMEWHERE. THIS WAS A HABIT NOTED BY POLICE DISPATCHER MURRAY JACKSON, TIPPIT'S LIEUTENANT JAY FINLAY, AND ALSO FELLOW PATROLMEN CHARLES WALKER AND BILL MENTZELL. TIPPIT WAS ALSO NOTED BY OFFICERS TO BE AN "EASY-GOING","GOOD-OL-BOY", "UNEDUCATED", AND "A LITTLE SLOW." LT. RIO SAM PIERCE NOTED THAT TIPPIT'S INABILITY TO MAKE EYE CONTACT AND DO WELL ON TESTS KEPT HIM FROM BEING PROMOTED. PROMOTION REQUIRED A WRITTEN EXAM AND A FACE-TO-FACE INTERVIEW. TIPPIT SERVED 11 YEARS ON THE DALLAS POLICE FORCE AND WAS AWARDED SEVERAL RAISES. HE WAS HOWEVER NEVER PROMOTED.

*SADLY ENOUGH, ALL THESE CHARACTERISTICS COULD HAVE BEEN THE VERY REASON HE WAS CHOSEN BY THE SET-UP CONSPIRATOR ROSCOE WHITE, VIA JACK RUBY, TO BE THE OFFICER TO DRIVE WHO HE THOUGHT TO BE **HARVEY** TO THE AIRFIELD. TIPPIT'S SELECTION BY ROSCOE WHITE AS THE VICTIM WHOSE DEATH WOULD HOPEFULLY PROMPT A FATAL SHOOTOUT BETWEEN THE POLICE AND **HARVEY** IN THE TEXAS THEATER COULD HAVE BEEN BASED SOLELY ON THIS FATAL CHARACTER FLAW IF TIPPIT HAD SURVIVED THE SHOOTING, IT IS POSSIBLE, BECAUSE OF HIS UNORTHODOX STYLE, THAT HE WOULD NOT HAVE BEEN ABLE TO IDENTIFY HIS SHOOTER. ONE OBSERVER OF THE TIPPIT MURDER,, CAB DRIVER WILLIAM SCOGGINS, NOTED THAT THE SHOOTER MUTTERED: "POOR DUMB COP" OR "POOR DAMN COP." POOR COP INDEED. BUT, THE POSSIBILITY THAT TIPPIT WOULD NOT IDENTIFY **HARVEY** AS HIS ASSAILANT WOULD NOT BE LEFT TO CHANCE. THE FINAL SHOT OF THE 4 SHOT SERIES WAS AN EXECUTION-STYLE SHOT TO THE HEAD.*

IN NOVEMBER 1952, TIPPIT WAS GIVEN A RORSCHACH INK BLOT TEST DURING HIS PROBATIONARY PATROLMAN PERIOD. THE ADMINISTRATOR OF THE TEST WAS AMAZINGLY ACCURATE IN HIS INTERPRETATION OF THE RESULTS AS HE NOTED THAT "HIS (TIPPIT'S) GRIP ON REALITY IS BELOW AVERAGE" AND THAT "ERRORS OF JUDGEMENT MAY BE EXPECTED." TIPPIT COMPLETED HIS FORMAL EDUCATION IN THE 8TH GRADE.

AFFADAVITS TAKEN BY THE FBI AND THE DALLAS POLICE OF WITNESSES WHO EITHER HEARD, SAW, OR ARRIVED AT THE SCENE OF THE SHOOTING VARY WIDELY IN THEIR ESTIMATES AS TO WHEN TIPPIT WAS SHOT.

SAM GUINYARD
"ABOUT 1:00 PM I HEARD SOME SHOOTING NEAR PATTON AND 10TH ST."

FRANK CIMINO
HE STATED THAT ABOUT 1:00 PM HE WAS AT HIS APARTMENT..."I HEARD 4 LOUD NOISES WHICH SOUNDED LIKE SHOTS."

FRANK KINNETH
HE ADVISED THAT "AT APPROXIMATELY 1:00 PM HE HEARD 2 OR 3 SHOTS."

BARBARA DAVIS
"AT APPROXIMATELY A FEW MINUTES AFTER 1:00PM I WAS LYING ON THE BED IN MY HOME. AT THAT TIME I HEARD A GUNSHOT OUTSIDE THE HOUSE."

T. F. BOWLEY
"I STOPPED MY CAR AND GOT OUT TO GO TO THE SCENE. I LOOKED AT MY WATCH AND IT SAID 1:10PM."

VIRGINIA DAVIS
"AT APPROXIMATELY 1:30PM I WAS IN THE HOME OF MY SISTER-IN-LAW BARBARA DAVIS. WE HEARD A LOUD BANG."

B. M. PATTERSON
ADVISED THAT AT APPROXIMATELY 1:30PM HE WAS STANDING ON REYNOLD'S USED CAR LOT WITH L. J. LEWIS AND HAROLD RUSSELL WHEN THEY HEARD SHOTS.

HELEN MARKHAM
"I WOULDN'T BE AFRAID TO BET IT WASN'T 7 MINUTES AFTER 1:00"

ACCORDING TO THE WARREN COMMISSION, **HARVEY** WAS AT HIS APARTMENT AT 1:00PM. BY 1:33 PM HE IS ABOUT TO ENTER THE TEXAS THEATER. IN MY TIMELINE HOWEVER, **HARVEY** ENTERS THE THEATER AT 1:08PM. ABOUT 1:15PM HE BUYS POPCORN FROM BUTCH BURROUGHS. ABOUT 1:18PM HE ENTERS THE LOWER LEVEL OF THE THEATER. AND, BY APPROXIMATELY 1:30PM, **HARVEY** HAS CHANGED SEATS 4 TIMES AND IS NOW SITTING ALONE. IT IS **LEE** WHO WILL ENTER THE THEATER AT APPROXIMATELY 1:33 PM.

IT IS INTERESTING TO NOTE THE DISCREPANCY BETWEEN BARBARA DAVIS AND VIRGINIA DAVIS. THEY WERE IN THE SAME HOUSE AND IN THE SAME ROOM IN THAT HOUSE. YET THEY NOTED THE TIME OF THE SHOTS THAT KILLED TIPPIT TO BE AS MUCH AS 25 MINUTES APART IN THEIR OCCURANCE.

IF WE LOOK AT THE <u>EARLIEST</u> TIMES NOTED BY THE 8 WITNESSES, 1:00 – 1:10, **HARVEY** WAS EITHER AT HIS ROOMING HOUSE, STANDING AT THE CORNER BUS STOP AT ZANG AND NORTH BECKLEY, OR ALREADY INSIDE THE THEATER. IF WE LOOK AT THE LATTER TIME, 1:30PM, **HARVEY** WAS CLEARLY IN THE THEATER AS HE HAD ARRIVED AT APPROXIMATELY 1:08PM.

THE W.C. HAS YET ANOTHER DILEMMA. FIVE OF THE 7 WITNESSES TO TIPPIT'S SHOOTING HAVE THE SHOOTING PLACE SHORTLY AFTER 1:00 (1:00-1:10 PM). THIS OF COURSE DOES NOT ALLOW **HARVEY** ENOUGH TIME TO DEPART FROM THE BUS STOP (1:04 PM) AND TAKE THE 17 MINUTE WALK TO 10TH AND PATTON. THIS 17 MINUTE STROLL WOULD HAVE HIM ARRIVING AT THE SCENE OF THE SHOOTING AT 1:21.

ON THE OTHER HAND, IF WE USE THE "APPROXIMATELTY 1:30 PM" TIME NOTED BY THE 2 REMAINING WITNESSES **HARVEY** IS ALREADY IN THE TEXAS THEATER WITH AN APPROXIMATELY 1:08 ARRIVAL TIME. THE ONLY TIMELINE THAT EVEN REMOTELY WORKS FOR THE W.C. IS TO PUT THE TIPPIT SHOOTING AT APPROXIMATELY 1:15 WITHOUT EXPLAINING HOW **HARVEY** GOT THERE A MERE 11MINUTES AFTER HIS 1:04 DEPARTURE FROM THE BUS STOP AND IGNORING BUTCH BURROUGHS 1:08 ARRIVAL TIME FOR **HARVEY** AT THE THEATER AND THE 1:15 SALE OF POPCORN TO **HARVEY**. THEY WOULD ALSO HAVE TO EXPLAIN THE 1:33 OBSERVATION OF JOHNNY BREWER OF A MAN SLIPPING INTO THE TEXAS THEATER. UNFORTUNATELY BREWER HAD SEEN **LEE** ENTER THE THEATER AT 1:33, NOT **HARVEY**.

AN INTERESTING THOUGHT CAME TO MIND REGARDING TIPPIT BEING SHOT BY **LEE**. IMMEDIATELY AFTER THE ASSASSINATION **LEE** BECAME, FOR THOSE RESPONSIBLE FOR THE PRESIDENTIAL SHOOTING, AND "INCONVENIENCE." HE HAD SERVED HIS PURPOSE WELL. HE FACILITATED THE MERGING OF **HARVEY** AND **LEE**, ASSISTED IN THE SET-UP OF **HARVEY**, ASSISTED IN THE ASSASSINATION, AND NOW, WITH THE SHOOTING OF TIPPIT, INCREASED DRAMATICALLY THE LIKELIHOOD THAT **HARVEY** WOULD NOT BE TAKEN ALIVE HAVING NOW APPARENTLY SHOT AN OFFICER AS WELL AS THE PRESIDENT. **HARVEY** WOULD BE TAKEN CARE OF IN THE TEXAS THEATER. IF A SHOOTOUT WERE TO OCCUR BETWEEN **LEE** AND TIPPIT, THE NOW EXPENDABLE **LEE** COULD BE ELIMINATED AS WELL. IF TIPPIT HAD KILLED **LEE** AT 1:15 AND **HARVEY** BEEN SHOT IN THE THEATER AT 1:52, IT WOULD HAVE VERY TIDILY WRAPPED UP A 10-12 YEAR SAGA OF **HARVEY** BECOMING **LEE**

IN A MERE 37 MINUTES. THE SET-UP CONSPIRATORS COULD NOT HAVE SCRIPTED A BETTER OUTCOME.

1:15 PM FRIDAY

MRS. FRANK WRIGHT, WHO COULD SEE THE FALLEN TIPPIT FROM HER HOME, DIALED THE OPERATOR AND ASKED THE OPERATOR TO CALL THE POLICE. HER HUSBAND RAN TO THE STREET AFTER HEARING THE GUNFIRE.

1:15 PM FRIDAY

HARVEY, ACCORDING TO BUTCH BURROUGHS, RETURNS FROM THE LOWER LEVEL TO THE LOBBY AND BUYS POPCORN FROM THE TEXAS THEATER CONCESSION STAND.

APPROXIMATELY 1:15 PM FRIDAY

LT. CARL DAY AND DETECTIVE R. L. STUDEBAKER, DPD CRIME LAB UNIT, ARRIVE AT THE TSBD. THE THREE 6TH FLOOR SHELL CASINGS FOUND BY DEPUTY SHERIFF LUKE MOONEY AT 1:05 PM WERE DUSTED BY LT. DAY. NO PRINTS WERE FOUND.

OFFICER ROGER CRAIG WOULD LATER NOTE IN REGARDS TO THE 3 CASINGS FOUND BENEATH THE 6TH FLOOR WINDOW: "THEY WERE LINED UP UNIFORMLY ALL FACING THE SAME DIRECTION." HARDLY WHAT ONE WOULD EXPECT IF THEY HAD BEEN HASTILY EJECTED FROM A RIFLE ALLEGEDLY USED TO ASSASSINATE THE PRESIDENT OF THE UNITED STATES.

HOOVER WOULD LATER NOTE IN A LETTER TO LEE RANKIN THAT FBI TESTS SHOWED THAT WHEN AN EMPTY CASING IS EJECTED FROM A MANNLICHER-CARCANO THAT THE SHELLS TYPICALLY LANDED 55 TO 115 INCHES FROM THE LOCATION OF THE RIFLE AT THE TIME OF EJECTION. UPON HITTING THE FLOOR, THEY COULD THEN BOUNCE AND EVENTUALLY LAND UP TO 10 FEET AWAY FROM THE INITIAL CONTACT POINT WITH THE FLOOR."

1:16 PM FRIDAY

DOMINGO BENAVIDES TRIES UNSUCCESSFULLY TO USE TIPPIT'S SQUAD CAR RADIO.

1:16 PM FRIDAY

THE OPERATOR FORWARDED THE CALL FROM MRS. WRIGHT TO THE POLICE

1:17 PM FRIDAY

AFTER REPEATED, FAILED ATTEMPTS TO UTILIZE THE SQUAD CAR'S RADIO BY DOMINGO BENAVIDES, T. F. BOWLEY, A CIVILIAN, CALLS DISPATCH USING TIPPIT'S RADIO TO REPORT HE SHOOTING.

DISPATCH TRIES 3 TIMES TO CONTACT #78, OFFICER TIPPIT IN AN APPARENT EFFORT TO EITHER SEND HIM TO THIS LOCATION OR TO POSSIBLY VERIFY IF IT IS INDEED TIPPIT IN SQUAD CAR #10 WHO IS DOWN.

1:18 PM FRIDAY

THE POLICE CONTACTED THE AMBULANCE DISPATCHER FOR SOUTH DALLAS. THE AMBULANCE DISPATCH LOCATION WAS THE DUDLEY HUGHES FUNERAL HOME.

1:18 PM FRIDAY

DUDLEY HUGHES JR., DISPATCHES AN AMBULANCE TO THE SCENE OF THE TIPPIT SHOOTING.

THERE WAS CONSIDERABLE VARIANCE REGARDING THE DESCRIPTIONS OF THE 2 MEN PRESENT AT THE TIPPIT SHOOTING:

HELEN MARKHAM GAVE 3 DIFFERENT DESCRIPTIONS:

(1)--25 Y/O --5'8"---BROWN HAIR---RUDDY COMPLEXION---LIGHT SHIRT---DARK PANTS WHITE JACKET

(2)--18 Y/O------------------------BLACK HAIR--TAN JACKET

(3)--BUSHY HAIR----------------SHORT, HEAVY---NO JACKET

ACQUILLA CLEMONS
SAW TWO MEN; ONE SHORT AND HEAVY, THE OTHER TALL AND THIN.

FRANK WRIGHT
MEDIUM HEIGHT, LONG COAT, AND LEFT IN GREY 1951 CAR.

TED CALLOWAY
DARK WAVY HAIR, FAIR COMPLEXION, BLACK TROUSERS, WHITE SHIRT, LIGHT TAN JACKET.

WILLIAM SMITH
DARK HAIR, LIGHT BROWN JACKET.

BARBARA DAVIS-
5'8----WHITE JACKET

JACK TATUM
LIGHT-COLORED JACKET, DARK PANTS, WHITE T-SHIRT.

DOMINGO BENAVIDEZ
ABOUT 5'10, AVERAGE WEIGHT, SOMEWHAT DARK COMPLEXION, LIGHT BEIGE JACKET

VIRGINIA DAVIS
LESS THAN 20 YEARS OLD, LIGHT BROWN HAIR, SLIM, LIGHT TAN JACKET, AND BLACK PANTS.

***HELEN MARKHAM**, IN ONE OF HER 3 DESRIPTIONS, WOULD NOTE THAT THE MAN SHE THOUGHT TO BE THE SHOOTER HAD BUSHY HAIR AND WAS SHORT AND HEAVY. ROSCOE WHITE WORE A BLACK BUSHY <u>TOUPEE</u>. INTERESTINGLY, DOMINGO BENVENIDES NOTED REGARDING TIPPIT'S ASSAILANT THAT "THE BACK OF HIS HEAD SEEMED LIKE HIS HAIRLINE SORT OF WENT SQUARE INSTEAD OF TAPERING OFF." ALTHOUGH THIS IS WHAT ONE MIGHT EXPECT IF ONE WERE WEARING A TOUPEE, MUCH THE SAME COULD BE SAID ABOUT **LEE** WHO HAD HIS HAIR CUT EVERY OTHER WEEK.*

*MARKHAM'S "BUSHY HAIR", "SHORT/HEAVY", "NO JACKET" DESCRIPTION FITS ROSCOE WHITE. THE MAN WITH THE "WHITE OR TAN" JACKET WOULD BE **LEE**.*

***ACQUILLA CLEMONS** ALSO SAW TWO MEN. THE "SHORT AND HEAVY" DESCRIPTION MORE POINTEDLY DESCRIBES ROSCOE WHITE RATHER THAN **LEE**. THE "LIGHT SHIRT", "DARK PANTS", "WHITE JACKET" AND "TALL AND THIN" WOULD INDEED DESCRIBE **LEE'S** PHYSIQUE RELATIVE TO ROSCOE WHITE'S AND HIS ATTIRE. SHE HOWEVER DESCRIBED THE "SHORT AND HEAVY" MAN AS THE SHOOTER. SHE NOTED THAT HE WORE A LONG COAT.*

***FRANK WRIGHT** WOULD DISTINGUISH HIMSELF AS A WITNESS HOWEVER BY NOTING THAT THE MAN HE SAW STANDING IN FRONT OF TIPPIT'S SQUAD DID NOT <u>RUN</u> FROM THE SHOOTING SCENE BUT <u>DROVE</u> AWAY IN A CAR. WRIGHT DESCRIBED THE CAR AS A 1950-1951 MODEL, GREY IN COLOR, AND LIKELY A PLYMOUTH. HE WOULD ALSO NOTE THAT THE ASSAILANT WORE A LONG COAT. **LEE** HAD ON A SHORT VERY LIGHT COLORED JACKET.*

***TED CALLOWAY'S** DESCRIPTION MORE POINTEDLY FITS **LEE** SINCE ROSCOE WHITE WAS APPARENTLY WEARING A LONG COAT.*

***WILLIAM SMITH'S** DESCRIPTION ALSO FITS **LEE**.*

BARBARA DAVIS' DESCRIPTION IS THAT OF **LEE**.

JACK TATUM'S DESCRIPTION DESCRIBES **LEE'S** ATTIRE.

DOMINGO BENAVIDEZ *DESCRIPTION ALSO MORE POINTEDLY DESCRIBES* **LEE** *IN STATURE AND ATTIRE.*

VIRGINIA DAVIS *DESCRIPTION ACCURATELY DESCRIBES* **LEE** *IN STATURE AND ATTIRE.*

NONE OF THE WITNESSES DESCRIBE THE ASSAILANT AS WEARING THE LONG SLEEVE REDDISH-BROWN SHIRT THAT **HARVEY** *WORE TO WORK THAT DAY AND WAS LATER ARRESTED IN.*

ALTHOUGH IT APPEARS THAT ONE MAN LEFT THE SCENE IN A GREY CAR, THE "DECOY" HOWEVER WOULD OF COURSE NOW BE ON FOOT AS HE NOW LED THE OFFICERS TO THE TEXAS THEATER. THE "DECOY" IN THIS CASE WOULD BE **LEE**. *NEITHER FRANK WRIGHT NOR ACQUILA CLEMONS WERE QUESTIONED BY THE WARREN COMMISSION.*

CAB DRIVER ***WILLIAM SCOGGINS****, WHO ALSO WITNESSED THE SHOOTING OF TIPPIT, NOTED THAT THE ASSAILANT RAN FROM THE SCENE HOLDING "A GUN IN HIS <u>LEFT</u> HAND WITH THE BARREL POINTED UP." TED CALLOWAY, STANDING LESS THAN 60 FEET FROM 10TH AND PATTON, WITNESSED THE ASSAILANT RUN ACROSS PATTON. HE HOWEVER NOTED THAT THE MAN "HAD A GUN IN HIS <u>RIGHT</u> HAND, HOLDING IT IN A RAISED POSITION." HE WENT ON TO EXPLAIN THAT "HIS <u>LEFT</u> HAND WAS GOING TOWARD THE BUTT OF THE GUN LIKE THE WAY YOU WOULD LOAD AN AUTOMATIC."* **LEE** *WAS LEFT HANDED AND* **HARVEY** *WAS RIGHT HANDED. AT 1:38PM, CAPTAIN W. R. WESTBROOK WOULD OFFER HIS OPINION THAT THE ASSAILANT USED AN AUTOMATIC WEAPON.*

OF THE 13 DESCRIPTIONS (IF WE COUNT 3 FROM MRS. MARKHAM AND TWO FROM AQUILA CLEMONS) OF TIPPIT'S ASSAILANT OR OF THE TWO MEN WHO WERE AT THE SCENE IMMEDIATELY AFTER THE SHOOTING, 3 MORE ACCURATELY DESCRIBE ROSCOE WHITE'S PHYSIQUE/APPEARANCE AND ATTIRE, AND 10 MORE ACCURATELY DESCRIPE **LEE'S** *PHYSIQUE/APPEARANCE AND ATTIRE.*

I AM VERY MUCH INCLINED TO CONCLUDE THAT BOTH ROSCOE WHITE <u>AND</u> LEE WERE AT THE SCENE OF THE TIPPIT SHOOTING THUS THE VARIED DESCRIPTIONS. LEE WOULD BE THE ASSAILANT WHO ARRIVED AND LEFT THE SCENE ON FOOT, WHITE WOULD BOTH ARRIVE AND DEPART THE SCENE IN A GREY VEHICLE, A 1950, 2 DOOR, SINGLE SEAT, PLYOUTH COUPE.

1:18 PM FRIDAY
LEE NOW TURNS SOUTH ON PATTON. HE IS ONLY 1 BLOCK FROM JEFFERSON BLVD.

1:19 PM FRIDAY
DISPATCH REPORTS: "SUSPECT RUNNING <u>WEST</u> ON JEFFERSON FROM THE LOCATION, NO PHYSICAL DESCRIPTION."

IT IS INTERESTING TO NOTE THAT IN THE TRANSCRIPT OF THE DALLAS POLICE TAPE THAT THERE IS NO INDICATION <u>HOW</u> DISPATCH RECEIVED THIS INFORMATION. MORE POINTEDLY, THERE IS NO <u>CLOTHING</u> DESCRIPTION, NOR IS THERE A <u>PHYSICAL</u> DESCRIPTION. THE "SUSPECT" COULD HAVE BEEN ANYONE. IT WAS HOWEVER **LEE**. *I FEEL THAT IT IS ROSCOE WHITE PROVIDING THE ANONYMOUS INFORMATION AND HE PURPOSEFULLY DOES* **NOT** *GIVE A CLOTHING DESCRIPTION SINCE* **LEE** *AND* **HARVEY** *ARE NOT SIMILARLY DRESSED.*

THIS IS THE SECOND "ANONYMOUS" OR UNIDENTIFIED LEAD THE DPD HAS RECEIVED REGARDING THEIR "SUSPECT." THE FIRST UNIDENTIFIED LEAD WAS THE 12:45 APB ISSUED

REGARDING A SUSPECT IN THE PRESIDENTIAL SHOOTING. I STRONGLY SUSPECT THAT THIS PARTICULAR LEAD WAS ALSO PROVIDED BY ROSCOE WHITE OR VIA ROSCOE WHITE.

1:19 PM FRIDAY
AMBULANCE DRIVERS CLAYTON BUTLER AND EDDIE KINSLEY ARRIVE ON THE SCENE OF THE TIPPIT SHOOTING.

1:19 PM FRIDAY
HARVEY RETURNS TO THE LOWER LEVEL AND SITS NEXT TO A PREGNANT WOMAN.

HARVEY HAS YET TO FIND HIS CONTACT FOR WHAT HE PERCEIVES AS HIS RIDE TO RED BIRD AIRPORT. AFTER HIS ARREST, A TORN BOX TOP WAS FOUND IN HIS POCKET. IT IS A COMMON INTELLIGENCE PRACTICE TO VERIFY A CONTACT BY MATCHING THE TORN HALVES OF AN ITEM.. HIS BOARDING HOUSE ROOM CONTAINED TORN HALVES OF ONE DOLLAR BILLS.

1:19 PM FRIDAY
DPD RESERVE SERGEANT KEN CROY ARRIVES AT THE SCENE OF THE TIPPIT SHOOTING. HE IS THE FIRST LAW ENFORCEMENT OFFICER TO ARRIVE AT THE SCENE.

1:20 PM FRIDAY
THE AMBULANCE DEPARTS THE SCENE OF THE SHOOTING WITH OFFICER TIPPIT'S BODY.

T. F. BOWLEY, WHO HAD MADE THE 1:17 CALL TO DISPATCH INFORMING THEM OF TIPPIT'S SHOOTING, NOTED IN A SWORN AFFADAVIT ON DECEMBER 2ND, 1963, THAT AFTER HE HELPED LOAD TIPPIT INTO THE AMBULANCE THAT TIPPIT'S REVOLVER HAD BEEN LYING UNDER THE BODY. HE NOTED THAT SOMEONE PICKED UP THE PISTOL AND PLACED IT ON THE HOOD OF THE SQUAD CAR. HE IN TURN PLACED THE GUN INSIDE THE CAR. HE CONTINUED, NOTING THAT AN UNIDENTIFIED MALE THEN RETRIEVED THE GUN FROM THE CAR AND ENTERED A CAB WHICH THEN PROCEEDED TO DRIVE AWAY. THE CAB DRIVER, WILLIAM SCOGGINS, THOUGHT THE MAN WAS EITHER A DETECTIVE OR SECRET SERVICE. SCOGGINS THEN TOOK THE UNIDENTIFIED MAN AND DROVE HIM ABOUT THE NEIIGHBORHOOD IN HIS CAB. SCOGGINS WAS NOT ASKED TO DESCRIBE THE MAN NOW IN POSSESSION OF TIPPIT'S HANDGUN NOR WAS HE ASKED WHERE THE MAN EVENTUALLY EXITED HIS CAB. IT WOULD APPEAR, ACCORDING TO W.C. TESTIMONY, THAT THE MAN NOW IN POSSESSION OF TIPPIT'S GUN AND TAKEN IN SCOGGINS CAB WAS KENNETH HUDSON CROY. SCOGGINS GUESSED CORRECTLY THAT HE THOUGHT THE MAN WAS A DETECTIVE OR SS. CROY WAS A SERGEANT IN THE DPD RESERVE. BUT CROY CLAIMS THAT HE HEARD THAT A CABDRIVER (SCOGGINS?) HAD PICKED UP THE PISTOL AND LEFT THE SCENE IN PURSUIT OF TIPPIT'S ASSAILANT. HE WENT ON TO STATE THAT WHEN THE CAB DRIVER RETURNED THAT HE TOOK TIPPIT'S REVOLVER FROM THE TAXI DRIVER AND TURNED THE DRIVER OVER TO OFFICERS ON THE SCENE FOR QUESTIONING. AS IT STANDS, T.F. BOWLEY STATED THAT SOMEONE TOOK THE REVOLVER FROM THE SQUAD CAR AND LEFT IN A CAB IN PURSUIT. SCOGGINS STATED THAT HE INDEED DROVE SOMEONE IN POSSESSION OF THE REVOLVER AROUND THE NEIGHBORHOOD WHO SOUNDS SUSPICIOUSLY LIKE KENNETH CROY. CROY HOWEVER DENIED THE CAB PURSUIT AND STATED THAT HE DIDN'T RECEIVE THE REVOLVER UNTIL THE CAB DRIVER (SCOGGINS?) RETURNED TO THE SCENE.

EITHER BOWLEY AND SCOGGINS ARE LYING OR CROY'S TESTIMONY CURIOUSLY OMITTED THE CAB PURSUIT. I FIND IT DIFFICULT TO BELIEVE THAT A SERGEANT IN THE DPD RESERVE WOULD TAKE A PISTOL FROM A CRIME SCENE AT WHICH A DPD OFFICER HAD BEEN MORTALLY WOUNDED. THE CHAIN OF EVIDENCE OF THE GUN TAKES YET ANOTHER CURIOUS TURN WHEN OFFICER CALVIN BUD OWENS GIVES HIS W.C. TESTIMONY. IN DESCRIBING HIS ARRIVAL AT 10TH AND PATTON, HE ABRUPTLY INTERJECTS "NOW RIGHT THERE, HERE'S WHERE I'M NOT QUITE SURE....I DON'T KNOW WHETHER I WAS GIVEN THE GUN AND ALL....BUT I BELIEVE I WAS GIVEN A GUN AND THIS WAS TIPPIT'S GUN AND SHELLS." WHEN ASKED WHO HAD GIVEN HIM THE GUN HE REPLIED "SOME OFFICER, I DON'T KNOW WHO IT WAS." WHEN ASKED WHAT HE HAD DONE WITH THE GUN HE

REPLIED "I COULDN'T SAY POSITIVELY WHO I GAVE THEM (GUN AND SHELLS) TO." THE GUN APPARENTLY EVENTUALLY MADE IT TO THE DPD PROPERTY ROOM.

1:20 PM FRIDAY
OFFICER H. W. SUMMERS ARRIVES AT THE SCENE OF THE TIPPIT SHOOTING.

1:21 PM FRIDAY
DISPATCH NOW BROADCASTS THAT "SUSPECT LAST SEEN RUNNING WEST ON JEFFERSON. NO DESCRIPTION AT THIS TIME." AFTER A FEW SECONDS PAUSE, DISPATCH ADDS: "SUSPECT JUST PASSED 401 EAST JEFFERSON."
APPARENTLY ROSCOE WHITE IS FOLLOWING **LEE** AS **LEE** MAKES HIS WAY TO THE TEXAS THEATER.

1:22 PM FRIDAY
A RIFLE INITIALLY DESCRIBED BY DEPUTY CONSTABLE SEYMOUR WEITZMAN AS A 7.65 MM GERMAN MAUSER WITH A 4/18 SCOPE IS DISCOVERED ON THE 6TH FLOOR OF THE TSBD BY DEPUTY SHERIFF E. L. BOONE, DEPUTY CONSTABLE WEITZMAN, AND CAPTAIN WILL FRITZ. BOONE WOULD ALSO DESCRIBE THE RIFLE AS A 7.65 MAUSER WITH A SCOPE. THERE IS NO DISCUSSION REGARDING AN AMMO CLIP. LT. CARL DAY PICKS UP THE RIFLE, BUT IT IS CAPTAIN FRITZ WHO OPENS THE BOLT. ONE LIVE ROUND IS EJECTED.

ONE WOULD HAVE TO QUESTION THE NEED FOR ANY CONFUSION AS TO JUST WHAT MAKE OF RIFLE WAS DISCOVERED SINCE THE CARCANO HAS CLEARLY STAMPED ON IT "MADE ITALY CAL 6.5." DEPUTY SHERIFF ROGER CRAIG WAS ALSO PRESENT AND NOTED LATER HOWEVER THAT THE WORD "MAUSER" WAS PRINTED IN THE METAL OF THIS PARTICULAR RIFLE. THIS RIFLE WAS NEVER TO BE SEEN AGAIN.

THE "MAUSER" DESCRIPTION FOR THE INITIAL 7.65 CALIBER RIFLE FOUND IN THE TSBD WAS STILL IN USE BY THE CIA ON NOVEMBER 25TH. IN FACT, A CIA DOCUMENT DATED 25 NOVEMBER STATED THAT "EMPLOYED IN THIS CRIMINAL ATTACK IS A MODEL 91 RIFLE, 7.35 CALIBER, 1938 MODIFICATION…..THE DESCRIPTION OF A MANNLICHER-CARCANO RIFLE IN THE FOREIGN PRESS IS IN ERROR. IT WAS A MAUSER." BUT, A CIA MEMO AS LATE AS NOVEMBER 28TH NOW DESCRIBED THE SAME RIFLE AS AN "ITALIAN MODEL, MODEL 91, 7.35 CALIBER." ONCE AGAIN THIS IS NOT CORRECT SINCE THE ALLEGED ASSASSINATION WEAPON WAS A 6.5 CALIBER.

DEPUTY SHERIFF BOONE, BEFORE THE WARREN COMMISSION IN MARCH 1964 WAS NOT ASKED ABOUT HIS "MAUSER" DESCRIPTION. HE WAS SHOWN HOWEVER THE 6.5 MANNLICHER. BOONE REPLIED TO THE COMMISSION COUNSEL "IT LOOKS LIKE THE SAME RIFLE. I HAVE NO WAY OF BEING POSITIVE." WEITZMAN, WHO WAS <u>KNOWN</u> TO BE QUITE FAMILIAR WITH RIFLES WAS <u>NOT</u> SHOWN THE 6.5 MANNLICHER.

A RIFLE WAS ALSO DISCOVERED ON THE <u>ROOF</u> OF THE TSBD. THIS DISCOVERY WAS FILMED, AND A FILM WAS MADE AVAILABLE BY THE DALLAS CINEMA ASSOCIATES. CAPTIONED UNDER THE FILM SEGMENT SHOWING THIS RIFLE BEING HELD ALOFT IS THE NOTATION: "THE ASSASSIN'S RIFLE HAS NO TELESCOPIC SIGHT ON IT." NOTING THAT THE ALLEGED ASSASSIN'S RIFLE WAS DISPLAYED <u>WITH</u> A SCOPE, THIS <u>SECOND</u> RIFLE WAS NOT TO BE SEEN AGAIN EITHER. THE ROOFTOOP RIFLE ALSO HAD NO SLING.

1:22 PM FRIDAY
PATROLMAN R. W. WALKER ARRIVES ON THE SCENE OF THE TIPPIT SHOOTING AND CONTACTS DISPATCH. HE PROVIDES DISPATCH WITH A DESCRIPTION GIVEN BY WARREN REYNOLDS OF THE SUSPECT <u>APPARENTLY</u> WANTED IN CONNECTION WITH THE TIPPIT SHOOTING. HIS REPORT: "HAVE A DESCRIPTION ON THE SUSPECT ON JEFFERSON. LAST SEEN ABOUT 300 BLOCK EAST JEFFERSON. A WHITE MALE, ABOUT 30, 5'8, BLACK HAIR, SLENDER BUILD, WEARING A <u>WHITE</u> JACKET, A <u>WHITE</u> SHIRT, AND <u>DARK</u> SLACKS."

*HARVEY IS IN THE TEXAS THEATER. HE IS WEARING A DARK REDDISH-BROWN SHIRT AND GREY SLACKS. **LEE** HOWEVER IS INDEED WEARING A LIGHT-COLORED JACKET, A WHITE SHIRT, AND DARK SLACKS.*

ONE HAS TO APPRECIATE JUST WHAT IS TAKING PLACE HERE. SINCE 1:19, DISPATCH, WITH NO APPARENT INPUT FROM ANY PATROLMAN OR CITIZEN AND NO PHYSICAL DESCRIPTION FROM A PATROLMAN OR CITIZEN, HAS BEEN ABLE TO TRACK A "SUSPECT" FROM "RUNNING WEST ON JEFFERSON" AT 1:19 TO "JUST PASSED 401 EAST JEFFERSON" AT 1:21. NOW, <u>WITH</u> A DESCRIPTION, THE SUSPECT IS "LAST SEEN ABOUT 300 BLOCK EAST JEFFERSON." AT 1:22

*<u>SOMEONE</u> IS APPARENTLY PROVIDING INFORMATION TO DISPATCH TO ALLOW FOR THE AMAZING "TRACKING" OF THE SUSPECT VIA THE 1:19, 1:21, AND 1:22 BROADCASTS. THE TRACK IS QUICKLY LEADING WEST ON JEFFERSON TO THE TEXAS THEATER WHERE, ACCORDING TO BUTCH BURROUGHS, **HARVEY** ENTERED ABOUT 1:08 PM. I STRONGLY SUSPECT ONCE AGAIN THAT IT IS ROSCOE WHITE WHO IS PROVIDING THE ANONYMOUS "GUIDANCE" THAT ENABLES DISPATCH TO TRACK THE "SUSPECT." IN THIS CASE, THE "SUSPECT" IS **LEE**. IT IS **LEE** WHO WILL LEAD THE PURSUING OFFICERS TO THE TEXAS THEATER.*

IT IS INTERESTING THAT DISPATCH ASKS OFFICER WALKER IN REGARDS TO THE SUSPECT "ARMED WITH WHAT?" WALKER REPLIES "UNKNOWN." BUT, IF WALKER GOT HIS DESCRIPTIION FROM WARREN REYNOLDS, WHY DID HE NOT INCLUDE THE PISTOL THAT REYNOLDS NOTED THE SUSPECT WAS CARRYING WHILE FLEEING THE SCENE?

1:23 PM FRIDAY
OFFICERS J.M. POE AND L.E. JEZ ARRIVE AT THE SCENE OF THE TIPPIT SHOOTING. D.A. WILLIAM ALEXANDER AND CAPTAIN WESTBROOK ARE DRIVEN BY SERGEANT CALVIN OWENS TO THE SCENE.

1:23 PM FRIDAY
THE POLICE DISPATCHER BROADCAST THIS DESCRIPTION: "WANTED FOR INVESTIGATION FOR ASSAULT TO MURDER A POLICE OFFICER: A WHITE MALE, APPROXIMATELY 30, 5'8", SLENDER BUILD, BLACK HAIR, A WHITE JACKET, A WHITE SHIRT, AND DARK TROUSERS.

*INTERESTINGLY THE <u>PHYSICAL</u> PORTIONS OF THIS DESCRIPTION CLOSELY RESEMBLES THE APB ISSUED AT 12"45 FOR A MAN WANTED IN CONNECTION WITH JFK'S SHOOTING. BUT, IT ALSO VERY ACCURATELY DESCRIBES THE <u>ATTIRE</u> **LEE** HAD ON AT THE SCENE OF THE TIPPIT SHOOTING. THE 12:45 APB PROVIDED NO CLOTHING DESCRIPTION.*

1:24 PM FRIDAY
OFFICERS OWENS AND HILL WERE APPROACHED BY AN UNKNOWN CIVILIAN. THE CIVILIAN TOLD OFFICERS THAT THE GUNMAN HAD THROWN DOWN HIS JACKET IN A PARKING LOT ACROSS FROM DUDLEY-HUGHES FUNERAL HOME.

*WE NOW HAVE <u>**UNKNOWN CIVILIANS**</u> WHO HAVE **(1)** PROVIDED A DESCRIPTION OF THE PRESIDENTIAL SHOOTER THAT PROMPTED THE INITIAL APB AT 12:45, **(2)** PROVIDED DISPATCH WITH DIRECTIONS IN WHICH THE TIPPIT ASSAILANT WAS HEADING, AND **(3)** ALSO ATTEMPTING TO LINK A JACKET DISCARDED BY THE ASSAILANT TO **HARVEY** AS WELL. WAS THE UNKNOWN CIVILIAN WHO TIPPED OFF OWENS AND HILL THE SAME UNIDENTIFIED CIVILIAN WHO PROVIDED THE DESCRIPTION FOR THE 12:45 APB AND GRACIOUSLY GAVE DISPATCH THE ROUTE OF TIPPIT'S ASSAILANT? THESE THREE PIECES OF "EVIDENCE" ARE CRUCIAL TO THE TIPPIT SHOOTING, THE PRESIDENTIAL SHOOTING, AND GUIDING THE POLICE PURSUIT OF TIPPIT'S ASSAILANT **(LEE)** TO THE TEXAS THEATER.*

1:25 PM FRIDAY
DISPATCH REPEATS THE 1:22 BROADCAST ADDING "GOING WEST ON JEFFERSON FROM THE 300 BLOCK."

*ROSCOE WHITE CONTINUES TO MONITOR **LEE'S** PROGRESS.*

1:25 PM FRIDAY
OFFICER J. C. GRIFFIN RADIOS DISPATCH ABOUT THE FINDING OF A "WHITE" JACKET NEAR THE SHOOTING IN THE PARKING LOT ACROSS FROM DUDLEY-HUGHES FUNERAL HOME ON EAST JEFFERSON.

*NOT ONLY IS THE JACKET IN QUESTION DESCRIBED BY MORE COLORS AND SHADES OF COLORS THAN CONTAINED IN A LARGE CRAYOLA CRAYON BOX, THERE IS CONSIDERABLE DOUBT NOT ONLY AS TO WHETHER **HARVEY** WORE A JACKET AFTER LEAVING HIS ROOMING HOUSE AT APPROXIMATELY 1:03, AND, IF HE DID, AT WHAT POINT DID HE SHED IT.*

LET'S START WITH THE <u>EARLIEST</u> POINT AT WHICH HARVEY <u>COULD</u> HAVE DONNED A JACKET:

MARINA *NOTED THAT SHE DID NOT KNOW IF **HARVEY** LEFT THE HOUSE WITH A JACKET.*

LINNIE MAE RANDLE, *AS **HARVEY** APPROACHED HER HOUSE FOR HIS RIDE TO WORK WITH BUEL FRAZIER, NOTED THAT HIS JACKET (GREY) WAS CLOSER IN COLOR TO THE <u>BLUE</u> JACKET LATER FOUND IN THE TSBD LUNCHROOM ON DECEMBER 16TH.*

BUELL FRAZIER, *WHO DROVE **HARVEY** TO WORK, DESCRIBED THE JACKET AS A "FLANNEL WOOL-LOOKING" JACKET.*

THE WARREN COMMISSION INSISTS THAT HARVEY WAS <u>NOT</u> WEARING A JACKET WHEN HE LEFT THE TSBD.

CECIL MCWATTERS, *THE DRIVER OF THE BUS **HARVEY** BOARDED, NOTED THAT HE <u>WAS</u> WEARING A JACKET.*

WILLIAM WHALEY, *WHO GAVE **HARVEY** THE CAB RIDE TO NORTH BECKLEY NOTED THAT HE <u>WAS</u> WEAING A FADED <u>BLUE</u> JACKET.*

EARLENE ROBERTS *NOTED THAT **HARVEY** ARRIVED AT HIS BOARDING HOUSE WITH <u>NO</u> JACKET AND LEFT WITH A DARK JACKET.*

DPD CAPTAIN WESTBROOK *CLAIMED TO HAVE ACTUALLY RETRIEVED THE JACKET FROM UNDER THE CAR. HE NOTED THIS IN HIS COMMISSION TESTIMONY ABOUT THE JACKET. WHEN ASKED WHERE IT WAS FOUND, HE REPLIED: "...BEHIND THE TEXACO SERVICE STATION, AND SOME OFFICER, I FEEL SURE IT WAS AN OFFICER, I STILL CAN'T BE POSITIVE...POINTED THIS JACKET OUT TO ME...." WESTBROOK'S INABILITY TO RECALL WHETHER THE MAN WAS AN OFFICER IS SADLY REMINISCENT OF INSPECTOR SAWYER'S GROSS INABILITY TO DESCRIBE THE MAN WHO GAVE HIM THE INITIAL DESCRIPTION PROMPTING THE EARLIER 12:45 APB REGARDING THE PRESIDENT'S SHOOTING. WESTBROOK WOULD LATER JOIN THE CIA IN 1965.*

OFFICER THOMAS HUTSON *NOTED THAT THE JACKET WAS PICKED UP BY ANOTHER OFFICER WITH CAPTAIN WESTBROOK SIMPLY WITNESSING THE EVENT. HUTSON DID HOWEVER NOTE THAT THE JACKET WAS <u>WHITE.</u> THE JACKET FOUND UNDER THE CAR IN THE PARKING LOT NEAR THE TIPPIT SHOOTING WAS ALSO DESCRIBED AS <u>WHITE</u> IN COLOR BY WESTBROOK AS WELL.*

THOSE WITNESSES AT THE TIPPIT SHOOTING HOWEVER NOTED THAT TIPPIT'S ASSAILANT EITHER HAD ON <u>NO</u> JACKET, A <u>WHITE</u> JACKET, A <u>TAN</u> JACKET, A <u>FADED BLUE</u> JACKET, A <u>LIGHT TAN</u> JACKET, A <u>LIGHT BROWN</u> JACKET, A <u>DARK</u> JACKET, OR A <u>LIGHT GREY</u> JACKET.

*TO SUMMARIZE THE JACKET EITHER ALLEGEDLY WORN BY **HARVEY** THAT DAY OR ALLEGEDLY WORN BY **LEE**, TIPPIT'S ASSAILANT:*

WITNESS	JACKET/NO	JACKET/YES	COLOR
MARINA OSWALD	NOT SURE		
LINNIE MAE RANDLE		YES	DARK BLUE
BUELL FRAZIER		YES	FLANNEL, WOOL-LOOKING
CECIL MCWATTERS		YES	
WILLIAM WHALEY		YES	FADED BLUE
EARLENE ROBERTS	(UPON ARRIVAL)	(UPON DEPARTURE)	DARK
HELEN MARKHAM		YES	WHITE
WILLIAM SCOGGINS		YES	GREYISH-TAN
FRANK WRIGHT	LONG COAT		
DOMINGO BENEVIDES		YES	LIGHT BEIGE
TED CALLAWAY		YES	LIGHT TAN
WILLIAM A SMITH		YES	LIGHT BROWN
WARREN REYNOLDS		YES	BLUISH
CAPTAIN WESTBROOK	(JACKET FOUND)		WHITE
THOMAS HUTSON	(JACKET FOUND)		WHITE

ELEVEN *WITNESSES NOTE A JACKET* <u>WORN</u> *BY EITHER **HARVEY** OR **LEE** IF ONE DISCOUNTS THE LONG COAT DESCRIBED BY FRANK WRIGHT AND MARINA'S UNCERTAINTY.*

TWELVE *WITNESSES NOTE A COLOR OF THE JACKET WORN BY EITHER **HARVEY** OR **LEE**. THE JACKET IS DESCRIBED HOWEVER BY AS MANY AS **5** DISTINCT <u>COLORS</u> RANGING FROM WHITE TO DARK BLUE TO FADED BLUE TO GREYISH-TAN TO LIGHT BEIGE/TAN.*

*THE WARREN COMMISSION CHOSE TO CONVENIENTLY DESCRIBE IT AS <u>LIGHT GREY</u> WHICH CONFORMS TO MARINA'S OFFERING THAT **HARVEY** HAD ONLY 2 JACKETS: ONE DARK BLUE AND ONE A LIGHT GREY. BUT, THEIR INCLUSION OF THE LAUNDRY TAG, b9738, IS DISPUTED BY MARINA WHO DENIES EVER SENDING ANY OF **HARVEY'S** CLOTHING TO A LAUNDRY SERVICE. THE WARREN COMMISSION JACKET WAS NOTED TO BE A "MEDIUM". **HARVEY'S** TYPICAL CLOTHING SIZE WAS "SMALL." **HARVEY'S** BLUE JACKET WAS FOUND IN THE TSBD LUNCHROOM ON DECEMBER 16TH, 1963.*

*IT IS IMPORTANT TO NOTE ONCE AGAIN THAT THE APB ISSUED AT 12:45 P.M. DID <u>NOT</u> INCLUDE THE USUAL DESCRIPTION OF CLOTHING WORN BY A SUSPECT. **HARVEY** HAS, SINCE THE 12:30 SHOOTING, CHANGED HIS SLACKS AND NOW HAS APPARENTLY (IF ONE IS TO FOLLOW THE BAIT OF SET-UP CONSPIRATORS ROSCOE WHITE AND **LEE**), SHED A JACKET AS WELL. WITH **HARVEY** HAVING FOR CERTAIN CHANGED HIS SLACKS ABOUT 1:00-1:03 PM, AND NOW ALLEGEDLY SHED A JACKET, A CLOTHING DESCRIPTION (HAD IT BEEN INCLUDED IN THE 12:45 APB) WOULD NOW HAVE BEEN VIRTUALLY USELESS SHORTLY AFTER THE 1:15 SHOOTING OF OFFICER TIPPIT. ROSCOE WHITE WAS ACUTELY AWARE OF*

THIS AND THERFORE DID <u>NOT</u> PROVIDE A CLOTHING DESCRIPTION IN HIS "ANONYMOUS" OFFERING OF THE DETAILS INCLUDED IN THE DESCRIPTION OF THE SUSPECT GIVEN AT 12:45 P.M..

*HAD **HARVEY** ACTUALLY SHED THE WHITE JACKET FOUND IN THE PARKING LOT, HE WOULD STILL BE WEARING THE DARK REDDISH-BROWN LONG SLEEVED SHIRT NOT A WHITE SHIRT NOTED TO DISPATCH AT 1:22 BY PATROLMAN WALKER.*

*IF THE W.C. IS TO BE BELIEVED, **HARVEY** HAS COMMITTED THE CRIME OF THE CENTURY. HE HAS ALSO, IN HIS POST-ASSASSINATION WAKE, LEFT BEHIND IN THE TSBD THE ALLEGED ASSASSINATION WEAPON, SPENT SHELL CASINGS, AND, AT THE SCENE OF THE TIPPIT SHOOTING, MORE SHELL CASINGS, HIS JACKET, AND HIS WALLET. ONE MIGHT, IN HASTE, LEAVE **ONE** OF THESE SELF-INCRIMINATING ITEMS BEHIND. BUT, IT IS BEYOND THE SCOPE OF COMPREHENSION THAT HE WOULD LEAVE **5** ITEMS BEHIND POSSIBLY LINKING HIM TO TWO DIFFERENT MURDERS. IN EACH INSTANCE IT IS MY FIRM OPINION THAT EACH DISCARDED ITEM AT BOTH CRIME SCENES WAS DONE FOR THE SOLE PURPOSE OF INCRIMINATING **HARVEY** REGARDLESS OF HIS ACTUAL LEVEL OF INVOLVEMENT IN THE MURDERS.*

1:26 PM FRIDAY
THE AMBULANCE ARRIVES AT METHODIST HOSPITAL BEARING THE BODY OF J.D. TIPPIT.

1:28 PM FRIDAY
SETH KANTOR, A WRITER FOR SCRIPPS-HOWARD IN DALLAS, REPORTED THAT HE HAD TALKED TO RUBY AT PARKLAND AT APPROXIMATELY 1:28 PM, PRIOR TO THE 1:30 PRESS CONFERENCE BY MALCOLM KILDUFF. RUBY HOWEVER TOLD THE WARREN COMMISSION THAT AFTER HE HAD LEFT THE DALLAS MORNING NEWS BUILDING AT APPROXIMATELY 12:43 THAT HE HAD GONE HOME TO CALL HIS SISTER EVA. KANTOR NOTED LATER THAT RUBY APPEARED TO BE "GRIM AND PALE." THE COMMISSION CHOSE TO ACCEPT RUBY'S VERSION OVER KANTOR'S.

RUBY NOW REALIZED THAT SOMETHING HAS TRANSPIRED FAR BEYOND WHAT HAD ORIGINALLY BEEN PLANNED.

1:28 PM FRIDAY
DOMINGO BENEVIDES GIVES TWO .38 CALIBER SHELLS TO OFFICER POE WHO IN TURN SHOWS THE SHELLS TO SERGEANT GERALD HILL.

1:30 PM FRIDAY
OFFICER J.D. TIPPIT IS PRONOUNCED DEAD AT METHODIST HOSPITAL BY DR. RICHARD LIGUORI. HE IS TRANSFERRED TO PARKLAND FOR HIS AUTOPSY.

1:30 PM FRIDAY
A SEARCH OF THE TSBD FINDS A 3RD RIFLE, A MANNLICHER-CARCANO ON THE 4TH FLOOR. THE SPENT CARTRIDGES EJECTED FROM THE ALLEGED ASSASSINATION RIFLE WERE FOUND ON THE 6TH FLOOR.

1:30 PM FRIDAY
MALCOLM KILDUFF, WHITE HOUSE PRESS SPOKESMAN, ANNOUNCES THE PRESIDENT'S DEATH AT A PRESS CONFERENCE AT PARKLAND.

APPROXIMATELY 1:32 PM FRIDAY
ADRIAN HAMBY, AN EMPLOYEE AT THE JEFFERSON BRANCH LIBRARY IN OAK CLIFF, JOINED OTHER EMPLOYEES IN THE BASEMENT OF THE LIBRARY. THEY WERE TOLD BY THE POLICE NOT TO LET ANYONE ENTER OR LEAVE THE LIBRARY UNTIL IT WAS SECURED AS A "SUSPECT" IN THE TIPPIT SHOOTING HAD BEEN SEEN RUNNING INTO THE LIBRARY. HAMBY HOWEVER TOOK A CHANCE AND PEERED OUT THE BASEMENT DOOR. ACCORDING TO HAMBY, THE OFFICERS TOLD HIM "IF I DIDN'T COME OUT THEY WOULD OPEN FIRE." APPARENTLY THE OFFICERS THOUGHT HAMBY WAS THEIR SUSPECT. HAMBY'S DILEMMA WAS SOON RESOLVED. DETECTIVE MARVIN BUHK

NOTED THAT A "SECRET SERVICE MAN" OFFERED THAT "HE HAD ALREADY TALKED TO HIM (HAMBY) A FEW MINUTES PREVIOUSLY."

*THERE ARE 2 INTERESTING THINGS TO NOTE ABOUT THIS INCIDENT. THE POLICE ATTITUDE WAS JUST WHAT THE SET-UP CONSPIRATORS HAD HOPED FOR; THE OFFICERS WOULD, WITHOUT HESITATION, GUNDOWN SOMEONE WHOM THEY <u>SUSPECTED</u> OF SHOOTING A FELLOW OFFICER. THE TIPPIT MURDER WAS DESIGNED TO DRAW THE IRE OF THE DALLAS POLICE FORCE. IT APPARENTLY SUCCEEDED. IF AN UNARMED HAMBY WAS AT RISK, CERTAINLY AN ARMED **HARVEY** WOULD BE AT AN EVEN HIGHER LEVEL OF RISK WHEN HE WOULD BE ENCOUNTERED BY THE POLICE IN THE TEXAS THEATER.*

DALLAS POLICE OFFICER BILL ANGLIN SUMMED UP THE SITUATION PRECISELY: "WE WERE ALL PRETTY WELL PUMPED UP WITH THE PRESIDENT SHOT AND THEN ONE OF OUR OWN HAD FALLEN."

*THE SECOND ODDITY ABOUT HAMBY'S ENCOUNTER WITH THE POLICE WAS THE COMMENT BY DETECTIVE BUHK REGARDING THE "SECRET SERVICE AGENT." I FIND IT VIRTUALLY IMPOSSIBLE TO BELIEVE THAT AN AGENT OF THE SECRET SERVICE WOULD BE INVOLVED IN THE PURSUIT OF A SUSPECT WANTED FOR THE SHOOTING OF A DALLAS POLICE OFFICER. THE SECRET SERVICE'S RESPONSIBILITY AND CONCERN WOULD BE FOR THE PRESIDENTS; THE DECEASED JFK AND THE NEW PRESIDENT LYNDON JOHNSON. THIS STRIKES ME AS EERILY SIMILAR TO THE ENCOUNTER DALLAS DEPUTY SHERIFF SEYMOUR WEITZMAN HAD AS HE CLIMBED THE FENCE AT THE GRASSY KNOLL ONLY SECONDS AFTER THE SHOTS HAD BEEN FIRED IN DEALEY PLAZA. HE NOTED THAT HE ENCOUNTERED A MAN WHO SHOWED AN I.D. AND CLAIMED TO BE SECRET SERVICE. ONCE AGAIN, THERE WERE NO AGENTS ASSIGNED TO DEALEY PLAZA OTHER THAN THOSE RIDING IN THE MOTORCADE. THE "AGENT" DETECTIVE BUHK ENCOUNTERED WAS AN IMPOSTER. HIS EFFORT WAS DESIGNED SOLELY TO KEEP THE DALLAS POLICE FORCE FROM BEING DISTRACTED BY ANY "SUSPECTS" OTHER THAN THE DECOY/**LEE** THAT WOULD LEAD THEM TO THE TEXAS THEATER WHERE **HARVEY** WAS PATIENTLY WAITING FOR HIS RIDE.*

EARLY AFTERNOON FRIDAY
WFAA TV REPORTS "THE POLICE HAVE ARRESTED A WHITE MALE IN THE RIVERSIDE SECTION OF FT. WORTH IN CONNECTION WITH THE SHOOTING OF A DALLAS POLICEMAN."

1:33 PM FRIDAY
A MAN IS NOTICED SLIPPING INTO THE TEXAS THEATER BY JOHNNY C. BREWER, A NEARBY SHOESTORE EMPLOYEE AT HARDY'S SHOE STORE. BREWER INFORMS THE THEATER CASHIER, JULIA POSTAL.

*KEEP IN MIND THAT BUTCH BURROUGHS OFFERED THAT **HARVEY** ENTERED THE THEATER "SHORTLY AFTER 1:00" AND THAT HE (**HARVEY**) INITIALLY WENT TO THE BALCONY. HE RETURNED FROM THE BALCONY TO THE LOBBY AND BOUGHT POPCORN ABOUT 1:15. BY 1:33, **HARVEY**, ACCORDING TO BURROUGHS HAS BEEN IN THE THEATER FOR APPROXIMATELY 25 MINUTES IF ONE ALLOWS FOR THE 1:08 ENTRY THAT BURROUGHS CITES AS THE APPROXIMATE TIME **HARVEY** ENTERS THE THEATER. THE "SUSPECT" JOHNNY BREWER NOTICES IS THE DECOY, **LEE**, LEADING THE SQUAD CARS TO THE TEXAS THEATER. **LEE** DID NOT PURCHASE A TICKET. **LEE** WOULD GO IMMEDIATELY TO THE BALCONY.*

*JULIA POSTAL NOTED IN HER AFFADAVIT THAT **HARVEY** ENTERED THE THEATER SHORTLY AFTER 1:30 PM. KEEP IN MIND THAT BOTH SHE AND JOHNNY BREWER HAD WITNESSED **LEE'S** ENTRY INTO THE THEATER, **NOT HARVEY'S**. IT IS 6/10THS OF A MILE AND APPROXIMATELY A 13 MINUTE WALK FROM THE 10TH AND PATTON LOCATION OF TIPPIT'S MURDER TO THE TEXAS THEATER. IF TIPPIT IS SHOT AT APPROXIMATELY 1:15, A 13 MINUTE WALK TO THE THEATER WOULD TRANSLATE TO A 1:28 ARRIVAL TIME. THIS TIME IS REASONABLY CLOSE TO POSTAL'S "SHORTLY AFTER 1:30" APPROXIMATION AND BREWER'S 1:33 TIME.*

1:37 PM FRIDAY
OFFICER H. W. SUMMERS ISSUES A DESCRIPTION OF THE SUSPECT IN THE TIPPIT SHOOTING NOTING THAT HE WAS "APPARENTLY ARMED WITH A .32 DARK-FINISH AUTOMATIC PISTOL WHICH HE HAD IN HIS RIGHT HAND."

1:37 PM FRIDAY
LT. CARL DAY IS PHOTOGRAPHED OUTSIDE THE TSBD HOLDING A MANNLICHER-CARCANO RIFLE <u>WITH</u> A CLIP ON BOARD. DAY IS THEN DRIVEN TO CITY HALL BY FBI AGENT BARDWELL ODOM. AT THIS TIME, LT. DAY HAS IN HIS POSSESSION THE 3 SPENT HULLS FOUND EARLIER UNDER THE SO-CALLED SNIPER'S WINDOW AND THE ONE LIVE ROUND EJECTED BY CAPTAIN FRITZ.

LET US EXAMINE THE DISCOVERY PROCESS
REGARDING THE RIFLE(S) AND THE CASINGS.

1:05 PM
THE "SNIPER'S NEST" ALONG WITH 3 SPENT CASINGS IS DISCOVERED ON THE 6TH FLOOR. THE CASINGS ARE <u>6.5MM</u>.

1:22 PM
A <u>7.65MM</u> MAUSER IS FOUND ON THE 6TH FLOOR. THE RIFLE HAS <u>NO CLIP</u>.

EARLY AFTERNOON
A RIFLE IS FOUND ON THE **ROOF** OF THE TSBD. THE RIFLE HAS <u>NO SCOPE</u>.

1:30 PM
A <u>6.5MM</u> MANNLICHER-CARCANO IS FOUND ON THE 4TH **FLOOR** OF THE TSBD.

1:37 PM
LT. CARL DAY DISPLAYS A <u>6.5MM</u> MANNLICHER-CARCANO <u>WITH A CLIP</u>.

WE OBVIOUSLY HAVE SEVERAL DISCREPANCIES HERE:

6TH FLOOR------------------7.65MM MAUSER, NO CLIP, BUT 6.5MM CASINGS.
4TH FLOOR------------------6.5MM MANNLICHER-CARCANO, NO CASINGS, NO CLIP
ROOF------------------------RIFLE WITH NO SCOPE
IN FRONT OF TSBD-----6.5MM MANNLICHER <u>WITH</u> A CLIP

*IN ESSENCE, YOU INITIALLY HAVE THE <u>WRONG</u> RIFLE (7.65MM MAUSER) ON THE <u>6TH</u> FLOOR BUT WITH 6.5MM CASINGS, THE <u>RIGHT</u> (ALLEGEDLY) RIFLE (6.5MM CARCANO) ON THE <u>WRONG</u> FLOOR (4TH), AND A RIFLE FOUND ON THE ROOF WITHOUT A SCOPE. THE WARREN COMMISSION SIMPLY CHOSE TO IGNORE ANY AND ALL DISCREPANCIES THAT DISPUTED THEIR NOTION THAT **HARVEY** WAS ON THE 6TH FLOOR AND THAT THE RIFLE "TRACED" TO HIM WAS A 6.5MM MANNLICHER-CARCANO WITH A SCOPE..*

1:40 PM FRIDAY
SERGEANT GERALD HILL, AT THE SCENE OF THE TIPPIT SHOOTING, RADIOS: "THE SHELLS AT THE SCENE INDICATE THE SUSPECT IS ARMED WITH AN AUTOMATIC .38 RATHER THAN A PISTOL." **HARVEY'S** HANDGUN WAS A REVOLVER.

A TOTAL OF 4 SHELL CASINGS WERE FOUND AT OR NEAR THE SITE OF THE TIPPIT SHOOTING. SERGEANT HILL'S COMMENT WAS UNDOUBTEDLY BASED ON THE PRESUMPTION THAT TIPPIT'S ASSAILANT WOULD NOT NORMALLY LEAVE BEHIND INCRIMINATING CASINGS UNLESS HE WAS INDEED USING AN AUTOMATIC AND IN HIS HASTE TO DEPART THE SCENE SIMPLY DID NOT PAUSE TO COLLECT THE SPENT SHELL CASINGS.

A REVOLVER <u>RETAINS</u> THE SHELL CASING AFTER BEING FIRED. AN AUTOMATIC WOULD EJECT THE CASING AFTER EACH ROUND FIRED. MORE ON THIS IN CHAPTER 16.

*HAD **HARVEY** BEEN TIPPIT'S ASSAILANT, HE WOULD HAVE HAD TO <u>MANUALLY</u> REMOVE THE SHELL CASINGS AND <u>DELIBERATELY</u> TOSS THEM ON THE GROUND. AS YOU WELL KNOW, THERE WERE ALSO SHELL CASINGS LEFT ON THE 6TH FLOOR OF THE TSBD. AS A RESULT, ONE IS LEFT TO CONCLUDE THAT IF **HARVEY** <u>HAD</u> BEEN THE SHOOTER IN <u>BOTH</u> INSTANCES, HE WAS EITHER EXTREMELY CARELESS OR HE WAS BEING TIED TO BOTH CRIME SCENES BY EVIDENCE DELIBERATELY LEFT BEHIND BY THE SET-UP CONSPIRATORS. IT WOULD MAKE LITTLE SENSE FOR **HARVEY** TO HAVE <u>PICKED UP</u> SHELL CASINGS AT THE RIFLE RANGES AS WAS REPORTED EARLIER YET <u>LEAVE THEM</u> EJECTED ON THE FLOOR OF THE TSBD AND CONSCIOUSLY <u>TOSS THEM</u> ON THE GROUND AT THE SITE OF TIPPIT'S SHOOTING.*

*WHITE AND **LEE** WERE KEENLY AWARE THAT IT WOULD BE DIFFICULT FOR A WITNESS TO PLACE **HARVEY** AT THE SCENE OF THE TIPPIT SHOOTING AS **HARVEY** WOULD, AT THAT MOMENT, BE VISUALLY SEARCHING THE DARKENED TEXAS THEATER FOR HIS CONTACT. BALLISTIC EVIDENCE, NO MATTER HOW FLIMSY, WOULD HAVE TO BE THE TIE THAT BINDS **HARVEY** TO THE TIPPIT CRIME SCENE. WITH THE DECISION HAVING ALREADY BEEN MADE THAT THE ALLEGED PRESIDENTIAL ASSASSIN WOULD BE SO CARELESS AS TO <u>NOT</u> PICK UP THE SPENT SHELLS AT THE TSBD, LEAVING SPENT SHELLS AT THE SCENE OF THE TIPPIT SHOOTING WOULD SEEM TO THE CASUAL OBSERVER AS A CONTINUANCE OF THE ASSASSIN'S WRECKLESSNESS. BUT THERE IS STILL ONE NAGGING PROBLEM: THE SHELLS AT THE TSBD WOULD AT LEAST HAVE BEEN <u>AUTOMATICALLY EJECTED</u> FROM THE CARBINE AS THEY WERE FIRED AND SIMPLY <u>NOT RETRIEVED</u> BY THE ASSASSIN. THE SPENT SHELLS AT THE TIPPIT SHOOTING WOULD HAVE HAD TO HAVE BEEN <u>MANUALLY</u> REMOVED FROM THE REVOLVER AND <u>INTENTIONALLY</u> STREWN ON THE GROUND AS **HARVEY'S** PISTOL WAS A REVOLVER WHICH, BY DESIGN, WOULD NOT HAVE AUTOMATICALLY EJECTED THE SHELLS.*

IT IS ONE MATTER TO FRANTICALLY LEAVE THE 6TH FLOOR OF THE TSBD AFTER ALLEGEDLY SHOOTING THE PRESIDENT OF THE UNITED STATES AND IN YOUR HASTE NEGLECT TO PICK UP YOUR SPENT SHELLS. IT IS HOWEVER ANOTHER MATTER ENTIRELY TO SHOOT A POLICE OFFICER THEN DELIBERATELY UNLOAD THE SPENT SHELLS AND TOSS THEM ON THE GROUND AT THE SITE OF THE SHOOTING. THE FIRST ACT COULD EASILY BE CONSTRUED AS A MOMENT OF FORGETFULL PANIC. THE SECOND ACT WOULD BE FOOLISH UNLESS COMMITTED BY SOMEONE FOR THE SOLE PURPOSE OF SETTING UP AN INDIVIDUAL <u>OTHER</u> THAN THE ACTUAL SHOOTER. AND, ACCORDING TO BARBARA AND VIRGINIA DAVIS WHO WATCHED TIPPIT'S ASSAILANT RUN ACROSS THEIR FRONT YARD, THAT IS EXACTLY WHAT THEY WITNESSED. BARBARA DAVIS WOULD NOTE IN HER FBI INTERVIEW THAT "THE CHAMBER OF THE PISTOL WAS OPEN AND THIS YOUNG WHITE MAN WAS SHAKING IT AS HE WALKED."

*WERE WHITE/**LEE** AND PERHAPS OTHER CO-CONSPIRATORS IN THE SET-UP OF **HARVEY** SO DESPERATE TO TIE HIM <u>BALLISTICALLY</u> TO THE TIPPIT SHOOTING THAT THEY WERE WILLING TO TAKE THE CHANCE THAT NO ONE WOULD LATER APPRECIATE THE DISTINCTION BETWEEN <u>CARELESSLY</u> LEFT SPENT SHELLS <u>EJECTED</u> <u>AUTOMATICALLY</u> FROM A RIFLE AND <u>PURPOSELY</u> LEFT SPENT SHELLS <u>MANUALLY</u> STREWN FROM A REVOLVER? OR, DID **LEE** MAKE A SET-UP-JEOPARDIZING MISTAKE?*

*THE SET-UP CONSPIRATORS PLAN, IF WORKED TO PERFECTION, WOULD CULMINATE IN THE DEATH OF **HARVEY** IN A SHOOTOUT WITH DALLAS POLICE IN THE TEXAS THEATER IF NOT PREVIOUSLY ACCOMPLISHED. I AM VERY MUCH INCLINED TO SUGGEST THAT THE REVOLVER/EJECTED SHELLS PROBLEM WAS, TO THEM, OF MINIMAL IMPORTANCE. **HARVEY** WOULD BE UNABLE TO DEFEND HIMSELF AGAINST THE MOUNTING "EVIDENCE" NO MATTER HOW QUESTIONABLE AND CIRCUMSTANTIAL. THE SET-UP CONSPIRATORS FELT QUITE CONFIDENT THAT THE INVESTIGATION WOULD BE MINIMAL WITH THE DEATH*

OF THE ALLEGED PRESIDENTIAL ASSASSIN. THERE WOULD BE LITTLE NEED TO EXPAND THE INVESTIGATION AND CLOSELY EXAMINE THE TIPPIT SHOOTING AS WELL.

A CITY OF DALLAS POLICE ARREST REPORT FILLED OUT AT 1:40 PM ON 11/22/63 LISTED UNDER DETAILS OF ARREST: "THIS MAN SHOT AND KILLED PRESIDENT JOHN F. KENNEDY AND POLICE OFFICER J. D. TIPPIT. HE ALSO SHOT AND WOUNDED GOVENOR JOHN CONNALLY." AT 1:40 PM, **HARVEY** HAS YET TO BE EVEN <u>APPREHENDED</u> AS HE IS STILL INSIDE THE TEXAS THEATER. CERTAINLY A RUSH TO JUDGEMENT SINCE IT WOULD BE 7:00 PM THAT EVENING WHEN **HARVEY** IS FORMALLY CHARGED WITH TIPPIT'S MURDER AND NOT UNTIL 1:35 AM, SATURDAY, NOVEMBER 23RD THAT HE IS CHARGED WITH THE PRESIDENT'S, AND PRESUMABLY GOVENOR CONNALLY'S SHOOTING.

1:40 PM FRIDAY
THE BRONZE CEREMONIAL CASKET FOR THE PRESIDENT ARRIVES AT PARKLAND.

1:42 PM FRIDAY
W. E. BARNES, DPD CRIME SCENE SECTION, ARRIVES AT 10TH AND PATTON AND DUSTS TIPPIT'S PATROL CAR FOR PRINTS. NONE OF THE PRINTS TAKEN FROM THE VEHICLE MATCHED **HARVEY**. DETECTIVE JIM LEAVELLE ARRIVES AT THE SCENE AS WELL AS FBI AGENT BARRETT. DETECTIVE PAUL BENTLEY AND CAPTAIN GEORGE DOUGHTY ALSO ARRIVE AT THE SITE OF THE TIPPIT SHOOTING.

1:44 PM FRIDAY
THE CASHIER AT THE TEXAS THEATER, JULIA POSTAL, CALLS THE POLICE. SHE TELLS THE POLICE: "I THINK WE HAVE YOUR MAN." WHEN ASKED "WHY DO YOU THINK IT'S OUR MAN?" SHE GIVES THEM A DESCRIPTION PROVIDED BY JOHNNY BREWER AND ADDED THAT BREWER HAD PREVIOUSLY NOTED THAT "EVERY TIME THE SIRENS GO BY HE DUCKS." BREWER'S DESCRIPTION, ACCORDING TO POSTAL, IS OF A MAN WITH A WHITE SHIRT AND A <u>WHITE</u> JACKET WHO ACTED "SCARED" AND LOOKED "MESSED UP." **HARVEY** WAS WEARING A REDDISH-BROWN SHIRT WITH A WHITE T-SHIRT UNDERNEATH. POSTAL WOULD ALSO TELL THE POLICE THAT THE MAN WAS HIDING IN THE BALCONY. **LEE** WAS IN THE BALCONY.

*IN HIS W.C. TESTIMONY HOWEVER, BREWER STATED THAT THE SUSPECT (**LEE**) WAS NOT WEARING A JACKET AND WAS WEARING A BROWN SPORT SHIRT WITH A WHITE T-SHIRT UNDERNEATH.*

*IF POSTAL'S RECOLLECTION OF BREWER'S DESCRIPTION OF THE DECOY/**LEE** IS CORRECT, I.E. WEARING A <u>WHITE</u> JACKET, THEN ONE HAS TO QUESTION THE "FLEEING SUSPECT'S" WHITE JACKET THAT WAS FOUND AT 1:25 BY OFFICER J.T. GRIFFIN AND CAPTAIN WESTBROOK. **LEE** SEEMS TO HAVE THE SAME PROBLEM WITH JACKETS THAT **HARVEY** HAS WITH WALLETS: HE HAS MORE THAN HE NEEDS.*

*I FIND IT INTERESTING THAT THE MAN WHO ALLEGEDLY SHOT THE PRESIDENT OF THE UNITED STATES WAS FOUND APPROXIMATELY 90 SECONDS OR LESS AFTER THE SHOOTING CALMLY ENJOYING HIS LUNCH AND A COKE. BUT, THE SAME MAN, AFTER ALLEGEDLY SHOOTING A DALLAS PATROL OFFICER, IS NOW DESCRIBED AS "DUCKING EVERY TIME THE SIRENS GO BY." THE MAN WHO "DUCKED" WITH THE APPROACHING SIRENS AND THEN SLIPPED INTO THE THEATER WITHOUT PAYING WAS THE DECOY/**LEE**. AT THAT TIME, THE POLICE HAD A DESCRIPTION FAVORING **HARVEY** THAT PROMPTED THE 12:45 APB REGARDING A SUSPECT WANTED FOR QUESTIONING IN CONNECTION WITH THE SHOOTING OF THE PRESIDENT. THEY ALSO HAD ANOTHER APB ISSUED AT 1:24 WITH A SIMILAR DESCRIPTION OF A SUSPECT WANTED IN THE SHOOTING OF A POLICEMAN. BUT, THE POLICE HAD <u>NO IDEA</u> WHERE **HARVEY** WAS, <u>OR</u> ANY REASON TO CHECK THE TEXAS THEATER. THE NERVOUS DECOY/**LEE** GAVE THEM THEIR MUCH NEEDED ASSISTANCE IN LOCATING **HARVEY**. THE TRAP WAS SET BY ROSCOE WHITE AND **LEE** WITH THE ASSISTANCE OF THE UNSUSPECTING AND NOW DECEASED TIPPIT. THE DECOY/**LEE**, WHO ACTED "SCARED", "MESSED UP", AND "LOOKED FUNNY", AS DESCRIBED BY JOHNNY*

BREWER, WOULD LEAD THE NOW AGITATED POLICE (HAVING LOST A FELLOW OFFICER) TO THEIR PREY.

FBI AGENT BOB BARRETT ARRIVED AT THE SCENE OF THE TIPPIT SHOOTING <u>AFTER</u> THE AMBULANCE CREW HAD LEFT WITH TIPPIT'S BODY. ALTHOUGH CAPTAIN WESTBROOK AND THE DALLAS POLICE WERE IN CHARGE, BARRETT DECIDED TO INSPECT THE CRIME SCENE AS WELL. NEAR THE CAR WHERE TIPPIT HAD FALLEN, A MAN'S WALLET HAD BEEN FOUND. IN IT WAS A DEPARTMENT OF DEFENSE MILITARY I.D. FOR "LEE OSWALD" ALONG WITH A SELECTIVE SERVICE CARD FOR A "ALEX J. HIDELL." THE "CHAIN OF EVIDENCE", ACCORDING TO DPD SERGEANT CROY, HAS THE WALLET BEING FOUND BY YET ANOTHER <u>UNKNOWN CIVILIAN</u> WHO IN TURN GIVES IT TO HIM. IN TURN, SERGEANT CROY GIVES THE WALLET TO SERGEANT BUD OWENS WHO IN TURN GAVE IT TO CAPTAIN GEORGE DOUGHTY WHO IN TURN HANDS IT TO CAPTAIN WESTBROOK.

AGENT BARETT NOTED THAT CAPTAIN WESTBROOK ASKED HIM "DO YOU KNOW WHO LEE HARVEY OSWALD IS?" AND "DO YOU KNOW WHO ALEX HIDELL IS?" IF IT WAS <u>NOT</u> **HARVEY'S** WALLET AND INDEED NOT TIPPIT'S WALLET, WHY DOES THE TIPPIT CRIME SCENE HAVE WHAT APPEARS TO BE A WALLET CONTAINING **HARVEY'S** S DOD MILITARY I.D. AND A SELECTIVE SERVICE CARD IN THE NAME OF ALEX J. HIDELL? THE WALLET, LEFT BEHIND BY **LEE**, WAS INTENDED TO IMPLY THAT IT WAS **HARVEY** WHO HAD SHOT TIPPIT.

ONE THING HOWEVER IS CERTAIN; **HARVEY** IS NOW AT LEAST CIRCUMSTANTIALLY LINKED TO THE TIPPIT SHOOTING AND ALSO APPEARS TO BE MISSING FROM THE TSBD FROM WHERE IT IS BELIEVED THE MOTORCADE SHOTS WERE FIRED.

THE DOD CARD, #N4,271,617, WAS A DDFORM 1173 CARD. IT WAS ISSUED 9/11/59 AT EL TORO AIR STATION IN SANTA ANA, CALIFORNIA ON THE DAY **HARVEY** WAS DISCHARGED. THIS TYPE OF CARD WAS ROUTINELY CALLED A "DEPENDENT'S CARD" SINCE IT WAS THE TYPE OF CARD ISSUED TO DEPENDENTS OF ACTIVE DUTY MILITARY PERSONNEL. HOWEVER IT WAS SOMETIMES ISSUED TO <u>CIVILIAN</u> EMPLOYEES OF THE GOVERNMENT REQUIRING MILITARY I.D. OVERSEAS. THIS SAME TYPE OF CARD WAS FOUND ON CIA CONTRACT AGENT GARY POWERS WHEN HE WAS SHOT DOWN OVER RUSSIA. MANY RESEARCHERS FEEL THAT POSSESSION OF THIS CARD WOULD BE THE LOGICAL EXPLANATAION AS TO HOW **HARVEY,** ENROUTE TO MOSCOW WHERE HE "DEFECTED", MANAGED TO FLY TO HELSINKI FROM LONDON WHEN NO COMMERCIAL FLIGHTS WERE AVAILABLE TO ALLOW FOR HIS ARRIVAL TIME IN FINLAND. **HARVEY** MAY HAVE SIMPLY CAUGHT A MILITARY TRANSPORT FLIGHT COURTESY OF THE DD 1173 CARD IN HIS POSSESSION.

THESE CARDS CARRIED A "IF FOUND DROP IN ANY MAILBOX" PROMPT. THE POSTMASTER WOULD THEN "RETURN TO DOD, WASH. 25, D.C." **HARVEY'S** DOD 1173 CARD HAD A POSTMARK OF 10/23/1963, ONE WEEK <u>AFTER</u> HIS START DATE AT THE TSBD. THIS DATE WOULD HAVE BEEN 10 MONTHS <u>AFTER</u> THE CARDS EXPIRATION DATE OF 12/7/1962. IF THE CARD HAD INDEED BEEN FOUND AND DROPPED IN A MAILBOX THEN THE DOD WOULD HAVE <u>RETURNED AN</u> <u>EXPIRED</u> CARD TO A <u>FORMER DEFECTOR</u>. ONE HAS TO WONDER WHY THEY WOULD DO THIS AND, MORE POINTEDLY, HOW WERE THEY ABLE TO LOCATE THE NOMADIC **HARVEY** WITH HIS FREQUENT MOVES AND P.O. BOXES LESS THAN 1 MONTH PRIOR TO THE ASSASSINATION.

THE ANSWER OF COURSE WOULD BE THAT THEY DID <u>NOT</u> RETURN THE CARD TO **HARVEY**. HUNT AND PHILLIPS HOWEVER WOULD BE IN A POSITION TO OBTAIN EITHER THE ORIGINAL CARD OR A REPLICA OF THE CARD. THE CARD WOULD THEN BE FORWARDED TO **LEE** WHO WOULD, AS TIPPIT'S ASSAILANT, CERTAINLY BE IN A POSITION TO DEPOSIT A WALLET AND THE ENCLOSED DOD CARD AT THE SCENE. THE CARD WOULD ALLOW THE LOCAL DALLAS AUTHORITIES TO QUICKLY ASSIGN A NAME TO THE TIPPIT MURDERER. THIS NAME WOULD CONVENIENTLY BE THE SAME NAME AS AN EMPLOYEE AT THE TSBD WHO HAD NOT BEEN PRESENT FOR A ROLL CALL SHORTLY AFTER THE ASSASSINATION.

ONE HAS TO WONDER THOUGH IF **LEE** WAS AWARE THAT **HARVEY** HAD LEFT <u>HIS</u> WALLET ON THE DRESSER PRIOR TO LEAVING FOR WORK THAT DAY. APPARENTLY THERE WAS NO WAY HE COULD HAVE PREDICTED THIS THUS NECESSITATING THE INCRIMINATING WALLET PLANTED AT THE SCENE OF THE TIPPIT SHOOTING. FBI AGENT ROBERT BARRETT NOTED THAT ONE OF THE WITNESSES AT THE TIPPET CRIME SCENE HAD TOLD HIM THAT THE ASSAILANT HAD HANDED TIPPIT SOMETHING THROUGH THE OPEN WING VENT WINDOW AS SOON AS HE HAD APPROACHED THE SQUAD CAR. IF THIS WAS INDEED THE WALLET FOUND BESIDE TIPPIT'S FALLEN BODY, IT MAY HAVE INDICATED TO TIPPIT THAT SOMETHING WAS AMISS. ONE OF THE ID'S IN THE WALLET WAS THAT OF **HARVEY**. THE OTHER ID WAS FOR A **HIDELL**. TIPPIT LIKELY WONDERED JUST WHO HE HAD STOPPED, **HARVEY** OR HIDELL PROMPTING HIS EXIT FROM THE PATROL CAR FOR SOME FURTHER QUESTIONING.

1:45 PM FRIDAY

DISPATCH BROADCASTS: "WE HAVE INFORMATION THAT A SUSPECT JUST WENT IN THE TEXAS THEATER ON WEST JEFFERSON. THE SUSPECT IS SUPPOSED TO BE HIDING IN THE BALCONY."

1:48 PM FRIDAY

POLICE ARRIVE AT THE TEXAS THEATER. OFFICERS CHARLES WALKER, THOMAS HUTSON, RAY HAWKINS, NICK MCDONALD, CAPTAIN C.E. TALBERT, AND E.R. BAGGETT STAY ON THE MAIN FLOOR COVERING THE REAT EXITS. SA BARRETT, DETECTIVE PAUL BENTLEY, OFFICER BOB APPLE, AND SERGEANT GERALD HILL ARRIVE AT THE FRONT ENTRANCE. BENTLEY SEARCHED THE RESTROOMS GERALD HILL SEARCHED THE BALCONY. BARRETT ASKED A MAN TO TURN UP THE HOUSE LIGHTS. THE MAN HAD IDENTIFIED HIMSELF AS THE ASSISTANT MANAGER. THE MAN REPLIED TO BARRETT "I DON'T KNOW HOW. THIS IS MY FIRST DAY ON THE JOB." THERE WAS NO ASSISTANT MANAGER AT THE THEATER AT THAT TIME. THE ONLY THEATER EMPLOYEES THERE WHEN THE POLICE ARRIVED WERE JULIA POSTAL, THE TICKET SELLER, BUTCH BURROUGHS, THE TICKET TAKER AND CONCESSION OPERATOR, AND THE PROJECTIONIST WHO WAS IN THE PROJECTION BOOTH.

THIS "ASSISTANT MANAGER" WAS NEVER IDENTIFIED.

DETECTIVE ROBERT CARROLL AND DPD OFFICER K. E. LYONS ENTERED THE FRONT OF THE THEATER. THEY ENCOUNTERED JULIA POSTAL WHO TOLD THEM THE MAN WAS UPSTAIRS. THEY THEN WENT UP TO THE BALCONY.

DEPUTY SHERIFF BILL COURSON WAS ALSO DIRECTED TO THE BALCONY BY POSTAL. HE HAD ENCOUNTERED **LEE** EXITING THE BALCONY AS HE ENTERED. **HARVEY** WAS ON THE MAIN LEVEL OF THE THEATER.

LT. CUNNINGHAM AND DETECTIVES J.B. TONEY AND E.E. TAYLOR ALSO ENTERED THE THEATER VIA THE FRONT ENTRANCE. THEY TOO WERE SENT TO THE BALCONY BY JULIA POSTAL. CUNNINGHAM AND TONEY STARTED UP THE STAIRS AND FOUND A YOUNG MAN SMOKING ON THE STAIRWAY. WHILE QUESTIONING THE MAN, THEY WERE APPROACHED BY A MAN DESCRIBING HIMSELF AS THE "MANAGER ON DUTY." THE "MANAGER" ASSURED THEM THAT THE YOUNG MAN HAD "BEEN IN THE THEATER SINCE ABOUT 12:05." THIS TIME OF COURSE WOULD HAVE CLEARED THE YOUNG MAN IN REGARDS TO THE SHOOTING OF OFFICER TIPPIT. THE THEATER HOWEVER DID NOT OPEN UNTIL 12:45.

*WE NOW HAVE AN UNIDENTIFIED "ASSISTANT MANAGER" WHO IS UNABLE TO TURN ON THE HOUSE LIGHTS AND AN UNIDENTIFIED "MANAGER ON DUTY" WHO VOUCHES FOR **LEE**. THE ROLE OF DECOY FOR **LEE** HAS COME TO AN END. IT IS HIS PRIORITY NOW TO EXIT THE THEATER PRIOR TO **HARVEY'S** ARREST. IF THE "ASSISTANT MANAGER" AND THE "MANAGER ON DUTY" ARE NOT THE SAME INDIVIDUAL, THEN THE TALLY FOR **UNIDENTIFIED** YET CRUCIAL INDIVIDUALS WHO ASSIST LAW ENFORCEMENT IN THEIR ATTEMPT TO LOCATE **HARVEY** HAS GROWN TO SIX:*

1) THE INDIVIDUAL WHO PROVIDED THE DESCRIPTION FOR THE 12:45 APB.

2) THE INDIVIDUAL WHO FOUND **HARVEY'S** WALLET AT 10TH AND PATTON.

3) THE INDIVIDUAL WHO FOUND THE DISCARDED JACKET.

4) THE INDIVIDUAL WHO PROVIDED THE ROUTE OF TIPPIT'S ASSAILANT FROM 10TH AND PATTON TO JEFFERSON STREET.

5) THE "ASSISTANT MANAGER" ON HIS FIRST DAY OF WORK.

6) THE "MANAGER ON DUTY" WHO VOUCHES FOR **LEE**.

ALSO ARRIVING WAS CAPTAIN WESTBROOK WHO WAS LOOKING FOR EITHER A "LEE OSWALD" OR A "ALEX J. HIDELL" BY VIRTUE OF THE WALLET FOUND AT THE TIPPIT MURDER SCENE.

1:51 PM FRIDAY

JOHNNY BROWN CHECKS THE EXIT DOOR OF THE THEATER BEHIND THE STAGE. HE FINDS 4 POLICEMEN ARMED WITH HANGUNS AND SHOTGUNS.

OFFICER MCDONALD IS STANDING BESIDE THE MOVIE SCREEN. IN AN ASSOCIATED PRESS ARTICLE MCDONALD NOTED: "A MAN SITTING NEAR THE FRONT, AND I STILL DON'T KNOW WHO IT WAS, TIPPED ME THAT THE MAN I WANTED WAS SITTING IN THE 3RD ROW FROM THE REAR AND <u>NOT</u> IN THE BALCONY." THE WELL-INFORMED STRANGER REMAINS UNIDENTIFIED. THE ABOVE NOTED LIST OF WELL INFORMED "UNIDENTIFIEDS" HAS JUST GROWN TO SEVEN.

IT IS ALL TOO PLAIN TO SEE THAT THE TIPPIT SHOOTING WAS DESIGNED SOLELY TO PUT THE DALLAS POLICE (THERE WERE NOW 19 IN OR JUST OUTSIDE THE THEATER) IN A SITUATION WHEREBY THEY WOULD QUITE LIKELY SHOOT TO KILL WITH THE SLIGHTEST OF PROVOCATION:

1) A MAN WHO CLOSELY FITTED THE DESCRIPTION OF A SUSPECT WANTED IN CONNECTION WITH THE SHOOTING OF A PRESIDENT SIMPLY BECAUSE HE MISSED A ROLL CALL AT THE TSBD.

2) A MAN NOW IDENTIFIED AS "LEE OSWALD" OR "HIDELL" BY THE I.D.S FOUND AT THE SCENE OF THE SLAYING OF A FELLOW OFFICER

3) A MAN WHO LOOKED "MESSED UP", "ACTED SCARED", AND "DUCKED" WITH APPROACHING SIRENS.

TIPPIT WAS ONLY THE 2ND DALLAS POLICEMAN IN NEARLY 12 YEARS TO BE KILLED IN THE LINE OF DUTY. THE FUROR THAT WOULD ARISE AS A RESULT OF LOSING A FELLOW OFFICER WAS PRECISELY WHAT THE SET-UP CONSPIRATORS HAD HOPED FOR. THE JFK SHOOTING COULD BE LINKED TO **HARVEY** POST MORTEM. IT WAS HOWEVER IMPERATIVE TO SILENCE **HARVEY** <u>PRIOR</u> TO HIS ARREST AS THERE WAS NO PREDICTING WHAT HE WOULD DIVULGE (PRIMARILY HIS INTELLIGENCE BACKGROUND THUS IMPLICATING THE FBI/CIA) IF HE WERE QUESTIONED IN CUSTODY. HE WOULD ALSO, IF PRESSED BY THE LOCAL POLICE DEPARTMENT WITHOUT ANY LEGAL ASSISTANCE FROM THE INTELLIGENCE COMMUNITY, POSSIBLY REVEAL DETAILS ABOUT WHAT HE HAD BEEN LED TO BELIEVE WAS HIS PARTICIPATION IN WHAT WAS LIKELY A LEGITIMATE CIA EFFORT TO KILL CASTRO. KEEP IN MIND THAT THE REMOVAL OF CASTRO WAS A HIGHLY CLASSIFIED PROJECT. THE PUBLIC DID NOT BECOME AWARE OF THE EFFORTS OF THE CIA, WITH THE ASSISTANCE OF THE MAFIA, TO KILL CASTRO UNTIL THE 1978 HSCA HEARINGS.

1:52 PM FRIDAY

HARVEY IS CAPTURED IN THE TEXAS THEATER. HE COMMENTS: "I AM NOT RESISTING ARREST" AND "THIS IS IT… IT'S ALL OVER WITH NOW."

JOHNNY BREWER, THE SHOE STORE EMPLOYEE WHO LED THE POLICE TO **HARVEY** BY BEING SUSPICIOUS OF **LEE'S** BEHAVIOUR, HEARD ONE OF THE ARRESTING OFFICERS REMARK: "KILL THE PRESIDENT, WILL YOU?" AT THAT TIME, THE <u>ONLY</u> CRIME THAT **HARVEY** COULD POSSIBLY BE ACCUSED OF WAS SNEAKING INTO THE TEXAS THEATER WITHOUT PAYING. HE WOULD NOT BE CHARGED WITH TIPPIT'S MURDER UNTIL 7:10 THAT EVENING AND NOT CHARGED WITH JFK'S DEATH UNTIL 1:30 AM ON SATURDAY, THE 23RD. I SUSPECT THAT THE COMMENT BY THE OFFICER WAS INTENDED TO INCREASE THE LIKLIHOOD OF ONE OF THE POLICMEN SHOOTING **HARVEY** IN THE THEATER AS WAS THE INTENTION OF THE SET-UP CONSPIRATORS. BREWER WAS UNABLE TO IDENTIFY THE OFFICER MAKING THE COMMENT.

JULIA POSTAL NOTED THAT AS **HARVEY** WAS BEING ESCORTED OUT OF THE THEATER THAT AN OFFICER ENTERED THE BOX OFFICE TO USE THE PHONE. SHE NOTED THAT THE OFFICER COMMENTED DURING HIS PHONE CALL "I THINK WE GOT OUR MAN ON BOTH COUNTS." HE ALSO IDENTIFIED THE SUSPECT AS "OSWALD." THE WALLET **HARVEY** APPARENTLY HAD ON HIS PERSON WHEN HE WAS ARRESTED HOWEVER WAS NOT EXAMINED UNTIL <u>AFTER</u> HE WAS PLACED IN THE SQUAD CAR. WHEN POSTAL INQUIRED "WHAT TWO COUNTS?" HE REPLIED "OFFICER TIPPITS' AS WELL." I WOULD OFFER THAT THIS PARTICULAR OFFICER WAS LIKELY THE SAME OFFICER WHO JOHNNY BREWER NOTED TO HAVE MADE THE "KILL THE PRESIDENT WILL YOU?" COMMENT ONLY MINUTES AFTER **HARVEY'S** ARREST. A DPD OFFICER HAD ALREADY FORMED THE OPINION THAT **HARVEY** WAS GUILTY OF MURDERING BOTH OFFICER TIPPIT AND THE PRESIDENT.

GEORGE APPLIN WAS STANDING BEHIND THE BACK ROW WHEN THE LIGHTS CAME ON JUST MOMENTS BEFORE **HARVEY'S** ARREST. HE NOTICED A MAN SITTING IN THE LAST ROW. DURING THE STRUGGLE BETWEEN **HARVEY** AND THE POLICE, APPLIN TAPPED THE MAN ON THE SHOULDER AND TOLD HIM HE MIGHT WANT TO MOVE WITH ALL THE GUNS WAVING. "HE JUST TURNED AROUND AND LOOKED AT ME, THEN HE TURNED BACK AROUND AND STARTED WATCHING THEM.." ON TUESDAY, NOVEMBER 26TH, RUBY'S PICTURE WAS SHOWN IN THE DALLAS PAPERS. APPLIN FELT THAT THE MAN WHO HAD SHOT **HARVEY** WAS THE SAME MAN HE HAD ENCOUNTERED IN THE THEATER. ACCORDING TO APPLIN, THE MAN IN THE THEATER RAPTLY WATCHING **HARVEY'S** ARREST WAS JACK RUBY.

IF APPLIN IS CORRECT, ROSCOE WHITE WOULD BE THE LIKELY CANDIDATE TO INFORM RUBY THAT HE, RUBY, SHOULD PROCEED TO THE THEATER. RUBY, IN ALL LIKELIHOOD, IS ALSO TOLD BY WHITE <u>NOT</u> TO APPROACH **HARVEY** IN THE THEATER BUT TO ONLY <u>OBSERVE</u> **HARVEY'S** EFFORT TO MEET HIS CONTACT IN THE THEATER FOR WHAT BOTH **HARVEY** AND RUBY PERCEIVE AS **HARVEY'S** RIDE TO THE AIRPORT. AS YOU WILL SEE LATER, **HARVEY** APPROACHES SEVERAL PEOPLE IN THE THEATER INCLUDING A WOMAN LOOKING FOR HIS CONTACT/RIDE TO THE AIRPORT. THERE IS NO INDICATION THAT HE NOTICED RUBY'S PRESENCE IN THE THEATER, AND APPARENTLY DID NOT SEEK HIM OUT.

RUBY WAS LAST SIGHTED ABOUT 1:28PM AT PARKLAND BY SETH KANTOR. RUBY DENIED GOING TO PARKLAND AND CLAIMED HE HAD GONE HOME AFTER LEAVING THE DALLAS MORNING NEWS BUILDING AT ABOUT 12:43. A 1:28 SIGHTING AT PARKLAND WOULD HAVE ALLOWED RUBY ABOUT 24 MINUTES TO TRAVEL FROM THE HOSPITAL TO THE THEATER TO WITNESS **HARVEY'S** 1:52 ARREST. IT WAS ONLY A 12 MINUTE DRIVE FROM PARKLAND TO THE THEATER. RUBY HOWEVER IS ALSO THOUGHT TO HAVE BEEN AT THE DALLAS MORNING NEWS OR THE CAROUSEL CLUB AT APPROXIMATELY THIS SAME TIME.

IF IT IS INDEED RUBY IN THE THEATER, THE NEED FOR HIS PRESENCE WAS SIMPLE: THE SET-UP CONSPIRATORS WANTED RUBY TO KNOW AT THE FIRST POSSIBLE MOMENT THAT **HARVEY** WAS NOW CONSIDERED A PRESIDENTIAL ASSASSIN. THE EARLIER RUBY KNEW THIS, THE LONGER RUBY WOULD HAVE TO CONTEMPLATE THE ERRONEOUS POSSIBILITY THAT **HARVEY** HAD BEEN "TURNED." THE COMMENT OVERHEARD BY JOHNNY BREWER "KILL THE PRESIDENT, WILL YOU?" COULD IN ITSELF BE ENOUGH TO REMOVE ANY

HESITANCY ON THE PART OF A POLICE OFFICER TO SHOOT **HARVEY** DURING THE STRUGGLE SINCE THE OFFICERS WOULD NOW PRESUME THAT THE SUSPECT HAD NOT ONLY SHOT A FELLOW OFFICER BUT THE PRESIDENT AS WELL.HOWEVER THIS COMMENT WOULD ALSO SIGNAL TO RUBY THAT SOMETHING UNEXPECTEDLY HAD GONE WRONG, VERY WRONG. HAD **HARVEY** BEEN "TURNED" BY HIS ASSOCIATION WITH PRO-CASTRO ACTIVIST? HAD HE ACTUALLY KILLED THE PRESIDENT? AT THIS TIME ONE CAN ONLY WONDER WHAT RUBY MUST HAVE THOUGHT.

THE W.C. HOWEVER MAINTAINS THAT RUBY DID NOT GO HOME ABOUT 1:40 AS HE CLAIMED AFTER LEAVING THE DALLAS MORNING NEWS AT 12:43. THEY NOTE THAT HE ARRIVED AT THE CAROUSEL CLUB WHERE HE MADE NUMEROUS PHONE CALLS. THE FIRST LONG DISTANCE CALL, ACCORDING TO PHONE RECORDS, WAS AT 1:51 P.M. IF SO, THIS WOULD REFUTE APPLIN'S CLAIM THAT RUBY WAS IN THE THEATER WITNESSING **HARVEY'S** 1:52 ARREST. MORE RESEARCH IS NECESSARY REGARDING RUBY'S WHERABOUTS AT 1:52 P.M.

THE "TRAIL" TO HARVEY IS QUITE EASY TO FOLLOW:

1. AN APB IS BROADCAST AT 12:45 FOR A MAN WHOSE PHYSICAL DESCRIPTION MORE CLOSELY FITS **LEE**. THE MAN IS BEING SOUGHT APPARENTLY BECAUSE HE MISSED A ROLL-CALL OF TSBD EMPLOYEES. NO CLOTHING DESCRIPTION IS PROVIDED.

2. AT 1:07 PM, CAR # 107 DELIVERS **HARVEY** TO THE TEXAS THEATER, <u>NOT</u> REDBIRD AIRFIELD.

3. AT 1:19 PM, DISPATCH REPORTS: "<u>SUSPECT</u> RUNNING WEST ON JEFFERSON."

4. AT 1:21 PM, DISPATCH REPORTS: "<u>SUSPECT</u> JUST PASSED 401 EAST JEFFERSON."

5. AT 1:25 PM, DISPATCH REPORTS: "<u>SUSPECT</u> GOING WEST ON JEFFERSON FROM THE 300 BLOCK."

6. AT APPROXIMATELY 1:33PM, A DECOY, THE ABOVE "SUSPECT", ACTING "SCARRED" AND LOOKING "MESSED UP" SNEAKS INTO THE TEXAS THEATER. THE "SUSPECT" IS **LEE**.

7. AT 1:43 PM, THE POLICE ARE CALLED AND TOLD: "I THINK WE HAVE YOUR MAN." THEY ARRIVE ENMASS SIMPLY BECAUSE THIS SAME MAN, YET TO BE IDENTIFIED, ALLEGEDLY ENTERED THE THEATER WITHOUT PAYING.

8. AT APPROXIMATELY 1:45-1:50 PM, A WALLET IS FOUND AT THE TIPPIT SHOOTING WITH AN <u>EXPIRED</u> MILITARY I.D. BEARING THE NAME "LEE OSWALD."

9. AT 1:45 PM, DISPATCH REPORTS: "WE HAVE INFORMATION THAT A <u>SUSPECT</u> JUST WENT IN THE TEXAS THEATER ON WEST JEFFERSON."

10. AT 1:52 PM, POLICE, WITH GUNS DRAWN, SUBDUE **HARVEY** WITH ONE OFFICER OFFERING AN INFLAMMATORY "KILL THE PRESIDENT WILL YOU?" COMMENT.

WHITE WOULD HAVE KNOWN <u>EXACTLY</u> WHERE **HARVEY** WAS SINCE HE HAD ARRANGED FOR HIS DELIVERY TO THE THEATER VIA SQUAD CAR #107. WHITE WOULD ALSO KNOW THAT TIPPIT HAD BEEN KILLED, THAT AN I.D. WITH THE NAME "LEE OSWALD" ON IT WOULD BE FOUND AT THE SITE OF THE TIPPIT SHOOTING, AND WHITE WOULD UNDERSTAND THAT DALLAS POLICE WOULD NOT HESITATE TO SHOOT A SUSPECT WHO WAS NOW KNOWN TO THEM AS THE LIKELY KILLER NOT ONLY OF A FELLOW OFFICER, BUT,

THANKS TO THE "KILL THE PRESIDENT, WILL YOU?" COMMENT THE PRESIDENT AS WELL. FORTUNATELY, FOR THE TIME BEING, COOLER HEADS PREVAILED. BUT, IT WOULD ONLY CHANGE THE SITE AND THE ASSAILANT THAT WOULD BE CHOSEN TO SILENCE **HARVEY**.

ROSCOE WHITE HAD SOME LEGITIMATE CONCERNS AS TO WHETHER TIPPIT COULD BE RELIED UPON TO DELIVER **HARVEY** TO RED BIRD AIRPORT. IF **HARVEY** OR TIPPIT MISSED THE LAST POSSIBLE RENDEZVOUZ AT ZANG AND NORTH BECKLEY, WHICH THEY DID, IT WAS LIKELY THAT **HARVEY** WOULD HAVE MADE HIS WAY BY TAXI OR BUS TO THE AIRPORT RATHER THAN THE TEXAS THEATER FOR THE CONTINUANCE OF WHAT HE PERCEIVED AS A LEGITIMATE ASSIGNMENT. WHITE HAD DECIDED THAT **HARVEY** WOULD INSTEAD BE TAKEN FROM HIS ROOMING HOUSE TO THE THEATER BY THE UNIDENTIFIED CAR #107. A DECOY, **LEE,** WOULD NOW LEAD THE DPD TO THE THEATER RATHER THAN THE AIRPORT.

THE DEPARTURE PLANNED THAT DAY BY THE SET-UP CONSPIRATORS THAT WOULD HAVE TAKEN **HARVEY** FROM DALLAS TO GALVESTON OR HOUSTON WHERE HE WOULD BE PICKED UP BY DAVID FERRIE FOR THE FLIGHT TO MEXICO AND CUBA WAS CREATED SOLELY TO GIVE THE IMPRESSION THAT AFTER THE ASSASSINATION THE "ALLEGED" PRESIDENTIAL ASSASSIN WAS INDEED FLEEING THE COUNTRY. THE FORMER "DEFECTOR", FPFC "ADVOCATE" WOULD NOW BE PERCEIVED AS ATTEMPTING TO ESCAPE TO CUBA WHERE IT WOULD BE PERCEIVED BY THE PUBLIC THAT THE ASSASSINATION PLANS HAD BEEN LAUNCHED. IT WAS THE PERFECT INVITATION TO INVADE CUBA THAT THE CIA RENEGADES, THE ANTI-CASTRO MILITANTS, AND ORGANIZED CRIME HAD FOR YEARS SOUGHT. IT WOULD BE THE PERFECT INTRO TO THE C-DAY COUP.

AT THE AIRPORT, HAD **HARVEY** INITIALLY ARRIVED THERE, HE WOULD NOW BE PERCEIVED AS "FLEEING THE CITY" AFTER THE ASSASSINATION. IF HE WERE TO AVOID THE TEXAS THEATER SET-UP AND/OR AVOID A LATER ENCOUNTER AT RED BIRD, HE WOULD HAVE CERTAINLY BEEN KILLED IN HOUSTON OR GALVESTON WITH THE EVER-TALKATIVE DAVID FERRIE. THEY WOULD NOW BOTH BE PERCEIVED AS ATTEMPTING TO "FLEE THE COUNTRY" AFTER THE SHOOTING OF THE PRESIDENT AND ON THEIR WAY TO CUBA VIA MEXICO.

THE ENTIRE POST-ASSASSINATION MOVEMENT OF **HARVEY** WAS DICTATED BY THE FACT THAT HE SIMPLY WENT WHERE HE HAD BEEN TOLD TO GO. HOWEVER WITH EACH PLANNED "STOP" ON HIS ITINERARY; THE TEXAS THEATER AND/OR REDBIRD AIRPORT, HOUSTON OR GALVESTON, THEN MEXICO AND CUBA, IT WOULD INVOLVE AND REQUIRE MORE MANIPULATION AND "GUIDANCE" BY THE SET-UP CONSPIRATORS (IN THIS CASE ROSCOE WHITE, HUNT AND PHILLIPS) TO INSURE THAT DALLAS AND QUITE POSSIBLY HOUSTON OR GALVESTON POLICE FORCES WOULD FIND **HARVEY** AND KILL HIM IN HIS POST-ASSASSINATION FLIGHT. THE SAME QUESTIONABLE "DIVINE GUIDANCE" THAT LED DALLAS POLICE TO THE TEXAS THEATER WOULD NOW BE REQUIRED TO SEND THEM TO REDBIRD AIRPORT. IF **HARVEY** WASN'T SILENCED THERE, THEN LOCAL AUTHORITIES WOULD NOW HAVE TO BE "GUIDED" TO HOUSTON, GALVESTON, AND POSSIBLY MEXICO. THE PREVIOUSLY DISCUSSED VISIT TO RED BIRD AIRFIELD THE MORNING OF NOVEMBER 20TH BY **LEE,** ANOTHER MALE, AND A FEMALE DESIRING TO CHARTER A SMALL AIRCRAFT WOULD BE THE INITIAL EVENT IN WHAT WOULD APPEAR TO BE **HARVEY'S** EFFORT TO TRAVEL TO CUBA. ANY FURTHERANCE OF THE DISTANCE REQUIRED TO CAPTURE OR KILL **HARVEY** WOULD NOT ONLY LEAVE TOO MUCH TO CHANCE, BUT LEAD TO LATER QUESTIONS AS TO WHY A YET TO BE IDENTIFIED MAN WHO AT THAT TIME HAD DONE NOTHING MORE THAN ALLEGEDLY ENTER A THEATER WITHOUT PAYING WAS BEING PURSUED FROM A DALLAS THEATER TO A NEARBY AIRPORT AND THEN ON TO HOUSTON OR GALVESTON, THE YUCATAN, AND THEN CUBA.

BUT, THERE COULD STILL BE SOME MERIT DERIVED BY THE SET-UP CONSPIRATORS IF **HARVEY** WERE TO SOMEHOW DEPART THE THEATER PRIOR TO THE ARRIVAL OF THE DALLAS POLICE OR IF HE SIMPLY PROCEEDED DIRECTLY TO REDBIRD AIRPORT. WITH EACH PROGRESSIVE STOP IN HIS "ESCAPE" PLAN, IT COULD LATER BE IMPLIED THAT HE WAS NOT ONLY TRYING TO ESCAPE THE CITY OF DALLAS, BUT THE STATE OF TEXAS IN HIS

EFFORTS TO FLEE TO CUBA VIA MEXICO. THIS WOULD DOVETAIL NICELY WITH HIS PREVIOUS PRO-CASTRO "ACTIVITY" AND HIS FORMER "DEFECTION." BUT, THE FURTHER THE PROGRESSION OF **HARVEY'S** "FLIGHT FROM JUSTICE", THE LESS CONTROL THE SET-UP CONSPIRATORS WOULD ENJOY. IT WOULD BE MUCH EASIER TO MANAGE THE SILENCING OF **HARVEY** "LOCALLY" AT THE FIRST OPPORTUNITY POSSIBLE; THE TEXAS THEATER. IN MY OPINION, THE SILENCING OF **HARVEY** AT THE THEATER WAS "PLAN A." A SHOOT-OUT AT REDBIRD AIRPORT WOULD HAVE BEEN "PLAN B" SINCE THE SAME DALLAS POLICE FORCE COULD HAVE PURSUED HIM TO THAT POINT AS WELL. HOUSTON, GALVESTON, AND THE RENDEZVOUZ WITH THE LOOSE-LIPPED DAVID FERRIE WOULD THEN BE RELEGATED TO "PLAN C" AS THE SITE OF WHAT THE SET-UP CONSPIRATORS HOPED WOULD BE THE INEVITABLE SHOOTOUT WITH A SUSPECT WHO HAD NOW ALLEGEDLY SHOT A POLICE OFFICER AND THE PRESIDENT.

WITH **HARVEY** CAPTURED RATHER THAN KILLED AT THE THEATER, RUBY'S ROLE WOULD TAKE A DRAMATIC TURN. RATHER THAN SIMPLY OBSERVE **HARVEY** MEETING HIS CONTACT FOR HIS RIDE TO THE AIRPORT FOR WHAT WOULD BE HIS DEPARTURE POINT FOR THE PERCEIVED LEGITIMATE "CARCINOGENS TO CUBA" ASSIGNMENT, RUBY WOULD NOW BE CALLED UPON TO SOLVE A PREDICAMENT THAT THE SET-UP CONSPIRATORS MAY NOT HAVE FORESEEN; THE NECESSITY TO KILL **HARVEY** WHILE HE IS IN POLICE CUSTODY AND WITHIN THE CONFINES OF THE DALLAS JAIL.

ON THE RIDE TO THE POLICE STATION, PAUL BENTLEY DISCOVERS YET ANOTHER WALLET. IT WAS TAKEN FROM **HARVEY'S** LEFT HIP POCKET. A SOCIAL SECURITY CARD WITH THE NAME "LEE HARVEY OSWALD" IS IN THE WALLET. LATER THE NEXT DAY A SELECTIVE SERVICE CARD WITH THE NAME "ALEK J. HIDELL" SURFACES. THE PHOTO ON THE SELECTIVE SERVICE CARD IS IDENTICAL TO THE PHOTO ON THE DOD CARD N4,271,617 FOUND FOUND AT THE SITE OF THE TIPPIT SHOOTING. BENTLEY STATED IN HIS REPORT: "ON THE WAY TO CITY HALL I REMOVED THE SUSPECT'S WALLET AND OBTAINED HIS NAME." SINCE BENTLEY'S REPORT TO CHIEF CURRY MENTIONS NO OTHER NAME OR ALIAS, ONE WOULD HAVE TO ASSUME THAT BENTLEY'S IDENTIFICATION OF **HARVEY** WAS BASED ON **HARVEY'S** SOCIAL SECURITY CARD. BENTLEY, IN AN EFFORT TO RECTIFY THE PROBLEM AS TO JUST WHEN THE HIDELL SELECTIVE SERVICE CARD WAS FOUND, CLAIMED THAT HE RADIO'D IN THE HIDELL CARD ON THE WAY TO CITY HALL ON FRIDAY AND SIMPLY FORGOT TO INCLUDE THIS IN HIS WRITTEN REPORT. THERE IS HOWEVER NO RECORD OF A CALL REGARDING EITHER A WALLET OR A HIDELL ALIAS IN THE POLICE RADIO TRANSCRIPTS GATHERED BY THE FBI. IT APPEARS THAT BENTLEY WAS UNDER SOME PRESSURE TO SUGGEST THAT THE HIDELL SELECTIVE SERVICE CARD HAD INDEED BEEN FOUND ON THE DRIVE TO CITY HALL IMMEDIATELY AFTER **HARVEY'S** ARREST. FINDING THE CARD WITH THE INCRIMINATING HIDELL MONIKER THE NEXT DAY WOULD RAISE QUESTIONS AS TO WHY IT WAS NOT PRODUCED ON FRIDAY WITH **HARVEY'S** SOCIAL SECURITY CARD.

POSTAL INSPECTOR HARRY HOLMES WOULD LATER NOTE THAT THE SELECTIVE SERVICE CARD HAD BEEN ERASED. I SUSPECT THAT **HARVEY'S** NAME HAD BEEN ERASED AND THE NAME HIDELL HAD BEEN TYPED IN ITS PLACE. THE NAME "ALEC HIDELL" OR "A.J. HIDELL" WAS USED TO TIE THE MAIL ORDER OF THE REVOLVER AND RIFLE TO **HARVEY'S** P.O BOX BY THE SET-UP CONSPIRATORS. **HARVEY** HAD USED THE NAME "HIDELL" ONLY TWICE; ONCE WAS ON HIS FPFC NEW ORLEANS CHAPTER MEMBERSHIP CARD WHERE HE LISTED A A. J. HIDELL AS "CHAPTER PRESIDENT" (MARINA ADMITTED TO HAVING FORGED THIS SIGNATURE), AND ANOTHER TIME AS AN EMPLOYMENT REFERENCE AT THE REILY COMPANY IN NEW ORLEANS. AS PREVIOUSLY DISCUSSED, SINCE THE FPFC WAS, ACCORDING TO THE FBI, ALSO LISTED AS ENTITLED TO RECEIVE MAIL AT THE FIRST DALLAS P.O. BOX, ANYONE WITH FPFC CREDENTIALS OR AN I.D. PROCLAIMING THEM AS "HIDELL," COULD HAVE CLAIMED THE RIFLE OR THE REVOLVER.

ALTHOUGH IT IS POSSIBLE THAT **HARVEY** CLAIMED THE REVOLVER, THERE IS NO EVIDENCE THAT HE CLAIMED THE RIFLE THAT WOULD LATER BE USED TO FRAME HIM IN THE PRESIDENT'S DEATH. SECRET SERVICE AGENT KELLEY, IN A LATER INTERROGATION

SESSION WITH **HARVEY**, HAD THIS EXCHANGE AS RECALLED BY DETECTIVE JAMES LEAVELLE: "WHEN ASKED BY KELLEY 'DID YOU EVER USE THAT NAME (HIDELL)? HE ANSWERED 'NO.' KELLEY REPLIED: 'WELL ISN'T IT TRUE THAT WHEN YOU WERE ARRESTED YOU HAD AN I.D. CARD WITH YOUR PICTURE AND THE NAME ON IT…?' **HARVEY** REPLIED, 'I THINK THAT'S RIGHT.' KELLEY PUSHED ON, 'WELL, HOW DO YOU EXPLAIN THAT?' **HARVEY** REPLIED 'I DON'T.'" SINCE THE HIDELL NAME WAS USED IN CONJUNCTION WITH HIS GUY BANISTER INSPIRED, NEW ORLEANS BASED, PRO-CASTRO FPFC POSTURING AND PART OF **HARVEY'S** PERCEIVED PREPARATION FOR A NEW CIA ASSIGNMENT, HE WAS UNWILLING TO BLOW HIS COVER.

*IN CASE YOU HAVE LOST COUNT, THE WALLET HOLDING THESE CARDS WOULD MAKE THE 3^D **WALLET FOUND THAT DAY.**

*THE ONE THE WARREN COMMISSION CLAIMS **HARVEY** LEFT IN MARINA'S DRESSER PRIOR TO LEAVING FOR WORK.

*THE ONE FOUND AT THE SCENE OF THE TIPPIT SHOOTING.

*AND NOW THIS ONE FOUND ON **HARVEY'S** PERSON ON THE RIDE TO THE POLICE STATION.

ON NOVEMBER 26TH, 1963, THE FBI TOOK POSSESSION OF **HARVEY'S** PERSONAL BELONGINGS FROM RUTH PAINE. THEIR INVENTORY LIST NOTED 2 WALLETS; ITEMS #382, A RED BILLFOLD, AND ITEM #114, A BROWN BILLFOLD. NEITHER OF THESE WALLETS WERE THE WALLET TAKEN FROM **HARVEY** BY PAUL BENTLEY UPON **HARVEY'S** ARREST NOR WERE THEY THE WALLET FOUND AT THE SCENE OF THE TIPPIT SHOOTING. IF WE ALLOW ONE OF THESE WALLETS, ITEM #382 OR #114, TO BE THE ONE **HARVEY** HAD LEFT IN MARINA'S DRESSER, THE WALLET COUNT IS NOW **FOUR**. IF NOT, THE WALLET COUNT REMAINS AT **FIVE**.

BUT ON NOVEMBER 27TH, MARINA TURNED OVER A BLACK WALLET TO THE SECRET SERVICE. IF THIS WAS THE WALLET LEFT IN THE DRESSER THE MORNING OF THE ASSASSINATION BY **HARVEY** THE WALLET COUNT REMAINS **FIVE**. IF THIS IS YET AN ADDITIONAL WALLET THE COUNT HAS NOW REACHED **SIX**.

HARVEY IS EITHER VERY FOND OF WALLETS, OR WE HAVE TOO MANY HARVEYS

1:54 PM FRIDAY
HARVEY IS PLACED IN A SQUAD CAR AT THE ENTRANCE TO THE TEXAS THEATER. SERGEANT GERALD HILL RADIO'S DISPATCH: "SUSPECT ON THE SHOOTING OF POLICE OFFICER IS APPREHENDED, ON ROUTE TO STATION."

UNLIKE THE OFFICER WHO USED JULIA POSTAL'S BOX OFFICE TELEPHONE, IT APPEARS THAT SERGEANT HILL'S OPINION IS THAT **HARVEY** IS, AT THIS TIME, ONLY A SUSPECT IN REGARDS TO ONE SHOOTING; THAT OF OFFICER TIPPIT.

SERGEANT HILL LATER NOTED THAT **HARVEY** "SHOWED ABSOLUTELY NO EMOTION…HE WAS SILENT ALMOST THE ENTIRE TIME. THIS IS ONE OF THE THINGS THAT STUCK OUT MOST ABOUT HIM IN MY MIND, HOW QUIET HE DID KEEP."

BUTCH BURROUGHS, WHO HAD SOLD **HARVEY** POPCORN AT APPROXIMATELY 1:15, NOTED THAT HE WITNESSED A 2ND ARREST APPROXIMATELY 3-4 MINUTES AFTER **HARVEY** WAS APPREHENDED. BURROUGHS NOTED THAT THE MAN WAS "AN OSWALD LOOKALIKE." THIS SUSPECT HOWEVER WAS TAKEN OUT THE REAR ALLEY EXIT OF THE THEATER. BURROUGH'S STORY IS SUPPORTED BY BERNARD HAIRE PROPRIETOR OF A BUSINESS TWO DOORS FROM THE THEATER. HE TOO WITNESSED THE APPREHENSION OF A YOUNG MAN AT THE REAR EXIT OF THE THEATER. HAIRE NOTED THAT THE MAN WAS WEARING A LIGHT-

*COLORED PULL OVER SHIRT AND DARK PANTS. INTERESTINGLY, THE HOMICIDE REPORT ON TIPPIT'S DEATH NOTED "SUSPECT WAS ARRESTED IN THE BALCONY OF THE TEXAS THEATER." SINCE IT WAS INDEED **LEE** WHO WAS QUESTIONED IN THE BALCONY AND APPARENTLY **LEE** ESCORTED OUT THE ALLEY EXIT OF THE THEATER AND TAKEN AWAY IN A SQUAD CAR ONE HAS TO QUESTION WHY THERE IS NOT ANY DPD DOCUMENTATION ON THIS SUSPECT IN REGARDS TO HIS BEING TAKEN TO THE JAIL AND BOOKED.*

*I FEEL FAIRLY COMFORTABLE IN SPECULATING THAT **LEE** WAS TAKEN AWAY IN THE MYSTERIOUS CAR #107. THIS IS SAME CAR THAT PROVIDED **HARVEY** WITH THE RIDE FROM HIS ROOMING HOUSE TO THE TEXAS THEATER. THIS WOULD EXPLAIN THE INABILITY OF THE DPD TO PROVIDE THE NAMES OF THE OFFICER(S) WHO DEPARTED THE THEATER WITH **LEE** IN TOW AND THE LACK OF AN ARREST RECORD. **LEE** WAS SIMPLY RELEASED BY THE UNIDENTIFIED MEN IN CAR #107.*

APPROXIMATELY 1:54PM FRIDAY

FORD KAUFMAN, AN ASSOCIATED PRESS PHOTOGRAPHER RECEIVES AN ANONYMOUS PHONE CALL PLACED TO HIS DALLAS MORNING NEWS DESK. THE CALLER COMMENTS: "THEY'VE APPREHENDED A SUSPECT AT THE TEXAS THEATER."

COULD THIS PHONE CALL HAVE BEEN FROM THE SAME OFFICER WHO USED THE PHONE IN THE TEXAS THEATER BOX OFFICE OF JULIA POSTAL?

2:00 PM FRIDAY

T.F. WHITE, WHO WORKED AT MACK'S AUTOMOBILE SERVICE ON WEST 7TH ST. NOTICED A 1961 RED FORD FALCON SPEEDING WEST ON DAVIS ST. A FEW MINUTES LATER, HE NOTICED THE CAR AT THE EL CHICO RESTAURANT. THE CAR HAD BEEN PARKED BEHIND A BILLBOARD. WHITE APPROACHED THE CAR. THE DRIVER, WHO HAD THE ENGINE RUNNING, WAS WEARING A WHITE T-SHIRT. THE CAR SPED AWAY WITH WHITE NOTING THE LICENSE NUMBER. WHITE WOULD LATER TELL FBI AGENT CHARLES BROWN THAT THE MAN WAS IDENTICAL TO **HARVEY**. THE LICENSE PLATE HOWEVER, #PP4537, WAS REGISTERED TO A 1957 PLYMOUTH BELONGING TO A CARL MATHER. MATHER WAS EMPLOYED BY COLLINS RADIO, A FIRM CONTRACTED TO THE CIA. MATHER'S WORK WITH COLLINS INVOLVED HIGH LEVEL SECURE COMUNICATIONS. AFTER THE ASSASSINATION MATHER WAS QUESTIONED BY THE FBI. HE OFFERED LITTLE INFORMATION OF USE SO THE FBI QUESTIONED HIS WIFE. SHE HOWEVER WAS MUCH MORE FORTHRIGHT WITH THE FBI. SHE NOTED THAT HER HUSBAND WAS A CLOSE FRIEND OF J.D. TIPPIT. SHE WENT ON TO OFFER THAT AFTER OFFICER TIPPIT WAS MURDERED THAT MRS. TIPPIT CALLED THE MATHER'S HOME. THE HSCA INTERVIEWED MATHER IN 1977. IN EXCHANGE FOR HIS TESTIMONY HE WAS GRANTED IMMUNITY. ONE IS STILL LEFT TO WONDER HOW HIS PLATES WERE ATTACHED TO A VEHICLE DRIVEN BY **LEE** ONLY 90 MINUTES AFTER THE ASSASSINATION.

2:00PM—2:15 PM FRIDAY

THE "MAGIC BULLET" WAS FOUND BY SENIOR PLANT ENGINEER DARELL TOMLINSON ABOUT 30 MINUTES AFTER RUBY WAS SIGHTED AT PARKLAND BY SETH KANTOR. TOMLINSON INFORMS O.P. WRIGHT, PERSONNEL OFFICER AT PARKLAND, OF THE FINDING. WRIGHT TAKES POSSESSION OF THE SHELL AND IN TURN TURNS IT OVER TO SA RICHARD JOHNSEN. TOMLINSON LATER DESCRIBES THE BULLET AS COPPER-COLORED. HE ALSO NOTED THAT IT DID NOT SHOW ANY TRACES OF BLOOD OR TISSUE AND THAT THE BULLET THEY FOUND THAT DAY HAD A ROUNDED NOSE. THE "MAGIC BULLET, CE-399 HAD A ROUNDED NOSE. A LATER FBI MEMO STATED THAT NEITHER TOMLINSON OR WRIGHT COULD IDENTIFY CE-399 AS THE BULLET THEY FOUND ON THE STRETCHER ON NOVEMBER 22ND. THE BULLET WAS FOUND UNDER THE CORNER OF MATTRESS ON A STRETCHER. THE STRETCHER WAS LOCATED IN THE HALLWAY OF THE EMERGENCY DEPARTMENT. WE WILL DISCUSS CE-399 AND IT'S NECESSITY IN CHAPTER 20.

*I WOULD OFFER THE POSSIBILITY THAT RUBY'S SOLE PURPOSE AT PARKLAND WAS TO PLANT A BULLET THAT WOULD HOPEFULLY TIE THE RIFLE FOUND IN THE TSBD TO THE WOUNDS INFLICTED ON THE PRESIDENT AND GOVENOR CONNALLY. BUT, DID RUBY KNOW THAT THE ALLEGED ASSASSINATION WEAPON WOULD IN TURN BE TIED TO **HARVEY**? BY THIS TIME RUBY IS AWARE OF TWO THINGS: THE PRESIDENT'S DEATH AND, IF MY THEORY ABOUT **HARVEY** IS CORRECT, THAT **HARVEY** IS ABOUT TO EMBARK ON AN "INTELLIGENCE ASSIGNMENT" TO CUBA VIA MEXICO CITY. I DO NOT BELIEVE HOWEVER THAT RUBY, AT THIS POINT, REALIZES THAT THE RECIPIENT OF HIS INCRIMINATING ACTION IS **HARVEY** OR THAT **HARVEY** IS BEING PURSUED AS THE SUSPECTED ASSASSIN OF THE PRESIDENT AND AS THE ALLEGED ASSAILANT OF OFFICER TIPPIT. RUBY'S PERSPECTIVE MAY WELL BE THAT HE IS SIMPLY PLANTING EVIDENCE THAT WILL TIE CASTRO SUPPORTERS TO THE SHOTS FIRED ON THE MOTORCADE THUS ENHANCING THE POSSIBITY OF A RETALIATORY REMOVAL OF CASTRO. RUBY HOWEVER WOULD LATER DENY HAVING BEEN AT PARKLAND WHEN QUESTIONED BY THE COMMISSION.*

IF RUBY DID NOT PLANT WHAT WAS LATER LABELLED C.E. 399 THE ONLY OTHER LOGICAL CONCLUSION IS THAT THE BULLET WAS THE LOW VELOCITY BULLET THAT STRUCK THE PRESIDENT IN THE UPPER BACK WITH NO POINT OF EXIT OTHER THAN THE INITIAL POINT OF ENTRY. ALTHOUGH THIS NOTION IS CONSIDERABLY MORE PLAUSIBLE THAN THE 7-WOUND-2-VICTIM SCENARIO OFFERED BY THE W.C., IT WOULD BE VIRTUALLY IMPOSSIBLE FOR THIS MISSLE TO BE VOID OF ANY HUMAN BLOOD OR TISSUE. I AM MUCH MORE INCLINED TO BELIEVE THAT CE399 WAS THE BULLET RETRIEVED BY FBI AGENT ROBERT BARRETT FROM THE SOUTH SIDE OF DEALEY PLAZA THAT HAD IMBEDDED ITSELF IN THE GRASS. THIS WOULD EXPLAIN THE LACK OF HUMAN TISSUE OR BLOOD AS THIS NEAR PRISTINE BULLET STRUCK NEITHER THE PRESIDENT OR CONNALLY.

THERE ARE HOWEVER 2 OTHER POSSIBILITIES REGARDING THE PLANTING OF CE399. THE SECRET SERVICE HAD TO RESTRAIN AN FBI AGENT NAMED DOYLE WILLIAMS FROM FORCING HIS WAY INTO THE ER ROOM CONTAINING THE DECEASED PRESIDENT. WILLIAM'S SOMEWHAT QUESTIONABLE EXCUSE WAS THAT HE HAD TO INFORM THE SECRET SERVICE THAT THE FBI WAS STANDING BY AND READY TO ASSIST THEM. THE W.C. DID NOT PURSUE QUESTIONING SA WILLIAMS NOR DID THEY QUESTION WITNESSES TO THE INCIDENT. NOTED RESEARCHER HAROLD WEISBERG STATED THAT THERE WAS A POLITICALLY-ACTIVE CUBAN EMPLOYED AT PARKLAND IN NOVEMBER OF 1963. NEITHER THE W.C. OR THE SECRET SERVICE SOUGHT TO IDENTIFY THIS INDIVIDUAL. ONE WOULD HAVE TO INCLUDE THE POSSIBILITY THAT EITHER OF THESE INDIVIDUALS COULD HAVE BEEN RESPONSIBLE FOR THE APPEARANCE OF CE 399.

DONALD BYRON THOMAS' EXCELLENT BOOK "HEAR NO EVIL" OFFERS A PLAUSIBLE SEQUENCE OF EVENTS AS TO HOW CE399 <u>AND</u> A BONE FRAGMENT FROM THE PRESIDENT'S SKULL WERE TRANSPORTED FROM DEALEY PLAZA TO PARKLAND. HE PROPOSES THAT THE BULLET WAS RETRIEVED FROM THE LAWN OF DEALEY PLAZA BY FBI AGENT ROBERT BARRETT. THE MISSLE IS THEN PASSED ON TO FBI AGENT DOYLE WILLIAMS. THE BONE FRAGMENT, DISCOVERED BY CONSTABLE SEYMOUR WEITZMANN ON THE SOUTH SIDE OF ELM STREET WAS, BY HIS ACCOUNT, TURNED OVER TO THE SECRET SERVICE IN DEALEY PLAZA. THERE WERE HOWEVER NO SS AGENTS IN DEALEY PLAZA; THEY WOULD REMAIN WITH THE MOTORCADE. IT IS FBI AGENT ROBERT BARRETT WHO RECEIVES THE BONE FRAGMENT FROM WEITZMANN. BARRETT WOULD IN THEN TURN THE FRAGMENT OVER TO FBI AGENT DOYLE WILLIAMS. WILLIAMS WOULD NOW TRANSPORT BOTH THE FRAGMENT <u>AND</u> THE BULLET TO PARKLAND. IT WOULD BE WILLIAMS WHO PLACES THE BULLET ON THE STRETCHER OUTSIDE THE OR AT PARKLAND WHERE IT IS DISCOVERED BY DARELL TOMLINSON WHO PROMPTLY GIVES IT TO O.P. WRIGHT THE PERSONNEL OFFICER AT PARKLAND. WRIGHT IN TURN GIVES IT TO SS AGENT RICHARD JOHNSEN. WILLIAMS HOWEVER IS STILL IN POSSESSION OF THE SKULL FRAGMENT. THIS PROMPTS WILLIAM'S ATTEMPT TO FORCE HIS WAY INTO THE ER TO RETURN THE FRAGMENT TO A SITE NEAR THE PRESIDENT'S BODY WHERE IT COULD NOT POSSIBLY BE MISSED.

THOMAS NOTES THAT IT IS LIKELY THAT FBI AGENT ROBERT BARRETT DELIBERATELY AND FALSELY IDENTIFIED HIMSELF AS A SS AGENT WHEN RECEIVING THE SKULL FRAGMENT FROM WEITZMANN AND THAT FBI AGENT DOYLE WILLIAMS MADE EVERY EFFORT TO <u>NOT</u> IDENTIFY HIMSELF AS FBI WHEN HE TRIED TO FORCE HIS WAY INTO THE ER AT PARKLAND. IT APPEARS THAT THE FBI WAS DETERMINED TO TURN OVER WHAT WOULD BE CONSIDERED VALUABLE EVIDENCE IN THE SHOOTING, BUT WAS DELIBERATELY TRYING TO CONCEAL THE FACT THAT AGENTS BARRETT AND WILLIAMS WERE IN DEALEY PLAZA, AND THAT WILLIAMS AND POSSIBLY BARRETT WERE AT PARKLAND. THE FBI WOULD SOON BE FACED WITH THE PROBLEM OF **HARVEY** AND HIS RELATIONSHIP TO THE AGENCY. THEY COULD ILL AFFORD TO TIE TWO OF THEIR AGENTS TO RECEIVING CRUCIAL EVIDENCE IN DEALEY PLAZA AND TRANSPORTING IT TO PARKLAND PARTICULARLY SINCE THERE WERE NO FBI AGENTS ASSIGNED TO DEALY PLAZA THAT DAY. THE AGENTS ARRIVED AFTER THE SHOOTING.

2:02 PM FRIDAY

THE SQUAD CAR CONTAINING OFFICERS C.T. WALKER, BOB CARROLL, PAUL BENTLEY, GERALD HILL, K. E. LYONS AND **HARVEY** ARRIVE AT THE BASEMENT OF CITY HALL.

ALTHOUGH NOTHING WAS RECORDED, HARVEY DID INDEED COMMENT ON HIS ARREST BOTH PRIOR TO ENTERING THE SQUAD CAR AND IN TRANSIT TO THE POLICE STATION:

"I AM NOT RESISTING ARREST."

"WHY AM I BEING ARRESTED?"

"WHAT IS THIS ALL ABOUT?"

"I DON'T KNOW WHY YOU ARE TREATING ME LIKE THIS."

"I DON'T SEE WHY YOU HANDCUFFED ME."

"I PROTEST THIS POLICE BRUTALITY…I FOUGHT BACK THERE, **BUT I KNOW I WASN'T SUPPOSED TO BE CARRYING A GUN.**"

I AM NOT BEING HANDLED RIGHT."

"I HAVE BEEN IN THE MARINE CORP, HAVE A DISHONORABLE DISCHARGE, AND WENT TO RUSSIA."

"I HAD SOME TROUBLE WITH POLICE IN NEW ORLEANS FOR PASSING OUT PRO-CASTRO LITERATURE."

"NO, HIDELL IS NOT MY REAL NAME."

"THE ONLY THING I HAVE DONE IS CARRY A PISTOL INTO A MOVIE."

"I DIDN'T KILL ANYBODY………….I HAVEN'T SHOT ANYBODY."
"I WANT A LAWYER."

IT IS INTERESTING THAT **HARVEY'S** COMMENT REGARDING THE GUN SUPPORTS THE COMMENT BY MICHAEL PAINE THAT **HARVEY** WAS NOT SUPPOSED TO BE CARRYING A GUN THAT AFTERNOON.

WAS **HARVEY** INDEED RELUCTANTLY ARMED BY RUBY IN SPITE OF HIS UNDERSTANDING THAT HE WAS NOT SUPPOSED TO BE CARRYING A GUN AS NOTED BY PAINE? IF SO, EITHER RUBY, WHO OFTEN CARRIED A PISTOL, SINCERELY BELIEVED HE WAS OFFERING **HARVEY**

SOME LEVEL OF PROTECTION FOR HIS UPCOMING "ASSIGNMENT" OR HE WAS UNWITTINGLY SETTING UP **HARVEY** FOR A AS-SOON-AS-POSSIBLE FATAL ENCOUNTER WITH LAW ENFORCEMENT.

HARVEY, IN PROFESSING BOTH HIS IGNORANCE OF WHAT HAD TAKEN PLACE SINCE 12:30 AND HIS INSISTANCE THAT HE DID NOT KNOW WHY HE WAS BEING ARRESTED ENCOURAGED HIM TO BE CANDID IN REGARDS TO HIS DISCHARGE STATUS FROM THE MARINES, HIS RUSSIAN TRIP, AND HIS PRO-CASTRO LEANINGS. OFFICER L.T. WALKER WOULD NOTE THAT **HARVEY** OFFERED LITTLE OF SUBSTANCE BUT THAT "HE WAS JUST DENYING HE KILLED OFFICER TIPPIT." SERGEANT HILL ALSO THOUGHT IT NOTEWORTHY THAT **HARVEY** WAS FOR THE MOST PART QUIET AND "SHOWED ABSOLUTELY NO EMOTION." HILL WOULD ALSO NOTE THAT AS THEY PULLED INTO THE BASEMENT OF THE STATION, HE ASKED **HARVEY** IF HE WISHED TO HAVE HIS FACE HIDDEN UPON EXITING THE CAR. HE REPLIED: "WHY SHOULD I HIDE MY FACE? I HAVEN'T DONE ANYTHING TO BE ASHAMED OF."

THE "I AM NOT BEING HANDLED RIGHT" COMMENT CLEARLY REFLECTS **HARVEY'S** NOTION THAT HE EXPECTED SOMEONE FROM EITHER THE FBI, THE CIA, OR THE ONI TO OFFER HIM ASSISTANCE.

CHAPTER 12: DALLAS JAIL: FRIDAY

*AT CITY HALL, EMPLOYEES FROM THE TSBD WERE SITTING IN CHAIRS IN THE HALLWAY WAITING TO BE INTERVIEWED AS **HARVEY** WAS BROUGHT IN. TWO EMPLOYEES COMMENTED: "HELLO LEE. WHAT ARE YOU DOING HERE?" AT THIS POINT, OFFICERS REALIZED THAT **HARVEY** WORKED AT THE TSBD.*

2:05 PM FRIDAY
RUBY, WHO HAS ARRIVED AT THE CAROUSEL CLUB, TELEPHONES HIS SISTER IN CHICAGO. HE WOULD MAKE SEVERAL MORE CALLS PRIOR TO LEAVING THE CLUB.

2:06 PM FRIDAY
HARVEY IS <u>INFORMALLY</u> QUESTIONED IN THE 3RD FLOOR HOMICIDE AND ROBBERY OFFICE BY OFFICER C.T. WALKER. WALKER NOTED THAT HE HAD ASKED **HARVEY**, IN DEFFERENCE TO THE SELECTIVE SERVICE CARD WITH ALEK JAMES HIDELL'S NAME AND **HARVEY'S** PHOTO, "THAT IS YOUR REAL NAME ISN'T IT?" **HARVEY** REPLIED "NO, THAT IS NOT MY REAL NAME." WALKER WENT ON TO NOTE THAT HE APPEARED "CALM…..NOT A BIT NERVOUS."

2:12-2:15 PM FRIDAY
HARVEY'S <u>INFORMAL</u> QUESTIONING CONTINUES JOINED BY OFFICERS GUY F. ROSE AND RICHARD STOVALL. NO NOTES WERE TAKEN.

2:15-2:22 PM FRIDAY
HARVEY IS <u>INFORMALLY</u> QUESTIONED BY DETECTIVE JIM LEAVELLE ALSO. LEAVELLE WOULD NOTE THAT **HARVEY** WAS "CALM…AND GENERALLY VERY COOL IN THE SITUATION HE FOUND HIMSELF IN." HE ADDED THAT **HARVEY** COMMENTED "IF YOU WANT ME TO ADMIT THAT I HIT A COP IN THE MOUTH AT THE THEATER, I'LL ADMIT THAT. BUT, I'M NOT GOING TO ADMIT TO SHOOTING ONE." HE DENIED SHOOTING TIPPIT OR EVEN BEING AT THE SCENE OF THE SHOOTING. LT. LEAVELLE NOTED TO **HARVEY** THAT "WE HAVE WITNESSES THAT SAW YOU LEAVING THAT LOCATION." HE REPLIED "WELL YOU'LL JUST HAVE TO BRING THEM IN."

2:15 PM FRIDAY
LT. CARL DAY COMPLETES A CRIME SCENE SEARCH FORM. ON THE FORM DAY LISTS ONE 6.5 RIFLE AND 2 SPENT HULLS. THERE IS NO MENTION OF THE 1 LIVE ROUND NOR IS THERE MENTION OF A 3RD SPENT HULL. DAY HAD DUSTED 3 SPENT HULLS (CASINGS) AT THE TSBD AT APPROXIMATELY 1:15 PM. THESE WERE THE 3 CASINGS FOUND BY DEPUTY SHERIFF LUKE MOONEY AT 1:05 PM. TWO CASINGS, ONE LIVE ROUND, WHICH WAS FOUND IN THE MANNLICHER-CARCANO BY CAPTAIN FRITZ, AND THE RIFLE ITSELF WERE THEN GIVEN TO FBI AGENT VINCENT DRAIN AND AGENT CHARLES BROWN BY LT. DAY. AGENTS BROWN AND DRAIN THEN FORWARDED THE 2 HULLS, THE ONE LIVE ROUND, AND THE RIFLE TO THE DALLAS FBI OFFICE WHERE AGENT DOYLE WILLIAMS RECEIVED AND PHOTOGRAPHED THE 2 HULLS, THE LIVE ROUND, AND THE RIFLE.

SOMEWHERE BETWEEN 1:15PM, WHEN LT. CARL DAY DUSTS THE 3 SHELL CASINGS AT THE TSBD AND HIS 2:15PM COMPLETION OF THE CRIME SCENE SEARCH FORM, WE HAVE MANAGED TO <u>LOSE</u> ONE OF THE 3 EMPTY CASINGS FOUND BY SHERIFF MOONEY AT 1:05 PM BENEATH THE 6TH FLOOR WINDOW. WE HAVE ALSO MANAGED TO <u>ADD</u> TO THE CRIME SCENE SEARCH FORM 1 LIVE ROUND. THIS MAY HOWEVER BE THE ONE FOUND <u>IN</u> THE RIFLE FOUND AT 1:22 PM ON THE 6TH FLOOR BY DEPUTY SHERIFF E.L. BOONE, DEPUTY CONSTABLE SEYMOUR WEITZMAN, AND CAPTAIN WILL FRITZ. WHAT IS BOTHERSOME IS THE "LOSING" OF THE 3RD EMPTY CASING. IF THERE ARE NOW ONLY TWO EMPTY CASINGS RATHER THAN THE 3 FOUND AT 1:05 PM IS ONE TO ASSUME THAT ONLY TWO SHOTS WERE FIRED FROM THE ALLEGED ASSASSIN'S WINDOW?

MY SUSPICION IS THAT THE 3ʳᴅ EMPTY CASING WAS TAKEN BY AGENT BARDWELL ODOM. IT WAS ODOM WHO, FOR SOME REASON, DROVE LT. DAY TO CITY HALL. WAS THERE AN INHERENT "ADVANTAGE" IN LOSING THE 3ʳᴅ EMPTY HULL? COULD IT LATER BE ARGUED THAT IF 3 SHOTS, (FOUR SHOTS WITH THE LATER DISCOVERED MISSED JAMES TAGUE SHOT) WERE NEXT TO IMPOSSIBLE IN 5.6 SECONDS THAT REDUCING THE NUMBER OF SHOTS FIRED TO 2 WOULD BE MORE PLAUSABLE? MORE RESEARCH NEEDS TO BE DONE REGARDING AGENT ODOM AND THE MISSING 3ʳᴅ SHELL CASING.

2:23 PM FRIDAY

HARVEY'S 1ˢᵀ <u>FORMAL</u> INTERROGATION SESSION WITH HOMICIDE CAPTAIN WILL FRITZ BEGINS. DETECTIVES SIMS, BOYD, AND SS INSPECTOR KELLEY WERE ALSO PRESENT.

COMMENTS <u>ATTRIBUTED</u> TO HARVEY DURING THIS SESSION:

"MY NAME IS LEE HARVEY OSWALD…I WORK AT THE TSBD BUILDING."

"I LIVED IN MINSK AND IN MOSCOW….I WORKED IN A FACTORY."

"I WAS NEVER IN MEXICO CITY… I HAVE BEEN TO TIJUANA." "WHAT MAKES YOU THINK I'VE BEEN TO MEXICO CITY?"

"I OBSERVED A RIFLE IN THE TSBD WHERE I WORK ON NOVEMBER 20ᵀᴴ, 1963…MR. ROY TRULY, THE SUPERVISOR, DISPLAYED THE RIFLE TO INDIVIDUALS IN HIS OFFICE ON THE FIRST FLOOR."

"I NEVER OWNED A RIFLE MYSELF."

"I WAS SECRETARY OF THE FPFC COMMITTEE IN NEW ORLEANS A FEW MONTHS AGO."

"I HAVE A WIFE AND SOME CHILDREN."

"MY RESIDENCE IS 1026 NORTH BECKLEY, DALLAS, TEXAS."

"I WAS PRESENT IN THE TSBD BUILDING…., I HAVE BEEN EMPLOYED THERE SINCE OCTOBER 15ᵀᴴ, 1963 AS A LABORER, I HAVE ACCESS TO THE ENTIRE BUILDING….MY USUAL PLACE OF WORK IS ON THE FIRST FLOOR ..HOWEVER I FREQUENTLY USE THE 4, 5, 6 AND 7ᵀᴴ FLOORS TO GET BOOKS. I WAS ON ALL THE FLOORS THIS MORNING."

"BECAUSE OF ALL THE CONFUSION, I FIGURED THERE WOULD BE NO WORK IN THE AFTERNOON SO I DECIDED TO GO HOME…."

"I AM NOT A MALCONTENT. NOTHING IRRITATED ME ABOUT THE PRESIDENT."

"I DIDN'T SHOOT PRESIDENT KENNEDY OR OFFICER TIPPIT."

I TOOK THE BUS AND WENT HOME…I CHANGED MY CLOTHING AND WENT TO A MOVIE." (HE NOTED THAT THE CLOTHES HE TOOK OFF, THE "DIRTY CLOTHING" WERE A LONG SLEEVE RED SHIRT AND GREY TROUSERS).

NOTE: CAPTAIN WILL FRITZ'S **<u>WRITTEN</u>** NOTES ON THIS TOPIC READ "HOME BY BUS, CHANGED BRITCHES." IF **HARVEY** DID <u>NOT</u> CHANGE SHIRTS, THEN THE SHIRT HE WAS ARRESTED IN IS NEARLY IDENTICAL TO OR IS INDEED THE ONE IN THE ALTGEN'S PHOTO VIRTUALLY ELIMINATING THE POSSIBILITY THAT THE MAN IN THE PHOTO WAS LOVELADY. IT WOULD SEEM TO ME THAT FRITZ'S <u>WRITTEN</u> NOTES WOULD BE MORE RELIABLE THAN COMMENTS MERELY <u>ATTRIBUTED</u> TO **HARVEY** DURING QUESTIONING SINCE IT APPEARS THAT NO ONE TOOK NOTES OTHER THAN FRITZ. FRITZ'S NOTES ALSO READ "HAD LUNCH OUT WITH BILL SHELLEY IN FRONT." THIS IS NO DOUBT IN RESPONSE TO **HARVEY'S** BEING

QUESTIONED ABOUT HIS LOCATION IMMEDIATELY PRIOR TO OR DURING THE SHOOTING SEQUENCE.

*LATER IN FRITZ'S NOTES HE WRITES: "AT APT. CHANGED SHIRT AND TR. (TROUSERS) PUT IN DIRTY CLOTHES LONG SLEEVE RED SHIRT AND GREY TR." WAS FRITZ AT SOME POINT MADE AWARE OF THE IMPORTANCE OF **HARVEY'S** WORK SHIRT AS A RESULT OF THE ALTGEN'S PHOTO AND CORRECTED HIS INITIAL NOTE STATING "CHANGED BRITCHES" TO "CHANGED SHIRT AND TR.?" THE IMPORTANCE OF THE CHANGING OF THE SHIRT CANNOT BE UNDERSTATED. IF **HARVEY** DID INDEED CHANGE HIS SHIRT, THEN HE WOULD HAVE HAD TO HAVE PUT ON A SHIRT IDENTICAL TO OR NEARLY IDENTICAL TO THE ONE HE WORE TO WORK THAT DAY, MISSING BUTTONS AND ALL INCLUDING THE BUS TRANSFER IN THE POCKET. ALTHOUGH THE SHIRT CHANGE TO AN IDENTICAL SHIRT WOULD SEEM UNLIKELY, IT MAY HAVE BEEN THOUGHT TO BE A BETTER ALTERNATIVE THAN TO <u>NOT</u> HAVE HIM CHANGE HIS SHIRT THUS BEING ARRESTED IN A SHIRT IDENTICAL TO THE ONE IN THE ALTGEN'S PHOTO ELIMINATING THE POSSIBILITY THAT THE MAN ON THE STEPS OF THE TSBD AS BEING LOVELADY.*

*ONCE AGAIN, **HARVEY** WAS QUITE CANDID REGARDING HIS TIME IN RUSSIA AND THE FPFC COMMITTEE. HE HOWEVER DENIED HAVING BEEN IN MEXICO CITY AND HAVING EVER OWNED A RIFLE. HE ALSO CLAIMED HE HAD LUNCH WITH BILL SHELLEY "OUT FRONT" AND WAS IN THE 2ND FLOOR BREAK AREA WHEN CONFRONTED BY OFFICER BAKER.*

EARLY AFTERNOON FRIDAY
FBI AGENT DON ADAMS IS INSTRUCTED BY THE ATLANTA OFFICE TO RETURN TO QUITMAN, GEORGIA AND INTERVIEW JOSEPH MILTEER. HE WAS TO DETAIN MILTEER FOR THE SECRET SERVICE. ADAMS WAS GIVEN 6 QUESTIONS TO POSE TO MILTEER. HE WAS VERY POINTEDLY TOLD THAT HE WAS NOT TO PURSUE ANY QUESTIONING BEYOND THE 6 QUESTIONS GIVEN TO HIM BY THE ATLANTA OFFICE. AGENT ADAMS DROVE FROM THOMASVILLE TO BOTH QUITMAN AND VALDOSTA, GEORGIA IN PURSUIT OF MILTEER. ADAMS WOULD FINALLY LOCATE MILTEER ON NOVEMBER 27TH AND CONDUCT THE STRANGELY LIMITED INTERVIEW.

2:27 PM FRIDAY
LESLIE MONTGOMERY, DPD HOMICIDE DETECTIVE, IS PHOTOGRAPHED IN FRONT OF THE TSBD HOLDING THE BAG THAT **HARVEY** ALLEGEDLY USED TO CARRY THE ALLEGED ASSASSINATION RIFLE INTO THE TSBD.

2:30 PM FRIDAY
CARLOS MARCELLO IS ACQUITED IN REGARDS TO HIS DEPORTATION TRIAL IN NEW ORLEANS. FERRIE, HIS PRIVATE PILOT, IS IN THE COURTROOM WITH MARCELLO.

2:38 PM FRIDAY
LBJ IS SWORN IN ON AIR FORCE ONE.

2:46 PM FRIDAY
AIR FORCE ONE LEAVES LOVE FIELD ENROUTE TO WASHINGTON.

2:50 PM FRIDAY
JACK REVILL, DPD LIEUTENANT, ENCOUNTERS FBI AGENT HOSTY AT THE POLICE STATION. HE WOULD NOTE THAT HOSTY TOLD HIM THAT **HARVEY** "WAS A MEMBER OF THE COMMUNIST PARTY."

3:00 PM FRIDAY
RUBY, AFTER CLOSING DOWN THE CAROUSEL CLUB, STOPS AT THE MERCHANT'S STATE BANK.

3:00 PM FRIDAY
HARVEY'S ROOM AT 1026 NORTH BECKLEY IS SEARCHED BY OFFICERS F.M. TURNER, AND N.M. MOORE AND DETECTIVES W.E. POTTS AND B. L. SENKEL.

3:00 PM FRIDAY
WORD REACHES LBJ ON AIR FORCE 1 THAT **HARVEY** HAS A FILE IN THE STATE DEPARTMENT.

3:01 PM FRIDAY
DIRECTOR HOOVER WOULD NOTE THAT HE HAD CALLED THE ATTORNEY GENERAL, ROBERT KENNEDY AND TOLD HIM THAT "OSWALD WENT TO RUSSIA AND STAYED 3 YEARS; CAME BACK TO THE U.S IN JUNE 1962, AND WENT TO CUBA ON SEVERAL OCCASIONS…"

HARVEY HAD NEVER BEEN TO CUBA. THIS REVELATION TO THE ATTORNEY GENERAL WAS MADE ONLY 1 HOUR AFTER HARVEY'S ARREST. HOOVER MOST CERTAINLY WOULD HAVE HAD TO BEEN REFERRING TO LEE IN REGARDS TO THE CUBA VISITS. LEE VISITED CUBA IN EARLY 1961. ACCORDING TO ARMSTRONG, ARMY INTELLIGENCE WAS AWARE OF THIS. HARVEY AT THAT SAME TIME WAS IN RUSSIA.

3:10 PM FRIDAY
UPI QUOTES DR. MALCOLM PERRY: "THERE WAS AN ENTRANCE WOUND BELOW THE ADAM'S APPLE."

3:15 PM FRIDAY
FBI AGENTS JAMES BOOKOUT AND JAMES HOSTY JOIN CAPTAIN FRITZ AS HE INTERROGATES **HARVEY**.

3:15 PM FRIDAY
PARKLAND PHYSICIAN EARL ROSE STARTS THE AUTOPSY ON SLAIN OFFICER J.D. TIPPIT. TIPPIT WAS SHOT 4 TIMES: ONCE IN THE HEAD, TWICE IN THE CHEST, AND ONCE IN THE ABDOMEN. DR. ROSE'S REPORT WOULD BE ISSUED ON DECEMBER 9TH, 1963.

3:15 PM FRIDAY
AT A PRESS CONFERENCE AT PARKLAND, DR. MALCOLM PERRY REITERATES HIS OPINION THAT THE WOUND IN THE PRESIDENT'S NECK IS A WOUND OF ENTRY. DR. KEMP CLARK SUPPORTED PERRY'S ENTRANCE WOUND ANALYSIS.

APPROXIMATELY 3:15 FRIDAY
RUBY DRIVES TO THE APARTMENT OF HIS SISTER, EVA GRANT.

3:30 PM FRIDAY
"MARGUERITE" ARRIVES AT THE DPD. SHE IS SOON JOINED BY MARINA.

ARMSTRONG POINTS OUT THAT "MARGUERITE"IS SHORTER THEN MARINA WHO IS 5'1. THERE ARE SEVERAL PHOTOS TAKEN IN JAIL THAT SUPPORT THS. LEE'S MOTHER MARGUERITE IS 5'7".

3:30 PM FRIDAY
THE PAINE RESIDENCE AT 2515 5TH STREET IS SEARCHED BY DETECTIVE N. STOVALL, DETECTIVE G.F. ROSE, DETECTIVE J.P. ADAMCIK, AND DEPUTY SHERIFFS HARRY WEATHERFORD AND J.L. OXFORD.

RUTH PAINE'S ODD RESPONSE TO THER ARRIVAL WAS "I'VE BEEN EXPECTING YOU ALL." SHE LATER NOTED "JUST AS SOON AS I HEARD WHERE THE SHOOTING HAPPENED I KNEW THERE WOULD BE SOMEONE OUT." MICHAEL PAINE ARRIVED WITHIN MINUTES OF THE OFFICERS. HE STATED TO RUTH "JUST AS SOON AS I FOUND WHERE IT HAPPENED I KNEW YOU WOULD NEED SOME HELP." I AM VERY MUCH INCLINED TO BELIEVE THAT THE PAINE'S WERE PRIVY TO WHAT WAS TO BE AN "ATTEMPT" ON THE PRESIDENT'S LIFE. I DO NOT HOWEVER FEEL THAT THEY SUSPECTED HARVEY WOULD BE INVOLVED IN WHAT WOULD PROVE TO BE A SUCCESSFUL ASSASSINATION.

3:35 PM FRIDAY
LIEUTENANT REVILL PREPARES A MEMO FOR CAPTAIN GANNAWAY REFLECTING AGENT HOSTY'S COMMENTS ABOUT **HARVEY**. GANNAWAY WOULD IN TURN FORWARD THIS TO DPD CHIEF CURRY.

3:54 PM FRIDAY
BILL RYAN, A NBC NEWS COMMENTATOR, REMARKED ON A NATIONAL BROADCAST: "LEE HARVEY OSWALD SEEMS TO BE THE PRIME SUSPECT IN THE ASSASSINATION OF JOHN FITZGERALD KENNEDY."

4:00 PM FRIDAY
RUBY STOPPED AT THE RITZ DELICATESSEN. HE THEN RETURNED TO HIS SISTER'S APARTMENT. SHE NOTED LATER THAT WHEN HE ARRIVED "HE DIDN'T SAY NOTHING. HE WENT INTO THE BATHROOM AND THREW UP."

BY THIS TIME RUBY HAS HAD A CHANCE TO ABSORB WHAT HAS TRANSPIRED THAT AFTERNOON:

- *THE PLANNED DIVERSIONARY "FIREWORKS" HAD DISGUISED UNEXPECTED FATAL GUNFIRE…AT LEAST UNEXPECTED TO RUBY AND **HARVEY***

- *THE GUNFIRE HAD KILLED THE PRESIDENT*

- *HIS FRIEND J.D. TIPPIT HAD BEEN SLAIN*

- *THE GUNMAN IN BOTH INSTANCES APPEARS TO HAVE BEEN **HARVEY**.*

*I ALSO FEEL THAT WITH **HARVEY** HAVING AVOIDED A POTENTIAL SHOOTOUT ON THE MARSALIS BUS AND AN EVEN MORE LIKELY SHOOTOUT IN THE TEXAS THEATER THAT THE NEXT ATTEMPT, SINCE HE WAS NOW IN CUSTODY, WOULD HAVE TO BE UNDERTAKEN BY SOMEONE OUTSIDE THE REALM OF LAW ENFORCEMENT. RUBY MAY HAVE ALREADY BEEN INFORMED THAT THIS TASK WOULD FALL TO HIM.*

4:00 PM FRIDAY
LBJ RECEIVES WORD FROM THE SITUATION ROOM AT THE WHITE HOUSE THAT THE ASSASSINATION IS THE ACT OF ONE LONE INDIVIDUAL AND THAT NO CONSPIRACY EXISTS.

*AT THIS TIME **HARVEY** HAS NOT BEEN CHARGED WITH EITHER THE TIPPIT MURDER OR THE PRESIDENT'S DEATH.*

4:00 – 4:30 PM FRIDAY
FERDINAND KAUFMAN, AN AP PHOTOGRAPHER NOTED THAT HE ENCOUNTERED RUBY ON THE 3RD FLOOR AT CITY HALL.

4:01 PM FRIDAY
HOOVER CALLS RFK TO REPORT THAT: "WE THINK WE HAVE THE MAN WHO KILLED THE PRESIDENT DOWN IN DALLAS." HOOVER WENT ON TO DESCRIBE **HARVEY** AS AN EX-MARINE, A DEFECTOR, A PRO-COMMUNIST, AND A "MEAN-MINDED INDIVIDUAL…IN THE CATEGORY OF A NUT."

*ONCE AGAIN NOTE THAT **HARVEY** HAS STILL NOT BEEN FORMALLY CHARGED WITH ANY CRIME. IN FACT, HIS 1ST FORMAL INTERROGATION SESSION WILL NOT END UNTIL 4:05 PM. AT THAT TIME THE DALLAS POLICE WERE STILL UNCERTAIN AS TO WHETHER THEY HAD A "LEE HARVEY OSWALD" OR A "HIDELL" IN CUSTODY. HOOVER SEEMED TO NOT ONLY ALREADY HAVE A GREAT DEAL OF INFORMATION ON **HARVEY**, BUT IS WILLING TO OFFER TO THE SLAIN PRESIDENT'S BROTHER THAT **HARVEY** IS THE PRESIDENT'S ASSASSIN.*

4:05 PM FRIDAY
HARVEY'S 1ST FORMAL INTERROGATION SESSION ENDS. SOME RESEARCHERS CONSIDER THIS MORE OF AN "INTERRUPTION" OF HIS 1ST FORMAL INTERROGATION. HE DENIED SHOOTING THE PRESIDENT AND OFFICER TIPPIT. HE IS THEN SEARCHED FOR THE FIRST TIME SINCE ARRIVING AT CITY HALL. THE SEARCH IS CONDUCTED BY DETECTIVES SIMS AND BOYD. THEY FIND FIVE .38 CALIBER BULLETS, A BUS TRANSFER, #004459, A PAY CHECK STUB, A P.O. BOX KEY, AND CASH AMOUNTING TO $13.87. THE

PAY STUB IS DATED AUGUST 22ND, 1960 AND IS FROM AMERICAN BAKERIES COMPANY. **HARVEY** HOWEVER IS IN RUSSIA AT THAT TIME.

*DURING THIS SESSION CAPTAIN FRITZ COMMENTED TO **HARVEY**: "WE FOUND THIS PAPER IN YOUR WALLET. IT TALKS ABOUT SOMETHING CALLED 'FAIR PLAY FOR CUBA.' NOW WHAT IS THIS LEE?" **HARVEY** NODDED HIS HEAD TOWARDS FBI AGENT JAMES HOSTY AND SAID: "WHY DON'T YOU ASK AGENT HOSTY." THIS WOULD LIKELY BE IN REFERENCE TO HIS BEING QUESTIONED BY THE FBI IN NEW ORLEANS AFTER HIS ARREST FOR HIS SCUFFLE WITH CARLOS BRINGUIER WHILE PASSING OUT FPFC PAMPHLETS. HOWEVER IT IS IMPORTANT TO NOTE THAT THE NEW ORLEANS FPFC POSTURING WAS LIKELY SIMPLY A ROLE DESIGNED FOR HIM BY SET-UP CONSPIRATOR GUY BANISTER. CAPTAIN FRITZ THEN LOOKED OVER TO AGENT HOSTY WHO MERELY <u>GESTURED</u> FOR CAPTAIN FRITZ TO CONTINUE HIS QUESTIONING.*

*THE FBI'S RELUCTANCE TO ACKNOWLEDGE **HARVEY** WOULD BE FURTHER CEMENTED BY WORD FROM WASHINGTON. LATER THAT AFTERNOON, AGENT HARLAN BROWN ENCOUNTERED AGENT HOSTY IN THE HALLWAY OF THE POLICE STATION. BROWN SAID TO HIM: "YOU ARE <u>NOT</u> TO GO BACK IN ON THE INTERROGATION OF OSWALD, AND YOU ARE NOT TO PROVIDE ANY INFORMATION WE HAVE ABOUT OSWALD TO THE POLICE." HOSTY WOULD LATER COMMENT: "I HAVE SINCE DETERMINED THAT THOSE ORDERS CAME DIRECTLY FROM ASSISTANT DIRECTOR WILLIAM SULLIVAN WHO WAS IN CHARGE OF FOREIGN COUNTER- INTELLIGENCE AND DIRECT LIASON TO THE NATIONAL SECURITY COUNCIL." ONE HAS TO WONDER WHY THE QUESTIONING OF A MAN BY LOCAL AUTHORITIES WHO, AT THIS POINT, WAS GUILTY OF NOTHING MORE THAN MISSING A ROLLCALL AND POSSIBLY NOT PAYING FOR ADMISSION TO A THEATER, WOULD WARRANT THE ATTENTION OF THE FBI'S ASSISTANT DIRECTOR. THE FACT THAT SULLIVAN WAS IN CHARGE OF <u>FOREIGN</u> COUNTER INTELLIGENCE IS OF PARTICULAR SIGNIFICANCE IN **HARVEY'S** CASE.*

*LATER IN AN AFFADAVIT TO THE WARREN COMMISSION, HOOVER STATED THAT **HARVEY'S** INTERROGATION BY THE FBI THAT DAY WAS: "TO OBTAIN ANY INFO HE MIGHT HAVE BEEN ABLE TO FURNISH OF A <u>SECURITY NATURE</u>." THIS IS CERTAINLY THE TYPE OF INFORMATION ONE WOULD EXPECT FROM A PAID INFORMANT.*

*HOOVER WOULD LATER ADMIT THAT <u>SEVEN</u> AGENTS INTERVIEWED **HARVEY** AFTER HIS ARREST. NONE TOOK NOTES AND NONE TAPED THE INTERROGATION SESSIONS.*

*DETECTIVE RICHARD SIMS WAS ALSO PRESENT DURING THIS SESSION. SIMS NOTED "HE (**HARVEY**) CONDUCTED HIMSELF, I BELIEVE, BETTER THAN ANYONE I HAVE EVER SEEN DURING INTERROGATION. HE WAS CALM AND WASN'T NERVOUS."*

NOTE
*IT IS IMPERATIVE TO POINT OUT THAT AMONG **HARVEY'S** POSSESSIONS IS BUS TRANSFER #004459. HE OBTAINED THE TRANSFER WHEN HE DEPARTED CECIL MCWATTER'S #1213 MARSALIS BUS AT 12:39 PM. THIS TRANSFER WAS IDENTIFIED BY MCWATTERS AS THE ONE HE GAVE TO **HARVEY** AS MCWATTERS NOTED THAT THE STAMP ON THE TRANSFER WAS HIS. IF THIS TRANSFER WAS FOUND IN THE SHIRT POCKET OF THE SHIRT **HARVEY** WAS WEARING WHEN <u>ARRESTED</u> THEN IT IS THE SAME SHIRT HE WORE <u>TO WORK</u> THAT DAY AND MORE IMPORTANTLY THE SAME SHIRT HE WAS WEARING <u>ON THE STEPS OF THE TSBD</u> AT THE TIME OF THE SHOOTING WHEN HE WAS CAPTURED BY PHOTOGRAPHER JAMES ALTGENS. **HARVEY** WAS NOT ON THE 6TH FLOOR. HE WAS CLEARLY ON THE STEPS OF THE TSBD AT 12:30 PM. **HARVEY** DID <u>NOT</u> CHANGE SHIRTS AT HIS ROOMING HOUSE AS CAPTAIN FRITZ ALLUDED TO IN HIS HANDWRITTEN NOTES.*

4:15 PM FRIDAY
IN ANOTHER NOTE, DIRECTOR HOOVER STATED "OSWALD MADE SEVERAL TRIPS TO CUBA, UPON HIS RETURN EACH TIME WE INTERVIEWED HIM ABOUT WHAT HE WENT TO CUBA FOR AND HE ANSWERED THAT IT WAS NONE OF OUR BUSINESS."

*ONCE AGAIN, THIS WOULD MOST CERTAINLY HAVE BEEN IN REGARDS TO **LEE**, NOT **HARVEY**. BUT, MORE IMPORTANTLY IT REVEALS THAT THE FBI HAD INTERVIEWED BOTH **HARVEY** AND **LEE** REGARDING THEIR RESPECTIVE CUBA CONNECTIONS.*

4:30 -7:30 PM FRIDAY

WFAA REPORTER W.C. ROBERTSON NOTED THAT HE SAW RUBY ATTEMPT TO ENTER THE 3RD FLOOR HOMICIDE OFFICE. TWO OFFICERS, R.B. COUNTS AND C.F. GOODSON STOPPED RUBY'S ATTEMPT TO ENTER THE OFFICE WITH THIS ADMONITION: "YOU CAN'T GO IN THERE JACK." GOODSON AND COUNTS HOWEVER LATER DENIED HAVING SEEN RUBY ANYWHERE DURING THIS TIME FRAME.

A REPORTER, JOHN RUTLEDGE, AND DETECTIVE, RAY STANDIFER NOTED THAT THEY SAW RUBY AT THE DALLAS POLICE STATION IN VARIOUS LOCALES AND AT VARIOUS TIMES DURING THIS 3 HOUR INTERVAL. VICTOR ROBERTSON, A REPORTER FOR WFAA ALSO NOTED RUBY'S PRESENCE. HOWEVER HE NOTED THAT RUBY APPEARED TO BE "JOVIAL, JOKING AND LAUGHING."

EVA GRANT, RUBY'S SISTER INSISTS HOWEVER THAT RUBY WAS AT HER APARTMENT AT 4:30 AND REMAINED UNTIL 7:15 PM.

*I WOULD STRONGLY SUSPECT THAT BY THIS POINT RUBY HAD BEEN TASKED WITH THE ASSIGNMENT TO SILENCE **HARVEY**. ONE COULD HAVE CONVINCED HIM ON THE GROUNDS THAT **HARVEY** MIGHT POSSIBLY REVEAL THE "CUBAN ASSIGNMENT" IF HE WERE NOT ELIMINATED SOON. RUBY'S UNWAVERING SENSE OF PATRIOTISM AND PERHAPS MORE IMPORTANTLY THE OPPORTUNITY TO GARNER THE ELUSIVE RECOGNITION HE HAD LONG SOUGHT WOULD PROVE TO BE AN IRRESISTABLE ATTRACTION. PERHAPS IT WAS THIS TASK THAT HAD APPARENTLY TRANSFORMED THE "DOLE AND SOMBER" RUBY OF EARLIER THAT DAY TO THE "JOVIAL, JOKING AND LAUGHING" RUBY WITNESSED BY VICTOR ROBERTSON LATER THAT AFTERNOON.*

4:35 PM FRIDAY

HARVEY IS TAKEN TO HIS FIRST LINEUP AND THEN RETURNED TO CAPTAIN FRITZ OFFICE FOR FURTHER QUESTIONING.

*THIS PARTICULAR LINEUP WAS FOR HELEN MARKHAM, ONE OF THE WITNESSES TO THE TIPPIT MURDER. **HARVEY** COMMENTED REPEATEDLY IN REGARDS TO THE LINEUP:"YOU ARE DOING ME AN INJUSTICE BY PUTTING ME OUT THERE DRESSED DIFFERENT THAN THESE OTHER MEN.....I AM OUT THERE, THE ONLY ONE WITH A BRUISE ON HIS HEAD....I DON'T BELIEVE THE LINEUP IS FAIR, AND I DESIRE TO PUT ON A JACKET SIMILAR TO THOSE WORN BY SOME OF THE OTHER INDIVIDUALS IN THE LINEUP....ALL OF YOU HAVE A SHIRT ON AND I HAVE A T-SHIRT ON. I WANT A SHIRT....THIS SHIRT IS UNFAIR......"*

NOTE: *WHERE IS **HARVEY'S** REDDISH-BROWN SHIRT? WAS IT REMOVED BECAUSE OF ITS MARKED SIMILARITY TO THE ONE WORN BY THE MAN ON THE TOP STEP OF THE TSBD AS THE MOTORCADE PASSED?*

THE OTHER 3 PARTICIPANTS IN THIS LINE-UP WERE DON ABLES, A JAIL GUARD, BILL PERRY, DPD DETECTIVE, AND RICHARD CLARK, ALSO A DPD DETECTIVE. ABLE WORE A WHITE SHIRT AND A SWEATER, PERRY WAS WEARING A SPORT COAT, AND CLARK WAS WEARING A SPORT SHIRT AND A VEST.

*WHEN QUESTIONED BY THE W.C. MARKHAM STATED THAT AT THE LINEUP SHE COMMENTED "I DIDN'T KNOW NOBODY.....I HAD NEVER SEEN NONE OF THEM." SHE THEN PROCEEDS TO SAY "NUMBER 2 (**HARVEY**) WAS THE MAN I SAW SHOOT THE POLICEMAN." BUT SHE FOLLOWS THAT STATEMENT BY SAYING "WHEN I SAW THIS MAN, I WASN'T SURE, BUT I HAD COLD CHILLS JUST RUN ALL OVER ME."*

IT IS WORTH NOTING THAT COMMISSION LAWYER WESLEY LIEBLER STATED LATER THAT MARKHAM'S TESTIMONY WAS "CONTRADICTORY AND WORTHLESS." COMMISSION

COUNSEL JOSEPH BALL WAS LESS KIND IN STATING THAT SHE WAS AN "UTTER SCREWBALL."

4:45 PM FRIDAY
HARVEY'S <u>SECOND</u> **FORMAL INTERROGATION SESSION BEGINS.**

NOTE: SOME RESEARCHERS CONSIDER THIS AS MORE OF A CONTINUATION OF HIS <u>FIRST</u> FORMAL INTERROGATION AS THE FIRST ONE WAS INTERRUPTED FOR THE HELEN MARKUM LINEUP.

AT THIS SESSION FURTHER COMMENTS ARE <u>ATTRIBUTED</u> TO HARVEY REGARDING HIS ACTIVITIES THAT AFTERNOON:

"WHEN I LEFT THE TSBD, I WENT TO MY ROOM WHERE I CHANGED MY TROUSERS AND SHIRT,* GOT A PISTOL, AND WENT TO A PICTURE SHOW."

"YOU KNOW HOW BOYS DO WHEN THEY HAVE A GUN, THEY CARRY IT..."

"YES I HAD WRITTEN TO THE RUSSIAN EMBASSY..."

"THE ONLY PACKAGE I BROUGHT TO WORK WAS MY LUNCH..."

"I NEVER ORDERED ANY GUNS."

"HOW COULD I AFFORD A RIFLE ON THE BOOK DEPOSITORY SALARY OF $1.25 AN HOUR."

"ABT WILL UNDERSTAND WHAT THIS CASE IS ALL ABOUT."

"AS I SAID, THE FPFC COMMITTEE HAS DEFINITELY BEEN INVESTIGATED, THAT IS VERY TRUE....THE RESULTS OF THAT INVESTIGATION WERE ZERO, THE FPFC COMMITTEE IS <u>NOT</u> ON THE ATTORNEY GENERAL'S SUBVERSIVE LIST."

HARVEY'S COMMENTS REGARDING THE FPFC ARE INTERESTING. IF WHAT HE STATES IS VALID, THEN THE FPFC WAS INDEED NOTHING MORE THAN A MEANS BY WHICH THE SET-UP CONSPIRATORS CHOSE TO TIE HIM TO A PRO-CASTRO ORGANIZATION VIA THE NAME *"HIDELL"* WHICH WOULD IN TURN BE TIED TO THE MAIL-ORDER OF THE WEAPONS USED ON NOVEMBER 22ND.

* ONCE AGAIN, **HARVEY'S** ALLEGED COMMENTS REGARDING HIS STOP AT HIS ROOMING HOUSE TO CHANGE CLOTHES ARE WORTH NOTING. HE WAS ALLEGED TO HAVE DESCRIBED THE DIRTY CLOTHES HE CHANGED <u>FROM</u> AS A REDDISH-COLORED LONG SLEEVE SHIRT WITH A BUTTON DOWN COLLAR AND GREY SLACKS. HE ALLEGEDLY TOLD THOSE PRESENT THAT HE PLACED THOSE CLOTHES IN THE BOTTOM DRAWER OF HIS DRESSER. AN INVENTORY OF **HARVEY'S** POSSESSIONS FOUND AT 1026 NORTH BECKLEY INCLUDED A REDDISH-BROWN LONG SLEEVE SHIRT WITH A BUTTON DOWN COLLAR AND A PAIR OF GREY PANTS. BUT THE FACT THAT THESE TWO ITEMS OF CLOTHING WERE APPARENTLY FOUND IN HIS DRESSER DOES NOT PROVE THAT HE HAD ACTUALLY "CHANGED" FROM THOSE TWO PARTICULAR ITEMS OF CLOTHING TO WHAT WOULD PROVE TO BE TWO VIRTUALLY IDENTICAL ITEMS OF CLOTHING THAT HE WAS WEARING AT THE TIME OF HIS ARREST.

A LATER **TYPED** REPORT BY CAPTAIN FRITZ REGARDING THE INTERROGATION OF **HARVEY** WOULD NOTE THAT ON FRIDAY **HARVEY** ONLY MENTIONED CHANGING HIS <u>TROUSERS</u> DURING HIS 1:00 PM STOP AT HIS ROOMING HOUSE. ONCE AGAIN THE COMMENTS <u>ATTRIBUTED</u> TO **HARVEY** REGARDING THE CLOTHING CHANGE VARY FROM THE HANDWRITTEN AND LATER TYPED NOTES OF CAPTAIN FRITZ.

LATE AFTERNOON FRIDAY

GUY BANISTER SPENT THE AFTERNOON DRINKING WITH HIS PART-TIME INVESTIGATOR JACK MARTIN. AFTER **HARVEY'S** ARREST, MARTIN MENTIONED **HARVEY'S** NUMEROUS APPEARANCES AT THE CAMP ST. OFFICE THAT SUMMER. BANISTER'S VIOLENT RESPONSE WAS TO PISTOL-WHIP HIM. MARTIN WENT TO CHARITY HOSPITAL. MARTIN SPOKE WITH POLICE THAT EVENING BUT DID NOT FILE CHARGES AGAINST BANISTER. BANISTER'S VIOLENT OUTBURST HAD THE DESIRED EFFECT. MARTIN CHOSE <u>NOT</u> TO LINK BANISTER WITH **HARVEY**. HE DID HOWEVER LINK DAVID FERRIE TO **HARVEY**.

*MARTIN NOTED THAT EARLIER IN THE DAY BANISTER APPEARED TO BE SOMEWHAT PLEASED THAT THE PRESIDENT HAD BEEN SHOT. HOWEVER AS REPORTS SOON MENTIONED THAT THE SUSPECT WAS **HARVEY** MARTIN NOTED THAT BANISTER BECAME UPSET AND INCREASINGLY ANGRY. DID BANISTER PERHAPS FEEL THAT **HARVEY** HAD DECEIVED HIM AND HAD BEEN "TURNED" DURING HIS PRO-CASTRO POSTURING? OR, DID BANISTER SENSE THAT BOTH HE AND FERRIE HAD BEEN USED BY THE SET-UP CONSPIRATORS PHILLIPS AND HUNT?*

5:30 – 7:30 PM FRIDAY
RONALD JENKINS, AN ANNOUNCER FOR KBOX RADIO IN DALLAS NOTED THAT HE SAW RUBY OUTSIDE CAPTAIN FRITZ'S OFFICE. **HARVEY** IS BEING INTERROGATED FROM 4:45 UNTIL 6:20 PM IN FRITZ'S OFFICE.

5:43 PM FRIDAY
AN FBI TELETYPE FROM THE ATLANTA OFFICE TO THE DIRECTOR CLAIMS THAT JOSEPH MILTEER WAS IN QUITMAN, GEORGIA THAT DAY.

THIS OF COURSE CONTRADICTS AGENT ADAMS WHO HAD BEEN SENT TO QUITMAN TO INTERVIEW MILTEER THAT VERY DAY. ADAMS NOTES THAT HE WAS UNABLE TO LOCATE MILTEER UNTIL NOVEMBER 27TH. THE TELETYPE WILL ALSO PROVE TO BE CONTRADICTORY TO THE PHOTO TAKEN EARLIER IN THE DAY WHICH SHOWS MILTEER IN DEALY PLAZA. WHO AT THE ATLANTA OFFICE WAS VOUCHING FOR MILTEER'S PRESENCE IN GEORGIA WITHOUT CORROBORATION FROM AGENT ADAMS, THE FBI IN WASHINGTON, AND, IN SPITE OF THE PHOTOGRAPHIC EVIDENCE WHICH CLEARLY SHOWS MILTEER IN DEALY PLAZA? EVEN MORE AMAZING IS THAT SOMEONE AT THE FBI OFFICE IN ATLANTA VOUCHED FOR HIS PRESENCE IN QUITMAN WHEN MILTEER ADMITTED TO INFORMANT SOMERSETT THAT HE WAS INDEED IN DALLAS WHEN HE CALLED SOMERSETT THE MORNING OF THE ASSASSINATION.

5:59 PM FRIDAY
AIR FORCE ONE ARRIVES IN WASHINGTON LANDING AT ANDREWS AIR FORCE BASE. THOSE ON BOARD WERE TOLD THAT THERE WAS NO CONSPIRACY AND THAT A LEE HARVEY OSWALD HAD BEEN ARRESTED. AIR FORCE ONE WAS INFORMED OF THIS BY THE WHITE HOUSE SITUATION ROOM. **HARVEY** WOULD NOT BE CHARGED WITH THE PRESIDENT'S DEATH UNTIL 11:26 PM DALLAS TIME.

6:00-7:00 PM FRIDAY
DETECTIVE AUGUST EBERHARDT RECALLED CONVERSING WITH JACK RUBY ON THE THIRD FLOOR OF THE POLICE STATION.

6:09 PM FRIDAY
HARVEY IS INTERVIEWED FOR THE FIRST TIME BY POSTAL INSPECTOR HARRY HOLMES.

6:16 PM FRIDAY
THE RIFLE ALLEGEDLY USED IN THE ASSASSINATION IS SHOWN TO THE PRESS IN THE HALLWAY AT THE POLICE STATION. THERE IS NO SCOPE ON THE RIFLE.

6:20 PM FRIDAY

HARVEY'S SECOND FORMAL INTERROGATION SESSION ENDS AND HE IS TAKEN TO HIS SECOND LINEUP. HE IS THEN RETURNED TO CAPTAIN FRITZ'S OFFICE. THIS LINE-UP CONSISTED OF THE SAME MEN WHO PARTICIPATED IN THE FIRST LINE-UP.

STATEMENTS ATTRIBUTED TO HARVEY DURING THIS SESSION:

"MR. HOSTY (FBI AGENT JAMES HOSTY) YOU HAVE BEEN ACCOSTING MY WIFE…YOU MISTREATED HER ON TWO DIFFERENT OCCASIONS….HE PRACTICALLY TOLD HER THAT SHE WOULD HAVE TO GO BACK TO RUSSIA…."

"I WANT THAT ATTORNEY IN NEW YORK, MR. ABT….I DON'T KNOW HIM PERSONALLY, BUT I KNOW ABOUT A CASE THAT HE HANDLED SOME YEARS AGO WHERE HE REPRESENTED THE PEOPLE WHO HAD VIOLATED THE SMITH ACT."

"IF I CAN'T GET HIM, THEN I MAY GET THE ACLU TO SEND ME AN ATTORNEY."

"I WENT TO SCHOOL IN NEW YORK AND FORT WORTH."
"I SUPPORT THE CASTRO REVOLUTION."

"THE ONLY PACKAGE I BROUGHT TO WORK WAS MY LUNCH."

"I BOUGHT A PISTOL IN FORT WORTH SEVERAL MONTHS AGO…I REFUSE TO TELL YOU WHERE THE PISTOL WAS PURCHASED."

"I NEVER ORDERED ANY GUNS."

"AS I SAID, THE FPFC HAS DEFINITELY BEEN INVESTIGATED…THE RESULTS OF THAT INVESTIGATION WERE ZERO…THE FPFC IS NOW NOT ON THE ATTORNEY GENERAL'S SUBVERSIVE LIST."

ON HIS WAY FROM THE LINEUP TO THE ARRAIGNMENT, **HARVEY** SHOUTS TO REPORTERS IN THE HALLWAY:

"I DIDN'T SHOOT ANYONE….I DIDN'T KILL ANYBODY."

"YES I DID RIDE IN THE CAB. I TOLD YOU WRONG ABOUT TAKING THE BUS HOME. THE BUS I GOT ON NEAR WHERE I WORK GOT INTO HEAVY TRAFFIC AND WAS TRAVELLING TOO SLOW. I GOT OFF AND CAUGHT A CAB…THE FARE WAS 85 CENTS."

"THE ONLY LAW I HAVE VIOLATED WAS IN THE SHOW….I HIT THE OFFICER IN THE SHOW…HE HIT ME IN THE EYE AND I GUESS I DESERVED IT….THAT WAS THE ONLY THING I HAVE DONE WRONG."

CAPTAIN FRITZ WOULD LATER NOTE: *"I DON'T BELIEVE HE WAS AFRAID AT ALL…..HE WAS ABOVE AVERAGE FOR INTELLIGENCE. HE DIDN'T TALK LIKE A NUT…HE KNEW EXACTLY WHEN TO QUIT TALKING…HE SEEMED TO ANTICIPATE WHAT I WAS GOING TO ASK."* FRITZ WENT ON TO NOTE *"YOU DIDN'T HAVE TO SIT THERE VERY LONG AND LISTEN TO THEM TALK TO OSWALD TO REALIZE THAT THIS GUY HAD BEEN TRAINED IN INTERROGATION. BY THAT I MEAN RESISTING INTERROGATION."*

6:20 PM FRIDAY

HARVEY IS TAKEN TO HIS THIRD LINEUP. THIS LINEUP INVOLVES SAM GUINYARD, CECIL MCWATTERS, TED CALLAWAY, AND HOWARD BRENNAN. THOSE IN THE LINEUP WITH **HARVEY** ARE BILL PERRY, OFFICER R.L. CLARK, AND DON ABLES, THE JAIL CLERK.

*GUINYARD IDENTIFIED **HARVEY** AS TIPPIT'S ASSAILANT. HE WAS HOWEVER NEVER LESS THAN 50 FEET FROM **LEE** WHO HAD ACTUALLY COMMITED THE CRIME. CALLAWAY, WHO*

*NOTED THAT TIPPIT'S ASSAILANT WAS WEARING A WHITE, SHORT EISENHOWER-TYPE JACKET AND A WHITE T-SHIRT, POINTED OUT TO OFFICERS WITNESSING THE LINEUP THAT THE "OSWALD" AT THE TIPPIT SHOOTING WAS <u>NOT</u> WEARING A BROWN SHIRT AS WAS **HARVEY** IN THE LINEUP. MCWATTERS IDENTIFIED **HARVEY** AS BEING <u>CLOSEST</u> IN APPEARANCE TO THE MAN WHO HAD BOARDED HIS BUS. WHEN BRENNAN WAS ASKED IF **HARVEY** WAS THE MAN WHO HE SAID HE HAD SEEN FIRING THE SHOTS FROM THE TSBD HE REPLIED "I AM SORRY, BUT I CAN'T DO IT. I JUST CAN'T BE POSITIVE. I CANNOT POSITIVELY SAY." THE W.C. PAINTED A SLIGHTLY DIFFERENT PORTRAIT OF BRENNAN'S REMARKS: "BRENNAN TESTIFIED THAT LEE HARVEY OSWALD, WHOM HE VIEWED IN A POLICE LINEUP ON THE NIGHT OF THE ASSASSINATION, WAS THE MAN HE SAW FIRE THE SHOTS FROM THE SIXTH FLOOR WINDOW OF THE DEPOSITORY BUILDING."*

IN THE OCTOBER 2ND, 1964 ISSUE OF LIFE MAGAZINE, BRENNAN WAS DESCRIBED BY COMMISSION MEMBER GERALD FORD AS "THE MOST IMPORTANT WITNESS TO APPEAR BEFORE THE WARREN COMMISSION."

6:37 PM FRIDAY
HARVEY'S <u>THIRD</u> LINEUP IS COMPLETED. HE IS RETURNED TO CAPTAIN FRITZ'S OFFICE.

7:00 PM FRIDAY
JOHN RUTLEDGE, A NIGHT BEAT REPORTER FOR THE DALLAS MORNING NEWS, NOTED RUBY'S PRESENCE IN THE HOMICIDE AND BURGLARY OFFICE. RUBY WAS IDENTIFYING VARIOUS DALLAS OFFICERS FOR THE OUT-OF-STATE PRESS. RUTLEDGE NOTICED RUBY APPROACHING ROOM 317 WHERE **HARVEY** HAD BEEN INTERROGATED. MIKE EVERHARDT, A DALLAS POLICE DETECTIVE, INQUIRED AS TO WHAT RUBY WAS DOING ON THE THIRD FLOOR. RUBY RESPONDED THAT HE WAS ACTING AS AN INTERPRETER FOR THE FOREIGN PRESS. DETECTIVE ROY STANDIFER ALSO SAW RUBY ON THE 3RD FLOOR ABOUT THIS TIME.

ABOUT 7:00 PM FRIDAY
DAVID FERRIE LEAVES NEW ORLEANS FOR KENNER, LOUISIANA. HE IS ACCOMPANIED BY ALVIN BEAUBOEUF AND MELVIN COFFEY. THE TRIO HAS DINNER AT JOHN PAUL'S RESTAURANT IN KENNER.

7:05 PM FRIDAY
HARVEY IS FORMALLY CHARGED WITH THE MURDER OF OFFICER J.D. TIPPIT IN AN AFFADAVIT SIGNED BY JUDGE DAVID JOHNSTON IN CAPTAIN FRITZ'S OFFICE.

7:10 PM FRIDAY
JUDGE JOHNSTON READS THE FORMAL COMPLAINT TO **HARVEY**.

7:15 PM FRIDAY
HARVEY IS INTERROGATED FOR THE 3TH TIME. SIX SECRET SERVICE AGENTS AND 4 FBI AGENTS ARE PRESENT. <u>NONE</u> WERE QUESTIONED BY THE WARREN COMMISSION.

*CHIEF CURRY WOULD LATER STATE REGARDING THE QUESTIONING OF **HARVEY**: "ONE WOULD THINK OSWALD HAD BEEN TRAINED IN INTERROGATION TECHNIQUES..." IN FACT, CAPTAIN FRITZ WOULD POINT BLANK ASK **HARVEY** IF HE HAD ANY INTERROGATION TRAINING. DISTRICT ATTORNEY WILLIAM ALEXANDER WOULD ADD: "IT WAS ALMOST AS IF HE HAD BEEN REHEARSED OR PROGRAMMED TO MEET THE SITUATION HE FOUND HIMSELF IN....THE ONLY RESPONSIBLE DEDUCTION YOU CAN MAKE IS THAT OSWALD WAS A DOUBLE AGENT. OSWALD WAS OBVIOUSLY TRAINED TO RESIST INTERROGATION, HE COULDN'T HAVE KNOWN HOW TO DO IT ON HIS OWN." TRAINED INDEED. THIS SORT OF INTERROGATION TRAINING WOULD OF COURSE BEEN INTEGRAL TO HIS PREPARATION FOR HIS RUSSIAN ASSIGNMENT AS IT WOULD BE A CERTAINTY THAT HE WOULD BE INTERROGATED BY THE SOVIETS IN REGARD TO THE LEGITIMACY OF HIS "DEFECTION" AND HIS OFFERING OF "RADAR SECRETS."*

HARVEY CONTINUED TO REFUSE TO DISCUSS "HIDELL" IN SPITE OF THE FACT THAT NO ONE FROM THE INTELLIGENCE COMMUNITY HAS COME FORTH TO VOUCH FOR HIM. HE CONTINUES TO PROTECT WHO HE CONSIDERS HIS CIA HANDLERS.

7:30 PM FRIDAY
VICTOR ROBERTSON, JR., A REPORTER FOR WFAA T.V., ENCOUNTERS RUBY AS WELL. HE WATCHES AS RUBY TRIES TO ENTER THE INTERROGATION ROOM. RUBY IS STOPPED BY TWO DPD OFFICERS.

RUBY WOULD LATER NOTE THAT HE DID NOT ARRIVE AT THE POLICE STATION UNTIL ABOUT 11:15PM. THE WARREN COMMISSION CHOSE TO ACCEPT RUBY AT HIS WORD AND IGNORE THE ENCOUNTERS NOTED BY THE DETECTIVES AND THE REPORTERS.

*AT THIS POINT IT IS APPARENT THAT RUBY IS STALKING **HARVEY**. HOWEVER IT IS IMPORTANT THAT THE COMMISSION IGNORE EARLIER SIGHTINGS OF RUBY AT THE STATION IF THEY ARE TO OFFER THAT THE SUNDAY MORNING SHOOTING OF **HARVEY** BY RUBY WAS PURELY A SPONTANEOUS ACT.*

7:40 PM FRIDAY
RUBY APPARENTLY HAS LEFT THE DPD STATION. HE THEN STOPPED BY THE CAROUSEL CLUB.

7:40 PM FRIDAY
HARVEY IS TAKEN TO HIS <u>FOURTH</u> LINEUP. THE LINEUP PARTICIPANTS ARE RICHARD BORCHARDT, ELLIS BRAZEL.AND DON ABLES. BORCHARD AND BRAZEL ARE JAIL PRISONERS, ABLES IS THE JAIL CLERK. THIS LINEUP IS FOR THE BENEFIT OF BARBARA DAVIS AND HER SISTER VIRGINIA RUTH DAVIS.

*BARBARA DAVIS, WHO HAD RECALLED THAT THE MAN WHO HAD SHOT TIPPIT WAS WEARING A LIGHT COLORED SHIRT AND A DARK COAT NEVERTHELESS IDENTIFIED **HARVEY** AS THE SHOOTER. VIRGINIA DAVIS WHO HAD RECALLED THAT THE ASSAILANT HAD WORN A BROWNISH-TAN JACKET AND BLACK TROUSERS ALSO IDENTIFIED **HARVEY** AS THE SHOOTER. **LEE** HAD BEEN WEARING DARK SLACKS AND A WHITE T-SHIRT WHEN HE SHOT TIPPIT.*

HARVEY CONTINUES TO COMPLAIN ABOUT THE LINEUPS: "I HAVE BEEN DRESSED DIFFERENTLY THAN THE OTHER THREE....I STILL HAVE ON THE SAME CLOTHES I WAS ARRESTED IN...THE OTHER TWO WERE PRISONERS ALREADY IN JAIL."

HE ALSO COMMENTS: "I INSIST UPON MY CONSTITUTIOINAL RIGHTS. THE WAY YOU ARE TREATING ME, I MIGHT AS WELL BE IN RUSSIA. I WAS NOT GRANTED MY REQUEST TO PUT ON A JACKET SIMILAR TO THOSE WORN BY OTHER INDIVIDUALS IN SOME PREVIOUS LINEUPS."

7:55 PM FRIDAY
HARVEY'S <u>FOURTH</u> FORMAL INTERROGATION SESSION BEGINS.

*BY THIS TIME **HARVEY** APPARENTLY FEELS THAT HE HAS ANSWERED, PERHAPS REPEATEDLY, EVERY QUESTION THAT COULD POSSIBLY BE ASKED REGARDING HIS BACKGROUND AND HIS MOVEMENTS ON NOVEMBER 22ND: "I HAVE TALKED LONG ENOUGH" HE SAID "I DON'T HAVE ANYTHING ELSE TO SAY...I DON'T CARE TO TALK ANYMORE...I AM WAITING FOR SOMEONE TO COME FORWARD TO GIVE ME LEGAL ASSISTANCE."*

HE WENT ON TO COMMENT: "AS TO HOW I GOT HOME...I TOOK A BUS, BUT DUE TO A TRAFFIC JAM, I LEFT THE BUS AND GOT A TAXI CAB."

*IF **HARVEY** IS EXPECTING LEGAL ASSISTANCE FROM THE INTELLIGENCE COMMUNITY, HIS HOPES WILL BE IN VAIN. HOWEVER HE IS ONCE AGAIN CANDID AS TO HIS TRAVELS THAT DAY.*

*SETH KANTOR, A WRITER FOR SCRIPPS-HOWARD IN DALLAS, NOTED THAT IT WAS AT THIS TIME THAT **HARVEY** FIRST UTTERED HIS PROPHETIC "I'M JUST A PATSY." COMMENT.*

8:32 PM FRIDAY
THE NEW ORLEANS PD INFORM THE FBI THAT DAVID FERRIE IS ACQUAINTED WITH **HARVEY** AND IS ASSOCIATED WITH AN ANTI-CASTRO MOVEMENT.

8:55 PM FRIDAY
J. B. HICKS AND ROBERT STUDEBAKER JOIN **HARVEY** IN CAPTAIN FRITZ'S OFFICE TO PERFORM A FINGERPRINT TEST.

HARVEY OBJECTS TO THE TESTS: *"I WILL NOT SIGN THE FINGERPRINT CARD UNTIL I TALK TO MY ATTORNEY....WHAT ARE YOU TRYING TO PROVE WITH THIS PARAFFIN TEST, THAT I FIRED A GUN?.....YOU ARE WASTING YOUR TIME....I DON'T KNOW ANYTHING ABOUT WHAT YOU ARE ACCUSING ME."* THE UNSIGNED FINGERPRINT CARD WILL BECOME AN ISSUE LATER THAT WEEKEND.

9:00 PM FRIDAY
ACCORDING TO HIS DIARY, RUBY IS BACK AT HIS APARTMENT.

9:00 PM FRIDAY
DETECTIVE PETE BARNES JOINS THE FINGERPRINT TEAM AND PERFORMS A PARRAFIN MASK OF **HARVEY'S** HANDS AND RIGHT CHEEK. THE TEST COMES BACK POSITIVE FOR HANDS, BUT NEGATIVE FOR HIS CHEEK. THIS SUGGESTS THAT HE <u>MAY</u> HAVE FIRED A PISTOL, BUT HE HAD <u>NOT</u> FIRED A RIFLE.

IT IS IMPORTANT TO NOTE THE PARRAFIN TEST ON THE HANDS CAME BACK POSITIVE ON <u>BOTH</u> HANDS. THIS ALL BUT EXCLUDES A PISTOL AS BEING THE SOURCE OF THE POWDER SINCE A PISTOL GENERALLY WILL ONLY CONTAMINATE THE HAND IN WHICH THE GUN IS HELD WHILE FIRING.

*THE FBI WOULD TELL THE WARREN COMMISSION THAT THE PARRAFIN TEST WAS UNRELIABLE AND ONLY CONDUCTED BY THE DPD TO GAIN A PSYCHOLOGICAL ADVANTAGE OVER THE SUSPECT. BUT, THE PARRAFIN CASTS WERE THEN SENT TO THE FBI LAB FOR SPECTROSCOPIC ANALYSIS. ONCE AGAIN, THE RIGHT CHEEK CAST WAS NEGATIVE. THE CAST WAS THEN SENT TO THE AEC LAB AT OAK RIDGE, TENNESSEE FOR NEUTRON ACTIVATION ANALYSIS. IT WAS DETERMINED THERE THAT THE RIGHT CHEEK CASTING "COULD NOT BE SPECIFICALLY ASSOCIATED WITH THE RIFLE NOR COULD THE HAND CASTINGS BE LINKED TO REVOLVER CARTRIDGES." THE MOST SENSITIVE OF THE 3 TESTS PERFORMED COULD NOT DEMONSTRATE THAT **HARVEY** HAD FIRED A RIFLE THAT DAY NOR COULD IT DEMONSTRATE THAT HE HAD FIRED A REVOLVER.*

POLICE CHIEF CURRY WOULD LATER COMMENT: ***"WE DON'T HAVE ANY PROOF THAT OSWALD FIRED THE RIFLE AND NEVER DID. NOBODY'S BEEN ABLE TO PUT HIM IN THAT BUILDING WITH A GUN IN HIS HAND."***

WHEN ASKED "DO YOU HAVE ANY EYEWITNESSES TO THE SHOOTING?" CHIEF CURRY'S REPLY WAS: "NO SIR, WE DO NOT."

ABOUT 9:00 PM FRIDAY
FERRIE, COFFEY, AND BEAUBOEUF LEAVE JOHN PAUL'S RESTAURANT IN KENNER, LOUSIANA AND DRIVE TO HOUSTON.

9:10 PM FRIDAY
HARVEY IS INFORMED THAT HE HAS BEEN CHARGED WITH TIPPIT'S MURDER.

APPROXIMATELY 9:45 PM FRIDAY
RUBY REPORTEDLY VISITED A SYNAGOGUE, CONGREGATION SHEARITH ISRAEL.

10:00 PM FRIDAY
COPIES OF A PHOTO OF A MAN PURPORTED TO BE **HARVEY** EXITING THE SOVIET EMBASSY IN MEXICO CITY AND A TAPE OF A PHONE CALL PURPORTEDLY MADE BY **HARVEY** TO THE EMBASSY ON OCTOBER 1ST ARE ENROUTE TO DALLAS.

10:30 PM FRIDAY
RUBY VISITS PHIL'S DELI TO PICK UP SANDWICHES.

11:00 PM FRIDAY
RONALD JENKINS, ANNOUNCER FOR RADIO STATION KBOX, NOTES THE PRESENCE OF RUBY ON THE 3RD FLOOR OF CITY HALL.

RUBY, IN SPITE OF THE NUMEROUS SIGHTINGS EARLIER THAT EVENING WILL INSIST THAT HE DID NOT ARRIVE AT CITY HALL UNTIL ABOUT 11:45 PM. THE W.C. WOULD NOT HAVE HIM ARRIVING AT CITY HALL UNTIL 10:30 PM. THE W.C. WAS NOT ONLY WILLING TO IGNORE THE WITNESSES WHO HAD NOTED RUBY'S PRESENCE AS EARLY AS 6:00 PM, BUT WAS ALSO WILLING TO ACCEPT RUBY'S INSISTANCE THAT HE DID NOT ARRIVE UNTIL ABOUT 11:45 PM.

11:00-11:20 PM FRIDAY
HARVEY IS INFORMALLY "TALKED TO" BY OFFICER JOHN ADAMCIK AND AGENT M. CLEMENTS.

DURING THIS SESSION COMMENTS ATTRIBUTED TO HARVEY WERE:

"I WAS IN RUSSIA TWO YEARS AGO AND LIKED IT IN RUSSIA...."

"I AM 5'9", WEIGH 140 POUNDS, HAVE BROWN HAIR, BLUE-GREY EYES AND HAVE NO TATTOOS OR PERMANENT SCARS."

NOTE: *HARVEY WAS WEIGHED UPON HIS ARREST IN NEW ORLEANS ON AUGUST 9TH, 1963. HIS WEIGHT WAS RECORDED AS 140 POUNDS. HIS ARREST WEIGHT IN DALLAS WAS 132 POUNDS. HE LIKELY RECALLED THE NEW ORLEANS WEIGHT AS HE WOULD HAVE LITTLE REASON TO HAVE WEIGHED HIMSELF SINCE THAT TIME.*

11:26 PM FRIDAY
HARVEY IS FORMALLY CHARGED WITH THE MURDER OF THE PRESIDENT IN AN AFFIDAVIT SIGNED BY JUDGE DAVID JOHNSON.

11:30 PM FRIDAY
DISTRICT ATTORNEY WADE HELD A PRESS CONFERENCE. RUBY, WHEN ASKED BY DETECTIVE A.M. EBERHART WHAT HE WAS DOING THERE AT FIRST SAID: "I BROUGHT THE SANDWICHES." THEN, HOLDING UP A PAD AND PENCIL SAID: "I'M A REPORTER TONIGHT." WADE TELLS THE PRESS THAT **HARVEY** HAD TIES TO THE ANTI-CASTRO "FREE CUBA COMMITTEE." RUBY IMMEDIATELY CORRECTS WADE SHOUTING OUT: "HENRY, THAT'S THE FAIR PLAY FOR CUBA COMMITTEEEE." THE FPFC IS A PRO-CASTRO GROUP.

*THIS WOULD INDICATE THAT RUBY WAS MORE THAN JUST PASSINGLY FAMILIAR WITH **HARVEY** AND HIS BACKGROUND SINCE THIS INFORMATION ABOUT **HARVEY** WAS VIRTUALLY UNKNOWN IN DALLAS AS OF THAT FRIDAY EVENING. HOWEVER BETTY OLIVER, A DANCER FOR RUBY, CLAIMED THAT RUBY INTRODUCED HER TO "MY GOOD FRIEND, **LEE**" AT THE CAROUSEL CLUB 2 WEEKS BEFORE THE ASSASSINATION, .ANOTHER DANCER, JADA, ALSO RECOGNIZED **HARVEY** AS HAVING BEEN IN RUBY'S CLUB. JADA HOWEVER WAS MISTAKEN. IT HAD BEEN **LEE** WHO HAD BEEN A FREQUENT VISITOR TO THE CAROUSEL CLUB, NOT **HARVEY**. RUBY'S CARELESS UTTERANCE WAS LIKELY NOT WELL RECEIVED BY THOSE MANIPULATING **HARVEY** AND THOSE WHO WOULD LATER COERCE RUBY INTO SILENCING **HARVEY**.*

A NEWS PHOTOGRAPHER, TONY RECORD, NOTED THAT PRIOR TO THE START OF THE PRESS CONFERENCE, RUBY HAD ELBOWED HIS WAY TO AND WAS STANDING ON TOP OF A TABLE AT THE REAR OF THE ROOM. RECORD NOTED THAT RUBY WAS INSISTANT ON STANDING ON THE TABLE DESPITE THE FACT THAT HE HAD NO CAMERA.

11:35 PM FRIDAY

CAPTAIN FRITZ FILES A COMPLAINT CHARGING **HARVEY** WITH THE PRESIDENT'S DEATH. THE FBI PHOTOGRAPHS **HARVEY'S** POSSESSIONS THAT HAD BEEN TAKEN FROM HIS NORTH BECKLEY ROOMING HOUSE AND RUTH PAINE'S HOME.

11:45 PM FRIDAY

THE FBI HAS THE MANNLICHER-CARCANO RIFLE, THE TWO SHELL CASINGS, 1 LIVE ROUND, THE 38 S&W PISTOL. BULLET FRAGMENTS, A BLANKET, **HARVEY'S** SHIRT, AND TAPE AND PAPER FROM THE TSBD FLOWN TO THE FBI LAB IN WASHINGTON. FBI AGENT VINCENT DRAIN ACCOMPANIES THE EVIDENCE. THERE WAS NO WRITTEN INVENTORY OF THE ITEMS TURNED OVER TO AGENT DRAIN. THE TOTAL NUMBER OF ITEMS ACTUALLY NUMBERED 400-500.

*ONCE IN WASHINGTON, THE FBI LAB PERFORMED TESTS ON FIBERS FOUND ON THE BUTT OF THE RIFLE TO DETERMINE IF THEY MATCHED THOSE OF THE SHIRT **HARVEY** WAS WEARING WHEN <u>ARRESTED</u> THE FBI NOTED "THE FIBERS MATCH IN MICROSCOPIC CHARATERISTICS THE SHIRT OF THE SUSPECT." EITHER ONE LOOKS AT THIS COMMENT AS PROOF THAT **HARVEY** DID <u>NOT</u> CHANGE SHIRTS UPON VISITING HIS ROOMING HOUSE OR THE COMMENT CAN ONLY <u>INSINUATE</u> THAT THE SHIRT WORN BY **HARVEY** WHEN HE WAS ARRESTED HAD, AT SOME POINT IN TIME, MADE CONTACT WITH THE RIFLE BUTT.*

NEAR MIDNIGHT FRIDAY

WILLIAM DUNCAN, JR., A NEWSMAN FOR RADIO STATION KLIF IN DALLAS, RECEIVES A PHONE CALL FROM RUBY ASKING IF HE WOULD BE INTERESTED IN AN INTERVIEW WITH DISTRICT ATTORNEY WADE. DUNCAN SAID YES AND RUBY CALLS WADE TO THE PHONE.

CHAPTER 13: DALLAS JAIL: SATURDAY

12:03 AM SATURDAY
HARVEY'S <u>FOURTH</u> FORMAL INTERROGATION SESSION ENDS.

12:05—12:19 AM SATURDAY
A SHORT PRESS CONFERENCE IS HELD WITH **HARVEY** PRESENT. DALLAS DISTRICT ATTORNEY HENRY WADE, WHEN ASKED THE MAKE OF THE RIFLE USED TO ASSASSINATE THE PRESIDENT REPLIES: "IT'S A MAUSER, I BELIEVE."

VARIOUS COMMENTS MADE BY HARVEY EARLY THAT SATURDAY MORNING SHOW A STEADY RESOLVE TO CLEAR HIS NAME IN THE SHOOTINGS OF THE PRESIDENT AND OFFICER TIPPIT:

PRIOR TO ENTERING THE CORRIDOR, **HARVEY** *WAS ONCE AGAIN TOLD HE COULD HIDE HIS FACE. HE REPEATED HIS EARLIER REPLY: "WHY SHOULD I HIDE MY FACE? I HAVEN'T DONE ANYTHING TO BE ASHAMED OF."*

DURING THIS CONFERENCE HE WAS QUESTIONED BY NEWSMEN. HIS COMMENTS WERE BROKEN AS WERE THE RAPID-FIRE QUESTIONS BY THE REPORTERS.

"WELL, I WAS QUESTIONED BY JUDGE JOHNSTON. HOWEVER I PROTESTED AT THAT TIME THAT I WAS NOT ALLOWED LEGAL REPRESENTATION DURING THAT SHORT AND SWEET HEARING."

"I POSITIVELY KNOW NOTHING ABOUT THIS SITUATION.....I WOULD LIKE TO HAVE LEGAL REPRESENTATION....I REALLY DON'T KNOW WHAT THIS SITUATION IS ABOUT...NOBODY HAS TOLD ME ANYTHING EXCEPT THAT I AM ACCUSED OF MURDERING A POLICEMAN...I KNOW NOTHING MORE THAN THAT....AND I DO REQUEST THAT SOMEONE COME FORWARD TO GIVE ME LEGAL ASSISTANCE...."

HARVEY *WAS VISITED BY LOCAL ACLU OFFICIALS WHILE IN CUSTODY. ALTHOUGH HE HAD BEEN CONVINCED, POSSIBLY BY MICHAEL PAINE, TO LIST THE ACLU ON HIS LAST P.O. BOX UNDER "NAME OF FIRM OR CORPORATION" ENTITLED TO USE THE BOX, HE DECLINED THEIR OFFER OF LEGAL ASSISTANCE. HE APPARENTLY CONTINUED TO HARBOR SOME HOPE THAT THE INTELLIGENCE COMMUNITY WOULD INTERCEDE ON HIS BEHALF PRIOR TO HAVING TO RESORT TO THE LOCAL ACLU FOR LEGAL COUNSEL.*

LATER, THE CIA WOULD ADMIT TO HAVING A "201" FILE ON **HARVEY***. A "201" FILE IS OPENED ON ANYONE IN WHICH THE CIA TAKES AN INTEREST. ALTHOUGH A "201" FILE DOES NOT PROVE THAT HE WAS AN AGENT OF THE CIA, IT CERTAINLY OFFERS NO ASSURANCE THAT HE WAS NOT.*

IN **HARVEY'S** *"201" FILE THERE WERE 1,196 INDIVIDUAL DOCUMENTS. SOME OF THESE DOCUMENTS ARE <u>HUNDREDS</u> OF PAGES LONG. 260 OF THE 1,196 DOCUMENTS ARE STILL CLASSIFIED. OF THE REMAINING 926 DOCUMENTS THAT ARE NOT STILL CLASSIFIED, MANY ARE HEAVILY CENSORED. IF* **HARVEY** *WERE NOT AN AGENT, AND THE CIA APPARENTLY HAD SO LITTLE INTEREST IN HIM, WHY THE MASSIVE AMOUNT OF DOCUMENTATION?*

*COLONEL FLETCHER PROUTY WAS THE POINT OFFICER BETWEEN THE CIA AND THE PENTAGON. HE LATER NOTED: "LEE (**HARVEY**) OSWALD WAS NOT AN ORDINARY MARINE. HE WAS A MARINE ON COVER ASSIGNMENT."*

BOTH FBI AGENTS HOSTY AND BOOKOUT REPORTED THAT "OSWALD FRANTICALLY DENIED SHOOTING POLICE OFFICER TIPPIT OR SHOOTING PRESIDENT JOHN F. KENNEDY."

WHEN ASKED DID YOU KILL THE PRESIDENT? HE REPLIED "NO, I HAVE NOT BEEN CHARGED WITH THAT. IN FACT NOBODY HAS SAID THAT TO ME YET. THE FIRST THING I HEARD ABOUT IT WAS WHEN THE NEWSPAPER REPORTERS IN THE HALL ASKED ME THAT QUESTION."

WHEN ASKED "HOW DID YOU HURT YOUR EYE?" HE REPLIED "A POLICEMAN HIT ME."

DURING HIS WALK FROM THE PRESS CONFERENCE BACK TO HIS CELL, A BRIEF EXCHANGE TOOK PLACE BETWEEN HARVEY AND THE SURROUNDING REPORTERS:

HARVEY: "I'D LIKE SOME LEGAL REPRESENTATION. THESE POLICE OFFICERS HAVE NOT ALLOWED ME TO HAVE ANY. I DON'T KNOW WHAT THIS IS ALL ABOUT."

REPORTER: "DID YOU KILL THE PRESIDENT?"

HARVEY: "NO SIR I DIDN'T. PEOPLE KEEP ASKING ME THAT."

2ND REPORTER: "HOW DID YOU GET THE BLACK EYE?"

HARVEY: (NOT UNDERSTANDING THE QUESTION) "SIR?"

3RD REPORTER: "DID YOU SHOOT THE PRESIDENT?"

HARVEY: (LIKELY IN RESPONSE TO A QUESTION BY ANOTHER REPORTER) "I WORK IN THAT BUILDING."

SAME REPORTER: "WERE YOU IN THE BUILDING AT THE TIME?"

HARVEY: "NATURALLY, IF I WORK IN THAT BUILDING. YES SIR."

3RD REPORTER REPEATING HIS QUESTION: "DID YOU SHOOT THE PRESIDENT?"

HARVEY: "NO, THEY HAVE TAKEN ME IN BECAUSE OF THE FACT THAT I LIVED IN THE SOVIET UNION."

QUESTION REPEATED: "DID YOU SHOOT THE PRESIDENT?"

HARVEY: "I'M JUST A PATSY."

THE CONTINUED INSISTANCE BY **HARVEY** THAT HE WAS "JUST A PATSY" NOT ONLY FURTHER SEALED HIS FATE BUT ADDED A SENSE OF URGENCY TO THOSE WHO WOULD ARRANGE FOR RUBY TO DO SO. **HARVEY** HAD MADE IT PERFECTLY CLEAR THAT HE WOULD NOT BE A SCAPEGOAT FOR THE PREVIOUS DAYS EVENTS. IT WAS IMPERATIVE THAT HE BE SILENCED AT THE NEXT AVAILABLE OPPORTUNITY.

D. A. HENRY WADE, STILL BEING QUESTIONED BY REPORTERS, WAS ASKED "ARE YOU WILLING TO SAY WHETHER YOU THINK THIS MAN WAS INSPIRED AS A COMMUNIST OR WHETHER HE IS SIMPLY A NUT OR A MIDDLEMAN?" WADE'S REPLY, ALTHOUGH SOMEWHAT CRYPTIC, REVEALED HIS TRUE THOUGHTS ON THE MATTER: "I'LL PUT IT THIS WAY, I DON'T THINK HE'S A NUT."

12:20 AM SATURDAY
HARVEY IS PLACED IN MAXIMUM SECURITY CELL F2 ON THE FIFTH FLOOR OF CITY HALL.

12:35 AM SATURDAY
HARVEY IS FINGERPRINTED ONCE AGAIN AND THEN PHOTOGRAPHED IN THE IDENTIFICATION BUREAU ON THE 4TH FLOOR. HE REFUSED TO SIGN THE FINGERPRINT CARD.

1:10 AM SATURDAY
HARVEY IS RETURNED TO HIS CELL.

1:35 AM SATURDAY
HARVEY IS TAKEN TO THE 4TH FLOOR I.D. BUREAU WHERE HE IS FORMALLY ARRAIGNED AND CHARGED WITH THE PRESIDENT'S DEATH "IN FURTHERANCE OF AN INTERNATIONAL COMMUNIST CONSPIRACY."

***HARVEY** COMMENTS:" I DON'T KNOW WHAT YOU ARE TALKING ABOUT. WHAT'S THE IDEA OF THIS? WHAT ARE YOU DOING THIS FOR?" "WELL SIR, I GUESS THIS IS THE TRIAL…I WANT TO CONTACT MY LAWYER, MR. ABT, IN NEW YORK CITY. I WOULD LIKE TO HAVE THIS GENTLEMAN. HE IS WITH THE ACLU." ALTHOUGH MR. ABT WAS NOT WITH THE ACLU, HIS EXPERTISE IN CASES INVOLVING ALLEGED TREASON AND CONSPIRACY MAKES HIM MORE POINTEDLY THE LAWYER **HARVEY** DESIRES.*

ABOUT 1:45 AM SATURDAY
RUBY APPEARS AT RADIO STATION KLIF. HE HAD BROUGHT SANDWICHES AND SODA FOR THE NEWSMEN. KLIF IS OWNED BY GORDON MCCLENDON, A CLOSE ASSOCIATE OF DAVID ATLEE PHILLIPS.

MCCLENDON SERVED IN WWII AS A NAVAL INTELLIGENCE OFFICER. HIS LIBERTY RADIO, WITH KLIF AS THE DALLAS FLAGSHIP STATION, WAS KNOWN TO BE OPENLY ANTI-COMMUNIST.

1:45 AM SATURDAY
HARVEY IS RETURNED TO HIS CELL.

2:05 AM SATURDAY
RUBY LEAVES THE NEWSROOM AT KLIF.

APPROXIMATELY 2:15-3:15 AM SATURDAY
RUBY IS REPORTEDLY MEETING AT SIMON'S PARKING GARAGE WITH DALLAS POLICE OFFICER HARRY OLSEN AND THE OFFICER'S GIRLFRIEND, KAY COLEMAN AKA KATHY KAY. COLEMAN IS A DANCER AT RUBY'S CAROUSEL CLUB. OLSEN CLAIMED THAT THE MEETING LASTED ABOUT 1 HOUR.

3:10 AM SATURDAY
AGENT DRAIN DEPARTS FROM CARSWELL AFB ENROUTE TO WASHINGTON WITH THE POSSESSIONS OF **HARVEY**.

THE ITEMS WOULD BE QUIETLY RETURNED TO DPD ON NOVEMBER 26TH. ONCE AGAIN, THERE WAS NO INVENTORY LIST OF THE ITEMS <u>RETURNED</u> TO THE DPD. IT WAS THEN AND ONLY THEN THAT THE ITEMS WERE PHOTOGRAPHED AND INVENTORIED. THE INVENTORY LIST WAS THEN INITIALED BY BOTH DPD OFFICERS AND FBI AGENTS. THE DPD THEN "CEREMONIOUSLY" TURNED OVER THE EVIDENCE TO THE FBI WITH CAMERAS AND REPORTERS PRESENT.

3:30 AM SATURDAY
RUBY ARRIVES AT THE DALLAS TIMES HERALD. HE TAKES OUT AN AD NOTING THAT HIS CLUB WILL BE CLOSED BOTH SATURDAY AND SUNDAY. HE WOULD LATER DENY HAVING STOPPED AT SIMPSON'S PARKING GARAGE FOR THE ONE HOUR TALK WITH OLSEN AND COLEMAN.

APPROXIMATELY 3:30 AM SATURDAY
FERRIE, BEAUBOEUF, AND COFFEY ARRIVE AT THE ALAMOTEL IN HOUSTON AND CHECK INTO ROOM 19. THE ALAMOTEL IS OWNED BY CARLOS MARCELLO. THE TRIO WOULD CHECK OUT ABOUT 7:00 PM.

3:46 AM SATURDAY

THE PHOTOS AND TAPE RECORDINGS OF A MAN IDENTIFYING HIMSELF AS "LEE HARVEY OSWALD" ARRIVE AT DALLAS. THEY WERE COURIERED BY FBI AGENT ELDON RUDD FROM MEXICO CITY. THE PACKAGE IS THEN FLOWN TO WASHINGTON.

*THE DALLAS FBI AGENTS WHO HAD BEEN INTERVIEWING **HARVEY** WOULD SOON REALIZE THAT NEITHER THE PHOTOS NOR THE VOICE RECORDINGS FROM MEXICO CITY WERE A MATCH FOR THE MAN THEY HAD IN CUSTODY.*

4:20 AM SATURDAY
RUBY RETURNS TO HIS APARTMENT AND WAKES UP ROOMMATE GEORGE SENATOR. SENATOR NOTED: "HE HAD A LOOK ON HIS FACE LIKE I'D NEVER SEEN BEFORE…LIKE HE WAS OUT IN SPACE." SENATOR AND RUBY THEN PICKED UP CAROUSEL CLUB EMPLOYEE LARRY CRAFARD AND DROVE TO A BILLBOARD IN DALLAS THAT CALLED FOR THE IMPEACHMENT OF EARL WARREN. RUBY HAD CRAFARD TAKE POLAROID PICTURES OF THE BILLBOARD. THE TRIO THEN STOPS FOR COFFEE AT WEBB'S WAFFLE SHOP. THEY THEN DROVE TO THE POST OFFICE WHERE RUBY TRIED TO DETERMINE THE OWNER OF THE P.O.BOX LISTED ON THE BILLBOARD.

5:00 AM SATURDAY
THE TRIO THEN MADE A STOP AT THE TIMES-HERALD OFFICE WHERE RUBY TALKED WITH A PRINTER, ARNOLD GADASH, FOR ABOUT 10 MINUTES. RUBY AND SENATOR THEN DROPPED CRAFARD OFF AT THE CAROUSEL CLUB AND RETURNED TO THEIR APARTMENT AT APPROXIMATELY 6:30 AM.

6:30 AM SATURDAY
AGENT SEBASTIAN LATONA, AN FBI FIREARMS EXPERT AT THE WASHINGTON OFFICE, EXAMINED THE RIFLE. HE WAS NOT ABLE TO FIND ANY IDENTIFIABLE PRINTS OR EVEN PARTIAL PRINTS THAT COULD BE ASSIGNED TO **HARVEY**. THE "CHECK-IN" INVENTORY IN WASHINGTON LISTS 2 CASINGS, 1 LIVE ROUND, AND THE RIFLE.

8:30 AM SATURDAY
RUBY IS AWAKENED BY A PHONE CALL FROM LARRY CRAFARD. RUBY'S DOGS WERE BEING TENDED TO BY CRAFARD AT THE CAROUSEL CLUB.

EARLY AM SATURDAY
DAVID PHILLIP'S' DRE/AMSPELL OPERATION WASTED NO TIME IN INITIATING A **HARVEY**/CASTRO CONNECTION. THE WASHINGTON POST MORNING EDITION QUOTES DRE SPOKESMAN CARLOS BRINGUIER IN REGARDS TO **HARVEY'S** NEW ORLEANS FPFC ACTIVITY AND HIS ENSUING RADIO DEBATE WITH **HARVEY**.

10:01 AM SATURDAY
HOOVER CALLS LBJ REGARDING THE TAPES AND PHOTOS FROM MEXICO CITY. HOOVER TELLS LBJ: "WE HAVE UP HERE THE TAPE AND THE PHOTO OF THE MAN WHO WAS AT THE SOVIET EMBASSY USING OSWALD'S NAME. THAT PICTURE AND THE TAPE DO NOT CORRESPOND TO THE MAN'S (**HARVEY**) VOICE, NEITHER TO HIS APPEARANCE. IN OTHER WORDS IT APPEARS THAT THERE IS A SECOND PERSON WHO WAS AT THE SOVIET EMBASSY DOWN THERE." HOOVER WOULD ALSO NOTE TO LBJ THAT "THE EVIDENCE THAT THEY HAVE AT THE PRESENT TIME IS NOT VERY STRONG." HE WAS OF COURSE REFERRING TO THE EVIDENCE AGAINST **HARVEY** IN REGARDS TO THE PRESIDENT'S SHOOTING. HOOVER CONTINUED: "THE CASE, AS IT STANDS NOW, ISN'T STRONG ENOUGH TO GET A CONVICTION." IN THIS SAME CONVERSATION HOOVER ALSO MAKES AN INTERESTING COMMENT REGARDING THE RIFLE: "WE HAVE JUST DISCOVERED THAT PLACE WHERE THE GUN WAS PURCHASED AND THE SHIPMENT OF THE GUN FROM CHICAGO TO DALLAS TO A P.O. BOX DALLAS, TO A MAN, NO TO A WOMAN BY THE NAME OF 'A. HIDELL'."

HOOVER WOULD ALSO REFERENCE THE LETTER WHICH ARRIVED AT THE SOVIET EMBASSY IN WASHINGTON ON NOVEMBER 18TH. HOOVER HOWEVER DID <u>NOT</u> MENTION

THE CUBAN/SOVIET OVERTURES IN THE LETTER, PARTICULARLY THE COMMENT REGARDING THE AUTHOR, "LEE H. OSWALD" HAVING MET WITH VALERY KOSTIKOV IN MEXICO CITY. HOOVER, BY ALL INDICATIONS, HARBORED SERIOUS DOUBTS AS TO WHETHER **HARVEY** WAS IN MEXICO CITY.

*IN MY EXTENSIVE READING, I HAVE NEVER SEEN ANY FURTHER COMMENT OR CLARIFICATION AS TO HOW OR WHY HOOVER WOULD DESCRIBE "A. HIDELL" AS A WOMAN. COULD THERE HAVE BEEN A WOMAN INVOLVED IN THE SET-UP OF **HARVEY** AS WELL? THERE WERE INDEED SEVERAL INSTANCES WHERE THE "OSWALDS" WERE SEEN AS A COUPLE. THESE INSTANCES TYPICALLY RESULTED IN AN ACT THAT WOULD LATER PROVE TO BE CIRCUMSTANTIALLY INCRIMINATING TO **HARVEY**. ONE MUST ALSO RECALL THE INCIDENT AT REDBIRD AIRFIELD WHERE A WOMAN ACCOMPANIED A MAN WHO HAD ATTEMPTED TO CHARTER A SMALL PLANE FOR TRAVEL TO MEXICO AND POSSIBLY CUBA. THERE CERTAINLY WERE ENOUGH SITUATIONS WHERE ONE MIGHT SUSPECT THE INVOLVEMENT OF A WOMAN IN THE SET-UP OF **HARVEY**. ALTHOUGH HOOVER'S COMMENT WOULD DO LITTLE TO SUPRESS THAT SUSPICION, IT WOULD ALSO SHED LITTLE LIGHT ON THE IDENTITY OF THE WOMAN.*

HOOVER ALSO NOTED THAT ONLY ONE FULL BULLET WAS FOUND. BUT, HE NOTES THAT IT WAS "ON THE STRETCHER THAT THE PRESIDENT WAS ON." THE LATER NECESSITY OF THE MAGIC BULLET HAD NOT YET DEMANDED THAT THE FINDING OF THIS BULLET BE RELEGATED TO <u>CONNALLY'S</u> STRETCHER <u>NOT</u> THE PRESIDENT'S .

APPROXIMATELY 10:30 AM SATURDAY

IN A PHONE CONVERSATION WITH JOSEPH MILTEER, FBI INFORMANT SOMERSETT NOTES MILTEER'S JUBILANT COMMENTS: "EVERYTHING RAN TRUE TO FORM....I GUESS YOU THOUGHT I WAS KIDDING YOU WHEN I SAID HE WOULD BE KILLED FROM A WINDOW WITH A HIGH-POWERED RIFLE....I DON'T DO ANY GUESSING."

10:30 AM TO 11:33 AM SATURDAY

HARVEY IS QUESTIONED AGAIN. THIS WILL BE THE <u>5TH</u> FORMAL INTERROGATION SESSION.

*THIS WILL ACTUALLY BE THE 7TH TIME **HARVEY** IS QUESTIONED; 2 TIMES INFORMALLY, AND 5 OFFICIAL SESSIONS.*

HARVEY AGAIN ENDURES QUESTIONS PREVIOUSLY ASKED. HE COMMENTS: "I NEVER OWNED A RIFLE...THE FBI HAS THOROUGHLY INTERVIEWED ME AT VARIOUS OTHER TIMES....THEY HAVE USED THEIR HARD AND SOFT APPROACH TO ME, THE USE THE BUDDY SYSTEM....I AM FAMILIAR WITH ALL TYPES OF QUESTIONING AND HAVE NO INTENTION OF MAKING ANY STATEMENT..." ONCE AGAIN, **HARVEY** ALLUDES TO THE LIKLIHOOD THAT HE HAD INDEED BEEN TRAINED IN INTERROGATION TECHNIQUES.

HARVEY WENT ON TO RECONFIRM HIS ARREST IN NEW ORLEANS WHILE PASSING OUT FPFC PAMPHLETS. HE ALSO REFUSED TO TAKE A POLYGRAPH. IN FACT HE COMMENTED: "IT HAS ALWAYS BEEN MY PRACTICE NOT TO AGREE TO TAKE A POLYGRAPH." *I WOULD OFFER THAT IT WAS NOT **HARVEY'S** "PRACTICE" NOT TO TAKE A POLYGRAPH, BUT THE "PRACTICE" OF THE CIA AND THE ONI TO INSTRUCT THEIR OPERATIVES <u>NOT</u> TO TAKE THE TEST.*

INTERESTINGLY, HE DENIES HAVING TOLD BUELL FRAZIER ANYTHING REGARDING BRINGING BACK SOME CURTAIN RODS. HE NOTED THAT FRIDAY MORNING HE CARRIED HIS LUNCH: "A CHEESE SANDWICH AND FRUIT WHICH I MADE AT THE PAINE'S HOUSE." ONE HAS TO WONDER WHETHER HE IS REFERRING TO HAVING NOT MENTIONED CURTAIN RODS TO FRAZIER AT <u>ANY</u> TIME, OR <u>ONLY</u> ON NOVEMBER 21ST PRIOR TO HIS VISIT TO MARINA THAT EVENING. THE PACKAGE HE CARRIED TO WORK THE MORNING OF THE 22ND DID NOT AND COULD NOT HAVE CONTAINED THE ALLEGED ASSASSINATION WEAPON. TO

PARAPHRASE JOHNNY COCHRAN, "IF THE GUN DON'T FIT YOU MUST AQUIT." SORRY, I COULDN'T RESIST.

WHEN QUESTIONED REGARDING A "HIDELL" HE RESPONDED: "THE NAME ALEX HIDELL WAS PICKED UP WHILE WORKING IN NEW ORLEANS IN THE FPFC ORGANIZATION." **HARVEY** HAD, IN NEW ORLEANS, UNSUSPECTINGLY TIED HIMSELF TO THE NAME "HIDELL" WHICH HAD BEEN PREVIOUSLY USED BY THE SET-UP CONSPIRATORS TO ASSOCIATE HIM WITH THE MONEY ORDER PURCHASES OF BOTH THE PISTOL ALLEGEDLY USED IN TIPPIT'S MURDER AND THE RIFLE ALLEGEDLY USED IN THE JFK SHOOTING. **HARVEY** ONCE AGAIN DENIED ORDERING ANY GUNS.

HE ALSO STATED: "I HAVE NO VIEWS ON THE PRESIDENT. MY WIFE AND I LIKED THE PRESIDENT'S FAMILY VERY WELL. I HAVE MY OWN VIEWS ON THE PRESIDENT'S NATIONAL POLICY. I HAVE A RIGHT TO EXPRESS MY VIEWS, BUT BECAUSE OF THE CHARGES I DO NOT THINK I SHOULD COMMENT FURTHER."

FRITZ'S <u>TYPED</u> INTERROGATION REPORT ALLEGES THAT DURING THIS SESSION **HARVEY** NOW CLAIMED THAT HE CHANGED <u>BOTH</u> HIS TROUSERS AND SHIRT. ONCE AGAIN, WAS THIS A RESPONSE REQUIRED BY THE ALTGEN'S PHOTO SHOWING WHAT APPEARED TO BE **HARVEY** ON THE TSBD STEPS WEARING A SHIRT REMARKABLY SIMILAR TO IF NOT INDEED THE SAME ONE HE WAS WEARING WHEN ARRESTED? IF SO, IT FAILED MISERABLY IN IT'S CLUMSY EFFORT TO DISPROVE THAT IT WAS **HARVEY** IN THE PHOTO FOR THE SHIRT WHEN **HARVEY** WAS ARRESTED (IF IT WAS INDEED CHANGED) LOOKS IDENTICAL TO THE ONE WORN BY THE MAN IN THE ALTGEN'S PHOTO. AN FBI REPORT DATED 11/23/63 NOTES ONLY THAT HE "CHANGED HIS CLOTHES." IT DOES <u>NOT</u> SPECIFY SHIRT OR SLACKS. HOWEVER AN FBI REPORT DATED 11/25/63 NOW ALLEGES THAT **HARVEY** CHANGED HIS "SHIRT AND TROUSERS." ONCE AGAIN, DID THE ALTGEN'S PHOTO HAVE SOME BEARING ON THE INCLUSION OF A SHIRT IN REGARDS TO JUST WHAT ARTICLE(S) OF CLOTHING WERE CHANGED BY **HARVEY** WHEN HE STOPPED AT HIS ROOMING HOUSE?

THE DARK REDDISH-BROWN SHIRT, MISSING BUTTONS AND ALL, THAT **HARVEY** WAS ARRESTED IN APPEARS TO BE <u>IDENTICAL</u> TO THE ONE WORN BY THE MAN ON THE TSBD STEPS IN THE ALTGEN'S PHOTO. IF IT IS <u>NOT</u> THE <u>SAME SHIRT</u>, THEN **HARVEY** WOULD HAVE HAD TO CHANGE FROM THE REDDISH-BROWN, MISSING-BUTTONS SHIRT HE WORE TO WORK THAT DAY TO A VIRTUALLY IDENTICAL REDDISH-BROWN, MISSING-BUTTONS SHIRT AT THE ROOMING HOUSE. HE WOULD ALSO HAVE TO REMEMBER TO REMOVE THE BUS TRANSFER HE OBTAINED FROM THE #1213 MARSALIS BUS FROM HIS <u>WORK</u> SHIRT AND PLACE IT IN THE POCKET OF HIS "NEW" SHIRT. WHY WOULD SOMEONE WHO HAD ALLEGEDLY SHOT THE PRESIDENT BOTHER TO CHANGE FROM THE CRIME SCENE SHIRT TO A NEARLY IDENTICAL (MISSING BUTTONS INCLUDED) SHIRT AND ALSO BOTHER TO RETRIEVE THE TRANSFER AND PLACE IT IN THE "NEW" SHIRT? SHORT ANSWER: HE DIDN'T

11:25 AM SATURDAY
POLICE CHIEF CURRY IS QUESTIONED BY UPI REPORTERS. CURRY NOTED TO THE REPORTERS THAT THE FBI HAD INTERVIEWED **HARVEY** RECENTLY AND HAD KNOWLEDGE OF HIS PREVIOUS FPCC AND LEFT WING ACTIVITIES.

HOOVER, UPON LEARNING OF CURRY'S COMMENTS TO REPORTERS, INFORMED SAIC GORDON SHANKLIN THAT UNLESS HE OBTAINED A RETRACTION FROM CURRY HE WOULD BE DISMISSED FROM THE BUREAU. SHANKLIN, NEEDLESS TO SAY, PHONED CURRY AND PRACTICALLY BEGGED CURRY TO ISSUE ANOTHER STATEMENT REJECTING HIS EARLIER CLAIM. AT 1:15 PM, CURRY ANNOUNCED ON NBC TV THAT "FROM HIS OWN PERSONAL KNOWLEDGE, THE FBI DID <u>NOT</u> HAVE ANY PREVIOUS INFORMATION REGARDING OSWALD <u>NOR</u> ABOUT OSWALD BEING A COMMUNIST." ALL IT TOOK WAS A PHONE CALL FROM J. EDGAR.

11:30 AM SATURDAY
RUBY LEAVES HIS APARTMENT.

11:33 AM SATURDAY

283

HARVEY IS RETURNED TO HIS CELL.

APPROXIMATELY 11:50 AM SATURDAY
RUBY ENTERS A WBAP TV TRUCK PARKED OUTSIDE CITY HALL. NBC NEWS PRODUCER FRED RHEINSTEIN ASKS THE UNINVITED RUBY TO LEAVE.

11:57 AM SATURDAY
HOOVER SENDS A MEMO TO ALL FBI OFFICES: "LHO HAS BEEN DEVELOPED AS THE PRINCIPAL SUSPECT IN THE ASSASSINATION OF PRESIDENT KENNEDY."

*HOOVER HAD PREVIOUSLY SUGGESTED TO LBJ THE POSSIBILITY OF A CONSPIRACY INVOLVING CUBA AND RUSSIA. HOWEVER HE IS NOW INFORMING ALL FBI OFFICES THAT IT APPEARS THAT THE ASSASSINATION IS THE WORK OF A LONE GUNMAN, **HARVEY**. I TRULY THINK THAT THE REMARKS BY HOOVER TO LBJ REGARDING MEXICO CITY WERE INTENDED TO GIVE LBJ AT LEAST A REASONABLE RATIONALE FOR HIS LATER PLEA TO EARL WARREN THAT THE WARREN COMMISSION MUST, FOR THE SAKE OF THE COUNTRY, RUBBER STAMP THE FBI FINDING OF **HARVEY** AS A LONE GUNMAN TO PREVENT THE POSSIBILITY OF A NUCLEAR WAR WITH RUSSIA. THE CIA AND FBI WERE ALREADY IN THE EARLY STAGES OF DENYING ANY AND ALL INVOLVEMENT WITH **HARVEY**. IF EARL WARREN AND HIS COMMISSION COULD BE COERCED BY LBJ TO ACCEPT THE "LONE ASSASSIN" CONCLUSION OF THE FBI FOR THE APARRENT GOOD OF THE COUNTRY, ALL THAT WOULD BE LEFT WOULD BE TO SELL THE COMMISSION FINDINGS TO THE AMERICAN PUBLIC.*

THE PRESS WOULD PROVE TO BE OF CONSIDERABLE HELP IN THAT REGARD. ON SUNDAY, NOVEMBER 23RD, THE NEW YORK HERALD TRIBUNE RAN AN EDITORIAL WITH THE NOTATION "AMERICANS CAN TAKE COMFORT IN THE FACT THAT THE MURDERERS OF THEIR PRESIDENTS HAVE, IN NEARLY EVERY CASE, BEEN CRAZED INDIVIDUALS." THE EDITORIAL CITED OTHER EXCERPTS FROM A BOOK BY ROBERT DONOVAN SUPPORTING THIS PREMISE TITLED "THE ASSASSINS." ALLEN DULLES WOULD TAKE THIS SAME ROBERT DONOVAN TO THE FIRST MEETING OF THE WARREN COMMISSION. DONOVAN LATER WROTE AN INTRODUCTION FOR A CONDENSED VERSION OF THE COMMISSION FINDINGS

*THE SELLING OF **HARVEY** AS THE LONE GUNMAN TO THE AMERICAN PUBLIC WAS "ON." ON NOVEMBER 25TH, THE NEW YORK TIMES CHIMED IN WITH A STORY: "LONE ASSASSIN THE RULE IN U.S; PLOTTING MORE PREVALENT ABROAD." NOT TO BE IGNORED, THE WALL STREET JOURNAL EDITORIALIZED U.S. ASSASSINATIONS AS BEING THE WORK OF INDIVIDUALS RATHER THAN POLITICAL COUPS.*

12:00 PM SATURDAY
REPORTER PHILLIPPE LABRO ENCOUNTERS RUBY AT THE POLICE STATION. RUBY OFFERS THE REPORTER A BUSINESS CARD FOR THE CAROUSEL CLUB.

APPROXIMATELY 12:15 PM SATURDAY
RUBY LEAVES CITY HALL AND RETURNS TO HIS APARTMENT. HE PHONED KLIF RADIO AND ASKED KENNETH DOWE IF HE HAD ANY INDICATION AS TO WHEN **HARVEY** WOULD BE TRANSFERRED TO COUNTY JAIL.

APPROXIMATELY 12:30 PM SATURDAY
DAVID FERRIE PHONES CARLOS MARCELLO'S OFFICE AT THE TOWN AND COUNTRY HOTEL.

LATER, NEW ORLEANS FBI AGENT J. SMITH WOULD ASK MARCELLO'S ATTORNEY G. WRAY GILL FOR RECORDS OF FERRIE'S PHONE CALLS TO HIS, MARCELLO'S OFFICE. GILL SURRENDERED PHONE RECORDS FROM SEPTEMBER AND OCTOBER. GILL CLAIMED PHONE RECORDS FROM NOVEMBER WERE "UNAVAILABLE."

12:30 PM SATURDAY

LBJ MEETS WITH CIA DIRECTOR JOHN MCCONE. THE NEW PRESIDENT IS WRESTLING WITH THE RAMIFICATIONS OF CUBAN/SOVIET INVOLVEMENT WITH **HARVEY** AND THE POTENTIAL NUCLEAR SHOWDOWN THAT MAY RESULT IF THE CONNECTION IS REVEALED TO THE AMERICAN PUBLIC.

12:35 PM SATURDAY
HARVEY IS BROUGHT TO CAPTAIN FRITZ'S OFFICE FOR A <u>6TH</u> FORMAL INTERROGATION SESSION. HE IS RETURNED TO HIS CELL AT 1:10 PM.

1:15 –1:30 PM SATURDAY
HARVEY'S WIFE AND MOTHER "MARGUERITE" ARE ALLOWED TO SEE HIM.

IN A CONVERSATION WITH HIS WIFE HARVEY TELLS HER:

"THEY ARE TREATING ME FINE…"

"…YOU'RE NOT TO WORRY ABOUT THAT"…

"DID YOU BRING JUNE AND RACHEL?"

"….OF COURSE WE CAN SPEAK ABOUT ABSOLUTELY ANYTHING AT ALL"

"….IT'S A MISTAKE…I'M NOT GUILTY."

"THERE ARE PEOPLE WHO WILL HELP ME…BE SURE TO BUY SHOES FOR JUNE."

"EVERYTHING IS GOING TO BE ALRIGHT…YOU ARE NOT TO WORRY."

"YOU HAVE FRIENDS..THEY WILL HELP YOU."

"YOU MUSN'T WORRY ABOUT ME."

"THERE IS A LAWYER IN NEW YORK ON WHOM I AM COUNTING FOR HELP."

"DON'T CRY…THERE IS NOTHING TO CRY ABOUT."

THESE CALM, CONFIDENT REMARKS ARE NOT WHAT ONE MIGHT EXPECT FROM A MAN WHO HAS BEEN EXCLUSIVELY CHARGED WITH THE MURDER OF THE CENTURY AND THE SLAYING OF A POLICE OFFICER. HARVEY'S CANDOR AND SEEMINGLY LACK OF CONCERN REGARDING HIS FATE LIKELY HINGED ON HIS EXPECTATION THAT "SOMEONE" WOULD STEP FORWARD AND CLEAR HIM. WITH "SOMEONE" BEING THE CIA/ONI OR PERHAPS THE FBI. HIS HOPE WAS FUTILE. HE WAS ON HIS OWN.

APPROXIMATELY 1:30 PM SATURDAY
RUBY LEAVES HIS APARTMENT AND WALKS TO THE ALLRIGHT PARKING GARAGE. HE ONCE AGAIN PHONES KEN DOWE AT KLIF RADIO. RUBY ASKS DOWE IF HE AWARE OF WHO HE IS TALKING WITH. DOWE DOES NOT, PROMPTING RUBY TO IDENTIFY HIMSELF.

1:40 PM SATURDAY
HARVEY MAKES HIS FIRST ATTEMPT TO CALL ATTORNEY JOHN ABT IN NEW YORK.

*ABT IS KNOWN FOR HIS PREVIOUS HANDLING OF POLITICAL CONSPIRACY CASES. MORE POINTEDLY, ABT DEFENDS POLITICAL MINORITIES WHO SUSPECT THEY HAVE BEEN FRAMED BY THE FBI. **HARVEY** IS WELL AWARE OF HIS PREDICAMENT. THE CHOICE OF ABT DEMONSTRATES THAT **HARVEY** IS ALSO ACCUTELY AWARE OF THE FACT THAT THERE IS MUCH MORE INVOLVED IN THE EVENTS OF A WEEKEND THAT WAS SUPPOSED TO START WITH HIS DEPARTURE ON A CIA "ASSIGNMENT" AND ENDED WITH HIM BEING CHARGED WITH THE DEATH OF A PRESIDENT.*

*HOOVER HIMSELF KNEW OF ABT'S HISTORY OF DEFENDING THOSE ACCUSED BY THE FBI OF BEING COMMUNISTS. A HSCA DOCUMENT QUOTES A HOOVER MEMO DATED 11/24/63 AFTER **HARVEY'S** DEATH.*

HOOVER: "THEY REALLY DIDN'T HAVE A CASE AGAINST OSWALD UNTIL WE GAVE THEM OUR INFORMATION....ALL THE DPD HAD WAS THREE WITNESSES WHO TENTATIVELY IDENTIFIED HIM....WITH ONLY THAT KIND OF EVIDENCE, (ABT) HE COULD HAVE TURNED THE CASE AROUND....."

EARLY AFTERNOON SATURDAY

DPD DETECTIVES ADAMCIK, STOVALL, ROSE AND MOORE, ACCOMPANIED BY IRVING POLICE DEPARTMENT DETECTIVE JOHN MCCABE, SEARCH THE GARAGE AT RUTH PAINE'S HOUSE ON 2515 WEST 5TH STREET IN IRVING, TEXAS. IT IS AT THIS POINT THAT IT IS DISCOVERED THAT THE RIFLE ALLEGEDLY USED TO KILL THE PRESIDENT IS NO LONGER IN THE BLANKET STORED IN THE PAINE'S GARAGE AS MARINA HAD CLAIMED. BUT, AS WESLEY LIEBELER, W.C. COUNCIL POINTED OUT, "NOT ONE PERSON ALIVE TODAY SAW THAT RIFLE IN THE PAINE GARAGE IN SUCH A WAY THAT IT COULD BE IDENTIFIED AS THAT (THE ALLEGED ASSASSINATION WEAPON) RIFLE."

AFTERNOON SATURDAY

THE STILL HOSPITALIZED JACK MARTIN CONTACTS NEW ORLEANS PD MAJOR PRESLEY TROSCLAIR. HE INFORMS THE MAJOR ABOUT CONNECTIONS BETWEEN FERRIE AND **HARVEY**.

APPROXIMATELY 1:45 PM SATURDAY

GARNETT HALLMARK, MANAGER OF THE PARKING LOT WHERE RUBY NORMALLY LEFT HIS CAR, LATER TESTIFIED THAT RUBY TRIED TO CALL WESLEY WISE, A NEWSMAN AT RADIO STATION KLRD. UNABLE TO GET WISE (WISE WAS AT THE TSBD), RUBY CALLED KEN DOWE, AN ANNOUNCER AT RADIO STATION KLIF. RUBY NOTED TO MR. DOWE THAT **HARVEY'S** SCHEDULED 4:00 PM TRANSFER WOULD PROBABLY BE POSTPONED.

2:15 PM SATURDAY

HARVEY APPEARS IN YET ANOTHER LINE-UP. THIS WOULD BE HIS 5TH LINEUP.

ONCE AGAIN HARVEY COMPLAINS ABOUT THE LINEUP:

"I REFUSE TO ANSWER QUESTIONS."

" I HAVE MY T-SHIRT ON, THE OTHER MEN ARE DRESSED DIFFERENTLY..."

"THIS IS UNFAIR.."

"IT ISN'T RIGHT TO PUT ME IN A LINE-UP WITH 3 TEENAGERS...

"YOU KNOW WHAT YOU ARE DOING AND YOU ARE TRYING TO RAILROAD ME."

THE THREE PARTICIPANTS IN THIS PARTICULAR LINE-UP WERE 17 YEAR OLD JOHN HORN, 18 YEAR OLD DAVID KNAPP, AND DANIEL LUJAN, AGE 26.

2:30 PM SATURDAY

HARVEY IS RETURNED TO HIS CELL.

APPROXIMATELY 2:30 PM SATURDAY

RUBY STOPS AT SOL'S BAR AND DELI. HE WOULD LEAVE AT ABOUT 2:50 PM.

2:45 PM SATURDAY

OFFICERS JACK DONAHUE AND BOBBY BROWN TAKE FINGERNAIL SCRAPINGS AND HAIR SPECIMENS FROM **HARVEY**. THE SAMPLES ARE GIVEN TO SA C. RAY HALL OF THE FBI.

APPROXIMATELY 2:50 PM SATURDAY

RUBY RETURNS TO ALLRIGHT PARKING GARAGE. HE PHONES KEN DOWE AGAIN. HE INFORMS DOWE THAT HE IS GOING TO CITY HALL TO WITNESS **HARVEY'S** TRANSFER TO THE COUNTY JAIL.

MID AFTERNOON SATURDAY
FERRIE CALLS MARTENS WHO IS AT FERRIES RESIDENCE IN NEW ORLEANS. MARTENS INFORMS FERRIE THAT THE N.O. POLICE, THE FBI, AND THE SECRET SERVICE ARE WANTING TO INTERVIEW HIM. THIS IS LIKELY THE RESULT OF JACK MARTIN HAVING CONTACTED THE NEW ORLEANS PD.

3:00 PM SATURDAY
D. V. HARKNESS, A SERGEANT ON THE DALLAS POLICE FORCE SPOTS RUBY AT THE VEHICLE ENTRANCE OF THE JAIL. OFFICER JAMES OWNEY SPOTS RUBY ALSO.

3:30 PM SATURDAY
WESLEY WISE WAS IN A MOBILE T.V. UNIT NEAR THE TSBD WHEN RUBY RAPPED ON THE WINDOW OF THE VAN. RUBY TOLD WISE THAT BOTH CAPTAIN WILL FRITZ AND CHIEF CURRY WERE NEARBY AND SUGGESTED TO WISE THAT HE MIGHT WANT TO TAKE SOME PICTURES.

3:30 PM SATURDAY
FERRIE, ACCORDING TO CHUCK ROLAND, OWNER OF THE WINTERLAND SKATING RINK IN HOUSTON, SPENT APPROXIMATELY 2 HOURS MAKING AND RECEIVING PHONE CALLS FROM A PUBLIC PHONE AT THE RINK. ACCORDING TO WITNESSES, FERRIE AND COMPANY APPARENTLY WENT TO A SECOND RINK, THE BELAIR. THEY DID NOT SKATE AT THIS RINK EITHER. BUT, FERRIE CONTINUED MAKING ADDITIONAL PHONE CALLS. ROLAND NOTED THAT FERRIE HAD INTRODUCED HIMSELF 4 OR 5 TIMES. APPARENTLY FERRIE WANTED ROLAND TO REMEMBER HIS PRESENCE IN HOUSTON

3:37 PM SATURDAY
HARVEY SPENDS 10 MINUTES WITH HIS "BROTHER" ROBERT.

HARVEY COMMENTS TO HIS "BROTHER" "I CANNOT OR WOULD NOT SAY ANYTHING BECAUSE THE LINE IS APPARENTLY TAPPED.....I DON'T KNOW WHAT IS GOING ON...I JUST DON'T KNOW WHAT THEY ARE TALKING ABOUT...DON'T BELIEVE ALL THE SO-CALLED EVIDENCE."

ROBERT NOTED: "ALL THE TIME WE WERE TALKING I SEARCHED HIS EYES FOR ANY SIGN OF GUILT. THERE WAS NOTHING THERE...NO GUILT, NO SHAME, NO NOTHING. **HARVEY**, FINALLY AWARE OF MY LOOKING INTO HIS EYES SAID.....'BROTHER...YOU WILL FIND NOTHING THERE." **HARVEY** CONTINUED: "MY FRIENDS WILL TAKE CARE OF MARINA AND THE TWO CHILDREN." WHEN ROBERT SAID THAT HE DIDN'T THINK THE PAINE'S WERE HIS FRIENDS, **HARVEY** REPLIED: "YES THEY ARE...."

I FIND ROBERT'S USE OF THE TERM "BROTHER" AND IMPLYING THAT IT WAS **HARVEY** WHO USED THE TERM INTERESTING. I THINK IT WAS INSERTED IN THE CONVERSATION BY ROBERT TO REINFORCE THE NOTION THAT FOR PUBLIC CONSUMPTION, HE WAS **HARVEY'S** "BROTHER" NOT **LEE'S** WHEN IN FACT JUST THE OPPOSITE WAS TRUE.

APPROXIMATELY 3:45 PM SATURDAY
RUBY PROCEEDS TO MAKE HIS WAY TO THE 3RD FLOOR OF THE CITY JAIL. THAYER WALDO, A FORT WORTH REPORTER, ENCOUNTERS RUBY AT THE JAIL. HE ALSO RECEIVES A CAROUSEL CLUB CARD FROM RUBY. PHILIPPE LABRO AND FRANCOIS PELOV, BOTH FRENCH REPORTERS, ALSO ENCOUNTER RUBY. RUBY WAS ALSO SIGHTED BY UPI PHOTOGRAPHER FRANK JOHNSTON.
IT HAD EARLIER BEEN THOUGHT THAT **HARVEY** MIGHT BE TRANSFERRED AT 4:00 PM THAT AFTERNOON. RUBY ONCE AGAIN WAS IN THE IMMEDIATE VICINITY. A CROWD HAD ASSEMBLED OUTSIDE THE JAIL SHORTLY AFTER 3:00 AND OFFICER D.V. HARKNESS NOTED THAT RUBY WAS IN THE CROWD. IN ALL LIKELIHOOD, RUBY <u>KNEW</u> **HARVEY** WOULD NOT BE TRANSFERRED OR HE WOULD HAVE BEEN <u>INSIDE</u> THE JAIL AS HE HAD BEEN THE PREVIOUS

EVENING, NOT <u>OUTSIDE</u>. IT IS READILY APPARENT THAT RUBY HAS A CONTACT INSIDE THE DPD KEEPING HIM ABREAST OF THE PENDING MOVE OF **HARVEY**.

ABOUT 4:00 PM SATURDAY

CLAY SHAW, LIKE GUY BANISTER, ALSO RESPONDS TO THE ASSASSINATION AND SUBSEQUENT ARREST OF **HARVEY**. HIS RESPONSE HOWEVER IS MARKEDLY DIFFERENT FROM BANISTER'S VIOLENT OUTBURST. SHAW CALLS ATTORNEY DEAN ANDREWS WHO IS IN A HOSPITAL IN NEW ORLEANS AND TELLS HIM TO GO TO DALLAS AND DEFEND **HARVEY**. ANDREWS IS FAMILIAR WITH **HARVEY** AND HAD BEEN ASSISTING HIM IN AN EFFORT TO OVERTURN HIS UNDESIRABLE DISCHARGE FROM THE MARINES. ANDREWS WOULD LATER DENY THE CALL FROM SHAW ATTRIBUTING HIS FAULTY RECOLLECTION OF THE CALL TO THE EFFECTS OF HIS MEDICATIONS AT THE HOSPITAL. A CHECK OF HOSPITAL RECORDS BY FBI AGENT RICHARD BUCARO FOUND THAT ON THE DAY THAT ANDREWS RECEIVED THE CALL FROM SHAW HE WAS GIVEN NO MEDICATION UNTIL <u>8:00 PM</u> THAT EVENING.

*ONE HAS TO WONDER WHY SHAW WOULD OFFER LEGAL ASSISTANCE TO **HARVEY**. DOES HE SIMPLY THINK **HARVEY** IS A VICTIM OF CIRCUMSTANCES BEYOND HIS CONTROL, OR DOES HE BELIEVE THAT **HARVEY** DID INDEED ASSASSINATE THE PRESIDENT? IF SHAW WAS UNAWARE OF THE CONSEQUENCES OF **HARVEY'S** MANIPULATION IN NEW ORLEANS AND LATER DALLAS, HE MIGHT BE SINCERE IN HIS OFFER TO LEND A HAND LEGALLY VIA DEAN ANDREWS. BUT, IF SHAW WAS AWARE OF THE FINAL OUTCOME OF **HARVEY'S** MANIPULATION, SENDING ANDREWS AS A LEGITIMATE LEGAL OPTION FOR **HARVEY** WAS POSTURING ON SHAW'S PART. ANDREWS WAS LITTLE MORE THAN AN AMBULANCE CHASER. HIS CASES TYPICALLY INVOLVED GETTING YOUNG HOMOSEXUAL FRIENDS OF SHAW OUT OF TROUBLE. IF ANDREWS WERE EVENTUALLY **HARVEY'S** LEGAL COUNSEL IN A COURT CASE, HE WOULD HAVE VIRTUALLY NO CHANCE AGAINST THE LAWYERS OF THE JUSTICE DEPARTMENT. SHAW MAY HAVE ALSO CHOSEN ANDREWS IF HE WERE AWARE THAT BY SUNDAY MORNING **HARVEY** WOULD NO LONGER NEED THE SERVICES OF AN ATTORNEY.*

EVA SPRINGER, ANDREW'S SECRETARY, NOTED TO THE FBI THAT ANDREWS CALLED HER AT HOME SHORTLY AFTER 4:00 PM THAT DAY. SHE REFUSED ANDREWS REQUEST THAT SHE GO WITH HIM TO DALLAS. SHE ASKED ANDREWS WHO HAD REQUESTED HIS SERVICES. HE REPLIED "BERTRAND." SHAW OF COURSE WAS ALSO KNOWN AS CLAY BERTRAND.

4:10 PM SATURDAY

HARVEY IS ALLOWED TO PLACE A CALL IN AN EFFORT TO REACH ATTORNEY ABT. HIS ATTEMPT IS WITHOUT SUCCESS.

4:25 PM SATURDAY

WILLIAM SOMERSETT MET WITH JOSEPH MILTEER AT THE UNION TRAIN STATION IN JACKSONVILLE, FLORIDA. THEY THEN DROVE TO COLUMBIA, SOUTH CAROLINA. MILTEER OFFERED FURTHER COMMENTS REGARDING THE EVENTS OF THE PREVIOUS DAY: "WELL I TOLD YOU SO, IT HAPPENED LIKE I TOLD YOU DIDN'T IT? HAPPENED FROM A WINDOW WITH A HIGH-POWERED RIFLE."

5:30 PM SATURDAY

HARVEY SPENDS 5 MINUTES WITH THE PRESIDENT OF THE DALLAS BAR ASSOCIATION, H. LOUIS NICHOLS. HE ONCE AGAIN REITERATES HIS INNOCENCE AND PUZZLEMENT AS TO WHAT IS GOING ON. HE COMMENTS TO NICHOLS: "WELL, I REALLY DON'T KNOW WHAT THIS IS ALL ABOUT….." WHEN NICHOLS OFERS TO FIND HIM A LAWYER, **HARVEY** REPLIES: "NO, NOT NOW. YOU MIGHT COME BACK NEXT WEEK. AND, IF I DON'T GET SOME OF THESE OTHER PEOPLE TO ASSIST ME, I MIGHT ASK YOU TO GET SOMEBODY TO REPRESENT ME."

HARVEY CONTINUES TO HOLD ON TO THE NOTION THAT SOMEONE, "OTHER PEOPLE" FROM THE INTELLIGENCE COMMUNITY, WILL COME FORWARD TO ASSIST HIM. AT THIS POINT, BOTH THE FBI AND THE CIA ARE DOING EVERYTHING POSSIBLE TO DISTANCE THEIR ORGANIZATIONS FROM **HARVEY**.

APPROXIMATELY 5:30 PM SATURDAY
RUBY LEAVES POLICE HEADQUARTERS. HE WOULD THEN GO TO ENQUIRE SHINE AND PRESS SHOP NEAR THE CAROUSEL CLUB.

6:15 PM SATURDAY
CHARGES ARE FILED AGAINST **HARVEY** IN REGARDS TO THE SHOOTING OF GOVENOR CONNALLY.

6:15 PM SATURDAY
RUBY, ACCORDING TO BARTENDER ANDREW ARMSTRONG, STOPS BY THE CAROUSEL CLUB.

6:30—7:15 PM SATURDAY
HARVEY IS <u>FORMALLY</u> INTERROGATED FOR THE 7TH TIME. IN THIS SESSION HE CONTINUES TO INSIST THAT HE IS INNOCENT AND NOTES HIS SUSPICION OF CERTAIN EVIDENCE. HE COMMENTS:

"THERE WAS ANOTHER RIFLE IN THE BUILDING, I HAVE SEEN IT.....WARREN CASTER HAD 2 RIFLES, A 30.06 MAUSER, AND A .22 FOR HIS SON...."

IN REGARDS TO THE SOON TO BE INFAMOUS "BACKYARD PHOTOS": *"I WILL NOT DISCUSS THE PHOTOGRAPHS WITHOUT ADVICE OF AN ATTORNEY....THAT PICTURE IS NOT MINE, BUT THE FACE IS ME. THE PICTURE HAS BEEN MADE BY SUPERIMPOSING MY FACE. THE OTHER PART OF THE PICTURE IS NOT ME AT ALL AND I HAVE NOT SEEN THIS PICTURE BEFORE. I UNDERSTAND PHOTOGRAPHY REAL WELL AND IN TIME I WILL BE ABLE TO SHOW YOU THAT THIS IS NOT MY PICTURE AND THAT IT HAS BEEN MADE BY SOMEONE ELSE."*

ROSCOE WHITE HAD A REPUTATION AS A TRICK PHOTOGRAPHER. HE ALSO HAD AN ASSIGNMENT WITH THE PHOTO SECTION OF THE DPD CRIME LAB. IT IS NOT A CERTAINTY THAT WHITE WAS THE CREATOR OF THE BACKYARD PHOTOS. BUT, IF HE WAS INDEED A SET-UP CONSPIRATOR AND PRESENT AT THE TIPPIT MURDER, THEN ONE WOULD HAVE TO STRONGLY CONSIDER THE POSSIBILITY THAT HE HAD ALSO CREATED THE PHOTOS THAT **HARVEY** QUESTIONED.

HARVEY WENT ON TO DISCUSS THE GUNS INVOLVED IN THE PREVIOUS DAYS'S EVENTS:

"I NEVER KEPT A RIFLE AT MRS. PAINE'S GARAGE....I HAVE NO RECEIPTS FOR PURCHASE OF ANY GUN, AND I HAVE NEVER ORDERED ANY GUNS." "I DO NOT OWN A RIFLE, NEVER POSSESSED A RIFLE."

"THE ADDRESS BOOK IN MY POSSESSION HAS THE NAMES OF RUSSIAN IMMIGRANTS IN DALLAS, TEXAS WHOM I HAVE VISITED."

HARVEY ALSO COMMENTS ON THE "HIDELL" MONIKER:

"I WILL NOT SAY WHO WROTE A.J. HIDELL ON MY SELECTIVE SERVICE CARD....I WILL NOT TELL YOU THE PURPOSE OF CARRYING THE CARD OR THE USE I MADE OF IT."

ALTHOUGH HE REFUSES TO SHED ANY LIGHT ON THE "HIDELL" NAME IN REFERENCE TO THE SELECTIVE SERVICE CARD, HE DOES NOT AT THIS TIME REALIZE THAT THE GUNS IN QUESTION WERE ORDERED BY A "HIDELL" AND THAT AUTHORITIES WILL ATTEMPT TO CONNECT "HIDELL" TO THE SAME POST OFFICE BOXES USED BY **HARVEY.**

7:00 PM SATURDAY
RUBY LEAVES THE CAROUSEL CLUB.

7:15 PM SATURDAY
HARVEY IS RETURNED TO HIS CELL.

7:15 PM SATURDAY
RUBY ONCE AGAIN STOPS AT HIS SISTER EVA'S APARTMENT

ABOUT 7:20 PM SATURDAY
"MARGUERITE" OSWALD LATER RELATED TO THE PRESS THAT 2 FBI AGENTS CAME TO THE DOOR OF HER ROOM AT THE EXECUTIVE INN IN DALLAS WHERE SHE AND MARINA WERE BEING KEPT. ONE OF THE AGENTS SHOWED HER A PHOTO AND SAID: "TELL ME ONE THING, HAVE YOU EVER SEEN THIS MAN BEFORE?" THE PHOTO WAS, ACCORDING TO "MARGUERITE", OF JACK RUBY.

LATER, ON JULY 10TH, 1964, FBI AGENT BARDWELL D. ODUM GAVE AN AFFADIVIT TO THE WARREN COMMISSION STATING THAT HE DID INDEED SHOW A PICTURE TO "MARGUERITE" AND MARINA. HE SAID THE PHOTO WAS FURNISHED TO THE FBI BY THE CIA. THE PHOTO, ACCORDING TO THE CIA, IS BELIEVED TO BE THE PHOTO TAKEN OUTSIDE THE RUSSIAN EMBASSY IN MEXICO CITY. IF THEY ARE CORRECT, THEN THE PHOTO IS NOT OF JACK RUBY BUT POSSIBLY DAVID L.CHRIST AKA DANIEL CARSWELL. BUT IF IT IS NOT JACK RUBY THEN WHY WAS "MARGUERITE" ASKED IF SHE HAD SEEN THE MAN BEFORE AS IT IS VIRTUALLY A CERTAINTY THAT SHE DID NOT KNOW A DAVID L. CHRIST OR A DANIEL CARSWELL?

"MARGUERITE" NOTED THAT THE FBI EITHER KNEW OF A CONNECTION BETWEEN RUBY AND HER "SON" OR HAD SUSPECTED THAT RUBY MIGHT BE STALKING **HARVEY** IN AN EFFORT TO SILENCE HIM. IF SO THEY APPARENTLY SHARED LITTLE OF THIS INFORMATION WITH THE DALLAS POLICE. HOWEVER ONE MUST NOT BE ALARMED BY THIS SINCE RUBY'S ASSIGNMENT, IF SUCCESSFUL, WOULD RELIEVE THE FBI OF ANY POTENTIAL EMBARASSMENT IF IT WERE LATER DISCLOSED BY **HARVEY** THAT THE ACCUSED PRESIDENTIAL ASSASSIN WAS ALSO AN FBI INFORMANT

8:00 PM SATURDAY
HARVEY IS PERMITTED TO USE THE PHONE ONCE AGAIN. HE OCCUPIED THE PHONE BOOTH FOR ABOUT 30 MINUTES. IT IS UNCERTAIN TO WHOM HE PLACED HIS CALL(S). BUT, RUTH PAINE LATER NOTED THAT IT WAS SHE WHO TALKED WITH **HARVEY** ABOUT THAT TIME. BUT, SHE REMEMBERS THE CALL BEING CLOSER TO 9:30 THAN 8:00. IT IS POSSIBLE THAT SHE IS MISTAKEN ON THE EXACT TIME SINCE **HARVEY'S** TWO EVENING PHONE SESSIONS WERE LOGGED AT 8:00 AND 10:45 BY DALLAS POLICE. RUTH PAINE, IN HER CONVERSATION WITH **HARVEY**, TELLS HIM THAT HIS WIFE IS NO LONGER THERE.

*A SEARCH OF **HARVEY'S** POSSESSIONS WAS CONDUCTED AT THE PAINE RESIDENCE ON FRIDAY, THEE 22ND.* ^{D} *A PHOTOGRAPH TAKEN, WHICH WAS <u>NOT</u> INCLUDED IN THE WARREN COMMISSION EXHIBITS, SHOWS A MINOX CAMERA, S/N 27259. KURT LUHN, WHO WAS IN CHARGE OF DISTRIBUTION FOR MINOX IN NEW YORK IN 1963, NOTED THAT THE MINOX WAS USED DURING WWII AS A SPY CAMERA. OFFICER GUS ROSE, WHO HELPED CONDUCT THE 2 SEARCHES OF THE PAINE RESIDENCE, STATED THAT HE FOUND THE CAMERA WITH FILM IN IT INSIDE ONE OF **HARVEY'S** SEABAGS. OFFICER RICHARD STOVALL, WHO HELPED COMPILE THE INITIAL INVENTORY LIST, NOTED ON THE LIST A "SMALL GERMAN CAMERA." INDEED THE FBI INVENTORY LIST COMPILED ON 11/26/63 OF THE POSSESSIONS GIVEN TO THEM BY THE DALLAS POLICE LISTED UNDER ITEM 375 "ONE MINOX CAMERA." HOWEVER, WHEN THOSE SAME ITEMS ARE <u>RE-INVENTORIED</u> IN WASHINGTON, ITEM 375 BECOMES A "MINOX LIGHT METER." BUT, THE SECOND LIST <u>STILL</u> INCLUDED 2 ROLLS OF MINOX FILM. IN THEIR CONCERN OVER THE CAMERA, THE FBI NEGLECTED TO DELETE THE FILM ROLLS.*

*AFTER THE FBI TOOK POSSESSION OF **HARVEY'S** INVENTORIED BELONGINGS, THEY TRIED 3 TIMES TO PRESSURE GUS ROSE INTO CHANGING THE <u>POLICE</u> INVENTORY LIST TO INCLUDE A MINOX LIGHT <u>METER</u>, <u>NOT</u> A MINOX <u>CAMERA.</u> WHEN OFFICER ROSE REFUSED, THE FBI SIMPLY CLAIMED THAT THE MINOX CAMERA BELONGED TO THE PAINES AND WAS OBTAINED FROM THEM ON JANUARY 31, 1964. HOWEVER RUTH PAINE NOTED THAT THERE HAD BEEN <u>NO SEARCH</u> OF THEIR HOUSE <u>AFTER</u> NOVEMBER 23RD, 1963 AND THAT NEITHER*

SHE NOR HER HUSBAND MICHAEL GAVE THE FBI A CAMERA. ONE SHOULD HAVE SERIOUS CONCERNS AS TO:

- WHY THE FBI DENIED THE CAMERA'S EXISTENCE IN **HARVEY'S** POSSESSIONS.

- WHY THE FBI TRIED 3 TIMES TO PRESSURE THE DALLAS POLICE INTO CHANGING THEIR INVENTORY LIST TO EXCLUDE THE MINOX CAMERA IN **HARVEY'S** POSSESSIONS

- WHY THE FBI THEN TRIED TO CLAIM IT WAS THE PAINE'S CAMERA IN LIGHT OF THE FACT THAT THEY HAD INITIALLY DENIED EVEN THE EXISTANCE OF THE CAMERA.

IN MY OPINION, CONSIDERING THE ZEAL IN WHICH THE FBI TRIED TO MAKE THE CAMERA DISAPPEAR, IT COULD HAVE BEEN THE FBI WHO ACTUALLY ISSUED **HARVEY** THE CAMERA FOR USE IN HIS UNDERCOVER INFILTRATION OF THE SHAW/BANISTER/FERRIE GROUP IN NEW ORLEANS. BUT, IT IS JUST AS LIKELY OR MORE LIKELY THAT THE CAMERA MAY HAVE BEEN ISSUED TO HIM BY THE CIA/ONI IN CONJUNCTION WITH EVENTS LEADING UP TO HIS "DEFECTION."

ALSO LISTED IN **HARVEY'S** POSSESSIONS WAS A 15X WOLLENSAK TELESCOPE, 2 PAIRS OF BINOCULARS, SEVERAL CAMERA FILTERS, TW0 35MM CAMERAS, AN ANESCO FLASH ATTACHMENT, A 7X18 TELESCOPE, A LENS HOOD, A COMPASS, AND A PEDOMETER. IT IS NO WONDER THAT CAPTAIN FRITZ HAD HIS SUSPICIONS THAT **HARVEY** HAD SOME TIE TO THE INTELLIGENCE COMMUNITY.

THERE WERE A TOTAL OF 451 ITEMS CONFISCATED AND INVENTORIED IN THE SEARCHES OF THE PAINE HOUSE AND **HARVEY'S** APARTMENT. ONLY 251 ITEMS WERE RETURNED TO THE DALLAS POLICE DEPARTMENT BY THE FBI. FBI SECTION CHIEF BULL BRANIGAN WAS CONCERNED THAT THIS DISCREPANCY WOULD BE QUESTIONED BY THE WARREN COMMISSION. HE WROTE A MEMO TO THE DALLAS FBI OFFICE STATING THAT: "DALLAS SHOULD EITHER FURNISH AMMENDED PAGES AND RE-NUMBER THE EXHIBITS SO THAT ALL THE EXHIBITS ARE ACCOUNTED FOR, OR THEY SHOULD EXPLAIN WHY SOME OF THE EXHIBITS ARE MISSING." THE DALLAS OFFICE RESPONDED TO HIS REQUEST BY RE-NUMBERING THE EXHIBITS TO SHOW ONLY 251 ITEMS. THE REMAINING 200 ITEMS WERE HELD IN WASHINGTON.

8:15 PM SATURDAY

CHIEF CURRY INFORMS THE PRESS THAT **HARVEY** WILL NOT BE MOVED THAT EVENING. HE ALSO TELLS THE REPORTERS THAT IF THEY ARE BACK BY 10:00 AM SUNDAY THAT THEY WILL BE THERE IN TIME TO VIEW THE TRANSFER.

SATURDAY EVENING

FERRIE'S CONCERNS PROMPT A PHONE CALL TO JUDYTH VARY/BAKER THAT EVENING. SHE CLAIMS A FRANTIC FERRIE CALLED HER AND TOLD HER TO STAY CALM, KEEP QUIET, AND THAT "EVERYTHING IS GOING WRONG." HE TOLD VARY/BAKER THAT THE ORIGINAL PLAN WAS FOR HIM TO DRIVE TO HOUSTON TO A LITTLE AIRPORT AT ALICE AND PICK UP **HARVEY**. IF THIS WERE TRUE, THEN **HARVEY** WOULD HAVE HAD A DIFFERENT COURIER TO TAKE HIM FROM RED BIRD IN DALLAS TO HOUSTON. FERRIE WOULD THEN HAVE GONE TO HALL FIELD IN ALICE AND WOULD THEN FLY **HARVEY** TO NEW LAREDO, TEXAS. TWO WEEKS AFTER **HARVEY'S** DEATH, FERRIE WOULD CALL VARY/BAKER ONCE AGAIN. THIS TIME HE TELLS HER THAT TRAFFICANTE'S MIAMI-BASED GROUP IS MONITORING HER BEHAVIOUR. HE WARNS HER TO MAINTAIN A VERY LOW PROFILE AND TO SPEAK NOTHING OF HER SCIENCE WORK IN NEW ORLEANS OR OF **HARVEY**.

8:45 PM SATURDAY

RUBY LEAVES HIS SISTER'S APARTMENT AND DRIVES TO THE EMPIRE ROOM. HE CONVERSES WITH THE PIANO PLAYER AND APPARENTLY WAS IN A GENEROUS MOOD AS HE GAVE SEVERAL WAITRESSES A $5 TIP.

9:00 PM SATURDAY
BILLY GRAMMER, THE COMMUNICATIONS OFFICER ON DUTY AT THE DPD STATED THAT HE RECEIVED AN ANONYMOUS CALL FROM SOMEONE WHO APPARENTLY HAD KNOWLEDGE OF THE DETAILS OF THE TRANSFER OF **HARVEY**. THE CALLER INFORMED GRAMMER THAT: "YOU'RE GOING TO HAVE TO MAKE SOME OTHER PLANS OR WE ARE GOING TO KILL HIM." THE VOICE SOUNDED FAMILIAR TO GRAMMER.

*HOURS LATER, LATE SUNDAY MORNING, GRAMMER WAS AWAKENED BY HIS WIFE AND TOLD THAT **HARVEY** HAD BEEN SHOT BY JACK RUBY. GRAMMER WOULD LATER STATE THAT IT WAS THEN THAT HE REALIZED THAT IT WAS INDEED RUBY'S VOICE WHO HE HAD RECOGNIZED THE PREVIOUS EVENING.*

9:00 PM SATURDAY
FERRIE, COFFEY, AND BEAUBOUEF LEAVE HOUSTON FOR GALVESTON. HOTEL RECORDS HOWEVER SHOW THAT THEY DIDN'T CHECK OUT UNTIL 10:00 AM, SUNDAY MORNING.

9:45 PM SATURDAY
RUBY DEPARTS THE EMPIRE ROOM.

10:00 PM SATURDAY
RUBY RETURNS TO HIS APARTMENT.

10:00 PM SATURDAY
HARVEY IS QUESTONED BY CAPTAIN FRITZ. THIS WOULD BE HIS 8TH FORMAL INTERROGATION.

10:15 PM SATURDAY
A PHONE CALL IS PLACED TO THE JAIL BY A "MR. HURT" IN AN ATTEMPT TO CONVERSE WITH **HARVEY**. THE PHONE CALL IS NOT PUT THROUGH. MR. HURT DID HOWEVER LEAVE A NUMBER AT WHICH **HARVEY** COULD CONTACT HIM.

10:15 PM SATURDAY
GEORGE SENATOR, RUBY'S ROOMMATE, RETURNS TO THEIR RESIDENCE. ACCORDING TO SENATOR, RUBY LEFT SHORTLY AFTER HE (SENATOR) RETURNED.

10:20 PM SATURDAY
RUBY CALLS HIS SISTER EVA. HE THEN CALLS LITTLE LYNN CARLIN (KAREN BENNETT). SHE IS A FORMER STRIPPER AT THE CAROUSEL CLUB. RUBY APPARENTLY FIRED HER JUST THE EVENING BEFORE. CARLIN IS AT THE NICHOL'S PARKING GARAGE. RUBY HAS HUEY REEVES, THE PARKING LOT ATTENDANT, LOAN CARLIN $5 SO THAT SHE CAN RETURN HOME TO FT. WORTH.

10:40 PM SATURDAY
RUBY STOPS BRIEFLY AT HIS SISTER EVA'S WHERE HE WILL CALL HIS BUSINESS PARTNER RALPH PAUL.

10:45 PM SATURDAY
HARVEY CALLED RUTH PAINE TWICE. IN EACH CALL, HE SPOKE TO HER ABOUT OBTAINING LEGAL REPRESENTATION AND ASKED HER TO TRY TO CONTACT JOHN ABT IN NEW YORK.

*TWO MEN WERE PRESENT IN THE ROOM NEXT TO THE SWITCHBOARD ROOM AS **HARVEY** MADE ANOTHER PHONE CALL HE GAVE THE OPERATOR, MRS. LOUISE SWINNEY, TWO NUMBERS TO TRY: 919-834-7430 AND 919-833-1253. MRS. SWEENEY CONSULTED THE TWO MEN AND WAS TOLD TO TELL **HARVEY** THAT THE NUMBERS DIDN'T ANSWER.*

SHE UNPLUGED AND DISCONNECTED **HARVEY** WITHOUT HAVING MADE AN <u>ATTEMPT</u> TO PUT THE CALLS THROUGH. MRS. SWEENEY SAID THAT **HARVEY** HAD BEEN TRYING TO CONTACT A MAN NAMED "HURT" IN RALEIGH, NORTH CAROLINA.

THE HSCA REVEALED LATER THAT THERE WERE 2 "MR. HURTS" IN THAT AREA AT THE TIME. ALTHOUGH BOTH HURTS DENIED KNOWING **HARVEY**, ONE, A MR. JOHN DAVID HURT, HAD BEEN IN MILITARY INTELLIGENCE DURING THE SECOND WORLD WAR. WAS THIS THE MAN **HARVEY** WAS TRYING TO CONTACT?

IN THE LATE 1950'S, THE ONI, OFFICE OF NAVAL INTELLIGENCE, RAN A PROGRAM TO TRAIN INFILTRATORS FOR IRON CURTAIN COUNTRIES AT NAGS HEAD, NORTH CAROLINA. VICTOR MARCHETTI, FORMER CIA OFFICER AND MILITARY ANALYST, RELATED TO AUTHOR ANTHONY SUMMERS THAT THE ONI DID INDEED HAVE A PROGRAM IN WHICH 35-40 YOUNG MEN WERE TRAINED AS "DEFECTORS" AND SENT TO RUSSIA OR EASTERN EUROPEAN COUNTRIES. ALTHOUGH THEY WERE TRAINED AT VARIOUS NAVAL INSTALLATIONS BOTH STATESIDE AND OVERSEAS, MARCHETTI CLAIMED THAT THE OPERATION WAS RUN OUT OF NAG'S HEAD, NORTH CAROLINA.

JOHN DAVID HURT DIED IN 1987. HIS WIFE LATER RECALLED THAT ON THE EVENING OF THE ASSASSINATION HER HUSBAND DRANK EXCESSIVELY AND CALLED THE DALLAS JAIL IN AN ATTEMPT TO SPEAK TO **HARVEY**. HIS CALL WAS NOT PUT THROUGH.

ONE WOULD HAVE TO SURMISE THAT THE TWO MEN SCREENING **HARVEY'S** ATTEMPTED CALLS WOULD HAVE INTELLIGENCE BACKGROUNDS AND THAT THE CALL **HARVEY** WANTED TO MAKE TO A "MR. HURT" WAS INDEED THE MR. JOHN DAVID HURT WHO HAD WORKED ON THE ONI PROGRAM IN NORTH CAROLINA. THIS WOULD BE ONE OF MANY EFFORTS BY THE INTELLIGENCE COMMUNITY TO DISAVOW AND DISRUPT ANY ATTEMPTS AT A CONNECTION BETWEEN THEIR ORGANIZATIONS AND **HARVEY**.

THIS ATTEMPTED CALL, COMBINED WITH THE EARLIER "I'M JUST A PATSY" COMMENT WOULD FURTHER SIGNIFY THAT **HARVEY** WAS, IN INTELLIGENCE PARLANCE, A "LOOSE CANNON." HIS SILENCING WOULD NOW TAKE ON AN EVEN HIGHER DEGREE OF URGENCY.

THE W.C. DID NOT QUESTION LOUISE SWEENEY OR ALVEETA TREON, THE OPERATOR WHO WOULD RELIEVE SWEENEY FOR THE NIGHT SHIFT. ONLY THE CALLS TO THE PAINE RESIDENCE AND TO ATTORNEY JOHN ABT WERE NOTED IN THEIR LOGS.

ABOUT 11:00 PM SATURDAY
DAVID FERRIE CHECKS INTO ROOM 117 AT THE DRIFTWOOD MOTEL IN GALVESTON, TEXAS. TRAVELING WITH FERRIE IS ALVIN BEAUBOEUF AND MELVIN COFFEY.

11:10 PM SATURDAY
RUBY ARRIVES AT THE NICHOL'S GARAGE. HE REIMBURSES HUEY REEVES THE $5:00 THAT HE HAD REEVES GIVE STRIPPER LITTLE LYNN CARLIN. CARLIN HAD CALLED RUBY EARLIER FROM THE GARAGE AND HAD ASKED FOR THE LOAN.

ABOUT 11:15PM SATURDAY
RUBY STOPS AT THE CAROUSEL CLUB. HE WOULD MAKE SEVERAL PHONE CALLS AND LEAVE JUST BEFORE MIDNIGHT. TWO OF THE CALLS WERE TO HIS BUSINESS PARTNER RALPH PAUL.

LATE SATURDAY EVENING
FERRIE CALLS HIS NEW ORLEANS ROOMMATE LAYTON MARTENS. MARTENS TELLS FERRIE THAT HE HAD BEEN VISITED BY WRAY GILL, MARCELLO'S ATTORNEY. GILL, ACCORDING TO MARTENS STATED THAT AMONG **HARVEY'S** POSSESSIONS WHEN ARRESTED WAS A LIBRARY CARD IN FERRIE'S NAME. ONE WOULD THINK THAT APPARENTLY **HARVEY** NEVER FORWARDED FERRIE'S CARD TO VARY/BAKER OR THAT SHE HAD USED IT AND RETURNED IT TO **HARVEY** WHO APPARENTLY NEVER RETURNED IT TO FERRIE. BUT, WRAY GILL HAD LIED TO MARTENS REGARDING A

LIBRARY CARD FOUND IN **HARVEY'S** POSSESSION. MARTENS IN TURN UNKNOWINGLY RELATED THE LIE TO FERRIE. THERE WAS NOT A LIBRARY CARD IN FERRIE'S NAME FOUND AMONG **HARVEY'S** POSSESSIONS. WHY WOULD WREY LIE TO MARTENS? WAS WRAY'S LIE TO MARTENS REGARDING THE LIBRARY CARD AN EFFORT TO PUT FERRIE ON NOTICE THAT HE WAS INDEED INVOLVED IN THE EVENTS OF THAT WEEKEND UP TO AND INCLUDING THE ASSASSINATION?

CHAPTER 14: THE SUNDAY SILENCING OF HARVEY

MIDNIGHT TO 12:15 AM SUNDAY
RUBY VISITS THE PAGO CLUB AND BRIEFLY TALKS WITH BOB NORTON THE MANAGER.

APPROXIMATELY 12:45 AM SUNDAY
RUBY RETURNS TO HIS APARTMENT WHERE HE ONCE AGAIN CALLS HIS SISTER, EVA.

2:15 AM SUNDAY
DEPUTY C.C. MCCOY REPORTED TO SHERIFF BILL DECKER: "AT APPROXIMATELY 2:15 AM, I RECEIVED A CALL FROM A PERSON THAT STATED HE WAS A MEMBER OF A GROUP OF 100 AND THAT HE WANTED THE SHERIFF'S OFFICE TO KNOW THAT THEY HAD VOTED 100% TO KILL OSWALD WHILE HE WAS TRANSFERRED….WANTED THIS DEPARTMENT TO HAVE THE INFORMATION SO THAT NONE OF THE DEPUTIES WOULD GET HURT." THE DALLAS POLICE WOULD RECEIVE A SIMILAR CALL AT APPROXIMATELY THE SAME TIME.

*IN THE NOW FAMOUS PHOTO OF **HARVEY** BEING SHOT BY RUBY, IT IS QUITE APPARENT THAT THE PHONE CALL HAD THE DESIRED EFFECT. THERE WERE NO DETECTIVES STANDING IN <u>FRONT</u> OF **HARVEY** AS HE WAS BEING ESCORTED TO THE AREA WHERE THE TRANSFER VEHICLE WAS SCHEDULED TO BE AWAITING HIS ARRIVAL. IN FACT, WHEN PARKLAND HOSPITAL HEARD **HARVEY** WAS TO BE MOVED THAT SUNDAY MORNING, THEY ACTUALLY MADE ARRANGEMENTS TO RECEIVE HIM.*

*PARKLAND ADMINISTRATOR STEVE LANDREGAN NOTED THAT HE HAD RECEIVED A CALL EARLY SUNDAY MORNING THAT WARNED THAT A CROWD WAS GATHERING FOR **HARVEY'S** TRANSFER AND THAT IT WAS SUGGESTED TO HIM THAT "WE MIGHT WANT TO ALERT THE EMERGENCY ROOM." LANDREGAN WAS ALSO TOLD THAT THE TELEPHONE SERVICEMEN WERE ON STAND-BY AT PARKLAND. WHEN THE HOSPITAL RECEIVED WORD THAT THE WOUNDED **HARVEY** WAS ENROUTE THE SERVICEMEN PROMTLY HOOKED UP 25 EXTRA PHONE LINES FOR THE PRESS.*

2:30 AM SUNDAY
THE FBI RECEIVES A CALL SIMILAR IN CONTENT TO THE 2:15 AM CALL RECEIVED BY THE SHERIFF'S OFFICE.

3:00 AM SUNDAY
BILLY GRAMMER, DPD, RECEIVED A CALL INFORMING HIM THAT **HARVEY** WOULD BE KILLED IF THE TRANSFER DIDN'T TAKE PLACE WITHOUT PUBLIC KNOWLEDGE. GRAMMER NOTED THAT THE VOICE SOUNDED FAMILIAR TO HIM.

*ARMSTRONG SUSPECTS THAT THE CALLER INVOLVED IN ALL THREE INSTANCES IS RUBY. RUBY IS NOW APPARENTLY TRYING TO AVOID ELIMINATING **HARVEY** AS HE WAS INSTRUCTED. HAS HE HAD CONTACT WITH DAVID FERRIE? DOES RUBY, LIKE FERRIE, NOW HAVE SOME SUSPICION THAT **HARVEY** DID NOT SHOOT EITHER THE PRESIDENT OR OFFICER TIPPIT?*

3:45 AM SUNDAY
THE FBI NOTIFIES THE SHERIFF'S OFFICE OF THE THREATENING CALL THAT THEY HAD RECEIVED. THE CALL WAS TAKEN BY VERNON GLOSSUP, A NIGHT DESK CLERK AT THE DALLAS FBI OFFICE. FBI SA NEWSOM CALLS DPD CAPTAIN W.B.FRAZIER AND INFORMS HIM OF THE EARLIER THREATENING PHONE CALL.

EARLY AM SUNDAY
ANOTHER **HARVEY**/CASTRO CONNECTION ARTICLE APPEARED IN THE NEW YORK TIMES IN THE SUNDAY, NOVEMBER 24TH EDITION. ONCE AGAIN DAVID PHILLIPS' DRE/AMSPELL, VIA CARLOS BRINGUIER, NOTES **HARVEY'S** PRO-CASTRO SYMPATHIES AND HIS INVOLVEMENT IN THE FPCC.

PHILLIIPS IS NOT ONLY ABLE TO SWAY THE EARLY THEORIES OF THE ASSASSINATION TOWARDS A CASTRO CONNECTION BUT HE IS ABLE TO SUCCESSFULLY ISOLATE THE CIA FROM THIS MANIPULATION BY UTILIZING HIS AMSPELL/DRE MOUTHPIECE CARLOS BRINGUIER.

5:00 AM SUNDAY
DPD CAPTAIN FRAZIER CALLS DPD CAPTAIN FRITZ AND INFORMS HIM OF THE EARLIER PHONE THREAT. FRITZ WOULD LATER NOTE "I HAVE ALWAYS FELT THAT THAT WAS RUBY WHO MADE THAT CALL."

5:30 AM SUNDAY
A DALLAS DEPUTY SHERIFF PHONES THE DALLAS POLICE AND INFORMS THEM THAT SHERIFF DECKER WANTS **HARVEY** TRANSFERRED TO THE COUNTY JAIL AS SOON AS IT CAN BE ARRANGED.

6:00 AM SUNDAY
DPD CAPTAIN FRAZIER CALLS CHIEF CURRY'S HOME BUT IS UNABLE TO CONTACT CURRY. UNDETERRED, THE DPD SENDS A SQUAD CAR TO CURRY'S HOME.

7:00 AM SUNDAY
RUBY, OPERATING ON VERY LITTLE SLEEP, ARRIVES AT THE ALLRIGHT PARKING LOT WHERE HE LEAVES HIS 1960 OLDSMOBILE. HE HAD LEFT HIS WALLET AND KEYS TO THE AUTOMOBILE TRUNK IN THE GLOVE BOX. IN THE TRUNK WERE THE IGNITION KEYS AND $873 IN CASH.

8:00 AM SUNDAY
WARREN RICHEY, A CAMERAMAN AT WBAP-TV REPORTED SEEING RUBY IN FRONT OF THE POLICE STATION. IRA WARNER AND JOHN SMITH, BOTH NEWSMEN FOR WBAP, CONFIRMED RICHEY'S SIGHTINGS OF RUBY.

9:00 AM SUNDAY
FERRIE, COFFEY AND BEAUBOUEF CHECK OUT OF THE DRIFTWOOD MOTEL AND LEAVE GALVESTON. ONCE AGAIN THERE IS A DISCREPANCY REGARDING THEIR CHECK-OUT TIME. HOTEL RECORDS SHOW THEY DIDN'T CHECK OUT UNTIL 2:00 PM

9:30 AM SUNDAY
RAY RUSHING, A PLANO, TEXAS PREACHER TOLD DALLAS POLICE LT. JACK REVILL THAT HE HAD A BRIEF CONVERSATION WITH RUBY AT ABOUT THIS TIME AT CITY HALL.

SUNDAY MID MORNING
THE EVIDENCE TAKEN FROM **HARVEY'S** ROOMING HOUSE AND THE PAINE RESIDENCE IS RETURNED TO THE DALLAS POLICE FROM THE FBI IN WASHINGTON. THE DPD OFFERED THAT THEY HAD FOUND **HARVEY'S** PALM PRINT ON THE RIFLE. LATER, ON NOVEMBER 26TH AT 2:00 PM, THE EVIDENCE WAS ONCE AGAIN TRANSFERRED TO THE FBI'S AGENT VINCENT DRAIN.

*AGENT DRAIN RELATED IN 1984 THAT HE DOUBTED WHETHER THERE WAS ACTUALLY SUCH A PRINT: "ALL I CAN FIGURE IS THAT IT (**HARVEY'S**) PRINT) WAS SOME KIND OF CUSHION BECAUSE THEY (DALLAS PD) WERE GETTING A LOT OF HEAT BY SUNDAY NIGHT. YOU COULD TAKE THE PRINT OFF OSWALD'S CARD AND PUT IT ON THE RIFLE. SOMETHING LIKE THAT HAPPENED."*

ONCE AGAIN, THE DPD'S PROPERTY CLERK LISTED AMONG THOSE ITEMS TRANSFERRED TO AGENT DRAIN ON NOVEMBER 26TH, THE RIFLE, ONE LIVE ROUND, AND 2 SPENT HULLS. THE "2 SPENT 6.5 HULLS" NOTATION ALSO INCLUDED THE COMMENT "FOUND UNDER WINDOW." THE ABSENCE OF THE 3RD SPENT HULL ORIGINALLY FOUND "UNDER THE WINDOW" IN THE TSBD REMAINS.

BUT, AT 1:00 AM ON NOVEMBER 27TH CAPTAIN WILL FRITZ TRANSFERS TO FBI AGENT JAMES HOSTY "ONE 6.5MM RIFLE HULL RECOVERED AT TSBD ON 11-22-63." ALAS, THE 3RD RIFLE HULL RETURNS. THE QUESTION REMAINS HOWEVER WHERE HAD IT BEEN SINCE THE AFTERNOON OF NOVEMBER 22ND AND WHAT WAS THE REASON FOR ITS ABSENCE?

9:30-11:10 AM SUNDAY

HARVEY IS INTERROGATED FOR THE LAST TIME BY SECRET SERVICE AGENT THOMAS J. KELLY, CAPTAIN FRITZ, AND POSTAL INSPECTOR HARRY HOLMES. THIS WILL BE THE 10TH AND FINAL TIME THAT **HARVEY** IS INTERROGATED EITHER FORMALLY OR INFORMALLY.

APPARENTLY THE TOPIC OF THE PACKAGE HE CARRIED TO WORK ON NOVEMBER 22ND CAME UP ONCE AGAIN AS **HARVEY** REMARKED: "I DON'T RECALL THE SHAPE (OF THE BAG), IT MAY HAVE BEEN A SMALL SACK, OR A LARGE SACK; YOU DON'T ALWAYS FIND ONE THAT JUST FITS YOUR SANDWICHES." HE WENT ON TO NOTE: "THE SACK WAS IN THE CAR BESIDE ME, ON MY LAP AS IT ALWAYS IS…IT WAS <u>NOT</u> ON THE BACK SEAT."

FRAZIER'S COMMENTS REGARDING THE PACKAGE WAS THAT IT WAS ON THE <u>BACK</u> SEAT AND THAT **HARVEY** CLAIMED IT CONTAINED CURTAIN RODS. **HARVEY** DENIED THE "CURTAIN ROD" STORY AND MAINTAINED THAT THE PACKAGE REMAINED ON THE <u>FRONT</u> SEAT ON OR NEAR HIS LAP. THE PACKAGE FRAZIER DESCRIES AS ALLEGEDLY CONTAINING THE MANNLICHER-CARCANO WOULD OBVIOUSLY BE TOO LONG TO PLACE ON THE FRONT SEAT BETWEEN HIM AND **HARVEY**. IT WAS THEREFORE NECESSARY FOR FRAZIER TO RELEGATE THE PACKAGE TO THE <u>BACK</u> SEAT.

THE PACKAGE **HARVEY** DESCRIBES AS CONTAINING HIS LUNCH WAS OBVIOUSLY TOO SMALL TO ACCOMMODATE THE RIFLE ALLEGEDLY USED IN THE PRESIDENTIAL SHOOTING. AUTHORITIES WOULD HAVE TO FIND ANOTHER WAY AND ANOTHER DAY FOR **HARVEY** TO HAVE TAKEN A RIFLE INTO THE TSBD.

CHIEF JESSE CURRY NOTED LATER: "WE WERE VIOLATING EVERY PRINCIPLE OF INTERROGATION………IT WAS JUST AGAINST ALL PRINCIPLES OF GOOD INTERROGATION PRACTICE." **HARVEY** WAS INTERROGATED FOR A TOTAL OF APPROXIMATELY 12 HOURS FROM FRIDAY AFTERNOON UNTIL HIS DEATH ON SUNDAY MORNING.

POSTAL INSPECTOR HARRY HOLMES NOTED THAT **HARVEY** "HAD BEEN TRAINED TO EVADE QUESTIONS AND BE ABLE TO KEEP HIMSELF COMPOSED TO GUARD WHAT HE WANTED TO KEEP SECRET." INDEED THIS TECHNIQUE WOULD HAVE BEEN PRACTICED PRIOR TO HIS CIA-SPONSORED "DEFECTION" AS IT WAS A CERTAINTY THAT HE WOULD BE SUBJECTED TO INTERROGATION BY THE KGB.

HARVEY ALSO HAD A MAP OF A PORTION OF DALLAS WITH "X'S" MARKED ON IT. HOLMES RECALLED **HARVEY'S** COMMENTS ON THE MAP: "WELL, THIS OVER HERE IS WHERE I LIVE ON BECKLEY. YOU'LL NOTICE THOSE X'S ARE ON BUS LINES BETWEEN THERE AND WHERE MY WIFE STAYED WITH MRS. PAINE OVER IN IRVING. EVERY ONE OF THESE X'S ARE ON A BUS LINE. I HAD NO TRANSPORTATION, SO I WOULD CHECK THEM OUT. EVERY X IS WHERE I INTERVIEWED FOR A JOB. IN FACT HERE'S AN X ON THE SCHOOL BOOK DEPOSITORY AND THAT'S WHERE I GOT A JOB." HOLMES NOTED THAT HE HAD NO REASON NOT TO BELIEVE HIM SINCE **HARVEY** WAS VERY FORTHRIGHT ABOUT IT AND THAT HIS EXPLANATIONS DID INDEED MAKE SENSE.

HOLMES QUESTIONS HIM ABOUT HIS FIRST DALLAS P.O. BOX, #2915. HOLMES IS SOMEWHAT SURPRISED ABOUT **HARVEY'S** CANDOR REGARDING THE BOX SINCE ITHIS IS THE P.O. BOX THAT THE ALLEGED ASSASSINATION RIFLE WAS SENT TO. I WOULD OFFER THAT **HARVEY'S** OPENNESS REGARDING THE P.O. BOX STEMS FROM THE LIKELIHOOD THAT HE WAS COMPLETELY UNAWARE THAT ANY RIFLE HAD BEEN SENT TO THAT P.O. BOX.

ONCE AGAIN HE IS QUESTIONED ABOUT "HIDELL" BY POSTAL INSPECTOR HOLMES. HOLMES: "ISN'T IT A FACT THAT WHEN YOU WERE ARRESTED YOU HAD AN I.D. CARD WITH HIS NAME ON IT IN YOUR POSSESSION?" **HARVEY** REPLIED "THAT'S RIGHT." HOLMES: "HOW DO YOU EXPLAIN THAT?" **HARVEY**: "I DON'T EXPLAIN IT." HE ONCE AGAIN REFUSES TO ELABORATE ON "HIDELL", THE APPARENT INTELLIGENCE "MIDDLE-MAN"

BETWEEN **HARVEY** AND HUNT/PHILLIPS. I SUSPECT THAT **HARVEY** IS EITHER AWARE THAT LEE IS "HIDELL" OR STRONGLY SUSPECTS THE SAME.

9:45 AM SUNDAY

JOHN SMITH AND IRA WARNER, THE WBAP NEWSMEN, NOTED THAT RUBY APPROACHED THEM AND ASKED: "HAS HE (**HARVEY**) BEEN BROUGHT DOWN YET?" KEEP IN MIND THAT CHIEF CURRY HAD, ON SATURDAY EVENING, TOLD THE PRESS THAT **HARVEY** WOULD BE TRANSFERRED AT 10:00 AM SUNDAY.

*RUBY APPARENTLY RETURNED TO HIS APARTMENT SHORTLY AFTER THIS MISSED ENCOUNTER WITH **HARVEY** AS HE WAS AT HIS RESIDENCE AT 10:19 TO RECEIVE THE UPCOMING CALL FROM LITTLE LYNN CARLIN.*

10:19 AM SUNDAY

ACCORDING TO LITTLE LYNN CARLIN, A NOW <u>FORMER</u> STRIPPER AT THE CAROUSEL CLUB, SHE CALLS RUBY AT HIS APARTMENT REQUESTING A SALARY ADVANCE OF $25.00. SINCE SHE IS NOW APPARENTLY HOME IN FT. WORTH, THE MONEY WILLL HAVE TO BE WIRED TO HER.

*KEEP IN MIND THAT CARLIN HAD BORROWED $5 FROM RUBY LESS THAN 12 HOURS AGO VIA THE TEMPORARY LOAN THROUGH HUEY REEVES. WHY WOULD SHE BE CALLING RUBY EARLY SUNDAY MORNING FOR 5 TIMES THAT AMOUNT? IT IS MY SUSPICION THAT THE PHONE CALL, IF INDEED IT WAS MADE, WAS NECESSARY TO SET THE STAGE FOR RUBY'S PRESENCE NEAR THE POLICE STATION WHERE **HARVEY** WAS BEING HELD. THE WESTERN UNION OFFICE IS ONLY 100 YARDS FROM THE POLICE STATION.*

RUBY HAD, THE PREVIOUS EVENING AT APPROXIMATELY 11:10 PM, REIMBURSED <u>HUEY REEVES</u> AT THE NICHOL'S GARAGE THE $5 IN CASH THAT REEVES HAD LOANED TO CARLIN ON RUBY'S BEHALF. REEVES HAD GIVEN CARLIN THE $5 AT APPROXIMATELY 10:20 PM. IT WOULD SEEM THAT NOT ONLY COULD CARLIN HAVE WAITED 50 MINUTES FOR RUBY TO ARRIVE AT THE GARAGE WHERE HE COULD HAVE <u>PERSONALLY</u> HANDED HER THE $5, BUT THAT SHE WOULD ALSO BE AWARE THAT THE $5 LOAN WAS NOT NEAR ENOUGH AS SHE WOULD ONLY 12 HOURS LATER ASK FOR AN ADDITIONAL $25.

*IT IS MY SUSPICION THAT RUBY WAS DELIBERATELY TRYING TO AVOID PERSON-TO-PERSON CONTACT WITH CARLIN LATE THAT SATURDAY NIGHT. SHE WOULD THEN LEAVE DALLAS TO RETURN TO FT. WORTH. FROM THAT DISTANCE THERE WOULD BE NO PERSONAL CONTACT WITH RUBY, NOR AN ADDITIONAL LOAN VIA HUEY REEVES. THE ONLY OPTION IN FULFILLING CARLIN'S REQUEST FOR THE ADDITIONAL FUNDS WAS VIA A WIRED MONEY ORDER FROM A WESTERN UNION OFFICE CONVENIENTLY LOCATED 100 YARDS FROM WHERE **HARVEY** WAS JAILED.*

*ON NOVEMBER 24TH, AFTER **HARVEY** HAD BEEN SHOT, CARLIN WAS INTERVIEWED BY SA WARNER OF THE SS. WARNER'S AFFADAVIT TO THE W.C. NOTED THAT CARLIN WAS "HIGHLY AGITATED AND RELUCTANT TO MAKE ANY STATEMENT TO ME…SHE SEEMED ON THE POINT OF HYSTERIA." CARLIN HAD CLEARLY STUMBLED INTO A SCENARIO THAT WOULD NECESSITATE HER LYING ABOUT THE NECESSITY OF THE $25 WIRED MONEY ORDER. HER "HYSTERIA" OVER HER FORCED INVOLVEMENT WAS UNDERSTANDABLE IN LIGHT OF WHAT HAD TRANSPIRED IN DALLAS THAT WEEKEND.*

10:45 AM SUNDAY

RUBY LEAVES HIS APARTMENT ENROUTE TO THE WESTERN UNION OFFICE TO WIRE THE MONEY TO LYNN CARLIN.

11:15 AM SUNDAY

THE TRANSFER PARTY WITH **HARVEY** IN TOW BEGINS TO LEAVE CAPTAIN FRITZ'S OFFICE.

IN HS STATEMENT OF 26 NOVEMBER, CAPTAIN FRITZ NOTED THAT HE HAD INSTRUCTED DETECTIVE JAMES LEAVELLE TO CUFF HIS LEFT HAND TO THE RIGHT HAND OF **HARVEY**. DETECTIVE L.C. GRAVES WOULD BE ON **HARVEY'S** LEFT SIDE. DETECTIVE LESLIE MONTGOMERY WAS TO FOLLOW BEHIND **HARVEY**. FRITZ WAS TO WALK IN FRONT OF **HARVEY**. THEY PROCEEDED IN JUST THIS FASHION FROM THE HOMICIDE AND ROBBERY BUREAU OFFICE TO THE JAIL OFFICE IN THE BASEMENT. UPON REACHING THE EXIT DOOR OF THE JAIL THAT OPENED INTO THE PARKING GARAGE, FRITZ EXITED FIRST AND NOTED THAT HE ASKED AN OFFICER IF "EVERYTHING WAS SECURE." THE OFFICER REPLIED "YES" AND FRITZ THEN TURNED AND TOLD THE TRANSFER PARTY TO "FOLLOW HIM." FRITZ THEN APPARENTLY QUICKENED HIS PACE TO THE DEGREE THAT HE HAD ALREADY REACHED THE DOOR OF THE TRANSFER VEHICLE WHEN HE NOTED THAT HE HEARD A SHOT, THEN TURNED AND LOOKED BACK TO SEE THE MAYHEM THAT ENSUED FOLLOWING RUBY'S SHOOTING OF **HARVEY**. APPARENTLY THE "FRITZ IN FRONT" NOTION ONLY EXTENDED TO THE POINT WHERE THE TRANSFER PARTY REACHED THE JAIL EXIT DOOR, NOT THE COMPLETE JOURNEY TO THE AWATING TRANSFER VEHICLE.

THE OFFICER IN CHARGE OF BASEMENT SECURITY WAS SERGEANT P.T. DEAN. DEAN WAS KNOWN TO BE A CLOSE ASSOCIATE OF DALLAS MAFIA HEAD JOSEPH CIVELLO. CIVELLO OF COURSE WAS CARLOS MARCELLO'S REPRESENTATIVE IN DALLAS AS MARCELLO'S TERRITORY COVERED BOTH LOUISIANA AND TEXAS. UPON RETURNING FROM THE 1957 MAFIA SUMMIT IN APALACHIN, NEW YORK, CIVELLO HAD DINNER WITH SERGEANT DEAN. I WOULD SUSPECT THAT IT WAS SERGEANT DEAN WHO HAD KEPT RUBY INFORMED AS TO EXACTLY WHEN **HARVEY** WOULD BE MOVED AND ASSISTED RUBY IN GAINING A TIMELY ENTRANCE TO THE BASEMENT OF THE JAIL.

DEAN WAS THE NEXTDOOR NEIGHBOR OF DOYLE LANE, THE MANAGER OF THE WESTERN UNION OFFICE WHERE RUBY IS ABOUT TO PURCHASE THE MONEY ORDER FOR LYNN CARLIN.

11:17 AM SUNDAY
RUBY RECEIVES A RECEIPT FROM DOYLE LANE FOR THE $25 MONEY ORDER HE HAD WIRED TO LYNN CARLIN AT THE WESTERN UNION OFFICE IN FT. WORTH.

11:19 AM SUNDAY
RUBY CROSSES THE STREET, WALKS THE APPROXIMATELY 100 YARD DISTANCE FROM THE WESTERN UNION OFFICE, AND ENTERS THE JAIL BASEMENT

11:19 AM SUNDAY
TOM HOWARD, SOON TO BE RUBY'S INITIAL LAWYER, ENTERS THE POLICE STATION AND LOOKS THROUGH THE WINDOW AS **HARVEY** IS BEING TAKEN OFF THE ELEVATOR. H. L. MCGEE, A DALLAS P.D. DISPATCHER LATER STATED: "AT THE TIME OSWALD WAS BROUGHT OFF THE JAIL ELEVATOR, TOM HOWARD TURNED AWAY FROM THE WINDOW AND WENT BACK TOWARD THE HARWOOD STREET DOOR. HE WAVED AT ME AS HE WENT BY AND SAID: 'THAT'S ALL I WANTED TO SEE.' SHORTLY AFTER THAT I HEARD A SHOT."

11:21 AM SUNDAY
IKE PAPPAS, A REPORTER FROM WNEW-AM IN NEW YORK CITY, ASKS **HARVEY** "DO YOU HAVE ANYTHING TO SAY IN YOUR DEFENSE?" ALMOST SIMULTANEOUSLY, RUBY SHOOTS **HARVEY**.

RICHER, WALKER, AND SMITH, THE WBAP NEWSMEN, WOULD LATER VIEW RUBY'S MUG SHOT. WALKER WOULD LATER TELL THE WARREN COMMISSION: "WELL, ABOUT 4 OF US POINTED AT HIM AT THE SAME TIME IN THE TRUCK. I MEAN WE ALL RECOGNIZED HIM AT THE SAME TIME." RUBY WOULD LATER TELL THE COMMISSION: "WHO EVER COULD HAVE TIMED IT SO PERFECTLY BY SECONDS.... IF IT WERE TIMED THAT WAY, THEN SOMEONE IN THE DALLAS POLICE DEPARTMENT IS GUILTY OF GIVING THE INFO AS TO WHEN OSWALD WAS COMING DOWN....."

SATURDAY NIGHT CHIEF CURRY HAD REMARKED TO REPORTERS: "OKAY, YOU CAN GO GET SOME SLEEP. WE WON'T TRANSFER HIM BEFORE 10:00 TOMORROW MORNING." THE NEWSMEN HOWEVER TOOK THE REMARK TO MEAN THAT THE MOVE WOULD BE EXACTLY AT 10:00. **HARVEY** DID NOT ENTER THE PARKING GARAGE UNTIL 11:20. RUBY APPARENTLY HAD BETTER SOURCES THAN THE NEWSMEN.

CHIEF CURRY INSISTED THAT RUBY ENTERED THE BASEMENT VIA THE MAIN ST. RAMP. HE OFFERED THAT OFFICER ROY VAUGHN, STATIONED AT THE TOP OF THE RAMP, WAS DISTRACTED BY THE ARRIVAL OF A "DECOY" CAR DRIVEN BY LT. RIO SAM PIERCE. VAUGHN AND PIERCE INSISTED HOWEVER THAT RUBY DID NOT ENTER VIA THE MAIN ST. RAMP. IN CUSTODY, RUBY WAS QUESTIONED BY S.A. FORREST SORRELS, DISTRICT SECRET SERVICE CHIEF. ON NOVEMBER 26TH, DPD SERGEANT P.T. DEAN NOTED IN A REPORT: "I QUESTIONED RUBY AS TO HOW HE HAD ENTERED THE BASEMENT.....RUBY THEN STATED TO ME IN THE PRESENCE OF MR. SORRELS THAT HE HAD ENTERED THE BASEMENT THROUGH THE RAMP ENTERING ON MAIN STREET." S.A. SORRELS KNEW THIS TO BE A LIE. RUBY DID NOT STATE THAT HE HAD ENTERED THE BASEMENT VIA THE MAIN STREET RAMP. RUBY WAS ALSO QUESTIONED BY FBI AGENT C. RAY HALL WHO WOULD LATER TELL THE W.C. THAT RUBY "DID NOT WISH TO SAY HOW HE GOT INTO THE BASEMENT."

IN CUSTODY, RUBY INITIALLY WOULD ONLY OFFER THAT HE HAD ENTERED THE BASEMENT VIA MAIN STREET. HE WOULD NOT AND DID NOT SAY SPECIFICALLY THAT IT WAS VIA THE MAIN STREET RAMP. AFTER RUBY HAD MET WITH SORRELS, P.T. DEAN, AND HALL, HE MET WITH HIS LAWYER, TOM HOWARD AT 1:56 PM SUNDAY. AT 3:15 RUBY WAS INTERROGATED BY CAPTAIN WILL FRITZ. RUBY NOW OFFERED THAT HE ENTERED VIA THE MAIN STREET RAMP. I SUSPECT HE WAS TOLD BY HOWARD THAT IT WOULD BE PRUDENT NOT TO REVEAL HOW HE ACTUALLY ENTERED THE BASEMENT BUT TO ADHERE TO THE VERSION TENDERED BY CHIEF CURRY AND P.T. DEAN THAT HAD HIM USING THE MAIN STREET RAMP. DEAN WOULD BE PARTICULARLY RELIEVED BY THIS DECISION AS HE WAS RESPONSIBLE FOR SECURING ALL ENTRANCES TO THE BASEMENT DURING THE TRANSFER OF **HARVEY**.

RATHER THAN DISCLOSE THAT HE WAS ASSISTED IN HIS ENTRANCE TO THE BASEMENT VIA THE SUPPOSEDLY LOCKED STAIRWELL FROM THE MAIN STREET LOBBY ENTRANCE TO THE BASEMENT, RUBY WAS SIMPLY TOLD TO ADMIT TO HAVE USED THE MAIN STREET RAMP. THE DPD NOT ONLY ALLOWED RUBY TO SILENCE **HARVEY**, BUT THEY FACILITATED HIS ABILITY TO DO SO.

THE W.C. CHOSE TO BELIEVE CHIEF CURRY'S AND P.T. DEAN'S VERSION OF RUBY HAVING ENTERED THE BASEMENT VIA THE MAIN ST. RAMP.

RUBY'S ASSIGNMENT WAS TO SHOOT **HARVEY**. IT HAD BEEN HIS TASK ALL WEEKEND. RUBY HAD EITHER BEEN CONVINCED BY THE SET-UP CONSPIRATORS THAT **HARVEY**, THROUGH HIS INFILTRATION OF BOTH PRO AND ANTI-CASTRO GROUPS, HAD BEEN "TURNED" AND HAD ACTUALLY SHOT THE PRESIDENT, OR THAT EVEN IF HE HAD NOT SHOT THE PRESIDENT, THERE WAS THE RISK THAT HE WOULD REVEAL THE PURPOSE OF WHAT BOTH HE AND **HARVEY** HAD PERCEIVED AS A LEGITIMATE "CARCINOGENS TO CUBA" INTELLIGENCE MISSION AND POSSIBLY JEOPARDIZE THE PLANNED DECEMBER 1ST C-DAY COUP. RUBY COULD EASILY BE PURSUADED TO SILENCE **HARVEY** FOR THE "GOOD OF THE COUNTRY." RUBY STRIVED TO BE CONSIDERED AN IMPORTANT FIGURE. IF RUBY THOUGHT HE WAS SILENCING **HARVEY** IN THE SERVICE OF HIS GOVERNMENT HE WOULD PERFORM WHAT WAS ASKED OF HIM WITHOUT HESITATION

HYMAN RUBENSTEIN, THE ELDER BROTHER OF JACK RUBY, WOULD NOTE LATER: "OUR BROTHER DID THIS FOR ONLY ONE REASON...HE'S A GOOD PATRIOTIC AMERICAN AND HE GOT CARRIED AWAY." RUBY'S YOUNGER BROTHER WOULD OFFER THAT RUBY KILLED **HARVEY** BECAUSE HE WAS "ALWAYS AGGRESSIVELY PATRIOTIC."IT WAS TOLD THAT RUBY HAD ONCE INSISTED THAT A FRIEND PUT OUT A CIGARETTE PRIOR TO THE PLAYING OF THE NATIONAL ANTHEM AT A SPORTING EVENT.

THIS "AGGRESSIVE PATRIOTISM" COULD INDEED BE THE VERY TRAIT THAT WOULD MAKE IT A RELATIVELY EASY TASK FOR THE SET-UP CONSPIRATORS TO ENLIST RUBY'S ASSISTANCE IN SILENCING **HARVEY**. ONE MUST ALSO CONSIDER THE VERY REAL POSSIBILITY THAT RUBY PERFORMED THE TASK AT THE REQUEST OF ORGANIZED CRIME IN THAT RUBY WAS "CONVINCED" BY CARLOS MARCELLO THAT IT WOULD BE IN HIS "BEST INTEREST" TO PERFORM THE TASK AS A FAVOR TO THE MAFIA DON.

TIES BETWEEN HARVEY AND JACK RUBY

IN 1964 THE WARREN COMMISSION STATED: "THERE IS NO EVIDENCE THAT OSWALD AND RUBY KNEW EACH OTHER OR HAD ANY ASSOCIATION THROUGH A THIRD PARTY OR PARTIES." THE HSCA HOWEVER ARRIVED AT AN ENTIRELY DIFFERENT CONCLUSION IN STATING: "...THE COMMITTEE'S INVESTIGATION OF OSWALD AND RUBY SHOWED A VARIETY OF RELATIONSHIPS THAT MAY HAVE MATURED INTO AN ASSASSINATION CONSPIRACY.

NEITHER **HARVEY** NOR RUBY TURNED OUT TO BE THE "LONERS" DESCRIBED IN THE 1964 INVESTIGATION. BUT THE HSCA, LIKE THE W.C., DID NOT OFFER THAT THERE WAS BOTH A LEE **HARVEY** OSWALD AND A **LEE** HARVEY OSWALD. BOTH INVESTIGATIONS CHOSE TO REFERENCE A "COMPOSITE" OSWALD TO AVOIDING EXPOSING THE EFFORTS OF THE CIA TO REPLACE **LEE** WITH **HARVEY**. MORE IMPORTANTLY, THEY DID NOT REVEAL THAT RUBY KNEW BOTH **LEE** AND **HARVEY**.

THERE IS MUCH TO SUPPORT THE HSCA CONCLUSION:

MADELEINE BROWN
LBJ'S MISTRESS, WORKED FOR AN AD AGENCY IN DALLAS IN 1963. SHE AND HER CO-WORKERS WOULD OFTEN UNWIND AFTER WORK. OCCASSIONALLY THEY VISITED THE CAROUSEL CLUB. BROWN LATER TOLD AUTHOR JIM MARRS: "I ASKED AROUND AND FOUND OUT THAT MANY PEOPLE KNEW THAT OSWALD AND RUBY KNEW EACH OTHER."

"OSWALD" IN THIS CASE ACTUALLY COULD HAVE BEEN <u>EITHER</u> **LEE** OR **HARVEY**.

RAYMOND CUMMINGS
A DALLAS CAB DRIVER, NOTICED AN ARTICLE RELEASED DURING GARRISON'S INVESTIGATION THAT NOTED THAT DAVID FERRIE DENIED EVER HAVING BEEN IN DALLAS. CUMMINGS CONTACTED GARRISON'S OFFICE TO INFORM THEM THAT HE HAD DRIVEN FERRIE AND OSWALD TO RUBY'S CAROUSEL CLUB IN EARLY 1963.

"OSWALD" IN THIS INSTANCE WAS LIKELY **LEE**.

WILLIAM D. CROWE JR.
A MAGICIAN/ENTERTAINER AT THE CAROUSEL CLUB, NOTED THAT ONE WEEK PRIOR TO THE ASSASSINATION HE HAD COERCED OSWALD TO BE A PARTICIPANT IN HIS MAGIC ACT AT THE CLUB. SHORTLY AFTER THIS REVELATION, CROWE WAS CONTACTED BY FBI AGENTS WHO ADVISED HIM TO GET OUT DALLAS AND GO INTO HIDING.

CROWE HAD LIKELY INTERACTED WITH **LEE**.

BEVERLY OLIVER
A SINGER AT THE COLONY CLUB, WOULD OFTEN VISIT THE CAROUSEL CLUB TO VISIT ANOTHER DANCER, JADA. OLIVER NOTICED JADA SITTING AT A TABLE WITH RUBY AND AN OTHER MAN. AS OLIVER JOINED THEM, SHE NOTED "RUBY INTRODUCED ME TO THIS MAN. HE SAID: 'BEVERLY, THIS IS MY FRIEND, **LEE**." **LEE** HAD BEEN IN RUBY'S CLUB SO MUCH THAT SHE THOUGHT HE WAS THE ASSISTANT MANAGER.

*OLIVER HAD BEEN INTRODUCED TO **LEE**.*

JANET ADAMS CONFERTO
STAGE NAME "JADA", TOLD DALLAS REPORTERS THAT SHE HAD SEEN OSWALD IN THE CAROUSEL CLUB."

*ADAMS LIKELY SAW **LEE** AT THE CLUB.*

BILL WILLS
A CAROUSEL CLUB MUSICIAN, ALSO NOTED OSWALD'S PRESENCE AT THE CLUB.

*WILLS HAD LIKELY SEEN **LEE** AT THE CLUB.*

KATHY KAY
ONE OF RUBY'S STRIPPERS, ALSO RECALLED SEEING OSWALD AT THE CLUB. HER ACCOUNT IS SUPPORTED BY ANOTHER DANCER, BOBBIE LOWE MESEROLE WHO RECALLED HOW EMBARASSED OSWALD WAS AFTER RUBY HAD KATHY KAY DANCE A "BUMP AND GRIND" WITH HIM.

*KAY AND MESEROLE HAD LIKELY SEEN **LEE**. IT IS HOWEVER **HARVEY** WHO WOULD HAVE BEEN MORE LIKELY TO BE EMBARRASSED THAN **LEE**.*

WALTER "WALLY" WESTON
HUSBAND OF DANCER BOBBIE MESEROLE, WAS THE M.C. AT THE CAROUSEL CLUB UNTIL NOVEMBER 17TH, 1963. WESTON SAID HE SAW OSWALD IN THE CLUB AT LEAST TWICE PRIOR TO NOVEMBER 17TH.

*WESTON HAD LIKELY SEEN **LEE**.*

CARROLL JARNACIN
AN ATTORNEY, NOTED TO AUTHOR JIM MARRS THAT HE VISITED THE CLUB ON OCTOBER 4TH, 1963 TO DISCUSS A CASE WITH ONE OF RUBY'S DANCERS. JARNACIN STATED THAT HE OVERHEARD RUBY IN CONVERSATION WITH NOTHER MAN. JARNACIN HEARD THE OTHER MAN TELL RUBY: "DON'T USE MY REAL NAME. I'M GOING BY THE NAME OF O.H. LEE." **HARVEY** HAD RENTED A ROOM FROM MARY BLEDSOE AT 621 MARSALIS ON OCTOBER 7TH. HE REGISTERED UNDER THE NAME O.H. LEE.

*ALTHOUGH IT IS POSSIBLE THAT THIS MAY HAVE INDEED BEEN **HARVEY**, IT IS MORE LIKELY THAT IT IS **LEE**. **LEE** APPARENTLY WAS AWARE OF THE FACT THAT **HARVEY** WOULD BE RENTING A ROOM FROM BLEDSOE USING THE NAME O.H. LEE. JARNACIN'S VISIT TO THE CAROUSEL CLUB WAS 3 DAYS <u>PRIOR</u> TO **HARVEY'S** RENTAL OF THE ROOM AT 621 MARSALIS.*

ROSE CHERAMIE
WAS A STRIPPER AT THE CAROUSEL CLUB. SHE STATED TO AUTHORITIES THAT RUBY AND OSWALD HAD INDEED KNOWN EACH OTHER.

*ALTHOUGH CHERAMIE COULD HAVE BEEN REFERRING TO EITHER **LEE** OR **HARVEY**, IT IS MOST LIKELY **LEE** SINCE HER COMMENTS REGARDING "OSWALD" AND RUBY WERE IN PROBABLE REFERENCE TO THEIR MEETINGS IN DALLAS NOT NEW ORLEANS.*

BILL DEMARR
AN MC AND MAGICIAN AT THE CLUB, NOTED TO DAN RATHER, THEN A REPORTER IN DALLAS, THAT HE "SAW OSWALD IN THE AUDIENCE LAST WEEK." THIS INTERVIEW TOOK PLACE ON SUNDAY, NOVEMBER 24TH, 1963.

*DEMARR WAS LIKELY REFERRING TO **LEE**.*

CLYDE LIMBOUGH
A CAROUSEL CLUB EMPLOYEE, NOTED IN TESTIMONY TO JIM GARRISON THAT HE HAD SEEN OSWALD ON 3 SEPARATE OCCASSIONS IN RUBY'S OFFICE.

*THIS WAS LIKELY **LEE**.*

*DEPUTY CHIEF JESSE CURRY IN HIS BOOK NOTED: "WITNESSESS TO THE SHOOTING (OF **HARVEY**) WONDERED IF THERE WASN'T A GLEAN OF RECOGNITION IN OSWALD'S EYE WHEN RUBY STEPPED OUT FROM THE NEWSMEN..." **HARVEY'S** KNOWLEDGE OF RUBY PROBABLY OCCURRED IN NEW ORLEANS WHILE WORKING FOR BANISTER.*

11:25 AM SUNDAY
THE AMBULANCE ARRIVES FROM O'NEALS FUNERAL HOME TO PICK UP THE WOUNDED **HARVEY**. THE AMBULANCE IS MANNED BY HAROLD WOLFE AND DRIVER MICHAEL HARDIN.

11:34 AM SUNDAY
HARVEY'S ARRIVES VIA AMBULANCE AT PARKLAND.

11:40 AM SUNDAY
AGENT JIM HOSTY OF THE FBI GETS A CALL FROM A CAPTAIN GANNOWAY OF THE DALLAS POLICE ASKING WHAT THE FBI HAD ON A "JACK RUBENSTEIN." HOSTY, CHECKING THE INDEX SYSTEM, FOUND SEVERAL REFERENCES TO ORGANIZED CRIME. HE ALSO FOUND THAT RUBY HAD A FILE, FILE #137-681. RUBY WAS AN FBI CRIMINAL INFORMANT.

11:54 AM SUNDAY
LBJ CALLS PARKLAND AND ASKS DR. CRENSHAW IF **HARVEY** HAD OFFERED A "DEATHBED CONFESSION."

ABOUT NOON SUNDAY
DAVID FERRIE AND HIS COMPANIONS LEAVE GALVESTON TO RETURN TO NEW ORLEANS.

SUNDAY AFTERNOON
ACCORDING TO VARY/BAKER, JACK MARTIN INCREASES THE LEVEL OF SUSPICION THAT THERE WAS INDEED A CONNECTION BETWEEN **HARVEY** AND FERRIE. BOTH SUNDAY AND MONDAY, MARTIN WILL CONTACT THE FBI, THE SECRET SERVICE, NEWSPAPERS, AND BOTH RADIO AND TV STATIONS REGARDING WHAT HE KNOWS ABOUT DAVID FERRIE.

1:00 PM SUNDAY
G. WRAY GILL STOPS AT FERRIE'S APARTMENT AND TELLS MARTENS THAT **HARVEY** HAD IN HIS POSSESSION A LIBRARY CARD WITH FERRIE'S NAME ON IT.

*THE SECRET SERVICE MUST ALSO HAVE BEEN AWARE OF THIS CARD OR THE RUMOR CONCERNING THE CARD SINCE THEY HAD ASKED MARINA IF **HARVEY** KNEW A "MR. FARRY." THE LIBRARY CARD ALLEGEDLY IN **HARVEY'S** POSSESSION WAS NEVER PRODUCED. I WOULD SUSPECT THAT THE EFFORT TO FRIGHTEN FERRIE WITH THE POSSIBILITY OF A CONNECTION BETWEEN HIM AND **HARVEY** WAS DONE IN AN ATTEMPT TO INSURE FERRIE'S SILENCE. AT THIS TIME FERRIE WOULD BE AT A LOSS TO EXPLAIN OR UNDERSTAND JUST WHAT HAD GONE WRONG WITH THEIR "ASSIGNMENT." FERRIE'S CONCERN HOWEVER WOULD BE HEIGHTENED IF INDEED THE ALLEGED PRESIDENTIAL ASSASSIN WERE INDEED IN POSSESSION OF HIS LIBRARY CARD.*

*ONE HAS TO WONDER IF THE TRIP TO TEXAS BY FERRIE WAS AN EFFORT TO RETRIEVE SAID CARD FROM SOMEONE WHO HAD ACCESS TO **HARVEY** IN DALLAS SINCE THE CUBAN "ASSIGNMENT" WAS NO LONGER ON THE TABLE FOR EITHER FERRIE OR THE JAILED **HARVEY**.*

1:07 PM SUNDAY
HARVEY IS PRONOUNCED DEAD AT PARKLAND. HIS AUTOPSY WAS PERFORMED BY DR EARL ROSE. DR. ROSE NOTED THE SCARS ON **HARVEY'S** WRIST FROM THE OCTOBER

21ST, 1959 "SUICIDE" ATTEMPT IN MOSCOW. BUT, HE DID NOT NOTE THE 1 INCH MASTOID SCAR BEHIND THE LEFT EAR, NOR DID HE NOTE THE WOUNDS CAUSED BY THE ACCIDENTAL SHOOTING OF OCTOBER 27TH, 1957. HE DID NOT NOTE ANY TATTOO'S ON EITHER ARM. IT WAS **LEE** WHO WAS ADORNED WITH THE MASTOID SCAR, THE WOUND SCARS, AND THE TATTOO. AFTER THE AUTOPSY, THE BODY OF **HARVEY** WAS TAKEN TO THE MORTICIAN WHO WOULD PREPARE THE BODY FOR BURIAL. PAUL GROODS, THE MORTICIAN, ALSO DID NOT NOTICE A MASTOID SCAR, WOUND SCARS, OR ANY TATTOOS.

*ON AUGUST 8TH, 1980, MARINA OSWALD CONSENTED TO HAVE **HARVEY'S** BODY EXUMED TO CONFIRM THAT IT WAS INDEED **HARVEY**. ROBERT OSWALD HOWEVER ATTEMPTED TO PREVENT THE EXHUMATION. ROBERT WAS ACUTELY AWARE THAT IT WAS NOT HIS BROTHER **LEE** IN THE CASKET, BUT HIS "BROTHER" **HARVEY**. ON OCTOBER 4TH, 1981, DR. LINDA NEWTON CONCLUDED THAT BY MATCHING TEETH FOUND IN THE REMAINS OF THE COFFIN WITH MARINE DENTAL RECORDS, THAT IT WAS INDEED **HARVEY'S** REMAINS.*

1:56 PM SUNDAY
RUBY MEETS WITH HIS LAWYER, TOM HOWARD.

EARLY SUNDAY AFTERNOON
CASTRO, IN RESPONSE TO THE DRE'S ALLEGATIONS THAT **HARVEY** WAS A "CASTRO-COMMUNIST" TOOK TO THE AIRWAVES IN HAVANA.

CASTRO WAS ACCUTELY AWARE OF WHAT CERTAIN ELEMENTS OF THE U.S. GOVERNMENT WOULD MAKE OF THE DRE'S PRONOUNCEMENTS. HE WISELY AND CORRECTLY INTERPRETED THE DRE'S INTENTIONS: A U.S. INVASION OF CUBA IN RESPONSE TO THE ASSASSINATION.

ABOUT 2:30 PM SUNDAY
DON RAY ARCHER PLACES RUBY IN HIS CELL. HE WOULD LATER NOTE THAT RUBY WAS: "VERY HYPER….SWEATING PROFUSELY…I COULD SEE HIS HEART BEATING." WHEN ARCHER WAS INFORMED THAT **HARVEY** HAD DIED HE SAID TO RUBY: "JACK, IT LOOKS LIKE IT'S GOING TO BE THE ELECTRIC CHAIR FOR YOU." ARCHER NOTED THAT ALMOST IMMEDIATELY RUBY "BECAME CALM, HE QUIT SWEATING, HIS HEART SLOWED DOWN. I WOULD SAY HIS LIFE HAD DEPENDED ON HIM GETTING OSWALD."

*ATTORNEY TOM HOWARD HAD VISITED RUBY IN HIS CELL. LATER DURING HIS TRIAL, RUBY PASSED HIS NEW ATTORNEY A NOTE: "JOE, YOU SHOULD KNOW THAT TOM (HOWARD) TOLD ME TO SAY THAT I SHOT OSWALD SO THAT CAROLINE AND MRS. KENNEDY WOULDN'T HAVE TO COME TO DALLAS TO TESTIFY." RUBY OF COURSE, WOULD NOT OFFER THAT HE HAD SHOT **HARVEY** TO SILENCE HIM.*

*RUBY WAS TAKEN TO THE SAME CELL THAT **HARVEY** HAD JUST VACATED. I DOUBT THAT THIS WAS A COINCIDENCE. I WOULD SUSPECT THAT THIS PARTICULAR CELL WAS BUGGED TO MONITOR ANY DISCUSSIONS THAT TOOK PLACE INVOLVING **HARVEY** OR RUBY AND THEIR RESPECTIVE VISITORS.*

PRIOR TO HIS DEATH, RUBY WAS VISITED BY A DR. LOUIS J. WEST. DR. WEST'S FIRST VISIT TO RUBY WAS ON APRIL 29TH, 1964. HIS NEXT VISIT WAS NOT UNTIL 1965. RUBY WAS ALSO VISITED BY A ROBERT STUBBLEFIELD ON APRIL 30TH, 1964. BOTH DR. WEST AND ROBERT STUBBLEFIELD WERE INVOLVED WITH THE CIA MIND AND BEHAVIOUR MODIFICATION PROGRAM KNOWN AS MK ULTRA. NEITHER MAN HAD ANY RELATIONSHIP WITH EITHER THE DEFENSE OR THE PROSECUTION LAWYERS INVOLVED IN JACK RUBY'S MURDER TRIAL.

RUBY WOULD LATER WIN AN APPEAL FOR A NEW TRIAL. TWO DAYS AFTER THE DECEMBER 7TH, 1966 APPEAL WAS GRANTED, RUBY WAS ADMITTED TO PARKLAND HOSPITAL SUFFERING FROM PNEUMONIA. THE FOLLOWING DAY HE WAS DIAGNOSED WITH CANCER WHICH HAD SPREAD TO HIS LUNGS, LIVER, AND BRAIN. HE DIED A MERE 24 DAYS LATER ON JANUARY 3RD, 1967.

AGENT BELMONT OF THE FBI NOTED IN A MEMO PREPARED ON SUNDAY, NOVEMBER 24TH, 1963 FOR DEPUTY DIRECTOR CLYDE TOLSON THAT IT WAS READILY CONCLUSIVE THAT **HARVEY** WAS THE LONE ASSASSIN AND ESSENTIALLY DEEMED THE INVESTIGATION COMPLETE. IT WOULD BE LATER, DECEMBER 9TH, 1963 THAT THE FIRST FBI SUMMARY REPORT WOULD BE RELEASED. IT APPEARS HOWEVER THAT THE "INVESTIGATION" TOOK LESS THAN 2 DAYS. THE WARREN COMMISSION WOULD NOT MEET FOR THE FIRST TIME UNTIL TWO WEEKS LATER. AGENT BELMONT DID NOT WISH TO SEND AN FBI REPRESENTATIVE TO THE FIRST SESSION. ALTHOUGH THE COMMISSION HAD JUST <u>BEGUN</u> THEIR INVESTIGATION, THE FBI HAD APPARENTLY ALREADY <u>COMPLETED</u> THEIRS.

AT THE FUNERAL HOME, **HARVEY** WAS FINGERPRINTED AND PALM PRINTED ONCE AGAIN BY THE FBI. SPECIAL AGENT RICHARD HARRISON WENT TO MILLER'S FUNERAL HOME WITH THE ALLEGED ASSASSINATION RIFLE AND A FINGERPRINT KIT. THE FINGERPRINT CARD PORTION REQUIRING THE SIGNATURE OF THE PRINTEE HAD THE NOTATION "REFUSED TO SIGN."

3:15 PM SUNDAY
RUBY IS INTERVIEWED BY CAPTAIN WILL FRITZ.

ABOUT 3:30 PM SUNDAY
FERRIE AND COMPANY ARRIVE IN ALEXANDRIA, LOUSIANA. ONCE AGAIN, FERRIE TRIES TO CONTACT GILL.

LATE SUNDAY AFTERNOON
FERRIE, STILL IN A PANIC, TRIES REPEATEDLY TO CONTACT GILL. HE FINALLY CALLS HIS APARTMENT WHERE LAYTON MARTENS INFORMS HIM THAT REPORTERS FROM WWL-TV HAD VISITED AND QUESTIONED HIM ABOUT THE LIBRARY CARD AND FERRIE'S CONNECTION TO **HARVEY**. FERRIE FINALLY CONTACTS GILL WHO ADVISES HIM TO RETURN IMMEDIATELY TO NEW ORLEANS.

9:00 PM SUNDAY
FERRIE AND HIS COMPANIONS ARRIVE IN NEW ORLEANS. FERRIE DROPS OFF BEAUBOEUF NEAR HIS (FERRIE'S) APARTMENT. FERRIE AND COFFEY THEN GO TO FERRIE'S APARTMENT.

9:15 PM SUNDAY
BEAUBOUEF AND MARTENS ARE ARRESTED AT DAVID FERRIE'S APARTMENT. FERRIE CONTACTS GILL WHO UPDATES HIM ON HIS FRIENDS ARREST.

MONDAY NOVEMBER 25TH

1:30 AM MONDAY NOVEMBER 25TH
FERRIE PANICS AND DRIVES TO HAMMOND, LOUSIANA. HE ARRIVES ABOUT 5:30 AM AT THE DORM ROOM OF THOMAS COMPTON AT SOUTHEASTERN LOUISIANA COLLEGE.

8:30 AM MONDAY NOVEMBER 25TH
COMPTON NOTES THAT FERRIE LEFT HIS DORM. FERRIE HOWEVER WILL LATER TELLTHE FBI THAT HE DIDN'T LEAVE HAMMOND UNTIL ABOUT 1:30 OR SO THAT AFTERNOON.

4:30 PM MONDAY NOVEMBER 25TH
UPON RETURNING TO NEW ORLEANS, FERRIE STOPS BRIEFLY AT HIS APARTMENT BEFORE GOING TO HIS ATTORNEY'S OFFICE. BOTH GILL AND FERRIE APPEARED AT D.A.'S OFFICE WHERE FERRIE IS INTERVIEWED BY THE SECRET SERVICE, THE FBI, AND THE NEW ORLEANS POLICE.

THE FBI REPORT NOTES REGARDING THE NOVEMBER 25TH INTERVIEW ARE INTERESTING.

FERRIE IS INTERVIEWED BY SA'S ERNEST WALL AND L.M. SHEARER IN NEW ORLEANS. PREDICTABLY, FERRIE STATED THAT HE DID NOT KNOW A LEE **HARVEY**, OSWALD. WHEN ASKED ABOUT THE FRIDAY DRIVE TO TEXAS, FERRIE STATED THAT WHEN HE LEFT HIS HOME AT ABOUT 6:30 PM THAT FRIDAY THAT HE DIDN'T KNOW EXACTLY WHERE HE WAS GOING. HE ALSO OFFERED THAT AFTER PICKING UP BEAUBOUEF AND COFFEY THAT HE WAS NOT CARRYING ANY FIREARMS. IRONICALLY THOUGH HE VOICED CONCERN ABOUT TRANSPORTING FIREARMS ACROSS STATE LINES; A LOGICAL CONCERN FOR SOMEONE WHO WAS INVOLVED IN RUNNING GUNS TO CUBA. FERRIE NOTED THAT HE REPEATEDLY TRIED TO CONTACT HIS EMPLOYER, G. WRAY GILL THAT WEEKEND. ON THE EVENING OF THE 24TH, HE TALKED TO HIS ROOMATE LAYTON MARTENS WHO NOTED TO HIM THAT REPORTERS FROM WWL-TV HAD VISITED HIS RESIDENCE AND STATED THAT FERRIE WAS BEING IMPLICATED IN THE ASSASSINATION. WHEN FERRIE FINALLY CONTACTED GILL, HE IS TOLD THAT THE RUMOR WAS APPARENTLY STARTED BY JACK MARTIN, AN ASSOCIATE OF GUY BANISTER. MARTIN HAD STATED THAT FERRIE NOT ONLY KNEW **HARVEY** BUT TRAINED HIM AS WELL. THE REFERENCE TO "TRAINING" HOWEVER MAY HAVE BEEN IN REGARD TO TRAINING **LEE** AT THE CAMP NEAR LAKE PONTCHARTRAIN. GILL HAD ADVISED FERRIE TO RETURN IMMEDIATELY TO NEW ORLEANS. FERRIE DID INDEED RETURN TO NEW ORLEANS LATE THAT DAY MONDAY, VISITED GILL, THEN PROCEEDED TO THE D.A.'S OFFICE TO TURN HIMSELF IN. FERRIE NOTED THAT HE AND MARTIN HAD PREVIOUS DISAGREEMENTS AND THAT HAD PROMPTED MARTIN'S "RUMORS" REGARDING FERRIE AND LEE **HARVEY** OSWALD.

IN REGARDS TO THE TROUBLESOME LIBRARY CARD, FERRIE NOTED THAT HIS <u>PUBLIC</u> LIBRARY CARD HAD EXPIRED ON MARCH 13TH, 1963. BUT, WHAT ACTUALLY CONCERNED FERRIE WAS THE POSSIBILITY THAT THE LIBRARY CARD IN QUESTION WAS NOT A PUBLIC LIBRARY CARD, BUT A <u>MEDICAL</u> LIBRARY CARD SHARED BY THOSE WHO WORKED ON THE "PROJECT." THIS CARD WOULD TIE **HARVEY**/VARY-BAKER/DR. SHERMAN, AND FERRIE TO THE OCHSNER CLINIC AND IN TURN TO THE "PROJECT." FERRIE WENT ON TO DENY KNOWING OF THE FPFC COMMITTEE AND ALSO DENIED KKNOWING EITHER A JACK RUBY OR JACK RUBENSTEIN.

ON MONDAY, NOVEMBER 25TH, 1963, IN A PHONE CONVERSATION WITH HOOVER, LBJ WOULD OFFER HIS OBJECTIONS TO A PRESIDENTIAL COMMISSION TO INVESTIGATE THE SHOOTING. HE FAVORED AN INVESTIGATION BY EITHER THE FBI, WITH THE ASSISTANCE OF A TEXAS COURT OF INQUIRY, OR AN INVESTIGATION BY A TEXAS COURT OF INQUIRY WITH ASSISTANCE FROM THE FBI. IN BOTH INSTANCES, LBJ WOULD BE ABLE TO CONTROL THE SCOPE OF THE INVESTIGATION WITH HIS POLITICAL LEVERAGE IN TEXAS AND ALSO IN REGARDS TO HOOVER AND THE FBI. HE DID NOT WANT AN INVESTIGATION SPEARHEADED BY THE WHITE HOUSE AS THE WASHINGTON POST DEMANDED IN AN EDITORIAL THAT WAS PUBLISHED THE FOLLOWING DAY. JOHNSON DID NOT WANT TO GET PERSONALLY INVOLVED IN THE INVESTIGATION. HE COMMENTED TO HOOVER: "….THE PRESIDENTIAL COMMISSION, WHICH WE THINK WOULD BE VERY BAD AND PUT IT RIGHT AT THE WHITE HOUSE…..WE CAN'T BE CHECKING UP ON EVERY SHOOTING SCRAPE IN THE COUNTRY…" FURTHER VOICING HIS VIEWS, JOHNSON WOULD IN TURN COMMENT TO COLUMNIST JOSEPH ALSOP: "MY LAWYERS JOE TELL ME THAT….THE PRESIDENT MUST NOT INJECT HIMSELF INTO LOCAL KILLINGS."

I FIND LITTLE COMFORT IN THE FACT THAT THE NEW PRESIDENT WOULD REFER TO THE ASSASSINATION OF JOHN F. KENNEDY, <u>HIS</u> PRESIDENT, AS A "SHOOTING SCRAPE" AND A "LOCAL KILLING."

TUESDAY NOVEMBER 26TH

AFTERNOON, NOVEMBER 26TH

FERRIE VISITS **HARVEY'S** OLD RESIDENCE ON MAGAZINE STREET IN NEW ORLEANS. ACCORDING TO MRS. GARNER THE LANDLADY, HE WAS IN SEARCH OF THE LIBRARY CARD THAT SEEMS TO BE RAISING SO MANY QUESTIONS. THE CARD HE WAS LIKELY IN PURSUIT OF WAS THE CARD HE HAD GIVEN TO **HARVEY** TO LOAN TO VARY/BAKER ON JUNE 4TH, 1963. IF **HARVEY** HAD NOT GIVEN VARY/BAKER THE CARD OR IF SHE HAD RETURNED IT TO HIM, IT WAS POSSIBLE THAT THE CARD WAS STILL IN **HARVEY'S** POSSESSION OR AT THE ROOMING HOUSE.

A PRESS RELEASE BY HOOVER NOTES: "NOT A SHRED OF EVIDENCE HAS BEEN DEVELOPED TO LINK ANY OTHER PERSON IN A CONSPIRACY WITH OSWALD TO ASSASSINATE PRESIDENT KENNEDY."

VARY/BAKER AGREES THAT THE LIBRARY CARD THAT CONCERNED FERRIE WAS NOT AN ORDINARY PUBLIC LIBRARY CARD. THIS PARTICULAR CARD WAS A CARD TO THE MEDICAL LIBRARY AT TULANE. THIS CARD COULD BE LINKED TO THE "PROJECT" SINCE IT WAS ISSUED BY THE OCHSNER CLINIC. THE CARD BORE NO NAME, ONLY AN ID# ASSIGNED TO THE CLINIC. THIS CARD COULD HAVE LINKED **HARVEY** TO FERRIE AND IN TURN BOTH MEN TO THE "PROJECT" AND THE OCSHNER CLINIC.

6:00 PM TUESDAY NOVEMBER 26TH

ACCORDING TO VARY/BAKER, FERRIE CONTACTS HER ONLY TO FIND OUT THAT SHE DID INDEED HAVE THE MEDICAL LIBRARY CARD. HE TOLD HER TO TEAR IT UP IMMEDIATELY.

WEDNESDAY NOVEMBER 27TH

FERRIE RETRIEVES HIS EXPIRED PUBLIC LIBRARY CARD FROM THE POLICE. HE HAD TURNED IT OVER TO THEM ON MONDAY. LATER THAT DAY HE IS RE-INTERVIERWED BY THE FBI.

NOTES REGARDING THE 2ND FBI INTERVIEW ARE ALSO WORTH REVIEWING.

THIS INTERVIEW TOOK PLACE AT FERRIE'S APARTMENT IN NEW ORLEANS. FERRIE WAS INTERVIEWED BY SA'S ERNEST WALL AND THEODORE VLATER. ONCE AGAIN HE IS ASKED ABOUT THE PUBLIC LIBRARY CARD AND DENIES EVER HAVING LOANED THIS CARD TO **HARVEY**. HE THEN PRODUCED HIS EXPIRED PUBLIC LIBRARY CARD WHICH HE HAD RETRIEVED FROM THE NEW ORLEANS PD. NEEDLESS TO SAY, FERRIE IS CONSIDERABLY MORE COMFORTABLE IN THIS INTERVIEW IN REGARDS TO THE LIBRARY CARD AS HE HAD LEARNED THAT VARY/BAKER HAD THE INCRIMINATING MEDICAL LIBRARY CARD. HE CONTINUES TO DENY KNOWING **HARVEY**, OWNING A RIFLE WITH A TELESCOPIC SIGHT, OR TRAINING **HARVEY** WITH THE SAME. HE DENIED FLYING **HARVEY** TO DALLAS TEXAS OR ANY OTHER CITY IN TEXAS. WITH THE LIBRARY CARD INCIDENT BEHIND HIM, FERRIE'S SOLE CONCERN NOW IS DISAVOWING ANY KNOWLEDGE OF LEE **HARVEY** OSWALD. FOR THAT MATTER, HE WOULD ALSO DISAVOW ANY KNOWLEDGE OF A **LEE** HARVEY OSWALD. HIS STANCE WOULD BE MUCH THE SAME AS THAT ALREADY TAKEN BY THE CIA AND THE FBI.

THEODORE VORHEES, CHANCELLOR ELECT OF THE PHILADELPHIA BAR ASSOCIATION, RELATED TO THE PRESS THAT IN HIS OPINION, LEE HARVEY OSWALD HAD BEEN "LYNCHED." QUITE AN ASTUTE OBSERVATION.

CHAPTER 15: BALLISTIC EVIDENCE IN THE TIPPIT SHOOTING

FBI AGENT CORTLANDT CUNNINGHAM INITIALLY RECEIVED ONLY 1 CASING FROM THE DALLAS POLICE. THE FBI SAID IT WAS NOT FROM OSWALD'S **(HARVEY'S)** GUN. BUT LATER IN MARCH 1964, 3 MORE CASINGS WERE FOUND IN POSSESSION OF THE DALLAS POLICE. WHEN AGENT CUNNINGHAM EXAMINED THE OTHER 3 CASINGS HE SAID IT WAS NOT POSSIBLE TO TELL IF THESE 3 HAD BEEN FIRED BY OSWALD'S **(HARVEY'S)** GUN.

THERE WERE NOW 4 CASINGS IN THE POSSESSION OF THE WARREN COMMISSION: ONE WAS A REMINGTON, THE OTHER 3 WERE WESTERN-WINCHESTERS. HOWEVER OF THE CASINGS RECOVERED AT THE SCENE OF THE TIPPIT SHOOTING THERE WERE 2 REMINGTONS FOUND NEAR TIPPIT'S BODY, AND 2 WESTERN WINCHESTERS FOUND IN THE FRONT YARD OF BARBARA DAVIS' APARTMENT.

OSWALD'S (**HARVEY'S**) GUN WAS A REVOLVER NOT AN AUTOMATIC; THEREFORE IT WOULD NOT HAVE "EJECTED" THE SHELL CASINGS AT THE SCENE OF THE TIPPIT SHOOTING. THE SHELL CASINGS WOULD HAVE TO HAVE BEEN MANUALLY REMOVED FROM A REVOLVER AND DELIBERATELY LEFT AT THE SCENE. THEY WERE OF COURSE LEFT BY **LEE**.

OFFICER J.M. POE THOUGHT BUT WAS NOT CERTAIN THAT HE HAD MARKED "JMP" ON 2 REMINGTON CASINGS FOUND AT THE TIPPIT SCENE. OFFICER W. E. BARNES HOWEVER RECALLED MARKING A "B" INSIDE EACH OF THE 2 CASINGS GIVEN TO HIM BY OFFICER POE. NEITHER OF THEM HOWEVER COULD FIND THEIR MARKINGS ON THE 4 CASINGS IN POSSESSION OF THE WARREN COMMISSION.

THE FIRST OF TWO WESTERN-WINCHESTER CASINGS FOUND IN BARBARA DAVIS' FRONT YARD WAS FOUND ABOUT 2:00 PM AND MARKED BY GEORGE M. DOUGHTY. THE SECOND CASING, FOUND ABOUT 5 HOURS LATER, APPROXIMATELY 6:45 PM, BY VIRGINIA DAVIS, WAS NOT MARKED BY THE DALLAS POLICE. IT WAS RETRIEVED FROM MISS DAVIS BY DALLAS POLICE DETECTIVE C.N. DHORITY AND C. W. BROWN.

ALTHOUGH **HARVEY'S** REVOLVER COULD NOT BE ELIMINATED AS HAVING BEEN THE WEAPON THAT FIRED THE BULLETS THAT KILLED OFFICER TIPPIT, MOST OF THE EXPERTS WHO EXAMINED THE BULLETS REFUSED TO STATE THAT THERE WAS ANY DEGREE OF CERTAINTY THAT THE BULLETS REMOVED FROM TIPPIT HAD BEEN FIRED FROM **HARVEY'S** REVOLVER.

THE EXPERTS WHO EXAMINED THE CASINGS HOWEVER WERE CERTAIN THAT THE CASINGS HAD INDEED BEEN FIRED FROM **HARVEY'S** REVOLVER. BUT, IT IS IMPORTANT TO NOTE THAT THE CASINGS "MATCH" SIMPLY MEAN THAT AT SOME POINT IN TIME THAT THE CASINGS STREWN ABOUT AT THE TIPPIT CRIME SCENE HAD BEEN FIRED THROUGH **HARVEY'S** REVOLVER. IT COULD HAVE BEEN THAT DAY, OR ANY DAY PRIOR TO TIPPIT'S SLAYING. MORE IMPORTANTLY, IT IS NECESSARY TO STRESS THAT THERE IS NO BALLISTIC "LINK" BETWEEN THE BULLETS FOUND IN TIPPIT AND THE CASINGS FOUND AT THE SCENE.

ALTHOUGH YOU CAN BALISTICALLY LINK THE CASINGS TO THE REVOLVER WITH NO REGARD AS TO WHEN THEY WERE FIRED, IT IS NOT POSSIBLE TO LINK THE BULLETS REMOVED FROM TIPPIT TO THE CASINGS. WITHOUT THIS LINK YOU CANNOT LINK THE BULLETS TO **HARVEY'S** HANDGUN, AND THEREFORE NOT BALISTICALLY LINK **HARVEY** TO THE SLAYING OF OFFICER TIPPIT.

A W.C. EXCHANGE BETWEEN MR. EISENBERG AND AGENT CORTLANDT CUNNINGHAM CEMENTS THIS FACT:

EISENBERG:
NOW WERE YOU ABLE TO DETERMINE WHETHER THESE BULLETS HAD BEEN IN THIS WEAPON?

CUNNINGHAM:
NO I WAS NOT.

CUNNINGHAM WENT ON TO NOTE THAT C.E. #602 WAS TOO MUTILATED TO DETERMINE WHETHER IT HAD BEEN FIRED FROM THE PISTOL ALLEGEDLY USED BY **HARVEY** TO SHOOT TIPPIT. REGARDING THE OTHER 3 BULLETS, C.E.'S # 603, #604, AND #605, CUNNINGHAM NOTED "IT WAS NOT POSSIBLE TO DETERMINE WHETHER OR NOT THEY HAD BEEN FIRED FROM OSWALD'S REVOLVER."

THE W.C. HOWEVER WOULD NOT BE DENIED THEIR PREORDAINED CONCLUSION THAT **HARVEY** SHOT TIPPIT. THE COMMISSION NOTED THAT THE BULLETS REMOVED FROM OFFICER TIPPIT HAD INDEED BEEN FIRED FROM **HARVEY'S** PISTOL. MORE POINTEDLY, THEY TIED THE TIPPIT BULLETS TO HIS PISTOL "TO THE EXCLUSION OF ALL OTHER WEAPONS." NO REASON TO LET EXPERT FBI OPINION REFUTE THEIR DESIRED CONCLUSION.

CHAPTER 16: THE PHOTOGRAPHIC SET-UP

THERE WERE APPARENTLY PHOTOS TAKEN OF **HARVEY** SHOWING HIM POSING WITH THE RIFLE AND HANDGUN ALLEGEDLY USED TO SHOOT JFK AND TIPPIT RESPECTIVELY. THERE ARE MANY QUESTIONS CONCERNING THE LEGITIMACY OF THESE PHOTOS.

- THE SHADOW BENEATH THE NOSE WAS CAST DIRECTLY BENEATH THE NOSE AS ONE WOULD EXPECT IN A SHADOW CAST BY A MID-DAY, DIRECTLY OVERHEAD SUN. HOWEVER THE SHADOW CAST BY THE SUBJECT'S BODY FOLLOWED A DIFFERENT ANGLE AS ONE WOULD EXPECT BY A PHOTO TAKEN MUCH LATER IN THE DAY OR EARLY EVENING.

- THE TWO PHOTOS WERE TAKEN AT DIFFERENT DISTANCES. WHILE THE SIZE OF THE HEAD REMAINED CONSTANT, THE SIZE OF THE BODY DECREASED AS ONE WOULD EXPECT IF A PHOTO WAS TAKEN AT A FURTHER DISTANCE.

- **HARVEY** HAS A ALMOST POINTED CHIN WITH A SMALL DIMPLE. THE CHIN ON BOTH PHOTOS IS QUITE SQUARE WITH NO DIMPLE.

A BRITISH FORENSIC PHOTO EXPERT, DETECTIVE INSPECTOR MALCOLM THOMSON, DECLARED THAT BOTH PHOTOS HAD BEEN RETOUCHED, PARTICULARLY IN THE CHIN AREA.

AN EXPERT FROM THE CANADIAN DEPARTMENT OF DEFENSE ALSO CONCLUDED THAT THE PHOTOS HAD BEEN TAMPERED WITH.

AFTER GEORGE DEMOHRENSDCHILDT'S "SUICIDE", YET ANOTHER PHOTO SHOWED UP IN HIS POSSESSIONS. IT WAS SIGNED: "TO MY DEAR FRIEND GEORGE FROM LEE." APPARENTLY TO INSURE THAT GEORGE WAS PERFECTLY CLEAR ON JUST WHO "LEE" WAS, IT WAS ALSO SIGNED "LEE HARVEY OSWALD." DE MOHRENSCHILDT'S WIFE JEANNE CLAIMED NEITHER SHE NOR HER LATE HUSBAND HAD EVER SEEN THE PHOTO. THIS PARTICULAR PHOTO TURNED UP WHEN JEANNE RETURNED TO DALLAS TO RECOVER SOME STORED ITEMS THAT THEY HAD LEFT BEHIND IN DALLAS. JEANNE SAID SHE THOUGHT THE PHOTO HAD BEEN PLANTED.

INDEED ANOTHER COPY SHOWED UP IN LATER YEARS IN THE PERSONAL EFFECTS OF ROSCOE WHITE, THE DALLAS POLICE OFFICER AND DALLAS-BASED SET-UP CONSPIRATOR. IT IS MY OPINION AND THE OPINION OF MANY RESEARCHERS THAT WHITE WAS AT THE SCENE OF THE TIPPIT SHOOTING. ARMSTRONG SUGGESTS THAT IT WAS ACTUALLY **LEE** WHO HAD SHOT OFFICER TIPPIT, NOT WHITE.

CHAPTER 17: THE RIFLE SET-UP AND THE "HIDELL" CONNECTION

THE MANNLICHER-CARCANO RIFLE ALLEGEDLY BOUGHT BY **HARVEY** WAS PURCHASED VIA MAIL ORDER FROM KLEIN'S OF CHICAGO AND BOUGHT UNDER THE NAME OF "A. HIDDELL." IT WAS PURCHASED WITH A MONEY ORDER DATED 12 MARCH 1963 THAT WAS BOUGHT AT A DALLAS POST OFFICE.

WAS THE NAME "HIDELL" USED BY **HARVEY** AS AN ACTUAL ALIAS IN WHAT HE PERCEIVED AS LEGITIMATE CIA COVER WORK, OR WAS IT SIMPLY A MONIKER THAT **HARVEY** WOULD USE ON ONLY TWO OCCASSIONS AND ONE THAT THE SET-UP CONSPIRATORS WOULD USE TO TIE **HARVEY** TO THE RIFLE?

LET US REVISIT THE THREE P.O. BOXES RENTED BY **HARVEY**; TWO IN DALLAS, AND ONE IN NEW ORLEANS AND THE ALLEGED RELATIONSHIP BETWEEN A "HIDELL" AND THESE 3 BOXES.

ON OCTOBER 9TH, 1962, **HARVEY** RENTED P.O. BOX 2915 IN DALLAS. HE NOTED THAT THIS BOX WAS LISTED IN HIS NAME ONLY. IT WAS ALLEGED HOWEVER THAT ON PART 3 OF THE APPLICATION LISTED AS INDIVIDUALS "OTHER THAN THE APPLICANT" ELIGIBLE TO RECEIVE MAIL THE NAME "HIDELL." ON JANUARY 27TH, 1963 A HANDGUN IS ORDERED BY A "HIDELL", AND ON MARCH 12TH, 1963, THE RIFLE ALLEGEDLY USED IN THE ASSASSINATION IS ORDERED BY A "HIDELL."

ON APRIL 24TH, 1963, **HARVEY** MOVED TO NEW ORLEANS. LISTED AS A REFERENCE ON HIS JOB APPLICATION AT REILY COFFEE WAS A "SERGEANT ROBERT HIDELL." ON MAY 26TH, 1963, **HARVEY**, AT BANISTER'S REQUEST, FORMED A NEW ORLEANS CHAPTER OF THE FPFC COMMITTEE. HIS CHAPTER CARD SHOWS A "A.J. HIDELL" AS CHAPTER PRESIDENT. ON JUNE 3RD, **HARVEY** OPENS P.O. BOX 30061. ACCORDING TO **HARVEY**, THE BOX IS OPENED IN HIS NAME AND MARINA'S NAME ONLY. BUT ON THIS BOXES' PART 3, LISTED UNDER "NAMES OF PERSONS ENTITLED TO RECEIVE MAIL THROUGH BOX" WAS A "A.J. HIDELL."

*IT IS INTERESTING TO NOTE THAT MARINA'S LAST NAME IS WRITTEN "OSWALD" IN ALL CAPITAL LETTERS, BUT THE HIDELL NAME IS WRITTEN "HideLL" WITH ONLY THE "H" AND THE DOUBLE LL'S IN CAPITAL LETTERS. ARMSTRONG CONTENDS, AND I TEND TO AGREE, THAT IT IS **LEE** WHO IS PLAYING THE ROLE OF "HIDELL."*

ON OCTOBER 3RD, **HARVEY** MOVES BACK TO DALLAS. ON NOVEMBER 1ST HE OPENS P.O. BOX 6225. THIS TIME THERE IS NO "HIDELL" LISTED ON THE APPLICATION.

NOW, LET US EXAMINE WHAT WAS FOUND AND WHAT WAS LEARNED ABOUT THE RELATIONSHIP BETWEEN **HARVEY**, A "HIDELL", THE P.O BOXES, AND THE ORDERING OF THE WEAPONS ALLEGEDLY USED THAT NOVEMBER WEEKEND.

THE LINK BETWEEN **HARVEY** AND A "HIDELL" WAS BASED ON A SELECTIVE SERVICE I.D. CARD WITH THE NAME "ALEK JAMES HIDELL" ALLEGEDLY FOUND IN **HARVEY'S** POSSESSION WHEN HE WAS ARRESTED. ALTHOUGH THE FBI CLAIMED THAT THE HIDELL I.D. CARD WAS THE ONLY ONE FOUND ON **HARVEY**, THERE IS NO MENTION OF IT AS BEING FOUND IN HIS POSSESSION ON FRIDAY THE DAY HE IS ARRESTED. POSTAL INSPECTOR HARRY O. HOLMES NOTED THAT THE CARD HAD BEEN ERASED AND RE-TYPED. THE ONLY I.D. FOUND ON **HARVEY** THAT FRIDAY WAS A SOCIAL SECURITY CARD IN HIS NAME, LEE **HARVEY** OSWALD. THE INCRIMINATING I.D. CARD, CRUCIAL TO ESTABLISHING A LINK BETWEEN A "HIDELL", **HARVEY,** THE FIRST DALLAS P.O. BOX, AND THE ORDERING OF THE RIFLE AND HANDGUN, DIDN'T SHOW UP UNTIL SATURDAY. HOWEVER A WALLET FOUND AT THE SITE OF THE TIPPIT SHOOTING ALSO CONTAINED A SELECTIVE SERVICE CARD FOR A "ALEX JAMES HIDELL." THE SET-UP CONSPIRATORS, ALTHOUGH CARELESS REGARDING THE MULTI-WALLET SCENARIO,

WERE INDEED AWARE OF THE IMPORTANCE OF LINKING **HARVEY** TO A "HIDELL" SINCE THEY HAD CHOSEN "HIDELL" AS THE PURCHASER OF THE WEAPONS.

HOLMES, THE DALLAS POSTAL INSPECTOR, LATER TOLD THE WARREN COMMISSION THAT IT WAS POSSIBLE THAT A PERSON OTHER THAN **HARVEY** (HIDELL) COULD HAVE RECEIVED A PACKAGE (RIFLE) AT THE SAME DALLAS P.O. BOX , #2915, AS THE ONE REGISTERED TO **HARVEY**. IT WOULD ALL HINGE ON PART THREE OF THE REGISTRATION FORM **HARVEY** HAD FILLED OUT WHEN OBTAINING THE P.O. BOX. PART THREE IS USED TO IDENTIFY INDIVIDUALS OTHER THAN THE APPLICANT WHO ARE AUTHORIZED TO RECEIVE MAIL AT THAT PARTICULAR P.O. BOX. **HARVEY** INSISTED HOWEVER THAT THIS BOX WAS REGISTERED IN HIS NAME ONLY. ALTHOUGH POSTAL REGULATIONS REQUIRE THAT PART 3 BE RETAINED FOR 2 YEARS AFTER THE BOX IS CLOSED, **HARVEY'S** PART 3 WAS DESTROYED ON MAY 14TH, 1963. IT SHOULD NOT HAVE BEEN DESTROYED UNTIL OCTOBER 9TH, 1964. MORE IMPORTANTLY, THE SIGNED RECEIPT FOR THE PICKUP OF THE RIFLE AND HANDGUN WAS NOT FOUND EITHER. POSTAL REGULATIONS REQUIRE THAT THIS BE KEPT FOR 4 YEARS. THIS FORM THEN SHOULD HAVE BEEN KEPT UNTIL MARCH 20TH, 1967. ***WITHOUT THESE TWO FORMS, THE LATER ATTEMPT TO LINK HARVEY AND THE RIFLE PURCHASE BY A "HIDELL" VIA THE INITIAL DALLAS P.O. BOX WAS BROKEN.*** ANYONE COULD HAVE ORDERED THE RIFLE, HAD IT DELIVERED TO **HARVEY'S** P.O. BOX, THEN PICKED IT UP BY SIMPLY ARRIVING AT THE POST OFFICE WITH AN I.D. SHOWING THEM TO BE "A. HIDELL" OR, ACCORDING TO INSPECTOR HOLMES, NO I.D. AT ALL BUT SIMPLY IN POSSESSION OF THE NOTICE LEFT IN THE BOX THAT STATED THAT A PACKAGE HAD BEEN DELIVERED FOR THAT PARTICULAR POST OFFICE BOX. ONCE AGAIN, I TEND TO AGREE WITH ARMSTRONG THAT THE LIKELY CANDIDATE FOR THIS EFFORT WAS **LEE**.

IN CUSTODY, **HARVEY** ADMITTED FREELY TO LISTING A "SERGEANT ROBERT HIDELL" ON HIS JOB APPLICATION AT REILY COFFEE. IN REGARDS TO THE NEW ORLEANS CHAPTER OF THE FPFC CARD, A CARD LISTING A "A. J. HIDELL" AS CHAPTER PRESIDENT, THE FBI DETERMINED THAT THE HIDELL SIGNATURE WAS NOT **HARVEY'S**. ALTHOUGH MARINA WOULD LATER ADMIT TO HAVING SIGNED THE CARD, **HARVEY** WOULD NOT SAY WHO HAD WRITTEN "ALEX J. HIDELL" ON THIS CARD, THE PURPOSE OF THE CARD, OR THE USE HE MADE OF THE CARD. THIS IS NOT SURPRISING SINCE HE WAS STILL UNDER THE IMPRESSION THAT HIS NEW ORLEANS FPFC ACTIVITY WAS A LEGITIMATE CIA ENDEAVOR. THE 112 MILITARY INTELLIGENCE GROUP ADMITTED THAT UNTIL 1973 THAT THEY HAD A FILE ON **HARVEY** UNDER THE NAME "A. J. HIDELL." **HARVEY** WOULD NOT BLOW HIS COVER EVEN IN CUSTODY FOR THE ASSASSINATION OF THE PRESIDENT OF THE UNITED STATES.

HARVEY'S LAST POST OFFICE BOX, DALLAS # 6225, DID NOT HAVE A "HIDELL" LISTED ON PART 3 OF THE APPLICATION. THE SET-UP CONSPIRATORS HAD, TO THEIR SATISFACTION, MADE THE FATEFULL CONNECTION BETWEEN **HARVEY**, "HIDELL", AND IN TURN, THE RIFLE AND HANDGUN PURCHASE VIA WHAT WOULD BE LATER THE "MISSING" PART 3 OF THE INITIAL DALLAS P.O. BOX, #2915; THE BOX TO WHICH THE WEAPONS WERE DELIVERED. THESE MISSING FORMS WOULD NOW NECESSITATE TYING **HARVEY** TO A "HIDELL" MAIL DROP VIA HIS NEW ORLEANS P.O. BOX SINCE THAT PART 3 APPARENTLY DID NOT SUFFER THE SAME FATE AS THE DALLAS BOX, 2915 PART 3. IT IS HOWEVER INTERESTING TO NOTE THAT ON THIS LAST BOX, #6225, THE ACLU WAS LISTED. THIS MAY HAVE BEEN GENUINELY LISTED BY **HARVEY** SINCE HE MAY HAVE HAD SOME CONCERNS AS TO WHAT LEGAL ASSISTANCE HE COULD EXPECT IF HE WERE INDEED CAPTURED DURING WHAT HE PERCEIVED AS HIS CIA ASSIGNMENT TO DELIVER THE CARCINOGENS TO CUBA. **HARVEY** WOULD BE ACUTELY AWARE THAT IF HE WERE INDEED TAKEN INTO CUSTODY THAT THE CIA WOULD DISAVOW ANY KNOWLEDGE OF HIM OR HIS "MISSION." I WOULD BE REMISS HOWEVER IF I DID NOT ALSO OFFER THE POSSIBILITY THAT THE INCLUSION OF THE ACLU WAS ALSO AN ACT OF THE SET-UP CONSPIRATORS AS IT WOULD LEND CREEDENCE TO THE NOTION THAT **HARVEY** HAD INDEED PLANNED TO KILL THE PRESIDENT AND WOULD INDEED NEED LEGAL ASSISTANCE.

OVER THE COURSE OF **HARVEY'S** NUMEROUS INTERROGATION SESSIONS THAT WEEKEND HE DENIED <u>LISTING</u>, <u>KNOWING</u>, OR <u>USING</u> THE NAME "A.J. HIDELL" AS AN <u>ALIAS</u>. IF WE DISSECT THIS STATEMENT, IT DOES INDEED DOVETAIL WITH WHAT WE KNOW ABOUT THE LINK BETWEEN **HARVEY** AND THE NAME "HIDELL."

HARVEY CLAIMS HE DID NOT LIST A "HIDELL" ON <u>ANY</u> P.O. BOXES. AT ANY RATE, A.J. HIDELL WAS NOT AN <u>ALIAS</u> IF INDEED IT WAS CONNECTED TO THE FIRST DALLAS POST OFFICE BOX, #2915, IN <u>ANY</u> FASHION. THE INCLUSION OF "HIDELL" WOULD HAVE BEEN MADE BY THE SET-UP CONSPIRATORS ON "PART 3" OF THE <u>FIRST</u> DALLAS BOX, #2915 APPLICATION AND THE SIGNED RECEIPT WHEN THE RIFLE AND HANDGUN WERE PICKED UP AT THAT SAMEBOX. KEEP IN MIND HOWEVER THAT THESE TWO ITEMS WERE EITHERDESTROYED OR LOST.

*THE PART 3 OF THE <u>NEW ORLEANS</u> P.O. BOX HOWEVER <u>WAS</u> RETAINED AND DID INDEED LIST A "A.J. HIDELL." **HARVEY** STATED THAT HE "DIDN'T RECALL ANYTHING ABOUT THAT."*

THE JOB APPLICATION AT REILLY COFFEE LISTED A "SERGEANT ROBERT HIDELL", NOT A "ALEX J. HIDELL."

THE NEW ORLEANS FPFC CARD WAS SIGNED BY A "A. J. HIDELL" AS THE CHAPTER PRESIDENT. THE CARD MEMBER HOWEVER WAS "LEE H. OSWALD", THEREFORE **HARVEY** DID NOT USE "A. J. HIDELL" AS AN <u>ALIAS.</u>

A VACCINATION CARD FOUND IN **HARVEY'S** ROOM ON BECKLEY WAS SIGNED AND STAMPED BY A DR. A. J. HIDEEL AT THE U.S. PUBLIC HEALTH SERVICE OFFICE ON JUNE 8TH, 1963. THE CARD WAS TO NOTE THAT **HARVEY** HAD RECEIVED THE SMALLPOX VACCINATION. THE P.O. BOX **HARVEY** OPENED IN NEW ORLEANS WAS 30061. THE P.O. BOX OF DR. HIDEEL IS HOWEVER NOTED ON THE CARD AS #30016.

*THERE ARE TWO ITEMS OF NOTE REGARDNG THIS CARD. ON THE SAME DATE, JUNE 8TH, 1963, MARINA VISITED CHARITY HOSPITAL AS SHE WAS 5 MONTHS PREGNANT WITH HER SECOND DAUGHTER RACHEL. WHY WOULD **HARVEY** NOT OBTAIN HIS SMALLPOX VACCINATION AT CHARITY HOSPITAL IN CONJUNCTION WITH MARINA'S VISIT? IT WAS ALSO NOTED BY THE WARREN COMMISSION THAT THE FBI VISITED THE U.S. PUBLIC SERVICE HOSPITAL ON BOTH NOVEMBER 25TH AND THE 26TH LOOKING FOR INFORMATION ON BOTH **HARVEY** <u>AND</u> A DR. A.J. HIDEEL. ONCE AGAIN, NO PROOF THAT THE NAME "HIDELL" OR "HIDEEL" WAS USED FOR THE PURPOSE OF AN <u>ALIAS</u>.*

THE CIA NOTED IN A CABLE THAT THE "FBI HAD NOT ESTABLISHED AS OF NOON ON NOVEMBER 23RD WHETHER HIDELL EXISTS OR WHETHER IT IS AN ALIAS USED BY OSWALD."

HARVEY HAD, ON VARIOUS OCCASSIONS DURING 1963 ADMITEDLY <u>CORRESPONDED</u> WITH A "HIDELL" AND <u>SPOKEN</u> WITH A "HIDELL" ON THE PHONE. BUT HE NEVER CLAIMED TO HAVE <u>MET</u> A "HIDELL" FACE TO FACE OTHER THAN A SERGEANT ROBERT HIDELL FROM HIS MARINE CORP SERVICE.

NEITHER "A. HIDELL", "ALEX J. HIDELL", "A.J. HIDEEL" NOR "A.J. HIDELL" WERE USED BY **HARVEY** AS AN <u>ALIAS</u>. ONE WOULD LIKELY BE MORE ACCURATE IN LABELLING THE VARIOUS "HIDELLS" AS **HARVEY'S** HANDLER(S)., OR AS NOTED IN MY SCENARIO, ONE OF HIS SET-UP CONSPIRATORS. THE CONSPIRATOR IN QUESTION WAS LIKELY **LEE**.

VARY/BAKER HAS NOTED THAT **HARVEY** TOLD HER THAT "HIDELL" WAS A "PROJECT NAME." MORE IMPORTANTLY, HE TOLD HER THAT THE NAME "HIDELL" WAS NOT USED EXCLUSIVELY BY HIM LENDING CREEDENCE TO THE NOTION THAT **LEE** MAY HAVE BEEN "HIDELL" AS ARMSTRONG NOTES. THIS WOULD INDEED BE THE CASE IF INDEED "HIDELL" WAS A PROJECT NAME.

THERE WERE OTHER PROBLEMS REGARDING THE ASSOCIATION OF **HARVEY** TO THE ALLEGED ASSASSINATION RIFLE OUTSIDE THE REALM OF THE ATTEMPTED PAPERWORK CONNECTION. THE SCOPE ON THE RIFLE WOULD OFFER LITTLE ASSISTANCE TO **HARVEY** HAD HE INDEED BEEN THE SHOOTER. AN EXAMINATION OF THE GUN BY THE ABERDEEN PROVING GROUND FOUND THE SCOPE HAD BEEN ADJUSTED AND MOUNTED FOR A LEFT-HANDED SHOOTER. **HARVEY** WAS RIGHT-HANDED.

INDEED, NO ONE EVER SAW **HARVEY** WITH THE RIFLE. A PARAFFIN TEST, CONDUCTED AFTER THE ARREST OF **HARVEY**, PROVED TO BE NEGATIVE FOR NITRATES. IT IS VIRTUALLY IMPOSSIBLE TO TEST NEGATIVE FOR FACIAL NITRATES AFTER FIRING A RIFLE.

CHAPTER 18: FPFC: FBI FACT OR SET-UP FICTION

IN MUCH THE SAME FASHION AS WE EXAMINED THE USE OF "HIDELL" WITH THE RIFLE SET-UP WE WILL VISIT THE FPFC AND ITS MANIPULATIVE VALUE TO THE SET-UP CONSPIRATORS.

ON OCTOBER 9TH, 1962, **HARVEY** OPENED HIS FIRST P.O. BOX #2915 IN DALLAS. AS NOTED PREVIOUSLY, HE HAD OPENED THE BOX IN HIS NAME ONLY. LATER, ON PART 3, THE PORTION OF THE FORM LISTING INDIVIDUALS "OTHER THAN THE APPLICANT" ELIGIBLE TO RECEIVE MAIL, IT WAS CLAIMED BY THE FBI THAT THE FPFC WAS LISTED. BUT, AS WE KNOW, THERE IS NO WAY TO VERIFY THIS SINCE THAT PART OF THE FORM WAS DESTROYED OR LOST. THE INCLUSION OF THE FPFC AT THIS JUNCTURE MAY HAVE BEEN AT THE REQUEST OF THE FBI SINCE IT IS LIKELY THAT **HARVEY** HAD BEEN ENLISTED AS A DOMESTIC ASSET BY THEM IN THEIR ATTEMPTS TO INFILTRATE VARIOUS SUBVERSIVE GROUPS. INDEED THERE ARE NUMEROUS GROUPS CONTACTED BY **HARVEY** IN THE MONTHS PRIOR TO AND AFTER HE HAD OPENED THIS P.O. BOX OTHER THAN THE FPFC:

* JUNE 26TH, 1962, **HARVEY** IS INTERVIEWED BY THE FBI.
* AUGUST 5TH, 1962, **HARVEY** SUBSCRIBES TO THE WORKER.
* AUGUST 12TH, 1962, **HARVEY** WRITES TO THE SOCIALISTS WORKERS PARTY.
* AUGUST 28TH, 1962, **HARVEY** WRITES TO THE SWP ABOUT PAMPHLETS.
* OCTOBER 9TH, 1962, **HARVEY** OPENS DALLAS P.O. BOX #2915.
* OCTOBER 30TH, 1962, **HARVEY** APPLIES FOR MEMBERSHIP IN SWP.
* DECEMBER 15TH, 1962, **HARVEY** SUBSCRIBES TO THE MILITANT.
* JANUARY 1963, **HARVEY** SUBSCRIBES TO THE OGONEK, KKROKODR, AND THE AGITATOR.

HARVEY'S INVOLVEMENT WITH THESE GROUPS IS LIKELY PART OF HIS CONFIDENTIAL INFORMANT STATUS WITH THE FBI. HOWEVER ON APRIL 16TH, 1963, HE APPARENTLY WRITES THE FPFC. ALTHOUGH IT IS POSSIBLE THAT THIS TOO IS IN REGARD TO HIS FBI INFORMANT STATUS, I AM MORE INCLINED TO BELIEVE THAT IT IS PART OF THE INITIAL STAGES OF THE SET-UP AS IT IS ONLY 27 DAYS AFTER THE HANDGUN AND THE RIFLE ARRIVE IN DALLAS AND 8 DAYS BEFORE HIS DEPARTURE FOR NEW ORLEANS. THE PAMPHLETS ARE MAILED TO **HARVEY** ON APRIL 19TH. THERE IS HOWEVER NO CERTAINTY THAT THE PAMPHLETS ARRIVED PRIOR TO HIS APRIL 24TH DEPARTURE FOR NEW ORLEANS.

AS WE WILL SEE, **HARVEY** WILL ALLEGEDLY ORDER 1000 FPFC PAMPHLETS ON MAY 29TH, 1963 ADDING CREEDENCE TO THE POSSIBILITY THAT HIS INITIAL REQUEST HAD NOT ARRIVED BEFORE APRIL 24TH, HIS DEPARTURE DATE FOR NEW ORLEANS. IF THEY DID, THEY ARE LIKELY THE PAMPHLETS THAT HE WOULD LATER HAND OUT IN NEW ORLEANS STAMPED WITH THE CAMP STREET ADDRESS OF BANISTER'S OFFICE BUT, **HARVEY** WOULD LATER IN CUSTODY STATE THAT HE HAD NO INTEREST OR INVOLVEMENT IN THE FPFC UNTIL AFTER HE ARRIVED IN NEW ORLEANS. HE MAY HAVE EITHER FORGOTTEN ABOUT THE ORDERED PAMPHLETS IN DALLAS PRIOR TO NEW ORLEANS, OR SIMPLY MAY HAVE PERCEIVED HIS MORE ACTIVE PAMPHLET DISTRIBUTING IN HIS NEW ORLEANS FPFC ROLE AS HIS *INITIAL*, MORE HANDS-ON INVOLVEMENT WITH THE FPFC.

IT IS INTERESTING TO NOTE THE FBI'S INSISTANCE THAT THE FPFC WAS LISTED ON PART 3 OF BOTH **HARVEY'S** 2 DALLAS P.O. BOXES. SINCE THE OTHER SUBVERSIVE ORGANIZATIONS AND NEWSPAPERS (WORKER, SWP, MILITANT, OGONEK, KROKODR AND THE AGITATOR) WERE NOT LISTED ON ANY OF THE P.O BOXES PART 3, WHY WOULD THE FPFC BE INCLUDED? I THINK THAT THE FBI SUSPECTED THAT THE FPFC/**HARVEY** RELATIONSHIP WAS NOT OF THEIR MAKING BUT THAT OF THE CIA. THE SET-UP CONSPIRATORS KNEW THE FBI WOULD DESTROY THE PART 3'S SINCE IT WOULD MORE LIKELY BE PERCEIVED THAT A

*FPFC/**HARVEY**/FBI CONNECTION EXISTED RATHER THAN A FPFC/**HARVEY**/CIA CONNECTION DUE TO THE FBI'S ADOPTION OF **HARVEY** AS AN INFORMANT OF OTHER SUBVERSIVE COMMUNIST GROUPS.*

IN NEW ORLEANS, ON MAY 26TH, 1963, BANISTER HAD **HARVEY** START A NEW ORLEANS CHAPTER OF THE FPFC. HIS CHAPTER CARD LISTS HIM AS A MEMBER, AND A "A.J. HIDELL" AS CHAPTER PRESIDENT. THE FBI NOTED LATER THAT THE HANDWRITTEN SIGNATURE BY "A.J. HIDELL" WAS NOT IN **HARVEY'S** HANDWRITING. MARINA WOULD LATER ADMIIT TO HAVING SIGNED THE CARD FOR HIM. **HARVEY** WAS SIMPLY TRYING TO AVOID ANY OBVIOUS SIMILARITIES BETWEEN HIS SIGNATURE ON THE CARD AS A MEMBER AND THE SIGNATURE OF THE CHAPTER PRESIDENT, A.J. HIDELL.

ON MAY 29TH IN NEW ORLEANS, **HARVEY** ALLEGEDLY ORDERS 1000 FPFC LEAFLETS. THE LEAFLETS ARE ORDERED BY A "LEE OSBORNE." WHY WOULD **HARVEY** USE AN ALIAS TO OBTAIN A PRINTING OF FPFC PAMPHLETS WHEN HE HAD FREELY ASSOCIATED HIS NAME WITH THE GROUP ON THE CARD DEPICTING HIS MEMBERSHIP IN THE BANISTER-INSPIRED NEW ORLEANS CHAPTER AND HAD APPARENTLY ALREADY CONTACTED THE FPFC ON APRIL 16TH PRIOR TO LEAVING DALLAS? IN MY OPINION IT WAS THE DESIRE OF THE SET-UP CONSPIRATORS TO ISOLATE **HARVEY'S** ASSOCIATION WITH THE FPFC IN NEW ORLEANS IN CONJUNCTION WITH THEIR EFFORTS FROM **HARVEY'S** LEGITIMATE SUBVERSIVE ACTIVITY MONITORING WITH THE FBI. IT WOULD BE MORE PRUDENT FOR THE SET-UP CONSPIRATORS TO ORDER THE FPFC PAMPHLETS VIA AN ALIAS AND NOT INCLUDE THE FPFC ON PART 3 OF THE NEW ORLEANS P.O. BOX SINCE THE SET-UP CONSPIRATORS WERE WELL AWARE THAT THE FBI WAS MONITORING **HARVEY'S** MAIL. THIS WOULD IN EFFECT KEEP THE FBI IN THE DARK, AT LEAST TEMPORARILY, IN REGARDS TO THE EFFORTS OF THE SET-UP CONSPIRATORS; PARTICULARLY THOSE EFFORTS TO CONNECT **HARVEY** WITH THE FPFC IN NEW ORLEANS.

ON JUNE 3RD, 1963 **HARVEY**, OPENS P.O. BOX 30051 IN NEW ORLEANS. ONCE AGAIN HE CLAIMS THAT IT WAS OPENED IN HIS NAME ONLY. LATER IN CUSTODY HE REMARKED THAT ONLY HE AND MARINA HAD ACCESS TO THIS BOX. THE FPFC WAS NOT LINKED TO THIS BOX.

ON THIS SAME DATE, **HARVEY** ALLEGEDLY ORDERS ANOTHER PRINTING OF FPFC MATERIAL. THIS TIME IT IS FOR 500 COPIES OF AN APPLICATION FORM. ONCE AGAIN THE ORDER IS PLACED BY A "LEE OSBORNE." THIS IS THE 2ND FPFC ORDER IN THE LAST 6 DAYS. ONCE AGAIN I AM INCLINED TO BELIEVE THAT **HARVEY** LEFT DALLAS PRIOR TO RECEIVING THE FPFC PAMPHLETS REQUESTED ON APRIL 16TH.

THE PAMPHLETS HOWEVER WERE APPARENTLY NOT PICKED UP BY **HARVEY** ACCORDING TO MYRA SILVER AN EMPLOYEE OF JONES PRINTING COMPANY. DOUGLAS JONES, THE OWNER OF JONES PRINTING, DESCRIBED THE RECIPIENT OF THE PAMPHLETS AS A "HUSKY" TYPE PERSON. I AM INCLINED TO BELIEVE THAT THE PERSON WHO PRESENTED HIMSELF AT JONES PRINTING AS "LEE OSBORNE" FOR THE PICK-UP OF THE PAMPHLETS WAS EITHER ROSCOE WHITE OR THE RELATIVE-TO-HARVEY "HUSKY" **LEE**. WHITE WILL RETURN TO DALLAS ONLY 4 DAYS AFTER **HARVEY** RETURNS FROM HIS VISIT TO NEW ORLEANS.

ON JUNE 10TH, 1963, **HARVEY** WOULD WRITE TO THE WORKER. ON SEPTEMBER 1ST, HE WOULD WRITE TO THE COMMUNIST PARTY USA AND THE SOCIALIST WORKERS PARTY. THESE CONTACTS WOULD LIKELY BE IN CONJUNCTION WITH HIS CONFIDENTIAL INFORMANT STATUS FOR THE FBI.

TO REVIEW THE P.O. BOX SITUATION, THE FIRST DALLAS P.O. BOX #2915 SUPPOSEDLY HAD LISTED ON THE DESTROYED PART 3 BOTH HIDELL AND THE FPFC. THE ADDITION BY THE SET-UP CONSPIRATORS OF "HIDELL" WOULD BE FOR THE SOLE PURPOSE OF TYING **HARVEY** TO A NAME TO BE LATER USED IN THE ORDERING OF THE ALLEGED

ASSASSINATION WEAPON. THE ADDITION OF THE FPFC TO PART 3 WOULD ALSO HAVE TO HAVE BEEN DONE BY THE SET-UP CONSPIRATORS SINCE **HARVEY** DID NOT MAKE HIS INITIAL WRITTEN CONTACT WITH THE FPFC UNTIL APRIL 16TH, 1963, OVER 5 MONTHS LATER.

THE NEW ORLEANS P.O. BOX, #30061 SUPPOSEDLY LISTED "HIDELL" ONCE AGAIN BUT DID NOT INCLUDE THE FPFC. THE SET-UP CONSPIRATORS WOULD AVOID THE P.O. BOX LINK BETWEEN **HARVEY** AND THE FPFC AND USE THE ALIAS "OSBORNE" TO ORDER PAMPHLETS AND ADDITIONAL FORMS. THEY WOULD BE MORE ACTIVELY IMPLICATING **HARVEY** WITH THE CAUSE OF THE FPFC BY VIRTUE OF HIS PAMPHLET DISTRIBUTING AND HIS ENCOUNTERS WITH BRINGUIER BOTH ON THE STREET AND IN THEIR RADIO DEBATE.

HARVEY'S LAST P.O. BOX, #6225, OPENED ON NOVEMBER 1ST, 1963, ALLEGEDLY LISTED THE FPFC AND THE ACLU. THESE INCLUSIONS MAY HAVE BEEN LEGITIMATE AS HE ALSO ON THIS DATE SENT IN HIS APPLICATION FOR MEMBERSHIP IN THE ACLU. HE WOULD HAVE NO REASON NOT TO INCLUDE THE FPFC AT THIS POINT SINCE HE HAD POINTEDLY ASSOCIATED HIMSELF WITH THIS ORGANIZATION WHILE IN NEW ORLEANS. IN FACT ON NOVEMBER 2ND, HE WOULD SEND A CHANGE OF ADDRESS CARD TO THE FPFC. BUT IN CUSTODY, HE DENIED ALLOWING ANYONE ACCESS TO THIS BOX OTHER THAN MARINA. WE WILL LIKELY NEVER KNOW IF THE ACLU AND THE FPFC WERE INDEED INCLUDED BY **HARVEY** OR ADDED WITHOUT HIS KNOWLEDGE BY THE SET-UP CONSPIRATORS SINCE THE PORTION OF THIS APPLICATION LISTING "OTHER PERSONS" ELIGIBLE TO RECEIVE MAIL AT THE P.O. BOX HAD BEEN "LOST." IN MUCH THE SAME FASHION AS THE FIRST DALLAS P.O. BOX, THERE IS NO CONCLUSIVE WAY TO DETERMINE JUST WHO HAD ACCESS TO EITHER OF **HARVEY'S** DALLAS POST OFFICE BOXES.

THE INCLUSION OR EXCLUSION OF THE FPFC ON **HARVEY'S** VARIOUS P.O. BOXES IS NOT AS CRITICAL TO THE SET-UP CONSPIRATORS AS THE INCLUSION OF "HIDELL." THE LINK BETWEEN **HARVEY** AND THE FPFC ON THE FIRST DALLAS BOX WOULD BE ERASED WITH THE DESTROYED "PART 3" ALONG WITH THE ALLEGED CONNECTION BETWEEN **HARVEY**, THE P.O. BOX WHERE THE RIFLE WAS DELIVERED, AND A "HIDELL." THE FPFC WAS NOT LISTED ON THE SECOND BOX, THE NEW ORLEANS BOX, AND WAS EITHER LEGITIMATELY INCLUDED BY **HARVEY** ON HIS LAST DALLAS BOX ALONG WITH THE ACLU OR ADDED BY THE SET-UP CONSPIRATORS AND CONVENIENTLY "LOST" WHEN THE POSTAL SERVICE, LIKELY WITH THE ENCOURAGEMENT OF THE FBI, WAS UNABLE TO LOCATE THE "PART 3" OF THAT PARTICULAR POST OFFICE BOX APPLICATION.

ONE WOULD CERTAINLY HAVE TO WONDER WHY, ON **HARVEY'S** TWO DALLAS POST OFFICE BOXES, THAT EVIDENCE THAT COULD IN ESSENCE LINK HIM TO A "HIDELL" AND IN TURN A RIFLE ORDER AND THE FPFC WOULD BE DESTROYED OR LOST. I WOULD OFFER THAT IT WAS THE INCLUSION BY THE SET-UP CONSPIRATORS OF THE FPFC ON BOTH THE DALLAS P.O. BOX APPLICATIONS THAT NECESSITATED THE "ABSENCE" OF THESE CRITICAL DOCUMENTS. IF INDEED THE FBI WAS UTILIZING **HARVEY** AS A CRIMINAL INFORMANT, AND IF THE FPFC WAS INDEED ON THE LIST OF "SUBVERSIVE" GROUPS MONITORED BY THE FBI, THE INTEGRITY OF THE FBI'S INFORMANT PROGRAM WOULD TRULY BE IN JEOPARDY – NOT TO MENTION THE REPUTATION OF THE FBI - SINCE IT WOULD NOW APPEAR AS THOUGH ONE OF THEIR OWN HAD KILLED THE PRESIDENT.

THE SET-UP CONSPIRATORS WERE WELL AWARE THAT THE FBI WOULD RESORT TO ANY MEANS NECESSARY TO DESTROY ANY POSSIBLE PAPER TRAIL THAT COULD EXPOSE A LEGITIMATE CONNECTION WITH **HARVEY**. HOWEVER THE FBI WOULD ALSO, IN THE CASE OF THE FIRST DALLAS P.O. BOX, ALSO DESTROY ANY LINK BETWEEN **HARVEY**, A "HIDELL", AND THE RIFLE PURCHASE; A LINK THE SET-UP CONSPIRATORS WOULD HAVE PREFERRED TO MAINTAIN. THE SET-UP CONSPIRATORS WOULD HAVE

TO "RE-ESTABLISH" THIS LINK BETWEEN **HARVEY** AND "HIDELL" BY VIRTUE OF THE FRAUDULENT SELECTIVE SERVICE CARD "DISCOVERED" ON SATURDAY, NOVEMBER 23RD.

CHAPTER 19: NOTED HARVEY IMPOSTORS USED IN THE SET-UP

SUMMER 1963

MRS. LAVELL PENN OWNED LAND ON THE OUTSKIRTS OF DALLAS. SHE SAW 2 MEN, ONE LATIN OR CUBAN WITH ANOTHER MAN SHE CLAIMED LOOKED LIKE **HARVEY** FIRING A RIFLE ON HER PROPERTY. LATER A CARTRIDGE FROM A 6.5 MANNLICHER WAS FOUND. BUT, THE FBI DETERMINED THAT IT HAD <u>NOT</u> BEEN FIRED FROM THE RIFLE THAT **HARVEY** ALLEGEDLY USED IN THE ASSASSINATION.

*MRS. PENN LIKELY WITNESSED **LEE**.*

SEPTEMBER 27TH, 1963

A MAN CLAIMING TO BE OSWALD VISITS THE CUBAN EMBASSY. BOTH CONSUL ASSISTANT SILVIA DURAN AND CONSUL EUSEDIO AZCUE DENY THAT THE MAN IS **HARVEY**. A PHOTO TAKEN BY SURVEILLANCE CAMERAS OUTSIDE THE SOVIET EMBASSY PURPORTING TO SHOW **HARVEY** WAS CLEARLY NOT **HARVEY**. THE VOICE TAPE OF HIS TELEPHONE CONVERSATIONS WAS CLEARLY NOT THE VOICE OF **HARVEY**. HOOVER HIMSELF WOULD TELL LBJ "IT APPEARS THAT THERE IS A SECOND PERSON WHO WAS AT THE SOVIET EMBASSY DOWN THERE."

*ARMSTRONG NOTES THAT IT WAS LIKELY **LEE** IN MEXICO CITY. THE PHOTO TAKEN OUTSIDE THE SOVIET EMBASSY HOWEVER IS NEITHER **LEE** NOR **HARVEY**.*

OCTOBER 4TH, 1963

STATION MANAGER OF KPOY, ALICE, TEXAS WAS VISITED BY SOMEONE HE THOUGHT TO BE **HARVEY** ACCOMPANIED BY HIS "WIFE", AND A BABY NAMED "JUNE." THEY ARRIVED IN A 1953 CAR. **HARVEY** NEITHER DROVE NOR OWNED A CAR. ALICE IS 350 MILES FROM DALLAS.

*THE VISITOR WAS LIKELY **LEE**.*

NOVEMBER 2ND, 1963

DEWEY BRADFORD TOLD THE FBI THAT HE SAW "OSWALD" AT MORGAN'S GUNSHOP IN FORT WORTH ATTEMPTING TO BUY AMMO. "OSWALD" SAID HE HAD BEEN IN THE MARINES AND WAS NOTED BY BRADFORD TO BE "RUDE AND IMPERTINENT." THERE IS NO RECORD OF <u>ANY</u> AMMO <u>EVER</u> BEING PURCHASED FOR THE ALLEGED ASSASSINATION RIFLE AND THERE WAS NONE FOUND IN **HARVEY'S** POSSESSION AFTER THE ASSASSINATION.

*BRADFORD HAD LIKELY ENCOUNTERED **LEE**.*

NOVEMBER 6TH, 1963

AN "OSWALD" VISITED A GUNSHOP IN IRVING, TEXAS ONLY TO FIND OUT IT WAS NOW A FURNITURE SHOP. "OSWALD" HAD BROUGHT HIS "WIFE" IN AND THEY CONVERSED IN A "FOREIGN LANGUAGE." MARINA WOULD LATER SAY THAT SHE HAD NOT BEEN THERE.

*ONCE AGAIN, THE VISITOR WAS LIKELY **LEE**.*

NOVEMBER 8TH 1963

A BARBER IN IRVING IS VISITED BY AN "OSWALD" WITH A 14 YEAR OLD BOY. THEY BOTH MAKE "LEFTIST REMARKS." WHEN "OSWALD" LEFT HE ENTERED A NEARBY GROCERY AND ASKED THE MANAGER LEONARD HUTCHINSON TO CASH A CHECK FOR $189 MADE OUT TO "HARVEY OSWALD."

*THE BARBER HAD LIKELY ENCOUNTERED **LEE**.*

NOVEMBER 9ᵀᴴ, 1963

AN "OSWALD" WAS SEEN ALMOST EVERY NIGHT AT EITHER THE SPORTSDROME RIFLE RANGE IN DALLAS OR AT A RANGE IN IRVING. THIS "OSWALD" FIRED AT OTHER PEOPLES TARGETS, BEHAVED OBNOXIOUSLY, AND FIRED A 6.5MM ITALIAN CARBINE THAT EMITTED "A BALL OF FIRE" WHEN FIRED. EXPERIENCED RIFLEMEN HOWEVER NOTED THAT THE GUN WAS <u>NOT</u> A MANNLICHER AND THAT THIS "OSWALD" PICKED UP <u>EVERY</u> SPENT SHELL. WHY WOULD **HARVEY** OR "OSWALD" DO THIS <u>PRACTICING</u>, BUT NOT AT THE TSBD AFTER HAVING ALLEGEDLY SHOT THE PRESIDENT AND NOT AT THE SCENE OF THEN TIPPIT SHOOTING?

INTERESTINGLY, THE FBI REPORT ON THE SHELLS PICKED UP IN THE TSBD NOTED THAT THOSE SHELLS HAD DOUBLE MARKINGS AS THOUGH THEY HAD BEEN LOADED TWICE.

*THE SHOOTER AT THE RIFLE RANGES WAS LIKELY **LEE**.*

NOVEMBER 9ᵀᴴ, 1963

A MAN CLAIMING TO BE LEE OSWALD VISITED THE DOWNTOWN LINCON-MERCURY DEALERSHIP AND TOLD SALESMAN ALBERT GUY BOGARD THAT HE WOULD "BE COMING INTO A LOT OF MONEY SOON" AND THAT "WORKERS IN RUSSIA RECEIVED BETTER TREATMENT." HE WAS ALSO HEARD TO HAVE MUTTERED "MAYBE I'M GOING TO HAVE TO GO BACK TO RUSSIA TO BUY A CAR." BOGARD HAD WRITTEN THE PROSPECTIVE BUYER'S NAME ON THE BACK OF A BUSINESS CARD AS "LEE OSWALD." THE MAN ALSO WENT ON A TEST DRIVE WITH BOGARD AT SPEEDS UP TO 70 MPH ON THE STEMMONS FREEWAY. **HARVEY** DIDN'T DRIVE. THE WARREN COMMISSION SAID THAT IT COULD NOT BE **HARVEY**. BOGARD, AFTER SEEING **HARVEY** ON TV AFTER THE ASSASSINATION, SAID THAT **HARVEY** WAS NOT THE SAME MAN AT THE DEALERSHIP.

*IT WAS LIKELY **LEE** WHO HAD TAKEN THE INCRIMINATING TEST DRIVE.*

NOVEMBER 1963

IN AN IRVING SPORTS SHOP, A MAN BROUGHT IN A RIFLE TO HAVE <u>3 HOLES</u> DRILLED FOR A SCOPE. THE WORK TICKET WAS ASSIGNED TO AN "OSWALD." BUT, **HARVEY'S** ALLEGED ASSASSINATION RIFLE NEEDED ONLY <u>2 HOLES</u> TO MOUNT A SCOPE. AND, MORE IMPORTANTLY, THE GUN **HARVEY** HAD ALLEGEDLY ORDERED WAS SHIPPED WITH A SCOPE <u>ALREADY</u> <u>MOUNTED</u>.

*ONCE AGAIN, MOST LIKELY **LEE**.*

NOVEMBER 1963

A MAN ASKS HUBERT MORROW ABOUT A JOB AS A PARKING ATTENDANT AT THE SOUTHLAND HOTEL IN CENTRAL DALLAS. MORROW WRITES DOWN HIS NAME AS "OSBORNE" BUT WAS IMMEDIATELY CORRECTED BY THE MAN TO CHANGE THE NAME TO "OSWALD." "OSWALD" ALSO ASKED HOW TALL THE HOTEL WAS AND WHAT KIND OF VIEW IT HAD OF DALLAS

*INTERESTINGLY, THE NAME "OSBORNE" IS THE SAME NAME USED IN NEW ORLEANS TO ORDER THE PAMPHLETS AND APPLICATIONS FOR THE FPFC. WAS THE INITIAL UTTERANCE OF "OSBORNE" A SLIP OF THE TONGUE BY **LEE**? IN A SET-UP OF THIS COMPLEXITY, IT WOULD NOT BE UNEXPECTED THAT ACCOMPLICES WOULD OCCASSIONALLY FORGET JUST WHO THEY WERE IMPLICATING, **HARVEY** OR "OSBORNE." **LEE** IS THE LIKELY CANDIDATE FOR THIS ATTEMPT. **LEE** MAY ALSO HAVE BEEN THE PERSON TO ORDER THE FPFC PAMPHLETS IN NEW ORLEANS.*

NOVEMBER 24ᵀᴴ, 1963

WFAA-TV IN DALLAS RECEIVED A PHONE CALL SAYING AN "OSWALD" HAD A GUN SIGHTED. ONCE AGAIN, THE ALLEGED ASSASSINATION RIFLE AS ORDERED WAS SHIPPED <u>WITH</u> A SCOPE. THE FBI WOULD RECEIVE THE SAME PHONE CALL.

IT IS INTERESTING TO NOTE THAT VIRTUALLY ALL, 10 OF 11, OF THESE SIGHTINGS TAKE PLACE <u>AFTER</u> THE SEPTEMBER 24TH DEPARTURE OF **HARVEY** FROM NEW ORLEANS. IF ONE DISCOUNTS THE POSSIBILITY THAT **HARVEY** ACTUALLY MADE THE MEXICO CITY TRIP, HE WOULD RETURN TO TEXAS ON SEPTEMBER 25TH. THE ANNOUNCEMENT OF JFK'S TRIP TO DALLAS WILL BE MADE THE FOLLOWING DAY, SEPTEMBER 26TH.

THE SET-UP PLOT WAS IN ITS FINAL STAGE

IN INSTANCES WHERE **HARVEY** OR AN "OSWALD" (MOST LIKELY **LEE**) APPEARED TO BE IN TWO PLACES AT ONCE, THE WARREN COMMISSON SIMPLY STATED THAT THE WITNESSES WERE WRONG; IT WASN'T **HARVEY**. THE COMMISSION NEVER PURSUED JUST <u>WHO</u> HAD IMPERSONATED **HARVEY** OR MORE IMPORTANTLY <u>WHY.</u>

THE SET-UP CONSPIRATOR ORCHESTRATING THE TEXAS BASED SIGHTINGS, MOST LIKELY ROSCOE WHITE AND **LEE**, MADE MANY MISTAKES:

* **HARVEY** DID NOT OWN A CAR, A VALID DRIVERS LICENSE, NOR DID HE DRIVE

* **HARVEY'S** ALLEGED ASSASSINATION RIFLE DID NOT NEED A FIRING PIN

* THE ALLEGED ASSASSINATION RIFLE NEEDED ONLY 2 HOLES FOR A SCOPE NOT 3

* THE ALLEGED ASSASSINATION RIFLE HAD BEEN ORDERED AND APPARENTLY DELIVERED WITH A SCOPE ALREADY MOUNTED

* BYSTANDERS NOTED THAT THE RIFLE USED IN THE SHOOTING RANGE INCIDENTS WAS NOT A MANNLICHER.

EITHER THE TEXAS BASED SET-UP CONSPIRATORS WERE EXTREMELY CARELESS IN ALLOWING "OSWALD" TO BE IN DIFFERENT LOCATIONS AT THE SAME TIME OR THEY WERE NOT AT ALL CONCERNED ABOUT THE POSSIBILITY OF **HARVEY** LATER BEING PERCEIVED AS HAVING BEEN "SET-UP" AS PART OF A LARGER CONSPIRACY WITH NUMEROUS PARTICIPANTS. THE LONE GUNMAN THEORY ADAMANTLY PURSUED BY THE WARREN COMMISSION AND THE FBI AND THEIR SUPPRESSION OF ANY EVIDENCE POINTING TO A CONSPIRACY PROVED THE SET-UP CONSPIRATORS LACK OF CONCERN TO BE A CORRECT ONE.

CHAPTER 20: WOUND EVIDENCE AND THE BIRTH OF THE MAGIC BULLET

THE SECRET SERVICE REPORT OF 28 NOVEMBER 1963 FROM INSPECTOR TOM KERRY TO CHIEF ROWLEY READS IN PART: "....PRESIDENT KENNEDY, WHO WAS SEATED ON THE RIGHT REAR SEAT, WAS SHOT. IMMEDIATELY THEREAFTER, GOVENOR CONNALLY, SEATED IN THE RIGHT JUMP SEAT, WAS SHOT ONCE. THE PRESIDENT WAS THEN SHOT THE SECOND TIME."

NOTE THERE IS NO REFERENCE TO THE DIRECTION OR SOURCE OF THE SHOTS. BUT THE REPORT DOES INDICATE THAT CONNALLY WAS NOT HIT BY A BULLET THAT HAD FIRST STRUCK THE PRESIDENT

IN A PHONE CONVERSATION WITH LBJ AT 1:40 PM ON FRIDAY NOVEMBER 29TH, 1963, HOOVER REITERATES THIS FIRING SEQUENCE: "....THE PRESIDENT – HE WAS HIT BY THE FIRST AND THIRD. THE SECOND SHOT HIT THE GOVENOR...." HOOVER HOWEVER PLACES THE MAGIC BULLET FOUND AT PARKLAND ON THE PRESIDENT'S STRETCHER, NOT CONNALLY'S. HE TELLS LBJ: "THE 3RD SHOT IS A COMPLETE BULLET AND THAT ROLLED OUT OF THE PRESIDENT'S HEAD."

AN EVEN MORE INTERESTING COMMENT BY HOOVER COMES LATER IN THIS SAME CONVERSATION. LBJ INQUIRED AS TO HOW CONNALLY WAS HIT. HOOVER NOTES THAT CONNALLY WAS HIT AS HE TURNED TO SEE THE PRESIDENT.

THESE DIRECT QUOTES ARE TAKEN FROM LBJ'S WHITE HOUSE TAPES:

LBJ: *"IF HE HADN'T TURNED, HE PROBABLY WOULDN'T HAVE GOT HIT?"*

HOOVER: *"I THINK THAT IS VERY LIKELY."*

LBJ: *"WOULD THE PRESIDENT HAVE GOT HIT WITH THE SECOND ONE?"*

HOOVER: *"NO, THE PRESIDENT WASN'T HIT WITH THE SECOND ONE."*

LBJ: *"I SAY, IF CONNALLY HADN'T BEEN IN HIS WAY?"*

HOOVER: *"OH, YES, YES, THE PRESIDENT WOULD NO DOUBT HAVE BEEN HIT."*

LBJ: *"HE WOULD HAVE BEEN HIT 3 TIMES."*

THE ONLY WAY CONNALLY COULD HAVE BEEN IN A POSITION TO PREVENT THE PRESIDENT FROM GETTING HIT 3 TIMES BY ABSORBING THE 2ND SHOT HIMSELF WAS IF THE SHOOTER WAS IN FRONT OF CONNALLY AND THE PRESIDENT. WAS THE CONVERSATION AN INDICATION THAT BOTH LBJ AND HOOVER FELT THAT SHOTS WERE INDEED FIRED FROM THE OVERPASS OR GRASSY KNOLL?

AN FBI SUMMARY REPORT DATED 9 DECEMBER 1963 STATED: "THREE SHOTS RANG OUT. TWO BULLETS STRUCK PRESIDENT KENNEDY AND ONE WOUNDED GOVENOR CONNALLY."

ONCE AGAIN NO REFERENCE OR IMPLICATION OF THE DIRECTION OR SOURCE OF THE SHOTS AND NO INDICATION THAT CONNALLY WAS HIT BY A BULLET THAT HAD FIRST STRUCK THE PRESIDENT.

THE FIRST VOLUME OF THE 4 VOLUME SUMMARY REPORT ALSO NOTED THAT "ONE OF THE BULLETS HAD ENTERED JUST BELOW HIS (JFK'S) SHOULDER TO THE RIGHT OF THE

SPINAL COLUMN AT AN ANGLE OF 45 TO 60 DEGREES DOWNWARD. THERE WAS NO POINT OF EXIT AND THE BULLET WAS NOT IN THE BODY."

IT IS READILY APPARENT THAT THE FBI'S INITIAL CONCLUSION IS IN STARK CONTRAST TO THE LATER PROPOSED WARREN COMMISSION CONCLUSION THAT THIS BACK SHOT NOT ONLY STRUCK THE PRESIDENT IN A DIFFERENT LOCATION, BUT DID INDEED EXIT THE PRESIDENT INFLICTING ALL THE WOUNDS ON GOVENOR CONNALLY.

THE FBI ISSUED ANOTHER REPORT, A 5TH VOLUME ADDITION TO THE PREVIOUSLY ISSUED 4 VOLUME SUMMARY REPORT ON 13 JANUARY 1964 STILL SUPPPORTING THEIR REPORT OF 12/9/63 THAT EACH OF THE 3 SHOTS STRUCK EITHER THE PRESIDENT OR GOVENOR CONNALLY. PAGE 14 OF THE REPORT READS:

A) SHOT ONE HIT THE TARGET FROM A DISTANCE OF 167 FEET
B) SHOT TWO HIT THE TARGET FROM A DISTANCE OF 262 FEET
C) SHOT THREE HIT THE TARGET FROM A DISTANCE OF 307 FEET

THIS REPORT ALSO NOTED THAT THE BULLET WHICH ENTERED THE PRESIDENT'S BACK, SHOT #1, HAD PENETRATED TO A DISTANCE OF LESS THAN A FINGER LENGTH AND DID NOT EXIT THE BODY.

THUSFAR WE HAVE 3 REPORTS; TWO BY THE FBI. ONE A 4 VOLUME SUMMARY REPORT OF DECEMBER 9TH, 1963, AND AN ADDITIONAL VOLUME TO THAT REPORT DATED JANUARY 13TH, 1964. THE FBI NOTES THAT THERE IS NO POINT OF EXIT FOR THE PRESIDENT'S BACK WOUND. THE THIRD REPORT WAS BY THE SECRET SERVICE STATING THAT THERE WERE 3 AND ONLY 3 SHOTS FIRED AND THAT EACH OF THEM HIT THEIR TARGET, EITHER THE PRESIDENT OR GOVENOR CONNALLY. ALL 3 REPORTS ARE IN STARK CONTRADICTION TO THE COMMISSION CONCLUSIONS.

THE 5 VOLUME SUMMARY REPORT BY THE FBI WAS NOT MADE PUBLIC.

BYSTANDER JAMES TAGUE IS ABOUT TO BECOME THE FLY IN THE OINTMENT. THE WOUNDING OF MR. TAGUE WAS KNOWN THE DAY OF THE ASSASSINATION. TAGUE SAID HE CALLED THE DALLAS FBI OFFICE THE AFTERNOON OF THE ASSASSINATION BUT THAT "THEY DIDN'T WANT MY TESTIMONY ABOUT THE STRAY BULLET." IN FACT, THE FIRST DOCUMENTED EVIDENCE OF WARREN COMMISSION AND THEREFORE ARLEN SPECTER'S ACKNOWLEDGEMENT OF THE MISSED SHOT WAS IN A MEMO TO LEE RANKIN FROM SPECTER DATED JUNE 11TH, 1964. IT READ IN PART: "IF ADDITIONAL DEPOSITIONS ARE TAKEN IN DALLAS, I SUGGEST JIM TAGUE AND VIRGIE RICHLEY BE DEPOSED TO DETERMINE KNOWLEDGE ON WHERE THE MISSING BULLET STRUCK THESE 2 WITNESSES WHO WERE MENTIONED IN EARLY FBI REPORTS BUT HAVE NEVER BEEN DISPOSED."

WHEN THE EXAMINATION OF THE ZAPRUDER FILM REVEALED THAT THERE WAS ONLY 5.6 SECONDS TO FIRE THE SHOTS, SPECTER AND OTHER COMMISSION MEMBERS REALIZED THAT THE NOTION OF WOUNDS HAVING BEEN INFLICTED ON BOTH MEN BY A SINGLE BULLET WOULD NOT SUFFICE AS JUST A "THEORY" BUT THAT THIS "THEORY" MUST NOW BECOME AN *ABSOLUTE NECESSITY* WITH THE ADDITION OF A 4TH SHOT THAT MISSED THE PRESIDENTIAL LIMO ENTIRELY AND CAUSED THE TAGUE WOUND.

IRONICALLY IF THIS SHOT (4TH) HAD INDEED BEEN FIRED FROM THE ALLEGED 6TH FLOOR SNIPER'S NEST WINDOW, IT WOULD HAVE CROSSED THE MOTORCADE 30 FEET ABOVE THE LIMO IN ORDER TO STRIKE THE MAIN STREET CURB. ALTHOUGH I HAVE READ MANY "SINGLE-BULLET THEORY" APOLOGISTS' MUSINGS REGARDING THE ACCURACY WHICH **HARVEY** *ALLEGEDLY EXHIBITED IN A 3 SHOT/ 3 HIT SCENARIO, I HAVE READ NO VALID EXPLANATION REGARDING THE AMAZING INACCURACY OF A BADLY MISSED 4TH SHOT.*

*WITH THE ADDITION OF A 4TH SHOT (THE TAGUE SHOT), THE W.C. NOW INSISTS THAT YOU BELIEVE THAT **HARVEY**, IN AN AMAZING FEAT OF ACCURACY, IS ABLE TO INFLICT 7 WOUNDS ON <u>TWO</u> INDIVIDUALS WITH <u>ONE</u> SHOT. IT ALSO MUST INSIST THAT YOU BELIEVE THAT THE EXTREMELY <u>LOW VELOCITY</u> BULLET THAT PENETRATED THE PRESIDENT'S BACK TO ONLY A FINGER'S DEPTH NOW BECOME AN APPARENT <u>HIGH</u> <u>VELOCITY</u> BULLET IN ORDER TO INFLICT THE 7 WOUNDS ON THE PRESIDENT AND GOVERNOR CONNALLY.*

ALLTHOUGH WE WILL MOST VIVIDLY REMEMBER VIEWING THE HEAD SHOT(S) THAT TOOK THE PRESIDENT'S LIFE, IT IS IN MY OPINION THE MISSED TAGUE SHOT THAT IS THE MOST IMPORTANT SHOT INFLICTED UPON THE MOTORCADE. IT IS <u>THIS</u> SHOT THAT WILL INITIATE THE MANIPULATION OF THE SHOOTING SEQUENCE AND THE WOUND LOCATIONS AND EVENTUALLY DISCREDIT THE W.C. FINDINGS.

THE DEGREE TO WHICH THE WARREN COMMISSION FOUND IT IMPERATIVE TO TIE THE "MAGIC" BULLET TO CONNALLY'S STRETCHER IS EVIDENT BY THE EXCHANGE BETWEEN COMMISSION ATTORNEY ARLAN SPECTER AND DARRELL TOMLINSON. THE FIRST TIME SPECTER ASKS TOMLINSON WHICH STRETCHER THE BULLET HAD FALLEN FROM TOMLINSON REPLIED: "I BELIEVE IT WAS B." ("B" WAS JFK'S STRETCHER) AFTER FURTHER QUESTIONING BY SPECTER, TOMLINSON SOFTENED A BIT AND CONCEDED THAT HE WASN'T SURE. THIS HOWEVER WAS NOT ENOUGH FOR SPECTER. HE NEEDED A <u>FIRM</u> CONFIRMATION FROM TOMLINSON THAT THE BULLET HAD FALLEN FROM THE STRETCHER DESIGNATED "A"; CONNALLY'S STRETCHER. SPECTER'S PURSUIT OF THE "RIGHT" ANSWER BORDERED ON COMICAL IF NOT CRIMINAL. HE COMMENTS TO TOMLINSON: "NOW, JUST BEFORE WE STARTED THIS DEPOSITION....YOU AND I HAD A BRIEF TALK DID WE NOT?" TOMLINSON ANSWERED IN THE AFFIRMATIVE. SPECTER CONTINUED: "AND AT THE TIME WE STARTED OUR DISCUSSION IT WAS YOUR RECOLLECTION THAT THE BULLET CAME OFF STRETCHER "A" (CONNALLY'S) WAS IT NOT?". TOMLINSON REPLIED: "B". (JFK'S STRETCHER) SPECTER COULD NOT COERCE TOMLINSON TO CHANGE HIS OPINION. TOMLINSON WOULD CLOSE BY STATING "I'M NOT GOING TO TELL YOU SOMETHING I CAN'T LAY DOWN AND SLEEP AT NIGHT WITH."

SPECTER'S EFFORTS TO BOLSTER THE CREDIBILITY OF THE BULLET RECEIVED A SOLID REBUKE FROM DR. ROBERT SHAW. DR. SHAW NOTED: "I FEEL THERE WOULD BE SOME DIFFICULTY IN EXPLAINING ALL THE WOUNDS AS BEING INFLICTED BY EXHIBIT 399 WITHOUT CAUSING MORE IN THE WAY OF LOSS OF SUBSTANCE TO THE BULLET OR DEFORMATION OF THE BULLET." IN FACT, THERE WERE MORE REMNANTS OF CE399 <u>REMAINING</u> IN GOVENOR CONNALLY'S BODY THAN WAS <u>MISSING</u> FROM THE SAME PROJECTILE.

BULLETS FROM THE MANLICHER-CARCANO TYPICALLY WEIGH 160-161 GRAINS. THE COMMISSION EXHIBIT, #399, WEIGHED 158.6 GRAINS; ONLY 2.4 GRAINS LESS THAN THE <u>UPPER</u> WEIGHT RANGE OF 6.5 CALIBER AMMO. SHAW WOULD FURTHER NOTE: "...THE EXAMINATION OF THE WRIST BY BOTH X-RAY AND AT THE TIME OF SURGERY SHOWED SOME FRAGMENTS OF METAL THAT MADE IT DIFFICULT TO BELIEVE THAT THE SAME MISSLE (#399) COULD HAVE CAUSED THESE TWO WOUNDS. THERE SEEMS TO BE <u>MORE</u> THAT 3 GRAINS OF METAL MISSING IN THE WRIST."

DR. SHAW'S SENTIMENTS WOULD BE ECHOED BY DR. CHARLES GREGORY. WHEN ASKED IF THE BULLET COULD HAVE CAUSED ALL THE WOUNDS IN BOTH THE PRESIDENT AND CONNALLY, DR. GREGORY OFFERED: "ONE WOULD HAVE TO CONCEDE THE POSSIBILITY, BUT I FIRMLY BELIEVE THAT THE POSSIBILITY IS MUCH DIMINISHED."

NURSE AUDREY BELL WAS EVEN MORE POINTED IN HER OPINION OF THE FRAGMENTS RECOVERED FROM CONALLY'S WRIST AND THIGH: "WHAT WE TOOK OFF CONNALLY WAS GREATER THAN WHAT IS MISSING FROM THE BULLET....THE SMALLEST (FRAGMENT) WAS THE SIZE OF THE STRIKING END OF A MATCH AND THE LARGEST WAS AT LEAST TWICE THAT BIG."

NAVY PATHOLOGIST DR. JAMES HUMES WAS SKEPTICAL OF CE399'S (THE MAGIC BULLET) CREDIBILITY. WHEN ASKED BY SPECTER IF THE BULLET COULD HAVE CAUSED THE WOUNDS INFLICTED UPON CONNALLY'S WRIST HE REPLIED "I THINK THAT IS MOST UNLIKELY."

THE STRETCHER ON WHICH THE BULLET WAS FOUND WAS USED BY NEITHER JFK OR CONNALLY. THIS BULLET WAS CLEARLY PLANTED BY THE SET-UP CONSPIRATORS TO MERELY ESTABLISH BALLISTIC EVIDENCE BETWEEN A BULLET AND THE ALLEGED ASSASSIN'S RIFLE. I DO NOT THINK IT WAS INTENDED NOR PREDICTED BY THE SET-UP CONSPIRATORS THAT THE WARREN COMMISSION WOULD PRESS THIS PARTICULAR BULLET INTO SERVICE AS A SOLUTION TO THE PROBLEM CREATED BY THE MISSED SHOT THAT GRAZED JAMES TAGUE.

CONSIDERING THE NEARLY PRISTINE CONDITION OF THE BULLET FOUND ON THE STRETCHER AT PARKLAND, AND THAT WHEN THIS BULLET, COMBINED WITH THE FRAGMENTS INVOLVING GOVENOR CONNALLY'S WOUNDS, EXCEEDED THE MAXIMUM WEIGHT OF AN UNUSED BULLET, THE CHOICE OF THIS PARTICULAR MISSLE TO SOLVE THE PROBLEM CREATED BY THE MISSED SHOT WOULD PROVE TO BE A POOR CHOICE INDEED. IN FACT, CE399 BORE NO BONE, CLOTHING FIBERS, OR BLOOD RESIDUE FROM EITHER THE PRESIDENT OR GOVENOR CONNALLY. THE BULLET NOT ONLY WAS "NEAR PRISTINE" IN ITS SIZE AND SHAPE, BUT IT WAS MIRACULOUSLY VOID OF ANY CONTAMINATION RESIDUE THAT WOULD NORMALLY BE ACQUIRED UPON PASSING THROUGH ONE OR BOTH OF THE SHOOTING VICTIMS.

BEFORE WE CONTINUE, LET US COMPARE THE INTERPRETATION OF THE WOUNDS AND HOW THEY CHANGED FROM WHAT THE PARKLAND PHYSICIANS SAW TO WHAT WAS NECESSARY FOR DR HUMES TO SEE TO ACCOMMODATE THE MAGIC BULLET NECCESITATED BY THE ADDITION OF THE 4TH SHOT.

THROAT WOUND AS PERCEIVED AT PARKLAND

DR. MALCOLM PERRY-----------------------ENTRANCE WOUND TO THE NECK 3-5 MM IN SIZE
DR. JAMES CARRICO--SMALL PENETRATING WOUND
DR. PAUL PETERS---WOUND OF ENTRY IN THROAT
DR. CHARLES BAXTER--------------------------A SPHERICAL WOUND…4-5cm…VERY SMALL
DR. RONALD JONES---SMALL HOLE MIDLINE THOUGHT TO BE A WOUND OF ENTRANCE
DR. CHARLES CRENSHAW--SMALL ROUNDED WELL DEMARCATED ENTRANCE WOUND
DR. ROBERT MCCLELLAND----------------------LESS THAN A QUARTER INCH IN DIAMETER
MARGARET HINCHCLIFFE-------------------------------------ENTRANCE WOUND IN THE THROAT
DR. KEMP CLARK-------------------SMALL ENTRANCE WOUND BELOW THE ADAM'S APPLE
DR. GENE COLEMAN----------------------------------MUST HAVE BEEN AN ENTRANCE WOUND
DPD CHIEF CURRY--A SMALL NEAT WOUND IN THE THROAT
DR. RICHARD DELANY---IT WAS AN ENTRY WOUND
DR. GENE AKIN---MUST HAVE BEEN AN ENTRANCE WOUND

THROAT WOUND IN BETHESDA AUTOPSY REPORT

DR. JAMES HUMES
7-8cm PRESUMABLY OF EXIT BUT OBSCURED BYTHE TRACHEOTOMY.

NOTE: THE TRACHEOTOMY INCISION AT PARKLAND WAS ONLY 2-3cm

DR. HUMES WAS ACUTELY AWARE THAT SOMETHING WAS UNDERFOOT THAT EVENING AT THE AUTOPSY. I BELIEVE THAT WAS WHY HE QUALIFIED HIS STATEMENT BY USING THE TERM "PRESUMABLY".

IN A TELEVISED REPORT ON NOVEMBER 22ND, KRLD-TV REPORTER DAN RATHER STATED THAT THE WOUND "<u>ENTERED</u> AT THE BASE OF THE THROAT AND CAME OUT AT THE BASE OF THE NECK ON THE BACK SIDE."

LIFE MAGAZINE WOULD ATTEMPT TO BOLSTER THE OBSERVATION OF DAN RATHER. THE NOVEMBER 29TH, 1963 ISSUE SHOWED 37 FRAMES OF THE ZAPRUDER FILM. ONE FRAME SHOWS THE PRESIDENT WITH BOTH HANDS DRAWN TOWARDS HIS THROAT, PRESUMABLY IN RESPONSE TO THE SHOT THAT HAD STRUCK HIS NECK. HE IS HOWEVER FACING <u>FORWARD</u>. NOW BOTH RATHER AND LIFE MAGAZINE HAVE INSINUATED THAT A SHOT WAS INDEED FIRED FROM THE FRONT. IN THE FOLLOWING WEEKS ISSUE OF LIFE, DECEMBER 6TH, THE MAGAZINE BRAZINGLY SOUGHT TO RECTIFY THIS OBVIOUS PROBLEM BY NOTING THAT "THE 8MM FILM SHOWS THE PRESIDENT TURNING HIS BODY FAR AROUND TO THE RIGHT AS HE WAVES TO SOMEONE IN THE CROWD. HIS THROAT IS EXPOSED TOWARDS THE SNIPER'S NEST JUST BEFORE HE CLUTCHES IT."

ONE HAS TO BE OFFENDED BY THE MAGAZINE'S OUTRAGEOUS ATTEMPT TO DISTORT AND DECEIVE THE PUBLIC PARTICULARLY WHEN THEIR EARLIER ISSUE OFFERED NOTHING PHOTOGRAPHICALLY TO SUPPORT THEIR INSINUATION IN THE LATER ISSUE THAT THE PRESIDENT TURNED TOWARDS THE TSBD THUS ALLOWING FOR THE THROAT SHOT TO INDEED BE A WOUND OF ENTRY.

THERE WAS NO APPARENT EXIT WOUND FOR THE FRONTAL NECK ENTRY WOUND AS DESCRIBED BY THE PARKLAND DOCTORS. THERE WAS HOWEVER DAMAGE TO THE CHROME STRIP SURROUNDING THE INSIDE PORTION OF THE WINDSHIELD JUST LEFT OF THE REAR VIEW MIRROR AS VIEWED FROM THE FRONT SEAT OF THE LIMO AND ALSO A THROUGH-AND-THROUGH SHOT THROUGH THE WINDSHIELD ORIGINATING FROM A LOCALE IN FRONT OF THE LIMO. I AM INCLINED TO BELIEVE THAT A GLASS OR BULLET FRAGMENT FROM THE SHOT THROUGH THE WINDSHIELD CAUSIED THE ENTRY/NO EXIT WOUND TO THE PRESIDENT'S THROAT.

THIS SHOT THROUGH THE WINDSHIELD WOULD HAVE BEEN EARLY IN THE SEQUENCE AND LIKELY EITHER THE FIRST OR SECOND SHOT FIRED. IT IS UNBELIEVEABLY IRONIC THAT LIFE MAGAZINE BLATANTLY LIED ABOUT THE PRESIDENT TURNING 180 DEGREES SO THAT HE WOULD BE FACING THE TSBD IN SUPPORT OF WHAT DAN RATHER HAD REPORTED AS A THROAT ENTRY WOUND. ALTHOUGH BOTH LIFE AND RATHER WERE CORRECT IN LABELLING THE THROAT WOUND AS AN ENTRY WOUND, LIFE ALONE TOOK THE EXTRAORDINARY STEP OF ACTUALLY TURNING THE PRESIDENT TOWARDS THE TSBD AS IT WAS CONSIDERED THE SOLE SOURCE OF THE SHOTS FIRED AT THE MOTORCADE. LIFE'S EARLY EFFORT TO FOCUS AS THE SOURCE OF SHOTS THE TSBD BY TURNING THE PRESIDENT 180 DEGREES WOULD LATER BE TOSSED ASIDE AS THE NECK WOUND WOULD HAVE TO BE TRANSFORMED FROM ENTRY TO EXIT AS THE TAGUE SHOT BECAME A 4TH SHOT THAT THE W.C. WOULD NOW HAVE TO RELUCTANTLY DEAL WITH.

THE BELOW LISTED SHOTSAND THE RESULTANT WOUNDS ARE NOT IN A PARTICULAR FIRING SEQUENCE.

- MISSED THE LIMO COMPLETELY WITH A FRAGMENT HITTING JAMES TAGUE

- SHOT THROUGH THE WINDSHIELD POSSIBLY CAUSING THE PRESIDENT'S FRONTAL THROAT WOUND WITH A GLASS OR BULLET FRAGMENT

- MISSED THE LIMO IMBEDDING ITSELF IN THE GRASS ON THE SOUTH SIDE OF DEALEY PLAZA

- HIT THE PRESIDENT IN THE UPPER BACK WITH NO APPARENT POINT OF EXIT

- HIT ONLY GOVENOR CONNALLY

- STRUCK THE PRESIDENT NEAR THE COWLICK OF THE SCALP WITH A POSSIBLE FRAGMENT HITTING THE CHROME STRIP SURROUDING THE WINDSHIELD

- THE FATAL FRONT HEAD SHOT THROUGH THE RIGHT TEMPLE

- A SHOT CAUSING NO WOUNDS BUT DAMAGING THE CHROME ON THE UPPER PART OF THE WINDSHIELD (IF THIS DAMAGE WAS <u>NO</u>T CAUSED BY THE REAR COWLICK HEAD SHOT)

ONLY 2 SHOTS WERE FIRED FROM THE FRONT: THE FATAL HEAD SHOT THAT ARRIVED ALMOST SIMULTANEOUSLY WITH THE REAR HEAD SHOT AND THE SHOT THAT PENETRATED THE WINDSHIELD. THE FRONTAL HEAD SHOT HIT THE PRESIDENT IN THE RIGHT TEMPLE NEAR THE HAIRLINE. A MINIMUM OF 7 SHOTS WERE FIRED IN THE VOLLEY. THE 2 SHOTS THAT MISSED THE LIMO, THE SHOT THAT CAUSED THE DAMAGE TO THE CHROME STRIP ABOVE THE WINDSHIELD, AND THE SHOT THAT CAUSED THE FINGER-DEPTH NO EXIT WOUND ON THE PRESIDENT WERE LIKELY LOW VELOCITY SHOTS FIRED FROM THE REAR AND LIKELY FIRED FROM TWO DIFFERENT LOCATIONS. THE SHOT THAT HIT ONLY GOVENOR CONNALLY AND THE SHOT THAT STRUCK THE PRESIDENT IN THE COWLICK WITH A FRAGMENT POSSIBLY CAUSING THE DENT IN THE CHROME WINDSHIELD TRIM WERE LIKELY HIGH VELOCITY SHOTS FIRED FROM THE REAR AND POSSIBLY FROM THE SAME LOCATIONS AS THE OTHER FOUR SHOTS THAT WERE FIRED FROM BEHIND THE LIMO. THE FATAL FRONTAL HEAD SHOT WAS ALSO A HIGH VELOCITY SHOT AND OBVIOUSLY NOT FROM THE RIFLE USED FOR HIGH VELOCITY SHOTS FROM LOCATIONS BEHIND THE LIMO. THE LIKELY LOCATION OF THIS SHOT WAS THE GRASSY KNOLL. THE WINDSHIELD FRONTAL SHOT WAS FIRED FROM A LOCATION SOUTH OF ELM. IN MY OPINION, THERE WERE 4 DIFFERENT SHOOTERS; TWO FIRING FROM LOCATIONS BEHIND THE LIMO AND TWO FROM LOCATIONS IN FRONT OF THE LIMO.

THE REAR HEAD SHOT AND THE FRONTAL HEAD SHOT OCCURRED NEARLY SIMULTANEOUSLY WITH THE REAR HEAD SHOT ARRIVING FRACTIONS OF A SECOND BEFORE THE FRONTAL HEAD SHOT. THIS WOULD EXPLAIN THE BARELY PERCEPTABLE FORWARD MOVEMENT OF THE PRESIDENT'S SKULL PRIOR TO THE MORE VISIBLE REARWARD AND LEFTWARD MOVEMENT CAUSED BY THE FRONTAL SHOT.

SINCE THE PRESIDENT WAS NOT TURNED OVER TO EXAMINE HIS BACK AT PARKLAND, LET US EXAMINE WHAT WAS PERCEIVED REGARDING THE BACK WOUND AT BETHESDA.

BACK WOUND IN BETHESDA AUTOPSY REPORT

DR. JAMES HUMES
14cm INFERIOR TO THE MASTOID TIP AND 14cm FROM THE ACROMION PROCESS. PRESUMABLY OF ENTRANCE, BUT WELL <u>BELOW</u> THE NECK WOUND.

NOTE THAT HUMES ONCE AGAIN QUALIFIES HIS FINDING WITH THE TERM "PRESUMABLY." BUT IT IS CONSIDERABLY MORE IMPORTANT THAT HE NOTES THAT IT IS <u>WELL BELOW THE NECK WOUND.</u>

*IT WAS ALSO NOTED BY HUMES THAT THE BACK WOUND WAS DOWNWARD IN AN ANGLE OF 45-60 DEGREES. THIS ALONE WOULD MAKE IT **IMPOSSIBLE** TO HAVE EXITED THE PRESDENT'S THROAT AND A CERTAINTY THAT THIS SAME BULLET DID NOT CAUSE THE GOVENOR'S WOUNDS.*

DR. GEORGE BURKLEY, THE PRESIDENT'S PHYSICIAN, SIGNED THE PRESIDEN'TS DEATH CERTIFICATE. THE CERTIFICATE NOTES THE BACK WOUND TO BE AT THE LEVEL OF THE 3RD THORACIC VERTEBRAE, WELL BELOW THE THROAT "EXIT" WOUND NOTED BY THE W.C.

NOW WE WILL COMPARE OBSERVATIONS REGARDING THE REAR EXIT HEAD WOUND AS PERCEIVED AT PARKLAND

DR. CHARLES CRENSHAW
THE WOUND WAS THE SIZE OF A BASEBALL.

DR. MALCOLM PERRY
LARGE AVULSIVE WOUND OF RIGHT POSTERIOR CRANIUM. IT EXTENDED FROM THE APPROXIMATE CENTER OF THE SKULL IN THE BACK TO JUST BEHIND THE RIGHT EAR.

DR. JAMES CARRICO
LARGE GAPING WOUND LOCATED IN RIGHT OCCIPITAL-PARIETAL AREA

DR. PAUL PETERS
LARGE OCCIPITAL WOUND WITH CONSIDERABLE PORTION OF BRAIN MISSING

DR. CHARLES BAXTER
OCCIPITAL BONES WERE MISSING AND THE BRAIN LYING ON THE TABLE

DR. RONALD JONES
LARGE DEFECT BACK OF THE HEAD

DR. ROBERT MCCLELLAND
ONE QUARTER OF RIGHT BACK OF HEAD AND BRAIN TISSUE HAD BEEN BLASTED OUT.

DR. KEMP CLARK
A LARGE GAPING OCCIPITAL/PARIETAL WOUND WITH CONSIDERABLE LOSS OF TISSUE

AUBREY RIKE
THE BACK OF HIS HEAD FELT LIKE A WET SPONGE…IT WAS REAL SOFT. PART OF HIS SKULL WAS MISSING.

DR. GENE AKIN-
OCCIPPITAL-PARIETAL AREA SHATTERED WITH BRAIN SUBSTANCE EXTRUDING.

DIANA BOWRON, RN
GAPING WOUND IN THE BACK OF HIS HEAD.

DORIS NELSON, RN
THERE WASN'T EVEN HAIR BACK THERE…IT WAS BLOWN AWAY.

PAT HUTTON, RN
MASSIVE OPENING ON THE BACK OF THE HEAD.

AUDREY BELL, RN
LARGE OCCIPITAL HEAD WOUND.

MARGARET HINCHCLIFFE, RN
GAPING WOUND IN THE BACK OF THE HEAD.

DR RICHARD DULANEY
THEY LIFTED UP HIS HEAD AND THE WHOLE BACK SIDE WAS GONE.

DR. MARION JENKINS
A GREAT LACERATION ON THE RIGHT SIDE OF THE HEAD, TEMPORAL AND OCCIPITAL.

DR. GENE COLEMAN
THE RIGHT OCCIPITAL-PARIETAL REGION WAS THE EXIT.

DR. ROBERT GROSSMAN
A LARGE HOLE IN THE OCCIPUT, FAR TOO LARGE FOR A BULLET ENTRY WOUND.

DR. ROBERT SELDIN
THE BULLET STRUCK THE PRESIDENT IN THE FOREHEAD AND LITERALLY EXPLODED IN HIS SKULL.

DR. WILLIAM ZEDLITZ
A MASSIVE HEAD INJURY TO THE RIGHT OCCIPITAL-PARIETAL AREA.

HURCHEL JACKS (DROVE LBJ'S LIMO)
IT APPEARED THAT THE BULLET HAD STRUCK HIM ABOVE THE RIGHT EAR OR NEAR THE TEMPLE.

DPD CHIEF JESSE CURRY
DR. PERRY INSISTED THAT THE PRESIDENT WAS SHOT FROM THE FRONT, ENTERING AT THE THROAT AND EXITING OUT THE BACK OF THE HEAD.

AGENT CLINT HILL, WHO CLIMBED ONTO THE PRESIDENTIAL LIMO JUST AS THE SHOOTING CEASED, DESCRIBED THE WOUND HE HAD SEEN: "THE RIGHT REAR BOTTOM OF THE HEAD WAS MISSING. IT WAS LYING IN THE REAR SEAT OF THE CAR. HIS BRAIN WAS EXPOSED."

HEAD WOUND IN BETHESDA AUTOPSY REPORT

DR. HUMES
SMALL ENTRY WOUND TO RIGHT OF OCCIPITAL PROTUBERANCE.

THE PREVIOUS DESCRIPTIONS SPEAK FOR THEMSELVES. THE PARKLAND PHYSICIANS, EXPERIENCED WITH GUNSHOT WOUNDS, DESCRIBED IT AS A <u>LARGE</u> WOUND EXUDING CONSIDERABLE BRAIN TISSUE AND LOCATED PRIMARILY AT THE <u>BACK</u> OF THE HEAD. THE WOUND AS THEY COLLECTIVELY DESCRIBE IT WOULD LEAD ONE TO CONSIDER THE WOUND AS A WOUND OF <u>EXIT</u>: THAT IS A WOUND CAUSED BY A SHOT FROM THE <u>FRONT</u>. HUMES, WHO HAD NEVER PERFORMED A FORENSIC AUTOPSY, SOMEHOW FELT JUSTIFIED OR MORE LIKELY PRESSURED INTO DESCRIBING THE WOUND AS BOTH SMALL, AND MORE POINTEDLY, A WOUND OF ENTRANCE.

AS THE AUTOPSY PHOTOS TAKEN OF THE NECK WOULD LATER BE ALTERED TO BOLSTER HUMES DESCRIPTION, THE AUTOPSY PHOTOS TAKEN OF THE HEAD WOULD PREDICTABLY BE ALTERED TO COMPLEMENT HUMES DESCRIPTION AS WELL. THESE PHOTOS SHOW WHAT WAS DESCRIBED AS A SMALL WOUND "4 INCHES HIGHER, AND IN THE COWLICK AREA OF THE PARIETAL BONE...NO INVOLVEMENT OF THE OCCIPITAL BONE.."

WHEN THE AUTOPSY PHOTOS OF THE BACK OF THE HEAD WERE LATER SHOWN TO 16 DOCTORS WHO WERE IN ATTENDANCE AT PARKLAND ON NOVEMBER 22ND, <u>NONE</u> OF THE 16 CLAIMED THAT THE <u>PHOTOS</u> DEPICTED THE EXTENSIVE WOUND THEY HAD NOTED AT PARKLAND.

LATER, THE HSCA STATED THAT OF THE 22 WITNESSES THEY INTERVIEWED WHO WERE IN ATTENDANCE AT THE <u>AUTOPSY</u>, 20 AGREED THAT THE AUTOPSY <u>PHOTOS</u> SHOWED A LARGE <u>EXIT</u> WOUND IN THE RIGHT <u>FRONT</u> PART OF THE SKULL AND NO LARGE EXIT WOUND IN THE <u>REAR</u> PORTION OF THE SKULL, BUT, WHEN THEIR <u>INTERVIEWS</u> WERE REVEALED IN THE EARLY 1990'S DETAILING WHAT THEY HAD SEEN IN THE MORGUE THE EVENING OF THE AUTOPSY, THEY ALL AGREED THAT THE WOUNDS WERE <u>EXACTLY</u> AS THE

*PARKLAND DOCTORS HAD DESCRIBED; SMALL FRONTAL ENTRANCE AND LARGE OCCIPITAL EXIT. THE HSCA IGNORED THEIR VERBAL STATEMENTS REGARDING WHAT THEY HAD SEEN FIRSTHAND AT THE AUTOPSY AND CHOSE TO RELY ON THEIR DESCRIPTION OF THE FORGED PHOTOS TO REFUTE THE PARKLAND DOCTORS. THE HSCA WENT ON TO NOTE THAT IF THE PRESIDENT WAS INDEED FIRED UPON FROM THE FRONT THAT THE SHOTS MISSED. IN ESSENCE, THE HSCA ADMITTED TO THE PROBABILITY OF A CONSPIRACY BUT MAINTAINED, IN SUPPORT OF THE WARREN COMMISSON, THAT THE REMAINING SHOTS WERE FIRED FROM THE REAR BY **HARVEY** TO THE EXCLUSION OF ALL OTHERS.*

ALTHOUGH BOTH THE PHOTOS AND HUMES AUTOPSY REPORT REFUTE WHAT WAS SEEN BY THE EMERGENCY ROOM PHYSICIANS AT PARKLAND, THEY DO INDEED LEND MUCH NEEDED CREEDENCE TO WHAT THE WARREN COMMISSION WOULD NOW REQUIRE OF THE WOUNDS TO SUPPORT THE MAGIC BULLET THEORY THAT WAS PRESSED INTO SERVICE WHEN IT WAS DISCOVERED THAT THERE WAS A 4TH SHOT CAUSING THE SCRATCH ON JAMES TAGUE'S CHEEK.

EVERY EFFORT WAS MADE VIA THE AUTOPSY REPORT AND THE AUTOPSY PHOTOS TO MINIMIZE ANY CORROBORATION OF SHOTS FROM THE FRONT. LATER, THE AUTOPSY X-RAYS WERE ALSO ALTERED. THE ALTERED PHOTOS AND X-RAYS WERE DESIGNED TO SUPERCEDE THE LESS THAN CONVINCING AUTOPSY REPORT BY DR. HUMES. IT WAS NOT A CERTAINTY THAT THE MUCH BADGERED DR. HUMES AND HIS AUTOPSY REPORT COULD HOLD UP UNDER WHAT WOULD CERTAINLY BE MORE CLOSE SCRUTINY WHEN COMPARED TO THE PARKLAND FINDINGS. IT WAS HOWEVER HOPED BY THE WARREN COMMISSION THAT THE ALTERED PHOTOS AND X-RAYS WOULD BE MORE DIFFICULT TO DISPUTE THAN THE RELUCTANTLY ACCOMODATING DR. HUMES.

THE WOUNDS INFLICTED UPON THE PRESIDENT WOULD DO LITTLE TO LESSEN THE QUESTIONABLE ATTRIBUTES OF THE MAGIC BULLET:

THE SMALL, ROUND, NECK WOUND DESCRIBED AT PARKLAND AS A WOUND OF ENTRY WOULD NOW HAVE TO BE TRANSFORMED IN THE FINAL AUTOPSY REPORT TO A LARGE, JAGGED WOUND PRESUMABLY OF EXIT.

THE LARGE OCCIPITAL-PARIETAL EXIT WOUND NOTED AT PARKLAND NOW WOULD HAVE TO BE TRANSFORMED TO A SMALLER ENTRY WOUND, MOVED 4 INCHES HIGHER TO THE COWLICK AREA AND NOW INVOLVE PRIMARILY ONLY THE RIGHT PARIETAL BONE WITH NO INVOLVEMENT OF THE OCCIPITAL BONE.

THE BACK WOUND OF THE PRESIDENT NOT NOTED AT PARKLAND BUT NOTED TO BE WELL BELOW (6 INCHES) THE COLLAR LINE IN HUMES' AUTOPYS NOTES (WHICH WOULD HAVE PLACED IT BELOW THE NECK WOUND) WOULD NOW HAVE TO BE MOVED UP TO ACCOMMODATE NOT ONLY A SHOT FROM ABOVE THAT RESULTED IN THE LOWER "EXIT" WOUND ON THE FRONT OF THE NECK, BUT ALSO TO ALLOW THE BULLET CAUSING THESE TWO WOUNDS TO ALSO ACCOUNT FOR ALL OF GOVENOR CONNALLY'S WOUNDS AS WELL.

AMAZINGLY THE PRESIDENT'S DEATH CERTIFICATE, AS SIGNED BY HIS PERSONAL PHYSICIAN, ADMIRAL BURKLEY ON NOVEMBER 23RD, NOTED THAT THE PRESIDENT "WAS STRUCK IN THE HEAD BY AN ASSASSIN'S BULLET AND A SECOND WOUND OCCURRED IN THE POSTERIOR BASE AT ABOUT THE LEVEL OF THE THIRD THORACIC VERTEBRAE." THE 3RD THORACIC VERTEBRAE IS SEVERAL INCHES BELOW THE FRONTAL NECK WOUND. THIS DOCUMENT ALONE COMPLETELY VOIDS THE SINGLE BULLET THEORY. PREDICTABLY, ADMIRAL BURKLEY WAS NOT CALLED BEFORE THE COMMISSION.

THE MISSED SHOT CHANGED EVERYTHING. THREE SHOTS COULD CONCEIVABLY BE FIRED IN THE 5.6 SECONDS ALLOWED **IF** ONE USED A CLIP; FOUR SHOTS COULD NOT.

HARVEY THUS COULD NOT HAVE FIRED <u>ALL</u> THE SHOTS IF INDEED HE FIRED <u>ANY</u> OF THE SHOTS.

THERE WERE 4 LIVE-FIRE TESTS PERFORMED BY A TOTAL OF 7 SHOOTERS WITH THE ACTUAL RIFLE ALLEGEDLY USED IN THE ASSASSINATION.

TEST #1
THE FBI USED 3 MARKSMEN (AGENTS CUNNINGHAM, FRAZIER, AND KILLION) WHO FIRED 3 SHOTS EACH ONLY <u>15 YARDS AWAY</u> FROM A <u>FIXED</u> TARGET. NONE WERE ABLE TO ACHIEVE A TIME LESS THAN 6 SECONDS. THE AGENTS TIMES WERE 6, 7, AND 9 SECONDS. NONE ACHIEVED THE 5.6 SECONDS ALLOWED TO **HARVEY** TO FIRE THE 3 SHOTS. THE DISPERSION AND ACCURACY OF THE SHOOTERS WAS ALSO LESS THAN WHAT WOULD BE REQUIRED TO DUPLICATE **HARVEY'S** ALLEGED FEAT. THE 3 SHOOTERS ACCURACY OUTCOMES WERE 2.5 INCHES HIGH AND 1 INCH TO THE RIGHT, 4 INCHES HIGH AND 1 INCH TO THE RIGHT, AND 4 INCHES HIGH AND 1 INCH TO THE RIGHT. KEEP IN MIND THEY WERE SHOOTING AT A <u>STATIONARY TARGET</u> ONLY <u>15 YARDS</u> AWAY.

TEST #2
ROBERT FRAZIER FROM THE FBI FIRED 6 MORE SHOTS. BUT, HE ALSO TOOK MORE THAN 5.6 SECONDS. HIS FIXED TARGET HOWEVER WAS NOW AT 25 YARDS. HIS FIRST SERIES OF 3 SHOTS LANDED NEARLY 5 INCHES HIGH AND NEARLY 2 INCHES TO THE RIGHT. THE 2ND SERIES OF 3 SHOTS WERE ON AVERAGE ABOUT 3 INCHES HIGH.

TEST #3
FRAZIER ALSO FIRED AT FIXED TARGETS AT 100 YARDS. HIS FIRST 3 SHOTS WERE 5 INCHES HIGH. HIS SECOND 3 SHOTS LANDED 4 INCHES HIGH AND 3.5 INCHES TO THE RIGHT. HIS LAST SEQUENCE OF 3 SHOTS LANDED 2.5 INCHES HIGH AND 2 INCHES TO THE RIGHT. WHEN QUESTIONED BY THE W.C. AS TO WHY SHOTS WERE CONSISTANTLY HIGH AND TO THE RIGHT, AGENT FRAZIER NOTED "THE ELEVATION AND ADJUSTMENT IN THE TELESCOPE WAS NOT SUFFICIENT TO BRING THE POINT OF IMPACT TO THE AIMING POINT."

TEST #4
AT ABERDEEN PROVING GROUND, 3 MARKSMEN WHO WERE RATED BY THE NRA AS MASTER RIFLEMEN FIRED AT <u>FIXED</u> TARGETS SET UP AT THE SAME DISTANCES THAT **HARVEY** ALLEGEDLY FIRED HIS SHOTS. EACH OF THE MARKSMEN FIRED 2 SEQUENCES OF 3 SHOTS WITH THE USE OF THE SCOPE AT EACH OF THE THREE TARGET DISTANCES. EACH OF THE 3 SHOOTERS HIT THE FIRST <u>TARGET</u> AT 175 FEET.

THE SECOND TARGET WAS SET AT 240 FEET. ACCORDING TO A MR. SIMMONS, THE SHOOTERS MISSED THE SECOND TARGET. SIMMONS POINTS OUT "THERE WAS A CONSCIOUS EFFORT MADE ON THE ADDITIONAL ROUNDS TO HIT THE SECOND TARGET." ONE WOULD ASSUME THAT THIS WAS THE PURPOSE OF THE TEST. CONVENIENTLY HOWEVER HE DOES NOT NOTE THE SUCCESS OF THEIR "ADDITIONAL ROUNDS" AS COMPARED TO THE MISSED SHOTS ON THEIR <u>INITIAL</u> ATTEMPT TO HIT THE 240 FOOT TARGET. KEEP IN MIND THE SHOOTERS HAD THE BENEFIT OF SHIMS ON THE DEFECTIVE SCOPE.

THE THIRD TARGET WAS SET AT 265 FEET. THE TIMES FOR THE THREE SHOOTERS WERE NOTED. ONE SHOOTER'S TIMES WERE 7 SECONDS AND 8.25 SECONDS. ANOTHER SHOOTER'S TIMES WERE 6.45 AND 6.75 SECONDS AND THE THIRD SHOOTER'S TIMES WERE 4.6 SECONDS AND 5.15 SECONDS. KEEP IN MIND ALL THE SHOOTERS WERE SHOOTING AT <u>FIXED</u> TARGETS. MORE IMPORTANTLY THEY USED A CLIP-FED RIFLE AND WERE ALLOWED TO SHIM THE DEFECTIVE SCOPE. FURTHER DISCUSSION ABOUT THE <u>ACCURACY</u> OF THE SHOOTERS FOR ALL 3 TARGET DISTANCES WAS ALSO DETAILED. THIS EXPLANATION IS AS CONVOLUTED AND CONFUSING AS ANY W.C. TESTIMONY I HAVE READ TO DATE.

A MR. EISENBERG FOR THE W.C. WAS QUESTIONING RONALD SIMMONS FROM THE ABERDEEN PROVING GROUNDS. THE EXCHANGE IS FASCINATING:

MR. SIMMONS
"THERE WERE NO MARKINGS ON THE TARGET VISIBLE TO THE FIRER."

MR. EISENBERG:
"DID I UNDERSTAND YOU JUST TOLD THE FIRERS TO AIM AT THE TARGET WITHOUT REFERRING TO…(UNDOUBTEDLY CROSSHAIRS ON THE TARGET)

MR. SIMMONS:
"YES."

MR. EISENBERG:
"THERE IS AN APPARENT CROSSLINE RUNNING DARKLY THROUGH THAT PHOTOGRAPH."

MR. SIMMONS:
"THESE LINES WERE DRAWN IN AFTERWARDS, IN ORDER FOR US TO MAKE MEASUREMENTS FROM THE ACTUAL IMPACT POINT."

NOTE

"DRAWN IN AFTERWARDS"….IF I UNDERSTAND MR. SIMMONS CORRECTLY, IT APPEARS THAT THE SHOOTERS WERE FREE TO SIMPLY SHOOT AND HIT THE TARGET AND THE LINES THAT WOULD DETERMINE THEIR <u>ACCURACY</u> WERE DRAWN IN <u>AFTER</u> THEY COMPLETED SHOOTING. THIS MEANS THAT THE LINES COULD BE DRAWN IN A LOCATION ON THE TARGET THAT WOULD GIVE THEM THE BEST POSSIBLE ACCURACY SCORE.

MR. EISENBERG:
"…DID YOU MAKE A DETERMINATION OF THE AMOUNT OF ERROR ….AMOUNT OF ERROR IN THE AIM OF THESE RIFLEMEN?"

MR. SIMMONS:
"…AGAINST THE FIRST TARGET (175 FEET) THE ACCURACY OBSERVED WAS ABOUT .7 MILS, IN STANDARD DEVIATION. AGAINST THE SECOND TARGET (240 FEET), THE ACCURACY WAS 1.4 MILS AND AGAINST THE THIRD TARGET (265 FEET) IT WAS 1.2 MILS."

AT THIS POINT MR. EISENBERG IS AS CONFUSED AS I AM AS HE ASKS FOR FURTHER SIMPLIFICATION OF MR. SIMMONS VENTURE INTO STANDARD DEVIATIONS.

MR. SIMMONS:
"…COULD YOU CONVERT THOSE AT A HUNDRED YARDS TO INCHES?"

MR. SIMMONS:
"0.7 OF MIL AT 100 YARDS IS APPROXIMATELY 2 INCHES, 1.4 MILS IS APPROXIMATELY 4 INCHES, AND 1.2 MILS IS APPROXIMATELY 3.5 INCHES.

KEEP IN MIND THAT WHEN THE 3 FBI AGENTS WERE QUESTIONED ABOUT THEIR ACCURACY IT WAS CLEARLY EXPLAINED IN A "HIGH AND TO THE RIGHT/LEFT" FASHION THAT NOTED IN INCHES HOW HIGH AND HOW LEFT OR RIGHT EACH SHOT IN A GIVEN SEQUENCE LANDED. NOW WE HAVE MR. EISENBERG AND MR. SIMMONS CONVERTING MILS TO INCHES. NOT ONLY THAT, EISENBERG HAS HIM EQUATE THE INCHES TO A TARGET PRESUMABLY AT <u>100 YARDS</u> WHEN THE 3 TARGETS THE MARKSMEN WERE SHOOTING AT WERE AT 175, 240, AND 265 <u>FEET</u>. THIS LINE OF QUESTIONING HAD TO BE REHEARSED. I FIND IT IMPOSSIBLE TO BELIEVE THAT MR. SIMMONS COULD SIMULTANEOUSLY CONVERT 3 SHOTS AT 175, 240, AND 265 FEET TO 100 YARD EQUIVALENTS WHILE SIMULTANEOUSLY

CONVERTING .7, 1.4, AND 1.2 MILS TO INCHES. I HAVE READ THIS TESTIMONY REPEATEDLY.....I WISH YOU SUCCESS IN INTERPRETING WHAT IS AN OBVIOUS ATTEMPT TO CONFUSE WHAT SHOULD HAVE BEEN A SIMPLE HIGH-LOW-LEFT-OR-RIGHT-IN-INCHES EXPLANATION AS TO THE ACCURACY OF THE ABERDEEN SHOOTERS.

SEARCHING THE INTERNET FOR AN EXPLANATION REGARDING MILS, I CAME ACROSS A SITE AUTHORED BY ROBERT J. SIMEONE. HIS NOTES REGARDING MILS IS REVEALING:

"HAS ANYONE EVER WONDERED HOW THEY CAME UP WITH THESE? WELL I'VE WONDERED. I'VE READ NUMEROUS ACCOUNTS ON THE INTERNET ON "MILS"BUT NONE OF THEM EXPLAINED HOW TO ACTUALLY DERIVE THESE EQUATIONS. THEY JUST SEEM TO PULL THEM OUT OF THE AIR AT SOME POINT IN THEIR EXPLANATION OF "MILS" WITHOUT ACTUALLY SHOWING US HOW OR WHERE THEY CAME FROM. I SEARCHED THE INTERNET FAR AND WIDE, BUT TO NO AVAIL. I WAS STARTING TO WONDER IF THEY WERE DERIVED SO LONG AGO THAT NOBODY KNEW HOW TO DO IT ANYMORE. A "MIL" IS A UNIT OF ANGULAR MEASUREMENT. THE MODERN "MIL" IS SHORT FOR MILLIRADIAN, A TRIGONOMETRIC UNIT OF ANGULAR MEASUREMENT. IN SHOOTING WE CAN USE MILS TO FIND THE DISTANCE TO A TARGET. IT IS ALSO USED TO ADJUST SHOTS FOR WINDS AND THE MOVEMENT OF A TARGET."

WITH WHAT MR. SIMEONE HAS TAUGHT US ABOUT MILS, WHY WOULD MR. SIMMONS NEED TO CALCULATE THE <u>DISTANCE</u> TO A TARGET WHEN THE DISTANCES, 175 FEET, 240 FEET, AND 265 FEET WERE PREDETERMINED? WHY ALSO WOULD MR. SIMMONS HAVE TO ADJUST FOR THE <u>MOVEMENT</u> OF A TARGET WHEN ALL THREE TARGETS WERE STATIONARY?

USING A FORMULA PROVIDED BY MR. SIMEONE, I WAS HOWEVER ABLE TO RE-CALCULATE MR. SIMMONS ABOVE REFERENCE TO MILS PER 100 YARDS. EVEN THESE AREN'T QUITE ACCURATE:

0.7 MILS AT 100 YARDS PER SIMMONS: "2 INCHES"---------ACTUAL: 2.5 INCHES
1.2 MILS AT 100 YARDS PER SIMMONS: "3.5 INCHES"------ACTUAL: 4.3 INCHES
1.4 MILS AT 100 YARDS PER SIMMONS: "4 INCHES"-------ACTUAL: 5 INCHES

TO BE QUITE CANDID, THIS TOO IS PROBABLY IRRELEVANT SINCE THE ENTIRE "MIL" PROCESS EQUATED TO 100 YARDS IS USELESS WHEN ONE IS ACCUSTOMED TO THE "INCHES" APPROACH PER ACTUAL GIVEN TARGET DISTANCES (175, 240, AND 265 FEET) USED BY THE FBI.

THE TIMING OF THE SHOOTERS IS ALSO WORTH A SECOND LOOK. IF ONE AVERAGES THE 6 TIMES OF THE THREE SHOOTERS; 8.25, 7.00, 6.45, 6.75, 4.60, AND 5.15 SECONDS, THEIR AVERAGE TIME FOR A SEQUENCE OF 3 SHOTS IS 6.37 SECONDS, NEARLY 8/10'S OF A SECOND <u>SLOWER</u> THAN **HARVEY** WHO DID NOT HAVE THE ASSISTANCE AND ADVANTAGE OF A SHIMMED SCOPE AND A CLIP.

KEEP IN MIND THAT THE FBI SUMMARY REPORT OF 12/9/63 STATED THAT THE 3 SHOTS ALLEGEDLY FIRED BY **HARVEY** WERE AT DISTANCES OF 167 FEET (JFK'S BACK WOUND), 262 FEET (CONNALLY'S BACK-TO-THIGH WOUND), AND 307 FEET (JFK'S FATAL HEAD SHOT).

THE 3 FBI TESTS CHOSE TO USE DISTANCES OF 45 FEET (122 FEET CLOSER), 75 FEET (187 FEET CLOSER), AND 300 FEET (7 FEET CLOSER) THAN THE DISTANCES ESTIMATED BY THE 12/9/63 FBI REPORT. THET ALSO APPARRNTLY DID NOT "SEQUENCE" THEIR SHOTS AS **HARVEY** WOULD HAVE HAD TO DO WITH A MOVING TARGET. THEY FIRED AT STATIONARY TARGETS ONE AT A TIME.

THE 4TH TEST CONDUCTED BY NRA CERTFIED SHOOTERS ALSO CHOSE DISTANCES THAT DID NOT MATCH THE ESTIMATED DISTANCES IN THE FBI REPORT. ALTHOUGH THEIR 175 FOOT DISTANCE WAS 8 FEET MORE THAN THE FBI ESTIMATE FOR THE FIRST SHOT, THE 2ND ATTEMPTS (AT 240 FEET) WERE 22 FEET CLOSER THAN THE FBI ESTIMATE OF 262 FEET

FOR **HARVEY'S** 2ND SHOT. AND, AMAZINGLY, THEIR 3RD SHOT ATTEMPTS (265 FFEET) WERE 42 FEET SHORT OF WHAT THE FBI DETERMINED AS 307 FEET FOR **HARVEY'S** LAST SHOT. IT DOES APPEAR HOWEVER THAT THE NRA SHOOTERS IN TEST 4 DID ATTEMPT TO "SEQUENCE" THEIR SHOTS AS **HARVEY** WOULD HAVE HAD TO DO. BUT, SEQUENCING 3 SHOTS AT 3 STATIONARY TARGETS SHOULD BE A FAR EASIER TASK THAN SEQUENCING 3 SHOTS AT A MOVING TARGET.

THE 4 FBI/NRA TESTS WERE A SHAM. IF ONE COULD NOT DUPLICATE WHAT THE FBI ALLEGED **HARVEY** ACCOMPLISHED WITH THE BENEFIT OF SHORTER DISTANCES, STATIONARY TARGETS, AND A SHIMMED SCOPE WITH ONLY 3 SHOTS, THEY CERTAINLY COULD NOT DUPLICATE HIS FEAT WITH 4 OR MORE SHOTS. THE TEAGUE SHOT (4TH SHOT) CHANGED EVERYTHING.

EVEN GOVERNOR CONALLY'S COMMENTS IN HIS WARREN COMMISSION TESTIMONY NOTED THE RAPIDITY IN WHICH THE SHOTS WERE FIRED: "THE THOUGHT IMMEDIATELY PASSED THROUGH MY MIND THAT THERE WERE EITHER 2 OR 3 PEOPLE INVOLVED OR SOMEONE WAS SHOOTING WITH AN AUTOMATIC RIFLE."

FURTHER CLOUDING THE W.C.'S DESIRE FOR A 3 SHOT/5.6 SECOND SCENARIO WERE THE WINDSHIELD DAMAGE AND THE DAMAGE TO THE CHROME WINDSHIELD TRIM.

TWO DPD OFFICERS TESTIFIED IN REGARDS TO THE WINDSHIELD:

DPD OFFICER STAVIS ELLIS
"A HOLE IN THE LEFT FRONT WINDSHIELD….YOU COULD PUT A PENCIL THROUGH IT."
(THE LEFT FRONT AS SEEN FROM INSIDE THE LIMO.)

DPD OFFICER H.R. FREEMAN
"I COULD'A TOUCHED IT….IT WAS A BULLET HOLE."

THE DAMAGE TO THE WINDSHIELD WAS ALSO NOTED BY A SENIOR MANAGER AT FORD MOTOR COMPANY

GEORGE WHITAKER SR.
"THE WINDSHIELD HAD A BULLET HOLE IN IT….RIGHT STRAIGHT THROUGH THE FRONT. THE HOLE WAS 4-6 INCHES TO THE RIGHT OF THE REAR VIEW MIRROR.*THE IMPACT HAD COME FROM THE FRONT OF THE WINDSHIELD."
*(WHEN ONE IS STANDING IN FRONT OF THE VEHICLE.)

DAMAGE WAS ALSO NOTED BY A SECRET SERVICE AGENT

SS AGENT CHARLES TAYLOR JR
"A SMALL HOLE JUST LEFT OF CENTER IN THE WINDSHIELD." (*AS VIEWED FROM INSIDE THE LIMO.)

RICHARD DUDMAN, A REPORTER FROM THE ST. LOUIS DISPATCH ALSO OBSERVED THE DAMAGE TO THE WINDSHIELD AS HE NOTED: "A FEW OF US NOTED THE HOLE IN THE WINDSHIELD."

AN FBI REPORT TO CHIEF CURRY DATED NOVEMBER 23RD, 1963 MAKES REFERENCE TO A "SCRAPING FROM INSIDE SURFACE OF WINDSHIELD." THE FBI REFERENCES THE WINDSHIELD SHOT. THE WC WOULD HOWEVER WOULD NOT.

THE WINDSHIELD ON DISPLAY AT THE NATIONAL ARCHIVES DOES NOT SHOW A BULLET HOLE BUT RATHER ELONGATED HAIRLINE CRACKS ON THE INSIDE SURFACE.

IN MY OPINION, BASED ON EXTENSIVE REVIEWS OF THE MANY SHOOTING SCENARIOS, I HAVE COME TO THE CONCLUSION THAT AT LEAST 7SHOTS WERE FIRED.

THE SHOTS LISTED AND THEIR ORIGIN AND VELOCITY
ARE NOT ARRANGED IN A PARTICULAR FIRING SEQUENCE

SHOT	ORIGIN	VELOCITY	WOUNDS
SHOT 1	REAR	LOW	FRAGMENT/CONCRETE GRAZED CHEEK OF JAMES TAGUE
SHOT 2	LEFT FRONT	HIGH	PENETRATES WINDSHIELD, THROAT ENTRY WOUND TO JFK CAUSED BY BULLET FRAGMENT OR GLASS FRAGMENT FROM THE WINDSHIELD
SHOT 3	REAR	HIGH	ALL GOVENOR CONNALLY'S WOUNDS
SHOT 4	REAR	LOW	JFK'S SHALLOW UPPER BACK WOUND NO EXIT
SHOT 5	RIGHT FRONT	HIGH	JFK'S RIGHT TEMPLE---A TANGENTIAL SHOT THAT EXITS TO THE REAR OF THE RIGHT PARIETAL BONE IN THE WOUND CAUSED BY THE NEAR SIMULTANEOUS REAR HEAD SHOT
SHOT 6	REAR	HIGH	COWLICK AREA OF SKULL OF THE PRESIDENT
SHOT 7	REAR	LOW	NONE, DAMAGE TO WINDSHIELD FRAME ABOVE REARVIEW MIRROR
SHOT 8	REAR	LOW	NONE, ENTERS THE GRASS SOUTH OF ELM

NOTE: A FRAGMENT FROM SHOT #6 COULD HAVE CAUSED THE WINDSHIELD FRAME DAMAGE NOTED IN SHOT #7. IF SO, THERE WOULD HAVE BEEN 7 SHOTS FIRED.

THE NEED TO QUELL ANY RUMORS OF A CONSPIRACY HOWEVER MADE IT IMPERATIVE TO FIND **HARVEY** THE SOLE SHOOTER. INDEED THIS WOULD BE THE ULTIMATE DESIRED OUTCOME OF THE WARREN COMMISSION. JOHNSON HAD SOLD THE "40 MILLION LIVES AT STAKE" DILEMMA TO CHIEF JUSTICE WARREN. IT WAS NOW WARREN'S TURN TO SWAY THE LAWYERS OF THE COMMISSION. HE TOLD THE ASSEMBLED STAFF AT THEIR FIRST MEETING THAT THEY HAD A RESPONSIBILITY TO SILENCE THE RUMORS SWIRLING AROUND THE ASSASSINATION. REITERATING WHAT JOHNSON HAD POINTEDLY IMPRESSED UPON HIM, WARREN COMMENTED "SOME OF THOSE RUMORS COULD CONCEIVABLY LEAD THE COUNTRY INTO A WAR WHICH COULD COST 40 MILLION LIVES." THE NECESSITY OF A COVER-UP HAD BEEN DULY EXPRESSED. BUT, WITH THE HIGHLY DESIRED AND LATER WIDELY PROMULGATED NOTION THAT THERE WAS BUT A SINGLE SHOOTER FIRING FROM THE REAR AND THAT THE SHOOTER WAS **HARVEY** TO THE EXCLUSION OF ALL OTHERS, THE ONLY WAY THE COMMISSION COULD SUPPORT THIS CONSPIRACY-SILENCING CONCLUSION WOULD BE TO ALTER <u>ANY</u> AND <u>ALL</u> EVIDENCE THAT DID NOT SUPPORT IT. THE ERRANT SHOT THAT STRUCK JAMES TAGUE FORCED THE COMMISSION TO ALTER ANY EVIDENCE THAT DID NOT SUPPORT THEIR DESIRED RESULT; THEIR DESIRED RESULT BEING THAT ALL SHOTS WERE FIRED FROM THE REAR BY **HARVEY** AND **HARVEY** ALONE. SOME COMMISSION MEMBERS WERE RELUCTANT TO PURSUE SUCH METHODS, BUT, WITH THE ERRANT SHOT, THEY WOULD HAVE LITTLE CHOICE IF THE CASE AGAINST

HARVEY WERE TO START AND END WITH HIM BEING THE SOLE PERPETRATOR OF THE PRESIDENTIAL MURDER AND THE WOUNDING OF GOVENOR CONNALLY.

THE COMMISSION STARTED BY ALTERING THE NUMBER OF SHOTS ALLOWED FROM 4 TO 3 TO FIT THE 5.6 SECOND TIMEFRAME OFFERED BY THE ZAPRUDER FILM. THE MISSED SHOT THAT STRUCK JAMES TAGUE COULD NOW BE ALLOWED IN THE SAME 5.6 SECOND TIMEFRAME. BUT, THIS WOULD REQUIRE 1 BULLET TO ACCOUNT FOR THE PRESIDENT'S BACK/NECK WOUNDS AND ALL OF GOVENOR CONNALLY'S WOUNDS. THIS BEGAT THE BIRTH OF AND THE NECESSITY OF THE MAGIC BULLET. FOR THIS ONE BULLET TO INFLICT ALL THE WOUNDS ON BOTH MEN WITH THE EXCEPTION OF JFK'S FATAL HEAD WOUND, THE DIRECTION OF THE WOUNDS, (ENTRANCE TO EXIT ON THE PRESIDENT'S THROAT WOUND) THE LOCATION OF THE WOUNDS, (HIGHER IN REGARDS TO BOTH THE BACK AND HEAD WOUNDS OF JFK) AND THE PATH OF THE WOUNDS WOULD ALL HAVE TO BE ALTERED. ALL EVIDENCE NOT IN SUPPORT OF THE COMMISSION'S DESIRED CONCLUSION, i.e. THE AUTOPSY PHOTOS AND X-RAYS, WOULD HAVE TO BE ALTERED AS WELL.

CONNIE KRITZBERG, A REPORTER FOR THE DALLAS TIMES HERALD, INTERVIEWED DR. KEMP CLARK AND DR. MALCOLM PERRY ONLY HOURS AFTER THE SHOOTING. BOTH DESCRIBED THE NECK WOUND **AND** A GAPING WOUND AT THE BACK OF THE HEAD THAT COULD HAVE BEEN AN **EXIT** WOUND OR A TANGENTIAL **ENTRANCE/EXIT** WOUND. THE NEXT DAY WHEN THE ARTICLE APPEARED, A LINE HAD BEEN INSERTED NOTING THAT "A DOCTOR ADMITTED THAT IT WAS POSSIBLE THERE WAS ONLY ONE WOUND." THIS WAS IN REFERENCE TO THE MASSIVE REAR HEAD WOUND. KRITZBERG CALLED THE CITY DESK AT THE TIMES HERALD TO INQUIRE AS TO WHO HAD CHANGED HER STORY. SHE WAS TOLD THAT IT HAD BEEN CHANGED BY THE FBI.

IN ESSENCE, THE "OFFICIAL" EVIDENCE HAD TO BE ALTERED TO SUPPORT WHAT WOULD LATER BE THE "OFFICIAL" WARREN COMMISSION FINDINGS. HAD THE AUTOPSY BEEN CONDUCTED AT PARKLAND WITH PRACTICING FORENSIC PATHOLOGISTS, HISTORY WOULD HAVE BEEN WRITTEN FAR DIFFERENTLY THAN THE WARREN COMMISSION HAD INTENDED.

AN EXCELLENT BOOK ON THE DESCRIPTION OF THE WOUNDS AS OBSERVED AT BOTH PARKLAND AND BETHESDA IS "JFK: FROM PARKLAND TO BETHESDA" BY VINCENT PALMARA.

CHAPTER 21: WITNESSES AND THEIR FATE

ROGER CRAIG
OFFICER CRAIG WOULD NOT CHANGE HIS TESTIMONY ABOUT HIS DESCRIPTION OF THE ALLEGED SHOOTER'S RIFLE AS A MAUSER. HE WOULD ALSO REFUSE TO CHANGE HIS TESTIMONY ABOUT SEEING "OSWALD" FLEEING THE BACK OF THE TSBD, RUNNING DOWN THE GRASSY KNOLL, AND ENTERING A GREEN RAMBLER STATION WAGON WITHIN MINUTES OF THE SHOOTING. CRAIG WOULD BE FIRED IN 1967 FOR TALKING TO REPORTERS ABOUT THE ASSASSINATION. A FEW YEARS LATER, HE WOULD BE FIRED AT WITH THE BULLET GRAZING HIS HEAD. IN 1973 HE WOULD BE RUN OFF THE ROAD. IN 1974 HIS CAR WAS BOMBED. IN 1975 HE WAS ONCE AGAIN SHOT; THIS TIME IN THE SHOULDER. ON MAY 15TH, 1975 CRAIG WOULD COMMIT "SUICIDE" AT THE AGE OF 39.

DOMINGO BENAVIDES
HE RUSHED TO TIPPIT'S SIDE AFTER TIPPIT WAS SHOT. LATER IN FEBRUARY 1965, BENAVIDES BROTHER, EDDIE, WAS SHOT TO DEATH IN A BAR IN DALLAS. THE BROTHERS WERE CLOSE ENOUGH IN APPEARANCE TO HAVE BEEN TWINS.

WARREN REYNOLDS
HE SAW A MAN FLEEING THE TIPPIT SHOOTING BUT CLAIMED THAT IT WAS NOT **HARVEY**. SHORTLY AFTER THE SHOOTING OF TIPPIT, THERE WAS AN ATTEMPT TO ABDUCT REYNOLDS 10 YEAR OLD DAUGHTER. HE WAS ALSO SHOT IN THE HEAD IN JANUARY 1964 WHILE HE WAS IN HIS OFFICE. HE WAS SHOT BY DARRELL WAYNE GARNER. (SEE ENTRY ON NANCY JANE MOONEY) THIS TOOK PLACE ONLY 2 DAYS AFTER HE FAILED TO IDENTIFY **HARVEY** AS TIPPIT'S ASSAILANT. THREE MONTHS LATER BEFORE THE WARREN COMMISSION REYNOLDS IDENTIFIED **HARVEY** AS TIPPIT'S ASSAILANT.

BILL HUNTER
HUNTER WAS A JOURNALIST WHO INTERVIEWED TOM HOWARD, RUBY'S LAWYER, IN DALLAS. HUNTER, ALONG WITH JIM KOETHE, WENT TO RUBY'S APARTMENT AFTER **HARVEY** WAS SHOT. THEY WERE ACCOMPANIED BY HOWARD AND OTHER ATTORNEYS. HUNTER WAS SHOT TO DEATH IN AN ACCIDENT IN A <u>POLICE STATION</u> IN LONG BEACH, CALIFORNIA ON APRIL 22ND, 1964.

JIM KEOTHE
KEOTHE, WHO ACCOMPANIED HOWARD AND HUNTER TO RUBY'S APARTMENT, ALSO INTERVIEWED TOM HOWARD. IN SEPTEMBER 1964, KEOTHE STEPPED OUT OF HIS SHOWER AND WAS KILLED BY A KARATE CHOP TO THE THROAT.

THOMAS KILLAN
HIS WIFE WORKED FOR RUBY AND KNEW OF A LINK BETWEEN RUBY AND **LEE**. HE WAS FOUND IN AN ALLEY IN MARCH 1964 WITH HIS THROAT CUT.

DOROTHY KILGALLEN
THE NOTED PANELIST ON THE GAME SHOW "TO TELL THE TRUTH" INTERVIEWED RUBY IN PRISON IN NOVEMBER 1965. WHEN SHE RETURNED TO NEW YORK, SHE TOLD HER FRIEND, MRS. FLORENCE. SMITH, A JOURNALIST, THAT SHE WAS "GOING TO BREAK THE ASSASSINATION MYSTERY WIDE OPEN." KILGALLEN HAD GIVEN HER DOCUMENTS TO SMITH FOR SAFE KEEPING. SHE WAS FOUND DEAD 2 DAYS LATER ON NOVEMBER 8TH OF AN "OVERDOSE." TWO DAYS AFTER THAT, HER FRIEND MRS. SMITH WAS FOUND DEAD ALSO; AN APPARENT "SUICIDE."

NANCY JANE MOONEY
MOONEY GAVE AN ALIBI FOR DARRELL WAYNE GARNER WHO WAS ACCUSED OF SHOOTING A MR. WARREN REYNOLDS. REYNOLDS HAD SEEN A MAN, <u>NOT</u> **HARVEY**, RUN FROM THE SCENE OF THE TIPPIT SHOOTING. GARNER WAS RELEASED ON THE ALIBI PROVIDED BY NANCY MOONEY. BUT, SHE WAS PICKED UP ON A MINOR OFFENSE

AND WAS FOUND HANGED IN HER JAIL CELL BY HER OWN SLACKS. MOONEY WORKED AT RUBY'S CAROUSEL CLUB.

WILLIAM WHALEY

WHALEY HAD GIVEN **HARVEY** THE CAB RIDE FROM THE BUS STATION TO NEAR HIS ROOMING HOUSE THE DAY OF THE ASSASSINATION. WHALEY DIED ON DECEMBER 18TH, 1965 IN AN AUTO ACCIDENT. UP TO THAT TIME, THERE HAD BEEN NO OTHER ON-DUTY DALLAS TAXI DRIVER TO DIE WHILE ON DUTY SINCE 1937.

MARILYN MAGYAR

MAGYAR WAS MURDERED IN 1964. ALTHOUGH HER HUSBAND WAS CONVICTED OF THE CRIME, IT WAS ALSO KNOWN THAT SHE WAS PLANNING A BOOK ON THE ASSASSINATION. MAGYAR WAS A STRIPPER AT JACK RUBY'S CAROUSEL CLUB.

ROSE CHERAMIE

SEE THE TIMELINE ENTRY ON ROSE CHERAMIE RECORDED ON NOVEMBER 20TH, 1963.

KAREN BENNETT CARLIN

A STRIPPER AT THE CAROUSEL CLUB. CARLIN WAS SHOT TO DEATH IN A HOTEL IN HOUSTON IN AUGUST OF 1964. CARLIN'S SON, MICHAEL, WOULD HOWEVER RELAY TO RESEARCHER GARY SHAW THAT CARLIN HAD ACTUALLY DIED IN SEPTEMBER 2010. IT WAS BELIEVED THAT SHE HAD APPARENTLY FAKED HER EARLIER DEATH DUE TO HER CONNECTION TO THE EVENTS OF NOVEMBER 1963.

LEE J. BOWERS

BOWERS WORKED IN THE RAILROAD TOWER BEHIND THE GRASSY KNOLL. HE WITNESSED 3 CARS CIRCLING THE LOT BEHIND THE FENCE JUST BEFORE THE SHOOTING ON NOVEMBER 22ND. BOWERS DIED WHEN HIS CAR LEFT THE ROAD ON AUGUST 9TH, 1966 AND SLAMMED INTO A BRIDGE SUPPORT. THERE WERE NO SKID MARKS TO INDICATE THAT BOWERS ATTEMPTED TO BRAKE. HE WAS 41 YEARS OLD. THE DOCTORS CLAIMED THAT HE WAS IN A STATE OF "STRANGE SHOCK" WHEN HE DIED. HE WAS CREAMATED THE NEXT DAY. NO AUTOPSY WAS PERFORMED.

RICHARD CARR

CARR SAW A HEAVY SET MAN ON THE 6TH FLOOR JUST BEFORE THE SHOOTING. HE THEN WITNESSED 2 MEN RUNNING FROM BEHIND THE TSBD JUST AFTER THE SHOOTING. HE THEN SAW THE SAME MAN HE HAD SEEN IN THE 6TH FLOOR WINDOW WALKING EAST ON COMMERCE IN AN "EXTREME HURRY AND LOOKING OVER HIS SHOULDER." THIS SAME MAN WOULD THEN ENTER A RAMBLER STATION WAGON ON RECORD STREET. CARR WAS LATER INTERVIEWED BY THE FBI AND TOLD "IF YOU DIDN'T SEE LHO UP IN THE TSBD WITH A RIFLE, YOU DIDN'T WITNESS IT." CARR WAS TOLD TO KEEP HIS MOUTH SHUT. SHORTLY THEREAFTER HIS HOME WAS RAIDED BY A DOZEN OR MORE DALLAS POLICE DETECTIVES. THEY CLAIMED TO BE LOOKING FOR "STOLEN ARTICLES." BOTH CARR AND HIS WIFE WERE JAILED THE NEXT DAY. CARR RECEIVED A CALL TELLING HIM TO "GET OUT OF TEXAS." CARR THEN MOVED TO MONTANA. HE FOUND DYNAMITE WIRED TO HIS CAR THE DAY PRIOR TO HIS TESTIMONY IN THE CLAY SHAW TRIAL. HE WAS ALSO SHOT AT AFTER TESTIFYING IN THE SHAW TRIAL. CARR WAS ATTACKED AND STABBED TWICE IN ATLANTA IN THE 1970'S.

ALBERT BOGARD

ON NOVEMBER 9TH, 1963, A MAN CLAIMING TO BE **HARVEY** VISITED BOGARD'S DOWNTOWN LINCOLN-MERCURY DEALERSHIP AND TOLD HIM THAT HE WOULD "BE COMING INTO A LOT OF MONEY SOON" AND THAT "WORKERS IN RUSSIA RECEIVED BETTER TREATMENT." ON A TEST DRIVE, THE MAN DROVE AT HIGH SPEEDS ON STEMMONS FREEWAY. **HARVEY** DIDN'T DRIVE. THE WARREN COMMISSION SAID IT SIMPLY COULD NOT BE **HARVEY**. BOGARD, AFTER SEEING **HARVEY** ON T.V. SAID IT WAS NOT THE SAME MAN AT THE DEALERSHIP. BOGARD WAS FOUND DEAD ON FEBRUARY 14TH, 1966 IN HIS CAR IN A CEMETERY IN HALLSVILLE, LOUISIANA. A HOSE HAD BEEN CONNECTED TO THE EXHAUST AND RAN INTO THE CAR. ORAN BROWN ALSO

WORKED AT THE SAME DEALERSHIP. HE TOLD AN INVESTIGATOR ON APRIL 4TH, 1966: "YOU KNOW I AM AFRAID TO TALK…..I THINK WE MAY HAVE SEEN SOMETHING IMPORTANT AND I THINK THAT THERE ARE SOME WHO DON'T WANT US TO TALK." BROWN DID NOT KNOW AT THE TIME THAT BOGARD WAS ALREADY DEAD.

JAMES WORRELL
WORRELL SAW A MAN RUNNING TROM THE BACK OF THE TSBD IMMEDIATELY AFTER THE SHOOTING. IT WAS NOT **HARVEY**. WORRELL DIED IN A ROAD ACCIDENT ON NOVEMBER 9TH, 1966.

HAROLD RUSSELL
RUSSELL SAW THE ESCAPE OF THE MAN WHO HE CLAIMS SHOT TIPPITT. IT WAS NOT **HARVEY**. IN JULY 1966 AT A PARTY, RUSSELL BECAME HYSTERICAL SAYING HE WAS GOING TO BE KILLED. THE HOSTS OF THE PARTY CALLED THE POLICE. WHEN THE POLICE ARRIVED, ONE STRUCK RUSSELL IN THE HEAD. HE DIED SEVERAL DAYS LATER OF HEAD INJURIES.

GARY UNDERHILL
UNDERHILL WAS A CIA AGENT WHO CLAIMED TO HAVE INSIDE INFO ON THE ASSASSINATION. HE WAS FOUND SHOT IN THE LEFT SIDE OF HIS HEAD ON MAY 8TH, 1964. HIS DEATH WAS LABELLED A SUICIDE. UNDERHILL WAS RIGHT HANDED.

DAVID FERRIE
FERRIE DIED ON FEBRUARY 22ND, 1967 OF AN OVERDOSE WHILE BEING RE-INVESTIGATED BY JIM GARRISON IN NEW ORLEANS. FERRIE HAD ALSO BEEN QUESTIONED ON MONDAY, NOVEMBER 25TH 1963 BY GARRISON IN REGARDS TO THE ASSASSINATION.

ELADIO DEL VALLE
DEL VALLE WAS A CLOSE FRIEND OF DAVID FERRIE. HE WAS SHOT AND HIS SKULL SPLIT OPEN BY WHAT WAS APPARENTLY A MACHETE. HE TOO WAS BEING SOUGHT BY JIM GARRISON IN REGARDS TO THE CLAY SHAW TRIAL. HIS MURDER WOULD OCCUR ONLY HOURS AFTER DAVID FERRIE WAS FOUND DEAD.

CLYDE JOHNSON
JOHNSON WAS SUPOENED BY JIM GARRISON. HE WAS SHOT TO DEATH.

ROBERT PERRIN
PERRIN WAS THE HUSBAND OF NANCY RICH PERRIN. MRS. PERRIN HAD TESTIFIED TO THE WARREN COMMISSION ON RUBY'S BACKGROUND. ROBERT PERRIN DIED OF ARSENIC POISONING IN AUGUST OF 1962.

DR. MARY SHERMAN
ON JULY 21ST, 1964, SHE WAS SHOT AND HAD HER BED SET ON FIRE. DR. SHERMAN WAS INVOLVED IN CANCER RESEARCH AT THE OCHSNER CLINIC IN NEW ORLEANS. IT IS BELIEVED THAT SHE WAS INVOLVED IN RESEARCH FUNDED BY THE CIA TO DEVELOP CARCINOGENS IN AN EFFORT TO USE THEM TO KILL CASTRO. THIS IS THE PROJECT THAT **HARVEY** WAS LEAD TO BELIEVE HE WAS INVOLVED IN.

DR. NICHOLAS CHETTA
DR. CHEETA WAS THE CORONER IN NEW ORLEANS DURING THE GARRISON INVESTIGATION AND PERFORMED THE AUTOPSIES ON DAVID FERRIE AND ROBERT PERRIN AN ASSOCIATE OF JACK RUBY. DR. CHETTA DIED OF AN APPARENT HEART ATTACK ON MAY 25TH, 1968

DR. HENRY DELAUNE
DR. DELAUNE WAS AN ASSISTANT TO DR. NICHOLAS CHETTA. DELAUNE WAS MURDERED ON JANUARY 26TH, 1969.

GUY BANISTER

BANISTER, CLOSELY ASSOCIATED WITH DAVID FERRIE AND **HARVEY** IN NEW ORLEANS, WAS ALSO QUESTIONED BY GARRISON. BANISTER DIED IN JUNE 1964 OF AN APPARENT HEART ATTACK. ONE WEEK BEFORE HIS DEATH HE TOLD GUY JOHNSON, ONI CHIEF IN NEW ORLEANS "IF I'M DEAD IN A WEEK, NO MATTER THE CIRCUMSTANCES, IT WON'T BE FROM NATURAL CAUSES." HE DIED AT THE OCHSNER CLINIC IN NEW ORLEANS.

GEORGE DE MOHRENSCHILDT

HE BEFRIENDED **HARVEY** IN DALLAS' RUSSIAN COMMUNITY. HE HAD LINKS TO THE CIA AND ARMY INTELLIGENCE. HE AND HIS WIFE WROTE A BOOK "I'M A PATSY!" ABOUT **HARVEY**. ON MARCH 29TH, 1971, THE SAME DAY THAT A HSCA COMMITTEE INVESTIGATOR PAID HIM A VISIT, HE WAS FOUND SHOT TO DEATH. HIS DEATH WAS RULED A SUICIDE. HE WAS TO TESTIFY TO THE HSCA TWO DAYS AFTER HIS DEATH.

SAM GIANCANA

GIANCANA WAS INVOLVED IN CIA-SPONSORED PLOTS TO KILL CASTRO. HE WAS SCHEDULED TO TESTIFY BEFORE THE CHURCH COMMITTEE REGARDING THE PLOTS. HE WAS FOUND SHOT IN THE HEAD IN HIS HOME ON JUNE 19TH, 1975 WHILE THE COMMITTEE WAS STILL IN SESSION. HE WAS SCHEDULED TO TESTIFY 5 DAYS LATER. HE HAD BEEN SHOT ONCE IN THE BACK OF THE HEAD AND 6 TIMES IN A CIRCULAR FASHION AROUND HIS MOUTH. THE GUNSHOTS AROUND THE MOUTH WERE KNOWN TO BE A MAFIA REMINDER TO THOSE WITH LOOSE LIPS.

JOHNNY ROSELLI

ROSELLI, WHO HAD TESTIFIED BEFORE THE SENATE INTELLIGENCE COMMITTEE IN JUNE 1976, WAS KILLED ON AUGUST 9TH, 1976. ROSELLI WAS STRANGLED, STABBED, AND HIS BODY DISMEMBERED TO THE EXTENT THAT IT WAS FOUND STUFFED IN AN OIL DRUM OFF THE COAST OF FLORIDA.

WILLIAM SULLIVAN

SULLIVAN WAS HOOVER'S RIGHT HAND MAN IN THE FBI. HE WAS HEAVILY INVOLVED WITH THE ASSASSINATION INVESTIGATION. HE DIED IN A HUNTING ACCIDENT IN 1977.

HOWARD L. BRENNAN

BRENNAN WAS SITTING ACROSS ELM STREET ACROSS FROM THE TSBD ON THE DAY OF THE ASSASSINATION. HE CLAIMED TO WITNESS **HARVEY** ON THE 6TH FLOOR FIRING HIS RIFLE. BRENNAN'S BOSS, SANDY SPEAKER NOTED: "THEY (FBI?) TOOK HIM OFF WORK FOR ABOUT 3 WEEKS. HE CAME BACK A NERVOUS WRECK. WITHIN 1 YEAR HIS HAIR HAD TURNED SNOW WHITE. HE WOULDN'T TALK ABOUT IT AFTER THAT. HE WAS SCARRED TO DEATH. THEY MADE HIM SAY WHAT THEY WANTED HIM TO SAY."

BIBLIOGRAPHY

RUSH TO JUDGEMENT	*MARK LANE*
CITIZEN'S DISSENT	*MARK LANE*
OPERATION OVERFLIGHT	*FRANCIS GARY POWERS*
THE INVISIBLE GOVERNMENT	*DAVID WISE*
THE U-2 AFFAIR	*DAVID WISE*
THE ASSASSINATION TAPES	*GEORGE O'TOOLE*
HERITAGE OF STONE	*JIM GARRISON*
THE WARREN REPORT	*THE ASSOCIATED PRESS*
THE OSWALD FILE	*MICHAEL ENDOWES*
THE FINAL ASSASSINATIONS REPORT	*SELECT COMMITTEE ON ASSASSINATIONS*
LEGEND	*EDWARD JAY EPSTEIN*
CLEARING THE AIR	*DANIEL SCHORR*
THE TEAMSTERS	*STEVEN BRILL*
BEST EVIDENCE	*DAVID LIFTON*
THE DAY KENNEDY WAS SHOT	*JIM BISHOP*
CONSPIRACY	*ANTHONY SUMMERS*
MARINA AND LEE	*PRISCILLA JOHNSON MCMILLAN*
THE PLOT TO KILL THE PRESIDENT	*G. ROBERT BLAKELY / ROBERT BILLINGS*
THE WITNESSES	*THE NEW YORK TIMES*
FOUR DAYS	*THEODORE WHITE*
CONTRACT ON AMERICA	*DAVID E. SCHEIM*
THEY'VE KILLED THE PRESIDENT	*ROBERT SAM ANSON*
LIBRA	*DON DELILLO*
HIGH TREASON	*ROBERT GRODEN / HARRISON LIVINGSTON*
ON THE TRAIL OF THE ASSASSINS	*JIM GARRISON*
CONSPIRACY OF ONE	*JIM MOORE*

THE TEXAS CONNECTION	CRAIG ZIRBEL
PLAUSIBLE DENIAL	MARK LANE
CROSS FIRE: THE PLOT THAT KILLED KENNEDY	JIM MARRS
HIGH TREASON 2	HARRISON LIVINGSTON
COUP D'ETAT IN AMERICA	ALAN J. WEBERMAN / MICHAEL CANFIELD
INQUEST	EDWARD J. EPSTEIN
COUNTERPLOT	EDWARD J. EPSTEIN
THE KILLING OF THE PRESIDENT	ROBERT GRODEN
THE LAST INVESTIGATION	GAETON FONZI
MORTAL ERROR	BONAR MENNINGER
ACT OF TREASON	MARK NORTH
THE MAN WHO KNEW TOO MUCH	DICK RUSSELL
KILLING THE TRUTH	HARRISON LIVINGSTON
REASONABLE DOUBT	HENRY HURT
JFK: THE CIA, VIETNAM, AND THE PLOT TO ASSASSINATE JFK	L. FLETCHER PROUTY
KILLING KENNEDY	HARRISON LIVINGSTON
TREACHERY IN DALLAS	WALT BROWN
UMBRELLA MAN	R. B. CUTLER
NEVER AGAIN	HAROLD WEISBERG
THE PEOPLE VS LEE HARVEY OSWALD	WALT BROWN
OSWALD TALKED	RAY AND MARY LAFONTAINE
ASSIGNMENT OSWALD	JAMES P. HOSTY, JR.
PASSPORT TO ASSASSINATION	COLONEL OLEG NECHIPORENKO
TRIANGLE OF FIRE	BOB GOODMAN
OSWALD AND THE CIA	JOHN NEWMAN
THE SEARCH FOR LEE HARVEY OSWALD	ROBERT J. GRODEN
JFK: FOR A NEW GENERATION	CONOVER HUNT
BLOODY TREASON	NOEL TWYMAN
AMERICAN GROTESQUE	JAMES KIRKWOOD

DESTINY BETRAYED	*JAMES DIEUGENIO*
NO MORE SILENCE	*LARRY A. SNEED*
HISTORY WILL NOT ABSOLVE US	*E. MARTIN SCHOTZ*
FAREWELL AMERICA	*JAMES HEPBURN*
JFK: FIRST DAY EVIDENCE	*GARY SAVAGE*
SQUARE PEG FOR A ROUND HOLE	*J. W. HUGHES*
SELECTIONS FROM WHITEWASH	*HAROLD WEISBERG*
THE WEB	*JAMES R. DUFFY*
DOUBLE CROSS	*SAM AND CHUCK GIANCANA*
DEADLY SECRETS	*WARREN HINCKLE / WILLIAM TURNER*
NOVEMBER PATRIOTS	*CONSTANCE KRITZBERG / LARRY HANCOCK*
PICTURES OF THE PAIN	*RICHARD B. TRASK*
FIRST HAND KNOWLEDGE	*ROBERT D. MORROW*
COVER UP	*STEWART GALANOR*
REAL ANSWERS	*GARY CORNWELL*
THE TRIAL OF JACK RUBY	*JOHN KAPLAN / JON WALTZ*
OSWALD'S TALE	*NORMAN MAILER*
JACK RUBY	*GARRY WILLS / OVID DEMARIS*
THE TORCH IS PASSED	*KANSAS CITY STAR*
MURDER IN DEALY PLAZA	*JAMES FETZER*
ASSASSINATION SCIENCE	*JAMES FETZER*
SAY GOODBYE TO AMERICA	*MATTHEW SMITH*
REGICIDE	*GREGORY DOUGLAS*
THE SECOND PLOT	*MATTHEW SMITH*
BLOOD, MONEY AND POWER	*BARR MCCLELLAN*
SOMEONE WOULD HAVE TALKED	*LARRY HANCOCK*
WHO'S WHO IN THE ASSASSINATION	*MICHAEL BENSON*
TRUTH WITHHELD	*JAMES TAGUE*
THE PEOPLE VS THE WARREN REPORT	*RODGER REMINGTON*

OSWALD IN NEW ORLEANS----------------------HAROLD WEISBERG

IN THE EYE OF HISTORY-------------------------WILLIAM MATSON LAW

NO CASE TO ANSWER------------------------------IAN GRIGGS

DR. MARY'S MONKEY------------------------------EDWARD HASLAM

DEEP POLITICS II----------------------------------PETER DALE SCOTT

FILES ON JFK--WIM DANKBAAR

THE CUBA FILES------------------------------------FABIAN ESCALANTE

WITH MALICE--DALE MYERS

THE RADICAL RIGHT AND THE MURDER OF JFK-----------------HARRISON LIVINGSTONE

THE ROAD TO DALLAS--------------------------DAVID KAISER

THE MIND OF OSWALD--------------------------DIANE HOLLOWAY

LEGACY OF SECRECY-----------------------------LAMAR WALDRON

ON THE TRAIL OF THE JFK ASSASSINS---DICK RUSSELL

THE MISSING CHAPTER-------------------------JACK SWIKE

OUR MAN IN MEXICO-----------------------------JEFFERSON MORLEY

MAFIA KINGFISH------------------------------------JOHN H. DAVIS

THE RUBY/ OSWALD AFFAIR------------------ALAN ADELSON

THE SECOND OSWALD--------------------------RICHARD POPKIN

SPY SAGA---PHILIP MELANSON

JFK AND THE UNSPEAKABLE----------------JAMES DOUGLAS

THE KENNEDY ASSASSINATION/24 HOURS AFTER-----STEVEN GILLON

JFK: THE LAST DISSENTING WITNESS------BILL SLOAN

ME AND LEE---JUDYTH VARY BAKER

WITHOUT SMOKING GUN-------------------------KENT HEINER

HEAD SHOT--G. PAUL CHAMBERS

LBJ: THE MASTERMIND OF JFK'S ASSASSINATION------PHILLIP NELSON

MATRIX FOR ASSASSINATION-------------------RICHARD GILBRIDE

MRS. PAINE'S GARAGE-------------------------THOMAS MALLON

THE KENNEDY ASSASSINATION TAPES--------MAX HOLLAND

FAREWELL TO JUSTICE----------------------------*JOAN MELLEN*

PRAISE FOR A FUTURE GENERATION------*JOHN KELEN*

COINCIDENCE OR CONSPIRACY--------------*BERNARD FENSTERWALD*

CASE CLOSED--*GERALD POSNER*

FROM AN OFFICE BUILDING WITH A HIGH-POWERED RIFLE--------*DON ADAMS*

HARVEY AND LEE------------------------------------*JOHN ARMSTRONG*

THE GIRL ON THE STAIRS------------------------*BARRY ERNEST*

LBJ AND THE CONSPIRACY TO KILL KENNEDY-------*JOSEPH FARRELL*

THE MAN WHO KILLED KENNEDY---------------------------*ROGER STONE*

THE HIDDEN HISTORY OF THE JFK ASSASSINATION-----*LAMAR WALDRON*

THE MAN WHO KILLED JFK: THE CASE AGAINST LBJ----*ROGER STONE*

SILENCING THE LONE ASSASSIN---------------------------------*JOHN CANAL*

DAVID FERRIE---*JUDYTH VARY BAKER*

CARLOS MARCELLO-THE MAN BEHIND THE JFK ASASSINATION---*STEFAN O VACCARA*

THE PRESIDENT'S MORTICIAN--*TIM FLEMING*

KENNEDY'S LAST STAND--*MIHAEL E. SALLA*

THE MEN AT SYLVIA'S DOOR------------------------*J. TIMOTHY GRATZ/MARK HOWELL*

EDWIN KAISER'S COVERT LIFE--*SCOTT KAISER*

THE MEN ON THE SIXTH FLOOR-------------------------*GLEN SAMPLE/ MARK COLLOM*

CIA ROGUES AND THE KILLING OF THE KENNEDY'S-----------------*PATRICK NOLAN*

TRIANGLE OF DEATH--*BRAD O'LEARY / L. E. SEYMOUR*

BEYOND THE FENCE LINE-----------------------------*CASEY J. QUINLIN / BRIAN K EDWARDS*

A SECRET ORDER (VOL.I)----------------------------------*H.P. ALBARELLI JR.*

WHITE WASH III--*HAROLD WEISBERG*

THE RUBY COVER-UP-------------------------------------*SETH KANTOR*

THE OSWALD CODE--*A. J. WEBERMAN*

PRESUMED GUILTY-------------------------------------*HOWARD ROFFMAN*

A CERTAIN ARROGANCE-----------------------------------*GEORGE MICHAEL EVICA*

EXTRAORDINARY EVIDENCE----------------------------*CRAIG FRALEY*

JFK FROM PARKLAND TO BETHESDA-----------VINCENT PALAMARA

WHERE ANGELS TREAD LIGHTLY (VOL. 1)----JOHN M. NEWMAN

AMBUSH IN DEALEY PLAZE-------------------------ROBERT MURDOCH

WHO REALLY KILLED KENNEDY------------------JEROME R. CORSI

HIT LIST--RICHARD BELZER AND DAVID WAYNE

FLIGHT FROM DALLAS-------------------------------JAMES P. JOHNSTON AND JON ROE

I AM A PATSY---GEORGE DEMOHRENSCHILDT

DOPPELGANGER--------------------------------------GEORGE SCHWIMMER, PhD

THE MEN THAT DON'T FIT IN---------------------FREDERICK A. MACKENZIE, III

COUNTDOWN TO DARKNESS (vol. II)-------------JOHN M. NEWMAN

OSWALD'S ODYSSEY-----------------------------------ANDREW CULVER

THE INNOCENCE OF OSWALD---------------------GARY FANNIN

AN AMERICAN COUP D'ETAT-----------------------COLONEL JOHN HUGHES=WILSON

HEAR NO EVIL---DONALD BYRON THOMAS

PRAYER MAN---STAN DANE

THE LIFE AND TIMES OF GERALD PATRICK HEMMING----ALAN JULES WEBERMAN

THROUGH THE "OSWALD" WINDOW-------------DAVE OBRIEN

PIECES OF THE PUZZLE-----------------------------GAYLE NIX JACKSON

THE LEE HARVEY OSWALD FILES-------------FLIP DE MAY

VIDEO

THE MEN WHO KILLED KENNEDY---------------------------------------HISTORY CHANNEL

THE MEN WHO KILLED KENNEDY: THE FINAL CHAPTER----HISTORY CHANNEL

JFK ASSASSINATION: A VISUAL INVESTIGATION----------------MEDIO

THE MURDER OF JFK/A REVISIONIST HISTORY-----------------MPI HOME VIDEO

I CURRENTLY HAVE IN MY LIBRARY A COPY OF NEARLY ALL OF THE NOTED VOLUMES AND EACH OF THE VIDEO SELECTIONS NOTED. THEY WERE INSTRUMENTAL IN THE DEVELOPMENT OF THIS WORK AS WELL AS INPUT FROM INTERNET SOURCES SUCH AS JFK LANCER, MARY FERRELL'S SITE, JFK ASSASSINATION FORUM, JFK RESEARCH ARCHIVE, MAGAZINE ARTICLES, THE 22NOVEMBER1963 SITE, JOHN ARMSTRONG'S SITE, HAROLD WEISBERG'S SITE, THE EDUCATION FORUM, HISTORY MATTERS, THE ASSASSINATION ARCHIVES AND RESEARCH CENTER, THE NARA SITE AND A MEMORABLE VISIT TO DEALEY PLAZA, THE TEXAS SCHOOL BOOK DEPOSITORY, AND THE CONSPIRACY MUSEUM.

JOEL THOMAS GOLLAR IS A NATIVE OF LOUISVILLE, KENTUCKY. AFTER COMPLETING HIS HIGH SCHOOL EDUCATION HE SERVED 4 YEARS IN THE NAVY AS A MORSE INTERCEPT OPERATOR UNDER THE GUIDANCE OF THE NAVAL SECURITY GROUP, THE DEFENSE INTELLIGENCE AGENCY AND THE NSA. HE WAS STATIONED AT THE NAVAL COMMUNICATION STATION IN ROTA, SPAIN IN THE EARLY 1970'S. UPON COMPLETION OF HIS NAVAL ENLISTMENT HE RETURNED TO KENTUCKY WHERE HE RECEIVED HIS BHS IN NUCLEAR MEDICINE TECHNOLOGY AND HIS MS IN INTEGRATED COMMUNITY DEVELOPMENT AND HEALTH PROMOTION AND DISEASE PREVENTION FROM THE UNIVERSITY OF LOUISVILLE.

www.ingramcontent.com/pod-product-compliance
Lightning Source LLC
Chambersburg PA
CBHW060454170426
43199CB00011B/1205